ACCOUNTING TRENDS & TECHNIQUES

U.S. GAAP Financial Statements

Best Practices in Presentation and Disclosure

15122B-360

AICPA®

SIXTY-EIGHTH EDITION

ISSN 1531-4340

ISBN 978-1-94023-580-6

Director, Content and Product Development: Linda Cohen
Senior Technical Manager: Doug Bowman
Technical Manager: Liese Faircloth
Content Development Specialist: David Cohen
Project Manager: Charlotte Ingles

The 2014 edition of *U.S. GAAP Financial Statements—Best Practices in Presentation and Disclosure* was developed by

RAYMOND J. PETRINO, CPA
CONTENT MATTER EXPERT

DAVID J. COHEN
DEVELOPMENTAL EDITOR
AICPA LEARNING DESIGN AND DEVELOPMENT

LIESE FAIRCLOTH, CPA
TECHNICAL MANAGER
AICPA ACCOUNTING AND AUDITING CONTENT DEVELOPMENT

About This Edition of *U.S. GAAP Financial Statements—Best Practices in Presentation and Disclosure*

This book remains the best source for reporting and disclosure examples from real world financial statements, providing accounting professionals with an invaluable resource for incorporating new and existing accounting and reporting guidance into financial statements using presentation techniques adopted by companies across numerous industries, all of which are headquartered in the United States.

Organization and Content

This 2014 edition surveyed annual reports of 350 entities of various sizes representing over 100 industries with fiscal periods ending between January and December 2013. The industry classifications of survey entities (as shown in the Appendix of Survey Entity Industries) were obtained from Morningstar, Inc.

To provide you with the most useful and comprehensive look at current financial reporting presentation and disclosure, this book is topically organized and offers the following:
- Examples taken from the surveyed annual reports illustrating financial statement presentation and virtually every required U.S. GAAP disclosure.
- Descriptive guidance that includes current reporting requirements under U.S. generally accepted accounting principles (GAAP). U.S. GAAP is generally considered to be the requirements of the Financial Accounting Standards Board (FASB) *Accounting Standards Codification*™ (ASC). Select Securities and Exchange Commission (SEC) guidance is also included.
- Detailed indexes.

ILLUSTRATIVE REPORTING EXAMPLES

AICPA leverages its decades of experience as the CPA national membership organization to select the most useful, comprehensive presentation and disclosure examples, which comprise the majority of this book. Every edition of *Best Practices in Presentation and Disclosure* includes all new annual report excerpts that were chosen to be particularly relevant and useful to financial statement preparers in illustrating current reporting practices.

Because survey entities may present disclosures on specific topics within different footnotes in their annual filings, including those ostensibly about a separate accounting topic, the excerpts presented herein to illustrate a given topic may have been taken from footnotes about other topics.

GUIDANCE

Discerning, plain English guidance covers the significant U.S. GAAP accounting and financial statement reporting requirements in narrative form. These narratives use common headings (recognition and measurement, presentation, and disclosure) to achieve a consistent presentation throughout all the sections. Although not a substitute for the authoritative accounting and reporting standards, the reporting guidance herein encapsulates the complex requirements to facilitate your understanding of the content. The related authoritative sources for each requirement are cited within the narratives (for example, FASB ASC 310, *Receivables*, or Regulation S-K).

SEC rules and interpretative releases may expand, modify, or decrease accounting and disclosure requirements for foreign private issuers, regardless of whether they file their annual financial statements with the SEC in Forms 10-K, 20-F, or 40-F (Canadian issuers). Therefore, it is critical to consider SEC requirements, as well as those of FASB ASC, when reviewing the financial statements of SEC registrants. A general reference to FASB ASC in this publication does not include the SEC materials. When requirements are taken from an SEC rule or regulation, that rule or regulation will be cited directly.

INDEXES

Indexes in this edition include the "Appendix of 350 Entities," which alphabetically lists each of the 350 survey entities included in the current edition and notes where in the text excerpts from their annual reports can be found; the "Appendix of Survey Entity Industries," which lists the industries represented by the 350 survey entities and lists the entities within each industry classification; the "Index of Authoritative Accounting & Auditing Guidance," which provides for easy cross-referencing of pronouncements to the applicable descriptive narratives; and a detailed "Subject Index," which is fully cross-referenced to all significant topics included throughout the narratives.

FASB ASC

Because FASB ASC is the source of authoritative U.S. GAAP for nongovernmental entities, in addition to guidance issued by the SEC, the guidance herein refers only to the appropriate FASB ASC reference for all standards.

Note that the effective dates of recently released guidance affect the timing of its inclusion in the financial statements of the survey entities, thereby affecting the availability of illustrative excerpts for potential inclusion in each edition of *Best Practices in Presentation and Disclosure*. This 2014 edition includes survey entities having fiscal years ending within calendar year 2013. Technical guidance for which this edition supplies illustrative annual report excerpts includes the following, among other recently issued guidance:
- ASU No. 2013-04, *Liabilities (Topic 405): Obligations Resulting from Joint and Several Liability Arrangements for Which the Total Amount of the Obligation Is Fixed at the Reporting Date*
- ASU No. 2013-07, *Presentation of Financial Statements (Topic 205): Liquidation Basis of Accounting*
- ASU No. 2013-11, *Income Taxes (Topic 740): Presentation of an Unrecognized Tax Benefit When a Net Operating Loss Carryforward, a Similar Tax Loss, or a Tax Credit Carryforward Exists*

Related Products

U.S. GAAP Financial Statements—Best Practices in Presentation and Disclosure is the flagship product in the AICPA's *Accounting Trends & Techniques* series; it is also available in an interactive, online format. Other titles in the *Accounting Trends & Techniques* series include
- *Employee Benefit Plans Financial Statements—Best Practices in Presentation and Disclosure*
- *Not-for-Profit Entities Financial Statements—Best Practices in Presentation and Disclosure*

Notice

This book is a nonauthoritative practice aid and is not designed to provide a comprehensive understanding of all the requirements contained in U.S. GAAP. The guidance provided herein may not discuss all relevant accounting guidance on a given topic and should not be relied upon for its completeness. Users are encouraged to consult FASB ASC for complete, authoritative discussion of U.S. GAAP. Users are also encouraged to consult the complete body of SEC rules and regulations for regulatory requirements. In addition, this book does not include reporting requirements relating to other matters such as internal control or agreed-upon procedures.

Authoritative guidance on accounting treatments in accordance with U.S. GAAP can be made only by reference to the FASB ASC, which is copyright of the FAF and can be acquired directly from FASB.

This book has not been reviewed, approved, disapproved, or otherwise acted on by any senior technical committee of the AICPA and does not represent official positions or pronouncements of the AICPA.

The use of this publication requires the exercise of individual professional judgment. It is not a substitute for the original authoritative accounting and auditing guidance. Users are urged to refer directly to applicable authoritative pronouncements, when appropriate. As an additional resource, users may call the AICPA Technical Hotline at 1.877.242.7212.

Feedback

We hope that you find this edition to be informative and useful. Please let us know! What features do you like? What do you think can be improved or added? We encourage you to submit your comments and questions to Anjali Patel, using the following contact information. All feedback is greatly appreciated and kept strictly confidential.

Liese Faircloth— Accounting and Auditing Content Development

AMERICAN INSTITUTE OF CERTIFIED PUBLIC ACCOUNTANTS

220 Leigh Farm Road

Durham, NC 27707-8110

Telephone: 919.402.4819

E-mail: lfaircloth@aicpa.org

You can also contact the Accounting and Auditing Content Development team of the AICPA directly via e-mail at

A&Apublications@aicpa.org

TABLE OF CONTENTS

Survey Entities

1.01 All 350 entities included in the survey are registered with the SEC. All of the survey entities have securities traded on one of the major stock exchanges: 84 percent on the New York Stock Exchange and 16 percent on NASDAQ.

1.02 Each year, entities are selected across various industry classifications with the purpose of highlighting those entities that exhibit the best practices.

General Financial Statement Considerations

RECOGNITION AND MEASUREMENT

1.03 FASB *Accounting Standards Codification®* (ASC) 105-10-05-2 explains that if the necessary guidance for a transaction or event is not specified within a source of authoritative generally accepted accounting principles (GAAP), an entity should first consider accounting principles for similar transactions or events within a source of authoritative GAAP for that entity and then consider nonauthoritative guidance from other sources. When those accounting principles either prohibit the application of the accounting treatment to the particular transaction or event or indicate that the accounting treatment should not be applied by analogy, an entity should not follow those accounting principles.

1.04 FASB ASC 105-10-05-3 explains that accounting and financial reporting practices not included in FASB ASC are nonauthoritative. FASB Concepts Statements are not considered authoritative sources of GAAP, and no preference is given to the FASB Concepts Statements over other nonauthoritative sources. FASB ASC does not state that consistency with the FASB Concept Statements in connection with an entity's application of an accounting treatment is necessary. Sources of nonauthoritative accounting guidance include the following:
- Practices that are widely recognized and prevalent, either generally or in the industry
- FASB Concepts Statements
- AICPA Issues Papers
- International Financial Reporting Standards (IFRSs) of the International Accounting Standards Board (IASB)
- Pronouncements of professional associations or regulatory agencies
- Technical Questions and Answers included in AICPA *Technical Practice Aids*
- Accounting textbooks, handbooks, and articles

The appropriateness of other sources of accounting guidance depends on its relevance to particular circumstances, the specificity of the guidance, the general recognition of the issuer or author as an authority, and the extent of its use in practice.

1.05 As discussed in FASB ASC 105-10-05-1, GAAP, as codified in FASB ASC, includes the rules and interpretive releases of the SEC as sources of authoritative GAAP as a convenience only to SEC registrants. In addition to the SEC's rules and interpretive releases, the SEC staff issues Staff Accounting Bulletins that represent practices that the staff follows when administering SEC disclosure requirements. SEC staff announcements and observer comments made at meetings of the Emerging Issues Task Force announce the staff's views on certain accounting issues for SEC registrants.

1.06 In June 2009, FASB issued the last FASB statement referenced in that form: FASB Statement No. 168, *The FASB Accounting Standards Codification® and the Hierarchy of Generally Accepted Accounting Principles—a replacement of FASB Statement No. 162*. This standard established FASB ASC as the source of authoritative U.S. accounting and reporting standards for nongovernmental companies, in addition to guidance issued by the SEC, and was effective for financial statements issued for interim and annual periods ending after September 15, 2009.

1.07 In FASB ASC's Notice to Constituents (NTC), FASB suggests the use of plain English references to describe broad FASB ASC topics going forward in financial statements and related footnote disclosures. FASB provides the following example of plain English references in the NTC when referring to the requirements of FASB ASC 815, *Derivatives and Hedging*: "as required by the Derivatives and Hedging Topic of the FASB Accounting Standards Codification."

1.08 A natural business year is the period of 12 consecutive months that ends when the business activities of an entity have reached the lowest point in their annual cycle. In many instances, the natural business year of an entity ends December 31.

PRESENTATION

1.09 Rule 14 a-3 of the Securities Exchange Act of 1934 states that annual reports furnished to stockholders in connection with the annual meetings of stockholders should include audited financial statements: balance sheets as of the end of the two most recent fiscal years and statements of income and cash flows for each of the three most recent fiscal years. Rule 14 a-3 also states that the following information, as specified in SEC Regulation S-K should be included in the annual report to stockholders:
- Selected quarterly financial data
- Changes in, and disagreements with, accountants on accounting and financial disclosure
- Summary of selected financial data for the last five years
- Description of business activities
- Segment information
- Listing of company directors and executive officers
- Market price of, and dividends on, the company's common stock for each quarterly period within the two most recent fiscal years
- Management's discussion and analysis (MD&A) of financial condition and results of operations
- Quantitative and qualitative disclosures about market risk

1.10 FASB ASC 205-10-45-2 states that it is ordinarily desirable for an entity to present the statement of financial position; the income statement; and the statement of changes in equity for one or more preceding years, in addition to those of the current year.

1.11 Paragraphs 3–4 of FASB ASC 205-10-45 require these statements to be comparable, and any exceptions to comparability should be described as required by FASB ASC 250, *Accounting Changes and Error Corrections*. An entity is required to repeat, or at least refer to, any notes to financial statements, other explanations, or accountants' reports that contain qualifications for prior years that appeared in the comparative statements when originally issued, to the extent this information remains significant. Multiple rules set forth in SEC Regulation S-X provide guidance to SEC registrants on the form and ordering of financial statements, the presentation of amounts, the omission of certain items, and requirements for supplemental schedules. Rule 14 a-3 requires that annual reports to stockholders should include comparative balance sheets and statements of income and cash flows for each of the three most recent fiscal years. All the survey entities are SEC registrants and conformed to the aforementioned requirements of Rule 14 a-3.

1.12 FASB ASC permits an entity to offset a liability with an asset only when the following certain conditions discussed in FASB ASC 210-20-45-1 are met:
- Each of two parties owes the other determinable amounts.
- The reporting party has the right to set off the amount owed with the amount owed by the other party.
- The reporting party intends to set off.
- The right of setoff is enforceable at law.

Author's Note

In December 2011, FASB issued Accounting Standards Update (ASU) No. 2011-11, *Balance Sheet (Topic 210): Disclosures about Offsetting Assets and Liabilities*, to enhance comparability of financial statements prepared in accordance with GAAP and IFRS. The amendments in this update will enhance disclosures by requiring improved information about financial instruments and derivative instruments that are either (*a*) offset in accordance with either FASB ASC 210-20-45 or 815-10-45 or (*b*) subject to an enforceable master netting arrangement or similar agreement, irrespective of whether they are offset in accordance with either of the aforementioned FASB ASC sections. The additional disclosures will enable financial statement users to better understand the effect of such arrangements on their financial position. Entities are required to apply the amendments in this ASU for annual reporting periods beginning on or after January 1, 2013, and interim periods within those annual periods. As a result of the effective date of this ASU, the excerpts appearing later in this section may not reflect all or some of these revisions.

In January 2013, FASB issued ASU No. 2013-01, Balance Sheet (Topic 210): Clarifying the Scope of Disclosures about Offsetting Assets and Liabilities, to address implementation issues about the scope of ASU No. 2011-11. Stakeholders have told the board that because

---

the scope in ASU No. 2011-11 is unclear, diversity in practice may result. Recent feedback from stakeholders is that standard commercial provisions of many contracts would equate to a master netting arrangement. Stakeholders questioned whether it was the board's intent to require disclosures for such a broad scope, which would significantly increase the cost of compliance. The objective of this update is to clarify the scope of the offsetting disclosures and address any unintended consequences. Entities are required to apply the amendments in this ASU for annual reporting periods beginning on or after January 1, 2013, and interim periods within those annual periods.

DISCLOSURE

1.13 SEC Regulations S-X and S-K and paragraphs .19–.20 and .A22–.A23 of AU-C section 705, *Modifications to the Opinion in the Independent Auditor's Report* (AICPA, *Professional Standards*), state the need for adequate disclosure in financial statements. Normally, the financial statements alone cannot present all information necessary for adequate disclosure without considering appended notes that disclose information. All surveyed entities provided footnote disclosures to their financial statements.

1.14 FASB ASC 235, *Notes to Financial Statements*, sets forth guidelines about the content and format of disclosures of accounting policies. FASB ASC 235-10-50-1 requires that the significant accounting policies of an entity be presented as an integral part of the financial statements of the entity. FASB ASC 235-10-50-6 states that the preferable format is to present a summary of significant accounting policies preceding notes to financial statements, or as the initial note, under the same or a similar title.

1.15 FASB ASC 205-10-50-1 requires an entity to provide information explaining changes due to reclassifications or other reasons that affect the manner of, or basis for, presenting corresponding items for two or more periods. FASB ASC 250-10 does not require an entity to present an opening balance sheet of the earliest period presented when an entity retrospectively applies a change in accounting policy or restates to correct an error.

1.16 FASB ASC 275, *Risks and Uncertainties*, requires reporting entities to disclose information about the risks and uncertainties resulting from the nature of their operations, the use of estimates in preparing financial statements, and significant concentrations in certain aspects of the entity's operations.

PRESENTATION AND DISCLOSURE EXCERPTS

QUARTERLY FINANCIAL DATA

1.17 STANLEY BLACK & DECKER, INC. (DEC)
SELECTED QUARTERLY FINANCIAL DATA (unaudited)

(Millions of dollars, except per share amounts)	Quarter				
	First	**Second**	**Third**	**Fourth**	**Year**
2013					
Net sales	$2,476.5	$2,859.4	$2,759.3	$2,906.0	$11,001.2
Gross profit	908.6	1,005.9	987.7	1,030.7	3,932.9
Selling, general and administrative expenses	664.7	677.2	669.6	703.1	2,714.6
Net earnings from continuing operations	84.7	197.4	169.6	65.6	517.3
Less: Net loss attributable to non-controlling interest	(0.4)	(0.3)	(0.3)	(0.1)	(1.0)
Net earnings from continuing operations attributable to Stanley Black & Decker, Inc.	85.1	197.7	169.9	65.7	518.3
Net loss from discontinued operations	(4.0)	(10.6)	(3.9)	(9.6)	(28.0)
Net earnings attributable to Stanley Black & Decker, Inc.	$ 81.1	$ 187.1	$ 166.0	$ 56.1	$ 490.3
Basic earnings (loss) per common share:					
Continuing operations	$ 0.55	$ 1.27	$ 1.10	$ 0.42	$ 3.34
Discontinued operations	(0.03)	(0.07)	(0.02)	(0.06)	(0.18)
Total basic earnings per common share	$ 0.52	$ 1.21	$ 1.07	$ 0.36	$ 3.16
Diluted earnings (loss) per common share:					
Continuing operations	$ 0.53	$ 1.25	$ 1.07	$ 0.41	$ 3.26
Discontinued operations	(0.02)	(0.07)	(0.02)	(0.06)	(0.18)
Total diluted earnings per common share	$ 0.51	$ 1.18	$ 1.04	$ 0.35	$ 3.09

(continued)

(Millions of dollars, except per share amounts)	Quarter				
	First	Second	Third	Fourth	Year
2012					
Net sales	$2,414.0	$2,557.2	$2,517.2	$2,659.5	$10,147.9
Gross profit	908.6	928.9	911.9	946.1	3,695.5
Selling, general and administrative expenses	632.6	621.5	609.2	636.6	2,499.9
Net earnings from continuing operations	107.9	128.4	90.0	137.7	464.0
Less: Net (loss) earnings attributable to non-controlling interest	(0.7)	(0.3)	(0.2)	0.4	(0.8)
Net earnings from continuing operations attributable to Stanley Black & Decker, Inc.	108.6	128.7	90.2	137.3	464.8
Net earnings from discontinued operations	13.2	26.1	25.0	354.8	419.0
Net earnings attributable to Stanley Black & Decker, Inc.	$ 121.8	$ 154.8	$ 115.2	$ 492.1	$ 883.8
Basic earnings per common share:					
Continuing operations	$ 0.66	$ 0.78	$ 0.55	$ 0.85	$ 2.85
Discontinued operations	0.08	0.16	0.15	2.20	2.57
Total basic earnings per common share	$ 0.74	$ 0.94	$ 0.71	$ 3.05	$ 5.41
Diluted earnings per common share:					
Continuing operations	$ 0.64	$ 0.77	$ 0.54	$ 0.83	$ 2.79
Discontinued operations	0.08	0.15	0.15	2.16	2.51
Total diluted earnings per common share	$ 0.72	$ 0.92	$ 0.69	$ 2.99	$ 5.30

The quarterly amounts above have been adjusted for the divestiture of HHI as well as for two small businesses within the Security and Industrial segments, which have been excluded from continuing operations and are reported as discontinued operations. Refer to *Note T, Discontinued Operations*, of the *Notes to Consolidated Financial Statements* in *Item 8* for further discussion.

During 2013, the Company recognized $394 million ($273 million after tax, or $1.72 per diluted share), in charges on continuing operations primarily associated with merger and acquisitions-related charges pertaining to the Black & Decker merger and Niscayah and Infastech acquisitions, including facility closure-related charges, employee-related charges and integration costs, as well as cost containment charges and a restructuring reversal in the second quarter due to the termination of a previously approved restructuring action. Other charges relate to the loss on extinguishment of debt.

The impact of these merger and acquisition-related charges and effect on diluted earnings per share by quarter was as follows:

Merger and Acquisition-Related Charges	Diluted EPS Impact
• Q1 2013—$106 million ($81 million after-tax)	$0.51 per diluted share
• Q2 2013—$5 million (($4) million after-tax)	($0.02) per diluted share
• Q3 2013—$67 million ($51 million after-tax)	$0.32 per diluted share
• Q4 2013—$215 million ($144 million after-tax)	$0.91 per diluted share

During 2012, the Company recognized $442 million ($329 million after tax), or $1.97 per diluted share, in charges on continuing operations primarily associated with merger and acquisitions-related charges (including facility closure-related charges, integration-related administration costs and consulting fees, as well as transaction cost), the charges associated with the $200 million in cost actions implemented in 2012, as well as the charges associated with the extinguishment of debt during the third quarter of 2012. The impact of these merger and acquisition-related charges and effect on diluted earnings per share by quarter was as follows:

Merger and Acquisition-Related Charges	Diluted EPS Impact
• Q1 2012—$80 million ($59 million after-tax)	$0.35 per diluted share
• Q2 2012—$74 million ($63 million after-tax)	$0.37 per diluted share
• Q3 2012—$157 million ($113 million after-tax)	$0.68 per diluted share
• Q4 2012—$131 million ($95 million after-tax)	$0.58 per diluted share

In the third and fourth quarter of 2012, the Company recognized an income tax benefit attributable to the settlement of certain tax contingencies of $7 million, or $0.04 per diluted share, and $42 million, or $0.25 per diluted share, respectively.

SELECTED INFORMATION FOR FIVE YEARS

1.18 J. C. PENNEY COMPANY, INC. (JAN)
SELECTED FINANCIAL DATA

Five-Year Financial Summary

($ in millions, except per share data)	2012	2011	2010	2009	2008
Results for the year					
Total net sales	$12,985	$17,260	$17,759	$17,556	$18,486
Sales percent increase/(decrease):					
Total net sales	(24.8)%[1]	(2.8)%	1.2%	(5.0)%	(6.9)%
Comparable store sales[2]	(25.2)%	0.2%	2.5%	(6.3)%	(8.5)%
Operating income/(loss)	(1,310)	(2)	832	663	1,135
As a percent of sales	(10.1)%	(0.0)%	4.7%	3.8%	6.1%
Adjusted operating income/(loss) (non-GAAP)[3]	(939)	536	1,085	961	1,002
As a percent of sales (non-GAAP)[3]	(7.2)%	3.1%	6.1%	5.5%	5.4%
Income/(loss) from continuing operations	(985)	(152)	378	249	567
Adjusted income/(loss) from continuing operations (non-GAAP)[3]	(766)	207	533	433	484
Per common share					
Income/(loss) from continuing operations, diluted	$(4.49)	$(0.70)	$1.59	$1.07	$2.54
Adjusted income/(loss) from continuing operations, diluted (non-GAAP)[3]	(3.49)	0.94	2.24	1.86	2.17
Dividends declared[4]	0.20	0.80	0.80	0.80	0.80
Financial position and cash flow					
Total assets	$9,781	$11,424	$13,068	$12,609	$12,039
Cash and cash equivalents	930	1,507	2,622	3,011	2,352
Long-term debt, including capital leases, note payable and current maturities	2,982	3,102	3,099	3,392	3,505
Free cash flow (non-GAAP)[3]	(906)	23	158	677	22

[1] Includes the effect of the 53rd week in 2012. Excluding sales of $163 million for the 53rd week in 2012, total net sales decreased 25.7%.

[2] Comparable store sales are presented on a 52-week basis and include sales from new and relocated stores that have been opened for 12 consecutive full fiscal months and Internet sales. Stores closed for an extended period are not included in comparable store sales calculations, while stores remodeled and minor expansions not requiring store closures remain in the calculations. Our definition and calculation of comparable store sales may differ from other companies in the retail industry.

[3] See Non-GAAP Financial Measures beginning on the following page for additional information and reconciliation to the most directly comparable GAAP financial measure.

[4] On May 15, 2012, we announced that we had discontinued the quarterly $0.20 per share dividend.

Five-Year Operations Summary

	2012	2011	2010	2009	2008
Number of department stores:					
Beginning of year	1,102	1,106	1,108	1,093	1,067
Openings	9	3	2	17	35
Closings[1]	(7)	(7)	(4)	(2)	(9)
End of year	1,104	1,102	1,106	1,108	1,093
Gross selling space *(square feet in millions)*	111.6	111.2	111.6	111.7	109.9
Sales per gross square foot[2]	$ 116	$ 154	$ 153	$ 149	$ 160
Sales per net selling square foot[2]	$ 161	$ 212	$ 210	$ 206	$ 223
Number of the Foundry Big and Tall Supply Co. stores[3]	10	10	—	—	—

[1] Includes relocations of 3, –, –, 1, and 7 respectively.

[2] Calculation includes the sales and square footage of jcpenney department stores that were open for the full fiscal year and sales for jcp.com.

[3] All stores opened during 2011. Gross selling space was 51 thousand square feet as of February 2, 2013 and January 28, 2012.

Non-GAAP Financial Measures

We report our financial information in accordance with generally accepted accounting principles in the United States (GAAP). However, we present certain financial measures and ratios identified as non-GAAP under the rules of the Securities and Exchange Commission (SEC) to assess our results. We believe the presentation of these non-GAAP financial measures and ratios is useful in order to better understand our financial performance as well as to facilitate the comparison of our results to the results of our peer companies. It is important to view non-GAAP financial measures in addition to, rather than as a substitute for, those measures and ratios prepared in accordance with GAAP. We have provided reconciliations of the most directly comparable GAAP measures to our non-GAAP financial measures presented.

Non-GAAP Measures Excluding Markdowns Related to the Alignment of Inventory with Our New Strategy, Restructuring and Management Transition Charges, the Non-Cash Impact of Our Qualified Defined Benefit Pension Plan Expense and the Net Gain on the Sale or Redemption of Non-Operating Assets

The following non-GAAP financial measures are adjusted to exclude the impact of markdowns related to the alignment of inventory with our new strategy, restructuring and management transition charges, the non-cash impact of our qualified defined benefit pension plan (Primary Pension Plan) expense and the net gain on the sale or redemption of non-operating assets. Unlike other operating expenses, markdowns related to the alignment of inventory with our new strategy, restructuring and management transition charges and the net gain on the sale or redemption of non-operating assets are not directly related to our ongoing core business operations. Additionally, Primary Pension Plan expense is determined using numerous complex assumptions about changes in pension assets and liabilities that are subject to factors beyond our control, such as market volatility. We believe it is useful for investors to understand the impact of markdowns related to the alignment of inventory with our new strategy, restructuring and management transition charges, the non-cash impact of our Primary Pension Plan expense and the net gain on the sale or redemption of non-operating assets on our financial results and therefore are presenting the following non-GAAP financial measures: (1) adjusted operating income/(loss); (2) adjusted net income/(loss); and (3) adjusted diluted earnings/(loss) per share (EPS).

Adjusted Operating Income/(Loss). The following table reconciles operating income/(loss), the most directly comparable GAAP financial measure, to adjusted operating income/(loss), a non-GAAP financial measure:

($ in millions)	2012	2011	2010	2009	2008
Operating income/(loss) (GAAP)	$(1,310)	$ (2)	$ 832	$663	$1,135
As a percent of sales	(10.1)%	(0.0)%	4.7%	3.8%	6.1%
Add: markdowns—inventory strategy alignment	155	—	—	—	—
Add: restructuring and management transition charges	298	451	32	—	—
Add/(deduct): primary pension plan expense/(income)	315	87	221	298	(133)
Less: Net gain on sale or redemption of non-operating assets	(397)	—	—	—	—
Adjusted operating income/(loss) (non-GAAP)	$ (939)	$536	$1,085	$961	$1,002
As a percent of sales	(7.2)%	3.1%	6.1%	5.5%	5.4%

Adjusted Net Income/(Loss) and Adjusted Diluted EPS from Continuing Operations. The following table reconciles net income/(loss) and diluted EPS from continuing operations, the most directly comparable GAAP financial measures, to adjusted net income/(loss) and adjusted diluted EPS from continuing operations, non-GAAP financial measures:

($ in millions, except per share data)	2012	2011	2010	2009	2008
Income/(loss) from continuing operations (GAAP)	$ (985)	$ (152)	$ 378	$ 249	$ 567
Diluted EPS from continuing operations (GAAP)	$(4.49)	$(0.70)	$1.59	$1.07	$2.54
Add: markdowns—inventory strategy alignment, net of tax of $60, $-, $-, $- and $-	95	—	—	—	—
Add: restructuring and management transition charges, net of tax of $116, $145, $12, $- and $-	182	306	20	—	—
Add/(deduct): primary pension plan expense/(income), net of tax of $122, $34, $86, $114, and $(50)	193	53	135	184	(83)
Less: Net gain on sale or redemption of non-operating assets, net of tax of $(146), $-, $-, $- and $-	(251)	—	—	—	—
Adjusted income/(loss) from continuing operations (non-GAAP)	$ (766)	$ 207	$ 533	$ 433	$ 484
Adjusted diluted EPS from continuing operations (non-GAAP)	$(3.49)	$ 0.94[1]	$2.24	$1.86	$2.17

[1] Weighted average shares—diluted of 220.7 million was used for this calculation as 2011 adjusted income from continuing operations was positive. 3.3 million shares were added to weighted average shares—basic of 217.4 million for assumed dilution for stock options, restricted stock awards and stock warrant.

Free Cash Flow

Free cash flow is a key financial measure of our ability to generate additional cash from operating our business and in evaluating our financial performance. We define free cash flow as cash flow from operating activities, less capital expenditures and dividends paid, plus the proceeds from the sale of operating assets. Free cash flow is a relevant indicator of our ability to repay maturing debt, revise our dividend policy or fund other uses of capital that we believe will enhance stockholder value. Free cash flow is considered a non-GAAP financial measure under the rules of the SEC. Free cash flow is limited and does not represent remaining cash flow available for discretionary expenditures due to the fact that the measure does not deduct payments required for debt maturities, pay-down of off-balance sheet pension debt, and other obligations or payments made for business acquisitions. Therefore, it is important to view free cash flow in addition to, rather than as a substitute for, our entire statement of cash flows and those measures prepared in accordance with GAAP.

The following table reconciles net cash provided by /(used in) operating activities, the most directly comparable GAAP measure, to free cash flow, a non-GAAP financial measure.

($ in millions)	2012	2011	2010	2009	2008
Net cash provided by/(used in) operating activities (GAAP)	$ (10)	$820	$592	$1,573	$1,156
Less:					
Capital expenditures	(810)	(634)	(499)	(600)	(969)
Dividends paid, common stock	(86)	(178)	(189)	(183)	(178)
Tax benefit from pension contribution	—	—	(152)	(126)[1]	—
Plus:					
Discretionary cash pension contribution	—	—	392	—	—
Proceeds from sale of operating assets	—	15	14	13	13
Free cash flow (non-GAAP)	$(906)	$ 23	$158	$ 677	$ 22

[1] Related to the discretionary contribution of $340 million of Company common stock in 2009.

FORWARD-LOOKING INFORMATION

1.19 CITIGROUP INC. (DEC)
FORWARD-LOOKING STATEMENTS

Certain statements in this Form 10-K, including but not limited to statements included within the Management's Discussion and Analysis of Financial Condition and Results of Operations, are "forward-looking statements" within the meaning of the U.S. Private Securities Litigation Reform Act of 1995. In addition, Citigroup also may make forward-looking statements in its other documents filed or furnished with the SEC, and its management may make forward-looking statements orally to analysts, investors, representatives of the media and others.

Generally, forward-looking statements are not based on historical facts but instead represent Citigroup's and its management's beliefs regarding future events. Such statements may be identified by words such as *believe, expect, anticipate, intend, estimate, may increase, may fluctuate*, and similar expressions, or future or conditional verbs such as *will, should, would* and *could*.

Such statements are based on management's current expectations and are subject to risks, uncertainties and changes in circumstances. Actual results and capital and other financial conditions may differ materially from those included in these statements due to a variety of factors, including without limitation the precautionary statements included throughout this Form 10-K and the risks and uncertainties listed and described under "Risk Factors" above and summarized below:
- regulatory changes and uncertainties faced by Citi in the U.S. and non-U.S. jurisdictions in which it operates and the potential impact these changes and uncertainties could have on Citi's business planning, compliance risks and costs and overall results of operations;
- continued uncertainty arising from numerous aspects of the regulatory capital requirements applicable to Citi, including Citi's continued implementation of the final U.S. Basel III rules and the ongoing regulatory review of Citi's risk models, and the potential impact these uncertainties could have on Citi's ability to meet its capital requirements as it projects or as required;
- the potential impact of U.S. and international derivatives regulation on Citi's competitiveness, compliance costs and regulatory and reputational risks and results of operations;
- ongoing implementation of proprietary trading restrictions under the "Volcker Rule" and similar international proposals and the potential impact of these reforms on Citi's global market-making businesses, results of operations and compliance risks and costs;
- the potential impact to Citi's businesses and capital and funding structure as a result of regulatory requirements in the U.S. and in non-U.S. jurisdictions to facilitate the future orderly resolution of large financial institutions;
- additional regulations with respect to securitizations and the potential impact to Citi and its businesses;
- continued uncertainty relating to the sustainability and pace of economic recovery and growth in the U.S. and globally and the potential impact fiscal and monetary actions taken by U.S. and non-U.S. authorities may have on economic recovery and growth, global trading markets, and the emerging markets, as well as Citi's businesses and results of operations;
- any significant global economic downturn or disruption, including a significant decline in global trade volumes, on Citi's businesses, results of operations and financial condition, particularly as compared to Citi's competitors;
- uncertainty arising from the level of U.S. government debt or a potential U.S. government default or downgrade of the U.S. government credit rating on Citi's businesses, results of operations, capital, funding and liquidity;
- risks arising from Citi's extensive operations outside of the U.S., including in the emerging markets, including foreign exchange controls, limitations on foreign investments, sociopolitical instability, fraud, nationalization, closure of branches or subsidiaries and confiscation of assets, as well as increased compliance and regulatory risks and costs;
- ongoing economic and fiscal issues in the Eurozone and the potential outcomes that could occur, including the exit of one or more countries from the European Monetary Union and any resulting redenomination/revaluation, and the potential impact, directly or indirectly, on Citi's businesses, results of operations or financial condition;

- uncertainty regarding the future quantitative liquidity requirements applicable to Citi and the potential impact these requirements could have on Citi's liquidity ratios, planning, management and funding;
- potential impacts on Citi's liquidity and/or costs of funding as a result of external factors, such as market disruptions, governmental fiscal and monetary policies and changes in Citi's credit spreads;
- reductions in Citi's or its more significant subsidiaries' credit ratings and the potential impact on Citi's funding and liquidity, as well as the results of operations for certain of its businesses;
- the potential impact on Citi's businesses, business practices, reputation, financial condition or results of operations from the extensive legal and regulatory proceedings, investigations and inquiries to which Citi is subject, including those related to Citi's U.S. mortgage-related activities, Citi's contribution to, or trading in products linked to, various rates or benchmarks, and its anti-money laundering programs;
- the potential impact to Citi's delinquency rates, loan loss reserves and net credit losses as Citi's revolving home equity lines of credit begin to "reset";
- results from the Comprehensive Capital Analysis and Review (CCAR) process and evolving supervisory stress tests and the potential impacts on Citi's ability to return capital to shareholders and market perceptions of Citi;
- Citi's ability to successfully execute on and achieve its ongoing execution priorities and the potential impact its inability to do so could have on the achievement of its 2015 financial targets;
- Citi's ability to utilize its deferred tax assets (DTAs), including the foreign tax credit components of its DTAs, and thus utilize the regulatory capital supporting its DTAs for more productive purposes;
- the potential impact on the value of Citi's DTAs if corporate tax rates in the U.S. or certain state or foreign jurisdictions decline, or if other changes are made to the U.S. tax system, such as changes to the tax treatment of foreign business income;
- the possibility that Citi's interpretation or application of the extensive tax laws to which it is subject, such as with respect to withholding tax obligations and stamp and other transactional taxes, could differ from that of the relevant governmental taxing authorities;
- Citi's failure to maintain its contractual relationships with various third-party retailers and merchants within its U.S. credit card businesses in *NA RCB*, and the potential impact any such failure could have on the results of operations or financial condition of those businesses;
- the potential impact to Citi from continually evolving cybersecurity and other technological risks and attacks, including additional costs, reputational damage, regulatory penalties and financial losses;
- the potential impact on Citi's performance, including its competitive position and ability to execute its strategy, if Citi is unable to hire or retain qualified employees;
- incorrect assumptions or estimates in Citi's financial statements, and the potential impact of regulatory changes to financial accounting and reporting standards on how Citi records and reports its financial condition and results of operations;
- changes in the administration of or method for determining LIBOR on the value of any LIBOR-linked securities and other financial obligations held or issued by Citi; and
- the effectiveness of Citi's risk management and mitigation processes and strategies, including the effectiveness of its risk models.

Any forward-looking statements made by or on behalf of Citigroup speak only as to the date they are made, and Citi does not undertake to update forward-looking statements to reflect the impact of circumstances or events that arise after the date the forward-looking statements were made.

LIQUIDITY AND CAPITAL RESOURCES

1.20 AMERICAN GREETINGS CORPORATION (FEB)
MANAGEMENT'S DISCUSSION AND ANALYSIS OF FINANCIAL CONDITION AND RESULTS OF OPERATIONS (in part)

Liquidity and Capital Resources

Operating Activities

During the year, cash flow from operating activities provided cash of $162.8 million compared to $123.8 million in 2012, an increase of $39.0 million. Cash flow from operating activities for 2012 compared to 2011 resulted in a decrease of $59.4 million from $183.2 million in 2011.

Accounts receivable, net of the effect of acquisitions and dispositions, was a use of cash of $9.8 million in 2013 compared to a source of cash of $4.5 million in 2012 and a source of cash of $11.5 million in 2011. As a percentage of the prior twelve months' net sales, net accounts receivable was 5.7% at February 28, 2013 compared to 6.8% at February 29, 2012. The year-over-year fluctuations are primarily due to the timing of collections from, or credits issued to, certain customers occurring in a different pattern in the current period compared to the prior periods.

Inventories, net of the effect of acquisitions and dispositions, were a use of cash of $31.6 million in 2013 compared to a use of cash of $23.3 million in 2012 and a use of cash of $13.1 million in 2011. The use of cash in the current year was driven primarily by our new Retail Operations segment that grew inventory by approximately $27 million since its acquisition in June 2012. The use of cash in 2012 and 2011 was primarily due to the inventory build of cards associated with expanded distribution.

Other current assets, net of the effect of acquisitions and dispositions, were a use of cash of $23.4 million during 2013, compared to a source of cash of $7.0 million in 2012 and a use of cash of $2.1 million in 2011. The use of cash in the current year was driven primarily by prepaid rents within our new Retail Operations segment that was not present in prior years. The source of cash in 2012 compared to the use of cash in 2011 was primarily due to the use of trust assets to pay medical claim expenses as we terminated the active employees' medical trust fund as of February 29, 2012.

Deferred costs—net generally represents payments under agreements with retailers net of the related amortization of those payments. During 2013, amortization exceeded payments by $27.1 million. During 2012, payments exceeded amortization by $31.3 million. In 2011, amortization exceeded payments by $14.3 million. See Note 10, "Deferred Costs," to the Consolidated Financial Statements under Part II, Item 8 of this Annual Report for further detail of deferred costs related to customer agreements.

Accounts payable and other liabilities, net of the effect of acquisitions and dispositions, were a source of cash of $58.6 million in 2013, compared to uses of cash of $13.6 million in 2012 and $31.0 million in 2011. The growth in accounts payable and other liabilities, and thus an increase in cash flow in the current period, was primarily due to our new Retail Operations segment as well as activities related to our information technology systems refresh project and other strategic projects.

Investing Activities

Investing activities used $163.2 million of cash in 2013 compared to $70.3 million of cash used in 2012 and $4.8 million of cash provided in 2011. The use of cash in the current year was primarily related to cash outlays of $114.1 million associated with capital expenditures. The increase in capital expenditures compared to the prior year related primarily to assets acquired in connection with our information technology systems refresh project and investments in our new Retail Operations segment. In addition, during the first quarter of 2013 we paid $56.6 million of cash to acquire all of the outstanding senior secured debt of Clinton Cards.

The use of cash during 2012 was primarily related to cash payments for capital expenditures of $78.2 million as well as business acquisitions of $5.9 million. The increase in capital expenditures compared to the 2011 period related primarily to assets acquired in connection with our information technology systems refresh project and our new world headquarters project, as well as machinery and equipment purchased for our card-producing facilities. During 2012, cash paid for the Watermark acquisition, net of cash acquired, was $5.9 million. Partially offsetting these uses of cash in 2012 were cash receipts of $6.0 million from the sale of the land and building related to our DesignWare party goods product lines in our North American Social Expression Products segment, $4.5 million from the sale of certain minor characters in our intellectual properties portfolio and approximately $2.4 million from the sale of the land, building and certain equipment associated with a distribution facility in our International Social Expression Products segment.

The source of cash during 2011 included $25.2 million received from the sale of certain assets, equipment and processes of the DesignWare party goods product lines, which occurred in the fourth quarter of 2010. The 2011 results also included a $5.7 million return of capital related to our investment in Party City. In addition, we received approximately $12 million related to the sale of the land and buildings associated with the closure of our Mexican facility and a manufacturing facility within the International Social Expression Products segment during 2011. Partially offsetting these sources of cash in 2011 were cash payments for capital expenditures of $39.8 million.

Financing Activities

Financing activities used $42.0 million of cash during 2013 compared to $136.9 million in 2012 and $117.2 million in 2011. The current year use of cash primarily related to share repurchases and dividend payments. We paid $81.0 million to repurchase approximately 5.3 million Class A common shares under our repurchase programs during the current year, which includes $2.2 million of cash settlements related to the repurchase of approximately 0.1 million Class A common shares that were initiated during 2012. In addition, we paid cash dividends of $19.9 million during 2013. Partially offsetting these uses of cash, were borrowings under our credit agreement, which provided $61.2 million of cash during the current year.

The 2012 use of cash primarily related to the tender offers and redemption of our 7.375% senior notes due 2016 of $222.0 million, our 7.375% notes due 2016 of $32.7 million and a charge of $9.1 million for the consent payments, tender fees, call premium and other fees associated with these transactions. Share repurchases and dividend payments also contributed to the use of the cash in 2012. We paid $72.4

million to repurchase approximately 4.4 million Class A common shares under our repurchase program and $10.1 million to purchase approximately 0.4 million Class B common shares in accordance with our Amended and Restated Articles of Incorporation. Repurchases of $2.2 million for approximately 0.1 million Class A common shares initiated at the end of 2012 were not included in the above repurchase amount in the Consolidated Statement of Cash Flows because the cash settlement for these transactions did not occur until 2013. However, this $2.2 million was included in the shares repurchased amount within our Consolidated Statement of Shareholders' Equity under Part II, Item 8 of this Annual Report. In addition, we paid cash dividends of $23.9 million during 2012. Partially offsetting these uses of cash was a cash receipt of $225.0 million from the issuance of the 7.375% senior notes due 2021. Refer to Note 11, "Debt," to the Consolidated Financial Statements under Part II, Item 8 of this Annual Report for further information. Also, proceeds from the exercise of stock options and tax benefits from share-based payment awards provided $13.6 million of cash during 2012.

The use of cash in 2011 related primarily to the repayment of the term loan under our senior secured credit facility in the amount of $99.3 million as well as share repurchases and dividend payments. During 2011, we paid $13.5 million to repurchase approximately 0.5 million Class B common shares in accordance with our Amended and Restated Articles of Incorporation and paid dividends of $22.4 million. Partially offsetting these uses of cash were proceeds from the exercise of stock options and tax benefits from share-based payment awards, which provided $21.1 million of cash during 2011.

Credit Sources

Substantial credit sources are available to us. In total, we had available sources of approximately $450 million at February 28, 2013, which included our $400 million senior secured credit facility and our $50 million accounts receivable securitization facility. Borrowings under the accounts receivable securitization facility are limited based on our eligible receivables outstanding. At February 28, 2013, we had $61.2 million of borrowings under the senior secured credit facility and no borrowings outstanding under the accounts receivable securitization facility. As of February 28, 2013, we had an aggregate of $27.5 million outstanding under letters of credit, which reduced total availability under our credit sources.

Credit Facility

We are a party to a $400 million senior secured credit agreement (the "Credit Agreement"), under which there were $61.2 million of borrowings outstanding as of February 28, 2013. Under the original terms of the Credit Agreement, we were permitted to borrow, on a revolving basis, up to $350 million (with an ability to increase this amount by $50 million to $400 million) during a five year term from June 11, 2010 through June 11, 2015. On January 18, 2012, we amended our Credit Agreement, to, among other things, extend the expiration date of the Credit Agreement from June 11, 2015 to January 18, 2017, and increase the maximum principal amount that can be borrowed, on a revolving basis, from $350 million to $400 million, with the continued ability to further increase such maximum principal amount from $400 million to $450 million, subject to customary conditions.

The amendment also:
- decreased the applicable margin paid on United States dollar loans bearing interest based on the London Inter-Bank Offer Rate ("LIBOR") and Canadian dollar loans bearing interest based on the Canadian Dollar Offer Rate, from a range of 2.25% to 3.50% per year to a range of 1.25% to 2.25%;
- decreased the applicable margin paid on United States dollar loans bearing interest based on the United States base rate and the Canadian base rate from a range of 1.25% to 2.50% per year to a range of 0.25% to 1.25%; and
- reduced commitment fees paid on the unused portion of the revolving credit facility from a range of 0.375% to 0.500% per annum to a range of 0.250% to 0.400%.

On December 19, 2012, we further amended the Credit Agreement to modify the definition of EBITDA to permit, as of February 28, 2013, certain add-backs for specific non-recurring expenses associated with the Clinton Cards acquisition.

The obligations under our Credit Agreement are guaranteed by our material domestic subsidiaries and are secured by substantially all of our personal property and each of our material domestic subsidiaries, including a pledge of all of the capital stock in substantially all of our domestic subsidiaries and 65% of the capital stock of our first tier international subsidiaries.

The Credit Agreement also contains certain restrictive covenants that are customary for similar credit arrangements. For example, the Credit Agreement contains covenants relating to financial reporting and notification, compliance with laws, preserving existence, maintenance of books and records, how we may use proceeds from borrowings, and maintenance of properties and insurance. In addition, the Credit Agreement includes covenants that limit our ability to incur additional debt; declare or pay dividends; make distributions on or repurchase or redeem capital stock; make certain investments; enter into transactions with affiliates; grant or permit liens; sell assets; enter into sale and leaseback transactions; and consolidate, merge or sell all or substantially all of our assets. There are also financial performance covenants that require us to maintain a maximum leverage ratio and a minimum interest coverage ratio. The Credit Agreement also requires us to make certain mandatory prepayments of outstanding indebtedness using the net cash proceeds received from certain dispositions, events of loss and additional indebtedness that we may incur from time to time. These restrictions are subject to customary baskets.

Accounts Receivable Facility

We are also a party to an accounts receivable facility that provides funding of up to $50 million, under which there were no borrowings outstanding as of February 28,2014;however, outstanding letters of credit issued under the accounts receivable program totaled $27.5 million as of February 28, 2013, which reduced the total credit availability thereunder. Until the facility was amended on September 21, 2012, our accounts receivable facility provided funding of up to $70 million. Also, on September 21, 2012, the liquidity commitments under the accounts receivable facility were renewed for an additional year and the facility's term was extended an additional three years from September 21, 2012 to October 1, 2015.

Under the terms of the accounts receivable facility, we sell accounts receivable to AGC Funding Corporation (our wholly-owned, consolidated subsidiary), which in turn sells undivided interests in eligible accounts receivable to third party financial institutions as part of a process that provides us funding similar to a revolving credit facility.

The interest rate under the accounts receivable securitization facility is based on (i) commercial paper interest rates, (ii) LIBOR rates plus an applicable margin or (iii) a rate that is the higher of the prime rate as announced by the applicable purchaser financial institution or the federal funds rate plus 0.50%. We pay an annual commitment fee that ranges from 35 to 45 basis points on the unfunded portion of the accounts receivable securitization facility, based on the level of utilization, together with customary administrative fees on letters of credit that have been issued and on outstanding amounts funded under the facility. Funding under the facility may be used for working capital, general corporate purposes and the issuance of letters of credit.

The accounts receivable facility contains representations, warranties, covenants and indemnities customary for facilities of this type, including our obligation to maintain the same consolidated leverage ratio as is required to be maintained under our Credit Agreement.

7.375% Senior Notes Due 2021

On November 30, 2011, we closed a public offering of $225 million aggregate principal amount of 7.375% senior notes due 2021 (the "2021 Senior Notes"). The net proceeds from this offering were used to finance the cash tender offers for all the existing 7.375% senior notes and notes due 2016 which include the original $200.0 million of 7.375% senior notes issued on May 24, 2006 (the "Original Senior Notes"), the additional $22.0 million of 7.375% senior notes issued on February 24, 2009 (the "Additional Senior Notes," together with the Original Senior Notes, the "2016 Senior Notes") and the $32.7 million of 7.375% notes issued on February 24, 2009 (the "2016 Notes," together with the 2016 Senior Notes, the "Notes"). The cash tenders were commenced on November 15, 2011, where, in the fourth quarter of 2012, we purchased $180.4 million and $24.5 million aggregate principal amount of 2016 Senior Notes and 2016 Notes, respectively, representing approximately 81% and 75% of the aggregate principal amount of the outstanding 2016 Senior Notes and 2016 Notes, respectively. On December 15, 2011, we redeemed the remaining $49.8 million of the Notes that were not repurchased pursuant to the tender offers. In connection with these transactions, we wrote off the remaining unamortized discount and deferred financing costs related to the Notes, totaling $21.7 million, as well as recorded a charge of $9.1 million for the consent payments, tender fees, call premium and other fees incurred in connection with these transactions.

The 2021 Senior Notes will mature on December 1, 2021 and bear interest at a fixed rate of 7.375% per year. The 2021 Senior Notes constitute our general unsecured senior obligations. The 2021 Senior Notes rank senior in right of payment to all our future obligations that are, by their terms, expressly subordinated in right of payment to the 2021 Senior Notes and pari passu in right of payment with all our existing and future unsecured obligations that are not so subordinated. The 2021 Senior Notes are effectively subordinated to our secured indebtedness, including borrowings under our revolving credit facility described above, to the extent of the value of the assets securing such indebtedness. The 2021 Senior Notes also contain certain restrictive covenants that are customary for similar credit arrangements, including covenants that limit our ability to incur additional debt; declare or pay dividends; make distributions on or repurchase or redeem capital stock; make certain investments; enter into transactions with affiliates; grant or permit liens; sell assets; enter into sale and leaseback transactions; and consolidate, merge or sell all or substantially all of our assets. These restrictions are subject to customary baskets and financial covenant tests. We anticipate that if the Merger is consummated as contemplated by the Merger Agreement, the 2021 Senior Notes will remain outstanding.

The total fair value of our publicly traded debt, based on quoted market prices, was $233.6 million (at a carrying value of $225.2 million) and $239.6 million (at a carrying value of $225.2 million) at February 28, 2013 and February 29, 2012, respectively.

At February 28, 2013, the Corporation was in compliance with the financial covenants under its borrowing agreements, as amended.

Capital Deployment and Investments

Throughout fiscal 2014 and thereafter, we will continue to consider all options for capital deployment including growth options, acquisitions and other investments in third parties, expanding customer relationships, expenditures or investments related to our current product leadership initiatives or other future strategic initiatives, capital expenditures, the information technology systems refresh project, our new world headquarters project and, as appropriate, preserving cash.

As we have stated, our objective is to continue to expand our position as a leading creator, manufacturer and distributor of social expression products. As such, we have and expect to continue to focus resources on our core greeting card business, developing new, and growing existing, business, including by expanding Internet and other channels of electronic distribution to make American Greetings the natural and preferred social expressions solution, as well as by capturing any shifts in consumer demand. As a continuation of 2012, we increased our year-over-year marketing spend by approximately $7 million in 2013. This incremental spending was in support of our product leadership strategy, primarily related to promotional efforts related to our Web site Cardstore.com and other marketing initiatives within our North American Social Expression Products segment. As we seek to develop Cardstore.com and other channels of distribution, we expect that we will continue to make investments to support these efforts; however, the timing and amount are difficult to estimate. In addition, to the extent we are successful in expanding distribution and revenue in connection with expanding our leadership, additional capital may be deployed as we may incur incremental costs associated with this expanded distribution, including upfront costs prior to any incremental revenue being generated. If incurred, these costs may be material.

Over roughly the next five or six years, we expect to allocate resources, including capital, to refresh our information technology systems by modernizing our systems, redesigning and deploying new processes, and evolving new organization structures, all of which are intended to drive efficiencies within the business and add new capabilities. Amounts that we spend could be material in any fiscal year and over the life of the project. During 2013, we spent approximately $59 million, including capital of approximately $50 million and expense of approximately $9 million, on these information technology systems. The total amount spent through fiscal 2013 on this project was approximately $84 million. Including the amount that has already been spent, we currently expect to spend at least an aggregate of $150 million on these information technology systems over the life of the project, the majority of which we expect will be capital expenditures. We believe these investments are important to our business, help us drive further efficiencies and add new capabilities; however, there can be no assurance that we will not spend more or less than $150 million over the life of the project, or that we will achieve the anticipated efficiencies or any cost savings.

During March 2011, we also announced that in fiscal 2012 we expected that we would begin to invest in the development of a world headquarters in the Northeast Ohio area. The state of Ohio has committed certain tax credits, loans and other incentives totaling up to $93.5 million to assist us in the development of a new headquarters in Ohio. We are required to make certain investments and meet other criteria to receive these incentives over time. Although the project to build a new world headquarters is currently on hold, based on preliminary estimates, the gross costs associated with a new world headquarters building, before any tax credit, loans or other incentives that we may receive, will be between approximately $150 million and $200 million over a number of years following our resumption of the project.

During 2013, we repurchased $47.1 million of our Class A common shares, representing the remaining amount authorized under the $75 million stock repurchase authorized by our Board of Directors in January 2012. Also, during 2013, we repurchased $31.6 million of our Class A common shares under the $75 million stock repurchase program announced on July 24, 2012. Under this program, the share repurchases may be made through open market purchases or privately negotiated transactions as market conditions warrant, at prices we deem appropriate, and subject to applicable legal requirements and other factors. There is no set expiration date for this program. However, purchases under this stock repurchase program were suspended due to the Going Private Proposal referred to in Note 19, "Proposal by Members of the Weiss Family and Related Entities to Acquire the Corporation," to the Consolidated Financial Statements under Part II, Item 8 of this Annual Report.

Our future operating cash flow and borrowing availability under our credit agreement and our accounts receivable securitization facility are expected to meet currently anticipated funding requirements. The seasonal nature of our business results in peak working capital requirements that may be financed through short-term borrowings when cash on hand is insufficient.

Contractual Obligations

The following table presents our contractual obligations and commitments to make future payments as of February 28, 2013:

| (Dollars in thousands) | Payment Due by Period as of February 28, 2013 | | | | | | |
	2014	2015	2016	2017	2018	Thereafter	Total
Long-term debt	$ —	$ —	$ —	$ 61,200	$ —	$225,181	$286,381
Operating leases[(1)]	52,349	48,736	44,056	39,303	32,187	75,361	291,992
Commitments under customer agreements	61,282	48,940	42,678	185	350	—	153,435
Commitments under royalty agreements	7,151	6,745	10,118	2,980	2,880	—	29,874
Interest payments	18,975	17,702	17,702	17,702	16,605	66,491	155,177
Severance	5,435	594	—	—	—	—	6,029
Commitments under purchase agreements	4,500	1,996	—	—	—	—	6,496
	$149,692	$124,713	$114,554	$121,370	$52,022	$367,033	$929,384

(1) Approximately $12 million of the operating lease commitments in the table above relate to retail stores acquired by Schurman that are being subleased to Schurman. The failure of Schurman to operate the retail stores successfully could have a material adverse effect on us because if Schurman is not able to comply with its obligations under the subleases, we remain contractually obligated, as primary lessee, under those leases. Also, we are currently negotiating lease terms with a number of landlords related to the Clinton Cards acquisition. As of February 28, 2013, we have completed 295 lease assignments. The estimated future minimum rental payments for noncancelable operating leases related to these lease assignments are approximately $255 million. In addition, assuming that the remaining landlords consent to terms proposed by us and we are able to successfully complete assignments for all of the approximately 400 stores, the estimated future minimum rental payments for noncancelable operating leases will be approximately $105 million higher, resulting in a total estimated future minimum rental payments for noncancelable operating leases of approximately $360 million related to acquired stores. Subsequent to year-end, we have completed an additional 62 lease assignments. As such, the total number of lease assignments was 357 as of April 24, 2013. The negotiations with landlords are expected to take approximately twelve months from the closing of the transaction on June 6, 2012.

The interest payments in the above table are determined assuming the same level of debt outstanding in the future years as was outstanding at February 28, 2013 under our credit agreement and accounts receivable facility at the current average interest rates for those facilities.

In addition to the contracts noted in the table, we issue purchase orders for products, materials and supplies used in the ordinary course of business. These purchase orders typically do not include long-term volume commitments, are based on pricing terms previously negotiated with vendors and are generally cancelable with the appropriate notice prior to receipt of the materials or supplies. Accordingly, the foregoing table excludes open purchase orders for such products, materials and supplies as of February 28, 2013. Also, we provide credit support to Schurman through a liquidity guaranty of up to $10 million in favor of the lenders under Schurman's senior revolving credit facility as described in Note 1 to the Consolidated Financial Statements under Part II, Item 8 of this Annual Report, which are not included in the table as no amounts have been drawn and therefore we cannot determine the amount of usage in the future.

Although we do not anticipate that contributions will be required in 2014 to the defined benefit pension plan that we assumed in connection with our acquisition of Gibson Greetings, Inc. in 2001, we may make contributions in excess of the legally required minimum contribution level. Refer to Note 12 to the Consolidated Financial Statements under Part II, Item 8 of this Annual Report. We do anticipate that contributions will be required beginning in fiscal 2015, but those amounts have not been determined as of February 28, 2013.

NEW ACCOUNTING STANDARDS

1.21 PACCAR INC (DEC)
NOTES TO CONSOLIDATED FINANCIAL STATEMENTS (in part)

A. Significant Accounting Policies (in part)

New Accounting Pronouncements: In July 2013, the Financial Accounting Standards Board (FASB) issued Accounting Standards Update (ASU) 2013-11, *Presentation of an Unrecognized Tax Benefit When a Net Operating Loss Carryforward, a Similar Tax Loss, or a Tax Credit Carryforward Exists*. This ASU requires an unrecognized tax benefit, or a portion of an unrecognized tax benefit, to be presented in the consolidated financial statements as a reduction to a deferred tax asset for a net operating loss carryforward, a similar tax loss, or a tax credit carryforward if available under the applicable tax jurisdiction. The ASU is effective for annual periods beginning after December 15, 2013 and interim periods within those annual periods. The Company does not expect the adoption of the ASU to have a material impact on its consolidated financial statements.

In July 2013, the FASB issued ASU 2013-10, *Inclusion of the Fed Funds Effective Swap Rate (or Overnight Index Swap Rate) as a Benchmark Interest Rate for Hedge Accounting Purposes*. The amendments in this ASU permit the Fed Funds Effective Swap Rate (OIS) to be used as a U.S. benchmark interest rate for hedge accounting purposes in addition to U.S. government and London Interbank Offered Rate. The amendments also remove the restriction on using different benchmark rates for similar hedges. The ASU is effective for qualifying new or redesignated hedging relationships entered on or after July 17, 2013. The Company adopted ASU 2013-10 in the third quarter of 2014; the implementation of this amendment did not have an impact on the Company's consolidated financial statements.

In February 2013, the FASB issued ASU 2013-02, *Reporting of Amounts Reclassified Out of Accumulated Other Comprehensive Income*. This ASU requires disclosure of additional information about reclassification adjustments from other comprehensive income. The ASU is effective for annual periods beginning on or after January 1, 2013 and interim periods within those annual periods. The Company adopted ASU 2013-02 in the first quarter of2014;the implementation of this amendment resulted in additional disclosures (see Note N), but did not have an impact on the Company's consolidated financial statements.

In January 2013, the FASB issued ASU 2013-01, *Clarifying the Scope of Disclosures about Offsetting Assets and Liabilities*, an update to ASU 2011-11, *Disclosures about Offsetting Assets and Liabilities*. The ASUs require entities with derivatives, repurchase agreements and securities borrowing and lending transactions that are either offset on the balance sheet, or subject to a master netting arrangement, to provide expanded disclosures about the nature of the rights of offset. The updated ASU is effective for annual periods beginning on or after January 1, 2013 and interim periods within those annual periods. The Company adopted ASU 2013-01 in the first quarter of 2013; the implementation of this amendment resulted in additional disclosures (see Note O), but did not have an impact on the Company's consolidated financial statements.

MARKET RISK INFORMATION

1.22 BB&T CORPORATION (DEC)
MANAGEMENT'S DISCUSSION AND ANALYSIS OF FINANCIAL CONDITION AND RESULTS OF OPERATIONS (in part)

Market Risk Management

The effective management of market risk is essential to achieving BB&T's strategic financial objectives. As a financial institution, BB&T's most significant market risk exposure is interest rate risk in its balance sheet; however, market risk also includes product liquidity risk, price risk and volatility risk in BB&T's LOBs. The primary objectives of market risk management are to minimize any adverse effect that changes in market risk factors may have on net interest income, net income and capital and to offset the risk of price changes for certain assets recorded at fair value. At BB&T, market risk management also includes the enterprise-wide IPV function.

Interest Rate Market Risk (Other than Trading)

BB&T actively manages market risk associated with asset and liability portfolios with a focus on the strategic pricing of asset and liability accounts and management of appropriate maturity mixes of assets and liabilities. The goal of these activities is the development of appropriate maturity and repricing opportunities in BB&T's portfolios of assets and liabilities that will produce reasonably consistent net interest income during periods of changing interest rates. These portfolios are analyzed for proper fixed-rate and variable-rate mixes under various interest rate scenarios.

The asset/liability management process is designed to achieve relatively stable NIM and assure liquidity by coordinating the volumes, maturities or repricing opportunities of earning assets, deposits and borrowed funds. Among other things, this process gives consideration to prepayment trends related to securities, loans and leases and certain deposits that have no stated maturity. Prepayment assumptions are developed using a combination of market data and internal historical prepayment experience for residential mortgage-related loans and securities, and internal historical prepayment experience for client deposits with no stated maturity and loans that are not residential mortgage related. These assumptions are subject to monthly back-testing, and are adjusted as deemed necessary to reflect changes in interest rates relative to the reference rate of the underlying assets or liabilities. On a monthly basis, BB&T evaluates the accuracy of its Simulation model, which includes an evaluation of its prepayment assumptions, to ensure that all significant assumptions inherent in the model appropriately reflect changes in the interest rate environment and related trends in prepayment activity. It is the responsibility of the MRLCC to determine and achieve the most appropriate volume and mix of earning assets and interest-bearing liabilities, as well as to ensure an adequate level of liquidity and capital, within the context of corporate performance goals. The MRLCC also sets policy guidelines and establishes long-term strategies with respect to interest rate risk exposure and liquidity. The MRLCC meets regularly to review BB&T's interest rate risk and liquidity positions in relation to present and prospective market and business conditions, and adopts funding and balance sheet management strategies that are intended to ensure that the potential impacts on earnings and liquidity as a result of fluctuations in interest rates are within acceptable tolerance guidelines.

BB&T uses derivatives primarily to manage economic risk related to securities, commercial loans, MSRs and mortgage banking operations, long-term debt and other funding sources. BB&T also uses derivatives to facilitate transactions on behalf of its clients. As of December 31, 2013, BB&T had derivative financial instruments outstanding with notional amounts totaling $59.3 billion, with a net fair value of a loss of $106 million. See Note 18 "Derivative Financial Instruments" in the "Notes to Consolidated Financial Statements" herein for additional disclosures.

The majority of BB&T's assets and liabilities are monetary in nature and, therefore, differ greatly from most commercial and industrial companies that have significant investments in fixed assets or inventories. Fluctuations in interest rates and actions of the FRB to regulate the availability and cost of credit have a greater effect on a financial institution's profitability than do the effects of higher costs for goods and services. Through its balance sheet management function, which is monitored by the MRLCC, management believes that BB&T is positioned to respond to changing needs for liquidity, changes in interest rates and inflationary trends.

Management uses the Simulation to measure the sensitivity of projected earnings to changes in interest rates. The Simulation model projects net interest income and interest rate risk for a rolling two-year period of time. The Simulation takes into account the current contractual agreements that BB&T has made with its customers on deposits, borrowings, loans, investments and commitments to enter into those transactions. Furthermore, the Simulation considers the impact of expected customer behavior. Management monitors BB&T's interest sensitivity by means of a model that incorporates the current volumes, average rates earned and paid, and scheduled maturities and payments of asset and liability portfolios, together with multiple scenarios that include projected prepayments, repricing opportunities and anticipated volume growth. Using this information, the model projects earnings based on projected portfolio balances under multiple interest rate scenarios. This level of detail is needed to simulate the effect that changes in interest rates and portfolio balances may have on the earnings of BB&T. This method is subject to the accuracy of the assumptions that underlie the process, but management believes that it provides a better illustration of the sensitivity of earnings to changes in interest rates than other analyses such as static or dynamic gap. In addition to the Simulation, BB&T uses EVE analysis to focus on projected changes in capital given potential changes in interest rates. This measure also allows BB&T to analyze interest rate risk that falls outside the analysis window contained in the Simulation model. The EVE model is a discounted cash flow of the portfolio of assets, liabilities, and derivative instruments. The difference in the present value of assets minus the present value of liabilities is defined as the economic value of equity.

The asset/liability management process requires a number of key assumptions. Management determines the most likely outlook for the economy and interest rates by analyzing external factors, including published economic projections and data, the effects of likely monetary and fiscal policies, as well as any enacted or prospective regulatory changes. BB&T's current and prospective liquidity position, current balance sheet volumes and projected growth, accessibility of funds for short-term needs and capital maintenance are also considered. This data is combined with various interest rate scenarios to provide management with the information necessary to analyze interest sensitivity and to aid in the development of strategies to reach performance goals.

The following table shows the effect that the indicated changes in interest rates would have on net interest income as projected for the next twelve months assuming a gradual change in interest rates as described below. Key assumptions in the preparation of the table include prepayment speeds of mortgage-related and other assets, cash flows and maturities of derivative financial instruments, loan volumes and pricing, deposit sensitivity, customer preferences and capital plans. The resulting change in net interest income reflects the level of sensitivity that interest sensitive income has in relation to changing interest rates.

Table 31
Interest Sensitivity Simulation Analysis

Linear Change in Prime Rate	Interest Rate Scenario Prime Rate December 31,		Annualized Hypothetical Percentage Change in Net Interest Income December 31,	
	2013	2012	2013	2012
Up 200 bps	5.25%	5.25%	2.27%	3.16%
Up 100	4.25	4.25	1.35	2.04
No Change	3.25	3.25	—	—
Down 25	3.00	3.00	0.39	(0.13)

The MRLCC has established parameters related to interest sensitivity that prescribe a maximum negative impact on net interest income under different interest rate scenarios. In the event the results of the Simulation model fall outside the established parameters, management will make recommendations to the MRLCC on the most appropriate response given the current economic forecast. The following parameters and interest rate scenarios are considered BB&T's primary measures of interest rate risk:
- Maximum negative impact on net interest income of 2% for the next 12 months assuming a linear change in interest rates totaling 100 basis points over four months followed by a flat interest rate scenario for the remaining eight month period.
- Maximum negative impact on net interest income of 4% for the next 12 months assuming a linear change of 200 basis points over eight months followed by a flat interest rate scenario for the remaining four month period.

If a rate change of 200 basis points cannot be modeled due to a low level of rates, a proportional limit applies. Management currently only models a negative 25 basis point decline because larger declines would have resulted in a Federal funds rate of less than zero. In a situation such as this, the maximum negative impact on net interest income is adjusted on a proportional basis. Regardless of the proportional limit, the negative risk exposure limit will be the greater of 1% or the proportional limit.

Management has also established a maximum negative impact on net interest income of 4% for an immediate 100 basis points change in rates and 8% for an immediate 200 basis points change in rates. These "interest rate shock" limits are designed to create an outer band of acceptable risk based upon a significant and immediate change in rates.

Management must also consider how the balance sheet and interest rate risk position could be impacted by changes in balance sheet mix. Liquidity in the banking industry has been very strong during the current economic cycle. Much of this liquidity increase has been due to a significant increase in noninterest-bearing demand deposits. Consistent with the industry, Branch Bank has seen a significant increase in this funding source. The behavior of these deposits is one of the most important assumptions used in determining the interest rate risk position of BB&T. A loss of these deposits in the future would reduce the asset sensitivity of BB&T's balance sheet as the company increases interest-bearing funds to offset the loss of this advantageous funding source.

Beta represents the correlation between overall market interest rates and the rates paid by BB&T on interest-bearing deposits. BB&T applies an average beta of approximately 80% to its managed rate deposits for determining its interest rate sensitivity. Managed rate deposits are high beta, premium money market and interest checking accounts, which attract significant client funds when needed to support balance sheet growth. BB&T regularly conducts sensitivity on other key variables to determine the impact they could have on the interest rate risk position. This allows BB&T to evaluate the likely impact on its balance sheet management strategies due to a more extreme variation in a key assumption than expected.

The following table shows the effect that the loss of demand deposits and an associated increase in managed rate deposits would have on BB&T's interest-rate sensitivity position. For purposes of this analysis, BB&T modeled the incremental beta for the replacement of the lost demand deposits at 100%.

Table 32
Deposit Mix Sensitivity Analysis

Increase in Rates	Base Scenario at December 31, 2013[1]		Results Assuming a Decrease in Noninterest Bearing Demand Deposits	
			$1 Billion	$5 Billion
Up 200 bps	2.27%		2.01%	0.98%
Up 100	1.35		1.19	0.56

[1] The base scenario is equal to the annualized hypothetical percentage change in net interest income at December 31, 2013 as presented in the preceding table.

If rates increased 200 basis points, BB&T could absorb the loss of $8.8 billion, or 25.3%, of noninterest bearing demand deposits and replace them with managed rate deposits with a beta of 100% before becoming neutral to interest rate changes.

The following table shows the effect that the indicated changes in interest rates would have on EVE. Key assumptions in the preparation of the table include prepayment speeds of mortgage-related and other assets, cash flows and maturities of derivative financial instruments, loan volumes and pricing and deposit sensitivity. The resulting change in the EVE reflects the level of sensitivity that EVE has in relation to changing interest rates.

Table 33
EVE Simulation Analysis

Change in Rates	EVE/Assets December 31,		Hypothetical Percentage Change in EVE December 31,	
	2013	2012	2013	2012
Up 200 bps	10.3%	7.5%	(4.5)%	16.6%
Up 100	10.6	7.2	(1.4)	11.9
No Change	10.8	6.4	—	—
Down 25	10.8	6.2	(0.4)	(4.1)

Market Risk from Trading Activities

BB&T also manages market risk from trading activities which consists of acting as a financial intermediary to provide its customers access to derivatives, foreign exchange and securities markets. Trading market risk is managed through the use of statistical and non-statistical risk measures and limits. BB&T utilizes a historical VaR methodology to measure and aggregate risks across its covered trading LOBs. This methodology uses two years of historical data to estimate economic outcomes for a one-day time horizon at a 99% confidence level. The average 99% one-day VaR and the maximum daily VaR for the year ended December 31, 2013 were less than $1 million. For the year ended December 31, 2012, the average 99% one-day VaR was less than $1 million and the maximum daily VaR was approximately $3 million.

Market risk disclosures under Basel II.5 are available in the Additional Disclosures section of the Investor Relations site on www.bbt.com/about.

CRITICAL ACCOUNTING POLICIES AND ESTIMATES

1.23 CISCO SYSTEMS, INC. (JUL)

MANAGEMENT'S DISCUSSION AND ANALYSIS OF FINANCIAL CONDITION AND RESULTS OF OPERATIONS (in part)

Critical Accounting Estimates

The preparation of financial statements and related disclosures in conformity with accounting principles generally accepted in the United States requires us to make judgments, assumptions, and estimates that affect the amounts reported in the Consolidated Financial Statements and accompanying notes. Note 2 to the Consolidated Financial Statements describes the significant accounting policies and methods used in the preparation of the Consolidated Financial Statements. The accounting policies described below are significantly affected by critical accounting estimates. Such accounting policies require significant judgments, assumptions, and estimates used in the preparation of the Consolidated Financial Statements, and actual results could differ materially from the amounts reported based on these policies.

Revenue Recognition

Revenue is recognized when all of the following criteria have been met:
- *Persuasive evidence of an arrangement exists.* Contracts, Internet commerce agreements, and customer purchase orders are generally used to determine the existence of an arrangement.
- *Delivery has occurred.* Shipping documents and customer acceptance, when applicable, are used to verify delivery.
- *The fee is fixed or determinable.* We assess whether the fee is fixed or determinable based on the payment terms associated with the transaction and whether the sales price is subject to refund or adjustment.
- *Collectibility is reasonably assured.* We assess collectibility based primarily on the creditworthiness of the customer as determined by credit checks and analysis, as well as the customer's payment history.

In instances where final acceptance of the product, system, or solution is specified by the customer, revenue is deferred until all acceptance criteria have been met. When a sale involves multiple deliverables, such as sales of products that include services, the multiple deliverables are evaluated to determine the unit of accounting, and the entire fee from the arrangement is allocated to each unit of accounting based on the relative selling price. Revenue is recognized when the revenue recognition criteria for each unit of accounting are met.

The amount of product and service revenue recognized in a given period is affected by our judgment as to whether an arrangement includes multiple deliverables and, if so, our valuation of the units of accounting for multiple deliverables. According to the accounting guidance prescribed in Accounting Standards Codification (ASC) 605, *Revenue Recognition*, we use vendor-specific objective evidence of selling price (VSOE) for each of those units, when available. We determine VSOE based on our normal pricing and discounting practices for the specific product or service when sold separately. In determining VSOE, we require that a substantial majority of the historical standalone transactions have the selling prices for a product or service fall within a reasonably narrow pricing range, generally evidenced by approximately 80% of such historical standalone transactions falling within plus or minus 15% of the median rates. When VSOE does not exist, we apply the selling price hierarchy to applicable multiple-deliverable arrangements. Under the selling price hierarchy, third-party evidence of selling price (TPE) will be considered if VSOE does not exist, and estimated selling price (ESP) will be used if neither VSOE nor TPE is available. Generally, we are not able to determine TPE because our go-to-market strategy differs from that of others in our markets, and the extent of our proprietary technology varies among comparable products or services from those of our peers. In determining ESP, we apply significant judgment as we weigh a variety of factors, based on the facts and circumstances of the arrangement. We typically arrive at an ESP for a product or service that is not sold separately by considering company-specific factors such as geographies, competitive landscape, internal costs, profitability objectives, pricing practices used to establish bundled pricing, and existing portfolio pricing and discounting.

Some of our sales arrangements have multiple deliverables containing software and related software support components. Such sales arrangements are subject to the accounting guidance in ASC 985-605, *Software-Revenue Recognition*.

As our business and offerings evolve over time, our pricing practices may be required to be modified accordingly, which could result in changes in selling prices, including both VSOE and ESP, in subsequent periods. There were no material impacts during fiscal 2013, nor do we currently expect a material impact in the next 12 months on our revenue recognition due to any changes in our VSOE, TPE, or ESP.

Revenue deferrals relate to the timing of revenue recognition for specific transactions based on financing arrangements, service, support, and other factors. Financing arrangements may include sales-type, direct-financing, and operating leases, loans, and guarantees of third-party financing. Our deferred revenue for products was $4.0 billion and $3.7 billion as of July 27, 2013 and July 28, 2012, respectively. Technical support services revenue is deferred and recognized ratably over the period during which the services are to be performed, which typically is from one to three years. Advanced services revenue is recognized upon delivery or completion of performance. Our deferred revenue for services was $9.4 billion and $9.2 billion as of July 27, 2013 and July 28, 2012, respectively.

We make sales to distributors which we refer to as two-tier systems of sales to the end customer. Revenue from distributors is recognized based on a sell-through method using information provided by them. Our distributors participate in various cooperative marketing and other programs, and we maintain estimated accruals and allowances for these programs. If actual credits received by our distributors under these programs were to deviate significantly from our estimates, which are based on historical experience, our revenue could be adversely affected.

Allowances for Receivables and Sales Returns

The allowances for receivables were as follows (in millions, except percentages):

	July 27, 2013	July 28, 2012
Allowance for doubtful accounts	$228	$207
Percentage of gross accounts receivable	*4.0%*	*4.5%*
Allowance for credit loss—lease receivables	$238	$247
Percentage of gross lease receivables	*6.3%*	*7.2%*
Allowance for credit loss—loan receivables	$ 86	$122
Percentage of gross loan receivables	*5.2%*	*6.8%*

The allowance for doubtful accounts is based on our assessment of the collectibility of customer accounts. We regularly review the adequacy of these allowances by considering internal factors such as historical experience, credit quality and age of the receivable balances, as well as external factors such as economic conditions that may affect a customer's ability to pay and expected default frequency rates, which are published by major third-party credit-rating agencies and are generally updated on a quarterly basis. We also consider the concentration of receivables outstanding with a particular customer in assessing the adequacy of our allowances for doubtful accounts. If a major customer's creditworthiness deteriorates, if actual defaults are higher than our historical experience, or if other circumstances arise, our estimates of the recoverability of amounts due to us could be overstated, and additional allowances could be required, which could have an adverse impact on our operating results.

The allowance for credit loss on financing receivables is also based on the assessment of collectibility of customer accounts. We regularly review the adequacy of the credit allowances determined either on an individual or a collective basis. When evaluating the financing receivables on an individual basis, we consider historical experience, credit quality and age of receivable balances, and economic conditions that may affect a customer's ability to pay. When evaluating financing receivables on a collective basis, we use expected default frequency rates published by a major third-party credit-rating agency as well as our own historical loss rate in the event of default, while also systematically giving effect to economic conditions, concentration of risk and correlation. Determining expected default frequency rates and loss factors associated with internal credit risk ratings, as well as assessing factors such as economic conditions, concentration of risk, and correlation, are complex and subjective. Our ongoing consideration of all these factors could result in an increase in our allowance for credit loss in the future, which could adversely affect our operating results.

Both accounts receivable and financing receivables are charged off at the point when they are considered uncollectible.

A reserve for future sales returns is established based on historical trends in product return rates. The reserve for future sales returns as of July 27, 2013 and July 28, 2012 was $119 million and $129 million, respectively, and was recorded as a reduction of our accounts receivable. If the actual future returns were to deviate from the historical data on which the reserve had been established, our revenue could be adversely affected.

Inventory Valuation and Liability for Purchase Commitments with Contract Manufacturers and Suppliers

Our inventory balance was $1.5 billion and $1.7 billion as of July 27, 2013 and July 28, 2012, respectively. Inventory is written down based on excess and obsolete inventories, determined primarily by future demand forecasts. Inventory write-downs are measured as the difference between the cost of the inventory and market, based upon assumptions about future demand, and are charged to the provision for inventory, which is a component of our cost of sales. At the point of the loss recognition, a new, lower cost basis for that inventory is established, and subsequent changes in facts and circumstances do not result in the restoration or increase in that newly established cost basis.

We record a liability for firm, noncancelable, and unconditional purchase commitments with contract manufacturers and suppliers for quantities in excess of our future demand forecasts consistent with the valuation of our excess and obsolete inventory. As of July 27, 2013, the liability for these purchase commitments was $172 million, compared with $193 million as of July 28, 2012, and was included in other current liabilities.

Our provision for inventory was $114 million, $115 million, and $196 million for fiscal 2013, 2012, and 2011, respectively. The provision for the liability related to purchase commitments with contract manufacturers and suppliers was $106 million, $151 million, and $114 million in fiscal 2013, 2012, and 2011, respectively. The decrease in our provision for the liability related to purchase commitments with contract manufacturers and suppliers for fiscal 2013 was primarily due to the increase in demand for our products resulting in lower inventory levels with our contract manufacturers during fiscal 2013. If there were to be a sudden and significant decrease in demand for our products, or if there were a higher incidence of inventory obsolescence because of rapidly changing technology and customer requirements, we could be required to increase our inventory write-downs, and our liability for purchase commitments with contract manufacturers and suppliers, and accordingly our profitability, could be adversely affected. We regularly evaluate our exposure for inventory write-downs and the adequacy of our liability for purchase commitments. Inventory and supply chain management remain areas of focus as we balance the need to maintain supply chain flexibility to help ensure competitive lead times with the risk of inventory obsolescence, particularly in light of current macroeconomic uncertainties and conditions and the resulting potential for changes in future demand forecast.

Warranty Costs

The liability for product warranties, included in other current liabilities, was $431 million as of July 27, 2013, compared with $415 million as of July 28, 2012. See Note 12 to the Consolidated Financial Statements. Our products are generally covered by a warranty for periods ranging from 90 days to five years, and for some products we provide a limited lifetime warranty. We accrue for warranty costs as part of our cost of sales based on associated material costs, technical support labor costs, and associated overhead. Material cost is estimated based primarily upon historical trends in the volume of product returns within the warranty period and the cost to repair or replace the equipment. Technical support labor cost is estimated based primarily upon historical trends in the rate of customer cases and the cost to support the customer cases within the warranty period. Overhead cost is applied based on estimated time to support warranty activities.

The provision for product warranties issued during fiscal 2013, 2012, and 2011 was $664 million, $661 million, and $456 million, respectively. If we experience an increase in warranty claims compared with our historical experience, or if the cost of servicing warranty claims is greater than expected, our profitability could be adversely affected.

Share-Based Compensation Expense

Share-based compensation expense is presented as follows (in millions):

Years Ended	July 27, 2013	July 28, 2012	July 30, 2011
Share-based compensation expense	$1,120	$1,401	$1,620

Restricted stock units are valued using the market value of our common stock on the date of grant, discounted for the present value of expected dividends. Restricted stock unit awards with market-based conditions are valued using a Monte Carlo simulation. See Note 14 to the Consolidated Financial Statements.

The determination of the fair value of employee stock options and employee stock purchase rights on the date of grant using an option-pricing model is affected by our stock price as well as assumptions regarding a number of highly complex and subjective variables. For employee stock options and employee stock purchase rights, these variables include, but are not limited to, the expected stock price volatility over the term of the awards, the risk-free interest rate, and expected dividends as of the grant date. For employee stock options, we historically have used the implied volatility for two-year traded options on our stock as the expected volatility assumption required in the lattice-binomial model. For employee stock purchase rights, we used the implied volatility for traded options (with lives corresponding to the expected life of the employee stock purchase rights) on our stock. The selection of the implied volatility approach was based upon the availability of actively traded options on our stock and our assessment that implied volatility is more representative of future stock price trends than historical volatility. The valuation of employee stock options (granted in prior fiscal years, but for which expense was recognized during the fiscal years presented) is also impacted by kurtosis and skewness, which are technical measures of the distribution of stock price returns and the actual and projected employee stock option exercise behaviors.

Because share-based compensation expense is based on awards ultimately expected to vest, it has been reduced for forfeitures. If factors change and we employ different assumptions in the application of our option-pricing model in future periods or if we experience different forfeiture rates, the compensation expense that is derived may differ significantly from what we have recorded in the current year.

Fair Value Measurements

Our fixed income and publicly traded equity securities, collectively, are reflected in the Consolidated Balance Sheets at a fair value of $42.7 billion as of July 27, 2013, compared with $38.9 billion as of July 28, 2012. Our fixed income investment portfolio, as of July 27, 2013, consisted primarily of high quality investment-grade securities. See Note 8 to the Consolidated Financial Statements.

As described more fully in Note 2 to the Consolidated Financial Statements, a valuation hierarchy is based on the level of independent, objective evidence available regarding the value of the investments. It encompasses three classes of investments: Level 1 consists of securities for which there are quoted prices in active markets for identical securities; Level 2 consists of securities for which observable inputs other than Level 1 inputs are used, such as quoted prices for similar securities in active markets or quoted prices for identical securities in less active markets and model-derived valuations for which the variables are derived from, or corroborated by, observable market data; and Level 3 consists of securities for which there are unobservable inputs to the valuation methodology that are significant to the measurement of the fair value.

Our Level 2 securities are valued using quoted market prices for similar instruments or nonbinding market prices that are corroborated by observable market data. We use inputs such as actual trade data, benchmark yields, broker/dealer quotes, and other similar data, which are obtained from independent pricing vendors, quoted market prices, or other sources to determine the ultimate fair value of our assets and liabilities. We use such pricing data as the primary input, to which we have not made any material adjustments during fiscal 2013 and 2012, to make our assessments and determinations as to the ultimate valuation of our investment portfolio. We are ultimately responsible for the financial statements and underlying estimates.

The inputs and fair value are reviewed for reasonableness, may be further validated by comparison to publicly available information, and could be adjusted based on market indices or other information that management deems material to its estimate of fair value. The assessment of fair value can be difficult and subjective. However, given the relative reliability of the inputs we use to value our investment portfolio, and because substantially all of our valuation inputs are obtained using quoted market prices for similar or identical assets, we do not believe that the nature of estimates and assumptions affected by levels of subjectivity and judgment was material to the valuation of the investment portfolio as of July 27, 2013. We had no Level 3 investments in our total portfolio as of July 27, 2013.

Other-than-Temporary Impairments

We recognize an impairment charge when the declines in the fair values of our fixed income or publicly traded equity securities below their cost basis are judged to be other than temporary. The ultimate value realized on these securities, to the extent unhedged, is subject to market price volatility until they are sold.

If the fair value of a debt security is less than its amortized cost, we assess whether the impairment is other than temporary. An impairment is considered other than temporary if (i) we have the intent to sell the security, (ii) it is more likely than not that we will be required to sell the security before recovery of its entire amortized cost basis, or (iii) we do not expect to recover the entire amortized cost of the security. If an impairment is considered other than temporary based on (i) or (ii) described in the prior sentence, the entire difference between the amortized cost and the fair value of the security is recognized in earnings. If an impairment is considered other than temporary based on condition (iii), the amount representing credit loss, defined as the difference between the present value of the cash flows expected to be collected and the amortized cost basis of the debt security, will be recognized in earnings, and the amount relating to all other factors will be recognized in other comprehensive income (OCI). In estimating the amount and timing of cash flows expected to be collected, we consider all available information, including past events, current conditions, the remaining payment terms of the security, the financial condition of the issuer, expected defaults, and the value of underlying collateral.

For publicly traded equity securities, we consider various factors in determining whether we should recognize an impairment charge, including the length of time and extent to which the fair value has been less than our cost basis, the financial condition and near-term prospects of the issuer, and our intent and ability to hold the investment for a period of time sufficient to allow for any anticipated recovery in market value.

Impairment charges on our investments in publicly traded equity securities were not material in fiscal 2013, 2012, and 2011. There were no impairment charges on investments in fixed income securities in fiscal 2013, 2012, and 2011. Our ongoing consideration of all the factors described previously could result in additional impairment charges in the future, which could adversely affect our net income.

We also have investments in privately held companies, some of which are in the startup or development stages. As of July 27, 2013, our investments in privately held companies were $833 million, compared with $858 million as of July 28, 2012, and were included in other assets. We monitor these investments for events or circumstances indicative of potential impairment and will make appropriate reductions in carrying values if we determine that an impairment charge is required, based primarily on the financial condition and near-term prospects of these companies. These investments are inherently risky because the markets for the technologies or products these companies are developing are typically in the early stages and may never materialize. Our impairment charges on investments in privately held companies were $33 million, $23 million, and $10 million in fiscal 2013, 2012, and 2011, respectively.

Goodwill and Purchased Intangible Asset Impairments

Our methodology for allocating the purchase price relating to purchase acquisitions is determined through established valuation techniques. Goodwill represents a residual value as of the acquisition date, which in most cases results in measuring goodwill as an excess of the purchase consideration transferred plus the fair value of any noncontrolling interest in the acquired company over the fair value of net assets acquired, including contingent consideration. We perform goodwill impairment tests on an annual basis in the fourth fiscal quarter and between annual tests in certain circumstances for each reporting unit. The assessment of fair value for goodwill and purchased intangible assets is based on factors that market participants would use in an orderly transaction in accordance with the new accounting guidance for the fair value measurement of nonfinancial assets.

The goodwill recorded in the Consolidated Balance Sheets as of July 27, 2013 and July 28, 2012 was $21.9 billion and $17.0 billion, respectively. The increase in goodwill for fiscal 2013 was due in large part to our acquisitions of NDS and Meraki. In response to changes in industry and market conditions, we could be required to strategically realign our resources and consider restructuring, disposing of, or otherwise exiting businesses, which could result in an impairment of goodwill. There was no impairment of goodwill resulting from our annual impairment testing in fiscal 2013, 2012, and 2011. For the annual impairment testing in fiscal 2013, the excess of the fair value over the carrying value for each of our reporting units was $38.7 billion for the Americas, $15.5 billion for EMEA, and $17.8 billion for APJC. We performed a sensitivity analysis for goodwill impairment with respect to each of our respective reporting units and determined that a hypothetical 10% decline in the fair value of each reporting unit as of July 27, 2013 would not result in an impairment of goodwill for any reporting unit.

We make judgments about the recoverability of purchased intangible assets with finite lives whenever events or changes in circumstances indicate that an impairment may exist. Recoverability of purchased intangible assets with finite lives is measured by comparing the carrying amount of the asset to the future undiscounted cash flows the asset is expected to generate. We review indefinite-lived intangible assets for impairment annually or whenever events or changes in circumstances indicate the carrying value may not be recoverable. Recoverability of indefinite-lived intangible assets is measured by comparing the carrying amount of the asset to the future discounted cash flows the asset is expected to generate. If the asset is considered to be impaired, the amount of any impairment is measured as the difference between the carrying value and the fair value of the impaired asset. Assumptions and estimates about future values and remaining useful lives of our purchased intangible assets are complex and subjective. They can be affected by a variety of factors, including external factors such as industry and economic trends, and internal factors such as changes in our business strategy and our internal forecasts. There was no impairment charge related to purchased intangible assets during fiscal 2013. Our impairment charges related to purchased intangible assets were $12 million and $164 million during fiscal 2012 and 2011, respectively. Our ongoing consideration of all the factors described previously could result in additional impairment charges in the future, which could adversely affect our net income.

Income Taxes

We are subject to income taxes in the United States and numerous foreign jurisdictions. Our effective tax rates differ from the statutory rate, primarily due to the tax impact of state taxes, foreign operations, R&D tax credits, domestic manufacturing deductions, tax audit settlements, nondeductible compensation, international realignments, and transfer pricing adjustments. Our effective tax rate was 11.1%, 20.8%, and 17.1% in fiscal 2013, 2012, and 2011, respectively.

Significant judgment is required in evaluating our uncertain tax positions and determining our provision for income taxes. Although we believe our reserves are reasonable, no assurance can be given that the final tax outcome of these matters will not be different from that which is reflected in our historical income tax provisions and accruals. We adjust these reserves in light of changing facts and circumstances, such as the closing of a tax audit or the refinement of an estimate. To the extent that the final tax outcome of these matters is different than the amounts recorded, such differences will impact the provision for income taxes in the period in which such determination is made. The provision for income taxes includes the impact of reserve provisions and changes to reserves that are considered appropriate, as well as the related net interest and penalties.

Significant judgment is also required in determining any valuation allowance recorded against deferred tax assets. In assessing the need for a valuation allowance, we consider all available evidence, including past operating results, estimates of future taxable income, and the feasibility of tax planning strategies. In the event that we change our determination as to the amount of deferred tax assets that can be realized, we will adjust our valuation allowance with a corresponding impact to the provision for income taxes in the period in which such determination is made.

Our provision for income taxes is subject to volatility and could be adversely impacted by earnings being lower than anticipated in countries that have lower tax rates and higher than anticipated in countries that have higher tax rates; by changes in the valuation of our deferred tax assets and liabilities; by expiration of or lapses in the R&D tax credit or domestic manufacturing deduction laws; by expiration of or lapses in tax incentives; by transfer pricing adjustments, including the effect of acquisitions on our intercompany R&D cost-sharing arrangement and legal structure; by tax effects of nondeductible compensation; by tax costs related to intercompany realignments; by changes in accounting principles; or by changes in tax laws and regulations, including possible U.S. changes to the taxation of earnings of our foreign subsidiaries, the deductibility of expenses attributable to foreign income, or the foreign tax credit rules. Significant judgment is required to determine the recognition and measurement attributes prescribed in the accounting guidance for uncertainty in income taxes. The accounting guidance for uncertainty in income taxes applies to all income tax positions, including the potential recovery of previously paid taxes, which if settled unfavorably could adversely impact our provision for income taxes or additional paid-in capital. Further, as a result of certain of our ongoing employment and capital investment actions and commitments, our income in certain countries is subject to reduced tax rates and in some cases is wholly exempt from tax. Our failure to meet these commitments could adversely impact our provision for income taxes. In addition, we are subject to the continuous examination of our income tax returns by the IRS and other tax authorities. We regularly assess the likelihood of adverse outcomes resulting from these examinations to determine the adequacy of our provision for income taxes. There can be no assurance that the outcomes from these continuous examinations will not have an adverse impact on our operating results and financial condition.

Loss Contingencies

We are subject to the possibility of various losses arising in the ordinary course of business. We consider the likelihood of loss or impairment of an asset or the incurrence of a liability, as well as our ability to reasonably estimate the amount of loss, in determining loss contingencies. An estimated loss contingency is accrued when it is probable that an asset has been impaired or a liability has been incurred and the amount of loss can be reasonably estimated. We regularly evaluate current information available to us to determine whether such accruals should be adjusted and whether new accruals are required.

Third parties, including customers, have in the past and may in the future assert claims or initiate litigation related to exclusive patent, copyright, trademark, and other intellectual property rights to technologies and related standards that are relevant to us. These assertions have increased over time as a result of our growth and the general increase in the pace of patent claims assertions, particularly in the United States. If any infringement or other intellectual property claim made against us by any third party is successful, or if we fail to develop non-infringing technology or license the proprietary rights on commercially reasonable terms and conditions, our business, operating results, and financial condition could be materially and adversely affected.

SUMMARY OF SIGNIFICANT ACCOUNTING POLICIES

1.24 SPECTRUM BRANDS HOLDINGS, INC. (SEP)
NOTES TO CONSOLIDATED FINANCIAL STATEMENTS (in part)

(Amounts in thousands, except per share figures)

(2) Significant Accounting Policies and Practices

(a) Principles of Consolidation and Fiscal Year End

The consolidated financial statements include the financial statements of SB Holdings and its majority owned subsidiaries and have been prepared in accordance with U.S. Generally Accepted Accounting Principles ("GAAP"). All intercompany transactions have been eliminated. The Company's fiscal year ends September 30. References herein to Fiscal 2013, Fiscal 2012 and Fiscal 2011 refer to the fiscal years ended September 30, 2013, 2012 and 2011, respectively.

(b) Change in Accounting Principle

During Fiscal 2013, the Company made a change in accounting principle to present tax withholdings for share-based payment awards paid to taxing authorities on behalf of employees as a financing activity within the Consolidated Statements of Cash Flows. Such amounts were previously presented within operating activities. The Company believes this change is preferable as the predominant characteristic of the transaction is a financing activity. The Company has reclassified the following amounts within its previously reported Consolidated Statements of Cash Flows on a retrospective basis to reflect this change in accounting principle:

	Fiscal 2012	Fiscal 2011
Net cash used by operating activities—Accounts payable and accrued liabilities:		
As previously reported	$ 1,424	$(60,505)
Reclassification of share based award tax withholding payments	3,936	2,482
As reclassified	$ 5,360	$(58,023)
Net cash used by financing activities—Share based award tax withholding payments:		
As previously reported	$ —	$ —
Reclassification of share based award tax withholding payments	(3,936)	(2,482)
As reclassified	$(3,936)	$ (2,482)

(c) Revenue Recognition

The Company recognizes revenue from product sales generally upon delivery to the customer at the shipping point in situations where the customer picks up the product or where delivery terms so stipulate. This represents the point at which title and all risks and rewards of ownership of the product are passed, provided that: there are no uncertainties regarding customer acceptance; there is persuasive evidence that an arrangement exists; the price to the buyer is fixed or determinable; and collectibility is deemed reasonably assured. The Company is generally not obligated to allow for, and its general policy is not to accept, product returns for battery sales. The Company does accept returns in specific instances related to its shaving, grooming, personal care, home and garden, small appliances and pet products. The provision for customer returns is based on historical sales and returns and other relevant information. The Company estimates and accrues the cost of returns, which are treated as a reduction of Net sales.

The Company enters into various promotional arrangements, primarily with retail customers, including arrangements entitling such retailers to cash rebates from the Company based on the level of their purchases, which require the Company to estimate and accrue the estimated costs of the promotional programs. These costs are treated as a reduction of Net sales.

The Company also enters into promotional arrangements that target the ultimate consumer. The costs associated with such arrangements are treated as either a reduction in Net sales or an increase in Cost of goods sold, based on the type of promotional program. The income statement presentation of the Company's promotional arrangements complies with Accounting Standards Codification ("ASC") Topic 605: " Revenue Recognition." For all types of promotional arrangements and programs, the Company monitors its commitments and uses various measures, including past experience, to determine amounts to be recorded for the estimate of the earned, but unpaid, promotional costs. The terms of the Company's customer-related promotional arrangements and programs are tailored to each customer and are documented through written contracts, correspondence or other communications with the individual customers.

The Company also enters into various arrangements, primarily with retail customers, which require the Company to make upfront cash, or "slotting" payments, in order to secure the right to distribute through such customers. The Company capitalizes slotting payments; provided the payments are supported by a time or volume based arrangement with the retailer, and amortizes the associated payment over the appropriate time or volume based term of the arrangement. The amortization of slotting payments is treated as a reduction in Net sales and a corresponding asset is reported in Deferred charges and other in the accompanying Consolidated Statements of Financial Position.

(d) Use of Estimates

The preparation of financial statements in conformity with GAAP requires management to make estimates and assumptions that affect the reported amounts of assets and liabilities and disclosure of contingent assets and liabilities at the date of the financial statements and the reported amounts of revenues and expenses during the reporting period. Actual results could differ from those estimates.

(e) Cash Equivalents

For purposes of the accompanying Consolidated Statements of Financial Position and Consolidated Statements of Cash Flows, the Company considers all highly liquid debt instruments purchased with original maturities of three months or less to be cash equivalents.

(f) Concentrations of Credit Risk and Major Customers

Trade receivables subject the Company to credit risk. Trade accounts receivable are carried at net realizable value. The Company extends credit to its customers based upon an evaluation of the customer's financial condition and credit history, but generally does not require collateral. The Company monitors its customers' credit and financial condition based on changing economic conditions and will make adjustments to credit policies as required. Provisions for losses on uncollectible trade receivables are determined based on ongoing evaluations of the Company's receivables, principally on the basis of historical collection experience and evaluations of the risks of nonpayment for a given customer.

The Company has a broad range of customers including many large retail outlet chains, one of which accounts for a significant percentage of its sales volume. This major customer represented approximately 18%, 23% and 24% of the Company's Net sales during Fiscal 2013, Fiscal 2012 and Fiscal 2011, respectively. This major customer also represented approximately 11% and 13% of the Company's Trade accounts receivable, net as of September 30, 2013 and September 30, 2012, respectively.

Approximately 41%, 46% and 44% of the Company's Net sales during Fiscal 2013, Fiscal 2012 and Fiscal 2011, respectively, occurred outside of the United States. These sales and related receivables are subject to varying degrees of credit, currency, and political and economic risk. The Company monitors these risks and makes appropriate provisions for collectibility based on an assessment of the risks present.

(g) Displays and Fixtures

Temporary displays are generally disposable cardboard displays shipped to customers to facilitate display of the Company's products. Temporary displays are generally disposed of after a single use by the customer.

Permanent fixtures are more lasting in nature, are generally made from wire or other longer-lived materials, and are shipped to customers for use in displaying the Company's products. These permanent fixtures are restocked with the Company's product multiple times over the fixture's useful life.

The costs of both temporary and permanent displays are capitalized as a prepaid asset until shipped to the customer and are included in Prepaid expenses and other in the accompanying Consolidated Statements of Financial Position. The costs of temporary displays are expensed in the period in which they are shipped to customers and the costs of permanent fixtures are amortized over an estimated useful life of one to two years from the date they are shipped to customers. The unamortized cost of permanent fixtures is reflected in Deferred charges and other in the accompanying Consolidated Statements of Financial Position.

(h) Inventories

The Company's inventories are valued at the lower of cost or net realizable value. Cost of inventories is determined using the first-in, first-out (FIFO) method.

(i) Property, Plant and Equipment

Property, plant and equipment are recorded at cost or at fair value if acquired in a purchase business combination. Depreciation on plant and equipment is calculated on the straight-line method over the estimated useful lives of the assets. Depreciable lives by major classification are as follows:

Building and improvements	20–40 years
Machinery, equipment and other	2–15 years

Plant and equipment held under capital leases are amortized on a straight-line basis over the shorter of the lease term or estimated useful life of the asset; such amortization is included in depreciation expense.

The Company reviews long-lived assets for impairment whenever events or changes in circumstances indicate that the carrying amount of an asset may not be recoverable. The Company evaluates recoverability of assets to be held and used by comparing the carrying amount of an asset to future net cash flows expected to be generated by the asset. If such assets are considered to be impaired, the impairment to be recognized is measured by the amount by which the carrying amount of the assets exceeds the fair value of the assets. Assets to be disposed of are reported at the lower of the carrying amount or fair value less costs to sell.

(j) Intangible Assets

Intangible assets are recorded at cost or at fair value if acquired in a purchase business combination. In connection with fresh-start reporting, Intangible Assets were recorded at their estimated fair value on August 30, 2009. Customer lists, proprietary technology and certain trade name intangibles are amortized, using the straight-line method, over their estimated useful lives of up to 20 years. Excess of cost over fair value of net assets acquired (goodwill) and indefinite-lived intangible assets (certain trade name intangibles) are not amortized. Goodwill is tested for impairment at least annually, at the reporting unit level with such groupings being consistent with the Company's reportable segments. If impairment is indicated, a write-down to fair value (normally measured by discounting estimated future cash flows) is recorded. Indefinite-lived trade name intangibles are tested for impairment at least annually by comparing the fair value, determined using a relief from royalty methodology, with the carrying value. Any excess of carrying value over fair value is recognized as an impairment loss in income from operations.

ASC Topic 350: *"Intangibles-Goodwill and Other,"* ("ASC 350") requires that goodwill and indefinite-lived intangible assets be tested for impairment annually, or more often if an event or circumstance indicates that an impairment loss may have been incurred. The Company's management uses its judgment in assessing whether assets may have become impaired between annual impairment tests. Indicators such as unexpected adverse business conditions, economic factors, unanticipated technological change or competitive activities, loss of key personnel, and acts by governments and courts may signal that an asset has become impaired.

During Fiscal 2013, Fiscal 2012 and Fiscal 2011, the Company's goodwill and trade name intangibles were tested for impairment as of the Company's August financial period end, the Company's annual testing date, as well as in certain interim periods where an event or circumstance occurred that indicated an impairment loss may have been incurred.

Intangibles with Indefinite Lives

In accordance with ASC 350, the Company conducts impairment testing on the Company's goodwill. To determine fair value during Fiscal 2013, Fiscal 2012 and Fiscal 2011, the Company used the discounted estimated future cash flows methodology. Assumptions critical to the Company's fair value estimates under the discounted estimated future cash flows methodology are: (i) the present value factors used in determining the fair value of the reporting units and trade names; (ii) projected average revenue growth rates used in estimating future cash flows for the reporting unit; and (iii) projected long-term growth rates used in the derivation of terminal year values. These and other assumptions are impacted by economic conditions and expectations of management and will change in the future based on period specific facts and circumstances. The Company also tested the aggregate estimated fair value of its reporting units for reasonableness by comparison to the total market capitalization of the Company, which includes both its equity and debt securities.

In addition, in accordance with ASC 350, as part of the Company's annual impairment testing, the Company tested its indefinite-lived trade name intangible assets for impairment by comparing the carrying amount of such trade names to their respective fair values. Fair value was determined using a relief from royalty methodology. Assumptions critical to the Company's fair value estimates under the relief from royalty methodology were: (i) royalty rates, (ii) projected average revenue growth rates, and (iii) applicable discount rates.

In connection with the Company's annual goodwill impairment testing performed during Fiscal 2013, Fiscal 2012 and Fiscal 2011, the first step of such testing indicated that the fair value of the Company's reporting segments were in excess of their carrying amounts and, accordingly, no further testing of goodwill was required.

During Fiscal 2013, the Company concluded that the fair value of its intangible assets exceeded their carrying value.

During Fiscal 2012, the Company concluded that the fair value of its intangible assets exceeded their carrying value. Additionally, during Fiscal 2012 the Company reclassified $3,450 of certain trade names from indefinite lived to definite lived.

These trade names are being amortized over their remaining useful lives, which have been estimated to be 1-3 years.

In connection with its annual impairment testing of indefinite-lived intangible assets during Fiscal 2011, the Company concluded that the fair values of certain trade name intangible assets were less than the carrying amounts of those assets. As a result, during Fiscal 2011 the Company recorded a non-cash pretax intangible asset impairment charge of approximately $32,450 which was equal to the excess of the carrying amounts of the intangible assets over the fair value of such assets. This non-cash impairment of trade name intangible assets has been recorded as a separate component of Operating expenses. This impairment of trade name intangible assets was primarily attributed to lower forecasted profits, reflecting more conservative growth rates versus those originally assumed by the Company at the time of acquisition or upon adoption of fresh start reporting.

A triggering event occurred in Fiscal 2011 which required the Company to test its indefinite-lived intangible assets for impairment between annual impairment dates. On October 1, 2010, the Company realigned its operating segments, which constituted a triggering event for impairment testing. In connection with this interim test, the Company compared the fair value of its reporting segments to their carrying amounts both before and after the change in segment composition, and determined the fair values were in excess of their carrying amounts and, accordingly, no further testing of goodwill was required. The Company also tested the recoverability of its identified indefinite-lived intangibles in connection with the realignment of its operating segments and concluded that the fair values of these assets exceeded their carrying values.

Intangibles with Definite or Estimable Useful Lives

The Company assesses the recoverability of intangible assets with definite or estimable useful lives whenever an event or circumstance occurs that indicates an impairment loss may have been incurred. The Company assesses the recoverability of these intangible assets by determining whether their carrying value can be recovered through projected undiscounted future cash flows. If projected undiscounted future cash flows indicate that the carrying value of the assets will not be recovered, an adjustment would be made to reduce the carrying value to an amount equal to estimated fair value determined based on projected future cash flows discounted at the Company's incremental borrowing rate. The cash flow projections used in estimating fair value are based on historical performance and management's estimate of future performance, giving consideration to existing and anticipated competitive and economic conditions.

Impairment reviews are conducted at the judgment of management when it believes that a change in circumstances in the business or external factors warrants a review. Circumstances such as the discontinuation of a product or product line, a sudden or consistent decline in the sales forecast for a product, changes in technology or in the way an asset is being used, a history of operating or cash flow losses, or an adverse change in legal factors or in the business climate, among others, may trigger an impairment review.

(k) Debt Issuance Costs

Debt issuance costs are capitalized and amortized to interest expense using the effective interest method over the lives of the related debt agreements.

(l) Accounts Payable

Included in accounts payable are book overdrafts, net of deposits on hand, on disbursement accounts that are replenished when checks are presented for payment.

(m) Income Taxes

Income taxes are accounted for under the asset and liability method. Deferred tax assets and liabilities are recognized for the future tax consequences attributable to differences between the financial statement carrying amounts of existing assets and liabilities and their respective tax bases and operating loss and tax credit carryforwards. Deferred tax assets and liabilities are measured using enacted tax rates expected to apply to taxable income in the years in which those temporary differences are expected to be recovered or settled. The effect on deferred tax assets and liabilities of a change in tax rates is recognized in income in the period that includes the enactment date.

The Company recognizes the effect of income tax positions only if those positions are more likely than not of being sustained. Recognized income tax positions are measured at the largest amount that is greater than 50% likely of being realized. Changes in recognition or measurement are reflected in income tax expense in the period in which the change in judgment occurs. Accrued interest expense and penalties related to uncertain tax positions are recorded in Income tax expense.

(n) Foreign Currency Translation

Local currencies are considered the functional currencies for most of the Company's operations outside the United States. Assets and liabilities of the Company's foreign subsidiaries are translated at the rate of exchange existing at year-end, with revenues, expenses, and cash flows translated at the average of the monthly exchange rates. Adjustments resulting from translation of the financial statements are recorded as a component of Accumulated other comprehensive income (loss) ("AOCI"). Also included in AOCI are the effects of exchange rate changes on intercompany balances of a long-term nature.

As of September 30, 2013 and September 30, 2012, accumulated (losses) gains related to foreign currency translation adjustments of $(7,050) and $(225), respectively, were reflected in the accompanying Consolidated Statements of Financial Position in AOCI.

Foreign currency transaction gains and losses related to assets and liabilities that are denominated in a currency other than the functional currency are reported in the Consolidated Statements of Operations in the period they occur. Exchange losses on foreign currency transactions aggregating $9,388, $1,654 and $3,370 for Fiscal 2013, Fiscal 2012 and Fiscal 2011, respectively, are included in Other expense, net, in the accompanying Consolidated Statements of Operations.

(o) Shipping and Handling Costs

The Company incurred shipping and handling costs of $246,090, $198,152 and $201,480 during Fiscal 2013, Fiscal 2012 and Fiscal 2011, respectively. Shipping and handling costs, which are included in Selling expenses in the accompanying Consolidated Statements of Operations, include costs incurred with third-party carriers to transport products to customers and salaries and overhead costs related to activities to prepare the Company's products for shipment at the Company's distribution facilities.

(p) Advertising Costs

The Company incurred advertising costs of $22,971, $20,706 and $30,673 during Fiscal 2013, Fiscal 2012 and Fiscal 2011, respectively. Such advertising costs are included in Selling expenses in the accompanying Consolidated Statements of Operations and include agency fees and other costs to create advertisements, as well as costs paid to third parties to print or broadcast the Company's advertisements.

(q) Research and Development Costs

Research and development costs are charged to expense in the period they are incurred.

(r) Net (Loss) Income Per Common Share

Basic net (loss) income per common share is computed by dividing net (loss) income available to common shareholders by the weighted-average number of common shares outstanding for the period. Basic net (loss) income per common share does not consider the effect of dilutive common stock equivalents. As long as their effect is not antidilutive, diluted net (loss) income per common share reflects the dilution that would occur if employee stock units and restricted stock awards were exercised or converted into common shares or resulted in the issuance of common shares that then shared in the net (loss) income of the entity. The computation of diluted net (loss) income per common share uses the "treasury stock" method to reflect dilution. The difference between the number of shares used in the calculations of basic and diluted net (loss) income per share is due to the effects of restricted stock and assumed conversion of employee stock unit awards.

Net (loss) income per common share is calculated based upon the following shares:

	Fiscal 2013	Fiscal 2012	Fiscal 2011
Basic	52,034	51,608	51,092
Effect of restricted stock	—	1,701	—
Diluted	52,034	53,309	51,092

During Fiscal 2013 and Fiscal 2011, the Company has not assumed the exercise of common stock equivalents as the impact would be antidilutive due to the net losses reported.

(s) Environmental Expenditures

Environmental expenditures that relate to current ongoing operations or to conditions caused by past operations are expensed or capitalized as appropriate. The Company determines its liability for environmental matters on a site-by-site basis and records a liability at the time when it is probable that a liability has been incurred and such liability can be reasonably estimated. The estimated liability is not reduced for possible recoveries from insurance carriers. Estimated environmental remediation expenditures are included in the determination of the net realizable value recorded for assets held for sale.

(t) Reclassifications

Certain prior year amounts have been reclassified to conform to the current year presentation. These reclassifications had no effect on previously reported results of cash flows, operations or accumulated deficit.

(u) Comprehensive (Loss) Income

Comprehensive (loss) income includes foreign currency translation gains and losses on assets and liabilities of foreign subsidiaries, effects of exchange rate changes on intercompany balances of a long-term nature and transactions designated as a hedge of a net investment in a foreign subsidiary, deferred gains and losses on derivative financial instruments designated as cash flow hedges and amortization of deferred gains and losses associated with the Company's pension plans. The foreign currency translation gains and losses for Fiscal 2013, Fiscal 2012 and Fiscal 2011 were primarily attributable to the impact of translation of the net assets of the Company's European and Latin

American operations, which primarily have functional currencies in Euros, Pounds Sterling, Mexican Peso and Brazilian Real. Except for gains and losses resulting from exchange rate changes on intercompany balances of a long-term nature, and prior to September 30, 2011, the Company did not provide income taxes on currency translation adjustments, as earnings from international subsidiaries were considered to be permanently reinvested. As of the beginning of Fiscal 2012, the Company is no longer considering current and future earnings from international subsidiaries to be permanently reinvested, except for in locations where the Company is precluded by certain restrictions from repatriating earnings.

For information pertaining to the reclassification of unrealized gains and losses on derivative instruments, see Note 7, "Derivative Financial Instruments."

The following is a roll forward of the amounts recorded in AOCI:

	Fiscal 2013	Fiscal 2012	Fiscal 2011
Foreign Currency Translation Adjustments:			
Beginning balance	$ (225)	$ 8,377	$ 18,984
Gross change before reclassification adjustment	(6,622)	(8,602)	(12,857)
Gross change after reclassification adjustment	$ (6,622)	$ (8,602)	$(12,857)
Deferred tax effect	—	—	2,742
Deferred tax valuation allowance	—	—	(492)
Other Comprehensive Loss	$ (6,622)	$ (8,602)	$(10,607)
Noncontrolling interest	203	—	—
Ending balance	$ (7,050)	$ (225)	$ 8,377
Unrealized Gains (Losses) on Cash Flow Hedges:			
Beginning balance	$ 218	$ (1,327)	$ (5,755)
Gross change before reclassification adjustment	(2,013)	(1,824)	(5,992)
Net reclassification adjustment for (gains) losses included in earnings	(920)	3,097	13,422
Gross change after reclassification adjustment	$ (2,933)	$ 1,273	$ 7,430
Deferred tax effect	(234)	(636)	(2,671)
Deferred tax valuation allowance	658	908	(331)
Other Comprehensive Income	$ (2,509)	$ 1,545	$ 4,428
Ending balance	$ (2,291)	$ 218	$ (1,327)
Defined Benefit Pension Plans:			
Beginning balance	$(33,428)	$(21,496)	$(20,726)
Gross change before reclassification adjustment	8,097	(15,682)	(6,344)
Net reclassification adjustment for losses (gains) included in Cost of goods sold	1,571	900	(174)
Net reclassification adjustment for (gains) losses included in Selling expenses	(584)	—	69
Net reclassification adjustment for losses included in General and administrative expenses	373	—	113
Gross change after reclassification adjustment	$ 9,457	$(14,782)	$ (6,336)
Deferred tax effect	(5,123)	3,632	2,037
Deferred tax valuation allowance	(86)	(782)	3,529
Other Comprehensive (Loss) Income	$ 4,248	$(11,932)	$ (770)
Ending balance	$(29,180)	$(33,428)	$(21,496)
Total Other Comprehensive Loss, net of tax	$ (4,883)	$(18,989)	$ (6,949)
Total ending AOCI	$(38,521)	$(33,435)	$(14,446)

(v) Stock Compensation

The Company measures the cost of its stock-based compensation plans, which include restricted stock awards and restricted stock units, based on the fair value of the awards at the date of grant and recognizes these costs over the requisite service period of the awards.

In September 2009, SB Holdings' board of directors (the "Board") adopted the 2009 Spectrum Brands Inc. Incentive Plan (the "2009 Plan"). Prior to October 21, 2010, up to 3,333 shares of common stock, net of forfeitures and cancellations, could have been issued under the 2009 Plan. After October 21, 2010, no further awards may be made under the 2009 Plan.

In June 2010, SB Holdings adopted the Spectrum Brands Holdings, Inc. 2007 Omnibus Equity Award Plan (formerly known as the Russell Hobbs Inc. 2007 Omnibus Equity Award Plan, as amended on June 24, 2008) (the "RH Plan"). Prior to October 21, 2010, up to 600 shares of common stock, net of forfeitures and cancellations, could have been issued under the RH Plan. After October 21, 2010, no further awards may be made under the RH Plan.

On October 21, 2010, the Board adopted the Spectrum Brands Holdings, Inc. 2011 Omnibus Equity Award Plan (the "2011 Plan"), which was approved at the Annual Meeting of Stockholders on March 1, 2011. Up to 4,626 shares of common stock of SB Holdings, net of cancellations, may be issued under the 2011 Plan.

Total stock compensation expense associated with restricted stock units recognized by the Company during Fiscal 2013 was $43,861. The amounts before tax are included in General and administrative expenses in the accompanying Consolidated Statements of Operations.

Total stock compensation expense associated with restricted stock units recognized by the Company during Fiscal 2012 was $29,164. The amounts before tax are included in General and administrative expenses in the accompanying Consolidated Statements of Operations, of which $131, related to the accelerated vesting of certain awards to terminated employees.

Total stock compensation expense associated with restricted stock units recognized by the Company during Fiscal 2011 was $30,389. The amounts before tax are included in General and administrative expenses in the accompanying Consolidated Statements of Operations, of which $467, related to the accelerated vesting of certain awards to terminated employees.

The Company granted approximately 700 restricted stock units during Fiscal 2013. Of these grants, 48 restricted stock units are time-based and vest over a period of one year. Of the remaining 652 restricted stock units, 90 are performance-based and vest over a one year period and 562 are both performance and time-based and vest over a one year performance-based period followed by a one year time-based period. The total market value of the restricted stock units on the date of the grant was approximately $32,176.

The Company granted approximately 863 restricted stock units during Fiscal 2012. Of these grants, 160 restricted stock units are time-based and vest over a period ranging from one to two years. The remaining 703 restricted stock units are both performance and time-based and vest over a one year performance-based period followed by a one year time-based period. The total market value of the restricted stock units on the date of the grant was approximately $24,408.

A summary of the Company's restricted stock and restricted stock unit award activity for Fiscal 2013 and Fiscal 2012, and the non-vested awards outstanding as of September 30, 2013 is as follows:

Restricted Stock Awards	Shares	Weighted Average Grant Date Fair Value	Fair Value at Grant Date
Restricted stock awards at September 30, 2011	123	$24.20	$ 2,977
Vested	(110)	23.75	(2,613)
Restricted stock awards at September 30, 2012	13	$28.00	$364
Vested	(13)	28.00	(364)
Restricted stock awards at September 30, 2013	—	$ —	$ —

Restricted Stock Units	Shares	Weighted Average Grant Date Fair Value	Fair Value at Grant Date
Non-vested restricted stock units at September 30, 2011	1,645	$28.97	$47,656
Granted	863	28.28	24,408
Forfeited	(57)	28.49	(1,624)
Vested	(520)	29.83	(15,509)
Non-vested restricted stock units at September 30, 2012	1,931	$28.45	$54,931
Granted	700	45.97	32,176
Forfeited	(302)	30.36	(9,168)
Vested	(1,211)	28.25	(34,216)
Non-vested restricted stock units at September 30, 2013	1,118	$39.11	$43,723

(w) Restructuring and Related Charges

Restructuring charges are recognized and measured in accordance with the provisions of ASC Topic 420: *"Exit or Disposal Cost Obligations,"* ("ASC 420"). Under ASC 420, restructuring charges include, but are not limited to, termination and related costs consisting primarily of one-time termination benefits such as severance costs and retention bonuses, and contract termination costs consisting primarily of lease termination costs. Related charges, as defined by the Company, include, but are not limited to, other costs directly associated with exit and integration activities, including impairment of property and other assets, departmental costs of full-time incremental integration employees, and any other items related to the exit or integration activities. Costs for such activities are estimated by management after evaluating detailed analyses of the costs to be incurred. The Company presents restructuring and related charges on a combined basis. (See also Note 14, "Restructuring and Related Charges", for a more complete discussion of restructuring initiatives and related costs.)

(x) Acquisition and Integration Related Charges

Acquisition and integration related charges reflected in Operating expenses include, but are not limited to, transaction costs such as banking, legal, accounting and other professional fees directly related to both consummated acquisitions and acquisition targets, termination and related costs for transitional and certain other employees, integration related professional fees and other post business combination expenses associated with mergers and acquisitions.

The following table summarizes acquisition and integration related charges incurred by the Company during Fiscal 2013, Fiscal 2012 and Fiscal 2011:

	2013	2012	2011
Russell Hobbs			
Integration costs	$ 3,452	$10,168	$23,084
Employee termination charges	217	3,900	8,105
Legal and professional fees	39	1,495	4,883
Russell Hobbs Acquisition and integration related charges	$ 3,708	$15,563	$36,072
HHI Business			
Legal and professional fees	27,712	—	—
Integration costs	8,864	—	—
Employee termination charges	356	—	—
HHI Business Acquisition and integration related charges	$36,932	$ —	$ —
Shaser	4,828	—	—
FURminator	2,270	7,938	—
Black Flag	154	3,379	—
Other	553	4,186	531
Total Acquisition and integration related charges	$48,445	$31,066	$36,603

NATURE OF OPERATIONS

1.25 CSX CORPORATION (DEC)
NOTES TO CONSOLIDATED FINANCIAL STATEMENTS

Note 1. Nature of Operations and Significant Accounting Policies (in part)

Business

CSX Corporation ("CSX"), and together with its subsidiaries (the "Company"), based in Jacksonville, Florida, is one of the nation's leading transportation companies. The Company provides rail-based transportation services including traditional rail service and the transport of intermodal containers and trailers.

The Company's annual average number of employees was approximately 31,000 in 2013, which includes approximately 26,000 union employees. Most of the Company's employees provide or support transportation services.

CSX Transportation, Inc.

CSX's principal operating subsidiary, CSX Transportation, Inc. ("CSXT"), provides an important link to the transportation supply chain through its approximately 21,000 route mile rail network, which serves major population centers in 23 states east of the Mississippi River, the District of Columbia and the Canadian provinces of Ontario and Quebec. It has access to over 70 ocean, river and lake port terminals along the Atlantic and Gulf Coasts, the Mississippi River, the Great Lakes and the St. Lawrence Seaway. The Company's intermodal business, also part of CSXT, links customers to railroads via trucks and terminals. CSXT also serves thousands of production and distribution facilities through track connections to approximately 240 short-line and regional railroads.

Lines of Business

During 2013, CSXT's transportation services generated $12.0 billion of revenue and served three primary lines of business:
- The merchandise business shipped nearly 2.8 million carloads and generated approximately 59% of revenue and 42% of volume in 2013. The Company's merchandise business is the most diverse market and transports aggregates (which include crushed stone, sand and gravel), metal, phosphate, fertilizer, food, consumer (manufactured goods and appliances), agricultural, automotive, paper and chemical products.
- The coal business shipped 1.2 million carloads and accounted for 24% of revenue and 18% of volume in 2013. The Company transports domestic coal, coke and iron ore to electricity-generating power plants, steel manufacturers and industrial plants as well as export coal to deep-water port facilities. Almost half of export coal and nearly all of the domestic coal that the Company transports is used for generating electricity.

- The intermodal business accounted for approximately 14% of revenue and 40% of volume in 2013. The intermodal line of business combines the superior economics of rail transportation with the short-haul flexibility of trucks and offers a competitive cost advantage over long-haul trucking. Through a network of more than 50 terminals, the intermodal business serves all major markets east of the Mississippi and transports mainly manufactured consumer goods in containers, providing customers with truck-like service for longer shipments.

Other revenue accounted for approximately 3% of the Company's total revenue in 2013. This revenue category includes revenue from regional subsidiary railroads, demurrage, revenue for customer volume commitments not met, switching and other incidental charges. Revenue from regional railroads includes shipments by railroads that the Company does not directly operate. Demurrage represents charges assessed when freight cars are held beyond a specified period of time. Switching revenue is primarily generated when CSXT switches cars for a customer or another railroad.

Other Entities

In addition to CSXT, the Company's subsidiaries include CSX Intermodal Terminals, Inc. ("CSX Intermodal Terminals"), Total Distribution Services, Inc. ("TDSI"), Transflo Terminal Services, Inc. ("Transflo"), CSX Technology, Inc. ("CSX Technology") and other subsidiaries. CSX Intermodal Terminals owns and operates a system of intermodal terminals, predominantly in the eastern United States and also performs drayage services (the pickup and delivery of intermodal shipments) for certain CSXT customers and trucking dispatch operations. TDSI serves the automotive industry with distribution centers and storage locations. Transflo connects non-rail served customers to the many benefits of rail by transferring products from rail to trucks. Today, the biggest Transflo markets are chemicals and agriculture, such as minerals and ethanol. CSX Technology and other subsidiaries provide support services for the Company.

CSX's other holdings include CSX Real Property, Inc., a subsidiary responsible for the Company's real estate sales, leasing, acquisition and management and development activities. These activities are classified in other income—net because they are not considered to be operating activities by the Company. Results of these activities fluctuate with the timing of non-operating real estate transactions.

USE OF ESTIMATES

1.26 SERVICE CORPORATION INTERNATIONAL (DEC)
MANAGEMENT'S DISCUSSION AND ANALYSIS OF FINANCIAL CONDITION AND RESULTS OF OPERATIONS (in part)

Critical Accounting Policies, Recent Accounting Pronouncements, and Accounting Changes (in part)

Use of Estimates

The preparation of financial statements in conformity with Generally Accepted Accounting Principles in the United States (GAAP) requires management to make certain estimates and assumptions. These estimates and assumptions affect the carrying values of assets and liabilities and disclosures of contingent assets and liabilities at the balance sheet date. Actual results could differ from such estimates due to uncertainties associated with the methods and assumptions underlying our critical accounting measurements. Key estimates used by management include:

Allowances—We provide various allowances and/or cancellation reserves for our funeral and cemetery preneed and atneed receivables, as well as for our preneed funeral and preneed cemetery deferred revenues. These allowances are based on an analysis of historical trends and include, where applicable, collection and cancellation activity. We also record an estimate of general agency revenues that may be canceled in their first year and revenue would be charged back by the insurance company. These estimates are impacted by a number of factors, including changes in economy, relocation, and demographic or competitive changes in our areas of operation.

Valuation of trust investments—The trust investments include marketable securities that are classified as available-for-sale in accordance with the Investments in Debt and Equity Securities Topic of the ASC. When available, we use quoted market prices for specific securities. When quoted market prices are not available for the specific security, fair values are estimated by using either quoted market prices for securities with similar characteristics or a fair value model with observable inputs that include a combination of interest rates, yield curves, credit risks, prepayment terms, rating, and tax exempt status.

The valuation of private equity and other investments requires significant management judgment due to the absence of quoted market prices, inherent lack of liquidity, and the long-term nature of such assets. The fair value of these investments is estimated based on the market value of the underlying real estate and private equity instruments. The underlying real estate value is determined using the most recent appraisals. The private equity instruments are valued based on reported net asset values discounted by 0% and 20% for risk and 0% to 10% for liquidity. See Fair Value Measurements below for additional information.

Legal liability reserves—Contingent liabilities, principally for legal matters, are recorded when it is probable that a liability has been incurred and the amount of the loss can be reasonably estimated in accordance with the Contingencies Topic of the ASC. Liabilities accrued for legal matters require judgments regarding projected outcomes and a range of loss based on historical experience and recommendations of legal counsel. However, litigation is inherently unpredictable and excessive verdicts do occur. As disclosed in Note 12 in Part II, Item 8. Financial Statements and Supplementary Data, our legal exposures and the ultimate outcome of these legal proceedings could be material to operating results or cash flows in any given quarter or year.

Depreciation of long-lived assets—We depreciate our long-lived assets ratably over their estimated useful lives. These estimates of useful lives may be affected by such factors as changing market conditions or changes in regulatory requirements.

Valuation of assets acquired and liabilities assumed—We have applied the guidance in the Business Combinations Topic of the ASC to our business combinations. Tangible and intangible assets and liabilities assumed are recorded at their fair value and goodwill is recognized for any difference between the price of acquisition and our fair value determination. We have customarily estimated our purchase costs and other related transactions known to us at closing of the acquisition. To the extent that information not available to us at the closing date subsequently became available during the allocation period, we have adjusted our goodwill, assets, or liabilities associated with the acquisition.

Income taxes—We compute income taxes using the liability method. Our ability to realize the benefit of our federal, state, and foreign deferred tax assets requires us to achieve certain future earnings levels. We have established a valuation allowance against a portion of our deferred tax assets and we could be required to further adjust that valuation allowance if market conditions change materially and future earnings are, or are projected to be, significantly different than our current estimates.

We intend to permanently reinvest these undistributed foreign earnings in those businesses outside the United States. It is not practicable to determine the amount of federal income taxes, if any, that might become due if such earnings are repatriated.

We file income tax returns, including tax returns for our subsidiaries, with U.S. federal, state, local, and foreign jurisdictions. Our tax returns are subject to routine compliance review by the various federal, state, and foreign taxing authorities in the jurisdictions in which we have operated and filed tax returns in the ordinary course of business. We accrue tax expense to reduce our tax benefits in those situations where it is more likely than not that we will not prevail against the tax authorities should they challenge the tax return position that gave rise to the benefit. We believe that our tax returns are materially correct as filed, and we will vigorously defend any challenges and proposed adjustments to those filings made by the tax authorities. A number of years may elapse before particular tax matters, for which we have established accruals, are audited and finally resolved. The number of tax years that may be subject to a tax audit varies depending on the tax jurisdiction. While we have effectively concluded our 2003—2005 tax years with respect to our affiliate the COOP, SCI and Subsidiaries' tax years 1999—2005 remain under review at the IRS Appeals level. SCI and Subsidiaries received a letter of no change to its tax liability for the years 2008—2010. Furthermore, SCI and its affiliates are under audit by various state and foreign jurisdiction for years through 2010. While it is often difficult to predict the final outcome or the timing of resolution of any particular tax matter, we believe that our accruals reflect the probable outcome of known tax contingencies. Unfavorable settlement of any particular issue would reduce a deferred tax asset or require the payment of cash. Favorable resolution could result in reduced income tax expense reported in the financial statements in the future. Our tax accruals for uncertain tax positions are presented in the balance sheet within *Other liabilities*.

Pension cost—Our pension plans are frozen with no benefits accruing to participants except interest. Pension costs and liabilities are actuarially determined based on certain assumptions, including the discount rate used to compute future benefit obligations. Weighted-average discount rates used to determine net periodic pension cost were 2.90% and 4.05% as of December 31, 2013 and 2012, respectively. We verify the reasonableness of the discount rate by comparing our rate to the rate earned on high-quality fixed income investments, such as the Moody's Aa index.

Insurance loss reserves—We purchase comprehensive general liability, morticians and cemetery professional liability, automobile liability, and workers' compensation insurance coverages structured with high deductibles. This high-deductible insurance program means we are primarily self-insured for claims and associated costs and losses covered by these policies. Historical insurance industry experience indicates a high degree of inherent variability in assessing the ultimate amount of losses associated with casualty insurance claims. This is especially true with respect to liability and workers' compensation exposures due to the extended period of time that transpires between when the claim might occur and the full settlement of such claim, often many years. We continually evaluate loss estimates associated with claims and losses related to these insurance coverages falling within the deductible of each coverage. Assumptions based on factors such as claim settlement patterns, claim development trends, claim frequency and severity patterns, inflationary trends, and data reasonableness will generally affect the analysis and determination of the "best estimate" of the projected ultimate claim losses. The results of these evaluations are used to both analyze and adjust our insurance loss reserves.

As of December 31, 2013, reported losses within our retention for workers' compensation, general liability, and auto liability incurred during the period May 1, 1991 through December 31, 2013 were approximately $391.1 million over 22.7 years. The selected fully developed ultimate settlement value estimated was $437.4 million for the same period. Paid losses were $380.9 million indicating a reserve requirement of $78.0 million, including $21.5 million in reserves assumed as part of the acquisition of Stewart.

At December 31, 2013 and 2012, the balances in our reserve for workers' compensation, general, and auto liability and the related activity were as follows:

	(Dollars in millions)
Balance at December 31, 2011	$52.6
Additions	31.4
Payments	(26.5)
Balance at December 31, 2012	$57.5
Additions	26.2
Acquisition	21.5
Payments	(27.2)
Balance at December 31, 2013	$78.0

VULNERABILITY DUE TO CERTAIN CONCENTRATIONS

1.27 JPMORGAN CHASE & CO. (DEC)
NOTES TO CONSOLIDATED FINANCIAL STATEMENTS

Note 5—Credit risk concentrations

Concentrations of credit risk arise when a number of customers are engaged in similar business activities or activities in the same geographic region, or when they have similar economic features that would cause their ability to meet contractual obligations to be similarly affected by changes in economic conditions.

JPMorgan Chase regularly monitors various segments of its credit portfolios to assess potential concentration risks and to obtain collateral when deemed necessary. Senior management is significantly involved in the credit approval and review process, and risk levels are adjusted as needed to reflect the Firm's risk appetite.

In the Firm's consumer portfolio, concentrations are evaluated primarily by product and by U.S. geographic region, with a key focus on trends and concentrations at the portfolio level, where potential risk concentrations can be remedied through changes in underwriting policies and portfolio guidelines. In the wholesale portfolio, risk concentrations are evaluated primarily by industry and monitored regularly on both an aggregate portfolio level and on an individual customer basis. Management of the Firm's wholesale exposure is accomplished through loan syndications and participations, loan sales, securitizations, credit derivatives, use of master netting agreements, and collateral and other risk-reduction techniques. For additional information on loans see Note 14 on pages 258–283 of this Annual Report.

The Firm does not believe that its exposure to any particular loan product (e.g., option adjustable rate mortgages ("ARMs")), industry segment (e.g., commercial real estate) or its exposure to residential real estate loans with high loan-to-value ratios results in a significant concentration of credit risk. Terms of loan products and collateral coverage are included in the Firm's assessment when extending credit and establishing its allowance for loan losses.

Customer receivables representing primarily margin loans to prime and retail brokerage clients of $26.9 billion and $23.8 billion at December 31, 2013 and 2012, respectively, are included in the table below. These margin loans are generally over-collateralized through a pledge of assets maintained in clients' brokerage accounts and are subject to daily minimum collateral requirements. In the event that the collateral value decreases, a maintenance margin call is made to the client to provide additional collateral into the account. If additional collateral is not provided by the client, the client's positions may be liquidated by the Firm to meet the minimum collateral requirements. As a result of the Firm's credit risk mitigation practices, the Firm did not hold any reserves for credit impairment on these receivables as of December 31, 2013 and 2012.

The table below presents both on—balance sheet and off—balance sheet consumer and wholesale-related credit exposure by the Firm's three credit portfolio segments as of December 31, 2013 and 2012.

December 31, (In millions)	2013 Credit Exposure	On-Balance Sheet Loans	Derivatives	Off-Balance Sheet[b]	2012 Credit Exposure	On-Balance Sheet Loans	Derivatives	Off-Balance Sheet[b]
Total consumer, excluding credit card	$ 345,259	$289,063	$ —	$ 56,057	$ 352,889	$292,620	$ —	$ 60,156
Total credit card	657,174	127,791	—	529,383	661,011	127,993	—	533,018
Total consumer	1,002,433	416,854	—	585,440	1,013,900	420,613	—	593,174
Wholesale-related								
Real Estate	87,102	69,151	460	17,491	76,198	60,740	1,084	14,374
Banks & Finance Cos	66,881	25,482	18,888	22,511	73,318	26,651	19,846	26,821
Oil & Gas	46,934	14,383	2,203	30,348	42,563	14,704	2,345	25,514
Healthcare	45,910	13,319	3,202	29,389	48,487	11,638	3,359	33,490
State & Municipal Govt	35,666	8,708	3,319	23,639	41,821	7,998	5,138	28,685
Consumer Products	34,145	9,099	715	24,331	32,778	9,151	826	22,801
Asset Managers	33,506	5,656	7,175	20,675	31,474	6,220	8,390	16,864
Utilities	28,983	5,582	2,248	21,153	29,533	6,814	2,649	20,070
Retail & Consumer Services	25,068	7,504	273	17,291	25,597	7,901	429	17,267
Technology	21,403	4,426	1,392	15,585	18,488	3,806	1,192	13,490
Central Govt	21,049	1,754	9,998	9,297	21,223	1,333	11,232	8,658
Machinery & Equipment Mfg	19,078	5,969	476	12,633	18,504	6,304	592	11,608
Metals/Mining	17,434	5,825	560	11,049	20,958	6,059	624	14,275
Business Services	14,601	4,497	594	9,510	13,577	4,550	190	8,837
Transportation	13,975	6,845	621	6,509	19,827	12,763	673	6,391
All other[a]	308,519	120,063	13,635	174,821	301,673	119,590	16,414	165,669
Subtotal	820,254	308,263	65,759	446,232	816,019	306,222	74,983	434,814
Loans held-for-sale and loans at fair value	13,301	13,301	—	—	6,961	6,961	—	—
Receivables from customers and other	26,744	—	—	—	23,648	—	—	—
Total wholesale-related	860,299	321,564	65,759	446,232	$846,628	$313,183	74,983	434,814
Total exposure[c]	$1,862,732	$738,418	$65,759	$1,031,672	$1,860,528	$733,796	$74,983	$1,027,988

[a] For more information on exposures to SPEs included within All other see Note 16 on pages 288–299 of this Annual Report.

[b] Represents lending-related financial instruments.

[c] For further information regarding on-balance sheet credit concentrations by major product and/or geography, see Notes 6, 14 and 15 on pages 220–233, 258–283 and 284–287, respectively, of this Annual Report. For information regarding concentrations of off-balance sheet lending-related financial instruments by major product, see Note 29 on pages 318–324 of this Annual Report.

1.28 GENCORP INC. (NOV)
NOTES TO CONSOLIDATED FINANCIAL STATEMENTS

Note 1. Summary of Significant Accounting Policies (in part)

w. Concentrations

Dependence upon government programs and contracts

Sales to the U.S. government and its agencies, including sales to the Company's significant customers discussed below, were as follows (dollars in millions):

	U.S. Government Sales	Percentage of Net Sales
Fiscal 2013	$1,311.0	95%
Fiscal 2012	936.9	94
Fiscal 2011	855.8	93

The Standard Missile program, which is included in the U.S. government sales, represented 22%, 25%, and 24% of net sales for fiscal 2013, 2012, and 2011, respectively. The demand for certain of the Company's services and products is directly related to the level of funding of government programs.

Major customers

Customers that represented more than 10% of net sales for the fiscal years presented are as follows:

	Year Ended		
	2013	2012	2011
Raytheon Company ("Raytheon")	32%	37%	36%
Lockheed Martin Corporation ("Lockheed Martin")	23	32	28
United Launch Alliance ("ULA")	18	*	*
* Less than 10%.			

Credit Risk

Aside from investments held in the Company's defined benefit pension plan, financial instruments that could potentially subject the Company to concentration of credit risk consist primarily of cash, cash equivalents, and trade receivables. The Company's cash and cash equivalents are held and managed by recognized financial institutions and are subject to the Company's investment policy. The investment policy outlines minimum acceptable credit ratings for each type of investment and limits the amount of credit exposure to any one security issue. The Company does not believe significant concentration of credit risk exists with respect to these investments.

Customers that represented more than 10% of accounts receivable for the periods presented are as follows:

	As of November 30,	
	2013	2012
NASA	22%	*
Raytheon	20	48%
Lockheed Martin	19	31
ULA	18	*
* Less than 10%.		

Dependence on Single Source and Other Third Party Suppliers

The Company uses a significant quantity of raw materials that are highly dependent on market fluctuations and government regulations. Further, as a U.S. government contractor, the Company is often required to procure materials from suppliers capable of meeting rigorous customer and government specifications. As market conditions change for these companies, they often discontinue materials with low sales volumes or profit margins. The Company is often forced to either qualify new materials or pay higher prices to maintain the supply. To date the Company has been successful in establishing replacement materials and securing customer funding to address specific qualification needs of the programs. Prolonged disruptions in the supply of any of the Company's key raw materials, difficulty qualifying new sources of supply, implementing use of replacement materials or new sources of supply, and/or a continuing volatility in the prices of raw materials could have a material adverse effect on the Company's operating results, financial condition, and/or cash flows.

Workforce

As of November 30, 2013, 14% of the Company's 5,386 employees were covered by collective bargaining agreements.

Segment Reporting

PRESENTATION

1.29 FASB ASC 280, *Segment Reporting*, requires that a public business enterprise report a measure of segment profit or loss, certain specific revenue and expense items, and segment assets. FASB ASC 280-10 requires that all public business enterprises report information about the revenues derived from the enterprise's products or services or groups of similar products and services; about the countries in which the enterprise earns revenues and holds assets; and about major customers, regardless of whether that information is used in making operating decisions. Even if a public company has only one operating segment, FASB ASC 280 requires that it report information about geographic areas and major customers. However, FASB ASC does not require an enterprise to report information that is impracticable to present because the necessary information is not available, and the cost to develop it would be excessive.

1.30 According to FASB ASC 280-10-50-1, an operating segment of a public entity has all of the following characteristics:
- It engages in business activities from which it may earn revenues and incur expenses, including revenues and expenses relating to transactions with other components of the same public entity.
- Its operating results are regularly reviewed by the public entity's chief operating decision maker to make decisions about resources to be allocated to the segment and assess its performance.
- Its discrete financial information is available.

1.31 FASB ASC 280 uses the management approach to identify operating segments and measure the financial information disclosed based on information reported internally to the Chief Operating Decision Maker (CODM) to make resource allocation and performance assessment decisions. However, according to FASB ASC 280-10-50-9, entities that have a matrix organization should identify operating segments based on products and services when more than one type of component is reviewed by the CODM.

1.32 FASB ASC 280-10-50-30 requires reconciliations of total segment revenues, total segment profit or loss, total segment assets, and other amounts disclosed for segments to corresponding amounts in the enterprise's general-purpose financial statements. FASB ASC 350-20-50-1 states that entities that report segment information should provide information about the changes in the carrying amount of goodwill during the period for each reportable segment.

PRESENTATION AND DISCLOSURE EXCERPTS

SEGMENT INFORMATION

1.33 SCHNITZER STEEL INDUSTRIES, INC. (AUG)
NOTES TO THE CONSOLIDATED FINANCIAL STATEMENTS

Note 21—Segment Information

The accounting standards for reporting information about operating segments define an operating segment as a component of an enterprise that engages in business activities from which it may earn revenues and incur expenses for which discrete financial information is available that is evaluated regularly by the chief operating decision maker in deciding how to allocate resources and in assessing performance. The Company's chief operating decision maker is the Chief Executive Officer. The Company is organized by line of business. While the Chief Executive Officer evaluates results in a number of different ways, the line of business management structure is the primary basis for which the allocation of resources and financial results are assessed. Under the aforementioned criteria, the Company operates in three operating and reporting segments: metal purchasing, processing, recycling and selling (MRB), used auto parts (APB) and mini-mill steel manufacturing (SMB). Additionally, the Company is a noncontrolling partner in joint ventures, which are either in the metals recycling business or are suppliers of unprocessed metal.

MRB buys and processes ferrous and nonferrous metal for sale to foreign and other domestic steel producers or their representatives and to SMB. MRB also purchases ferrous metal from other processors for shipment directly to SMB.

APB purchases used and salvaged vehicles, sells parts from those vehicles through its retail facilities and wholesale operations, and sells the remaining portion of the vehicles to metal recyclers, including MRB.

SMB operates a steel mini-mill that produces a wide range of finished steel products using recycled metal and other raw materials.

Intersegment sales from MRB to SMB are made at rates that approximate export market prices for shipments from the West Coast of the U.S. In addition, the Company has intersegment sales of autobodies from APB to MRB at rates that approximate market prices. These intercompany sales tend to produce intercompany profits which are not recognized until the finished products are ultimately sold to third parties.

The information provided below is obtained from internal information that is provided to the Company's chief operating decision maker for the purpose of corporate management. The Company uses segment operating income (loss) to measure segment performance. The Company does not allocate corporate interest income and expense, income taxes, other income and expenses related to corporate activity or corporate expense for management and administrative services that benefit all three segments. In addition, the Company does not allocate restructuring charges to the segment operating income (loss) because management does not include this information in its measurement of the performance of the operating segments. Because of this unallocated income and expense, the operating income (loss) of each reporting segment does not reflect the operating income (loss) the reporting segment would report as a stand-alone business. All amounts presented exclude the results of operations of the Company's discontinued full-service used auto parts operation.

The following is a summary of the Company's total assets as of August 31 (in thousands):

	2013	2012
Total assets:		
Metals Recycling Business[1]	$1,316,202	$1,696,296
Auto Parts Business	359,977	329,327
Steel Manufacturing Business	330,282	322,398
Total segment assets	2,006,461	2,348,021
Corporate and eliminations	(600,949)	(584,448)
Total assets	$1,405,512	$1,763,573
Property, plant and equipment, net[2]	$ 564,426	$ 564,185

[1] MRB total assets include $15 million and $17 million as of August 31, 2013 and 2012, respectively, for investments in joint venture partnerships.

[2] Property, plant and equipment, net includes $85 million and $67 million as of August 31, 2013 and 2012, respectively, at our Canadian locations.

The table below illustrates the Company's results by reporting segment for the years ended August 31 (in thousands):

	2013	2012	2011
Metals Recycling Business:			
Revenues	$2,210,484	$2,948,707	$3,070,004
Less: Intersegment revenues	(178,341)	(183,906)	(169,331)
MRB external customer revenues	2,032,143	2,764,801	2,900,673
Auto Parts Business:			
Revenues	313,306	316,884	319,833
Less: Intersegment revenues	(75,992)	(73,974)	(78,795)
APB external customer revenues	237,314	242,910	241,038
Steel Manufacturing Business:			
Revenues	352,454	333,227	317,483
Total revenues	$2,621,911	$3,340,938	$3,459,194
Depreciation and amortization:			
Metals Recycling Business	$ 58,964	$ 57,855	$ 49,773
Auto Parts Business	11,793	10,920	10,131
Steel Manufacturing Business	9,072	9,436	10,782
Segment depreciation and amortization	79,829	78,211	70,686
Corporate	3,241	4,045	4,180
Total depreciation and amortization	$ 83,070	$ 82,256	$ 74,866
Capital expenditures:			
Metals Recycling Business	$ 61,930	$ 60,212	$ 88,917
Auto Parts Business	12,769	7,525	7,099
Steel Manufacturing Business	7,582	5,556	3,328
Segment capital expenditures	82,281	73,293	99,344
Corporate	8,100	5,267	5,620
Total capital expenditures	$ 90,381	$ 78,560	$ 104,964
Reconciliation of the Company's segment operating income (loss) to income (loss) from continuing operations before income taxes:			
Metals Recycling Business[1]	$ (311,549)	$ 63,872	$164,646
Auto Parts Business	24,539	33,304	64,027
Steel Manufacturing Business	6,541	(2,081)	2,562
Segment operating income (loss)	(280,469)	95,095	231,235
Restructuring charges	(7,906)	(5,012)	—
Corporate and eliminations	(39,414)	(36,415)	(45,271)
Operating income (loss)	(327,789)	53,668	185,964
Interest expense	(9,743)	(11,880)	(8,436)
Other income, net	83	1,168	3,277
Income (loss) from continuing operations before income taxes	$ (337,449)	$ 42,956	$ 180,805

[1] MRB operating income (loss) includes $1 million, $2 million and $5 million in income from joint ventures accounted for by the equity method in fiscal 2013, 2012 and 2011, respectively. The MRB operating loss for fiscal 2013 also includes a goodwill impairment charge of $321 million and other asset impairment charges of $13 million.

The following revenues from external customers are presented based on the sales destination and by major product for the years ended August 31 (in thousands):

	2013	2012	2011
Revenues based on sales destination:			
Foreign	$1,657,736	$2,284,152	$2,471,737
Domestic	964,175	1,056,786	987,457
Total revenues from external customers	$2,621,911	$3,340,938	$3,459,194
Major product information:			
Ferrous scrap metal	$1,500,115	$2,117,055	$2,259,229
Nonferrous scrap metal and other	532,028	647,746	641,444
Auto parts	237,314	242,910	241,038
Finished steel products	346,982	332,719	317,338
Semi-finished steel products	5,472	508	145
Total revenues from external customers	$2,621,911	$3,340,938	$3,459,194

In fiscal 2013, 2012 and 2011, there were no external customers that accounted for more than 10% of the Company's consolidated revenues. Sales to customers in foreign countries are a significant part of the Company's business. The schedule below identifies those foreign countries in which the Company's sales exceeded 10% of consolidated revenues in any of the last three years ended August 31 (in thousands):

	2013	% of Revenue	2012	% of Revenue	2011	% of Revenue
China	$562,558	21.5 %	$719,979	22.0 %	$884,744	25.6 %
Turkey	341,418	13.0 %	435,558	13.0 %	N/A	N/A
South Korea	N/A	N/A	$397,525	12.0 %	N/A	N/A

[1] N/A—sales were less than the 10% threshold and as such disclosure is not applicable.

1.34 CARLISLE COMPANIES INCORPORATED (DEC)
NOTES TO CONSOLIDATED FINANCIAL STATEMENTS

Note 2—Segment Information

The Company's operations are reported in the following segments:

Carlisle Construction Materials ("CCM" or the "Construction Materials segment") —the principal products of this segment are rubber (EPDM), thermoplastic polyolefin (TPO), and polyvinyl chloride (PVC) roofing membranes used predominantly on non-residential low-sloped roofs, related roofing accessories, including flashings, fasteners, sealing tapes, coatings and waterproofing, and insulation products. The markets served include new construction, re-roofing and maintenance of low-sloped roofs, water containment, HVAC sealants, and coatings and waterproofing.

Carlisle Interconnect Technologies ("CIT" or the "Interconnect Technologies segment") —the principal products of this segment are high-performance wire, cable, connectors, contacts, and cable assemblies primarily for the aerospace, defense electronics, industrial, medical, and test and measurement equipment markets.

Carlisle Brake & Friction ("CBF" or the "Brake & Friction segment") —the principal products of this segment include high-performance brakes and friction material, and clutch and transmission friction material for the mining, construction, aerospace, agriculture, motor sports, and alternative energy markets.

Carlisle FoodService Products ("CFSP" or the "FoodService Products segment") —the principal products of this segment include commercial and institutional foodservice permanentware, table coverings, cookware, catering equipment, fiberglass and composite material trays and dishes, industrial brooms, brushes, mops, and rotary brushes for commercial and non-commercial foodservice operators and sanitary maintenance professionals.

Corporate —includes other unallocated costs, primarily general corporate expenses. Corporate assets consist primarily of cash and cash equivalents, facilities, deferred taxes, and other invested assets. Corporate assets also include assets of ceased operations not classified as held for sale.

On October 21, 2013, the Company entered into a definitive agreement to sell the Transportation Products business for total cash consideration of $375 million, subject to working capital and other customary adjustments. On December 31, 2013, the Company completed the divestiture of the Transportation Products business. All prior period results of operations have been retrospectively adjusted to reflect the

Transportation Products business as discontinued operations. See Note 4 for further information related to the sale of the Transportation Products business.

Geographic Area Information —sales from continuing operations are attributable to the United States and to all foreign countries based on the country to which the product was delivered. Sales by region for the years ended December 31 are as follows (in millions):

Country	2013	2012	2011
United States	$2,260.8	$2,206.0	$1,997.6
International:			
Europe	330.4	315.9	233.5
Asia	126.3	117.3	104.4
Canada	90.1	82.6	76.6
Mexico and Latin America	69.7	65.8	26.5
Middle East and Africa	47.4	46.6	43.4
Other	18.3	17.0	10.4
Net sales	$2,943.0	$2,851.2	$2,492.4

Long-lived assets, comprised of net property, plant and equipment, goodwill and other intangible assets, investments and other long-term assets, located in the United States and foreign countries are as follows (in millions):

Country	2013	2012	2011
Long-lived asset held and used:			
United States	$1,479.6	$1,735.1	$1,428.1
Europe	343.5	331.6	334.6
Asia	77.1	127.4	130.8
United Kingdom	55.7	55.5	27.4
Canada	1.1	1.2	1.4
Mexico	1.0	1.2	1.5
Total long-lived asset	$1,958.0	$2,252.0	$1,923.8

Financial information for operations by reportable business segment is included in the following summary:

In millions	Sales[1]	EBIT	Assets[2]	Depreciation and Amortization	Capital Spending
2013					
Carlisle Construction Materials	$1,776.5	$264.0	$886.9	$31.0	$64.5
Carlisle Interconnect Technologies	577.7	89.4	1,017.5	34.4	12.2
Carlisle Brake & Friction	350.5	33.5	603.7	21.3	10.4
Carlisle FoodService Products	238.8	27.0	193.2	7.7	10.8
Corporate	—	(47.1)	791.4	1.7	—
Total	$2,943.0	$366.8	$3,492.7	$96.1	$97.9
2012					
Carlisle Construction Materials	$1,695.8	$273.4	$860.4	$27.9	$81.5
Carlisle Interconnect Technologies	463.1	69.1	1,075.7	24.6	19.2
Carlisle Brake & Friction	449.0	75.6	625.7	20.2	19.8
Carlisle FoodService Products	243.3	12.3	190.1	9.1	4.9
Corporate	—	(58.5)	132.3	1.7	1.6
Total	$2,851.2	$371.9	$2,884.2	$83.5	$127.0
2011					
Carlisle Construction Materials	1,484.0	177.9	774.4	$23.7	$21.1
Carlisle Interconnect Technologies	299.6	41.9	782.1	12.9	14.8
Carlisle Brake & Friction	473.0	77.2	665.8	20.2	16.8
Carlisle FoodService Products	235.8	13.2	206.8	9.2	5.1
Corporate	—	(44.2)	116.4	1.7	0.2
Total	$2,492.4	$266.0	$2,545.5	$67.7	$58.0

[1] Excludes intersegment sales
[2] Corporate assets include assets of discontinued operations not classified as held for sale

A reconciliation of assets, depreciation, and amortization and capital spending reported above to the amounts presented on the Consolidated Statements of Cash Flows is as follows:

	2013	2012
Assets per table above	$3,492.7	$2,884.2
Assets held for sale of discontinued operations (Note 4)	0.3	573.1
Total Assets per Consolidated Balance Sheets	$3,493.0	$3,457.3

	2013	2012	2011
Depreciation and amortization per table above	$ 96.1	$ 83.5	$67.7
Depreciation and amortization of discontinued operations	17.8	21.4	20.3
Total depreciation and amortization	$113.9	$104.9	$88.0

	2013	2012	2011
Capital spending per table above	$ 97.9	$127.0	$58.0
Capital spending of discontinued operations	12.9	13.4	21.6
Total capital spending	$110.8	$140.4	$79.6

Accounting Changes and Error Corrections

Author's Note

In April 2013, FASB issued ASU No. 2013-07, *Presentation of Financial Statements (Topic 205): Liquidation Basis of Accounting*, to address when and how a public or private company or a not-for-profit organization should apply the liquidation basis of accounting. The new standard also provides principles for the recognition and measurement of assets and liabilities and disclosures, as well as related financial statement presentation requirements. The amendments are effective for annual reporting periods beginning after December 15, 2013, and interim reporting periods therein. Organizations should apply the requirements prospectively from the day that liquidation becomes imminent. Early adoption is permitted. If an organization has already been reporting under the liquidation basis in accordance with existing GAAP as of the effective date, it would not need to apply the new standard. The most common example of this would be for terminating employee benefit plans.

PRESENTATION

1.35 FASB ASC 250 defines various types of accounting changes, including changes in accounting principles and accounting estimates, and provides guidance on the accounting for and reporting of each type of change.

1.36 FASB ASC 250-10-45-1 include the presumption that, once adopted, an entity should not change an accounting principle (policy) to account for events and transactions of a similar type. FASB ASC 250-10-45-2 permits an entity to change an accounting principle in certain circumstances, such as when required to do so by new authoritative accounting guidance that mandates the use of a new accounting principle, interprets an existing principle, expresses a preference for an accounting principle, or rejects a specific principle. This paragraph also permits an entity to change an accounting principle if it can justify the use of an allowable alternative accounting principle on the basis that it is preferable.

1.37 FASB ASC 250-10-45-1 does not consider the following to be changes in accounting principle:
- Initial adoption of an accounting principle for new events or transactions
- Initial adoption of an accounting principle for new events or transactions that previously were immaterial in their effect
- Adoption or modification of an accounting principle for substantively different transactions or events from those occurring previously

1.38 FASB ASC 250-10-45-5 requires an entity to apply a change in accounting principle retrospectively to all prior periods, unless it is impracticable to do so. Retrospective application requires cumulative adjustments to the carrying amounts of assets and liabilities at the beginning of the earliest period presented; an adjustment, if any, to the opening balance of retained earnings or other relevant equity account; and adjusted financial statements for each individual prior period presented to reflect the period-specific effects of applying the new accounting principle. FASB ASC 250-10-45-7 provides an exception if it is impracticable to determine the cumulative effect of applying a change in accounting principle to any prior period; the new accounting principle should be applied as if the change was made prospectively as of the earliest date practicable. FASB ASC 250-10-45-8 permits only direct effects of the change in accounting principle, including any related income tax effects, to be included in the retrospective adjustment and prohibits an entity from including indirect effects that would have been recognized if the newly adopted accounting principle had been followed in prior periods. If indirect effects are actually incurred and recognized, an entity should only report for those indirect effects in the period in which the accounting change is made.

1.39 FASB ASC 250-10-45-17 requires an entity to account for a change in accounting estimate prospectively in the period of change if the change affects that period only or in the period of change and future periods if the change affects both.

1.40 Paragraphs 18–19 of FASB ASC 250-10-45 recognize that it may be difficult to distinguish between a change in an accounting principle and a change in an accounting estimate. Additional guidance is provided for those circumstances when an entity's change in estimate is affected by a change in accounting principle, recognizing that the effect of a change in accounting principle or the method of applying it may be inseparable from the effect of the change in accounting estimate. An example of such change is a change in the method of depreciation, amortization, or depletion for long-lived nonfinancial assets. Although an entity is permitted to apply this change prospectively as a change in accounting estimate, an entity should only make a change in accounting estimate affected by a change in accounting principle if the entity can justify the new accounting principle on the basis that it is preferable.

1.41 Paragraphs 23–24 of FASB ASC 250-10-45 require an entity to correct any error in the financial statements of a prior period discovered after the financial statements are issued or are available to be issued by restating the prior-period financial statements. Such errors are required to be reported as an error correction by restating the prior-period financial statements retrospectively with adjustments to the financial statements.

DISCLOSURE

1.42 As discussed in FASB ASC 250-10-50, among the required disclosures for a change in accounting principle, the reason should be disclosed, including an explanation about why the new method is preferable. Specific disclosures are also required for a change in accounting estimate, a change in reporting entity, correction of an error in previously-issued financial statements, and error corrections related to prior interim periods of the current fiscal year.

PRESENTATION AND DISCLOSURE EXCERPTS

CHANGE IN ACCOUNTING PRINCIPLE—EMPLOYEE RETIREMENT PLANS

1.43 CORNING INCORPORATED (DEC)
NOTES TO CONSOLIDATED FINANCIAL STATEMENTS

1. Summary of Significant Accounting Policies (in part)

Employee Retirement Plans

In the first quarter of 2013, we elected to change our method of recognizing actuarial gains and losses for our defined benefit pension plans. Previously, we recognized the actuarial gains and losses as a component of Stockholders' Equity on our consolidated balance sheets on an annual basis. These amounts were amortized into our operating results over the average remaining service period of employees expected to receive benefits under the plan, to the extent such gains and losses were outside of the corridor, where the corridor is equal to 10% of the greater of the benefit obligation or the market-related value of plan assets at the beginning of the year. In addition, we used a calculated market-related value of plan assets for purposes of calculating the expected return on plan assets that spread asset gains and losses over a 3-year period. We have elected to recognize the change in the fair value of plan assets in full for purposes of calculating the expected return on plan assets and net actuarial gains and losses outside of the corridor in pension costs annually in the fourth quarter of each year and whenever the plan is remeasured or valuation estimates are finalized. The remaining components of pension expense are recorded on a quarterly basis. While the historical policy of recognizing pension expense was considered acceptable, we believe that the new policy is preferable as it recognizes the change in the fair value of plan assets in full for purposes of calculating the expected return on plan assets and eliminates the delay in recognition of net actuarial gains and losses outside of the corridor. We have applied these changes retrospectively, adjusting all prior periods, as if the new accounting methodology was in effect during those periods.

Following are the changes to financial statement line items as a result of the accounting methodology change for the periods presented in the accompanying consolidated financial statements:

(In millions, except share and per share amounts)	Year Ended December 31, 2013		
	Previous Accounting Method	Reported	Effect of Accounting Change
Cost of sales	$4,564	$4,495	$ (69)
Gross margin	3,255	3,324	69
Selling, general and administrative expenses	1,161	1,126	(35)
Research, development and engineering expenses	731	710	(21)
Operating income	1,246	1,371	125
Income before income taxes	2,348	2,473	125
Provision for income taxes	(466)	(512)	(46)
Net income attributable to Corning Incorporated	$1,882	$1,961	$ 79
Earnings per common share attributable to Corning Incorporated—Basic	$ 1.30	$ 1.35	$0.05
Earnings per common share attributable to Corning Incorporated—Diluted	$ 1.29	$ 1.34	$0.05

(In millions, except share and per share amounts)	Three Months Ended December 31, 2013 (unaudited)		
	Previous Accounting Method	Reported	Effect of Accounting Change
Cost of sales	$1,215	$1,186	$ (29)
Gross margin	741	770	29
Selling, general and administrative expenses	351	332	(19)
Research, development and engineering expenses	178	169	(9)
Operating income	131	184	53
Income before income taxes	514	567	53
Provision for income taxes	(126)	(146)	(20)
Net income attributable to Corning Incorporated	$ 388	$ 421	$ 33
Earnings per common share attributable to Corning Incorporated—Basic	$ 0.27	$ 0.30	$0.03
Earnings per common share attributable to Corning Incorporated—Diluted	$ 0.27	$ 0.30	$0.03

(In millions, except share and per share amounts)	Year Ended December 31, 2012		
	Previously Reported (before Accounting Change)	Revised (after Accounting Change)	Effect of Accounting Change
Cost of sales	$4,615	$4,693	$ 78
Gross margin	3,397	3,319	(78)
Selling, general and administrative expenses	1,165	1,205	40
Research, development and engineering expenses	745	769	24
Operating income	1,321	1,179	(142)
Income before income taxes	2,117	1,975	(142)
Provision for income taxes	(389)	(339)	50
Net income attributable to Corning Incorporated	$1,728	$1,636	$ (92)
Earnings per common share attributable to Corning Incorporated—Basic	$ 1.16	$ 1.10	$(0.06)
Earnings per common share attributable to Corning Incorporated—Diluted	$ 1.15	$ 1.09	$(0.06)

(In millions, except share and per share amounts)	Three Months Ended December 31, 2012 (unaudited)		
	Previously Reported (before Accounting Change)	Revised (after Accounting Change)	Effect of Accounting Change
Cost of sales	$1,239	$1,348	$ 109
Gross margin	907	798	(109)
Selling, general and administrative expenses	301	356	55
Research, development and engineering expenses	185	219	34
Operating income	277	79	(198)
Income before income taxes	381	183	(198)
Provision for income taxes	(98)	(28)	70
Net income attributable to Corning Incorporated	$ 283	$ 155	$ (128)
Earnings per common share attributable to Corning Incorporated—Basic	$ 0.19	$ 0.11	$(0.08)
Earnings per common share attributable to Corning Incorporated—Diluted	$ 0.19	$ 0.10	$(0.09)

(In millions, except share and per share amounts)	Year Ended December 31, 2011		
	Previously Reported (before Accounting Change)	Revised (after Accounting Change)	Effect of Accounting Change
Cost of sales	$4,324	$4,314	$ (10)
Gross margin	3,566	3,576	10
Selling, general and administrative expenses	1,033	1,028	(5)
Research, development and engineering expenses	671	668	(3)
Operating income	1,694	1,712	18
Income before income taxes	3,213	3,231	18
Provision for income taxes	(408)	(414)	(6)
Net income attributable to Corning Incorporated	$2,805	$2,817	$ 12
Earnings per common share attributable to Corning Incorporated—Basic	$ 1.80	$ 1.80	
Earnings per common share attributable to Corning Incorporated—Diluted	$ 1.77	$ 1.78	$0.01

Consolidated Statements of Comprehensive Income

(In millions)	Year Ended December 31, 2013		
	Previous Accounting Method	Reported	Effect of Accounting Change
Net income attributable to Corning Incorporated	$1,882	$1,961	$79
Other comprehensive loss, net of tax	(240)	(312)	(72)
Comprehensive income attributable to Corning Incorporated	$1,642	$1,649	$ 7

(In millions)	Year Ended December 31, 2012		
	Previously Reported (before Accounting Change)	Revised (after Accounting Change)	Effect of Accounting Change
Net income attributable to Corning Incorporated	$1,728	$1,636	$(92)
Other comprehensive loss, net of tax	(211)	(120)	91
Comprehensive income attributable to Corning Incorporated	$1,517	$1,516	$ (1)

(In millions)	Year Ended December 31, 2011		
	Previously Reported (before Accounting Change)	Revised (after Accounting Change)	Effect of Accounting Change
Net income attributable to Corning Incorporated	$2,805	$2,817	$12
Other comprehensive loss, net of tax	(132)	(144)	(12)
Comprehensive income attributable to Corning Incorporated	$2,673	$2,673	$ 0

Consolidated Balance Sheets

(In millions)	December 31, 2013		
	Previous Accounting Method	Reported	Effect of Accounting Change
Retained earnings	$11,904	$11,320	$(584)
Accumulated other comprehensive (loss) income	$ (540)	$ 44	$ 584

(In millions)	December 31, 2012		
	Previously Reported (before Accounting Change)	Revised (after Accounting Change)	Effect of Accounting Change
Retained earnings	$10,588	$9,932	$(656)
Accumulated other comprehensive (loss) income	$ (300)	$ 356	$ 656

(In millions)	December 31, 2011		
	Previously Reported (before Accounting Change)	Revised (after Accounting Change)	Effect of Accounting Change
Retained earnings	$9,332	$8,767	$(565)
Accumulated other comprehensive (loss) income	$ (89)	$ 476	$ 565

(In millions)	December 31, 2010		
	Previously Reported (before Accounting Change)	Revised (after Accounting Change)	Effect of Accounting Change
Retained earnings	$6,881	$6,304	$(577)
Accumulated other comprehensive income	$ 43	$ 620	$ 577

Consolidated Statements of Cash Flows

(In millions)	Year Ended December 31, 2013		
	Previous Accounting Method	Reported	Effect of Accounting Change
Cash flows from operating activities:			
Net income	$1,882	$1,961	$ 79
Deferred tax provision	$ 143	$ 189	$ 46
Employee benefit payments less than expense	$ 177	$ 52	$(125)

(In millions)	Year Ended December 31, 2012		
	Previously Reported (before Accounting Change)	Revised (after Accounting Change)	Effect of Accounting Change
Cash flows from operating activities:			
Net income	$1,728	$1,636	$ (92)
Deferred tax provision	$ 68	$ 18	$ (50)
Employee benefit payments less than expense	$ 36	$ 178	$142

(In millions)	Year Ended December 31, 2011		
	Previously Reported (before Accounting Change)	Revised (after Accounting Change)	Effect of Accounting Change
Cash flows from operating activities:			
Net income	$2,805	$2,817	$ 12
Deferred tax provision	$ 115	$ 121	$ 6
Employee benefit payments less than expense	$ 132	$ 114	$(18)

CHANGE IN ACCOUNTING PRINCIPLE—INVESTMENTS

1.44 MEDTRONIC, INC. (APR)

CONSOLIDATED BALANCE SHEETS (in part)

(In millions, except per share data)	April 26, 2013	April 27, 2012
Assets		
Current assets:		
Cash and cash equivalents	$ 860	$ 1,172
Investments	10,211	8,178
Accounts receivable, less allowances of $98 and $100, respectively	3,727	3,808
Inventories	1,712	1,800
Tax assets	539	703
Prepaid expenses and other current assets	744	675
Total current assets	17,793	16,336
Property, plant, and equipment, net	2,490	2,473
Goodwill	10,329	9,934
Other intangible assets, net	2,673	2,647
Long-term tax assets	232	176
Other assets	1,324	1,252
Total assets	$34,841	$32,818

1. Summary of Significant Accounting Policies (in part)

Investments —Investments in marketable equity securities and debt securities are classified and accounted for as available-for-sale at April 26, 2013 and April 27, 2012. Debt securities include corporate debt securities, U.S. and foreign government and agency securities, certificates of deposit, mortgage-backed securities, other asset-backed securities, and auction rate securities. These investments are recorded at fair value in the consolidated balance sheets. The change in fair value for available-for-sale securities is recorded, net of taxes, as a component of *accumulated other comprehensive loss* on the consolidated balance sheets.

Investments in securities that are classified and accounted for as trading securities at April 26, 2013 and April 27, 2012 include exchange-traded funds and are recorded at fair value on the consolidated balance sheets. The Company's trading securities seek to offset changes in liabilities related to equity and other market risks of certain deferred compensation arrangements. The change in fair value for trading securities is recorded as a component of *interest expense, net* on the consolidated statements of earnings. Management determines the appropriate classification of its investments in debt and equity securities at the time of purchase and reevaluates such determinations at each balance sheet date.

Effective April 26, 2013, the Company changed the method of classification of certain investments previously classified as long-term investments to current. The prior period balances have been reclassified to conform to the current year presentation. This new method classifies these securities as current or long-term based on the nature of the securities and availability for use in current operations while the prior classification was based on the maturities of the investments. The Company believes this method is preferable because it is consistent with how the Company manages its capital structure and liquidity. In conjunction with this change in classification of investments, the Company changed the classification of deferred taxes related to the unrealized gains and losses on investments previously classified as long-term from non-current assets to current assets.

Certain of the Company's investments in equity and other securities are long-term, strategic investments in companies that are in varied stages of development. The Company accounts for these investments under the cost or the equity method of accounting, as appropriate. These investments are included in *other assets* on the consolidated balance sheets. The valuation of equity and other securities accounted for under the cost method considers all available financial information related to the investee, including valuations based on recent third-party equity investments in the investee. If an unrealized loss for any investment is considered to be other-than-temporary, the loss will be recognized in the consolidated statements of earnings in the period the determination is made. Equity securities accounted for under the equity method are initially recorded at the amount of the Company's investment and adjusted each period for the Company's share of the investee's income or loss and dividends paid. Equity securities accounted for under both the cost and equity methods are reviewed quarterly for changes in circumstance or the occurrence of events that suggest the Company's investment may not be recoverable. See Note 5 for discussion of the gains and losses recognized on equity and other securities.

5. Investments

The Company holds investments consisting primarily of marketable debt and equity securities. The carrying amounts of cash and cash equivalents approximate fair value due to their short maturities.

Information regarding the Company's investments at April 26, 2013 is as follows:

(In millions)	Cost	Unrealized Gains	Unrealized Losses	Fair Value
Available-for-Sale Securities:				
Corporate debt securities	$ 4,587	$ 78	$ (4)	$ 4,661
Auction rate securities	118	—	(15)	103
Mortgage-backed securities	1,050	8	(5)	1,053
U.S. government and agency securities	3,882	17	(1)	3,898
Foreign government and agency securities	38	—	—	38
Certificates of deposit	6	—	—	6
Other asset-backed securities	539	2	—	541
Marketable equity securities	82	75	(2)	155
Trading Securities:				
Exchange-traded funds	45	5	—	50
Cost method, equity method, and other investments	549	—	—	NA
Total investments	$10,896	$185	$(27)	$10,505

Information regarding the Company's investments at April 27, 2012 is as follows:

(In millions)	Cost	Unrealized Gains	Unrealized Losses	Fair Value
Available-for-Sale Securities:				
Corporate debt securities	$3,501	$ 47	$ (7)	$3,541
Auction rate securities	153	—	(26)	127
Mortgage-backed securities	840	9	(10)	839
U.S. government and agency securities	3,122	38	—	3,160
Foreign government and agency securities	67	—	—	67
Certificates of deposit	47	—	—	47
Other asset-backed securities	535	3	(1)	537
Marketable equity securities	100	158	(5)	253
Trading Securities:				
Exchange-traded funds	45	2	(1)	46
Cost method, equity method, and other investments	508	—	—	NA
Total investments	$8,918	$257	$(50)	$8,617

Information regarding the Company's consolidated balance sheets presentation at April 26, 2013 and April 27, 2012 is as follows:

(In millions)	April 26, 2013 Investments	April 26, 2013 Other Assets	April 27, 2012 Investments	April 27, 2012 Other Assets
Available-for-sale securities	$10,161	$294	$8,132	$439
Trading securities	50	—	46	—
Cost method, equity method, and other investments	$ —	$549	$ —	$508
Total	$10,211	$843	$8,178	$947

The Company revised the classification, to investments, of certain amounts previously presented as cash and cash equivalents in the prior period consolidated balance sheets. These revisions, which are immaterial, also increased purchases and sales and maturities of marketable securities in the consolidated statements of cash flows for prior periods.

The following tables show the gross unrealized losses and fair values of the Company's available-for-sale securities that have been in a continuous unrealized loss position deemed to be temporary for less than 12 months and for more than 12 months, aggregated by investment category as of April 26, 2013 and April 27, 2012:

(In millions)	April 26, 2013 Less Than 12 Months Fair Value	April 26, 2013 Less Than 12 Months Unrealized Losses	April 26, 2013 More Than 12 Months Fair Value	April 26, 2013 More Than 12 Months Unrealized Losses
Corporate debt securities	$ 544	$(1)	$ 13	$ (3)
Auction rate securities	—	—	103	(15)
Mortgage-backed securities	195	(1)	44	(4)
U.S. government and agency securities	291	(1)	—	—
Marketable equity securities	14	(2)	—	—
Total	$1,044	$(5)	$160	$(22)

(In millions)	April 27, 2012 Less Than 12 Months Fair Value	April 27, 2012 Less Than 12 Months Unrealized Losses	April 27, 2012 More Than 12 Months Fair Value	April 27, 2012 More Than 12 Months Unrealized Losses
Corporate debt securities	$664	$ (4)	$ 16	$ (3)
Auction rate securities	—	—	127	(26)
Mortgage-backed securities	218	(2)	57	(8)
Other asset-backed securities	55	—	9	(1)
Marketable equity securities	24	(5)	—	—
Total	$961	$(11)	$209	$(38)

Activity related to the Company's investment portfolio is as follows:

| (In millions) | Fiscal Year | | | | | |
| | 2013 | | 2012 | | 2011 | |
	Debt[a]	Equity[b]	Debt[a]	Equity[b][c]	Debt[a]	Equity[b][d]
Proceeds from sales	$10,350	$161	$7,675	$113	$9,318	$ 31
Gross realized gains	$ 59	$ 94	$ 52	$ 93	$ 28	$ 85
Gross realized losses	$ (17)	$ —	$ (16)	$ —	$ (15)	$ —
Impairment losses recognized	$ —	$ (21)	$ (2)	$(10)	$ (5)	$(24)

[a] Includes available-for-sale debt securities.
[b] Includes marketable equity securities, cost method, equity method, exchange-traded funds, and other investments.
[c] As a result of the Salient and PEAK acquisitions that occurred during fiscal year 2012, the Company recognized a non-cash gain of $38 million on its previously-held minority investments.
[d] As a result of the Ardian acquisition that occurred during fiscal year 2011, the Company recognized a non-cash gain of $85 million on its previously-held minority investment.

The total other-than-temporary impairment losses on available-for-sale debt securities for the fiscal year ended April 26, 2013 were not significant. The total other-than-temporary impairment losses on available-for-sale debt securities for the fiscal year ended April 27, 2012 and April 29, 2011 were $6 million and $18 million, of which $4 million and $13 million, respectively, were recognized in other comprehensive income and $2 million and $5 million, respectively, were recognized in earnings. These charges relate to credit losses on certain mortgage-backed securities and auction rate securities. The amount of credit losses represents the difference between the present value of cash flows expected to be collected on these securities and the amortized cost. Based on the Company's assessment of the credit quality of the underlying collateral and credit support available to each of the remaining securities in which invested, the Company believes it has recorded all necessary other-than-temporary impairments as the Company does not have the intent to sell, nor is it more likely than not that the Company will be required to sell, before recovery of the amortized cost.

The following table shows the credit loss portion of other-than-temporary impairments on debt securities held by the Company as of the dates indicated and the corresponding changes in such amounts:

(In millions)	
Balance as of April 29, 2011	$ 20
Credit losses recognized on securities previously not impaired	1
Additional credit losses recognized on securities previously impaired	1
Reductions for securities sold during the period	(2)
Balance as of April 27, 2012	$ 20
Credit losses recognized on securities previously not impaired	—
Additional credit losses recognized on securities previously impaired	—
Reductions for securities sold during the period	(11)
Balance as of April 26, 2013	$ 9

The April 26, 2013 balance of available-for-sale debt securities by contractual maturity is shown in the following table at fair value. Within the table, maturities of mortgage-backed securities have been allocated based upon timing of estimated cash flows, assuming no change in the current interest rate environment. Actual maturities may differ from contractual maturities because the issuers of the securities may have the right to prepay obligations without prepayment penalties.

(In millions)	April 26, 2013
Due in one year or less	$ 2,169
Due after one year through five years	7,040
Due after five years through 10 years	978
Due after 10 years	113
Total debt securities	$10,300

As of April 26, 2013 and April 27, 2012, the aggregate carrying amount of equity and other securities without a quoted market price and accounted for using the cost or equity method was $549 million and $508 million, respectively. The total carrying value of these investments is reviewed quarterly for changes in circumstance or the occurrence of events that suggest the Company's investment may not be recoverable. The fair value of cost or equity method investments is not adjusted if there are no identified events or changes in circumstances that may have a material adverse effect on the fair value of the investment.

Gains and losses realized on trading securities and available-for-sale debt securities are recorded in interest expense, net in the consolidated statements of earnings. Gains and losses realized on marketable equity securities, cost method, equity method, and other investments are recorded in *other expense, net* in the consolidated statements of earnings. In addition, unrealized gains and losses on available-for-sale debt securities are recorded in *other comprehensive income (loss)* and unrealized gains and losses on trading securities are recorded in *interest expense, net* in the consolidated statements of earnings. Gains and losses from the sale of investments are calculated based on the specific identification method.

1.45 THE CHILDREN'S PLACE RETAIL STORES, INC. (JAN)
CONSOLIDATED BALANCE SHEETS (in part)

(In thousands, except par value)

Assets	February 2, 2013	January 28, 2012 (As Adjusted)
Current assets:		
Cash and cash equivalents	$194,128	$176,655
Short-term investments	15,000	—
Accounts receivable	18,490	17,382
Inventories	266,976	237,786
Prepaid expenses and other current assets	40,927	49,184
Deferred income taxes	9,714	7,921
Total current assets	545,235	488,928
Long-term assets:		
Property and equipment, net	330,101	323,863
Deferred income taxes	43,678	49,054
Other assets	4,396	4,407
Total assets	$923,410	$866,252

NOTES TO CONSOLIDATED FINANCIAL STATEMENTS

1. Basis of Presentation and Summary of Significant Accounting Policies (in part)

Inventories

Inventories, which consist primarily of finished goods, are stated at the lower of cost or market, with cost determined on an average cost basis. The Company capitalizes supply chain costs in inventory and these costs are reflected in cost of sales as the inventories are sold. Inventory includes items that have been marked down to the Company's best estimate of their lower of cost or market value and an estimate for inventory shrinkage. The Company bases its decision to mark down merchandise upon its current rate of sale, the season and the sell-through of the item. The Company adjusts its inventory based upon an annual physical inventory and shrinkage is estimated in interim periods based upon the historical results of physical inventories in the context of current year facts and circumstances.

In accordance with provisions of the FASB ASC topic on *"Accounting Changes and Error Corrections"* all prior periods presented have been retrospectively adjusted to apply the changes in accounting principle. For a summary of the retrospective adjustments, see Note 2.

2. Changes in Accounting Principle

During the fourth quarter of Fiscal 2012, the Company elected to change its method of accounting for inventories from the retail inventory method to the average cost method. In addition, the Company has elected to capitalize additional supply chain costs, which were previously expensed as incurred. We believe that the changes are preferable because they better reflect the value of inventory as of the balance sheet dates, provide a better reflection of periodic net income and improve comparability with our peers.

The Company has applied the changes in method of inventory costing to all prior periods presented within the consolidated financial statements in accordance with accounting principles relating to accounting changes. The cumulative impact of the retrospective application of the changes in accounting principle as of January 30, 2010 was a $22.1 million increase in retained earnings. The impact of these changes in accounting principle to our income from continuing operations, net income and earnings per share for the year ended February 2, 2013 were increases of $0.5 million, $0.5 million and $0.03 respectively. The following tables detail the impact of the retrospective application on previously reported periods included in the consolidated financial statements (in thousands, except per share amounts).

Consolidated Balance Sheets

January 28, 2012	As Reported	Effect of Change	As Adjusted
Inventories	$212,916	$24,870	$237,786
Deferred income taxes	17,188	(9,267)	7,921
Accumulated other comprehensive income	12,685	195	12,880
Retained earnings	$384,051	$15,408	$399,459

Consolidated Statements of Operations

	Fiscal Year Ended					
	January 28, 2012			January 29, 2011		
	As Reported	Effect of Change	As Adjusted	As Reported	Effect of Change	As Adjusted
Cost of sales	$1,051,649	$ 4,564	$1,056,213	$1,006,752	$ 7,126	$1,013,878
Gross profit	664,213	(4,564)	659,649	667,247	(7,126)	660,121
Income from continuing operations before income taxes	109,317	(4,564)	104,753	134,806	(7,126)	127,680
Provision for income taxes	32,092	(1,684)	30,408	51,219	(3,299)	47,920
Income from continuing operations	77,225	(2,880)	74,345	83,587	(3,827)	79,760
Net income	$ 77,225	$(2,880)	$ 74,345	$ 83,124	$(3,827)	$ 79,297
Basic Earnings Per Share Amounts						
Income from continuing operations	$ 3.03	(0.11)	$ 2.92	$ 3.09	(0.15)	$ 2.94
Net income	$ 3.03	(0.11)	$ 2.92	$ 3.07	(0.14)	$ 2.93
Diluted Earnings Per Share Amounts						
Income from continuing operations	$ 3.01	(0.11)	$ 2.90	$ 3.05	(0.14)	$ 2.91
Net income	$ 3.01	(0.11)	$ 2.90	$ 3.03	(0.14)	$ 2.89

Consolidated Statements of Comprehensive Income

	Fiscal Year Ended					
	January 28, 2012			January 29, 2011		
	As Reported	Effect of Change	As Adjusted	As Reported	Effect of Change	As Adjusted
Net income	$77,225	$(2,880)	$74,345	$83,124	$(3,827)	$79,297
Other Comprehensive Income (Loss):						
Foreign currency translation adjustment	(472)	53	(419)	5,596	102	5,698
Comprehensive income	$76,753	$(2,827)	$73,926	$88,720	$(3,725)	$84,995

Consolidated Statements of Cash Flows

	Fiscal Year Ended					
	January 28, 2012			January 29, 2011		
	As Reported	Effect of Change	As Adjusted	As Reported	Effect of Change	As Adjusted
Net income	$77,225	$(2,880)	$74,345	$83,124	$(3,827)	$79,297
Reconciliation of income from continuing operations to net cash provided by operating activities of continuing operations:						
Deferred taxes	3,953	(1,684)	2,269	27,473	(3,299)	24,174
Inventories	(2,760)	4,564	1,804	(2,476)	7,126	4,650

As the Company elected to change its method of accounting for inventory during the fourth quarter of Fiscal 2012, the following table shows the effect of the change on the unaudited quarterly results of operations for the first three quarters of Fiscal 2012 and the Fiscal 2011 interim periods (in thousands, except per share amounts). Refer to Note 15 for the adjusted quarterly financial information.

Consolidated Statements of Operations (Unaudited)

| | Fiscal Year Ended February 2, 2013 | | | | | | | | |
| | First Quarter | | | Second Quarter | | | Third Quarter | | |
	As Reported	Effect of Change	As Adjusted	As Reported	Effect of Change	As Adjusted	As Reported	Effect of Change	As Adjusted
Gross profit	$176,918	$1,728	$178,646	$114,606	$98	$114,704	$206,246	$3,287	$209,533
Income (loss) from continuing operations before income taxes	35,282	1,728	37,010	(26,919)	98	(26,821)	50,216	3,287	53,503
Provision (benefit) for income taxes	11,690	585	12,275	(8,930)	33	(8,897)	15,192	1,006	16,198
Income (loss) from continuing operations	23,592	1,143	24,735	(17,989)	65	(17,924)	35,024	2,281	37,305
Diluted earnings (loss) per share from continuing operations	$ 0.96	$ 0.04	$ 1.00	$ (0.74)	$—	$ (0.74)	$ 1.44	$ 0.10	$ 1.54

Consolidated Statements of Operations (Unaudited)

| | Fiscal Year Ended January 28, 2012 | | | | | |
| | First Quarter | | | Second Quarter | | |
	As Reported	Effect of Change	As Adjusted	As Reported	Effect of Change	As Adjusted
Gross profit	$183,587	$(2,158)	$181,429	$116,126	$1,448	$117,574
Income (loss) from continuing operations before income taxes	48,505	(2,158)	46,347	(16,092)	1,448	(14,644)
Provision (benefit) for income taxes	19,421	(844)	18,577	(6,315)	558	(5,757)
Income (loss) from continuing operations	29,084	(1,314)	27,770	(9,777)	890	(8,887)
Diluted earnings (loss) per share from continuing operations	$ 1.10	$ (0.05)	$ 1.05	$ (0.38)	$ 0.03	$ (0.35)

| | Third Quarter | | | Fourth Quarter | | |
	As Reported	Effect of Change	As Adjusted	As Reported	Effect of Change	As Adjusted
Gross profit	$200,539	$(2,513)	$198,026	$163,961	$(1,341)	$162,620
Income (loss) from continuing operations before income taxes	54,378	(2,513)	51,865	22,526	(1,341)	21,185
Provision (benefit) for income taxes	20,686	(958)	19,728	(1,700)	(440)	(2,140)
Income (loss) from continuing operations	33,692	(1,555)	32,137	24,226	(901)	23,325
Diluted earnings (loss) per share from continuing operations	$ 1.33	$ (0.06)	$ 1.27	$ 0.97	$ (0.04)	$ 0.93

CHANGE IN ACCOUNTING PRINCIPLE—INCENTIVE FEE REVENUE

1.46 PRUDENTIAL FINANCIAL, INC. (DEC)
NOTES TO CONSOLIDATED FINANCIAL STATEMENTS

2. Significant Accounting Policies and Pronouncements (in part)

Asset Management Fees and Other Income (in part)

In 2013, the Company adopted retrospectively a discretionary change in accounting principle for recognition of performance based incentive fee revenue. In certain asset management fee arrangements, the Company is entitled to receive performance based incentive fees when the return on assets under management exceeds certain benchmark returns or other performance targets. The Company may be required to return all, or part, of such performance based incentive fee depending on future performance of these assets relative to performance benchmarks. Under the newly adopted accounting principle, the Company records performance based incentive fee revenue when the contractual terms of the asset management fee arrangement have been satisfied such that the performance fee is no longer subject to clawback or contingency. Under this principle the Company records a deferred performance based incentive fee liability to the extent it receives cash related to the performance based incentive fee prior to meeting the revenue recognition criteria delineated above.

Under the prior accounting principle, the Company accrued performance based incentive fee revenue quarterly based on measuring fund performance to date versus the performance benchmark stated in the investment management agreement, as if the contracts containing the fee arrangements were terminated as of the applicable balance sheet date. Certain performance based incentive fees were also subject to future adjustment based on cumulative fund performance in relation to these specified benchmarks.

The new method is recognized as preferable in authoritative accounting literature. In addition, the Company believes that new method improves the quality of earnings by eliminating the potential that revenue will be recognized in one quarter and reversed in a future quarter. Finally, the Company believes that the new accounting principle provides a more meaningful comparison to competitors.

The following tables present: 1) pro-forma amounts as of, or for the year ended, December 31, 2013 under the prior accounting method, the effect on those amounts of the change in account principle, and amounts as reported in the Company's Consolidated Financial Statements; and 2) amounts as of, or for the years ended December 31, 2012 and 2011, as previously reported, the effect on those amounts of the change in accounting principle, and amounts as reported in the Company's Consolidated Financial Statements.

Consolidated Statement of Financial Position:

(In millions)	December 31, 2013		
	Previous Accounting Method	Effect of Change in Accounting Principle	As Reported
Assets			
Other assets	$ 13,893	$(60)	$ 13,833
Total assets	731,841	(60)	731,781
Liabilities and Equity			
Liabilities			
Income taxes	5,462	(40)	5,422
Other liabilities	13,749	176	13,925
Total liabilities	695,764	136	695,900
Equity			
Retained earnings	14,602	(71)	14,531
Total Prudential Financial, Inc. equity	35,349	(71)	35,278
Noncontrolling interests	728	(125)	603
Total equity	36,077	(196)	35,881
Total liabilities and Equity	$731,841	$(60)	$731,781

(In millions)	December 31, 2012		
	As Previously Reported	Effect of Change in Accounting Principle	As Currently Reported
Assets			
Other assets	$ 11,887	$(63)	$ 11,824
Total Assets	709,298	(63)	709,235
Liabilities and Equity			
Liabilities			
Income taxes	8,551	(39)	8,512
Other liabilities	11,683	155	11,838
Total liabilities	670,007	116	670,123
Equity			
Retained earnings	16,138	(72)	16,066
Total Prudential Financial, Inc. equity	38,575	(72)	38,503
Noncontrolling interests	716	(107)	609
Total equity	39,291	(179)	39,112
Total liabilities and equity	$709,298	$(63)	$709,235

Consolidated Statement of Operations:

(In millions)	Year Ended December 31, 2013		
	Previous Accounting Method	Effect of Change in Accounting Principle	As Reported
Revenues			
Asset management fees and other income	$ 304	$ (18)	$ 286
Total revenues	41,479	(18)	41,461
Income (Loss) from continuing operations before income taxes and equity in earnings of operating joint ventures	(1,666)	(18)	(1,684)
Income taxes:			
Deferred	(1,091)	(1)	(1,092)
Income tax expense	(1,057)	(1)	(1,058)
Income (Loss) from continuing operations before equity in earnings of operating joint ventures	(609)	(17)	(626)
Income (Loss) from continuing operations	(550)	(17)	(567)
Net income (Loss)	(543)	(17)	(560)
Less: Income (loss) attributable to noncontrolling interests	125	(18)	107
Net income (Loss) attributable to Prudential Financial, Inc.	$ (668)	$ 1	$ (667)
Earnings per Share			
Financial Services Businesses			
Basic earnings per share—Common Stock:			
Income (loss) from continuing operations attributable to Prudential Financial, Inc.	$ (1.57)	$0.00	$ (1.57)
Net income (Loss) attributable to Prudential Financial, Inc.	$ (1.55)	$0.00	$ (1.55)
Diluted earnings per share—Common Stock:			
Income (Loss) from continuing operations attributable to Prudential Financial, Inc.	$ (1.57)	$0.00	$ (1.57)
Net income (Loss) attributable to Prudential Financial, Inc.	$ (1.55)	$0.00	$ (1.55)

(In millions)	Year Ended December 31, 2012		
	As Previously Reported	Effect of Change in Accounting Principle	As Currently Reported
Revenues			
Asset management fees and other income	$ 2,752	$ 32	$ 2,784
Total revenues	84,815	32	84,847
Income (Loss) from continuing operations before income taxes and equity in earnings of operating joint ventures	676	32	708
Income taxes:			
Deferred	(884)	9	(875)
Income tax expense	204	9	213
Income (Loss) from continuing operations before equity in earnings of operating joint ventures	472	23	495
Income (Loss) from continuing operations	532	23	555
Net income (Loss)	547	23	570
Less: Income (Loss) attributable to noncontrolling interests	78	(28)	50
Net income (Loss) attributable to Prudential Financial, Inc.	$ 469	$ 51	$ 520
Earnings per Share			
Financial Services Businesses			
Basic earnings per share—Common Stock:			
Income (Loss) from continuing operations attributable to Prudential Financial, Inc.	$ 0.91	$0.11	$ 1.02
Net income (Loss) attributable to Prudential Financial, Inc.	$ 0.95	$0.11	$ 1.06
Diluted earnings per share—Common Stock:			
Income (Loss) from continuing operations attributable to Prudential Financial, Inc.	$ 0.91	$0.10	$ 1.01
Net income (Loss) attributable to Prudential Financial, Inc.	$ 0.94	$0.11	$ 1.05

(In millions)	Year Ended December 31, 2011		
	As Previously Reported	Effect of Change in Accounting Principle	As Currently Reported
Revenues			
Asset management fees and other income	$ 4,850	$ 55	$ 4,905
Total revenues	49,030	55	49,085
Income (Loss) from continuing operations before income taxes and equity in earnings of operating joint ventures	4,909	55	4,964
Income taxes:			
Deferred	1,041	27	1,068
Income tax expense	1,488	27	1,515
Income (Loss) from continuing operations before equity in earnings of operating joint ventures	3,421	28	3,449
Income (Loss) from continuing operations	3,603	28	3,631
Net Income (Loss)	3,638	28	3,666
Less: Income (loss) attributable to noncontrolling interests	72	(38)	34
Net Income (Loss) Attributable To Prudential Financial, Inc.	$ 3,566	$ 66	$ 3,632
Earnings per Share			
Financial Services Businesses			
Basic earnings per share—Common Stock:			
Income (loss) from continuing operations attributable to Prudential Financial, Inc.	$ 7.01	$0.13	$ 7.14
Net income (loss) attributable to Prudential Financial, Inc.	$ 7.08	$0.13	$ 7.21
Diluted earnings per share—Common Stock:			
Income (loss) from continuing operations attributable to Prudential Financial, Inc.	$ 6.92	$0.13	$ 7.05
Net income (loss) attributable to Prudential Financial, Inc.	$ 6.99	$0.13	$ 7.12

Consolidated Statement of Cash Flows:

(In millions)	Year Ended December 31, 2013		
	Previous Accounting Method	Effect of Change in Accounting Principle	As Reported
Cash Flows From Operating Activities			
Net income (loss)	$ (543)	$(17)	$ (560)
Adjustments to reconcile net income to net cash provided by operating activities:			
Change in:			
Other, net	$(2,683)	$ 17	$(2,666)

(In millions)	Year Ended December 31, 2012		
	As Previously Reported	Effect of Change in Accounting Principle	As Currently Reported
Cash Flows From Operating Activities			
Net income (loss)	$547	$ 23	$570
Adjustments to reconcile net income to net cash provided by operating activities:			
Change in:			
Other, net	$193	$(23)	$170

(In millions)	Year Ended December 31, 2011		
	As Previously Reported	Effect of Change in Accounting Principle	As Currently Reported
Cash Flows From Operating Activities			
Net income (loss)	$3,638	$ 28	$3,666
Adjustments to reconcile net income to net cash provided by operating activities:			
Change in:			
Other, net	$1,509	$(28)	$1,481

CHANGE IN ACCOUNTING PRINCIPLE—COMPREHENSIVE INCOME

1.47 AGCO CORPORATION (DEC)
CONSOLIDATED STATEMENTS OF STOCKHOLDERS' EQUITY

(In millions, except share amounts)

	Common Stock Shares	Common Stock Amount	Additional Paid-in Capital	Retained Earnings	Accumulated Other Comprehensive Loss — Defined Benefit Pension Plans	Accumulated Other Comprehensive Loss — Cumulative Translation Adjustment	Accumulated Other Comprehensive Loss — Deferred (Losses) Gains on Derivatives	Accumulated Other Comprehensive Loss — Accumulated Other Comprehensive Loss	Non-controlling Interests	Total Stockholders' Equity	Temporary Equity
Balance, December 31, 2010	93,143,542	$0.9	$1,051.3	$1,738.3	$(179.1)	$ 48.4	$(1.4)	$(132.1)	$ 0.8	$2,659.2	$ —
Net income	—	—	—	583.3	—	—	—	—	2.0	585.3	
Issuance of restricted stock	12,034	—	0.7	—	—	—	—	—	—	0.7	
Issuance of performance award stock	51,590	—	(1.5)	—	—	—	—	—	—	(1.5)	
Stock options and SSARs exercised	60,992	—	(0.7)	—	—	—	—	—	—	(0.7)	
Stock compensation	—	—	23.7	—	—	—	—	—	—	23.7	
Conversion of 1³/₄% convertible senior subordinated notes	3,926,574	0.1	(0.1)	—	—	—	—	—	—	—	
Investments by noncontrolling interests	—	—	—	—	—	—	—	—	34.6	34.6	
Distribution to noncontrolling interest	—	—	—	—	—	—	—	—	(1.5)	(1.5)	
Change in fair value of noncontrolling interest	—	—	(0.2)	—	—	—	—	—	0.2	—	
Defined benefit pension plans, net of taxes:											
Prior service cost arising during year	—	—	—	—	(5.0)	—	—	(5.0)	—	(5.0)	
Net actuarial loss arising during year	—	—	—	—	(61.8)	—	—	(61.8)	—	(61.8)	
Amortization of prior service cost included in net periodic pension cost	—	—	—	—	0.1	—	—	0.1	—	0.1	
Amortization of net actuarial losses included in net periodic pension cost	—	—	—	—	5.6	—	—	5.6	—	5.6	
Deferred gains and losses on derivatives, net	—	—	—	—	—	—	(5.4)	(5.4)	—	(5.4)	
Deferred gains and losses on derivatives held by affiliates, net	—	—	—	—	—	—	2.5	2.5	—	2.5	
Change in cumulative translation adjustment	—	—	—	—	—	(204.5)	—	(204.5)	(0.1)	(204.6)	
Balance, December 31, 2011	97,194,732	1.0	1,073.2	2,321.6	(240.2)	(156.1)	(4.3)	(400.6)	36.0	3,031.2	—

	Common Stock		Additional Paid-in Capital	Retained Earnings	Accumulated Other Comprehensive Loss				Non-controlling Interests	Total Stock-holders' Equity	Tempo-rary Equity
	Shares	Amount			Defined Benefit Pension Plans	Cumulative Translation Adjustment	Deferred (Losses) Gains on Derivatives	Accumulated Other Comprehen-Loss			
Net income (loss)	—	—	—	522.1	—	—	—	—	3.0	525.1	(8.7)
Issuance of restricted stock	13,986	—	1.0	—	—	—	—	—	—	1.0	
Stock options and SSARs exercised	16,287	—	(0.3)	—	—	—	—	—	—	(0.3)	
Stock compensation	—	—	35.8	—	—	—	—	—	—	35.8	
Investments by redeemable noncontrolling interest	—	—	—	—	—	—	—	—	—	—	17.6
Distribution to noncontrolling interest	—	—	—	—	—	—	—	—	(1.7)	(1.7)	
Changes in noncontrolling interests	—	—	—	—	—	—	—	—	(4.0)	(4.0)	
Purchases and retirement of common stock	(409,007)	—	(17.6)	—	—	—	—	—	—	(17.6)	
Defined benefit pension plans, net of taxes:											
Prior service cost arising during year	—	—	—	—	(2.5)	—	—	(2.5)	—	(2.5)	
Net actuarial loss arising during year	—	—	—	—	(28.2)	—	—	(28.2)	—	(28.2)	
Amortization of prior service cost included in net periodic pension cost	—	—	—	—	0.4	—	—	0.4	—	0.4	
Amortization of net actuarial losses included in net periodic pension cost	—	—	—	—	7.6	—	—	7.6	—	7.6	
Deferred gains and losses on derivatives, net	—	—	—	—	—	—	5.0	5.0	—	5.0	
Reclassification to temporary equity-Equity component of convertible senior subordinated notes	—	—	(9.2)	—	—	—	—	—	—	(9.2)	9.2
Change in cumulative translation adjustment	—	—	—	—	—	(61.1)	—	(61.1)	—	(61.1)	(1.6)
Balance, December 31, 2012	96,815,998	1.0	1,082.9	2,843.7	(262.9)	(217.2)	0.7	(479.4)	33.3	3,481.5	16.5
Net income (loss)	—	—	—	597.2	—	—	—	—	4.4	601.6	(9.3)
Payment of dividends to shareholders	—	—	—	(38.9)	—	—	—	—	—	(38.9)	
Issuance of restricted stock	12,059	—	0.6	—	—	—	—	—	—	0.6	
Issuance of performance award stock	491,692	—	(14.7)	—	—	—	—	—	—	(14.7)	

(continued)

| | Common Stock | | Additional Paid-in Capital | Retained Earnings | Accumulated Other Comprehensive Loss | | | | Non-controlling Interests | Total Stock-holders' Equity | Tempo-rary Equity |
| | | | | | Defined Benefit Pension Plans | Cumulative Translation Adjustment | Deferred (Losses) Gains on Derivatives | Accumulated Other Comprehen-sive Loss | | | |
	Shares	Amount									
SSARs exercised	61,941	—	(2.2)	—	—	—	—	—	—	(2.2)	
Stock compensation	—	—	34.0	—	—	—	—	—	—	34.0	
Excess tax benefit of stock awards	—	—	11.4	—	—	—	—	—	—	11.4	
Conversion of 1¼% convertible senior subordinated notes	286	—	—	—	—	—	—	—	—	—	
Distribution to noncontrolling interest	—	—	—	—	—	—	—	—	(3.1)	(3.1)	
Changes in noncontrolling interest	—	—	(2.3)	—	—	—	—	—	—	(2.3)	2.3
Purchases and retirement of common stock	(19,510)	—	(1.0)	—	—	—	—	—	—	(1.0)	
Defined benefit pension plans, net of taxes:											
Net actuarial gain arising during year	—	—	—	—	45.2	—	—	45.2	—	45.2	
Amortization of prior service cost included in net periodic pension cost	—	—	—	—	0.6	—	—	0.6	—	0.6	
Amortization of net actuarial losses included in net periodic pension cost	—	—	—	—	10.7	—	—	10.7	—	10.7	
Deferred gains and losses on derivatives, net	—	—	—	—	—	—	(0.9)	(0.9)	—	(0.9)	
Reclassification from temporary equity- Equity component of convertible senior subordinated notes	—	—	9.2	—	—	—	—	—	—	9.2	(9.2)
Change in cumulative translation adjustment	—	—	—	—	—	(86.9)	—	(86.9)	—	(86.9)	(0.3)
Balance, December 31, 2013	97,362,466	$1.0	$1,117.9	$3,402.0	$(206.4)	$(304.1)	$(0.2)	$(510.7)	$34.6	$4,044.8	$—

See accompanying notes to Consolidated Financial Statements.

NOTES TO CONSOLIDATED FINANCIAL STATEMENTS

1. Operations and Summary of Significant Accounting Policies (in part)

Recent Accounting Pronouncements (in part)

In February 2013, the FASB issued ASU 2013-02, "Comprehensive Income (Topic 220): Reporting of Amounts Reclassified Out of Accumulated Other Comprehensive Income" ("ASU 2013-02"). ASU 2013-02 does not change the current requirements for reporting net income or other comprehensive income in financial statements. The standard requires an entity to provide information about the amounts reclassified out of accumulated other comprehensive income ("AOCI") by component. The standard also requires an entity to present, either on the face of the statement where net income is presented or in the footnotes, significant amounts reclassified out of AOCI by the respective line items of net income, but only if the amount reclassified is required to be reclassified to net income in its entirety in the same reporting period. For amounts that are not required to be reclassified in their entirety to net income, the standard requires an entity to cross-reference other disclosures that provide additional detail on those amounts. The Company adopted ASU 2013-02 as of January 1, 2013 by presenting the required amounts in its footnote disclosures (Note 8).

8. Stockholders' Equity (in part)

The following table sets forth changes in accumulated other comprehensive loss by component, net of tax, attributed to AGCO Corporation and its subsidiaries for the year ended December 31, 2013 (in millions):

	Defined Benefit Pension Plans	Cumulative Translation Adjustment	Deferred Net Gains (Losses) on Derivatives	Total
Accumulated other comprehensive (loss) income, December 31, 2012	$(262.9)	$(217.2)	$ 0.7	$(479.4)
Other comprehensive gain (loss) before reclassifications	45.2	(86.9)	(1.4)	(43.1)
Net losses reclassified from accumulated other comprehensive loss	11.3	—	0.5	11.8
Other comprehensive income (loss), net of reclassification adjustments	56.5	(86.9)	(0.9)	(31.3)
Accumulated other comprehensive loss, December 31, 2013	$(206.4)	$(304.1)	$(0.2)	$(510.7)

The following table sets forth reclassification adjustments out of accumulated other comprehensive loss by component attributed to AGCO Corporation and its subsidiaries for the year ended December 31, 2013 (in millions):

Details about Accumulated Other Comprehensive Loss Components	Amount Reclassified from Accumulated Other Comprehensive Loss Year ended December 31, 2013[1]	Affected Line Item within the Consolidated Statements of Operations
Net losses on cash flow hedges	$ 0.7	Cost of goods sold
Tax	(0.2)	Income tax provision
Reclassification net of tax	$ 0.5	
Defined benefit pension plans:		
Amortization of net actuarial loss	$14.5	[2]
Amortization of prior service cost	1.1	[2]
Reclassification before tax	15.6	
Tax	(4.3)	Income tax provision
Reclassification net of tax	$11.3	
Net losses reclassified from accumulated other comprehensive loss	$11.8	

[1] Losses included within the Consolidated Statements of Operations for the year ended December 31, 2013.

[2] These accumulated other comprehensive loss components are included in the computation of net periodic pension and postretirement benefit cost. See Note 7 to the Company's Consolidated Financial Statements.

CHANGE IN ACCOUNTING PRINCIPLE—OFFSETTING ASSETS AND LIABILITIES

1.48 3M COMPANY (DEC)
NOTES TO CONSOLIDATED FINANCIAL STATEMENTS

Note 1. Significant Accounting Policies (in part)

New Accounting Pronouncements (in part)

In December 2011, the FASB issued ASU No. 2011-11, *Disclosures About Offsetting Assets and Liabilities*, and in January 2013 issued ASU No. 2013-01, *Clarifying the Scope of Disclosures About Offsetting Assets and Liabilities*. These standards created new disclosure requirements regarding the nature of an entity's rights of setoff and related arrangements associated with its derivative instruments, repurchase agreements, and securities lending transactions. Certain disclosures of the amounts of certain instruments subject to enforceable master netting arrangements are required, irrespective of whether the entity has elected to offset those instruments in the statement of financial position. For 3M, these ASUs were effective January 1, 2013 with retrospective application required. The additional disclosures required by these ASUs are included in Note 11. Since these standards impact disclosure requirements only, their adoption did not have a material impact on 3M's consolidated results of operations or financial condition.

Note 11. Derivatives (in part)

Credit Risk and Offsetting of Assets and Liabilities of Derivative Instruments

The Company is exposed to credit loss in the event of nonperformance by counterparties in interest rate swaps, currency swaps, commodity price swaps, and forward and option contracts. However, the Company's risk is limited to the fair value of the instruments. The Company actively monitors its exposure to credit risk through the use of credit approvals and credit limits, and by selecting major international banks and financial institutions as counterparties. 3M enters into master netting arrangements with counterparties when possible to mitigate credit risk in derivative transactions. A master netting arrangement may allow each counterparty to net settle amounts owed between a 3M entity and the counterparty as a result of multiple, separate derivative transactions. As of December 31, 2013, 3M has International Swaps and Derivatives Association (ISDA) agreements with 11 applicable banks and financial institutions which contain netting provisions. In addition to a master agreement with 3M supported by a primary counterparty's parent guarantee, 3M also has associated credit support agreements in place with 10 of its primary derivative counterparties which, among other things, provide the circumstances under which either party is required to post eligible collateral (when the market value of transactions covered by these agreements exceeds specified thresholds or if a counterparty's credit rating has been downgraded to a predetermined rating). The Company does not anticipate nonperformance by any of these counterparties.

3M has elected to present the fair value of derivative assets and liabilities within the Company's consolidated balance sheet on a gross basis even when derivative transactions are subject to master netting arrangements and may otherwise qualify for net presentation. However, the following tables provide information as if the Company had elected to offset the asset and liability balances of derivative instruments, netted in accordance with various criteria in the event of default or termination as stipulated by the terms of netting arrangements with each of the counterparties. For each counterparty, if netted, the Company would offset the asset and liability balances of all derivatives at the end of the reporting period based on the 3M entity that is a party to the transactions. Derivatives not subject to master netting agreements are not eligible for net presentation. As of the applicable dates presented below, no cash collateral had been received or pledged related to these derivative instruments.

Offsetting of Financial Assets/Liabilities under Master Netting Agreements with Derivative Counterparties

December 31, 2013

(Millions)	Gross Amount of Derivative Assets Presented in the Consolidated Balance Sheet	Gross Amounts not Offset in the Consolidated Balance Sheet that are Subject to Master Netting Agreements		Net Amount of Derivative Assets
		Gross Amount of Eligible Offsetting Recognized Derivative Liabilities	Cash Collateral Received	
Derivatives subject to master netting agreements	$83	$51	$—	$32
Derivatives not subject to master netting agreements	1			1
Total	$84			$33

December 31, 2013

(Millions)	Gross Amount of Derivative Liabilities Presented in the Consolidated Balance Sheet	Gross Amounts not Offset in the Consolidated Balance Sheet that are Subject to Master Netting Agreements		Net Amount of Derivative Liabilities
		Gross Amount of Eligible Offsetting Recognized Derivative Assets	Cash Collateral Pledged	
Derivatives subject to master netting agreements	$110	$51	$—	$59
Derivatives not subject to master netting agreements	—			—
Total	$110			$59

December 31, 2012

(Millions)	Gross Amount of Derivative Assets Presented in the Consolidated Balance Sheet	Gross Amounts not Offset in the Consolidated Balance Sheet that are Subject to Master Netting Agreements		Net Amount of Derivative Assets
		Gross Amount of Eligible Offsetting Recognized Derivative Liabilities	Cash Collateral Received	
Derivatives subject to master netting agreements	$67	$25	$—	$42
Derivatives not subject to master netting agreements	5			5
Total	$72			$47

December 31, 2012

(Millions)	Gross Amount of Derivative Liabilities Presented in the Consolidated Balance Sheet	Gross Amounts not Offset in the Consolidated Balance Sheet that are Subject to Master Netting Agreements		Net Amount of Derivative Liabilities
		Gross Amount of Eligible Offsetting Recognized Derivative Assets	Cash Collateral Pledged	
Derivatives subject to master netting agreements	$106	$25	$—	$81
Derivatives not subject to master netting agreements	—			—
Total	$106			$81

1.49 COOPER TIRE & RUBBER COMPANY (DEC)
NOTES TO CONSOLIDATED FINANCIAL STATEMENTS

(Dollar amounts in thousands except per share amounts)

Note 1—Significant Accounting Policies (in part)

Accounting Pronouncements—Recently Adopted (in part)

In December 2011, the FASB issued Accounting Standards Update ("ASU") 2011-11, "Disclosures about Offsetting Assets and Liabilities," which requires an entity to disclose information about offsetting and related arrangements. The amendments in this update are effective for annual and interim periods beginning on or after January 1, 2013, with retrospective application. In January 2013, the FASB issued ASU 2013-01, "Clarifying the Scope of Disclosures about Offsetting Assets and Liabilities." The Company has adopted these ASUs and has included the expanded disclosures in Footnote 11—Fair Value of Financial Instruments.

Note 11—Fair Value of Financial Instruments (in part)

Derivative financial instruments are utilized by the Company to reduce foreign currency exchange risks. The Company has established policies and procedures for risk assessment and the approval, reporting and monitoring of derivative financial instrument activities. The Company does not enter into financial instruments for trading or speculative purposes. The derivative financial instruments include fair value and cash flow hedges of foreign currency exposures. Exchange rate fluctuations on the foreign currency-denominated intercompany loans and obligations are offset by the change in values of the fair value foreign currency hedges. The Company presently hedges exposures in the Euro, Canadian dollar, British pound sterling, Swiss franc, Swedish kronar, Mexican peso and Chinese yuan generally for transactions expected to occur within the next 12 months. The notional amount of these foreign currency derivative instruments at December 31, 2012 and 2013 was $186,217 and $148,036, respectively. The counterparties to each of these agreements are major commercial banks. Management believes that the probability of losses related to credit risk on derivative financial instruments is unlikely.

The Company uses foreign currency forward contracts as hedges of the fair value of certain non-U.S. dollar denominated asset and liability positions, primarily accounts receivable and debt. Gains and losses resulting from the impact of currency exchange rate movements on these forward contracts are recognized in the accompanying Consolidated Statements of Income in the period in which the exchange rates change and offset the foreign currency gains and losses on the underlying exposure being hedged.

Foreign currency forward contracts are also used to hedge variable cash flows associated with forecasted sales and purchases denominated in currencies that are not the functional currency of certain entities. The forward contracts have maturities of less than twelve months pursuant to the Company's policies and hedging practices. These forward contracts meet the criteria for and have been designated as cash flow hedges. Accordingly, the effective portion of the change in fair value of such forward contracts (approximately ($1,461) and $398 as of

December 31, 2012 and 2013, respectively) are recorded as a separate component of stockholders' equity in the accompanying consolidated balance sheets and reclassified into earnings as the hedged transaction affects earnings.

The Company assesses hedge ineffectiveness quarterly using the hypothetical derivative methodology. In doing so, the Company monitors the actual and forecasted foreign currency sales and purchases versus the amounts hedged to identify any hedge ineffectiveness. Any hedge ineffectiveness is recorded as an adjustment in the accompanying Consolidated Statements of Income in the period in which the ineffectiveness occurs. The Company also performs regression analysis comparing the change in value of the hedging contracts versus the underlying foreign currency sales and purchases, which confirms a high correlation and hedge effectiveness.

The derivative instruments are subject to master netting arrangements with the counterparties to the contracts. The following table presents the location and amounts of derivative instrument fair values in the Consolidated Balance Sheets:

Assets/(Liabilities)		December 31, 2012		December 31, 2013
Designated as hedging instruments:				
Gross amounts recognized		$(2,610)		$ 2,702
Gross amounts offset		1,100		(2,232)
Net amounts		(1,510)		470
Not designated as hedging instruments:				
Gross amounts recognized		245		(121)
Gross amounts offset		—		—
Net amounts		245		(121)
Net amounts presented	Accrued liabilities	$(1,265)	Other current assets	$ 349

CHANGE IN ACCOUNTING PRINCIPLE—CUMULATIVE TRANSLATION ADJUSTMENT

1.50 SAFEWAY INC. (DEC)
NOTES TO CONSOLIDATED FINANCIAL STATEMENTS

Note A: The Company and Significant Accounting Policies (in part)

On November 3, 2013, Safeway completed the sale of substantially all of the net assets of Canada Safeway Limited ("CSL" now known as CSL IT Services ULC) to Sobeys Inc. ("Sobeys"), a wholly-owned subsidiary of Empire Company Limited. As a result, the operating results of CSL are reported as discontinued operations in the consolidated statements of income for all periods presented. See Note B to the consolidated financial statements for additional information.

Accumulated Other Comprehensive Loss Accumulated other comprehensive loss, net of applicable taxes, consisted of the following at year-end (in millions):

	2013	2012	2011
Translation adjustments	$(139.0)	$ 399.0	$ 402.1
Pension and post-retirement benefits adjustment to funded status	(403.0)	(737.8)	(658.1)
Recognition of pension and post-retirement benefits actuarial loss	272.5	265.5	196.0
Other	(1.6)	(0.5)	(1.5)
Total	$(271.1)	$ (73.8)	$ (61.5)

At the closing of the Sale of Canadian Operations, the Company recorded the related balance of cumulative translation adjustment, pension and post-retirement benefit adjustment to funded status and recognition of pension and post-retirement benefits actuarial loss which related to CSL as part of the gain on the sale. See Note B.

New Accounting Pronouncements (in part)

In March 2013, the FASB issued ASU No. 2013-05, "Parent's Accounting for the Cumulative Translation Adjustment upon Derecognition of Certain Subsidiaries or Groups of Assets within a Foreign Entity or of an Investment in a Foreign Entity." The ASU clarifies that when a parent entity ceases to have a controlling financial interest in a subsidiary or group of assets that is a nonprofit activity or a business (other than a sale of in substance real estate or conveyance of oil and gas mineral rights) within a foreign entity, the parent is required to apply the guidance in Accounting Standards Codification 830-30 to release any related cumulative translation adjustment into net income. The ASU provides that the cumulative translation adjustment should be released into net income only if the sale or transfer results in the complete or substantially complete liquidation of the foreign entity in which the subsidiary or group of assets had resided. The Company early adopted ASU No. 2013–05 and the effect is included in the gain on the sale of CSL in Note B.

Note B: Assets and Liabilities Held for Sale and Discontinued Operations (in part)

Discontinued Operations (in part)

Sale of Canadian Operations   On November 3, 2013, Safeway completed the Sale of Canadian Operations to Sobeys for CAD5.8 billion (USD 5.6 billion) in cash plus the assumption of certain liabilities.

The notes to the consolidated financial statements exclude discontinued operations, unless otherwise noted. Historical financial information for CSL and Dominick's presented in the consolidated income statements has been reclassified to discontinued operations to conform to current-year presentation. The historical operating results of Genuardi's stores have not been reflected in discontinued operations because the historical financial operating results were not material to the Company's consolidated financial statements for all periods presented. Financial information for discontinued operations is shown below (in millions):

	2013	2012	2011
Sales and Other Revenue:			
CSL[1]	$ 5,447.9	$6,695.8	$6,726.9
Dominick's	1,394.8	1,465.2	1,568.6
Total	$ 6,842.7	$8,161.0	$8,295.5
Income (loss) from discontinued operations, before income taxes:			
CSL[1]	$ 286.2	$ 442.3	$ 462.3
Dominick's	(92.0)	(50.4)	(38.7)
Total	$ 194.2	$ 391.9	$ 423.6
Gain (loss) on sale or disposal of operations, net of lease exit costs, before income taxes:			
CSL[2]	$ 4,783.1	$ —	$ —
Dominick's	(493.1)	—	—
Genuardi's	—	52.4	—
Total	$ 4,290.0	$ 52.4	$ —
Total income from discontinued operations before income taxes	$ 4,484.2	$ 444.3	$ 423.6
Income taxes on discontinued operations	(1,208.3)	(140.8)	(272.6)
Income from discontinued operations, net of tax	$ 3,275.9	$ 303.5	$ 151.0

[1] For CSL, 2013 reflects 44 weeks of activity compared to 52 weeks in 2012 and 2011.

[2] In accordance with ASU No. 2013-05, "Parent's Accounting for the Cumulative Translation Adjustment upon Derecognition of Certain Subsidiaries or Groups of Assets within a Foreign Entity or of an Investment in a Foreign Entity," the Company transferred the cumulative translation adjustment relating to Canadian operations from Accumulated Other Comprehensive Loss on the balance sheet to gain on the Sale of Canadian Operations.

CHANGE IN ACCOUNTING ESTIMATES

1.51 HARRIS CORPORATION (JUN)
MANAGEMENT'S DISCUSSION AND ANALYSIS OF FINANCIAL CONDITION AND RESULTS OF OPERATIONS (in part)

Operations Review (in part)

Integrated Network Solutions Segment (in part)

(Dollars in millions)	2013	2012	2013/2012 Percent Increase/ (Decrease)	2011	2012/2011 Percent Increase/ (Decrease)
Revenue	$1,538.6	$1,571.2	(2.1)%	$1,445.3	8.7 %
Cost of product sales and services	(1,239.2)	(1,235.2)	0.3%	(1,192.7)	3.6 %
Gross margin	299.4	336.0	(10.9)%	252.6	33.0 %
% of revenue	19.5 %	21.4 %		17.5 %	
ESA expenses	(221.9)	(266.1)	(16.6)%	(161.9)	64.4 %
% of revenue	14.4 %	16.9 %		11.2 %	
Segment operating income	$77.5	$69.9	10.9 %	$90.7	(22.9)%
% of revenue	5.0 %	4.4 %		6.3 %	

Fiscal 2013 Compared With Fiscal 2012:   The decrease in segment revenue in fiscal 2013 compared with fiscal 2012 was primarily due to an 11 percent decrease in IT Services revenue, primarily from the loss of the Patriot program, partially offset by revenue growth in Harris CapRock Communications and Healthcare Solutions of 8 percent and 7 percent, respectively.

The decrease in segment gross margin and gross margin percentage in fiscal 2013 compared with fiscal 2012 was primarily attributable to a decrease in gross margin percentage on satellite and terrestrial communications services, increased costs associated with delivering software products and increased costs on a service contract with a government healthcare customer. The decreases in segment ESA expenses and ESA expenses as a percentage of revenue in fiscal 2013 compared with fiscal 2012 were primarily due to lower general and administrative expenses, including the impact of ongoing cost-reduction efforts and $58 million of charges recorded in fiscal 2012 for integration and other costs associated with our acquisitions of CapRock, Schlumberger GCS and Carefx, partially offset by $44 million of charges recorded in fiscal 2013 for asset impairments and a write-off of capitalized software due to a change in accounting estimate. The increases in segment operating income and operating margin percentage in fiscal 2013 compared with fiscal 2012 were attributable to the decreases in segment ESA expenses and ESA expenses as a percentage of revenue discussed above, partially offset by the decrease in segment gross margin percentage discussed above.

NOTES TO CONSOLIDATED FINANCIAL STATEMENTS

Note 1: Significant Accounting Policies (in part)

Capitalized Software to Be Sold, Leased or Otherwise Marketed —Costs incurred to acquire or create a computer software product are expensed when incurred as research and development until technological feasibility has been established for the product, at which point such costs are capitalized. Technological feasibility is normally established upon completion of a detailed program design or, in its absence, a working model of the software product. Capitalization of computer software costs ceases when the product is available for general release to customers, at which point amortization begins based on the greater of the amount computed using (a) the ratio that current gross revenues for a product bear to the total of current and anticipated future gross revenues for that product or (b) the straight-line method over the remaining estimated economic life of the product. Costs of reproduction, documentation, training materials, physical packaging, maintenance and customer support are charged to cost of products sold as incurred. Capitalized software to be sold, leased or otherwise marketed is evaluated for impairment periodically by comparing the unamortized capitalized costs of a computer software product to the net realizable value of that product. Capitalized costs, net of accumulated amortization, are reflected in the "Other non-current assets" line item in our Consolidated Balance Sheet. The amortization of capitalized software is included in the "Cost of product sales" line item in our Consolidated Statement of Income.

In the fourth quarter of fiscal 2013, we recorded a $17.8 million write-off of the capitalized software in Healthcare Solutions as a change in accounting estimate, resulting from high-risk development issues and substantial revisions to the logic of Carefx's primary software product based on the realization that the software would require more features and better functionality. These changes to the software were such that the initial detail program design was no longer sufficient to establish technological feasibility.

CORRECTION OF ERRORS

1.52 BARNES & NOBLE, INC. (APR)
NOTES TO CONSOLIDATED FINANCIAL STATEMENTS

(Thousands of dollars, except per share data)

For the 52 weeks ended April 27, 2013 (fiscal 2013), April 28, 2012 (fiscal 2012) and April 30, 2011 (fiscal 2011)

2. Restatement of Prior Period Financial Statements

The Company has restated its previously reported consolidated financial statements for the years ended April 28, 2012 and April 30, 2011, including the opening stockholders' equity balance, in order to correct certain previously reported amounts.

In fiscal 2013, management determined that the Company had incorrectly overstated certain accruals for the periods prior to April 27, 2013, as a result of inadequate controls over its Distribution Center accrual reconciliation process. In accordance with ASC 250-10-S99-2, *Considering the Effects of Prior Year Misstatements when Quantifying Misstatements in Current Year Financial Statements* (ASC 250), the Company recorded an adjustment to decrease cost of sales by $6,700 ($4,027 after tax) and $8,460 ($5,084 after tax) to correctly present the statement of operations for fiscal 2012 and 2011, respectively. The Company also decreased accounts payable by $89,500 and $96,200 at April 30, 2011 and April 28, 2012, respectively; increased income taxes payable included in Accrued Liabilities in the consolidated Balance Sheets by $14,939 and $18,598 at April 30, 2011 and April 28, 2012, respectively; and increased retained earnings by $74,561 and $78,588, net of tax at April 30, 2011 and April 28, 2012, respectively.

In addition, in reviewing the Company's components of deferred income tax assets and liabilities, management determined that deferred income tax liability in the amount of $26,026, net, was related to a transaction in which gain was reported for both accounting and tax purposes prior to 2010. Accordingly, management concluded that this deferred income tax liability should be reversed. In accordance with

ASC 250, the Company recorded an adjustment to decrease deferred tax liability and increase retained earnings by $26,026 at May 1, 2010. The cumulative effect of these adjustments increased previously reported retained earnings by $95,503 at May 1, 2010.

In fiscal 2013, management determined that the Company had not accrued a tenant allowance related to one of its properties in fiscal 2012. The Company recorded an adjustment to increase receivable, net and other long-term liabilities by $9,450 in fiscal 2012.

The following tables set forth the correction to each of the individual affected line items in the consolidated balance sheets as of April 30, 2011 and April 28, 2012 and the consolidated statement of operations for fiscal 2011 and 2012. The restated amounts presented below reflect the impact of these corrections, as well as adjustments of $52,072 and $47,026 related to the current portion of deferred rent and tenant allowances on the April 30, 2011 and April 28, 2012 balance sheet, respectively. The Company did not present tables for the adjustments within the consolidated cash flow statement since all of the adjustments were within the operating section of the consolidated cash flow statement. The above corrections and adjustments did not effect total cash flows from operating activities, financing activities or investing activities for any period presented.

The financial information included in the accompanying financial statements and notes thereto reflect the affects of the corrections and other adjustments described in the preceding discussion and tables.

Balance Sheet Data:

| (In thousands, except per share data) | As of April 30, 2011 | | | |
	As Previously Reported	Corrections	Other Adjustments	Restated
Assets				
Current assets:				
Cash and cash equivalents	$ 59,429	—	—	$ 59,429
Receivables, net	150,294	—	—	150,294
Merchandise inventories, net	1,375,362	—	—	1,375,362
Prepaid expenses and other current assets	161,936	—	—	161,936
Total current assets	$ 1,747,021	—	—	$ 1,747,021
Property and equipment:				
Land and land improvements	8,617	—	—	8,617
Buildings and leasehold improvements	1,204,108	—	—	1,204,108
Fixtures and equipment	1,670,488	—	—	1,670,488
	2,883,213	—	—	2,883,213
Less accumulated depreciation and amortization	2,178,562	—	—	2,178,562
Net property and equipment	704,651	—	—	704,651
Goodwill	524,113	—	—	524,113
Intangible assets, net	566,578	—	—	566,578
Other noncurrent assets	54,103	—	—	54,103
Total assets	$ 3,596,466	—	—	$ 3,596,466
Liabilities and Shareholders' Equity				
Current liabilities:				
Accounts payable	$ 949,010	(89,500)	—	$ 859,510
Accrued liabilities	474,575	14,939	52,072	541,586
Gift card liabilities	311,092	—	—	311,092
Total current liabilities	1,734,677	(74,561)	52,072	1,712,188
Long-term debt	313,100	—	—	313,100
Deferred taxes	280,132	(26,026)	—	254,106
Other long-term liabilities	448,647	—	(52,072)	396,575
Shareholders' equity:				
Common stock; $.001 par value; 300,000 shares authorized; 90,465 shares issued	90	—	—	90
Additional paid-in capital	1,323,263	—	—	1,323,263
Accumulated other comprehensive loss	(11,630)	—	—	(11,630)
Retained earnings	562,379	100,587	—	662,966
Treasury stock, at cost, 33,410 shares	(1,054,192)	—	—	(1,054,192)
Total Shareholders' equity	819,910	100,587	—	920,497
Commitments and contingencies	—	—	—	—
Total liabilities and shareholders' equity	$ 3,596,466	—	—	$ 3,596,466

Balance Sheet Data:

(In thousands, except per share data)	As Previously Reported	Corrections	Other Adjustments	Restated
		As of April 28, 2012		
Assets				
Current assets:				
Cash and cash equivalents	$ 54,131	—	—	$ 54,131
Receivables, net	160,497	9,450	—	169,947
Merchandise inventories, net	1,561,841	—	—	1,561,841
Prepaid expenses and other current assets	221,324	—	—	221,324
Total current assets	$ 1,997,793	9,450	—	$ 2,007,243
Property and equipment:				
Land and land improvements	2,541	—	—	2,541
Buildings and leasehold improvements	1,196,764	—	—	1,196,764
Fixtures and equipment	1,784,492	—	—	1,784,492
	2,983,797	—	—	2,983,797
Less accumulated depreciation and amortization	2,361,142	—	—	2,361,142
Net property and equipment	622,655	—	—	622,655
Goodwill	519,685	—	—	519,685
Intangible assets, net	564,054	—	—	564,054
Other noncurrent assets	61,062	—	—	61,062
Total assets	$ 3,765,249	9,450	—	$ 3,774,699
Liabilities and Shareholders' Equity				
Current liabilities:				
Accounts payable	$ 959,423	(96,200)	—	$ 863,223
Accrued liabilities	546,495	18,598	47,026	612,119
Gift card liabilities	321,362	—	—	321,362
Total current liabilities	1,827,280	(77,602)	47,026	1,796,704
Long-term debt	324,200	—	—	324,200
Deferred taxes	268,774	(26,026)	—	242,748
Other long-term liabilities	405,065	8,464	(47,026)	366,503
Redeemable Preferred Shares; $.001 par value; 5,000 shares authorized; 204 shares issued	192,273	—	—	192,273
Shareholders' equity:				
Common stock; $.001 par value; 300,000 shares authorized; 91,376 shares issued	91	—	—	91
Additional paid-in capital	1,340,909	—	—	1,340,909
Accumulated other comprehensive loss	(16,635)	—	—	(16,635)
Retained earnings	481,574	104,614	—	586,188
Treasury stock, at cost, 33,722 shares	(1,058,282)	—	—	(1,058,282)
Total Shareholders' equity	747,657	104,614	—	852,271
Commitments and contingencies	—	—	—	—
Total liabilities and shareholders' equity	$ 3,765,249	9,450	—	$ 3,774,699

Statement of Operations Data:

(In thousands, except per share data)	As Previously Reported	Corrections	Restated
		Fiscal 2011	
Sales	$6,998,565	—	$6,998,565
Cost of sales and occupancy	5,205,712	(8,460)	5,197,252
Gross profit	1,792,853	8,460	1,801,313
Selling and administrative expenses	1,629,465	—	1,629,465
Depreciation and amortization	228,647	—	228,647
Operating income (loss)	(65,259)	8,460	(56,799)
Interest expense, net and amortization of deferred financing fees	(57,350)	—	(57,350)
Income (loss) before income taxes (benefit)	(122,609)	8,460	(114,149)
Income taxes (benefit)	(48,652)	3,376	(45,276)
Net income (loss)	(73,957)	5,084	(68,873)
Net loss attributable to noncontrolling interests	37	—	37
Net income (loss) attributable to Barnes & Noble, Inc.	$ (73,920)	5,084	$ (68,836)
Diluted income (loss) per common share			
Net income (loss) attributable to Barnes & Noble, Inc.	$ (1.31)	0.09	$ (1.22)

Statement of Operations Data:

(In thousands, except per share data)	Fiscal 2012 As Previously Reported	Corrections	Restated
Sales	$7,129,199	—	$7,129,199
Cost of sales and occupancy	5,218,383	(6,700)	5,211,683
Gross profit	1,910,816	6,700	1,917,516
Selling and administrative expenses	1,739,452	—	1,739,452
Depreciation and amortization	232,667	—	232,667
Operating income (loss)	(61,303)	6,700	(54,603)
Interest expense, net and amortization of deferred financing fees	(35,304)	—	(35,304)
Income (loss) before income taxes (benefit)	(96,607)	6,700	(89,907)
Income taxes (benefit)	(27,740)	2,673	(25,067)
Net income (loss)	$ (68,867)	4,027	$ (64,840)
Diluted income (loss) per common share			
Net income (loss)	$ (1.41)	0.07	$ (1.34)

1.53 COMPUTER SCIENCES CORPORATION (MAR)
NOTES TO CONSOLIDATED FINANCIAL STATEMENTS

Note 2—Investigations and Out of Period Adjustments

Summary of Audit Committee and SEC Investigations Related to the Out of Period Adjustments

As previously disclosed in fiscal 2012 and fiscal 2011, the Company initiated an investigation into out of period adjustments resulting from certain accounting errors in our Managed Services Sector (MSS) segment, primarily involving accounting irregularities in the Nordic region. Initially, the investigation was conducted by Company personnel, but outside Company counsel and forensic accountants retained by such counsel later assisted in the Company's investigation. On January 28, 2011, the Company was notified by the SEC's Division of Enforcement that it had commenced a formal civil investigation relating to these matters, which investigation has been expanded to other matters subsequently identified by the SEC, including matters specified in subpoenas issued to the Company from time to time by the SEC's Division of Enforcement as well as matters under investigation by the Audit Committee, as further described below. The Company is cooperating in the SEC's investigation.

On May 2, 2011, the Audit Committee commenced an independent investigation into the matters relating to the MSS segment and the Nordic region, matters identified by subpoenas issued by the SEC's Division of Enforcement, and certain other accounting matters identified by the Audit Committee and retained independent counsel to represent CSC on behalf of, and under the exclusive direction of, the Audit Committee in connection with such independent investigation. Independent counsel retained forensic accountants to assist with their work. Independent counsel also represents CSC on behalf of, and under the exclusive direction of, the Audit Committee in connection with the investigation by the SEC's Division of Enforcement.

The Audit Committee's investigation was expanded to encompass (i) the Company's operations in Australia, (ii) certain aspects of the Company's accounting practices within its Americas Outsourcing operation, and (iii) certain of the Company's accounting practices that involve the percentage-of-completion accounting method, including the Company's contract with the U.K. National Health Service (NHS). In the course of the Audit Committee's expanded investigation, accounting errors and irregularities were identified. As a result, certain personnel have been reprimanded, suspended, terminated and/or have resigned. The Audit Committee determined in August 2012 that its independent investigation was complete. The Audit Committee instructed its independent counsel to cooperate with the SEC's Division of Enforcement by completing production of documents and providing any further information requested by the SEC's Division of Enforcement.

In addition to the matters noted above, the SEC's Division of Enforcement is continuing its investigation involving its concerns with certain of the Company's prior disclosure and accounting determinations with respect to the Company's contract with the NHS and the possible impact of such matters on the Company's financial statements for years prior to the Company's current fiscal year. The Company and the Audit Committee and its independent counsel are investigating these matters and are continuing to cooperate with the SEC's Division of Enforcement in its investigation of prior disclosures of the Company's contract with the NHS. The SEC's investigative activities are ongoing.

In addition, the SEC's Division of Corporation Finance has issued comment letters to the Company requesting, among other things, additional information regarding its previously disclosed adjustments in connection with the above-referenced accounting errors, the Company's conclusions relating to the materiality of such adjustments, and the Company's analysis of the effectiveness of its disclosure controls and procedures and its internal control over financial reporting. The SEC's Division of Corporation Finance's comment letter process is ongoing, and the Company is continuing to cooperate with that process.

The investigation being conducted by the SEC's Division of Enforcement and the review of our financial disclosures by the SEC's Division of Corporation Finance are continuing and could identify other accounting errors, irregularities or other areas of review. As a result, we have incurred and may continue to incur significant legal and accounting expenditures. We are unable to predict how long the SEC's Division of Enforcement's investigation will continue or whether, at the conclusion of its investigation, the SEC will seek to impose fines or take other actions against the Company. In addition, we are unable to predict the timing of the completion of the SEC's Division of Corporation Finance's review of our financial disclosures or the outcome of such review. Publicity surrounding the foregoing or any enforcement action as a result of the SEC's investigation, even if ultimately resolved favorably for us, could have an adverse impact on the Company's reputation, business, financial condition, results of operations or cash flows. The Company is unable to estimate any possible loss or range of loss associated with these matters.

Out of Period Adjustments Financial Impact Summary

Cumulative Impact of Out of Period Adjustments

The rollover impact on income (loss) from continuing operations before taxes of the recorded out of period adjustments in fiscal 2013, 2012 and 2011 is attributable to the following prior fiscal years:

	Increase/(Decrease)			
(Amounts in millions)	Fiscal 2011 Adjustments	Fiscal 2012 Adjustments	Fiscal 2013 Adjustments	Total Adjustments
Fiscal 2013	$—	$—	$ 6	$ 6
Fiscal 2012	—	79	7	86
Fiscal 2011	52	(29)	(22)	1
Fiscal 2010	(48)	(9)	14	(43)
Prior fiscal years (unaudited)	(4)	(41)	(4)	(49)

See Note 16 for a summary of the effect of the pre-tax out of period adjustments on the Company's segment results for fiscal 2013, 2012 and 2011.

Fiscal 2013 Adjustments Financial Impact Summary

During fiscal 2013, the Company identified and recorded net adjustments decreasing income from continuing operations before taxes by $6 million that should have been recorded in prior fiscal years. This net impact on income from continuing operations before taxes for fiscal 2013 is comprised of the following:
- net adjustments decreasing fourth quarter pre-tax income by $9 million resulting primarily from the correction of inappropriately capitalized operating costs originating from MSS, a software revenue recognition correction originating from the Company's Business Solutions and Services (BSS) segment and the correction of understated payroll and related expenses at Corporate;
- net adjustments decreasing third quarter pre-tax income by $1 million primarily resulting from the correction of useful lives of property and equipment in service at a BSS contract that were inconsistent with established CSC accounting conventions;
- net adjustments increasing second quarter pre-tax income by $5 million primarily resulting from the correction of accounting errors identified by the Company related to costs incurred under the NHS contract (see below for more discussion of out of period adjustments related to the Company ' s NHS contract); and
- net adjustments decreasing first quarter pre-tax income by $1 million primarily resulting from the corrections of fiscal 2012 revenue recognized on a software contract in the Company's BSS segment, corrections of fiscal 2012 restructuring cost accruals originating primarily from the Company's BSS and MSS segments and corrections to record adjustments originating primarily from the Company's North American Public Sector (NPS) and MSS segments that were identified late in the close process but not included in the Company's consolidated fiscal 2012 financial statements

Adjustments recorded during fiscal 2013 that should have been recorded in prior fiscal years increased income from continuing operations by $7 million. This increase is attributable to the tax effect of the adjustments described above and $5 million of discrete tax benefits that should have been recorded in prior fiscal years. The discrete tax benefits are primarily attributable to the adjustment of the deferred tax liability related to intellectual property assets.

As previously disclosed in fiscal 2012 and in the first quarter of fiscal 2013, the Company had identified certain additional items related to the investigation of the Company's use of the percentage-of-completion accounting method used on the NHS contract. During the second quarter of fiscal 2013, based on its analysis of these items, the Company recorded net credits of $9 million in pre-tax out of period adjustments impacting prior fiscal years. During the third quarter of fiscal 2013, the Company identified additional prior period errors. Such errors identified in the third quarter, which were self-correcting in the third quarter of fiscal 2012, have no impact on income from continuing operations before taxes for fiscal 2013. The accounting errors identified during fiscal 2013 are primarily related to either costs incurred under the contract or the estimation of contract revenues and costs at completion, which resulted in the overstatement of income from continuing operations before taxes. The Company has concluded that there is no cumulative impact of this overstatement as a result of the $1.5 billion specified contract charge recorded as of December 30, 2011 being overstated by the same amount.

The Company has concluded that the errors identified during fiscal 2013 do not appear to have any impact on amounts charged to the NHS. Based on information provided by independent counsel, the Company believes that a small portion of such adjustments should be characterized as intentional accounting irregularities. The impact on income (loss) from continuing operations before taxes of the out of period adjustments identified in fiscal 2013 related to the Company's NHS contract is attributable to the following prior fiscal years:

(Amounts in millions)	Increase/(Decrease) Fiscal 2013 Adjustments
Fiscal 2013	$ (9)
Fiscal 2012	10
Fiscal 2011	(15)
Fiscal 2010	18
Prior fiscal years (unaudited)	(4)

The following table summarizes the cumulative effect on net income attributable to CSC common shareholders of the consolidated out of period adjustments recorded during fiscal 2013 under the rollover method. The amounts noted below also include certain adjustments that only impacted quarters (unaudited) within fiscal 2013, but had no net impact on the full year fiscal 2013 results:

(Amounts in millions)	Fiscal 2013 Quarter Ended				
	June 29, 2012	September 28, 2012	December 28, 2012	March 29, 2013	Total
NHS adjustments	$—	$(9)	$—	$—	$(9)
Other adjustments	3	12	4	(4)	15
Effect on income from continuing operations before taxes	3	3	4	(4)	6
Taxes on income	(2)	(1)	(4)	(1)	(8)
Other income tax adjustments	(2)	—	(2)	(1)	(5)
Effect on income from discontinued operations, net of taxes	—	—	(28)	28	—
Effect on net income attributable to CSC common shareholders	$ (1)	$ 2	$(30)	$ 22	$(7)

Out of period adjustments recorded in fiscal 2013 had the following impact on select line items of the Consolidated Statements of Operations for the twelve months ended March 29, 2013 under the rollover method:

(Amounts in millions, except per-share amounts)	Twelve Months Ended March 29, 2013		
	As Reported	Adjustments Increase/ (Decrease)	Amount Adjusted for Removal of Errors
Revenues	$14,993	14	$15,007
Costs of services (excludes depreciation and amortization and restructuring costs)	11,851	6	11,857
Selling, general and administrative (excluding restructuring costs)	1,195	(1)	1,194
Depreciation and amortization	1,076	(2)	1,074
Restructuring costs	264	5	269
Interest expense	183	—	183
Other (income) expense	(34)	—	(34)
Income from continuing operations before taxes	480	6	486
Taxes on income	(35)	13	(22)
Income from continuing operations	515	(7)	508
Income from discontinued operations, net of taxes	464	—	464
Net income attributable to CSC common shareholders	961	(7)	954
EPS—Diluted			
Continuing operations	$ 3.20	$(0.04)	$ 3.16
Discontinued operations	2.98	—	2.98
Total	$ 6.18	$(0.04)	$ 6.14

The out of period adjustments affecting income from continuing operations before taxes during the twelve months ended March 29, 2013 under the rollover method are related to the following consolidated balance sheet line items:

- Accounts receivable ($1 million decrease);
- Prepaid expenses and other current assets ($15 million increase);
- Outsourcing contract costs ($1 million decrease);
- Other assets ($6 million decrease);
- Property and equipment ($5 million decrease);
- Accrued payroll and related costs ($9 million increase);
- Accrued expenses and other current liabilities ($12 million decrease); and
- Deferred revenue ($13 million increase).

The Company has determined that the impact of the consolidated out of period adjustments recorded in fiscal 2013 is immaterial to the consolidated results, financial position and cash flows for fiscal 2013 and prior years. Consequently, the cumulative effect of these adjustments was recorded during fiscal 2013.

Fiscal 2012 Adjustments Financial Impact Summary

As previously disclosed, during fiscal 2012, the Company recorded various pre-tax adjustments that should have been recorded in prior fiscal years. The aggregate fiscal 2012 adjustments increased the loss from continuing operations before taxes by $79 million ($63 million net of tax) and were comprised of $13 million of charges relating to operations in the Nordic region, $23 million of charges relating to the Company's operations in Australia, and $25 million of charges originating from the NHS contract in the Company's BSS segment. Additionally, $16 million and $2 million of charges were recorded in the NPS segment and other operations of the Company, respectively. The fiscal 2012 out of period adjustments primarily related to the Company's MSS and BSS segments, with $37 million and $26 million of adjustments within MSS and BSS, respectively. Further adjustments were identified and recorded in fiscal 2013 related to fiscal 2012 that increased the net error by $7 million.

Nordic Region

The Company attributes the $13 million in pre-tax adjustments recorded in the Nordic region in fiscal 2012 to miscellaneous errors and not to any accounting irregularities or intentional misconduct other than a $1 million operating lease adjustment noted in the first quarter of fiscal 2012 which was a refinement of an error previously corrected and reported in fiscal 2011.

Australia

As previously disclosed, in the course of the Australia investigation initiated in fiscal 2012, accounting errors and irregularities were identified. As a result, certain personnel in Australia have been reprimanded, terminated and/or resigned. The Company attributes the $23 million of pre-tax adjustments recorded in fiscal 2012 to either intentional accounting irregularities (intentional irregularities) or other accounting errors (Other Errors). Other Errors include both unintentional errors and errors for which the categorization is unclear. The categorizations were provided to the Company through the independent investigation. The impact of the adjustments on income (loss) from continuing operations before taxes is attributable to the following prior fiscal years:

| | Increase/(Decrease) | | | | |
(Amounts in millions)	Fiscal 2008 & Prior (unaudited)	Fiscal 2009 (unaudited)	Fiscal 2010	Fiscal 2011	Total
Intentional irregularities	$10	$ (7)	$(4)	$ 1	$—
Other Errors	(7)	(16)	3	(3)	(23)
	$ 3	$(23)	$(1)	$(2)	$(23)

NHS

As previously disclosed, in fiscal 2012, $25 million of out of period adjustments reducing income from continuing operations related to the Company's NHS contract were identified and recorded. During the course of the investigation in fiscal 2012 of the percentage-of-completion accounting method used on the Company's NHS contract, certain accounting errors were identified related to costs incurred under the contract, which resulted in errors in the recognition of income from continuing operations that would have reduced by approximately $24 million the $1.5 billion write-off recorded by the Company in the third quarter of fiscal 2012. Although the Company has concluded that these errors do not appear to have any impact on amounts charged to the NHS, the errors have impacted the operating income recognized on the NHS contract. The exclusion of certain costs incurred under the contract caused the estimated margin at completion, which determines the operating income that is booked when revenue milestones are achieved, to be overstated. Although the Company has concluded that there is no cumulative impact as a result of the $1.5 billion charge relating to the NHS contract recorded as of December 30, 2011, operating income from fiscal year 2007 through and including fiscal 2011 has been overstated by a total of approximately $24 million and, therefore, the charge taken by the Company as of December 30, 2011 was overstated by approximately the same amount.

Certain additional items had been identified related to the NHS contract that could have had an effect on the amount and the allocation of the out of period adjustments for fiscal 2012 and prior fiscal years. These additional items were subject to further investigation and therefore were not recorded in fiscal 2012. See our discussion of fiscal 2013 adjustments above for further information regarding the impact of such items.

Certain CSC finance employees based in the U. K. were aware prior to fiscal 2012 of the aforementioned errors, but those employees failed to appropriately correct the errors. Therefore, the Company has classified these errors as intentional. Such categorization was provided to the Company through the independent investigation. As a result, certain personnel have been suspended.

The impact on income (loss) from continuing operations before taxes of the $25 million of out of period adjustments identified in fiscal 2012 related to the Company's NHS contract is attributable to the following prior fiscal years:

(Amounts in millions)	Increase/(Decrease) Fiscal 2012 Adjustments
Fiscal 2012	$25
Fiscal 2011	(7)
Fiscal 2010	(4)
Prior fiscal years (unaudited)	(14)

NPS

As previously reported, in fiscal 2012 the Company identified and recorded pre-tax adjustments reducing income from continuing operations before taxes by $16 million. Such adjustments were identified by the Company and were primarily related to the percentage-of-completion accounting adjustments.

Americas Outsourcing

As previously disclosed, in the course of the independent investigation of Americas Outsourcing accounting practices, accounting conventions used by Americas Outsourcing relating to intraperiod cost allocations were determined to be unintentional accounting errors. The errors did not have an impact on a fiscal year basis. The Company also determined that other operating units employed similar practices and made necessary corrections.

The following table summarizes the cumulative effect on the fiscal 2012 net loss attributable to CSC common shareholders of the consolidated out of period adjustments recorded during fiscal 2012 and fiscal 2013 under the rollover method. The amounts noted below also include certain adjustments that only impacted quarters (unaudited) within fiscal 2012, but had no net impact on the full year fiscal 2012 results:

	Fiscal 2012				
	Quarter Ended				
(Amounts in millions)	July 1, 2011	September 30, 2011	December 30, 2011	March 30, 2012	Total
Operating costs inappropriately capitalized	$ 1	$—	$—	$—	$ 1
Misapplication of US GAAP	1	(1)	2	(1)	1
Miscellaneous errors	2	7	—	2	11
Total Nordic adjustments	4	6	2	1	13
Operating costs inappropriately capitalized	—	11	—	—	11
Misapplication of US GAAP	—	8	—	1	9
Miscellaneous errors	—	2	2	(1)	3
Total Australia adjustments	—	21	2	—	23
NHS adjustments	(2)	(2)	46	(7)	35
NPS adjustments	3	1	(5)	11	10
Other adjustments	2	(11)	5	9	5
Effect on income (loss) from continuing operations before taxes	7	15	50	14	86
Taxes on income	(2)	(3)	(2)	(4)	(11)
Other income tax adjustments	1	14	(10)	(5)	—
Effect on net income (loss) attributable to CSC common shareholders	$ 6	$ 26	$ 38	$ 5	$ 75

Out of period adjustments recorded during fiscal 2012 and fiscal 2013 had the following impact on select line items of the Consolidated Statements of Operations for the twelve months ended March 30, 2012 under the rollover method:

(Amounts in millions, except per-share amounts)	Twelve Months Ended March 30, 2012		
	As Reported	Adjustments Increase/ (Decrease)	Amount Adjusted for Removal of Errors
Revenues	$15,364	$ 56	$15,420
Costs of services (excludes depreciation and amortization, specified contract charge, settlement charge and restructuring costs)	13,019	(27)	12,992
Cost of services—specified contract charge (excludes amount charged to revenue of $204)	1,281	3	1,284
Selling, general and administrative (excludes restructuring costs)	1,128	2	1,130
Depreciation and amortization	1,147	(2)	1,145
Restructuring costs	140	(5)	135
Interest expense	175	(3)	172
Other (income) expense	(6)	2	(4)
Loss from continuing operations before taxes	(4,454)	86	(4,368)
Taxes on income	(84)	11	(73)
Loss from continuing operations	(4,370)	75	(4,295)
Income from discontinued operations, net of taxes	145	—	145
Net loss attributable to CSC common shareholders	(4,242)	75	(4,167)
EPS—Diluted			
Continuing operations	$ (28.31)	$0.48	$ (27.83)
Discontinued operations	0.94		0.94
Total	$ (27.37)	$0.48	$ (26.89)

The out of period adjustments affecting loss from continuing operations before taxes during the twelve months ended March 30, 2012 under the rollover method are related to the following consolidated balance sheet line items:

- Accounts receivable ($66 million decrease);
- Prepaid expenses and other current assets ($44 million increase);
- Other assets ($6 million increase);
- Property and equipment ($29 million decrease);
- Accrued payroll and related costs ($2 million decrease);
- Accrued expenses and other current liabilities ($46 million increase); and
- Deferred revenue ($3 million decrease).

The Company has determined that the impact of the consolidated out of period adjustments recorded in fiscal 2012 and fiscal 2013 is immaterial to the consolidated results, financial position and cash flows for fiscal 2012 and prior years. Consequently, the cumulative effect of these adjustments was recorded during fiscal 2012 and fiscal 2013.

Fiscal 2011 Adjustments Financial Impact Summary

As previously reported, during fiscal 2011, the Company recorded $52 million of pre-tax adjustments that should have been recorded in prior fiscal years. The total out of period adjustments recorded in fiscal 2011 were comprised of $92 million of charges reducing income from continuing operations before taxes originating out of the Company's MSS operations in the Nordic region, and $40 million of adjustments increasing income from continuing operations before taxes, with $36 million of the $40 million within MSS. Further adjustments were identified and recorded in fiscal 2012 and 2013 related to fiscal 2011 that reduced the net error by $29 million and $22 million, respectively.

Nordic Region

As noted above, during fiscal 2011, the Company commenced an investigation into accounting irregularities in the Nordic region. Based upon the Company's investigation, review of underlying documentation for certain transactions and balances, review of contract documentation and discussions with Nordic personnel, the Company attributes the majority of the $92 million of pre-tax adjustments recorded in the Nordic region in fiscal 2011 to accounting irregularities arising from suspected intentional misconduct by certain former employees in our Danish subsidiaries. These accounting irregularities included the inappropriate capitalization of operating costs, the misapplication of U.S. GAAP and miscellaneous errors.

The following table summarizes the cumulative effect on the fiscal 2011 net income attributable to CSC common shareholders of the consolidated out of period adjustments recorded during fiscal 2011, 2012 and 2013. The amounts noted below also include certain adjustments that only impacted quarters (unaudited) within fiscal 2011, but had no net impact on the full year fiscal 2011 results:

(Amounts in millions)	July 2, 2010	October 1, 2010	December 31, 2010	April 1, 2011	Total
Fiscal 2011 / Quarter Ended					
Operating costs inappropriately capitalized	$ 15	$ 38	$ 8	$ 6	$ 67
Misapplication of US GAAP	4	3	6	(1)	12
Miscellaneous errors	1	(1)	9	(2)	7
Total Nordic adjustments	20	40	23	3	86
Operating costs inappropriately capitalized	—	(1)	(1)	—	(2)
Misapplication of US GAAP	—	1	3	(1)	3
Miscellaneous errors	(4)	5	(2)	(3)	(4)
Total Australia adjustments	(4)	5	—	(4)	(3)
NHS adjustments	(10)	(2)	(5)	(5)	(22)
NPS adjustments	4	2	(10)	(7)	(11)
Other adjustments	(9)	(8)	(18)	(14)	(49)
Effect on income from continuing operations before taxes	1	37	(10)	(27)	1
Taxes on income	4	1	9	10	24
Other income tax adjustments	(1)	(13)	(6)	18	(2)
Effect on net income attributable to CSC common shareholders	$ 4	$ 25	$ (7)	$ 1	$ 23

Out of period adjustments recorded during fiscal 2011, 2012 and 2013 had the following impact on select line items of the Consolidated Statements of Operations for the twelve months ended April 1, 2011 under the rollover method:

(Amounts in millions, except per-share amounts)	As Reported	Adjustments Increase/(Decrease)	Amount Adjusted for Removal of Errors
Twelve Months Ended April 1, 2011			
Revenues	$15,582	$ 1	$15,583
Costs of services (excludes depreciation and amortization)	12,578	(4)	12,574
Selling, general and administrative	949	1	950
Depreciation and amortization	1,068	3	1,071
Interest expense	167	—	167
Other (income) expense	(21)	—	(21)
Income from continuing operations before taxes	878	1	879
Taxes on income	202	(22)	180
Income from continuing operations	676	23	699
Income from discontinued operations, net of taxes	83	—	83
Net income attributable to CSC common shareholders	740	23	763
EPS—Diluted			
Continuing operations	$ 4.20	$0.15	$ 4.35
Discontinued operations	0.53	—	0.53
Total	$ 4.73	$0.15	$ 4.88

The Company has determined that the impact of the consolidated out of period adjustments recorded in fiscal 2013, 2012, and 2011 is immaterial to the consolidated results, financial position and cash flows for fiscal 2011 and prior years. Consequently, the cumulative effect of these adjustments was recorded during fiscal 2011.

Consolidation

RECOGNITION AND MEASUREMENT

1.54 FASB ASC 810-10-10 states that the purpose of consolidated financial statements is to present, primarily for the benefit of the owners and creditors of the parent, the results of operations and the financial position of a parent and all its subsidiaries as if the consolidated group were a single economic entity. It is presumed that consolidated financial statements are more meaningful than separate financial statements and are usually necessary for a fair presentation when one of the entities in the consolidated group directly or indirectly has a controlling financial interest in the other entities.

1.55 As noted in the "Pending Content" in FASB ASC 810-10-05–8,

[t]he Variable Interest Entities Subsections clarify the application of the General Subsections to certain legal entities in which equity investors do not have sufficient equity at risk for the legal entity to finance its activities without additional subordinated financial support or, as a group, the holders of the equity investment at risk lack any one of the following three characteristics:

a. The power, through voting rights or similar rights, to direct the activities of a legal entity that most significantly impact the entity's economic performance

b. The obligation to absorb the expected losses of the legal entity

c. The right to receive the expected residual returns of the legal entity.

Consolidated financial statements are usually necessary for a fair presentation if one of the entities in the consolidated group directly or indirectly has a controlling financial interest, typically a majority voting interest, in the other entities. Application of the majority voting interest requirement to certain types of entities may not identify the party with a controlling financial interest because that interest may be achieved through other arrangements. The "Pending Content" in FASB ASC 810-10-25-38A explains that a reporting entity with a variable interest in a variable interest entity (VIE) should assess whether the reporting entity has a controlling financial interest in the VIE and, thus, is the VIE's primary beneficiary. The reporting enterprise with a variable interest(s) that provides the reporting entity with a controlling financial interest in a VIE will have both the following characteristics: (*a*) the power to direct the activities of a VIE that most significantly affect the VIE's economic performance and (*b*) the obligation to absorb losses of the VIE that could potentially be significant to the VIE or the right to receive benefits from the VIE that could potentially be significant to the VIE. Only one reporting entity, if any, is expected to be identified as the primary beneficiary of a VIE. Although more than one reporting entity could have the obligation to absorb losses previously mentioned, only one reporting entity (if any) will have the power to direct the activities of a VIE that most significantly affect the VIE's economic performance. Further, the concept of a qualifying special-purpose entity no longer exists in FASB ASC.

1.56 FASB ASC 810 also establishes accounting and reporting standards for the noncontrolling interest in a subsidiary and the deconsolidation of a subsidiary. A *noncontrolling interest* is the portion of equity (net assets) in a subsidiary not directly or indirectly attributable to a parent. FASB ASC 810-10-45-16 requires the entity to present any noncontrolling interest within the "Equity" or "Net Assets" section of the consolidated statement of financial position separately from the parent's equity or net assets.

1.57 It is preferable under FASB ASC that the subsidiary's financial statements have the same or nearly the same fiscal period as the parent. However, FASB ASC 810-10-45-12 states that for consolidation purposes, it is usually acceptable to use the subsidiary's financial statements if the difference in fiscal period is not more than approximately three months. In addition, when a difference in the fiscal periods exists, FASB ASC does not require adjustments to be made for the effects of significant transactions that occurred between the parents' and subsidiaries' fiscal year-ends. FASB ASC 810-10-45-12 does require recognition by disclosure or otherwise of the effect of intervening events that materially affect the financial position or results of operations.

1.58 FASB ASC 810-10-45-11 recognizes that an entity may need to prepare parent-entity (separate) financial statements in addition to consolidated financial statements. This paragraph provides guidance on how an entity may choose to present these statements. For example, consolidating financial statements, in which one column is used for the parent and other columns for particular subsidiaries or groups of subsidiaries, is an effective means of presenting the pertinent information.

PRESENTATION

1.59 FASB ASC 810-10-45-23 requires that a change in a parent's ownership interest while the parent retains its controlling financial interest in its subsidiary should be accounted for as equity transactions (investments by owners and distributions to owners acting in their capacity as owners). Therefore, no gain or loss shall be recognized in consolidated net income or comprehensive income. The carrying amount of the noncontrolling interest should be adjusted to reflect the change in its ownership interest in the subsidiary. Any difference between the fair value of the consideration received or paid and the amount by which the noncontrolling interest is adjusted should be recognized in equity attributable to the parent.

1.60 The "Pending Content" paragraphs 4–5 of FASB ASC 810-10-40 state that a parent should deconsolidate a subsidiary or derecognize a group of assets specified in FASB ASC 810-10-40-3A as of the date the parent ceases to have a controlling financial interest in that subsidiary or group of assets. If a parent deconsolidates a subsidiary or derecognizes a group of assets through a nonreciprocal transfer to owners, such as a spinoff, the guidance in FASB ASC 845-10 applies. Otherwise, a parent should account for the deconsolidation of a subsidiary or derecognition of a group of assets by recognizing a gain or loss in net income attributable to the parent. This gain or loss is measured as the difference between (*a*) the aggregate of the fair value of any consideration received; the fair value of any retained noncontrolling interest in the former subsidiary or group of assets at the date the subsidiary is deconsolidated or the group of assets is derecognized, and the carrying amount of any noncontrolling interest in the former subsidiary, including any accumulated other comprehensive income attributable to the noncontrolling interest, at the date the subsidiary is deconsolidated and (*b*) the carrying amount of the former subsidiary's assets and liabilities or the carrying amount of the group of assets.

DISCLOSURE

1.61 FASB ASC 810-10-50-1 states in part that consolidated financial statements should disclose the consolidation policy that is being followed. In most cases, this can be made apparent by the headings or other information in the financial statements, but in other cases, a footnote is required.

1.62 FASB ASC 810-10-50-1A also requires disclosure on the face of the consolidated financial statements of the amounts of consolidated net income and consolidated comprehensive income attributable to the parent and noncontrolling interest. Disclosures in the consolidated financial statements should clearly identify and distinguish between the interests of the parent's owners and the interests of the noncontrolling owners of a subsidiary. Those disclosures include a reconciliation of the beginning and ending balances of the equity attributable to the parent and noncontrolling owners and a schedule showing the effects of changes in a parent's ownership interest in a subsidiary on the equity attributable to the parent.

PRESENTATION AND DISCLOSURE EXCERPTS

CONSOLIDATION

1.63 CITIGROUP INC. (DEC)
CONSOLIDATED BALANCE SHEET

Citigroup Inc. and Subsidiaries

	December 31,	
In millions of dollars	2013	2012
Assets		
Cash and due from banks (including segregated cash and other deposits)	$ 29,885	$ 36,453
Deposits with banks	169,005	102,134
Federal funds sold and securities borrowed or purchased under agreements to resell (including $141,481 and $160,589 as of December 31, 2013 and December 31, 2012, respectively, at fair value)	257,037	261,311
Brokerage receivables	25,674	22,490
Trading account assets (including $106,695 and $105,458 pledged to creditors at December 31, 2013 and December 31, 2012, respectively)	285,928	320,929
Investments (including $26,989 and $21,423 pledged to creditors at December 31, 2013 and December 31, 2012, respectively, and $291,216 and $294,463 as of December 31, 2013 and December 31, 2012, respectively, at fair value)	308,980	312,326
Loans, net of unearned income		
Consumer (including $957 and $1,231 as of December 31, 2013 and December 31, 2012, respectively, at fair value)	393,831	408,671
Corporate (including $4,072 and $4,056 as of December 31, 2013 and December 31, 2012, respectively, at fair value)	271,641	246,793
Loans, net of unearned income	$ 665,472	$ 655,464
Allowance for loan losses	(19,648)	(25,455)
Total loans, net	$ 645,824	$ 630,009
Goodwill	25,009	25,673
Intangible assets (other than MSRs)	5,056	5,697
Mortgage servicing rights (MSRs)	2,718	1,942
Other assets (including $7,123 and $13,299 as of December 31, 2013 and December 31, 2012, respectively, at fair value)	125,266	145,660
Assets of discontinued operations held for sale	—	36
Total assets	$1,880,382	$1,864,660

The following table presents certain assets of consolidated variable interest entities (VIEs), which are included in the Consolidated Balance Sheet above. The assets in the table below include only those assets that can be used to settle obligations of consolidated VIEs on the following page and are in excess of those obligations. Additionally, the assets in the table below include third-party assets of consolidated VIEs only and exclude intercompany balances that eliminate in consolidation.

	December 31,	
In millions of dollars	2013	2012
Assets of consolidated VIEs that can only be used to settle obligations of consolidated VIEs		
Cash and due from banks	$ 360	$ 498
Trading account assets	977	481
Investments	10,416	10,751
Loans, net of unearned income		
Consumer (including $910 and $1,191 as of December 31, 2013 and December 31, 2012, respectively, at fair value)	63,493	93,936
Corporate (including $14 and $157 as of December 31, 2013 and December 31, 2012, respectively, at fair value)	31,919	23,684
Loans, net of unearned income	$ 95,412	$117,620
Allowance for loan losses	(3,502)	(5,854)
Total loans, net	$ 91,910	$111,766
Other assets	1,233	674
Total assets of consolidated VIEs that can only be used to settle obligations of consolidated VIEs	$104,896	$124,170

In millions of dollars, except shares and per share amounts	December 31, 2013	December 31, 2012
Liabilities		
Non-interest-bearing deposits in U.S. offices	$ 128,399	$ 129,657
Interest-bearing deposits in U.S. offices (including $988 and $889 as of December 31, 2013 and December 31, 2012, respectively, at fair value)	284,164	247,716
Non-interest-bearing deposits in offices outside the U.S.	69,406	65,024
Interest-bearing deposits in offices outside the U.S. (including $689 and $558 as of December 31, 2013 and December 31, 2012, respectively, at fair value)	486,304	488,163
Total deposits	$ 968,273	$ 930,560
Federal funds purchased and securities loaned or sold under agreements to repurchase (including $51,545 and $116,689 as of December 31, 2013 and December 31, 2012, respectively, at fair value)	203,512	211,236
Brokerage payables	53,707	57,013
Trading account liabilities	108,762	115,549
Short-term borrowings (including $3,692 and $818 as of December 31, 2013 and December 31, 2012, respectively, at fair value)	58,944	52,027
Long-term debt (including $26,877 and $29,764 as of December 31, 2013 and December 31, 2012, respectively, at fair value)	221,116	239,463
Other liabilities (including $2,011 and $2,910 as of December 31, 2013 and December 31, 2012, respectively, at fair value)	59,935	67,815
Liabilities of discontinued operations held for sale	—	—
Total liabilities	$1,674,249	$1,673,663
Stockholders' equity		
Preferred stock ($1.00 par value; authorized shares: 30 million), issued shares: 269,520 as of December 31, 2013 and 102,038 as of December 31, 2012, at aggregate liquidation value	$ 6,738	$ 2,562
Common stock ($0.01 par value; authorized shares: 6 billion), issued shares: 3,062,098,976 as of December 31, 2013 and 3,043,153,204 as of December 31, 2012	31	30
Additional paid-in capital	107,193	106,391
Retained earnings	111,168	97,809
Treasury stock, at cost: December 31, 2013—32,856,062 shares and December 31, 2012—14,269,301 shares	(1,658)	(847)
Accumulated other comprehensive income (loss)	(19,133)	(16,896)
Total Citigroup stockholders' equity	$ 204,339	$ 189,049
Noncontrolling interest	1,794	1,948
Total equity	$ 206,133	$ 190,997
Total liabilities and equity	$1,880,382	$1,864,660

The following table presents certain liabilities of consolidated VIEs, which are included in the Consolidated Balance Sheet above. The liabilities in the table below include third-party liabilities of consolidated VIEs only and exclude intercompany balances that eliminate in consolidation. The liabilities also exclude amounts where creditors or beneficial interest holders have recourse to the general credit of Citigroup.

In millions of dollars	December 31, 2013	December 31, 2012
Liabilities of consolidated VIEs for which creditors or beneficial interest holders do not have recourse to the general credit of Citigroup		
Short-term borrowings	$21,793	$15,637
Long-term debt (including $909 and $1,330 as of December 31, 2013 and December 31, 2012, respectively, at fair value)	34,743	26,346
Other liabilities	999	1,224
Total liabilities of consolidated VIEs for which creditors or beneficial interest holders do not have recourse to the general credit of Citigroup	$57,535	$43,207

The Notes to the Consolidated Financial Statements are an integral part of these Consolidated Financial Statements.

NOTES TO CONSOLIDATED FINANCIAL STATEMENTS

1. Summary of Significant Accounting Policies (in part)

Principles of Consolidation

The Consolidated Financial Statements include the accounts of Citigroup and its subsidiaries prepared in accordance with U.S. Generally Accepted Accounting Principles (GAAP). The Company consolidates subsidiaries in which it holds, directly or indirectly, more than 50% of the voting rights or where it exercises control. Entities where the Company holds 20% to 50% of the voting rights and/or has the ability to exercise significant influence, other than investments of designated venture capital subsidiaries or investments accounted for at fair value under the fair value option, are accounted for under the equity method, and the pro rata share of their income (loss) is included in *Other revenue*. Income from investments in less than 20% owned companies is recognized when dividends are received. As discussed in more detail in Note 22 to the Consolidated Financial Statements, Citigroup consolidates entities deemed to be variable interest entities when

Citigroup is determined to be the primary beneficiary. Gains and losses on the disposition of branches, subsidiaries, affiliates, buildings, and other investments are included in *Other revenue*.

Throughout these Notes, "Citigroup," "Citi" and the "Company" refer to Citigroup Inc. and its consolidated subsidiaries.

Certain reclassifications have been made to the prior periods' financial statements and notes to conform to the current period's presentation.

Citibank, N.A. is a commercial bank and wholly owned subsidiary of Citigroup Inc. Citibank's principal offerings include: Consumer finance, mortgage lending, and retail banking products and services; investment banking, commercial banking, cash management, trade finance and e-commerce products and services; and private banking products and services.

Variable Interest Entities

An entity is referred to as a variable interest entity (VIE) if it meets the criteria outlined in ASC 810, *Consolidation* (formerly Statement of Financial Accounting Standards(SFAS) No. 167, *Amendments to FASB (Financial Accounting Standards Board) Interpretation No. 46(R))* (SFAS 167), which are: (i) the entity has equity that is insufficient to permit the entity to finance its activities without additional subordinated financial support from other parties; or (ii) the entity has equity investors that cannot make significant decisions about the entity's operations or that do not absorb their proportionate share of the entity's expected losses or expected returns.

The Company consolidates a VIE when it has both the power to direct the activities that most significantly impact the VIE's economic success and a right to receive benefits or the obligation to absorb losses of the entity that could be potentially significant to the VIE (that is, it is the primary beneficiary).

Along with the VIEs that are consolidated in accordance with these guidelines, the Company has variable interests in other VIEs that are not consolidated because the Company is not the primary beneficiary. These include multi-seller finance companies, certain collateralized debt obligations (CDOs), many structured finance transactions, and various investment funds.

However, these VIEs and all other unconsolidated VIEs are monitored by the Company to determine if any events have occurred that could cause its primary beneficiary status to change. These events include:
- additional purchases or sales of variable interests by Citigroup or an unrelated third party, which cause Citigroup's overall variable interest ownership to change;
- changes in contractual arrangements in a manner that reallocates expected losses and residual returns among the variable interest holders;
- changes in the party that has power to direct the activities of a VIE that most significantly impact the entity's economic performance; and
- providing support to an entity that results in an implicit variable interest.

All other entities not deemed to be VIEs with which the Company has involvement are evaluated for consolidation under other subtopics of ASC 810 (formerly Accounting Research Bulletin (ARB) No. 51, *Consolidated Financial Statements*, SFAS No. 94, *Consolidation of All Majority-Owned Subsidiaries*, and EITF Issue No. 04-5, *Determining Whether a General Partner, or the General Partners as a Group, Controls a Limited Partnership or Similar Entity When the Limited Partners Have Certain Rights*).

Securitizations

The Company primarily securitizes credit card receivables and mortgages. Other types of securitized assets include corporate debt instruments (in cash and synthetic form) and student loans.

There are two key accounting determinations that must be made relating to securitizations. Citi first makes a determination as to whether the securitization entity would be consolidated. Second, it determines whether the transfer of financial assets to the entity is considered a sale under GAAP. If the securitization entity is a VIE, the Company consolidates the VIE if it is the primary beneficiary (as discussed in "Variable Interest Entities" above). For all other securitization entities determined not to be VIEs in which Citigroup participates, a consolidation decision is based on which party has voting control of the entity, giving consideration to removal and liquidation rights in certain partnership structures. Only securitization entities controlled by Citigroup are consolidated.

Interests in the securitized and sold assets may be retained in the form of subordinated or senior interest-only strips, subordinated tranches, spread accounts and servicing rights. In credit card securitizations, the Company retains a seller's interest in the credit card receivables transferred to the trusts, which is not in securitized form. In the case of consolidated securitization entities, including the credit card trusts, these retained interests are not reported on Citi's Consolidated Balance Sheet. The securitized loans remain on the balance sheet. Substantially all of the Consumer loans sold or securitized through non-consolidated trusts by Citigroup are U.S. prime residential mortgage loans. Retained interests in non-consolidated mortgage securitization trusts are classified as *Trading account assets,* except for MSRs, which are included in *Mortgage servicing rights* on Citigroup's Consolidated Balance Sheet.

22. Securitizations and Variable Interest Entities (in part)

Uses of Special Purpose Entities

A special purpose entity (SPE) is an entity designed to fulfill a specific limited need of the company that organized it. The principal uses of SPEs are to obtain liquidity and favorable capital treatment by securitizing certain of Citigroup's financial assets, to assist clients in securitizing their financial assets and to create investment products for clients. SPEs may be organized in various legal forms including trusts, partnerships or corporations. In a securitization, the company transferring assets to an SPE converts all (or a portion) of those assets into cash before they would have been realized in the normal course of business through the SPE's issuance of debt and equity instruments, certificates, commercial paper and other notes of indebtedness. These issuances are recorded on the balance sheet of the SPE, which may or may not be consolidated onto the balance sheet of the company that organized the SPE.

Investors usually have recourse only to the assets in the SPE and often benefit from other credit enhancements, such as a collateral account or over-collateralization in the form of excess assets in the SPE, a line of credit, or a liquidity facility, such as a liquidity put option or asset purchase agreement. Because of these enhancements, the SPE issuances can typically obtain a more favorable credit rating from rating agencies than the transferor could obtain for its own debt issuances. This results in less expensive financing costs than unsecured debt. The SPE may also enter into derivative contracts in order to convert the yield or currency of the underlying assets to match the needs of the SPE investors or to limit or change the credit risk of the SPE. Citigroup may be the provider of certain credit enhancements as well as the counterparty to any related derivative contracts.

Most of Citigroup's SPEs are variable interest entities (VIEs), as described below.

Variable Interest Entities

VIEs are entities that have either a total equity investment that is insufficient to permit the entity to finance its activities without additional subordinated financial support, or whose equity investors lack the characteristics of a controlling financial interest (i.e., ability to make significant decisions through voting rights and right to receive the expected residual returns of the entity or obligation to absorb the expected losses of the entity). Investors that finance the VIE through debt or equity interests or other counterparties providing other forms of support such as guarantees, subordinated fee arrangements or certain types of derivative contracts, are variable interest holders in the entity.

The variable interest holder, if any, that has a controlling financial interest in a VIE is deemed to be the primary beneficiary and must consolidate the VIE. Citigroup would be deemed to have a controlling financial interest and be the primary beneficiary if it has both of the following characteristics:
- power to direct activities of a VIE that most significantly impact the entity's economic performance; and
- obligation to absorb losses of the entity that could potentially be significant to the VIE, or right to receive benefits from the entity that could potentially be significant to the VIE.

The Company must evaluate its involvement in each VIE and understand the purpose and design of the entity, the role the Company had in the entity's design and its involvement in the VIE's ongoing activities. The Company then must evaluate which activities most significantly impact the economic performance of the VIE and who has the power to direct such activities.

For those VIEs where the Company determines that it has the power to direct the activities that most significantly impact the VIE's economic performance, the Company then must evaluate its economic interests, if any, and determine whether it could absorb losses or receive benefits that could potentially be significant to the VIE. When evaluating whether the Company has an obligation to absorb losses that could potentially be significant, it considers the maximum exposure to such loss without consideration of probability. Such obligations could be in various forms, including, but not limited to, debt and equity investments, guarantees, liquidity agreements and certain derivative contracts.

In various other transactions, the Company may: (i) act as a derivative counterparty (for example, interest rate swap, cross-currency swap, or purchaser of credit protection under a credit default swap or total return swap where the Company pays the total return on certain assets to the SPE); (ii) act as underwriter or placement agent; (iii) provide administrative, trustee or other services; or (iv) make a market in debt securities or other instruments issued by VIEs. The Company generally considers such involvement, by itself, not to be variable interests and thus not an indicator of power or potentially significant benefits or losses.

Citigroup's involvement with consolidated and unconsolidated VIEs with which the Company holds significant variable interests or has continuing involvement through servicing a majority of the assets in a VIE, each as of December 31, 2013 and 2012, is presented below:

| In millions of dollars | As of December 31, 2013 | | | Maximum Exposure to Loss in Significant Unconsolidated VIEs [1] | | | | |
| | | | | Funded Exposures [2] | | Unfunded Exposures [3] | | |
	Total Involve-ment with SPE Assets	Consoli-dated VIE / SPE Assets	Significant Unconsolidated VIE Assets [5]	Debt Invest-ments	Equity Invest-ments	Funding Commit-ments	Guarantees and Derivatives	Total
Citicorp								
Credit card securitizations[5]	$ 52,229	$ 52,229	$ —	$ —	$ —	$ —	$ —	$ —
Mortgage securitizations[6]								
U.S. agency-sponsored	239,204	—	239,204	3,583	—	—	36	3,619
Non-agency-sponsored	7,711	598	7,113	583	—	—	—	583
Citi-administered asset-backed commercial paper conduits (ABCP)	31,759	31,759	—					
Collateralized debt obligations (CDOs)	4,204	—	4,204	34	—	—	—	34
Collateralized loan obligations (CLOs)	16,883	—	16,883	1,938	—	—	—	1,938
Asset-based financing	45,884	971	44,913	17,452	74	1,132	195	18,853
Municipal securities tender option bond trusts (TOBs)	12,716	7,039	5,677	29	—	3,881	—	3,910
Municipal investments	15,962	223	15,739	1,846	2,073	1,173	—	5,092
Client intermediation	1,778	195	1,583	145	—	—	—	145
Investment funds[7]	31,787	2,557	29,230	191	264	81	—	536
Trust preferred securities	4,822	—	4,822	—	51	—	—	51
Other	2,439	225	2,214	143	649	20	78	890
Total	$467,378	$ 95,796	$371,582	$25,944	$3,111	$6,287	$309	$35,651
Citi Holdings								
Credit card securitizations	$ 1,867	$ 1,448	$ 419	$ —	$ —	$ —	$ —	$ —
Mortgage securitizations								
U.S. agency-sponsored	73,549	—	73,549	549	—	—	77	626
Non-agency-sponsored	13,193	1,695	11,498	35	—	—	2	37
Student loan securitizations	1,520	1,520	—	—	—	—	—	—
Collateralized debt obligations (CDOs)	3,625	—	3,625	88	—	—	87	175
Collateralized loan obligations (CLOs)	2,733	—	2,733	358	—	—	111	469
Asset-based financing	3,508	3	3,505	629	3	258	—	890
Municipal investments	7,304	—	7,304	3	204	939	—	1,146
Client intermediation	—	—	—	—	—	—	—	—
Investment funds	1,237	—	1,237	—	61	—	—	61
Other	4,494	4,434	60	—	—	—	—	—
Total	$113,030	$ 9,100	$103,930	$ 1,662	$ 268	$1,197	$277	$ 3,404
Total Citigroup	$580,408	$104,896	$475,512	$27,606	$3,379	$7,484	$586	$39,055

[1] The definition of maximum exposure to loss is included in the text that follows this table.

[2] Included in Citigroup's December 31, 2013 Consolidated Balance Sheet.

[3] Not included in Citigroup's December 31, 2013 Consolidated Balance Sheet.

[4] A significant unconsolidated VIE is an entity where the Company has any variable interest considered to be significant, regardless of the likelihood of loss or the notional amount of exposure.

[5] As part of its liquidity and funding strategy, during the first quarter of 2013, the Company elected to remove approximately $27 billion of randomly selected credit card receivables from the Master Trust ($12 billion) and Omni Trust ($15 billion) that represented a portion of the excess seller's interest in each trust. Subsequently, during the second half of 2013, Citi elected to add approximately $7.4 billion of credit card receivables to the Master Trust from the U.S. Citi-branded cards business' portfolio of eligible unsecuritized credit card receivables (for a discussion of Citi's credit card securitizations, see "Credit Card Securitizations" below). These credit card receivables continue to be included in *Consumer loans* on the Consolidated Balance Sheet as of December 31, 2013.

[6] Citicorp mortgage securitizations also include agency and non-agency (private-label) re-securitization activities. These SPEs are not consolidated. See "Re-securitizations" below for further discussion.

[7] Substantially all of the unconsolidated investment funds' assets are related to retirement funds in Mexico managed by Citi. See "Investment Funds" below for further discussion.

In millions of dollars	Total Involvement with SPE Assets	Consolidated VIE / SPE Assets	Significant Unconsolidated VIE Assets [4]	Maximum Exposure to Loss in Significant Unconsolidated VIEs [1]				Total
				Funded Exposures [2]		Unfunded Exposures [3]		
				Debt Investments	Equity Investments	Funding Commitments	Guarantees and Derivatives	
Citicorp								
Credit card securitizations	$ 77,770	$ 77,770	$ —	$ —	$ —	$ —	$ —	$ —
Mortgage securitizations[5]								
U.S. agency-sponsored	232,741	—	232,741	3,042	—	—	45	3,087
Non-agency-sponsored	8,810	1,188	7,622	382	—	—	—	382
Citi-administered asset-backed commercial paper conduits (ABCP)	30,002	22,387	7,615	—	—	7,615	—	7,615
Collateralized debt obligations (CDOs)	5,539	—	5,539	24	—	—	—	24
Collateralized loan obligations (CLOs)	15,120	—	15,120	642	19	—	—	661
Asset-based financing	41,399	1,125	40,274	14,798	84	2,081	159	17,122
Municipal securities tender option bond trusts (TOBs)	15,163	7,573	7,590	352	—	4,628	—	4,980
Municipal investments	19,693	255	19,438	2,003	3,049	1,669	—	6,721
Client intermediation	2,486	151	2,335	319	—	—	—	319
Investment funds[6]	30,264	2,196	28,068	—	223	—	—	223
Trust preferred securities	12,221	—	12,221	—	126	—	—	126
Other	2,023	115	1,908	113	382	22	76	593
Total	$493,231	$112,760	$380,471	$21,675	$3,883	$16,015	$ 280	$41,853
Citi Holdings								
Credit card securitizations	$ 2,177	$ 1,736	$ 441	$ —	$ —	$ —	$ —	$ —
Mortgage securitizations								
U.S. agency-sponsored	106,888	—	106,888	700	—	—	163	863
Non-agency-sponsored	17,192	2,127	15,065	43	—	—	2	45
Student loan securitizations	1,681	1,681	—	—	—	—	—	—
Collateralized debt obligations (CDOs)	4,752	—	4,752	139	—	—	124	263
Collateralized loan obligations (CLOs)	4,676	—	4,676	435	—	13	108	556
Asset-based financing	4,166	3	4,163	984	6	243	—	1,233
Municipal investments	7,766	—	7,766	90	235	992	—	1,317
Client intermediation	13	13	—	—	—	—	—	—
Investment funds	1,083	—	1,083	—	47	—	—	47
Other	6,005	5,851	154	—	3	—	—	3
Total	$156,399	$ 11,411	$144,988	$ 2,391	$ 291	$ 1,248	$ 397	$ 4,327
Total Citigroup	$649,630	$124,171	$525,459	$24,066	$4,174	$17,263	$ 677	$46,180

[1] The definition of maximum exposure to loss is included in the text that follows this table.

[2] Included in Citigroup's December 31, 2012 Consolidated Balance Sheet.

[3] Not included in Citigroup's December 31, 2012 Consolidated Balance Sheet.

[4] A significant unconsolidated VIE is an entity where the Company has any variable interest considered to be significant, regardless of the likelihood of loss or the notional amount of exposure.

[5] Citicorp mortgage securitizations also include agency and non-agency (private-label) re-securitization activities. These SPEs are not consolidated. See "Re-securitizations" below for further discussion.

[6] Substantially all of the unconsolidated investment funds' assets are related to retirement funds in Mexico managed by Citi. See "Investment Funds" below for further discussion.

The previous tables do not include:

- certain venture capital investments made by some of the Company's private equity subsidiaries, as the Company accounts for these investments in accordance with the Investment Company Audit Guide (codified in ASC 946);
- certain limited partnerships that are investment funds that qualify for the deferral from the requirements of ASC 810 where the Company is the general partner and the limited partners have the right to replace the general partner or liquidate the funds;
- certain investment funds for which the Company provides investment management services and personal estate trusts for which the Company provides administrative, trustee and/or investment management services;
- VIEs structured by third parties where the Company holds securities in inventory, as these investments are made on arm's-length terms;
- certain positions in mortgage-backed and asset-backed securities held by the Company, which are classified as *Trading account assets* or *Investments*, where the Company has no other involvement with the related securitization entity deemed to be significant (for more information on these positions, see Notes 13 and 14 to the Consolidated Financial Statements);
- certain representations and warranties exposures in legacy *Securities and Banking*-sponsored mortgage-backed and asset-backed securitizations, where the Company has no variable interest or continuing involvement as servicer. The outstanding balance of

mortgage loans securitized during 2005 to 2008 where the Company has no variable interest or continuing involvement as servicer was approximately $16 billion and $19 billion at December 31, 2013 and 2012, respectively; and

- certain representations and warranties exposures in Citigroup residential mortgage securitizations, where the original mortgage loan balances are no longer outstanding.

The asset balances for consolidated VIEs represent the carrying amounts of the assets consolidated by the Company. The carrying amount may represent the amortized cost or the current fair value of the assets depending on the legal form of the asset (e.g., security or loan) and the Company's standard accounting policies for the asset type and line of business.

The asset balances for unconsolidated VIEs where the Company has significant involvement represent the most current information available to the Company. In most cases, the asset balances represent an amortized cost basis without regard to impairments in fair value, unless fair value information is readily available to the Company. For VIEs that obtain asset exposures synthetically through derivative instruments (for example, synthetic CDOs), the tables generally include the full original notional amount of the derivative as an asset balance.

The maximum funded exposure represents the balance sheet carrying amount of the Company's investment in the VIE. It reflects the initial amount of cash invested in the VIE adjusted for any accrued interest and cash principal payments received. The carrying amount may also be adjusted for increases or declines in fair value or any impairment in value recognized in earnings. The maximum exposure of unfunded positions represents the remaining undrawn committed amount, including liquidity and credit facilities provided by the Company, or the notional amount of a derivative instrument considered to be a variable interest. In certain transactions, the Company has entered into derivative instruments or other arrangements that are not considered variable interests in the VIE (e.g., interest rate swaps, cross-currency swaps, or where the Company is the purchaser of credit protection under a credit default swap or total return swap where the Company pays the total return on certain assets to the SPE). Receivables under such arrangements are not included in the maximum exposure amounts.

Funding Commitments for Significant Unconsolidated VIEs—Liquidity Facilities and Loan Commitments

The following table presents the notional amount of liquidity facilities and loan commitments that are classified as funding commitments in the VIE tables above as of December 31, 2013 and 2012:

	December 31, 2013		December 31, 2012	
In millions of dollars	Liquidity Facilities	Loan Commitments	Liquidity Facilities	Loan Commitments
Citicorp				
Citi-administered asset-backed commercial paper conduits (ABCP)	$ —	$ —	$ 7,615	$ —
Asset-based financing	5	1,127	6	2,075
Municipal securities tender option bond trusts (TOBs)	3,881	—	4,628	—
Municipal investments	—	1,173	—	1,669
Investment funds	—	81	—	—
Other	—	20	—	22
Total Citicorp	$3,886	$2,401	$12,249	$3,766
Citi Holdings				
Collateralized loan obligations (CLOs)	$ —	$ —	$ 13	$ —
Asset-based financing	—	258	—	243
Municipal investments	—	939	—	992
Total Citi Holdings	$ —	$1,197	$ 13	$1,235
Total Citigroup funding commitments	$3,886	$3,598	$12,262	$5,001

Citicorp and Citi Holdings Consolidated VIEs

The Company engages in on-balance-sheet securitizations, which are securitizations that do not qualify for sales treatment; thus, the assets remain on the Company's balance sheet. The consolidated VIEs included in the tables below represent hundreds of separate entities with which the Company is involved. In general, the third-party investors in the obligations of consolidated VIEs have legal recourse only to the assets of the VIEs and do not have such recourse to the Company, except where the Company has provided a guarantee to the investors or is the counterparty to certain derivative transactions involving the VIE. In addition, the assets are generally restricted only to pay such liabilities.

Thus, the Company's maximum legal exposure to loss related to consolidated VIEs is significantly less than the carrying value of the consolidated VIE assets due to outstanding third-party financing. Intercompany assets and liabilities are excluded from the table. All assets are restricted from being sold or pledged as collateral. The cash flows from these assets are the only source used to pay down the associated liabilities, which are non-recourse to the Company's general assets.

The following table presents the carrying amounts and classifications of consolidated assets that are collateral for consolidated VIE and SPE obligations as of December 31, 2013 and 2012:

In billions of dollars	December 31, 2013			December 31, 2012		
	Citicorp	Citi Holdings	Citigroup	Citicorp	Citi Holdings	Citigroup
Cash	$ 0.2	$0.2	$ 0.4	$ 0.3	$ 0.2	$ 0.5
Trading account assets	1.0	—	1.0	0.5	—	0.5
Investments	10.4	—	10.4	10.7	—	10.7
Total loans, net	83.2	8.7	91.9	100.8	11.0	111.8
Other	1.1	0.2	1.3	0.5	0.2	0.7
Total assets	$95.9	$9.1	$105.0	$112.8	$11.4	$124.2
Short-term borrowings	$24.3	$—	$ 24.3	$ 17.9	$ —	$ 17.9
Long-term debt	32.8	2.0	34.8	23.8	2.6	26.4
Other liabilities	0.9	0.1	1.0	1.1	0.1	1.2
Total liabilities	$58.0	$2.1	$ 60.1	$ 42.8	$ 2.7	$ 45.5

Citicorp and Citi Holdings Significant Interests in Unconsolidated VIEs—Balance Sheet Classification

The following table presents the carrying amounts and classification of significant variable interests in unconsolidated VIEs as of December 31, 2013 and 2012:

In billions of dollars	December 31, 2013			December 31, 2012		
	Citicorp	Citi Holdings	Citigroup	Citicorp	Citi Holdings	Citigroup
Trading account assets	$ 4.8	$0.4	$ 5.2	$ 4.0	$0.5	$ 4.5
Investments	3.7	0.4	4.1	5.4	0.7	6.1
Total loans, net	18.3	0.6	18.9	14.6	0.9	15.5
Other	2.2	0.5	2.7	1.6	0.5	2.1
Total assets	$29.0	$1.9	$30.9	$25.6	$2.6	$28.2

1.64 AK STEEL HOLDING CORPORATION (DEC)

CONSOLIDATED BALANCE SHEETS

December 31, 2013 and 2012

(dollars in millions, except per share data)

	2013	2012
Assets		
Current assets:		
Cash and cash equivalents	$ 45.3	$ 227.0
Accounts receivable, net	525.2	473.9
Inventory, net	586.6	609.2
Deferred tax assets, current	69.6	73.2
Other current assets	46.5	59.4
Total current assets	1,273.2	1,442.7
Property, plant and equipment	5,871.9	5,943.9
Accumulated depreciation	(3,991.8)	(3,931.6)
Property, plant and equipment, net	1,880.1	2,012.3
Other non-current assets:		
Investment in Magnetation LLC	187.8	150.0
Other non-current assets	264.6	298.1
Total Assets	$ 3,605.7	$ 3,903.1

	2013	2012
Liabilities and Equity (Deficit)		
Current liabilities:		
Accounts payable	$ 601.8	$ 538.3
Accrued liabilities	142.9	164.8
Current portion of long-term debt	0.8	0.7
Current portion of pension and other postretirement benefit obligations	85.9	108.6
Total current liabilities	831.4	812.4
Non-current liabilities:		
Long-term debt	1,506.2	1,411.2
Pension and other postretirement benefit obligations	965.4	1,661.7
Other non-current liabilities	110.0	108.8
Total Liabilities	3,413.0	3,994.1
Equity (deficit):		
Common stock, authorized 200,000,000 shares of $.01 par value each; issued 149,691,388 and 149,094,571 shares in 2013 and 2012; outstanding 136,380,078 and 135,944,172 shares in 2013 and 2012	1.5	1.5
Additional paid-in capital	2,079.2	2,069.7
Treasury stock, common shares at cost, 13,311,310 and 13,150,399 shares in 2013 and 2012	(174.0)	(173.3)
Accumulated deficit	(2,451.1)	(2,404.3)
Accumulated other comprehensive income	323.4	1.1
Total stockholders' equity (deficit)	(221.0)	(505.3)
Noncontrolling interests	413.7	414.3
Total Equity (Deficit)	192.7	(91.0)
Total Liabilities And Equity (Deficit)	$ 3,605.7	$ 3,903.1

The Consolidated Balance Sheets as of December 31, 2013 and 2012, include the following amounts related to consolidated variable interest entities, prior to intercompany eliminations. See Note 14 for more information concerning variable interest entities.

	2013	2012
SunCoke Middletown		
Cash and cash equivalents	$ 14.2	$ —
Accounts receivable, net	—	1.0
Inventory, net	22.1	28.3
Property, plant and equipment	418.5	414.5
Accumulated depreciation	(29.0)	(15.0)
Accounts payable	13.3	15.4
Other assets (liabilities), net	(0.7)	(1.2)
Noncontrolling interests	411.8	412.2
Other variable interest entities		
Cash and cash equivalents	$1.0	$1.2
Property, plant and equipment	11.5	11.4
Accumulated depreciation	(9.2)	(8.9)
Other assets (liabilities), net	0.6	0.6
Noncontrolling interests	1.9	2.1

See notes to consolidated financial statements.

NOTES TO CONSOLIDATED FINANCIAL STATEMENTS

(dollars in millions, except per share amounts or as otherwise specifically noted)

Note 1—Summary of Significant Accounting Policies (in part)

Basis of Presentation: These financial statements consolidate the operations and accounts of AK Steel Holding Corporation ("AK Holding"), its wholly-owned subsidiary AK Steel Corporation ("AK Steel," and together with AK Holding, the "Company"), all subsidiaries in which the Company has a controlling interest, and two variable interest entities for which the Company is the primary beneficiary. The Company also operates European trading companies that buy and sell steel and steel products and other materials. The Company manages its operations on a consolidated, integrated basis in order to utilize the most appropriate equipment and facilities for the production of a product, regardless of product line, and concludes that it operates in a single business segment. All intercompany transactions and balances have been eliminated.

Note 14—Variable Interest Entities

SunCoke Middletown

The Company is a party to supply contracts with SunCoke Middletown, an affiliate of SunCoke, to provide the Company with about 550,000 tons of metallurgical-grade lump coke and approximately 45 megawatts of electrical power annually. Under those agreements, the Company will purchase all of SunCoke Middletown's coke and electrical power through at least 2031. SunCoke Middletown is a variable interest entity. The Company has committed to purchase all of the expected production of SunCoke Middletown and the Company has been determined to be the primary beneficiary. Thus, the financial results of SunCoke Middletown are required to be consolidated with the results of the Company, even though the Company has no ownership interest in SunCoke Middletown. Included in the Consolidated Statements of Operations were income (loss) before taxes related to SunCoke Middletown of $64.3, $46.0 and $(7.8) for the years ended December 31, 2013, 2012 and 2011, respectively.

Vicksmetal/Armco Associates

The Company indirectly owns a 50% interest in Vicksmetal/Armco Associates ("VAA"), a joint venture with Vicksmetal Company, which is owned by Sumitomo Corporation. VAA slits electrical steel primarily for AK Steel, though also for third parties. AK Steel has determined that VAA meets the definition of a variable interest entity and the financial results of VAA are consolidated with the results of the Company, as the primary beneficiary.

Note 19—Supplemental Guarantor Information

AK Steel's Secured Notes, 2020 Notes, 2022 Notes and Exchangeable Notes (the "Senior Notes") are governed by indentures entered into by AK Holding and its 100% owned subsidiary, AK Steel. Under the terms of the indentures, AK Holding fully and unconditionally, jointly and severally, guarantees the payment of interest, principal and premium, if any, on each of the notes comprising the Senior Notes. AK Holding is the sole guarantor of the Senior Notes.

The presentation of the supplemental guarantor information reflects all investments in subsidiaries under the equity method of accounting. Net income (loss) of the subsidiaries accounted for under the equity method is therefore reflected in their parents' investment accounts. The principal elimination entries eliminate investments in subsidiaries and inter-company balances and transactions. The following supplemental condensed consolidating financial statements present information about AK Holding, AK Steel and the other non-guarantor subsidiaries.

Condensed Statements of Comprehensive Income (Loss)					
	Year Ended December 31, 2013				
	AK Holding	AK Steel	Other Non-Guarantor Subsidiaries	Eliminations	Consolidated Company
Net sales	$ —	$5,339.3	$830.3	$(599.2)	$5,570.4
Cost of products sold (exclusive of items shown separately below)	—	5,012.1	652.3	(556.6)	5,107.8
Selling and administrative expenses (exclusive of items shown separately below)	4.4	205.0	36.7	(40.8)	205.3
Depreciation	—	169.4	20.7	—	190.1
Pension and OPEB expense (income)	—	(68.6)	—	—	(68.6)
Total operating costs	4.4	5,317.9	709.7	(597.4)	5,434.6
Operating profit (loss)	(4.4)	21.4	120.6	(1.8)	135.8
Interest expense	—	125.9	1.5	—	127.4
Other income (expense)	—	(5.9)	4.5	—	(1.4)
Income (loss) before income taxes	(4.4)	(110.4)	123.6	(1.8)	7.0
Income tax expense (benefit)	—	(27.8)	18.1	(0.7)	(10.4)
Equity in net income (loss) of subsidiaries	(42.4)	40.2	—	2.2	—
Net income (loss)	(46.8)	(42.4)	105.5	1.1	17.4
Less: Net income (loss) attributable to noncontrolling interests	—	—	64.2	—	64.2
Net income (loss) attributable to AK Steel Holding Corporation	(46.8)	(42.4)	41.3	1.1	(46.8)
Other comprehensive income (loss)	322.3	322.3	1.2	(323.5)	322.3
Comprehensive income (loss) attributable to AK Steel Holding Corporation	$275.5	$ 279.9	$ 42.5	$(322.4)	$ 275.5

Condensed Statements of Comprehensive Income (Loss)

	Year Ended December 31, 2012				
	AK Holding	AK Steel	Other Non-Guarantor Subsidiaries	Eliminations	Consolidated Company
Net sales	$ —	$ 5,676.6	$906.3	$(649.2)	$ 5,933.7
Cost of products sold (exclusive of items shown separately below)	—	5,416.8	738.0	(615.7)	5,539.1
Selling and administrative expenses (exclusive of items shown separately below)	4.4	212.9	35.3	(43.9)	208.7
Depreciation	—	172.8	19.2	—	192.0
Pension and OPEB expense (income) (exclusive of corridor charge shown below)	—	(35.3)	—	—	(35.3)
Pension corridor charge	—	157.3	—	—	157.3
Total operating costs	4.4	5,924.5	792.5	(659.6)	6,061.8
Operating profit (loss)	(4.4)	(247.9)	113.8	10.4	(128.1)
Interest expense	—	85.9	0.8	—	86.7
Other income (expense)	—	(9.6)	15.8	—	6.2
Income (loss) before income taxes	(4.4)	(343.4)	128.8	10.4	(208.6)
Income tax expense (benefit)	—	735.9	49.9	4.2	790.0
Equity in net income (loss) of subsidiaries	(1,022.9)	56.4	—	966.5	—
Net income (loss)	(1,027.3)	(1,022.9)	78.9	972.7	(998.6)
Less: Net income (loss) attributable to noncontrolling interests	—	—	28.7	—	28.7
Net income (loss) attributable to AK Steel Holding Corporation	(1,027.3)	(1,022.9)	50.2	972.7	(1,027.3)
Other comprehensive income (loss)	(1.6)	(1.6)	0.7	0.9	(1.6)
Comprehensive income (loss) attributable to AK Steel Holding Corporation	$(1,028.9)	$(1,024.5)	$ 50.9	$ 973.6	$(1,028.9)

Condensed Statements of Comprehensive Income (Loss)

	Year Ended December 31, 2011				
	AK Holding	AK Steel	Other Non-Guarantor Subsidiaries	Eliminations	Consolidated Company
Net sales	$ —	$6,205.9	$756.7	$(494.6)	$6,468.0
Cost of products sold (exclusive of items shown separately below)	—	5,854.1	635.1	(452.4)	6,036.8
Selling and administrative expenses (exclusive of items shown separately below)	4.4	222.3	36.4	(47.7)	215.4
Depreciation	—	177.4	7.6	—	185.0
Pension and OPEB expense (income) (exclusive of corridor charge shown below)	—	(36.0)	—	—	(36.0)
Pension corridor charge	—	268.1	—	—	268.1
Total operating costs	4.4	6,485.9	679.1	(500.1)	6,669.3
Operating profit (loss)	(4.4)	(280.0)	77.6	5.5	(201.3)
Interest expense	—	47.3	0.2	—	47.5
Other income (expense)	—	(8.4)	3.1	—	(5.3)
Income (loss) before income taxes	(4.4)	(335.7)	80.5	5.5	(254.1)
Income tax expense (benefit)	(1.8)	(125.6)	31.2	2.2	(94.0)
Equity in net income (loss) of subsidiaries	(153.0)	57.1	—	95.9	—
Net income (loss)	(155.6)	(153.0)	49.3	99.2	(160.1)
Less: Net income (loss) attributable to noncontrolling interests	—	—	(4.5)	—	(4.5)
Net income (loss) attributable to AK Steel Holding Corporation	(155.6)	(153.0)	53.8	99.2	(155.6)
Other comprehensive income (loss)	(89.9)	(89.9)	(0.7)	90.6	(89.9)
Comprehensive income (loss) attributable to AK Steel Holding Corporation	$(245.5)	$ (242.9)	$ 53.1	$ 189.8	$ (245.5)

Condensed Balance Sheets

	December 31, 2013				
	AK Holding	AK Steel	Other Non-Guarantor Subsidiaries	Eliminations	Consolidated Company
Assets					
Current assets:					
Cash and cash equivalents	$ —	$ 16.8	$ 28.5	$ —	$ 45.3
Accounts receivable, net	—	492.4	61.1	(28.3)	525.2
Inventory, net	—	520.0	77.7	(11.1)	586.6
Deferred tax assets, current	—	69.4	0.2	—	69.6
Other current assets	0.3	43.9	2.3	—	46.5
Total current assets	0.3	1,142.5	169.8	(39.4)	1,273.2

(continued)

Condensed Balance Sheets

December 31, 2013

	AK Holding	AK Steel	Other Non-Guarantor Subsidiaries	Eliminations	Consolidated Company
Property, plant and equipment	—	5,258.4	613.5	—	5,871.9
Accumulated depreciation	—	(3,881.7)	(110.1)	—	(3,991.8)
Property, plant and equipment, net	—	1,376.7	503.4	—	1,880.1
Other non-current assets:					
Investment in Magnetation LLC	—	—	187.8	—	187.8
Investment in affiliates	(2,772.4)	1,393.8	—	1,378.6	—
Inter-company accounts	2,551.1	(3,479.7)	896.7	31.9	—
Other non-current assets	—	141.0	123.6	—	264.6
Total Assets	$ (221.0)	$ 574.3	$1,881.3	$1,371.1	$ 3,605.7
Liabilities and Equity (Deficit)					
Current liabilities:					
Accounts payable	$ —	$ 550.5	$ 51.9	$(0.6)	$ 601.8
Accrued liabilities	—	133.6	9.3	—	142.9
Current portion of long-term debt	—	0.8	—	—	0.8
Current portion of pension and other postretirement benefit obligations	—	85.4	0.5	—	85.9
Total current liabilities	—	770.3	61.7	(0.6)	831.4
Non-current liabilities:					
Long-term debt	—	1,506.2	—	—	1,506.2
Pension and other postretirement benefit obligations	—	960.6	4.8	—	965.4
Other non-current liabilities	—	109.6	0.4	—	110.0
Total Liabilities	—	3,346.7	66.9	(0.6)	3,413.0
Total stockholders' equity (deficit)	(221.0)	(2,772.4)	1,400.7	1,371.7	(221.0)
Noncontrolling interests	—	—	413.7	—	413.7
Total Equity (Deficit)	(221.0)	(2,772.4)	1,814.4	1,371.7	192.7
Total Liabilities and Equity (Deficit)	$ (221.0)	$ 574.3	$1,881.3	$1,371.1	$ 3,605.7

Condensed Balance Sheets

December 31, 2012

	AK Holding	AK Steel	Other Non-Guarantor Subsidiaries	Eliminations	Consolidated Company
Assets					
Current assets:					
Cash and cash equivalents	$ —	$ 203.6	$ 23.4	$ —	$ 227.0
Accounts receivable, net	—	484.4	54.3	(64.8)	473.9
Inventory, net	—	504.2	114.4	(9.4)	609.2
Deferred tax assets, current	—	73.0	0.2	—	73.2
Other current assets	0.2	57.6	1.6	—	59.4
Total current assets	0.2	1,322.8	193.9	(74.2)	1,442.7
Property, plant and equipment	—	5,355.1	588.8	—	5,943.9
Accumulated depreciation	—	(3,841.9)	(89.7)	—	(3,931.6)
Property, plant and equipment, net	—	1,513.2	499.1	—	2,012.3
Other non-current assets:					
Investment in Magnetation LLC	—	—	150.0	—	150.0
Investment in affiliates	(2,660.7)	1,337.4	—	1,323.3	—
Inter-company accounts	2,155.2	(3,066.5)	843.8	67.5	—
Other non-current assets	—	167.7	130.4	—	298.1
Total Assets	$ (505.3)	$ 1,274.6	$1,817.2	$1,316.6	$ 3,903.1
Liabilities and Equity (Deficit)					
Current liabilities:					
Accounts payable	$ —	$ 494.8	$ 44.4	$ (0.9)	$ 538.3
Accrued liabilities	—	155.0	9.8	—	164.8
Current portion of long-term debt	—	0.7	—	—	0.7
Current portion of pension and other postretirement benefit obligations	—	108.1	0.5	—	108.6
Total current liabilities	—	758.6	54.7	(0.9)	812.4
Non-current liabilities:					
Long-term debt	—	1,411.2	—	—	1,411.2
Pension and other postretirement benefit obligations	—	1,657.2	4.5	—	1,661.7
Other non-current liabilities	—	108.3	0.5	—	108.8
Total Liabilities	—	3,935.3	59.7	(0.9)	3,994.1
Total stockholders' equity (deficit)	(505.3)	(2,660.7)	1,343.2	1,317.5	(505.3)
Noncontrolling interests	—	—	414.3	—	414.3
Total Equity (Deficit)	(505.3)	(2,660.7)	1,757.5	1,317.5	(91.0)
Total Liabilities and Equity (Deficit)	$ (505.3)	$ 1,274.6	$1,817.2	$1,316.6	$ 3,903.1

Condensed Statements of Cash Flows

	AK Holding	AK Steel	Other Non-Guarantor Subsidiaries	Eliminations	Consolidated Company
			Year Ended December 31, 2013		
Net cash flows from operating activities	$(3.5)	$(251.1)	$ 180.0	$(35.6)	$(110.2)
Cash flows from investing activities:					
Capital investments	—	(39.2)	(24.4)	—	(63.6)
Investments in acquired businesses	—	—	(50.0)	—	(50.0)
Other investing items, net	—	8.5	6.6	—	15.1
Net cash flows from investing activities	—	(30.7)	(67.8)	—	(98.5)
Cash flows from financing activities:					
Net borrowings (repayments) under credit facility	—	90.0	—	—	90.0
Proceeds from issuance of long-term debt	—	31.9	—	—	31.9
Redemption of long-term debt	—	(27.4)	—	—	(27.4)
Debt issuance costs	—	(3.4)	—	—	(3.4)
Inter-company activity	4.1	3.9	(43.6)	35.6	—
SunCoke Middletown advances from (distributions to) noncontrolling interest owners	—	—	(64.8)	—	(64.8)
Other financing items, net	(0.6)	—	1.3	—	0.7
Net cash flows from financing activities	3.5	95.0	(107.1)	35.6	27.0
Net increase (decrease) in cash and cash equivalents	—	(186.8)	5.1	—	(181.7)
Cash and equivalents, beginning of year	—	203.6	23.4	—	227.0
Cash and equivalents, end of year	$ —	$ 16.8	$ 28.5	$ —	$ 45.3

Condensed Statements of Cash Flows

	AK Holding	AK Steel	Other Non-Guarantor Subsidiaries	Eliminations	Consolidated Company
			Year Ended December 31, 2012		
Net cash flows from operating activities	$ (3.5)	$(360.0)	$113.1	$(20.4)	$(270.8)
Cash flows from investing activities:					
Capital investments	—	(38.3)	(25.8)	—	(64.1)
Investments in acquired businesses	—	—	(60.6)	—	(60.6)
Other investing items, net	—	6.7	(0.6)	—	6.1
Net cash flows from investing activities	—	(31.6)	(87.0)	—	(118.6)
Cash flows from financing activities:					
Net borrowings (repayments) under credit facility	—	(250.0)	—	—	(250.0)
Proceeds from issuance of long-term debt	—	873.3	—	—	873.3
Redemption of long-term debt	—	(74.0)	—	—	(74.0)
Proceeds from issuance of common stock	96.4	—	—	—	96.4
Debt issuance costs	—	(22.3)	—	—	(22.3)
Common stock dividends paid	(11.0)	—	—	—	(11.0)
Inter-company activity	(80.2)	48.8	11.0	20.4	—
SunCoke Middletown advances from (distributions to) noncontrolling interest owners	—	—	(36.6)	—	(36.6)
Other financing items, net	(1.7)	(0.5)	0.8	—	(1.4)
Net cash flows from financing activities	3.5	575.3	(24.8)	20.4	574.4
Net increase (decrease) in cash and cash equivalents	—	183.7	1.3	—	185.0
Cash and equivalents, beginning of year	—	19.9	22.1	—	42.0
Cash and equivalents, end of year	$ —	$ 203.6	$ 23.4	$ —	$ 227.0

	Year Ended December 31, 2011				
	AK Holding	AK Steel	Other Non-Guarantor Subsidiaries	Eliminations	Consolidated Company
Net cash flows from operating activities	$ (1.7)	$(216.9)	$ 39.7	$(1.6)	$(180.5)
Cash flows from investing activities:					
Capital investments	—	(98.9)	(197.2)	—	(296.1)
Investments in acquired businesses	—	—	(125.4)	—	(125.4)
Other investing items, net	—	1.4	(0.1)	—	1.3
Net cash flows from investing activities	—	(97.5)	(322.7)	—	(420.2)
Cash flows from financing activities:					
Net borrowings (repayments) under credit facility	—	250.0	—	—	250.0
Redemption of long-term debt	—	(0.7)	—	—	(0.7)
Debt issuance costs	—	(10.1)	—	—	(10.1)
Common stock dividends paid	(22.0)	—	—	—	(22.0)
Inter-company activity	25.0	(106.4)	79.8	1.6	—
SunCoke Middletown advances from (distributions to) noncontrolling interest owners	—	—	210.7	—	210.7
Other financing items, net	(1.3)	0.1	(0.8)	—	(2.0)
Net cash flows from financing activities	1.7	132.9	289.7	1.6	425.9
Net increase (decrease) in cash and cash equivalents	—	(181.5)	6.7	—	(174.8)
Cash and equivalents, beginning of year	—	201.4	15.4	—	216.8
Cash and equivalents, end of year	$ —	$ 19.9	$ 22.1	$ —	$ 42.0

Business Combinations

RECOGNITION AND MEASUREMENT

1.65 FASB ASC 805, *Business Combinations*, requires that the acquisition method be used for all business combinations. An acquirer is required to recognize the identifiable acquired assets, the liabilities assumed, and any noncontrolling interest in the acquiree at the acquisition date, measured at their fair values as of that date. Additionally, FASB ASC 805-10-25-23 requires acquisition-related costs to be recognized as expenses as incurred, rather than included in the cost allocated to the acquired assets and assumed liabilities. However, the costs to issue debt or equity securities should be recognized in accordance with other applicable GAAP. In a business combination achieved in stages, the "Pending Content" in FASB ASC 805-10-25-10 also requires the acquirer to remeasure its previously held equity interest in the acquiree at its acquisition date fair value and recognize the resulting gain or loss, if any, in earnings. For all business combinations, the guidance requires the acquirer to recognize goodwill as of the acquisition date, measured as the excess of (a) over (b):

a. The aggregate of the following:
   i. The transferred consideration measured in accordance with FASB ASC 805-30, which generally requires acquisition-date fair value
   ii. The fair value of any noncontrolling interest in the acquiree
   iii. In a business combination achieved in stages, the acquisition-date fair value of the acquirer's previously-held equity interest in the acquiree
b. The net of the acquisition-date amounts of the identifiable acquired assets and the assumed liabilities, measured in accordance with FASB ASC 805

If the amounts in (b) are in excess of those in (a), a bargain purchase has occurred. Before recognizing a gain on a bargain purchase, FASB ASC 805-30-30-5 requires the acquirer to reassess whether it has correctly identified all the acquired assets and assumed liabilities and to recognize any additional assets or liabilities identified in that review. If an excess still remains, the acquirer should recognize the resulting gain in earnings on the acquisition date.

DISCLOSURE

1.66 FASB ASC 805-10-50 requires the acquirer to disclose information that enables financial statement users to evaluate the nature and financial statement effect of a business combination that occurs during the current reporting period or after the reporting date but before the financial statements are issued or are available to be issued. To meet this objective, the following items should be disclosed:

- The name and a description of the acquiree
- The acquisition date
- The percentage of voting equity interests acquired

- The primary reasons for the business combination and a description of how control was obtained
- For public business entities
  — The amounts of revenue and earnings of the acquiree since the acquisition date included in the consolidated income statement for the reporting period
  — Pro forma information that differs depending upon whether the entity presents comparative financial statements. If an entity presents comparative financial statements, it should provide pro forma disclosures for the comparative prior period for revenue and earnings of the combined entity
  — Nature and amount of any material, nonrecurring pro forma adjustments directly attributable to the business combination, that are included in the reported pro forma revenue and earnings
- For a business combination achieved in stages:
  — The acquisition-date fair value of the equity interest in the acquiree held by the acquirer immediately before the acquisition date
  — The amount of any gain or loss recognized as a result of remeasuring to fair value the equity interest in the acquiree that the acquirer held immediately before the business combination
  — The valuation technique(s) used to measure the acquisition-date fair value of the equity interest in the acquiree that the acquirer held immediately before the business combination
  — Other information helpful to users in assessing the inputs used to develop the fair value measurement of the equity interest in the acquiree held by the acquirer immediately before the business combination.

If any of the preceding disclosures for public business entities are impracticable, the acquirer should disclose that fact and explain why. Additional disclosures are required for transactions that are recognized separately from the acquisition of assets and assumptions of liabilities in the business combination.

PRESENTATION AND DISCLOSURE EXCERPTS

BUSINESS COMBINATIONS

1.67 SPECTRUM BRANDS HOLDINGS, INC. (SEP)
NOTES TO CONSOLIDATED FINANCIAL STATEMENTS

(Amounts in Thousands, Except Per Share Figures)

(15) Acquisitions

In accordance with ASC Topic 805, *"Business Combinations"* ("ASC 805"), the Company accounts for acquisitions by applying the acquisition method of accounting. The acquisition method of accounting requires, among other things, that the assets acquired and liabilities assumed in a business combination be measured at their fair values as of the closing date of the acquisition.

HHI Business

On December 17, 2012, the Company completed the cash acquisition of the HHI Business from Stanley Black & Decker. A portion of the HHI Business, consisting of the purchase of certain assets of TLM Taiwan, closed on April 8, 2013.

The following table summarizes the preliminary consideration paid for the HHI Business:

Negotiated sales price, excluding TLM Taiwan	$1,300,000
Working capital and other adjustments at December 17, 2012 close	(10,738)
Final working capital adjustment	(7,669)
Final purchase price, excluding TLM Taiwan	$1,281,593
Negotiated sales price, TLM Taiwan	100,000
Final TLM Taiwan working capital and other adjustments	(6,500)
Total HHI Business purchase price	$1,375,093

The HHI Business is a major manufacturer and supplier of residential locksets, residential builders' hardware and faucets with a portfolio of recognized brand names, including Kwikset, Weiser, Baldwin, National Hardware, Stanley, FANAL and Pfister, as well as patented technologies such as the SmartKey, a re-keyable lockset technology, and Smart Code Home Connect. Customers of the HHI Business include retailers, non-retail distributors and homebuilders. Headquartered in Lake Forest, California, the HHI Business has a global sales force and operates manufacturing and distribution facilities in the U.S., Canada, Mexico and Asia.

The results of the HHI Business are included in the Company's Consolidated Statements of Operations as of and subsequent to December 17, 2012, the date of the Hardware Acquisition. The results of the TLM Business are included in the Company's Consolidated Statements of Operations as of and subsequent to its acquisition on April 8, 2013. The financial results of the HHI Business are reported as a separate business segment, Hardware & Home Improvement.

Preliminary Valuation of Assets and Liabilities

The preliminary fair values of the net tangible and intangible assets acquired and liabilities assumed in connection with the purchase of the HHI Business, excluding TLM Taiwan, have been recognized in the Consolidated Statement of Financial Position based upon their preliminary values at December 17, 2012. The preliminary fair values of the net tangible and intangible assets acquired and liabilities assumed in connection with the TLM Taiwan purchase have been recognized in the Consolidated Statement of Financial Position based upon their preliminary values at April 8, 2013. The excess of the purchase price over the preliminary fair values of the net tangible and intangible assets was recorded as goodwill, and includes value associated with greater product diversity, stronger relationships with core retail partners, cross-selling opportunities in all channels and a new platform for potential future global growth using the Company's existing international infrastructure, most notably in Europe. The majority of goodwill recorded is not expected to be deductible for income tax purposes. The preliminary fair values recorded were based upon a preliminary valuation and the estimates and assumptions used in such valuation are subject to change, which could be significant, within the measurement period (up to one year from the acquisition date). The primary areas of the preliminary valuation that are not yet finalized relate to the fair values of amounts for income taxes including deferred tax accounts, amounts for uncertain tax positions and net operating loss carryforwards inclusive of associated limitations and valuation allowances and the final amount of residual goodwill. Additionally, finalized fair values associated with deferred tax accounts could have a material effect on the Company's estimated reversal of its consolidated U.S. valuation allowances against deferred tax assets recognized during the measurement period. See Note 9, "Income Taxes," for further information. The Company expects to continue to obtain information to assist it in determining the fair values of the net assets acquired at the acquisition date during the measurement period. The preliminary valuation of the assets acquired and liabilities assumed for the HHI Business, including a reconciliation to the preliminary valuation reported as of December 30, 2012, is as follows:

	HHI Business Preliminary Valuation December 30, 2012	TLM Taiwan Preliminary Valuation June 30, 2013	Adjustments/ Reclassifications	Preliminary Valuation September 30, 2013
Cash	$ 17,406	$ 843	$ 5,836	$ 24,085
Accounts receivable	104,641	11	4,007	108,659
Inventory	207,160	1,135	62	208,357
Prepaid expenses and other	13,311	2,148	(6,176)	9,283
Property, plant and equipment	104,502	36,750	(2,861)	138,391
Intangible assets	470,000	17,100	2,000	489,100
Other long-term assets	3,051	124	4,339	7,514
Total assets acquired	$ 920,071	$58,111	$ 7,207	$ 985,389
Accounts payable	130,140	—	7,967	138,107
Deferred tax liability—current	7,081	—	83	7,164
Accrued liabilities	37,530	241	4,966	42,737
Deferred tax liability—long-term	104,708	1,930	9,791	116,429
Other long-term liabilities	11,231	8,089	453	19,773
Total liabilities assumed	$ 290,690	$10,260	$ 23,260	$ 324,210
Total identifiable net assets	629,381	47,851	(16,053)	661,179
Noncontrolling interest	(2,235)	—	(1,704)	(3,939)
Goodwill	662,116	45,649	10,088	717,853
Total net assets	$1,289,262	$93,500	$ (7,669)	$1,375,093

Since the preliminary valuation on December 30, 2012, the Company recorded $45,649 to goodwill related to the acquisition of TLM Taiwan on April 8, 2013, and recorded adjustments to the preliminary valuation of assets and liabilities, excluding TLM Taiwan, resulting in a net increase to goodwill of $10,088. The preliminary goodwill increased $9,791 as a result of recording certain state and foreign valuation allowances against deferred tax assets, $2,861 resulting from a reduction in certain property, plant and equipment asset values and $7,022 from changes in working capital and other asset and liability accounts based on new information obtained by the Company. The preliminary goodwill decreased $7,669 as a result of the final working capital adjustment related to the December 17, 2012 close and $2,000 as a result of new information related to intangible assets which increased their value. The changes in estimates were the result of additional accounting information provided by Stanley Black & Decker during the period, as well as items identified by management. The Company believes that the information gathered to date provides a reasonable basis for estimating the fair values of assets acquired and liabilities assumed, but the Company is waiting for additional information necessary to finalize those fair values. Thus, the provisional measurements of fair value set forth above are subject to change further. The Company expects to complete the purchase accounting process as soon as practicable but no later than one year from the acquisition date.

Preliminary Pre-Acquisition Contingencies Assumed

The Company has evaluated and continues to evaluate pre-acquisition contingencies relating to the HHI Business that existed as of the acquisition date. Based on the evaluation to date, the Company has preliminarily determined that certain pre-acquisition contingencies are probable in nature and estimable as of the acquisition date. Accordingly, the Company has recorded its best estimates for these contingencies as part of the preliminary valuation of the assets and liabilities acquired for the HHI Business. The Company continues to gather information relating to all pre-acquisition contingencies that it has assumed from the HHI Business. Any changes to the pre-acquisition contingency amounts recorded during the measurement period will be included in the final valuation and related amounts recognized. Subsequent to the end of the measurement period, any adjustments to pre-acquisition contingency amounts will be reflected in the Company's results of operations.

Preliminary Valuation Adjustments

The Company performed a preliminary valuation of the assets and liabilities of the HHI Business, excluding TLM Taiwan, on December 17, 2012. The Company performed a preliminary valuation of the assets and liabilities of TLM Taiwan on April 8, 2013. Significant adjustments as a result of the preliminary valuation and the bases for their determination are summarized as follows:

- Inventories—An adjustment of $31,000 was recorded to adjust inventory to fair value. Finished goods were valued at estimated selling prices less the sum of costs of disposal and a reasonable profit allowance for the selling effort.
- Property, plant and equipment—An adjustment of $10,007 was recorded to adjust the net book value of property, plant and equipment to fair value giving consideration to the highest and best use of the assets. The valuation of the Company's property, plant and equipment was based on the cost approach.
- Certain indefinite-lived intangible assets were valued using a relief from royalty methodology. Customer relationships and certain definite-lived intangible assets were valued using a multi-period excess earnings method. The total fair value of indefinite and definite lived intangibles was $489,100. A summary of the significant key inputs is as follows:
  - The Company valued customer relationships using the income approach, specifically the multi-period excess earnings method. In determining the fair value of the customer relationships, the multi-period excess earnings approach values the intangible asset at the present value of the incremental after-tax cash flows attributable only to the customer relationship after deducting contributory asset charges. The incremental after-tax cash flows attributable to the subject intangible asset are then discounted to their present value. Only expected sales from current customers were used, which included an annual expected growth rate of 2.5%–15.5%. The Company assumed a customer retention rate of approximately 95%, which was supported by historical retention rates. Income taxes were estimated at 17%–35% and amounts were discounted using a rate of 12%. The customer relationships were valued at $90,000 under this approach and will be amortized over 20 years.
  - The Company valued indefinite-lived trade names and trademarks using the income approach, specifically the relief from royalty method. Under this method, the asset value was determined by estimating the hypothetical royalties that would have to be paid if the trade name was not owned. Royalty rates were selected based on consideration of several factors, including prior transactions of the HHI Business, related trademarks and trade names, other similar trademark licensing and transaction agreements and the relative profitability and perceived contribution of the trademarks and trade names. Royalty rates used in the determination of the fair values of trade names and trademarks ranged from 3%–5% of expected net sales related to the respective trade names and trademarks. The Company anticipates using the majority of the trade names and trademarks for an indefinite period as demonstrated by the sustained use of each subject trademark. In estimating the fair value of the trademarks and trade names, Net sales for significant trade names and trademarks were estimated to grow at a rate of 2.5%–5% annually with a terminal year growth rate of 2.5%. Income taxes were estimated at 35% and amounts were discounted using a rate of 12%. Trade name and trademarks were valued at $331,000 under this approach.
  - The Company valued definite lived trade names using the income approach, specifically the relief from royalty method. Under this method, the asset value was determined by estimating the hypothetical royalties that would have to be paid if the trade name was not owned. Royalty rates were selected based on consideration of several factors, including prior transactions of the HHI Business, related trademarks and trade names, other similar trademark licensing and transaction agreements and the relative profitability and perceived contribution of the trademarks and trade names. The royalty rates used in the determination of the fair values of the trade names ranged from 1%–3.5% of expected net sales related to the respective trade name. The Company assumed an 8 year useful life of the trade name. In estimating the fair value of the trade name, Net sales for the trade name were estimated to grow at a rate of 2.5%–15.5% annually. Income taxes were estimated at 17%–35% and amounts were discounted using a rate of 12%. The trade names were valued at $4,100 under this approach.
  - The Company valued a trade name license agreement using the income approach, specifically the relief from royalty method. Under this method, the asset value was determined by estimating the hypothetical royalties that would have to be paid if the trade name was not owned. Royalty rates were selected based on consideration of several factors, including prior transactions of the HHI Business, related trademarks and trade names, other similar trademark licensing and transaction agreements and the relative profitability and perceived contribution of the trademarks and trade names. The royalty rate used in the determination of the fair value of the trade name license agreement was 4% of expected Net sales related to the respective trade name. In

estimating the fair value of the trade name license agreement, Net sales were estimated to grow at a rate of 2.5%–5% annually. The Company assumed a 5 year useful life of the trade name license agreement. Income taxes were estimated at 35% and amounts were discounted using a rate of 12%. The trade name license agreement was valued at $13,000 under this approach.

— The Company valued technology using the income approach, specifically the relief from royalty method. Under this method, the asset value was determined by estimating the hypothetical royalties that would have to be paid if the technology was not owned. Royalty rates were selected based on consideration of several factors, including prior transactions of the HHI Business, related licensing agreements and the importance of the technology and profit levels, among other considerations. Royalty rates used in the determination of the fair values of technologies ranged from 4%–5% of expected Net sales related to the respective technology. The Company anticipates using these technologies through the legal life of the underlying patent; therefore, the expected life of these technologies was equal to the remaining legal life of the underlying patents which was 10 years. In estimating the fair value of the technologies, Net sales were estimated to grow at a rate of 2.5%–31% annually. Income taxes were estimated at 35% and amounts were discounted using the rate of 12%. The technology assets were valued at $51,000 under this approach.

- Deferred tax liabilities, net—An adjustment of $123,593 was recorded to adjust deferred taxes for the preliminary fair value adjustments made in accounting for the purchase.

Supplemental Pro Forma Information (Unaudited)

The following reflects the Company's pro forma results had the results of the HHI Business been included for all periods presented.

	2013	2012	2011
Net Sales:			
Reported net sales	$4,085,581	$3,252,435	$3,186,916
HHI business adjustment[1]	191,777	973,648	975,096
Pro forma net sales	$4,277,358	$4,226,083	$4,162,012
Net (Loss) Income:			
Reported net (loss) income[2] [3]	$ (55,313)	$ 48,572	$ (75,171)
HHI business adjustment[1]	4,942	76,120	77,035
Pro forma net (loss) income	$ (50,371)	$ 124,692	$ 1,864
Basic (Loss) Income Per Share:			
Reported basic (loss) income per share	$ (1.06)	$ 0.94	$ (1.47)
HHI business adjustment[1]	0.09	1.47	1.51
Pro forma basic (loss) income per share	$ (0.97)	$ 2.41	$ 0.04
Diluted (Loss) Income Per Share[4]:			
Reported diluted (loss) income per share	$ (1.06)	$ 0.91	$ (1.47)
HHI business adjustment[1]	0.09	1.43	1.51
Pro forma diluted (loss) income per share	$ (0.97)	$ 2.34	$ 0.04

[1] The results related to the HHI Business adjustment do not reflect the TLM Taiwan business as stand alone financial data is not available for the periods presented. The TLM Taiwan business is not deemed material to the operating results of the Company.

[2] Included in Reported Net (loss) income for Fiscal 2013, is an adjustment of $49,848 to record the income tax benefit resulting from the reversal of U.S. valuation allowances on deferred tax assets as a result of the HHI Business acquisition. For information pertaining to the income tax benefit, see Note 9, "Income Taxes."

[3] Included in Reported Net (loss) income for Fiscal 2013, is $36,932, of Acquisition and integration related charges as a result of the HHI Business acquisition. For information pertaining to Acquisition and integration related charges, see Note 2, "Significant Accounting Policies—Acquisition and Integration Related Charges."

[4] For Fiscal 2013, the Company has not assumed the exercise of common stock equivalents as the impact would be antidilutive due to the loss reported.

Shaser

On November 8, 2012, the Company completed the cash acquisition of approximately a 56% interest in Shaser Biosciences, Inc. ("Shaser"). Shaser is a global technology leader in developing energy-based, aesthetic dermatological technology for home use devices. This acquisition was not significant individually.

The following table summarizes the consideration paid for Shaser:

Negotiated sales price	$50,000
Preliminary working capital adjustment	(423)
Final working capital adjustment	58
Final purchase price	$49,635

The purchase agreement provides the Company with an option, exercisable solely at the Company's discretion, to acquire the remaining 44% interest of Shaser (the "Call Option"). The Call Option is exercisable any time between January 1, 2017 and March 31, 2017 at a price equal to 1.0x trailing revenues or 7.0x adjusted trailing EBITDA, as defined, for the calendar year ending December 31, 2016.

The results of Shaser's operations since November 8, 2012 are included in the Company's Consolidated Statements of Operations and are reported as part of the Global Batteries & Appliances segment.

Valuation of Assets and Liabilities

The assets acquired and liabilities assumed in the Shaser acquisition have been measured at their fair values at November 8, 2012 as set forth below. The excess of the purchase price over the fair values of the net tangible assets and identifiable intangible assets was recorded as goodwill, which includes value associated with the assembled workforce including an experienced research team, and is not expected to be deductible for income tax purposes. The fair values recorded were determined based upon a valuation and the estimates and assumptions used in such valuation are final and the measurement period has closed.

The fair values recorded for the assets acquired and liabilities assumed for Shaser, including a reconciliation to the preliminary valuation reported as of December 30, 2012, are as follows:

	Preliminary Valuation December 30, 2012	Adjustments/ Reclassifications	Final Valuation September 30, 2013
Cash	$ 870	$ —	$ 870
Intangible asset	35,500	(6,200)	29,300
Other assets	2,679	(2,531)	148
Total assets acquired	$ 39,049	$(8,731)	$ 30,318
Total liabilities assumed	14,398	(5,566)	8,832
Total identifiable net assets	24,651	(3,165)	21,486
Noncontrolling interest	(38,954)	(46)	(39,000)
Goodwill	63,880	3,269	67,149
Total identifiable net assets	$ 49,577	$ 58	$ 49,635

Subsequent to the preliminary purchase accounting, the Company recorded adjustments to the preliminary valuation of assets and liabilities resulting in a net increase to goodwill of $3,269. Goodwill increased as a result of further information to support a key valuation factor that impacted the valuation of the technology asset acquired, and the resulting changes to the deferred tax asset and liabilities. This revised information was provided by Shaser during the period.

Pre-Acquisition Contingencies Assumed

The Company has evaluated pre-acquisition contingencies relating to Shaser that existed as of the acquisition date. Based on the evaluation, the Company has determined that certain pre-acquisition contingencies are probable in nature and estimable as of the acquisition date. Accordingly, the Company has recorded its best estimates for these contingencies as part of the purchase accounting for Shaser.

Valuation Adjustments

The Company performed a valuation of the acquired proprietary technology assets, the non-controlling interest and the Call Option related to Shaser at November 8, 2012. A summary of the significant key inputs is as follows:
- The Company valued the technology assets using the income approach, specifically the relief from royalty method. Under this method, the asset value was determined by estimating the hypothetical royalties that would have to be paid if the technology was not owned. Royalty rates were selected based on consideration of several factors, including prior transactions of Shaser, related licensing agreements and the importance of the technology and profit levels, among other considerations. The royalty rate used in the determination of the fair value of the technology asset was 10.5% of expected Net sales related to the technology. The Company anticipates using the technology through the legal life of the underlying patent and therefore the expected life of the technology was equal to the remaining legal life of the underlying patent which was 13 years. In estimating the fair value of the technology, Net sales were estimated to grow at a long-term rate of 3% annually. Income taxes were estimated at 35% and amounts were discounted using the rate of 11%. The technology asset was valued at approximately $29,300 under this approach.
- The Company valued the non-controlling interest in Shaser, a private company, by applying both income and market approaches. Under these methods, the non-controlling value was determined by using a discounted cash flow method, a guideline companies method, and a recent transaction approach. In estimating the fair value of the non-controlling interest, key assumptions include (i) cash flow projections based on market participant data and estimates by Company management, with Net sales estimated to grow at a terminal growth rate of 3% annually, income taxes estimated at 35%, and amounts discounted using a rate of 17%, (ii) financial multiples of companies deemed to be similar to Shaser, and (iii) adjustments because of lack of control or lack of marketability that market participants would consider when estimating the fair value of the non-controlling interest in Shaser. The non-controlling interest was valued at $39,000 under this approach.
- The Company, in connection with valuing the non-controlling interest in Shaser, also valued the Call Option. In addition to the valuation methods and key assumptions discussed above, the Company compared the forecasted revenue and EBITDA multiples, as defined, associated with the Call Option to current guideline companies. The Call Option was determined to have an immaterial value under this approach.

(2) Business Combination

On March 18, 2013, the Company completed the Sealy Acquisition. Pursuant to the merger agreement, each share of common stock of Sealy issued and outstanding immediately prior to the effective time of the Sealy Acquisition was cancelled and (other than shares held by Sealy or Tempur-Pedic or their subsidiaries or Sealy stockholders who properly exercised their appraisal rights) converted into the right to receive $2.20 in cash. The total purchase price was $1,172.9 million, which was funded using available cash and financing consisting of the Company's 2012 Credit Agreement and Senior Notes (see Note 5, "Debt" for the definition of these terms and further discussion). The purchase price of Sealy consisted of the following items:

(In millions)	
Cash consideration for stock	$ 231.2[1]
Cash consideration for share-based awards	14.2[2]
Cash consideration for 8.0% Sealy Notes	442.1[3]
Cash consideration for repayment of Sealy Senior Notes	260.7[4]
Cash consideration for repayment of Sealy 2014 Notes	276.9[5]
Total consideration	1,225.1
Cash acquired	(52.2)[6]
Net consideration transferred	$1,172.9

[1] The cash consideration for outstanding shares of Sealy common stock is the product of the agreed-upon cash per share price of $2.20 and total Sealy shares of 105.1 million.

[2] The cash consideration for share-based awards is the product of the agreed-upon cash per share price of $2.20 and the total number of RSUs and DSUs outstanding and the "in the money" stock options net of the weighted average exercise price.

[3] The cash consideration for Sealy's 8.0% Senior Secured Third Lien Convertible Notes due 2016 ("8.0% Sealy Notes") is the result of applying the adjusted equity conversion rate to the 8.0% Sealy Notes tendered for conversion and multiplying the result by the agreed-upon cash per share price of $2.20. The 8.0% Sealy Notes that were converted represented the right to receive the same merger consideration that would have been payable to a holder of 201.0 million shares of Sealy common stock, subject to adjustment in accordance with the terms of the supplemental indenture governing the 8.0% Sealy Notes.

[4] The cash consideration for Sealy's 10.875% Senior Notes due 2016 ("Sealy Senior Notes") reflects the repayment of the outstanding obligation.

[5] The cash consideration for Sealy's 8.25% Senior Subordinated Notes due 2014 ("Sealy 2014 Notes") reflects the repayment of the outstanding obligation.

[6] Represents the Sealy cash balance acquired at acquisition.

The Company incurred $18.7 million of direct transaction costs for the year ended December 31, 2013, respectively. These costs are included in general, administrative and other expenses in the accompanying Consolidated Statements of Income. In addition, the Company incurred $19.9 million of incremental interest expense for the year ended December 31, 2013. This includes interest and other fees on the Senior Notes and the 2012 Credit Agreement for the period prior to March 18, 2013. The incremental interest expense also included commitment fees associated with financing for the closing of the Sealy Acquisition, and the write off of deferred financing costs associated with the 2011 Credit Facility.

The Sealy segment manufactures and markets a complete line of bedding products under the Sealy®, Sealy Posturepedic®, Optimum TM and Stearns & Foster® brands. The results of operations of Sealy and Sealy's historical subsidiaries are reported within the Company's Sealy reportable business segment.

The Company accounted for the Sealy Acquisition using the acquisition method. The preliminary allocation of the purchase price is based on estimates of the fair value of assets acquired and liabilities assumed as of March 18, 2013. The Company is continuing to obtain information to determine the acquired assets and liabilities, including tax assets, liabilities and other attributes. The components of the preliminary purchase price allocation are as follows:

(In millions)	
Accounts receivable	$ 185.0
Inventory	75.1
Prepaid expenses and other current assets	22.8
Accounts payable	(77.9)
Accrued expenses	(137.2)
Property, plant and equipment	242.9
Other assets	32.6
Identifiable intangible assets:	
Indefinite-lived trade names	521.2
Contractual retailer/distributor relationships	91.1
Developed technology, including patents	87.1

(continued)

Customer databases	3.9
Optimum™ trade name	2.3
Deferred income taxes, net	(232.8)
Sealy 8.0% Notes	(96.2)
Redeemable non-controlling interest	(11.3)
Other liabilities	(77.5)
Goodwill	541.8
Net consideration transferred	$1,172.9

The preliminary fair value of the intangible assets has been estimated using the income approach through a discounted cash flow analysis (except as noted below with respect to the trade names) with the cash flow projections discounted using rates ranging from 11.0% to 12.0%. The cash flows are based on estimates used to price the Sealy Acquisition, and the discount rates applied were benchmarked with reference to the implied rate of return from the Company's pricing model and the weighted average cost of capital.

The indefinite-lived trade names represent Sealy brand names as marketed through Sealy®, Sealy Posturepedic® and Stearns & Foster® brands. The Company applied the income approach through an excess earnings analysis to determine the preliminary fair value of the trade name assets.

The contractual retailer/distributor relationships pertain to Sealy's distribution network with their retailers, which are governed by contract. The Company used the income approach through an excess earnings analysis to determine the preliminary fair value of this asset.

The developed technology assets are comprised of know-how, patents and technologies embedded in Sealy's products and processes and relate to currently manufactured and marketed products. The Company applied the income approach through a relief-from-royalty analysis to determine the preliminary fair value of this asset.

The Company is amortizing the identifiable intangible assets, other than the indefinite-lived trade name, on a straight-line basis over the weighted average lives ranging from 5 to 15 years.

The table below sets forth the preliminary valuation and amortization period of identifiable intangible assets:

(In millions)	Preliminary Valuation	Amortization Period
Identifiable intangible assets:		
Trade names	$521.2	Indefinite
Contractual retailer/distributor relationships	91.1	15 years
Developed technology, including patents	87.1	10 years
Customer databases	3.9	5 years
Optimum™ trade name	2.3	5 years
Total	$705.6	

The Company estimated the preliminary fair value of the acquired property, plant and equipment using a combination of the cost and market approaches, depending on the component. The preliminary fair value of property, plant and equipment consisted of real property of $101.1 million and personal property of $141.8 million.

The excess of the purchase price over the preliminary estimated fair value of the tangible net assets and identifiable intangible assets acquired was recorded as goodwill. The factors contributing to the recognition of the amount of goodwill are based on several strategic and synergistic benefits that are expected to be realized from the Sealy Acquisition. These benefits include a comprehensive portfolio of iconic brands, complementary product offerings, enhanced global footprint, and attractive synergy opportunities and value creation. None of the goodwill is expected to be deductible for income tax purposes and is entirely allocated to the Sealy reportable business segment.

The following unaudited pro forma information presents the combined financial results for the Company and Sealy as if the Sealy Acquisition had been completed at the beginning of the Company's prior year, January 1, 2012. Prior to the Sealy Acquisition, Sealy used a 52–53 week fiscal year ending on the closest Sunday to November 30, but no later than December 2. The pro forma financial information set forth below for the year ended December 31, 2013 includes Sealy's pro forma information for the combined twelve month period from December 3, 2012 through March 3, 2013 and April 1, 2013 through December 29, 2013 and the twelve month period November 28, 2011 through December 2, 2012, respectively.

	Year Ended December 31,	
(In millions, except earnings per common share)	2013	2012
Net sales	$2,757.2	$2,750.8
Net income	$ 90.9	$ 51.2
Earnings per common share—Diluted	$ 1.49	$ 0.81

The information above does not include the pro forma adjustments that would be required under Regulation S-X for pro forma financial information, and does not reflect future events that may occur after December 31, 2013 or any operating efficiencies or inefficiencies that may result from the Sealy Acquisition and related financing. Therefore, the information is not necessarily indicative of results that would have been achieved had the businesses been combined during the periods presented or the results that the Company will experience going forward.

(5) Debt (in part)

Debt for the Company consists of the following:

(In millions)	December 31, 2013	December 31, 2012
$375.0 million Senior Notes, interest at 6.875%, due December 15, 2020	$ 375.0	$ 375.0
Revolving credit facility, interest at Base Rate plus applicable margin, 2.25% or LIBOR plus applicable margin, 3.25% as of December 31, 2013, commitment through and due March 18, 2018	74.5	—
Term A Facility, interest at Base Rate plus applicable margin 1.5%, or LIBOR plus applicable margin, 2.5% as of December 31, 2013, commitment through and due March 18, 2018	522.5	—
Term B Facility, interest at Base Rate plus applicable margin 1.75%, or LIBOR plus applicable margin, 2.75% as of December 31, 2013, commitment through and due March 18, 2020	737.3	—
8.0% Sealy Notes, due July 15, 2016	99.6	—
Capital lease obligations and other	27.6	—
2011 Domestic long-term revolving credit facility payable to lenders, interest at Base Rate or LIBOR plus applicable margin, 2.05% as of December 31, 2012, extinguished as of March 18, 2013	—	650.0
	1,836.5	1,025.0
Less current portion	(39.6)	—
	$1,796.9	$1,025.0

Senior Notes

On December 19, 2012, Tempur Sealy International issued $375.0 million aggregate principal amount of 6.875% senior notes due 2020 (the "Senior Notes") to qualified institutional buyers pursuant to Rule 144A of the Securities Act, and to certain non-U.S. persons in accordance with Regulation S under the Securities Act. The Senior Notes were issued pursuant to an indenture, dated as of December 19, 2012 (the "Indenture"), among the Company, certain subsidiaries of Tempur Sealy International as guarantors (the "Guarantors"), and The Bank of New York Mellon Trust Company, N.A., as trustee (the "Trustee"). The Senior Notes are general unsecured senior obligations of Tempur Sealy International and are guaranteed on a senior unsecured basis by the Guarantors. The Senior Notes mature on December 15, 2020, and interest is payable semi-annually in arrears on each June 15 and December 15, beginning on June 15, 2013. The gross proceeds from the Senior Notes, were funded into escrow and these funds were released from escrow on March 18, 2013 and used as part of the funding of the Sealy Acquisition. Following the completion of the Sealy Acquisition, Sealy and certain of its subsidiaries became Guarantors of the Senior Notes.

2012 Credit Agreement (in part)

On December 12, 2012, Tempur Sealy International and certain subsidiaries of Tempur Sealy International as borrowers and guarantors, entered into a credit agreement (the "2012 Credit Agreement") with a syndicate of banks. The 2012 Credit Agreement initially provided for (i) a revolving credit facility of $350.0 million (the "Revolver"), (ii) a term A facility of $550.0 million (the "Term A Facility") and (iii) a term B facility of $870.0 million (the "Term B Facility"). The Revolver includes a sublimit for letters of credit and swingline loans, subject to certain conditions and limits. The Revolver and the Term A Facility will mature on March 18, 2018 and the Term B Facility will mature on March 18, 2020. The Revolver, the Term A Facility and the Term B Facility closed and funded in connection with the Sealy Acquisition on March 18, 2013. In the first and second quarters of 2013, the outstanding balance of the Term A Facility and the Term B Facility were reduced by regularly scheduled payments. Additionally, on May 16, 2013, the outstanding balance of the Term B Facility was reduced by a voluntary prepayment of $125.0 million. After giving effect to $90.0 million in borrowings under the revolver portion of the 2012 Credit Agreement and letters of credit outstanding of $22.9 million, total availability under the revolver was $252.6 million as of December 31, 2013.

8.0% Sealy Notes (in part)

In conjunction with the Sealy Acquisition, Sealy's obligations under its 8.0% Sealy Notes were amended. As a result of the Sealy Acquisition, the 8.0% Sealy Notes became convertible solely into cash, in an amount that declined slightly every day during the Make-Whole Period (as defined under the Supplemental Indenture governing the 8.0% Sealy Notes) that followed the Sealy Acquisition, and then became fixed thereafter. The Make-Whole Period effectively expired on April 12, 2013. As of April 12, 2013, approximately 83.0% of all the 8.0% Sealy Notes outstanding prior to the Sealy Acquisition were converted into cash and paid to the holders. Holders of the 8.0% Sealy Notes who converted on March 19, 2013 received approximately $2,325.43 per $1,000 Accreted Principal Amount of the 8.0% Sealy Notes being converted. The holders of the 8.0% Sealy Notes who convert after April 12, 2013 will receive $2,200 per $1,000 Accreted Principal Amount of the 8.0% Sealy Notes being converted. The Company calculated the preliminary fair value of the remaining 8.0% Sealy Notes as part of its preliminary purchase price allocation by first calculating the future payout of the remaining 17.0% aggregate principal amount of the 8.0% Sealy Notes still outstanding and the cumulative semi-annual interest payments at the July 15, 2016 maturity, and then calculated the present value using a market discount rate, which resulted in a fair value of $96.2 million at the date of the opening balance sheet. As of December 31, 2013, the fair value of the 8.0% Sealy Notes are $99.9 million, which includes $3.7 million of accreted discount. The discount is accreted through non-cash interest expense over the life of the 8.0% Sealy Notes using the effective interest method. As of December 31, 2013, the 8.0% Sealy Notes had a carrying value of $99.6 million, which includes $3.7 million of accreted discount less conversion payments made to holders of certain 8.0% Sealy Notes that were tendered for conversion.

2011 Credit Facility

In conjunction with the closing of the Sealy Acquisition on March 18, 2013, the Company repaid all outstanding borrowings on the 2011 Credit Facility and terminated this facility. The 2011 Credit Facility consisted of domestic and foreign credit facilities (the "2011 Revolvers") that provided for the incurrence of indebtedness up to an aggregate principal amount of $770.0 million. The domestic credit facility was a five -year, $745.0 million revolving credit facility.

Commitments

DISCLOSURE

1.69 FASB ASC 440, *Commitments*, requires the disclosure of commitments such as those for unused letters of credit; long-term leases; assets pledged as security for loans; pension plans; cumulative preferred stock dividends in arrears; plant acquisition, obligations to reduce debts, maintain working capital, and restrict dividends; and unconditional purchase obligations.

PRESENTATION AND DISCLOSURE EXCERPTS

RESTRICTIVE COVENANTS

1.70 GREIF, INC. (OCT)
CONSOLIDATED BALANCE SHEETS (in part)

(Dollars in millions)

	As of October 31,	
	2013	2012
Liabilities and Shareholders' Equity (in part)		
Current liabilities		
Accounts payable	$ 431.3	$ 466.1
Accrued payroll and employee benefits	103.0	96.1
Restructuring reserves	3.0	8.0
Current portion of long-term debt	10.0	25.0
Short-term borrowings	64.1	76.1
Deferred tax liabilities	11.5	8.1
Other current liabilities	178.8	187.9
	801.7	867.3
Long-term liabilities		
Long-term debt	1,207.2	1,175.3
Deferred tax liabilities	238.1	197.0
Pension liabilities	82.5	123.4
Postretirement benefit obligations	18.5	19.3
Liabilities held by special purpose entities	43.3	43.3
Other long-term liabilities	92.9	117.0
	1,682.5	1,675.3

Note 9—Long-Term Debt (in part)

Long-term debt is summarized as follows (Dollars in millions):

	October 31, 2013	October 31, 2012
Amended Credit Agreement	$ 222.9	$ —
2010 Credit Agreement	—	255.0
Senior Notes due 2017	301.8	302.3
Senior Notes due 2019	244.4	243.6
Senior Notes due 2021	272.9	256.0
Amended Receivables Facility	140.0	—
Prior Receivables Facility	—	110.0
Other long-term debt	35.2	33.4
	1,217.2	1,200.3
Less current portion	(10.0)	(25.0)
Long-term debt	$1,207.2	$1,175.3

Credit Agreement

On December 19, 2012, the Company and two of its international subsidiaries amended and restated the Company's existing $1.0 billion senior secured credit agreement with a syndicate of financial institutions (the "Amended Credit Agreement"). The Amended Credit Agreement provides the Company with an $800 million revolving multicurrency credit facility and a $200 million term loan, both expiring in December 2017, with an option to add $250 million to the facilities with the agreement of the lenders. The $200 million term loan is scheduled to amortize by the payment of principal in the amount of $2.5 million each quarter-end for the first eight quarters, beginning January 2013, the payment of $5.0 million each quarter-end for the next twelve quarters and the payment of the remaining balance on the maturity date. The revolving credit facility under the Amended Credit Agreement is available to fund ongoing working capital and capital expenditure needs, for general corporate purposes and to finance acquisitions. Interest is based on a Eurodollar rate or a base rate that resets periodically plus an agreed upon margin amount. The total available borrowing under this facility was $753.8 million as of October 31, 2013, which has been reduced by $13.3 million for outstanding letters of credit.

The Amended Credit Agreement contains financial covenants that require the Company to maintain a certain leverage ratio and an interest coverage ratio. The leverage ratio generally requires that at the end of any fiscal quarter the Company will not permit the ratio of (a) the Company's total consolidated indebtedness, to (b) the Company's consolidated net income plus depreciation, depletion and amortization, interest expense (including capitalized interest), income taxes, and minus certain extraordinary gains and non-recurring gains (or plus certain extraordinary losses and non-recurring losses) and plus or minus certain other items for the preceding twelve months ("adjusted EBITDA") to be greater than 4.00 to 1. The interest coverage ratio generally requires that at the end of any fiscal quarter the Company will not permit the ratio of (a) the Company's consolidated adjusted EBITDA to (b) the Company's consolidated interest expense to the extent paid or payable, to be less than 3.00 to 1, during the preceding twelve month period (the "Interest Coverage Ratio Covenant"). As of October 31, 2013, the Company was in compliance with these covenants.

The terms of the Amended Credit Agreement limit the Company's ability to make "restricted payments," which include dividends and purchases, redemptions and acquisitions of the Company's equity interests. The repayment of amounts borrowed under the Amended Credit Agreement are secured by a security interest in the personal property of Greif, Inc. and certain of the Company's United States subsidiaries, including equipment and inventory and certain intangible assets, as well as a pledge of the capital stock of substantially all of the Company's United States subsidiaries. The repayment of amounts borrowed under the Amended Credit Agreement is also secured, in part, by capital stock of the non-U.S. subsidiaries that are parties to the Amended Credit Agreement. However, in the event that the Company receives and maintains an investment grade rating from either Moody's Investors Service, Inc. or Standard & Poor's Corporation, the Company may request the release of such collateral. The payment of outstanding principal under the Amended Credit Agreement and accrued interest thereon may be accelerated and become immediately due and payable upon the Company's default in its payment or other performance obligations or its failure to comply with the financial and other covenants in the Amended Credit Agreement, subject to applicable notice requirements and cure periods as provided in the Amended Credit Agreement.

During the twelve months ended October 31, 2013 the Company recorded debt extinguishment charges of $1.3 million resulting from the write off of unamortized deferred financing costs associated with the 2010 Credit Agreement, as defined below. The Company recorded no debt extinguishment charges for the twelve months ended October 31, 2012 and 2011. Financing costs associated with the Amended Credit Agreement totaling $3.4 million have been capitalized and included in other long term assets.

On October 29, 2010, the Company obtained a $1.0 billion senior secured credit facility pursuant to an Amended and Restated Credit Agreement with a syndicate of financial institutions (the "2010 Credit Agreement"). The 2010 Credit Agreement provided for a $750 million revolving multicurrency credit facility and a $250 million term loan, both expiring October 29, 2015, with an option to add $250 million to the facilities with the agreement of the lenders. The $250 million term loan was scheduled to amortize by $3.1 million each quarter-end for the first eight quarters, $6.3 million each quarter-end for the next eleven quarters and the remaining balance due on the maturity date. The 2010 Credit Agreement was replaced by the Amended Credit Agreement.

The Amended Credit Agreement is available to fund ongoing working capital and capital expenditure needs, for general corporate purposes and to finance acquisitions. Interest under the Amended Credit Agreement is based on a Eurodollar rate or a base rate that resets periodically plus a calculated margin amount. As of October 31, 2013, $222.9 million was outstanding under the Amended Credit Agreement. The current portion of the Amended Credit Agreement was $10.0 million and the long-term portion was $212.9 million. The weighted average interest rate on the Amended Credit Agreement was 1.86% for the year ended October 31, 2013. The actual interest rate on the Amended Credit Agreement was 1.87% as of October 31, 2013.

1.71 AUTONATION, INC. (DEC)
NOTES TO CONSOLIDATED FINANCIAL STATEMENTS

7. Long-Term Debt (In Part)

Restrictions and Covenants

Our credit agreement, the indentures for our 6.75% Senior Notes due 2018 and 5.5% Senior Notes due 2020, our vehicle floorplan facilities, and our mortgage facility contain numerous customary financial and operating covenants that place significant restrictions on us, including our ability to incur additional indebtedness or prepay existing indebtedness, to create liens or other encumbrances, to sell (or otherwise dispose of) assets, and to merge or consolidate with other entities.

Under our credit agreement we are required to remain in compliance with a maximum leverage ratio and maximum capitalization ratio. The leverage ratio is a contractually defined amount principally reflecting non-vehicle debt divided by a contractually defined measure of earnings with certain adjustments. The capitalization ratio is a contractually defined amount principally reflecting vehicle floorplan payable and non-vehicle debt divided by our total capitalization including vehicle floorplan payable. Under the credit agreement, the maximum leverage ratio is 3.75 x and the maximum capitalization ratio is 65.0%. In calculating our leverage and capitalization ratios, we are not required to include letters of credit in the definition of debt (except to the extent of letters of credit in excess of $150.0 million). In addition, in calculating our capitalization ratio, we are permitted to add back to shareholders' equity all goodwill, franchise rights, and long-lived asset impairment charges subsequent to September 30, 2011 plus $1.52 billion.

The indentures for our 6.75% Senior Notes due 2018 and 5.5% Senior Notes due 2020 contain certain limited covenants, including limitations on liens and sale and leaseback transactions. Our mortgage facility contains covenants regarding maximum cash flow leverage and minimum interest coverage.

Our failure to comply with the covenants contained in our debt agreements could permit acceleration of all of our indebtedness. Our debt agreements have cross-default provisions that trigger a default in the event of an uncured default under other material indebtedness of AutoNation.

Under the terms of our credit agreement, at December 31, 2013, our leverage ratio and capitalization ratio were as follows:

	December 31, 2013	
	Requirement	Actual
Leverage ratio	≤ 3.75x	2.25x
Capitalization ratio	≤ 65.0%	57.6%

Both the leverage ratio and the capitalization ratio limit our ability to incur additional non-vehicle debt. The capitalization ratio also limits our ability to incur additional vehicle floorplan indebtedness.

In the event of a downgrade in our credit ratings, none of the covenants described above would be impacted. In addition, availability under our credit agreement described above would not be impacted should a downgrade in the senior unsecured debt credit ratings occur.

1.72 CHESAPEAKE ENERGY CORPORATION (DEC)
NOTES TO CONSOLIDATED FINANCIAL STATEMENTS

4. Contingencies and Commitments (in part)

Commitments (in part)

Rig, Compressor and Other Operating Leases

As of December 31, 2013, we leased 45 rigs under master lease agreements with an aggregate undiscounted future lease commitment of $76 million. The lease commitments are guaranteed by Chesapeake and certain of its subsidiaries. Under the leases, we can exercise an early purchase option or we can purchase the rigs at the expiration of the lease for the fair market value at the time. In addition, in most cases, we have the option to renew a lease for negotiated new terms at the expiration of the lease. During 2013, we purchased 23 leased rigs from various lessors for an aggregate purchase price of approximately $141 million and paid approximately $22 million in lease termination costs. Through these transactions, we lowered our minimum aggregate undiscounted future rig lease payments by approximately $142 million. See Note 23 for further discussion related to additional leased rigs purchased subsequent to December 31, 2013.

As of December 31, 2013, we leased 1,781 compressors under master lease agreements with an aggregate undiscounted future lease commitment of $260 million. The lease commitments are guaranteed by Chesapeake and certain of its subsidiaries. Under the leases, we can exercise an early purchase option or we can purchase the compressors at the expiration of the lease for the fair market value at the time. In addition, in most cases we have the option to renew a lease for negotiated new terms at the expiration of the lease. During 2013, we purchased 541 leased compressor units from various lessors for an aggregate purchase price of approximately $97 million, lowering our minimum aggregate undiscounted future compressor lease payments by approximately $73 million. See Note 23 for further discussion related to additional leased compressors purchased subsequent to December 31, 2013.

Future operating lease commitments related to rigs, compressors and other equipment or property are not recorded in the accompanying consolidated balance sheets. The aggregate undiscounted minimum future lease payments are presented below.

($ in millions)	December 31, 2013			
	Rigs	**Compressors**	**Other**	**Total**
2014	$51	$ 53	$13	$117
2015	11	50	11	72
2016	6	104	9	119
2017	7	23	3	33
2018	1	29	2	32
After 2018	—	1	1	2
Total	$76	$260	$39	$375

Rent expense for rigs, compressors and other equipment, including short-term rentals, for the years ended December 31, 2013, 2012 and 2011 was $158 million, $185 million and $184 million, respectively.

16. Impairments (in part)

Drilling Rigs and Equipment. In 2013, we negotiated the purchase of 23 leased rigs (two of which were classified as held for sale assets as of December 31, 2013) from various lessors for an aggregate purchase price of $141 million and paid approximately $22 million in early lease termination costs, which is included in impairments of fixed assets and other in the consolidated statement of operations. In addition, we impaired approximately $22 million of leasehold improvements and other costs associated with these transactions. See Note 4 for a description of the master lease agreements. In addition, in 2013, we recognized $27 million of impairment losses on certain of our drilling rigs that qualified as held for sale during 2013 for the difference between the carrying amount and fair value, less the anticipated costs to sell. We estimated the fair value using prices expected to be received. In 2012, we negotiated the purchase of 25 leased rigs from various lessors for an aggregate purchase price of $36 million and paid approximately $25 million in early lease termination costs, which is included in impairments of fixed assets and other in the consolidated statement of operations. In addition, in 2012, we recognized $26 million of impairment losses on certain of our drilling rigs that we expected would have insufficient cash flow to recover carrying values because of a change in business climate resulting from depressed natural gas prices. We estimated the fair value of the drilling rigs using prices expected to be received from the sale of each rig in an orderly transaction between market participants. Also in 2012, we recognized $9 million of impairment losses primarily related to drill pipe and other oilfield services equipment. The drilling rigs and equipment are included in our oilfield services operating segment.

23. Subsequent Events (in part)

Subsequent to December 31, 2013, we acquired ten rigs subject to the master lease agreements described in Note 4. In conjunction with the purchases, we also terminated approximately $9 million of remaining lease commitments associated with these rigs. Total consideration paid was approximately $31 million and we anticipate recording a charge in the 2014 first quarter for lease termination cost.

Subsequent to December 31, 2013, we acquired 576 compressors subject to the master lease agreements described in Note 4. In conjunction with these purchases, we also terminated approximately $126 million of remaining lease commitments associated with these compressors. Total consideration paid was approximately $168 million.

ROYALTY AND LICENSING AGREEMENTS

1.73 ELECTRONIC ARTS INC. (MAR)

CONSOLIDATED STATEMENTS OF OPERATIONS (in part)

| | Year Ended March 31, | | |
	2013	2012	2011
(In millions, except per share data)			
Net revenue:			
Product	$2,738	$3,415	$3,181
Service and other	1,059	728	408
Total net revenue	3,797	4,143	3,589
Cost of revenue:			
Product	1,085	1,374	1,407
Service and other	303	224	92
Total cost of revenue	1,388	1,598	1,499
Gross profit	2,409	2,545	2,090
Operating expenses:			
Research and development	1,153	1,180	1,124
Marketing and sales	788	883	781
General and administrative	354	377	296
Acquisition-related contingent consideration	(64)	11	(17)
Amortization of intangibles	30	43	57
Restructuring and other charges	27	16	161
Total operating expenses	2,288	2,510	2,402
Operating income (loss)	121	35	(312)
Gains on strategic investments, net	39	—	23
Interest and other income (expense), net	(21)	(17)	10
Income (loss) before provision for (benefit from) income taxes	139	18	(279)
Provision for (benefit from) income taxes	41	(58)	(3)
Net income (loss)	$ 98	$ 76	$ (276)

NOTES TO CONSOLIDATED FINANCIAL STATEMENTS

(1) Description of Business and Summary of Significant Accounting Policies (in part)

Royalties and Licenses

Royalty-based obligations with content licensors and distribution affiliates are either paid in advance and capitalized as prepaid royalties or are accrued as incurred and subsequently paid. These royalty-based obligations are generally expensed to cost of revenue generally at the greater of the contractual rate or an effective royalty rate based on the total projected net revenue for contracts with guaranteed minimums. Significant judgment is required to estimate the effective royalty rate for a particular contract. Because the computation of effective royalty rates requires us to project future revenue, it is inherently subjective as our future revenue projections must anticipate a number of factors, including (1) the total number of titles subject to the contract, (2) the timing of the release of these titles, (3) the number of software units we expect to sell, which can be impacted by a number of variables, including product quality, the timing of the title's release and competition, and (4) future pricing. Determining the effective royalty rate for our titles is particularly challenging due to the inherent difficulty in predicting the popularity of entertainment products. Furthermore, if we conclude that we are unable to make a reasonably reliable forecast of projected net revenue, we recognize royalty expense at the greater of contract rate or on a straight-line basis over the term of the contract. Accordingly, if our future revenue projections change, our effective royalty rates would change, which could impact the amount and timing of royalty expenses that we recognize.

Each quarter, we evaluate the expected future realization of our royalty-based assets, as well as any unrecognized minimum commitments not yet paid to determine amounts we deem unlikely to be realized through product sales. Any impairments or losses determined before the launch of a product are charged to research and development expense. Impairments or losses determined post-launch are charged to cost of revenue. We evaluate long-lived royalty-based assets for impairment generally using undiscounted cash flows when impairment indicators exist. Unrecognized minimum royalty-based commitments are accounted for as executory contracts and, therefore, any losses on these commitments are recognized when the underlying intellectual property is abandoned (*i.e.*, cease use) or the contractual rights to use the intellectual property are terminated.

(8) Royalties and Licenses

Our royalty expenses consist of payments to (1) content licensors, (2) independent software developers, and (3) co-publishing and distribution affiliates. License royalties consist of payments made to celebrities, professional sports organizations, movie studios and other organizations for our use of their trademarks, copyrights, personal publicity rights, content and/or other intellectual property. Royalty payments to independent software developers are payments for the development of intellectual property related to our games. Co-publishing and distribution royalties are payments made to third parties for the delivery of products.

Royalty-based obligations with content licensors and distribution affiliates are either paid in advance and capitalized as prepaid royalties or are accrued as incurred and subsequently paid. These royalty-based obligations are generally expensed to cost of revenue generally at the greater of the contractual rate or an effective royalty rate based on the total projected net revenue for contracts with guaranteed minimums. Prepayments made to thinly capitalized independent software developers and co-publishing affiliates are generally made in connection with the development of a particular product and, therefore, we are generally subject to development risk prior to the release of the product. Accordingly, payments that are due prior to completion of a product are generally expensed to research and development over the development period as the services are incurred. Payments due after completion of the product (primarily royalty-based in nature) are generally expensed as cost of revenue.

Our contracts with some licensors include minimum guaranteed royalty payments, which are initially recorded as an asset and as a liability at the contractual amount when no performance remains with the licensor. When performance remains with the licensor, we record guarantee payments as an asset when actually paid and as a liability when incurred, rather than recording the asset and liability upon execution of the contract. Royalty liabilities are classified as current liabilities to the extent such royalty payments are contractually due within the next 12 months.

Each quarter, we also evaluate the expected future realization of our royalty-based assets, as well as any unrecognized minimum commitments not yet paid to determine amounts we deem unlikely to be realized through product sales. Any impairments or losses determined before the launch of a product are charged to research and development expense. Impairments or losses determined post-launch are charged to cost of revenue. We evaluate long-lived royalty-based assets for impairment generally using undiscounted cash flows when impairment indicators exist. Unrecognized minimum royalty-based commitments are accounted for as executory contracts and, therefore, any losses on these commitments are recognized when the underlying intellectual property is abandoned (*i.e.*, cease use) or the contractual rights to use the intellectual property are terminated. During fiscal year 2013, we recognized losses of $15 million on previously unrecognized royalty-based commitments, inclusive of $9 million in license termination costs related to our fiscal 2013 restructuring. During fiscal year 2012, we recognized losses of $21 million, representing an adjustment to our fiscal 2011 restructuring. During fiscal year 2011, we recognized losses of $85 million, inclusive of 75 million related to the fiscal 2011 restructuring, on previously unrecognized minimum royalty-based commitments. In addition, we recognized impairment charges of $40 million, inclusive of $27 million related to the fiscal 2011 restructuring, on royalty-based assets. The losses and impairment charges related to restructuring and other restructuring plan-related activities are presented in Note 7 of the Notes to Consolidated Financial Statements.

The current and long-term portions of prepaid royalties and minimum guaranteed royalty-related assets, included in other current assets and other assets, consisted of (in millions):

	As of March 31,	
	2013	2012
Other current assets	$ 63	$ 85
Other assets	93	102
Royalty-related assets	$156	$187

At any given time, depending on the timing of our payments to our co-publishing and/or distribution affiliates, content licensors and/or independent software developers, we recognize unpaid royalty amounts owed to these parties as accrued liabilities. The current and long-term portions of accrued royalties, included in accrued and other current liabilities and other liabilities, consisted of (in millions):

	As of March 31,	
	2013	**2012**
Accrued royalties	$103	$ 98
Other accrued expenses	21	23
Other liabilities	46	52
Royalty-related liabilities	$170	$173

As of March 31, 2013, $1 million of restructuring accruals related to the fiscal 2013 restructuring plan, and $57 million of restructuring accruals related to the fiscal 2011 restructuring plan is included in royalty-related liabilities in the table above. See Note 7 for details of restructuring and other restructuring plan-related activities and Note 9 for the details of our accrued and other current liabilities.

In addition, as of March 31, 2013, we were committed to pay approximately $1,144 million to content licensors, independent software developers, and co-publishing and/or distribution affiliates, but performance remained with the counterparty (*i.e.*, delivery of the product or content or other factors) and such commitments were therefore not recorded in our Consolidated Financial Statements.

MARKETING AGREEMENT

1.74 THE SCOTTS MIRACLE-GRO COMPANY (SEP)
NOTES TO CONSOLIDATED FINANCIAL STATEMENTS

Note 6. Marketing Agreement

The Company is Monsanto's exclusive agent for the marketing and distribution of consumer Roundup® herbicide products (with additional rights to new products containing glyphosate or other similar non-selective herbicides) in the consumer lawn and garden market within the United States and other specified countries, including Australia, Austria, Belgium, Canada, France, Germany, the Netherlands and the United Kingdom. Under the terms of the Marketing Agreement, the Company is entitled to receive an annual commission from Monsanto as consideration for the performance of the Company's duties as agent. The annual gross commission under the Marketing Agreement is calculated as a percentage of the actual earnings before interest and income taxes (EBIT) of the consumer Roundup® business in the markets covered by the Marketing Agreement and is based on the achievement of two earnings thresholds, as defined in the Marketing Agreement. The Marketing Agreement also requires the Company to make annual payments to Monsanto as a contribution against the overall expenses of the consumer Roundup® business. The annual contribution payment is defined in the Marketing Agreement as $20 million.

In consideration for the rights granted to the Company under the Marketing Agreement for North America, the Company was required to pay a marketing fee of $32 million to Monsanto. The Company has deferred this amount on the basis that the payment will provide a future benefit through commissions that will be earned under the Marketing Agreement. The economic useful life over which the marketing fee is being amortized is 20 years, with a remaining amortization period of five years as of September 30, 2013.

Under the terms of the Marketing Agreement, the Company performs certain functions, primarily manufacturing conversion, distribution and logistics, and selling and marketing support, on behalf of Monsanto in the conduct of the consumer Roundup® business. The actual costs incurred for these activities are charged to and reimbursed by Monsanto. The Company records costs incurred under the Marketing Agreement for which the Company is the primary obligor on a gross basis, recognizing such costs in "Cost of sales" and the reimbursement of these costs in "Net sales," with no effect on gross profit or net income.

The gross commission earned under the Marketing Agreement, the contribution payments to Monsanto and the amortization of the initial marketing fee paid to Monsanto are included in the calculation of net sales in the Company's Consolidated Statements of Operations. The elements of the net commission earned under the Marketing Agreement and reimbursements associated with the Marketing Agreement and included in "Net sales" were as follows:

(In millions)	Year Ended September 30		
	2013	**2012**	**2011**
Gross commission	$ 81.8	$ 81.3	$ 77.9
Contribution expenses	(20.0)	(20.0)	(20.0)
Amortization of marketing fee	(0.8)	(0.8)	(0.8)
Net commission income	61.0	60.5	57.1
Reimbursements associated with Marketing Agreement	62.0	79.6	63.7
Total net sales associated with Marketing Agreement	$123.0	$140.1	$120.8

The Marketing Agreement has no definite term except as it relates to the European Union countries (the "EU term"). The current EU term extends through September 30, 2015. Thereafter, the Marketing Agreement provides that the parties may agree to renew the EU term for an additional three years.

The Marketing Agreement provides Monsanto with the right to terminate the Marketing Agreement upon an event of default (as defined in the Marketing Agreement) by the Company, a change in control of Monsanto or the sale of the consumer Roundup® business. The Marketing Agreement provides the Company with the right to terminate the Marketing Agreement in certain circumstances, including an event of default by Monsanto or the sale of the consumer Roundup® business. Unless Monsanto terminates the Marketing Agreement due to an event of default by the Company, Monsanto is required to pay a termination fee to the Company that varies by program year. The termination fee is calculated as a percentage of the value of the Roundup® business exceeding a certain threshold, but in no event will the termination fee be less than $16 million. Monsanto may also be able to terminate the Marketing Agreement within a given region, including North America, without paying a termination fee if unit volume sales to consumers in that region decline: (1) over a cumulative three-fiscal-year period; or (2) by more than 5% for each of two consecutive years. If the Marketing Agreement was terminated for any reason, the Company would also lose all, or a substantial portion, of the significant source of earnings and overhead expense absorption the Marketing Agreement provides.

Under the Marketing Agreement, Monsanto must provide the Company with notice of any proposed sale of the consumer Roundup® business, allow the Company to participate in the sale process and negotiate in good faith with the Company with respect to any such proposed sale. In the event the Company acquires the consumer Roundup® business in such a sale, the Company would receive as a credit against the purchase price the amount of the termination fee that would have been paid to the Company if Monsanto had exercised its right to terminate the Marketing Agreement in connection with a sale to another party. If Monsanto decides to sell the consumer Roundup® business to another party, the Company must let Monsanto know whether the Company intends to terminate the Marketing Agreement and forfeit any right to a termination fee. For additional details regarding the Marketing Agreement, see "ITEM 1A. RISK FACTORS—If Monsanto were to terminate the Marketing Agreement for consumer Roundup® products, we would lose a substantial source of future earnings and overhead expense absorption" of this Annual Report on Form 10-K.

Contingencies

RECOGNITION AND MEASUREMENT

1.75 The FASB ASC glossary defines a *contingency* as an existing condition, situation, or set of circumstances involving uncertainty about possible gain (gain contingency) or loss (loss contingency) to an entity that will ultimately be resolved when one or more future events occur or fail to occur. FASB ASC 450-20 sets forth guidance for the recognition and disclosure of loss contingencies. An estimated loss from a loss contingency should be accrued by a charge to income if both of the following conditions are met:
- Information available before the financial statements are issued or are available to be issued indicates that it is probable that an asset had been impaired or a liability had been incurred at the date of the financial statements. It is implicit in this condition that it must be probable that one or more future events will occur confirming the fact of the loss.
- The amount of loss can be reasonably estimated.

1.76 Disclosure is preferable to accrual when a reasonable estimate of loss cannot be made. Even losses that are reasonably estimable should not be accrued if it is not probable that an asset has been impaired or a liability has been incurred at the date of the entity's financial statements because those losses relate to a future period, rather than the current period. In accordance with FASB ASC 450-20-30-1, if some amount within a range of loss appears at the time to be a better estimate than any other amount within the range, that amount should be accrued. When no amount within the range is a better estimate than any other amount, however, the minimum amount in that range should be accrued. Select loss contingency disclosures do not apply to loss contingencies arising from an entity's recurring estimation of its allowance for credit losses. FASB ASC 450-30-25-1 usually does not permit recognition of gain contingencies because to do so might be to recognize revenue before its realization. When contingency disclosures exist, public companies generally present a balance sheet caption for contingencies, in accordance with Rule 5-02 of Regulation S-X.

1.77 FASB ASC 460-10-25-5 considers warranties to fall within the definition of a contingency. Therefore, an entity should meet the two conditions described in paragraph 1.75 before recognizing a loss and related liability. FASB ASC 460-10 contains additional guidance concerning the items that an entity should consider in order to meet the probability recognition criteria, including references to the entity's own and others' experience. FASB ASC also provides more specific guidance for extended warranties and product maintenance contracts.

PRESENTATION AND DISCLOSURE EXCERPTS

LEGAL MATTERS

1.78 ANADARKO PETROLEUM CORPORATION (DEC)

CONSOLIDATED BALANCE SHEETS (in part)

	December 31,	
Millions	2013	2012
Liabilities and Equity (in part)		
Current Liabilities		
Accounts payable	$ 3,530	$ 2,989
Current asset retirement obligations	409	298
Accrued expenses	1,264	707
Current portion of long-term debt	500	—
Total	5,703	3,994
Long-term Debt	13,065	13,269
Other Long-term Liabilities		
Deferred income taxes	9,245	8,759
Asset retirement obligations	1,613	1,587
Tronox-related contingent liability	850	—
Other	1,655	3,098
Total	13,363	13,444

NOTES TO CONSOLIDATED FINANCIAL STATEMENTS

Years Ended December 31, 2013, 2012, and 2011

17. Contingencies (in part)

Liability Accrual Analysis Applicable accounting guidance requires the Company to accrue a liability if (a) it is probable that a liability has been incurred and (b) the amount of that liability can be reasonably estimated. That guidance also requires a liability accrual at the low end of an estimated range of probable loss when no amount within the range is a better estimate than any other amount. The Company believes that a loss in the Adversary Proceeding is probable, based on the Bankruptcy Court's finding of liability in its Opinion. The Company considers a reasonable estimate of the range of probable loss, after all appellate processes have concluded, to be $850 million to $5.15 billion, and recorded a liability of $850 million, equal to the low end of that range. Although the Company does not believe a loss in excess of $5.15 billion to be probable, it is reasonably possible that the loss could be as high as $14.52 billion, including $61 million for attorneys' fees and costs, but excluding any potential interest and appreciation.

The Company's $850 million contingent liability accrual is based on the application of accounting guidance to currently available information and the Company's judgment concerning the application of law to that information. Furthermore, the Company's liability accrual and estimated range of probable loss do not include any amounts for interest, appreciation, or attorneys' fees and costs, and reflects its assessment that resolution through settlement is not probable at this time. The ultimate outcome of the Adversary Proceeding is subject to significant uncertainty; accordingly, the Company's liability accrual could change materially in the near term as events unfold and more information becomes available. In quantifying an estimated range of probable loss, the Company considered the following components of a possible award for which it could ultimately be responsible: damages, pre-judgment interest and appreciation, post-judgment interest, and attorneys' fees and costs.

Damages The Company estimates a range of probable damages ultimately awarded to the plaintiffs to be $850 million to $5.15 billion. This estimate is based on currently available information and the Company's opinion regarding the ultimate outcome of the Adversary Proceeding. As described below, the degree of uncertainty regarding the determination of Kerr-McGee's allowable 502(h) Claim and the Recovery Percentage prevents the Company from determining any one amount within the estimated range of probable loss to be a better estimate than any other amount.

Critical factors in assessing the estimated range of probable loss with respect to damages are the as-yet unresolved issues of the amount of Kerr-McGee's 502(h) Claim, and the extent to which such an offset amount would reduce damages. The Bankruptcy Court provisionally stated that the 502(h) Claim could be $10.459 billion. This 502(h) Claim amount represents the difference between (i) $14.459 billion, which is the Bankruptcy Court's finding as to damages based on the net value of the transferred assets as of the date of IPO, and (ii) $4.0 billion, which is the mid-point in the plaintiffs' post-petition estimate of potential legacy environmental and tort liabilities as of 2010. To calculate the offset amount that could reduce damages, the Bankruptcy Court indicated that the Recovery Percentage to be applied to Kerr-McGee's 502(h) Claim could be either 89% or 2.8%. The Bankruptcy Court noted in its Opinion that the Plan provides that Kerr-McGee's 502(h) Claim must be multiplied by "the percentage recovery to Allowed Class 3 General Unsecured Creditors" (Class 3 Recovery). Additionally, the Bankruptcy Court noted that 89% represents the estimated average Class 3 Recovery as stated in the Disclosure Statement filed by Tronox in its bankruptcy case. Under this scenario, the damages paid to the plaintiffs would be reduced by approximately $9.3 billion, resulting in a net damage award to plaintiffs of $5.15 billion.

The Bankruptcy Court also suggested that the Recovery Percentage might be determined after including Kerr-McGee's 502(h) Claim with the Class 3 claims allowed under the Plan, which would have the effect of diluting Kerr-McGee's Recovery Percentage. Under this scenario, the Recovery Percentage to be applied to Kerr-McGee's 502(h) Claim would be 2.8%, resulting in an allowed 502(h) Claim of $293 million and a net damages award to plaintiffs of approximately $14.16 billion.

The Company believes that Kerr-McGee's 502(h) Claim should be computed by reference to the Bankruptcy Court's own findings in the Opinion and the language of the Plan, as opposed to being computed by reference to the plaintiffs' post-petition estimate of the amount of legacy environmental and tort liabilities as of 2010. Accordingly, the Company believes that Kerr-McGee's 502(h) Claim should be computed by reference to $850 million, which represents the Bankruptcy Court's finding as to the amount of the net creditor shortfall at the IPO date, which considers the fair value of all of Tronox's assets and liabilities including the legacy environmental and tort liabilities.

Using the Bankruptcy Court's framework for calculating the amount of Kerr-McGee's 502(h) Claim that may be allowed, but applying the Bankruptcy Court's finding of the $850 million net creditor shortfall instead of the plaintiffs' post-petition estimate of legacy environmental and tort liabilities used in the Bankruptcy Court's calculation, results in a 502(h) Claim of $13.609 billion. Furthermore, it is Kerr-McGee's position that the applicable Recovery Percentage should be determined by the Plan, which states that Kerr-McGee is entitled to the same Class 3 Recovery actually received in the bankruptcy, which exceeded 100%. In accordance with the principles of law and equity outlined in the Opinion, the Company believes that Kerr-McGee is entitled to a Recovery Percentage of 100%, resulting in a net damage award to plaintiffs of $850 million. While it is possible that damages could be determined using a Recovery Percentage of less than 89%, the Company does not believe that this outcome is probable, and therefore a lower Recovery Percentage is not included in the Company's estimated range of probable loss.

The following summarizes the Company's estimated range of probable loss:

Billions, except percentages	Low End of Range of Probable Loss	High End of Range of Probable Loss
Value of Transferred Assets as of IPO date[1]	$ 14.459	$14.459
Net Creditor Shortfall/Legacy Liabilities	(0.850)	(4.000)
Allowable 502(h) Claim	$ 13.609	$10.459
Recovery Percentage	100%	89%
Offset Amount	$ 13.609	$ 9.309
Value of Transferred Assets as of IPO date[1]	$ 14.459	$14.459
Offset Amount	(13.609)	(9.309)
Net Damages	$ 0.850	$ 5.150

[1] As determined by the Bankruptcy Court.

The Company's estimate of the range of probable loss requires significant assumptions. As summarized above, the Company's estimated range of probable loss uses the net creditor shortfall of $850 million on the low end and plaintiffs' estimated legacy environmental and tort liabilities of $4.0 billion on the high end. Alternatively, the Bankruptcy Court could use $1.757 billion, which represents the Bankruptcy Court's findings of fact related to the net present value of the environmental and tort liabilities at the IPO date. Further, the Company's estimated range of probable loss uses a Recovery Percentage of 100% for the low end and 89% for the high end. Combinations of the above factors would result in damage estimates that are within the Company's estimated range of probable loss.

If no 502(h) Claim is allowed, the Company could incur a liability for damages of $14.459 billion, which is materially higher than the Company's estimated range of probable loss.

Pre-Judgment Interest and Appreciation   The Bankruptcy Court did not address pre-judgment interest or appreciation in its Opinion. The Bankruptcy Court has discretion in deciding whether to award pre-judgment interest and how such interest may be calculated. The interest rate that may be charged, the date from which such interest is calculated, and whether any such interest is compounded or computed as simple interest may vary. If the Bankruptcy Court chooses to award pre-judgment interest, the amount could be material depending on the amount of net damages awarded in a judgment and the interest rates, dates, and compounding method applied for purposes of calculating the amount of pre-judgment interest.

As noted above, the plaintiffs argued that, in addition to the value of the transferred assets as of 2005, the plaintiffs should recover appreciation in the value of those assets from November 2005 until June 2012. In connection with their appreciation argument, the plaintiffs also are seeking pre-judgment interest applied at a rate of 6% compounded annually from June 2012 until the date of judgment. Appreciation was not addressed by the Bankruptcy Court in its Opinion and it is unclear how any such argument by the plaintiffs will be addressed by the Bankruptcy Court, if at all.

The inherent uncertainty and lack of information, including the lack of a court-provided framework for whether or how the Bankruptcy Court would consider pre-judgment interest or appreciation, prevent the Company from formulating a reasonable estimate of the amount of pre-judgment interest or appreciation that could be included as part of a judgment. Accordingly, the Company is unable to estimate a range of probable or reasonably possible loss from pre-judgment interest or appreciation at this time, and the Company's liability accrual does not include any such amounts. The Company will continue to evaluate the extent to which a reasonable estimate of such amounts can be made as additional information regarding the above factors becomes available. Developments that could assist the Company in estimating interest or appreciation include a judgment by the Bankruptcy Court or matters raised in potential hearings regarding the remaining issues being briefed.

Post-Judgment Interest   Post-judgment interest is mandated by federal law. Post-judgment interest would not begin to accrue until the date a judgment is entered, and would continue until that judgment is paid in full. Because no judgment had been issued as of December 31, 2013, a liability for post-judgment interest has not been incurred. Accordingly, no amount for post-judgment interest has been included in the Company's accrual or estimated range of probable loss. Further, the Company cannot estimate a range of future liability related to post-judgment interest at this time. At December 31, 2013, the annual interest rate for post-judgment interest was 0.13%.

Attorneys' Fees and Costs   In its Opinion, the Bankruptcy Court stated that the plaintiffs could request reimbursement of attorneys' fees and costs. Based on the Company's review of relevant law, aside from certain de minimis costs the Company believes there is no basis in law or contract that would permit the plaintiffs to recover attorneys' fees and costs. Accordingly, the Company has not included any amount related to attorneys' fees and costs in its estimated range of probable loss. However, it is reasonably possible that a loss related to attorneys' fees and costs could be as high as the $61 million requested by the plaintiffs.

Tax Deductibility   The Company has concluded that it is more likely than not that 88% of the $850 million loss recognized in 2013 will be deductible for U.S. tax purposes. Accordingly, the Company recognized a deferred tax benefit of $274 million in its 2013 financial statements. If additional losses are accrued in the future, the Company will evaluate the tax deductibility of any such accrual based on the facts and circumstances related to that accrual.

Liability Outlook   A separate action pending before the U.S. Supreme Court to which Anadarko is not a party, *Executive Benefits Insurance Agency v. Arkison*, raises certain legal issues including, but not limited to, whether a bankruptcy court has authority to enter a judgment or to make a report and recommendation in a fraudulent transfer case. The Company is uncertain, at this time, what impact any ruling in that case would have on the Adversary Proceeding.

As discussed above, the Company's $850 million accrued contingent liability as of December 31, 2013, has been established based on the application of accounting guidance to currently available information and the Company's judgment concerning the application of law to that information. A wide range of possible ultimate outcomes currently exists, and the Company may ultimately incur a liability related to the Adversary Proceeding materially in excess of the current accrued liability. The Company's liability accrual could also change materially in the near term as events unfold and more information becomes available. Further, it is possible that the Company's ultimate liability could exceed the currently estimated range of probable loss of $850 million to $5.15 billion. A judgment could also include an award of pre-judgment interest and appreciation, which could be material, as well as attorneys' fees and costs. In addition, the Company does not believe that the current contingent liability of $850 million accrued at December 31, 2013, is representative of the amount it could be required to pay to reach final resolution of the Adversary Proceeding through settlement. Although the Company does not believe final resolution through settlement to be probable at this time, it expects that any such settlement would require payment of an amount substantially greater than the current accrued liability.

Following a judgment, the Company would be required either to pay the damage award or appeal the judgment. If the Company pursues its rights through the appellate process, the Company may be required to post a bond or provide sufficient security to stay execution of the judgment by the plaintiffs pending the outcome of the appellate process. As the Bankruptcy Court has not yet issued a judgment, the Company is unable to estimate whether the Company would be required to provide a bond or other security or the potential form or amount of any such bond or other security. However, depending on the amount of the judgment and other factors relating to the appellate process, satisfying any security requirements could have a potentially material negative impact on the Company's consolidated financial position in the short term.

TAX CONTINGENCIES

1.79 IAC/INTERACTIVECORP (DEC)
MANAGEMENT'S DISCUSSION AND ANALYSIS OF FINANCIAL CONDITION AND RESULTS OF OPERATIONS (in part)

Critical Accounting Policies and Estimates (in part)

Income Taxes

Estimates of deferred income taxes and the significant items giving rise to the deferred assets and liabilities are shown in Note 4 to the consolidated financial statements, and reflect management's assessment of actual future taxes to be paid on items reflected in the consolidated financial statements, giving consideration to both timing and the probability of realization. As of December 31, 2013, the balance of deferred tax liabilities, net, is $286.6 million. Actual income taxes could vary from these estimates due to future changes in income tax law, state income tax apportionment or the outcome of any review of our tax returns by the various tax authorities, as well as actual operating results of the Company that vary significantly from anticipated results.

We recognize liabilities for uncertain tax positions based on the two-step process. The first step is to evaluate the tax position for recognition by determining if the weight of available evidence indicates it is more likely than not that the position will be sustained on audit, including resolution of related appeals or litigation processes, if any. A tax position that meets the more likely than not recognition threshold is then measured for purposes of financial statement recognition as the largest amount of benefit which is more than 50% likely of being realized upon ultimate settlement. This measurement step is inherently difficult and requires subjective estimations of such amounts to determine the probability of various possible outcomes. We consider many factors when evaluating and estimating our tax positions and tax benefits, which may require periodic adjustments and which may not accurately anticipate actual outcomes. At December 31, 2013, the Company has unrecognized tax benefits of $408.8 million, including interest. Changes to reserves from period to period and differences between amounts paid, if any, upon resolution of issues raised in audits and amounts previously provided may be material. Differences between the reserves for income tax contingencies and the amounts owed by the Company are recorded in the period they become known.

NOTES TO CONSOLIDATED FINANCIAL STATEMENTS

Note 4—Income Taxes (in part)

The Company is routinely under audit by federal, state, local and foreign authorities in the area of income tax. These audits include questioning the timing and the amount of income and deductions and the allocation of income and deductions among various tax jurisdictions. Various jurisdictions are currently under examination, the most significant of which are France, California, New York and New York City for various tax years beginning with 2006. Income taxes payable include reserves considered sufficient to pay assessments that may result from examination of prior year tax returns. Changes to reserves from period to period and differences between amounts paid, if any, upon the resolution of audits and amounts previously provided may be material. Differences between the reserves for income tax contingencies and the amounts owed by the Company are recorded in the period they become known.

On August 28, 2013, the Joint Committee of Taxation completed its review and approved the audit settlement previously agreed to with the Internal Revenue Service ("IRS") for the years ended December 31, 2001 through 2009. The statute of limitations for the years 2001 through 2009 expires on July 1, 2014. The resolution of this IRS examination resulted in a net liability to the IRS of $7.1 million. At December 31, 2013 and 2012, unrecognized tax benefits, including interest, are $408.8 million and $496.8 million, respectively. Unrecognized tax benefits, including interest, for the year ended December 31, 2013 decreased by $88.0 million due principally to the settlement of the audit of the federal income tax returns for the years ended December 31, 2001 through 2009. The reduction of unrecognized tax benefits was substantially offset by a reduction of receivables related to the same period. Of the total unrecognized tax benefits at December 31, 2013, $405.5 million is included in "Income taxes payable," $3.0 million relates to deferred tax assets included in "Deferred income taxes" and $0.3 million is included in "Accrued expenses and other current liabilities" in the accompanying consolidated balance sheet. Included in unrecognized tax benefits at December 31, 2013 is $44.7 million relating to tax positions for which the ultimate deductibility is highly certain, but for which there is uncertainty about the timing of such deductibility. If unrecognized tax benefits at December 31, 2013 are subsequently recognized, $120.9 million and $173.8 million, net of related deferred tax assets and interest, would reduce income tax expense from continuing operations and discontinued operations, respectively. The comparable amounts as of December 31, 2012 are $110.8 million and $222.3 million, respectively. The Company believes that it is reasonably possible that its unrecognized tax benefits could decrease within twelve months of the current reporting date. An estimate of changes in unrecognized tax benefits, while potentially significant, cannot be made.

Note 17—Contingencies

In the ordinary course of business, the Company is a party to various lawsuits. The Company establishes reserves for specific legal matters when it determines that the likelihood of an unfavorable outcome is probable and the loss is reasonably estimable. Management has also identified certain other legal matters where we believe an unfavorable outcome is not probable and, therefore, no reserve is established. Although management currently believes that resolving claims against us, including claims where an unfavorable outcome is reasonably possible, will not have a material impact on the liquidity, results of operations, or financial condition of the Company, these matters are subject to inherent uncertainties and management's view of these matters may change in the future. The Company also evaluates other contingent matters, including income and non-income tax contingencies, to assess the likelihood of an unfavorable outcome and estimated extent of potential loss. It is possible that an unfavorable outcome of one or more of these lawsuits or other contingencies could have a material impact on the liquidity, results of operations, or financial condition of the Company. See Note 4 for additional information related to income tax contingencies.

ENVIRONMENTAL MATTERS

1.80 ALLIANT TECHSYSTEMS INC. (MAR)
NOTES TO THE CONSOLIDATED FINANCIAL STATEMENTS

(Amounts in thousands except share and per share data and unless otherwise indicated)

1. Summary of Significant Accounting Policies (in part)

Environmental Remediation and Compliance. Costs associated with environmental compliance, restoration, and preventing future contamination that are estimable and probable are accrued and expensed, or capitalized as appropriate. Expected remediation, restoration, and monitoring costs relating to an existing condition caused by past operations, and which do not contribute to current or future revenue generation, are accrued and expensed in the period that such costs become estimable. Liabilities are recognized for remedial and resource restoration activities when they are probable and the cost can be reasonably estimated. ATK expects that a portion of its environmental remediation costs will be recoverable under U.S. Government contracts and has recorded a receivable equal to the present value of the amount that ATK expects to recover.

ATK's engineering, financial, and legal specialists estimate, based on current law and existing technologies, the cost of each environmental liability. Such estimates are based primarily upon the estimated cost of investigation and remediation required and the likelihood that other potentially responsible parties ("PRPs") will be able to fulfill their commitments at the sites where ATK may be jointly and severally liable. ATK's estimates for environmental obligations are dependent on, and affected by, the nature and extent of historical information and physical data relating to a contaminated site, the complexity of the site, methods of remediation available, the technology that will be required, the outcome of discussions with regulatory agencies and other PRPs at multi-party sites, the number and financial viability of other PRPs, changes in environmental laws and regulations, future technological developments, and the timing of expenditures; accordingly, ATK periodically evaluates and revises such estimates based on expenditures against established reserves and the availability of additional information.

8. Other Accrued Liabilities (in part)

The major categories of other current and long-term accrued liabilities are as follows:

	March 31	
	2013	**2012**
Employee benefits and insurance, including pension and other postretirement benefits	$ 75,882	$ 76,646
Warranty	19,669	24,221
Litigation Liability	—	25,500
Interest	1,887	15,293
Environmental remediation	6,847	5,135
Rebate	6,875	6,050
Deferred lease obligation	28,424	27,782
Commodity forward contracts	2,871	6,518
Federal excise tax	22,367	15,338
Other	97,199	105,159
Total other accrued liabilities—current	$262,021	$307,642

(continued)

	March 31	
	2013	**2012**
Environmental remediation	$ 49,373	$ 52,361
Management nonqualified deferred compensation plan	17,409	19,704
Non-current portion of accrued income tax liability	25,400	20,396
Deferred lease obligation	14,342	14,932
Other	19,934	15,609
Total other long-term liabilities	$126,458	$123,002

13. Contingencies (in part)

Environmental Liabilities. ATK's operations and ownership or use of real property are subject to a number of federal, state, and local environmental laws and regulations, including those for discharge of hazardous materials, remediation of contaminated sites, and restoration of damage to the environment. At certain sites that ATK owns or operates or formerly owned or operated, there is known or potential contamination that ATK is required to investigate or remediate. ATK could incur substantial costs, including remediation costs, resource restoration costs, fines, and penalties, or third party property damage or personal injury claims, as a result of liabilities associated with past practices or violations of environmental laws or non-compliance with environmental permits.

The liability for environmental remediation represents management's best estimate of the present value of the probable and reasonably estimable costs related to known remediation obligations. The receivable represents the present value of the amount that ATK expects to recover, as discussed below. Both the liability and receivable have been discounted to reflect the present value of the expected future cash flows, using a discount rate of 0.8% and 1.0% as of March 31, 2013 and 2012, respectively. ATK's discount rate is calculated using the 20-year Treasury constant maturities rate, net of an estimated inflationary factor of 1.9%, rounded to the nearest quarter percent. The following is a summary of the amounts recorded for environmental remediation:

	March 31, 2013		March 31, 2012	
	Liability	**Receivable**	**Liability**	**Receivable**
Amounts (payable) receivable	$(58,965)	$34,190	$(61,227)	$35,638
Unamortized discount	2,745	(1,446)	3,731	(1,925)
Present value amounts (payable) receivable	$(56,220)	$32,744	$(57,496)	$33,713

Amounts expected to be paid or received in periods more than one year from the balance sheet date are classified as non-current. Of the $56,220 discounted liability as of March 31, 2013, $6,847 was recorded within other current liabilities and $49,373 was recorded within other long-term liabilities. Of the $32,744 discounted receivable, ATK recorded $4,490 within other current assets and $28,254 within other non-current assets. As of March 31, 2013, the estimated discounted range of reasonably possible costs of environmental remediation was $56,220 to $83,245.

ATK expects that a portion of its environmental compliance and remediation costs will be recoverable under U.S. Government contracts. Some of the remediation costs that are not recoverable from the U.S. Government that are associated with facilities purchased in a business acquisition may be covered by various indemnification agreements, as described below.

- As part of its acquisition of the Hercules Aerospace Company in fiscal 1995, ATK generally assumed responsibility for environmental compliance at the facilities acquired from Hercules ("the Hercules Facilities"). ATK believes that a portion of the compliance and remediation costs associated with the Hercules Facilities will be recoverable under U.S. Government contracts. If ATK were unable to recover those environmental remediation costs under these contracts, ATK believes that these costs will be covered by Hercules Incorporated, a subsidiary of Ashland Inc., ("Hercules") under environmental agreements entered into in connection with the Hercules acquisition. Under these agreements, Hercules has agreed to indemnify ATK for environmental conditions relating to releases or hazardous waste activities occurring prior to ATK's purchase of the Hercules Facilities as long as they were identified in accordance with the terms of the agreement; fines relating to pre-acquisition environmental compliance; and environmental claims arising out of breaches of Hercules' representations and warranties. Hercules is not required to indemnify ATK for any individual claims below $50,000. Hercules is obligated to indemnify ATK for the lowest cost response of remediation required at the facility that is acceptable to the applicable regulatory agencies. ATK is not responsible for conducting any remedial activities with respect to the Clearwater, FL facility. In accordance with its agreement with Hercules, ATK notified Hercules of all known contamination on non-federal lands on or before March 31, 2000, and on federal lands on or before March 31, 2005.
- ATK generally assumed responsibility for environmental compliance at the Thiokol Facilities acquired from Alcoa Inc. ("Alcoa") in fiscal 2002. ATK expects that a portion of the compliance and remediation costs associated with the acquired Thiokol Facilities will be recoverable under U.S. Government contracts. In accordance with its agreement with Alcoa, ATK notified Alcoa of all known environmental remediation issues as of January 30, 2004. Of these known issues, ATK is responsible for any costs not recovered through U.S. Government contracts at Thiokol Facilities up to $29,000, ATK and Alcoa have agreed to split evenly any amounts between

$29,000 and $49,000, and ATK is responsible for any payments in excess of $49,000. At this time, ATK believes that costs not recovered through U.S. Government contracts will be immaterial.

ATK cannot ensure that the U.S. Government, Hercules, Alcoa, or other third parties will reimburse it for any particular environmental costs or reimburse ATK in a timely manner or that any claims for indemnification will not be disputed. U.S. Government reimbursements for cleanups are financed out of a particular agency's operating budget and the ability of a particular governmental agency to make timely reimbursements for cleanup costs will be subject to national budgetary constraints. ATK's failure to obtain full or timely reimbursement from the U.S. Government, Hercules, Alcoa, or other third parties could have a material adverse effect on its operating results, financial condition, or cash flows. While ATK has environmental management programs in place to mitigate these risks, and environmental laws and regulations have not had a material adverse effect on ATK's operating results, financial condition, or cash flows in the past, it is difficult to predict whether they will have a material impact in the future.

At March 31, 2013, the aggregate undiscounted amounts payable for environmental remediation costs, net of expected recoveries, are estimated to be:

Fiscal 2014	$2,357
Fiscal 2015	299
Fiscal 2016	304
Fiscal 2017	2,543
Fiscal 2018	2,063
Thereafter	17,209
Total	$24,775

There were no material insurance recoveries related to environmental remediation during any of the periods presented.

SELF-INSURANCE

1.81 PULTEGROUP, INC. (DEC)
CONSOLIDATED BALANCE SHEETS (in part)

For the years ended December 31, 2013, 2012, and 2011

(000's omitted, except per share data)

	2013	2012
Liabilities and Shareholders' Equity (in part)		
Liabilities:		
Accounts payable, including book overdrafts of $35,827 and $42,053 in 2013 and 2012, respectively	$ 202,736	$ 178,274
Customer deposits	134,858	101,183
Accrued and other liabilities	1,377,750	1,418,063
Income tax liabilities	206,015	198,865
Financial Services debt	105,664	138,795
Senior notes	2,058,168	2,509,613
Total liabilities	4,085,191	4,544,793

NOTES TO CONSOLIDATED FINANCIAL STATEMENTS

1. Summary of Significant Accounting Policies (in part)

Self-Insured Risks

We maintain, and require the majority of our subcontractors to maintain, general liability insurance coverage, including coverage for certain construction defects. We also maintain property, errors and omissions, workers compensation, and other business insurance coverage. These insurance policies protect us against a portion of the risk of loss from claims, subject to certain self-insured per occurrence and aggregate retentions, deductibles, and available policy limits. However, we retain a significant portion of the overall risk for such claims. We reserve for these costs on an undiscounted basis at the time product revenue is recognized for each home closing and evaluate the recorded liabilities based on actuarial analyses of our historical claims, which include estimates of claims incurred but not yet reported. Adjustments to estimated reserves are recorded in the period in which the change in estimate occurs. In certain instances, we have the ability to recover a portion of our costs under various insurance policies or from our subcontractors or other third parties. Estimates of such amounts are recorded when recovery is considered probable. See Note 13.

12. Other Assets and Accrued and Other Liabilities (in part)

Accrued and other liabilities are presented below ($000's omitted):

	December 31,	
	2013	2012
Self-insurance liabilities (Note 13)	$ 668,100	$ 721,284
Loan origination liabilities (Note 13)	124,956	164,280
Compensation-related	171,686	119,288
Warranty (Note 13)	63,992	64,098
Community development district obligations (Note 13)	26,124	33,119
Liability for land, not owned, under option agreements (Note 1)	24,024	31,066
Accrued interest	22,283	28,713
Other	276,585	256,215
	$1,377,750	$1,418,063

13. Commitments and Contingencies (in part)

Self-Insured Risks

We maintain, and require our subcontractors to maintain, general liability insurance coverage. We also maintain builders' risk, property, errors and omissions, workers compensation, and other business insurance coverage. These insurance policies protect us against a portion of the risk of loss from claims. However, we retain a significant portion of the overall risk for such claims either through policies issued by our captive insurance subsidiaries or through our own self-insured per occurrence and aggregate retentions, deductibles, and claims in excess of available insurance policy limits.

Our general liability insurance includes coverage for certain construction defects. While construction defect claims can relate to a variety of circumstances, the majority of our claims relate to alleged problems with siding, plumbing, foundations and other concrete work, windows, roofing, and heating, ventilation and air conditioning systems. The availability of general liability insurance for the homebuilding industry and its subcontractors has become increasingly limited, and the insurance policies available require companies to maintain significant per occurrence and aggregate retention levels. In certain instances, we may offer our subcontractors the opportunity to purchase insurance through one of our captive insurance subsidiaries or to participate in a project-specific insurance program provided by the Company. Policies issued by the captive insurance subsidiaries represent self-insurance of these risks by the Company. This self-insured exposure is limited by reinsurance policies that we purchase. General liability coverage for the homebuilding industry is complex, and our coverage varies from policy year to policy year. Our insurance coverage requires a per occurrence deductible up to an overall aggregate retention level. Beginning with the first dollar, amounts paid on insured claims satisfy our per occurrence and aggregate retention obligations. Any amounts incurred in excess of the occurrence or aggregate retention levels are covered by insurance up to our purchased coverage levels. Our insurance policies, including the captive insurance subsidiaries' reinsurance policies, are maintained with highly-rated underwriters for whom we believe counterparty default risk is not significant.

At any point in time, we are managing over 1,000 individual claims related to general liability, property, errors and omission, workers compensation, and other business insurance coverage. We reserve for costs associated with such claims (including expected claims management expenses) on an undiscounted basis at the time revenue is recognized for each home closing and evaluate the recorded liabilities based on actuarial analyses of our historical claims. The actuarial analyses calculate estimates of the ultimate net cost of all unpaid losses, including estimates for incurred but not reported losses ("IBNR"). IBNR represents losses related to claims incurred but not yet reported plus development on reported claims. These estimates comprise a significant portion of our liability and are subject to a high degree of uncertainty due to a variety of factors, including changes in claims reporting and resolution patterns, third party recoveries, insurance industry practices, the regulatory environment, and legal precedent. State regulations vary, but construction defect claims are reported and resolved over an extended period often exceeding ten years. In certain instances, we have the ability to recover a portion of our costs under various insurance policies or from subcontractors or other third parties. Estimates of such amounts are recorded when recovery is considered probable.

Our recorded reserves for all such claims totaled $668.1 million and $721.3 million at December 31, 2013 and 2012, respectively, the vast majority of which relates to general liability claims. The recorded reserves include loss estimates related to both (i) existing claims and related claim expenses and (ii) IBNR and related claim expenses. Liabilities related to IBNR and related claim expenses represented approximately 78% and 74% of the total general liability reserves at December 31, 2013 and 2012, respectively. The actuarial analyses that determine the IBNR portion of reserves consider a variety of factors, including the frequency and severity of losses, which are based on our historical claims experience supplemented by industry data. The actuarial analyses of the reserves also consider historical third party recovery rates and claims management expenses.

Adjustments to reserves are recorded in the period in which the change in estimate occurs. Because the majority of our reserves relate to IBNR, adjustments to reserve amounts for individual existing claims generally do not impact the recorded reserves materially. However, changes in the frequency and timing of reported claims and estimates of specific claim values can impact the underlying inputs and trends utilized in the actuarial analyses, which could have a material impact on the recorded reserves. Because of the inherent uncertainty in estimating future losses related to these claims, actual costs could differ significantly from estimated costs. Costs associated with our insurance programs are classified within selling, general, and administrative expenses. Changes in these liabilities were as follows ($000's omitted):

	2013	2012	2011
Balance, beginning of period	$ 721,284	$739,029	$787,918
Reserves provided	64,737	54,262	48,359
Payments	(117,921)	(72,007)	(97,248)
Balance, end of period	$ 668,100	$721,284	$739,029

The reserves provided reflected in the above table are classified within selling, general, and administrative expenses.

GOVERNMENT MATTERS

1.82 JOHNSON & JOHNSON (DEC)
NOTES TO CONSOLIDATED FINANCIAL STATEMENTS

21. Legal Proceedings (in part)

Government Proceedings

Like other companies in the pharmaceutical and medical devices and diagnostics industries, Johnson & Johnson and certain of its subsidiaries are subject to extensive regulation by national, state and local government agencies in the United States and other countries in which they operate. As a result, interaction with government agencies is ongoing. The most significant litigation brought by, and investigations conducted by, government agencies are listed below. It is possible that criminal charges and substantial fines and/or civil penalties or damages could result from government investigations or litigation.

Average Wholesale Price (AWP) Litigation

Johnson & Johnson and several of its pharmaceutical subsidiaries (the J&J AWP Defendants), along with numerous other pharmaceutical companies, are defendants in a series of lawsuits in state and federal courts involving allegations that the pricing and marketing of certain pharmaceutical products amounted to fraudulent and otherwise actionable conduct because, among other things, the companies allegedly reported an inflated Average Wholesale Price (AWP) for the drugs at issue. Payors alleged that they used those AWPs in calculating provider reimbursement levels. Many of these cases, both federal actions and state actions removed to federal court, were consolidated for pre-trial purposes in a Multi-District Litigation (MDL) in the United States District Court for the District of Massachusetts.

The plaintiffs in these cases included three classes of private persons or entities that paid for any portion of the purchase of the drugs at issue based on AWP, and state government entities that made Medicaid payments for the drugs at issue based on AWP. In June 2007, after a trial on the merits, the MDL Court dismissed the claims of two of the plaintiff classes against the J&J AWP Defendants. In March 2011, the Court dismissed the claims of the third class against the J&J AWP Defendants without prejudice.

AWP cases brought by various Attorneys General have proceeded to trial against other manufacturers. Several state cases against certain subsidiaries of Johnson & Johnson have been settled, including those filed by Kentucky, Kansas, Mississippi and Louisiana. The case filed by Illinois is set for trial in May 2014, and the Alaska case is set for trial in July 2014. Other state cases are likely to be set for trial in due course. In addition, an AWP case against the J&J AWP Defendants brought by the Commonwealth of Pennsylvania was tried in Commonwealth Court in October and November 2010. The Court found in the Commonwealth's favor with regard to certain of its claims under the Pennsylvania Unfair Trade Practices and Consumer Protection Law ("UTPL"), entered an injunction, and awarded $45 million in restitution and $6.5 million in civil penalties. The Court found in the J&J AWP Defendants' favor on the Commonwealth's claims of unjust enrichment, misrepresentation/fraud, civil conspiracy, and on certain of the Commonwealth's claims under the UTPL. The J&J AWP Defendants have appealed the Commonwealth Court's UTPL ruling to the Pennsylvania Supreme Court. The Company believes that the J&J AWP Defendants have strong arguments supporting their appeal. Because the Company believes that the potential for an unfavorable outcome is not probable, it has not established an accrual with respect to the verdict.

RISPERDAL®

Beginning in January 2004, Janssen Pharmaceutica Inc. (Janssen Pharmaceutica) (now Janssen Pharmaceuticals, Inc. (JPI)) received subpoenas from the Office of the Inspector General of the United States Office of Personnel Management, the Department of Justice and the United States Attorney's Office for the Eastern District of Pennsylvania seeking documents concerning sales and marketing of, payments to physicians in connection with sales and marketing of, and clinical trials for, RISPERDAL®. Numerous subpoenas seeking testimony from various witnesses before a grand jury were also received. JPI cooperated in responding to these requests for documents and witnesses. The United States Department of Justice and the United States Attorney's Office for the Eastern District of Pennsylvania (the Government) were pursuing both criminal and civil actions concerning these matters. In February 2010, the Government served Civil Investigative Demands seeking additional information relating to sales and marketing of RISPERDAL® and sales and marketing of INVEGA®. The focus of these matters was the alleged promotion of RISPERDAL® and INVEGA® for off-label uses. The Government had also notified JPI that there were pending qui tam actions alleging off-label promotion of RISPERDAL® in which the Government planned to intervene.

In 2011, discussions to resolve criminal penalties under the Food, Drug and Cosmetic Act related to the promotion of RISPERDAL® resulted in an agreement in principle with the United States Attorney's Office for the Eastern District of Pennsylvania on key issues relevant to a disposition of criminal charges pursuant to a single misdemeanor violation of the Food Drug, and Cosmetic Act. The settlement agreement was finalized in November 2013. Under its terms, JPI pled guilty to a single misdemeanor violation of the Food, Drug & Cosmetic Act and paid $400 million.

In 2012, the Company reached an agreement in principle with the United States Department of Justice to settle three civil False Claims Act matters pending in (1) the Eastern District of Pennsylvania concerning sales and marketing of RISPERDAL® and INVEGA®; (2) the Northern District of California regarding the sales and marketing of NATRECOR®, discussed separately below; and (3) the District of Massachusetts alleging that the defendants provided the Omnicare, Inc. (Omnicare) long-term care pharmacy with rebates and other payments regarding RISPERDAL® and other products, discussed separately below. These settlement agreements were finalized in November 2013. Under the terms of the settlements, the Company paid an amount of approximately $1.6 billion. The Company also entered into a five-year corporate integrity agreement with the Office of Inspector General of the Department of Health and Human Services. These civil settlements resolved the federal government's claims under the federal False Claims Act, resolved all pending state and federal government litigation regarding Omnicare and NATRECOR® (described below), and settled the RISPERDAL® Medicaid-related claims for the states that participated in the relevant settlement. To the extent any state has an outstanding Medicaid-related claim not resolved by these settlements, the Company has accrued an amount approximately equal to what that state would have received if it had participated in the relevant federal settlement.

In addition to the federal actions, the Attorneys General of several states brought actions against Janssen Pharmaceutica (now JPI), related to the sale and marketing of RISPERDAL®, seeking one or more of the following remedies: reimbursement of Medicaid or other public funds for RISPERDAL® prescriptions written for off-label use, compensation for treating their citizens for alleged adverse reactions to RISPERDAL®, civil fines or penalties, for violations of state false claims acts or consumer fraud statutes, punitive damages, or other relief relating to alleged unfair business practices. Certain of these actions also sought injunctive relief relating to the promotion of RISPERDAL®. The Attorneys General of multiple other states and the District of Columbia were pursuing investigations and potentially similar litigation against JPI. Many of the actions and claims brought by the state Attorneys General have been settled, either individually or as part of the federal settlements described above.

Following the federal and state settlements described above, as of year-end 2013, five states had remaining claims in litigation related to RISPERDAL®. Three of these (Arkansas, Louisiana, and South Carolina) are on appeal, and two (Kentucky and Mississippi) have not progressed to trial. The Company has not accrued amounts equal to the judgments obtained in the three cases on appeal. State cases that went to judgment after trial are discussed below.

In 2004, the Attorney General of West Virginia commenced a lawsuit against Janssen Pharmaceutica (now JPI) based on claims of alleged consumer fraud as to DURAGESIC®, as well as RISPERDAL®. JPI was found liable and damages were assessed at $4.5 million. JPI filed an appeal, and in November 2010, the West Virginia Supreme Court of Appeals reversed the trial court's decision. In December 2010, the Attorney General of West Virginia dismissed the case as it related to RISPERDAL® without any payment. Thereafter, JPI settled the case insofar as it related to DURAGESIC®.

In 2004, the Attorney General of Louisiana filed a multi-count Complaint against Janssen Pharmaceutica (now JPI). Johnson & Johnson was later added as a defendant. The case was tried in October 2010. The issue tried to the jury was whether Johnson & Johnson or JPI had violated the State's Medical Assistance Program Integrity Law (the Act) through misrepresentations allegedly made in the mailing of a November

2003 Dear Health Care Professional letter regarding RISPERDAL®. The jury returned a verdict that JPI and Johnson & Johnson had violated the Act and awarded $257.7 million in damages. The trial judge subsequently awarded the Attorney General counsel fees and expenses in the amount of $73 million. In August 2012, an intermediate appellate court affirmed the judgment. This judgment was appealed, and in January 2014, the Louisiana Supreme Court reversed the district court's judgment in favor of the Attorney General, and rendered judgment in favor of Johnson & Johnson and JPI. The Attorney General has filed a petition seeking a rehearing of the appellate arguments.

In 2007, the Office of General Counsel of the Commonwealth of Pennsylvania filed a lawsuit against Janssen Pharmaceutica (now JPI) on a multi-Count Complaint related to Janssen Pharmaceutica's sale of RISPERDAL® to the Commonwealth's Medicaid program. The trial occurred in June 2010. The trial judge dismissed the case after the close of the plaintiff's evidence. The Commonwealth filed an appeal and in July 2012, the Pennsylvania Appeals Court upheld the dismissal of the Commonwealth's case.

In 2007, the Attorney General of South Carolina filed a lawsuit against Johnson & Johnson and Janssen Pharmaceutica (now JPI) on several counts. In March 2011, the matter was tried to a jury on liability only, at which time the lawsuit was limited to claims of violation of the South Carolina Unfair Trade Practices Act, including, among others, questions of whether Johnson & Johnson or JPI engaged in unfair or deceptive acts or practices in the conduct of any trade or commerce by distributing the November 2003 Dear Health Care Professional letter regarding RISPERDAL® or in their use of the product's FDA-approved label. The jury found in favor of Johnson & Johnson and against JPI. In June 2011, the Court awarded civil penalties of approximately $327.1 million against JPI. JPI has appealed this judgment and the Company believes it has strong arguments supporting the appeal. Oral argument on the appeal took place before the South Carolina Supreme Court in March 2013 and the parties are awaiting a decision.

In April 2012, in the lawsuit brought by the Attorney General of Arkansas, the jury found against both JPI and Johnson & Johnson, and the Court imposed penalties in the amount of approximately $1.2 billion. In January 2013, the trial court awarded attorney fees of approximately $181 million. JPI and Johnson & Johnson have filed appeals from both awards and believe they have strong arguments in support of the appeals. Oral argument on the appeal has been scheduled for February 2014.

Omnicare

In September 2005, Johnson & Johnson received a subpoena from the United States Attorney's Office for the District of Massachusetts, seeking documents related to the sales and marketing of eight drugs to Omnicare, Inc. (Omnicare), a manager of pharmaceutical benefits for long-term care facilities. In April 2009, Johnson & Johnson and certain of its pharmaceutical subsidiaries were served in two civil qui tam cases asserting claims under the Federal False Claims Act and related state law claims alleging that the defendants provided Omnicare with rebates and other alleged kickbacks, causing Omnicare to file false claims with Medicaid and other government programs. In January 2010, the government intervened in both of these cases, naming Johnson & Johnson, Ortho-McNeil-Janssen Pharmaceuticals, Inc. (now Janssen Pharmaceuticals, Inc. (JPI)), and Johnson & Johnson Health Care Systems Inc. as defendants. Subsequently, the Commonwealths of Massachusetts, Virginia, and Kentucky, and the States of California and Indiana intervened in the action. In February 2011, the United States District Court for the District of Massachusetts dismissed one qui tam case entirely and dismissed the other case in part, rejecting allegations that the defendants had violated their obligation to report their "best price" to health care program officials. The remaining claims of the United States and intervening states were resolved in November 2013 as part of the federal civil settlements discussed in the RISPERDAL® section above.

NATRECOR®

In July 2005, Scios Inc. (Scios) received a subpoena from the United States Attorney's Office for the District of Massachusetts, seeking documents related to the sales and marketing of NATRECOR®. In August 2005, Scios was advised that the investigation would be handled by the United States Attorney's Office for the Northern District of California in San Francisco. In February 2009, two quitam complaints were unsealed in the United States District Court for the Northern District of California, alleging, among other things, improper activities in the promotion of NATRECOR®. In June 2009, the United States government intervened in one of the qui tam actions, and filed a complaint against Scios and Johnson & Johnson seeking relief under the Federal False Claims Act and asserting a claim of unjust enrichment. In October 2011, a criminal matter related to NATRECOR® was resolved. The remaining civil case was resolved in November 2013 as part of the federal civil settlements discussed in the RISPERDAL® section above.

McNeil Consumer Healthcare

Starting in June 2010, McNeil Consumer Healthcare Division of McNEIL-PPC, Inc. (McNeil Consumer Healthcare) and certain affiliates, including Johnson & Johnson (the Companies), received grand jury subpoenas from the United States Attorney's Office for the Eastern District of Pennsylvania requesting documents broadly relating to recalls of various products of McNeil Consumer Healthcare, and the FDA inspections of the Fort Washington, Pennsylvania and Lancaster, Pennsylvania manufacturing facilities, as well as certain documents relating to recalls of a small number of products of other subsidiaries. In addition, in February 2011, the government served McNEIL-PPC, Inc. (McNEIL-PPC) with a Civil Investigative Demand seeking records relevant to its investigation to determine if there was a violation of the Federal False Claims Act. The grand jury and False Claims investigations are continuing. The Companies are cooperating with the United States Attorney's Office in responding to these investigations.

The Companies have also received Civil Investigative Demands from multiple State Attorneys General Offices broadly relating to the McNeil recall issues. The Companies continue to cooperate with these inquiries, which are being coordinated through a multi-state coalition. If a resolution cannot be reached with this multi-state coalition, it is possible that individual State Attorneys General Offices may file civil money claims against the Companies. In January 2011, the Oregon Attorney General filed a civil complaint against Johnson & Johnson, McNEIL-PPC and McNeil Healthcare LLC in state court alleging civil violations of the Oregon Unlawful Trade Practices Act relating to an earlier recall of a McNeil OTC product. In November 2012, the state court granted a motion by the Companies to dismiss Oregon's complaint in its entirety, with prejudice. In December 2012, Oregon filed a Notice of Appeal in the Court of Appeals of the State of Oregon. Briefing on the appeal has concluded and the Court has not set a hearing date.

In March 2011, the United States filed a complaint for injunctive relief in the United States District Court for the Eastern District of Pennsylvania against McNEIL-PPC and two of its employees, alleging that McNEIL-PPC is in violation of FDA regulations regarding the manufacture of drugs at the facilities it operates in Lancaster, Pennsylvania, Fort Washington, Pennsylvania, and Las Piedras, Puerto Rico. On the same day, the parties filed a consent decree of permanent injunction resolving the claims set forth in the complaint. The Court approved and entered the consent decree on March 16, 2011.

The consent decree, which is subject to ongoing enforcement by the Court, requires McNEIL-PPC to take enhanced measures to remediate the three facilities. The Fort Washington facility, which was voluntarily shut down in April 2010, will remain shut down until a third-party consultant certifies that its operations will be in compliance with applicable law, and the FDA concurs with the third-party certification. The Lancaster and Las Piedras facilities may continue to manufacture and distribute drugs, provided that a third party reviews manufacturing records for selected batches of drugs released from the facilities, and certifies that any deviations reviewed do not adversely affect the quality of the selected batches. McNEIL-PPC submitted a workplan to the FDA for remediation of the Lancaster and Las Piedras facilities, and that plan was approved by the FDA in October 2012. Third-party batch record review may cease if the FDA has stated that the facilities appear to be in compliance with applicable law. Each facility is subject to a five-year audit period by a third party after the facility has been deemed by the FDA to be in apparent compliance with applicable law.

Other

In June 2008, Johnson & Johnson received a subpoena from the United States Attorney's Office for the District of Massachusetts relating to the marketing of biliary stents by Cordis Corporation (Cordis). In February 2012, the government informed Cordis that it was closing its investigation. In addition, in January 2010, a complaint was unsealed in the United States District Court for the Northern District of Texas, filed by Kevin Colquitt, seeking damages against Cordis and other parties for alleged violations of the Federal False Claims Act and several similar state laws in connection with the marketing of biliary stents. The United States Department of Justice and several states declined to intervene. In January 2013, the Court granted Cordis's motion to dismiss the claims against Cordis, with prejudice. Plaintiff appealed, and in May 2013, Plaintiff dismissed his appeal, concluding the matter.

In September 2011, Synthes, Inc. (Synthes) received a Civil Investigative Demand issued pursuant to the False Claims Act from the United States Attorney's Office for the Eastern District of Pennsylvania. The Demand sought information regarding allegations that fellowships had been offered to hospitals in exchange for agreements to purchase products. Synthes has produced documents and information in response to the Demand and is cooperating with the inquiry.

In October 2011, the European Commission (EC) announced that it opened an investigation concerning an agreement between Janssen-Cilag B.V. (Janssen-Cilag) and Sandoz B.V. relating to the supply of fentanyl patches in the Netherlands and whether the agreement infringes European competition law. In January 2013, the EC issued a Statement of Objections setting out facts regarding a potential violation of EU antitrust laws. Janssen-Cilag has submitted its response to the Statement of Objections. In December 2013, the EC issued its decision imposing a fine of approximately €10.8 million on Janssen-Cilag. Janssen-Cilag will not appeal the decision.

In April 2012, Janssen Pharmaceuticals, Inc. (JPI) received a letter requesting certain documents from the United States Department of Justice relating to the marketing and promotion of DORIBAX®. In 2012, JPI provided documents and will continue to cooperate with any further inquiries if and when they are received.

In May 2012, Acclarent, Inc. (Acclarent) received a subpoena from the United States Attorney's Office for the District of Massachusetts requesting documents broadly relating to the sales, marketing and promotion by Acclarent of RELIEVA STRATUS™ MicroFlow Spacer products. Acclarent is cooperating with the United States Attorney's Office in responding to the subpoena.

In August 2012, DePuy Orthopaedics, Inc., DePuy, Inc. (now DePuy Synthes, Inc. (DePuy Synthes)), and Johnson & Johnson Services, Inc. received an informal request from the United States Attorney's Office for the District of Massachusetts and the Civil Division of the United States Department of Justice for the production of materials relating to the ASR™ XL Hip device. The government has since made additional informal requests for the production of documents as to the device. The government is investigating whether any person or entity submitted or caused to be submitted false claims or false statements affecting federal health care programs in connection with the marketing and use of the ASR™ XL Hip device. DePuy Orthopaedics, Inc., DePuy Synthes, and Johnson & Johnson Services, Inc. have voluntarily produced documents in response to the government's informal requests and are fully cooperating with the government's civil investigation. In addition, the Company has received Civil Investigative Demands from a group of state Attorneys General relating to the development, sales and marketing of several of DePuy Orthopaedics, Inc.'s hip products. At least one state Attorney General has informed the Company of the intention to investigate these matters independently of the multi-state group. The Company is responding to these demands.

In October 2012, Johnson & Johnson was contacted by the California Attorney General's office regarding a multi-state Attorney General investigation of the marketing of surgical mesh products for hernia and urogynecological purposes by Johnson & Johnson's subsidiary, Ethicon, Inc. (Ethicon). Johnson & Johnson and Ethicon have since entered into a tolling agreement with the 44 states participating in the multi-state investigation and are in the process of responding to Civil Investigative Demands served by certain of the participating states.

In December 2012, Therakos, Inc. (Therakos), formerly a subsidiary of Johnson & Johnson and part of the Ortho-Clinical Diagnostics, Inc. (OCD) franchise, received a letter from the civil division of the United States Attorney's Office for the Eastern District of Pennsylvania informing Therakos that the United States Attorney's Office was investigating the sales and marketing of UVADEX® (methoxsalen) and the UVAR XTS® System during the period 2000 to the present. The United States Attorney's Office requested that OCD and Johnson & Johnson preserve documents that could relate to the investigation. Therakos was subsequently acquired by an affiliate of Gores Capital Partners III, L.P. OCD and Johnson & Johnson retain certain liabilities that may result from the investigation for activity that occurred prior to the sale of Therakos, and have taken appropriate steps to retain potentially relevant documents and will cooperate with the United States Attorney's Office's investigation with respect to such activity.

In May 2013, Janssen Pharmaceuticals, Inc. (JPI) received a subpoena from the Atlanta Regional Office of the Department of Health and Human Services, Office of Inspector General, seeking production of documents and information regarding: (1) the sales, marketing and promotional practices, including the remuneration of healthcare providers, related to NUCYNTA® IR and NUCYNTA® ER; and (2) any studies, reports and/or complaints regarding the safety and/or actual or potential side effects of NUCYNTA® IR and NUCYNTA® ER. JPI is in the process of responding to the subpoena.

In recent years, Johnson & Johnson has received numerous requests from a variety of United States Congressional Committees to produce information relevant to ongoing congressional inquiries. It is the policy of Johnson & Johnson to cooperate with these inquiries by producing the requested information.

GUARANTEES & PRODUCT WARRANTY

1.83 CATERPILLAR INC. (DEC)
NOTES TO CONSOLIDATED FINANCIAL STATEMENTS

21. Guarantees and Product Warranty

We have provided an indemnity to a third-party insurance company for potential losses related to performance bonds issued on behalf of Caterpillar dealers. The bonds are issued to insure governmental agencies against nonperformance by certain dealers. We also provided guarantees to a third-party related to the performance of contractual obligations by certain Caterpillar dealers. The guarantees cover potential financial losses incurred by the third-party resulting from the dealers' nonperformance.

We provide loan guarantees to third-party lenders for financing associated with machinery purchased by customers. These guarantees have varying terms and are secured by the machinery. In addition, Cat Financial participates in standby letters of credit issued to third parties on behalf of their customers. These standby letters of credit have varying terms and beneficiaries and are secured by customer assets.

We have provided a guarantee to one of our customers in Brazil related to the performance of contractual obligations by a supplier consortium to which one of our Caterpillar subsidiaries is a member. The guarantees cover potential damages (some of them capped) incurred by the customer resulting from the supplier consortium's non-performance. The guarantee will expire when the supplier consortium performs all its contractual obligations, which is expected to be completed in 2022.

We have provided guarantees to third-party lessors for certain properties leased by Cat Logistics Services, LLC, in which we sold a 65 percent equity interest in the third quarter of 2012. See Note 26 for further discussion on this divestiture. The guarantees are for the possibility that the third party logistics business would default on real estate lease payments. The guarantees were granted at lease inception, which was prior to the divestiture, and generally will expire at the end of the lease terms.

Cat Financial provided a limited indemnity to a third-party bank resulting from the assignment of certain leases to that bank. The indemnity was for the possibility that the insurers of these leases would become insolvent. The indemnity expired December 15, 2012.

No loss has been experienced or is anticipated under any of these guarantees. At December 31, 2013, 2012 and 2011, the related liability was $13 million, $14 million and $7 million, respectively. The maximum potential amount of future payments (undiscounted and without reduction for any amounts that may possibly be recovered under recourse or collateralized provisions) we could be required to make under the guarantees at December 31 are as follows:

(Millions of dollars)	2013	2012	2011
Caterpillar dealer guarantees	$193	$180	$140
Customer guarantees	62	77	96
Customer guarantees—supplier consortium	364	—	—
Third party logistics business guarantees	151	176	—
Limited indemnity	—	—	11
Other guarantees	35	53	28
Total guarantees	$805	$486	$275

Cat Financial provides guarantees to repurchase certain loans of Caterpillar dealers from a special-purpose corporation (SPC) that qualifies as a variable interest entity. The purpose of the SPC is to provide short-term working capital loans to Caterpillar dealers. This SPC issues commercial paper and uses the proceeds to fund its loan program. Cat Financial has a loan purchase agreement with the SPC that obligates Cat Financial to purchase certain loans that are not paid at maturity. Cat Financial receives a fee for providing this guarantee, which provides a source of liquidity for the SPC. Cat Financial is the primary beneficiary of the SPC as their guarantees result in Cat Financial having both the power to direct the activities that most significantly impact the SPC's economic performance and the obligation to absorb losses, and therefore Cat Financial has consolidated the financial statements of the SPC. As of December 31, 2013, 2012 and 2011, the SPC's assets of $1,005 million, $927 million and $586 million, respectively, are primarily comprised of loans to dealers, and the SPC's liabilities of $1,005 million, $927 million and $586 million, respectively, are primarily comprised of commercial paper. The assets of the SPC are not available to pay Cat Financial's creditors. Cat Financial may be obligated to perform under the guarantee if the SPC experiences losses. No loss has been experienced or is anticipated under this loan purchase agreement.

Cat Financial is party to agreements in the normal course of business with selected customers and Caterpillar dealers in which we commit to provide a set dollar amount of financing on a pre-approved basis. We also provide lines of credit to selected customers and Caterpillar dealers, of which a portion remains unused as of the end of the period. Commitments and lines of credit generally have fixed expiration dates or other termination clauses. It has been our experience that not all commitments and lines of credit will be used. Management applies the same credit policies when making commitments and granting lines of credit as it does for any other financing.

Cat Financial does not require collateral for these commitments/lines, but if credit is extended, collateral may be required upon funding. The amount of the unused commitments and lines of credit for dealers as of December 31, 2013, 2012 and 2011 was $10,503 million, $10,863 million and $6,469 million, respectively. The amount of the unused commitments and lines of credit for customers as of December 31, 2013, 2012 and 2011 was $4,635 million, $4,690 million and $2,785 million, respectively.

Our product warranty liability is determined by applying historical claim rate experience to the current field population and dealer inventory. Generally, historical claim rates are based on actual warranty experience for each product by machine model/engine size by customer or dealer location (inside or outside North America). Specific rates are developed for each product shipment month and are updated monthly based on actual warranty claim experience.

(Millions of dollars)	2013	2012	2011
Warranty liability, January 1	$1,477	$1,308	$1,035
Reduction in liability (payments)	(938)	(920)	(926)
Increase in liability (new warranties)	828	1,089	1,199
Warranty liability, December 31	$1,367	$1,477	$1,308

1.84 UNIVERSAL HEALTH SERVICES, INC. (DEC)
NOTES TO CONSOLIDATED FINANCIAL STATEMENTS

1) Business and Summary of Significant Accounting Policies (in part)

F) Accounting for Medicare and Medicaid Electronic Health Records Incentive Payments: In July 2010, the Department of Health and Human Services published final regulations implementing the health information technology provisions of the American Recovery and Reinvestment Act. The regulation defines the "meaningful use" of Electronic Health Records ("EHR") and established the requirements for the Medicare and Medicaid EHR payment incentive programs. The implementation period for these new Medicare and Medicaid incentive payments started in federal fiscal year 2011 and can end as late as 2016 for Medicare and 2021 for the state Medicaid programs. We recognize income related to Medicare and Medicaid incentive payments using a gain contingency model that is based upon when our eligible hospitals have demonstrated "meaningful use" of certified EHR technology for the applicable period and the cost report information for the full cost report year that will determine the final calculation of the incentive payment is available.

Medicare EHR incentive payments: Federal regulations require that Medicare EHR incentive payments be computed based on the Medicare cost report that begins in the federal fiscal period in which a hospital meets the applicable "meaningful use" requirements. Since the annual Medicare cost report periods for each of our acute care hospitals ends on December 31st, we will recognize Medicare EHR incentive income for each hospital during the fourth quarter of the year in which the facility meets the "meaningful use" criteria and during the fourth quarter of each applicable subsequent year.

Medicaid EHR incentive payments: Medicaid EHR incentive payments are determined based upon prior period cost report information available at the time our hospitals met the "meaningful use" criteria. Therefore, the majority of the Medicaid EHR incentive income recognition occurred in the period in which the applicable hospitals were deemed to have met initial "meaningful use" criteria. Upon meeting subsequent fiscal year "meaningful use" criteria, our hospitals may become entitled to additional Medicaid EHR incentive payments which will be recognized as incentive income in future periods. Medicaid EHR incentive payments received prior to our hospitals meeting the "meaningful use" criteria were included in other current liabilities (as deferred EHR incentive income) in our consolidated balance sheet.

Financial Instruments

RECOGNITION AND MEASUREMENT

1.85 FASB ASC 815, *Derivatives and Hedging*, establishes accounting and reporting standards for derivative instruments, including certain derivative instruments embedded in other contracts (collectively referred to as derivatives), and hedging activities. FASB ASC 815 requires that an entity recognize all derivatives as either assets or liabilities in the statement of financial position and measure those instruments at fair value. In addition, paragraphs 4–6 of FASB ASC 815-15-25 simplify the accounting for certain hybrid financial instruments by permitting an entity to irrevocably elect to initially and subsequently measure that hybrid financial instrument in its entirety at fair value, with changes recognized in earnings. This election is also available when a previously recognized financial instrument is subject to a remeasurement (new basis) event and the separate recognition of an embedded derivative.

1.86 FASB ASC 825, *Financial Instruments*, permits entities to choose to measure at fair value many financial instruments and certain other items that are not currently required to be measured at fair value. Further, under FASB ASC 825, a business entity should report unrealized gains and losses on eligible items for which the fair value option has been elected in earnings at each subsequent reporting date. The irrevocable election of the fair value option is made on an instrument by instrument basis, with certain exceptions, and applied to the entire instrument, not only to specified risks, specific cash flows, or portions of that instrument.

DISCLOSURE

1.87 The disclosures required by FASB ASC 815 for entities with derivative instruments or nonderivative instruments that are designated and qualify as hedging instruments are intended to enable users of financial statements to understand
- How and why an entity uses derivative or such nonderivative instruments.
- How derivative instruments or such nonderivative instruments and related hedged items are accounted for under FASB ASC 815.

- How derivative instruments or such nonderivative instruments and related hedged items affect an entity's financial position, financial performance, and cash flows.

1.88 To meet those objectives, FASB ASC 815-10-50-1A requires qualitative disclosures about an entity's objectives and strategies for using derivatives and such nonderivative instruments. An entity that holds or issues derivative instruments or such nonderivative instruments should disclose all of the following for each interim and annual reporting period for which a statement of financial position and statement of financial performance are presented:
- Its objectives for holding or issuing those instruments.
- The context needed to understand those objectives. This should be disclosed in the context of each instrument's primary underlying risk exposure.
- Its strategies for achieving those objectives. This should be disclosed in the context of each instrument's primary underlying risk exposure.
- Information that would enable users of its financial statements to understand the volume of its activity in those instruments.

1.89 These instruments should be disclosed in the context of each instrument's primary underlying risk exposure and should be distinguished among those used for risk management purposes, those used as economic hedges and other purposes related to risk exposure, and those used for other purposes. Those used for risk management purposes should be distinguished between those designated as hedging instruments and, further, whether they are fair value hedges, cash flow hedges, or foreign currency hedges. An entity should select the format and specifics for this that are most relevant and practicable for its individual facts and circumstances. For any derivatives not designated as hedging instruments under FASB ASC 815-20, the description should include the purpose of the derivative activity.

1.90 Paragraphs .4A-.4E of FASB ASC 815-10-50 explain the quantitative disclosures about derivatives and such nonderivative instruments. For every annual and interim reporting period for which a statement of financial position and statement of financial performance are presented, an entity that holds or issues derivative instruments is required to disclose the location and fair value amounts of derivative instruments and such nonderivative instruments reported in the statement of financial position. The fair value of those instruments should be presented on a gross basis, even when those instruments are subject to master netting arrangements and qualify for net presentation in the statement of financial position. Cash collateral payables and receivables associated with these instruments should not be added to, or netted against, the fair value amounts.

1.91 Fair value amounts should be presented as separate asset and liability values segregated between derivatives that are designated and qualifying as hedging instruments presented separately by type of contract and those that are not. The disclosure should also identify the line item(s) in the statement of financial position in which the fair value amounts for these categories of derivative instruments are included. Also, disclosure of the location and amount of the gains and losses on derivative instruments and such nonderivative instruments and related hedged items in the statement of financial performance or statement of financial position (for example, in other comprehensive income) is required. These gain and loss disclosures should be presented separately by type of contract. These quantitative disclosures are required to be presented in tabular format, except for disclosures regarding hedged items that can be presented in either tabular or nontabular format.

1.92 For derivative instruments not designated or qualifying as hedging instruments under FASB ASC 815-20, if the entity's policy is to include them in its trading activities, the entity can elect not to separately disclose gains and losses, provided that the entity discloses certain other information. Additionally, FASB ASC 815 requires specific disclosures for derivative instruments that contain credit-risk-related features and credit derivatives.

1.93 FASB ASC 825 requires certain reporting entities to disclose the fair value of financial instruments and disclosure requirements of credit risk concentrations of all financial instruments, and it provides guidance on the fair value option. FASB ASC 825 also establishes presentation and disclosure requirements designed to facilitate comparison between entities that choose different measurement attributes for similar types of assets and liabilities.

PRESENTATION AND DISCLOSURE EXCERPTS

FINANCIAL GUARANTEES AND INDEMNIFICATIONS—LINE OF CREDIT

1.94 PLUM CREEK TIMBER COMPANY, INC. (DEC)
CONSOLIDATED BALANCE SHEETS (in part)

(In millions, except per share amounts)	December 31, 2013	December 31, 2012
Liabilities		
Current liabilities:		
Current portion of long-term debt	$ —	$ 248
Line of credit	467	104
Accounts payable	24	26
Interest payable	22	26
Wages payable	29	29
Taxes payable	10	9
Deferred revenue	26	23
Other current liabilities	10	7
	588	472
Long-term debt	2,414	1,815
Note payable to Timberland Venture	783	783
Other liabilities	78	91
Total liabilities	3,863	3,161

NOTES TO CONSOLIDATED FINANCIAL STATEMENTS

Note 10. Borrowings (in part)

All of our borrowings, except the Note Payable to Timberland Venture, are made by Plum Creek Timberlands, L.P., the company's wholly-owned operating partnership ("the Partnership"). Furthermore, all of the outstanding indebtedness of the Partnership is unsecured. Outstanding borrowings consist of the following (in millions):

	December 31, 2013	December 31, 2012
Line of credit maturing 2019, 1.37% at 12/31/13, based on LIBOR plus 1.25%	$ 467	$ 104
Term credit agreement due 2019, 1.66% at 12/31/13, based on LIBOR plus 1.50%	225	450
Senior notes due 2013, 6.18%	—	174
Senior notes due 2013, 7.76% less unamortized discount of $0.1 at 12/31/12, effective rate of 8.05%	—	72
Senior notes due 2015, 5.875% less unamortized discount of $1.7 at 12/31/13, effective rate of 6.10%	438	456
Senior notes due 2016, mature serially 2013 to 2016, 8.05%	—	14
Senior notes due 2021, 4.70% less unamortized discount of $0.3 at 12/31/13, effective rate of 4.71%	568	575
Senior notes due 2023, 3.25% less unamortized discount of $2.4 at 12/31/13, effective rate of 3.34%	323	322
Installment note Payable due 2023, 5.207%	860	—
Note payable to Timberland Venture due 2018, 7.375%	783	783
Total long-term debt	3,664	2,950
Less: current portion of long-term debt	—	248
Less: line of credit	467	104
Long-term portion	$3,197	$2,598

Line of Credit. On November 8, 2013, the company amended its $700 million revolving line of credit agreement which extended the maturity to January 15, 2019. The weighted-average interest rate for the borrowings on the line of credit was 1.37% and 1.43% as of December 31, 2013 and December 31, 2012, respectively. The interest rate on the line of credit is based on LIBOR plus 1.25%, including the facility fee. This rate can range from LIBOR plus 1% to LIBOR plus 2% depending on our debt ratings. Subject to customary covenants, the line of credit allows for borrowings from time to time up to $700 million, including up to $60 million of standby letters of credit. Borrowings on the line of credit fluctuate daily based on cash needs. As of December 31, 2013, we had $467 million of borrowings and $1 million of standby letters of credit outstanding; $232 million remained available for borrowing under our line of credit. As of January 2, 2014, $416 million of the borrowings under our line of credit was repaid. The line of credit has been classified as a current liability in our Consolidated Balance Sheet as of December 31, 2013 because the company used a portion of its cash as of December 31, 2013 to repay the line.

1.95 MERCK & CO., INC. (DEC)

NOTES TO CONSOLIDATED FINANCIAL STATEMENTS

($ in millions except per share amounts)

5. Financial Instruments (in part)

Derivative Instruments and Hedging Activities (in part)

Interest Rate Risk Management

The Company may use interest rate swap contracts on certain investing and borrowing transactions to manage its net exposure to interest rate changes and to reduce its overall cost of borrowing. The Company does not use leveraged swaps and, in general, does not leverage any of its investment activities that would put principal capital at risk.

During 2013, the Company entered into 15 pay-floating, receive-fixed interest rate swap contracts designated as fair value hedges of fixed-rate notes in which the notional amounts match the amount of the hedged fixed-rate notes. There are four swaps maturing in 2016 with notional amounts of $250 million each that effectively convert the Company's 0.70% fixed-rate notes due in 2016 to floating-rate instruments; four swaps maturing in 2018 with notional amounts of $250 million each that effectively convert the Company's 1.30% fixed-rate notes due in 2018 to floating-rate instruments; four swaps maturing in 2017, one with a notional amount of $200 million, two with notional amounts of $250 million each, and one with a notional amount of $300 million, that effectively convert the Company's 6.00% fixed-rate notes due in 2017 to floating-rate instruments; and three swaps maturing in 2019, two with notional amounts of $200 million each, and one with a notional amount of $150 million, that effectively convert a portion of the Company's 5.00% notes due in 2019 to floating rate instruments. The interest rate swap contracts are designated hedges of the fair value changes in the notes attributable to changes in the benchmark London Interbank Offered Rate ("LIBOR") swap rate. The fair value changes in the notes attributable to changes in the LIBOR are recorded in interest expense and offset by the fair value changes in the swap contracts. The cash flows from these contracts are reported as operating activities in the Consolidated Statement of Cash Flows.

There were no interest rate swaps outstanding as of December 31, 2012. During 2011, the Company terminated pay-floating, receive-fixed interest rate swap contracts designated as fair value hedges of fixed-rate notes in which the notional amounts match the amount of the hedged fixed-rate notes. These swaps effectively converted certain of its fixed-rate notes to floating-rate instruments. The interest rate swap contracts were designated hedges of the fair value changes in the notes attributable to changes in the benchmark LIBOR swap rate. As a result of the swap terminations, the Company received $288 million in cash, which included $43 million in accrued interest. The corresponding $245 million basis adjustment of the debt associated with the terminated interest rate swap contracts was deferred and is being amortized as a reduction of interest expense over the respective term of the notes. The cash flows from these contracts are reported as operating activities in the Consolidated Statement of Cash Flows.

Presented in the table below is the fair value of derivatives on a gross basis segregated between those derivatives that are designated as hedging instruments and those that are not designated as hedging instruments as of December 31:

		2013			2012		
		Fair Value of Derivative		**U.S. Dollar**	**Fair Value of Derivative**		**U.S. Dollar**
	Balance Sheet Caption	**Asset**	**Liability**	**Notional**	**Asset**	**Liability**	**Notional**
Derivatives Designated as Hedging Instruments							
Interest rate swap contracts (non-current)	Other assets	$ 13	$ —	$ 1,550	$ —	$ —	$ —
Interest rate swap contracts (non-current)	Other noncurrent liabilities	—	25	2,000	—	—	—
Foreign exchange contracts (current)	Deferred income taxes and other current assets	493	—	4,427	281	—	6,646
Foreign exchange contracts (non-current)	Other assets	515	—	6,676	387	—	5,989
Foreign exchange contracts (current)	Accrued and other current liabilities	—	19	1,659	—	13	938
		$1,021	$ 44	$16,312	$668	$ 13	$13,573
Derivatives Not Designated as Hedging Instruments							
Foreign exchange contracts (current)	Deferred income taxes and other current assets	$ 69	$ —	$ 5,705	$ 55	$ —	$ 4,548
Foreign exchange contracts (non-current)	Other assets	—	—	—	8	—	232
Foreign exchange contracts (current)	Accrued and other current liabilities	—	140	7,892	—	216	8,203
		$ 69	$140	$13,597	$ 63	$216	$12,983
		$1,090	$184	$29,909	$731	$229	$26,556

As noted above, the Company records its derivatives on a gross basis in the Consolidated Balance Sheet. The Company has master netting agreements with several of its financial institution counterparties (see *Concentrations of Credit Risk* below). The following table provides information on the Company's derivative positions subject to these master netting arrangements as if they were presented on a net basis, allowing for the right of offset by counterparty and cash collateral exchanged per the master agreements and related credit support annexes at December 31:

	2013		2012	
	Asset	Liability	Asset	Liability
Gross amounts recognized in the consolidated balance sheet	$1,090	$ 184	$ 731	$ 229
Gross amount subject to offset in master netting arrangements not offset in the consolidated balance sheet	(147)	(147)	(195)	(195)
Cash collateral (received) posted	(652)	—	(305)	—
Net amounts	$ 291	$ 37	$ 231	$ 34

The table below provides information on the location and pretax gain or loss amounts for derivatives that are: (i) designated in a fair value hedging relationship, (ii) designated in a foreign currency cash flow hedging relationship, (iii) designated in a foreign currency net investment hedging relationship and (iv) not designated in a hedging relationship:

Years Ended December 31	2013	2012	2011
Derivatives Designated in a Fair Value Hedging Relationship			
Interest rate swap contracts			
Amount of loss (gain) recognized in *Other (income) expense, net* on derivatives [1]	$ 12	$ —	$(196)
Amount of (gain) loss recognized in *Other (income) expense, net* on hedged item [1]	(14)	—	196
Derivatives Designated in Foreign Currency Cash Flow Hedging Relationships			
Foreign exchange contracts			
Amount of loss reclassified from *AOCI* to *Sales*	45	50	85
Amount of (gain) loss recognized in *OCI* on derivatives	(306)	204	143
Derivatives Designated in Foreign Currency Net Investment Hedging Relationships			
Foreign exchange contracts			
Amount of gain recognized in *Other (income) expense, net* on derivatives [2]	(10)	(20)	(10)
Amount of (gain) loss recognized in *OCI* on derivatives	(363)	(208)	122
Derivatives not Designated in a Hedging Relationship			
Foreign exchange contracts			
Amount of loss (gain) recognized in *Other (income) expense, net* on derivatives [3]	183	382	(113)
Amount of loss recognized in *Sales*	8	30	—

[1] There was $2 million of ineffectiveness on the hedge during 2013.
[2] There was no ineffectiveness on the hedge. Represents the amount excluded from hedge effectiveness testing.
[3] These derivative contracts mitigate changes in the value of remeasured foreign currency denominated monetary assets and liabilities attributable to changes in foreign currency exchange rates.

At December 31, 2013, the Company estimates $66 million of pretax net unrealized gains on derivatives maturing within the next 12 months that hedge foreign currency denominated sales over that same period will be reclassified from *AOCI* to *Sales*. The amount ultimately reclassified to *Sales* may differ as foreign exchange rates change. Realized gains and losses are ultimately determined by actual exchange rates at maturity.

DERIVATIVE FINANCIAL INSTRUMENTS—FOREIGN CURRENCY CONTRACTS

1.96 BMC SOFTWARE, INC. (MAR)
CONSOLIDATED BALANCE SHEETS (in part)

(In millions, except par value data)

	March 31,	
	2013	2012
Assets (in part)		
Current assets:		
Cash and cash equivalents	$1,379.2	$1,496.9
Short-term investments	131.2	86.1
Trade accounts receivable, net	265.5	296.7
Trade finance receivables, net	110.4	108.0
Deferred tax assets	81.3	71.0
Other current assets	131.8	124.1
Total current assets	2,099.4	2,182.8

(1) Summary of Significant Accounting Policies (in part)

Foreign Currency Translation and Risk Management

We operate globally and transact business in various foreign currencies. The functional currency for many of our foreign subsidiaries is the respective local currency. Financial statements of these foreign operations are translated into United States dollars using the currency exchange rates in effect at the balance sheet dates. Revenue and expenses of these subsidiaries are translated using rates that approximate those in effect during the period. Translation adjustments are included in accumulated other comprehensive income (loss) within stockholders' equity. Our foreign currency exposures relate primarily to certain foreign currency denominated assets and liabilities. The substantial majority of our revenue derived from customers outside of the United States is billed in local currencies from regional headquarters, for which the functional currency is the United States dollar. Foreign currency transaction gains or losses are included in interest and other income, net, in the consolidated statements of comprehensive income.

To minimize the risk from changes in foreign currency exchange rates, we have established a program that utilizes foreign currency forward contracts to offset the risks associated with the effects of certain foreign currency exposures. Gains or losses on our foreign currency exposures are offset by gains or losses on the foreign currency forward contracts entered into under this program. Our foreign currency forward contracts generally have terms of one month or less and are entered into at the prevailing market exchange rate at the end of each month. All foreign currency forward contracts entered into by us are components of hedging programs and are entered into for the sole purpose of hedging an existing exposure, not for speculation or trading purposes. While these foreign currency forward contracts are utilized to hedge foreign currency exposures, they are not formally designated as hedges for accounting purposes, and therefore, the changes in the fair values of these contracts are recognized currently in earnings. We record these foreign currency forward contracts at fair value as either assets or liabilities depending on their net settlement position with each respective counterparty at the balance sheet date. All settlements of gains and losses related to the foreign currency forward contracts are included in cash flow from operating activities in the consolidated statements of cash flows.

(3) Financial Instruments (in part)

Derivative Financial Instruments (in part)

We operate globally and are exposed to foreign currency exchange rate fluctuations and interest rate changes in the normal course of business.

Our foreign currency exposures relate primarily to certain foreign currency denominated assets and liabilities, primarily non-U.S. dollar denominated accounts receivable, cash and intercompany balances held by U.S. dollar functional currency entities. To minimize the risk from changes in foreign currency exchange rates, we have established a program that utilizes foreign currency forward contracts to offset the risks associated with the effects of certain foreign currency exposures. Gains or losses on our foreign currency exposures are offset by gains or losses on the foreign currency forward contracts entered into under this program. These foreign currency forward contracts generally have terms of one month or less and are generally entered into at the prevailing market exchange rate at the end of each month. All foreign currency forward contracts entered into by us are components of hedging programs and are entered into for the sole purpose of hedging an existing exposure, not for speculation or trading purposes. While these foreign currency forward contracts are utilized to hedge foreign currency exposures, they are not formally designated as hedges for accounting purposes, and therefore, the changes in the fair values of these contracts are recognized currently in earnings. We record these foreign currency forward contracts at fair value as either assets or liabilities depending on their net settlement position with each respective counterparty at the balance sheet date.

The fair value of our outstanding foreign currency forward contracts that closed in a gain position at March 31, 2013 and 2012 was $5.5 million and $8.1 million, respectively, and was recorded within other current assets in our consolidated balance sheets. The fair value of our outstanding foreign currency forward contracts that closed in a loss position at March 31, 2013 and 2012 was $0.5 million and $0.6 million, respectively, and was recorded within accrued liabilities in our consolidated balance sheets. The notional amounts at contract exchange rates of our foreign currency forward contracts outstanding were:

(In millions)	Notional Amount March 31,	
	2013	2012
Foreign Currency Forward Contracts (receive United States dollar/pay foreign currency)		
Euro	$128.3	$214.2
British pound	18.8	19.2
Chinese yuan renminbi	16.3	11.7
Australian dollar	12.2	29.9
Swiss franc	10.1	6.8
Singapore dollar	6.7	3.8
Danish krone	5.0	3.9
New Zealand dollar	4.0	3.4
Brazilian real	3.8	8.7
South Korean won	3.0	2.6
Norwegian krone	2.0	2.9
Swedish krona	1.8	8.2
Mexican peso	1.4	3.2
Other	3.6	3.5
Total	$217.0	$322.0
Foreign Currency Forward Contracts (pay United States dollar/receive foreign currency)		
Israeli shekel	$178.1	$158.2
Indian rupee	14.7	15.0
Other	—	4.8
Total	$192.8	$178.0

Our use of foreign currency forward exchange contracts is intended to principally offset gains and losses associated with foreign currency exposures. Therefore, the notional amounts and currencies underlying our foreign currency forward contracts will fluctuate period to period as they are principally dependent on the balances and currency denomination of monetary assets and liabilities maintained by our global entities. The net effect of the foreign currency forward contracts for the years ended March 31, 2013, 2012 and 2011 was a gain of $16.8 million, a loss of $10.6 million and a gain of $3.3 million, respectively, which, after including gains and losses on our foreign currency exposures, resulted in net losses of $0.6 million, $3.3 million and $2.9 million, respectively, recorded in interest and other income, net.

CREDIT FACILITY

1.97 GENCORP INC. (NOV)

CONSOLIDATED BALANCE SHEETS (in part)

(In millions, except per share and share amounts)	November 30, 2013	November 30, 2012
Liabilities, Redeemable Common Stock, and Shareholders' Equity (Deficit) (in part)		
Current Liabilities		
Short-term borrowings and current portion of long-term debt	$ 2.9	$ 2.7
Accounts payable	122.5	56.1
Reserves for environmental remediation costs	36.6	39.5
Postretirement medical and life insurance benefits	7.3	7.5
Advance payments on contracts	104.4	100.1
Deferred income taxes	—	9.4
Other current liabilities	206.0	103.3
Total current liabilities	479.7	318.6
Noncurrent liabilities		
Senior debt	42.5	45.0
Second-priority senior notes	460.0	—
Convertible subordinated notes	193.2	200.2
Other debt	0.6	0.8
Deferred income taxes	—	2.2
Reserves for environmental remediation costs	134.7	150.0
Pension benefits	261.7	454.5
Postretirement medical and life insurance benefits	59.3	68.3
Other noncurrent liabilities	73.8	68.5
Total noncurrent liabilities	1,225.8	989.5
Total liabilities	1,705.5	1,308.1

Note 6. Long-Term Debt (in part)

(In millions)	As of November 30, 2013	2012
Senior debt	$ 45.0	$ 47.5
Senior secured notes	460.0	—
Convertible subordinated notes	193.4	200.2
Other debt	0.8	1.0
Total debt, carrying amount	699.2	248.7
Less: Amounts due within one year		
Senior debt	2.5	2.5
Other debt	0.4	0.2
Total long-term debt, carrying amount	$696.3	$246.0

As of November 30, 2013, the earlier of the Company's contractual debt principal maturities or the next debt redemption date that could be exercised at the option of the debt holder, are summarized by fiscal year as follows:

(In millions)	Total	2014	2015	2016	2017	2021
Term loan	$ 45.0	$2.5	$ 2.5	$40.0	$—	$ —
4 1/16% debentures	193.2	—	193.2	—	—	—
7 1/8% notes	460.0	—	—	—	—	460.0
2 1/4% debentures	0.2	0.2	—	—	—	—
Other debt	0.8	0.2	0.2	0.3	0.1	—
Total debt	$699.2	$2.9	$195.9	$40.3	$0.1	$460.0

a. Senior Debt:

(In millions)	As of November 30, 2013	2012
Term loan, bearing interest at variable rates (rate of 3.67% as of November 30, 2013), payable in quarterly installments of $0.6 million plus interest, maturing in November 2016	$45.0	$47.5

Senior Credit Facility

On November 18, 2011, the Company entered into the senior credit facility (the "Senior Credit Facility") with the lenders identified therein and Wells Fargo Bank, National Association, as administrative agent, which replaced the Company's prior credit facility.

On May 30, 2012, the Company executed an amendment (the "First Amendment") to the Senior Credit Facility with the lenders identified therein, and Wells Fargo Bank, National Association, as administrative agent. The First Amendment, among other things, (1) provided for an incremental facility of up to $50.0 million through additional borrowings under the term loan facility and/or increases under the revolving credit facility, (2) provided greater flexibility with respect to the Company's ability to incur indebtedness to support permitted acquisitions, and (3) increased the aggregate limitation on sale leasebacks from $20.0 million to $30.0 million during the term of the Senior Credit Facility.

On August 16, 2012, the Company executed an amendment (the "Second Amendment") to the Senior Credit Facility with the lenders identified therein, and Wells Fargo Bank, National Association, as administrative agent. The Second Amendment, among other things, (1) allowed for the incurrence of up to $510 million of second lien indebtedness in connection with the Acquisition, and (2) provided for a committed delayed draw term loan facility of $50 million under which the Company was entitled to draw in connection with the Acquisition or up through August 9, 2013. This delayed draw term loan facility expired undrawn in August 2013.

On January 14, 2013, the Company, executed an amendment (the "Third Amendment") to the Senior Credit Facility with the lenders identified therein, and Wells Fargo Bank, National Association, as administrative agent. The Third Amendment, among other things, allowed for the 7 1/8% Notes to be secured by a first priority security interest in the escrow account into which the proceeds of the 7 1/8% Notes offering were deposited pending the consummation of the Acquisition.

In connection with the consummation of the Acquisition, GenCorp added Pratt & Whitney Rocketdyne, Inc. ("PWR"), Arde, Inc. ("Arde") and Arde-Barinco, Inc. ("Arde-Barinco") as subsidiary guarantors under its Senior Credit Facility pursuant to that certain Joinder Agreement, dated as of June 14, 2013, by and among PWR, Arde, Arde-Barinco, GenCorp and Wells Fargo Bank, National Association, as administrative agent. In connection with the consummation of the Acquisition, the name of PWR was changed to Aerojet Rocketdyne of DE, Inc. and the name of Aerojet-General Corporation, an existing subsidiary guarantor at the time of the Acquisition, was changed to Aerojet Rocketdyne, Inc.

The Senior Credit Facility, as amended, provides for credit of up to $250.0 million in aggregate principal amount of senior secured financing, consisting of:
- a 5-year $50.0 million term loan facility;
- a 5-year $150.0 million revolving credit facility; and
- an incremental uncommitted facility under which the Company is entitled to incur, subject to certain conditions, up to $50.0 million of additional borrowings under the term loan facility and/or increases under the revolving credit facility.

The revolving credit facility includes a $100.0 million sublimit for the issuance of letters of credit and a $5.0 million sublimit for swingline loans. The term loan facility amortizes in quarterly installments at a rate of 5.0% of the original principal amount per annum, with the balance due on the maturity date. Outstanding indebtedness under the Senior Credit Facility may be voluntarily prepaid at any time, in whole or in part, in general without premium or penalty (subject to customary breakage costs).

As of November 30, 2013, the Company had $58.1 million outstanding letters of credit under the $100.0 million subfacility for standby letters of credit and had $45.0 million outstanding under the term loan facility.

In general, borrowings under the Senior Credit Facility bear interest at a rate equal to LIBOR plus 350 basis points (subject to downward adjustment), or the base rate as it is defined in the credit agreement governing the Senior Credit Facility plus 250 basis points (subject to downward adjustment). In addition, the Company is charged a commitment fee of 50 basis points per annum on unused amounts of the revolving credit facility and 350 basis points per annum (subject to downward adjustment), along with a fronting fee of 25 basis points per annum, on the undrawn amount of all outstanding letters of credit.

Aerojet Rocketdyne, Aerojet Rocketdyne of DE, Inc., Arde and Arde-Barinco guarantee the payment obligations under the Senior Credit Facility. All obligations under the Senior Credit Facility are further secured by (i) all equity interests owned or held by the loan parties, including interests in the Company's Easton subsidiary and 66% of the voting stock (and 100% of the non-voting stock) of all present and future first-tier foreign subsidiaries of the loan parties; (ii) substantially all of the tangible and intangible personal property and assets of the loan parties; and (iii) certain real property owned by the loan parties located in Orange, Virginia and Redmond, Washington. Except for certain real property located in Canoga Park, California acquired in connection with the consummation of the Acquisition, the Company's real property located in California, including the real estate holdings of Easton, is excluded from collateralization under the Senior Credit Facility.

The Company is subject to certain limitations including the ability to incur additional debt, make certain investments and acquisitions, and make certain restricted payments, including stock repurchases and dividends. The Senior Credit Facility includes events of default usual and customary for facilities of this nature, the occurrence of which could lead to an acceleration of the Company's obligations thereunder. Additionally, the Senior Credit Facility includes certain financial covenants, including that the Company maintain (i) a maximum total leverage ratio, calculated net of cash up to a maximum of $100.0 million, of 4.25 to 1.00 through fiscal periods ending November 30, 2014 and 4.00 to 1.00 thereafter; and (ii) a minimum interest coverage ratio of 2.40 to 1.00.

Financial Covenant	Actual Ratios as of November 30, 2013	Required Ratios
Interest coverage ratio, as defined under the Senior Credit Facility	4.54 to 1.00	Not less than: 2.4 to 1.00
Leverage ratio, as defined under the Senior Credit Facility	2.86 to 1.00	Not greater than: 4.25 to 1.00

The Company was in compliance with its financial and non-financial covenants as of November 30, 2013.

Fair Value

RECOGNITION AND MEASUREMENT

1.98 FASB ASC 820 defines fair value, establishes a framework for measuring fair value, and requires certain disclosures about fair value measurements. *Fair value* is defined as an exit price (that is, a price that would be received to sell, versus acquire, an asset or transfer a liability in an orderly transaction between market participants at the measurement date). Further, fair value is a market-based measurement, not an entity-specific measurement. It establishes a fair value hierarchy that distinguishes between assumptions developed based on market data obtained from independent external sources and the reporting entity's own assumptions. Further, fair value measurement should consider adjustment for risk, such as the risk inherent in a valuation technique or its inputs.

1.99 "Pending Content" FASB ASC 820-10-35-10A provides that a fair value measurement of a nonfinancial asset takes into account a market participant's ability to generate economic benefits by using the asset in its highest and best use or by selling it to another market participant that would use the asset in its highest and best use. Pending Content FASB ASC 820-10-35-10B states that the highest and best use for a nonfinancial asset takes into account the use of the asset that is physically possible, legally permissible, and financial feasible. Pending Content FASB ASC 820-10-35-10E states that the highest and best use of a nonfinancial asset might provide maximum value to market participants through its use in combination with other assets as a group (as installed or otherwise configured for use) or in combination with other assets and liabilities. The highest and best use of a nonfinancial asset is determined from the perspective of market participants, even if the reporting entity intends a different use. Because the highest and best use of the asset is determined based on its use by market participants, the fair value measurement considers the assumptions that market participants would use in pricing the asset, whether using an in-use or an in-exchange valuation premise.

1.100 According to "Pending Content" paragraphs 16–16AA of FASB ASC 820-10-35, a fair value measurement of a financial or nonfinancial liability or an instrument classified in a reporting entity's shareholders' equity is transferred to a market participant at the measurement date. Even when there is no observable market to provide pricing information about the transfer of a liability or an instrument classified in a reporting entity's shareholders' equity, there might be an observable market for such items if they are held by other parties as assets. In all cases, a reporting entity shall maximize the use of relevant observable inputs and minimize the use of unobservable inputs to meet the objective of a fair value measurement. A reporting entity is permitted, as a practical expedient, to estimate the fair value of an investment within the scope of paragraphs 4–5 of FASB ASC 820-10-15 using the net asset value per share (or its equivalent) of the investment if the net asset value per share or its equivalent is calculated in a manner consistent with the measurement principles of FASB ASC 946, *Financial Services—Investment Companies*, as of the reporting entity's measurement date.

DISCLOSURE

1.101 For assets and liabilities measured at fair value, whether on a recurring or nonrecurring basis, FASB ASC 820-10-50 specifies the required disclosures concerning the inputs used to measure fair value. "Pending Content" FASB ASC 820-10-50–1 explains that the reporting entity should disclose information that enables users of its financial statements to assess the following: (*a*) for assets and liabilities measured at fair value on a recurring basis in periods subsequent to initial recognition or measured on a nonrecurring basis in periods subsequent to initial recognition, the valuation techniques and inputs used to develop those measurements; and (*b*) for recurring fair value measurements using significant unobservable inputs (Level 3), the effect of the measurements on earnings for the period.

PRESENTATION AND DISCLOSURE EXCERPT

FAIR VALUE MEASUREMENTS

1.102 AMERICAN INTERNATIONAL GROUP, INC. (DEC)
NOTES TO CONSOLIDATED FINANCIAL STATEMENTS

5. Fair Value Measurements

Fair Value Measurements on a Recurring Basis

We carry certain of our financial instruments at fair value. We define the fair value of a financial instrument as the amount that would be received from the sale of an asset or paid to transfer a liability in an orderly transaction between market participants at the measurement date. We are responsible for the determination of the value of the investments carried at fair value and the supporting methodologies and assumptions.

The degree of judgment used in measuring the fair value of financial instruments generally inversely correlates with the level of observable valuation inputs. We maximize the use of observable inputs and minimize the use of unobservable inputs when measuring fair value. Financial instruments with quoted prices in active markets generally have more pricing observability and less judgment is used in measuring fair value. Conversely, financial instruments for which no quoted prices are available have less observability and are measured at fair value using valuation models or other pricing techniques that require more judgment. Pricing observability is affected by a number of factors, including the type of financial instrument, whether the financial instrument is new to the market and not yet established, the characteristics specific to the transaction, liquidity and general market conditions.

Fair Value Hierarchy

Assets and liabilities recorded at fair value in the Consolidated Balance Sheets are measured and classified in accordance with a fair value hierarchy consisting of three "levels" based on the observability of inputs available in the marketplace used to measure the fair values as discussed below:

- **Level 1:** Fair value measurements that are based on quoted prices (unadjusted) in active markets that we have the ability to access for identical assets or liabilities. Market price data generally is obtained from exchange or dealer markets. We do not adjust the quoted price for such instruments.
- **Level 2:** Fair value measurements based on inputs other than quoted prices included in Level 1 that are observable for the asset or liability, either directly or indirectly. Level 2 inputs include quoted prices for similar assets and liabilities in active markets, quoted prices for identical or similar assets or liabilities in markets that are not active, and inputs other than quoted prices that are observable for the asset or liability, such as interest rates and yield curves that are observable at commonly quoted intervals.
- **Level 3:** Fair value measurements based on valuation techniques that use significant inputs that are unobservable. Both observable and unobservable inputs may be used to determine the fair values of positions classified in Level 3. The circumstances for using these measurements include those in which there is little, if any, market activity for the asset or liability. Therefore, we must make certain assumptions about the inputs a hypothetical market participant would use to value that asset or liability. In certain cases, the inputs used to measure fair value may fall into different levels of the fair value hierarchy. In such cases, the level in the fair value hierarchy within which the fair value measurement in its entirety falls is determined based on the lowest level input that is significant to the fair value measurement in its entirety.

The following is a description of the valuation methodologies used for instruments carried at fair value. These methodologies are applied to assets and liabilities across the levels discussed above, and it is the observability of the inputs used that determines the appropriate level in the fair value hierarchy for the respective asset or liability.

Valuation Methodologies of Financial Instruments Measured at Fair Value

Incorporation of Credit Risk in Fair Value Measurements

- **Our Own Credit Risk.** Fair value measurements for certain liabilities incorporate our own credit risk by determining the explicit cost for each counterparty to protect against its net credit exposure to us at the balance sheet date by reference to observable AIG CDS or cash bond spreads. A derivative counterparty's net credit exposure to us is determined based on master netting agreements, when applicable, which take into consideration all derivative positions with us, as well as collateral we post with the counterparty at the balance sheet date. We calculate the effect of these credit spread changes using discounted cash flow techniques that incorporate current market interest rates.
- **Counterparty Credit Risk.** Fair value measurements for freestanding derivatives incorporate counterparty credit by determining the explicit cost for us to protect against our net credit exposure to each counterparty at the balance sheet date by reference to observable counterparty CDS spreads, when available. When not available, other directly or indirectly observable credit spreads will be used to derive the best estimates of the counterparty spreads. Our net credit exposure to a counterparty is determined based on master netting agreements, which take into consideration all derivative positions with the counterparty, as well as collateral posted by the counterparty at the balance sheet date.

Fair values for fixed maturity securities based on observable market prices for identical or similar instruments implicitly incorporate counterparty credit risk. Fair values for fixed maturity securities based on internal models incorporate counterparty credit risk by using discount rates that take into consideration cash issuance spreads for similar instruments or other observable information.

The cost of credit protection is determined under a discounted present value approach considering the market levels for single name CDS spreads for each specific counterparty, the mid market value of the net exposure (reflecting the amount of protection required) and the weighted average life of the net exposure. CDS spreads are provided to us by an independent third party. We utilize an interest rate based on the benchmark London Interbank Offered Rate (LIBOR) curve to derive our discount rates.

While this approach does not explicitly consider all potential future behavior of the derivative transactions or potential future changes in valuation inputs, we believe this approach provides a reasonable estimate of the fair value of the assets and liabilities, including consideration of the impact of non-performance risk.

Fixed Maturity Securities

Whenever available, we obtain quoted prices in active markets for identical assets at the balance sheet date to measure fixed maturity securities at fair value. Market price data is generally obtained from dealer markets.

We employ independent third-party valuation service providers to gather, analyze, and interpret market information to derive fair value estimates for individual investments, based upon market-accepted methodologies and assumptions. The methodologies used by these independent third-party valuation services are reviewed and understood by management, through periodic discussion with and information provided by the valuation services. In addition, as discussed further below, control processes are applied to the fair values received from third-party valuation services to ensure the accuracy of these values.

Valuation service providers typically obtain data about market transactions and other key valuation model inputs from multiple sources and, through the use of market-accepted valuation methodologies, which may utilize matrix pricing, financial models, accompanying model inputs and various assumptions, provide a single fair value measurement for individual securities. The inputs used by the valuation service providers include, but are not limited to, market prices from completed transactions for identical securities and transactions for comparable securities, benchmark yields, interest rate yield curves, credit spreads, currency rates, quoted prices for similar securities and other market-observable information, as applicable. If fair value is determined using financial models, these models generally take into account, among other things, market observable information as of the measurement date as well as the specific attributes of the security being valued, including its term, interest rate, credit rating, industry sector, and when applicable, collateral quality and other security or issuer-specific information. When market transactions or other market observable data is limited, the extent to which judgment is applied in determining fair value is greatly increased.

We have control processes designed to ensure that the fair values received from third party valuation services are accurately recorded, that their data inputs and valuation techniques are appropriate and consistently applied and that the assumptions used appear reasonable and consistent with the objective of determining fair value. We assess the reasonableness of individual security values received from valuation service providers through various analytical techniques, and have procedures to escalate related questions internally and to the third party valuation services for resolution. To assess the degree of pricing consensus among various valuation services for specific asset types, we have conducted comparisons of prices received from available sources. We have used these comparisons to establish a hierarchy for the fair values received from third party valuation services to be used for particular security classes. We also validate prices for selected securities through reviews by members of management who have relevant expertise and who are independent of those charged with executing investing transactions.

When our third-party valuation service providers are unable to obtain sufficient market observable information upon which to estimate the fair value for a particular security, fair value is determined either by requesting brokers who are knowledgeable about these securities to provide a price quote, which is generally non-binding, or by employing market accepted valuation models. Broker prices may be based on an income approach, which converts expected future cash flows to a single present value amount, with specific consideration of inputs relevant to particular security types. For structured securities, such inputs may include ratings, collateral types, geographic concentrations, underlying loan vintages, loan delinquencies and defaults, prepayments, and weighted average coupons and maturities. When the volume or level of market activity for a security is limited, certain inputs used to determine fair value may not be observable in the market. Broker prices may also be based on a market approach that considers recent transactions involving identical or similar securities. Fair values provided by brokers are subject to similar control processes to those noted above for fair values from third party valuation services, including management reviews. For those corporate debt instruments (for example, private placements) that are not traded in active markets or that are subject to transfer restrictions, valuations are adjusted to reflect illiquidity and non-transferability, and such adjustments generally are based on available market evidence. When observable price quotations are not available, fair value is determined based on discounted cash flow models using discount rates based on credit spreads, yields or price levels of comparable securities, adjusted for illiquidity and structure. Fair values determined internally are also subject to management review to ensure that valuation models and related inputs are reasonable.

The methodology above is relevant for all fixed maturity securities including residential mortgage backed securities (RMBS), commercial mortgage backed securities (CMBS), collateralized debt obligations (CDO), other asset-backed securities (ABS) and fixed maturity securities issued by government sponsored entities and corporate entities.

Equity Securities Traded in Active Markets

Whenever available, we obtain quoted prices in active markets for identical assets at the balance sheet date to measure equity securities at fair value. Market price data is generally obtained from exchange or dealer markets.

Mortgage and Other Loans Receivable

We estimate the fair value of mortgage and other loans receivable that are measured at fair value by using dealer quotations, discounted cash flow analyses and/or internal valuation models. The determination of fair value considers inputs such as interest rate, maturity, the borrower's creditworthiness, collateral, subordination, guarantees, past-due status, yield curves, credit curves, prepayment rates, market pricing for comparable loans and other relevant factors.

Other Invested Assets

We initially estimate the fair value of investments in certain hedge funds, private equity funds and other investment partnerships by reference to the transaction price. Subsequently, we generally obtain the fair value of these investments from net asset value information provided by the general partner or manager of the investments, the financial statements of which are generally audited annually. We consider observable market data and perform certain control procedures to validate the appropriateness of using the net asset value as a fair value measurement. The fair values of other investments carried at fair value, such as direct private equity holdings, are initially determined based on transaction price and are subsequently estimated based on available evidence such as market transactions in similar instruments, other financing transactions of the issuer and other available financial information for the issuer, with adjustments made to reflect illiquidity as appropriate.

Short-term Investments

For short-term investments that are measured at fair value, the carrying values of these assets approximate fair values because of the relatively short period of time between origination and expected realization, and their limited exposure to credit risk. Securities purchased under agreements to resell (reverse repurchase agreements) are generally treated as collateralized receivables. We report certain receivables arising from securities purchased under agreements to resell as Short-term investments in the Consolidated Balance Sheets. We use market-observable interest rates for receivables measured at fair value. This methodology considers such factors as the coupon rate and yield curves.

Separate Account Assets

Separate account assets are composed primarily of registered and unregistered open-end mutual funds that generally trade daily and are measured at fair value in the manner discussed above for equity securities traded in active markets.

Freestanding Derivatives

Derivative assets and liabilities can be exchange-traded or traded over-the-counter (OTC). We generally value exchange-traded derivatives such as futures and options using quoted prices in active markets for identical derivatives at the balance sheet date.

OTC derivatives are valued using market transactions and other market evidence whenever possible, including market-based inputs to models, model calibration to market clearing transactions, broker or dealer quotations or alternative pricing sources with reasonable levels of price transparency. When models are used, the selection of a particular model to value an OTC derivative depends on the contractual terms of, and specific risks inherent in the instrument, as well as the availability of pricing information in the market. We generally use similar models to value similar instruments. Valuation models require a variety of inputs, including contractual terms, market prices and rates, yield curves, credit curves, measures of volatility, prepayment rates and correlations of such inputs. For OTC derivatives that trade in liquid markets, such as generic forwards, swaps and options, model inputs can generally be corroborated by observable market data by correlation or other means, and model selection does not involve significant management judgment.

For certain OTC derivatives that trade in less liquid markets, where we generally do not have corroborating market evidence to support significant model inputs and cannot verify the model to market transactions, the transaction price may provide the best estimate of fair value. Accordingly, when a pricing model is used to value such an instrument, the model is adjusted so the model value at inception equals the transaction price. We will update valuation inputs in these models only when corroborated by evidence such as similar market transactions, third party pricing services and/or broker or dealer quotations, or other empirical market data. When appropriate, valuations are adjusted for various factors such as liquidity, bid/offer spreads and credit considerations. Such adjustments are generally based on available market evidence. In the absence of such evidence, management's best estimate is used.

Embedded Policy Derivatives

Certain variable annuity and equity-indexed annuity and life contracts contain embedded policy derivatives that we bifurcate from the host contracts and account for separately at fair value, with changes in fair value recognized in earnings. We have concluded these contracts contain (i) written option guarantees on minimum accumulation value, (ii) a series of written options that guarantee withdrawals from the highest anniversary value within a specific period or for life, or (iii) equity-indexed written options that meet the criteria of derivatives that must be bifurcated.

The fair value of embedded policy derivatives contained in certain variable annuity and equity-indexed annuity and life contracts is measured based on actuarial and capital market assumptions related to projected cash flows over the expected lives of the contracts. These cash flow estimates primarily include benefits and related fees assessed, when applicable, and incorporate expectations about policyholder behavior. Estimates of future policyholder behavior are subjective and based primarily on our historical experience.

With respect to embedded policy derivatives in our variable annuity contracts, because of the dynamic and complex nature of the expected cash flows, risk neutral valuations are used. Estimating the underlying cash flows for these products involves judgments regarding expected market rates of return, market volatility, correlations of market index returns to funds, fund performance, discount rates and policyholder behavior. With respect to embedded policy derivatives in our equity-indexed annuity and life contracts, option pricing models are used to estimate fair value, taking into account assumptions for future equity index growth rates, volatility of the equity index, future interest rates, and determinations on adjusting the participation rate and the cap on equity-indexed credited rates in light of market conditions and policyholder behavior assumptions. These methodologies incorporate an explicit risk margin to take into consideration market participant estimates of projected cash flows and policyholder behavior.

We also incorporate our own risk of non-performance in the valuation of the embedded policy derivatives associated with variable annuity and equity-indexed annuity and life contracts. Historically, the expected cash flows were discounted using the interest rate swap curve (swap curve), which is commonly viewed as being consistent with the credit spreads for highly-rated financial institutions (S&P AA-rated or above). A swap curve shows the fixed-rate leg of a non-complex swap against the floating rate (for example, LIBOR) leg of a related tenor. The swap curve was adjusted, as necessary, for anomalies between the swap curve and the U.S. Treasury yield curve.

Super Senior Credit Default Swap Portfolio

We value CDS transactions written on the super senior risk layers of designated pools of debt securities or loans using internal valuation models, third-party price estimates and market indices. The principal market was determined to be the market in which super senior credit default swaps of this type and size would be transacted, or have been transacted, with the greatest volume or level of activity. We have determined that the principal market participants, therefore, would consist of other large financial institutions who participate in sophisticated over-the-counter derivatives markets. The specific valuation methodologies vary based on the nature of the referenced obligations and availability of market prices.

The valuation of the super senior credit derivatives is complex because of the limited availability of market observable information due to the lack of trading and price transparency in certain structured finance markets. These market conditions have increased the reliance on management estimates and judgments in arriving at an estimate of fair value for financial reporting purposes. Further, disparities in the valuation methodologies employed by market participants and the varying judgments reached by such participants when assessing volatile markets have increased the likelihood that the various parties to these instruments may arrive at significantly different estimates as to their fair values.

Our valuation methodologies for the super senior credit default swap portfolio have evolved over time in response to market conditions and the availability of market observable information. We have sought to calibrate the methodologies to available market information and to review the assumptions of the methodologies on a regular basis.

Multi-sector CDO portfolios: We use a modified version of the Binomial Expansion Technique (BET) model to value our credit default swap portfolio written on super senior tranches of multi-sector CDOs of ABS. The BET model was developed in 1996 by a major rating agency to generate expected loss estimates for CDO tranches and derive a credit rating for those tranches, and remains widely used.

We have adapted the BET model to estimate the price of the super senior risk layer or tranche of the CDO. We modified the BET model to imply default probabilities from market prices for the underlying securities and not from rating agency assumptions. To generate the estimate, the model uses the price estimates for the securities comprising the portfolio of a CDO as an input and converts those estimates to credit spreads over current LIBOR-based interest rates. These credit spreads are used to determine implied probabilities of default and expected losses on the underlying securities. This data is then aggregated and used to estimate the expected cash flows of the super senior tranche of the CDO.

Prices for the individual securities held by a CDO are obtained in most cases from the CDO collateral managers, to the extent available. CDO collateral managers provided market prices for 46 percent and 59 percent of the underlying securities used in the valuation at December 31, 2013 and 2012. When a price for an individual security is not provided by a CDO collateral manager, we derive the price through a pricing matrix using prices from CDO collateral managers for similar securities. Matrix pricing is a mathematical technique used principally to value debt securities without relying exclusively on quoted prices for the specific securities, but rather by relying on the relationship of the security to other benchmark quoted securities. Substantially all of the CDO collateral managers who provided prices used dealer prices for all or part of the underlying securities, in some cases supplemented by third-party pricing services.

The BET model also uses diversity scores, weighted average lives, recovery rates and discount rates. We employ a Monte Carlo simulation to assist in quantifying the effect on the valuation of the CDO of the unique aspects of the CDO's structure such as triggers that divert cash flows to the most senior part of the capital structure. The Monte Carlo simulation is used to determine whether an underlying security defaults in a given simulation scenario and, if it does, the security's implied random default time and expected loss. This information is used to project cash flow streams and to determine the expected losses of the portfolio.

In addition to calculating an estimate of the fair value of the super senior CDO security referenced in the credit default swaps using our internal model, we also consider the price estimates for the super senior CDO securities provided by third parties, including counterparties to these transactions, to validate the results of the model and to determine the best available estimate of fair value. In determining the fair value of the super senior CDO security referenced in the credit default swaps, we use a consistent process that considers all available pricing data points and eliminates the use of outlying data points. When pricing data points are within a reasonable range an averaging technique is applied.

Corporate debt/Collateralized loan obligation (CLO) portfolios: For credit default swaps written on portfolios of investment-grade corporate debt, we use a mathematical model that produces results that are closely aligned with prices received from third parties. This methodology uses the current market credit spreads of the names in the portfolios along with the base correlations implied by the current market prices of comparable tranches of the relevant market traded credit indices as inputs.

We estimate the fair value of our obligations resulting from credit default swaps written on CLOs to be equivalent to the par value less the current market value of the referenced obligation. Accordingly, the value is determined by obtaining third-party quotations on the underlying super senior tranches referenced under the credit default swap contract.

Policyholder Contract Deposits

Policyholder contract deposits accounted for at fair value are measured using an earnings approach by taking into consideration the following factors:
- Current policyholder account values and related surrender charges;
- The present value of estimated future cash inflows (policy fees) and outflows (benefits and maintenance expenses) associated with the product using risk neutral valuations, incorporating expectations about policyholder behavior, market returns and other factors; and
- A risk margin that market participants would require for a market return and the uncertainty inherent in the model inputs.

The change in fair value of these policyholder contract deposits is recorded as Policyholder benefits and claims incurred in the Consolidated Statements of Income.

Long-Term Debt

The fair value of non-structured liabilities is generally determined by using market prices from exchange or dealer markets, when available, or discounting expected cash flows using the appropriate discount rate for the applicable maturity. We determine the fair value of structured liabilities and hybrid financial instruments (where performance is linked to structured interest rates, inflation or currency risks) using the appropriate derivative valuation methodology (described above) given the nature of the embedded risk profile. In addition, adjustments are made to the valuations of both non-structured and structured liabilities to reflect our own creditworthiness based on the methodology described under the caption "Incorporation of Credit Risk in Fair Value Measurements—Our Own Credit Risk" above.

Borrowings under obligations of guaranteed investment agreements (GIAs), which are guaranteed by us, are recorded at fair value using discounted cash flow calculations based on interest rates currently being offered for similar contracts and our current market observable implicit credit spread rates with maturities consistent with those remaining for the contracts being valued. Obligations may be called at various times prior to maturity at the option of the counterparty. Interest rates on these borrowings are primarily fixed, vary by maturity and range up to 9.8 percent.

Other Liabilities

Other liabilities measured at fair value include certain securities sold under agreements to repurchase and certain securities sold but not yet purchased. Liabilities arising from securities sold under agreements to repurchase are generally treated as collateralized borrowings. We estimate the fair value of liabilities arising under these agreements by using market-observable interest rates. This methodology considers such factors as the coupon rate, yield curves and other relevant factors. Fair values for securities sold but not yet purchased are based on current market prices.

Assets and Liabilities Measured at Fair Value on a Recurring Basis

The following table presents information about assets and liabilities measured at fair value on a recurring basis and indicates the level of the fair value measurement based on the observability of the inputs used:

(In millions)	Level 1	Level 2	Level 3	Counterparty Netting[a]	Cash Collateral[b]	Total
December 31, 2013						
Assets:						
Bonds available for sale:						
U.S. government and government sponsored entities	$ 133	$ 3,062	$ —	$ —	$ —	$ 3,195
Obligations of states, municipalities and political subdivisions	—	28,300	1,080	—	—	29,380
Non-U.S. governments	508	21,985	16	—	—	22,509
Corporate debt	—	143,297	1,255	—	—	144,552
RMBS	—	21,207	14,941	—	—	36,148
CMBS	—	5,747	5,735	—	—	11,482
CDO/ABS	—	4,034	6,974	—	—	11,008
Total bonds available for sale	641	227,632	30,001	—	—	258,274
Other bond securities:						
U.S. government and government sponsored entities	78	5,645	—	—	—	5,723
Obligations of states, municipalities and political subdivisions	—	121	—	—	—	121
Non-U.S. governments	—	2	—	—	—	2
Corporate debt	—	1,169	—	—	—	1,169
RMBS	—	1,326	937	—	—	2,263
CMBS	—	509	844	—	—	1,353
CDO/ABS	—	3,158	8,834	—	—	11,992
Total other bond securities	78	11,930	10,615	—	—	22,623
Equity securities available for sale:						
Common stock	3,218	—	1	—	—	3,219
Preferred stock	—	27	—	—	—	27
Mutual funds	408	2	—	—	—	410
Total equity securities available for sale	3,626	29	1	—	—	3,656
Other equity securities	750	84	—	—	—	834
Mortgage and other loans receivable	—	—	—	—	—	—
Other invested assets	1	2,667	5,930	—	—	8,598
Derivative assets:						
Interest rate contracts	14	3,716	41	—	—	3,771
Foreign exchange contracts	—	52	—	—	—	52
Equity contracts	151	106	49	—	—	306
Commodity contracts	—	—	1	—	—	1
Credit contracts	—	—	55	—	—	55
Other contracts	—	1	33	—	—	34
Counterparty netting and cash collateral	—	—	—	(1,734)	(820)	(2,554)
Total derivative assets	165	3,875	179	(1,734)	(820)	1,665
Short-term investments	332	5,981	—	—	—	6,313
Separate account assets	67,708	3,351	—	—	—	71,059
Other assets	—	418	—	—	—	418
Total	$73,301	$255,967	$46,726	$(1,734)	$ (820)	$373,440
Liabilities:						
Policyholder contract deposits	$ —	$ 72	$ 312	$ —	$ —	$ 384
Derivative liabilities:						
Interest rate contracts	—	3,661	141	—	—	3,802
Foreign exchange contracts	—	319	—	—	—	319
Equity contracts	—	101	—	—	—	101
Commodity contracts	—	5	—	—	—	5
Credit contracts	—	—	1,335	—	—	1,335
Other contracts	—	25	142	—	—	167
Counterparty netting and cash collateral	—	—	—	(1,734)	(1,484)	(3,218)
Total derivative liabilities	—	4,111	1,618	(1,734)	(1,484)	2,511
Long-term debt	—	6,377	370	—	—	6,747
Other liabilities	42	891	—	—	—	933
Total	$ 42	$ 11,451	$ 2,300	$(1,734)	$(1,484)	$ 10,575

(In millions)	Level 1	Level 2	Level 3	Counterparty Netting[a]	Cash Collateral[b]	Total
December 31, 2012						
Assets:						
Bonds available for sale:						
U.S. government and government sponsored entities	$ —	$ 3,483	$ —	$ —	$ —	$ 3,483
Obligations of states, municipalities and political subdivisions	—	34,681	1,024	—	—	35,705
Non-U.S. governments	1,004	25,782	14	—	—	26,800
Corporate debt	—	149,625	1,487	—	—	151,112
RMBS	—	22,730	11,662	—	—	34,392
CMBS	—	5,010	4,905	—	—	9,915
CDO/ABS	—	3,492	5,060	—	—	8,552
Total bonds available for sale	1,004	244,803	24,152	—	—	269,959
Other bond securities:						
U.S. government and government sponsored entities	266	6,528	—	—	—	6,794
Non-U.S. governments	—	2	—	—	—	2
Corporate debt	—	1,320	—	—	—	1,320
RMBS	—	1,331	396	—	—	1,727
CMBS	—	1,424	803	—	—	2,227
CDO/ABS	—	3,969	8,545	—	—	12,514
Total other bond securities	266	14,574	9,744	—	—	24,584
Equity securities available for sale:						
Common stock	3,002	3	24	—	—	3,029
Preferred stock	—	34	44	—	—	78
Mutual funds	83	22	—	—	—	105
Total equity securities available for sale	3,085	59	68	—	—	3,212
Other equity securities	578	84	—	—	—	662
Mortgage and other loans receivable	—	134	—	—	—	134
Other invested assets	125	1,542	5,389	—	—	7,056
Derivative assets:						
Interest rate contracts	2	5,521	956	—	—	6,479
Foreign exchange contracts	—	104	—	—	—	104
Equity contracts	104	63	54	—	—	221
Commodity contracts	—	144	1	—	—	145
Credit contracts	—	—	60	—	—	60
Other contracts	—	—	38	—	—	38
Counterparty netting and cash collateral	—	—	—	(2,467)	(909)	(3,376)
Total derivative assets	106	5,832	1,109	(2,467)	(909)	3,671
Short-term investments	285	7,771	—	—	—	8,056
Separate account assets	54,430	2,907	—	—	—	57,337
Other assets	—	696	—	—	—	696
Total	$59,879	$278,402	$40,462	$(2,467)	$ (909)	$375,367
Liabilities:						
Policyholder contract deposits	$ —	$ —	$ 1,257	$ —	$ —	$ 1,257
Derivative liabilities:						
Interest rate contracts	—	5,582	224	—	—	5,806
Foreign exchange contracts	—	174	—	—	—	174
Equity contracts	—	114	7	—	—	121
Commodity contracts	—	146	—	—	—	146
Credit contracts	—	—	2,051	—	—	2,051
Other contracts	—	6	200	—	—	206
Counterparty netting and cash collateral	—	—	—	(2,467)	(1,976)	(4,443)
Total derivative liabilities	—	6,022	2,482	(2,467)	(1,976)	4,061
Long-term debt	—	7,711	344	—	—	8,055
Other liabilities	30	1,050	—	—	—	1,080
Total	$ 30	$ 14,783	$ 4,083	$(2,467)	$(1,976)	$ 14,453

[a] Represents netting of derivative exposures covered by qualifying master netting agreements.

[b] Represents cash collateral posted and received. Securities collateral posted for derivative transactions that is reflected in Fixed maturity securities in the Consolidated Balance Sheet, and collateral received, not reflected in the Consolidated Balance Sheet, was $1.3 billion and $120 million, respectively, at December 31, 2013 and $1.9 billion and $299 million, respectively, at December 31, 2012.

Transfers of Level 1 and Level 2 Assets and Liabilities

Our policy is to record transfers of assets and liabilities between Level 1 and Level 2 at their fair values as of the end of each reporting period, consistent with the date of the determination of fair value. Assets are transferred out of Level 1 when they are no longer transacted with sufficient frequency and volume in an active market. Conversely, assets are transferred from Level 2 to Level 1 when transaction volume and frequency are indicative of an active market. During the years ended December 31, 2013 and 2012, we transferred $944 million and $464 million, respectively, of securities issued by Non-U.S. government entities from Level 1 to Level 2, because they are no longer considered actively traded. For similar reasons, during the years ended December 31, 2013 and 2012, we transferred $356 million and $888 million, respectively, of securities issued by the U.S. government and government-sponsored entities from Level 1 to Level 2. We had no material transfers from Level 2 to Level 1 during the years ended December 31, 2013 and 2012.

Changes in Level 3 Recurring Fair Value Measurements

The following tables present changes during the years ended December 31, 2013 and 2012 in Level 3 assets and liabilities measured at fair value on a recurring basis, and the realized and unrealized gains (losses) related to the Level 3 assets and liabilities in the Consolidated Balance Sheets at December 31, 2013 and 2012:

(In millions)	Fair Value Beginning of Year[a]	Net Realized and Unrealized Gains (Losses) Included in Income	Other Comprehensive Income (Loss)	Purchases, Sales, Issues and Settlements, Net	Gross Transfers In	Gross Transfers Out	Fair Value End of Year	Changes in Unrealized Gains (Losses) Included in Income on Instruments Held at End of Year
December 31, 2013								
Assets:								
Bonds available for sale:								
Obligations of states, municipalities and political subdivisions	$ 1,024	$ 29	$(175)	$ 403	$ —	$ (201)	$ 1,080	$ —
Non-U.S. governments	14	—	(1)	3	1	(1)	16	—
Corporate debt	1,487	8	(19)	(176)	450	(495)	1,255	—
RMBS	11,662	867	466	1,818	186	(58)	14,941	—
CMBS	5,124	24	100	375	161	(49)	5,735	—
CDO/ABS	4,841	161	9	1,946	901	(884)	6,974	—
Total bonds available for sale	24,152	1,089	380	4,369	1,699	(1,688)	30,001	—
Other bond securities:								
RMBS	396	66	—	208	267	—	937	(2)
CMBS	812	67	—	(200)	279	(114)	844	29
CDO/ABS	8,536	1,527	—	(2,044)	843	(28)	8,834	681
Total other bond securities	9,744	1,660	—	(2,036)	1,389	(142)	10,615	708
Equity securities available for sale:								
Common stock	24	7	(8)	(22)	—	—	1	—
Preferred stock	44	—	3	(47)	—	—	—	—
Total equity securities available for sale	68	7	(5)	(69)	—	—	1	—
Other invested assets	5,389	208	237	64	344	(312)	5,930	—
Total	$39,353	$2,964	$ 612	$2,328	$3,432	$(2,142)	$46,547	$708
Liabilities:								
Policyholder contract deposits	$ (1,257)	$ 744	$ (1)	$ 202	$ —	$ —	$ (312)	$104
Derivative liabilities, net:								
Interest rate contracts	732	19	—	(851)	—	—	(100)	35
Equity contracts	47	74	—	(20)	1	(53)	49	30
Commodity contracts	1	—	—	—	—	—	1	(1)
Credit contracts	(1,991)	567	—	144	—	—	(1,280)	711
Other contracts	(162)	42	15	(2)	(2)	—	(109)	7
Total derivative liabilities, net	(1,373)	702	15	(729)	(1)	(53)	(1,439)	782
Long-term debt	(344)	(137)	—	38	(2)	75	(370)	(30)
Total	$ (2,974)	$1,309	$ 14	$ (489)	$ (3)	$ 22	$ (2,121)	$856

(continued)

(In millions)	Fair Value Beginning of Year[a]	Net Realized and Unrealized Gains (Losses) Included in Income	Other Comprehensive Income (Loss)	Purchases, Sales, Issues and Settlements, Net	Gross Transfers In	Gross Transfers Out	Fair Value End of Year	Changes in Unrealized Gains (Losses) Included in Income on Instruments Held at End of Year
December 31, 2012								
Assets:								
Bonds available for sale:								
Obligations of states, municipalities and political subdivisions	$ 960	$ 48	$ 12	$ 84	$ 70	$ (150)	$ 1,024	$ —
Non-U.S. governments	9	1	(1)	1	4	—	14	—
Corporate debt	1,935	(44)	145	24	664	(1,237)	1,487	—
RMBS	10,877	522	2,121	(316)	952	(2,494)	11,662	—
CMBS	3,955	(135)	786	636	44	(162)	5,124	—
CDO/ABS	4,220	334	289	10	691	(703)	4,841	—
Total bonds available for sale	21,956	726	3,352	439	2,425	(4,746)	24,152	—
Other bond securities:								
Corporate debt	7	—	—	(7)	—	—	—	—
RMBS	303	76	2	(109)	128	(4)	396	42
CMBS	554	70	2	(159)	446	(101)	812	87
CDO/ABS	8,432	3,683	3	(3,968)	386	—	8,536	2,547
Total other bond securities	9,296	3,829	7	(4,243)	960	(105)	9,744	2,676
Equity securities available for sale:								
Common stock	57	22	(28)	(33)	6	—	24	—
Preferred stock	99	17	(35)	(36)	11	(12)	44	—
Total equity securities available for sale	156	39	(63)	(69)	17	(12)	68	—
Mortgage and other loans receivable	1	—	—	(1)	—	—	—	—
Other invested assets	6,618	(95)	290	(257)	1,204	(2,371)	5,389	—
Total	$38,027	$4,499	$3,586	$(4,131)	$4,606	$(7,234)	$39,353	$2,676
Liabilities:								
Policyholder contract deposits	$ (918)	$ (275)	$ (72)	$ 8	$ —	$ —	$ (1,257)	$ (276)
Derivative liabilities, net:								
Interest rate contracts	785	(11)	—	(42)	—	—	732	(56)
Foreign exchange contracts	2	—	—	(2)	—	—	—	—
Equity contracts	28	10	—	12	(3)	—	47	10
Commodity contracts	2	5	—	(6)	—	—	1	6
Credit contracts	(3,273)	638	—	644	—	—	(1,991)	1,172
Other contracts	33	(76)	(18)	15	(116)	—	(162)	(46)
Total derivatives liabilities, net	(2,423)	566	(18)	621	(119)	—	(1,373)	1,086
Long-term debt	(508)	(411)	(77)	242	(14)	424	(344)	(105)
Total	$ (3,849)	$ (120)	$ (167)	$ 871	$ (133)	$ 424	$ (2,974)	$ 705

*Total Level 3 derivative exposures have been netted in these tables for presentation purposes only.

Net realized and unrealized gains and losses included in income related to Level 3 assets and liabilities shown above are reported in the Consolidated Statements of Income as follows:

(In millions)	Net Investment Income	Net Realized Capital Gains (Losses)	Other Income	Total
December 31, 2013				
Bonds available for sale	$ 997	$ (17)	$ 109	$1,089
Other bond securities	187	9	1,464	1,660
Equity securities available for sale	—	7	—	7
Other invested assets	210	(42)	40	208
Policyholder contract deposits	—	744	—	744
Derivative liabilities, net	39	43	620	702
Long-term debt	—	—	(137)	(137)
December 31, 2012				
Bonds available for sale	$ 906	$(395)	$ 215	$ 726
Other bond securities	3,303	—	526	3,829
Equity securities available for sale	—	39	—	39
Other invested assets	54	(210)	61	(95)
Policyholder contract deposits	—	(275)	—	(275)
Derivative liabilities, net	3	26	537	566
Long-term debt	—	—	(411)	(411)

The following table presents the gross components of purchases, sales, issues and settlements, net, shown above:

(In millions)	Purchases	Sales	Settlements	Purchases, Sales, Issues and Settlements, Net [a]
December 31, 2013				
Assets:				
Bonds available for sale:				
Obligations of states, municipalities and political subdivisions	$ 541	$ (138)	$ —	$ 403
Non-U.S. governments	9	—	(6)	3
Corporate debt	487	(114)	(549)	(176)
RMBS	4,424	(266)	(2,340)	1,818
CMBS	1,023	(188)	(460)	375
CDO/ABS	2,662	(159)	(557)	1,946
Total bonds available for sale	9,146	(865)	(3,912)	4,369
Other bond securities:				
RMBS	350	(12)	(130)	208
CMBS	24	(71)	(153)	(200)
CDO/ABS	353	(72)	(2,325)	(2,044)
Total other bond securities	727	(155)	(2,608)	(2,036)
Equity securities available for sale	58	(12)	(115)	(69)
Other invested assets	882	(9)	(809)	64
Total assets	$10,813	$(1,041)	$ (7,444)	$ 2,328
Liabilities:				
Policyholder contract deposits	$ —	$ (26)	$ 228	$ 202
Derivative liabilities, net	10	(1)	(738)	(729)
Long-term debt[c]	—	—	38	38
Total liabilities	$ 10	$ (27)	$ (472)	$ (489)
December 31, 2012				
Assets:				
Bonds available for sale:				
Obligations of states, municipalities and political subdivisions	$ 477	$ (219)	$ (174)	$ 84
Non-U.S. governments	5	(3)	(1)	1
Corporate debt	283	(75)	(184)	24
RMBS	2,308	(723)	(1,901)	(316)
CMBS	1,137	(318)	(183)	636
CDO/ABS	1,120	(4)	(1,106)	10
Total bonds available for sale	5,330	(1,342)	(3,549)	439
Other bond securities:				
Corporate debt	—	—	(7)	(7)
RMBS	—	(45)	(64)	(109)
CMBS	225	(106)	(278)	(159)
CDO/ABS[b]	7,382	(21)	(11,329)	(3,968)
Total other bond securities	7,607	(172)	(11,678)	(4,243)
Equity securities available for sale	67	(56)	(80)	(69)
Mortgage and other loans receivable	—	—	(1)	(1)
Other invested assets	900	(100)	(1,057)	(257)
Total assets	$13,904	$(1,670)	$(16,365)	$(4,131)
Liabilities:				
Policyholder contract deposits	$ —	$ (25)	$ 33	$ 8
Derivative liabilities, net	11	(2)	612	621
Long-term debt[c]	—	—	242	242
Total liabilities	$ 11	$ (27)	$ 887	$ 871

[a] There were no issuances during year ended December 31, 2013 and 2012.

[b] Includes $7.1 billion of securities purchased through the FRBNY's auction of ML III assets.

[c] Includes GIAs, notes, bonds, loans and mortgages payable.

Both observable and unobservable inputs may be used to determine the fair values of positions classified in Level 3 in the tables above. As a result, the unrealized gains (losses) on instruments held at December 31, 2013 and 2012 may include changes in fair value that were attributable to both observable (e.g., changes in market interest rates) and unobservable (e.g., changes in unobservable long-dated volatilities) inputs.

Transfers of Level 3 Assets and Liabilities

We record transfers of assets and liabilities into or out of Level 3 at their fair values as of the end of each reporting period, consistent with the date of the determination of fair value. As a result, the Net realized and unrealized gains (losses) included in income or other comprehensive income and as shown in the table above excludes $15 million and $143 million of net losses related to assets and liabilities transferred into

Level 3 during 2013 and 2012, respectively, and includes $44 million and $92 million of net gains related to assets and liabilities transferred out of Level 3 during 2013 and 2012, respectively.

Transfers of Level 3 Assets

During the years ended December 31, 2013 and 2012, transfers into Level 3 assets primarily included certain investments in private placement corporate debt, RMBS, CMBS, CDO, ABS, and investments in hedge funds and private equity funds.

- The transfer of investments in RMBS, CMBS and CDO and certain ABS into Level 3 assets were due to decreases in market transparency and liquidity for individual security types.
- Transfers of private placement corporate debt and certain ABS into Level 3 assets were primarily the result of limited market pricing information that required us to determine fair value for these securities based on inputs that are adjusted to better reflect our own assumptions regarding the characteristics of a specific security or associated market liquidity.
- Certain investments in hedge funds were transferred into Level 3 as a result of limited market activity due to fund-imposed redemption restrictions.
- Certain private equity fund investments were transferred into Level 3 due to these investments being carried at fair value and no longer being accounted for using the equity method of accounting.

Assets are transferred out of Level 3 when circumstances change such that significant inputs can be corroborated with market observable data. This may be due to a significant increase in market activity for the asset, a specific event, one or more significant input(s) becoming observable or a long-term interest rate significant to a valuation becoming short-term and thus observable. In addition, transfers out of Level 3 assets also occur when investments are no longer carried at fair value as the result of a change in the applicable accounting methodology, given changes in the nature and extent of our ownership interest.

During the years ended December 31, 2013 and 2012, transfers out of Level 3 assets primarily related to certain investments in municipal securities, private placement corporate debt, RMBS, CMBS, CDO/ABS, and investments in hedge funds and private equity funds.

- Transfers of certain investments in municipal securities, RMBS, CMBS, CDO and certain ABS out of Level 3 assets were based on consideration of market liquidity as well as related transparency of pricing and associated observable inputs for these investments.
- Transfers of private placement corporate debt and certain ABS out of Level 3 assets were primarily the result of using observable pricing information that reflects the fair value of those securities without the need for adjustment based on our own assumptions regarding the characteristics of a specific security or the current liquidity in the market.
- The removal or easing of fund-imposed redemption restrictions, as well as certain fund investments becoming subject to the equity method of accounting resulted in the transfer of certain hedge fund and private equity fund investments out of Level 3 assets.

Transfers of Level 3 Liabilities

There were no significant transfers of derivative or other liabilities into or out of Level 3 for the year ended December 31, 2013.

Because we present carrying values of our derivative positions on a net basis in the table above, transfers into Level 3 liabilities for the year ended December 31, 2012 primarily related to certain derivative assets transferred out of Level 3 because of the presence of observable inputs on certain forward commitments and options. During the year ended December 31, 2012, certain notes payable were transferred out of Level 3 liabilities because input parameters for the pricing of these liabilities became more observable as a result of market movements and portfolio aging. There were no significant transfers of derivative liabilities out of Level 3 for the year ended December 31, 2012.

We use various hedging techniques to manage risks associated with certain positions, including those classified within Level 3. Such techniques may include the purchase or sale of financial instruments that are classified within Level 1 and/or Level 2. As a result, the realized and unrealized gains (losses) for assets and liabilities classified within Level 3 presented in the table above do not reflect the related realized or unrealized gains (losses) on hedging instruments that are classified within Level 1 and/or Level 2.

Quantitative Information about Level 3 Fair Value Measurements

The table below presents information about the significant unobservable inputs used for recurring fair value measurements for certain Level 3 instruments, and includes only those instruments for which information about the inputs is reasonably available to us, such as data from third-party valuation service providers and from internal valuation models. Because input information from third-parties with respect to certain Level 3 instruments (primarily CDO/ABS) may not be reasonably available to us, balances shown below may not equal total amounts reported for such Level 3 assets and liabilities:

(In millions)	Fair Value at December 31, 2013	Valuation Technique	Unobservable Input[a]	Range (Weighted Average)[a]
Assets:				
Corporate debt	$788	Discounted cash flow	Yield [b]	0.00%–14.29% (6.64%)
RMBS	14,419	Discounted cash flow	Constant prepayment rate [c]	0.00%–10.35% (4.97%)
			Loss severity [c]	42.60%–79.07% (60.84%)
			Constant default rate [c]	3.98%–12.22% (8.10%)
			Yield [c]	2.54%–7.40% (4.97%)
Certain CDO/ABS	5,414	Discounted cash flow	Constant prepayment rate [c]	5.20%–10.80% (8.20%)
			Loss severity [c]	48.60%–63.40% (56.40%)
			Constant default rate [c]	3.20%–16.20% (9.00%)
			Yield [c]	5.20%–11.50% (9.40%)
CMBS	5,847	Discounted cash flow	Yield [b]	0.00%–14.69% (5.58%)
CDO/ABS—Direct Investment Book	557	Binomial Expansion Technique (BET)	Recovery rate [b]	6.00%–63.00% (25.00%)
			Diversity score [b]	5–35 (12)
			Weighted average life [b]	1.07–9.47 years (4.86 years)
Liabilities:				
Policyholder contract deposits—GMWB	312	Discounted cash flow	Equity implied volatility [b]	6.00%–39.00%
			Base lapse rate [b]	1.00%–40.00%
			Dynamic lapse rate [b]	0.20%–60.00%
			Mortality rate [b]	0.50%–40.00%
			Utilization rate [b]	0.50%–25.00%
Derivative Liabilities—Credit contracts	996	BET	Recovery rate [b]	5.00%–34.00% (17.00%)
			Diversity score [b]	9–32 (13)
			Weighted average life [b]	4.50–9.47 years (5.63 years)

(In millions)	Fair Value at December 31, 2012	Valuation Technique	Unobservable Input[a]	Range (Weighted Average)[a]
Assets:				
Corporate debt	$ 775	Discounted cash flow	Yield [b]	0.08%–6.55% (3.31%)
RMBS	10,650	Discounted cash flow	Constant prepayment rate [c]	0.00%–10.76% (5.03%)
			Loss severity [c]	43.70%–78.72% (61.21%)
			Constant default rate [c]	4.21%–13.30% (8.75%)
			Yield [c]	2.23%–9.42% (5.82%)
Certain CDO/ABS [d]	7,844	Discounted cash flow	Constant prepayment rate [c]	0.00%–32.25% (11.82%)
			Loss severity [c]	0.00%–29.38% (6.36%)
			Constant default rate [c]	0.00%–4.05% (1.18%)
			Yield [c]	5.41%–10.67% (8.04%)
CMBS	3,251	Discounted cash flow	Yield [b]	0.00%–19.95% (7.76%)
CDO/ABS—Direct Investment Book	1,205	Binomial Expansion Technique (BET)	Recovery rate [b]	3.00%–63.00% (27.00%)
			Diversity score [b]	4–44 (13)
			Weighted average life [b]	1.27–9.11 years (4.91 years)
Liabilities:				
Policyholder contract deposits—GMWB	1,257	Discounted cash flow	Equity implied volatility [b]	6.00%–39.00%
			Base lapse rate [b]	1.00%–40.00%
			Dynamic lapse rate [b]	0.20%–60.00%
			Mortality rate [b]	0.50%–40.00%
			Utilization rate [b]	0.50%–25.00%
Derivative Liabilities—Credit contracts	1,436	BET	Recovery rate [b]	3.00%–37.00% (17.00%)
			Diversity score [b]	9–38 (14)
			Weighted average life [b]	5.10–8.45 years (5.75 years)

[a] The unobservable inputs and ranges for the constant prepayment rate, loss severity and constant default rate relate to each of the individual underlying mortgage loans that comprise the entire portfolio of securities in the RMBS and CDO securitization vehicles and not necessarily to the securitization vehicle bonds (tranches) purchased by us. The ranges of these inputs do not directly correlate to changes in the fair values of the tranches purchased by us because there are other factors relevant to the fair values of specific tranches owned by us including, but not limited to, purchase price, position in the waterfall, senior versus subordinated position and attachment points.

[b] Represents discount rates, estimates and assumptions that we believe would be used by market participants when valuing these assets and liabilities.

[c] Information received from third-party valuation service providers.

[d] Yield was the only input available for $6.6 billion of total fair value at December 31, 2012.

The ranges of reported inputs for Corporate debt, RMBS, CDO/ABS, and CMBS valued using a discounted cash flow technique consist of plus/minus one standard deviation in either direction from the value-weighted average. The preceding table does not give effect to our risk management practices that might offset risks inherent in these investments.

Sensitivity to Changes in Unobservable Inputs

We consider unobservable inputs to be those for which market data is not available and that are developed using the best information available to us about the assumptions that market participants would use when pricing the asset or liability. Relevant inputs vary depending on the nature of the instrument being measured at fair value. The following is a general description of sensitivities of significant unobservable inputs along with interrelationships between and among the significant unobservable inputs and their impact on the fair value measurements. The effect of a change in a particular assumption in the sensitivity analysis below is considered independently of changes in any other assumptions. In practice, simultaneous changes in assumptions may not always have a linear effect on the inputs discussed below. Interrelationships may also exist between observable and unobservable inputs. Such relationships have not been included in the discussion below. For each of the individual relationships described below, the inverse relationship would also generally apply.

Corporate Debt

Corporate debt securities included in Level 3 are primarily private placement issuances that are not traded in active markets or that are subject to transfer restrictions. Fair value measurements consider illiquidity and non-transferability. When observable price quotations are not available, fair value is determined based on discounted cash flow models using discount rates based on credit spreads, yields or price levels of publicly-traded debt of the issuer or other comparable securities, considering illiquidity and structure. The significant unobservable input used in the fair value measurement of corporate debt is the yield. The yield is affected by the market movements in credit spreads and U.S. Treasury yields. In addition, the migration in credit quality of a given security generally has a corresponding effect on the fair value measurement of the security. For example, a downward migration of credit quality would increase spreads. Holding U.S. Treasury rates constant, an increase in corporate credit spreads would decrease the fair value of corporate debt.

RMBS and Certain CDO/ABS

The significant unobservable inputs used in fair value measurements of RMBS and certain CDO/ABS valued by third-party valuation service providers are constant prepayment rates (CPR), loss severity, constant default rates (CDR), and yield. A change in the assumptions used for the probability of default will generally be accompanied by a corresponding change in the assumption used for the loss severity and an inverse change in the assumption used for prepayment rates. In general, increases in CPR, loss severity, CDR, and yield, in isolation, would result in a decrease in the fair value measurement. Changes in fair value based on variations in assumptions generally cannot be extrapolated because the relationship between the directional change of each input is not usually linear.

CMBS

The significant unobservable input used in fair value measurements for CMBS is the yield. Prepayment assumptions for each mortgage pool are factored into the yield. CMBS generally feature a lower degree of prepayment risk than RMBS because commercial mortgages generally contain a penalty for prepayment. In general, increases in the yield would decrease the fair value of CMBS.

CDO/ABS—Direct Investment book

The significant unobservable inputs used for certain CDO/ABS securities valued using the BET are recovery rates, diversity score, and the weighted average life of the portfolio. An increase in recovery rates and diversity score will increase the fair value of the portfolio. An increase in the weighted average life will decrease the fair value.

Policyholder contract deposits

Embedded derivatives within Policyholder contract deposits relate to guaranteed minimum withdrawal benefits (GMWB) within variable annuity products and certain enhancements to interest crediting rates based on market indices within equity-indexed annuities and guaranteed investment contracts (GICs). GMWB represents our largest exposure of these embedded derivatives, although the carrying value of the liability fluctuates based on the performance of the equity markets and therefore, at a point in time, can be low relative to the exposure. The principal unobservable input used for GMWBs and embedded derivatives in equity-indexed annuities measured at fair value is equity implied volatility. For GMWBs, other significant unobservable inputs include base and dynamic lapse rates, mortality rates, and utilization rates. Lapse, mortality, and utilization rates may vary significantly depending upon age groups and duration. In general, increases in volatility and utilization rates will increase the fair value of the liability associated with GMWB, while increases in lapse rates and mortality rates will decrease the fair value of the liability. Significant unobservable inputs used in valuing embedded derivatives within GICs include long-term forward interest rates and foreign exchange rates. Generally, the embedded derivative liability for GICs will increase as interest rates decrease or if the U.S. dollar weakens compared to the euro.

Derivative liabilities—credit contracts

The significant unobservable inputs used for Derivatives liabilities—credit contracts are recovery rates, diversity scores, and the weighted average life of the portfolio. AIG non-performance risk is also considered in the measurement of the liability.

An increase in recovery rates and diversity score will decrease the fair value of the liability. An increase in the weighted average life will increase the fair value measurement of the liability.

Investments in Certain Entities Carried at Fair Value Using Net Asset Value per Share

The following table includes information related to our investments in certain other invested assets, including private equity funds, hedge funds and other alternative investments that calculate net asset value per share (or its equivalent). For these investments, which are measured at fair value on a recurring basis, we use the net asset value per share as a practical expedient to measure fair value.

(In millions) **Investment Category**	**Investment Category Includes**	December 31, 2013		December 31, 2012	
		Fair Value Using Net Asset Value Per Share (or its equivalent)	**Unfunded Commitments**	**Fair Value Using Net Asset Value Per Share (or its equivalent)**	**Unfunded Commitments**
Private equity funds:					
Leveraged buyout	Debt and/or equity investments made as part of a transaction in which assets of mature companies are acquired from the current shareholders, typically with the use of financial leverage	$2,544	$578	$2,529	$669
Real Estate/ Infrastructure	Investments in real estate properties and infrastructure positions, including power plants and other energy generating facilities	346	86	251	52
Venture capital	Early-stage, high-potential, growth companies expected to generate a return through an eventual realization event, such as an initial public offering or sale of the company	140	13	157	16
Distressed	Securities of companies that are in default, under bankruptcy protection, or troubled	183	34	184	36
Other	Includes multi-strategy and mezzanine strategies	134	238	112	100
Total private equity funds		3,347	949	3,233	873
Hedge funds:					
Event-driven	Securities of companies undergoing material structural changes, including mergers, acquisitions and other reorganizations	976	2	788	2
Long-short	Securities that the manager believes are undervalued, with corresponding short positions to hedge market risk	1,759	11	1,318	—
Macro	Investments that take long and short positions in financial instruments based on a top-down view of certain economic and capital market conditions	612	—	320	—
Distressed	Securities of companies that are in default, under bankruptcy protection or troubled	594	15	316	—
Emerging markets	Investments in the financial markets of developing countries	287	—	—	—
Other	Includes multi-strategy and relative value strategies	157	—	66	—
Total hedge funds		4,385	28	2,808	2
Total		$7,732	$977	$6,041	$875

Private equity fund investments included above are not redeemable, as distributions from the funds will be received when underlying investments of the funds are liquidated. Private equity funds are generally expected to have 10-year lives at their inception, but these lives may be extended at the fund manager's discretion, typically in one or two-year increments. At December 31, 2013, assuming average original expected lives of 10 years for the funds, 62 percent of the total fair value using net asset value per share (or its equivalent) presented above would have expected remaining lives of three years or less, 34 percent between four and six years and 4 percent between seven and 10 years.

The hedge fund investments included above are generally redeemable monthly (14 percent), quarterly (44 percent), semi-annually (22 percent) and annually (20 percent), with redemption notices ranging from one day to 180 days. At December 31, 2013, however, investments representing approximately 57 percent of the total fair value of the hedge fund investments cannot be redeemed, either in whole or in part, because the investments include various contractual restrictions. The majority of these contractual restrictions, which may have been put in place at the fund's inception or thereafter, have pre-defined end dates and are generally expected to be lifted by the end of 2015. The fund investments for which redemption is restricted only in part generally relate to certain hedge funds that hold at least one investment that the fund manager deems to be illiquid.

Fair Value Option

Under the fair value option, we may elect to measure at fair value financial assets and financial liabilities that are not otherwise required to be carried at fair value. Subsequent changes in fair value for designated items are reported in earnings. We elect the fair value option for certain hybrid securities given the complexity of bifurcating the economic components associated with the embedded derivatives. Refer to Note 11 for additional information related to embedded derivatives.

Additionally, beginning in the third quarter of 2012 we elected the fair value option for investments in certain private equity funds, hedge funds and other alternative investments when such investments are eligible for this election. We believe this measurement basis is consistent with the applicable accounting guidance used by the respective investment company funds themselves. Refer to Note 6 herein for additional information.

The following table presents the gains or losses recorded related to the eligible instruments for which we elected the fair value option:

	Gain (Loss)		
Years Ended December 31, (In millions)	2013	2012	2011
Assets:			
Mortgage and other loans receivable	$ 3	$ 47	$ 11
Bond and equity securities	1,667	2,339	1,273
Other securities—ML II interest	—	246	42
Other securities—ML III interest	—	2,888	(646)
Retained interest in AIA	—	2,069	1,289
Alternative investments[a]	360	36	2
Other, including Short-term investments	11	20	33
Liabilities:			
Long-term debt [b]	327	(681)	(966)
Other liabilities	(15)	(33)	(67)
Total gain	$2,353	$6,931	$ 971

[a] Includes certain hedge funds, private equity funds and other investment partnerships.
[b] Includes GIAs, notes, bonds and mortgage payable.

Interest income and dividend income on assets measured under the fair value option are recognized and included in Net investment income in the Consolidated Statements of Income with the exception of activity within AIG's Other Operations, which is included in Other income. Interest on liabilities measured under the fair value option is recognized in interest expense in the Consolidated Statements of Income. See Note 6 herein for additional information about our policies for recognition, measurement, and disclosure of interest and dividend income and interest expense.

During 2013, 2012 and 2011, we recognized losses of $54 million, losses of $641 million and gains of $420 million, respectively, attributable to the observable effect of changes in credit spreads on our own liabilities for which the fair value option was elected. We calculate the effect of these credit spread changes using discounted cash flow techniques that incorporate current market interest rates, our observable credit spreads on these liabilities and other factors that mitigate the risk of nonperformance such as cash collateral posted.

The following table presents the difference between fair values and the aggregate contractual principal amounts of mortgage and other loans receivable and long-term borrowings for which the fair value option was elected:

	December 31, 2013			December 31, 2012		
(In millions)	Fair Value	Outstanding Principal Amount	Difference	Fair Value	Outstanding Principal Amount	Difference
Assets:						
Mortgage and other loans receivable	$ —	$ —	$ —	$ 134	$ 141	$ (7)
Liabilities:						
Long-term debt*	$6,747	$5,231	$1,516	$8,055	$5,705	$2,350

* Includes GIAs, notes, bonds, loans and mortgages payable.

There were no mortgage or other loans receivable for which the fair value option was elected that were 90 days or more past due or in non-accrual status at December 31, 2013 and 2012.

Fair Value Measurements on A Non-Recurring Basis

We measure the fair value of certain assets on a non-recurring basis, generally quarterly, annually or when events or changes in circumstances indicate that the carrying amount of the assets may not be recoverable. These assets include cost and equity-method investments, investments in life settlements, collateral securing foreclosed loans and real estate and other fixed assets, goodwill and other intangible assets. See Note 6 herein for additional information about how we test various asset classes for impairment.

The following table presents assets measured at fair value on a non-recurring basis at the time of impairment and the related impairment charges recorded during the periods presented:

(In millions)	Assets at Fair Value Non-Recurring Basis				Impairment Charges December 31,		
	Level 1	Level 2	Level 3	Total	2013	2012	2011
December 31, 2013							
Investment real estate	$—	$—	$ —	$ —	$ —	$—	$ 18
Other investments	—	—	1,615	1,615	112	151	327
Investments in life settlements	—	—	896	896	971	309	312
Other assets	—	11	48	59	31	11	3
Total	$—	$ 11	$2,559	$2,570	$1,114	$471	$660
December 31, 2012							
Other investments	$—	$—	$1,930	$1,930			
Investments in life settlements	—	—	120	120			
Other assets	—	3	18	21			
Total	$—	$ 3	$2,068	$2,071			

Fair Value Information about Financial Instruments Not Measured At Fair Value

Information regarding the estimation of fair value for financial instruments not carried at fair value (excluding insurance contracts and lease contracts) is discussed below:

- **Mortgage and other loans receivable:** Fair values of loans on real estate and other loans receivable were estimated for disclosure purposes using discounted cash flow calculations based on discount rates that we believe market participants would use in determining the price that they would pay for such assets. For certain loans, our current incremental lending rates for similar types of loans are used as the discount rates, because we believe this rate approximates the rates market participants would use. The fair values of policy loans are generally estimated based on unpaid principal amount as of each reporting date or, in some cases, based on the present value of the loans using a discounted cash flow model. No consideration is given to credit risk because policy loans are effectively collateralized by the cash surrender value of the policies.
- **Other invested assets:** The majority of Other invested assets that are not measured at fair value represent investments in life settlements. The fair value of investments in life settlements is determined using a discounted cash flow methodology that incorporates best available market assumptions for longevity as well as market yields based on reported transactions. Due to the individual life nature of each investment in life settlements and the illiquidity of the existing market, significant inputs to the fair value are unobservable.
- **Cash and short-term investments:** The carrying values of these assets approximate fair values because of the relatively short period of time between origination and expected realization, and their limited exposure to credit risk.
- **Policyholder contract deposits associated with investment-type contracts:** Fair values for policyholder contract deposits associated with investment-type contracts not accounted for at fair value were estimated using discounted cash flow calculations based on interest rates currently being offered for similar contracts with maturities consistent with those of the contracts being valued. When no similar contracts are being offered, the discount rate is the appropriate swap rate (if available) or current risk-free interest rate consistent with the currency in which the cash flows are denominated.
- **Other liabilities:** The majority of Other liabilities that are financial instruments not measured at fair value represent secured financing arrangements, including repurchase agreements. The carrying values of these liabilities approximate fair value, because the financing arrangements are short-term and are secured by cash or other liquid collateral.
- **Long-term debt:** Fair values of these obligations were determined by reference to quoted market prices, when available and appropriate, or discounted cash flow calculations based upon our current market-observable implicit-credit-spread rates for similar types of borrowings with maturities consistent with those remaining for the debt being valued.

The following table presents the carrying values and estimated fair values of our financial instruments not measured at fair value and indicates the level in the fair value hierarchy of the estimated fair value measurement based on the observability of the inputs used:

(In millions)	Estimated Fair Value				Carrying Value
	Level 1	Level 2	Level 3	Total	
December 31, 2013					
Assets:					
Mortgage and other loans receivable	$ —	$ 219	$ 21,418	$ 21,637	$ 20,765
Other invested assets	—	529	2,705	3,234	4,194
Short-term investments	—	15,304	—	15,304	15,304
Cash	2,241	—	—	2,241	2,241
Liabilities:					
Policyholder contract deposits associated with investment-type contracts	—	199	114,361	114,560	105,093
Other liabilities	—	4,869	1	4,870	4,869
Long-term debt	—	36,239	2,394	38,633	34,946
December 31, 2012					
Assets:					
Mortgage and other loans receivable	$ —	$ 823	$ 19,396	$ 20,219	$ 19,348
Other invested assets	—	237	3,521	3,758	4,932
Short-term investments	—	20,752	—	20,752	20,752
Cash	1,151	—	—	1,151	1,151
Liabilities:					
Policyholder contract deposits associated with investment-type contracts	—	245	123,860	124,105	105,979
Other liabilities	—	3,981	818	4,799	4,800
Long-term debt	—	43,966	1,925	45,891	40,445

Subsequent Events

RECOGNITION AND MEASUREMENT

1.103 The FASB ASC glossary defines *subsequent events* as events or transactions that occur subsequent to the balance sheet date but before financial statements are issued or are available to be issued. FASB ASC 855, *Subsequent Events,* includes general guidance applicable to all entities on accounting for, and disclosure of, events after the reporting period (subsequent events) that are not addressed specifically in other topics within FASB ASC. The following are the two types of subsequent events: the first type existed at the balance sheet date and includes the estimates inherent in the process of preparing financial statements (recognized subsequent events); the second type did not exist at the balance sheet date but arose subsequent to that date (nonrecognized subsequent events). The first type of subsequent event should be recognized in the entity's financial statements.

1.104 FASB ASC 855-10-25-1 requires an entity to recognize the effects of events that provide evidence of conditions that existed at the balance sheet date, including accounting estimates. FASB ASC 855-10-25-1A indicates that an SEC filer or a conduit bond obligor for conduit debt securities that are traded in a public market (a domestic or foreign stock exchange or an over-the-counter market, including local or regional markets) should evaluate subsequent events through the date the financial statements are issued. In addition, FASB ASC 855-10-25-2 requires all other entities that do not meet the criteria outlined in FASB ASC 855-10-25-1A to evaluate such events through the date the financial statements are available to be issued. As defined in the FASB ASC glossary, financial statements are considered available to be issued when they are complete in a form and format that complies with GAAP and all approvals necessary for issuance have been obtained, for example, from management, the board of directors, and all significant shareholders.

1.105 FASB ASC 855-10-25-3 prohibits an entity from recognizing subsequent events that provide evidence about conditions that did not exist at the date of the balance sheet but which arose after that date but before the financial statements are issued or are available to be issued.

1.106 FASB ASC 855-10-25-4 also addresses the potential for reissue of the financial statements in reports filed with regulatory agencies. In this circumstance, an entity should not recognize events occurring between the time the financial statements were originally issued or were available to be issued and the time the financial statements were reissued, unless U.S. GAAP or regulatory requirements require the adjustment. Similarly, an entity should not recognize events or transactions occurring after the financial statements were issued or were available to be issued in financial statements that are later reissued in comparative form along with financial statements of subsequent periods, unless the adjustment meets the criteria previously stated.

DISCLOSURE

1.107 FASB ASC 855-10-50-3 requires an entity to consider supplementing the historical financial statements with pro forma financial data when an unrecognized subsequent event occurs. An entity should present pro forma financial data when an unrecognized subsequent event is sufficiently significant that pro forma information provides the best disclosure. In preparing pro forma data, an entity should include the event as if it had occurred on the balance sheet date. An entity should also consider presenting pro forma statements, usually a statement of financial position only, in columnar form on the face of the historical statements.

1.108 Paragraphs 1 and 4 of FASB ASC 855-10-50 state that an entity, except an SEC registrant, should disclose the date through which subsequent events have been evaluated, as well as whether that date is the date the financial statements were issued or the date the financial statements were available to be issued. An entity, except an SEC registrant, should also disclose in the revised financial statements the date through which subsequent events have been evaluated in both the originally issued financial statements and the reissued financial statements.

PRESENTATION AND DISCLOSURE EXCERPTS

SALE OF BUSINESS

1.109 COACH, INC. (JUN)
NOTES TO CONSOLIDATED FINANCIAL STATEMENTS

(dollars and shares in thousands, except per share data)

19. Subsequent Events (in part)

Sale of Reed Krakoff Business

The Company announced that it has entered into a binding agreement (the "Purchase Agreement") to sell the Reed Krakoff business to Reed Krakoff Investments LLC ("the Buyer"), an investment group led by Mr. Krakoff. The Buyer will purchase the equity interests of the business and certain assets, including the Reed Krakoff brand name and related intellectual property rights from Coach. In consideration, the Buyer will assume certain liabilities of Coach, pay to Coach ten dollars in cash and issue to Coach an approximate 15% equity interest in the newly formed company. This equity interest is subject to adjustment under certain circumstances. Concurrent with the closing under the Purchase Agreement, the parties contemplate executing certain ancillary agreements, including under certain circumstances, a credit agreement whereby Coach will agree to loan Buyer up to $20 million for general corporate purposes for a term of two years.

The Purchase Agreement provides that the closing is subject to the satisfaction or waiver of certain conditions, including the accuracy of each party's representations and warranties at the closing, subject to materiality qualifiers, compliance in all material respects with each party's covenants under the Purchase Agreement, Buyer receiving additional equity financing, and other customary conditions. The Purchase Agreement is subject to termination under certain customary circumstances, including that both parties will have the right to terminate the Purchase Agreement if the closing has not occurred by August 31, 2013.

In connection with the Purchase Agreement and Mr. Krakoff's resignation from Coach, Mr. Krakoff agreed to waive his right to receive any compensation, salary, bonuses, equity vesting and certain other benefits if the closing occurs.

The sale is anticipated to close by the end of the first quarter 2014 and assuming the transaction closes, it is not expected to have a material impact on our first quarter results of operations.

LITIGATION

1.110 SEALED AIR CORPORATION (DEC)
CONSOLIDATED BALANCE SHEETS (in part)

(In millions, except share data)

	December 31,	
	2013	2012
Liabilities and Stockholders' Equity (in part)		
Current liabilities:		
Short-term borrowings	$ 81.6	$ 39.2
Current portion of long-term debt	201.5	1.8
Accounts payable	524.5	480.2
Deferred taxes	8.1	10.3
Settlement agreement and related accrued interest	925.1	876.9
Accrued restructuring costs	69.6	72.4
Liabilities held for sale	—	8.9
Other current liabilities	890.4	845.3
Total current liabilities	2,700.8	2,335.0

NOTES TO CONSOLIDATED FINANCIAL STATEMENTS

Note 18 Commitments and Contingencies (in part)

Cryovac Transaction Commitments and Contingencies (in part)

Settlement Agreement and Related Costs

On November 27, 2002, we reached an agreement in principle with the Committees appointed to represent asbestos claimants in the bankruptcy case of W. R. Grace & Co., known as Grace or WRG, to resolve all current and future asbestos-related claims made against the Company and our affiliates in connection with the Cryovac transaction described below (as memorialized by the parties in the Settlement agreement and as approved by the Bankruptcy Court, the "Settlement agreement"). The Settlement agreement provided for the resolution of the fraudulent transfer claims and successor liability claims, as well as indemnification claims by Fresenius Medical Care Holdings, Inc. and affiliated companies, in connection with the Cryovac transaction. On December 3, 2002, our Board of Directors approved the agreement in principle. We received notice that both of the Committees had approved the agreement in principle as of December 5, 2002. The parties subsequently signed the definitive Settlement agreement as of November 10, 2003 consistent with the terms of the agreement in principle. For a description of the Cryovac transaction, asbestos-related claims and the parties involved, see "Cryovac Transaction," "Discussion of Cryovac Transaction Commitments and Contingencies," "Fresenius Claims," "Canadian Claims" and "Additional Matters Related to the Cryovac Transaction" below.

We recorded a pre-tax charge of approximately $850 million as a result of the Settlement agreement on our consolidated statement of operations for the year ended December 31, 2002. The charge consisted of the following items:
- a charge of $513 million covering a cash payment that we were required to make under the Settlement agreement upon the effectiveness of an appropriate plan of reorganization in the Grace bankruptcy. Because we could not predict when a plan of reorganization would become effective, we recorded this liability as a current liability on our consolidated balance sheet at December 31, 2002. Under the terms of the Settlement agreement, this amount accrued interest at a 5.5% annual rate from December 21, 2002 to the date of payment. We recorded this interest in interest expense on our consolidated statements of operations and in Settlement agreement and related accrued interest on our consolidated balance sheets. The accrued interest, which was compounded annually, was $412 million at December 31, 2013 and $364 million at December 31, 2012.
- a non-cash charge of $322 million representing the fair market value at the date we recorded the charge of nine million shares of Sealed Air common stock would issue under the Settlement agreement upon the effectiveness of an appropriate plan of reorganization in the Grace bankruptcy, which was adjusted to eighteen million shares due to our two-for-one stock split in March 2007. These shares were subject to customary anti-dilution provisions that adjusted for the effects of stock splits, stock dividends and other events affecting our common stock. The fair market value of our common stock was $35.72 per pre-split share ($17.86 post-split) as of the close of business on December 5, 2002. We recorded this amount on our consolidated balance sheet at December 31, 2002 as follows: $0.9 million representing the aggregate par value of these shares of common stock reserved for issuance related to the Settlement agreement, and the remaining $321 million, representing the excess of the aggregate fair market value over the aggregate par value of these common shares, in additional paid-in capital.
- $16 million of legal and related fees as of December 31, 2002.

As discussed below, on February 3, 2014, the Company's subsidiary, Cryovac, Inc., made the payments contemplated by the Settlement agreement, consisting of aggregate cash payments in the amount of $929.7 million to the WRG Asbestos PI Trust and the WRG Asbestos PD Trust and the transfer of 18 million shares of Sealed Air common stock (the "Settlement Shares") to the PI Trust, in each case reflecting adjustments made in accordance with the Settlement agreement. In connection with the issuance of the Settlement Shares and their transfer to the PI Trust by Cryovac, the Company entered into a Registration Rights Agreement, dated as of February 3, 2014 (the "Registration Rights Agreement"), with the PI Trust as initial holder of the Settlement Shares. Under the Registration Rights Agreement, the Company will be required to use reasonable best efforts to prepare and file with the SEC a shelf registration statement covering resales of the Settlement Shares on or prior to 60 days after the Effective Date, and to use reasonable best efforts to cause such shelf registration statement to be declared effective by the SEC as soon as reasonably practicable.

Note 22 Subsequent Events (in part)

Settlement Agreement

On February 3, 2014, the remaining conditions to the effectiveness of the PI Settlement Plan and the Settlement agreement were satisfied or waived by the relevant parties and the PI Settlement Plan became effective with Grace emerging from bankruptcy (the "Effective Date"). Pursuant to the Settlement agreement and the PI Settlement Plan, on the Effective Date, Cryovac paid cash consideration, consisting of cash payments in the aggregate amount of $930 million, to the WRG Asbestos PI Trust and the WRG Asbestos PD Trust and transferred the Settlement Shares (described below) to the WRG Asbestos PI Trust, in each case reflecting adjustments made in accordance with the Settlement agreement. To fund the cash payment, we used $555 million of cash and cash equivalents and utilized borrowings of $260 million from our revolving credit facility and $115 million from our accounts receivable securitization programs.

In connection with the issuance of the Settlement Shares and their transfer to the WRG Asbestos PI Trust by Cryovac, the Company entered into a Registration Rights Agreement, dated as of February 3, 2014 (the "Registration Rights Agreement"), with the WRG Asbestos PI Trust as initial holder of the Settlement Shares. Under the Registration Rights Agreement, the Company will be required to use reasonable best efforts to prepare and file with the SEC a shelf registration statement covering resales of the Settlement Shares on or prior to 60 days after February 3, 2014, and to use reasonable best efforts to cause such shelf registration statement to be declared effective by the SEC as soon as reasonably practicable.

MERGER AGREEMENT

1.111 DELL INC. (JAN)
NOTES TO CONSOLIDATED FINANCIAL STATEMENTS

Note 18—Subsequent Event

Merger Agreement

On February 5, 2013, Dell announced that it had signed a definitive agreement and plan of merger (the "merger agreement") pursuant to which it will be acquired by Denali Holding Inc. ("Parent"), a Delaware corporation owned by Michael S. Dell, the Chairman, Chief Executive Officer and founder of Dell, and investment funds affiliated with Silver Lake Partners, a global private equity firm ("Silver Lake"). Following completion of the transaction, Mr. Dell will continue to lead Dell as Chairman and Chief Executive Officer and will maintain a significant equity investment in Dell by contributing his Dell shares to Parent and making a cash investment in Parent. Subject to the satisfaction or permitted waiver of closing conditions set forth in the merger agreement, the merger is expected to be consummated before the end of the second quarter of the fiscal year ending January 31, 2014.

At the effective time of the merger, each share of Dell's common stock issued and outstanding immediately before the effective time, other than certain excluded shares, will be converted into the right to receive $13.65 in cash, without interest (the "merger consideration"). Shares of common stock held by the Parent and its subsidiaries, shares held by Mr. Dell and certain of Mr. Dell's related parties (together with Mr. Dell, the "MD Investors"), and by Dell or any wholly-owned subsidiary of Dell will not be entitled to receive the merger consideration.

Dell's stockholders will be asked to vote on the adoption of the merger agreement and the merger at a special stockholders meeting that will be held on a date to be announced. The closing of the merger is subject to a non-waivable condition that the merger agreement be adopted by the affirmative vote of the holders of (1) at least a majority of all outstanding shares of common stock and (2) at least a majority of all outstanding shares of common stock held by stockholders other than Parent and its subsidiaries, the MD Investors, any other officers and directors of Dell or any other person having any equity interest in, or any right to acquire any equity interest in, Parent's merger subsidiary or any person of which the merger subsidiary is a direct or indirect subsidiary. Consummation of the merger is also subject to certain customary conditions. The merger agreement does not contain a financing condition.

The merger agreement places limitations on Dell's ability to engage in certain types of transactions without Parent's consent during the period between the signing of the merger agreement and the effective time of the merger. During this period, Dell may not repurchase shares of its common stock or declare dividends in excess of the quarterly rate of $0.08 per share authorized under its current dividend policy. In addition, with limited exceptions, Dell may not incur additional debt other than up to $1.8 billion under its existing commercial paper program, $2.0 billion under its revolving credit facilities, $1.5 billion under its structured financing debt facilities, and up to $25 million of additional indebtedness. Further, other than in transactions in the ordinary course of business or within specified dollar limits and certain other limited exceptions, Dell generally may not acquire other businesses, make investments in other persons, or sell, lease, or encumber its material assets.

Parent has obtained equity and debt financing commitments for the transactions contemplated by the merger agreement, the aggregate proceeds of which, together with the proceeds of a rollover investment of Dell shares in Parent by the MD Investors, an investment in subordinated securities and the available cash of Dell, will be sufficient for Parent to pay the aggregate merger consideration and all related fees and expenses. The commitment of financial institutions to provide debt financing for the transaction is subject to a number of customary conditions, including the execution and delivery by the borrowers and the guarantors of definitive documentation consistent with the debt commitment letter.

Pursuant to the terms of a "go-shop" provision in the merger agreement, during the period beginning on the date of the merger agreement and expiring after March 22, 2013, Dell and its subsidiaries and their respective representatives may initiate, solicit and encourage any alternative acquisition proposals from third parties, provide nonpublic information to such third parties and participate in discussions and negotiations with such third parties regarding alternative acquisition proposals. Under the terms and conditions set forth in the merger agreement, before the company stockholder approvals adopting the merger agreement, the Board of Directors may change its recommendation, including in order to approve, and may authorize Dell to enter into, an alternative acquisition proposal if the special committee of the Board of Directors that recommended approval of the merger has determined in good faith, after consultation with outside counsel and its financial advisors, that such alternative acquisition proposal would be more favorable to Dell's stockholders, taking into account all of the terms and conditions of such proposal (including, among other things, the financing, likelihood and timing of its consummation and any adjustments to the merger agreement).

The merger agreement contains certain termination rights for Dell and Parent. Among such rights, and subject to certain limitations, either Dell or Parent may terminate the merger agreement if the merger is not completed by November 5, 2013.

The terms of the merger agreement did not impact Dell's Consolidated Financial Statements as of and for the fiscal year ended February 1, 2013.

ACQUISITIONS

1.112 LOUISIANA-PACIFIC CORPORATION (DEC)
NOTES TO THE CONSOLIDATED FINANCIAL STATEMENTS

25. Proposed Acquisition of Ainsworth Lumber Co. Ltd.

In September of 2013 LP entered into an Arrangement Agreement (the "Arrangement") with Ainsworth Lumber Co. Ltd., a British Columbia corporation ("Ainsworth"), providing an arrangement under British Columbia law whereby a wholly owned subsidiary of the Company will acquire all of the outstanding shares of Ainsworth capital stock in exchange for 0.114 shares of LP common stock ("LP Shares") and C$1.94 in cash per Ainsworth common share ("Ainsworth Shares") subject to certain terms and conditions. Although the Arrangement provides for Ainsworth shareholders to elect among cash consideration, share consideration and mixed consideration, proration provisions will ensure that the aggregate amounts of cash and LP Shares issued in the Transaction are fixed at approximately C$467.0 million and 27.5 million LP Shares, respectively.

The requisite approvals of the Transaction by Ainsworth shareholders and the Supreme Court of British Columbia were obtained on October 29, 2013 and October 31, 2013, respectively. As of the date of this report, the consummation of the Transaction remained subject to other closing conditions, including the expiration or termination of the waiting period under the Hart-Scott-Rodino Antitrust Improvements Act of 1976 and the receipt of other regulatory approvals and clearances, including under the Canadian Competition Act and the Investment Act of Canada. LP and Ainsworth have agreed to endeavor to cause all closing conditions (including the receipt of regulatory approvals) to be satisfied, which under certain circumstances could require the taking of actions that could adversely affect the value of the Transaction to us.

On February 13, 2014, Ainsworth and LP announced that they have entered into timing agreements with each of the Canadian Competition Bureau (the "CCB") and the Antitrust Division of the U.S. Department of Justice (the "DOJ") pursuant to which Ainsworth and LP have agreed, subject to certain conditions, that they will not consummate LP's acquisition of Ainsworth before March 13, 2014 as the CCB and the DOJ continue their reviews.

As a consequence of the timing agreements described above, Ainsworth and LP also announced that they have agreed to extend the outside date for completion of the Arrangement from March 4, 2014 to April 18, 2014. The Arrangement permits either party to further extend the outside date for two additional 45 day periods if required to obtain certain regulatory approvals.

The closing of the Arrangement remains subject to a number of conditions, including the expiration or termination of the waiting period under the HSR Act and the receipt of other regulatory approvals and clearances including under the Canadian Competition Act. Subject to obtaining required regulatory approvals and clearances and the satisfaction or waiver of other closing conditions, it is now anticipated that the Arrangement will be completed before the end of the second quarter of 2014.

The Arrangement contains certain termination rights for each of LP and Ainsworth. Either party may terminate the Arrangement Agreement if: (i) the parties mutually agree; (ii) the Transaction has not been consummated by March 31, 2014 (subject to extension in certain circumstances); (iii) a governmental authority issues a law or order prohibiting the Transaction; (iv) the other party materially breaches its representations, warranties or covenants such that the applicable closing condition would not to be satisfied; or (v) the other party has incurred a Material Adverse Effect (as defined in the Arrangement Agreement).

LP expects to fund the purchase price payable in the Transaction and related fees and expenses through a combination of cash on hand at LP and Ainsworth and borrowings under our revolving credit facility. The obligations of the lenders to provide debt financing under the debt commitments are subject to customary conditions.

On October 17, 2013, Ainsworth issued a press release announcing that it had received the requisite consents in connection with its consent solicitation (the "Consent Solicitation") from holders of Ainsworth's 7.5% Senior Secured Notes due 2017 (the "Notes"). The press release also announced that Ainsworth has entered into a supplemental indenture relating to the Notes, which modified certain definitions in the indenture relating to the Notes (the "Indenture") so that the consummation of the Transaction pursuant to the Arrangement Agreement, and the designation by LP of members of Ainsworth's board of directors upon and after the consummation of the Transaction, will not constitute a "Change of Control" under the Indenture and Ainsworth will not be required to make a "Change of Control Offer" under the Indenture in connection with the Transaction. Subject to the satisfaction or waiver of the conditions set forth in the solicitation statement distributed by Ainsworth to holders of the Notes, LP will make the consent payments contemplated thereby as and when they become due. Promptly following the consummation of the Transaction, LP will unconditionally guarantee the prompt payment and performance of the obligations of Ainsworth under the Indenture and the Notes.

The Transaction is expected to have a material effect on LP's consolidated financial position, results of operations and cash flows. For additional information, see the Ainsworth Lumber Co. Ltd. Notice of Special Meeting and Management Proxy Circular furnished as Exhibit 99.1 to LP's Current Report on Form 8-K dated September 30, 2013.

Related Party Transactions

DISCLOSURE

1.113 FASB ASC 850, *Related Party Disclosures*, specifies the nature of information that should be disclosed in financial statements about related-party transactions and certain common control relationships. FASB ASC 850-10-50-1 requires an entity to disclose material related party transactions but exempts compensation arrangements, expense allowances, and other similar items in the ordinary course of business from disclosure requirements. However, Item 402, "Executive Compensation," of SEC Regulation S-K requires SEC registrants to provide compensation information outside the financial statements for specified members of management. The disclosures should include the nature of the relationship(s) involved, a description of the transactions, the dollar amounts of the transactions, and amounts due to or from related parties for each period for which the entity presents an income statement. FASB ASC 740-10-50-17 also includes guidance for entities with separately issued financial statements that are members of a consolidated tax return and the additional disclosures that are required. Further, if the reporting entity and one or more other companies are under common ownership or management control, and the existence of that control could result in operating results or a financial position of the reporting entity significantly different from those that would have been obtained if the companies were autonomous, FASB ASC 850-10-50-6 requires the nature of the control relationship to be disclosed even if there are no transactions between the entities.

PRESENTATION AND DISCLOSURE EXCERPTS

TRANSACTIONS WITH RELATED PARTIES

1.114 CABLEVISION SYSTEMS CORPORATION (DEC)
COMBINED NOTES TO CONSOLIDATED FINANCIAL STATEMENTS

(Dollars in thousands, except per share amounts)

Note 15. Related Party Transactions

Cablevision is controlled by Charles F. Dolan, certain members of his immediate family and certain family related entities (collectively the "Dolan Family"). Members of the Dolan Family are also the controlling stockholders of both AMC Networks and Madison Square Garden.

In connection with the AMC Networks Distribution and the MSG Distribution, the Company entered into various agreements with AMC Networks and Madison Square Garden, including distribution agreements, tax disaffiliation agreements, transition services agreements, employee matters agreements and certain related party arrangements. These agreements govern the Company's relationship with AMC Networks and Madison Square Garden subsequent to the AMC Networks Distribution and the MSG Distribution. These agreements also include arrangements with respect to transition services and a number of on-going relationships. The distribution agreements include agreements that the Company and AMC Networks and the Company and Madison Square Garden agree to provide each other with indemnities with respect to liabilities arising out of the businesses the Company transferred to AMC Networks and Madison Square Garden.

The following table summarizes the revenue and charges (credits) related to services provided to or received from AMC Networks reflected in continuing operations not discussed elsewhere in the accompanying combined notes to the consolidated financial statements:

	Years Ending December 31,		
	2013	2012	2011[a]
Revenues, net	$ 2,483	$ 3,246	$ 2,741
Operating expenses:			
Technical expenses, net of credits	$22,963	$22,751	$ 21,757
Selling, general and administrative expenses (credits):			
General and administrative expense allocations	(1,458)	1,777	(4,797)
Health and welfare plan allocations	—	—	(9,719)
Risk management and general insurance allocations	—	—	(836)
Other	(407)	(454)	(1,901)
Selling, general and administrative expenses (credits), subtotal	(1,865)	1,323	(17,253)
Operating expenses, net	21,098	24,074	4,504
Net charges	$18,615	$20,828	$ 1,763

[a] Amounts relating to AMC Networks for the period prior to the AMC Networks Distribution are eliminated in consolidation. Operating results of AMC Networks are reported in discontinued operations for all periods presented prior to the AMC Networks Distribution. Corporate overhead costs previously allocated to AMC Networks that were not eliminated as a result of the AMC Networks Distribution have been reclassified to continuing operations and are not reflected in the table above.

The following table summarizes the revenue and charges (credits) related to services provided to or received from Madison Square Garden reflected in continuing operations not discussed elsewhere in the accompanying combined notes to the consolidated financial statements:

	Years Ending December 31,		
	2013	2012	2011
Revenues, net	$ 3,103	$ 2,538	$ 2,455
Operating expenses:			
Technical expenses, net of credits	$156,028	$158,622	$155,559
Selling, general and administrative expenses (credits):			
General and administrative expense allocations	(2,282)	(2,755)	(3,170)
Other	7,133	5,046	3,429
Selling, general and administrative expenses, subtotal	4,851	2,291	259
Operating expenses, net	160,879	160,913	155,818
Net charges	$157,776	$158,375	$153,363

Revenues, Net

The Company recognizes revenue in connection with television advertisements and print advertising, as well as certain telecommunication services charged by its subsidiaries to AMC Networks and Madison Square Garden.

The Company and its subsidiaries, together with AMC Networks and Madison Square Garden, may enter into agreements with third parties in which the amounts paid/received by AMC Networks and Madison Square Garden, their subsidiaries, or the Company may differ from the amounts that would have been paid/received if such arrangements were negotiated separately. Where subsidiaries of the Company have incurred a cost incremental to fair value and Madison Square Garden or AMC Networks have received a benefit incremental to fair value from these negotiations, the Company and its subsidiaries will charge Madison Square Garden or AMC Networks for the incremental amount.

Technical Expenses

Technical expenses include costs incurred by the Company for the carriage of the MSG networks and Fuse program services, as well as for AMC, WE tv, IFC and Sundance Channel on Cablevision's cable systems. The Company also purchases certain programming signal transmission and production services from AMC Networks.

Selling, General and Administrative Expenses (Credits)

General and Administrative Expense Allocations

General and administrative costs, primarily costs of maintaining common support functions such as executive management, human resources, legal, finance, tax, accounting, audit, treasury, strategic planning, information technology, transportation services, creative and production services, etc., were allocated to AMC Networks through June 30, 2011. Corporate overhead costs allocated to AMC Networks prior to July 1, 2011 that were not eliminated as a result of the AMC Networks Distribution have been reclassified to continuing operations and are not included in the table above.

Amounts included in the tables above represent allocations to Madison Square Garden and AMC Networks for services performed by the Company on their behalf, including transition services. Amounts also include charges to the Company for services performed or paid by the affiliate on the Company's behalf.

Health and Welfare Plan Allocations

Employees of AMC Networks participated in health and welfare plans sponsored by the Company through December 31, 2011. Health and welfare benefit costs have generally been charged to AMC Networks based upon the proportionate number of participants in the plans.

Risk Management and General Insurance Allocations

The Company provided AMC Networks with risk management and general insurance related services through the date of the AMC Networks Distribution.

Other

The Company, AMC Networks and Madison Square Garden routinely enter into transactions with each other in the ordinary course of business. Such transactions may include, but are not limited to, sponsorship agreements and cross-promotion arrangements.

As the transactions discussed above are conducted between subsidiaries under common control, amounts charged for certain services may not represent amounts that might have been received or incurred if the transactions were based upon arm's length negotiations.

During 2013, 2012 and 2011, the Company provided services to or incurred costs on behalf of certain related parties, including from time to time, members of the Dolan family or to entities owned by members of the Dolan family. All costs incurred on behalf of these related parties are reimbursed to the Company.

Aggregate amounts due from and due to AMC Networks, Madison Square Garden and other affiliates at December 31, 2013 and 2012 are summarized below:

	December 31,	
Cablevision	**2013**	**2012**
Amounts due from affiliates	$1,520	$5,339
Amounts due to affiliates	30,941	36,397

	December 31,	
CSC Holdings	**2013**	**2012**
Amounts due from affiliates (principally Cablevision)	$115,538	$487,352
Amounts due to affiliates	30,887	33,311

1.115 VIACOM INC. (SEP)
NOTES TO CONSOLIDATED FINANCIAL STATEMENTS

Note 17. Related Party Transactions

NAI, directly and through a wholly-owned subsidiary, is the controlling stockholder of both Viacom and CBS. Sumner M. Redstone, the controlling stockholder, Chairman and Chief Executive Officer of NAI, serves as our Executive Chairman and Founder and as the Executive Chairman and Founder of CBS. Shari Redstone, who is Sumner Redstone's daughter, is the President and a director of NAI, and serves as non-executive Vice Chair of the Board of Directors of both Viacom and CBS. George Abrams, one of our directors, serves on the boards of both NAI and Viacom, and Frederic Salerno, another of our directors, serves on the boards of both Viacom and CBS. Philippe Dauman, our President and Chief Executive Officer, also serves on the boards of both NAI and Viacom. Transactions between Viacom and related parties are overseen by our Governance and Nominating Committee.

Viacom and NAI Related Party Transactions

NAI licenses films in the ordinary course of business for its motion picture theaters from all major studios, including Paramount. During the years ended September 30, 2013, 2012 and 2011, Paramount earned revenues from NAI in connection with these licenses in the aggregate amounts of approximately $19 million, $19 million and $44 million, respectively.

Viacom and CBS Corporation Related Party Transactions

In the ordinary course of business, we are involved in transactions with CBS and its various businesses that result in the recognition of revenues and expenses by us. Transactions with CBS are settled in cash.

Paramount earns revenues and recognizes expenses associated with its distribution of certain television products into the home entertainment market on behalf of CBS. Pursuant to its agreement with CBS, Paramount distributes CBS's library of television and other content on DVD and Blu-ray disc on a worldwide basis. Under the terms of the agreement, Paramount is entitled to retain a fee based on a percentage of gross receipts and is generally responsible for all out-of-pocket costs, which are recoupable prior to any participation payments to CBS. In April 2013, Paramount and CBS extended the term of the agreement. Paramount also earns revenues from CBS through leasing of studio space and licensing of certain film products.

The *Media Networks* segment recognizes advertising revenues and purchases television programming from CBS. The cost of the programming purchases is initially recorded as acquired program rights inventory and amortized over the estimated period that revenues will be generated.

Both of our segments recognize advertising expenses related to the placement of advertisements with CBS.

The following table summarizes the transactions with CBS as included in our Consolidated Financial Statements:

| CBS Related Party Transactions | Year Ended September 30, | | |
(In millions)	2013	2012	2011
Consolidated Statements of Earnings			
Revenues	$264	$285	$341
Operating expenses	$327	$347	$434
	September 30,		
	2013	2012	
Consolidated Balance Sheets			
Accounts receivable	$ 5	$ 7	
Other assets	—	1	
Total due from CBS	$ 5	$ 8	
Accounts payable	$ 3	$ 1	
Participants' share and residuals, current	115	143	
Program rights obligations, current	99	110	
Program rights obligations, noncurrent	139	169	
Other liabilities	15	24	
Total due to CBS	$371	$447	

Other Related Party Transactions

In the ordinary course of business, we are involved in related party transactions with equity investees, principally related to investments in unconsolidated VIEs as more fully described in Note 3. These related party transactions primarily relate to the provision of advertising services, licensing of film and programming content, distribution of films and provision of certain administrative support services, for which the impact on our Consolidated Financial Statements is as follows:

| Other Related Party Transactions | Year Ended September 30, | | |
(In millions)	2013	2012	2011
Consolidated Statements of Earnings			
Revenues	$216	$309	$239
Operating expenses	$ 63	$120	$ 83
Selling, general and administrative	$ (17)	$ (16)	$ (16)
	September 30,		
	2013	2012	
Consolidated Balance Sheets			
Accounts receivable	$ 84	$114	
Other assets	1	3	
Total due from other related parties	$ 85	$117	
Accounts payable	$ 4	$ 8	
Other liabilities	26	17	
Total due to other related parties	$ 30	$ 25	

All other related party transactions are not material in the periods presented.

1.116 CLIFFS NATURAL RESOURCES INC. (DEC)
NOTES TO CONSOLIDATED FINANCIAL STATEMENTS

Note 18—Related Parties

Three of our five U.S. iron ore mines and one of our two Eastern Canadian iron ore mines are owned with various joint venture partners that are integrated steel producers or their subsidiaries. We are the manager of each of the mines we co-own and rely on our joint venture partners to make their required capital contributions and to pay for their share of the iron ore pellets and concentrate that we produce. The joint venture partners are also our customers. The following is a summary of the mine ownership of these iron ore mines at December 31, 2013:

Mine	Cliffs Natural Resources	ArcelorMittal	U.S. Steel Canada	WISCO
Empire	79.0%	21.0%	—	—
Tilden	85.0%	—	15.0%	—
Hibbing	23.0%	62.3%	14.7%	—
Bloom Lake	82.8%	—	—	17.2%

ArcelorMittal has a unilateral right to put its interest in the Empire mine to us, but has not exercised this right to date.

Product revenues from related parties were as follows:

(In millions)	Year Ended December 31,		
	2013	2012	2011
Product revenues from related parties	$1,664.8	$1,660.8	$2,192.4
Total product revenues	5,346.6	5,520.9	6,321.3
Related party product revenue as a percent of total product revenue	31.1%	30.1%	34.7%

Amounts due from related parties recorded in *Accounts receivable, net* and *Other current assets*, including customer supply agreements and provisional pricing arrangements, were $132.0 million and $149.8 million at December 31, 2013 and 2012, respectively. Amounts due to related parties recorded in *Other current liabilities,* including provisional pricing arrangements and liabilities to related parties, were $25.1 million and $20.2 million at December 31, 2013 and 2012, respectively.

In 2002, we entered into an agreement with Ispat that restructured the ownership of the Empire mine and increased our ownership from 46.7 percent to 79.0 percent in exchange for the assumption of all mine liabilities. Under the terms of the agreement, we indemnified Ispat from obligations of Empire in exchange for certain future payments to Empire and to us by Ispat of $120.0 million, recorded at a present value of $11.3 million and $19.3 million at December 31, 2013 and December 31, 2012, respectively. At December 31, 2013, the remaining balance of $11.3 million was recorded in *Other current assets* and at December 31, 2012, $10.0 million of the remaining balance was recorded in *Other current assets*. The fair value of the receivable of $11.9 million and $21.3 million at December 31, 2013 and December 31, 2012, respectively, is based on a discount rate of 1.28 percent and 2.85 percent, respectively, which represents the estimated credit-adjusted risk-free interest rate for the period the receivable is outstanding.

Supply agreements with one of our customers include provisions for supplemental revenue or refunds based on the customer's annual steel pricing for the year the product is consumed in the customer's blast furnace. The supplemental pricing is characterized as an embedded derivative. Refer to NOTE 3—DERIVATIVE INSTRUMENTS AND HEDGING ACTIVITIES for further information.

Inflationary Accounting

DISCLOSURE

1.117 FASB ASC 255, *Changing Prices*, states that entities are encouraged to disclose supplementary information on the effects of changing prices (inflation). Entities are not discouraged from experimenting with other forms of disclosure.

1.118 However, the Item 303 of the SEC's Regulation S-K requires that registrants discuss in "Management's Discussion and Analysis of Financial Condition and Results of Operations" the effects of inflation and other changes in prices when considered material. The SEC also encourages experimentation with these disclosures in order to provide the most meaningful presentation of the impact of price changes on the registrant's financial statements.

PRESENTATION AND DISCLOSURE EXCERPT

INFLATIONARY ACCOUNTING

1.119 THE BRINK'S COMPANY (DEC)
NOTES TO CONSOLIDATED FINANCIAL STATEMENTS

Note 1—Summary of Significant Accounting Policies (in part)

Foreign Currency Translation

Our consolidated financial statements are reported in U.S. dollars. Our foreign subsidiaries maintain their records primarily in the currency of the country in which they operate.

The method of translating local currency financial information into U.S. dollars depends on whether the economy in which our foreign subsidiary operates has been designated as highly inflationary or not. Economies with a three-year cumulative inflation rate of more than 100% are considered highly inflationary.

Assets and liabilities of foreign subsidiaries in non-highly inflationary economies are translated into U.S. dollars using rates of exchange at the balance sheet date. Translation adjustments are recorded in other comprehensive income (loss). Revenues and expenses are translated at rates of exchange in effect during the year. Transaction gains and losses are recorded in net income.

Foreign subsidiaries that operate in highly inflationary countries use the U.S. dollar as their functional currency. Local currency monetary assets and liabilities are remeasured into U.S. dollars using rates of exchange as of each balance sheet date, with remeasurement adjustments and other transaction gains and losses recognized in earnings. Non-monetary assets and liabilities do not fluctuate with changes in local currency exchange rates to the dollar.

Venezuela

Brink's Venezuela accounted for $447 million or 11% of total Brink's revenues and represented a significant component of total segment operating profit in 2013. At December 31, 2013, we had investments in our Venezuelan operations of $125.3 million on an equity-method basis. At December 31, 2013, we had bolivar denominated net monetary assets of $120.4 million, including $93.8 million of cash and cash equivalents denominated in bolivars.

The economy in Venezuela has had significant inflation in the last several years. We consolidate our Venezuelan results using our accounting policy for subsidiaries operating in highly inflationary economies.

Since 2003, the Venezuelan government has controlled the exchange of local currency into other currencies, including the U.S. dollar. The Venezuelan government requires that currency exchanges be made at official rates established by the government instead of allowing open markets to determine currency rates. Different official rates exist for different industries and purposes. The government does not approve all requests to convert bolivars to other currencies.

The government devalued the official rate for essential services in February 2013 to 6.3 bolivars to the dollar. In January 2014, the government expanded an alternate process to obtain dollars for travel and certain other purposes. Rates obtained by the alternate process were reported to be 11.3 bolivars to U.S. dollars in December 2013.

Since the February 2013 devaluation, we have been unable to obtain dollars using either process. We do not expect to be able to obtain dollars using either process in the foreseeable future. There are other legal, but irregular and highly illiquid, mechanisms for converting bolivars.

As a result of these restrictions, we have been unable to obtain sufficient U.S. dollars to purchase certain imported supplies and fixed assets to fully operate our business in Venezuela, and as a result, have occasionally purchased more expensive, locally denominated supplies and fixed assets. The restrictions also prevent us from repatriating earnings and from being fully compensated for intercompany services.

Through January 31, 2013, we used an official rate of 5.3 bolivars to the dollar to remeasure our bolivar denominated monetary assets and liabilities into U.S. dollars and to translate our revenue and expenses. After the devaluation in February 2013, we began to use the 6.3 official exchange rate to remeasure bolivar denominated monetary assets and liabilities and to translate our revenue and expenses. As a result of the devaluation, we recognized a $13.4 million net remeasurement loss in 2013.

General Balance Sheet Considerations

PRESENTATION

2.01 FASB *Accounting Standards Codification®* (ASC) describes the benefits of presenting comparative financial statements instead of single-period financial statements and addresses the required disclosures and how the comparative information should be presented. SEC Regulation S-X, together with Financial Reporting Releases and Staff Accounting Bulletins, prescribe the form and content of, and requirements for, financial statements filed with the SEC. However, those requirements are modified for smaller reporting companies, as defined by SEC Regulation S-K, in Article 8 of Regulation S-X.

2.02 FASB ASC 810, *Consolidation*, and Rule 3A-02 of Regulation S-X state that a presumption exists that consolidated financial statements are more meaningful than separate financial statements and that they are usually necessary for a fair presentation when one of the entities in the consolidated group directly or indirectly has a controlling financial interest in the other entities. Rule 3-01(a) of Regulation S-X requires an entity to present consolidated balance sheets as of the end of each of the two most recent fiscal years, unless the entity has been in existence for less than one year.

2.03 FASB ASC does not require an entity to present a classified balance sheet or mandate any particular ordering of balance sheet accounts. However, FASB ASC 210-10-05-4 states that entities usually present a classified balance sheet to facilitate calculation of working capital. FASB ASC 210-10-05-5 indicates that in the statements of manufacturing, trading, and service entities, assets and liabilities are generally classified and segregated. Financial institutions generally present unclassified balance sheets. The FASB ASC glossary includes definitions of *current assets* and *current liabilities* for when an entity presents a classified balance sheet. FASB ASC 210-10-45 provides additional guidance for determining these classifications.

DISCLOSURE

Author's Note

In December 2011, FASB issued Accounting Standards Update (ASU) No. 2011-11, *Balance Sheet (Topic 210): Disclosures about Offsetting Assets and Liabilities*, to enhance comparability of financial statements prepared in accordance with GAAP and IFRS. The amendments in this update will enhance disclosures by requiring improved information about financial instruments and derivative instruments that are either (*a*) offset in accordance with either FASB ASC 210-20-45 or 815-10-45 or (*b*) subject to an enforceable master netting arrangement or similar agreement, irrespective of whether they are offset in accordance with either of the aforementioned FASB ASC sections. The additional disclosures will enable financial statement users to better understand the effect of such arrangements on their financial position. Entities are required to apply the amendments in this update for annual reporting periods beginning on or after January 1, 2013, and interim periods within those annual periods. Given the effective date of this update, no survey entity will have adopted these requirements in its 2013 financial statements.

In January 2013, FASB issued ASU No. 2013-01, *Balance Sheet (Topic 210): Clarifying the Scope of Disclosures about Offsetting Assets and Liabilities*, to help clarify the scope of ASU No. 2011-11. Stakeholders have told the board that because the scope in ASU No. 2011-11 is unclear, diversity in practice may result. Recent feedback from stakeholders is that standard commercial provisions of many contracts would equate to a master netting arrangement. Stakeholders questioned whether it was the board's intent to require disclosures for such a broad scope, which would significantly increase the cost of compliance. The objective of this update is to clarify the scope of the offsetting disclosures and address any unintended consequences. Entities are required to apply the amendments in this ASU for annual reporting periods beginning on or after January 1, 2013, and interim periods within those annual periods. The effective date is the same as the effective date of ASU No. 2011-11; therefore, no survey entity will have adopted these requirements in its 2013 financial statements.

2.04 FASB ASC sets forth disclosure guidelines regarding capital structure and other balance sheet items. SEC regulations also contain additional requirements for disclosures that registrants should provide outside the financial statements.

PRESENTATION AND DISCLOSURE EXCERPT

RECLASSIFICATIONS

2.06 PRICELINE.COM INCORPORATED (DEC)

CONSOLIDATED BALANCE SHEETS (in part)

(In thousands, except share and per share data)

	December 31,	
	2013	2012
Liabilities and Stockholders' Equity		
Current liabilities:		
Accounts payable	$ 247,345	$ 184,648
Accrued expenses and other current liabilities	545,342	387,911
Deferred merchant bookings	437,127	368,823
Convertible debt (See Note 11)	151,931	520,344
Total current liabilities	1,381,745	1,461,726
Deferred income taxes	326,425	45,159
Other long-term liabilities	75,981	68,944
Convertible debt (See Note 11)	1,742,047	881,996
Total liabilities	3,526,198	2,457,825
Commitments and Contingencies (See Note 16)		
Redeemable noncontrolling interests (See Note 13)	—	160,287
Convertible debt (See Note 11)	8,533	54,655
Stockholders' equity:		
Common stock, $0.008 par value, authorized 1,000,000,000 shares, 61,265,160 and 58,055,586 shares issued, respectively	476	450
Treasury stock, 9,256,721 and 8,184,787, respectively	(1,987,207)	(1,060,607)
Additional paid-in capital	4,592,979	2,612,197
Accumulated earnings	4,218,752	2,368,611
Accumulated other comprehensive income (loss)	84,729	(23,676)
Total stockholders' equity	6,909,729	3,896,975
Total liabilities and stockholders' equity	$10,444,460	$ 6,569,742

NOTES TO CONSOLIDATED FINANCIAL STATEMENTS

11. Debt (in part)

Convertible Debt (in part)

Convertible debt as of December 31, 2013 consisted of the following (in thousands):

December 31, 2013	Outstanding Principal Amount	Unamortized Debt Discount	Carrying Value
1.25% Convertible Senior Notes due March 2015	$ 160,464	$ (8,533)	$ 151,931
1.0% Convertible Senior Notes due March 2018	1,000,000	(96,797)	903,203
0.35% Convertible Senior Notes due June 2020	1,000,000	(161,156)	838,844
Outstanding convertible debt	$2,160,464	$(266,486)	$1,893,978

Convertible debt as of December 31, 2012 consisted of the following (in thousands):

December 31, 2012	Outstanding Principal Amount	Unamortized Debt Discount	Carrying Value
1.25% Convertible Senior Notes due March 2015	$ 574,999	$ (54,655)	$ 520,344
1.0% Convertible Senior Notes due March 2018	1,000,000	(118,004)	881,996
Outstanding convertible debt	$1,574,999	$(172,659)	$1,402,340

Based upon the closing price of the Company's common stock for the prescribed measurement periods during the three months ended December 31, 2013 and 2012, respectively, the contingent conversion threshold of the 2015 Notes (as defined below) was exceeded. Therefore, the 2015 Notes are convertible at the option of the holders. Accordingly, the Company reported the carrying value of the 2015

Notes as a current liability as of December 31, 2013 and 2012. Since these notes are convertible at the option of the holders and the principal amount is required to be paid in cash, the difference between the principal amount and the carrying value is reflected as convertible debt in the mezzanine section on the Company's Consolidated Balance Sheet. Therefore, with respect to the 2015 Notes, the Company reclassified amounts before tax of $8.5 million and $54.7 million from additional paid-in-capital to convertible debt in the mezzanine section on the Company's Consolidated Balance Sheet as of December 31, 2013 and 2012, respectively.

Debt discount after tax of $69.1 million ($115.2 million before tax) net of financing costs associated with the equity component of convertible debt of $1.6 million after tax were recorded in additional paid-in capital related to the 2015 Notes in March 2010. The Company reclassified before tax amounts of $8.5 million and $54.7 million out of additional paid-in-capital to the mezzanine section on the Company's Consolidated Balance Sheets at December 31, 2013 and 2012, respectively, because the 2015 Notes were convertible at the option of the holders. Debt discount after tax of $80.9 million ($135.2 million before tax) net of financing costs associated with the equity component of convertible debt of $2.8 million after tax were recorded in additional paid-in capital related to the 2018 Notes in March 2012. Debt discount after tax of $92.4 million ($154.3 million before tax) and financing costs associated with the equity component of convertible debt of $0.1 million after tax were recorded in additional paid-in capital related to the 2020 Notes at June 30, 2013.

Cash and Cash Equivalents

PRESENTATION

2.07 Cash is commonly considered to consist of currency and demand deposits. The FASB ASC glossary defines *cash equivalents* as short-term, highly liquid investments that are both readily convertible into known amounts of cash and so near their maturity that they present an insignificant risk of changes in value because of changes in interest rates. Generally, only investments with original maturities of three months or less qualify under that definition.

DISCLOSURE

2.08 Rule 5-02.1 of Regulation S-X states that separate disclosure should be made of the cash and cash items that are restricted regarding withdrawal or usage. The provisions of any restrictions should be described in a note to the financial statements. Restrictions may include legally restricted deposits held as compensating balances against short-term borrowing arrangements, contracts entered into with others, or company statements of intention with regard to particular deposits; however, time deposits and short-term certificates of deposit are not generally included in legally restricted deposits. Compensating balance arrangements that do not legally restrict the use of cash should be described in the notes to the financial statements; the amount involved, if determinable, for the most recent audited balance sheet and any subsequent unaudited balance sheet should be disclosed. Compensating balances maintained under an agreement to assure future credit availability should be disclosed, along with the amount and terms of such agreement.

Marketable Securities

RECOGNITION AND MEASUREMENT

2.09 FASB ASC 320, *Investments—Debt and Equity Securities*, provides guidance on accounting for and reporting investments in equity securities that have readily determinable fair values and all investments in debt securities.

2.10 FASB ASC 320-10-25-1 requires that at acquisition, entities classify certain debt and equity securities into one of three categories: held-to-maturity, trading, or available-for-sale. Investments in debt securities that the entity has the positive intent and ability to hold to maturity are classified as held to maturity and reported at amortized cost in the statement of financial position. Securities that are bought and held principally for the purpose of selling them in the near term (thus held for only a short period of time) are classified as trading securities and reported at fair value. Trading generally reflects active and frequent buying and selling, and trading securities are generally used with the objective of generating profits on short-term differences in price. Investments not classified as either held-to-maturity or trading securities are classified as available-for-sale securities and reported at fair value. FASB ASC 320-10-35-1 explains that unrealized holding gains and losses are included in earnings for trading securities and other comprehensive income for available-for-sale securities with the exception of an available-for-sale security designated as being hedged in a fair value hedge. All or a portion of that unrealized gain or loss should be recognized in earnings during the period of the hedge in accordance with paragraphs 1–4 of FASB ASC 815-25-35.

2.11 FASB ASC 320 indicates when certain investments are considered impaired, whether that impairment is other than temporary, and the measurement and recognition of an impairment loss. FASB ASC 320 also provides guidance on accounting considerations for debt securities subsequent to the recognition of an other-than-temporary impairment and requires certain disclosures about unrealized losses that have not been recognized as other-than-temporary impairments.

PRESENTATION

2.12 Under FASB ASC 320-10-45-2, an entity that presents a classified balance sheet should report individual held-to-maturity securities, individual available-for-sale securities, and individual trading securities as either current or noncurrent.

DISCLOSURE

2.13 FASB ASC 320-10-50 includes detailed disclosure requirements for various marketable securities, including matters such as the nature and risks of the securities; cost, fair value, contractual maturities; impairment of securities; and certain transaction information.

2.14 By definition, investments in debt and equity securities are financial instruments. FASB ASC 825, *Financial Instruments*, requires disclosure of the fair value of those investments for which it is practicable to estimate that value, the methods and assumptions used in estimating the fair value of marketable securities, and a description of any changes in the methods and assumptions during the period. Under FASB ASC 825-10-50-3, the fair value disclosures are optional for certain nonpublic entities with assets less than $100 million.

2.15 FASB ASC 820, *Fair Value Measurement*, defines *fair value*, establishes a framework for measuring fair value, and requires certain disclosures about fair value measurements. *Fair value* is defined as an exit price (that is, a price that would be received to sell, versus acquire, an asset or transfer a liability in an orderly transaction between market participants at the measurement date). Further, fair value is a market-based measurement, not an entity-specific measurement. It establishes a fair value hierarchy that distinguishes between assumptions developed based on market data obtained from independent external sources and the reporting entity's own assumptions. Fair value measurement should consider adjustment for risk, such as the risk inherent in a valuation technique or its inputs.

2.16 For assets and liabilities measured at fair value, whether on a recurring or nonrecurring basis, FASB ASC 820 specifies the required disclosures concerning the inputs used to measure fair value. FASB ASC 820-10-50-1 explains that the reporting entity should disclose information that enables users of its financial statements to assess the following: (*a*) for assets and liabilities measured at fair value on a recurring basis in periods subsequent to initial recognition or measured on a nonrecurring basis in periods subsequent to initial recognition, the valuation techniques and inputs used to develop those measurements; and (*b*) for recurring fair value measurements using significant unobservable inputs (Level 3), the effect of the measurements on earnings for the period. Pending Content.

2.17 Pending Content in FASB ASC 820-10-50-2 states that the reporting entity should disclose all of the following information for each interim and annual period separately for each class of assets and liabilities:
   a. The fair value measurement at the reporting date.
   b. The level within the fair value hierarchy in which the fair value measurement in its entirety falls (quoted prices in active markets for identical assets or liabilities—Level 1, significant other observable inputs—Level 2; significant unobservable inputs—Level 3).
   c. The amounts of significant transfers between Level 1 and Level 2 and the reasons for the transfers.
   d. For Level 3 measurements, a reconciliation of beginning and ending balances showing gains and losses for the period (realized and unrealized), purchases, sales, issuances, and settlements, and transfers in or out of Level 3 and reasons for those transfers.
   e. the amount of total gains or losses for the period that are attributable to the change in unrealized gains or losses relating to those assets and liabilities still held at the reporting date and a description of where those unrealized gains or losses are reported in the statement of income (or activities).
   f. for Level 2 and Level 3 measurements, a description of the valuation technique and the inputs used in determining the fair values of each class of assets or liabilities.

2.18 FASB ASC 825 permits entities to choose to measure at fair value many financial instruments and certain other items that are not currently required to be measured at fair value. Further, under FASB ASC 825, a business entity should report unrealized gains and losses on eligible items for which the fair value option has been elected in earnings at each subsequent reporting date. The irrevocable election of the fair value option is made on an instrument-by-instrument basis, with certain exceptions, and applied to the entire instrument, not only to specified risks, specific cash flows, or portions of that instrument. FASB ASC 825 also establishes presentation and disclosure requirements designed to facilitate comparison between entities that choose different measurement attributes for similar types of assets and liabilities. The required disclosures are optional for certain nonpublic entities.

PRESENTATION AND DISCLOSURE EXCERPTS

MARKETABLE SECURITIES—AVAILABLE-FOR-SALE SECURITIES

2.19 AMERICAN INTERNATIONAL GROUP, INC. (DEC)
CONSOLIDATED BALANCE SHEETS (in part)

(In millions, except for share data)	December 31, 2013	December 31, 2012
Assets (in part):		
Investments:		
Fixed maturity securities:		
Bonds available for sale, at fair value (amortized cost: 2013—$248,531; 2012—$246,149)	$258,274	$269,959
Other bond securities, at fair value (See Note 6)	22,623	24,584
Equity Securities:		
Common and preferred stock available for sale, at fair value (cost: 2013—$1,726; 2012—$1,640)	3,656	3,212
Other common and preferred stock, at fair value (See Note 6)	834	662
Mortgage and other loans receivable, net of allowance (portion measured at fair value: 2013—$0; 2012—$134)	20,765	19,482
Other invested assets (portion measured at fair value: 2013—$8,598; 2012—$7,056)	28,659	29,117
Short-term investments (portion measured at fair value: 2013—$6,313; 2012—$8,056)	21,617	28,808
Total investments	356,428	375,824

NOTES TO CONSOLIDATED FINANCIAL STATEMENTS

6. Investments (in part)

Fixed Maturity and Equity Securities

Bonds held to maturity are carried at amortized cost when we have the ability and positive intent to hold these securities until maturity. When we do not have the ability or positive intent to hold bonds until maturity, these securities are classified as available for sale or are measured at fair value at our election. None of our fixed maturity securities met the criteria for held to maturity classification at December 31, 2013 or 2012.

Fixed maturity and equity securities classified as available for sale are carried at fair value. Unrealized gains and losses from available for sale investments in fixed maturity and equity securities are reported as a separate component of Accumulated other comprehensive income, net of deferred policy acquisition costs and deferred income taxes, in shareholders' equity. Realized and unrealized gains and losses from fixed maturity and equity securities measured at fair value at our election are reflected in Net investment income (for insurance subsidiaries) or Other income (for Other Operations). Investments in fixed maturity and equity securities are recorded on a trade-date basis.

Premiums and discounts arising from the purchase of bonds classified as available for sale are treated as yield adjustments over their estimated holding periods, until maturity, or call date, if applicable. For investments in certain RMBS, CMBS and CDO/ABS, (collectively, structured securities), recognized yields are updated based on current information regarding the timing and amount of expected undiscounted future cash flows. For high credit quality structured securities, effective yields are recalculated based on actual payments received and updated prepayment expectations, and the amortized cost is adjusted to the amount that would have existed had the new effective yield been applied since acquisition with a corresponding charge or credit to net investment income. For structured securities that are not high credit quality, effective yields are recalculated and adjusted prospectively based on changes in expected undiscounted future cash flows. For purchased credit impaired (PCI) securities, at acquisition, the difference between the undiscounted expected future cash flows and the recorded investment in the securities represents the initial accretable yield, which is to be accreted into net investment income over the securities' remaining lives on a level-yield basis. Subsequently, effective yields recognized on PCI securities are recalculated and adjusted prospectively to reflect changes in the contractual benchmark interest rates on variable rate securities and any significant increases in undiscounted expected future cash flows arising due to reasons other than interest rate changes.

Securities Available for Sale

The following table presents the amortized cost or cost and fair value of our available for sale securities:

(In millions)	Amortized Cost or Cost	Gross Unrealized Gains	Gross Unrealized Losses	Fair Value	Other-Than-Temporary Impairments in AOCI[a]
December 31, 2013					
Bonds available for sale:					
U.S. government and government sponsored entities	$ 3,084	$ 150	$ (39)	$ 3,195	$ —
Obligations of states, municipalities and political subdivisions	28,704	1,122	(446)	29,380	(15)
Non-U.S. governments	22,045	822	(358)	22,509	—
Corporate debt	139,461	7,989	(2,898)	144,552	74
Mortgage-backed, asset-backed and collateralized:					
RMBS	33,520	3,101	(473)	36,148	1,670
CMBS	11,216	558	(292)	11,482	125
CDO/ABS	10,501	649	(142)	11,008	62
Total mortgage-backed, asset-backed and collateralized	55,237	4,308	(907)	58,638	1,857
Total bonds available for sale[b]	248,531	14,391	(4,648)	258,274	1,916
Equity securities available for sale:					
Common stock	1,280	1,953	(14)	3,219	—
Preferred stock	24	4	(1)	27	—
Mutual funds	422	12	(24)	410	—
Total equity securities available for sale	1,726	1,969	(39)	3,656	—
Total	$250,257	$16,360	$(4,687)	$261,930	$1,916
December 31, 2012					
Bonds available for sale:					
U.S. government and government sponsored entities	$ 3,161	$ 323	$ (1)	$ 3,483	$ —
Obligations of states, municipalities and political subdivisions	33,042	2,685	(22)	35,705	2
Non-U.S. governments	25,449	1,395	(44)	26,800	—
Corporate debt	135,728	15,848	(464)	151,112	115
Mortgage-backed, asset-backed and collateralized:					
RMBS	31,330	3,379	(317)	34,392	1,330
CMBS	9,449	770	(304)	9,915	(79)
CDO/ABS	7,990	806	(244)	8,552	82
Total mortgage-backed, asset-backed and collateralized	48,769	4,955	(865)	52,859	1,333
Total bonds available for sale[b]	246,149	25,206	(1,396)	269,959	1,450
Equity securities available for sale:					
Common stock	1,492	1,574	(37)	3,029	—
Preferred stock	55	23	—	78	—
Mutual funds	93	12	—	105	—
Total equity securities available for sale	1,640	1,609	(37)	3,212	—
Total	$247,789	$26,815	$(1,433)	$273,171	$1,450

[a] Represents the amount of other-than-temporary impairment losses recognized in Accumulated other comprehensive income. Amount includes unrealized gains and losses on impaired securities relating to changes in the value of such securities subsequent to the impairment measurement date.

[b] At December 31, 2013 and 2012, bonds available for sale held by us that were below investment grade or not rated totaled $32.6 billion and $29.6 billion, respectively.

Securities Available for Sale in a Loss Position

The following table summarizes the fair value and gross unrealized losses on our available for sale securities, aggregated by major investment category and length of time that individual securities have been in a continuous unrealized loss position:

(In millions)	Less Than 12 Months		12 Months or More		Total	
	Fair Value	Gross Unrealized Losses	Fair Value	Gross Unrealized Losses	Fair Value	Gross Unrealized Losses
December 31, 2013						
Bonds available for sale:						
U.S. government and government sponsored entities	$ 1,101	$ 34	$ 42	$ 5	$ 1,143	$ 39
Obligations of states, municipalities and political subdivisions	6,134	379	376	67	6,510	446
Non-U.S. governments	4,102	217	710	141	4,812	358
Corporate debt	38,495	2,251	4,926	647	43,421	2,898
RMBS	8,543	349	1,217	124	9,760	473
CMBS	3,191	176	1,215	116	4,406	292
CDO/ABS	2,845	62	915	80	3,760	142
Total bonds available for sale	64,411	3,468	9,401	1,180	73,812	4,648
Equity securities available for sale:						
Common stock	96	14	—	—	96	14
Preferred stock	5	1	—	—	5	1
Mutual funds	369	24	—	—	369	24
Total equity securities available for sale	470	39	—	—	470	39
Total	$64,881	$3,507	$9,401	$1,180	$74,282	$4,687
December 31, 2012						
Bonds available for sale:						
U.S. government and government sponsored entities	$ 153	$ 1	$ —	$ —	$ 153	$ 1
Obligations of states, municipalities and political subdivisions	692	11	114	11	806	22
Non-U.S. governments	1,555	19	442	25	1,997	44
Corporate debt	8,483	201	3,229	263	11,712	464
RMBS	597	28	1,661	289	2,258	317
CMBS	404	8	1,481	296	1,885	304
CDO/ABS	393	3	1,624	241	2,017	244
Total bonds available for sale	12,277	271	8,551	1,125	20,828	1,396
Equity securities available for sale:						
Common stock	247	36	18	1	265	37
Mutual funds	3	—	—	—	3	—
Total equity securities available for sale	250	36	18	1	268	37
Total	$12,527	$ 307	$8,569	$1,126	$21,096	$1,433

At December 31, 2013, we held 7,652 and 126 individual fixed maturity and equity securities, respectively, that were in an unrealized loss position, of which 848 individual fixed maturity securities were in a continuous unrealized loss position for longer than 12 months. We did not recognize the unrealized losses in earnings on these fixed maturity securities at December 31, 2013, because we neither intend to sell the securities nor do we believe that it is more likely than not that we will be required to sell these securities before recovery of their amortized cost basis. For fixed maturity securities with significant declines, we performed fundamental credit analysis on a security-by-security basis, which included consideration of credit enhancements, expected defaults on underlying collateral, review of relevant industry analyst reports and forecasts and other available market data.

Contractual Maturities of Fixed Maturity Securities Available for Sale

The following table presents the amortized cost and fair value of fixed maturity securities available for sale by contractual maturity:

(in millions)	Total Fixed Maturity Securities Available for Sale		Fixed Maturity Securities Available for Sale in a Loss Position	
	Amortized Cost	Fair Value	Amortized Cost	Fair Value
December 31, 2013				
Due in one year or less	$ 10,470	$ 10,678	$ 739	$ 726
Due after one year through five years	50,698	53,410	7,620	7,471
Due after five years through ten years	70,096	72,386	22,534	21,445
Due after ten years	62,030	63,162	28,734	26,244
Mortgage-backed, asset-backed and collateralized	55,237	58,638	18,833	17,926
Total	$248,531	$258,274	$78,460	$73,812

Actual maturities may differ from contractual maturities because certain borrowers have the right to call or prepay certain obligations with or without call or prepayment penalties.

The following table presents the gross realized gains and gross realized losses from sales or maturities of our available for sale securities:

| | Years Ended December 31, | | | | | |
| | 2013 | | 2012 | | 2011 | |
(In millions)	Gross Realized Gains	Gross Realized Losses	Gross Realized Gains	Gross Realized Losses	Gross Realized Gains	Gross Realized Losses
Fixed maturity securities	$2,634	$202	$2,778	$171	$2,042	$129
Equity securities	130	19	515	31	199	35
Total	$2,764	$221	$3,293	$202	$2,241	$164

For the year ended December 31, 2013, 2012 and 2011, the aggregate fair value of available for sale securities sold was $35.9 billion, $40.3 billion and $44.0 billion, which resulted in net realized capital gains of $2.5 billion, $3.1 billion and $2.1 billion, respectively.

MARKETABLE SECURITIES—HELD-TO-MATURITY SECURITIES

2.20 PRUDENTIAL FINANCIAL, INC. (DEC)
CONSOLIDATED STATEMENTS OF FINANCIAL POSITION (in part)

December 31, 2013 and 2012 (in millions, except share amounts)

	2013	2012
Assets		
Fixed maturities, available-for-sale, at fair value (amortized cost: 2013—$268,727; 2012—$277,654)(1)	$286,866	$301,336
Fixed maturities, held-to-maturity, at amortized cost (fair value: 2013—$3,553; 2012—$4,511)(1)	3,312	4,268
Trading account assets supporting insurance liabilities, at fair value(1)	20,827	20,590
Other trading account assets, at fair value(1)	6,453	6,328
Equity securities, available-for-sale, at fair value (cost: 2013—$7,003; 2012—$6,759)	9,910	8,277
Commercial mortgage and other loans (includes $158 and $162 measured at fair value under the fair value option at December 31, 2013 and December 31, 2012, respectively)(1)	41,008	36,733
Policy loans	11,766	11,575
Other long-term investments (includes $873 and $465 measured at fair value under the fair value option at December 31, 2013 and December 31, 2012, respectively)(1)	10,328	10,028
Short-term investments	7,703	6,447
Total investments	398,173	405,582

NOTES TO CONSOLIDATED FINANCIAL STATEMENTS

2. Significant Accounting Policies and Pronouncements (in part)

Investments and Investment-Related Liabilities (in part)

The Company's principal investments are fixed maturities; equity securities; commercial mortgage and other loans; policy loans; other long-term investments, including joint ventures (other than operating joint ventures), limited partnerships, and real estate; and short-term investments. Investments and investment-related liabilities also include securities repurchase and resale agreements and securities lending transactions. The accounting policies related to each are as follows:

Fixed maturities are comprised of bonds, notes and redeemable preferred stock. Fixed maturities classified as "available-for-sale" are carried at fair value. See Note 20 for additional information regarding the determination of fair value. Fixed maturities that the Company has both the positive intent and ability to hold to maturity are carried at amortized cost and classified as "held-to-maturity." The amortized cost of fixed maturities is adjusted for amortization of premiums and accretion of discounts to maturity.

The Company's available-for-sale and held-to-maturity securities with unrealized losses are reviewed quarterly to identify other-than-temporary impairments in value. In evaluating whether a decline in value is other-than-temporary, the Company considers several factors including, but not limited to the following: (1) the extent and the duration of the decline; (2) the reasons for the decline in value (credit event, currency or interest-rate related, including general credit spread widening); and (3) the financial condition of and near-term prospects of the issuer. With regard to available-for-sale equity securities, the Company also considers the ability and intent to hold the investment for a period of time to allow for a recovery of value. When it is determined that a decline in value of an equity security is other-than-temporary, the carrying value of the equity security is reduced to its fair value, with a corresponding charge to earnings.

4. Investments (in part)

Fixed Maturities and Equity Securities

The following tables provide information relating to fixed maturities and equity securities (excluding investments classified as trading) as of the dates indicated:

| (In millions) | December 31, 2013 | | | |
	Amortized Cost	Gross Unrealized Gains	Gross Unrealized Losses	Fair Value
Fixed Maturities, Held-to-Maturity				
Foreign government bonds	$ 938	$117	$ 0	$1,055
Corporate securities[4]	904	50	24	930
Asset-backed securities[1]	693	46	0	739
Commercial mortgage-backed securities	166	18	0	184
Residential mortgage-backed securities[2]	611	34	0	645
Total fixed maturities, held-to-maturity[4]	$3,312	$265	$24	$3,553

[1] Includes credit-tranched securities collateralized by sub-prime mortgages, auto loans, credit cards, education loans and other asset types.

[2] Includes publicly-traded agency pass-through securities and collateralized mortgage obligations.

[3] Represents the amount of other-than-temporary impairment losses in AOCI, which were not included in earnings. Amount excludes $875 million of net unrealized gains on impaired available-for-sale securities and $1 million on impaired held-to-maturity securities relating to changes in the value of such securities subsequent to the impairment measurement date.

[4] Excludes notes with amortized cost of $2,400 million (fair value, $2,461 million) which have been offset with the associated payables under a netting agreement.

| (In millions) | December 31, 2012 | | | |
	Amortized Cost	Gross Unrealized Gains	Gross Unrealized Losses	Fair Value
Fixed Maturities, Held-to-Maturity				
Foreign government bonds	$1,142	$108	$ 0	$1,250
Corporate securities[4]	1,065	37	67	1,035
Asset-backed securities[1]	1,001	66	0	1,067
Commercial mortgage-backed securities	302	49	0	351
Residential mortgage-backed securities[2]	758	50	0	808
Total fixed maturities, held-to-maturity[4]	$4,268	$310	$67	$4,511

[1] Includes credit-tranched securities collateralized by sub-prime mortgages, auto loans, credit cards, education loans, and other asset types.

[2] Includes publicly-traded agency pass-through securities and collateralized mortgage obligations.

[3] Represents the amount of other-than-temporary impairment losses in AOCI, which were not included in earnings. Amount excludes $778 million of net unrealized gains on impaired available-for-sale securities and $1 million of net unrealized gains on impaired held-to-maturity securities relating to changes in the value of such securities subsequent to the impairment measurement date.

[4] Excludes notes with amortized cost of $1,500 million (fair value, $1,660 million) which have been offset with the associated payables under a netting agreement.

The amortized cost and fair value of fixed maturities by contractual maturities at December 31, 2013, are as follows:

| (in millions) | Available-for-Sale | | Held-to-Maturity | |
	Amortized Cost	Fair Value	Amortized Cost	Fair Value
Due in one year or less	$ 9,160	$ 9,591	$ 0	$ 0
Due after one year through five years	47,219	51,622	55	56
Due after five years through ten years	57,745	62,682	323	331
Due after ten years[1]	123,914	131,806	1,464	1,597
Asset-backed securities	10,691	10,589	693	739
Commercial mortgage-backed securities	13,633	13,873	166	184
Residential mortgage-backed securities	6,365	6,703	611	646
Total	$268,727	$286,866	$3,312	$3,553

[1] Excludes notes with amortized cost of $2,400 million (fair value, $2,461 million) which have been offset with the associated payables under a netting agreement.

2.21 CITIGROUP INC. (DEC)

CONSOLIDATED BALANCE SHEET (in part)

	December 31,	
(In millions of dollars)	2013	2012
Assets		
Cash and due from banks (including segregated cash and other deposits)	$ 29,885	$ 36,453
Deposits with banks	169,005	102,134
Federal funds sold and securities borrowed or purchased under agreements to resell (including $141,481 and $160,589 as of December 31, 2013 and December 31, 2012, respectively, at fair value)	257,037	261,311
Brokerage receivables	25,674	22,490
Trading account assets (including $106,695 and $105,458 pledged to creditors at December 31, 2013 and December 31, 2012, respectively)	285,928	320,929
Investments (including $26,989 and $21,423 pledged to creditors at December 31, 2013 and December 31, 2012, respectively, and $291,216 and $294,463 as of December 31, 2013 and December 31, 2012, respectively, at fair value)	308,980	312,326
Loans, net of unearned income		
Consumer (including $957 and $1,231 as of December 31, 2013 and December 31, 2012, respectively, at fair value)	393,831	408,671
Corporate (including $4,072 and $4,056 as of December 31, 2013 and December 31, 2012, respectively, at fair value)	271,641	246,793
Loans, net of unearned income	$ 665,472	$ 655,464
Allowance for loan losses	(19,648)	(25,455)
Total loans, net	$ 645,824	$ 630,009
Goodwill	25,009	25,673
Intangible assets (other than MSRs)	5,056	5,697
Mortgage servicing rights (MSRs)	2,718	1,942
Other assets (including $7,123 and $13,299 as of December 31, 2013 and December 31, 2012, respectively, at fair value)	125,266	145,660
Assets of discontinued operations held for sale	—	36
Total assets	$1,880,382	$1,864,660
Liabilities		
Non-interest-bearing deposits in U.S. offices	$ 128,399	$ 129,657
Interest-bearing deposits in U.S. offices (including $988 and $889 as of December 31, 2013 and December 31, 2012, respectively, at fair value)	284,164	247,716
Non-interest-bearing deposits in offices outside the U.S.	69,406	65,024
Interest-bearing deposits in offices outside the U.S. (including $689 and $558 as of December 31, 2013 and December 31, 2012, respectively, at fair value)	486,304	488,163
Total deposits	$ 968,273	$ 930,560
Federal funds purchased and securities loaned or sold under agreements to repurchase (including $51,545 and $116,689 as of December 31, 2013 and December 31, 2012, respectively, at fair value)	203,512	211,236
Brokerage payables	53,707	57,013
Trading account liabilities	108,762	115,549
Short-term borrowings (including $3,692 and $818 as of December 31, 2013 and December 31, 2012, respectively, at fair value)	58,944	52,027
Long-term debt (including $26,877 and $29,764 as of December 31, 2013 and December 31, 2012, respectively, at fair value)	221,116	239,463
Other liabilities (including $2,011 and $2,910 as of December 31, 2013 and December 31, 2012, respectively, at fair value)	59,935	67,815
Liabilities of discontinued operations held for sale	—	—
Total liabilities	$1,674,249	$1,673,663

NOTES TO CONSOLIDATED FINANCIAL STATEMENTS

1. Summary of Significant Accounting Policies (in part)

Trading Account Assets and Liabilities

Trading account assets include debt and marketable equity securities, derivatives in a receivable position, residual interests in securitizations and physical commodities inventory. In addition, as described in Note 26 to the Consolidated Financial Statements, certain assets that Citigroup has elected to carry at fair value under the fair value option, such as loans and purchased guarantees, are also included in *Trading account assets*.

Trading account liabilities include securities sold, not yet purchased (short positions), and derivatives in a net payable position, as well as certain liabilities that Citigroup has elected to carry at fair value (as described in Note 26 to the Consolidated Financial Statements).

Other than physical commodities inventory, all trading account assets and liabilities are carried at fair value. Revenues generated from trading assets and trading liabilities are generally reported in *Principal transactions* and include realized gains and losses as well as unrealized gains and losses resulting from changes in the fair value of such instruments. Interest income on trading assets is recorded in *Interest revenue* reduced by interest expense on trading liabilities.

Physical commodities inventory is carried at the lower of cost or market with related losses reported in *Principal transactions*. Realized gains and losses on sales of commodities inventory are included in *Principal transactions*. Investments in unallocated precious metals accounts (gold, silver, platinum and palladium) are accounted for as hybrid instruments containing a debt host contract and an embedded non-financial derivative instrument indexed to the price of the relevant precious metal. The embedded derivative instrument is separated from the debt host contract and accounted for at fair value. The debt host contract is accounted for at fair value under the fair value option, as described in Note 26 to the Consolidated Financial Statements.

Derivatives used for trading purposes include interest rate, currency, equity, credit, and commodity swap agreements, options, caps and floors, warrants, and financial and commodity futures and forward contracts. Derivative asset and liability positions are presented net by counterparty on the Consolidated Balance Sheet when a valid master netting agreement exists and the other conditions set out in ASC 210-20, *Balance Sheet-Offsetting,* are met. See Note 23 to the Consolidated Financial Statements.

The Company uses a number of techniques to determine the fair value of trading assets and liabilities, which are described in Note 25 to the Consolidated Financial Statements.

13. Trading Account Assets and Liabilities

Trading account assets and *Trading account liabilities*, at fair value, consisted of the following at December 31:

(In millions of dollars)	2013	2012
Trading account assets		
Mortgage-backed securities[1]		
U.S. government-sponsored agency guaranteed	$ 23,955	$ 31,160
Prime	1,422	1,248
Alt-A	721	801
Subprime	1,211	812
Non-U.S. residential	723	607
Commercial	2,574	2,441
Total mortgage-backed securities	$ 30,606	$ 37,069
U.S. Treasury and federal agency securities		
U.S. Treasury	$ 13,537	$ 17,472
Agency obligations	1,300	2,884
Total U.S. Treasury and federal agency securities	$ 14,837	$ 20,356
State and municipal securities	$ 3,207	$ 3,806
Foreign government securities	74,856	89,239
Corporate	30,534	35,224
Derivatives[2]	52,821	54,620
Equity securities	61,776	56,998
Asset-backed securities[1]	5,616	5,352
Other trading assets[3]	11,675	18,265
Total trading account assets	$285,928	$320,929
Trading account liabilities		
Securities sold, not yet purchased	$ 61,508	$ 63,798
Derivatives[2]	47,254	51,751
Total trading account liabilities	$108,762	$115,549

[1] The Company invests in mortgage-backed and asset-backed securities. These securitizations are generally considered VIEs. The Company's maximum exposure to loss from these VIEs is equal to the carrying amount of the securities, which is reflected in the table above. For mortgage-backed and asset-backed securitizations in which the Company has other involvement, see Note 22 to the Consolidated Financial Statements.

[2] Presented net, pursuant to enforceable master netting agreements. See Note 23 to the Consolidated Financial Statements for a discussion regarding the accounting and reporting for derivatives.

[3] Includes investments in unallocated precious metals, as discussed in Note 26 to the Consolidated Financial Statements. Also includes physical commodities accounted for at the lower of cost or fair value.

Current Receivables

PRESENTATION

2.22 FASB ASC 310, *Receivables*, indicates that loans or trade receivables may be presented on the balance sheet as aggregate amounts. However, major categories of loans or trade receivables should be presented separately either in the balance sheet or in the notes to the financial statements. Also, any such receivables held for sale should be a separate balance sheet category. Receivables from officers, employees, or affiliated companies should be shown separately and not included under a general heading, such as accounts receivable. Valuation allowance for credit losses or doubtful accounts and any unearned income included in the face amount of receivables should be shown as a deduction from the related receivables.

DISCLOSURE

2.23 FASB ASC 310 states that allowances for doubtful accounts should be deducted from the related receivables and appropriately disclosed. FASB ASC 310-10-50-4 requires, as applicable, any unearned income, unamortized premiums and discounts, and net unamortized deferred fees and costs be disclosed in the financial statements. Under FASB ASC 825, fair value disclosure is not required for trade receivables when the carrying amount of the trade receivable approximates its fair value.

PRESENTATION AND DISCLOSURE EXCERPTS

INCOME TAX RECEIVABLE

2.24 VISA INC. (SEP)
CONSOLIDATED BALANCE SHEETS (in part)

(In millions, except par value data)	September 30, 2013	September 30, 2012
Assets (in part)		
Cash and cash equivalents	$2,186	$ 2,074
Restricted cash—litigation escrow (Note 3)	49	4,432
Investment securities (Note 4):		
Trading	75	66
Available-for-sale	1,994	677
Income tax receivable (Note 19)	142	179
Settlement receivable	799	454
Accounts receivable	761	723
Customer collateral (Note 11)	866	823
Current portion of client incentives	282	209
Deferred tax assets (Note 19)	481	2,027
Prepaid expenses and other current assets (Note 5)	187	122
Total current assets	7,822	11,786

NOTES TO CONSOLIDATED FINANCIAL STATEMENTS

Note 1—Summary of Significant Accounting Policies (in part)

Income taxes. The Company's income tax expense consists of two components: current and deferred. Current income tax expense represents taxes paid or payable for the current period. Deferred tax assets and liabilities are recognized to reflect the future tax consequences attributable to temporary differences between the financial statement carrying amounts and the respective tax basis of existing assets and liabilities, and operating loss and credit carryforwards. Deferred tax assets and liabilities are measured using enacted tax rates expected to apply to taxable income in the years in which those temporary differences are expected to be recovered or settled. In assessing whether deferred tax assets are realizable, management considers whether it is more likely than not that some portion or all of the deferred tax assets will not be realized. A valuation allowance is recorded for the portions that are not expected to be realized based on the level of historical taxable income, projections of future taxable income over the periods in which the temporary differences are deductible, and qualifying tax planning strategies.

Where interpretation of the tax law may be uncertain, the Company recognizes, measures and discloses income tax uncertainties. The Company accounts for interest expense and penalties related to uncertain tax positions in non-operating income in the consolidated statements of operations. The Company files a consolidated federal income tax return and, in certain states, combined state tax returns.

Foreign taxes paid have historically been deducted to reduce federal income taxes payable. The Company elects to claim foreign tax credits in any given year if such election is beneficial to the Company. See *Note 19—Income Taxes*.

Note 19—Income Taxes

The Company's income before taxes by fiscal year consisted of the following:

(In millions)	2013	2012	2011
U.S.	$5,992	$1,030	$4,650
Non-U.S.	1,265	1,177	1,006
Total income before taxes and non-controlling interest	$7,257	$2,207	$5,656

U.S. income before taxes included $2.0 billion, $1.6 billion and $1.3 billion from non-U.S. clients for fiscal 2013, 2012 and 2011, respectively.

Income tax provision by fiscal year consisted of the following:

(in millions)	2013	2012	2011
Current:			
U.S. federal	$ 568	$ 1,376	$1,365
State and local	(58)	165	311
Non-U.S.	239	214	168
Total current taxes	749	1,755	1,844
Deferred:			
U.S. federal	1,401	(1,276)	160
State and local	114	(415)	(2)
Non-U.S.	13	1	8
Total deferred taxes	1,528	(1,690)	166
Total income tax provision	$2,277	$ 65	$2,010

The tax effect of temporary differences that give rise to significant portions of deferred tax assets and liabilities at September 30, 2013 and 2012, are presented below:

(In millions)	2013	2012
Deferred Tax Assets:		
Accrued compensation and benefits	$ 154	$ 103
Comprehensive (income) loss	(8)	102
Investments in joint ventures	14	11
Accrued litigation obligation	1	1,654
Client incentives	226	227
Net operating loss carryforward	31	33
Tax credits	22	23
Federal benefit of state taxes	176	90
Federal benefit of foreign taxes	13	16
Other	108	92
Valuation allowance	(25)	(13)
Deferred tax assets	712	2,338
Deferred Tax Liabilities:		
Property, equipment and technology, net	(310)	(288)
Intangible assets	(4,003)	(4,027)
Foreign taxes	(55)	(44)
Other	(12)	(10)
Deferred tax liabilities	(4,380)	(4,369)
Net deferred tax liabilities	$(3,668)	$(2,031)

Total net deferred tax assets and liabilities are included in the Company's consolidated balance sheets as follows:

(In millions)	September 30, 2013	September 30, 2012
Current deferred tax assets	$ 481	$ 2,027
Non-current deferred tax liabilities	(4,149)	(4,058)
Net deferred tax liabilities	$(3,668)	$(2,031)

The decrease in the deferred tax asset for accrued litigation obligation reflects the $1.6 billion reduction in tax payable due to the fiscal 2013 tax deductions of the $4.4 billion covered litigation payments. See *Note 3—Retrospective Responsibility Plan* and *Note 20—Legal Matters*.

In assessing the realizability of deferred tax assets, management considers whether it is more likely than not that all or some portion of the deferred tax assets will not be realized. The ultimate realization of the deferred tax assets is dependent upon the generation of future taxable income during the periods in which those temporary differences are deductible. The fiscal 2013 and 2012 valuation allowances relate primarily to foreign net operating losses from subsidiaries acquired in recent years.

As of September 30, 2013, the Company had $56 million state and $115 million foreign net operating loss carryforwards. The state net operating loss carryforwards will expire in fiscal 2025 through 2031. The foreign net operating loss may be carried forward indefinitely. The Company expects to fully utilize the state net operating loss carryforwards in future years.

As of September 30, 2013, the Company also had federal and state research and development tax credit carryforwards of $2 million and $21 million, respectively. The federal carryforwards will expire in fiscal 2029. The state carryforwards may be carried forward indefinitely. The Company also has federal alternative minimum tax credits of approximately $1 million, which do not expire. The Company expects to realize the benefit of the credit carryforwards in future years.

The income tax provision differs from the amount of income tax determined by applying the applicable U.S. federal statutory rate of 35% to pretax income, as a result of the following:

| | For the Years Ended September 30, | | | | | |
| | 2013 | | 2012 | | 2011 | |
(In millions, except percentages)	Dollars	Percent	Dollars	Percent	Dollars	Percent
U.S. federal income tax at statutory rate	$2,540	35 %	$ 772	35 %	$1,980	35 %
State income taxes, net of federal benefit	42	1 %	36	2 %	203	4 %
Non-U.S. tax effect, net of federal benefit	(328)	(5)%	(257)	(12)%	(150)	(2)%
Reversal of tax reserves related to the deductibility of covered litigation expense	—	— %	(299)	(14)%	—	— %
Remeasurement of deferred taxes due to:						
California state apportionment rule changes	—	— %	(208)	(9)%	—	— %
Other state apportionment changes	(6)	— %	11	1 %	(3)	— %
Revaluation of Visa Europe put option	—	— %	—	— %	(43)	(1)%
Other, net	29	— %	10	— %	23	— %
Income tax provision	$2,277	31 %	$ 65	3 %	$2,010	36 %

The effective income tax rate in fiscal 2013 differs from the rates in fiscal 2012 and 2011 mainly due to:
- the decrease in overall ongoing state tax rate beginning in fiscal 2012 as a result of changes in California apportionment rules adopted in that year;
- a tax benefit recognized in fiscal 2013 as a result of new guidance issued by the state of California regarding apportionment rules for years prior to fiscal 2012;
- certain foreign tax credit benefits related to prior years recognized in fiscal 2013; and
- the absence of the following in fiscal 2013 :
  — the fiscal 2012 reversal of previously recorded tax reserves associated with uncertainties related to the deductibility of covered litigation expense;
  — a fiscal 2012 one-time, non-cash benefit from the remeasurement of existing net deferred tax liabilities due to the changes in California apportionment rules adopted in that year;
  — the effect of applying the aforementioned fiscal 2012 tax benefits to a fiscal 2012 pre-tax income that was reduced by the $4.1 billion covered litigation provision; and
  — the nontaxable revaluation of the Visa Europe put option recorded in fiscal 2011.

Current income taxes receivable were $142 million and $179 million at September 30, 2013 and 2012, respectively. Non-current income taxes receivable of $253 million were included in other assets at September 30, 2013. See *Note 5—Prepaid Expenses and Other Assets*. At September 30, 2013 and 2012, income taxes payable of $64 million and $58 million, respectively, were included in accrued income taxes as part of accrued liabilities, and accrued income taxes of $453 million and $171 million, respectively, were included in other long-term liabilities. See *Note 8—Accrued and Other Liabilities*.

2.25 CISCO SYSTEMS, INC. (JUL)

CONSOLIDATED BALANCE SHEETS (in part)

(In millions, except par value)

	July 27, 2013	July 28, 2012
Assets		
Current assets:		
Cash and cash equivalents	$ 7,925	$ 9,799
Investments	42,685	38,917
Accounts receivable, net of allowance for doubtful accounts of $228 at July 27, 2013 and $207 at July 28, 2012	5,470	4,369
Inventories	1,476	1,663
Financing receivables, net	4,037	3,661
Deferred tax assets	2,616	2,294
Other current assets	1,312	1,230
Total current assets	65,521	61,933
Property and equipment, net	3,322	3,402
Financing receivables, net	3,911	3,585
Goodwill	21,919	16,998
Purchased intangible assets, net	3,403	1,959
Other assets	3,115	3,882
Total Assets	$101,191	$91,759

NOTES TO CONSOLIDATED FINANCIAL STATEMENTS

2. Summary of Significant Accounting Policies (in part)

(f) Financing Receivables The Company provides financing arrangements, including leases, financed service contracts, and loans, for certain qualified end-user customers to build, maintain, and upgrade their networks. Lease receivables primarily represent sales-type and direct-financing leases. Leases have on average a four-year term and are usually collateralized by a security interest in the underlying assets, while loan receivables generally have terms of up to three years. Financed service contracts typically have terms of one to three years and primarily relate to technical support services.

The Company determines the adequacy of its allowance for credit loss by assessing the risks and losses inherent in its financing receivables by portfolio segment. The portfolio segment is based on the types of financing offered by the Company to its customers: lease receivables, loan receivables, and financed service contracts and other.

The Company assesses the allowance for credit loss related to financing receivables on either an individual or a collective basis. The Company considers various factors in evaluating lease and loan receivables and the earned portion of financed service contracts for possible impairment on an individual basis. These factors include the Company's historical experience, credit quality and age of the receivable balances, and economic conditions that may affect a customer's ability to pay. When the evaluation indicates that it is probable that all amounts due pursuant to the contractual terms of the financing agreement, including scheduled interest payments, are unable to be collected, the financing receivable is considered impaired. All such outstanding amounts, including any accrued interest, will be assessed and fully reserved at the customer level. The Company's internal credit risk ratings are categorized as 1 through 10, with the lowest credit risk rating representing the highest quality financing receivables. Typically, the Company also considers receivables with a risk rating of 8 or higher to be impaired and will include them in the individual assessment for allowance. The Company evaluates the remainder of its financing receivables portfolio for impairment on a collective basis and records an allowance for credit loss at the portfolio segment level. When evaluating the financing receivables on a collective basis, the Company uses expected default frequency rates published by a major third-party credit-rating agency as well as its own historical loss rate in the event of default, while also systematically giving effect to economic conditions, concentration of risk, and correlation.

Expected default frequency rates are published quarterly by a major third-party credit-rating agency, and the internal credit risk rating is derived by taking into consideration various customer-specific factors and macroeconomic conditions. These factors, which include the strength of the customer's business and financial performance, the quality of the customer's banking relationships, the Company's specific historical experience with the customer, the performance and outlook of the customer's industry, the customer's legal and regulatory environment, the potential sovereign risk of the geographic locations in which the customer is operating, and independent third-party evaluations, are updated regularly or when facts and circumstances indicate that an update is deemed necessary.

Financing receivables are written off at the point when they are considered uncollectible and all outstanding balances, including any previously earned but uncollected interest income, will be reversed and charged against the allowance for credit loss. The Company does not typically have any partially written-off financing receivables.

Outstanding financing receivables that are aged 31 days or more from the contractual payment date are considered past due. The Company does not accrue interest on financing receivables that are considered impaired or more than 90 days past due unless either the receivable has not been collected due to administrative reasons or the receivable is well secured and in the process of collection. Financing receivables may be placed on nonaccrual status earlier if, in management's opinion, a timely collection of the full principal and interest becomes uncertain. After a financing receivable has been categorized as nonaccrual, interest will be recognized when cash is received. A financing receivable may be returned to accrual status after all of the customer's delinquent balances of principal and interest have been settled and the customer remains current for an appropriate period.

The Company facilitates arrangements for third-party financing extended to channel partners, consisting of revolving short-term financing, generally with payment terms ranging from 60 to 90 days. In certain instances, these financing arrangements result in a transfer of the Company's receivables to the third party. The receivables are derecognized upon transfer, as these transfers qualify as true sales, and the Company receives a payment for the receivables from the third party based on the Company's standard payment terms. These financing arrangements facilitate the working capital requirements of the channel partners, and, in some cases, the Company guarantees a portion of these arrangements. The Company also provides financing guarantees for third-party financing arrangements extended to end-user customers related to leases and loans, which typically have terms of up to three years. The Company could be called upon to make payments under these guarantees in the event of nonpayment by the channel partners or end-user customers. Deferred revenue relating to these financing arrangements is recorded in accordance with revenue recognition policies or for the fair value of the financing guarantees.

7. Financing Receivables and Guarantees

(a) Financing Receivables

Financing receivables primarily consist of lease receivables, loan receivables, and financed service contracts and other. Lease receivables represent sales-type and direct-financing leases resulting from the sale of the Company's and complementary third-party products and are typically collateralized by a security interest in the underlying assets. Loan receivables represent financing arrangements related to the sale of the Company's products and services, which may include additional funding for other costs associated with network installation and integration of the Company's products and services. Lease receivables consist of arrangements with terms of four years on average, while loan receivables generally have terms of up to three years. The financed service contracts and other category includes financing receivables related to technical support and advanced services, as well as receivables related to financing of certain indirect costs associated with leases. Revenue related to the technical support services is typically deferred and included in deferred service revenue and is recognized ratably over the period during which the related services are to be performed, which typically ranges from one to three years.

A summary of the Company's financing receivables is presented as follows (in millions):

July 27, 2013	Lease Receivables	Loan Receivables	Financed Service Contracts and Other	Total Financing Receivables
Gross	$3,780	$1,649	$3,136	$8,565
Unearned income	(273)	—	—	(273)
Allowance for credit loss	(238)	(86)	(20)	(344)
Total, net	$3,269	$1,563	$3,116	$7,948
Reported as:				
Current	$1,418	$ 898	$1,721	$4,037
Noncurrent	1,851	665	1,395	3,911
Total, net	$3,269	$1,563	$3,116	$7,948

July 28, 2012	Lease Receivables	Loan Receivables	Financed Service Contracts and Other	Total Financing Receivables
Gross	$3,429	$1,796	$2,651	$7,876
Unearned income	(250)	—	—	(250)
Allowance for credit loss	(247)	(122)	(11)	(380)
Total, net	$2,932	$1,674	$2,640	$7,246
Reported as:				
Current	$1,200	$ 968	$1,493	$3,661
Noncurrent	1,732	706	1,147	3,585
Total, net	$2,932	$1,674	$2,640	$7,246

As of July 27, 2013 and July 28, 2012, the deferred service revenue related to the financed service contracts and other was $2,036 million and $1,838 million, respectively.

Contractual maturities of the gross lease receivables at July 27, 2013 are summarized as follows (in millions):

Fiscal Year	Amount
2014	$1,656
2015	1,114
2016	632
2017	301
2018	75
Thereafter	2
Total	$3,780

Actual cash collections may differ from the contractual maturities due to early customer buyouts, refinancings, or defaults.

(b) Credit Quality of Financing Receivables

Financing receivables categorized by the Company's internal credit risk rating as of July 27, 2013 and July 28, 2012 are summarized as follows (in millions):

July 27, 2013	Internal Credit Risk Rating			Total	Residual Value	Gross Receivables, Net of Unearned Income
	1 to 4	5 to 6	7 and Higher			
Lease receivables	$1,681	$1,482	$93	$3,256	$251	$3,507
Loan receivables	842	777	30	1,649	—	1,649
Financed service contracts and other	1,876	1,141	119	3,136	—	3,136
Total	$4,399	$3,400	$242	$8,041	$251	$8,292

July 28, 2012	Internal Credit Risk Rating			Total	Residual Value	Gross Receivables, Net of Unearned Income
	1 to 4	5 to 6	7 and Higher			
Lease receivables	$1,532	$1,342	$31	$2,905	$274	$3,179
Loan receivables	831	921	44	1,796	—	1,796
Financed service contracts and other	1,552	1,030	69	2,651	—	2,651
Total	$3,915	$3,293	$144	$7,352	$274	$7,626

The Company determines the adequacy of its allowance for credit loss by assessing the risks and losses inherent in its financing receivables by portfolio segment. The portfolio segment is based on the types of financing offered by the Company to its customers: lease receivables, loan receivables, and financed service contracts and other.

The Company's internal credit risk ratings of 1 through 4 correspond to investment-grade ratings, while credit risk ratings of 5 and 6 correspond to non-investment grade ratings. Credit risk ratings of 7 and higher correspond to substandard ratings and constitute a relatively small portion of the Company's financing receivables.

In circumstances when collectibility is not deemed reasonably assured, the associated revenue is deferred in accordance with the Company's revenue recognition policies, and the related allowance for credit loss, if any, is included in deferred revenue. The Company also records deferred revenue associated with financing receivables when there are remaining performance obligations, as it does for financed service contracts. Total allowances for credit loss and deferred revenue as of July 27, 2013 and July 28, 2012 were $2,453 million and $2,387 million, respectively, and were associated with financing receivables (net of unearned income) of $8,292 million and $7,626 million as of their respective period ends. The Company did not modify any financing receivables during the periods presented.

The following tables present the aging analysis of financing receivables as of July 27, 2013 and July 28, 2012 (in millions):

July 27, 2013	Days Past Due (Includes Billed and Unbilled)			Total Past Due	Current	Gross Receivables, Net of Unearned Income	Nonaccrual Financing Receivables	Impaired Financing Receivables
	31–60	61–90	91 +					
Lease receivables	$ 85	$48	$124	$257	$3,250	$3,507	$27	$22
Loan receivables	6	3	11	20	1,629	1,649	11	9
Financed service contracts and other	75	48	392	515	2,621	3,136	18	11
Total	$166	$99	$527	$792	$7,500	$8,292	$56	$42

| July 28, 2012 | Days Past Due (Includes Billed and Unbilled) | | | | | | | |
	31–60	61–90	91 +	Total Past Due	Current	Gross Receivables, Net of Unearned Income	Nonaccrual Financing Receivables	Impaired Financing Receivables
Lease receivables	$151	$ 69	$173	$393	$2,786	$3,179	$23	$14
Loan receivables	10	8	11	29	1,767	1,796	4	4
Financed service contracts and other	89	68	392	549	2,102	2,651	18	10
Total	$250	$145	$576	$971	$6,655	$7,626	$45	$28

Past due financing receivables are those that are 31 days or more past due according to their contractual payment terms. The data in the preceding tables are presented by contract and the aging classification of each contract is based on the oldest outstanding receivable, and therefore past due amounts also include unbilled and current receivables within the same contract. The preceding aging tables exclude pending adjustments on billed tax assessment in certain international markets. The balances of either unbilled or current financing receivables included in the category of 91 days plus past due for financing receivables were $406 million and $455 million as of July 27, 2013 and July 28, 2012, respectively.

As of July 27, 2013, the Company had financing receivables of $87 million, net of unbilled or current receivables from the same contract, that were in the category for 91 days plus past due but remained on accrual status. Such balance was $109 million as of July 28, 2012. A financing receivable may be placed on nonaccrual status earlier if, in management's opinion, a timely collection of the full principal and interest becomes uncertain.

(c) Allowance for Credit Loss Rollforward

The allowances for credit loss and the related financing receivables are summarized as follows (in millions):

| | Credit Loss Allowances | | | |
	Lease Receivables	Loan Receivables	Financed Service Contracts and Other	Total
Allowance for credit loss as of July 28, 2012	$ 247	$ 122	$ 11	$ 380
Provisions	21	(20)	10	11
Write-offs, net of recoveries	(30)	(15)	(1)	(46)
Foreign exchange and other	—	(1)	—	(1)
Allowance for credit loss as of July 27, 2013	$ 238	$ 86	$ 20	$ 344
Gross receivables as of July 27, 2013, net of unearned income	$3,507	$1,649	$3,136	$8,292

| | Credit Loss Allowances | | | |
	Lease Receivables	Loan Receivables	Financed Service Contracts and Other	Total
Allowance for credit loss as of July 30, 2011	$ 237	$ 103	$ 27	$ 367
Provisions	22	22	(13)	31
Write-offs, net of recoveries	(2)	—	(1)	(3)
Foreign exchange and other	(10)	(3)	(2)	(15)
Allowance for credit loss as of July 28, 2012	$ 247	$ 122	$ 11	$ 380
Gross receivables as of July 28, 2012, net of unearned income	$3,179	$1,796	$2,651	$7,626

| | Credit Loss Allowances | | | |
	Lease Receivables	Loan Receivables	Financed Service Contracts and Other	Total
Allowance for credit loss as of July 31, 2010	$ 207	$ 73	$ 21	$ 301
Provisions	31	43	8	82
Write-offs, net of recoveries	(13)	(18)	(2)	(33)
Foreign exchange and other	12	5	—	17
Allowance for credit loss as of July 30, 2011	$ 237	$ 103	$ 27	$ 367
Gross receivables as of July 30, 2011, net of unearned income	$2,861	$1,468	$2,637	$6,966

(d) Financing Guarantees

In the ordinary course of business, the Company provides financing guarantees for various third-party financing arrangements extended to channel partners and end-user customers. Payments under these financing guarantee arrangements were not material for the periods presented.

Channel Partner Financing Guarantees The Company facilitates arrangements for third-party financing extended to channel partners, consisting of revolving short-term financing, generally with payment terms ranging from 60 to 90 days. These financing arrangements facilitate the working capital requirements of the channel partners, and, in some cases, the Company guarantees a portion of these arrangements. The volume of channel partner financing was $23.8 billion, $21.3 billion, and $18.2 billion for fiscal 2013, 2012, and 2011, respectively. The balance of the channel partner financing subject to guarantees was $1.4 billion and $1.2 billion as of July 27, 2013 and July 28, 2012, respectively.

End-User Financing Guarantees The Company also provides financing guarantees for third-party financing arrangements extended to end-user customers related to leases and loans, which typically have terms of up to three years. The volume of financing provided by third parties for leases and loans as to which the Company had provided guarantees was $185 million for fiscal 2013, $227 million for fiscal 2012, and $247 million for fiscal 2011.

Financing Guarantee Summary The aggregate amounts of financing guarantees outstanding at July 27, 2013 and July 28, 2012, representing the total maximum potential future payments under financing arrangements with third parties along with the related deferred revenue, are summarized in the following table (in millions):

	July 27, 2013	July 28, 2012
Maximum potential future payments relating to financing guarantees:		
Channel partner	$ 438	$ 277
End user	237	232
Total	$ 675	$ 509
Deferred revenue associated with financing guarantees:		
Channel partner	$(225)	$(193)
End user	(191)	(200)
Total	$(416)	$(393)
Maximum potential future payments relating to financing guarantees, net of associated deferred revenue	$ 259	$ 116

INSURANCE CLAIMS

2.26 CRANE CO. (DEC)
CONSOLIDATED BALANCE SHEETS (in part)

	Balance at December 31,	
(In thousands, except shares and per share data)	2013	2012
Assets (in part)		
Current assets:		
Cash and cash equivalents	$ 270,643	$ 423,947
Current insurance receivable — asbestos	22,783	33,722
Accounts receivable, net	437,541	333,330
Inventories	368,886	352,725
Current deferred tax assets	31,651	21,618
Other current assets	17,588	15,179
Total current assets	1,149,092	1,180,521

NOTES TO CONSOLIDATED FINANCIAL STATEMENTS

Note 11–Commitments and Contingencies (in part)

Asbestos Liability (in part)

Insurance Coverage and Receivables. Prior to 2005, a significant portion of the Company's settlement and defense costs were paid by its primary insurers. With the exhaustion of that primary coverage, the Company began negotiations with its excess insurers to reimburse the Company for a portion of its settlement and/or defense costs as incurred. To date, the Company has entered into agreements providing for such reimbursements, known as "coverage-in-place", with eleven of its excess insurer groups. Under such coverage-in-place agreements, an insurer's policies remain in force and the insurer undertakes to provide coverage for the Company's present and future asbestos claims on specified terms and conditions that address, among other things, the share of asbestos claims costs to be paid by the insurer, payment terms, claims handling procedures and the expiration of the insurer's obligations. Similarly, under a variant of coverage-in-place, the Company has entered into an agreement with a group of insurers confirming the aggregate amount of available coverage under the subject policies and setting forth a schedule for future reimbursement payments to the Company based on aggregate indemnity and defense payments made. In addition, with ten of its excess insurer groups, the Company entered into policy buyout agreements, settling all asbestos and other coverage obligations for an agreed sum, totaling $82.5 million in aggregate. Reimbursements from insurers for past and ongoing settlement and defense costs allocable to their policies have been made in accordance with these coverage-in-place and other agreements. All of these agreements include provisions for mutual releases, indemnification of the insurer and, for coverage-in-place, claims handling procedures. With the agreements referenced above, the Company has concluded settlements with all but one of its solvent excess insurers whose policies are expected to respond to the aggregate costs included in the updated liability estimate. That insurer, which issued a single applicable policy, has been paying the shares of defense and indemnity costs the Company has allocated to it, subject to a reservation of rights. There are no pending legal proceedings between the Company and any insurer contesting the Company's asbestos claims under its insurance policies.

In conjunction with developing the aggregate liability estimate referenced above, the Company also developed an estimate of probable insurance recoveries for its asbestos liabilities. In developing this estimate, the Company considered its coverage-in-place and other settlement agreements described above, as well as a number of additional factors. These additional factors include the financial viability of the insurance companies, the method by which losses will be allocated to the various insurance policies and the years covered by those policies, how settlement and defense costs will be covered by the insurance policies and interpretation of the effect on coverage of various policy terms and limits and their interrelationships. In addition, the timing and amount of reimbursements will vary because the Company's insurance coverage for asbestos claims involves multiple insurers, with different policy terms and certain gaps in coverage. In addition to consulting with legal counsel on these insurance matters, the Company retained insurance consultants to assist management in the estimation of probable insurance recoveries based upon the aggregate liability estimate described above and assuming the continued viability of all solvent insurance carriers. Based upon the analysis of policy terms and other factors noted above by the Company's legal counsel, and incorporating risk mitigation judgments by the Company where policy terms or other factors were not certain, the Company's insurance consultants compiled a model indicating how the Company's historical insurance policies would respond to varying levels of asbestos settlement and defense costs and the allocation of such costs between such insurers and the Company. Using the estimated liability as of December 31, 2011 (for claims filed or expected to be filed through 2021), the insurance consultant's model forecasted that approximately 25% of the liability would be reimbursed by the Company's insurers. While there are overall limits on the aggregate amount of insurance available to the Company with respect to asbestos claims, those overall limits were not reached by the total estimated liability currently recorded by the Company, and such overall limits did not influence the Company in its determination of the asset amount to record. The proportion of the asbestos liability that is allocated to certain insurance coverage years, however, exceeds the limits of available insurance in those years. The Company allocates to itself the amount of the asbestos liability (for claims filed or expected to be filed through 2021) that is in excess of available insurance coverage allocated to such years. An asset of $225 million was recorded as of December 31, 2011 representing the probable insurance reimbursement for such claims expected through 2021. The asset is reduced as reimbursements and other payments from insurers are received. The asset was $171 million as of December 31, 2013.

The Company reviews the aforementioned estimated reimbursement rate with its insurance consultants on a periodic basis in order to confirm its overall consistency with the Company's established reserves. The reviews encompass consideration of the performance of the insurers under coverage-in-place agreements and the effect of any additional lump-sum payments under policy buyout agreements. Since December 2011, there have been no developments that have caused the Company to change the estimated 25% rate, although actual insurance reimbursements vary from period to period, and will decline over time, for the reasons cited above.

Uncertainties. Estimation of the Company's ultimate exposure for asbestos-related claims is subject to significant uncertainties, as there are multiple variables that can affect the timing, severity and quantity of claims and the manner of their resolution. The Company cautions that its estimated liability is based on assumptions with respect to future claims, settlement and defense costs based on past experience that may not prove reliable as predictors. A significant upward or downward trend in the number of claims filed, depending on the nature of the alleged injury, the jurisdiction where filed and the quality of the product identification, or a significant upward or downward trend in the costs of defending claims, could change the estimated liability, as would substantial adverse verdicts at trial that withstand appeal. A legislative solution, structured settlement transaction, or significant change in relevant case law could also change the estimated liability.

The same factors that affect developing estimates of probable settlement and defense costs for asbestos-related liabilities also affect estimates of the probable insurance reimbursements, as do a number of additional factors. These additional factors include the financial viability of the insurance companies, the method by which losses will be allocated to the various insurance policies and the years covered by those policies, how settlement and defense costs will be covered by the insurance policies and interpretation of the effect on coverage of various policy terms and limits and their interrelationships. In addition, due to the uncertainties inherent in litigation matters, no assurances can be given regarding the outcome of any litigation, if necessary, to enforce the Company's rights under its insurance policies or settlement agreements.

Many uncertainties exist surrounding asbestos litigation, and the Company will continue to evaluate its estimated asbestos-related liability and corresponding estimated insurance reimbursement as well as the underlying assumptions and process used to derive these amounts. These uncertainties may result in the Company incurring future charges or increases to income to adjust the carrying value of recorded liabilities and assets, particularly if the number of claims and settlement and defense costs change significantly, or if there are significant developments in the trend of case law or court procedures, or if legislation or another alternative solution is implemented; however, the Company is currently unable to estimate such future changes and, accordingly, while it is probable that the Company will incur additional charges for asbestos liabilities and defense costs in excess of the amounts currently provided, the Company does not believe that any such amount can be reasonably determined beyond 2021. Although the resolution of these claims may take many years, the effect on the results of operations, financial position and cash flow in any given period from a revision to these estimates could be material.

Receivables Sold or Collateralized

RECOGNITION AND MEASUREMENT

2.27 FASB ASC 860, *Transfers and Servicing*, establishes criteria for determining whether a transfer of financial assets in exchange for cash or other consideration should be accounted for as a sale or pledge of collateral in a secured borrowing. FASB ASC 860 also establishes the criteria for accounting for securitizations and other transfers of financial assets and collateral and requires certain disclosures.

2.28 FASB ASC 860 requires that all separately recognized servicing assets and liabilities be initially measured at fair value. Further, FASB ASC 860 permits, but does not require, the subsequent measurement of servicing assets and liabilities at fair value.

2.29 ASU No. 2009-16, *Transfers and Servicing (Topic 860): Accounting for Transfers of Financial Assets*, eliminated the exceptions for qualifying special-purpose entities from the consolidation guidance. Further, ASU No. 2009-16 provides clarifications of the requirements for isolation and limitations on portions of financial assets that are eligible for sale accounting. ASU No. 2009-16 was effective for fiscal years beginning after November 15, 2009.

DISCLOSURE

2.30 FASB ASC 860 requires additional disclosures and separate balance sheet presentation of the carrying amounts of servicing assets and liabilities that are subsequently measured at fair value. FASB ASC 860-50-50-2 requires disclosures including (*a*) a description of the risks inherent in servicing assets and servicing liabilities, (*b*) the amount of contractually specified servicing fees, late fees, and ancillary fees earned for each period, including a description of where each amount is reported in the statement of income, and (*c*) quantitative and qualitative information about the assumptions used to estimate fair value.

PRESENTATION AND DISCLOSURE EXCERPTS

RECEIVABLES SOLD OR COLLATERALIZED

2.31 TENNECO INC. (DEC)
CONSOLIDATED BALANCE SHEETS (in part)

	December 31,	
(Millions)	2013	2012
Assets		
Current assets:		
Cash and cash equivalents	$ 275	$ 223
Restricted cash	5	—
Receivables—		
Customer notes and accounts, net	1,041	966
Other	19	20
Inventories	656	667
Deferred income taxes	71	72
Prepayments and other	223	176
Total current assets	2,290	2,124

(continued)

(Millions)	December 31,	
	2013	2012
Other assets:		
Long-term receivables, net	14	4
Goodwill	69	72
Intangibles, net	30	35
Deferred income taxes	125	116
Other	127	135
	365	362
Plant, property, and equipment, at cost	3,498	3,365
Less—Accumulated depreciation and amortization	(2,323)	(2,243)
	1,175	1,122
Total Assets	$ 3,830	$ 3,608

NOTES TO CONSOLIDATED FINANCIAL STATEMENTS

5. Long-Term Debt, Short-Term Debt, and Financing Arrangements (in part)

Accounts Receivable Securitization. We securitize some of our accounts receivable on a limited recourse basis in North America and Europe. As servicer under these accounts receivable securitization programs, we are responsible for performing all accounts receivable administration functions for these securitized financial assets including collections and processing of customer invoice adjustments. In North America, we have an accounts receivable securitization program with three commercial banks comprised of a first priority facility and a second priority facility. We securitize original equipment and aftermarket receivables on a daily basis under the bank program. In March 2013, the North American program was amended and extended to March 21, 2014. The first priority facility continues to provide financing of up to $110 million and the second priority facility, which is subordinated to the first priority facility, continues to provide up to an additional $40 million of financing. Both facilities monetize accounts receivable generated in the U.S. and Canada that meet certain eligibility requirements. The second priority facility also monetizes certain accounts receivable generated in the U.S. or Canada that would otherwise be ineligible under the first priority securitization facility. The amount of outstanding third-party investments in our securitized accounts receivable under the North American program was $10 million at December 31, 2013 and $50 million at December 31, 2012.

Each facility contains customary covenants for financings of this type, including restrictions related to liens, payments, mergers or consolidations and amendments to the agreements underlying the receivables pool. Further, each facility may be terminated upon the occurrence of customary events (with customary grace periods, if applicable), including breaches of covenants, failure to maintain certain financial ratios, inaccuracies of representations and warranties, bankruptcy and insolvency events, certain changes in the rate of default or delinquency of the receivables, a change of control and the entry or other enforcement of material judgments. In addition, each facility contains cross-default provisions, where the facility could be terminated in the event of non-payment of other material indebtedness when due and any other event which permits the acceleration of the maturity of material indebtedness.

We also securitize receivables in our European operations with regional banks in Europe. The arrangements to securitize receivables in Europe are provided under six separate facilities provided by various financial institutions in each of the foreign jurisdictions. The commitments for these arrangements are generally for one year, but some may be cancelled with notice 90 days prior to renewal. In some instances, the arrangement provides for cancellation by the applicable financial institution at any time upon notification. The amount of outstanding third-party investments in our securitized accounts receivable in Europe was $134 million and $94 million at December 31, 2013 and December 31, 2012, respectively.

If we were not able to securitize receivables under either the North American or European securitization programs, our borrowings under our revolving credit agreement might increase. These accounts receivable securitization programs provide us with access to cash at costs that are generally favorable to alternative sources of financing, and allow us to reduce borrowings under our revolving credit agreement.

In our North American accounts receivable securitization programs, we transfer a partial interest in a pool of receivables and the interest that we retain is subordinate to the transferred interest. Accordingly, we account for our North American securitization program as a secured borrowing. In our European programs, we transfer accounts receivables in their entirety to the acquiring entities and satisfy all of the conditions established under ASC Topic 860, "Transfers and Servicing," to report the transfer of financial assets in their entirety as a sale. The fair value of assets received as proceeds in exchange for the transfer of accounts receivable under our European securitization programs approximates the fair value of such receivables. We recognized $2 million in interest expense for the year ended 2013 and $3 million in interest expense for each of the years ended 2012 and 2011, respectively, relating to our North American securitization program. In addition, we recognized a loss of $4 million, $4 million and $5 million for each of the years ended 2013, 2012 and 2011, on the sale of trade accounts receivable in our European accounts receivable securitization programs, representing the discount from book values at which these receivables were sold to our banks. The discount rate varies based on funding costs incurred by our banks, which averaged approximately three percent for each of the years ended 2013, 2012 and 2011, respectively.

2.32 ALLIANCE ONE INTERNATIONAL, INC. (MAR)
CONSOLIDATED BALANCE SHEETS (in part)

(In thousands)	March 31, 2013	March 31, 2012
Assets		
Current assets		
Cash and cash equivalents	$ 92,026	$ 119,743
Trade and other receivables, net	224,222	303,090
Accounts receivable, related parties	55,696	32,316
Inventories	903,947	839,902
Advances to tobacco suppliers	109,520	89,378
Recoverable income taxes	8,980	9,592
Current deferred taxes	16,776	23,855
Prepaid expenses	36,811	45,097
Current derivative asset	3,145	312
Other current assets	13,632	14,562
Total current assets	1,464,755	1,477,847
Other assets		
Investments in unconsolidated affiliates	25,169	24,530
Goodwill and other intangible assets	31,471	35,865
Deferred income taxes	56,045	73,378
Other deferred charges	12,971	12,467
Other noncurrent assets	50,190	66,079
	175,846	212,319
Property, plant and equipment, net	270,978	259,679
	$1,911,579	$1,949,845

NOTES TO CONSOLIDATED FINANCIAL STATEMENTS

(In thousands)

Note 17—Sale of Receivables

The Company sells trade receivables to unaffiliated financial institutions under three accounts receivable securitization programs. Under the first program, the Company continuously sells a designated pool of trade receivables to a special purpose entity, which in turn sells 100% of the receivables to an unaffiliated financial institution. This program allows the Company to receive a cash payment and a deferred purchase price receivable for sold receivables. Following the sale and transfer of the receivables to the special purpose entity, the receivables are isolated from the Company and its affiliates, and upon the sale and transfer of the receivables from the special purpose entity to the unaffiliated financial institutions effective control of the receivables is passed to the unaffiliated financial institution, which has all rights, including the right to pledge or sell the receivables. The investment limit of this facility was increased from $125,000 to $250,000 in March 2012. The cost for increasing this facility was $1,545 and included in Other Income in the Statements of Consolidated Operations in fiscal 2012. The Company incurred program costs of $2,100 during the year ending March 31, 2013 which were included in Other Income in the Statements of Consolidated Operations. The program requires a minimum level of deferred purchase price to be retained by the Company in connection with the sales. The Company continues to service, administer and collect the receivables on behalf of the special purpose entity and receives a servicing fee of .5% of serviced receivables per annum. As the Company estimates the fee it receives in return for its obligation to service these receivables is at fair value, no servicing assets or liabilities are recognized. Servicing fees recognized were not material and are recorded as a reduction of Selling, General and Administrative Expenses within the Statements of Consolidated Operations.

The agreements for the second and third securitization programs were executed on September 28, 2011 and March 28, 2013 between the Company and unaffiliated financial institutions. These programs also allow the Company to receive a cash payment and a deferred purchase price receivable for sold receivables. These are uncommitted programs, whereby the Company offers receivables for sale to the respective unaffiliated financial institution, which are then subject to acceptance by the unaffiliated financial institution. Following the sale and transfer of the receivables to the unaffiliated financial institution, the receivables are isolated from the Company and its affiliates, and effective control of the receivables is passed to the unaffiliated financial institution, which has all rights, including the right to pledge or sell the receivables. The Company receives no servicing fee from the unaffiliated financial institution and as a result, has established a servicing liability based upon unobservable inputs, primarily discounted cash flow. For the year ended March 31, 2013, the expense for the servicing liability was $221 and included in Other Income in the Statements of Consolidated Operations. The liability is recorded in Accrued Expenses and other Current Liabilities in the Consolidated Balance Sheets. As receivables sold under these facilities were settled in fiscal 2013, the servicing liability was reduced by $55 and included in Selling, General and Administrative Expenses in the Statements of Consolidated Operations. The investment limits under the September 28, 2011 and March 28, 2013 agreements are $35,000 and $85,000 respectively. The cost for entering the March 28, 2013 program was $1,220 and is included in Other Income in the Statements of Consolidated Operations in fiscal 2013.

Under the programs, all of the receivables sold for cash are removed from the Consolidated Balance Sheets and the net cash proceeds received by the Company are included as cash provided by operating activities in the Statements of Consolidated Cash Flows. A portion of the purchase price for the receivables is paid by the unaffiliated financial institutions in cash and the balance is a deferred purchase price receivable, which is paid as payments on the receivables are collected from account debtors. The deferred purchase price receivable represents a continuing involvement and a beneficial interest in the transferred financial assets and is recognized at fair value as part of the sale transaction. The deferred purchase price receivables are included in Trade and Other Receivables, Net in the Consolidated Balance Sheets and are valued using unobservable inputs (i.e., level three inputs), primarily discounted cash flow. As servicer of these facilities, the Company may receive funds that are due to the unaffiliated financial institutions which are net settled on the next settlement date. As of March 31, 2013, Trade and Other Receivables, Net in the Consolidated Balance Sheets has been reduced by $ 12,316 as a result of the net settlement. See Note 18 "Fair Value Measurements" to the "Notes to Consolidated Financial Statements" for further information.

The difference between the carrying amount of the receivables sold under these programs and the sum of the cash and fair value of the other assets received at the time of transfer is recognized as a loss on sale of the related receivables and recorded in Other Income in the Statements of Consolidated Operations.

	2013	2012
Receivables outstanding in facility as of March 31:	$156,633	$182,856
Beneficial interest as of March 31	$ 31,992	$ 25,864
Servicing Liability as of March 31	$ 166	$ 45
Cash proceeds for the twelve months ended March 31:		
Cash purchase price	$643,399	$638,975
Deferred purchase price	287,027	274,194
Service fees	644	562
Total	$931,070	$913,731

2.33 THE SCOTTS MIRACLE-GRO COMPANY (SEP)

CONSOLIDATED BALANCE SHEETS (in part)

(In millions, except stated value per share)

	September 30,	
	2013	2012
Assets		
Current assets:		
Cash and cash equivalents	$ 129.8	$ 131.9
Accounts receivable, less allowances of $9.5 in 2013 and $10.5 in 2012	206.6	330.9
Accounts receivable pledged	106.7	—
Inventories	324.9	414.9
Prepaid and other current assets	113.0	122.3
Total current assets	881.0	1,000.0
Property, plant and equipment, net	422.3	427.4
Goodwill	315.1	309.4
Intangible assets, net	284.4	307.1
Other assets	34.4	30.5
Total assets	$1,937.2	$2,074.4
Liabilities and Shareholders' Equity (in part)		
Current liabilities:		
Current portion of debt	$ 92.4	$ 1.5
Accounts payable	137.7	152.3
Other current liabilities	279.7	279.8
Total current liabilities	509.8	433.6
Long-term debt	478.1	781.1
Other liabilities	238.8	257.8
Total liabilities	1,226.7	1,472.5

Note 10. Debt (in part)

Master Accounts Receivable Purchase Agreement

The Company maintains a Master Accounts Receivable Purchase Agreement ("MARP Agreement"), which is uncommitted and provides for the discretionary sale by the Company, and the discretionary purchase by the banks, on a revolving basis, of accounts receivable generated by sales to three specified account debtors in an aggregate amount not to exceed $400 million. On October 25, 2013, the Company signed an amendment to the existing MARP Agreement which extended the termination date to August 29, 2014, or such later date as may be mutually agreed by the Company and the banks party thereto. Under the amended terms of the MARP Agreement, the banks have the opportunity to purchase those accounts receivable offered by the Company at a discount (from the agreed base value thereof) effectively equal to the one-week LIBOR plus 0.75%.

The Company accounts for the sale of receivables under its MARP Agreement as short-term debt and continues to carry the receivables on its Consolidated Balance Sheet, primarily as a result of the Company's right to repurchase receivables sold. There were $85.3 million of short-term borrowings as of September 30, 2013 and no short-term borrowings as of September 30, 2012 under the MARP Agreement. The carrying value of the receivables pledged as collateral was $ 106.7 million as of September 30, 2013.

Estimated Fair Values (in part)

A description of the methods and assumptions used to estimate the fair values of the Company's debt instruments is as follows:

Accounts Receivable Pledged

The interest rate on the short-term debt associated with accounts receivable pledged under the MARP Agreement fluctuates with the applicable LIBOR rate, and thus the carrying value is a reasonable estimate of fair value. The fair value measurement for the MARP agreement was classified in Level 2 of the fair value hierarchy.

The estimated fair values of the Company's debt instruments are as follows:

| | Year Ended September 30, | | | | |
| | 2013 | | | 2012 | |
(In millions)	**Carrying Amount**	**Fair Value**		**Carrying Amount**	**Fair Value**
Revolving loans	$ 73.0	$ 73.0		$377.1	$377.1
Senior Notes—7.25%	200.0	209.5		200.0	212.0
Senior Notes—6.625%	200.0	213.5		200.0	217.5
Master Accounts Receivable Purchase Agreement	85.3	85.3		—	—
Other	12.2	12.2		5.5	5.5

RECEIVABLES TRANSFERRED

2.34 DEERE & COMPANY (OCT)
CONSOLIDATED BALANCE SHEET (in part)

As of October 31, 2013 and 2012

(In millions of dollars except per share amounts)

	2013	2012
Assets		
Cash and cash equivalents	$ 3,504.0	$ 4,652.2
Marketable securities	1,624.8	1,470.4
Receivables from unconsolidated affiliates	31.2	59.7
Trade accounts and notes receivable—net	3,758.2	3,799.1
Financing receivables—net	25,632.7	22,159.1
Financing receivables securitized—net	4,153.1	3,617.6
Other receivables	1,464.0	1,790.9
Equipment on operating leases—net	3,152.2	2,527.8

(continued)

	2013	2012
Inventories	4,934.7	5,170.0
Property and equipment—net	5,466.9	5,011.9
Investments in unconsolidated affiliates	221.4	215.0
Goodwill	844.8	921.2
Other intangible assets—net	77.1	105.0
Retirement benefits	551.1	20.2
Deferred income taxes	2,325.4	3,280.4
Other assets	1,274.7	1,465.3
Assets held for sale	505.0	
Total assets	$59,521.3	$56,265.8
Liabilities and Stockholders' Equity (in part)		
Liabilities		
Short-term borrowings	$ 8,788.9	$ 6,392.5
Short-term securitization borrowings	4,109.1	3,574.8
Payables to unconsolidated affiliates	106.9	135.2
Accounts payable and accrued expenses	8,973.6	8,988.9
Deferred income taxes	160.3	164.4
Long-term borrowings	21,577.7	22,453.1
Retirement benefits and other liabilities	5,416.7	7,694.9
Liabilities held for sale	120.4	
Total liabilities	49,253.6	49,403.8

NOTES TO CONSOLIDATED FINANCIAL STATEMENTS

2. Summary of Significant Accounting Policies (in part)

Securitization of Receivables

Certain financing receivables are periodically transferred to special purpose entities (SPEs) in securitization transactions (see Note 13). These securitizations qualify as collateral for secured borrowings and no gains or losses are recognized at the time of securitization. The receivables remain on the balance sheet and are classified as "Financing receivables securitized—net." The company recognizes finance income over the lives of these receivables using the interest method.

13. Securitization of Financing Receivables

The company, as a part of its overall funding strategy, periodically transfers certain financing receivables (retail notes) into variable interest entities (VIEs) that are special purpose entities (SPEs), or a non-VIE banking operation, as part of its asset-backed securities programs (securitizations). The structure of these transactions is such that the transfer of the retail notes did not meet the criteria of sales of receivables, and is, therefore, accounted for as a secured borrowing. SPEs utilized in securitizations of retail notes differ from other entities included in the company's consolidated statements because the assets they hold are legally isolated. Use of the assets held by the SPEs or the non-VIE is restricted by terms of the documents governing the securitization transactions.

In securitizations of retail notes related to secured borrowings, the retail notes are transferred to certain SPEs or to a non-VIE banking operation, which in turn issue debt to investors. The resulting secured borrowings are recorded as "Short-term securitization borrowings" on the balance sheet. The securitized retail notes are recorded as "Financing receivables securitized—net" on the balance sheet. The total restricted assets on the balance sheet related to these securitizations include the financing receivables securitized less an allowance for credit losses, and other assets primarily representing restricted cash. For those securitizations in which retail notes are transferred into SPEs, the SPEs supporting the secured borrowings are consolidated unless the company does not have both the power to direct the activities that most significantly impact the SPEs' economic performance and the obligation to absorb losses or the right to receive benefits that could potentially be significant to the SPEs. No additional support to these SPEs beyond what was previously contractually required has been provided during the reporting periods.

In certain securitizations, the company consolidates the SPEs since it has both the power to direct the activities that most significantly impact the SPEs' economic performance through its role as servicer of all the receivables held by the SPEs, and the obligation through variable interests in the SPEs to absorb losses or receive benefits that could potentially be significant to the SPEs. The restricted assets (retail notes securitized, allowance for credit losses and other assets) of the consolidated SPEs totaled $2,626 million and $2,330 million at October 31, 2013 and 2012, respectively. The liabilities (short-term securitization borrowings and accrued interest) of these SPEs totaled $2,547 million and $2,262 million at October 31, 2013 and 2012, respectively. The credit holders of these SPEs do not have legal recourse to the company's general credit.

In certain securitizations, the company transfers retail notes to a non-VIE banking operation, which is not consolidated since the company does not have a controlling interest in the entity. The company's carrying values and interests related to the securitizations with the unconsolidated non-VIE were restricted assets (retail notes securitized, allowance for credit losses and other assets) of $353 million and $324 million at October 31, 2013 and 2012, respectively. The liabilities (short-term securitization borrowings and accrued interest) were $338 million and $310 million at October 31, 2013 and 2012, respectively.

In certain securitizations, the company transfers retail notes into bank-sponsored, multi-seller, commercial paper conduits, which are SPEs that are not consolidated. The company does not service a significant portion of the conduits' receivables, and therefore, does not have the power to direct the activities that most significantly impact the conduits' economic performance. These conduits provide a funding source to the company (as well as other transferors into the conduit) as they fund the retail notes through the issuance of commercial paper. The company's carrying values and variable interest related to these conduits were restricted assets (retail notes securitized, allowance for credit losses and other assets) of $1,274 million and $1,049 million at October 31, 2013 and 2012, respectively. The liabilities (short-term securitization borrowings and accrued interest) related to these conduits were $1,225 million and $1,004 million at October 31, 2013 and 2012, respectively.

The company's carrying amount of the liabilities to the unconsolidated conduits, compared to the maximum exposure to loss related to these conduits, which would only be incurred in the event of a complete loss on the restricted assets, was as follows at October 31 in millions of dollars:

	2013
Carrying value of liabilities	$1,225
Maximum exposure to loss	1,274

The total assets of unconsolidated VIEs related to securitizations were approximately $42 billion at October 31, 2013.

The components of consolidated restricted assets related to secured borrowings in securitization transactions at October 31 were as follows in millions of dollars:

	2013	2012
Financing receivables securitized (retail notes)	$4,167	$3,635
Allowance for credit losses	(14)	(17)
Other assets	100	85
Total restricted securitized assets	$4,253	$3,703

The components of consolidated secured borrowings and other liabilities related to securitizations at October 31 were as follows in millions of dollars:

	2013	2012
Short-term securitization borrowings	$4,109	$3,575
Accrued interest on borrowings	1	1
Total liabilities related to restricted securitized assets	$4,110	$3,576

The secured borrowings related to these restricted securitized retail notes are obligations that are payable as the retail notes are liquidated. Repayment of the secured borrowings depends primarily on cash flows generated by the restricted assets. Due to the company's short-term credit rating, cash collections from these restricted assets are not required to be placed into a segregated collection account until immediately prior to the time payment is required to the secured creditors. At October 31, 2013, the maximum remaining term of all securitized retail notes was approximately seven years.

Inventory

RECOGNITION AND MEASUREMENT

2.35 FASB ASC 330, *Inventory*, states that the primary basis of accounting for inventories is cost, but a departure from the cost basis of pricing the inventory is required when the utility of the goods is no longer as great as their cost. FASB ASC 330-10-35-1 requires an entity to measure inventories at the lower of cost or market. *Market*, as defined in the FASB ASC glossary, means current replacement cost, with the constraint that market should not exceed net realizable value and should not be lower than net realizable value less an allowance for an approximately normal profit margin.

2.36 FASB ASC 330-10-35-14 states that if inventories are written down below cost at the close of a fiscal year, such reduced amount is to be considered the cost for subsequent accounting purposes. Similarly, the Topic 5(BB), "Inventory Valuation Allowances," of the SEC's *Codification of Staff Accounting Bulletins* indicates that a write-down of inventory creates a new cost basis that subsequently cannot be marked up.

PRESENTATION

2.37 Rule 5-02.6 of Regulation S-X requires separate presentation in the balance sheet or notes of the amounts of major classes of inventory, such as finished goods, work in process, raw materials, and supplies. Additional disclosures are required for amounts related to long-term contracts or programs.

DISCLOSURE

2.38 FASB ASC 330 requires disclosure of the basis for stating inventories. Rule 5-02.6 of Regulation S-X requires disclosure of the method by which amounts are removed from inventory (for example, average cost; first in, first out (FIFO); last in, first out (LIFO); estimated average cost per unit).

2.39 Rule 5-02.6c of Regulation S-X requires that registrants using LIFO disclose the excess of replacement or current cost over stated LIFO value, if material.

PRESENTATION AND DISCLOSURE EXCERPTS

FIRST-IN FIRST-OUT

2.40 TEREX CORPORATION (DEC)
CONSOLIDATED BALANCE SHEET (in part)

(In millions, except par value)

	December 31,	
	2013	2012
Assets		
Current assets		
Cash and cash equivalents	$ 408.1	$ 678.0
Trade receivables (net of allowance of $47.6 and $38.5 at December 31, 2013 and 2012, respectively)	1,176.8	1,026.6
Inventories	1,613.2	1,632.2
Other current assets	312.0	319.6
Current assets—discontinued operations	129.3	141.0
Total current assets	3,639.4	3,797.4
Non-current assets		
Property, plant and equipment—net	789.4	806.8
Goodwill	1,245.6	1,245.3
Intangible assets—net	444.8	474.4
Other assets	401.9	410.8
Non-current assets—discontinued operations	15.6	11.5
Total assets	$6,536.7	$6,746.2

December 31, 2013

(dollar amounts in millions, unless otherwise noted, except per share amounts)

Note A—Basis of Presentation (in part)

Inventories. Inventories are stated at the lower of cost or market ("LCM") value. Cost is determined principally by the average cost method and the first-in, first-out ("FIFO") (approximately 55% and 45%, respectively). In valuing inventory, the Company is required to make assumptions regarding the level of reserves required to value potentially obsolete or over-valued items at the lower of cost or market. These assumptions require the Company to analyze the aging of and forecasted demand for its inventory, forecast future products sales prices, pricing trends and margins, and to make judgments and estimates regarding obsolete or excess inventory. Future product sales prices, pricing trends and margins are based on the best available information at that time including actual orders received, negotiations with the Company's customers for future orders, including their plans for expenditures, and market trends for similar products. The Company's judgments and estimates for excess or obsolete inventory are based on analysis of actual and forecasted usage. The valuation of used equipment taken in trade from customers requires the Company to use the best information available to determine the value of the equipment to potential customers. This value is subject to change based on numerous conditions. Inventory reserves are established taking into account age, frequency of use, or sale, and in the case of repair parts, the installed base of machines. While calculations are made involving these factors, significant management judgment regarding expectations for future events is involved. Future events that could significantly influence the Company's judgment and related estimates include general economic conditions in markets where the Company's products are sold, new equipment price fluctuations, actions of the Company's competitors, including the introduction of new products and technological advances, as well as new products and design changes the Company introduces. The Company makes adjustments to its inventory reserve based on the identification of specific situations and increases its inventory reserves accordingly. As further changes in future economic or industry conditions occur, the Company will revise the estimates that were used to calculate its inventory reserves. At December 31, 2013 and 2012, reserves for LCM, excess and obsolete inventory totaled $132.5 million and $131.9 million, respectively.

If actual conditions are less favorable than those the Company has projected, the Company will increase its reserves for LCM, excess and obsolete inventory accordingly. Any increase in the Company's reserves will adversely impact its results of operations. The establishment of a reserve for LCM, excess and obsolete inventory establishes a new cost basis in the inventory. Such reserves are not reduced until the product is sold.

Note F—Inventories

Inventories consist of the following (in millions):

	December 31,	
	2013	**2012**
Finished equipment	$ 450.0	$ 459.8
Replacement parts	168.4	178.7
Work-in-process	527.3	505.6
Raw materials and supplies	467.5	488.1
Inventories	$1,613.2	$1,632.2

Reserves for lower of cost or market value, excess and obsolete inventory were $132.5 million and $131.9 million at December 31, 2013 and 2012, respectively.

LAST-IN FIRST-OUT

2.41 THE BON-TON STORES, INC. (JAN)
CONSOLIDATED BALANCE SHEETS (in part)

(In thousands, except share and per share data)	**February 2, 2013**	**January 28, 2012**
Assets (in part)		
Current assets:		
Cash and cash equivalents	$ 7,926	$ 14,272
Merchandise inventories	758,400	699,504
Prepaid expenses and other current assets	70,601	69,032
Total current assets	836,927	782,808

(In thousands except share and per share data)

2. Summary of Significant Accounting Policies (in part)

Merchandise Inventories

Merchandise inventories are determined by the retail method. Inherent in the retail inventory method calculation are certain significant management judgments and estimates including, among others, merchandise markups, markdowns and shrinkage, which significantly impact both the ending inventory valuation and the resulting gross margin.

Factors considered in the determination of permanent markdowns include inventory obsolescence, excess inventories, current and anticipated demand, age of the merchandise, customer preferences and fashion trends. Pursuant to the retail inventory method, permanent markdowns result in the devaluation of inventory and the resulting gross margin reduction is recognized in the period in which the markdown is recorded.

The Company seeks return privileges from its vendors for damaged inventory or marks the goods out-of-stock. Historically, damaged inventory has been an immaterial factor in the Company's calculation of gross margin.

The Company regularly records a provision for estimated shrinkage, thereby reducing the carrying value of inventory. A physical inventory of each merchandise department is conducted annually in January, with the recorded amount of inventory adjusted to reflect this physical count. The differences between the estimated amount of shrinkage and the actual amount realized have been insignificant.

As of February 2, 2013 and January 28, 2012, approximately 32% of the Company's merchandise inventories were valued using a first-in, first-out ("FIFO") cost basis and approximately 68% of merchandise inventories were valued using a last-in, first-out ("LIFO") cost basis. There was no effect on costs of merchandise sold for LIFO valuations in 2012, 2011 and 2010. If the FIFO method of inventory valuation had been used for all inventories, the Company's merchandise inventories would have been lower by $6,837 at February 2, 2013 and January 28, 2012 due to the Company having recognized prior years' cost increases associated with its LIFO calculations. The Company's LIFO calculations yielded inventory increases due to deflation reflected in price indices used. The LIFO method values merchandise sold at the cost of more recent inventory purchases (which the deflationary indices indicated to be lower), resulting in the general inventory on-hand being carried at the older, higher costs. Given these higher values and the promotional retail environment, the Company has reduced the carrying value of its LIFO inventories to an estimated realizable value, with reductions of $38,867 to offset the $45,704 cumulative inventory increases generated by its computation of LIFO inventory as of February 2, 2013 and with reductions of $37,158 to offset the $43,995 cumulative inventory increases generated by its computation of LIFO inventory as of January 28, 2012.

Costs for merchandise purchases, product development and distribution are included in costs of merchandise sold.

AVERAGE COST

2.42 GENERAL CABLE CORPORATION (DEC)
CONSOLIDATED BALANCE SHEETS (in part)

(In millions, except share data)

Assets (in part)	Dec 31, 2013	Dec 31, 2012
Current assets:		
Cash and cash equivalents	$ 418.8	$ 622.3
Receivables, net of allowances of $39.2 million in 2013 and $38.3 million in 2012	1,171.7	1,182.1
Inventories	1,239.6	1,273.6
Deferred income taxes	50.2	39.5
Prepaid expenses and other	126.2	133.0
Total current assets	3,006.5	3,250.5

2. Summary of Significant Accounting Policies (in part)

Inventories

Approximately 85% of the Company's inventories are valued using the average cost method and all remaining inventories are valued using the first-in, first-out (FIFO) method. All inventories are stated at the lower of cost or market value.

The Company has consignment inventory at certain of its customer locations for purchase and use by the customer or other parties. General Cable retains title to the inventory and records no sale until it is ultimately sold either to the customer storing the inventory or to another party. In general, the value and quantity of the consignment inventory is verified by General Cable through either cycle counting or annual physical inventory counting procedures.

5. Inventories

Approximately 85% of the Company's inventories are valued using the average cost method and all remaining inventories are valued using the first-in, first-out (FIFO) method. All inventories are stated at the lower of cost or market value.

(In millions)	Dec 31, 2013	Dec 31, 2012
Raw materials	$ 319.1	$ 332.0
Work in process	190.1	211.8
Finished goods	730.4	729.8
Total	$1,239.6	$1,273.6

At December 31, 2013 and 2012, the Company had approximately $ 32.5 million and $ 27.3 million, respectively of consignment inventory at locations not operated by the Company with approximately 87% and 92%, respectively, of the consignment inventory located throughout the United States and Canada.

RETAIL METHOD

2.43 FRED'S, INC. (JAN)
CONSOLIDATED BALANCE SHEETS (in part)

(In thousands, except for number of shares)

	February 2, 2013	January 28, 2012
Assets (in part)		
Current assets:		
Cash and cash equivalents	$ 8,129	$ 27,130
Receivables, less allowance for doubtful accounts of $1,489 and $1,595, respectively	35,943	31,883
Inventories	353,266	331,882
Other non-trade receivables	33,273	32,090
Prepaid expenses and other current assets	13,134	12,321
Total current assets	443,745	435,306

Note 1—Description of Business and Summary of Significant Accounting Policies (in part)

Inventories. Merchandise inventories are valued at the lower of cost or market using the retail first-in, first-out method for goods in our stores and the cost first-in, first-out method for goods in our distribution centers. The retail inventory method is a reverse mark-up, averaging method which has been widely used in the retail industry for many years. This method calculates a cost-to-retail ratio that is applied to the retail value of inventory to determine the cost value of inventory and the resulting cost of goods sold and gross margin. The assumption that the retail inventory method provides for valuation at lower of cost or market and the inherent uncertainties therein are discussed in the following paragraphs.

In order to assure valuation at the lower of cost or market, the retail value of our inventory is adjusted on a consistent basis to reflect current market conditions. These adjustments include increases to the retail value of inventory for initial markups to set the selling price of goods or additional markups to adjust pricing for inflation and decreases to the retail value of inventory for markdowns associated with promotional, seasonal or other declines in the market value. Because these adjustments are made on a consistent basis and are based on current prevailing market conditions, they approximate the carrying value of the inventory at net realizable value. Therefore, after applying the cost to retail ratio, the cost value of our inventory is stated at the lower of cost or market as is prescribed by U.S. GAAP.

Because the approximation of net realizable value under the retail inventory method is based on estimates such as markups, markdowns and inventory losses, there exists an inherent uncertainty in the final determination of inventory cost and gross margin. In order to mitigate that uncertainty, the Company has a formal review by product class which considers such variables as current market trends, seasonality, weather patterns and age of merchandise to ensure that markdowns are taken currently, or a markdown reserve is established to cover future anticipated markdowns. This review also considers current pricing trends and inflation to ensure that markups are taken if necessary. The estimation of inventory losses is a significant element in approximating the carrying value of inventory at net realizable value, and as such the following paragraph describes our estimation method as well as the steps we take to mitigate the risk that this estimate has in the determination of the cost value of inventory.

The Company calculates inventory losses based on actual inventory losses occurring as a result of physical inventory counts during each fiscal period and estimated inventory losses occurring between yearly physical inventory counts. The estimate for shrink occurring in the interim period between physical counts is calculated on a store-specific basis and is based on history, as well as performance on the most recent physical count. It is calculated by multiplying each store's shrink rate, which is based on the previously mentioned factors, by the interim period's sales for each store. Additionally, the overall estimate for shrink is adjusted at the corporate level to a three-year historical average to ensure that the overall shrink estimate is the most accurate approximation of shrink based on the Company's overall history of shrink. The three-year historical estimate is calculated by dividing the "book to physical" inventory adjustments for the trailing 36 months by the related sales for the same period. In order to reduce the uncertainty inherent in the shrink calculation, the Company first performs the calculation at the lowest practical level (by store) using the most current performance indicators. This ensures a more reliable number, as opposed to using a higher level aggregation or percentage method. The second portion of the calculation ensures that the extreme negative or positive performance of any particular store or group of stores does not skew the overall estimation of shrink. This portion of the calculation removes additional uncertainty by eliminating short-term peaks and valleys that could otherwise cause the underlying carrying value of inventory to fluctuate unnecessarily. The methodology that we have applied in estimating shrink has resulted in variability in result that is not material to our financial statements. The Company has experienced improvement in reducing shrink as a percentage of sales from year to year due to improved inventory control measures, which includes the chain-wide utilization of the NEX/DEX technology.

Management believes that the Company's retail inventory method provides an inventory valuation which reasonably approximates cost and results in valuing inventory at the lower of cost or market. For pharmacy department inventories, which were approximately $33.8 million, and $40.4 million at February 2, 2013 and January 28, 2012, respectively, cost was determined using the retail LIFO ("last-in, first-out") method in which inventory cost is maintained using the retail inventory method, then adjusted by application of the highly inflationary Producer Price Index published by the U.S. Department of Labor for the cumulative annual periods. The current cost of inventories exceeded the LIFO cost by approximately $30.7 million at February 2, 2013 and $26.8 million at January 28, 2012. The LIFO reserve increased by approximately $3.9 million and $2.8 million during 2012 and 2011, respectively.

The Company has historically included an estimate of inbound freight and certain general and administrative costs in merchandise inventory as prescribed by U.S. GAAP. These costs include activities surrounding the procurement and storage of merchandise inventory such as merchandise planning and buying, warehousing, accounting, information technology and human resources, as well as inbound freight. The total amount of procurement and storage costs and inbound freight included in merchandise inventory at February 2, 2013 is $21.6 million compared to $20.3 million at January 28, 2012.

The Company did not record any below-cost inventory adjustments during the years ended February 2, 2013, January 28, 2012 and January 29, 2011 in connection with planned store closures (see Note 12—Exit and Disposal Activity).

Other Current Assets

PRESENTATION

2.44 Rule 5-02.8 of Regulation S-X requires that any amounts in excess of 5 percent of total current assets be stated separately on the balance sheet or disclosed in the notes.

PRESENTATION AND DISCLOSURE EXCERPTS

DEFERRED TAXES

2.45 SPECTRUM BRANDS HOLDINGS, INC. (SEP)
CONSOLIDATED STATEMENTS OF FINANCIAL POSITION (in part)

September 30, 2013 and September 30, 2012

(Amounts in thousands, except per share figures)

	September 30, 2013	September 30, 2012
Assets (in part)		
Current assets:		
Cash and cash equivalents	$ 207,257	$ 157,961
Receivables:		
Trade accounts receivable, net of allowances of $37,376 and $21,870, respectively	481,313	335,301
Other	65,620	38,116
Inventories	632,923	452,633
Deferred income taxes, net	32,959	28,143
Prepaid expenses and other	62,833	49,273
Total current assets	1,482,905	1,061,427

NOTES TO CONSOLIDATED FINANCIAL STATEMENTS

(Amounts in thousands, except per share figures)

(2) Significant Accounting Policies and Practices (in part)

(m) Income Taxes

Income taxes are accounted for under the asset and liability method. Deferred tax assets and liabilities are recognized for the future tax consequences attributable to differences between the financial statement carrying amounts of existing assets and liabilities and their respective tax bases and operating loss and tax credit carryforwards. Deferred tax assets and liabilities are measured using enacted tax rates expected to apply to taxable income in the years in which those temporary differences are expected to be recovered or settled. The effect on deferred tax assets and liabilities of a change in tax rates is recognized in income in the period that includes the enactment date.

The Company recognizes the effect of income tax positions only if those positions are more likely than not of being sustained. Recognized income tax positions are measured at the largest amount that is greater than 50% likely of being realized. Changes in recognition or measurement are reflected in income tax expense in the period in which the change in judgment occurs. Accrued interest expense and penalties related to uncertain tax positions are recorded in Income tax expense.

(9) Income Taxes (in part)

Income tax expense was calculated based upon the following components of (loss) income from continuing operations before income tax:

	2013	2012	2011
Pretax (loss) income:			
United States	$(212,168)	$ (66,102)	$(119,984)
Outside the United States	184,214	175,059	137,108
Total pretax (loss) income	$ (27,954)	$108,957	$ 17,124

The components of income tax expense are as follows:

	2013	2012	2011
Current:			
Foreign	$ 47,740	$38,113	$32,649
State	1,274	(361)	2,332
Total current	$ 49,014	$37,752	$34,981
Deferred:			
Federal	(23,397)	20,884	20,247
Foreign	2,146	5,190	28,054
State	(404)	(3,441)	9,013
Total deferred	$(21,655)	$22,633	$57,314
Income tax expense	$ 27,359	$60,385	$92,295

The following reconciles the total income tax expense, based on the Federal statutory income tax rate of 35%, with the Company's recognized income tax expense:

	2013	2012	2011
Statutory federal income tax (benefit) expense	$ (9,784)	$ 38,135	$ 5,994
Permanent items	10,104	8,595	8,654
Exempt foreign income	(5,921)	(5,760)	(380)
Foreign statutory rate vs. U.S. statutory rate	(19,182)	(15,211)	(14,132)
State income taxes, net of federal (benefit) expense	(11,686)	(2,164)	1,242
Residual tax on foreign earnings	(6,958)	29,844	18,943
FURminator purchase accounting benefit	—	(14,511)	—
HHI purchase accounting benefit	(49,848)	—	—
Valuation allowance	115,318	26,003	68,615
Unrecognized tax expense (benefits)	4,062	(4,386)	(2,793)
Inflationary adjustments	(245)	(803)	(1,472)
Correction of immaterial prior period error	—	—	4,873
Nondeductible share compensation	1,669	684	1,953
Other, net	(170)	(41)	798
Income tax expense	$ 27,359	$ 60,385	$ 92,295

The tax effects of temporary differences that give rise to significant portions of the deferred tax assets and deferred tax liabilities are as follows:

	September 30,	
	2013	2012
Current deferred tax assets:		
Employee benefits	$ 11,372	$ 16,399
Restructuring	7,085	8,054
Inventories and receivables	24,296	22,495
Marketing and promotional accruals	14,146	8,270
Other	23,261	14,440
Valuation allowance	(32,342)	(29,808)
Total current deferred tax assets	$ 47,818	$ 39,850
Current deferred tax liabilities:		
Inventories and receivables	(2,748)	(2,618)
Unrealized gains	(373)	(1,153)
Other	(11,738)	(7,936)
Total current deferred tax liabilities	$ (14,859)	$ (11,707)
Net current deferred tax assets	$ 32,959	$ 28,143
Noncurrent deferred tax assets:		
Employee benefits	$ 35,578	$ 34,927
Restructuring and purchase accounting	340	371
Net operating loss and credit carry forwards	668,679	572,857
Prepaid royalty	6,956	7,006
Property, plant and equipment	9,692	3,255
Unrealized losses	2,136	2,521
Long-term debt	668	3,976
Intangibles	3,917	4,282
Other	5,268	7,866
Valuation allowance	(422,244)	(354,992)
Total noncurrent deferred tax assets	$ 310,990	$ 282,069
Noncurrent deferred tax liabilities:		
Property, plant, and equipment	(27,478)	(15,337)
Unrealized gains	(13,126)	(15,803)
Intangibles	(735,506)	(596,199)
Taxes on unremitted foreign earnings	(18,581)	(29,231)
Other	(9,073)	(2,964)
Total noncurrent deferred tax liabilities	$(803,764)	$(659,534)
Net noncurrent deferred tax liabilities	$(492,774)	$(377,465)
Net current and noncurrent deferred tax liabilities	$(459,815)	$(349,322)

In Fiscal 2012, the Company began recording residual U.S. and foreign taxes on foreign earnings as a result of its change in position regarding future repatriation and the requirements of ASC 740. To the extent necessary, the Company intends to utilize earnings of foreign subsidiaries in order to support management's plans to voluntarily accelerate pay down of U.S. debt, fund distributions to shareholders, fund U.S. acquisitions, and satisfy ongoing U.S. operational cash flow requirements. As a result, earnings of the Company's non-U.S. subsidiaries after September 30, 2011 are generally not considered to be permanently reinvested, except in jurisdictions where repatriation is either precluded or restricted by law. The Company annually estimates the available earnings, permanent reinvestment classification, and availability and intent to use alternative mechanisms for repatriation for each jurisdiction in which the Company does business. Accordingly, the Company is providing residual U.S. and foreign deferred taxes on these earnings to the extent they cannot be repatriated in a tax-free manner. As of September 30, 2013, the Company has provided residual taxes on approximately $12,506 of Fiscal 2013 distributions of foreign earnings, and $45,735 of earnings not yet taxed in the U.S. resulting in a Fiscal 2013 increase in tax expense, net of a corresponding adjustment to the Company's domestic valuation allowance, of approximately $109. As of September 30, 2012, the Company recorded residual U.S. and foreign taxes on approximately $21,163 of Fiscal 2012 distributions and $76,475 of earnings not yet taxed in the U.S., resulting in a Fiscal 2012 increase in tax expense, net of a corresponding adjustment to the Company's domestic valuation allowance, of approximately $3,278. As of September 30, 2011, the Company recorded residual U.S. and foreign taxes on approximately $39,391 of actual and deemed distributions of foreign earnings resulting in a Fiscal 2011 increase in tax expense, net of a corresponding adjustment to the Company's domestic valuation allowance, of approximately $771. Fiscal 2013, 2012 and 2011 distributions were primarily non-cash deemed distributions under U.S. tax law.

Remaining undistributed earnings of the Company's foreign operations are approximately $409,589 at September 30, 2013, and are intended to remain permanently invested. Accordingly, no residual income taxes have been provided on those earnings at September 30, 2013. If at some future date these earnings cease to be permanently invested, the Company may be subject to U.S. income taxes and foreign withholding and other taxes on such amounts, which cannot be reasonably estimated at this time.

As of September 30, 2013, the Company has U.S. federal and state net operating loss carryforwards of approximately $1,515,344 and $1,551,341, respectively. These net operating loss carryforwards expire through years ending in 2033. As of September 30, 2013 the Company has foreign loss carryforwards of approximately $111,186 which will expire beginning in the Company's fiscal year ending 2014. Certain of the foreign net operating losses have indefinite carryforward periods. The Company is subject to an annual limitation on the use of its net operating losses that arose prior to its emergence from bankruptcy. The Company has had multiple changes of ownership, as defined under Section 382 of the Internal Revenue Code of 1986, as amended, that subject the Company's U.S. federal and state net operating losses and other tax attributes to certain limitations. The annual limitation is based on a number of factors including the value of the Company's stock (as defined for tax purposes), on the date of the ownership change, its net unrealized built in gain position on that date, the occurrence of realized built in gains in years subsequent to the ownership change, and the effects of subsequent ownership changes (as defined for tax purposes), if any. Due to these limitations, the Company estimates, as of September 30, 2013, that $301,202 of the total U.S. federal and $357,938 of the state net operating loss will expire unused even if the Company generates sufficient income to otherwise use all of its NOLs. In addition, separate return year limitations apply to limit the Company's utilization of the acquired Russell Hobbs U.S. federal and state net operating losses to future income of the Russell Hobbs subgroup. The Company also projects, as of September 30, 2013, that $102,576 of the total foreign loss carryforwards will expire unused. The Company has provided a full valuation allowance against these deferred tax assets.

A valuation allowance is recorded when it is more likely than not that some portion or all of the deferred tax assets will not be realized. The ultimate realization of the deferred tax assets depends on the ability of the Company to generate sufficient taxable income of the appropriate character in the future and in the appropriate taxing jurisdictions. As of September 30, 2013 and September 30, 2012, the Company's valuation allowance, established for the tax benefit that may not be realized, totaled approximately $454,586 and $384,800, respectively. As of September 30, 2013 and September 30, 2012, approximately $421,743 and $349,316, respectively, related to U.S. net deferred tax assets, and approximately $32,843 and $35,484, respectively, related to foreign net deferred tax assets. The net increase in the valuation allowance for deferred tax assets during Fiscal 2013 totaled approximately $69,786, of which approximately $72,427 related to an increase in the valuation allowance against U.S. net deferred tax assets, and approximately $2,641 related to a decrease in the valuation allowance against foreign net deferred tax assets. As a result of the purchase of HHI, the Company reversed $49,848 of U.S. valuation allowance during Fiscal 2013. The reversal was attributable to $49,848 of net deferred tax liabilities recorded on the HHI acquisition date balance sheet that offset other U.S. net deferred tax assets. As a result of the purchase of FURminator, the Company reversed $14,511 of U.S. valuation allowance during Fiscal 2012. The reversal was attributable to $14,511 of net deferred tax liabilities recorded on the FURminator acquisition date balance sheet that offset other U.S. net deferred tax assets. During Fiscal 2011, the Company determined that a valuation allowance was required against deferred tax assets related to net operating losses in Brazil, and thus recorded a $25,877 increase in the valuation allowance.

The total amount of unrecognized tax benefits on the Company's Consolidated Statements of Financial Position at September 30, 2013 and September 30, 2012 are $13,807 and $5,877, respectively. If recognized in the future, $10,115 of unrecognized tax benefits will affect the effective tax rate, and $3,692 of unrecognized tax benefits would create deferred tax assets against which the Company would have a full valuation allowance. The Company recognizes interest and penalties related to uncertain tax positions in income tax expense. As of September 30, 2013 and September 30, 2012 the Company had approximately $3,671 and $3,564, respectively, of accrued interest and penalties related to uncertain tax positions. The impact related to interest and penalties on the Consolidated Statement of Operations for Fiscal 2013 was a net increase to Income tax expense of $8. The impact related to interest and penalties on the Consolidated Statement of Operations for Fiscal 2012 was a net decrease to Income tax expense of $1,184. The impact related to interest and penalties on the Consolidated Statement of Operations for Fiscal 2011 was a net decrease to Income tax expense of $1,422.

As of September 30, 2013, certain of the Company's legal entities are undergoing income tax audits. The Company cannot predict the ultimate outcome of the examinations; however, it is reasonably possible that during the next 12 months some portion of previously unrecognized tax benefits could be recognized.

ADVANCES

2.46 ALLIANCE ONE INTERNATIONAL, INC. (MAR)

CONSOLIDATED BALANCE SHEETS (in part)

(In thousands)	March 31, 2013	March 31, 2012
Assets (in part)		
Current assets		
Cash and cash equivalents	$ 92,026	$ 119,743
Trade and other receivables, net	224,222	303,090
Accounts receivable, related parties	55,696	32,316
Inventories	903,947	839,902
Advances to tobacco suppliers	109,520	89,378
Recoverable income taxes	8,980	9,592
Current deferred taxes	16,776	23,855
Prepaid expenses	36,811	45,097
Current derivative asset	3,145	312
Other current assets	13,632	14,562
Total current assets	1,464,755	1,477,847

NOTES TO CONSOLIDATED FINANCIAL STATEMENTS

(In thousands)

Note 1—Significant Accounting Policies (in part)

Advances to Tobacco Suppliers

The Company purchases seeds, fertilizer, pesticides and other products related to growing tobacco and advances them to suppliers, which represents prepaid inventory and is recorded as advances to tobacco suppliers. The advances of current crop inputs generally include the original cost of the inputs plus a mark-up and interest as it is earned. Where contractually permitted, the Company charges interest to the suppliers during the period the current crop advance is outstanding. The Company generally advances the inputs at a price that is greater than its cost, which results in a mark-up on the inputs. The suppliers then utilize these inputs to grow tobacco, which the Company is contractually obligated to purchase. Upon delivery of tobacco, part of the purchase price to the supplier is paid in cash and part through a reduction of the advance balance. The advances applied to the delivery are reclassified out of advances and into unprocessed inventory. Advances to tobacco suppliers are accounted for utilizing a cost accumulation methodology.

The Company has current and noncurrent advances to tobacco suppliers. The current advances represent the cost of the seeds, fertilizer and other materials that are advanced for the current crop of inventory. The noncurrent advances generally represent the cost of advances to suppliers for infrastructure, such as curing barns, which is also recovered through the delivery of tobacco to the Company by the suppliers. As a result of various factors in a given crop year (weather, etc.) not all suppliers are able to settle the entire amount of advances that are due that year. In these situations, the Company may allow the suppliers to deliver tobacco over future crop years to recover its advances. The advance balances that are deferred over future crop years are also classified as noncurrent.

Advances to tobacco suppliers are carried at cost and evaluated for recoverability. The realizability evaluation process is similar to that of the LCM evaluation process for inventories. The Company evaluates its advances for recoverability by crop and country. The Company reclasses the advance to inventory at the time suppliers deliver tobacco. The purchase price for the tobacco delivered by the suppliers is based on market prices. Two primary factors determine the market value of the tobacco suppliers deliver: the quantity of tobacco delivered and the quality of the tobacco delivered. Therefore, the Company ensures its advances are appropriately stated at the lower of cost or estimated recoverable amounts.

Upon delivery of tobacco, part of the purchase price to the supplier is paid in cash and part through a reduction of the advance balance. If a sufficient value of tobacco is not delivered to allow the reduction of the entire advance balance, then the Company first determines how much of the deficiency for the current crop is recoverable through future crops. This determination is made by analyzing the suppliers' ability-to-deliver a sufficient supply of tobacco. This analysis includes historical quantity and quality of production with monitoring of crop information provided by field service technicians related to flood, drought and disease. The remaining recoverable advance balance would then be classified as noncurrent. Any increase in the estimate of unrecoverable advances associated with the noncurrent portion is charged to cost of goods and services sold in the income statement when determined. Amounts not expected to be recovered through current or future crops are then evaluated to determine whether the yield is considered to be normal or abnormal. If the yield adjustment is normal, then the Company capitalizes the applicable variance in the current crop of inventory. If the yield adjustment is considered abnormal, then the Company immediately charges the applicable variance to cost of goods and services sold in the income statement. A normal yield adjustment is based on the range of unrecoverability for the previous three years by country.

The Company accounts for its advances to tobacco suppliers using a cost accumulation model, which results in the reporting of its advances at the lower of cost or recoverable amounts exclusive of the mark-up and interest. The mark-up and interest on its advances are recognized upon delivery of tobacco as a decrease in the cost of the current crop. The mark-up and interest capitalized or to be capitalized into inventory for the current crop was $14,464 and $21,139 as of March 31, 2013 and 2012, respectively. Unrecoverable advances and other costs capitalized or to be capitalized into the current crop was $13,347 and $13,746 at March 31, 2013 and 2012, respectively. The following table reflects the classification of advances to tobacco suppliers:

	March 31, 2013	March 31, 2012
Current	$109,520	$89,378
Noncurrent	6,421	5,613
	$115,941	$94,991

Noncurrent advances to tobacco suppliers are recorded in Other Noncurrent Assets in the Consolidated Balance Sheets.

Unrecovered amounts expensed directly to cost of goods and services sold in the income statement for abnormal yield adjustments or unrecovered amounts from prior crops were $1,750 and $1,350 for the years ended March 31, 2013 and 2011, respectively. There were no abnormal yield adjustments for the year ended March 31, 2012. Normal yield adjustments are capitalized into the cost of the current crop and are expensed as cost of goods and services sold as that crop is sold.

ASSETS HELD FOR SALE

2.47 JOHNSON CONTROLS, INC. (SEP)

CONSOLIDATED STATEMENTS OF FINANCIAL POSITION (in part)

	September 30,	
(In millions, except par value and share data)	2013	2012
Assets (in part)		
Cash and cash equivalents	$ 1,055	$ 265
Accounts receivable, less allowance for doubtful accounts of $68 and $78, respectively	7,206	7,308
Inventories	2,325	2,343
Assets held for sale	804	—
Other current assets	2,308	2,827
Current assets	13,698	12,743

NOTES TO CONSOLIDATED FINANCIAL STATEMENTS

1. Summary of Significant Accounting Policies (in part)

Assets and Liabilities Held for Sale

The Company classifies assets and liabilities (disposal groups) to be sold as held for sale in the period in which all of the following criteria are met: management, having the authority to approve the action, commits to a plan to sell the disposal group; the disposal group is available for immediate sale in its present condition subject only to terms that are usual and customary for sales of such disposal groups; an active program to locate a buyer and other actions required to complete the plan to sell the disposal group have been initiated; the sale of the disposal group is probable, and transfer of the disposal group is expected to qualify for recognition as a completed sale within one year, except if events or circumstances beyond the Company's control extend the period of time required to sell the disposal group beyond one year; the disposal group is being actively marketed for sale at a price that is reasonable in relation to its current fair value; and actions required to complete the plan indicate that it is unlikely that significant changes to the plan will be made or that the plan will be withdrawn.

The Company initially measures a disposal group that is classified as held for sale at the lower of its carrying value or fair value less any costs to sell. Any loss resulting from this measurement is recognized in the period in which the held for sale criteria are met. Conversely, gains are not recognized on the sale of a disposal group until the date of sale. The Company assesses the fair value of a disposal group less any costs to sell each reporting period it remains classified as held for sale and reports any subsequent changes as an adjustment to the carrying value of the disposal group, as long as the new carrying value does not exceed the carrying value of the disposal group at the time it was initially classified as held for sale.

Upon determining that a disposal group meets the criteria to be classified as held for sale, the Company reports the assets and liabilities of the disposal group, if material, in the line items assets held for sale and liabilities held for sale, respectively, in the consolidated statement of financial position. Refer to Note 3, "Assets and Liabilities Held for Sale," of the notes to consolidated financial statements for further information.

3. Assets and Liabilities Held For Sale

At September 30, 2013, the Company determined that certain of its businesses met the criteria to be classified as held for sale. The Automotive Experience Electronics segment and certain product lines of the Automotive Experience Interiors segment are classified as held for sale as of September 30, 2013.

The following table summarizes the carrying value of the assets and liabilities held for sale (in millions):

	September 30, 2013
Cash and cash equivalents	$ 4
Accounts receivable	197
Inventories	124
Other current assets	91
Property, plant and equipment—net	167
Goodwill	74
Other intangibles assets—net	57
Investments in partially-owned affiliates	26
Other noncurrent assets	64
Assets held for sale	$804
Short-term debt	$5
Accounts payable	253
Accrued compensation and benefits	46
Other current liabilities	84
Pension and postretirement benefits	13
Other noncurrent liabilities	1
Liabilities held for sale	$402

Assets and liabilities classified as held for sale were required to be recorded at the lower of carrying value or fair value less any costs to sell. Accordingly, the Company recorded an impairment charge of $41 million within restructuring and impairment costs in the consolidated statement of income related to certain product lines of the Automotive Experience Interiors segment. Refer to Note 17, "Impairment of Long-Lived Assets" of the notes to consolidated financial statements for further information regarding the impairment charge. The divestiture of the businesses held for sale could result in a gain or loss on sale to the extent the ultimate selling price differs from the current carrying value of the net assets recorded.

The Automotive Experience Electronics business does not meet the criteria to be classified as a discontinued operation at September 30, 2013 primarily due to the uncertainty regarding the Company's potential continuing involvement in these operations following a divestiture. The Automotive Experience Interiors product lines classified as held for sale are immaterial to the Company individually and in the aggregate and do not constitute a distinguishable business in order to be classified as a discontinued operation.

COSTS AND ACCRUED EARNINGS IN EXCESS OF BILLINGS

2.48 URS CORPORATION (DEC)
CONSOLIDATED BALANCE SHEETS (in part)

(In millions, except per share data)

	January 3, 2014	December 28, 2012
Assets (in part)		
Current assets:		
Cash and cash equivalents	$ 283.7	$ 314.5
Accounts receivable, including retentions of $116.6 and $114.4, respectively	1,392.6	1,554.8
Costs and accrued earnings in excess of billings on contracts	1,521.5	1,384.3
Less receivable allowances	(65.1)	(69.7)
Net accounts receivable	2,849.0	2,869.4
Deferred tax assets	35.6	67.6
Inventory	49.2	61.5
Other current assets	173.2	204.2
Total current assets	3,390.7	3,517.2

NOTES TO CONSOLIDATED FINANCIAL STATEMENTS

Note 1. Business, Basis of Presentation, and Accounting Policies (in part)

Accounts Receivable and Costs and Accrued Earnings in Excess of Billings on Contracts

Accounts receivable in the accompanying Consolidated Balance Sheets are primarily comprised of amounts billed to clients for services already provided, but which have not yet been collected. Occasionally, under the terms of specific contracts, we are permitted to submit invoices in advance of providing our services to our clients and, to the extent they have not been collected, these amounts are also included in accounts receivable.

Costs and accrued earnings in excess of billings on contracts (also referred to as "Unbilled Accounts Receivable") in the accompanying Consolidated Balance Sheets represent unbilled amounts earned and reimbursable under contracts. These amounts become billable according to the contract terms, which usually consider the passage of time, achievement of milestones or completion of the project. Generally, such unbilled amounts will be billed and collected over the next twelve months.

Accounts receivable and costs and accrued earnings in excess of billings on contracts include certain amounts recognized related to unapproved change orders (amounts representing the value of proposed contract modifications, but which are unapproved as to either price or scope) and claims, (change orders that are unapproved as to both price and scope) that have not been collected and, in the case of balances included in costs and accrued earnings in excess of billings on contracts, may not be billable until an agreement or, in the case of claims, a settlement is reached. Most of those balances are not material and are typically resolved in the ordinary course of business.

Concentrations of Credit Risk

Our accounts receivable and costs and accrued earnings in excess of billings on contracts are potentially subject to concentrations of credit risk. Our credit risk on accounts receivable is limited due to the large number of contracts for clients that comprise our customer base and their dispersion across different business and geographic areas. We estimate and maintain an allowance for potential uncollectible accounts, and such estimates have historically been within management's expectations. See Note 4, "Accounts Receivable and Costs and Accrued Earnings in Excess of Billings on Contracts" for more details. Our cash and cash equivalents are maintained in accounts held by major banks and financial institutions located primarily in North America, Europe and Asia Pacific.

Note 4. Accounts Receivable and Costs and Accrued Earnings in Excess of Billings on Contracts (in part)

The following table summarizes the components of our accounts receivable and Unbilled Accounts Receivable with the U.S. federal government and with other customers as of January 3, 2014 and December 28, 2012:

(In millions)	January 3, 2014	December 28, 2012
Accounts receivable:		
U.S. federal government	$ 353.2	$ 376.2
Others	1,039.4	1,178.6
Total accounts receivable	$1,392.6	$1,554.8
Unbilled Accounts Receivable:		
U.S. federal government	$ 855.7	$ 892.7
Others	796.9	756.5
Total	1,652.6	1,649.2
Less: Amounts included in Other long-term assets	(131.1)	(264.9)
Unbilled Accounts Receivable	$1,521.5	$1,384.3

As of January 3, 2014 and December 28, 2012, $131.1 million and $264.9 million, respectively, of Unbilled Accounts Receivable are not expected to become billable within twelve months of the balance sheet date and, as a result, are included as a component of "Other long-term assets." As of January 3, 2014 and December 28, 2012, we reclassified unbilled amounts representing performance-based incentive fee receivables from our work managing chemical demilitarization and nuclear management and decommissioning programs from "Other long-term assets" to Unbilled Accounts Receivable.

We are required contractually to share a portion of the performance-based incentive fees with our employees and subcontractors for some of our projects. These liabilities are accrued concurrently with the related receivables and are not expected to be paid until after the fees are collected, and, as a result, are originally included as a component of "Other long-term liabilities." As the underlying performance-based incentive fee receivables become current and are reclassified from "Other long-term assets" to Unbilled Accounts Receivable, the corresponding liabilities are also reclassified from "Other long-term liabilities" to "Other current liabilities."

The following table summarizes the activities of Unbilled Accounts Receivable included in "Other long-term assets" and the corresponding liabilities included in "Other long-term liabilities" for our fiscal years 2013 and 2012:

(In millions)	Amounts Included in "Other Long-Term Assets"	Amounts Included in "Other Long-Term Liabilities"
Balances as of December 30, 2011	$ 185.0	$ 105.6
Additions	209.2	38.9
Reclassification from long-term to short-term	(129.3)	(37.5)
Balances as of December 28, 2012	264.9	107.0
Additions	241.7	59.7
Reclassification from long-term to short-term	(375.5)	(164.5)
Balances as of January 3, 2014	$ 131.1	$ 2.2

DERIVATIVES

2.49 INTERNATIONAL BUSINESS MACHINES CORPORATION (DEC)
CONSOLIDATED STATEMENT OF FINANCIAL POSITION (in part)

($ in millions except per share amounts)

At December 31:	Notes	2013	2012
Assets (in part)			
Current assets			
Cash and cash equivalents		$10,716	$10,412
Marketable securities	D	350	717
Notes and accounts receivable—trade (net of allowances of $291 in 2013 and $255 in 2012)		10,465	10,667
Short-term financing receivables (net of allowances of $308 in 2013 and $288 in 2012)	F	19,787	18,038
Other accounts receivable (net of allowances of $36 in 2013 and $17 in 2012)		1,584	1,873
Inventories	E	2,310	2,287
Deferred taxes	N	1,651	1,415
Prepaid expenses and other current assets		4,488	4,024
Total current assets		51,350	49,433

Note A. Significant Accounting Policies (in part)

Derivative Financial Instruments

Derivatives are recognized in the Consolidated Statement of Financial Position at fair value and are reported in prepaid expenses and other current assets, investments and sundry assets, other accrued expenses and liabilities or other liabilities. Classification of each derivative as current or noncurrent is based upon whether the maturity of the instrument is less than or greater than 12 months. To qualify for hedge accounting, the company requires that the instruments be effective in reducing the risk exposure that they are designated to hedge. For instruments that hedge cash flows, hedge designation criteria also require that it be probable that the underlying transaction will occur. Instruments that meet established accounting criteria are formally designated as hedges. These criteria demonstrate that the derivative is expected to be highly effective at offsetting changes in fair value or cash flows of the underlying exposure both at inception of the hedging relationship and on an ongoing basis. The method of assessing hedge effectiveness and measuring hedge ineffectiveness is formally documented at hedge inception. The company assesses hedge effectiveness and measures hedge ineffectiveness at least quarterly throughout the designated hedge period.

Where the company applies hedge accounting, the company designates each derivative as a hedge of: (1) the fair value of a recognized financial asset or liability, or of an unrecognized firm commitment (fair value hedge attributable to interest rate or foreign currency risk); (2) the variability of anticipated cash flows of a forecasted transaction, or the cash flows to be received or paid related to a recognized financial asset or liability (cash flow hedge attributable to interest rate or foreign currency risk); or (3) a hedge of a long-term investment (net investment hedge) in a foreign operation. In addition, the company may enter into derivative contracts that economically hedge certain of its risks, even though hedge accounting does not apply or the company elects not to apply hedge accounting. In these cases, there exists a natural hedging relationship in which changes in the fair value of the derivative, which are recognized currently in net income, act as an economic offset to changes in the fair value of the underlying hedged item(s).

Financial Instruments

In determining the fair value of its financial instruments, the company uses a variety of methods and assumptions that are based on market conditions and risks existing at each balance sheet date. See note D, "Financial Instruments," on pages 100 to 102 for further information. All methods of assessing fair value result in a general approximation of value, and such value may never actually be realized.

Note D. Financial Instruments (in part)

Derivative Financial Instruments

The company operates in multiple functional currencies and is a significant lender and borrower in the global markets. In the normal course of business, the company is exposed to the impact of interest rate changes and foreign currency fluctuations, and to a lesser extent equity and commodity price changes and client credit risk. The company limits these risks by following established risk management policies and procedures, including the use of derivatives, and, where cost effective, financing with debt in the currencies in which assets are denominated. For interest rate exposures, derivatives are used to better align rate movements between the interest rates associated with the company's lease and other financial assets and the interest rates associated with its financing debt. Derivatives are also used to manage the related cost of debt. For foreign currency exposures, derivatives are used to better manage the cash flow volatility arising from foreign exchange rate fluctuations.

As a result of the use of derivative instruments, the company is exposed to the risk that counterparties to derivative contracts will fail to meet their contractual obligations. To mitigate the counterparty credit risk, the company has a policy of only entering into contracts with carefully selected major financial institutions based upon their overall credit profile. The company's established policies and procedures for mitigating credit risk on principal transactions include reviewing and establishing limits for credit exposure and continually assessing the creditworthiness of counterparties. The right of set-off that exists under certain of these arrangements enables the legal entities of the company subject to the arrangement to net amounts due to and from the counterparty reducing the maximum loss from credit risk in the event of counterparty default.

The company is also a party to collateral security arrangements with most of its major derivative counterparties. These arrangements require the company to hold or post collateral (cash or U.S. Treasury securities) when the derivative fair values exceed contractually established thresholds. Posting thresholds can be fixed or can vary based on credit default swap pricing or credit ratings received from the major credit agencies. The aggregate fair value of all derivative instruments under these collateralized arrangements that were in a liability position at December 31, 2013 and 2012 was $216 million and $94 million, respectively, for which no collateral was posted at either date. Full collateralization of these agreements would be required in the event that the company's credit rating falls below investment grade or if its credit default swap spread exceeds 250 basis points, as applicable, pursuant to the terms of the collateral security arrangements. The aggregate fair value of derivative instruments in net asset positions as of December 31, 2013 and 2012 was $719 million and $918 million, respectively. This amount represents the maximum exposure to loss at the reporting date as a result of the counterparties failing to perform as contracted. This exposure was reduced by $251 million and $262 million at December 31, 2013 and 2012, respectively, of liabilities included in master netting arrangements with those counterparties. Additionally, at December 31, 2013 and 2012, this exposure was reduced by $29 million and $69 million of cash collateral, respectively, received by the company. At December 31, 2013 and 2012, the net exposure related to derivative assets recorded in the Statement of Financial Position was $439 million and $587 million, respectively. At December 31, 2013 and 2012, the net amount related to derivative liabilities recorded in the Statement of Financial Position was $250 million and $242 million, respectively.

In the Consolidated Statement of Financial Position, the company does not offset derivative assets against liabilities in master netting arrangements nor does it offset receivables or payables recognized upon payment or receipt of cash collateral against the fair values of the related derivative instruments. No amount was recognized in other receivables at December 31, 2013 and 2012 for the right to reclaim cash collateral. The amount recognized in accounts payable for the obligation to return cash collateral totaled $29 million and $69 million at December 31, 2013 and 2012, respectively. The company restricts the use of cash collateral received to rehypothecation, and therefore reports it in prepaid expenses and other current assets in the Consolidated Statement of Financial Position. No amount was rehypothecated at December 31, 2013 and 2012. At December 31, 2013 and 2012 the company held $0 million and $31 million in non-cash collateral in U.S. Treasury securities. Per accounting guidance, non-cash collateral is not recorded on the Statement of Financial Position.

The company may employ derivative instruments to hedge the volatility in stockholders' equity resulting from changes in currency exchange rates of significant foreign subsidiaries of the company with respect to the U.S. dollar. These instruments, designated as net investment hedges, expose the company to liquidity risk as the derivatives have an immediate cash flow impact upon maturity which is not offset by a cash flow from the translation of the underlying hedged equity. The company monitors this cash loss potential on an ongoing basis, and may discontinue some of these hedging relationships by de-designating or terminating the derivative instrument in order to manage the liquidity risk. Although not designated as accounting hedges, the company may utilize derivatives to offset the changes in the fair value of the de-designated instruments from the date of de-designation until maturity.

In its hedging programs, the company uses forward contracts, futures contracts, interest-rate swaps and cross-currency swaps, depending upon the underlying exposure. The company is not a party to leveraged derivative instruments.

A brief description of the major hedging programs, categorized by underlying risk, follows.

Interest Rate Risk

Fixed and Variable Rate Borrowings

The company issues debt in the global capital markets, principally to fund its financing lease and loan portfolio. Access to cost-effective financing can result in interest rate mismatches with the underlying assets. To manage these mismatches and to reduce overall interest cost, the company uses interest rate swaps to convert specific fixed-rate debt issuances into variable-rate debt (i.e., fair value hedges) and to convert specific variable-rate debt issuances into fixed-rate debt (i.e., cash flow hedges). At December 31, 2013 and 2012, the total notional amount of the company's interest rate swaps was $3.1 billion and $4.3 billion, respectively. The weighted-average remaining maturity of these instruments at December 31, 2013 and 2012 was approximately 10.6 years and 5.1 years, respectively.

Forecasted Debt Issuance

The company is exposed to interest rate volatility on future debt issuances. To manage this risk, the company may use forward-starting interest rate swaps to lock in the rate on the interest payments related to the forecasted debt issuance. These swaps are accounted for as cash flow hedges. The company did not have any derivative instruments relating to this program outstanding at December 31, 2013 and 2012.

At December 31, 2013 and 2012, net gains of approximately $1 million (before taxes), respectively, were recorded in AOCI in connection with cash flow hedges of the company's borrowings. Within these amounts, less than $1 million of gains, respectively, are expected to be reclassified to net income within the next 12 months, providing an offsetting economic impact against the underlying transactions.

Foreign Exchange Risk

Long-Term Investments in Foreign Subsidiaries (Net Investment)

A large portion of the company's foreign currency denominated debt portfolio is designated as a hedge of net investment in foreign subsidiaries to reduce the volatility in stockholders' equity caused by changes in foreign currency exchange rates in the functional currency of major foreign subsidiaries with respect to the U.S. dollar. The company also uses cross-currency swaps and foreign exchange forward contracts for this risk management purpose. At December 31, 2013 and 2012, the total notional amount of derivative instruments designated as net investment hedges was $3.0 billion and $3.3 billion, respectively. The weighted-average remaining maturity of these instruments at December 31, 2013 and 2012 was approximately 0.4 years for both periods.

Anticipated Royalties and Cost Transactions

The company's operations generate significant nonfunctional currency, third-party vendor payments and intercompany payments for royalties and goods and services among the company's non-U.S. subsidiaries and with the parent company. In anticipation of these foreign currency cash flows and in view of the volatility of the currency markets, the company selectively employs foreign exchange forward contracts to manage its currency risk. These forward contracts are accounted for as cash flow hedges. The maximum length of time over which the company is hedging its exposure to the variability in future cash flows is four years. At December 31, 2013 and 2012, the total notional amount of forward contracts designated as cash flow hedges of forecasted royalty and cost transactions was $10.2 billion and $10.7 billion, respectively, with a weighted-average remaining maturity of 0.7 years at both year-end dates.

At December 31, 2013 and 2012, in connection with cash flow hedges of anticipated royalties and cost transactions, the company recorded net losses of $252 million and $138 million (before taxes), respectively, in AOCI. Within these amounts $166 million and $79 million of losses, respectively, are expected to be reclassified to net income within the next 12 months, providing an offsetting economic impact against the underlying anticipated transactions.

Foreign Currency Denominated Borrowings

The company is exposed to exchange rate volatility on foreign currency denominated debt. To manage this risk, the company employs cross-currency swaps to convert fixed-rate foreign currency denominated debt to fixed-rate debt denominated in the functional currency of the borrowing entity. These swaps are accounted for as cash flow hedges. The maximum length of time over which the company hedges its exposure to the variability in future cash flows is approximately seven years. At December 31, 2013 the total notional amount of cross currency swaps designated as cash flow hedges of foreign currency denominated debt was $1.2 billion. At December 31, 2012, no instruments relating to this program were outstanding.

At December 31, 2013, in connection with cash flow hedges of foreign currency denominated borrowings, the company recorded net losses of $9 million (before taxes) in AOCI. Within this amount, $3 million of losses is expected to be reclassified to net income within the next 12 months, providing an offsetting economic impact against the underlying exposure.

Subsidiary Cash and Foreign Currency Asset/Liability Management

The company uses its Global Treasury Centers to manage the cash of its subsidiaries. These centers principally use currency swaps to convert cash flows in a cost-effective manner. In addition, the company uses foreign exchange forward contracts to economically hedge, on a net basis, the foreign currency exposure of a portion of the company's nonfunctional currency assets and liabilities. The terms of these forward and swap contracts are generally less than one year. The changes in the fair values of these contracts and of the underlying hedged exposures are generally offsetting and are recorded in other (income) and expense in the Consolidated Statement of Earnings. At December 31, 2013 and 2012, the total notional amount of derivative instruments in economic hedges of foreign currency exposure was $14.7 billion and $12.9 billion, respectively.

Equity Risk Management

The company is exposed to market price changes in certain broad market indices and in the company's own stock primarily related to certain obligations to employees. Changes in the overall value of these employee compensation obligations are recorded in SG&A expense in the Consolidated Statement of Earnings. Although not designated as accounting hedges, the company utilizes derivatives, including equity swaps and futures, to economically hedge the exposures related to its employee compensation obligations. The derivatives are linked to the total return on certain broad market indices or the total return on the company's common stock. They are recorded at fair value with gains or losses also reported in SG&A expense in the Consolidated Statement of Earnings. At December 31, 2013 and 2012, the total notional amount of derivative instruments in economic hedges of these compensation obligations was $1.3 billion and $1.2 billion, respectively.

Other Risks

The company may hold warrants to purchase shares of common stock in connection with various investments that are deemed derivatives because they contain net share or net cash settlement provisions. The company records the changes in the fair value of these warrants in other (income) and expense in the Consolidated Statement of Earnings. The company did not have any warrants qualifying as derivatives outstanding at December 31, 2013 and 2012.

The company is exposed to a potential loss if a client fails to pay amounts due under contractual terms. The company utilizes credit default swaps to economically hedge its credit exposures. These derivatives have terms of one year or less. The swaps are recorded at fair value with gains and losses reported in other (income) and expense in the Consolidated Statement of Earnings. The company did not have any derivative instruments relating to this program outstanding at December 31, 2013 and 2012.

The following tables provide a quantitative summary of the derivative and non-derivative instrument-related risk management activity as of December 31, 2013 and 2012 as well as for the years ended December 31, 2013, 2012 and 2011, respectively.

Fair Values of Derivative Instruments in the Consolidated Statement of Financial Position

($ in millions)

At December 31:	Fair Value of Derivative Assets			Fair Value of Derivative Liabilities		
	Balance Sheet Classification	2013	2012	Balance Sheet Classification	2013	2012
Designated as hedging instruments:						
Interest rate contracts	Prepaid expenses and other current assets	$ —	$ 47	Other accrued expenses and liabilities	$ 0	$ —
	Investments and sundry assets	308	557	Other liabilities	13	—
Foreign exchange contracts	Prepaid expenses and other current assets	187	135	Other accrued expenses and liabilities	331	267
	Investments and sundry assets	26	5	Other liabilities	112	78
	Fair value of derivative assets	$522	$744	Fair value of derivative liabilities	$ 456	$ 345
Not designated as hedging instruments:						
Foreign exchange contracts	Prepaid expenses and other current assets	$ 94	$142	Other accrued expenses and liabilities	$ 40	$ 152
	Investments and sundry assets	67	23	Other liabilities	1	—
Equity contracts	Prepaid expenses and other current assets	36	9	Other accrued expenses and liabilities	4	7
	Fair value of derivative assets	$197	$174	Fair value of derivative liabilities	$ 45	$ 159
Total debt designated as hedging instruments						
Short-term debt		N/A	N/A		$ 190	$ 578
Long-term debt		N/A	N/A		$6,111	$3,035
Total		$719	$918		$6,802	$4,116

N/A—Not applicable.

PREPAID EXPENSES

2.50 WILLIAMS-SONOMA, INC. (JAN)
CONSOLIDATED BALANCE SHEETS (in part)

(Dollars and shares in thousands, except per share amounts)	Feb. 3, 2013	Jan. 29, 2012
Assets (in part)		
Current assets		
Cash and cash equivalents	$ 424,555	$ 502,757
Restricted cash	16,055	14,732
Accounts receivable, net	62,985	45,961
Merchandise inventories, net	640,024	553,461
Prepaid catalog expenses	37,231	34,294
Prepaid expenses	26,339	24,188
Deferred income taxes, net	99,764	91,744
Other assets	9,819	9,229
Total current assets	1,316,772	1,276,366

Note A: Summary of Significant Accounting Policies (in part)

Advertising and Prepaid Catalog Expenses

Advertising expenses consist of media and production costs related to catalog mailings, e-commerce advertising and other direct marketing activities. All advertising costs are expensed as incurred, or upon the release of the initial advertisement, with the exception of prepaid catalog expenses. Prepaid catalog expenses consist primarily of third party incremental direct costs, including creative design, paper, printing, postage and mailing costs for all of our direct response catalogs. Such costs are capitalized as prepaid catalog expenses and are amortized over their expected period of future benefit. Such amortization is based upon the ratio of estimated direct-to-customer revenues for the period to the total estimated direct-to-customer revenues over the life of the catalog on an individual catalog basis. Estimated direct-to-customer revenues over the life of the catalog are based upon various factors such as the total number of catalogs and pages circulated, the probability and magnitude of consumer response and the assortment of merchandise offered. Each catalog is generally fully amortized over a six to nine month period, with the majority of the amortization occurring within the first four to five months. Prepaid catalog expenses are evaluated for realizability on a monthly basis by comparing the carrying amount associated with each catalog to the estimated probable remaining future profitability (remaining net revenues less merchandise cost of goods sold, selling expenses and catalog-related costs) associated with that catalog. If the catalog is not expected to be profitable, the carrying amount of the catalog is impaired accordingly.

Total advertising expenses (including catalog advertising, e-commerce advertising and all other advertising costs) were approximately $318,338,000, $301,316,000 and $293,623,000 in fiscal 2012, fiscal 2011 and fiscal 2010, respectively.

CONTRACTS

2.51 GENERAL DYNAMICS CORPORATION (DEC)
CONSOLIDATED BALANCE SHEETS (in part)

	December 31	
(Dollars in millions)	2012	2013
Assets (in part)		
Current assets:		
Cash and equivalents	$ 3,296	$ 5,301
Accounts receivable	4,204	4,402
Contracts in process	4,964	4,780
Inventories	2,776	2,968
Other current assets	504	435
Total current assets	15,744	17,886

(Dollars in millions, except per-share amounts or unless otherwise noted)

A. Summary of Significant Accounting Policies (in part)

Basis of Consolidation and Classification. The Consolidated Financial Statements include the accounts of General Dynamics Corporation and our wholly owned and majority-owned subsidiaries. We eliminate all inter-company balances and transactions in the Consolidated Financial Statements.

Consistent with defense industry practice, we classify assets and liabilities related to long-term production contracts as current, even though some of these amounts may not be realized within one year. In addition, some prior-year amounts have been reclassified among financial statement accounts to conform to the current-year presentation.

G. Contracts in Process

Contracts in process represent recoverable costs and, where applicable, accrued profit related to long-term contracts that have been inventoried until the customer is billed, and consisted of the following:

December 31	2012	2013
Contract costs and estimated profits	$ 8,162	$ 7,961
Other contract costs	1,089	1,178
	9,251	9,139
Advances and progress payments	(4,287)	(4,359)
Total contracts in process	$ 4,964	$ 4,780

Contract costs consist primarily of labor, material, overhead and G&A expenses. Contract costs also may include estimated contract recoveries for matters such as contract changes and claims for unanticipated contract costs. We record revenue associated with these matters only when the amount of recovery can be estimated reliably and realization is probable. Assumed recoveries for claims included in contracts in process were not material on December 31, 2012 or 2013.

Other contract costs represent amounts that are not currently allocable to government contracts, such as a portion of our estimated workers' compensation obligations, other insurance-related assessments, pension and other post-retirement benefits and environmental expenses. These costs will become allocable to contracts generally after they are paid. We expect to recover these costs through ongoing business, including existing backlog and probable follow-on contracts. If the backlog in the future does not support the continued deferral of these costs, the profitability of our remaining contracts could be adversely affected.

Excluding our other contract costs, we expect to bill all but approximately 15 percent of our year-end 2013 contracts-in-process balance during 2014. Of the amount not expected to be billed in 2014, approximately $315 relates to a single contract, the Canadian Maritime Helicopter Project (MHP), as the prime contract is behind schedule. Ultimately, we believe these delays will be resolved and the balance will be billed and collected.

Property, Plant, and Equipment

RECOGNITION AND MEASUREMENT

2.52 *Property, plant, and equipment* are the long-lived, physical assets of the entity acquired for use in the entity's normal business operations and not intended for resale by the entity. FASB ASC 360, *Property, Plant, and Equipment*, states that these assets are initially recorded at historical cost, which includes the costs necessarily incurred to bring them to the condition and location necessary for their intended use. FASB ASC 835-20 establishes standards for capitalizing interest cost as part of the historical cost of acquiring assets constructed by an entity for its own use or produced for the entity by others for which deposits or progress payments have been made.

2.53 An entity may acquire or develop computer software either for internal use or for sale or lease to others. If for internal use, FASB ASC 350-40 provides guidance on accounting for the costs of computer software and for determining whether the software is for internal use. Under FASB ASC 350-40, internal and external costs incurred to develop internal-use software during the application development stage should be capitalized and amortized over the software's estimated useful life. Accounting for software acquired or developed for sale or lease is addressed by FASB ASC 985-20. Whether for internal use or sale or lease, FASB ASC refers to capitalized software costs as amortizable intangible assets.

PRESENTATION

2.54 FASB ASC 210-10-45-4 indicates that property, plant, and equipment should be classified as noncurrent when a classified balance sheet is presented. Under FASB ASC 805-20-55-37, some use rights acquired in a business combination may have characteristics of tangible, rather than intangible, assets. An example is mineral rights.

2.55 Under FASB ASC 985-20-45-2, capitalized costs related to software for sale or lease having a life of more than one year or one operating cycle should be presented as an other asset. Under FASB ASC 985-20, amortization expense should be on a product-by-product basis and charged to cost of sales or a similar expense category because it relates to a software product that is marketed to others. Presentations of capitalized computer software costs by survey entities vary.

DISCLOSURE

2.56 FASB ASC 360-10-50-1 requires the following disclosures in the financial statements or notes thereto:

a. Depreciation expense for the period
b. Balances of major classes of depreciable assets, by nature or function, at the balance sheet date
c. Accumulated depreciation, either by major classes of depreciable assets or in total, at the balance sheet date
d. A general description of the method(s) used in computing depreciation with respect to major classes of depreciable assets.

FASB ASC 360 also provides accounting and disclosure guidance for the long-lived assets that are impaired or held for disposal. Rule 5-02 of Regulation S-X requires that registrants state the basis of determining the amounts of property, plant, and equipment.

PRESENTATION AND DISCLOSURE EXCERPTS

PROPERTY, PLANT, AND EQUIPMENT

2.57 COCA-COLA ENTERPRISES, INC. (DEC)
CONSOLIDATED BALANCE SHEETS (in part)

	December 31,	
(In millions, except share data)	**2013**	**2012**
Assets		
Current:		
Cash and cash equivalents	$ 343	$ 721
Trade accounts receivable, less allowances of $16 and $17, respectively	1,515	1,432
Amounts receivable from The Coca-Cola Company	89	66
Inventories	452	386
Other current assets	169	157
Total current assets	2,568	2,762
Property, plant, and equipment, net	2,353	2,322
Franchise license intangible assets, net	4,004	3,923
Goodwill	124	132
Other noncurrent assets	476	371
Total assets	$9,525	$9,510

NOTES TO CONSOLIDATED FINANCIAL STATEMENTS

Note 1—Business and Summary of Significant Accounting Policies (in part)

Property, Plant, and Equipment

Property, plant, and equipment is recorded at cost. Major property additions, replacements, and betterments are capitalized, while maintenance and repairs that do not extend the useful life of an asset or add new functionality are expensed as incurred. Depreciation is recorded using the straight-line method over the respective estimated useful lives of our assets. Our cold-drink equipment and containers, such as reusable crates, shells, and bottles, are depreciated using the straight-line method over the estimated useful life of each group of equipment, as determined using the group-life method. Under this method, we do not recognize gains or losses on the disposal of individual units of equipment when the disposal occurs in the normal course of business. We capitalize the costs of refurbishing our cold-drink equipment and depreciate those costs over the estimated period until the next scheduled refurbishment or until the equipment is retired. Leasehold improvements are amortized using the straight-line method over the shorter of the remaining lease term or the estimated useful life of the improvement.

The following table summarizes the classification of depreciation and amortization expense in our Consolidated Statements of Income for the periods presented (in millions):

Location—Statements of Income	2013	2012	2011
Selling, delivery, and administrative expenses	$190	$214	$200
Cost of sales	118	121	121
Total depreciation and amortization	$308	$335	$321

Our interests in assets acquired under capital leases are included in property, plant, and equipment and primarily relate to buildings and fleet assets. Amortization of capital lease assets is included in depreciation expense. Our net interests in assets acquired under capital leases totaled $31 million as of December 31, 2013 (gross cost of $91 million, net of accumulated amortization of $60 million). The net present values of amounts due under capital leases are recorded as liabilities and are included within our total debt. Refer to Note 6.

We assess the recoverability of the carrying amount of our property, plant, and equipment when events or changes in circumstances indicate that the carrying amount of an asset or asset group may not be recoverable. If we determine that the carrying amount of an asset or asset group is not recoverable based upon the expected undiscounted future cash flows of the asset or asset group, we record an impairment loss equal to the excess of the carrying amount over the estimated fair value of the asset or asset group.

We capitalize certain development costs associated with internal use software, including external direct costs of materials and services and payroll costs for employees devoting time to a software project. Costs incurred during the preliminary project stage, as well as costs for maintenance and training, are expensed as incurred.

The following table summarizes our property, plant, and equipment as of the dates presented (in millions):

	December 31,		
	2013	2012	Useful Life
Land	$ 166	$ 161	n/a
Building and improvements	1,024	948	20 to 40 years
Machinery, equipment, and containers	1,773	1,625	3 to 20 years
Cold-drink equipment	1,721	1,602	3 to 13 years
Vehicle fleet	110	122	3 to 12 years
Furniture, office equipment, and software	431	379	3 to 10 years
Property, plant, and equipment	5,225	4,837	
Accumulated depreciation and amortization	(3,050)	(2,756)	
	2,175	2,081	
Construction in process	178	241	
Property, plant, and equipment, net	$ 2,353	$ 2,322	

2.58 CHEVRON CORPORATION (DEC)
CONSOLIDATED BALANCE SHEET (in part)

Millions of dollars, except per-share amounts

	At December 31	
	2013	2012
Assets		
Cash and cash equivalents	$ 16,245	$ 20,939
Time deposits	8	708
Marketable securities	263	266
Accounts and notes receivable (less allowance: 2013—$62; 2012—$80)	21,622	20,997
Inventories:		
Crude oil and petroleum products	3,879	3,923
Chemicals	491	475
Materials, supplies and other	2,010	1,746
Total inventories	6,380	6,144
Prepaid expenses and other current assets	5,732	6,666
Total Current Assets	50,250	55,720
Long-term receivables, net	2,833	3,053
Investments and advances	25,502	23,718
Properties, plant and equipment, at cost	296,433	263,481
Less: Accumulated depreciation, depletion and amortization	131,604	122,133
Properties, plant and equipment, net	164,829	141,348
Deferred charges and other assets	5,120	4,503
Goodwill	4,639	4,640
Assets held for sale	580	—
Total Assets	$253,753	$232,982

Millions of dollars, except per-share amounts

Note 1—Summary of Significant Accounting Policies (in part)

Properties, Plant and Equipment The successful efforts method is used for crude oil and natural gas exploration and production activities. All costs for development wells, related plant and equipment, proved mineral interests in crude oil and natural gas properties, and related asset retirement obligation (ARO) assets are capitalized. Costs of exploratory wells are capitalized pending determination of whether the wells found proved reserves. Costs of wells that are assigned proved reserves remain capitalized. Costs also are capitalized for exploratory wells that have found crude oil and natural gas reserves even if the reserves cannot be classified as proved when the drilling is completed, provided the exploratory well has found a sufficient quantity of reserves to justify its completion as a producing well and the company is making sufficient progress assessing the reserves and the economic and operating viability of the project. All other exploratory wells and costs are expensed. Refer to Note 19, beginning on page FS-46, for additional discussion of accounting for suspended exploratory well costs.

Long-lived assets to be held and used, including proved crude oil and natural gas properties, are assessed for possible impairment by comparing their carrying values with their associated undiscounted, future net before-tax cash flows. Events that can trigger assessments for possible impairments include write-downs of proved reserves based on field performance, significant decreases in the market value of an asset, significant change in the extent or manner of use of or a physical change in an asset, and a more-likely-than-not expectation that a long-lived asset or asset group will be sold or otherwise disposed of significantly sooner than the end of its previously estimated useful life. Impaired assets are written down to their estimated fair values, generally their discounted, future net before-tax cash flows. For proved crude oil and natural gas properties in the United States, the company generally performs an impairment review on an individual field basis. Outside the United States, reviews are performed on a country, concession, development area or field basis, as appropriate. In Downstream, impairment reviews are performed on the basis of a refinery, a plant, a marketing/lubricants area or distribution area, as appropriate. Impairment amounts are recorded as incremental "Depreciation, depletion and amortization" expense.

Long-lived assets that are held for sale are evaluated for possible impairment by comparing the carrying value of the asset with its fair value less the cost to sell. If the net book value exceeds the fair value less cost to sell, the asset is considered impaired and adjusted to the lower value. Refer to Note 9, beginning on page FS-32, relating to fair value measurements.

The fair value of a liability for an ARO is recorded as an asset and a liability when there is a legal obligation associated with the retirement of a long-lived asset and the amount can be reasonably estimated. Refer also to Note 24, on page FS-56, relating to AROs.

Depreciation and depletion of all capitalized costs of proved crude oil and natural gas producing properties, except mineral interests, are expensed using the unit-of-production method, generally by individual field, as the proved developed reserves are produced. Depletion expenses for capitalized costs of proved mineral interests are recognized using the unit-of-production method by individual field as the related proved reserves are produced. Periodic valuation provisions for impairment of capitalized costs of unproved mineral interests are expensed.

The capitalized costs of all other plant and equipment are depreciated or amortized over their estimated useful lives. In general, the declining-balance method is used to depreciate plant and equipment in the United States; the straight-line method is generally used to depreciate international plant and equipment and to amortize all capitalized leased assets.

Gains or losses are not recognized for normal retirements of properties, plant and equipment subject to composite group amortization or depreciation. Gains or losses from abnormal retirements are recorded as expenses, and from sales as "Other income."

Expenditures for maintenance (including those for planned major maintenance projects), repairs and minor renewals to maintain facilities in operating condition are generally expensed as incurred. Major replacements and renewals are capitalized.

Note 13—Properties, Plant and Equipment[1]

| | At December 31 | | | | | | Year ended December 31 | | | | | |
| | Gross Investment at Cost | | | Net Investment | | | Additions at Cost[2,3] | | | Depreciation Expense[4] | | |
	2013	2012	2011	2013	2012	2011	2013	2012	2011	2013	2012	2011
Upstream												
United States	$ 89,555	$ 81,908	$ 74,369	$ 41,831	$ 37,909	$ 33,461	$ 8,188	$ 8,211	$14,404	$ 4,412	$ 3,902	$ 3,870
International	169,623	145,799	125,795	104,100	85,318	72,543	27,383	21,343	15,722	8,336	8,015	7,590
Total Upstream	259,178	227,707	200,164	145,931	123,227	106,004	35,571	29,554	30,126	12,748	11,917	11,460
Downstream												
United States	22,407	21,792	20,699	11,481	11,333	10,723	1,154	1,498	1,226	780	799	776
International	9,303	8,990	7,422	4,139	3,930	2,995	653	2,544	443	360	308	332
Total Downstream	31,710	30,782	28,121	15,620	15,263	13,718	1,807	4,042	1,669	1,140	1,107	1,108
All Other[5]												
United States	5,402	4,959	5,117	3,194	2,845	2,872	721	415	591	286	384	338
International	143	33	30	84	13	14	23	4	5	12	5	5
Total All Other	5,545	4,992	5,147	3,278	2,858	2,886	744	419	596	298	389	343
Total United States	117,364	108,659	100,185	56,506	52,087	47,056	10,063	10,124	16,221	5,478	5,085	4,984
Total International	179,069	154,822	133,247	108,323	89,261	75,552	28,059	23,891	16,170	8,708	8,328	7,927
Total	$296,433	$263,481	$233,432	$164,829	$141,348	$122,608	$38,122	$34,015	$32,391	$14,186	$13,413	$12,911

[1] Other than the United States, Australia and Nigeria, no other country accounted for 10 percent or more of the company's net properties, plant and equipment (PP&E) in 2013. Australia had $31,464, $21,770 and $12,423 in 2013, 2012, and 2011, respectively. Nigeria had PP&E of $18,429, $17,485 and $15,601 for 2013, 2012 and 2011, respectively.

[2] Net of dry hole expense related to prior years' expenditures of $89, $80 and $45 in 2013, 2012 and 2011, respectively.

[3] Includes properties acquired with the acquisition of Atlas Energy, Inc., in 2011.

[4] Depreciation expense includes accretion expense of $627, $629 and $628 in 2013, 2012 and 2011, respectively.

[5] Primarily mining operations, power and energy services, real estate assets and management information systems.

Equity Method and Joint Ventures

RECOGNITION AND MEASUREMENT

2.59 FASB ASC 323, *Investments—Equity Method and Joint Ventures*, stipulates that the equity method should be used to account for investments in corporate joint ventures and certain other noncontrolled entities when an investor has the ability to exercise significant influence over operating and financial policies of an investee, even though the investor holds 50 percent or less of the common stock. FASB ASC 323 considers an investor to have the ability to exercise significant influence when it owns 20 percent or more of the voting stock of an investee. FASB ASC 323 specifies the criteria for applying the equity method of accounting to 50 percent or less owned entities and lists circumstances under which, despite 20 percent ownership, an investor may not be able to exercise significant influence.

PRESENTATION

2.60 Under the equity method, FASB ASC 323–10–45–1 requires that an investment in common stock be shown in the balance sheet of an investor as a single amount.

DISCLOSURE

2.61 Under FASB ASC 323–10–50–2, the significance of an equity method investment to the investor's financial position and results of operations should be considered in evaluating the extent of disclosures of the financial position and results of operations of an investee. If the investor has more than one investment in common stock, disclosures wholly or partly on a combined basis may be appropriate. FASB ASC 323–10–50–3 details disclosures required for equity method investments, including name and percentage of ownership of the investee, investor accounting policies, any difference between the amount at which an investment is carried and the amount of underlying equity in net assets, and the accounting treatment of the difference.

PRESENTATION AND DISCLOSURE EXCERPTS

EQUITY METHOD

2.62 CONSTELLATION BRANDS, INC. (FEB)

CONSOLIDATED BALANCE SHEETS (in part)

(In millions, except share and per share data)

	February 28, 2013	February 29, 2012
Assets		
Current assets:		
Cash and cash investments	$ 331.5	$ 85.8
Accounts receivable, net	471.9	437.6
Inventories	1,480.9	1,374.5
Prepaid expenses and other	186.9	136.4
Total current assets	2,471.2	2,034.3
Property, Plant and Equipment, net	1,229.0	1,255.8
Goodwill	2,722.3	2,632.9
Intangible Assets, net	871.4	866.4
Other Assets, net	344.2	320.5
Total assets	$7,638.1	$7,109.9

NOTES TO CONSOLIDATED FINANCIAL STATEMENTS

1. Summary of Significant Accounting Policies (in part)

Equity Method Investments—

If the Company is not required to consolidate its investment in another entity, the Company uses the equity method if the Company (i) can exercise significant influence over the other entity and (ii) holds common stock and/or in-substance common stock of the other entity. Under the equity method, investments are carried at cost, plus or minus the Company's equity in the increases and decreases in the investee's net assets after the date of acquisition and certain other adjustments. The Company's share of the net income or loss of the investee is included in equity in earnings of equity method investees on the Company's Consolidated Statements of Comprehensive Income. Dividends received from the investee reduce the carrying amount of the investment.

Equity method investments are also reviewed for impairment whenever events or changes in circumstances indicate that the carrying amount of the investments may not be recoverable. No instances of impairment were noted on the Company's equity method investments for the years ended February 28, 2013, February 29, 2012, and February 28, 2011.

Other Assets—

Other assets include the following: (i) investments in equity method investees which are carried under the equity method of accounting (see Note 8); (ii) deferred financing costs which are stated at cost, net of accumulated amortization, and are amortized on an effective interest basis over the term of the related debt; (iii) an investment in Accolade (as defined in Note 8) consisting of cost method investments which are carried at cost and available-for-sale ("AFS") debt securities which are carried at fair value (see Note 8); (iv) deferred tax assets which are stated net of valuation allowances (see Note 11); and (v) derivative assets which are stated at fair value.

8. Other Assets (in part)

The major components of other assets are as follows:

(In millions)	February 28, 2013	February 29, 2012
Investments in equity method investees	$243.6	$248.3
Deferred financing costs	54.4	44.9
Investment in Accolade	42.8	37.1
Other	17.3	22.3
	358.1	352.6
Less—Accumulated amortization	(13.9)	(32.1)
	$344.2	$320.5

Investments in Equity Method Investees—

Crown Imports:

Constellation Beers Ltd. ("Constellation Beers"), an indirect wholly-owned subsidiary of the Company, and Diblo, S.A. de C.V. ("Diblo"), an entity owned 76.75% by Grupo Modelo, S.A.B. de C.V. ("Modelo") and 23.25% by Anheuser-Busch Companies, Inc., each have, directly or indirectly, equal interests in a joint venture, Crown Imports LLC ("Crown Imports"). Crown Imports has the exclusive right to import, market and sell primarily Modelo's Mexican beer portfolio (the "Modelo Brands") in the U.S. and Guam.

The Company accounts for the investment in Crown Imports under the equity method. Accordingly, the results of operations of Crown Imports are included in equity in earnings of equity method investees on the Company's Consolidated Statements of Comprehensive Income. As of February 28, 2013, and February 29, 2012, the Company's investment in Crown Imports was $169.3 million and $176.4 million, respectively. As of February 28, 2013, and February 29, 2012, the carrying amount of the investment is greater than the Company's equity in the underlying assets of Crown Imports by $13.6 million and $26.4 million, respectively, due to the difference in the carrying amounts of the indefinite lived intangible assets contributed to Crown Imports by each party and timing of receipt of certain cash distributions from Crown Imports. The Company received $230.2 million, $222.0 million and $210.0 million of cash distributions from Crown Imports for the years ended February 28, 2013, February 29, 2012, and February 28, 2011, respectively, all of which represent distributions of earnings.

Prior to January 1, 2012, Constellation Beers provided certain administrative services to Crown Imports. On January 1, 2012, in accordance with the terms of the original joint venture agreement, such administrative services were discontinued. Additionally, on January 1, 2012, a new services agreement was established whereby Constellation Beers continues to provide information technology services to Crown Imports. Amounts related to the performance of these services for the years ended February 28, 2013, February 29, 2012, and February 28, 2011, as appropriate, were not material. Amounts receivable from Crown Imports as of February 28, 2013, and February 29, 2012, were not material.

In June 2012, the Company signed an agreement to acquire the remaining 50% equity interest in Crown Imports for approximately $1.85 billion (the "Initial Purchase Agreement"). In February 2013, the Company signed an amended and restated agreement to acquire the remaining 50% equity interest in Crown Imports for the previously agreed approximately $1.85 billion (the "February 2013 Crown Purchase Agreement"). In addition, the Company signed an agreement to purchase (i) all of the outstanding capital stock of Compañia Cervecera de Coahuila, S.A. de C.V., the company which owns the Piedras Negras brewery located in Nava, Coahuila, Mexico (the "Brewery"), (ii) all of the outstanding capital stock of Servicios Modelo de Coahuila, S.A. de C.V., (the "Services Company"), and (iii) the perpetual brand rights for the Modelo Brands currently sold in the U.S. and certain extensions (collectively, the "February 2013 Purchased Shares and Licensed Rights") for approximately $2.9 billion, in aggregate, subject to a post-closing adjustment. The February 2013 Crown Purchase Agreement and the February 2013 Purchased Shares and Licensed Rights are collectively referred to as the "February 2013 Beer Business Acquisition."

In April 2013, the Company entered into amendments to the agreements regarding the February 2013 Beer Business Acquisition (the "First Amendments"), pursuant to which, among other things, the Company is required to build out and expand the Brewery to a nominal capacity of at least 20 million hectoliters of packaged beer annually by December 31, 2016. In addition, the First Amendments provide, among other things, that the United States will have approval rights, in its sole discretion, for amendments or modifications to the amended agreements and the United States will have a right of approval, in its sole discretion, of any extension of the term of interim supply arrangements beyond three years. The February 2013 Beer Business Acquisition together with the First Amendments is referred to as the "Beer Business Acquisition."

In August 2012, the Company entered into financing arrangements to fund the Initial Purchase Agreement consisting of the Term A-2 Facility and the August 2012 Senior Notes (both as defined in Note 10). Because of the differences between the terms relating to the February 2013 Beer Business Acquisition and the Initial Purchase Agreement, the Company determined that the conditions for the release of the Escrowed Property (as defined in Note 10) to the Company pursuant to the Escrow Agreement (as defined in Note 10) could not be satisfied. Accordingly, the Company gave notice to the escrow agent on February 19, 2013, to release the Escrowed Property for purposes of effecting the Special Mandatory Redemption (as defined in Note 10). As a result, the August 2012 Senior Notes were redeemed on February 20, 2013, and the Escrow Agreement was terminated in accordance with its terms. The Company expects permanent financing for the Beer Business Acquisition to consist of a combination of available cash and debt financings, including an amended delayed draw U.S. term loan facility (in favor of the Company), one or more new credit facilities (in favor of a European subsidiary of the Company) under an amended and restated senior credit facility, an accounts receivable securitization facility (see Note 10), the issuance of certain notes or debt securities, and revolver borrowings under an amended and restated senior credit facility. The Company has a fully committed, amended and restated bridge financing in place through December 30, 2013, upon which it could draw to fund a portion of the Beer Business Acquisition if any of its expected financing is unavailable. The Company currently expects to complete the Beer Business Acquisition around the end of the

Company's first quarter of fiscal 2014, or shortly thereafter, subject to the satisfaction of certain closing conditions, including the receipt of any required regulatory approvals and the consummation of certain transactions between Anheuser-Busch InBev SA/NV and Modelo and certain of its affiliates. The Company cannot guarantee, however, that this transaction will be completed upon the agreed upon terms, or at all. The results of operations of the Beer Business Acquisition will be reported in the Crown Imports segment and will be included in the consolidated results of operations from the date of acquisition. The Beer Business Acquisition is expected to be significant and the Company expects it to have a material impact on the Company's future results of operations, financial position and cash flows.

Ruffino:

Prior to the acquisition of Ruffino, the well-known Italian fine wine company, on October 5, 2011 (as further discussed below), the Company had a 49.9% interest in Ruffino. The Company did not have a controlling interest in Ruffino or exert any managerial control and the Company accounted for its investment in Ruffino under the equity method. Accordingly, the results of operations of Ruffino were included in equity in earnings of equity method investees on the Company's Consolidated Statements of Comprehensive Income through October 5, 2011. In addition, prior to October 5, 2011, the Company's Constellation Wines and Spirits segment distributed Ruffino's products primarily in the U.S. Amounts purchased from Ruffino under this arrangement for the years ended February 29, 2012, and February 28, 2011, were not material.

In connection with the Company's December 2004 investment in Ruffino, the Company granted separate irrevocable and unconditional options to the two other shareholders of Ruffino to put to the Company all of the ownership interests held by these shareholders for a price as calculated in the joint venture agreement. Each option was exercisable during the period starting from January 1, 2010, and ending on December 31, 2010. During the year ended February 28, 2010, the 9.9% shareholder of Ruffino exercised its option to put its entire equity interest in Ruffino to the Company. In May 2010, the Company settled this put option through a cash payment of €23.5 million ($29.6 million) to the 9.9% shareholder of Ruffino, thereby increasing the Company's equity interest in Ruffino from 40.0% to 49.9%. In December 2010, the Company received notification from the 50.1% shareholder of Ruffino that it was exercising its option to put its entire equity interest in Ruffino to the Company for €55.9 million. Prior to this notification, the Company had initiated arbitration proceedings against the 50.1% shareholder alleging various matters which should have affected the validity of the put option. However, subsequent to the initiation of the arbitration proceedings, the Company began discussions with the 50.1% shareholder on a framework for settlement of all legal actions. The framework of the settlement would include the Company's purchase of the 50.1% shareholder's entire equity interest in Ruffino on revised terms to be agreed upon by both parties. As a result, the Company recognized a loss for the fourth quarter of fiscal 2011 of €43.4 million ($60.0 million) on the contingent obligation. This loss is included in selling, general and administrative expenses on the Company's Consolidated Statements of Comprehensive Income.

On October 5, 2011, the Company acquired the 50.1% shareholder's entire equity interest in Ruffino for €50.3 million ($68.6 million). In conjunction with this acquisition, all of the aforementioned legal actions were settled. As a result of this acquisition, the Company assumed indebtedness of Ruffino, net of cash acquired, of €54.2 million ($73.1 million). The purchase price was financed with revolver borrowings under the Company's then existing senior credit facility. In accordance with the acquisition method of accounting, the identifiable assets acquired and the liabilities assumed have been measured at their acquisition-date fair values. The acquisition of Ruffino was not material for purposes of supplemental disclosure pursuant to the FASB guidance on business combinations. Prior to the acquisition of Ruffino, the Company recognized a net foreign currency loss of $2.1 million on the contingent obligation originally recorded in the fourth quarter of fiscal 2011. This net loss is included in selling, general and administrative expenses on the Company's Consolidated Statements of Comprehensive Income. In connection with the acquisition of Ruffino, the Company recognized net gains of $8.4 million related primarily to the gain on the revaluation of the Company's previously held 49.9% equity interest in Ruffino to the acquisition-date fair value (consisting largely of the reclassification of the related foreign currency translation adjustments previously recognized in other comprehensive income), and the revaluation of the Company's contingent obligation originally recorded in the fourth quarter of fiscal 2011. These net gains are included in selling, general and administrative expenses on the Company's Consolidated Statements of Comprehensive Income. The results of operations of the Ruffino business are reported in the Company's Constellation Wines and Spirits segment and are included in the consolidated results of operations of the Company from the date of acquisition.

Other:

In connection with prior acquisitions, the Company acquired several investments which are being accounted for under the equity method. The primary investment consists of Opus One Winery LLC ("Opus One"), a 50% owned joint venture arrangement. As of February 28, 2013, and February 29, 2012, the Company's investment in Opus One was $59.3 million and $56.4 million, respectively. The percentage of ownership of the remaining investments ranges from 20% to 50%.

The following table presents summarized financial information for the Company's Crown Imports equity method investment and the other material equity method investments discussed above. The amounts shown represent 100% of these equity method investments' financial position and results of operations for those investments accounted for under the equity method as of February 28, 2013. As the financial position and results of operations of Ruffino have been included in the Company's consolidated financial position and results of operations from the date of acquisition, amounts shown for Ruffino represent 100% of the equity method investment's results of operations prior to the date of acquisition.

| (In millions) | February 28, 2013 | | | February 29, 2012 | | |
	Crown Imports	Other	Total	Crown Imports	Other	Total
Current assets	$404.1	$27.4	$431.5	$372.3	$20.9	$393.2
Noncurrent assets	$ 36.4	$50.8	$ 87.2	$ 37.3	$50.6	$ 87.9
Current liabilities	$123.2	$ 4.7	$127.9	$105.0	$ 4.2	$109.2
Noncurrent liabilities	$ 6.0	$22.6	$ 28.6	$ 4.6	$25.4	$ 30.0

(In millions)	Crown Imports	Other	Total
For the Year Ended February 28, 2013			
Net sales	$2,588.1	$ 52.6	$2,640.7
Gross profit	$ 755.4	$ 39.0	$ 794.4
Income from continuing operations	$ 446.2	$ 24.8	$ 471.0
Net income	$ 446.2	$ 24.8	$ 471.0
For the Year Ended February 29, 2012			
Net sales	$2,469.5	$106.2	$2,575.7
Gross profit	$ 721.0	$ 61.5	$ 782.5
Income from continuing operations	$ 430.2	$ 28.1	$ 458.3
Net income	$ 430.2	$ 28.1	$ 458.3
For the Year Ended February 28, 2011			
Net sales	$2,392.9	$987.5	$3,380.4
Gross profit	$ 690.5	$170.4	$ 860.9
Income from continuing operations	$ 452.3	$ 40.4	$ 492.7
Net income	$ 452.3	$ 40.4	$ 492.7

2.63 ALCOA INC. (DEC)

CONSOLIDATED BALANCE SHEET (in part)

(in millions)

December 31,	2013	2012
Assets		
Current assets:		
Cash and cash equivalents (X)	$ 1,437	$ 1,861
Receivables from customers, less allowances of $20 in 2013 and $39 in 2012 (U)	1,221	1,399
Other receivables (U)	597	340
Inventories (G)	2,705	2,825
Prepaid expenses and other current assets	1,009	1,275
Total current assets	6,969	7,700
Properties, plants, and equipment, net (H)	17,639	18,947
Goodwill (A & E)	3,415	5,170
Investments (I)	1,907	1,860
Deferred income taxes (T)	3,184	3,790
Other noncurrent assets (J)	2,628	2,712
Total Assets	$35,742	$40,179

NOTES TO THE CONSOLIDATED FINANCIAL STATEMENTS

(Dollars in millions, except per-share amounts)

A. Summary of Significant Accounting Policies (in part)

Equity Investments. Alcoa invests in a number of privately-held companies, primarily through joint ventures and consortia, which are accounted for on the equity method. The equity method is applied in situations where Alcoa has the ability to exercise significant influence, but not control, over the investee. Management reviews equity investments for impairment whenever certain indicators are present suggesting that the carrying value of an investment is not recoverable. This analysis requires a significant amount of judgment from management to identify events or circumstances indicating that an equity investment is impaired. The following items are examples of impairment indicators: significant, sustained declines in an investee's revenue, earnings, and cash flow trends; adverse market conditions of the investee's industry or geographic area; the investee's ability to continue operations measured by several items, including liquidity; and other factors. Once an impairment indicator is identified, management uses considerable judgment to determine if the impairment is other than temporary, in which case the equity investment is written down to its estimated fair value. An impairment that is other than temporary could significantly and adversely impact reported results of operations.

I. Investments (in part)

December 31,	2013	2012
Equity investments	$1,777	$1,782
Other investments	130	78
	$1,907	$1,860

Equity Investments. As of December 31, 2013 and 2012, Equity investments included an interest in a project to develop a fully-integrated aluminum complex in Saudi Arabia (see below), hydroelectric power projects in Brazil (see Note N), a smelter operation in Canada (50% of Pechiney Reynolds Quebec, Inc.), bauxite mining interests in Guinea (45% of Halco Mining, Inc.) and Brazil (18.2% of Mineração Rio do Norte S.A.), and a natural gas pipeline in Australia (see Note N). Pechiney Reynolds Quebec, Inc. owns a 50.1% interest in the Bécancour smelter in Quebec, Canada thereby entitling Alcoa to a 25.05% interest in the smelter. Through two wholly-owned Canadian subsidiaries, Alcoa also owns 49.9% of the Bécancour smelter. Halco Mining, Inc. owns 100% of Boké Investment Company, which owns 51% of Compagnie des Bauxites de Guinée. The investments in the bauxite mining interests in Guinea and Brazil and the natural gas pipeline in Australia are held by wholly-owned subsidiaries of Alcoa World Alumina and Chemicals (AWAC), which is owned 60% by Alcoa and 40% by Alumina Limited. In 2013, 2012, and 2011, Alcoa received $89, $101, and $100, respectively, in dividends from its equity investments.

Alcoa and Saudi Arabian Mining Company (known as "Ma'aden") have a 30-year joint venture shareholders' agreement (automatic extension for an additional 20 years, unless the parties agree otherwise or unless earlier terminated) setting forth the terms for the development, construction, ownership, and operation of an integrated bauxite mine, alumina refinery, aluminum smelter, and rolling mill, in Saudi Arabia. Specifically, the project to be developed by the joint venture will consist of: (i) a bauxite mine for the extraction of approximately 4,000 kmt of bauxite from the Al Ba'itha bauxite deposit near Quiba in the northern part of Saudi Arabia; (ii) an alumina refinery with an initial capacity of 1,800 kmt; (iii) a primary aluminum smelter with an initial capacity of 740 kmt; and (iv) a rolling mill with an initial capacity of 380 kmt. The refinery, smelter, and rolling mill are being constructed in an industrial area at Ras Al Khair on the east coast of Saudi Arabia. The facilities will use critical infrastructure, including power generation derived from reserves of natural gas, as well as port and rail facilities, developed by the government of Saudi Arabia. First production from the rolling mill and the smelter occurred in December 2013 and 2012, respectively. For the mine and refinery, first production is expected in 2014.

In 2012, Alcoa and Ma'aden agreed to expand the capabilities of the rolling mill to include a capacity of 100 kmt dedicated to supplying aluminum automotive, building and construction, and foil stock sheet. First production related to the expanded capacity is expected in 2014. This expansion is not expected to result in additional equity investment (see below) due to significant savings anticipated from a change in the project execution strategy of the initial 380 kmt capacity of the rolling mill.

The joint venture is owned 74.9% by Ma'aden and 25.1% by Alcoa and consists of three separate companies as follows: one each for the mine and refinery, the smelter, and the rolling mill. Following the signing of the joint venture shareholders' agreement, Alcoa paid Ma'aden $80 representing the initial investment in the project. In addition, Alcoa paid $56 to Ma'aden, representing Alcoa's pro rata share of certain agreed upon pre-incorporation costs incurred by Ma'aden before formation of the joint venture.

Ma'aden and Alcoa have put and call options, respectively, whereby Ma'aden can require Alcoa to purchase from Ma'aden, or Alcoa can require Ma'aden to sell to Alcoa, a 14.9% interest in the joint venture at the then fair market value. These options may only be exercised in a six-month window that opens five years after the Commercial Production Date (as defined in the joint venture shareholders' agreement) and, if exercised, must be exercised for the full 14.9% interest.

The Alcoa affiliate that holds Alcoa's interests in the smelting company and the rolling mill company is wholly owned by Alcoa, and the Alcoa affiliate that holds Alcoa's interests in the mining and refining company is wholly owned by AWAC. Except in limited circumstances, Alcoa may not sell, transfer or otherwise dispose of or encumber or enter into any agreement in respect of the votes or other rights attached to its interests in the joint venture without Ma'aden's prior written consent.

A number of Alcoa employees perform various types of services for the smelting, rolling mill, and refining and mining companies as part of the construction of the fully-integrated aluminum complex. At December 31, 2013 and 2012, Alcoa had an outstanding receivable of $31 and $28, respectively, from the smelting, rolling mill, and refining and mining companies for labor and other employee-related expenses.

Capital investment in the project is expected to total approximately $10,800 (SAR 40.5 billion). Alcoa's equity investment in the joint venture will be approximately $1,100, and Alcoa will be responsible for its pro rata share of the joint venture's project financing. Alcoa has contributed $832, including $171 and $253 in 2013 and 2012, respectively, towards the $1,100 commitment. As of December 31, 2013 and 2012, the carrying value of Alcoa's investment in this project was $951 and $816, respectively.

In late 2010, the smelting and rolling mill companies entered into project financing totaling $4,035, of which $1,013 represents Alcoa's share (the equivalent of Alcoa's 25.1% interest in the smelting and rolling mill companies). Also, in late 2012, the smelting and rolling mill companies entered into additional project financing totaling $480, of which $120 represents Alcoa's share. In conjunction with the financings, Alcoa issued guarantees on behalf of the smelting and rolling mill companies to the lenders in the event that such companies default on their debt service requirements through June 2017 and December 2018, respectively, (Ma'aden issued similar guarantees for its 74.9% interest). Alcoa's guarantees for the smelting and rolling mill companies cover total debt service requirements of $121 in principal and up to a maximum of approximately $60 in interest per year (based on projected interest rates). At December 31, 2013 and 2012, the combined fair value of the guarantees was $10, which was included in Other noncurrent liabilities and deferred credits on the accompanying Consolidated Balance Sheet. Under the project financings, a downgrade of Alcoa's credit ratings below investment grade by at least two agencies would require Alcoa to provide a letter of credit or fund an escrow account for a portion or all of Alcoa's remaining equity commitment to the joint venture project in Saudi Arabia.

In late 2011, the refining and mining company entered into project financing totaling $1,992, of which $500 represents AWAC's 25.1% interest in the mining and refining company. In conjunction with the financing, Alcoa, on behalf of AWAC, issued guarantees to the lenders in the event that the mining and refining company defaults on its debt service requirements through June 2019 (Ma'aden issued similar guarantees for its 74.9% interest). Alcoa's guarantees for the mining and refining company cover total debt service requirements of $60 in principal and up to a maximum of approximately $25 in interest per year (based on projected interest rates). At December 31, 2013 and 2012, the combined fair value of the guarantees was $4, which was included in Other noncurrent liabilities and deferred credits on the accompanying Consolidated Balance Sheet. In the event Alcoa would be required to make payments under the guarantees, 40% of such amount would be contributed to Alcoa by Alumina Limited, consistent with its ownership interest in AWAC. Under the project financing, a downgrade of Alcoa's credit ratings below investment grade by at least two agencies would require Alcoa to provide a letter of credit or fund an escrow account for a portion or all of Alcoa's remaining equity commitment to the joint venture project in Saudi Arabia.

In June 2013, all three joint venture companies entered into a 20-year gas supply agreement with Saudi Aramco, replacing the previous authorized gas allocation of the Ministry of Petroleum and Mineral Resources of Saudi Arabia (the "Ministry of Petroleum"). The gas supply agreement provides sufficient fuel to meet manufacturing process requirements as well as fuel to the adjacent combined water and power plant being constructed by Saline Water Conversion Corporation, which is owned by the government of Saudi Arabia and is responsible for desalinating sea water and producing electricity for Saudi Arabia. The combined water and power plant will convert the three joint venture companies' gas into electricity and water at cost, which will be supplied to the refinery, smelter, and rolling mill. During 2013, the $350 letter of credit that was previously provided to the Ministry of Petroleum by Ma'aden (Alcoa was responsible for its pro rata share) under the gas allocation related to the completion of the refinery was terminated upon the mining and refining company entering into construction contracts. A $60 letter of credit previously provided to the Ministry of Petroleum by Ma'aden (Alcoa is responsible for its pro rata share) under the gas allocation related to the completion of certain auxiliary rolling facilities was outstanding as of December 31, 2013.

The parties subject to the joint venture shareholders' agreement may not sell, transfer, or otherwise dispose of, pledge, or encumber any interests in the joint venture until certain milestones have been met as defined in both agreements. Under the joint venture shareholders' agreement, upon the occurrence of an unremedied event of default by Alcoa, Ma'aden may purchase, or, upon the occurrence of an unremedied event of default by Ma'aden, Alcoa may sell, its interest for consideration that varies depending on the time of the default.

COST METHOD

2.64 MARRIOTT INTERNATIONAL, INC. (DEC)

CONSOLIDATED BALANCE SHEETS (in part)

Fiscal Year-End 2013 and 2012

($ in millions)

	December 31, 2013	December 28, 2012
Assets		
Current assets		
Cash and equivalents	$ 126	$ 88
Accounts and notes receivable, net[1]	1,081	1,028
Current deferred taxes, net	252	280
Prepaid expenses	67	57
Other	27	22
Assets held for sale	350	—
	1,903	1,475
Property and equipment	1,543	1,539
Intangible assets		
Goodwill	874	874
Contract acquisition costs and other[1]	1,131	1,115
	2,005	1,989
Equity and cost method investments[1]	222	216
Notes receivable, net[1]	142	180
Deferred taxes, net[1]	647	676
Other[1]	332	267
	$6,794	$6,342

NOTES TO CONSOLIDATED FINANCIAL STATEMENTS

1. Summary of Significant Accounting Policies (in part)

Investments

We consolidate entities that we control. We account for investments in joint ventures using the equity method of accounting when we exercise significant influence over the venture. If we do not exercise significant influence, we account for the investment using the cost method of accounting. We account for investments in limited partnerships and limited liability companies using the equity method of accounting when we own more than a minimal investment. Our ownership interest in these equity method investments varies generally from 10 percent to 49 percent. See Footnote No. 4, "Fair Value of Financial Instruments" for additional information on available-for-sale securities. When we sell available-for-sale securities, we determine the cost basis of the securities sold using specific identification, meaning that we track our securities individually.

Valuation of Investments in Ventures

We may hold a minority equity interest in ventures established to develop or acquire and own hotel properties. These ventures are generally limited liability companies or limited partnerships.

We evaluate an investment in a venture for impairment when circumstances indicate that we may not be able to recover the carrying value, for example due to loan defaults, significant under performance relative to historical or projected operating performance, or significant negative industry or economic trends.

We impair investments we account for using the equity and cost methods of accounting when we determine that there has been an "other-than-temporary" decline in the venture's estimated fair value compared to its carrying value. Additionally, a venture's commitment to a plan to sell some or all of its assets could cause us to evaluate the recoverability of the venture's individual long-lived assets and possibly the venture itself.

We calculate the estimated fair value of an investment in a venture using either a market approach or an income approach. We utilize the same assumptions and methodology for the income approach that we describe in the "Goodwill" caption. For the market approach, we use internal analyses based primarily on market comparables and assumptions about market capitalization rates, growth rates, and inflation.

For information on an impairment loss that we recorded in 2012 for a cost method investment, see Footnote No. 4, "Fair Value of Financial Instruments."

4. Fair Value of Financial Instruments (in part)

We believe that the fair values of our current assets and current liabilities approximate their reported carrying amounts. We show the carrying values and the fair values of noncurrent financial assets and liabilities that qualify as financial instruments, determined under current guidance for disclosures on the fair value of financial instruments, in the following table:

($ in millions)	At Year-End 2013		At Year-End 2012	
	Carrying Amount	Fair Value	Carrying Amount	Fair Value
Cost method investments	$ 16	$ 17	$ 21	$ 23
Senior, mezzanine, and other loans	142	145	180	172
Marketable securities and other debt securities	111	111	56	56
Total long-term financial assets	$ 269	$ 273	$ 257	$ 251
Senior Notes	$(2,185)	$(2,302)	$(1,833)	$(2,008)
Commercial paper	(834)	(834)	(501)	(501)
Other long-term debt	(123)	(124)	(130)	(139)
Other long-term liabilities	(50)	(50)	(69)	(69)
Total long-term financial liabilities	$(3,192)	$(3,310)	$(2,533)	$(2,717)

We estimate the fair value of our cost method investments by applying a cap rate to stabilized earnings (a market approach using Level 3 inputs). During the 2012 third quarter, we determined that a cost method investment was other-than-temporarily impaired and, accordingly, we recorded the investment at its fair value as of the end of the 2012 third quarter ($12 million) and reflected a $7 million loss in the "Gains (losses) and other income" caption of our Income Statement. We estimated the fair value of the investment using cash flow projections discounted at risk premiums commensurate with market conditions. We used Level 3 inputs for these discounted cash flow analyses and our assumptions included revenue forecasts, cash flow projections, and timing of the sale of each hotel in the underlying investment.

We estimate the fair value of our senior, mezzanine, and other loans, including the current portion, by discounting cash flows using risk-adjusted rates, both of which are Level 3 inputs.

We carry our marketable securities at fair value. Our marketable securities include debt securities of the U.S. Government, its sponsored agencies and other U.S. corporations invested for our self-insurance programs, as well as shares of a publicly traded company, which we value using directly observable Level 1 inputs. The carrying value of these marketable securities at year-end 2013 was $41 million.

In the 2013 second quarter, we acquired a $65 million mandatorily redeemable preferred equity ownership interest in an entity that owns three hotels that we manage. We account for this investment as a debt security (with an amortized cost of $70 million at year-end 2013, including accrued interest income), and we include it in the "Marketable securities and other debt securities" caption in the preceding table. We estimated the $70 million fair value of this security by discounting cash flows using risk-adjusted rates, both of which are Level 3 inputs. This security matures in 2015 subject to annual extensions through 2018. We do not intend to sell this security and it is not more likely than not that we will be required to sell the investment before recovery of the amortized cost basis, which may be at maturity.

In the 2013 second quarter, we received $22 million in net cash proceeds for the sale of a portion of our shares of a publicly traded company (with an amortized cost of $14 million at the date of sale) and recognized an $8 million gain in the "Gains (losses) and other income" caption of our Income Statement. This gain included recognition of unrealized gains that we previously recorded in other comprehensive income. See Footnote No. 12, "Comprehensive Income and Shareholders' (Deficit) Equity" for additional information on the reclassification of these unrealized gains from accumulated other comprehensive income.

Noncurrent Receivables

PRESENTATION

2.65 FASB ASC 210, *Balance Sheet*, states that the concept of current assets excludes receivables arising from unusual transactions that are not expected to be collected within 12 months, such as the sale of capital assets or loans or advances to affiliates, officers, or employees.

PRESENTATION AND DISCLOSURE EXCERPTS

LONG-TERM RECEIVABLES

2.67 AUTOMATIC DATA PROCESSING, INC. (JUN)
CONSOLIDATED BALANCE SHEETS (in part)

(In millions, except per share amounts)

June 30,	2013	2012
Assets		
Current assets:		
Cash and cash equivalents (A)	$ 1,699.1	$ 1,548.1
Short-term marketable securities	28.0	30.4
Accounts receivable, net	1,598.3	1,391.7
Other current assets	646.8	631.6
Assets held for sale	—	6.7
Assets of discontinued operations	—	125.0
Total current assets before funds held for clients	3,972.2	3,733.5
Funds held for clients	22,228.8	21,539.1
Total current assets	26,201.0	25,272.6
Long-term marketable securities (A)	314.0	86.9
Long-term receivables, net	138.7	129.8
Property, plant and equipment, net	728.7	706.3
Other assets	1,189.9	871.5
Goodwill	3,052.6	3,062.0
Intangible assets, net	643.2	688.3
Total assets	$32,268.1	$30,817.4

NOTES TO THE CONSOLIDATED FINANCIAL STATEMENTS

(Tabular dollars in millions, except per share amounts)

(Unaudited)

Note 1. Summary of Significant Accounting Policies (in part)

G. Long-term Receivables. Long-term receivables relate to notes receivable from the sale of computer systems, primarily to auto, truck, motorcycle, marine, recreational vehicle, and heavy equipment retailers and manufacturers. Unearned income from finance receivables represents the excess of gross receivables over the sales price of the computer systems financed. Unearned income is amortized using the effective-interest method to maintain a constant rate of return over the term of each contract.

Notes receivable aged over 30 days past due are considered delinquent and notes receivable aged over 60 days past due with known collection issues are placed on non-accrual status. Interest revenue is not recognized on notes receivable while on non-accrual status. Cash payments received on non-accrual receivables are applied towards the principal. When notes receivable on non-accrual status are again less than 60 days past due, recognition of interest revenue for notes receivable is resumed.

The allowance for doubtful accounts on long-term receivables is the Company's best estimate of the amount of probable credit losses related to the Company's existing note receivables.

Note 6. Receivables

Accounts receivable, net, includes the Company's trade receivables, which are recorded based upon the amount the Company expects to receive from its clients, net of an allowance for doubtful accounts. The Company's receivables also include notes receivable for the financing of the sale of computer systems, primarily from auto, truck, motorcycle, marine, recreational vehicle, and heavy equipment retailers and manufacturers. Notes receivable are recorded based upon the amount the Company expects to receive from its clients, net of an allowance for doubtful accounts and unearned income. The allowance for doubtful accounts is the Company's best estimate of probable credit losses related to trade receivables and notes receivable based upon the aging of the receivables, historical collection data, internal assessments of credit quality and the economic conditions in the automobile industry, as well as in the economy as a whole. The Company charges off uncollectable amounts against the reserve in the period in which it determines they are uncollectable. Unearned income on notes receivable is amortized using the effective interest method.

The Company's receivables, whose carrying value approximates fair value, are as follows:

	June 30, 2013		June 30, 2012	
	Current	Long-Term	Current	Long-Term
Trade receivables	$1,564.8	$ —	$1,355.7	$ —
Notes receivable	91.0	154.7	89.1	145.5
Less:				
Allowance for doubtful accounts—trade receivables	(45.6)	—	(40.7)	—
Allowance for doubtful accounts—notes receivable	(5.3)	(9.0)	(5.4)	(8.8)
Unearned income—notes receivable	(6.6)	(7.0)	(7.0)	(6.9)
	$1,598.3	$138.7	$1,391.7	$129.8

Long-term receivables at June 30, 2013 mature as follows:

2015	$ 67.2
2016	$ 47.6
2017	$ 28.8
2018	$ 11.1
Total	$154.7

The Company determines the allowance for doubtful accounts related to notes receivable based upon a specific reserve for known collection issues, as well as a non-specific reserve based upon aging, both of which are based upon history of such losses and current economic conditions. Based upon the Company's methodology, the notes receivable balances with specific and non-specific reserves and the specific and non-specific reserves associated with those balances are as follows:

	June 30, 2013			
	Notes Receivable		Reserve	
	Current	Long-Term	Current	Long-Term
Specific reserve	$ 0.3	$ 0.5	$0.3	$0.5
Non-specific reserve	90.7	154.2	5.0	8.5
	$91.0	$154.7	$5.3	$9.0

	June 30, 2012			
	Notes Receivable		Reserve	
	Current	Long-Term	Current	Long-Term
Specific reserve	$ 0.4	$ 0.6	$0.4	$0.6
Non-specific reserve	88.7	144.9	5.0	8.2
	$89.1	$145.5	$5.4	$8.8

The rollforward of the allowance for doubtful accounts related to notes receivable is as follows:

	Current	Long-Term
Balance at June 30, 2011	$ 5.7	$ 9.4
Incremental provision	0.6	0.2
Recoveries	—	0.4
Chargeoffs	(0.9)	(1.2)
Balance at June 30, 2012	$ 5.4	$ 8.8
Incremental provision	0.8	1.2
Recoveries	—	0.2
Chargeoffs	(0.9)	(1.2)
Balance at June 30, 2013	$ 5.3	$ 9.0

The allowance for doubtful accounts as a percentage of notes receivable was approximately 6% as of June 30, 2013 and 6% as of June 30, 2012.

On an ongoing basis, the Company evaluates the credit quality of its financing receivables, utilizing aging of receivables, collection experience and charge-offs. In addition, the Company evaluates economic conditions in the auto industry and specific dealership matters, such as bankruptcy. As events related to a specific client dictate, the credit quality of a client is reevaluated. Approximately 100% of notes receivable were current at June 30, 2013 and 2012.

2.68 TEXTRON INC. (DEC)
CONSOLIDATED BALANCE SHEETS (in part)

(In millions, except share data)	December 28, 2013	December 29, 2012
Assets		
Manufacturing group		
Cash and equivalents	$ 1,163	$ 1,378
Accounts receivable, net	979	829
Inventories	2,963	2,712
Other current assets	467	470
Total current assets	5,572	5,389
Property, plant and equipment, net	2,215	2,149
Goodwill	1,735	1,649
Other assets	1,697	1,524
Total Manufacturing group assets	11,219	10,711
Finance group		
Cash and equivalents	48	35
Finance receivables, net	1,493	1,990
Other assets	184	297
Total Finance group assets	1,725	2,322
Total assets	$12,944	$13,033

NOTES TO THE CONSOLIDATED FINANCIAL STATEMENTS

Note 1. Summary of Significant Accounting Policies (in part)

Finance Receivables

Finance receivables primarily include finance receivables classified as held for investment, and also include finance receivables classified as held for sale. Finance receivables are classified as held for investment when we have the intent and the ability to hold the receivable for the foreseeable future or until maturity or payoff. Finance receivables held for investment are generally recorded at the amount of outstanding principal less allowance for losses.

We maintain an allowance for losses on finance receivables at a level considered adequate to cover inherent losses in the portfolio based on management's evaluation. For larger balance accounts specifically identified as impaired, including large accounts in homogeneous portfolios, a reserve is established based on comparing the expected future cash flows, discounted at the finance receivable's effective interest rate, or the fair value of the underlying collateral if the finance receivable is collateral dependent, to its carrying amount. The expected future cash flows consider collateral value; financial performance and liquidity of our borrower; existence and financial strength of guarantors; estimated recovery costs, including legal expenses; and costs associated with the repossession and eventual disposal of collateral. When there is a range of potential outcomes, we perform multiple discounted cash flow analyses and weight the potential outcomes based on their relative likelihood of occurrence. The evaluation of our portfolio is inherently subjective, as it requires estimates, including the amount and timing of future cash flows expected to be received on impaired finance receivables and the estimated fair value of the underlying collateral, which may differ from actual results. While our analysis is specific to each individual account, critical factors included in this analysis include industry valuation guides, age and physical condition of the collateral, payment history and existence and financial strength of guarantors. We also establish an allowance for losses to cover probable but specifically unknown losses existing in the portfolio. This allowance is established as a percentage of non-recourse finance receivables, which have not been identified as requiring specific reserves. The percentage is based on a combination of factors, including historical loss experience, current delinquency and default trends, collateral values and both general economic and specific industry trends. Finance receivables are charged off at the earlier of the date the collateral is repossessed or when no payment has been received for six months, unless management deems the receivable collectible. Repossessed assets are recorded at their fair value, less estimated cost to sell.

Finance receivables are classified as held for sale based on the determination that we no longer intend to hold the receivables for the foreseeable future, until maturity or payoff, or we no longer have the ability to hold to maturity. Our decision to classify certain finance receivables as held for sale is based on a number of factors, including, but not limited to, contractual duration, type of collateral, credit strength of the borrowers, interest rates and perceived marketability of the receivables. These receivables are carried at the lower of cost or fair value. At the time of transfer to the held for sale classification, we establish a valuation allowance for any shortfall between the carrying value and fair value. In addition, any allowance for loan losses previously allocated to these finance receivables is transferred to the valuation allowance account and adjusted quarterly. Fair value changes can occur based on market interest rates, market liquidity, and changes in the credit quality of the borrower and value of underlying loan collateral.

Note 3. Accounts Receivable and Finance Receivables (in part)

Finance Receivables

Finance receivables by classification are presented in the following table.

(In millions)	December 28, 2013	December 29, 2012
Finance receivables held for investment	$1,483	$1,934
Allowance for losses	(55)	(84)
Total finance receivables held for investment, net	1,428	1,850
Finance receivables held for sale	65	140
Total finance receivables, net	$1,493	$1,990

Finance receivables held for investment primarily includes loans and finance leases provided to purchasers of new and used Cessna aircraft and Bell helicopters and also includes loans and finance leases secured by used aircraft produced by other manufacturers. These agreements typically have initial terms ranging from five to ten years and amortization terms ranging from eight to fifteen years. The average balance of loans and finance leases was $1 million at December 28, 2013. Loans generally require the customer to pay a significant down payment, along with periodic scheduled principal payments that reduce the outstanding balance through the term of the loan. Finance leases with no significant residual value at the end of the contractual term are classified as loans, as their legal and economic substance is more equivalent to a secured borrowing than a finance lease with a significant residual value. Finance receivables held for investment also includes leveraged leases secured by the ownership of the leased equipment and real property.

Finance receivables held for sale includes the non-captive loan portfolio at December 28, 2013. These finance receivables are carried at the lower of cost or fair value and are not included in the credit performance tables below. During 2013, we determined that we no longer had the intent to hold the remaining non-captive loan portfolio for the foreseeable future and, accordingly, transferred $34 million of the remaining non-captive loans, net of a $1 million allowance for losses, from the held for investment classification to the held for sale classification. We received total proceeds of $64 million and $109 million in 2013 and 2012, respectively, from the sale of finance receivables held for sale and $76 million and $207 million, respectively, from payoffs and collections.

Our finance receivables are diversified across geographic region and borrower industry. At December 28, 2013, 41% of our finance receivables were distributed throughout the U.S. compared with 45% at the end of 2012. At December 28, 2013 and December 29, 2012, finance receivables included $200 million and $341 million, respectively, of receivables that have been legally sold to a special purpose entity (SPE), which is a consolidated subsidiary of TFC. The assets of the SPE are pledged as collateral for its debt, which is reflected as securitized on-balance sheet debt in Note 7. Third-party investors have no legal recourse to TFC beyond the credit enhancement provided by the assets of the SPE.

Credit Quality Indicators and Nonaccrual Finance Receivables

We internally assess the quality of our finance receivables based on a number of key credit quality indicators and statistics such as delinquency, loan balance to estimated collateral value and the financial strength of individual borrowers and guarantors. Because many of these indicators are difficult to apply across an entire class of receivables, we evaluate individual loans on a quarterly basis and classify these loans into three categories based on the key credit quality indicators for the individual loan. These three categories are performing, watchlist and nonaccrual.

We classify finance receivables as nonaccrual if credit quality indicators suggest full collection of principal and interest is doubtful. In addition, we automatically classify accounts as nonaccrual once they are contractually delinquent by more than three months unless collection of principal and interest is not doubtful. Recognition of interest income is suspended for these accounts and all cash collections are used to reduce the net investment balance. We resume the accrual of interest when the loan becomes contractually current through payment according to the original terms of the loan or, if a loan has been modified, following a period of performance under the terms of the modification, provided we conclude that collection of all principal and interest is no longer doubtful. Previously suspended interest income is recognized at that time. Accounts are classified as watchlist when credit quality indicators have deteriorated as compared with typical underwriting criteria, and we believe collection of full principal and interest is probable but not certain. All other finance receivables that do not meet the watchlist or nonaccrual categories are classified as performing.

A summary of finance receivables categorized based on the credit quality indicators discussed above is as follows:

(In millions)	December 28, 2013	December 29, 2012
Performing	$1,285	$1,661
Watchlist	93	130
Nonaccrual	105	143
Total	$1,483	$1,934
Nonaccrual as a percentage of total finance receivables	7.08%	7.39%

We measure delinquency based on the contractual payment terms of our loans and leases. In determining the delinquency aging category of an account, any/all principal and interest received is applied to the most past-due principal and/or interest amounts due. If a significant portion of the contractually due payment is delinquent, the entire finance receivable balance is reported in accordance with the most past-due delinquency aging category.

Finance receivables by delinquency aging category are summarized in the table below:

(In millions)	December 28, 2013	December 29, 2012
Less than 31 days past due	$1,295	$1,757
31–60 days past due	108	87
61–90 days past due	37	56
Over 90 days past due	43	34
Total	$1,483	$1,934

Accrual status loans that were greater than 90 days past due totaled $5 million at December 28, 2013. There were no accrual status loans that were greater than 90 days past due at December 29, 2012. At December 28, 2013 and December 29, 2012, 60 + days contractual delinquency as a percentage of finance receivables was 5.39% and 4.65%, respectively.

Loan Modifications

Troubled debt restructurings occur when we have either modified the contract terms of finance receivables for borrowers experiencing financial difficulties or accepted a transfer of assets in full or partial satisfaction of the loan balance. The types of modifications we typically make include extensions of the original maturity date of the contract, extensions of revolving borrowing periods, delays in the timing of required principal payments, deferrals of interest payments, advances to protect the value of our collateral and principal reductions contingent on full repayment prior to the maturity date. The changes effected by modifications made during 2013 and 2012 to finance receivables held for investment were not material.

Impaired Loans

On a quarterly basis, we evaluate individual finance receivables for impairment in non-homogeneous portfolios and larger accounts in homogeneous loan portfolios. A finance receivable is considered impaired when it is probable that we will be unable to collect all amounts due according to the contractual terms of the loan agreement based on our review of the credit quality indicators discussed above. Impaired finance receivables include both nonaccrual accounts and accounts for which full collection of principal and interest remains probable, but the account's original terms have been, or are expected to be, significantly modified. If the modification specifies an interest rate equal to or greater than a market rate for a finance receivable with comparable risk, the account is not considered impaired in years subsequent to the modification. There was no significant interest income recognized on impaired loans in 2013 or 2012.

A summary of impaired finance receivables, excluding leveraged leases, at year end and the average recorded investment for the year is provided below:

(In millions)	December 28, 2013	December 29, 2012
Recorded investment:		
Impaired loans with no related allowance for credit losses	$ 78	$ 72
Impaired loans with related allowance for credit losses	59	99
Total	$137	$171
Unpaid principal balance	$141	$187
Allowance for losses on impaired loans	14	27
Average recorded investment	155	270

Allowance for Losses

A rollforward of the allowance for losses on finance receivables and a summary of its composition, based on how the underlying finance receivables are evaluated for impairment, is provided below. The finance receivables reported in this table specifically exclude $120 million and $122 million of leveraged leases at December 28, 2013 and December 29, 2012, respectively, in accordance with authoritative accounting standards.

(In millions)	December 28, 2013	December 29, 2012
Balance at beginning of period	$ 84	$ 156
Provision for losses	(23)	(3)
Charge-offs	(17)	(84)
Recoveries	12	15
Transfers	(1)	—
Balance at end of period	$ 55	$ 84
Allowance based on collective evaluation	$ 41	$ 57
Allowance based on individual evaluation	14	27
Finance receivables evaluated collectively	$1,226	$1,641
Finance receivables evaluated individually	137	171

Our Finance group provides financing for retail purchases and leases for new and used aircraft and equipment manufactured by our Manufacturing group. The finance receivables for these inventory sales that are included in the Finance group's balance sheets are summarized below:

(In millions)	December 28, 2013	December 29, 2012
Loans	$1,121	$1,389
Finance leases	80	107
Total	$1,201	$1,496

In 2013, 2012 and 2011, our Finance group paid our Manufacturing group $248 million, $309 million and $284 million, respectively, related to the sale of Textron-manufactured products to third parties that were financed by the Finance group. Operating agreements specify that our Finance group has recourse to our Manufacturing group for certain uncollected amounts related to these transactions. At December 28, 2013 and December 29, 2012, finance receivables and operating leases subject to recourse to the Manufacturing group totaled $75 million and $83 million, respectively. Our Manufacturing group has established reserves for losses on its balance sheet within accrued and other liabilities for the amounts it guarantees.

Intangible Assets

Author's Note
In July 2012, FASB issued ASU No. 2012-02, *Intangibles—Goodwill and Other (Topic 350): Testing Indefinite-Lived Intangible Assets for Impairment*, to reduce the cost and complexity of performing an impairment test for indefinite-lived intangible assets by simplifying how an entity tests those assets for impairment and to improve consistency in impairment testing guidance among long-lived asset categories. The amendments permit an entity first to assess qualitative factors to determine whether it is more likely than not that an indefinite-lived intangible asset is impaired as a basis for determining whether it is necessary to perform the quantitative impairment test in accordance with Subtopic 350-30, Intangibles—Goodwill and Other—General Intangibles Other than Goodwill. The more-likely-than-not threshold is defined as having a likelihood of more than 50 percent. The amendments are effective for annual and interim impairment tests performed for fiscal years beginning after September 15, 2012. Early adoption is permitted, including for annual and interim impairment tests performed as of a date before July 27, 2012, if a public entity's financial statements for the most recent annual or interim period have not yet been issued or, for nonpublic entities, have not yet been made available for issuance.

RECOGNITION AND MEASUREMENT

2.69 FASB ASC 350, *Intangibles—Goodwill and Other*, specifies that goodwill and intangible assets that have indefinite lives are not subject to amortization but, rather, should be tested at least annually for impairment. In addition, FASB ASC 350 provides specific guidance on how to determine and measure impairment of goodwill and intangible assets not subject to amortization. Intangible assets that have finite useful lives should be amortized over their useful lives.

2.70 FASB ASC 350-20-35 delineates a comprehensive two-step approach to impairment testing of a reporting unit that includes goodwill. If an entity chooses, it may assess qualitative factors to determine whether it is more likely than not that the fair value of a reporting unit is less than its carrying amount; the entity may use this determination as a basis for deciding whether it is necessary to perform the two-step goodwill impairment test. The *more-likely-than-not threshold* is defined as having a likelihood of more than 50 percent. An entity has an unconditional option to bypass the qualitative assessment described in the preceding paragraph for any reporting unit in any period and proceed directly to performing the first step of the goodwill impairment test. An entity may resume performing the qualitative assessment in any subsequent period.

2.71 If the entity decides that the quantitative impairment test is required, then the first step is to compare the fair value of a reporting unit with its carrying amount, including goodwill. When the carrying amount is greater than zero and its fair value exceeds its carrying amount, the entity should not consider the goodwill impaired and the second step is unnecessary. When the carrying amount of the reporting unit exceeds its fair value, an entity should proceed to step two to measure the loss by comparing the implied fair value of the goodwill with its carrying value. When the carrying amount of the reporting unit is zero or negative, an entity should proceed to step two to measure an impairment loss, if any, when it is more likely than not that a goodwill impairment exists. An entity should evaluate whether there are adverse qualitative factors in making that "more likely than not" assessment. FASB ASC 350-20-35-30 (a)–(g) provide examples of such qualitative factors.

2.72 FASB ASC 350 also provides guidance on accounting for the cost of computer software developed or obtained for internal use and website development costs.

PRESENTATION

2.73 FASB ASC 350-20-45-1 requires that the aggregate amount of goodwill be presented as a separate line item in the balance sheet. Under FASB ASC 350-30-45-1, at minimum, all intangible assets should be aggregated and presented as a separate line item in the balance sheet. However, that requirement does not preclude the presentation of individual intangible assets or classes of intangible assets as separate line items. Rule 5-02 of Regulation S-X also calls for separately stating each class of intangible assets in excess of 5 percent of total assets and for separate presentation of the amount of accumulated amortization of intangible assets.

DISCLOSURE

2.74 FASB ASC 350 requires additional disclosures for each period for which a balance sheet is presented, including information about gross carrying amounts and changes therein of goodwill and other intangible assets, accumulated amortization for amortizable assets, and estimates about intangible asset amortization expense for each of the five succeeding fiscal years. For intangibles, the balance sheet disclosures should be in total and by major intangible asset class.

PRESENTATION AND DISCLOSURE EXCERPTS

GOODWILL

2.75 ALCOA INC. (DEC)
CONSOLIDATED BALANCE SHEET (in part)

(In millions)

	December 31,	
	2013	2012
Assets		
Current assets:		
Cash and cash equivalents (X)	$ 1,437	$ 1,861
Receivables from customers, less allowances of $20 in 2013 and $39 in 2012 (U)	1,221	1,399
Other receivables (U)	597	340
Inventories (G)	2,705	2,825
Prepaid expenses and other current assets	1,009	1,275
Total current assets	6,969	7,700

(continued)

	December 31,	
	2013	**2012**
Properties, plants, and equipment, net (H)	17,639	18,947
Goodwill (A & E)	3,415	5,170
Investments (I)	1,907	1,860
Deferred income taxes (T)	3,184	3,790
Other noncurrent assets (J)	2,628	2,712
Total Assets	$35,742	$40,179

NOTES TO THE CONSOLIDATED FINANCIAL STATEMENTS

(Dollars in millions, except per-share amounts)

A. Summary of Significant Accounting Policies (in part)

Goodwill and Other Intangible Assets (in part). Goodwill is not amortized; instead, it is reviewed for impairment annually (in the fourth quarter) or more frequently if indicators of impairment exist or if a decision is made to sell or exit a business. A significant amount of judgment is involved in determining if an indicator of impairment has occurred. Such indicators may include deterioration in general economic conditions, negative developments in equity and credit markets, adverse changes in the markets in which an entity operates, increases in input costs that have a negative effect on earnings and cash flows, or a trend of negative or declining cash flows over multiple periods, among others. The fair value that could be realized in an actual transaction may differ from that used to evaluate the impairment of goodwill.

Goodwill is allocated among and evaluated for impairment at the reporting unit level, which is defined as an operating segment or one level below an operating segment. Alcoa has nine reporting units, of which five are included in the Engineered Products and Solutions segment. The remaining four reporting units are the Alumina segment, the Primary Metals segment, the Global Rolled Products segment, and the soft alloy extrusions business in Brazil, which is included in Corporate. More than 80% of Alcoa's total goodwill is allocated to two reporting units as follows: Alcoa Fastening Systems (AFS) ($1,166) and Alcoa Power and Propulsion (APP) ($1,617) businesses, both of which are included in the Engineered Products and Solutions segment. These amounts include an allocation of Corporate's goodwill.

In reviewing goodwill for impairment, an entity has the option to first assess qualitative factors to determine whether the existence of events or circumstances leads to a determination that it is more likely than not (greater than 50%) that the estimated fair value of a reporting unit is less than its carrying amount. If an entity elects to perform a qualitative assessment and determines that an impairment is more likely than not, the entity is then required to perform the existing two-step quantitative impairment test (described below), otherwise no further analysis is required. An entity also may elect not to perform the qualitative assessment and, instead, proceed directly to the two-step quantitative impairment test. The ultimate outcome of the goodwill impairment review for a reporting unit should be the same whether an entity chooses to perform the qualitative assessment or proceeds directly to the two-step quantitative impairment test.

Alcoa's policy for its annual review of goodwill is to perform the qualitative assessment for all reporting units not subjected directly to the two-step quantitative impairment test. Management will proceed directly to the two-step quantitative impairment test for a minimum of three reporting units (based on facts and circumstances) during each annual review of goodwill. This policy will result in each of the nine reporting units being subjected to the two-step quantitative impairment test at least once during every three-year period.

Under the qualitative assessment, various events and circumstances (or factors) that would affect the estimated fair value of a reporting unit are identified (similar to impairment indicators above). These factors are then classified by the type of impact they would have on the estimated fair value using positive, neutral, and adverse categories based on current business conditions. Additionally, an assessment of the level of impact that a particular factor would have on the estimated fair value is determined using high, medium, and low weighting. Furthermore, management considers the results of the most recent two-step quantitative impairment test completed for a reporting unit and compares the weighted average cost of capital (WACC) between the current and prior years for each reporting unit.

During the 2013 annual review of goodwill, management performed the qualitative assessment for two reporting units, the Global Rolled Products segment and one of the five reporting units in the Engineered Products and Solutions segment. Management concluded that it was not more likely than not that the estimated fair values of the two reporting units were less than their carrying values. As such, no further analysis was required.

Under the two-step quantitative impairment test, the evaluation of impairment involves comparing the current fair value of each reporting unit to its carrying value, including goodwill. Alcoa uses a DCF model to estimate the current fair value of its reporting units when testing for impairment, as management believes forecasted cash flows are the best indicator of such fair value. A number of significant assumptions and estimates are involved in the application of the DCF model to forecast operating cash flows, including markets and market share, sales volumes and prices, production costs, tax rates, capital spending, discount rate, and working capital changes. Most of these assumptions vary significantly among the reporting units. Cash flow forecasts are generally based on approved business unit operating plans for the early years and historical relationships in later years. The betas used in calculating the individual reporting units' WACC rate are estimated for each business with the assistance of valuation experts.

In the event the estimated fair value of a reporting unit per the DCF model is less than the carrying value, additional analysis would be required. The additional analysis would compare the carrying amount of the reporting unit's goodwill with the implied fair value of that goodwill, which may involve the use of valuation experts. The implied fair value of goodwill is the excess of the fair value of the reporting unit over the fair value amounts assigned to all of the assets and liabilities of that unit as if the reporting unit was acquired in a business combination and the fair value of the reporting unit represented the purchase price. If the carrying value of goodwill exceeds its implied fair value, an impairment loss equal to such excess would be recognized, which could significantly and adversely impact reported results of operations and shareholders' equity.

During the 2013 annual review of goodwill, management proceeded directly to the two-step quantitative impairment test for seven reporting units as follows: the Primary Metals segment, the Alumina segment, the soft alloy extrusions business in Brazil, and four of the five reporting units in the Engineered Products and Solutions segment, including AFS and APP. The estimated fair values of the four Engineered Products and Solutions businesses, and the soft alloy extrusions business were substantially in excess of their respective carrying value, resulting in no impairment.

During the 2012 annual testing of goodwill, the estimated fair value of the Alumina segment exceeded the carrying value by 7%. In connection with the 2013 testing, the estimated fair value of the Alumina segment exceeded the carrying value by 18%. This increase is attributable to several factors: improved pricing due to the continued implementation of the Alumina Price Index; operating and productivity improvements in the business; and a stronger U.S. dollar, all of which increased management's estimates of operating results and cash flows used in assessing Alumina's goodwill for impairment. These improvements were partially offset by an increase in the discount rate used in the DCF models. Unfavorable movements in one or more of these trends in the future could have a negative impact on the estimated fair value of the Alumina segment.

For Primary Metals, the estimated fair value as determined by the DCF model was lower than the associated carrying value. As a result, management performed the second step of the impairment analysis in order to determine the implied fair value of Primary Metals' goodwill. The results of the second-step analysis showed that the implied fair value of goodwill was zero. Therefore, in the fourth quarter of 2013, Alcoa recorded a goodwill impairment of $1,731 ($1,719 after noncontrolling interest). As a result of the goodwill impairment, there is no goodwill remaining for the Primary Metals reporting unit.

The impairment of Primary Metals' goodwill results from several causes: the prolonged economic downturn; a disconnect between industry fundamentals and pricing that has resulted in lower metal prices; and the increased cost of alumina, a key raw material, resulting from expansion of the Alumina Price Index throughout the industry. All of these factors, exacerbated by increases in discount rates, continue to place significant downward pressure on metal prices and operating margins, and the resulting estimated fair value, of the Primary Metals business. As a result, management decreased the near-term and long-term estimates of the operating results and cash flows utilized in assessing Primary Metals' goodwill for impairment. The valuation of goodwill for the second step of the goodwill impairment analysis is considered a level 3 fair value measurement, which means that the valuation of the assets and liabilities reflect management's own judgments regarding the assumptions market participants would use in determining the fair value of the assets and liabilities.

Goodwill impairment tests in prior years indicated that goodwill was not impaired for any of the Company's reporting units and there were no triggering events since that time that necessitated an impairment test.

Recently Adopted Accounting Guidance (in part)

Goodwill and Other Intangible Assets (in part). On January 1, 2011, Alcoa adopted changes issued by the FASB to the testing of goodwill for impairment. These changes require an entity to perform all steps in the test for a reporting unit whose carrying value is zero or negative if it is more likely than not (greater than 50%) that a goodwill impairment exists based on qualitative factors. This will result in the elimination of an entity's ability to assert that such a reporting unit's goodwill is not impaired and additional testing is not necessary despite the existence of qualitative factors that indicate otherwise. Based on the then most recent impairment review of Alcoa's goodwill (2011 fourth quarter), the adoption of these changes had no impact on the Consolidated Financial Statements.

In September 2011, the FASB issued changes to the testing of goodwill for impairment. These changes provide an entity the option to first assess qualitative factors to determine whether the existence of events or circumstances leads to a determination that it is more likely than not (greater than 50%) that the fair value of a reporting unit is less than its carrying amount. Such qualitative factors may include the following: macroeconomic conditions; industry and market considerations; cost factors; overall financial performance; and other relevant entity-specific events. If an entity elects to perform a qualitative assessment and determines that an impairment is more likely than not, the entity is then required to perform the existing two-step quantitative impairment test, otherwise no further analysis is required. An entity also may elect not to perform the qualitative assessment and, instead, proceed directly to the two-step quantitative impairment test. Under either option, the ultimate outcome of the goodwill impairment test should be the same. These changes were required to become effective for Alcoa for any goodwill impairment test performed on January 1, 2012 or later; however, early adoption is permitted. Alcoa elected to early adopt these changes in conjunction with management's annual review of goodwill in the fourth quarter of 2011 (see Goodwill and Other Intangible Assets policy in Note A above). The adoption of these changes had no impact on the Consolidated Financial Statements.

E. Goodwill and Other Intangible Assets (in part)

The following table details the changes in the carrying amount of goodwill:

	Alumina	Primary Metals	Global Rolled Products	Engineered Products and Solutions	Corporate*	Total
Balance at December 31, 2011:						
Goodwill	$11	$ 991	$208	$2,694	$1,281	$ 5,185
Accumulated impairment losses	—	—	—	(28)	—	(28)
	11	991	208	2,666	1,281	5,157
Acquisition of businesses	—	—	—	(1)	—	(1)
Translation	(1)	6	6	12	(9)	14
Balance at December 31, 2012:						
Goodwill	10	997	214	2,705	1,272	5,198
Accumulated impairment losses	—	—	—	(28)	—	(28)
	10	997	214	2,677	1,272	5,170
Impairment	—	(989)	—	—	(742)	(1,731)
Translation	(1)	(8)	4	(7)	(12)	(24)
Balance at December 31, 2013:						
Goodwill	9	989	218	2,698	1,260	5,174
Accumulated impairment losses	—	(989)	—	(28)	(742)	(1,759)
	$ 9	$ —	$218	$2,670	$ 518	$ 3,415

* As of December 31, 2013, $493 of the amount reflected in Corporate is allocated to three of Alcoa's four reportable segments ($158 to Alumina, $61 to Global Rolled Products, and $274 to Engineered Products and Solutions) included in the table above for purposes of impairment testing (see Note A). This goodwill is reflected in Corporate for segment reporting purposes because it is not included in management's assessment of performance by the three reportable segments.

In 2013, Alcoa recognized an impairment of goodwill in the amount of $1,731 ($1,719 after noncontrolling interest) related to the annual impairment review of the Primary Metals segment (see Goodwill and Other Intangible Assets policy in Note A).

TRADE NAMES

2.76 AGCO CORPORATION (DEC)
MANAGEMENT'S DISCUSSION AND ANALYSIS OF FINANCIAL CONDITION AND RESULTS OF OPERATIONS

Recent Acquisitions (in part)

In January 2012, we acquired 61% of Santal Equipamentos S.A. Comércio e Indústria ("Santal") for approximately R$36.7 million, net of approximately R$11.9 million cash acquired (or approximately $20.1 million, net). Santal, headquartered in Ribeirão Preto, Brazil, manufactures and distributes sugar cane planting, harvesting, handling and transportation equipment as well as replacement parts across Brazil. The acquisition of Santal provides our customers in Brazil with a wider range of agricultural products and services. The acquisition was funded with available cash on hand. We recorded approximately $28.0 million of goodwill and approximately $2.6 million of trade name, trademark and patent identifiable intangible assets associated with the acquisition.

(In millions, except share amounts)

	December 31, 2013	December 31, 2012
Assets		
Current assets:		
Cash and cash equivalents	$1,047.2	$ 781.3
Accounts and notes receivable, net	940.6	924.6
Inventories, net	2,016.1	1,703.1
Deferred tax assets	241.2	243.5
Other current assets	272.0	302.2
Total current assets	4,517.1	3,954.7
Property, plant and equipment, net	1,602.3	1,406.1
Investment in affiliates	416.1	390.3
Deferred tax assets	24.4	40.0
Other assets	134.6	131.2
Intangible assets, net	565.6	607.1
Goodwill	1,178.7	1,192.4
Total assets	$8,438.8	$7,721.8

NOTES TO CONSOLIDATED FINANCIAL STATEMENTS

Goodwill, Other Intangible Assets and Long-Lived Assets (in part)

The Company amortizes certain acquired identifiable intangible assets primarily on a straight-line basis over their estimated useful lives, which range from 5 to 50 years. The acquired intangible assets have a weighted average useful life as follows:

Intangible Asset	Weighted-Average Useful Life
Patents and technology	13 years
Customer relationships	14 years
Trademarks and Trade Names	21 years
Land use rights	47 years

For the years ended December 31, 2013, 2012 and 2011, acquired intangible asset amortization was $47.8 million, $49.3 million and $21.6 million, respectively. The Company estimates amortization of existing intangible assets will be $39.9 million for 2014, $39.9 million for 2015, $38.8 million for 2016, $38.4 million for 2017, and $38.3 million for 2018.

The Company has previously determined that two of its trademarks have an indefinite useful life. The Massey Ferguson trademark has been in existence since 1952 and was formed from the merger of Massey-Harris (established in the 1890's) and Ferguson (established in the 1930's). The Massey Ferguson brand is currently sold in over 140 countries worldwide, making it one of the most widely sold tractor brands in the world. The Company has also identified the Valtra trademark as an indefinite-lived asset. The Valtra trademark has been in existence since the late 1990's, but is a derivative of the Valmet trademark which has been in existence since 1951. The Valmet name transitioned to the Valtra name over a period of time in the marketplace. The Valtra brand is currently sold in approximately 50 countries around the world. Both the Massey Ferguson brand and the Valtra brand are primary product lines of the Company's business, and the Company plans to use these trademarks for an indefinite period of time. The Company plans to continue to make investments in product development to enhance the value of these brands into the future. There are no legal, regulatory, contractual, competitive, economic or other factors that the Company is aware of or that the Company believes would limit the useful lives of the trademarks. The Massey Ferguson and Valtra trademark registrations can be renewed at a nominal cost in the countries in which the Company operates.

Changes in the carrying amount of acquired intangible assets during 2013 and 2012 are summarized as follows (in millions):

	Trademarks and trade names	Customer Relationships	Patents and Technology	Land Use Rights	Total
Gross carrying amounts:					
Balance as of December 31, 2011	$118.1	$511.4	$85.7	$ 8.6	$723.8
Acquisition	1.5	—	1.1	—	2.6
Foreign currency translation	(0.7)	(3.6)	0.8	0.1	(3.4)
Balance as of December 31, 2012	118.9	507.8	87.6	8.7	723.0
Acquisition	—	—	—	6.0	6.0
Foreign currency translation	(0.3)	(5.1)	1.5	0.2	(3.7)
Balance as of December 31, 2013	$118.6	$502.7	$89.1	$14.9	$725.3

	Trademarks and Trade Names	Customer Relationships	Patents and Technology	Land Use Rights	Total
Accumulated amortization:					
Balance as of December 31, 2011	$13.1	$ 85.3	$50.3	$—	$148.7
Amortization expense	6.7	39.4	3.0	0.2	49.3
Impairment charge	5.6	5.4	—	2.3	13.3
Foreign currency translation	(0.5)	(3.5)	0.8	—	(3.2)
Balance as of December 31, 2012	24.9	126.6	54.1	2.5	208.1
Amortization expense	6.2	38.4	3.0	0.2	47.8
Foreign currency translation	(0.1)	(4.3)	1.9	—	(2.5)
Balance as of December 31, 2013	$31.0	$160.7	$59.0	$ 2.7	$253.4

	Trademarks and Trade Names
Indefinite-lived intangible assets:	
Balance as of December 31, 2011	$91.4
Foreign currency translation	0.8
Balance as of December 31, 2012	92.2
Foreign currency translation	1.5
Balance as of December 31, 2013	$93.7

CUSTOMER RELATIONSHIPS

2.77 CENTURYLINK, INC. (DEC)

CONSOLIDATED BALANCE SHEETS (in part)

	December 31,	
(Dollars in millions and shares in thousands)	2013	2012
Assets		
Current Assets		
Cash and cash equivalents	$ 168	211
Accounts receivable, less allowance of $155 and $158	1,977	1,917
Income tax receivable	—	42
Deferred income taxes, net	1,165	916
Other	597	552
Total current assets	3,907	3,638
Net Property, Plant and Equipment		
Property, plant and equipment	34,307	31,933
Accumulated depreciation	(15,661)	(13,024)
Net property, plant and equipment	18,646	18,909
Goodwill and Other Assets		
Goodwill	20,674	21,627
Customer relationships, net	5,935	7,052
Other intangible assets, net	1,802	1,918
Other, net	823	796
Total goodwill and other assets	29,234	31,393
Total assets	$ 51,787	53,940

NOTES TO CONSOLIDATED FINANCIAL STATEMENTS

Unless the context requires otherwise, references in this annual report to "CenturyLink," "we," "us" and "our" refer to CenturyLink, Inc. and its consolidated subsidiaries, including SAVVIS, Inc. and its consolidated subsidiaries (referred to as "Savvis") for periods on or after July 15, 2011 and Qwest Communications International Inc. and its consolidated subsidiaries (referred to as "Qwest") for periods on or after April 1, 2011.

(1) Basis of Presentation and Summary of Significant Accounting Policies (in part)

Goodwill, Customer Relationships and Other Intangible Assets (in part)

Intangible assets arising from business combinations, such as goodwill, customer relationships, capitalized software, trademarks and trade names, are initially recorded at estimated fair value. We amortize customer relationships primarily over an estimated life of 10 years to 15, using either the sum-of-the-years-digits or the straight-line methods, depending on the type of customer. We amortize capitalized software using the straight-line method over estimated lives ranging up to seven years, except for approximately $237 million of our capitalized software costs, which represents costs to develop an integrated billing and customer care system which is amortized using the straight-line method over a 20 year period. We amortize our other intangible assets predominantly using the sum-of-the-years-digits method over an estimated life of four years. Other intangible assets not arising from business combinations are initially recorded at cost. Where there are no legal, regulatory, contractual or other factors that would reasonably limit the useful life of an intangible asset, we classify the intangible asset as indefinite-lived and such intangible assets are not amortized.

Our long-lived intangible assets, other than goodwill, with indefinite lives are assessed for impairment annually, or, under certain circumstances, more frequently, such as when events or circumstances indicate there may be an impairment. These assets are carried at the estimated fair value at the time of acquisition and assets not acquired in acquisitions are recorded at historical cost. However, if their estimated fair value is less than the carrying amount, other indefinite-lived intangible assets are reduced to their estimated fair value through an impairment charge to our consolidated statements of operations.

We annually review the estimated lives and methods used to amortize our other intangible assets. The actual amounts of amortization expense may differ materially from our estimates, depending on the results of our annual review.

(3) Goodwill, Customer Relationships and Other Intangible Assets (in part)

Goodwill, customer relationships and other intangible assets consisted of the following:

(Dollars in millions)	December 31, 2013	December 31, 2012
Goodwill	$20,674	21,627
Customer relationships, less accumulated amortization of $3,641 and $2,524	5,935	7,052
Indefinite-life intangible assets	321	268
Other intangible assets subject to amortization		
Capitalized software, less accumulated amortization of $1,193 and $844	1,415	1,522
Trade names and patents, less accumulated amortization of $208 and $142	66	128
Total other intangible assets, net	$ 1,802	1,918

Total amortization expense for intangible assets for the years ended December 31, 2013, 2012 and 2011 was $1.589 billion, $1.710 billion and $1.433 billion, respectively.

We estimate that total amortization expense for intangible assets for the years ending December 31, 2014 through 2018 will be as follows:

	(Dollars in millions)
2014	$1,390
2015	1,249
2016	1,139
2017	1,027
2018	904

TECHNOLOGY

2.78 INTEL CORPORATION (DEC)

CONSOLIDATED BALANCE SHEETS (in part)

	December 28, 2013, and December 29, 2012	
(In millions, except par value)	2013	2012
Assets		
Current assets:		
Cash and cash equivalents	$ 5,674	$ 8,478
Short-term investments	5,972	3,999
Trading assets	8,441	5,685
Accounts receivable, net of allowance for doubtful accounts of $38 ($38 in 2012)	3,582	3,833
Inventories	4,172	4,734
Deferred tax assets	2,594	2,117
Other current assets	1,649	2,512
Total current assets	32,084	31,358
Property, plant and equipment, net	31,428	27,983
Marketable equity securities	6,221	4,424
Other long-term investments	1,473	493
Goodwill	10,513	9,710
Identified intangible assets, net	5,150	6,235
Other long-term assets	5,489	4,148
Total assets	$92,358	$84,351

Note 2: Accounting Policies (in part)

Identified Intangible Assets

Licensed technology and patents are generally amortized on a straight-line basis over the periods of benefit. We amortize all acquisition-related intangible assets that are subject to amortization over their estimated useful life based on economic benefit. Acquisition-related in-process R&D assets represent the fair value of incomplete R&D projects that had not reached technological feasibility as of the date of acquisition; initially, these are classified as "other intangible assets" that are not subject to amortization. Assets related to projects that have been completed are transferred from "other intangible assets" to "acquisition-related developed technology;" these are subject to amortization, while assets related to projects that have been abandoned are impaired and expensed to R&D. In the quarter following the period in which identified intangible assets become fully amortized, we remove the fully amortized balances from the gross asset and accumulated amortization amounts.

The estimated useful life ranges for substantially all identified intangible assets that are subject to amortization as of December 28, 2013, were as follows:

(In Years)	Estimated Useful Life
Acquisition-related developed technology	4–9
Acquisition-related customer relationships	5–8
Acquisition-related trade names	4–8
Licensed technology and patents	5–17

We perform a quarterly review of finite-lived identified intangible assets to determine whether facts and circumstances indicate that the useful life is shorter than we had originally estimated or that the carrying amount of assets may not be recoverable. If such facts and circumstances exist, we assess recoverability by comparing the projected undiscounted net cash flows associated with the related asset or group of assets over their remaining lives against their respective carrying amounts. Impairments, if any, are based on the excess of the carrying amount over the fair value of those assets. If an asset's useful life is shorter than originally estimated, we accelerate the rate of amortization and amortize the remaining carrying value over the new shorter useful life. We perform an annual impairment assessment in the fourth quarter of each year for indefinite-lived intangible assets, or more frequently if indicators of potential impairment exist, to determine whether it is more likely than not that the carrying value of the assets may not be recoverable. If necessary, a quantitative impairment test is performed to compare the fair value of the indefinite-lived intangible asset with its carrying value. Impairments, if any, are based on the excess of the carrying amount over the fair value of those assets.

For further discussion of identified intangible assets, see "Note 11: Identified Intangible Assets."

Note 11: Identified Intangible Assets

Identified intangible assets at the end of December 28, 2013, were as follows:

(In millions)	Gross Assets	Accumulated Amortization	Net
Acquisition-related developed technology	$2,922	$(1,691)	$1,231
Acquisition-related customer relationships	1,760	(828)	932
Acquisition-related trade names	65	(44)	21
Licensed technology and patents	3,093	(974)	2,119
Identified intangible assets subject to amortization	7,840	(3,537)	4,303
Acquisition-related trade names	818	—	818
Other intangible assets	29	—	29
Identified intangible assets not subject to amortization	847	—	847
Total identified intangible assets	$8,687	$(3,537)	$5,150

As a result of our acquisitions in 2013, we recorded acquisition-related developed technology of $114 million with a weighted average useful life of five years and acquisition-related customer relationships of $60 million with a weighted average useful life of seven years. During 2013, we purchased licensed technology and patents of $36 million with a weighted average useful life of 10 years.

Identified intangible assets at the end of December 29, 2012 were as follows:

(In millions)	Gross Assets	Accumulated Amortization	Net
Acquisition-related developed technology	$2,778	$(1,116)	$1,662
Acquisition-related customer relationships	1,712	(551)	1,161
Acquisition-related trade names	68	(33)	35
Licensed technology and patents	2,986	(699)	2,287
Other intangible assets	238	(86)	152
Identified intangible assets subject to amortization	7,782	(2,485)	5,297
Acquisition-related trade names	809	—	809
Other intangible assets	129	—	129
Identified intangible assets not subject to amortization	938	—	938
Total identified intangible assets	$8,720	$(2,485)	$6,235

As a result of our acquisitions in 2012, we recorded acquisition-related developed technology of $168 million with a weighted average useful life of 10 years. During 2012, we purchased licensed technology and patents of $815 million with a weighted average useful life of nine years, including wireless patents purchased from InterDigital, Inc. for $375 million to be amortized over approximately 10 years. Additionally, we recorded other intangible assets subject to amortization of $238 million associated with customer relationships, which was fully amortized in 2013.

In January 2011, we entered into a long-term patent cross-license agreement with NVIDIA. Under the agreement, we received a license to all of NVIDIA's patents with a capture period that runs through March 2017 while NVIDIA products are licensed to our patents, subject to exclusions for x86 products, certain chipsets, and certain flash memory technology products. The agreement also included settlement of the existing litigation between the companies, as well as broad mutual general releases. We agreed to make payments totaling $1.5 billion to NVIDIA over six years ($300 million in each of January 2011, 2012, and 2013; and $200 million in each of January 2014, 2015, and 2016), which resulted in a liability totaling approximately $1.4 billion, on a discounted basis. In the fourth quarter of 2010, we recognized an expense of $100 million related to the litigation settlement. In the first quarter of 2011, we recognized the remaining amount of $1.3 billion as licensed technology, which will be amortized into cost of sales over its estimated useful life of 17 years. The initial recognition of the intangible asset and associated liability for future payments to NVIDIA was treated as a non-cash transaction and, therefore, had no impact on our consolidated statements of cash flows. Future payments are treated as cash used for financing activities. As of December 28, 2013, the remaining liability of $587 million is classified within other accrued liabilities and other long-term liabilities, based on the expected timing of the underlying payments.

We recorded amortization expense on the consolidated statements of income as follows: amortization of acquisition-related developed technology and licensed technology and patents is included in cost of sales, amortization of acquisition-related customer relationships and trade names is included in amortization of acquisition-related intangibles, and amortization of other intangible assets is recorded as a reduction of revenue.

Amortization expenses for each period were as follows:

(In millions)	2013	2012	2011
Acquisition-related developed technology	$ 576	$ 557	$482
Acquisition-related customer relationships	279	296	250
Acquisition-related trade names	12	12	10
Licensed technology and patents	272	214	181
Other intangible assets	103	86	—
Total amortization expenses	$1,242	$1,165	$923

Based on identified intangible assets that are subject to amortization as of December 28, 2013, we expect future amortization expense for each period to be as follows:

(In millions)	2014	2015	2016	2017	2018
Acquisition-related developed technology	$ 579	$303	$211	$ 63	$ 41
Acquisition-related customer relationships	268	251	233	142	29
Acquisition-related trade names	10	9	3	—	—
Licensed technology and patents	270	252	238	199	158
Total future amortization expenses	$1,127	$815	$685	$404	$228

2.79 HARRIS CORPORATION (JUN)
CONSOLIDATED BALANCE SHEET (in part)

(In millions, except shares)	June 28, 2013	June 29, 2012
Assets		
Current assets		
Cash and cash equivalents	$ 321.0	$ 356.0
Receivables	696.8	750.2
Inventories	668.7	617.8
Income taxes receivable	36.2	12.0
Current deferred income taxes	121.2	160.5
Other current assets	77.2	71.2
Assets of discontinued operations	27.0	632.7
Total current assets	1,948.1	2,600.4
Non-current Assets		
Property, plant and equipment	653.2	659.4
Goodwill	1,692.0	1,695.3
Intangible assets	308.1	421.7
Non-current deferred income taxes	124.8	80.3
Other non-current assets	132.2	135.7
Total non-current assets	2,910.3	2,992.4
	$4,858.4	$5,592.8

NOTES TO CONSOLIDATED FINANCIAL STATEMENTS

Note 1: Significant Accounting Policies (in part)

Property, Plant and Equipment —Property, plant and equipment are carried on the basis of cost and include software capitalized for internal use. Depreciation of buildings, machinery and equipment is computed by the straight-line and accelerated methods. The estimated useful lives of buildings, including leasehold improvements, generally range between 2 and 45 years. The estimated useful lives of machinery and equipment generally range between 2 and 10 years. Amortization of internal-use software begins when the software is put into service and is based on the expected useful life of the software. The useful lives over which we amortize internal-use software generally range between 3 and 7 years. See *Note 7: Property, Plant and Equipment* for additional information regarding property, plant and equipment.

Capitalized Software to Be Sold, Leased or Otherwise Marketed —Costs incurred to acquire or create a computer software product are expensed when incurred as research and development until technological feasibility has been established for the product, at which point such costs are capitalized. Technological feasibility is normally established upon completion of a detailed program design or, in its absence, a working model of the software product. Capitalization of computer software costs ceases when the product is available for general release to customers, at which point amortization begins based on the greater of the amount computed using (a) the ratio that current gross revenues for a product bear to the total of current and anticipated future gross revenues for that product or (b) the straight-line method over the remaining estimated economic life of the product. Costs of reproduction, documentation, training materials, physical packaging, maintenance and customer support are charged to cost of products sold as incurred. Capitalized software to be sold, leased or otherwise marketed is evaluated for impairment periodically by comparing the unamortized capitalized costs of a computer software product to the net realizable value of that product. Capitalized costs, net of accumulated amortization, are reflected in the "Other non-current assets" line item in our Consolidated Balance Sheet. The amortization of capitalized software is included in the "Cost of product sales" line item in our Consolidated Statement of Income.

In the fourth quarter of fiscal 2013, we recorded a $17.8 million write-off of the capitalized software in Healthcare Solutions as a change in accounting estimate, resulting from high-risk development issues and substantial revisions to the logic of Carefx's primary software product based on the realization that the software would require more features and better functionality. These changes to the software were such that the initial detail program design was no longer sufficient to establish technological feasibility.

Note 7: Property, Plant and Equipment

Property, plant and equipment are summarized below:

(In millions)	2013	2012
Land	$ 13.0	$ 13.0
Software capitalized for internal use	110.5	93.1
Buildings	420.4	414.1
Machinery and equipment	1,022.0	1,014.2
	1,565.9	1,534.4
Less allowances for depreciation and amortization	(912.7)	(875.0)
	$ 653.2	$ 659.4

Depreciation and amortization expense related to property, plant and equipment was $146.4 million, $143.0 million and $121.6 million in fiscal 2013, 2012 and 2011, respectively.

Note 16: Research and Development

Company-sponsored research and development costs are expensed as incurred. These costs were $254.1 million, $218.9 million and $239.8 million in fiscal 2013, 2012 and 2011, respectively, and are included in the "Engineering, selling and administrative expenses" line item in our Consolidated Statement of Income. These costs in fiscal 2013 included a $17.8 million write-off of capitalized software in our Integrated Network Solutions segment—see the caption "Capitalized Software to Be Sold, Leased or Otherwise Marketed" in *Note 1: Significant Accounting Policies* for further discussion. Customer-sponsored research and development costs are incurred pursuant to contractual arrangements and are accounted for principally by the cost-to-cost percentage-of-completion method. Customer-sponsored research and development costs are incurred principally under U.S. Government-sponsored contracts and require us to provide a product or service meeting certain defined performance or other specifications (such as designs). Customer-sponsored research and development is included in our revenue and cost of product sales and services.

LICENSES

2.80 VERIZON COMMUNICATIONS INC. (DEC)
CONSOLIDATED BALANCE SHEETS (in part)

	At December 31,	
(Dollars in millions, except per share amounts)	2013	2012
Assets		
Current assets		
Cash and cash equivalents	$ 53,528	$ 3,093
Short-term investments	601	470
Accounts receivable, net of allowances of $645 and $641	12,439	12,576
Inventories	1,020	1,075
Prepaid expenses and other	3,406	4,021
Total current assets	70,994	21,235
Plant, property and equipment	220,865	209,575
Less accumulated depreciation	131,909	120,933
	88,956	88,642
Investments in unconsolidated businesses	3,432	3,401
Wireless licenses	75,747	77,744
Goodwill	24,634	24,139
Other intangible assets, net	5,800	5,933
Other assets	4,535	4,128
Total assets	$274,098	$225,222

NOTES TO CONSOLIDATED FINANCIAL STATEMENTS

Verizon Communications Inc. and Subsidiaries

Note 1—Description of Business and Summary of Significant Accounting Policies (in part)

Goodwill and Other Intangible Assets (in part)

Intangible Assets Not Subject to Amortization

A significant portion of our intangible assets are wireless licenses that provide our wireless operations with the exclusive right to utilize designated radio frequency spectrum to provide wireless communication services. While licenses are issued for only a fixed time, generally ten years, such licenses are subject to renewal by the Federal Communications Commission (FCC). License renewals have occurred routinely and at nominal cost. Moreover, we have determined that there are currently no legal, regulatory, contractual, competitive, economic or other factors that limit the useful life of our wireless licenses. As a result, we treat the wireless licenses as an indefinite-lived intangible asset. We reevaluate the useful life determination for wireless licenses each year to determine whether events and circumstances continue to support an indefinite useful life.

We test our wireless licenses for potential impairment annually. In 2013, we performed a qualitative assessment to determine whether it is more likely than not that the fair value of our wireless licenses was less than the carrying amount. As part of our assessment, we considered several qualitative factors including the business enterprise value of Wireless, macroeconomic conditions (including changes in interest rates and discount rates), industry and market considerations (including industry revenue and EBITDA (Earnings before interest, taxes, depreciation and amortization) margin projections), the projected financial performance of Wireless, as well as other factors. In 2012 and 2011, our quantitative assessment consisted of comparing the estimated fair value of our wireless licenses to the aggregated carrying amount as of the test date. Using the quantitative assessment, we evaluated our licenses on an aggregate basis using a direct value approach. The direct value approach estimates fair value using a discounted cash flow analysis to estimate what a marketplace participant would be willing to pay to purchase the aggregated wireless licenses as of the valuation date. If the fair value of the aggregated wireless licenses is less than the aggregated carrying amount of the licenses, an impairment is recognized.

Interest expense incurred while qualifying activities are performed to ready wireless licenses for their intended use is capitalized as part of wireless licenses. The capitalization period ends when the development is discontinued or substantially complete and the license is ready for its intended use.

Intangible Assets Subject to Amortization and Long-Lived Assets (in part)

For information related to the carrying amount of goodwill by segment, wireless licenses and other intangible assets, as well as the major components and average useful lives of our other acquired intangible assets, see Note 3.

Note 2—Acquisitions and Divestitures (in part)

   Wireless (in part)

Spectrum License Transactions

Since 2012, we have entered into several strategic spectrum transactions including:
- During the third quarter of 2012, after receiving the required regulatory approvals, Verizon Wireless completed the following previously announced transactions in which we acquired wireless spectrum that will be used to deploy additional 4G LTE capacity:
  — Verizon Wireless acquired Advanced Wireless Services (AWS) spectrum in separate transactions with SpectrumCo and Cox TMI Wireless, LLC for which it paid an aggregate of $3.9 billion at the time of the closings. Verizon Wireless has also recorded a liability of $0.4 billion related to a three-year service obligation to SpectrumCo's members pursuant to commercial agreements executed concurrently with the SpectrumCo transaction.
  — Verizon Wireless completed license purchase and exchange transactions with Leap Wireless, Savary Island Wireless, which is majority owned by Leap Wireless, and a subsidiary of T-Mobile USA, Inc. (T-Mobile USA). As a result of these transactions, Verizon Wireless received an aggregate $2.6 billion of AWS and Personal Communication Services (PCS) licenses at fair value and net cash proceeds of $0.2 billion, transferred certain AWS licenses to T-Mobile USA and a 700 megahertz (MHz) lower A block license to Leap Wireless, and recorded an immaterial gain.
- During the first quarter of 2013, we completed license exchange transactions with T-Mobile License LLC and Cricket License Company, LLC, a subsidiary of Leap Wireless, to exchange certain AWS licenses. These non-cash exchanges include a number of intra-market swaps that we expect will enable Verizon Wireless to make more efficient use of the AWS band. As a result of these exchanges, we received an aggregate $0.5 billion of AWS licenses at fair value and recorded an immaterial gain.
- During the third quarter of 2013, after receiving the required regulatory approvals, Verizon Wireless sold 39 lower 700 MHz B block spectrum licenses to AT&T Inc. (AT&T) in exchange for a payment of $1.9 billion and the transfer by AT&T to Verizon Wireless of AWS (10 MHz) licenses in certain markets in the western United States. Verizon Wireless also sold certain lower 700 MHz B block spectrum licenses to an investment firm for a payment of $0.2 billion. As a result, we received $0.5 billion of AWS licenses at fair value and we recorded a pre-tax gain of approximately $0.3 billion in Selling, general and administrative expense on our consolidated statement of income for the year ended December 31, 2013.
- During the fourth quarter of 2013, we entered into license exchange agreements with T-Mobile USA to exchange certain AWS and PCS licenses. These non-cash exchanges, which are subject to approval by the FCC and other customary closing conditions, are expected to

close in the first half of 2014. The exchange includes a number of swaps that we expect will result in more efficient use of the AWS and PCS bands. As a result of these agreements, $0.9 billion of Wireless licenses are classified as held for sale and included in Prepaid expenses and other on our consolidated balance sheet at December 31, 2013. Upon completion of the transaction, we expect to record an immaterial gain.

- Subsequent to the transaction with T-Mobile USA in the fourth quarter of 2013, on January 6, 2014, we announced two agreements with T-Mobile USA with respect to our remaining 700 MHz A block spectrum licenses. Under one agreement, we will sell certain of these licenses to T-Mobile USA in exchange for cash consideration of approximately $2.4 billion, and under the second agreement we will exchange the remainder of these licenses for AWS and PCS spectrum licenses. These transactions are subject to the approval of the FCC as well as other customary closing conditions. These transactions are expected to close in the middle of 2014.

Note 3—Wireless Licenses, Goodwill and Other Intangible Assets (in part)

Wireless Licenses

Changes in the carrying amount of Wireless licenses are as follows:

	(Dollars in millions)
Balance at January 1, 2012	$73,250
Acquisitions (Note 2)	4,544
Capitalized interest on wireless licenses	205
Reclassifications, adjustments and other	(255)
Balance at December 31, 2012	$77,744
Acquisitions (Note 2)	579
Dispositions (Note 2)	(2,361)
Capitalized interest on wireless licenses	566
Reclassifications, adjustments and other	(781)
Balance at December 31, 2013	$75,747

Reclassifications, adjustments and other includes $0.9 billion of Wireless licenses that are classified as held for sale and included in Prepaid expenses and other on our consolidated balance sheet at December 31, 2013 as well as the exchanges of wireless licenses in 2013 and 2012. See Note 2 for additional details.

At December 31, 2013 and 2012, approximately $7.7 billion and $7.3 billion, respectively, of wireless licenses were under development for commercial service for which we were capitalizing interest costs.

The average remaining renewal period of our wireless license portfolio was 5.1 years as of December 31, 2013. See Note 1 for additional details.

PURCHASED INTANGIBLE ASSETS

2.81 APPLIED MATERIALS, INC. (OCT)
CONSOLIDATED BALANCE SHEETS (in part)

(In millions, except per share amounts)	October 27, 2013	October 28, 2012
Assets		
Current assets:		
Cash and cash equivalents	$ 1,711	$ 1,392
Short-term investments	180	545
Accounts receivable, net	1,633	1,220
Inventories	1,413	1,272
Other current assets	705	673
Total current assets	5,642	5,102
Long-term investments	1,005	1,055
Property, plant and equipment, net	850	910
Goodwill	3,294	3,518
Purchased technology and other intangible assets, net	1,103	1,355
Deferred income taxes and other assets	149	162
Total assets	$12,043	$12,102

Note 1—Summary of Significant Accounting Policies (in part)

Intangible Assets

Goodwill and indefinite-lived assets are not amortized, but are reviewed for impairment annually during the fourth quarter of each fiscal year and whenever events or changes in circumstances indicate that the carrying value of an asset may not be recoverable. Purchased technology and other intangible assets are presented at cost, net of accumulated amortization, and are amortized over their estimated useful lives of 1 to 15 years using the straight-line method.

Note 9—Goodwill, Purchased Technology and Other Intangible Assets (in part)

Goodwill and Purchased Intangible Assets (in part)

Applied's methodology for allocating the purchase price relating to purchase acquisitions is determined through established and generally accepted valuation techniques. Goodwill is measured as the excess of the cost of the acquisition over the sum of the amounts assigned to tangible and identifiable intangible assets acquired less liabilities assumed. Applied assigns assets acquired (including goodwill) and liabilities assumed to one or more reporting units as of the date of acquisition. Typically, acquisitions relate to a single reporting unit and thus do not require the allocation of goodwill to multiple reporting units. If the products obtained in an acquisition are assigned to multiple reporting units, the goodwill is distributed to the respective reporting units as part of the purchase price allocation process.

Goodwill and purchased intangible assets with indefinite useful lives are not amortized, but are reviewed for impairment annually during the fourth quarter of each fiscal year and whenever events or changes in circumstances indicate that the carrying value of an asset may not be recoverable. The process of evaluating the potential impairment of goodwill and intangible assets requires significant judgment, especially in emerging markets. Applied regularly monitors current business conditions and other factors including, but not limited to, adverse industry or economic trends, restructuring actions and lower projections of profitability that may impact future operating results.

Applied also performed an impairment test for long-lived assets associated with the Energy and Environmental Solutions reporting unit and determined that the majority of intangible assets were impaired mostly due to the lower long-term revenue and profitability outlook associated with products related to these intangible assets. Accordingly, during the second quarter of fiscal 2013, Applied recorded an impairment charge of $54 million related to these intangible assets, which was the amount by which the carrying value of these intangible assets exceeded their estimated fair value, based on discounted projected cash flows.

Applied utilized an equal weighting of both the discounted cash flow method of the income approach and the guideline company method of the market approach to estimate the fair value of the Energy and Environmental Solutions reporting unit. The estimates used in the impairment testing were consistent with the discrete forecasts that Applied uses to manage its business, and considered the significant developments that occurred during the quarter. Under the discounted cash flow method, cash flows beyond the discrete forecasts were estimated using a terminal growth rate, which considered the long-term earnings growth rate specific to the Energy and Environmental Solutions reporting unit. The estimated future cash flows were discounted to present value using a discount rate that was the value-weighted average of the reporting unit's estimated cost of equity and debt derived using both known and estimated market metrics, and was adjusted to reflect risk factors that considered both the timing and risks associated with the estimated cash flows. The tax rate used in the discounted cash flow method reflected the international structure currently in place, which is consistent with the market participant perspective. Under the guideline company method, market multiples were applied to forecasted revenues and earnings before interest, taxes, depreciation and amortization. The market multiples used were consistent with comparable publicly-traded companies.

A summary of Applied's purchased technology and intangible assets is set forth below:

(In millions)	October 27, 2013	October 28, 2012
Purchased technology, net	$ 748	$ 945
Intangible assets—finite-lived, net	213	268
Intangible assets—indefinite-lived	142	142
Total	$1,103	$1,355

Finite-Lived Purchased Intangible Assets

Applied amortizes purchased intangible assets with finite lives using the straight-line method over the estimated economic lives of the assets, ranging from 1 to 15 years.

Applied evaluates long-lived assets for impairment whenever events or changes in circumstances indicate the carrying value of an asset group may not be recoverable. Applied assesses the fair value of the assets based on the amount of the undiscounted future cash flow that the assets are expected to generate and recognizes an impairment loss when estimated undiscounted future cash flow expected to result from the use of the asset, plus net proceeds expected from disposition of the asset, if any, are less than the carrying value of the asset. When Applied identifies an impairment, Applied reduces the carrying value of the group of assets to comparable market values, when available and appropriate, or to its estimated fair value based on a discounted cash flow approach.

Intangible assets, such as purchased technology, are generally recorded in connection with a business acquisition. The value assigned to intangible assets is usually based on estimates and judgments regarding expectations for the success and life cycle of products and technology acquired. Applied evaluates the useful lives of its intangible assets each reporting period to determine whether events and circumstances require revising the remaining period of amortization. In addition, Applied reviews intangible assets for impairment when events or changes in circumstances indicate their carrying value may not be recoverable. Management considers such indicators as significant differences in actual product acceptance from the estimates, changes in the competitive and economic environment, technological advances, and changes in cost structure. In the fourth quarter of fiscal 2013, Applied performed an impairment analysis on the carrying value of its intangible assets and determined that there was no impairment.

Details of finite-lived intangible assets were as follows:

	October 27, 2013			October 28, 2012		
(In millions)	Purchased Technology	Other Intangible Assets	Total	Purchased Technology	Other Intangible Assets	Total
Gross Carrying Amount:						
Silicon Systems Group	$1,301	$ 252	$1,553	$1,300	$ 252	$1,552
Applied Global Services	28	44	72	28	44	72
Display	110	33	143	110	33	143
Energy and Environmental Solutions	5	15	20	105	232	337
Gross carrying amount	$1,444	$ 344	$1,788	$1,543	$ 561	$2,104
Accumulated Amortization:						
Silicon Systems Group	$ (562)	$ (58)	$ (620)	$ (411)	$ (36)	$ (447)
Applied Global Services	(23)	(42)	(65)	(22)	(39)	(61)
Display	(110)	(29)	(139)	(106)	(27)	(133)
Energy and Environmental Solutions	(1)	(2)	(3)	(59)	(191)	(250)
Accumulated amortization	$ (696)	$(131)	$ (827)	$ (598)	$(293)	$ (891)
Carrying amount	$ 748	$ 213	$ 961	$ 945	$ 268	$1,213

During fiscal 2013, the impact of the impairment of certain intangible assets associated with the Energy and Environmental Solutions segment on the gross carrying amount and accumulated amortization of the finite-lived intangible assets was approximately $317 million and $262 million, respectively.

Details of amortization expense by segment for fiscal 2013, 2012 and 2011 were as follows:

(In millions)	2013	2012	2011
Silicon Systems Group	$172	$183	$13
Applied Global Services	5	9	7
Display	6	7	8
Energy and Environmental Solutions	16	25	24
Total	$199	$224	$52

For fiscal 2013, 2012 and 2011, amortization expense was charged to the following categories:

(In millions)	2013	2012	2011
Cost of products sold	$166	$185	$36
Research, development and engineering	1	1	—
Marketing and selling	26	30	16
General and administrative	6	8	—
Total	$199	$224	$52

As of October 27, 2013, future estimated amortization expense is expected to be as follows:

(In millions)	Amortization Expense
2014	181
2015	175
2016	169
2017	165
2018	163
Thereafter	108
Total	$961

Other Noncurrent Assets

RECOGNITION AND MEASUREMENT

2.82 FASB ASC 210 indicates that the concept of current assets excludes resources such as the following:
- Cash restricted regarding withdrawal or use for other than current operations, designated for expenditure in the acquisition or construction of noncurrent assets, or segregated for the liquidation of long-term debts
- Investments or advances for the purposes of control, affiliation, or other continuing business advantage
- Certain receivables (see the "Noncurrent Receivables" section)
- Cash surrender value of life insurance policies
- Land and other natural resources
- Long-term prepayments chargeable to operations over several years

DISCLOSURE

2.83 Rule 5-02 of Regulation S-X requires that any item not classed in another Regulation S-X caption and in excess of 5 percent of total assets be stated separately on the balance sheet or disclosed in the notes.

PRESENTATION AND DISCLOSURE EXCERPTS

ASSETS HELD FOR SALE

2.84 CATERPILLAR INC. (DEC)
CONSOLIDATED FINANCIAL POSITION (in part)

at December 31

(Dollars in millions)

	2013	2012	2011
Assets			
Current assets:			
Cash and short-term investments	$ 6,081	$ 5,490	$ 3,057
Receivables—trade and other	8,413	9,706	10,057
Receivables—finance	8,763	8,860	7,668
Deferred and refundable income taxes	1,553	1,547	1,580
Prepaid expenses and other current assets	900	988	994
Inventories	12,625	15,547	14,544
Total current assets	38,335	42,138	37,900
Property, plant and equipment—net	17,075	16,461	14,395
Long-term receivables—trade and other	1,397	1,316	1,130
Long-term receivables—finance	14,926	14,029	11,948
Investments in unconsolidated affiliated companies	272	272	133
Noncurrent deferred and refundable income taxes	594	2,011	2,157
Intangible assets	3,596	4,016	4,368
Goodwill	6,956	6,942	7,080
Other assets	1,745	1,785	2,107
Total assets	$84,896	$88,970	$81,218

1. Operations and Summary of Significant Accounting Policies (in part)

L. Assets Held for Sale

For those businesses where management has committed to a plan to divest, which is typically demonstrated by approval from the Board of Directors or Group President, each business is valued at the lower of its carrying amount or estimated fair value less cost to sell. If the carrying amount of the business exceeds its estimated fair value, an impairment loss is recognized. The fair values are estimated using accepted valuation techniques such as a discounted cash flow model, valuations performed by third parties, or indicative bids, when available. A number of significant estimates and assumptions are involved in the application of these techniques, including the forecasting of markets and market share, sales volumes and prices, costs and expenses, and multiple other factors. Management considers historical experience and all available information at the time the estimates are made; however, the fair values that are ultimately realized upon the sale of the businesses to be divested may differ from the estimated fair values reflected in the Consolidated Financial Statements.

26. Divestitures and Assets Held for Sale (in part)

Bucyrus Distribution Business Divestitures

In conjunction with our acquisition of Bucyrus in July 2011, we announced our intention to sell the Bucyrus distribution business to Caterpillar dealers that support mining customers around the world in a series of individual transactions. Bucyrus predominantly employed a direct to end customer model to sell and support products. The intention is for all Bucyrus products to be sold and serviced by Caterpillar dealers, consistent with our long-held distribution strategy. These transitions are occurring in phases based on the mining business opportunity within each dealer territory.

As portions of the Bucyrus distribution business are sold or classified as held for sale, they will not qualify as discontinued operations because Caterpillar expects significant continuing direct cash flows from the Caterpillar dealers after the divestitures. The gain or loss on disposal, along with the continuing operations of these disposal groups, will be reported in the Resource Industries segment. Goodwill will be allocated to each disposal group using the relative fair value method. The value of the customer relationship intangibles related to each portion of the Bucyrus distribution business to be sold will be included in the disposal groups. The disposal groups will be recorded at the lower of their carrying value or fair value less cost to sell. In 2013 and 2012, we recorded asset impairment charges of $11 million and $27 million respectively, related to disposal groups being sold to Caterpillar dealers. Fair value was determined based upon the negotiated sales price. The impairments were recorded in Other operating (income) expenses and included in the Resource Industries segment. The portions of the distribution business that were sold were not material to our results of operations, financial position or cash flow.

In 2013, we completed 19 sale transactions whereby we sold portions of the Bucyrus distribution business to Caterpillar dealers for an aggregate price of $466 million. A portion of these transactions are subject to certain working capital adjustments. For the full year 2013, after-tax profit was unfavorably impacted by $39 million as a result of the Bucyrus distribution divestiture activities. This is comprised of $95 million of income related to sales transactions, a $34 million unfavorable adjustment due to a change in estimate to increase the reserve for parts returns related to prior sale transactions (both included in Other operating (income) expenses), costs incurred related to the Bucyrus distribution divestiture activities of $104 million (included in Selling, general and administrative expenses) and an income tax benefit of $4 million.

Assets sold in 2013 included customer relationship intangibles of $127 million, other assets of $65 million, which consisted primarily of inventory and fixed assets, and allocated goodwill of $56 million related to the divested portions of the Bucyrus distribution business.

As part of the 2013 divestitures, Cat Financial provided $132 million of financing to five of the Caterpillar dealers.

In 2012, we completed 12 sale transactions whereby we sold portions of the Bucyrus distribution business to Caterpillar dealers for an aggregate price of $1,443 million, which included $38 million of working capital adjustments paid throughout 2013. For the full year 2012, after-tax profit was unfavorably impacted by $28 million as a result of the Bucyrus distribution divestiture activities. This is comprised of $310 million of income (included in Other operating (income) expenses) related to sales transactions, offset by costs incurred related to the Bucyrus distribution divestiture activities of $177 million (included in Selling, general and administrative expenses) and income tax of $161 million.

Assets sold in 2012 included customer relationship intangibles of $256 million, other assets of $254 million, which consisted primarily of inventory and fixed assets, and allocated goodwill of $405 million related to the divested portions of the Bucyrus distribution business.

As part of the 2012 divestitures, Cat Financial provided $739 million of financing to five of the Caterpillar dealers.

In December 2011, we completed one sale transaction whereby we sold a portion of the Bucyrus distribution business to a Caterpillar dealer for $337 million, which includes a $23 million working capital adjustment paid in the third quarter of 2012. After-tax profit was favorably impacted by $9 million in 2011 as a result of the Bucyrus distribution business divestiture activities. This is comprised of $96 million of income (included in Other operating (income) expenses) primarily related to the sale transaction, offset by costs incurred related to the Bucyrus distribution business divestiture activities of $32 million (included in Selling, general and administrative expenses) and income tax of $55 million. Assets sold included customer relationship intangibles of $63 million, other assets of $53 million, which consisted primarily of inventory and fixed assets, and allocated goodwill of $101 million.

As of December 31, 2013, ten divestiture transactions were classified as held for sale and are expected to close in 2014. Current assets held for sale were included in Prepaid expenses and other current assets and non-current assets held for sale were included in Other assets in Statement 3.

The major classes of assets held for sale for a portion of the Bucyrus distribution business were as follows:

	December 31,		
(Millions of dollars)	2013	2012	2011
Receivables—trade and other	$—	$—	$ 25
Inventories	14	30	109
Current assets held for sale	$ 14	$ 30	$134
Property, plant and equipment—net	$ 5	$—	$ 28
Intangible assets	44	32	186
Goodwill	45	52	296
Non-current assets held for sale	$ 94	$ 84	$510

RETIREMENT SAVINGS PLAN ASSETS

2.85 WELLPOINT, INC. (DEC)
NOTES TO CONSOLIDATED FINANCIAL STATEMENTS

December 31, 2013

(In Millions, Except Per Share Data or As Otherwise Stated Herein)

2. Basis of Presentation and Significant Accounting Policies (in part)

Retirement Benefits: We recognize the funded status of pension and other postretirement benefit plans on the consolidated balance sheets based on fiscal-year-end measurements of plan assets and benefit obligations. Prepaid pension benefits represent prepaid costs related to defined benefit pension plans and are reported with other noncurrent assets. Postretirement benefits represent outstanding obligations for retiree medical, life, vision and dental benefits. Liabilities for pension and other postretirement benefits are reported with current and noncurrent liabilities based on the amount by which the actuarial present value of benefits payable in the next twelve months included in the benefit obligation exceeds the fair value of plan assets.

11. Retirement Benefits (in part)

We sponsor various non-contributory employee defined benefit plans through certain subsidiaries.

The WellPoint Cash Balance Pension Plan, or the WellPoint Plan, is a cash balance pension plan covering certain eligible employees of the affiliated companies that participate in the WellPoint Plan. Effective January 1, 2006, benefits were curtailed, with the result that most participants stopped accruing benefits but continue to earn interest on benefits accrued prior to the curtailment. Certain participants subject to collective bargaining and certain other participants who met grandfathering rules continue to accrue benefits. Several pension plans acquired through various corporate mergers and acquisitions have been merged into the WellPoint Plan. Effective January 1, 2011, we split the WellPoint Plan, with no change in benefits for any participant. Current employees who are still receiving credits and/or benefit accruals were placed into a new plan, the WellPoint Cash Balance Pension Plan B. All other participants remain in the WellPoint Plan. Effective January 1, 2012, the WellPoint Plan was renamed the WellPoint Cash Balance Pension Plan A.

The UGS Pension Plan is a defined benefit pension plan with a cash balance component. The UGS Pension Plan covers eligible employees of the affiliated companies that participate in the UGS Pension Plan. Effective January 1, 2004, benefits were curtailed, with the result that most participants stopped accruing benefits but continue to earn interest on benefits previously accrued. Certain employees subject to collective bargaining and certain other employees who met grandfathering rules continue to accrue benefits.

The Employees' Retirement Plan of Blue Cross of California, or the BCC Plan, is a defined benefit pension plan that covers eligible employees of Blue Cross of California who are covered by a collective bargaining agreement. Effective January 1, 2007, benefits were curtailed under the BCC Plan with the result that no Blue Cross of California employees hired or rehired after December 31, 2006 are eligible to participate in the BCC Plan.

All of the plans' assets consist primarily of common stocks, fixed maturity securities, investment funds and short-term investments. The funding policies for all plans are to contribute amounts at least sufficient to meet the minimum funding requirements set forth in the Employee Retirement Income Security Act of 1974, as amended, or ERISA, including amendment by the Pension Protection Act of 2006, and in accordance with income tax regulations, plus such additional amounts as are necessary to provide assets sufficient to meet the benefits to be paid to plan participants.

We use a December 31 measurement date for determining benefit obligations and fair value of plan assets.

The following tables disclose consolidated "pension benefits," which include the defined benefit pension plans described above, and consolidated "other benefits," which include postretirement health and welfare benefits including medical, vision and dental benefits offered to certain employees. Calculations were computed using assumptions at the December 31 measurement dates.

The reconciliation of the benefit obligation is as follows:

	Pension Benefits		Other Benefits	
	2013	2012	2013	2012
Benefit obligation at beginning of year	$1,948.5	$1,851.3	$623.0	$651.3
Service cost	14.2	16.4	6.7	6.8
Interest cost	67.8	76.4	22.4	27.5
Actuarial (gain) loss	(129.9)	129.6	4.8	(28.4)
Benefits paid	(135.9)	(125.2)	(49.4)	(34.2)
Benefit obligation at end of year	$1,764.7	$1,948.5	$607.5	$623.0

The changes in the fair value of plan assets are as follows:

	Pension Benefits		Other Benefits	
	2013	2012	2013	2012
Fair value of plan assets at beginning of year	$1,817.9	$1,721.8	$320.3	$301.1
Actual return on plan assets	223.4	186.8	37.0	21.9
Employer contributions	38.6	34.5	31.3	38.4
Benefits paid	(135.9)	(125.2)	(38.8)	(41.1)
Fair value of plan assets at end of year	$1,944.0	$1,817.9	$349.8	$320.3

The net amount included in the consolidated balance sheets is as follows:

	Pension Benefits		Other Benefits	
	2013	2012	2013	2012
Noncurrent assets	$240.8	$ 3.0	$ —	$ —
Current liabilities	(3.5)	(11.5)	—	—
Noncurrent liabilities	(58.0)	(122.1)	(257.7)	(302.7)
Net amount at December 31	$179.3	$(130.6)	$(257.7)	$(302.7)

RESTRICTED CASH AND INVESTMENTS

2.86 FIRST SOLAR, INC. (DEC)
CONSOLIDATED BALANCE SHEETS (in part)

(In thousands, except share data)

	December 31, 2013	December 31, 2012
Assets		
Current assets:		
Cash and cash equivalents	$1,325,072	$ 901,294
Marketable securities	439,102	102,578
Accounts receivable trade, net	136,383	553,567
Accounts receivable, unbilled and retainage	521,323	400,987
Inventories	388,951	434,921
Balance of systems parts	133,731	98,903
Deferred project costs	556,957	21,390
Deferred tax assets, net	63,899	44,070
Assets held for sale	132,626	49,521
Note receivable, affiliate	—	17,725
Prepaid expenses and other current assets	94,720	207,368
Total current assets	3,792,764	2,832,324
Property, plant and equipment, net	1,385,084	1,525,382
Project assets and deferred project costs	720,916	845,478
Deferred tax assets, net	296,603	317,473
Restricted cash and investments	279,441	301,400
Goodwill	84,985	65,444
Inventories	129,664	134,375
Retainage	992	270,364
Other assets	193,053	56,452
Total assets	$6,883,502	$6,348,692

NOTES TO CONSOLIDATED FINANCIAL STATEMENTS

2. Summary of Significant Accounting Policies (in part)

Marketable Securities—current and noncurrent and Restricted Investments. We determine the classification of our marketable securities and restricted investments at the time of purchase and reevaluate such designation at each balance sheet date. We have classified our marketable securities and restricted investments as "available-for-sale." These marketable securities and restricted investments are recorded at fair value and unrealized gains and losses are recorded to accumulated other comprehensive income (loss) until realized. Realized gains and losses on sales of these marketable securities and restricted investments are reported in earnings, computed using the specific identification method.

We may sell marketable securities prior to their stated maturities after consideration of our liquidity requirements. We view unrestricted securities with maturities beyond 12 months as available to support current operations, and accordingly we classify all such securities as current assets under the caption marketable securities in the consolidated balance sheets. Restricted investments consist of long-term duration marketable securities that we hold through a custodial account to fund the estimated future costs of our solar module collection and recycling obligations and accordingly we classify all restricted investments as noncurrent assets under the caption restricted cash and investments in the consolidated balance sheets.

All of our available-for-sale marketable securities and restricted investments are subject to a periodic impairment review. We consider a marketable security or restricted investment to be impaired when its fair value is less than its carrying cost, in which case we would further review the marketable security or restricted investment to determine if it is other-than-temporarily impaired. When we evaluate a marketable security or restricted investment for other-than-temporary impairment, we review factors such as the length of time and extent to which its fair value has been below its cost basis, the financial conditions of the issuer and any changes thereto, our intent to sell, and whether it is more likely than not that we will be required to sell the marketable security or restricted investment before we have recovered its cost basis. If a marketable security or restricted investment were other-than-temporarily impaired, we would write it down through earnings to its impaired value and establish that as a new cost basis for the marketable security or restricted investment.

8. Restricted Cash and Investments

Restricted cash and investments consisted of the following at December 31, 2013 and 2012 (in thousands):

	2013	2012
Restricted cash, noncurrent	$ 167	$ 184
Restricted investments, noncurrent	279,274	301,216
Total restricted cash and investments, noncurrent[(1)]	$279,441	$301,400

[(1)] There was zero and $5.1 million of restricted cash included within prepaid expenses and other current assets at December 31, 2013 and 2012, respectively, primarily related to required cash collateral for certain letters of credit provided for projects under development in foreign jurisdictions.

At December 31, 2013 and 2012, our restricted investments consisted of long-term marketable securities that we hold through a custodial account to fund the estimated future costs of our collecting and recycling modules covered under our solar module collection and recycling program. We have classified our restricted investments as "available-for-sale." Accordingly, we record them at fair value and account for net unrealized gains and losses as a part of accumulated other comprehensive income (loss). We report realized gains and losses on the maturity or sale of our restricted investments in other income (expense), net computed using the specific identification method. Restricted investments are classified as noncurrent as the underlying accrued solar module collection and recycling liability is also noncurrent in nature.

We fund the estimated collection and recycling obligations incremental to amounts already pre-funded in prior years for the cumulative module sales covered by our solar module collection and recycling program within 90 days of the end of each year, assuming for this purpose a service life of 25 years for our solar modules. To ensure that our collection and recycling program for covered modules is available at all times and the pre-funded amounts are accessible regardless of our financial status in the future (even in the case of our own insolvency), we have established a trust structure (the "Trust") under which estimated required funds are put into custodial accounts with an established and reputable bank as the investment advisor in the name of the Trust, for which First Solar, Inc. ("FSI"), First Solar Malaysia Sdn. Bhd. ("FS Malaysia"), and First Solar Manufacturing GmbH are grantors. Only the trustee can distribute funds from the custodial accounts and these funds cannot be accessed for any purpose other than to cover qualified costs of module collection and recycling, either by us or a third party executing the required collection and recycling services. Investments in this custodial account must meet the criteria of the highest quality investments, such as highly rated government or agency bonds. We closely monitor our exposure to European markets and maintain holdings primarily consisting of German and French sovereign debt securities which are not currently at risk of default. Under the trust agreements, each year we determine the annual pre-funding requirement (if any) based upon the difference between the current estimated future costs of collecting and recycling all solar modules covered under our program combined with the rate of return restricted investments will earn prior to being utilized to cover qualified collection and recycling costs and amounts already pre-funded in prior years. Based primarily upon reductions in the estimated future costs of collecting and recycling solar modules covered under our program combined with the cumulative amounts pre-funded since the inception of our program, we have determined that no incremental funding will be required in the first quarter of 2014 for all historical covered module sales through December 31, 2013.

The following table summarizes unrealized gains and losses related to our restricted investments by major security type as of December 31, 2013 and 2012 (in thousands):

Security Type	As of December 31, 2013			
	Amortized Cost	Gross Unrealized Gains	Gross Unrealized Losses	Estimated Fair Value
Foreign government obligations	$205,484	$22,295	$1,489	$226,290
U.S. government obligations	55,916	1,372	4,304	52,984
Total	$261,400	$23,667	$5,793	$279,274

Security Type	As of December 31, 2012			
	Amortized Cost	Gross Unrealized Gains	Gross Unrealized Losses	Estimated Fair Value
Foreign government obligations	$188,350	$47,921	$—	$236,271
U.S. government obligations	53,368	11,577	—	64,945
Total	$241,718	$59,498	$—	$301,216

As of December 31, 2013, the contractual maturities of these restricted investments were between 14 years and 23 years. As of December 31, 2012, the contractual maturities of these restricted investments were between 15 years and 24 years. As of December 31, 2013, the gross unrealized loss of $5.8 million had been in a continuous loss position for less than 12 months.

DEPOSITS

2.87 INSPERITY, INC. (DEC)
CONSOLIDATED BALANCE SHEETS (in part)

(in thousands)

	December 31, 2013	December 31, 2012
Assets		
Current assets:		
Cash and cash equivalents	$ 225,755	$ 264,544
Restricted cash	51,928	47,149
Marketable securities	46,340	16,904
Accounts receivable, net:		
Trade	7,453	6,931
Unbilled	199,628	181,040
Other	2,928	2,415
Prepaid insurance	10,638	15,620
Other current assets	12,053	9,651
Income taxes receivable	409	—
Deferred income taxes	8,185	7,211
Total current assets	565,317	551,465
Property and equipment:		
Land	4,115	4,115
Buildings and improvements	67,939	68,583
Computer hardware and software	85,241	81,140
Software development costs	38,522	35,866
Furniture and fixtures	36,479	36,717
Aircraft	35,879	35,879
	268,175	262,300
Accumulated depreciation and amortization	(181,760)	(168,358)
Total property and equipment, net	86,415	93,942
Other assets:		
Prepaid health insurance	9,000	9,000
Deposits—health insurance	3,700	3,000
Deposits—workers' compensation	81,878	64,201
Goodwill and other intangible assets, net	18,434	23,775
Other assets	1,816	4,817
Total other assets	114,828	104,793
Total assets	$ 766,560	$ 750,200

NOTES TO CONSOLIDATED FINANCIAL STATEMENTS

December 31, 2013

1. Accounting Policies (in part)

Health Insurance Costs

We provide group health insurance coverage to our worksite employees through a national network of carriers including UnitedHealthcare ("United"), UnitedHealthcare of California, Kaiser Permanente, Blue Shield of California, HMSA BlueCross BlueShield, Unity Health Plan and Tufts, all of which provide fully insured policies or service contracts.

The policy with United provides the majority of our health insurance coverage. As a result of certain contractual terms, we have accounted for this plan since its inception using a partially self-funded insurance accounting model. Accordingly, we record the cost of the United portion of the plan, including an estimate of the incurred claims, taxes and administrative fees (collectively the "Plan Costs") as benefits expense in the Consolidated Statements of Operations. The estimated incurred claims are based upon: (i) the level of claims processed during each quarter; (ii) estimated completion rates based upon recent claim development patterns under the plan; and (iii) the number of participants in the plan, including both active and COBRA enrollees. Each reporting period, changes in the estimated ultimate costs resulting from claim trends, plan design and migration, participant demographics and other factors are incorporated into the benefits costs.

Additionally, since the plan's inception, under the terms of the contract, United establishes cash funding rates 90 days in advance of the beginning of a reporting quarter. If the Plan Costs for a reporting quarter are greater than the premiums paid and owed to United, a deficit in the plan would be incurred and a liability for the excess costs would be accrued in our Consolidated Balance Sheets. On the other hand, if the

Plan Costs for the reporting quarter are less than the premiums paid and owed to United, a surplus in the plan would be incurred and we would record an asset for the excess premiums in our Consolidated Balance Sheets. The terms of the arrangement require us to maintain an accumulated cash surplus in the plan of $9.0 million, which is reported as long-term prepaid insurance. In addition, United requires a deposit equal to approximately one day of claims funding activity, which was $3.5 million as of December 31, 2013, and is reported as a long-term asset.

As of December 31, 2013, Plan Costs were less than the net premiums paid and owed to United by $13.5 million. As this amount is in excess of the agreed-upon $9.0 million surplus maintenance level, the $4.5 million balance is included in prepaid insurance, a current asset, in our Consolidated Balance Sheets. The premiums owed to United at December 31, 2013, were $2.1 million, which is included in accrued health insurance costs, a current liability in our Consolidated Balance Sheets.

Workers' Compensation Costs

Our workers' compensation coverage has been provided through an arrangement with the ACE Group of Companies ("the ACE Program") since 2007. The ACE Program is fully insured in that ACE has the responsibility to pay all claims incurred regardless of whether we satisfy our responsibilities. Through September 30, 2010, we bore the economic burden for the first $1 million layer of claims per occurrence and the insurance carrier was and remains responsible for the economic burden for all claims in excess of such first $1 million layer.

Effective October 1, 2010, in addition to bearing the economic burden for the first $1 million layer of claims per occurrence, we also bear the economic burden for those claims exceeding $1 million, up to a maximum aggregate amount of $5 million per policy year.

Because we bear the economic burden for claims up to the levels noted above, such claims, which are the primary component of our workers' compensation costs, are recorded in the period incurred. Workers' compensation insurance includes ongoing health care and indemnity coverage whereby claims are paid over numerous years following the date of injury. Accordingly, the accrual of related incurred costs in each reporting period includes estimates, which take into account the ongoing development of claims and therefore requires a significant level of judgment.

We employ a third party actuary to estimate our loss development rate, which is primarily based upon the nature of worksite employees' job responsibilities, the location of worksite employees, the historical frequency and severity of workers compensation claims, and an estimate of future cost trends. Each reporting period, changes in the actuarial assumptions resulting from changes in actual claims experience and other trends are incorporated into our workers' compensation claims cost estimates. During the years ended December 31, 2013 and 2012, we reduced accrued workers' compensation costs by $9.3 million and $13.1 million, respectively, for changes in estimated losses related to prior reporting periods. Workers' compensation cost estimates are discounted to present value at a rate based upon the U.S. Treasury rates that correspond with the weighted average estimated claim payout period (the average discount rates utilized in 2013 and 2012 were 0.8% and 0.6%, respectively) and are accreted over the estimated claim payment period and included as a component of direct costs in our Consolidated Statements of Operations.

The following table provides the activity and balances related to incurred but not reported workers' compensation claims:

	Year ended December 31,	
(in thousands)	2013	2012
Beginning balance	$111,685	$104,791
Accrued claims	42,900	37,772
Present value discount	(1,169)	(868)
Paid claims	(32,583)	(30,010)
Ending balance	$120,833	$111,685
Current portion of accrued claims	$ 51,928	$ 47,149
Long-term portion of accrued claims	68,905	64,536
	$120,833	$111,685

The current portion of accrued workers' compensation costs at December 31, 2013 and 2012 includes $1.0 million and $2.3 million, respectively, of workers' compensation administrative fees.

As of December 31, the undiscounted accrued workers' compensation costs were $131.2 million in 2013 and $123.4 million in 2012.

At the beginning of each policy period, the insurance carrier establishes monthly funding requirements comprised of premium costs and funds to be set aside for payment of future claims ("claim funds"). The level of claim funds is primarily based upon anticipated worksite employee payroll levels and expected workers' compensation loss rates, as determined by the insurance carrier. Monies funded into the program for incurred claims expected to be paid within one year are recorded as restricted cash, a short-term asset, while the remainder of claim funds are included in deposits, a long-term asset in our Consolidated Balance Sheets. In 2013, we paid the insurance carrier an additional $5.0 million in claim funds for policy years prior to 2013, which increased deposits. As of December 31, 2013, we had restricted cash of $51.9 million and deposits of $81.9 million.

Our estimate of incurred claim costs expected to be paid within one year are recorded as accrued workers' compensation costs and included in short-term liabilities, while our estimate of incurred claim costs expected to be paid beyond one year are included in long-term liabilities on our Consolidated Balance Sheets.

4. Deposits

The contractual arrangement with United for health insurance coverage requires us to maintain an accumulated cash surplus in the plan of $9.0 million, which is reported as long-term prepaid health insurance. Please read Note 1, "Accounting Policies," for a discussion of our accounting policies for health insurance costs.

As of December 31, 2013, we had $3.7 million in health insurance long-term deposits. Please read Note 1 " Accounting Policies " for a discussion of our accounting policies for health insurance costs.

As of December 31, 2013, we had $81.9 million in workers' compensation long-term deposits. Please read Note 1 " Accounting Policies " for a discussion of our accounting policies for workers' compensation costs.

DEFERRED INCOME TAXES

2.88 THE CHILDREN'S PLACE RETAIL STORES, INC. (JAN)
CONSOLIDATED BALANCE SHEETS (in part)

(In thousands, except par value)

	February 2, 2013	January 28, 2012 (As adjusted)
Assets		
Current assets:		
Cash and cash equivalents	$194,128	$176,655
Short-term investments	15,000	—
Accounts receivable	18,490	17,382
Inventories	266,976	237,786
Prepaid expenses and other current assets	40,927	49,184
Deferred income taxes	9,714	7,921
Total current assets	545,235	488,928
Long-term assets:		
Property and equipment, net	330,101	323,863
Deferred income taxes	43,678	49,054
Other assets	4,396	4,407
Total assets	$923,410	$866,252

NOTES TO CONSOLIDATED FINANCIAL STATEMENTS

1. Basis of Presentation and Summary of Significant Accounting Policies (in part)

Income Taxes

We utilize the liability method of accounting for income taxes as set forth in the " Income Taxes " topic of the FASB ASC. Under the liability method, deferred taxes are determined based on the temporary differences between the financial statement and tax basis of assets and liabilities using tax rates expected to be in effect during the years in which the basis differences reverse. A valuation allowance is recorded when it is more likely than not that any of the deferred tax assets will not be realized. In determining the need for valuation allowances we consider projected future taxable income and the availability of tax planning strategies. If in the future we determine that we would not be able to realize our recorded deferred tax assets, an increase in the valuation allowance would decrease earnings in the period in which such determination is made.

We assess our income tax positions and record tax benefits for all years subject to examination based upon our evaluation of the facts, circumstances and information available at the reporting date. For those tax positions where it is more likely than not that a tax benefit will be sustained, we have recorded the largest amount of tax benefit with a greater than 50% likelihood of being realized upon ultimate settlement with a taxing authority that has full knowledge of all relevant information. For those income tax positions where it is not more likely than not that a tax benefit will be sustained, no tax benefit has been recognized in the financial statements.

12. Income Taxes

Prior years in the below tables have been adjusted for the accounting method change for inventory (see Note 2 for the impact of the change in accounting principle).

The components of income from continuing operations before taxes are as follows (in thousands):

	Fiscal Year Ended		
	February 2, 2013	January 28, 2012	January 29, 2011
U.S.	$36,948	$ 47,101	$ 61,095
Foreign	52,747	57,652	66,585
Total	$89,695	$104,753	$127,680

The components of the Company's provision for income taxes consisted of the following (in thousands):

	Fiscal Year Ended		
	February 2, 2013	January 28, 2012	January 29, 2011
Continuing Operations			
Current—			
Federal	$ 7,575	$ 6,984	$ (207)
State	5,230	6,462	7,240
Foreign	11,674	14,693	16,713
Total current	24,479	28,139	23,746
Deferred—			
Federal	3,045	1,542	22,517
State	(762)	1,590	981
Foreign	(310)	(863)	676
Total deferred	1,973	2,269	24,174
Tax provision as shown on the consolidated statements of operations	$26,452	$30,408	$47,920
Effective tax rate	29.5 %	29.0 %	37.5 %
Discontinued Operations			
Federal	$ —	$ —	$ (249)
State	—	—	(62)
Foreign	—	—	—
Total benefit	$ —	$ —	$ (311)

A reconciliation between the calculated tax provision on income based on statutory rates in effect and the effective tax rate for continuing operations is as follows (in thousands):

	Fiscal Year Ended		
	February 2, 2013	January 28, 2012	January 29, 2011
Calculated income tax provision at federal statutory rate	$31,393	$36,664	$44,688
State income taxes, net of federal benefit	2,904	5,234	5,344
Foreign tax rate differential	(9,044)	(7,064)	(6,850)
Deemed repatriation of foreign income and reversals thereof	—	(870)	5,359
Nondeductible expenses	1,611	1,373	771
Unrecognized tax benefit	(743)	(3,729)	(93)
Change in valuation allowance	1,395	—	—
Other	(1,064)	(1,200)	(1,299)
Total tax provision	$26,452	$30,408	$47,920

The tax effects of temporary differences which give rise to deferred tax assets and liabilities are as follows (in thousands):

	February 2, 2013	January 28, 2012
Current—		
Assets		
Inventory	1,538	1,783
Reserves	12,376	6,109
Foreign tax and other tax credits	—	4,052
Total current assets	13,914	11,944
Liabilities-prepaid expenses	(4,200)	(4,023)
Total current, net	9,714	7,921
Noncurrent—		
Property and equipment	18,519	22,631
Deferred rent	13,598	13,325
Equity compensation	4,401	6,500
Reserves and other	7,160	6,068
Net operating loss carryover and other tax credits	1,395	530
Capital loss carryover	1,560	1,560
Total noncurrent, gross	46,633	50,614
Valuation allowance	(2,955)	(1,560)
Net noncurrent	43,678	49,054
Total deferred tax asset, net	$53,392	$56,975

The Company evaluates its permanent reinvestment assertions with respect to foreign earnings at each reporting period. During the fourth quarter of fiscal 2011 the Company changed its permanent reinvestment assertion as it related to its Hong Kong and other Asian subsidiaries, whereby the Company no longer provides deferred taxes on the undistributed earnings of these subsidiaries. After this date the Company is fully reinvested in all its foreign subsidiaries. This had the effect of reducing the Company's anticipated income tax provision by approximately $6.9 million, of which approximately $0.9 million related to prior year non-repatriated foreign income for which U.S. income taxes were provided.

As of February 2, 2013, the Company has not provided Federal taxes on approximately $169.8 million of unremitted earnings of its foreign subsidiaries. The Company intends to reinvest these earnings to fund expansion in these and other markets outside the U.S. Accordingly, the Company has not provided any provision for income tax expense in excess of foreign jurisdiction income tax requirements relative to such unremitted earnings in the accompanying financial statements. Determining the unrecognized deferred tax liability for these undistributed foreign earnings is not practicable.

The Company has a capital loss carryforward ("CLC") of approximately $3.9 million, which will expire in 2015, if unused. The Company also has an Alternative Minimum Tax credit ("AMT") in Puerto Rico of approximately $1.0 million which does not expire.

In assessing the realizability of deferred tax assets, management considers whether it is more likely than not that some portion or all of the deferred tax assets will not be realized. The ultimate realization of deferred tax assets is dependent upon the generation of future taxable income during the periods in which those temporary differences become realizable.

Management considers the scheduled reversal of deferred tax liabilities, projected future taxable income, and tax planning strategies in making this assessment. The Company has concluded that it is more likely than not that certain deferred tax assets cannot be used in the foreseeable future, principally the CLC in the U.S. and the AMT credit in Puerto Rico. Accordingly, a valuation allowance has been established for these tax benefits. However, to the extent that tax benefits related to these are realized in the future, the reduction of the valuation allowance will reduce income tax expense accordingly.

Deferred tax assets relating to tax benefits of stock-based compensation have been reduced to reflect exercises of stock options and vesting of restricted shares during Fiscal 2011 to the extent recognized for financial statement purposes. Some exercises resulted in tax deductions in excess of previously recorded benefits at the time of grant. Although these additional tax benefits were reflected in the foreign tax credit ("FTC") disclosed above, pursuant to the provisions of the " *Compensation-Stock Compensation* " topic of FASB ASC, they are not recognized in the deferred tax balances until the deductions reduce taxes payable. The windfall deductions do not reduce our current federal taxes payable in Fiscal 2011 because of the FTC generated in the current and prior years. As such, these windfall tax benefits are not reflected in our FTC included in the deferred tax assets disclosed in the above table. Windfall deductions included in our FTC balance but not reflected in the deferred tax assets in the table above were approximately $6.8 million for Fiscal 2011. These windfall deductions were recognized directly into stockholders' equity during Fiscal 2012.

A reconciliation of the gross amounts of unrecognized tax benefits, excluding accrued interest and penalties, is as follows (in thousands):

	February 2, 2013	January 28, 2012
Beginning Balance	$ 6,935	$11,386
Additions for current year tax positions	475	430
Additions for prior year tax positions	100	112
Reductions for prior year tax positions	(158)	(3,344)
Settlements	(39)	(5)
Reductions due to a lapse of the applicable statute of limitations	(1,394)	(1,644)
	$ 5,919	$ 6,935

Approximately $6.1 million of unrecognized tax benefits at February 2, 2013 would affect the Company's effective tax rate if recognized. The Company believes it is reasonably possible that there may be a reduction of approximately $2.5 million of unrecognized tax benefits in the next 12 months as a result of settlements with taxing authorities and statute of limitations expirations.

The Company accrued interest and penalties related to unrecognized tax benefits as part of the provision for income taxes. At February 2, 2013 and January 28, 2012 accrued interest and penalties included in unrecognized tax benefits were approximately $1.9 million and $2.1 million, respectively. Interest, penalties and reversals, thereof, net of taxes, was a benefit of $0.2 million, $0.8 million and a cost of $0.2 million for Fiscal 2012, Fiscal 2011 and Fiscal 2010, respectively. Included in income tax expense for Fiscal 2011, the Company recorded a benefit of approximately $3.7 million related to unrecognized tax benefits primarily as a result of settlements with taxing authorities and statute of limitations expirations.

The Company is subject to tax in the United States and foreign jurisdictions, including Canada and Hong Kong. The Company, joined by its domestic subsidiaries, files a consolidated income tax return for Federal income tax purposes. During fiscal 2009, the Company completed the U.S. Federal income tax audit for fiscal years 2006 and prior. The Company, with certain exceptions, is no longer subject to income tax examinations by state and local or foreign tax authorities for tax years before fiscal 2008.

CASH SURRENDER VALUE OF LIFE INSURANCE

2.89 NORTHROP GRUMMAN CORPORATION (DEC)
CONSOLIDATED STATEMENTS OF FINANCIAL POSITION (in part)

	December 31	
$ in millions	2013	2012
Assets		
Cash and cash equivalents	$ 5,150	$ 3,862
Accounts receivable, net	2,685	2,858
Inventoried costs, net	698	798
Deferred tax assets	605	574
Prepaid expenses and other current assets	350	300
Total current assets	9,488	8,392
Property, plant and equipment, net of accumulated depreciation of $4,337 in 2013 and $4,146 in 2012	2,806	2,887
Goodwill	12,438	12,431
Non-current deferred tax assets	209	1,542
Other non-current assets	1,440	1,291
Total assets	$26,381	$26,543

NOTES TO CONSOLIDATED FINANCIAL STATEMENTS

1. Summary of Significant Accounting Policies (in part)

Cash Surrender Value of Life Insurance Policies

The company maintains whole life insurance policies on a group of executives, which are recorded at their cash surrender value as determined by the insurance carrier. The company also has split-dollar life insurance policies on former officers and executives from acquired businesses, which are recorded at the lesser of their cash surrender value or premiums paid. These policies are utilized as a partial funding source for deferred compensation and other non-qualified employee retirement plans. As of December 31, 2013 and 2012, the carrying values associated with these policies are $287 million and $271 million, respectively, and are recorded in other non-current assets in the consolidated statements of financial position.

DERIVATIVES

2.90 THE COCA-COLA COMPANY (DEC)

CONSOLIDATED BALANCE SHEETS (in part)

(In millions except par value)	December 31, 2013	December 31, 2012
Assets		
Current Assets		
Cash and cash equivalents	$10,414	$ 8,442
Short-term investments	6,707	5,017
Total Cash, Cash Equivalents and Short-Term Investments	17,121	13,459
Marketable securities	3,147	3,092
Trade accounts receivable, less allowances of $61 and $53, respectively	4,873	4,759
Inventories	3,277	3,264
Prepaid expenses and other assets	2,886	2,781
Assets held for sale	—	2,973
Total Current Assets	31,304	30,328
Equity Method Investments	10,393	9,216
Other Investments, Principally Bottling Companies	1,119	1,232
Other Assets	4,661	3,585
Property, Plant And Equipment—net	14,967	14,476
Trademarks With Indefinite Lives	6,744	6,527
Bottlers' Franchise Rights With Indefinite Lives	7,415	7,405
Goodwill	12,312	12,255
Other Intangible Assets	1,140	1,150
Total Assets	$90,055	$86,174

NOTES TO CONSOLIDATED FINANCIAL STATEMENTS

Note 1: Business and Summary of Significant Accounting Policies (in part)

Summary of Significant Accounting Policies (in part)

Derivative Instruments

Our Company, when deemed appropriate, uses derivatives as a risk management tool to mitigate the potential impact of certain market risks. The primary market risks managed by the Company through the use of derivative instruments are foreign currency exchange rate risk, commodity price risk and interest rate risk. All derivatives are carried at fair value in our consolidated balance sheets in the line items prepaid expenses and other assets; other assets; or accounts payable and accrued expenses; and other liabilities, as applicable. The cash flow impact of the Company's derivative instruments is primarily included in our consolidated statements of cash flows in net cash provided by operating activities. Refer to Note 5.

Note 5: Hedging Transactions and Derivative Financial Instruments (in part)

The Company is directly and indirectly affected by changes in certain market conditions. These changes in market conditions may adversely impact the Company's financial performance and are referred to as "market risks." Our Company, when deemed appropriate, uses derivatives as a risk management tool to mitigate the potential impact of certain market risks. The primary market risks managed by the Company through the use of derivative instruments are foreign currency exchange rate risk, commodity price risk and interest rate risk.

The Company uses various types of derivative instruments including, but not limited to, forward contracts, commodity futures contracts, option contracts, collars and swaps. Forward contracts and commodity futures contracts are agreements to buy or sell a quantity of a currency or commodity at a predetermined future date, and at a predetermined rate or price. An option contract is an agreement that conveys the purchaser the right, but not the obligation, to buy or sell a quantity of a currency or commodity at a predetermined rate or price during a period or at a time in the future. A collar is a strategy that uses a combination of options to limit the range of possible positive or negative returns on an underlying asset or liability to a specific range, or to protect expected future cash flows. To do this, an investor simultaneously buys a put option and sells (writes) a call option, or alternatively buys a call option and sells (writes) a put option. A swap agreement is a contract between two parties to exchange cash flows based on specified underlying notional amounts, assets and/or indices. We do not enter into derivative financial instruments for trading purposes.

All derivatives are carried at fair value in our consolidated balance sheets in the following line items, as applicable: prepaid expenses and other assets; other assets; accounts payable and accrued expenses; and other liabilities. The carrying values of the derivatives reflect the impact of legally enforceable master netting agreements and cash collateral held or placed with the same counterparties, as applicable. These master netting agreements allow the Company to net settle positive and negative positions (assets and liabilities) arising from different transactions with the same counterparty.

The accounting for gains and losses that result from changes in the fair values of derivative instruments depends on whether the derivatives have been designated and qualify as hedging instruments and the type of hedging relationships. Derivatives can be designated as fair value hedges, cash flow hedges or hedges of net investments in foreign operations. The changes in the fair values of derivatives that have been designated and qualify for fair value hedge accounting are recorded in the same line item in our consolidated statements of income as the changes in the fair values of the hedged items attributable to the risk being hedged. The changes in fair values of derivatives that have been designated and qualify as cash flow hedges or hedges of net investments in foreign operations are recorded in AOCI and are reclassified into the line item in our consolidated statement of income in which the hedged items are recorded in the same period the hedged items affect earnings. Due to the high degree of effectiveness between the hedging instruments and the underlying exposures being hedged, fluctuations in the value of the derivative instruments are generally offset by changes in the fair values or cash flows of the underlying exposures being hedged. The changes in fair values of derivatives that were not designated and/or did not qualify as hedging instruments are immediately recognized into earnings.

For derivatives that will be accounted for as hedging instruments, the Company formally designates and documents, at inception, the financial instrument as a hedge of a specific underlying exposure, the risk management objective and the strategy for undertaking the hedge transaction. In addition, the Company formally assesses, both at the inception and at least quarterly thereafter, whether the financial instruments used in hedging transactions are effective at offsetting changes in either the fair values or cash flows of the related underlying exposures. Any ineffective portion of a financial instrument's change in fair value is immediately recognized into earnings.

The Company determines the fair values of its derivatives based on quoted market prices or using standard valuation models. Refer to Note 16. The notional amounts of the derivative financial instruments do not necessarily represent amounts exchanged by the parties and, therefore, are not a direct measure of our exposure to the financial risks described above. The amounts exchanged are calculated by reference to the notional amounts and by other terms of the derivatives, such as interest rates, foreign currency exchange rates, commodity rates or other financial indices. The Company does not view the fair values of its derivatives in isolation, but rather in relation to the fair values or cash flows of the underlying hedged transactions or other exposures. Virtually all of our derivatives are straightforward over-the-counter instruments with liquid markets.

The following table presents the fair values of the Company's derivative instruments that were designated and qualified as part of a hedging relationship (in millions):

Derivatives Designated as Hedging Instruments	Balance Sheet Location[1]	Fair Value[1,2] December 31, 2013	December 31, 2012
Assets:			
Foreign currency contracts	Prepaid expenses and other assets	$211	$149
Foreign currency contracts	Other assets	109	—
Commodity contracts	Prepaid expenses and other assets	1	—
Interest rate contracts	Prepaid expenses and other assets	—	7
Interest rate contracts	Other assets	283	335
Total assets		$604	$491
Liabilities:			
Foreign currency contracts	Accounts payable and accrued expenses	$ 84	$ 55
Foreign currency contracts	Other liabilities	40	—
Commodity contracts	Accounts payable and accrued expenses	1	1
Interest rate contracts	Other liabilities	—	6
Total liabilities		$125	$ 62

[1] All of the Company's derivative instruments are carried at fair value in our consolidated balance sheets after considering the impact of legally enforceable master netting agreements and cash collateral held or placed with the same counterparties, as applicable. Current disclosure requirements mandate that derivatives must also be disclosed without reflecting the impact of master netting agreements and cash collateral. Refer to Note 16 for the net presentation of the Company's derivative instruments.

[2] Refer to Note 16 for additional information related to the estimated fair value.

The following table presents the fair values of the Company's derivative instruments that were not designated as hedging instruments (in millions):

Derivatives Not Designated as Hedging Instruments	Balance Sheet Location[1]	Fair Value[1,2]	
		December 31, 2013	December 31, 2012
Assets:			
Foreign currency contracts	Prepaid expenses and other assets	$ 21	$ 19
Foreign currency contracts	Other assets	171	42
Commodity contracts	Prepaid expenses and other assets	33	72
Commodity contracts	Other assets	1	—
Other derivative instruments	Prepaid expenses and other assets	9	6
Total assets		$235	$139
Liabilities:			
Foreign currency contracts	Accounts payable and accrued expenses	$ 24	$ 24
Foreign currency contracts	Other liabilities	—	1
Commodity contracts	Accounts payable and accrued expenses	23	43
Commodity contracts	Other liabilities	—	1
Interest rate contracts	Other liabilities	3	—
Other derivative instruments	Accounts payable and accrued expenses	—	2
Total liabilities		$ 50	$ 71

[1] All of the Company's derivative instruments are carried at fair value in our consolidated balance sheets after considering the impact of legally enforceable master netting agreements and cash collateral held or placed with the same counterparties, as applicable. Current disclosure requirements mandate that derivatives must also be disclosed without reflecting the impact of master netting agreements and cash collateral. Refer to Note 16 for the net presentation of the Company's derivative instruments.

[2] Refer to Note 16 for additional information related to the estimated fair value.

Credit Risk Associated with Derivatives

We have established strict counterparty credit guidelines and enter into transactions only with financial institutions of investment grade or better. We monitor counterparty exposures regularly and review any downgrade in credit rating immediately. If a downgrade in the credit rating of a counterparty were to occur, we have provisions requiring collateral in the form of U.S. government securities for substantially all of our transactions. To mitigate presettlement risk, minimum credit standards become more stringent as the duration of the derivative financial instrument increases. In addition, the Company's master netting agreements reduce credit risk by permitting the Company to net settle for transactions with the same counterparty. To minimize the concentration of credit risk, we enter into derivative transactions with a portfolio of financial institutions. Based on these factors, we consider the risk of counterparty default to be minimal.

Cash Flow Hedging Strategy (in part)

The Company uses cash flow hedges to minimize the variability in cash flows of assets or liabilities or forecasted transactions caused by fluctuations in foreign currency exchange rates, commodity prices or interest rates. The changes in the fair values of derivatives designated as cash flow hedges are recorded in AOCI and are reclassified into the line item in our consolidated statement of income in which the hedged items are recorded in the same period the hedged items affect earnings. The changes in fair values of hedges that are determined to be ineffective are immediately reclassified from AOCI into earnings. During the years ended December 31, 2013, 2012 and 2011, the Company did not record any gains or losses into earnings as a result of the discontinuance of cash flow hedges due to forecasted transactions that were no longer expected to occur. The maximum length of time for which the Company hedges its exposure to the variability in future cash flows is typically three years.

The Company maintains a foreign currency cash flow hedging program to reduce the risk that our eventual U.S. dollar net cash inflows from sales outside the United States and U.S. dollar net cash outflows from procurement activities will be adversely affected by changes in foreign currency exchange rates. We enter into forward contracts and purchase foreign currency options (principally euros and Japanese yen) and collars to hedge certain portions of forecasted cash flows denominated in foreign currencies. When the U.S. dollar strengthens against the foreign currencies, the decline in the present value of future foreign currency cash flows is partially offset by gains in the fair value of the derivative instruments. Conversely, when the U.S. dollar weakens, the increase in the present value of future foreign currency cash flows is partially offset by losses in the fair value of the derivative instruments. The total notional values of derivatives that have been designated and qualify for the Company's foreign currency cash flow hedging program were $ 8,450 million and $ 4,715 million as of December 31, 2013 and 2012, respectively.

The Company has entered into commodity futures contracts and other derivative instruments on various commodities to mitigate the price risk associated with forecasted purchases of materials used in our manufacturing process. The derivative instruments have been designated and qualify as part of the Company's commodity cash flow hedging program. The objective of this hedging program is to reduce the variability of cash flows associated with future purchases of certain commodities. The total notional values of derivatives that have been designated and qualify for this program were $ 26 million and $ 17 million as of December 31, 2013 and 2012, respectively.

Our Company monitors our mix of short-term debt and long-term debt regularly. From time to time, we manage our risk to interest rate fluctuations through the use of derivative financial instruments. The Company has entered into interest rate swap agreements and has designated these instruments as part of the Company's interest rate cash flow hedging program. The objective of this hedging program is to mitigate the risk of adverse changes in benchmark interest rates on the Company's future interest payments. The total notional values of these interest rate swap agreements that were designated and qualified for the Company's interest rate cash flow hedging program were $ 1,828 million and $ 1,764 million as of December 31, 2013 and 2012, respectively.

Fair Value Hedging Strategy (in part)

The Company uses interest rate swap agreements designated as fair value hedges to minimize exposure to changes in the fair value of fixed-rate debt that results from fluctuations in benchmark interest rates. The changes in fair values of derivatives designated as fair value hedges and the offsetting changes in fair values of the hedged items are recognized in earnings. The ineffective portions of these hedges are immediately recognized in earnings. As of December 31, 2013, such adjustments increased the carrying value of our long-term debt by $ 52 million. Refer to Note 10. When a derivative is no longer designated as a fair value hedge for any reason, including termination and maturity, the remaining unamortized difference between the carrying value of the hedged item at that time and the par value of the hedged item is amortized to earnings over the remaining life of the hedged item, or immediately if the hedged item has matured. The changes in fair values of hedges that are determined to be ineffective are immediately recognized into earnings. The total notional values of derivatives that related to our fair value hedges of this type were $ 5,600 million and $ 6,700 million as of December 31, 2013 and 2012, respectively.

During the first quarter of 2012, the Company began using fair value hedges to minimize exposure to changes in the fair value of certain available-for-sale securities from fluctuations in foreign currency exchange rates. The changes in fair values of derivatives designated as fair value hedges and the offsetting changes in fair values of the hedged items are recognized in earnings. The changes in fair values of hedges that are determined to be ineffective are immediately recognized into earnings. The total notional values of derivatives that related to our fair value hedges of this type were $ 996 million and $ 850 million as of December 31, 2013 and 2012, respectively.

Hedges of Net Investments in Foreign Operations Strategy (in part)

The Company uses forward contracts to protect the value of our investments in a number of foreign subsidiaries. For derivative instruments that are designated and qualify as hedges of net investments in foreign operations, the changes in fair values of the derivative instruments are recognized in net foreign currency translation gain (loss), a component of AOCI, to offset the changes in the values of the net investments being hedged. Any ineffective portions of net investment hedges are reclassified from AOCI into earnings during the period of change. The total notional values of derivatives under this hedging program were $ 2,024 million and $ 1,718 million as of December 31, 2013 and 2012, respectively.

The following table presents the pretax impact that changes in the fair values of derivatives designated as net investment hedges had on AOCI during the years ended December 31, 2013, 2012 and 2011 (in millions):

Economic (Non-Designated) Hedging Strategy (in part)

In addition to derivative instruments that are designated and qualify for hedge accounting, the Company also uses certain derivatives as economic hedges of foreign currency, interest rate and commodity exposure. Although these derivatives were not designated and/or did not qualify for hedge accounting, they are effective economic hedges. The changes in fair value of economic hedges are immediately recognized into earnings.

The Company uses foreign currency economic hedges to offset the earnings impact that fluctuations in foreign currency exchange rates have on certain monetary assets and liabilities denominated in nonfunctional currencies. The changes in fair value of economic hedges used to offset the monetary assets and liabilities are recognized into earnings in the line item other income (loss)—net in our consolidated statements of income. In addition, we use foreign currency economic hedges to minimize the variability in cash flows associated with changes in foreign currency exchange rates. The changes in fair value of economic hedges used to offset the variability in U.S. dollar net cash flows are recognized into earnings in the line items net operating revenues and cost of goods sold in our consolidated statements of income. The total notional values of derivatives related to our foreign currency economic hedges were $ 3,871 million and $ 3,865 million as of December 31, 2013 and 2012, respectively.

The Company also uses certain derivatives as economic hedges to mitigate the price risk associated with the purchase of materials used in the manufacturing process and for vehicle fuel. The changes in fair values of these economic hedges are immediately recognized into earnings in the line items net operating revenues, cost of goods sold, and selling, general and administrative expenses in our consolidated statements of income, as applicable. The total notional values of derivatives related to our economic hedges of this type were $ 1,441 million and $ 1,084 million as of December 31, 2013 and 2012, respectively.

SOFTWARE

2.91 THE DUN & BRADSTREET CORPORATION (DEC)
CONSOLIDATED BALANCE SHEETS (in part)

	December 31,	
(Amounts in millions, except per share data)	2013	2012
Assets		
Current Assets		
Cash and Cash Equivalents	$ 235.9	$ 149.1
Accounts Receivable, Net of Allowance of $23.9 at December 31, 2013 and $27.3 at December 31, 2012	518.5	514.3
Other Receivables	6.3	6.5
Prepaid Taxes	9.1	—
Deferred Income Tax	14.0	26.3
Other Prepaids	30.3	46.8
Other Current Assets	8.3	4.4
Total Current Assets	822.4	747.4
Non-Current Assets		
Property, Plant and Equipment, Net of Accumulated Depreciation of $83.9 at December 31, 2013 and $81.2 at December 31, 2012	39.6	40.6
Computer Software, Net of Accumulated Amortization of $474.1 at December 31, 2013 and $431.9 at December 31, 2012	107.9	140.9
Goodwill	589.1	611.1
Deferred Income Tax	148.4	247.8
Other Receivables	45.6	47.1
Other Intangibles (Note 15)	76.7	99.3
Other Non-Current Assets	60.6	57.6
Total Non-Current Assets	1,067.9	1,244.4
Total Assets	$1,890.3	$1,991.8

NOTES TO CONSOLIDATED FINANCIAL STATEMENTS

(Tabular dollar amounts in millions, except per share data)

Note 1. Description of Business and Summary of Significant Accounting Policies (in part)

Significant Accounting Policies (in part)

Computer Software. We develop various computer software applications for internal use including systems which support our databases and common business services and processes (back-end systems), our financial and administrative systems (backoffice systems) and systems which we use to deliver our information solutions to customers (customer-facing systems).

We expense costs as incurred during the preliminary development stage which includes conceptual formulation and review of alternatives. Once that stage is complete, we begin the application development stage which includes design, coding and testing. Direct internal and external costs incurred during this stage are capitalized. Capitalization of costs cease when the software is ready for its intended use and all substantial testing is completed. Upgrades and enhancements which provide added functionality are accounted for in the same manner. Maintenance costs incurred solely to extend the life of the software are expensed as incurred.

We periodically reassess the estimated useful lives of our computer software considering our overall technology strategy, the effects of obsolescence, technology, competition and other economic factors on the useful life of these assets.

Internal-use software is tested for impairment along with other long-lived assets (See Impairment of Long-Lived Assets).

We also develop software for sale to customers. Costs are expensed until technological feasibility is established after which costs are capitalized until the software is ready for general release to customers. Costs of enhancements that extend the life or improve the marketability of the software are capitalized once technological feasibility is reached. Maintenance and customer support are expensed as incurred.

Capitalized costs of software for sale are amortized on a straight-line basis over the estimated economic life of the software of three years. We continually evaluate recoverability of the unamortized costs, which are reported at the lower of unamortized cost or net realizable value.

The computer software amortization expense for the years ended December 31, 2013, 2012 and 2011 were $46.9 million, $49.2 million and $46.0 million, respectively. As of December 31, 2013 and 2012, we acquired $2.9 million and $4.2 million, respectively, of computer software, which was included in accounts payable and accrued liabilities on the accompanying consolidated balance sheets as of December 31, 2013 and 2012, and was therefore excluded from the consolidated statements of cash flows for the years ended December 31, 2013 and 2012, respectively.

Impairment of Long-Lived Assets (in part). Long-lived assets, including property, plant and equipment, internal-use software and other intangible assets held for use, are tested for impairment when events or circumstances indicate the carrying amount of the asset group that includes these assets is not recoverable. An asset group is the lowest level for which its cash flows are independent of the cash flows of other asset groups. The carrying value of an asset group is not considered recoverable if the carrying value exceeds the sum of the undiscounted cash flows expected to result from the use and eventual disposition of the asset group. The impairment loss is measured by the difference between the carrying value of the asset group and its fair value. We generally estimate the fair value of an asset group using an income approach.

During the fourth quarter of 2013, we recorded an impairment charge of $31.3 million primarily related to (i) technology and software assets that were primarily related to our data management infrastructure (data supply chain) in our North America segment. We can improve data collection through other commercially available means, as needed. We determined that the fair value of these assets is zero based on Level III inputs (see "Fair Value of Financial Instruments" below for discussion on Level inputs), as market data is not readily available. Of the $31.3 million impairment charge, $28.6 million was included in "Operating Costs" and $2.7 million was included in "Selling and Administrative Expenses" in our North America segment.

During the fourth quarter of 2013, we also recorded an impairment charge of $1.7 million related to our China Trade Portal ("Portal") asset resulting from lower than expected product revenue. We decided to sunset the Portal product and migrate our existing Portal customers to an enhanced version of our existing DUNS Registered Seal product. We determined that the fair value of these assets is zero based on Level III inputs (see "Fair Value of Financial Instruments" below for discussion on Level inputs) as market data is not readily available. The impairment charge was included in "Operating Costs" in our Asia Pacific segment.

During the first quarter of 2012, we recorded an impairment charge of $12.9 million related to the accounts receivable, intangible assets, prepaid costs and software for Roadway, an operation in our Greater China reporting unit. See Note 13 to the consolidated financial statements included in this Annual Report on Form 10-K for further discussion. We determined that the fair value of these intangible assets, prepaid costs and software is zero based on Level III inputs (see "Fair Value of Financial Instruments" below for discussion on Level inputs), as market data of these assets are not readily available. We wrote down the accounts receivable balance to its realizable value based on the probability of collecting from the customer accounts. Of the $12.9 million impairment charge, $4.1 million was included in "Operating Costs" and $8.8 million was included in "Selling and Administrative Expenses" in our Asia Pacific segment.

DEBT ISSUANCE COSTS

2.92 HANESBRANDS INC. (DEC)
CONSOLIDATED BALANCE SHEETS (in part)

(In thousands, except share and per share amounts)

	December 28, 2013	December 29, 2012
Assets		
Cash and cash equivalents	$ 115,863	$ 42,796
Trade accounts receivable, net	578,558	506,278
Inventories	1,283,331	1,253,136
Deferred tax assets	197,260	166,189
Other current assets	68,654	59,126
Total current assets	2,243,666	2,027,525
Property, net	579,883	596,158
Trademarks and other identifiable intangibles, net	377,751	120,114
Goodwill	626,392	433,300
Deferred tax assets	207,426	397,529
Other noncurrent assets	54,930	57,074
Total assets	$4,090,048	$3,631,700

Years ended December 28, 2013, December 29, 2012 and December 31, 2011

(Amounts in thousands, except per share data)

(10) Debt (in part)

Debt Issuance Costs

During 2013, 2012 and 2011, the Company incurred $5,630, $2,353 and $3,757, respectively, in capitalized debt issuance costs in connection with the amendments to the Senior Secured Credit Facility and the Accounts Receivable Securitization Facility. Debt issuance costs are amortized to interest expense over the respective lives of the debt instruments, which range from one to ten years. As of December 28, 2013, the net carrying value of unamortized debt issuance costs was $31,048 which is included in "Other Noncurrent Assets" in the Consolidated Balance Sheet. The Company's debt issuance cost amortization was $6,921, $9,168 and $10,367 in 2013, 2012 and 2011, respectively.

The Company recognizes charges in the "Other expenses" line of the Consolidated Statements of Income for fees incurred in financing transactions such as refinancing and amendments and for write-offs incurred in the early extinguishment of debt. In 2013 and 2012, the Company recognized charges of $14,749 and $33,906, respectively, for the call premium and acceleration of unamortized debt costs related to the redemption of the 8% Senior Notes. In addition, in 2012 the Company recognized combined charges of $3,272 of write-offs on early extinguishment of debt related to the Floating Rate Senior Notes and the Revolving Loan Facility. In 2011, the Company recognized charges of $3,297 of a write-off on early extinguishment of debt related to the Floating Rate Senior Notes.

Short-Term Debt

Author's Note
In February 2013, FASB issued ASU No. 2013-04, *Liabilities (Topic 405): Obligations Resulting from Joint and Several Liability Arrangements for Which the Total Amount of the Obligation Is Fixed at the Reporting Date*, to provide guidance for the recognition, measurement, and disclosure of obligations resulting from joint and several liability arrangements for which the total amount of the obligation within the scope of this guidance is fixed at the reporting date, except for obligations addressed within existing guidance in U.S. generally accepted accounting principles (GAAP). Examples of obligations within the scope of this update include debt arrangements, other contractual obligations, and settled litigation and judicial rulings. U.S. GAAP does not include specific guidance on accounting for such obligations with joint and several liability, which has resulted in diversity in practice. Some entities record the entire amount under the joint and several liability arrangement on the basis of the concept of a liability and the guidance that must be met to extinguish a liability. Other entities record less than the total amount of the obligation, such as an amount allocated, an amount corresponding to the proceeds received, or the portion of the amount the entity agreed to pay among its co-obligors, on the basis of the guidance for contingent liabilities. The guidance in this update also requires an entity to disclose the nature and amount of the obligation as well as other information about those obligations. For public entities, the amendments in this update are effective for fiscal years, and interim periods within those years, beginning after December 15, 2013. For nonpublic entities, the amendments are effective for fiscal years ending after December 15, 2014, and interim periods and annual periods thereafter. Given the effective date of this update, no survey entity will have adopted these requirements in its 2013 financial statements.

PRESENTATION

2.93 FASB ASC 470, *Debt*, addresses classification determination for specific debt obligations, such as the following:
- Short-term obligations expected to be refinanced on a long-term basis
- Due-on-demand loan arrangements
- Callable debt
- Sales of future revenue
- Increasing-rate debt
- Debt that includes covenants
- Revolving credit agreements subject to lock-box arrangements and subjective acceleration clauses

DISCLOSURE

2.94 Rule 5-02 of Regulation S-X calls for disclosure of the amount and terms of unused lines of credit for short-term financing, if significant. The weighted average interest rate on short-term borrowings outstanding as of the date of each balance sheet presented should be furnished. Further, the amount of these lines of credit that support commercial paper or similar borrowing arrangements should be separately identified.

2.95 By definition, *short-term notes payable*, *loans payable*, and *commercial paper* are financial instruments. FASB ASC 825 requires disclosure of both the fair value and bases for estimating the fair value of short-term notes payable, loans payable, and commercial paper, unless it is not practicable to estimate that value.

PRESENTATION AND DISCLOSURE EXCERPT

SHORT-TERM DEBT

2.96 DEERE & COMPANY (OCT)
CONSOLIDATED BALANCE SHEET (in part)

As of October 31, 2013 and 2012

(In millions of dollars except per share amounts)

	2013	2012
Liabilities and Stockholders' Equity (in part)		
Liabilities		
Short-term borrowings	$ 8,788.9	$ 6,392.5
Short-term securitization borrowings	4,109.1	3,574.8
Payables to unconsolidated affiliates	106.9	135.2
Accounts payable and accrued expenses	8,973.6	8,988.9
Deferred income taxes	160.3	164.4
Long-term borrowings	21,577.7	22,453.1
Retirement benefits and other liabilities	5,416.7	7,694.9
Liabilities held for sale	120.4	
Total liabilities	49,253.6	49,403.8

NOTES TO CONSOLIDATED FINANCIAL STATEMENTS

18. Total Short-Term Borrowings

Total short-term borrowings at October 31 consisted of the following in millions of dollars:

	2013	2012
Equipment Operations		
Commercial paper		$ 146
Notes payable to banks	$ 259	84
Long-term borrowings due within one year	821	195
Total	1,080	425
Financial Services		
Commercial paper	3,162	1,061
Notes payable to banks	139	117
Long-term borrowings due within one year	4,408*	4,790*
Total	7,709	5,968
Short-term borrowings	8,789	6,393
Financial Services		
Short-term securitization borrowings	4,109	3,575
Total short-term borrowings	$12,898	$9,968

* Includes unamortized fair value adjustments related to interest rate swaps.

The short-term securitization borrowings for financial services are secured by financing receivables (retail notes) on the balance sheet (see Note 13). Although these securitization borrowings are classified as short-term since payment is required if the retail notes are liquidated early, the payment schedule for these borrowings of $4,109 million at October 31, 2013 based on the expected liquidation of the retail notes in millions of dollars is as follows: 2014—$2,162, 2015—$1,177, 2016—$577, 2017—$166, 2018—$25 and 2019—$2.

The weighted-average interest rates on total short-term borrowings, excluding current maturities of long-term borrowings, at October 31, 2013 and 2012 were .8 percent and 1.0 percent, respectively.

Lines of credit available from U.S. and foreign banks were $6,498 million at October 31, 2013. At October 31, 2013, $2,939 million of these worldwide lines of credit were unused. For the purpose of computing the unused credit lines, commercial paper and short-term bank borrowings, excluding secured borrowings and the current portion of long-term borrowings, were primarily considered to constitute utilization. Included in the above lines of credit were long-term credit facility agreements for $2,500 million, expiring in April 2017, and $2,500 million, expiring in April 2018. The agreements are mutually extendable and the annual facility fees are not significant. These credit agreements require Capital Corporation to maintain its consolidated ratio of earnings to fixed charges at not less than 1.05 to 1 for each fiscal quarter and the ratio of senior debt, excluding securitization indebtedness, to capital base (total subordinated debt and stockholder's equity excluding accumulated other comprehensive income (loss)) at not more than 11 to 1 at the end of any fiscal quarter. The credit agreements also require the equipment operations to maintain a ratio of total debt to total capital (total debt and stockholders' equity excluding accumulated other comprehensive income (loss)) of 65 percent or less at the end of each fiscal quarter. Under this provision, the company's excess equity capacity and retained earnings balance free of restriction at October 31, 2013 was $9,756 million. Alternatively under this provision, the equipment operations had the capacity to incur additional debt of $18,119 million at October 31, 2013. All of these requirements of the credit agreements have been met during the periods included in the consolidated financial statements.

Deere & Company has an agreement with Capital Corporation pursuant to which it has agreed to continue to own, directly or through one or more wholly-owned subsidiaries, at least 51 percent of the voting shares of capital stock of Capital Corporation and to maintain Capital Corporation's consolidated tangible net worth at not less than $50 million. This agreement also obligates Deere & Company to make payments to Capital Corporation such that its consolidated ratio of earnings to fixed charges is not less than 1.05 to 1 for each fiscal quarter. Deere & Company's obligations to make payments to Capital Corporation under the agreement are independent of whether Capital Corporation is in default on its indebtedness, obligations or other liabilities. Further, Deere & Company's obligations under the agreement are not measured by the amount of Capital Corporation's indebtedness, obligations or other liabilities. Deere & Company's obligations to make payments under this agreement are expressly stated not to be a guaranty of any specific indebtedness, obligation or liability of Capital Corporation and are enforceable only by or in the name of Capital Corporation. No payments were required under this agreement during the periods included in the consolidated financial statements.

Trade Accounts Payable

RECOGNITION AND MEASUREMENT

2.97 FASB ASC 210 states that current liabilities generally include obligations for items that have entered into the operating cycle, such as payables incurred in the acquisition of materials and supplies to be used in the production of goods or in providing services to be offered for sale.

PRESENTATION

2.98 Rule 5.02 of Regulation S-X requires that amounts payable to trade creditors be separately stated.

DISCLOSURE

2.99 Under FASB ASC 825, fair value disclosure is not required for trade payables when the carrying amount of the trade payable approximates its fair value.

Employee-Related Liabilities

PRESENTATION

2.100 FASB ASC 715, *Compensation—Retirement Benefits*, requires that an entity recognize the overfunded or underfunded status of a single-employer defined benefit postretirement plan as an asset or a liability in its statement of financial position. FASB ASC 715 also requires that an employer that presents a classified balance sheet should classify the liability for an underfunded plan as a current liability, a noncurrent liability, or a combination of both. The current portion (determined on a plan-by-plan basis) is the amount by which the actuarial present value of benefits included in the benefit obligation that is payable in the next 12 months, or operating cycle if longer, exceeds the fair value of plan assets. The asset for an overfunded plan should be classified as a noncurrent asset in a classified balance sheet. The amount classified as a current liability is limited to the amount of the plan's unfunded status recognized in the employer's balance sheet.

DISCLOSURE

2.101 FASB ASC 715 requires that employers recognize changes in that funded status in comprehensive income and disclose in the notes to financial statements additional information about plan assets, the benefit obligation, reconciliations of beginning and ending balances of both plan assets and obligations, and net periodic benefit cost.

2.102 FASB ASC 715—80 requires additional discloses related to multiemployer plans. An entity should include details in these disclosures including plan names and identifying numbers for significant multiemployer plans, the level of employer's participation in the plans, the financial health of the plans, and the nature of the employer commitments to the plans.

PRESENTATION AND DISCLOSURE EXCERPTS

EMPLOYEE-RELATED LIABILITIES

2.103 THE BOEING COMPANY (DEC)
CONSOLIDATED STATEMENTS OF FINANCIAL POSITION (in part)

	December 31,	
(Dollars in millions, except per share data)	2013	2012
Liabilities and Equity (in part)		
Accounts payable	$ 9,498	$ 9,394
Accrued liabilities	14,131	12,995
Advances and billings in excess of related costs	20,027	16,672
Deferred income taxes and income taxes payable	6,267	4,485
Short-term debt and current portion of long-term debt	1,563	1,436
Total current liabilities	51,486	44,982
Accrued retiree health care	6,528	7,528
Accrued pension plan liability, net	10,474	19,651
Non-current income taxes payable	156	366
Other long-term liabilities	950	1,429
Long-term debt	8,072	8,973

NOTES TO THE CONSOLIDATED FINANCIAL STATEMENTS

Years ended December 31, 2013, 2012 and 2011

(Dollars in millions, except per share data)

Note 1—Summary of Significant Accounting Policies (in part)

Postretirement Plans

The majority of our employees are earning benefits under defined benefit pension plans. All nonunion and some union employees hired after December 31, 2008 are not covered by defined benefit plans. We also provide postretirement benefit plans other than pensions, consisting principally of health care coverage to eligible retirees and qualifying dependents. Benefits under the pension and other postretirement benefit plans are generally based on age at retirement and years of service and, for some pension plans, benefits are also based on the employee's annual earnings. The net periodic cost of our pension and other postretirement plans is determined using the projected unit credit method and several actuarial assumptions, the most significant of which are the discount rate, the long-term rate of asset return, and medical trend (rate of growth for medical costs). A portion of net periodic pension and other postretirement income or expense is not recognized in net earnings in the year incurred because it is allocated to production as product costs, and reflected in inventory at the end of a reporting period. Actuarial gains and losses, which occur when actual experience differs from actuarial assumptions, are reflected in Shareholders' equity (net of taxes). If actuarial gains and losses exceed ten percent of the greater of plan assets or plan liabilities we amortize them over the average future service period of employees. The funded status of our pension and postretirement plans is reflected on the Consolidated Statements of Financial Position.

Note 14—Postretirement Plans (in part)

The majority of our employees are earning benefits under defined benefit pension plans. All nonunion and some union employees hired after December 31, 2008 are not covered by defined benefit plans. We fund our major pension plans through trusts. Pension assets are placed in trust solely for the benefit of the plans' participants, and are structured to maintain liquidity that is sufficient to pay benefit obligations as well as to keep pace over the long-term with the growth of obligations for future benefit payments.

We also have other postretirement benefits (OPB) other than pensions which consist principally of health care coverage for eligible retirees and qualifying dependents, and to a lesser extent, life insurance to certain groups of retirees. Retiree health care is provided principally until age 65 for approximately half those retirees who are eligible for health care coverage. Certain employee groups, including employees covered by most United Auto Workers bargaining agreements, are provided lifetime health care coverage.

The funded status of the plans is measured as the difference between the plan assets at fair value and the projected benefit obligation (PBO). We have recognized the aggregate of all overfunded plans in Other assets, and the aggregate of all underfunded plans in either Accrued retiree health care or Accrued pension plan liability, net. The portion of the amount by which the actuarial present value of benefits included in the PBO exceeds the fair value of plan assets, payable in the next 12 months, is reflected in Accrued liabilities. The components of net periodic benefit cost were as follows:

	Pension			Other Postretirement Benefits		
Years Ended December 31,	**2013**	**2012**	**2011**	**2013**	**2012**	**2011**
Service cost	$ 1,886	$ 1,649	$ 1,406	$ 148	$ 146	$221
Interest cost	2,906	3,005	3,116	263	313	484
Expected return on plan assets	(3,874)	(3,831)	(3,741)	(6)	(7)	(6)
Amortization of prior service costs	196	225	244	(180)	(197)	(96)
Recognized net actuarial loss	2,231	1,937	1,254	95	119	178
Settlement and curtailment loss	104	25	64		(1)	3
Net periodic benefit cost	$ 3,449	$ 3,010	$ 2,343	$ 320	$ 373	$784
Net periodic benefit cost included in Earnings from operations	$ 3,036	$ 2,407	$ 1,648	$ 353	$ 543	$692

During the quarter ended September 30, 2011, we determined the accumulated benefit obligation (ABO) for certain other postretirement benefit plans was understated. As a result, we recognized an additional $294 of postretirement benefit obligations at September 30, 2011. This increased net periodic benefit cost during 2011 by $184, which includes service cost of $73, interest cost of $68 and recognized net actuarial loss of $43.

Under our accounting policy, a portion of net periodic benefit cost is allocated to production as inventoried costs. Of the $184 increase in net periodic benefit cost described above, the associated cost included in Earnings from operations was $161 for the quarter ended September 30, 2011, with the remaining cost of $23 classified as inventory.

The following tables show changes in the benefit obligation, plan assets and funded status of both pensions and OPB for the years ended December 31, 2013 and 2012. Benefit obligation balances presented below reflect the PBO for our pension plans, and accumulated postretirement benefit obligations (APBO) for our OPB plans.

	Pension		Other Postretirement Benefits	
	2013	**2012**	**2013**	**2012**
Change in Benefit Obligation				
Beginning balance	$75,895	$67,651	$7,981	$7,997
Service cost	1,886	1,649	148	146
Interest cost	2,906	3,005	263	313
Plan participants' contributions	8	9		
Amendments	111	13	4	12
Actuarial (gain)/loss	(9,205)	6,378	(905)	(53)
Settlement/curtailment/other	(81)	(76)	(57)	(1)
Gross benefits paid	(2,874)	(2,744)	(451)	(474)
Subsidies			32	37
Exchange rate adjustment	(21)	10	(7)	4
Ending balance	$68,625	$75,895	$7,008	$7,981

(continued)

	Pension		Other Postretirement Benefits	
	2013	2012	2013	2012
Change in Plan Assets				
Beginning balance at fair value	$56,178	$51,051	$110	$102
Actual return on plan assets	3,316	6,300	23	1
Company contribution	1,542	1,550	14	15
Plan participants' contributions	8	9	3	3
Settlement/curtailment/other	(103)	(71)	11	10
Benefits paid	(2,792)	(2,669)	(21)	(21)
Exchange rate adjustment	(18)	8		
Ending balance at fair value	$58,131	$56,178	$140	$110
Amounts Recognized in Statement of Financial Position at December 31 Consist of:				
Other assets	$ 60	$ 5		
Other accrued liabilities	(80)	(71)	($340)	($343)
Accrued retiree health care			(6,528)	(7,528)
Accrued pension plan liability, net	(10,474)	(19,651)		
Net amount recognized	($10,494)	($19,717)	($6,868)	($7,871)

Amounts recognized in Accumulated other comprehensive loss at December 31 were as follows:

	Pension		Other Postretirement Benefits	
	2013	2012	2013	2012
Net actuarial loss	$15,460	$26,387	$ 561	$1,651
Prior service costs/(credits)	788	904	(614)	(799)
Total recognized in Accumulated other comprehensive loss	$16,248	$27,291	($53)	$ 852

The estimated amount that will be amortized from Accumulated other comprehensive loss into net periodic benefit cost during the year ended December 31, 2014 is as follows:

	Pension	Other Postretirement Benefits
Recognized net actuarial loss	$1,032	$ 7
Amortization of prior service costs/(credits)	178	(141)
Total	$1,210	($134)

The ABO for all pension plans was $63,491 and $69,312 at December 31, 2013 and 2012. Key information for our plans with ABO in excess of plan assets as of December 31 is as follows:

	2013	2012
Projected benefit obligation	$63,445	$75,851
Accumulated benefit obligation	58,334	69,272
Fair value of plan assets	52,905	56,129

Assumptions

The following assumptions, which are the weighted average for all plans, are used to calculate the benefit obligation at December 31 of each year and the net periodic benefit cost for the subsequent year.

	December 31,		
	2013	2012	2011
Discount rate:			
Pension	4.80 %	3.80 %	4.40 %
Other postretirement benefits	4.20 %	3.30 %	4.00 %
Expected return on plan assets	7.50 %	7.50 %	7.75 %
Rate of compensation increase	4.00 %	4.00 %	3.90 %

The discount rate for each plan is determined based on the plans' expected future benefit payments using a yield curve developed from high quality bonds that are rated as Aa or better by at least half of the four rating agencies utilized as of the measurement date. The yield curve is fitted to yields developed from bonds at various maturity points. Bonds with the ten percent highest and the ten percent lowest yields are omitted. A portfolio of about 400 bonds is used to construct the yield curve. Since corporate bond yields are generally not available at maturities beyond 30 years, it is assumed that spot rates will remain level beyond that 30-year point. The present value of each plan's benefits is calculated by applying the spot/discount rates to projected benefit cash flows. All bonds are U.S. issues, with a minimum outstanding of $50.

The pension fund's expected return on plan assets assumption is derived from a review of actual historical returns achieved by the pension trust and anticipated future long-term performance of individual asset classes. While consideration is given to recent trust performance and historical returns, the assumption represents a long-term, prospective return. The expected return on plan assets component of the net periodic benefit cost for the upcoming plan year is determined based on the expected return on plan assets assumption and the market-related value of plan assets (MRVA). Since our adoption of the accounting standard for pensions in 1987, we have determined the MRVA based on a five-year moving average of plan assets. As of December 31, 2013, the MRVA is approximately $1,340 less than the fair market value of assets.

Assumed health care cost trend rates were as follows:

	December 31,		
	2013	2012	2011
Health care cost trend rate assumed next year	7.00%	7.50%	7.50%
Ultimate trend rate	5.00%	5.00%	5.00%
Year that trend reached ultimate rate	2018	2018	2018

Assumed health care cost trend rates have a significant effect on the amounts reported for the health care plans. To determine the health care cost trend rates we look at a combination of information including ongoing claims cost monitoring, annual statistical analyses of claims data, reconciliation of forecast claims against actual claims, review of trend assumptions of other plan sponsors and national health trends, and adjustments for plan design changes, workforce changes, and changes in plan participant behavior. A one-percentage-point change in assumed health care cost trend rates would have the following effect:

	Increase	Decrease
Effect on total of service and interest cost	$ 57	($47)
Effect on postretirement benefit obligation	681	(575)

2.104 BRIGGS & STRATTON CORPORATION (JUN)
CONSOLIDATED BALANCE SHEETS (in part)

As Of June 30, 2013 and July 1, 2012

(In thousands, except per share data)

Liabilities and Shareholders' Investment (in part)	2013	2012
Current liabilities:		
Accounts payable	$143,189	$151,153
Short-term debt	300	3,000
Accrued liabilities:		
Wages and salaries	35,163	44,756
Warranty	26,167	29,597
Accrued postretirement health care obligation	16,344	22,891
Other	53,592	54,512
Total accrued liabilities	131,266	151,756
Total current liabilities	274,755	305,909
Accrued pension cost	150,131	296,394
Accrued employee benefits	23,458	25,035
Accrued postretirement health care obligation	72,695	89,842
Accrued warranty	18,871	16,415
Other long-term liabilities	14,703	17,666
Long-term debt	225,000	225,000
Commitments and contingencies (Note 12)		

NOTES TO CONSOLIDATED FINANCIAL STATEMENTS

For The Fiscal Years Ended June 30, 2013, July 1, 2012 and July 3, 2011

(2) Summary of Significant Accounting Policies (in part)

Retirement Plans: The Company has noncontributory, defined benefit retirement plans and postretirement benefit plans covering certain employees. Retirement benefits represent a form of deferred compensation, which are subject to change due to changes in assumptions. Management reviews underlying assumptions on an annual basis. Refer to Note 16.

(16) Employee Benefit Costs (in part)

Retirement Plan and Other Postretirement Benefits

The Company has noncontributory, defined benefit retirement plans and other postretirement benefit plans covering certain employees. The Company uses a June 30 measurement date for all of its plans. The following provides a reconciliation of obligations, plan assets and funded status of the plans for the two years indicated (in thousands):

	Pension Benefits		Other Postretirement Benefits	
Actuarial Assumptions:	**2013**	**2012**	**2013**	**2012**
Discounted rate used to determine present value of projected benefit obligation	5.00%	4.45%	4.40%	3.75%
Expected rate of future compensation level increases	3.0–4.0%	3.0–4.0%	n/a	n/a
Expected long-term rate of return on plan assets	8.25%	8.50%	n/a	n/a
Change in Benefit Obligations:				
Projected benefit obligation at beginning of year	$1,236,747	$1,110,299	$ 136,854	$ 161,796
Service cost	13,222	13,764	358	407
Interest cost	50,154	56,762	4,754	6,468
Plan curtailments	(52,236)	(327)	—	1,357
Plan participant contributions	—	—	1,347	1,181
Actuarial (Gain) loss	(56,239)	130,173	(13,309)	(15,984)
Benefits paid	(75,793)	(73,924)	(18,498)	(18,371)
Projected benefit obligation at end of year	$1,115,855	$1,236,747	$ 111,506	$ 136,854
Change in Plan Assets:				
Fair value of plan assets at beginning of year	$ 937,745	$ 916,210	$ —	$ —
Actual return on plan assets	68,296	63,822	—	—
Plan participant contributions	—	—	1,347	1,181
Employer contributions	32,385	31,637	17,151	17,190
Benefits paid	(75,793)	(73,924)	(18,498)	(18,371)
Fair value of plan assets at end of year	$ 962,633	$ 937,745	$ —	$ —
Funded Status:				
Plan assets (less than) in excess of projected benefit obligation	$ (153,222)	$ (299,002)	$(111,506)	$(136,854)
Amounts Recognized on the Balance Sheets:				
Accrued pension cost	$ (150,131)	$ (296,394)	$ —	$ —
Accrued wages and salaries	(3,091)	(2,608)	—	—
Accrued postretirement health care obligation	—	—	(72,695)	(89,842)
Accrued liabilities	—	—	(16,113)	(22,827)
Accrued employee benefits	—	—	(22,698)	(24,185)
Net amount recognized at end of year	$ (153,222)	$ (299,002)	$(111,506)	$(136,854)
Amounts Recognized in Accumulated Other Comprehensive Income (Loss):				
Transition assets (obligation)	$ —	$ (5)	$ —	$ —
Net actuarial loss	(211,444)	(294,258)	(28,668)	(41,437)
Prior service credit (cost)	(660)	(2,051)	8,008	10,198
Net amount recognized at end of year	$ (212,104)	$ (296,314)	$ (20,660)	$ (31,239)

The accumulated benefit obligation for all defined benefit pension plans was $1,115 million and $1,186 million at June 30, 2013 and July 1, 2012, respectively.

The following table summarizes the plans' income and expense for the three years indicated (in thousands):

	Pension Benefits			Other Postretirement Benefits		
	2013	**2012**	**2011**	**2013**	**2012**	**2011**
Components of net periodic (income) expense:						
Service cost-benefits earned during the year	$ 13,222	$ 13,764	$ 13,475	$ 358	$ 407	$ 486
Interest cost on projected benefit obligation	50,154	56,762	56,696	4,754	6,468	7,088
Expected return on plan assets	(75,832)	(76,445)	(76,975)	—	—	—
Amortization of:						
Transition obligation	7	8	8	—	—	—
Prior service cost (credit)	366	2,856	3,059	(3,589)	(3,800)	(3,485)
Actuarial loss	34,821	20,230	17,771	7,624	8,942	10,268
Net curtailment loss	1,914	375	—	—	359	—
Net periodic expense	$ 24,652	$ 17,550	$ 14,034	$ 9,147	$12,376	$14,357

Significant assumptions used in determining net periodic expense for the fiscal years indicated are as follows:

	Pension Benefits			Other Postretirement Benefits		
	2013	2012	2011	2013	2012	2011
Discount rate	4.45%	5.35%	5.30%	3.75%	4.45%	4.60%
Expected return on plan assets	8.50%	8.50%	8.50%	n/a	n/a	n/a
Compensation increase rate	3.0–4.0%	3.0–4.0%	3.0–4.0%	n/a	n/a	n/a

The amounts in Accumulated Other Comprehensive Income that are expected to be recognized as components of net periodic (income) expense during the next fiscal year are as follows (in thousands):

	Pension Plans	Other Postretirement Plans
Transition obligation	$ —	$ —
Prior service cost (credit)	180	(2,895)
Net actuarial loss	25,076	5,837

The "Other Postretirement Benefit" plans are unfunded.

On May 14, 2010, the Company notified retirees and certain retirement eligible employees of various changes to the Company-sponsored retiree medical plans. The purpose of the amendments was to better align the plans offered to both hourly and salaried retirees. On August 16, 2010, a putative class of retirees who retired prior to August 1, 2006 and the United Steel Workers filed a complaint in the U.S. District Court for the Eastern District of Wisconsin (Merrill, Weber, Carpenter, et al; United Steel, Paper and Forestry, Rubber, Manufacturing, Energy, Allied Industrial and Service Workers International Union, AFL-CIO/CLC v. Briggs & Stratton Corporation; Group Insurance Plan of Briggs & Stratton Corporation; and Does 1 through 20, Docket No. 10-C-0700), contesting the Company's right to make these changes. In addition to a request for class certification, the complaint seeks an injunction preventing the alleged unilateral termination or reduction in insurance coverage to the class of retirees, a permanent injunction preventing defendants from ever making changes to the retirees' insurance coverage, restitution with interest (if applicable) and attorneys' fees and costs. The Company moved to dismiss the complaint and believes the changes are within its rights. On April 21, 2011, the district court issued an order granting the Company's motion to dismiss the complaint. The plaintiffs filed a motion with the court to reconsider its order on May 17, 2011, and on August 24, 2011 the court granted the motion and vacated the dismissal of the case. The Company then filed a motion with the court to appeal its decision directly to the U.S. Court of Appeals for the Seventh Circuit, but the court denied this motion on February 29, 2012. On October 9, 2012 the court granted the parties' unopposed motion for class certification. Discovery is underway in the case.

For measurement purposes an 8.1% annual rate of increase in the per capita cost of covered health care claims was assumed for the Company for the fiscal year 2013 decreasing gradually to 4.5% for the fiscal year 2028. The health care cost trend rate assumptions have a significant effect on the amounts reported. An increase of one percentage point, would increase the accumulated postretirement benefit by $2.3 million and would increase the service and interest cost by $0.1 million for fiscal 2013. A corresponding decrease of one percentage point, would decrease the accumulated postretirement benefit by $2.5 million and decrease the service and interest cost by $0.1 million for the fiscal year 2013.

In October 2012, the Board of Directors of the Company authorized an amendment to the Company's defined benefit retirement plans for U.S., non-bargaining employees. The amendment freezes accruals for all non-bargaining employees within the pension plan effective January 1, 2014. The Company recorded a pre-tax curtailment charge of $1.9 million in fiscal 2013 related to the defined benefit plan change.

As discussed in Note 17, the Company reduced its salaried headcount by approximately 10% in fiscal 2012. The termination of the employees associated with this restructuring action, and the related impact on unrecognized prior service costs, unrecognized losses and the projected benefit obligation resulted in a net curtailment loss of $0.7 million in fiscal 2012.

In fiscal 2012, as a result of the non-discrimination testing results of the qualified pension plan, approximately 90 employees were moved to the non-qualified pension plan. Benefits accrued prior to July 1, 2012 were unaffected; only benefits accruing for those affected employees after July 1, 2012 are being covered by the non-qualified plan.

2.105 HARLEY-DAVIDSON, INC. (DEC)

CONSOLIDATED BALANCE SHEETS (in part)

December 31, 2013 and 2012

(In thousands, except share amounts)

	2013	2012
Liabilities and Shareholders' Equity (in part)		
Current liabilities:		
Accounts payable	$ 239,794	$ 257,386
Accrued liabilities	427,335	513,591
Short-term debt	666,317	294,943
Current portion of long-term debt	1,176,140	437,162
Total current liabilities	2,509,586	1,503,082
Long-term debt	3,416,713	4,370,544
Pension liability	36,371	330,294
Postretirement healthcare liability	216,165	278,062
Deferred income taxes	49,499	—
Other long-term liabilities	167,220	131,167
Commitments and contingencies (Note 16)		

NOTES TO CONSOLIDATED FINANCIAL STATEMENTS

14. Employee Benefit Plans and Other Postretirement Benefits (in part)

The Company has a qualified defined benefit pension plan and several postretirement healthcare benefit plans, which cover employees of the Motorcycles segment. The Company also has unfunded supplemental employee retirement plan agreements (SERPA) with certain employees which were instituted to replace benefits lost under the Tax Revenue Reconciliation Act of 1993. During 2012, the Company consolidated four qualified defined benefit pension plans into one qualified pension plan. The consolidation had no impact on participant benefits.

Obligations and Funded Status:

The following table provides the changes in the benefit obligations, fair value of plan assets and funded status of the Company's pension, SERPA and postretirement healthcare plans as of the Company's December 31, 2013 and 2012 measurement dates (in thousands):

	Pension and SERPA Benefits		Postretirement Healthcare Benefits	
	2013	2012	2013	2012
Change in benefit obligation				
Benefit obligation, beginning of period	$1,871,575	$1,570,930	$ 403,227	$ 380,625
Service cost	35,987	33,681	7,858	7,413
Interest cost	79,248	83,265	15,599	18,310
Actuarial (gains) losses	(199,408)	276,069	(33,729)	23,367
Plan participant contributions	—	1,459	2,609	1,561
Benefits paid, net of Medicare Part D subsidy	(72,752)	(93,829)	(29,040)	(28,049)
Benefit obligation, end of period	1,714,650	1,871,575	366,524	403,227
Change in plan assets:				
Fair value of plan assets, beginning of period	1,539,018	1,253,916	123,106	109,160
Actual return on plan assets	277,388	160,731	24,769	13,946
Company contributions	176,947	216,741	27,849	27,675
Plan participant contributions	—	1,459	2,609	1,561
Benefits paid	(72,752)	(93,829)	(30,458)	(29,236)
Fair value of plan assets, end of period	1,920,601	1,539,018	147,875	123,106
Funded status of the plans, December 31	$ 205,951	$ (332,557)	$(218,649)	$(280,121)
Amounts recognized in the Consolidated Balance Sheets, December 31,:				
Prepaid benefit costs (long-term assets)	$ 244,871	$ —	$ —	$ —
Accrued benefit liability (current liabilities)	(2,549)	(2,263)	(2,484)	(2,059)
Accrued benefit liability (long-term liabilities)	(36,371)	(330,294)	(216,165)	(278,062)
Net amount recognized	$ 205,951	$ (332,557)	$(218,649)	$(280,121)

Benefit Costs:

Components of net periodic benefit costs for the years ended December 31 (in thousands):

	Pension and SERPA Benefits			Postretirement Healthcare Benefits		
	2013	2012	2011	2013	2012	2011
Service cost	$ 35,987	$ 33,681	$ 37,341	$ 7,858	$ 7,413	$ 7,630
Interest cost	79,248	83,265	80,805	15,599	18,310	19,644
Expected return on plan assets	(127,327)	(117,110)	(106,612)	(9,537)	(9,423)	(9,386)
Amortization of unrecognized:						
Prior service cost (credit)	1,746	2,958	2,981	(3,853)	(3,853)	(3,878)
Net loss	58,608	43,874	30,266	8,549	7,421	7,192
Net curtailment loss	—	—	236	—	—	—
Settlement loss	—	6,242	274	—	—	—
Net periodic benefit cost	$ 48,262	$ 52,910	$ 45,291	$18,616	$19,868	$21,202

Net periodic benefit costs are allocated among selling, administrative and engineering expense, cost of goods sold and inventory. The 2010 Restructuring Plan actions discussed in Note 4 resulted in the pension and postretirement healthcare plan net curtailment losses noted in the table above and were included in restructuring expense in the consolidated income statement.

Amounts included in accumulated other comprehensive income, net of tax, at December 31, 2013 which have not yet been recognized in net periodic benefit cost are as follows (in thousands):

	Pension and SERPA Benefits	Postretirement Healthcare Benefits	Total
Prior service cost (credit)	$ 2,390	$(13,495)	$ (11,105)
Net actuarial loss	326,588	48,563	375,151
	$328,978	$ 35,068	$364,046

Amounts expected to be recognized in net periodic benefit cost, net of tax, during the year ended December 31, 2014 are as follows (in thousands):

	Pension and SERPA Benefits	Postretirement Healthcare Benefits	Total
Prior service cost (credit)	$ 704	$(2,426)	$ (1,722)
Net actuarial loss	23,020	2,977	25,997
	$23,724	$ 551	$24,275

Assumptions:

Weighted-average assumptions used to determine benefit obligations and net periodic benefit cost at December 31 were as follows:

	Pension and SERPA Benefits			Postretirement Healthcare Benefits		
	2013	2012	2011	2013	2012	2011
Assumptions for benefit obligations:						
Discount rate	5.08%	4.23%	5.30%	4.70%	3.93%	4.90%
Rate of compensation	4.00%	4.00%	3.49%	n/a	n/a	n/a
Assumptions for net periodic benefit cost:						
Discount rate	4.23%	5.30%	5.79%	3.93%	4.90%	5.28%
Expected return on plan assets	7.75%	7.80%	8.00%	8.00%	8.00%	8.00%
Rate of compensation increase	4.00%	3.49%	3.49%	n/a	n/a	n/a

Plan Assets (in part)

Postretirement Healthcare Plan Assets—The Company's investment objective is to maximize the return on assets to help pay the benefits by prudently investing in equities, fixed income and alternative assets. The Company's current overall targeted asset allocation as a percentage of total market value was approximately 70% equities and 30% fixed-income. Equity holdings primarily include investments in small-, medium-, and large-cap companies in the U.S., investments in developed and emerging foreign markets and alternative investments such as private equity and real estate. Fixed-income holdings consist of U.S. government and agency securities, state and municipal bonds, corporate bonds from diversified industries and foreign obligations. In addition, cash equivalent balances are maintained at levels adequate to meet near-term plan expenses and benefit payments. Investment risk is measured and monitored on an ongoing basis through quarterly investment portfolio reviews.

The following tables present the fair values of the plan assets related to the Company's pension and postretirement healthcare plans within the fair value hierarchy as defined in Note 8.

The fair values of the Company's postretirement healthcare plan assets, which did not contain any Level 3 assets, as of December 31, 2013, were as follows (in thousands):

	Balance as of December 31, 2013	Quoted Prices in Active Markets for Identical Assets (Level 1)	Significant Other Observable Inputs (Level 2)
Assets:			
Cash and cash equivalents	$ 8,402	$ —	$ 8,402
Equity holdings:			
U.S. companies	29,365	29,365	—
Foreign companies	18,010	17,630	380
Pooled equity funds	61,134	61,134	—
Total equity holdings	108,509	108,129	380
Fixed-income holdings:			
U.S. Treasuries	9,488	9,488	—
Federal agencies	2,579	—	2,579
Corporate bonds	8,685	—	8,685
Pooled fixed income funds	8,977	—	8,977
Foreign bonds	941	—	941
Municipal bonds	294	—	294
Total fixed-income holdings	30,964	9,488	21,476
Total postretirement healthcare plan assets	$147,875	$117,617	$30,258

Postretirement Healthcare Cost

The weighted-average healthcare cost trend rate used in determining the accumulated postretirement benefit obligation of the healthcare plans was as follows:

	2013	2012
Healthcare cost trend rate for next year	8.0%	7.5%
Rate to which the cost trend rate is assumed to decline (the ultimate rate)	5.0%	5.0%
Year that the rate reaches the ultimate trend rate	2021	2019

This healthcare cost trend rate assumption can have a significant effect on the amounts reported. A one-percentage-point change in the assumed healthcare cost trend rate would have the following effects (in thousands):

	One Percent Increase	One Percent Decrease
Total of service and interest cost components in 2013	$ 729	$ (729)
Accumulated benefit obligation as of December 31, 2013	$13,318	$(12,368)

Future Contributions and Benefit Payments

No pension plan contributions are required in 2014. The Company expects it will continue to make on-going contributions related to current benefit payments for SERPA and postretirement healthcare plans in 2014 (1).

The expected benefit payments and Medicare subsidy receipts for the next five years and thereafter were as follows (in thousands):

	Pension Benefits	SERPA Benefits	Postretirement Healthcare Benefits	Medicare Subsidy Receipts
2014	$ 68,418	$ 2,549	$ 30,694	$ 1,507
2015	$ 69,178	$ 1,440	$ 31,047	$ 1,716
2016	$ 70,098	$ 1,895	$ 30,644	$ 1,988
2017	$ 71,508	$ 1,880	$ 29,817	$ 2,224
2018	$ 73,150	$ 2,014	$ 28,785	$ 2,466
2019–2023	$430,427	$16,506	$147,623	$16,125

Income Tax Liability

PRESENTATION

2.106 FASB ASC 210 provides general guidance for classification of accounts in balance sheets. FASB 740-10-45 addresses classification matters applicable to income tax accounts and is incremental to the general guidance.

DISCLOSURE

2.107 FASB ASC 740-10-50 provides detailed disclosures for income taxes, including the components of the net deferred tax liability or asset recognized in an entity's balance sheet.

PRESENTATION AND DISCLOSURE EXCERPT

INCOME TAXES PAYABLE

2.108 IAC/INTERACTIVECORP (DEC)
CONSOLIDATED BALANCE SHEET (in part)

	December 31,	
(In thousands, except share data)	2013	2012
Liabilities and Shareholders' Equity (in part)		
Liabilities:		
Current maturities of long-term debt	$ —	$ 15,844
Accounts payable, trade	77,653	98,314
Deferred revenue	158,206	155,499
Accrued expenses and other current liabilities	351,038	355,232
Total current liabilities	586,897	624,889
Long-term debt, net of current maturities	1,080,000	580,000
Income taxes payable	416,384	479,945
Deferred income taxes	320,748	323,403
Other long-term liabilities	58,393	31,830
Redeemable noncontrolling interests	42,861	58,126
Commitments and contingencies		

NOTES TO CONSOLIDATED FINANCIAL STATEMENTS

Note 2—Summary of Significant Accounting Policies (in part)

Income Taxes

The Company accounts for income taxes under the liability method, and deferred tax assets and liabilities are recognized for the future tax consequences attributable to differences between the financial statement carrying values of existing assets and liabilities and their respective tax bases. Deferred tax assets and liabilities are measured using enacted tax rates in effect for the year in which those temporary differences are expected to be recovered or settled. A valuation allowance is provided on deferred tax assets if it is determined that it is more likely than not that the deferred tax asset will not be realized. The Company records interest, net of any applicable related income tax benefit, on potential income tax contingencies as a component of income tax expense.

The Company recognizes liabilities for uncertain tax positions based on a two-step process. The first step is to evaluate the tax position for recognition by determining if the weight of available evidence indicates it is more likely than not that the position will be sustained on audit, including resolution of related appeals or litigation processes, if any. The second step is to measure the tax benefit as the largest amount which is more than 50% likely of being realized upon ultimate settlement.

Note 4—Income Taxes

U.S. and foreign earnings from continuing operations before income taxes are as follows:

(In thousands)	Years Ended December 31,		
	2013	2012	2011
U.S.	$331,520	$214,675	$142,623
Foreign	84,781	74,387	28,899
Total	$416,301	$289,062	$171,522

The components of the provision (benefit) for income taxes attributable to continuing operations are as follows:

(In thousands)	Years Ended December 31,		
	2013	2012	2011
Current Income Tax Provision (Benefit):			
Federal	$115,250	$ 56,439	$ 49,450
State	13,946	9,204	(26,510)
Foreign	14,402	16,496	8,496
Current income tax provision	143,598	82,139	31,436
Deferred Income Tax (Benefit) Provision:			
Federal	(821)	40,414	(23,293)
State	(2,117)	1,978	639
Foreign	(6,158)	(5,316)	(12,829)
Deferred income tax (benefit) provision	(9,096)	37,076	(35,483)
Income tax provision (benefit)	$134,502	$119,215	$ (4,047)

The current income tax payable was reduced by $32.9 million, $57.1 million and $22.2 million for the years ended December 31, 2013, 2012 and 2011, respectively, for excess tax deductions attributable to stock-based compensation. The related income tax benefits are recorded as increases to additional paid-in capital.

Income taxes (payable) receivable and deferred tax (liabilities) assets are included in the following captions in the accompanying consolidated balance sheet at December 31, 2013 and 2012 :

(In thousands)	December 31,	
	2013	2012
Income Taxes (Payable) Receivable:		
Other current assets	$ 12,242	$ 27,437
Other non-current assets	19,217	79,130
Accrued expenses and other current liabilities	(16,159)	(17,679)
Income taxes payable	(416,384)	(479,945)
Net income taxes payable	$(401,084)	$(391,057)
Deferred Tax (Liabilities) Assets:		
Other current assets	$ 34,381	$ 20,343
Other non-current assets	26	85
Accrued expenses and other current liabilities	(255)	—
Deferred income taxes	(320,748)	(323,403)
Net deferred tax liabilities	$(286,596)	$(302,975)

The tax effects of cumulative temporary differences that give rise to significant portions of the deferred tax assets and deferred tax liabilities are presented below. The valuation allowance is related to deferred tax assets for which it is more likely than not that the tax benefit will not be realized.

(In thousands)	December 31,	
	2013	2012
Deferred Tax Assets:		
Accrued expenses	$ 28,005	$ 13,708
Net operating loss carryforwards	52,336	27,177
Tax credit carryforwards	6,138	5,095
Stock-based compensation	69,101	66,962
Income tax reserves, including related interest	62,852	60,596
Fair value investments	1,151	12,189
Equity method investments	13,584	13,809
Other	11,444	13,374
Total deferred tax assets	244,611	212,910
Less valuation allowance	(62,353)	(60,783)
Net deferred tax assets	182,258	152,127

(continued)

(In thousands)	December 31,	
	2013	2012
Deferred Tax Liabilities:		
Property and equipment	(1,743)	(6,018)
Investment in subsidiaries	(377,483)	(373,652)
Intangible and other assets	(69,530)	(60,830)
Other	(20,098)	(14,602)
Total deferred tax liabilities	(468,854)	(455,102)
Net deferred tax liability	$(286,596)	$(302,975)

At December 31, 2013, the Company has federal and state net operating losses ("NOLs") of $54.9 million and $77.2 million, respectively. If not utilized, the federal NOLs will expire at various times between 2023 and 2033, and the state NOLs will expire at various times between 2014 and 2033. Utilization of federal NOLs will be subject to limitations under Section 382 of the Internal Revenue Code of 1986, as amended. In addition, utilization of certain state NOLs may be subject to limitations under state laws similar to Section 382 of the Internal Revenue Code of 1986. At December 31, 2013, the Company has foreign NOLs of $98.2 million available to offset future income. Of these foreign NOLs, $93.0 million can be carried forward indefinitely and $5.2 million will expire at various times between 2014 and 2033. During 2013, the Company recognized tax benefits related to NOLs of $10.6 million. Included in this amount is $10.4 million of tax benefits of acquired attributes, which was recorded as a reduction in goodwill. At December 31, 2013, the Company has $34.4 million of state capital losses. If not utilized, the federal and state capital losses will expire between 2014 and 2017. Utilization of capital losses will be limited to the Company's ability to generate future capital gains.

At December 31, 2013, the Company has tax credit carryforwards of $11.9 million. Of this amount, $5.5 million relates to federal credits for foreign taxes, $5.2 million relates to state tax credits for research activities, and $1.2 million relates to various state and local tax credits. Of these credit carryforwards, $6.4 million can be carried forward indefinitely and $5.5 million will expire within ten years.

During 2013, the Company's valuation allowance increased by $1.6 million primarily due to an increase in foreign net operating losses, partially offset by realized gains in long-term marketable equity securities. At December 31, 2013, the Company has a valuation allowance of $62.4 million related to the portion of tax loss carryforwards and other items for which it is more likely than not that the tax benefit will not be realized.

A reconciliation of the income tax provision (benefit) to the amounts computed by applying the statutory federal income tax rate to earnings from continuing operations before income taxes is shown as follows:

(In thousands)	Years Ended December 31,		
	2013	2012	2011
Income tax provision at the federal statutory rate of 35%	$145,705	$101,172	$ 60,033
Reversal of deferred tax liability associated with investment in Meetic	—	—	(43,696)
Change in tax reserves, net	1,791	17,703	(15,493)
Foreign income taxed at a different statutory tax rate	(17,428)	(16,240)	(11,774)
Net adjustment related to the reconciliation of income tax provision accruals to tax returns	(5,237)	(3,876)	(7,298)
Federal valuation allowance on equity method investments	214	979	4,595
State income taxes, net of effect of federal tax benefit	7,469	7,650	5,592
Other, net	1,988	11,827	3,994
Income tax provision (benefit)	$134,502	$119,215	$ (4,047)

No income taxes have been provided on indefinitely reinvested earnings of certain foreign subsidiaries aggregating $517.4 million at December 31, 2013. The amount of the unrecognized deferred income tax liability with respect to such earnings is $119.5 million.

Current Amount of Long-Term Debt

PRESENTATION

2.109 As noted in 2.93, FASB ASC 470 addresses classification determination for specific debt obligations.

DISCLOSURE

2.110 FASB ASC 470 includes disclosures required for long-term debt (see the "Long-Term Debt" section). FASB ASC 825 requires disclosure of both the fair value and bases for estimating the fair value of the current amount of long-term debt, unless it is not practicable to estimate that value.

PRESENTATION AND DISCLOSURE EXCERPT

CURRENT AMOUNT OF LONG-TERM DEBT

2.111 MOLSON COORS BREWING COMPANY (DEC)
CONSOLIDATED BALANCE SHEETS (in part)

	As of	
(In millions, except par value)	December 31, 2013	December 29, 2012
Liabilities and Equity (in part)		
Current liabilities:		
Accounts payable and other current liabilities (includes affiliate payable amounts of $22.8 and $34.1, respectively)	$1,336.4	$1,186.9
Derivative hedging instruments	73.9	6.0
Deferred tax liabilities	138.1	152.3
Current portion of long-term debt and short-term borrowings	586.9	1,245.6
Discontinued operations	6.8	7.9
Total current liabilities	2,142.1	2,598.7
Long-term debt	3,213.0	3,422.5
Pension and postretirement benefits	462.6	833.0
Derivative hedging instruments	3.0	222.2
Deferred tax liabilities	911.4	948.5
Unrecognized tax benefits	92.7	81.8
Other liabilities	74.2	93.9
Discontinued operations	17.3	20.0
Total liabilities	6,916.3	8,220.6

NOTES TO CONSOLIDATED FINANCIAL STATEMENTS

13. Debt (in part)

Debt Obligations

Our total long-term borrowings as of December 31, 2013, and December 29, 2012, were composed of the following:

	As of	
(In millions)	December 31, 2013	December 29, 2012
Senior notes:		
$575 million 2.5% convertible notes due 2013[1]	$ —	$ 575.0
€500 million 0.0% convertible note due 2013[2]	61.8	668.7
CAD 900 million 5.0% notes due 2015[3]	847.2	902.7
CAD 500 million 3.95% Series A notes due 2017[3]	470.7	501.5
$300 million 2.0% notes due 2017[4]	300.0	300.0
$500 million 3.5% notes due 2022[4]	500.0	500.0
$1.1 billion 5.0% notes due 2042[4]	1,100.0	1,100.0
€120 million term loan due 2016[5]	—	123.9
Other long-term debt	0.2	0.5
Long-term credit facilities[6]	—	—
Less: unamortized debt discounts[7]	(5.1)	(17.4)
Total long-term debt (including current portion)	3,274.8	4,654.9
Less: current portion of long-term debt	(61.8)	(1,232.4)
Total long-term debt	$3,213.0	$ 3,422.5
Short-term borrowings[8]	$ 525.1	$ 13.2
Current portion of long-term debt	61.8	1,232.4
Current portion of long-term debt and short-term borrowings	$ 586.9	$ 1,245.6

[1] On June 15, 2007, MCBC issued in a public offering $575 million of 2.5% Convertible Senior Notes (the "Notes") payable semi-annually in arrears. The Notes were senior unsecured obligations and ranked equal in rights of payment with all of our other senior unsecured debt and senior to all of our future subordinated debt. The Notes were guaranteed by MCBC and certain of our U.S. and Canadian subsidiaries. The Notes matured on July 30, 2013. The Notes contained certain customary anti-dilution and make-whole provisions to protect holders of the Notes as defined in the Indenture. As noted above, our $575 million convertible notes matured and were repaid on July 30, 2013, for their face value of $575 million. The required premium payment of $2.6 million, which was based on our weighted-average Class B common stock price exceeding the then-applicable conversion price on any of the 25 trading days following the maturity date, was paid in September 2013. This premium was hedged by call options that mitigated our exposure to increases in our stock price and resulted in proceeds of $2.6 million from these call options in September 2013, which fully offset the premium payment. The premium payment and call option proceeds were recorded in the stockholders' equity section of the consolidated balance sheets upon settlement in 2013. Separately, the warrants entered into concurrent with these call options, pursuant to which we would have been required to issue Class B common stock to the counterparty in the event our stock price reached $66.13 per share, began expiring in December 2013 and the final warrants expired February 6, 2014, all of which were out-of-the-money. The original conversion price for each $1,000 aggregate principal amount of notes was $54.76 per share of our Class B common stock, which represented a 25% premium above the stock price on the day of issuance of the notes and corresponded to the initial conversion ratio of 18.263 shares per each $1,000 aggregate principal amount of notes. The conversion ratio and conversion price were subject to adjustments for certain events and provisions, as defined in the indenture, including adjustments reflected for exceeding defined thresholds related to our dividend payments. At the maturity date our conversion price and ratio were $51.8284 and 19.2944 shares, respectively.

(continued)

(footnote continued)

We initially accounted for the Notes pursuant to guidance pertaining to convertible bonds with issuer option to settle for cash upon conversion, that is, we did not separate and assign values to the conversion feature of the Notes but rather accounted for the entire agreement as one debt instrument as the conversion feature met the requirements of guidance pertaining to accounting for derivative financial instruments indexed to, and potentially settled in, a company's own stock.

During the fiscal years 2013, 2012 and 2011, we incurred additional non-cash interest expense of $10.8 million, $18.1 million and $17.5 million, respectively. The additional non-cash interest expense impact (net of tax) to net income per basic share was a decrease of $0.04, $0.06 and $0.06 for the fiscal years 2013, 2012 and 2011, respectively. We also incurred interest expense related to the 2.5% coupon rate of $8.4 million, $14.4 million and $14.6 million for the fiscal years 2013, 2012 and 2011, respectively. The combination of non-cash and cash interest resulted in an effective interest rate of 5.73%, 5.75% and 5.90% for the fiscal years 2013 (through settlement), 2012 and 2011, respectively. As of December 31, 2013, there was no unamortized debt discount outstanding as we recorded the remaining discount amortization upon maturity in the third quarter of 2013. As of December 29, 2012, $10.8 million of the unamortized debt discount related to our $575 million convertible debt.

Convertible Note Hedge and Warrants:

In connection with the issuance of the Notes, we entered into a privately negotiated convertible note hedge transaction. The convertible note hedge (the "purchased call options") covered up to approximately 10.8 million shares of our Class B common stock. The purchased call options, if exercised by us, required the counterparty to deliver to us shares of Class B common stock adequate to meet our net share settlement obligations under the Notes and were expected to reduce the potential dilution to our Class B common stock to be issued upon conversion of the Notes, if any. Separately and concurrently, we also entered into warrant transactions with respect to our Class B common stock pursuant to which we were required to issue to the counterparty up to approximately 10.8 million shares of our Class B common stock. The warrant price is $67.82 which represents a 60% premium above the stock price on the date of the warrant transaction. These warrants began expiring in December 2013 and the final warrants expired February 6, 2014, during which time none of the warrants were exercised.

At issuance, we used a portion of the net proceeds from the issuance of the Notes to pay for the cost of the purchased call options, which was partially offset by the proceeds received from the warrant transaction, resulting in a net use of proceeds of approximately $50 million. The net cost of these transactions, net of tax, was recorded in the stockholders' equity section of the consolidated balance sheets.

(2) On June 15, 2012, we issued a €500 million Zero Coupon Senior Unsecured Convertible Note due December 31, 2013 (the "Convertible Note") to the Seller in conjunction with the closing of the Acquisition. The Seller had the ability to exercise a put right with respect to the Convertible Note as of March 14, 2013, (the "First Redemption Date") and ending on December 19, 2013, for the greater of the principal amount of the Convertible Note or the aggregate cash value of 12,894,044 shares of our Class B Common Stock, as adjusted for certain corporate events. In accordance with these terms, on August 13, 2013, the Seller exercised the conversion feature for an agreed upon value upon exercise of €510.9 million, consisting of €500 million in principal and €10.9 million for the conversion feature. At issuance, the total value of the Convertible Note was €511.1 million, consisting of the principal (€500 million), discount (€1.0 million), and conversion feature (€12.1 million), initially recorded as a component of the purchase price associated with the Acquisition.

On September 3, 2013, we paid the seller in cash a total of €466.0 million ($614.7 million) consisting of €455.1 million ($600.3 million) in principal and €10.9 million ($14.4 million) for the conversion feature. Separate from the Seller's notice to put, we have made claims with regard to the representations and warranties provided to us upon close of the Acquisition. As a result, we withheld €44.9 million ($61.8 million as of December 31, 2013) from the €500 million in principal related to these outstanding claims. The remaining balance as of December 31, 2013, continues to be classified as current portion of long-term debt pending the resolution of the unsettled claims. In January 2014, we settled one of the claims resulting in a payment to the Seller of €34.0 million ($46.3 million at settlement). We have not incurred, and do not expect to incur, any interest on the remaining amounts withheld.

The Convertible Note's embedded conversion feature was determined to meet the definition of a derivative required to be bifurcated and separately accounted for at fair value with changes in fair value recorded in earnings. During the fiscal year 2013 and 2012, we recognized a net loss of $6.5 million and a net gain of $7.3 million, respectively, on the conversion feature primarily related to the change from the previously recorded fair value to the value upon exercise. The Convertible Note was issued at a discount of $1.3 million, which has been recognized as interest expense over the period from issuance to the First Redemption Date. The non-cash interest, excluding the change in fair value of the convertible feature, resulted in an immaterial impact to our effective interest rate for the fiscal year 2013 and 2012. See Note 17, "Derivative Instruments and Hedging Activities" for further discussion.

(3) During the third quarter of 2005, Molson Coors Capital Finance ULC completed a CAD 900 million private placement in Canada due September 22, 2015. Additionally, during the fourth quarter 2010, Molson Coors International LP completed a CAD 500 million private placement in Canada due October 6, 2017. Prior to issuing the bonds, we entered into forward starting interest rate transactions for a portion of each Canadian offering. The bond forward transactions effectively established, in advance, the yield of the government of Canada bond rate over which the Company's private placement was priced. At the time of the private placement offerings and pricings, the government of Canada bond rates were trading at a yield lower than that locked in with the Company's interest rate locks. This resulted in a loss on the bond forward transactions of $4.0 million related to the CAD 900 million bonds, and $7.8 million on the CAD 500 million bonds. Per authoritative accounting guidance pertaining to derivatives and hedging, the losses are being amortized over the life of each respective Canadian issued private placement and will serve to increase our effective cost of borrowing compared to the stated coupon rates by 0.05% and 0.23% on the CAD 900 million and CAD 500 million bonds, respectively.

(4) On May 3, 2012, we issued $1.9 billion of senior notes with portions maturing in 2017, 2022 and 2042. The 2017 senior notes were issued in an initial aggregate principal amount of $300 million at 2.0% interest and will mature on May 1, 2017. The 2022 senior notes were issued in an initial aggregate principal amount of $500 million at 3.5% interest and will mature on May 1, 2022. The 2042 senior notes were issued in an initial aggregate principal amount of $1.1 billion at 5.0% interest and will mature on May 1, 2042. The issuance resulted in total proceeds to us, before expenses, of $1,880.7 million, net of underwriting fees and discounts of $14.7 million and $4.6 million, respectively. Total debt issuance costs capitalized in connection with these senior notes, including the underwriting fees and discounts, are approximately $18.0 million and will be amortized over the life of the notes. The issuance adds a number of guarantors to these debt securities as well as to our existing senior obligations, pursuant to requirements of our existing senior debt obligation agreements. These new guarantors consist principally of the U.K. operating entity. See Note 20, "Supplemental Guarantor Information" for further discussion and guarantor financial information reflective of this change.

Concurrent with the announcement of the Acquisition, we entered into a bridge loan agreement, which we terminated upon the issuance of the $1.9 billion senior notes. In connection with the issuance and subsequent termination of the bridge loan, we incurred costs of $13.0 million recorded in other expense in the second quarter of 2012. See Note 6, "Other Income and Expense" for further discussion.

Our risk management policy prohibits speculating on specific events, including the direction of interest rates. In advance of our issuance of the $1.9 billion senior notes, we systematically removed a portion of our interest rate market risk by entering into Treasury Locks. This resulted in an increase in the certainty of our yield to maturity when issuing the notes. In the second quarter of 2012, we recognized a cash loss of $39.2 million on settlement of the Treasury Locks recorded in interest expense. See Note 17, "Derivative Instruments and Hedging Activities" for further discussion.

(5) On April 3, 2012, we entered into a term loan agreement (the "Term Loan Agreement") that provides for a 4 -year term loan facility of $300 million, composed of one $150 million borrowing and one Euro-denominated borrowing equal to $150 million at issuance (or €120 million borrowing) both of which were funded upon close of the Acquisition on June 15, 2012. The Term Loan Agreement required quarterly principal repayments equal to 2.5% of the initial principal obligation, which commenced on September 30, 2012, with the remaining 62.5% principal balance due at the June 15, 2016 maturity date. The obligations under the Term Loan Agreement were our general unsecured obligations. The Term Loan Agreement contained customary events of default, specified representations and warranties and covenants, including, among other things, covenants that limited our and our subsidiaries' ability to incur certain additional priority indebtedness, create or permit liens on assets or engage in mergers or consolidations. Debt issuance costs capitalized in connection with the Term Loan Agreement were amortized over the life of the debt and totaled approximately $3 million.

During 2012, we repaid the $150 million borrowing and made principal repayments of €26.0 million on the €120 million borrowing. During the third quarter of 2012, we designated the €120 million term loan as a net investment hedge of our Central European operations. During 2013, we made principal repayments of $123.8 million (€93.7 million) on the remaining balance of our €120 million term loan. As a result, the term loan was fully repaid in the third quarter of 2013. See Note 17, "Derivative Instruments and Hedging Activities" for further discussion.

(6) On April 3, 2012, we entered into a revolving credit agreement (the "Credit Agreement"). The Credit Agreement provides for a 4 -year revolving credit facility of $300 million that was subsequently amended to increase the borrowing limit to $550 million. The Credit Agreement contains customary events of default and specified representations and warranties and covenants, including, among other things, covenants that limit our subsidiaries' ability to incur certain additional priority indebtedness, create or permit liens on assets, or engage in mergers or consolidations. In relation to the credit facilities issued during 2012, we incurred $5.5 million of total issuance costs and up-front fees, which are being amortized over the terms of each respective facility.

(continued)

(footnote continued)

In the second quarter of 2011, we entered into an agreement for a 4-year revolving multicurrency credit facility of $400 million, which provides a $100 million sub-facility available for the issuance of letters of credit.

There were no outstanding borrowings on these credit facilities as of December 31, 2013. These credit facilities support our commercial paper program discussed below.

[7] In addition to the unamortized debt discount on the $575 million convertible notes as of December 29, 2012, we have unamortized debt discounts on the additional debt balances of $5.1 million and $6.6 million as of December 31, 2013, and December 29, 2012, respectively.

[8] In the first quarter of 2013, a $950 million commercial paper program was approved and implemented. The commercial paper program is supported by our $550 million and $400 million revolving credit facilities. To fund the repayment of our €500 million Zero Coupon Senior Unsecured Convertible Note, we issued short-term commercial paper during the third quarter of 2013. As of December 31, 2013, the outstanding borrowings under the commercial paper program were $379.8 million at a weighted average effective interest rate and tenor of 0.49% and 47.2 days, respectively.

In the third quarter of 2012, we entered into a revolving credit agreement ("Euro Credit Agreement") to support the operations of our Europe segment. The Euro Credit Agreement provides for a 1-year revolving credit facility of €150 million on an uncommitted basis. In the third quarter of 2013, this revolving credit facility was renewed and restructured and will continue to provide €150.0 million on an uncommitted basis through September 2014. As of December 31, 2013, the outstanding borrowings under this revolving credit facility were $137.4 million. There were no outstanding borrowings under this revolving credit facility as of December 29, 2012.

Other short-term borrowing facilities consist of an overdraft facility of CAD $30.0 million at either USD Prime or CAD Prime depending on the borrowing currency, a GBP line of credit, which was temporarily increased to GBP 20.0 million as of December 31, 2013 and subsequently reduced to GBP 10.0 million in January 2014, and an overdraft facility for GBP 10.0 million, both at GBP LIBOR +1.5%, and a line of credit for Japanese Yen 1.5 billion (of which Japanese Yen 575.0 million is committed under an outstanding letter of credit, at a base rate of less than 1.0%). As of December 31, 2013, and December 29, 2012, we had outstanding borrowings of $3.1 million and $9.3 million, respectively, under the Japanese Yen line of credit, and no borrowings under the GBP and CAD facilities. See Note 19, "Commitments and Contingencies" for discussion related to letters of credit. Also included in short-term borrowings is $4.8 million and $3.9 million related to factoring arrangements and other short-term borrowings within our Europe business as of December 31, 2013, and December 29, 2012, respectively.

Debt Fair Value Measurements

We utilize market approaches to estimate the fair value of certain outstanding borrowings by discounting anticipated future cash flows derived from the contractual terms of the obligations and observable market interest and foreign exchange rates. As of December 31, 2013, and December 29, 2012, the fair value of our outstanding long-term debt (including current portion) was $3,359.1 million and $4,993.0 million, respectively. All senior notes are valued based on significant observable inputs and would be classified as Level 2 in the fair value hierarchy. The fair value measurement of the conversion feature embedded in the Convertible Note included significant unobservable inputs and was classified as Level 3 in the fair value hierarchy prior to settlement. See Note 17, "Derivative Instruments and Hedging Activities" for further discussion regarding the fair value of the conversion feature related to the Convertible Note which was settled in 2013. The carrying values of all other outstanding long-term borrowings and our short-term borrowings approximate their fair values.

Other Current Liabilities

PRESENTATION

2.112 Rule 5-02 of Regulation S-X requires that any items in excess of 5 percent of total current liabilities be stated separately on the balance sheet or disclosed in the notes. In addition, registrants should state separately amounts payable to the following:

- Banks for borrowings
- Factors or other financial institutions for borrowings
- Holders of commercial paper
- Trade creditors
- Related parties
- Underwriters, promoters, and employees (other than related parties)
- Others

Amounts applicable to the first three categories may be stated separately in the balance sheet or in a note thereto.

PRESENTATION AND DISCLOSURE EXCERPTS

DIVIDENDS

2.113 ILLINOIS TOOL WORKS INC. (DEC)
MARKET FOR REGISTRANT'S COMMON EQUITY, RELATED STOCKHOLDER MATTERS AND ISSUER PURCHASES OF EQUITY SECURITIES

Common Stock Price and Dividend Data—The common stock of Illinois Tool Works Inc. was listed on the New York Stock Exchange for 2013 and 2012. Quarterly market price and dividend data for 2013 and 2012 were as shown below:

	Market Price Per Share		Dividends Declared Per Share
	High	**Low**	
2013:			
Fourth quarter	$84.32	$73.60	$0.42
Third quarter	78.56	68.16	0.42
Second quarter	71.74	60.02	0.38
First quarter	65.60	59.71	0.38
2012:			
Fourth quarter	$63.33	$58.20	$0.38
Third quarter	62.09	49.07	0.38
Second quarter	58.27	50.35	0.36
First quarter	58.24	47.42	0.36

The approximate number of holders of record of common stock as of January 31, 2014 was 7,544. This number does not include beneficial owners of the Company's securities held in the name of nominees.

STATEMENT OF FINANCIAL POSITION (in part)

	December 31	
(In millions except shares)	**2013**	**2012**
Liabilities and Stockholders' Equity (in part)		
Current liabilities:		
Short-term debt	$3,551	$ 459
Accounts payable	634	676
Accrued expenses	1,272	1,392
Cash dividends payable	181	—
Income taxes payable	69	116
Deferred income taxes	10	8
Liabilities held for sale	317	—
Total current liabilities	6,034	2,651

NOTES TO FINANCIAL STATEMENTS

Cash Dividends declared were $1.60 per share in 2013, $1.48 per share in 2012 and $1.40 per share in 2011. Cash dividends paid were $1.18 per share in 2013, $1.84 per share in 2012 and $1.38 per share in 2011. The 2012 cash dividends included an accelerated dividend payment of $ 0.38 per share in December 2012, which was originally scheduled to be paid in January 2013.

DEPOSITS

2.114 BASSETT FURNITURE INDUSTRIES, INCORPORATED (NOV)
CONSOLIDATED BALANCE SHEETS (in part)

November 30, 2013 and November 24, 2012

(In thousands, except share and per share data)

	2013	2012
Liabilities and Stockholders' Equity (in part)		
Current liabilities		
Accounts payable	$19,892	$22,405
Accrued compensation and benefits	6,503	6,926
Customer deposits	16,214	12,253
Dividends payable	2,172	542
Other accrued liabilities	6,660	10,454
Total current liabilities	51,441	52,580

(In thousands, except share and per share data)

2. Significant Accounting Policies (in part)

Revenue Recognition

Revenue is recognized when the risks and rewards of ownership and title to the product have transferred to the buyer. This occurs upon the shipment of goods to independent dealers or, in the case of Company-owned retail stores, upon delivery to the customer. We offer terms varying from 30 to 60 days for wholesale customers. For retail sales, we typically collect a significant portion of the purchase price as a customer deposit upon order, with the balance typically collected upon delivery. These deposits are carried on our balance sheet as a current liability until delivery is fulfilled. Estimates for returns and allowances have been recorded as a reduction to revenue. The contracts with our licensee store owners do not provide for any royalty or license fee to be paid to us. Revenue is reported net of any taxes collected.

Staff Accounting Bulletin No. 104, *Revenue Recognition* ("SAB 104") outlines the four basic criteria for recognizing revenue as follows: (1) persuasive evidence of an arrangement exists, (2) delivery has occurred or services have been rendered, (3) the seller's price to the buyer is fixed or determinable, and (4) collectability is reasonably assured. SAB 104 further asserts that if collectability of all or a portion of the revenue is not reasonably assured, revenue recognition should be deferred until payment is received. During fiscal 2013, there were no dealers for which these criteria were not met. During fiscal 2012 and 2011, there were two and four dealers, respectively, for which these criteria were not met and therefore revenue was being recognized on a cost recovery basis. As of November 30, 2013 and November 24, 2012 there were no dealers that remained on a cost recovery basis, and as of November 26, 2011 there were two dealers that remained on the cost recovery basis. As of November 30, 2013 and November 24, 2012 there was no deferred gross profit resulting from the cost recovery method carried on our balance sheet as a reduction of accounts receivable. For fiscal 2013 and 2012, no revenue or cost was deferred during the year under the cost recovery method. During fiscal 2011, revenue of $1,678 and cost of $1,175 was deferred prior to any subsequent recognition due to the transaction meeting the revenue recognition requirements.

DEFERRED INCOME TAXES

2.115 VARIAN MEDICAL SYSTEMS, INC. (SEP)
CONSOLIDATED BALANCE SHEETS (in part)

(In thousands, except par values)	September 27, 2013	September 28, 2012
Liabilities and Stockholders' Equity (in part)		
Current liabilities:		
Accounts payable	$ 194,272	$ 180,736
Accrued expenses	320,884	336,568
Product warranty	39,050	52,799
Deferred revenue	389,479	369,456
Advance payments from customers	160,644	141,972
Short-term borrowings	—	155,000
Current maturities of long-term debt	56,250	—
Total current liabilities	1,160,579	1,236,531
Long-term debt	450,000	6,250
Other long-term liabilities	144,048	126,169
Total liabilities	1,754,627	1,368,950

13. Taxes on Earnings

The Company accounts for income taxes under an asset and liability approach where deferred income taxes are based upon enacted tax laws and rates applicable to the periods in which the taxes become payable.

Taxes on earnings from continuing operations were as follows:

(In millions)	Fiscal Years Ended		
	2013	2012	2011
Current provision:			
Federal	$110.1	$ 99.3	$ 80.4
State and local	13.4	8.5	11.7
Foreign	54.3	63.5	52.7
Total current	177.8	171.3	144.8
Deferred provision (benefit):			
Federal	(3.9)	(4.5)	32.9
State and local	(0.2)	0.1	6.0
Foreign	0.1	2.0	(3.6)
Total deferred	(4.0)	(2.4)	35.3
Taxes on earnings	$173.8	$168.9	$180.1

Earnings from continuing operations before taxes are generated from the following geographic areas:

(In millions)	Fiscal Years Ended		
	2013	2012	2011
United States	$308.0	$271.4	$299.3
Foreign	304.1	324.5	289.4
	$612.1	$595.9	$588.7

The effective tax rate differs from the U.S. federal statutory tax rate as a result of the following:

	Fiscal Years Ended		
	2013	2012	2011
Federal statutory income tax rate	35.0%	35.0%	35.0%
State and local taxes, net of federal tax benefit	1.3	1.3	2.5
Non-U.S. income taxed at different rates, net	(5.6)	(5.9)	(3.3)
Resolution of tax contingencies due to lapses of statutes of limitations	(1.2)	(1.8)	(2.8)
Other	(1.1)	(0.3)	(0.8)
Effective tax rate	28.4%	28.3%	30.6%

During fiscal years 2013, 2012 and 2011, the Company's effective tax rate was lower than the U.S. federal statutory rate primarily because the Company's foreign earnings are taxed at rates that, on average, are lower than the U.S. federal rate. This reduction is partly offset by the fact that the Company's domestic earnings are also subject to state income taxes. During fiscal years 2013 and 2012, and 2011, the benefit of the release of liabilities for uncertain tax positions as a result of the expiration of the statutes of limitation in various jurisdictions also contributed to the Company's effective tax rate being lower than the U.S. federal statutory rate.

Significant components of deferred tax assets and liabilities are as follows:

(In millions)	September 27, 2013	September 28, 2012
Deferred tax assets:		
Deferred revenues	$ 26.8	$ 26.8
Deferred compensation	34.9	32.7
Product warranty	13.9	13.7
Inventory adjustments	18.3	17.0
Equity-based compensation	33.3	41.8
Environmental reserve	5.7	5.9
Net operating loss carryforwards	78.6	54.2
Other	37.8	45.4
	249.3	237.5
Valuation allowance	(60.7)	(45.8)
Total deferred tax assets	188.6	191.7
Deferred tax liabilities:		
Tax-deductible goodwill	(27.3)	(27.4)
Fixed assets	(17.7)	(22.3)
Other	(30.4)	(28.8)
Total deferred tax liabilities	(75.4)	(78.5)
Net deferred tax assets	$ 113.2	$ 113.2
Reported as:		
Net current deferred tax assets	$ 122.3	$ 115.8
Net long-term deferred tax assets (included in "Other Assets")	10.5	13.8
Net current deferred tax liabilities (included in "Accrued Expenses")	(7.6)	(2.9)
Net long-term deferred tax liabilities (included in "Other long-term liabilities")	(12.0)	(13.5)
Net deferred tax assets	$ 113.2	$ 113.2

The Company has not provided for U.S. federal income and foreign withholding taxes on $1,412.2 million of cumulative undistributed earnings of non-U.S. subsidiaries. Such earnings are intended to be reinvested in the non-U.S. subsidiaries for an indefinite period of time. If such earnings were not considered to be reinvested indefinitely, additional deferred taxes of approximately $358.4 million would be provided.

The Company has federal net operating loss carryforwards of approximately $14.7 million expiring between 2018 and 2031. The federal net operating loss carryforwards are subject to an annual limitation of approximately $1.3 million per year. The Company has state net operating loss carryforwards of $31.1 million expiring between 2018 and 2032. The Company has foreign net operating loss carryforwards of $218.9 million with an indefinite life. Of this amount, $24.1 million is unavailable to the Company under local loss utilization rules.

Our valuation allowance relates primarily to net operating losses in certain foreign jurisdictions where, based on the weight of available evidence, it is more likely than not that the tax benefit of the net operating losses will not be realized. The valuation allowance increased by $14.9 million during fiscal year 2013, decreased by $1.1 million during fiscal year 2012, and increased by $8.4 million in fiscal year 2011.

Income taxes paid were as follows:

	Fiscal Years Ended		
(In millions)	2013	2012	2011
Federal income taxes paid, net	$119.1	$ 77.6	$ 70.0
State income taxes paid, net	14.9	9.3	11.9
Foreign income taxes paid, net	69.4	47.7	57.5
Total	$203.4	$134.6	$139.4

The Company accounts for uncertainty in income taxes following a two-step approach for recognizing and measuring uncertain tax positions. The first step is to evaluate the tax position for recognition by determining whether the weight of available evidence indicates that it is more likely than not that, based on the technical merits, the position will be sustained on audit, including resolution of related appeals or litigation processes, if any. The second step is to measure the tax benefit as the largest amount that is more than 50% likely of being realized upon settlement.

Changes in the Company's unrecognized tax benefits were as follows:

	Fiscal Years Ended		
(In millions)	2013	2012	2011
Unrecognized tax benefits balance—beginning of fiscal year	$38.8	$37.1	$ 46.4
Additions based on tax positions related to a prior year	2.5	3.8	1.0
Reductions based on tax positions related to a prior year	(0.7)	(0.9)	(0.4)
Additions based on tax positions related to the current year	6.6	6.8	8.6
Settlements	(4.2)	(0.4)	(5.1)
Reductions resulting from the expiration of the applicable statute of limitations	(6.0)	(7.6)	(13.4)
Unrecognized tax benefits balance—end of fiscal year	$37.0	$38.8	$ 37.1

As of September 27, 2013, the total amount of gross unrecognized tax benefits was $37.0 million. Of this amount, $32.8 million would affect the effective tax rate if recognized. The difference would be offset by changes to deferred tax assets and liabilities.

The Company includes interest and penalties related to income taxes within "Taxes on earnings" on the Consolidated Statements of Earnings. As of September 27, 2013, the Company had accrued $6.7 million for the payment of interest and penalties related to unrecognized tax benefits. A net expense of $1.2 million related to interest and penalties was included in "Taxes on earnings." As of September 28, 2012, the Company had accrued $5.5 million for the payment of interest and penalties related to unrecognized tax benefits. A net benefit of $2.2 million related to interest and penalties was included in "Taxes on earnings."

The Company files U.S. federal, U.S. state, and foreign tax returns. The Company's U.S. federal tax returns are generally no longer subject to tax examinations for years prior to 2010. The Company has significant operations in Switzerland. The Company's Swiss tax returns are generally no longer subject to tax examinations for years prior to 2009. For U.S. states and other foreign tax returns, the Company is generally no longer subject to tax examinations for years prior to 2007.

PRODUCTS LIABILITY

2.116 COOPER TIRE & RUBBER COMPANY (DEC)
CONSOLIDATED BALANCE SHEETS (in part)

December 31

(Dollar amounts in thousands, except par value amounts)

	2012	2013
Liabilities and Equity		
Current liabilities:		
Notes payable	$ 32,836	$ 22,105
Accounts payable	379,867	302,422
Accrued liabilities	221,822	211,090
Income taxes payable	18,297	11,098
Current portion of long-term debt	2,319	17,868
Total current liabilities	655,141	564,583
Long-term debt	336,142	320,959
Postretirement benefits other than pensions	291,546	238,653
Pension benefits	432,922	291,808
Other long-term liabilities	168,967	157,918
Deferred income tax liabilities	8,026	6,601

NOTES TO CONSOLIDATED FINANCIAL STATEMENTS

(Dollar amounts in thousands except per share amounts)

Note 1—Significant Accounting Policies (in part)

Products liability— The Company accrues costs for products liability at the time a loss is probable and the amount of loss can be estimated. The Company believes the probability of loss can be established and the amount of loss can be estimated only after certain minimum information is available, including verification that Company-produced products were involved in the incident giving rise to the claim, the condition of the product purported to be involved in the claim, the nature of the incident giving rise to the claim and the extent of the purported injury or damages. In cases where such information is known, each products liability claim is evaluated based on its specific facts and circumstances. A judgment is then made to determine the requirement for establishment or revision of an accrual for any potential liability. The liability often cannot be determined with precision until the claim is resolved.

Pursuant to applicable accounting rules, the Company accrues the minimum liability for each known claim when the estimated outcome is a range of possible loss and no one amount within that range is more likely than another. The Company uses a range of settlements because an average settlement cost would not be meaningful since the products liability claims faced by the Company are unique and widely variable. The cases involve different types of tires, models and lines, different circumstances surrounding the accident such as different applications, vehicles, speeds, road conditions, weather conditions, driver error, tire repair and maintenance practices, service life conditions, as well as different jurisdictions and different injuries. In addition, in many of the Company's products liability lawsuits the plaintiff alleges that his or her harm was caused by one or more co-defendants who acted independently of the Company. Accordingly, the claims asserted and the resolutions of those claims have an enormous amount of variability. The costs have ranged from zero dollars to $33 million in one case with no "average" that is meaningful. No specific accrual is made for individual unasserted claims or for premature claims, asserted claims where the minimum information needed to evaluate the probability of a liability is not yet known. However, an accrual for such claims based, in part, on management's expectations for future litigation activity and the settled claims history is maintained. Because of the speculative nature of litigation in the U.S., the Company does not believe a meaningful aggregate range of potential loss for asserted and unasserted claims can be determined. The Company's experience has demonstrated that its estimates have been reasonably accurate and, on average, cases are settled at amounts close to the reserves established. However, it is possible an individual claim from time to time may result in an aberration from the norm and could have a material impact.

The products liability expense reported by the Company includes amortization of insurance premium costs, adjustments to settlement reserves and legal costs incurred in defending claims against the Company. Legal costs are expensed as incurred and products liability insurance premiums are amortized over coverage periods.

Note 8—Accrued Liabilities

Accrued liabilities at December 31 were as follows:

	2012	2013
Products liability	$ 70,267	$ 70,472
Payroll and withholdings	71,054	59,158
Warranty	24,285	20,917
Other postretirement benefits	16,680	14,213
Advertising	13,991	12,146
Foreign currency derivative instruments	1,265	—
Other	24,280	34,184
	$221,822	$211,090

Note 20—Contingent Liabilities (in part)

Litigation (in part)

Products Liability Litigation

The Company is a defendant in various products liability claims brought in numerous jurisdictions in which individuals seek damages resulting from motor vehicle accidents allegedly caused by defective tires manufactured by the Company. Each of the products liability claims faced by the Company generally involve different types of tires, models and lines, different circumstances surrounding the accident such as different applications, vehicles, speeds, road conditions, weather conditions, driver error, tire repair and maintenance practices, service life conditions, as well as different jurisdictions and different injuries. In addition, in many of the Company's products liability lawsuits the plaintiff alleges that his or her harm was caused by one or more co-defendants who acted independently of the Company. Accordingly, both the claims asserted and the resolutions of those claims have an enormous amount of variability. The aggregate amount of damages asserted at any point in time is not determinable since often times when claims are filed, the plaintiffs do not specify the amount of damages. Even when there is an amount alleged, at times the amount is wildly inflated and has no rational basis.

Pursuant to applicable accounting rules, the Company accrues the minimum liability for each known claim when the estimated outcome is a range of possible loss and no one amount within that range is more likely than another. The Company uses a range of losses because an average cost would not be meaningful since the products liability claims faced by the Company are unique and widely variable, and accordingly, the resolutions of those claims have an enormous amount of variability. The costs have ranged from zero dollars to $33 million in one case with no "average" that is meaningful. No specific accrual is made for individual unasserted claims or for premature claims, asserted claims where the minimum information needed to evaluate the probability of a liability is not yet known. However, an accrual for such claims based, in part, on management's expectations for future litigation activity and the settled claims history is maintained. Because of the speculative nature of litigation in the U.S., the Company does not believe a meaningful aggregate range of potential loss for asserted and unasserted claims can be determined. The Company's experience has demonstrated that its estimates have been reasonably accurate and, on average, cases are settled at amounts close to the reserves established. However, it is possible an individual claim from time to time may result in an aberration from the norm and could have a material impact.

During 2012, the Company increased its products liability reserve by $72,478. The addition of another year of self-insured incidents accounted for $49,312 of this increase. The Company revised its estimates of future settlements for unasserted and premature claims. These revisions increased the reserve by $9,503. Finally, changes in the amount of reserves for cases where sufficient information is known to estimate a liability increased by $13,663.

During 2013, the Company increased its products liability reserve by $60,091. The addition of another year of self-insured incidents accounted for $50,436 of this increase. The Company revised its estimates of future settlements for unasserted and premature claims. These revisions increased the reserve by $8,298. Finally, changes in the amount of reserves for cases where sufficient information is known to estimate a liability increased by $1,357.

The time frame for the payment of a products liability claim is too variable to be meaningful. From the time a claim is filed to its ultimate disposition depends on the unique nature of the case, how it is resolved—claim dismissed, negotiated settlement, trial verdict and appeals process—and is highly dependent on jurisdiction, specific facts, the plaintiff's attorney, the court's docket and other factors. Given that some claims may be resolved in weeks and others may take five years or more, it is impossible to predict with any reasonable reliability the time frame over which the accrued amounts may be paid.

During 2012, the Company paid $73,482 to resolve cases and claims. The Company's products liability reserve balance at December 31, 2012 totaled $206,349 (current portion of $70,267).

During 2013, the Company paid $76,927 to resolve cases and claims. The Company's products liability reserve balance at December 31, 2013 totaled $189,513 (current portion of $70,472).

Products liability expenses totaled $97,504, $103,610 and $89,044 in 2011, 2012 and 2013, respectively.

BILLINGS IN EXCESS OF COSTS AND ESTIMATED EARNINGS

2.117 EMCOR GROUP, INC. (DEC)

CONSOLIDATED BALANCE SHEETS (in part)

(In thousands, except share and per share data)

	December 31, 2013	December 31, 2012
Liabilities and Equity (in part)		
Current liabilities:		
Borrowings under revolving credit facility	$ —	$ —
Current maturities of long-term debt and capital lease obligations	19,332	1,787
Accounts payable	487,738	490,621
Billings in excess of costs and estimated earnings on uncompleted contracts	381,295	383,527
Accrued payroll and benefits	237,779	224,555
Other accrued expenses and liabilities	172,599	194,029
Total current liabilities	1,298,743	1,294,519
Borrowings under revolving credit facility	—	150,000
Long-term debt and capital lease obligations	335,331	4,112
Other long-term obligations	352,215	301,260
Total liabilities	1,986,289	1,749,891

NOTES TO CONSOLIDATED FINANCIAL STATEMENTS

Note 2—Summary of Significant Accounting Policies (in part)

Costs and Estimated Earnings on Uncompleted Contracts

Costs and estimated earnings in excess of billings on uncompleted contracts arise in the consolidated balance sheets when revenues have been recognized but the amounts cannot be billed under the terms of the contracts. Such amounts are recoverable from customers upon various measures of performance, including achievement of certain milestones, completion of specified units, or completion of a contract. Also included in costs and estimated earnings on uncompleted contracts are amounts we seek or will seek to collect from customers or others for errors or changes in contract specifications or design, contract change orders in dispute or unapproved as to both scope and/or price or other customer-related causes of unanticipated additional contract costs (claims and unapproved change orders). Such amounts are recorded at estimated net realizable value when realization is probable and can be reasonably estimated. No profit is recognized on construction costs incurred in connection with claim amounts. Claims and unapproved change orders made by us involve negotiation and, in certain cases, litigation. In the event litigation costs are incurred by us in connection with claims or unapproved change orders, such litigation costs are expensed as incurred, although we may seek to recover these costs. We believe that we have established legal bases for pursuing recovery of our recorded unapproved change orders and claims, and it is management's intention to pursue and litigate such claims, if necessary, until a determination or settlement is reached. Unapproved change orders and claims also involve the use of estimates, and it is reasonably possible that revisions to the estimated recoverable amounts of recorded claims and unapproved change orders may be made in the near term. If we do not successfully resolve these matters, a net expense (recorded as a reduction in revenues) may be required, in addition to amounts that may have been previously provided for. We record the profit associated with the settlement of claims upon receipt of final payment. During 2012, we recognized approximately $9.5 million of profit from the settlement and payment of two claims within the United States electrical construction and facilities services segment. There was no significant profit recognized from settlements or payment of claims in 2013. Claims against us are recognized when a loss is considered probable and amounts are reasonably determinable.

Costs and estimated earnings on uncompleted contracts and related amounts billed as of December 31, 2013 and 2012 were as follows (in thousands):

	2013	2012
Costs incurred on uncompleted contracts	$7,794,620	$7,675,049
Estimated earnings, thereon	835,820	876,496
	8,630,440	8,551,545
Less: billings to date	8,921,008	8,842,011
	$(290,568)	$(290,466)

Such amounts were included in the accompanying Consolidated Balance Sheets at December 31, 2013 and 2012 under the following captions (in thousands):

	2013	2012
Costs and estimated earnings in excess of billings on uncompleted contracts	$ 90,727	$ 93,061
Billings in excess of costs and estimated earnings on uncompleted contracts	(381,295)	(383,527)
	$(290,568)	$(290,466)

As of December 31, 2013 and 2012, costs and estimated earnings in excess of billings on uncompleted contracts included unbilled revenues for unapproved change orders of approximately $19.2 million and $13.8 million, respectively, and claims of approximately $0.4 million and $0.7 million, respectively. In addition, accounts receivable as of December 31, 2013 and 2012 included claims of approximately $2.9 million and $0.8 million, respectively. Additionally, there are contractually billed amounts and retention related to such contracts of $56.1 million and $41.0 million as of December 31, 2013 and 2012, respectively. Generally, contractually billed amounts will not be paid by the customer to us until final resolution of related claims.

DISCONTINUED OPERATIONS

2.118 CAREER EDUCATION CORPORATION (DEC)

CONSOLIDATED BALANCE SHEETS (in part)

(In thousands, except share and per share amounts)

	As of December 31,	
	2013	2012
Liabilities and Stockholders' Equity (in part)		
Current liabilities:		
Short-term borrowings	$ —	$ 80,000
Accounts payable	24,651	32,070
Accrued expenses:		
Payroll and related benefits	34,172	38,772
Advertising and production costs	17,599	20,963
Income taxes	14,994	—
Other	43,275	34,999
Deferred tuition revenue	61,131	69,675
Liabilities of discontinued operations	11,610	76,236
Total current liabilities	207,432	352,715

NOTES TO CONSOLIDATED FINANCIAL STATEMENTS

December 31, 2013, 2012 and 2011

2. Summary of Significant Accounting Policies (in part)

j. Discontinued Operations

Discontinued operations are accounted for in accordance with the provisions of Financial Accounting Standards Board ("FASB") Accounting Standards Codification ("ASC") Section 360-10-35 *Property, Plant, and Equipment*. In accordance with FASB ASC Section 360-10-35, the net assets of discontinued operations are recorded on our consolidated balance sheets at estimated fair value. The results of operations of discontinued operations are segregated from continuing operations and reported separately as discontinued operations in our consolidated statements of (loss) income and comprehensive (loss) income. See Note 5 "Discontinued Operations" of the notes to our consolidated financial statements for further discussion.

5. Discontinued Operations (in part)

As of December 31, 2013, the results of operations for campuses that have ceased operations or schools that were sold, and are considered distinct operations as defined under FASB ASC Topic 205—*Presentation of Financial Statements,* are presented within discontinued operations. During the fourth quarter of 2013, we completed the sale of our International Segment. See Note 3 "Dispositions" of the notes to our consolidated financial statements for further discussion. During 2013, we completed the teach-out of our SBC Hazelwood, SBI Landover,

SBC Milwaukee and IADT Schaumburg campuses. All current and prior period financial statements include the results of operations and financial position of these campuses as components of discontinued operations.

Assets and Liabilities of Discontinued Operations

Assets and liabilities of discontinued operations on our consolidated balance sheets as of December 31, 2013 and 2012 include the following (dollars in thousands):

	As of December 31,	
	2013	2012
Assets:		
Current assets:		
Cash and cash equivalents	$ —	$127,738
Receivables, net	213	16,928
Other current assets	50	6,458
Deferred income tax assets, net	—	3,454
Total current assets	263	154,578
Non-current assets:		
Property and equipment, net	—	29,790
Goodwill	—	45,669
Intangible assets, net	—	5,675
Deferred income tax assets	—	17,804
Other assets, net	1,200	4,606
Total assets of discontinued operations	$ 1,463	$258,122
Liabilities:		
Current liabilities:		
Current maturities of capital lease obligations	$ —	$ 211
Accounts payable	10	6,378
Accrued expenses	325	18,110
Deferred tuition revenue	—	42,363
Remaining lease obligations	11,275	9,174
Total current liabilities	11,610	76,236
Non-current liabilities:		
Remaining lease obligations	27,507	33,103
Other	75	2,836
Total liabilities of discontinued operations	$39,192	$112,175

Remaining Lease Obligations

A number of the campuses that ceased operations have remaining lease obligations that expire over time with the latest expiration in 2019. A liability is recorded representing the fair value of the remaining lease obligation at the time the space is no longer being utilized. Changes in our future remaining lease obligations, which are reflected within current and non-current liabilities of discontinued operations on our consolidated balance sheets, for the years ended December 31, 2013, 2012 and 2011, were as follows (dollars in thousands):

	Balance, Beginning of Period	Charges Incurred[1]	Net Cash Payments[2]	Other[3]	Balance, End of Period
For the twelve months ended December 31, 2013	$42,277	$8,551	$(12,323)	$ 277	$38,782
For the twelve months ended December 31, 2012	$45,961	$7,371	$(11,055)	$ —	$42,277
For the twelve months ended December 31, 2011	$50,827	$7,636	$(11,035)	$(1,467)	$45,961

[1] Includes charges for newly vacated spaces and subsequent adjustments for accretion, revised estimates, and variances between estimated and actual charges, net of any reversals for terminated lease obligations.

[2] See Note 9 "Leases" of the notes to our consolidated financial statements for the future minimum lease payments under operating leases for discontinued operations as of December 31, 2013.

[3] Includes existing prepaid rent and deferred rent liability balances for newly vacated spaces that are netted with the losses incurred in the period recorded.

INSURANCE

2.119 UNIVERSAL HEALTH SERVICES, INC. (DEC)

CONSOLIDATED BALANCE SHEETS (in part)

	December 31,	
(Dollar amounts in thousands)	**2013**	**2012**
Liabilities and Stockholders' Equity (in part)		
Current liabilities:		
Current maturities of long-term debt	$ 99,312	$ 2,589
Accounts payable	276,911	247,033
Liabilities of facilities held for sale	0	850
Accrued liabilities		
Compensation and related benefits	278,206	259,646
Interest	9,577	10,774
Taxes other than income	59,473	49,829
Other	329,282	322,275
Current federal and state income taxes	7,127	1,062
Total current liabilities	1,059,888	894,058

NOTES TO CONSOLIDATED FINANCIAL STATEMENTS

1) Business and Summary of Significant Accounting Policies (in part)

M) Self-Insured Risks: We provide for self-insured risks, primarily general and professional liability claims and workers' compensation claims. Our estimated liability for self-insured professional and general liability claims is based on a number of factors including, among other things, the number of asserted claims and reported incidents, estimates of losses for these claims based on recent and historical settlement amounts, estimate of incurred but not reported claims based on historical experience, and estimates of amounts recoverable under our commercial insurance policies. All relevant information, including our own historical experience is used in estimating the expected amount of claims. While we continuously monitor these factors, our ultimate liability for professional and general liability claims could change materially from our current estimates due to inherent uncertainties involved in making this estimate. Our estimated self-insured reserves are reviewed and changed, if necessary, at each reporting date and changes are recognized currently as additional expense or as a reduction of expense. See Note 8 for discussion of adjustments to our prior year reserves for claims related to our self-insured general and professional liability and workers' compensation liability.

In addition, we also maintain self-insured employee benefits programs for employee healthcare and dental claims. The ultimate costs related to these programs include expenses for claims incurred and paid in addition to an accrual for the estimated expenses incurred in connection with claims incurred but not yet reported.

8) Commitments and Contingencies (in part)

Professional and General Liability, Workers' Compensation Liability and Property Insurance (in part)

Professional and General Liability and Workers Compensation Liability:

Effective January 1, 2008, most of our subsidiaries became self-insured for professional and general liability exposure up to $10 million per occurrence. Prior to our acquisition of Psychiatric Solutions, Inc. ("PSI") in November, 2010, our subsidiaries purchased several excess policies through commercial insurance carriers which provide for coverage in excess of $10 million up to $200 million per occurrence and in the aggregate. However, we are liable for 10% of the claims paid pursuant to the commercially insured coverage in excess of $10 million up to $60 million per occurrence and in the aggregate.

Prior to our acquisition in November, 2010, the PSI subsidiaries were commercially insured for professional and general liability insurance claims in excess of a $3 million self-insured retention to a limit of $75 million. PSI utilized its captive insurance company and that captive insurance company remains in place after our acquisition of PSI to manage the self-insured retention for all former PSI subsidiaries for claims incurred prior to January 1, 2011. The captive insurance company also continues to insure all professional and general liability claims, regardless of date incurred, for the former PSI subsidiaries located in Florida and Puerto Rico.

Since our acquisition of PSI on November 15, 2010, the former PSI subsidiaries are self-insured for professional and general liability exposure up to $3 million per occurrence and our legacy subsidiaries (which are not former PSI subsidiaries) are self-insured for professional and general liability exposure up to $10 million per occurrence. Effective November, 2010, our subsidiaries (including the former PSI subsidiaries) were provided with several excess policies through commercial insurance carriers which provide for coverage in excess of the applicable per occurrence self-insured retention (either $3 million or $10 million) up to $250 million per occurrence and in the aggregate. We remain liable for 10% of the claims paid pursuant to the commercially insured coverage in excess of $10 million up to $60 million per occurrence and in the aggregate. The 9 behavioral health facilities acquired from Ascend Health Corporation in October, 2012 have general and professional liability policies through commercial insurance carriers which provide for up to $20 million of aggregate coverage, subject to a $25,000 per occurrence deductible. These facilities, like our other facilities, are also provided excess coverage through commercial insurance carriers for coverage in excess of the underlying commercial policy limitations up to $250 million per occurrence and in the aggregate.

Our estimated liability for self-insured professional and general liability claims is based on a number of factors including, among other things, the number of asserted claims and reported incidents, estimates of losses for these claims based on recent and historical settlement amounts, estimates of incurred but not reported claims based on historical experience, and estimates of amounts recoverable under our commercial insurance policies. While we continuously monitor these factors, our ultimate liability for professional and general liability claims could change materially from our current estimates due to inherent uncertainties involved in making this estimate. Given our significant self-insured exposure for professional and general liability claims, there can be no assurance that a sharp increase in the number and/or severity of claims asserted against us will not have a material adverse effect on our future results of operations.

As of December 31, 2013, the total accrual for our professional and general liability claims was $206 million, of which $44 million is included in current liabilities. As of December 31, 2012, the total accrual for our professional and general liability claims was $279 million, of which $48 million is included in current liabilities.

We recorded reductions to our professional and general liability self-insurance reserves (relating to prior years) amounting to $81 million during 2013, $27 million during 2012 and $11 million during 2011. The favorable change in our estimated future claims payments recorded during 2013, relating to years prior to 2013, were due primarily to: (i) an increased weighting given to company-specific metrics (to 100% from 75%), and decreased general industry metrics (to 0% from 25%), related to projected incidents per exposure, historical claims experience and loss development factors; (ii) historical data which measured the realized favorable impact of medical malpractice tort reform experienced in several states in which we operate, and; (iii) a decrease in claims related to certain higher risk specialties (such as obstetrical) due to a continuation of the company-wide patient safety initiative undertaken during the last several years. As the number of our facilities and our patient volumes have increased, thereby providing for a statistically significant data group, and taking into consideration our long-history of company-specific risk management programs and claims experience, our reserve analyses have included a greater emphasis on our historical professional and general liability experience which has developed favorably as compared to general industry trends. The favorable change recorded during 2012 resulted from favorable changes in our estimated future claims payments pursuant to a reserve analysis. The favorable change recorded during 2011 consisted primarily of third-party recoveries and reserve reductions in connection with PHICO—related claims which we became liable for upon PHICO's (a former commercial insurance carrier) liquidation in 2002.

As of December 31, 2013, the total accrual for our workers' compensation liability claims was $64 million, of which $34 million is included in current liabilities. As of December 31, 2012, the total accrual for our workers' compensation liability claims was $66 million, of which $35 million is included in current liabilities. The adjustments recorded during the last three years to our prior year reserves for workers' compensation claims did not have a material impact on our consolidated results of operations for the years ended December 31, 2013, 2012 or 2011.

DEFERRED REVENUE

2.120 CA, INC. (MAR)
CONSOLIDATED BALANCE SHEETS (in part)

	March 31,	
(In millions, except share amounts)	2013	2012
Liabilities and Stockholders' Equity (in part)		
Current liabilities:		
Current portion of long-term debt	$ 16	$ 14
Accounts payable	93	95
Accrued salaries, wages and commissions	304	350
Accrued expenses and other current liabilities	406	444
Deferred revenue (billed or collected)	2,482	2,658
Taxes payable, other than income taxes payable	77	80
Federal, state and foreign income taxes payable	151	96
Deferred income taxes	12	14
Total current liabilities	$3,541	$3,751
Long-term debt, net of current portion	$1,274	$1,287
Federal, state and foreign income taxes payable	338	430
Deferred income taxes	120	44
Deferred revenue (billed or collected)	975	972
Other noncurrent liabilities	113	116
Total liabilities	$6,361	$6,600

Note 1—Significant Accounting Policies (in part)

(q) Deferred Revenue (Billed or Collected): The Company accounts for unearned revenue on billed amounts due from customers on a gross basis. Unearned revenue on billed installments (collected or uncollected) is reported as deferred revenue in the liabilities section of the Consolidated Balance Sheets.

Deferred revenue (billed or collected) excludes contractual commitments executed under license and maintenance agreements that will be billed in future periods. See Note 7, "Deferred Revenue," for additional information.

Note 7—Deferred Revenue

The current and noncurrent components of "Deferred revenue (billed or collected)" at March 31, 2013 and March 31, 2012 were as follows:

	At March 31,	
(in millions)	2013	2012
Current:		
Subscription and maintenance	$2,307	$2,479
Professional services	154	162
Software fees and other	21	17
Total deferred revenue (billed or collected)—current	$2,482	$2,658
Noncurrent:		
Subscription and maintenance	$ 940	$ 935
Professional services	33	35
Software fees and other	2	2
Total deferred revenue (billed or collected)—noncurrent	$ 975	$ 972
Total deferred revenue (billed or collected)	$3,457	$3,630

ENVIRONMENT

2.121 EASTMAN CHEMICAL COMPANY (DEC)
CONSOLIDATED STATEMENTS OF FINANCIAL POSITION (in part)

(Dollars in millions, except per share amounts)	December 31, 2013	December 31, 2012
Liabilities and Stockholders' Equity (in part)		
Current liabilities		
Payables and other current liabilities	$1,470	$1,360
Borrowings due within one year	—	4
Total current liabilities	1,470	1,364
Long-term borrowings	4,254	4,779
Deferred income tax liabilities	496	182
Post-employment obligations	1,297	1,856
Other long-term liabilities	453	501
Total liabilities	7,970	8,682

1. Significant Accounting Policies (in part)

Environmental Costs

The Company accrues environmental remediation costs when it is probable that the Company has incurred a liability at a contaminated site and the amount can be reasonably estimated. When a single amount cannot be reasonably estimated but the cost can be estimated within a range, the Company accrues the minimum amount. This undiscounted accrued amount reflects liabilities expected to be paid out within 30 years and the Company's assumptions about remediation requirements at the contaminated site, the nature of the remedy, the outcome of discussions with regulatory agencies and other potentially responsible parties at multi-party sites, and the number and financial viability of other potentially responsible parties.Changes in the estimates on which the accruals are based, unanticipated government enforcement action, or changes in health, safety, environmental, and chemical control regulations and testing requirements could result in higher or lower costs.

The Company also establishes reserves for closure/postclosure costs associated with the environmental and other assets it maintains. Environmental assets include but are not limited to waste management units, such as landfills, water treatment facilities, and ash ponds.

When these types of assets are constructed or installed, a reserve is established for the future costs anticipated to be associated with the closure of the site based on an expected life of the environmental assets and the applicable regulatory closure requirements. These expenses are charged into earnings over the estimated useful life of the assets. Currently, the Company estimates the useful life of each individual asset up to 50 years. If the Company changes its estimate of the environmental asset retirement obligation costs or its estimate of the useful lives of these assets, the expenses charged into earnings could increase or decrease. The Company also monitors conditional obligations and recognizes contingent liabilities associated with them when and to the extent that more detailed information becomes available concerning applicable retirement costs.

The current portion of accruals for environmental liabilities is included in payables and other current liabilities with the long-term portion included in other long-term liabilities. These accruals exclude claims for recoveries from insurance companies or other third parties. Environmental costs are capitalized if they extend the life of the related property, increase its capacity, and/or mitigate or prevent future contamination. The cost of operating and maintaining environmental control facilities is charged to expense.

For additional information see Note 13, "Environmental Matters".

Litigation and Contingent Liabilities

The Company and its operations from time to time are, and in the future may be, parties to or targets of lawsuits, claims, investigations, and proceedings, including product liability, personal injury, asbestos, patent and intellectual property, commercial, contract, environmental, antitrust, health and safety, and employment matters, which are handled and defended in the ordinary course of business. The Company accrues a liability for such matters when it is probable that a liability has been incurred and the amount can be reasonably estimated. When a single amount cannot be reasonably estimated but the cost can be estimated within a range, the Company accrues the minimum amount. The Company expenses legal costs, including those expected to be incurred in connection with a loss contingency, as incurred.

7. Payables and Other Current Liabilities

	December 31,	
(Dollars in millions)	2013	2012
Trade creditors	$ 762	$ 723
Accrued payrolls, vacation, and variable-incentive compensation	205	171
Accrued taxes	80	76
Post-employment obligations	59	62
Interest payable	46	59
Environmental contingent liabilities, current portion	40	35
Other	278	234
Total payables and other current liabilities	$1,470	$1,360

The current portion of post-employment obligations at December 31, 2013 is an estimate of 2014 payments. Included in "Other" above are certain accruals for payroll deductions and employee benefits, dividends payable, the current portion of hedging liabilities, divestitures, and other payables and accruals.

13. Environmental Matters

Certain Eastman manufacturing sites generate hazardous and nonhazardous wastes, the treatment, storage, transportation, and disposal of which are regulated by various governmental agencies. In connection with the cleanup of various hazardous waste sites, the Company, along with many other entities, has been designated a potentially responsible party ("PRP"), by the U.S. Environmental Protection Agency under the Comprehensive Environmental Response, Compensation and Liability Act, which potentially subjects PRPs to joint and several liability for such cleanup costs. In addition, the Company will be required to incur costs for environmental remediation and closure and postclosure under the federal Resource Conservation and Recovery Act. Reserves for environmental contingencies have been established in accordance with Eastman's policies described in Note 1, "Significant Accounting Policies". The Company's total reserve for environmental contingencies was $368 million and $394 million at December 31, 2013 and 2012, respectively. At December 31, 2013 and 2012, this reserve included $9 million and $8 million, respectively, related to sites previously closed and impaired by Eastman, as well as sites that have been divested by Eastman but for which the Company retains the environmental liability. Amounts at December 31, 2013 and 2012 included environmental contingencies assumed in the acquisition of Solutia on July 2, 2012. See Note 2, "Acquisitions and Investments in Joint Ventures."

Estimated future environmental expenditures for remediation costs ranged from the minimum or best estimate of $341 million to the maximum of $581 million and from the minimum or best estimate of $365 million to the maximum of $623 million at December 31, 2013 and 2012, respectively. The maximum estimated future costs are considered to be reasonably possible and include the amounts accrued at both December 31, 2013 and 2012. Although the resolution of uncertainties related to these environmental matters may have a material adverse effect on the Company's consolidated results of operations in the period recognized, because of expected sharing of costs, the availability of legal defenses, and the Company's preliminary assessment of actions that may be required, management does not believe that the Company's liability for these environmental matters, individually or in the aggregate, will be material to the Company's consolidated financial position or cash flows.

For facilities that have environmental asset retirement obligations, the best estimate accrued to date over the facilities' estimated useful lives for these asset retirement obligation costs were $27 million and $29 million at December 31, 2013 and 2012, respectively.

Reserves for environmental remediation that management believes to be probable and estimable are recorded as current and long-term liabilities in the Consolidated Statements of Financial Position. These reserves include liabilities expected to be paid out within 30 years. The amounts charged to pre-tax earnings for environmental remediation and related charges are included in cost of sales and other charges (income), net, and are summarized below:

(Dollars in millions)	
Balance at December 31, 2012	$365
Changes in estimates recorded to earnings and other	7
Cash reductions	(31)
Balance at December 31, 2013	$341

The Company's total environmental reserve for environmental contingencies, including remediation costs and asset retirement obligations, is recorded in the Consolidated Statements of Financial Position as follows:

	December 31,	
(Dollars in millions)	2013	2012
Environmental contingent liabilities, current	$ 40	$ 35
Environmental contingent liabilities, long-term	328	359
Total	$368	$394

Additionally, costs of certain remediation projects included in the assumed environmental reserve are subject to a cost-sharing arrangement with Monsanto Company ("Monsanto") under the provisions of the Amended and Restated Settlement Agreement effective February 28, 2008 (the "Effective Date"), into which Solutia entered with Monsanto upon its emergence from bankruptcy (the "Monsanto Settlement Agreement"). Under the provisions of the Monsanto Settlement Agreement, the Company shares responsibility with Monsanto for remediation at certain locations outside of the boundaries of plant sites in Anniston, Alabama and Sauget, Illinois (the "Shared Sites"). The Company is responsible for the funding of environmental liabilities at the Shared Sites up to a total of $325 million from the Effective Date. If remediation costs for the Shared Sites exceed this amount, such costs will thereafter be shared equally between the Company and Monsanto. Including payments by Solutia prior to its acquisition by Eastman, $56 million had been paid for costs at the Shared Sites as of December 31, 2013. As of December 31, 2013, an additional $215 million has been accrued for estimated future remediation costs at the Shared Sites, over a period of thirty years.

Environmental costs are capitalized if they extend the life of the related property, increase its capacity, and/or mitigate or prevent future contamination. The cost of operating and maintaining environmental control facilities is charged to expense. The Company's cash expenditures related to environmental protection and improvement were $285 million, $262 million, and $219 million in 2013, 2012, and 2011, respectively. These amounts were primarily for operating costs associated with environmental protection equipment and facilities, but also included $53 million and $34 million in expenditures for engineering and construction in 2013 and 2012, respectively.

In fourth quarter 2012, the Company recognized asset impairments of $17 million due to a change in approach to address recently finalized boiler air emissions regulations. See Note 16, "Asset Impairments and Restructuring Charges (Gains), Net" for additional information.

CONTINGENT CONSIDERATION

2.122 BOSTON SCIENTIFIC CORPORATION (DEC)
CONSOLIDATED BALANCE SHEETS (in part)

	As of December 31,	
(In millions, except share and per share data	2013	2012
Liabilities and Stockholders' Equity (in part)		
Current liabilities:		
Current debt obligations	$ 3	$ 4
Accounts payable	246	232
Accrued expenses	1,348	1,284
Other current liabilities	227	252
Total current liabilities	1,824	1,772
Long-term debt	4,237	4,252
Deferred income taxes	1,402	1,713
Other long-term liabilities	2,569	2,547
Commitments and contingencies		

Note A—Significant Accounting Policies (in part)

Valuation of Business Combinations

We allocate the amounts we pay for each acquisition to the assets we acquire and liabilities we assume based on their fair values at the dates of acquisition, including identifiable intangible assets and in-process research and development which either arise from a contractual or legal right or are separable from goodwill. We base the fair value of identifiable intangible assets acquired in a business combination, including in-process research and development, on detailed valuations that use information and assumptions provided by management, which consider management's best estimates of inputs and assumptions that a market participant would use. We allocate any excess purchase price over the fair value of the net tangible and identifiable intangible assets acquired to goodwill. Transaction costs associated with these acquisitions are expensed as incurred through selling, general and administrative costs.

In those circumstances where an acquisition involves a contingent consideration arrangement, we recognize a liability equal to the fair value of the contingent payments we expect to make as of the acquisition date. We re-measure this liability each reporting period and record changes in the fair value through a separate line item within our consolidated statements of operations. Increases or decreases in the fair value of the contingent consideration liability can result from changes in discount periods and rates, as well as changes in the timing and amount of revenue estimates or in the timing or likelihood of achieving regulatory, revenue or commercialization-based milestones.

Note B—Acquisitions (in part)

Vessix Vascular, Inc.

On November 19, 2012, we completed the acquisition of 100 percent of the fully diluted equity of Vessix Vascular, Inc. (Vessix). Vessix is a developer of a therapy to treat uncontrolled hypertension, or high blood pressure. The Vessix Vascular V2 Renal Denervation System™ has received CE Mark in Europe and TGA approval in Australia. Vessix has initiated the REDUCE-HTN post-market surveillance study and launched the product in CE Mark countries in 2013. We are integrating the operations of the Vessix business into our Peripheral Interventions business. Total consideration includes an initial $125 million at closing of the transaction and up to an additional $300 million of clinical and revenue-based milestones and revenue-based earnouts through 2016.

Purchase Price Allocation

The components of the aggregate purchase price for acquisitions consummated in 2012 are as follows (in millions):

Cash, net of cash acquired	$367
Fair value of contingent consideration	467
Fair value of prior interests	79
Fair value of debt assumed	9
	$922

Total consideration for the 2012 acquisitions included initial $367 million cash payments, net of cash acquired, at closing of the transactions, with potential payments of up to an additional $1.615 billion based upon achievement of certain regulatory- and commercialization-related milestones and revenue through 2018. As of the respective acquisition dates, we recorded total contingent consideration liabilities of $467 million, representing the estimated fair value of the contingent consideration we expected to pay to the former shareholders of the acquired companies. The fair value of the contingent consideration liabilities was estimated by discounting, to present value, contingent payments expected to be made. In certain circumstances, we utilized a probability-weighted approach or monte carlo revenue simulation model to determine the fair value of contingent consideration.

Note E—Fair Value Measurements (in part)

Other Fair Value Measurements (in part)

Recurring Fair Value Measurements (in part)

On a recurring basis, we measure certain financial assets and financial liabilities at fair value based upon quoted market prices, where available. Where quoted market prices or other observable inputs are not available, we apply valuation techniques to estimate fair value.

Topic 820 establishes a three-level valuation hierarchy for disclosure of fair value measurements. The categorization of financial assets and financial liabilities within the valuation hierarchy is based upon the lowest level of input that is significant to the measurement of fair value. The three levels of the hierarchy are defined as follows:

- Level 1—Inputs to the valuation methodology are quoted market prices for identical assets or liabilities.
- Level 2—Inputs to the valuation methodology are other observable inputs, including quoted market prices for similar assets or liabilities and market-corroborated inputs.
- Level 3—Inputs to the valuation methodology are unobservable inputs based on management's best estimate of inputs market participants would use in pricing the asset or liability at the measurement date, including assumptions about risk.

Assets and liabilities measured at fair value on a recurring basis consist of the following as of December 31, 2013 and December 31, 2012:

(In millions)	As of December 31, 2013				As of December 31, 2012			
	Level 1	Level 2	Level 3	Total	Level 1	Level 2	Level 3	Total
Assets								
Money market and government funds	$ 38	$ —	$ —	$ 38	$ 39	$ —	$ —	$ 39
Currency hedge contracts	—	264	—	264	—	121	—	121
Interest rate contracts	—	1	—	1	—	—	—	—
	$ 38	$265	$ —	$303	$ 39	$121	$ —	$160
Liabilities								
Currency hedge contracts	$—	$ 55	$ —	$ 55	$—	$ 57	$ —	$ 57
Accrued contingent consideration	—	—	501	501	—	—	663	663
Interest rate contracts	—	8	—	8	—	—	—	—
	$—	$ 63	$501	$564	—	$ 57	$663	$720

Our recurring fair value measurements using significant unobservable inputs (Level 3) relate solely to our contingent consideration liability. Refer to *Note B—Acquisitions* for a discussion of the changes in the fair value of our contingent consideration liability.

Note I—Supplemental Balance Sheet Information (in part)

Components of selected captions in our accompanying consolidated balance sheets are as follows:

Accrued Expenses

(In millions)	As of	
	December 31, 2013	December 31, 2012
Legal reserves	$ 84	$ 100
Payroll and related liabilities	488	452
Accrued contingent consideration	148	120
Other	628	612
	$1,348	$1,284

Other Long-Term Liabilities

(In millions)	As of	
	December 31, 2013	December 31, 2012
Legal reserves	$ 523	$ 391
Accrued income taxes	1,283	1,215
Accrued contingent consideration	353	543
Other long-term liabilities	410	398
	$2,569	$2,547

2.123 MASTERCARD INCORPORATED (DEC)

CONSOLIDATED BALANCE SHEET (in part)

	December 31,	
(In millions, except share data)	**2013**	**2012**
Liabilities and Equity (in part)		
Accounts payable	$ 338	$ 357
Settlement due to customers	1,433	1,064
Restricted security deposits held for customers	911	777
Accrued litigation	886	726
Accrued expenses	2,101	1,748
Other current liabilities	363	234
Total current liabilities	6,032	4,906
Deferred income taxes	117	104
Other liabilities	598	523
Total Liabilities	6,747	5,533
Commitments and contingencies		

NOTES TO CONSOLIDATED FINANCIAL STATEMENTS

Note 1. Summary of Significant Accounting Policies (in part)

Litigation—The Company is a party to certain legal and regulatory proceedings with respect to a variety of matters. The Company evaluates the likelihood of an unfavorable outcome of all legal or regulatory proceedings to which it is a party and accrues a loss contingency when the loss is probable and reasonably estimable. These judgments are subjective based on the status of the legal or regulatory proceedings, the merits of its defenses and consultation with in-house and external legal counsel. Legal costs are expensed as incurred and recorded in general and administrative expenses.

Restricted cash—The Company classifies cash as restricted when the cash is unavailable for withdrawal or usage for general operations. Restrictions may include legally restricted deposits, contracts entered into with others, or the Company's statements of intention with regard to particular deposits. In December 2012, the Company made a payment into a qualified cash settlement fund related to its U.S. merchant class litigation. The Company has presented these funds as restricted cash for litigation settlement since the use of the funds under the qualified cash settlement fund is restricted for payment under the settlement agreement. In January 2014, $164 million was returned to MasterCard from the qualified cash settlement fund related to the opt out merchants and will be reclassified to cash and cash equivalents. See Note 18 (Legal and Regulatory Proceedings) for further detail.

Note 10. Accrued Expenses and Accrued Litigation

Accrued expenses consisted of the following at December 31:

(In millions)	**2013**	**2012**
Customer and merchant incentives	$1,286	$1,058
Personnel costs	413	354
Advertising	149	122
Income and other taxes	95	94
Other	158	120
Total accrued expenses	$2,101	$1,748

As of December 31, 2013 and 2012, the Company's provision related to U.S. merchant litigations was $886 million and $726 million, respectively. These amounts are not included in the accrued expenses table above and are separately reported as accrued litigation on the consolidated balance sheet. In the fourth quarter of 2013, MasterCard recorded an incremental net pre-tax charge of $95 million related to the opt out merchants. The accrued litigation item also includes $68 million related to the timing of MasterCard's administration of the short-term reduction in default credit interchange from U.S. issuers. There is a corresponding equal amount presented in settlement due from customers. See Note 18 (Legal and Regulatory Proceedings) for further discussion of the U.S. merchant class litigation.

Note 18. Legal and Regulatory Proceedings (in part)

Interchange Litigation and Regulatory Proceedings (in part)

Interchange fees represent a sharing of payment system costs among the financial institutions participating in a four-party payment card system such as MasterCard's. Typically, interchange fees are paid by the acquirer to the issuer in connection with purchase transactions initiated with the payment system's cards. These fees reimburse the issuer for a portion of the costs incurred by it in providing services which are of benefit to all participants in the system, including acquirers and merchants. MasterCard or financial institutions establish default interchange fees in certain circumstances that apply when there is no other interchange fee arrangement between the issuer and the acquirer. MasterCard establishes a variety of interchange rates depending on such considerations as the location and the type of transaction, collects the interchange fee on behalf of the institutions entitled to receive it and remits the interchange fee to eligible institutions. MasterCard's interchange fees and other practices are subject to regulatory and/or legal review and/or challenges in a number of jurisdictions, including the proceedings described below. At this time, it is not possible to determine the ultimate resolution of, or estimate the liability related to, any of these interchange proceedings (except as otherwise indicated below), as the proceedings involve complex claims and/or substantial uncertainties and, in some cases, could include unascertainable damages or fines. Except as described below, no provision for losses has been provided in connection with them. Some of the proceedings described below could have a significant impact on our customers in the applicable country and on MasterCard's level of business in those countries. The proceedings reflect the significant and intense legal, regulatory and legislative scrutiny worldwide that interchange fees and acceptance practices have been receiving. When taken as a whole, the resulting decisions, regulations and legislation with respect to interchange fees and acceptance practices may have a material adverse effect on the Company's prospects for future growth and its overall results of operations, financial position and cash flows.

United States. In June 2005, the first of a series of complaints were filed on behalf of merchants (the majority of the complaints are styled as class actions, although a few complaints were filed on behalf of individual merchant plaintiffs) against MasterCard International Incorporated, Visa U.S.A., Inc., Visa International Service Association and a number of financial institutions. Taken together, the claims in the complaints are generally brought under both Sections 1 and 2 of the Sherman Act, which prohibit monopolization and attempts or conspiracies to monopolize a particular industry, and some of these complaints contain unfair competition law claims under state law. The complaints allege, among other things, that MasterCard, Visa, and certain financial institutions conspired to set the price of interchange fees, enacted point of sale acceptance rules (including the no surcharge rule) in violation of antitrust laws and engaged in unlawful tying and bundling of certain products and services. The cases have been consolidated for pre-trial proceedings in the U.S. District Court for the Eastern District of New York in MDL No. 1720. The plaintiffs have filed a consolidated class action complaint that seeks treble damages, as well as attorneys' fees and injunctive relief.

In July 2006, the group of purported merchant class plaintiffs filed a supplemental complaint alleging that MasterCard's initial public offering of its Class A Common Stock in May 2006 (the "IPO") and certain purported agreements entered into between MasterCard and financial institutions in connection with the IPO: (1) violate U.S. antitrust laws and (2) constituted a fraudulent conveyance because the financial institutions allegedly attempted to release, without adequate consideration, MasterCard's right to assess them for MasterCard's litigation liabilities. In November 2008, the district court granted MasterCard's motion to dismiss the plaintiffs' supplemental complaint in its entirety with leave to file an amended complaint. The class plaintiffs repled their complaint. The causes of action and claims for relief in the complaint generally mirror those in the plaintiffs' original IPO-related complaint although the plaintiffs have attempted to expand their factual allegations based upon discovery that has been garnered in the case. The class plaintiffs seek treble damages and injunctive relief including, but not limited to, an order reversing and unwinding the IPO. In July 2009, the class plaintiffs and individual plaintiffs served confidential expert reports detailing the plaintiffs' theories of liability and alleging damages in the tens of billions of dollars. The defendants served their expert reports in December 2009 rebutting the plaintiffs' assertions both with respect to liability and damages.

In February 2011, MasterCard and MasterCard International Incorporated entered into each of: (1) an omnibus judgment sharing and settlement sharing agreement with Visa Inc., Visa U.S.A. Inc. and Visa International Service Association and a number of financial institutions; and (2) a MasterCard settlement and judgment sharing agreement with a number of financial institutions. The agreements provide for the apportionment of certain costs and liabilities which MasterCard, the Visa parties and the financial institutions may incur, jointly and/or severally, in the event of an adverse judgment or settlement of one or all of the cases in the merchant litigations. Among a number of scenarios addressed by the agreements, in the event of a global settlement involving the Visa parties, the financial institutions and MasterCard, MasterCard would pay 12% of the monetary portion of the settlement. In the event of a settlement involving only MasterCard and the financial institutions with respect to their issuance of MasterCard cards, MasterCard would pay 36% of the monetary portion of such settlement.

In October 2012, the parties entered into a definitive settlement agreement with respect to the merchant class litigation and the defendants separately entered into a settlement agreement with the individual merchant plaintiffs (the terms of which were consistent with a memorandum of understanding that was executed by the parties in July 2012). The settlements included cash payments that were apportioned among the defendants pursuant to the omnibus judgment sharing and settlement sharing agreement described above. MasterCard also agreed to provide class members with a short-term reduction in default credit interchange rates and to modify certain of its business practices, including its No Surcharge Rule. The court granted final approval of the settlement in December 2013, which has been appealed by objectors to the settlement.

Merchants representing slightly more than 25% of the MasterCard and Visa purchase volume over the relevant period chose to opt out of the class settlement. MasterCard anticipates that most of the larger merchants who opted out of the settlement will initiate separate actions seeking to recover damages, and over 25 opt-out complaints have been filed on behalf of numerous merchants in various jurisdictions. Those cases are in the early stages and the defendants have consolidated all of these matters (except for one state court action) in front of the same court that is overseeing the approval of the settlement. In addition, certain competitors have raised objections to the settlement, including Discover. Discover's objections include a challenge to the settlement on the grounds that certain of the rule changes agreed to in the settlement constitute a restraint of trade in violation of Section 1 of the Sherman Act.

MasterCard recorded a pre-tax charge of $770 million in the fourth quarter of 2011 and an additional $20 million pre-tax charge in the second quarter of 2012 relating to the settlement agreements described above. In 2012, MasterCard paid $790 million with respect to the settlements, of which $726 million was paid into a qualified cash settlement fund related to the merchant class litigation. At December 31, 2013, MasterCard had $723 million in the qualified cash settlement fund classified as restricted cash on its balance sheet. The class settlement agreement provided for a return to the defendants of a portion of the class cash settlement fund based upon the percentage of purchase volume represented by the opt out merchants. This resulted in $164 million from the cash settlement fund being returned to MasterCard in January 2014 and reclassified at that time from restricted cash to cash and cash equivalents. In the fourth quarter of 2013, MasterCard recorded an incremental net pre-tax charge of $95 million related to these opt out merchants, representing a change in its estimate of possible losses relating to these matters. Accordingly, as of December 31, 2013, MasterCard had accrued a liability of $818 million as a reserve for both the merchant class litigation and the filed and anticipated opt out merchant cases.

The portion of the accrued liability relating to the opt out merchants does not represent an estimate of a loss, if any, if the opt out merchant matters were litigated to a final outcome, in which case MasterCard cannot estimate the potential liability. MasterCard's estimate involves significant judgment and may change depending on progress in settlement negotiations or depending upon decisions in any opt out merchant cases. In addition, in the event that the merchant class litigation settlement approval is overturned on appeal, a negative outcome in the litigation could have a material adverse effect on MasterCard's results of operations, financial position and cash flows.

DERIVATIVES

2.124 REGAL BELOIT CORPORATION (DEC)
CONSOLIDATED BALANCE SHEETS (in part)

(Dollars in Millions)

	December 28, 2013	December 29, 2012
Liabilities and Equity (in part)		
Current liabilities:		
Accounts payable	$304.6	$251.8
Dividends payable	9.0	8.5
Hedging obligations	11.3	6.3
Accrued compensation and employee benefits	85.6	80.0
Other accrued expenses	132.0	123.5
Current maturities of debt	158.4	63.8
Total current liabilities	700.9	533.9

NOTES TO THE CONSOLIDATED FINANCIAL STATEMENTS

(3) Accounting Policies (in part)

Derivative Financial Instruments

Derivative instruments are recorded on the consolidated balance sheet at fair value. Any fair value changes are recorded in net earnings or Accumulated Other Comprehensive Loss as determined under accounting guidance that establishes criteria for designation and effectiveness of the hedging relationships.

The Company uses derivative instruments to manage its exposure to fluctuations in certain raw material commodity pricing, fluctuations in the cost of forecasted foreign currency transactions, and variability in interest rate exposure on floating rate borrowings. The majority of derivative instruments have been designated as cash flow hedges (see also Note 13 of Notes to the Consolidated Financial Statements).

(13) Derivative Financial Instruments (in part)

The Company is exposed to certain risks relating to its ongoing business operations. The primary risks managed using derivative instruments are commodity price risk, currency exchange risk, and interest rate risk. Forward contracts on certain commodities are entered into to manage the price risk associated with forecasted purchases of materials used in the Company's manufacturing process. Forward contracts on certain currencies are entered into to manage forecasted cash flows in certain foreign currencies. Interest rate swaps are entered into to manage interest rate risk associated with the Company's floating rate borrowings.

The Company is exposed to credit losses in the event of non-performance by the counterparties to various financial agreements, including its commodity hedging transactions, foreign currency exchange contracts and interest rate swap agreements. Exposure to counterparty credit risk is managed by limiting counterparties to major international banks and financial institutions meeting established credit guidelines and continually monitoring their compliance with the credit guidelines. The Company does not obtain collateral or other security to support financial instruments subject to credit risk. The Company does not anticipate non-performance by its counterparties, but cannot provide assurances.

The Company recognizes all derivative instruments as either assets or liabilities at fair value in the statement of financial position. The Company designates commodity forward contracts as cash flow hedges of forecasted purchases of commodities, currency forward contracts as cash flow hedges of forecasted foreign currency cash flows and interest rate swaps as cash flow hedges of forecasted LIBOR-based interest payments. There were no significant collateral deposits on derivative financial instruments as of December 28, 2013.

For derivative instruments that are designated and qualify as a cash flow hedge, the effective portion of the gain or loss on the derivative is reported as a component of accumulated other comprehensive income (loss) and reclassified into earnings in the same period or periods during which the hedged transaction affects earnings. Gains and losses on the derivative representing either hedge ineffectiveness or changes in market value of derivatives not designated as hedges are recognized in current earnings. At December 28, 2013 and December 29, 2012 the Company had $(0.7) million and $0.3 million, net of tax, of derivative (losses) gains on closed hedge instruments in AOCI that will be realized in earnings when the hedged items impact earnings.

The Company had outstanding the following notional amounts to hedge forecasted purchases of commodities (in millions):

	December 28, 2013	December 29, 2012
Copper	$114.5	$132.8
Aluminum	9.7	8.5

As of December 28, 2013, the maturities of commodity forward contracts extended through December, 2014.

The Company had outstanding the following notional amounts of currency forward contracts (in millions):

	December 28, 2013	December 29, 2012
Mexican Peso	$203.0	$174.8
Chinese Renminbi	142.3	108.6
Indian Rupee	36.8	37.4
Euro	11.4	—
Thai Baht	4.1	17.3
Australian Dollar	1.5	7.1

As of December 28, 2013, the maturities of currency forward contracts extended through December 2015.

As of December 28, 2013 and December 29, 2012, the total notional amount of the Company's receive-variable/pay-fixed interest rate swaps was $250.0 million (with maturities extending to August 2017).

Fair values of derivative instruments were (in millions):

	December 28, 2013			
	Prepaid Expenses	Other Noncurrent Assets	Hedging Obligations (Current)	Hedging Obligations
Designated as hedging instruments:				
Interest rate swap contracts	$ —	$—	$ 5.7	$16.1
Currency contracts	8.4	0.7	3.0	0.7
Commodity contracts	4.0	—	1.7	—
Not designated as hedging instruments:				
Currency contracts	—	—	0.1	—
Commodity contracts	0.7	—	0.8	—
Total Derivatives	$13.1	$0.7	$11.3	$16.8

	December 29, 2012			
	Prepaid Expenses	Other Noncurrent Assets	Hedging Obligations (Current)	Hedging Obligations
Designated as hedging instruments:				
Interest rate swap contracts	$ —	$—	$—	$35.4
Currency contracts	6.8	2.3	4.6	0.3
Commodity contracts	3.6	0.2	1.2	—
Not designated as hedging instruments:				
Commodity contracts	0.6	—	0.5	—
Total Derivatives	$11.0	$2.5	$6.3	$35.7

CLAIMS AND DISCOUNTS

2.125 CVS CAREMARK CORPORATION (DEC)

CONSOLIDATED BALANCE SHEETS (in part)

	December 31,	
(In millions, except per share amounts)	2013	2012
Liabilities:		
Accounts payable	$5,548	$5,070
Claims and discounts payable	4,548	3,974
Accrued expenses	4,768	4,411
Short-term debt	—	690
Current portion of long-term debt	561	5
Total current liabilities	15,425	14,150
Long-term debt	12,841	9,133
Deferred income taxes	3,901	3,784
Other long-term liabilities	1,421	1,501
Commitments and contingencies (Note 12)	—	—

NOTES TO CONSOLIDATED FINANCIAL STATEMENTS

1. Significant Accounting Policies (in part)

Revenue Recognition

Pharmacy Services Segment—The PSS sells prescription drugs directly through its mail service dispensing pharmacies and indirectly through its retail pharmacy network. The PSS recognizes revenue from prescription drugs sold by its mail service dispensing pharmacies and under retail pharmacy network contracts where it is the principal using the gross method at the contract prices negotiated with its clients. Net revenues include: (i) the portion of the price the client pays directly to the PSS, net of any volume-related or other discounts paid back to the client (see "Drug Discounts" below), (ii) the price paid to the PSS by client plan members for mail order prescriptions ("Mail Co-Payments") and the price paid to retail network pharmacies by client plan members for retail prescriptions ("Retail Co-Payments"), and (iii) administrative fees for retail pharmacy network contracts where the PSS is not the principal as discussed below. Sales taxes are not included in revenue.

Revenue is recognized when: (i) persuasive evidence of an arrangement exists, (ii) delivery has occurred or services have been rendered, (iii) the seller's price to the buyer is fixed or determinable, and (iv) collectability is reasonably assured. The following revenue recognition policies have been established for the PSS:

- Revenues generated from prescription drugs sold by mail service dispensing pharmacies are recognized when the prescription is delivered. At the time of delivery, the PSS has performed substantially all of its obligations under its client contracts and does not experience a significant level of returns or reshipments.
- Revenues generated from prescription drugs sold by third party pharmacies in the PSS's retail pharmacy network and associated administrative fees are recognized at the PSS's point-of-sale, which is when the claim is adjudicated by the PSS's online claims processing system.

The PSS determines whether it is the principal or agent for its retail pharmacy network transactions on a contract by contract basis. In the majority of its contracts, the PSS has determined it is the principal due to it: (i) being the primary obligor in the arrangement, (ii) having latitude in establishing the price, changing the product or performing part of the service, (iii) having discretion in supplier selection, (iv) having involvement in the determination of product or service specifications, and (v) having credit risk. The PSS's obligations under its client contracts for which revenues are reported using the gross method are separate and distinct from its obligations to the third party pharmacies included in its retail pharmacy network contracts.

Pursuant to these contracts, the PSS is contractually required to pay the third party pharmacies in its retail pharmacy network for products sold, regardless of whether the PSS is paid by its clients. The PSS's responsibilities under its client contracts typically include validating eligibility and coverage levels, communicating the prescription price and the co-payments due to the third party retail pharmacy, identifying possible adverse drug interactions for the pharmacist to address with the prescriber prior to dispensing, suggesting generic alternatives where clinically appropriate and approving the prescription for dispensing. Although the PSS does not have credit risk with respect to Retail Co-Payments, management believes that all of the other applicable indicators of gross revenue reporting are present. For contracts under which the PSS acts as an agent, revenue is recognized using the net method.

Drug Discounts—The PSS deducts from its revenues any rebates, inclusive of discounts and fees, earned by its clients. Rebates are paid to clients in accordance with the terms of client contracts, which are normally based on fixed rebates per prescription for specific products dispensed or a percentage of manufacturer discounts received for specific products dispensed. The liability for rebates due to clients is included in "Claims and discounts payable" in the accompanying consolidated balance sheets.

Medicare Part D—The PSS, through its SilverScript Insurance Company subsidiary, participates in the Federal Government's Medicare Part D program as a Prescription Drug Plan ("PDP"). Net revenues include insurance premiums earned by the PDP, which are determined based on the PDP's annual bid and related contractual arrangements with the Centers for Medicare and Medicaid Services ("CMS"). The insurance premiums include a direct premium paid by CMS and a beneficiary premium, which is the responsibility of the PDP member, but is subsidized by CMS in the case of low-income members. Premiums collected in advance are initially deferred in accrued expenses and are then recognized in net revenues over the period in which members are entitled to receive benefits.

In addition to these premiums, net revenues include co-payments, coverage gap benefits, deductibles and co-insurance (collectively, the "Member Co-Payments") related to PDP members' actual prescription claims. In certain cases, CMS subsidizes a portion of these Member Co-Payments and pays the PSS an estimated prospective Member Co-Payment subsidy amount each month. The prospective Member Co-Payment subsidy amounts received from CMS are also included in net revenues. The Company assumes no risk for these amounts. If the prospective Member Co-Payment subsidies received differ from the amounts based on actual prescription claims, the difference is recorded in either accounts receivable or accrued expenses.

The PSS accounts for CMS obligations and Member Co-Payments (including the amounts subsidized by CMS) using the gross method consistent with its revenue recognition policies for Mail Co-Payments and Retail Co-Payments (discussed previously in this document).

Retail Pharmacy Segment—The RPS recognizes revenue from the sale of merchandise (other than prescription drugs) at the time the merchandise is purchased by the retail customer. Prior to the fourth quarter of 2013, revenue from the sale of prescription drugs was recognized at the time the prescription was filled as opposed to upon delivery as required under the Financial Accounting Standards Board ("FASB") Accounting Standards Codification 605, *Revenue Recognition*. For substantially all prescriptions, the fill date and the delivery date occur in the same reporting period. The effect on both revenue and income of recording prescription drug sales upon fill as opposed to delivery is immaterial. During the fourth quarter of 2013, the Company began recognizing revenue from the sale of prescription drugs when the prescription is picked up by the customer. This immaterial error correction is reflected in all annual and quarterly financial statements presented. For the year ended December 31, 2012, the correction reduced net revenues and net income attributable to CVS Caremark by $13 million and $13 million. For the year ended December 31, 2011, the correction reduced net revenues by $20 million and increased net income attributable to CVS Caremark by $1 million. Diluted earnings per share from net income attributable to CVS Caremark was reduced by $0.01 for the year ended December 31, 2012. There was no impact on diluted earnings per share from net income attributable to CVS Caremark in any other annual or interim period impacted by the immaterial error correction. The adjustment increased total assets and total liabilities by $309 million and $360 million as of December 31, 2012 and decreased retained earnings by $38 million and $39 million as of December 31, 2011 and 2010, respectively.

Customer returns are not material. Revenue generated from the performance of services in the RPS's health care clinics is recognized at the time the services are performed. Sales taxes are not included in revenue.

See Note 13 for additional information about the revenues of the Company's business segments.

Cost of Revenues

Pharmacy Services Segment—The PSS' cost of revenues includes: (i) the cost of prescription drugs sold during the reporting period directly through its mail service dispensing pharmacies and indirectly through its retail pharmacy network, (ii) shipping and handling costs, and (iii) the operating costs of its mail service dispensing pharmacies and client service operations and related information technology support costs including depreciation and amortization. The cost of prescription drugs sold component of cost of revenues includes: (i) the cost of the prescription drugs purchased from manufacturers or distributors and shipped to members in clients' benefit plans from the PSS' mail service dispensing pharmacies, net of any volume-related or other discounts (see "Vendor allowances and purchase discounts" below) and (ii) the cost of prescription drugs sold (including Retail Co-Payments) through the PSS' retail pharmacy network under contracts where it is the principal, net of any volume-related or other discounts.

Retail Pharmacy Segment—The RPS' cost of revenues includes: the cost of merchandise sold during the reporting period and the related purchasing costs, warehousing and delivery costs (including depreciation and amortization) and actual and estimated inventory losses.

See Note 13 for additional information about the cost of revenues of the Company's business segments.

Vendor Allowances and Purchase Discounts

The Company accounts for vendor allowances and purchase discounts as follows:

Pharmacy Services Segment—The PSS receives purchase discounts on products purchased. The PSS' contractual arrangements with vendors, including manufacturers, wholesalers and retail pharmacies, normally provide for the PSS to receive purchase discounts from established list prices in one, or a combination, of the following forms: (i) a direct discount at the time of purchase, (ii) a discount for the prompt payment of invoices, or (iii) when products are purchased indirectly from a manufacturer (e.g., through a wholesaler or retail pharmacy), a discount (or rebate) paid subsequent to dispensing. These rebates are recognized when prescriptions are dispensed and are generally calculated and billed to manufacturers within 30 days of the end of each completed quarter. Historically, the effect of adjustments resulting from the reconciliation of rebates recognized to the amounts billed and collected has not been material to the PSS' results of operations. The PSS accounts for the effect of any such differences as a change in accounting estimate in the period the reconciliation is completed. The PSS also receives additional discounts under its wholesaler contracts if it exceeds contractually defined annual purchase volumes. In addition, the PSS receives fees from pharmaceutical manufacturers for administrative services. Purchase discounts and administrative service fees are recorded as a reduction of "Cost of revenues".

Retail Pharmacy Segment—Vendor allowances received by the RPS reduce the carrying cost of inventory and are recognized in cost of revenues when the related inventory is sold, unless they are specifically identified as a reimbursement of incremental costs for promotional programs and/or other services provided. Amounts that are directly linked to advertising commitments are recognized as a reduction of advertising expense (included in operating expenses) when the related advertising commitment is satisfied. Any such allowances received in excess of the actual cost incurred also reduce the carrying cost of inventory. The total value of any upfront payments received from vendors that are linked to purchase commitments is initially deferred. The deferred amounts are then amortized to reduce cost of revenues over the life of the contract based upon purchase volume. The total value of any upfront payments received from vendors that are not linked to purchase commitments is also initially deferred. The deferred amounts are then amortized to reduce cost of revenues on a straight-line basis over the life of the related contract. The total amortization of these upfront payments was not material to the accompanying consolidated financial statements.

ASSET RETIREMENT OBLIGATION

2.126 FREEPORT-MCMORAN COPPER & GOLD INC. (DEC)

CONSOLIDATED BALANCE SHEETS (in part)

	December 31,	
(In millions, except par values)	2013	2012
Liabilities and Equity (in part)		
Current liabilities:		
Accounts payable and accrued liabilities	$ 3,700	$ 2,324
Dividends payable	333	299
Current portion of debt	312	2
Current portion of environmental and asset retirement obligations	236	241
Accrued income taxes	184	93
Current portion of deferred income taxes	8	384
Total current liabilities	4,773	3,343
Long-term debt, less current portion	20,394	3,525
Deferred income taxes	7,410	3,490
Environmental and asset retirement obligations, less current portion	3,259	2,127
Other liabilities	1,690	1,644
Total liabilities	37,526	14,129

NOTES TO CONSOLIDATED FINANCIAL STATEMENTS

Note 1. Summary of Significant Accounting Policies (in part)

Asset Retirement Obligations. FCX records the fair value of estimated asset retirement obligations (AROs) associated with tangible long-lived assets in the period incurred. Retirement obligations associated with long-lived assets are those for which there is a legal obligation to settle under existing or enacted law, statute, written or oral contract or by legal construction. These obligations, which are initially estimated based on discounted cash flow estimates, are accreted to full value over time through charges to cost of sales. In addition, asset retirement costs (ARCs) are capitalized as part of the related asset's carrying value and are depreciated over the asset's respective useful life.

For mining operations, reclamation costs for disturbances are recognized as an ARO and as a related ARC (included in property, plant, equipment and mining development costs) in the period of the disturbance and depreciated primarily on a UOP basis. FCX's AROs for mining operations consist primarily of costs associated with mine reclamation and closure activities. These activities, which are site specific, generally include costs for earthwork, revegetation, water treatment and demolition (refer to Note 12 for further discussion).

For oil and gas properties, the fair value of the legal obligation is recognized as an ARO and as a related ARC(included in oil and gas properties) in the period in which the well is drilled or acquired and is amortized on a UOP basis together with other capitalized costs. Substantially all of FCX's oil and gas leases require that, upon termination of economic production, the working interest owners plug and abandon non-producing wellbores, remove platforms, tanks, production equipment and flow lines, and restore the wellsite (refer to Note 12 for further discussion).

At least annually, FCX reviews its ARO estimates for changes in the projected timing of certain reclamation and closure/restoration costs, changes in cost estimates and additional AROs incurred during the period.

Note 12. Contingencies (in part)

Asset Retirement Obligations (AROs). FCX's ARO estimates are reflected on a third-party cost basis and comply with FCX's legal obligation to retire tangible, long-lived assets. A summary of changes in FCX's AROs for the years ended December 31 follows:

	2013	2012	2011
Balance at beginning of year	$1,146	$ 921	$856
Liabilities assumed in the acquisitions of PXP and MMR[a]	1,028	—	—
Liabilities incurred	45	6	9
Settlements and revisions to cash flow estimates, net	123	211	48
Accretion expense	95	55	58
Spending	(107)	(47)	(49)
Other	(2)	—	(1)
Balance at end of year	2,328	1,146	921
Less: current portion	(115)	(55)	(31)
Long-term portion	$2,213	$1,091	$890

[a] The fair value of AROs assumed in the acquisitions of PXP and MMR ($741 million and $287 million, respectively) were estimated based on projected cash flows, an estimated long-term annual inflation rate of 2.5 percent, and discount rates based on FCX's estimated credit-adjusted, risk-free interest rates ranging from 1.3 percent to 6.3 percent.

ARO costs may increase or decrease significantly in the future as a result of changes in regulations, changes in engineering designs and technology, permit modifications or updates, changes in mine plans, changes in drilling plans, settlements, inflation or other factors and as actual reclamation spending occurs. ARO activities and expenditures for mining operations generally are made over an extended period of time commencing near the end of the mine life; however, certain reclamation activities may be accelerated if legally required or if determined to be economically beneficial. The methods used or required to plug and abandon non-producing oil and gas wellbores, remove platforms, tanks, production equipment and flow lines, and restore wellsites could change over time.

New Mexico, Arizona, Colorado and other states require financial assurance to be provided for the estimated costs of mine reclamation and closure, including groundwater quality protection programs. FCX has satisfied financial assurance requirements by using a variety of mechanisms, primarily involving parent company performance guarantees and financial capability demonstrations, but also including trust funds, surety bonds, letters of credit and collateral. The applicable regulations specify financial strength tests that are designed to confirm a company's or guarantor's financial capability to fund estimated reclamation and closure costs. The amount of financial assurance FCX is required to provide will vary with changes in laws, regulations, reclamation and closure requirements, and cost estimates. At December 31, 2013, FCX's financial assurance obligations associated with these closure and reclamation/restoration costs totaled $2.4 billion, of which $1.7 billion was in the form of guarantees issued by FCX and financial capability demonstrations of FCX. At December 31, 2013, FCX had trust assets totaling $158 million (included in other assets), which are legally restricted to be used to satisfy its financial assurance obligations for its mining properties in New Mexico.

New Mexico Environmental and Reclamation Programs. FCX's New Mexico operations are regulated under the New Mexico Water Quality Act and regulations adopted under that act by the Water Quality Control Commission (WQCC). The New Mexico Environment Department (NMED) has required each of these operations to submit closure plans for NMED's approval. The closure plans must include measures to assure meeting groundwater quality standards following the closure of discharging facilities and to abate any groundwater or surface water contamination. In 2013, the WQCC adopted Supplemental Permitting Requirements for Copper Mining Facilities, which became effective on October 31, 2013. These rules identify closure requirements for copper mine facilities. The rules were adopted after an extensive stakeholder process in which FCX participated and were jointly supported by FCX and NMED. Although the rules are being challenged in the New Mexico courts by certain environmental organizations and the New Mexico Attorney General, their adoption, along with other commitments in a settlement agreement between NMED and FCX, have allowed NMED and FCX ' s Tyrone operation to dismiss its appeal of a WQCC Final Order, dated February 4, 2009, regarding closure conditions applicable to the Tyrone mine. Finalized closure plan requirements, including those resulting from the newly adopted rules, could result in increases in closure costs for FCX's New Mexico operations.

FCX's New Mexico operations also are subject to regulation under the 1993 New Mexico Mining Act (the Mining Act) and the related rules that are administered by the Mining and Minerals Division (MMD) of the New Mexico Energy, Minerals and Natural Resources Department. Under the Mining Act, mines are required to obtain approval of plans describing the reclamation to be performed following cessation of mining operations. At December 31, 2013, FCX had accrued reclamation and closure costs of $465 million for its New Mexico operations. As stated above, additional accruals may be required based on the state's review of FCX's updated closure plans and any resulting permit conditions, and the amount of those accruals could be material.

Arizona Environmental and Reclamation Programs. FCX's Arizona properties are subject to regulatory oversight in several areas. ADEQ has adopted regulations for its aquifer protection permit (APP) program that require permits for, among other things, certain facilities, activities and structures used for mining, concentrating and smelting and require compliance with aquifer water quality standards at an applicable point of compliance well or location. The APP program also may require mitigation and discharge reduction or elimination of some discharges.

An application for an APP requires a description of a closure strategy that will meet applicable groundwater protection requirements following cessation of operations and an estimate of the cost to implement the closure strategy. An APP may specify closure requirements, which may include post-closure monitoring and maintenance. A more detailed closure plan must be submitted within 90 days after a permitted entity notifies ADEQ of its intent to cease operations. A permit applicant must demonstrate its financial ability to meet the closure costs estimated in the APP.

Portions of Arizona mining facilities that operated after January 1, 1986, also are subject to the Arizona Mined Land Reclamation Act (AMLRA). AMLRA requires reclamation to achieve stability and safety consistent with post-mining land use objectives specified in a reclamation plan. Reclamation plans must be approved by the State Mine Inspector and must include an estimate of the cost to perform the reclamation measures specified in the plan.

FCX will continue to evaluate options for future reclamation and closure activities at its operating and non-operating sites, which are likely to result in adjustments to FCX's ARO liabilities. At December 31, 2013, FCX had accrued reclamation and closure costs of $237 million for its Arizona operations.

Colorado Reclamation Programs. FCX's Colorado operations are regulated by the Colorado Mined Land Reclamation Act (Reclamation Act) and regulations promulgated thereunder. Under the Reclamation Act, mines are required to obtain approval of reclamation plans describing the reclamation of lands affected by mining operations to be performed during mining or upon cessation of mining operations. As of December 31, 2013, FCX had accrued reclamation and closure costs of $50 million for its Colorado operations.

Chilean Reclamation and Closure Programs. In July 2011, the Chilean senate passed legislation regulating mine closure, which establishes new requirements for closure plans and became effective in November 2012. FCX's Chilean operations are required to update closure plans and provide financial assurance for these obligations. FCX cannot predict at this time the cost of these closure plans or the levels or forms of financial assurance that may be required. Revised closure plans for the Chilean mine sites are due in November 2014. At December 31, 2013, FCX had accrued reclamation and closure costs of $69 million for its Chilean operations.

Peruvian Reclamation and Closure Programs. Cerro Verde is subject to regulation under the Mine Closure Law administered by the Peruvian Ministry of Energy and Mines. Under the closure regulations, mines must submit a closure plan that includes the reclamation methods, closure cost estimates, methods of control and verification, closure and post-closure plans and financial assurance. The updated closure plan for the Cerro Verde mine expansion was submitted to the Peruvian regulatory authorities in November 2013. At December 31, 2013, Cerro Verde had accrued reclamation and closure costs of $79 million.

Indonesian Reclamation and Closure Programs. The ultimate amount of reclamation and closure costs to be incurred at PT-FI's operations will be determined based on applicable laws and regulations and PT-FI's assessment of appropriate remedial activities in the circumstances, after consultation with governmental authorities, affected local residents and other affected parties and cannot currently be projected with precision. Some reclamation costs will be incurred during mining activities, while most closure costs and the remaining reclamation costs will be incurred at the end of mining activities, which are currently estimated to continue for nearly 30 years. At December 31, 2013, PT-FI had accrued reclamation and closure costs of $249 million.

In 1996, PT-FI began contributing to a cash fund ($18 million balance at December 31, 2013, which is included in other assets) designed to accumulate at least $100 million (including interest) by the end of its Indonesia mining activities. PT-FI plans to use this fund, including accrued interest, to pay mine closure and reclamation costs. Any costs in excess of the $100 million fund would be funded by operational cash flow or other sources.

In December 2009, PT-FI submitted its revised mine closure plan to the Department of Energy and Mineral Resources for review and has addressed comments received during the course of this review process. In December 2010, the President of Indonesia issued a regulation regarding mine reclamation and closure, which requires a company to provide a mine closure guarantee in the form of a time deposit placed in a state-owned bank in Indonesia. In accordance with its Contract of Work, PT-FI is working with the Department of Energy and Mineral Resources to review these requirements, including discussion of other options for the mine closure guarantee.

Oil and Gas Properties. Substantially all of FM O&G's oil and gas leases require that, upon termination of economic production, the working interest owners plug and abandon non-producing wellbores, remove equipment and facilities from leased acreage and restore land in accordance with applicable local, state and federal laws. FM O&G operating areas include the GOM, offshore and onshore California, the Gulf Coast and the Rocky Mountain area. FM O&G AROs cover more than 6,600 wells and more than 200 platforms and other structures. At December 31, 2013, FM O&G had accrued $1.1 billion associated with its AROs.

Long-Term Debt

PRESENTATION

2.127 FASB ASC 470 addresses classification determination for specific debt obligations. FASB ASC 470-10-45-11 states that the current liability classification is intended to include long-term obligations that are or will be callable by the creditor either because the debtor's violation of a provision of the debt agreement at the balance sheet date makes the obligation callable, or the violation, if not cured within a specified grace period, will make the obligation callable. Accordingly, such callable obligations should be classified as current liabilities, unless one of the following conditions is met:

- The creditor has waived or subsequently lost the right to demand repayment for more than one year, or operating cycle if longer, from the balance sheet date. For example, the debtor may have cured the violation after the balance sheet date, and the obligation is not callable at the time the financial statements are issued or available to be issued.
- For long-term obligations containing a grace period within which the debtor may cure the violation, it is probable that the violation will be cured within that period, thus preventing the obligation from becoming callable.

DISCLOSURE

2.128 FASB ASC 470 requires, for each of the five years following the date of the latest balance sheet presented, disclosure of the combined aggregate amount of maturities and sinking fund requirements for all long-term borrowings. In addition, FASB ASC 440, *Commitments*, requires disclosure of terms and conditions provided in loan agreements, such as assets pledged as collateral and covenants to limit additional debt, maintain working capital, and restrict dividends. Regulation S-X has similar or expanded requirements for matters such as debt details, assets subject to lien, defaults, dividend restrictions, and changes in long-term debt.

2.129 FASB ASC 825 requires disclosure of both the fair value and bases for estimating the fair value of long-term debt, unless it is not practicable to estimate the value.

PRESENTATION AND DISCLOSURE EXCERPTS

UNSECURED

2.130 AK STEEL HOLDING CORPORATION (DEC)
CONSOLIDATED BALANCE SHEETS (in part)

December 31, 2013 and 2012

(Dollars in millions, except per share data)

	2013	2012
Liabilities and Equity (Deficit) (in part)		
Current liabilities:		
Accounts payable	$ 601.8	$ 538.3
Accrued liabilities	142.9	164.8
Current portion of long-term debt	0.8	0.7
Current portion of pension and other postretirement benefit obligations	85.9	108.6
Total current liabilities	831.4	812.4
Non-current liabilities:		
Long-term debt	1,506.2	1,411.2
Pension and other postretirement benefit obligations	965.4	1,661.7
Other non-current liabilities	110.0	108.8
Total liabilities	3,413.0	3,994.1

NOTES TO CONSOLIDATED FINANCIAL STATEMENTS

(Dollars in millions, except per share amounts or as otherwise specifically noted)

Note 5—Long-Term Debt and Other Financing (in part)

At December 31, 2013 and 2012, the Company's debt balances, including current portions, were as follows:

	2013	2012
Credit facility	$ 90.0	$ —
8.75% senior secured notes due December 2018	380.0	350.0
5.00% exchangeable senior notes due November 2019 (effective rate of 10.8%)	150.0	150.0
7.625% senior notes due May 2020	529.8	550.0
8.375% senior notes due April 2022	290.2	300.0
Industrial revenue bonds due 2014 through 2030	100.1	100.9
Unamortized debt discount/premium, net	(33.1)	(39.0)
Total debt	1,507.0	1,411.9
Less:		
Current portion of long-term debt	0.8	0.7
Total long-term debt	$1,506.2	$1,411.2

During the period, the Company was in compliance with all the terms and conditions of its debt agreements. At December 31, 2013, the maturities of long-term debt, including the amount outstanding on the Credit Facility, for the next five years are as follows:

Year	Debt Maturities
2014	$ 0.8
2015	—
2016	90.0
2017	—
2018	380.0

Senior Unsecured Notes

In November 2012, AK Steel issued $150.0 aggregate principal of 5.00% Exchangeable Senior Notes due November 2019 (the "Exchangeable Notes") and generated net proceeds of $144.8 after underwriting discounts and other expenses. AK Steel may not redeem the Exchangeable Notes prior to their maturity date. After August 15, 2019, holders may exchange their Exchangeable Notes at any time. Upon exchange, the Company will be obligated to (i) pay an amount in cash equal to the aggregate principal amount of the Exchangeable Notes to be exchanged and (ii) pay cash, deliver shares of AK Holding common stock or a combination thereof, at the Company's election, for the remainder, if any, of the exchange obligation in excess of the aggregate principal amount of the Exchangeable Notes being exchanged. Holders may exchange their Exchangeable Notes into shares of AK Holding common stock at their option at an initial exchange rate of 185.1852 shares of AK Holding common stock per $1,000 principal amount of Exchangeable Notes. The initial exchange rate is equivalent to a conversion price of approximately $5.40 per share of common stock, which equates to 27.8 million shares to be used to determine the aggregate equity consideration to be delivered upon exchange, subject to adjustment for certain dilutive effects from potential future events. Holders may exchange their Exchangeable Notes prior to August 15, 2019 only under certain circumstances. The indenture governing the Exchangeable Notes (the "Exchangeable Notes Indenture") does not contain any financial or operating covenants or restrictions on the payments of dividends, the incurrence of indebtedness or the issuance or repurchase of securities by the Company or its subsidiaries. If the Company undergoes a fundamental change, as defined in Exchangeable Notes Indenture (which, for example, would include various transactions pursuant to which the Company would undergo a change of control), holders may require AK Steel to repurchase the Exchangeable Notes in whole or in part for cash at a price equal to par plus any accrued and unpaid interest. In addition, in the event the Company undergoes a "make-whole fundamental change," as defined in the Exchangeable Notes Indenture, prior to the maturity date, in addition to requiring AK Steel to repurchase the Exchangeable Notes in whole or in part for cash at a price equal to par plus any accrued and unpaid interest, the exchange rate will be increased in certain circumstances for a holder who elects to exchange its notes in connection with such event. Based on the initial exchange rate, the Exchangeable Notes are exchangeable into a maximum of 37.5 million shares of AK Holding common stock. However, such maximum amount of shares would be exchanged only if, as a result of the occurrence of a "make-whole fundamental change" described above, the Company elects to satisfy the higher exchange rate by delivering to the holders shares of AK Holding common stock in consideration therefor. Although the Exchangeable Notes were issued at par, for accounting purposes the proceeds received from the issuance of the notes are allocated between debt and equity to reflect the fair value of the exchange option embedded in the notes and the fair value of similar debt without the exchange option. As a result, $38.7 of the gross proceeds of the Exchangeable Notes were recorded as an increase in additional paid-in capital with the offsetting amount recorded as a debt discount. The debt discount is being amortized over the term of the Exchangeable Notes using the effective interest method. As of December 31, 2013 and 2012, the remaining unamortized debt discount was $34.3 and $38.2, respectively, and the net carrying amount of the Exchangeable Notes was $115.7 and $111.8, respectively. The portion of underwriting discounts and other fees of $1.4 associated with the exchange option were recorded as a reduction to the gross proceeds included in additional paid-in capital. The carrying amount of the exchange option was $37.3 at December 31, 2013 and 2012. The value of the Exchangeable Notes if exchanged as of December 31, 2013, would have exceeded the principal amount by $35.3.

AK Steel's outstanding 7.625% Senior Notes are due May 2020 (the "2020 Notes"). Prior to May 15, 2015, AK Steel may redeem the 2020 Notes at a price equal to par plus a make-whole premium and all accrued and unpaid interest to the date of redemption. Subsequent to that date, they are redeemable at 103.813% until May 15, 2016, 102.542% thereafter until May 15, 2017, 101.271% thereafter until May 15, 2018 and 100.0% thereafter, together with all accrued and unpaid interest to the date of redemption.

In March 2012, AK Steel issued $300.0 of 8.375% Senior Notes due April 2022 (the "2022 Notes") and generated net proceeds of $293.2 after underwriting discounts and other fees. Prior to April 1, 2017, AK Steel may redeem the 2022 Notes at a price equal to par plus a make-whole premium and all accrued and unpaid interest to the date of redemption. Subsequent to that date, they are redeemable at 104.188% until April 1, 2018, 102.792% thereafter until April 1, 2019, 101.396% thereafter until April 1, 2020 and 100.0% thereafter, together with all accrued and unpaid interest to the date of redemption.

The 2020 Notes, the 2022 Notes, the Exchangeable Notes and the unsecured IRBs discussed below (collectively, the "Senior Unsecured Notes") are equal in right of payment. AK Holding fully and unconditionally, jointly and severally, guarantees the payment of interest, principal and premium, if any, on the Senior Unsecured Notes. The indentures governing the 2020 Notes, the 2022 Notes and the IRBs include covenants with customary restrictions on (a) the incurrence of additional debt by certain AK Steel subsidiaries, (b) the incurrence of liens by AK Steel and AK Holding's other subsidiaries, (c) the amount of sale/leaseback transactions, and (d) the ability of AK Steel and AK Holding to merge or consolidate with other entities or to sell, lease or transfer all or substantially all of the assets of AK Steel and AK Holding to another entity. The indentures governing the Senior Unsecured Notes also contain customary events of default. The Senior Unsecured Notes rank junior in priority to the Secured Notes to the extent of the value of the assets securing such indebtedness.

During 2013, the Company repurchased an aggregate principal amount of $20.2 and $9.8 of the 2020 Notes and the 2022 Notes, respectively, in private, open market transactions. These repurchases were unsolicited and completed at a discount to the Senior Unsecured Notes' par value. The Company recognized a gain on the repurchases of $2.9 for the year ended December 31, 2013, which is included in other income (expense).

COLLATERALIZED

2.131 THE BON-TON STORES, INC. (JAN)
CONSOLIDATED BALANCE SHEETS (in part)

(In thousands, except share and per share data)	February 2, 2013	January 28, 2012
Liabilities and Shareholders' Equity (in part)		
Current liabilities:		
Accounts payable	$ 193,898	$ 205,492
Accrued payroll and benefits	32,410	31,636
Accrued expenses	165,536	162,855
Current maturities of long-term debt	75,886	8,066
Current maturities of obligations under capital leases	3,925	4,365
Deferred income taxes	20,256	16,231
Income taxes payable	739	—
Total current liabilities	492,650	428,645
Long-term debt, less current maturities	768,864	814,271
Obligations under capital leases, less current maturities	52,478	56,677
Other long-term liabilities	209,611	187,003
Total liabilities	1,523,603	1,486,596

NOTES TO CONSOLIDATED FINANCIAL STATEMENTS

(In thousands except share and per share data)

10. Long-Term Debt (in part)

Long-term debt consisted of the following:

	February 2, 2013	January 28, 2012
Senior secured credit facility—expires on the earlier of (a) March 21, 2016 and (b) the date that is 60 days prior to the earlier of the maturity date of the senior notes and the mortgage loan facility; interest payable periodically at varying rates (2.93% weighted average for 2012)	$154,335	$119,435
Senior notes—mature on March 15, 2014; interest payable each March 15 and September 15 at 10.25%	133,983	464,000
Second lien senior secured notes—mature on July 15, 2017; interest payable each March 15 and September 15 at 10.625%	329,998	—
Mortgage loan facility—principal payable in varying monthly installments, with balance due April 1, 2016; interest payable monthly at 6.21%; secured by land and buildings	225,020	231,581
Mortgage notes payable—principal payable in varying monthly installments through June 2016; interest payable monthly at 9.62%; secured by land and buildings	1,414	7,321
Total debt	$844,750	$822,337
Less: current maturities	(75,886)	(8,066)
Long-term debt	$768,864	$814,271

On March 21, 2011, The Bon-Ton Department Stores, Inc.; The Elder-Beerman Stores Corp.; Carson Pirie Scott II, Inc.; Bon-Ton Distribution, Inc.; and McRIL, LLC, as borrowers (the "Borrowers"), and the Company and certain other subsidiaries as obligors (together with the Borrowers and the Company, the "Obligors") entered into the Second Amended Revolving Credit Facility with Bank of America, N.A., as Agent, and certain financial institutions as lenders that amends and restates the Company's prior $675,000 revolving credit facility, which was entered into on December 4, 2009 and scheduled to mature on June 4, 2013 (the "2009 Revolving Credit Facility"). The Second Amended Revolving Credit Facility initially provided for a revolving credit facility of $625,000 that expires on the earlier of (a) March 21,

2016 and (b) the date that is 60 days prior to the earlier of the maturity date of the Company's 10 ^{1}/4% Senior Notes due 2014 (the "Old Notes") and the mortgage loan facility. Unamortized deferred financing fees of $1,271 related to the 2009 Revolving Credit Facility were accelerated on the date of the agreement and recognized in loss on exchange/extinguishment of debt.

On October 25, 2012, the Obligors entered into a First Amendment (the "First Amendment") to the Second Amended Revolving Credit Facility, which (1) increased the Tranche A-1 revolving commitment (one of two borrowing tranches that comprise the Second Amended Revolving Credit Facility) from $50,000 to $100,000 (resulting in an increased borrowing limit totaling $675,000), (2) increased the margins applicable to borrowings under the Tranche A-1 revolving commitments, and (3) made certain other changes to the borrowing base calculations under the Second Amended Revolving Credit Facility. Unamortized deferred financing fees of $202 associated with the Second Amended Revolving Credit Facility were accelerated upon entry into the First Amendment and were recognized in loss on exchange/extinguishment of debt.

All borrowings under the Second Amended Revolving Credit Facility are limited by amounts available pursuant to a borrowing base calculation, which is based on percentages of eligible inventory, real estate and credit card receivables, in each case subject to reductions for applicable reserves. Under the terms of the Second Amended Revolving Credit Facility, the Borrowers are jointly and severally liable for all of the obligations incurred under the Second Amended Revolving Credit Facility and the other loan documents, which obligations are guaranteed on a joint and several basis by the Company, the other Obligors and all future domestic subsidiaries of the Obligors (subject to certain exceptions).

Commitments for loans under the Second Amended Revolving Credit Facility are in two tranches: Tranche A revolving commitments of $575,000 (which includes a $150,000 sub-line for letters of credit and $75,000 for swing line loans) and Tranche A-1 revolving commitments of $100,000. The Second Amended Revolving Credit Facility provides that the Borrowers may make requests to increase the Tranche A revolving commitments up to $800,000 in the aggregate upon the satisfaction of certain conditions, provided that the lenders are under no obligation to provide any such increases.

Borrowings under the Second Amended Revolving Credit Facility bear interest at either (1) Adjusted LIBOR (based on the British Bankers Association per annum LIBOR Rate for an interest period selected by the Borrowers) plus an applicable margin or (2) a base rate (based on the highest of (a) the Federal Funds Rate plus 0.5%, (b) the Bank of America prime rate, and (c) Adjusted LIBOR based on an interest period of one month plus 1.0%) plus the applicable margin. The applicable margin is based upon the excess availability under the Second Amended Revolving Credit Facility. The Borrowers are required to pay an unused line fee to the lenders for unused commitments at a rate of 0.375% to 0.50% per annum, based upon the unused portion of the total commitment under the Second Amended Revolving Credit Facility.

The Second Amended Revolving Credit Facility is secured by a first priority security position on substantially all of the current and future assets of the Borrowers and the other Obligors, including, but not limited to, inventory, general intangibles, trademarks, equipment, certain real estate and proceeds from any of the foregoing, subject to certain exceptions and permitted liens.

The financial covenant contained in the Second Amended Revolving Credit Facility requires that the minimum excess availability be an amount greater than or equal to the greater of (1) 10% of the lesser of: (a) the aggregate commitments at such time and (b) the aggregate borrowing base at such time and (2) $50,000. The affirmative covenants include requirements that the Obligors and their subsidiaries provide the lenders with certain financial statements, forecasts and other reports, borrowing base certificates and notices; comply with various federal, state and local rules and regulations, their organizational documents and their material contracts; maintain their properties; and take certain actions with respect to any future subsidiaries. In addition, there are certain limitations on the Obligors and their subsidiaries, including limitations on any debt the Obligors may have in addition to the existing debt, and the terms of that debt; acquisitions, joint ventures and investments; mergers and consolidations; dispositions of property; dividends by the Obligors or their subsidiaries (dividends paid may not exceed $10,000 in any year or $30,000 during the term of the agreement; however, additional dividends may be paid subject to meeting other requirements); transactions with affiliates; changes in the business or corporate structure of the Obligors or their subsidiaries; prepaying, redeeming or repurchasing certain debt; changes in accounting policies or reporting practices, unless required by generally accepted accounting principles; and speculative transactions. The Second Amended Revolving Credit Facility also provides that it is a condition precedent to borrowing that no event has occurred that could reasonably be expected to have a material adverse effect, as defined in the agreement, on the Company. If the Company fails to comply with the financial covenant or the other restrictions contained in the Second Amended Revolving Credit Facility, mortgage loan facility or the indentures that govern the senior notes, an event of default would occur. An event of default could result in the acceleration of the Company's debt due to the cross-default provisions within the debt agreements. The borrowing base calculation under the Second Amended Revolving Credit Facility contains an inventory advance rate subject to periodic review at the lenders' discretion.

As of February 2, 2013, the Company had borrowings of $154,335 under the Second Amended Revolving Credit Facility, with $517,612 of borrowing availability (before taking into account the minimum borrowing availability covenant under this facility) and letter-of-credit commitments of $3,053.

CONVERTIBLE

2.132 GENERAL CABLE CORPORATION (DEC)
CONSOLIDATED BALANCE SHEETS (in part)

(In millions, except share data)

Liabilities and Total Equity (in part)	Dec 31, 2013	Dec 31, 2012
Current liabilities:		
Accounts payable	$ 870.6	$1,003.0
Accrued liabilities	434.9	496.1
Current portion of long-term debt	250.3	511.2
Total current liabilities	1,555.8	2,010.3
Long-term debt	1,136.6	938.9
Deferred income taxes	233.8	223.9
Other liabilities	255.9	292.7
Total liabilities	3,182.1	3,465.8

NOTES TO CONSOLIDATED FINANCIAL STATEMENTS

2. Summary of Significant Accounting Policies (in part)

Long-Term Debt

In accordance with *ASC 470—Debt,* convertible debt instruments that may be settled in cash or other assets, or partially in cash, upon conversion, are separately accounted for as long-term debt and equity components (or conversion feature). The accounting applies to the Subordinated Convertible Notes. The debt component represents the Company's contractual obligation to pay principal and interest and the equity component represents the Company's option to convert the debt security into equity of the Company or the equivalent amount of cash. Upon issuance the Company allocated the debt component on the basis of the estimated fair value of an identical debt instrument that it would issue excluding the convertible option and the remaining proceeds are allocated to the equity component. The bifurcation of the debt and equity components resulted in a debt discount for each of the aforementioned notes. In accordance with *ASC 470—Debt,* the Company uses the interest method to amortize the debt discount to interest expense over the amortization period which is the expected life of the debt.

9. Long-Term Debt (in part)

(In millions)	Dec 31, 2013	Dec 31, 2012
North America		
5.75% Senior Notes due 2022	$ 600.0	$ 600.0
Subordinated Convertible Notes due 2029	429.5	429.5
Debt discount on Subordinated Convertible Notes due 2029	(261.5)	(263.0)
0.875% Convertible Notes due 2013	—	355.0
Debt discount on 0.875% Convertible Notes due 2013	—	(20.4)
Senior Floating Rate Notes	125.0	125.0
Revolving Credit Facility	225.0	—
Other	9.0	9.0
Europe and Mediterranean		
Spanish Term Loan	—	14.6
Credit facilities	17.0	14.7
Uncommitted accounts receivable facilities	—	4.0
Other	10.3	11.7
ROW		
Credit facilities	232.6	170.0
Total debt	1,386.9	1,450.1
Less current maturities	250.3	511.2
Long-term debt	$1,136.6	$ 938.9

Convertible Debt Instruments

The Company's convertible debt instruments outstanding as of December 31, 2013 and 2012 were as follows:

(In millions)	Subordinated Notes Due in 2029		0.875% Convertible Notes	
	Dec 31, 2013	Dec 31, 2012	Dec 31, 2013	Dec 31, 2012
Face value	$429.5	$429.5	$—	$355.0
Debt discount	(261.5)	(263.0)	—	(20.4)
Book value	168.0	166.5	—	334.6
Fair value (Level 1)	462.8	464.1	—	349.7
Maturity date	Nov 2029		Nov 2013	
Stated annual interest rate	4.50% until Nov 2019		0.875% until Nov 2013	
	2.25% until Nov 2029			
Interest payments	Semi-annually: May 15 & Nov 15		Semi-annually: May 15 & Nov 15	

The 0.875% Convertible Notes were unconditionally guaranteed, jointly and severally, on a senior unsecured basis, by the Company's wholly-owned U.S. subsidiaries.

Subordinated Convertible Notes

The Company's Subordinated Convertible Notes were issued on December 18, 2009 in the amount of $ 429.5 million. The notes and the common stock issuable upon conversion were registered on a Registration Statement on Form S-4, initially filed with the SEC on October 27, 2009, as amended and as declared effective by the SEC on December 18, 2009. At issuance, the Company separately accounted for the liability and equity components of the instrument, based on the Company's nonconvertible debt borrowing rate on the instrument's issuance date of 12.5%. At issuance, the liability and equity components were $ 162.9 million and $ 266.6 million, respectively. The equity component (debt discount) is being amortized to interest expense based on the effective interest method. There were no proceeds generated from the transaction and the Company incurred issuance fees and expenses of approximately $ 14.5 million as a result of the exchange offer which have been proportionately allocated to the liability and equity components of the new subordinate notes due in 2029. Additional terms have been summarized in the table below.

0.875% Convertible Notes

The Company's 0.875% Convertible Notes issued in November 2006 in the amount of $355.0 million matured on November 15, 2013. The Company fully satisfied and extinguished these notes at maturity. The Company used cash on hand and borrowings under its Revolving Credit Facility to fund the retirement of the notes.

Beginning January 1, 2009, as discussed in Note 2—Summary of Significant Accounting Policies, the Company separately accounted for the liability and equity components of the instrument, retrospectively, based on the Company's nonconvertible debt borrowing rate on the instrument's issuance date of 7.35%. At issuance, the liability and equity components were $ 230.9 million and $ 124.1 million, respectively. The equity component (debt discount) is being amortized to interest expense based on the effective interest method. Key terms have been summarized in the table below.

The Company's convertible debt instruments and terms are summarized in the tables below. For a discussion of the effects on earnings per share, refer to Note 16—Earnings Per Common Share.

	Subordinated Notes due in 2029 [1]
Conversion Rights—The notes are convertible at the option of the holder into the Company's common stock upon the occurrence of certain events, including	(i) during any calendar quarter commencing after March 31, 2010, in which the closing price of the Company's common stock is greater than or equal to 130% of the conversion price for at least 20 trading days during the period of 30 consecutive trading days ending on the last trading day of the preceding calendar quarter (establishing a contingent conversion price of $47.78);
	(ii) during any five business day period after any five consecutive trading day period in which the trading price per $1,000 principal amount of the notes for each day of that period is less than 98% of the product of the closing sale price of the Company's common stock and the applicable conversion rate;
	(iii) certain distributions to holders of the Company's common stock are made or upon specified corporate transactions including a consolidation or merger;
	(iv) a fundamental change as defined; and
	(v) at any time during the period beginning on August 31, 2029 and ending on the close of business on the business day immediately preceding the stated maturity date.
	(vi) On or after November 15, 2019, the Company may redeem all or a part of the notes for cash at a price equal to 100% of the principal amount of the notes, plus interest, if the price of our common stock has been at least 150% of the conversion price then in effect for at least 20 trading days during the 30 consecutive trading day period immediately preceding the date on which notice is given

(continued)

Initial conversion rate	$36.75 per share—approximating 27.2109 shares per $1,000 principal amount of notes
Upon conversion	A holder will receive, in lieu of common stock, an amount of cash equal to the lesser of (i) the principal amount of the notes, or (ii) the conversion value, determined in the manner set forth in the indenture governing the notes, of a number of shares equal to the conversion rate.
	If the conversion value exceeds the principal amount of the notes on the conversion date, the Company will also deliver, at the Company's election, cash or common stock or a combination of cash and common stock with respect to the conversion value upon conversion.
	If conversion occurs in connection with a "fundamental change" as defined in the notes indenture, the Company may be required to repurchase the notes for cash at a price equal to the principal amount plus accrued but unpaid interest.
	If conversion occurs in connection with certain changes in control, the Company may be required to deliver additional shares of the Company's common stock (a "make whole" premium) by increasing the conversion rate with respect to such notes.
Share issuable upon conversion	The Company may issue additional share up to 11,686,075 under almost all conditions and up to 14,315,419 under the "make-whole" premium
Guarantee	None

(1) In the event of a "fundamental change" or exceeding the aforementioned average pricing thresholds, the Company would be required to classify the amount outstanding as a current liability.

Credit Agreements

DISCLOSURE

2.133 Regulation S-X requires disclosure of the amounts and terms, including commitment fees and conditions for draw-downs, of unused commitments for short-term and long-term financing.

PRESENTATION AND DISCLOSURE EXCERPTS

CREDIT AGREEMENTS

2.134 AMERICAN GREETINGS CORPORATION (FEB)
CONSOLIDATED STATEMENT OF FINANCIAL POSITION (in part)

February 28, 2013 and February 29, 2012

Thousands of dollars except share and per share amounts

	2013	2012
Liabilities and Shareholders' Equity (in part)		
Current liabilities		
Accounts payable	$119,777	$ 86,166
Accrued liabilities	80,098	58,657
Accrued compensation and benefits	69,309	68,317
Income taxes payable	4,968	7,409
Deferred revenue	31,851	35,519
Other current liabilities	62,593	49,013
Total current liabilities	368,596	305,081
Long-term debt	286,381	225,181
Other liabilities	225,044	269,367
Deferred income taxes and noncurrent		
Income taxes payable	21,565	22,377

NOTES TO CONSOLIDATED FINANCIAL STATEMENTS

Years ended February 28, 2013, February 29, 2012 and February 28, 2011

Thousands of dollars except share and per share amounts

Note 11—Debt (in part)

There was no debt due within one year as of February 28, 2013 and February 29, 2012.

Long-term debt and their related calendar year due dates as of February 28, 2013 and February 29, 2012, respectively, were as follows:

	February 28, 2013	February 29, 2012
7.375% senior notes, due 2021	$225,000	$225,000
Revolving credit facility, due 2017	61,200	—
6.10% senior notes, due 2028	181	181
	$286,381	$225,181

At February 28, 2013, the balance outstanding on the revolving credit facility bears interest at a rate of approximately 1.5%. In addition to the balance outstanding on the aforementioned agreement, the Corporation also finances certain transactions with some of its vendors, which include a combination of various guaranties and letters of credit. At February 28, 2013, the Corporation had credit arrangements under a credit facility and an accounts receivable facility to support the letters of credit up to $130,800 with $27,505 of credit outstanding.

Aggregate maturities of long-term debt, by fiscal year, are as follows:

2014	$ —
2015	—
2016	—
2017	61,200
2018	—
Thereafter	225,181
	$286,381

Interest paid in cash on long-term debt was $19,184, $34,946 and $21,637 in 2013, 2012 and 2011, respectively.

Credit Facility

The Corporation is a party to a $400,000 senior secured credit agreement (the "Credit Agreement"), under which there were $61,200 borrowings outstanding as of February 28, 2013. There were no borrowings under the Credit Agreement as of February 29, 2012.

The total fair value of the Corporation's non-publicly traded debt, which was considered a Level 2 valuation as it was based on comparable privately traded debt prices, was $61,200 (at a carrying value of $61,200) at February 28, 2013.

Under the original terms of the Credit Agreement, the Corporation was permitted to borrow, on a revolving basis, up to $350,000 (with an ability to increase this amount by $50,000 to $400,000) during a five year term from June 11, 2010 through June 11, 2015. On January 18, 2012, the Corporation amended its Credit Agreement, to, among other things, extend the expiration date of the Credit Agreement from June 11, 2015 to January 18, 2017, and increase the maximum principal amount that can be borrowed, on a revolving basis, from $350,000 to $400,000, with the continued ability to further increase such maximum principal amount from $400,000 to $450,000, subject to customary conditions.

The amendment also:
- decreased the applicable margin paid on U.S. dollar loans bearing interest based on the London Inter-Bank Offer Rate ("LIBOR") and Canadian dollar loans bearing interest based on the Canadian Dollar Offer Rate, from a range of 2.25% to 3.50% per year to a range of 1.25% to 2.25%;
- decreased the applicable margin paid on U.S. dollar loans bearing interest based on the U.S. base rate and the Canadian base rate from a range of 1.25% to 2.50% per year to a range of 0.25% to 1.25%; and
- reduced commitment fees paid on the unused portion of the revolving credit facility from a range of 0.375% to 0.500% per annum to a range of 0.250% to 0.400%.

On December 19, 2012, the Corporation further amended its Credit Agreement to modify the definition of Earnings Before Interest, Taxes, Depreciation and Amortization ("EBITDA") to permit, as of February 28, 2013, certain add-backs for specific non-recurring expenses related to the Clinton Cards acquisition.

The obligations under the Credit Agreement are guaranteed by the Corporation's material domestic subsidiaries and are secured by substantially all of the personal property of the Corporation and each of its material domestic subsidiaries, including a pledge of all of the capital stock in substantially all of the Corporation's domestic subsidiaries and 65% of the capital stock of the Corporation's first tier international subsidiaries.

The Credit Agreement also contains certain restrictive covenants that are customary for similar credit arrangements. For example, the Credit Agreement contains covenants relating to financial reporting and notification, compliance with laws, preserving existence, maintenance of books and records, how the Corporation may use proceeds from borrowings, and maintenance of properties and insurance. In addition, the Credit Agreement includes covenants that limit the Corporation's ability to incur additional debt; declare or pay dividends; make distributions on or repurchase or redeem capital stock; make certain investments; enter into transactions with affiliates; grant or permit liens; sell assets; enter into sale and leaseback transactions; and consolidate, merge or sell all or substantially all of the Corporation's assets. There are also financial performance covenants that require the Corporation to maintain a maximum leverage ratio and a minimum interest coverage ratio. The Credit Agreement also requires the Corporation to make certain mandatory prepayments of outstanding indebtedness using the net cash proceeds received from certain dispositions, events of loss and additional indebtedness that the Corporation may incur from time to time. These restrictions are subject to customary baskets.

2.135 ALLIANCE ONE INTERNATIONAL, INC. (MAR)

CONSOLIDATED BALANCE SHEETS (in part)

(In thousands)	March 31, 2013	March 31, 2012
Liabilities and Stockholders' Equity (in part)		
Current liabilities		
Notes payable to banks	$356,836	$374,532
Accounts payable	135,260	120,148
Due to related parties	26,084	37,520
Advances from customers	16,817	14,876
Accrued expenses and other current liabilities	69,508	78,742
Current derivative liability	644	16
Income taxes	9,454	16,282
Long-term debt current	6,349	7,050
Total current liabilities	620,952	649,166
Long-term debt	830,870	821,453
Deferred income taxes	6,396	9,494
Liability for unrecognized tax benefits	8,617	18,183
Pension, postretirement and other long-term liabilities	102,713	121,128
	948,596	970,258

NOTES TO CONSOLIDATED FINANCIAL STATEMENTS

(In thousands)

Note 8—Long-Term Debt (in part)

Senior Secured Credit Facility

On July 2, 2009, the Company replaced its previous credit agreement by entering into a Credit Agreement (the "Credit Agreement"), with a syndicate of banks that provided for a senior secured credit facility (the "Credit Facility") of a three and one-quarter year $270,000 revolver (the "Revolver") which initially accrued interest at a rate of LIBOR plus 2.50%. The interest rate for the Revolver may increase or decrease according to a consolidated interest coverage ratio pricing matrix as defined in the Credit Agreement, plus an applicable percentage. As of April 7, 2010, the Company increased the Revolver to $290,000.

First Amendment. On August 24, 2009, the Company closed the First Amendment to the Credit Agreement which included allowing the issuance of up to an additional $100,000 of Senior Notes due 2016 within 90 days of the First Amendment Effective Date, amending the definition of Consolidated Total Senior Debt to exclude the Existing Senior Notes 2005, amending the definition of Applicable Percentage to clarify the effective date of the change in the Applicable Percentage and modifications to several schedules within the Credit Agreement.

Second Amendment. On June 9, 2010, the Company closed the Second Amendment to the Credit Agreement, which included adding back the Foreign Corrupt Practices Act estimate of $19,450 to Consolidated Net Income for the period ended March 31, 2011 and increasing the Maximum Consolidated Leverage Ratio to 5.25 to 1.00 for the period ending September 30, 2010 and to 5.00 to 1.00 for the period ending March 31, 2011. The Second Amendment also allowed a subsidiary of the Company to incur indebtedness of up to $25,000 after ceasing to be a wholly owned subsidiary, a guarantee by the Company of that indebtedness, the issuance of up to 30% equity interests in the subsidiary to officers, employees, directors, advisory boards and/or its third parties investors and allow certain restricted payments by the subsidiary.

Third Amendment. On June 6, 2011, the Company closed the Third Amendment to the Credit Agreement whereby the lenders agreed to extend the term of the facility to March 31, 2013. In addition, the Third Amendment modified certain financial covenants under the Credit Agreement, including establishing the financial maximum consolidated leverage ratio for each fiscal quarter through maturity, reducing the minimum consolidated interest coverage ratio for the quarter ended March 31, 2011 and the first three quarters of the fiscal year ending

March 31, 2012, permitting the exclusion of the effect of specified levels of restructuring and impairment charges for the fiscal year ended March 31, 2011 and the fiscal year ending March 31, 2012 for the financial covenants impacted by the Company's EBIT, and excluding the effect of noncash deferred compensation expense up to $2,200 for the quarter ended March 31, 2012 for these same covenants. The Third Amendment also increased the basket for capital expenditures for the year ending March 31, 2012 by $15,000 and permitted the Company to form a subsidiary for a specified business purpose to be funded by up to $1,000 in equity and $30,000 in subordinated note investments by the Company, provided the subsidiary receives either revolving credit financing of up to $200,000 from third parties or issues subordinated notes for an aggregate not to exceed $100,000. The Third Amendment increased the interest rates on base rate and LIBOR loans by 1.0 percentage point and the commitment fee on unborrowed amounts under the facility by 0.25 of a percentage point. In addition, pursuant to the Third Amendment, the Company agreed to grant the lenders a security interest on certain U.S. real estate.

Fourth Amendment. On November 3, 2011, the Company closed the Fourth Amendment to the Credit Agreement that expired March 31, 2013. The amendment permitted the exclusion of specified levels of restructuring and impairment charges from the financial covenants impacted by the Company's EBIT for fiscal quarters ending on or prior to March 31, 2012 and permitted the exclusion of specified levels of costs and expenses associated with the commercialization, sale or dissolution of the Company's Alert business from the financial covenants impacted by the Company's EBIT for fiscal quarters ending on or prior to December 31, 2011. The amendment also extended to April 30, 2012 the period in which the Company is permitted to form one or more subsidiaries for a specified business purpose to be funded by up to $1,000 in equity and $30,000 in subordinated note investments by the Company, provided the subsidiary or subsidiaries receive revolving credit financing of up to $200,000 from third parties and issue subordinated notes for an aggregate of up to $100,000.

Fifth Amendment. On June 13, 2012, the Company closed the Fifth Amendment to the Credit Agreement whereby the lenders agreed to reduce the Revolving Committed Amount by $40,000 to $250,000 and to extend the term of the facility to April 15, 2014. In addition, the amendment modified certain financial covenants under the Credit Agreement, including modifying the Minimum Consolidated Interest Coverage Ratio for the quarter ended June 30, 2012 and thereafter; modifying the Maximum Consolidated Leverage Ratio for each fiscal quarter through maturity, establishing a Minimum Consolidated EBITDA ratio for each fiscal quarter through maturity, increasing the basket related to Permitted Foreign Subsidiary credit lines to $675,000 with a reduction to $500,000 for each March 31 and eliminating the basket for future Restricted Payments as well as the exception permitting Restricted Payments used to acquire the Company's Senior Notes.

Financial Covenants. Certain financial covenants are based on a rolling twelve month basis and required financial ratios adjust over time in accordance with schedules in the Credit Agreement. After giving effect to all amendments to the Credit Agreement, the requirements of those covenants and financial ratios at March 31, 2013 are as follows:
- a minimum consolidated interest coverage ratio of not less than 1.90 to 1.00 (1.70 for the quarter ending June 2012 and 1.90 for the quarter ending September 30, 2012 to maturity);
- a maximum consolidated leverage ratio in an amount not more than a ratio specified for each fiscal quarter as set forth in a schedule, which ratio is 5.90 for the quarter ended March 31, 2013 (7.25 for the quarter ending June 30, 2012, 7.40 for the quarter ending September 30, 2012 and 6.50 for the quarter ending December 31, 2012);
- a maximum consolidated total senior debt to working capital amount ratio of not more than 0.80 to 1.00; and
- maximum annual capital expenditures of $59,353 during fiscal year ending March 31, 2013 and $40,000 during any fiscal year thereafter, in each case with a one -year carry-forward for capital expenditures in any fiscal year below the maximum amount.

The Company continuously monitors compliance with debt covenants. At March 31, 2013 and during the fiscal year, the Company was in compliance with the covenants under the Senior Secured Credit Facility agreement. Significant changes in market conditions or other factors could adversely affect the Company's business and future debt covenant compliance thereunder, which are more stringent than the prior year. As a result, the Company may not be able to maintain compliance with the covenants over the next twelve months. If the Company were unable to maintain compliance with the covenants in the Senior Secured Credit Facility agreement, as amended from time-to-time, the Company would seek modification to the existing agreement to further amend covenants and extend maturities. If the Company were unable to obtain modification, in a scenario where it is required during fiscal year 2014, the Company could decide to pay off outstanding amounts and terminate the agreement. In such case, the liquidity provided by the agreement would not be available and the Company believes that it has sufficient liquidity from operations and other available funding sources to meet future requirements.

Summary of Debt

All debt agreements contain cross-default or cross-acceleration provisions. The following table summarizes the Company's debt financing as of March 31, 2013:

| | Outstanding | | March 31, 2013 Lines and Letters Available | Interest Rate | | Long Term Debt Repayment Schedule by Fiscal Year | | | | | |
	March 31, 2012	March 31, 2013				2014	2015	2016	2017	2018	Later
Senior secured credit facility:											
Revolver[1]	$ —	$ 95,000	$155,000	6.0%	[2]	$ —	$ 95,000	$—	$ —	$—	$ —
Senior notes:											
10% senior notes due 2016[4]	615,189	619,016	—	10.0%		—	—	—	619,016	—	—
8 1/2% senior notes due 2012	6,000	—	—	8.5%		—	—	—	—	—	—
	621,189	619,016	—			—	—	—	619,016	—	—
5 1/2% convertible senior subordinated notes due 2014	115,000	115,000	—	5.5%		—	115,000	—	—	—	—
Long-term foreign seasonal borrowings	88,226	5,173	19,827	3.9%	[2]	5,173	—	—	—	—	—
Other long-term debt	4,088	3,030	1,121	7.2%	[2]	1,176	933	363	283	—	275
Notes payable to banks[3]	374,532	356,836	276,275	4.3%	[2]	—	—	—	—	—	—
Total debt	$1,203,035	$1,194,055	452,223			$6,349	$210,933	$363	$619,299	$—	$275
Short term	$ 374,532	$ 356,836									
Long term:											
Long term debt current	$ 7,050	$ 6,349									
Long term debt	821,453	830,870									
	$ 828,503	$ 837,219									
Letters of credit	$ 7,239	$ 4,138	10,557								
Total credit available			$462,780								

[1] As of March 31, 2013, pursuant to Section 2.1 (A) (iv) of the Credit Agreement, the full Revolving Committed Amount was available based on the calculation of the lesser of the Revolving Committed Amount and the Working Capital Amount.
[2] Weighted average rate for the twelve months ended March 31, 2013.
[3] Primarily foreign seasonal lines of credit.
[4] Repayment of $ 619,016 is net of original issue discount of $ 15,984. Total repayment will be $ 635,000.

Long-Term Leases

RECOGNITION AND MEASUREMENT

2.136 FASB ASC 840 establishes standards of financial accounting and reporting for leases on the financial statements of lessees and lessors. FASB ASC 840 classifies leases as capital or operating. Capital leases are accounted for as the acquisition of an asset and the incurrence of an obligation by the lessee and as a sale or financing by the lessor. All other leases are accounted for as operating leases.

PRESENTATION

2.137 Under FASB ASC 840-30-45-1, lessees should separately identify on the balance sheet or notes thereto assets recorded under capital leases, the accumulated amortization thereon, and obligations. Capital lease obligations are subject to the same considerations as other obligations in classifying them with current and noncurrent liabilities in classified balance sheets. Similarly, a lessor's net investment in a sales-type or direct financing lease is also subject to the same considerations as other assets in classification as current or noncurrent assets.

2.138 FASB ASC 840-20-45-2 requires that lessors include property subject to operating leases with or near property, plant, and equipment in the balance sheet. Accumulated depreciation should be deducted by lessors from the investments in the leased property, as explained in FASB ASC 840-20-45-3.

DISCLOSURE

2.139 FASB ASC 840-20-50 and 840-30-50 contain detailed disclosure requirements for lessors and lessees under operating and capital leases, respectively.

PRESENTATION AND DISCLOSURE EXCERPTS

LESSEE LEASES

2.140 RALPH LAUREN CORPORATION (MAR)
CONSOLIDATED BALANCE SHEETS (in part)

(Millions)	March 30, 2013	March 31, 2012
Liabilities and Equity (in part)		
Current liabilities:		
Current portion of long-term debt	$ 266.6	$ —
Accounts payable	146.9	180.6
Income tax payable	43.2	71.9
Accrued expenses and other current liabilities	664.6	693.7
Total current liabilities	1,121.3	946.2
Long-term debt	—	274.4
Non-current liability for unrecognized tax benefits	150.2	168.0
Other non-current liabilities	362.1	375.3
Commitments and contingencies (Note 17)		
Total liabilities	1,633.6	1,763.9

NOTES TO CONSOLIDATED FINANCIAL STATEMENTS

3. Summary of Significant Accounting Policies (in part)

Leases

The Company leases certain facilities and equipment, including the vast majority of its retail stores. Certain of the Company's leases contain renewal options, rent escalation clauses, and/or landlord incentives. Renewal terms generally reflect market rates at the time of renewal. Rent expense for noncancelable operating leases with scheduled rent increases and/or landlord incentives is recognized on a straight-line basis over the lease term, including any applicable rent holidays, beginning with the lease commencement date, or the date the Company takes control of the leased space, whichever is sooner. The excess of straight-line rent expense over scheduled payment amounts and landlord incentives is recorded as a deferred rent liability. As of the end of Fiscal 2013 and Fiscal 2012, deferred rent obligations of approximately $208 million and $193 million, respectively, were classified primarily within other non-current liabilities in the Company's consolidated balance sheets.

In certain lease arrangements, the Company is involved with the construction of the building (generally on land owned by the landlord). If the Company concludes that it has substantively all of the risks of ownership during construction of a leased property and therefore is deemed the owner of the project for accounting purposes, it records an asset and related financing obligation for the amount of the total project costs related to construction-in-progress and the pre-existing building. Once construction is complete, the Company considers the requirements for sale-leaseback treatment, including the transfer back of all risks of ownership and whether the Company has any continuing involvement in the leased property. If the arrangement does not qualify for sale-leaseback treatment, the Company continues to amortize the financing obligation and depreciate the building over the lease term.

4. Recently Issued Accounting Standards (in part)

Proposed Amendments to Current Accounting Standards

The FASB is currently working on amendments to existing accounting standards governing a number of areas including, but not limited to, accounting for leases. In May 2013, the FASB issued a new exposure draft, "Leases" (the "Exposure Draft"), which would replace the existing guidance in ASC topic 840, "Leases." Under the Exposure Draft, among other changes in practice, a lessee's rights and obligations under most leases, including existing and new arrangements, would be recognized as assets and liabilities, respectively, on the balance sheet. Other significant provisions of the Exposure Draft include (i) defining the "lease term" to include the noncancellable period together with periods for which there is a significant economic incentive for the lessee to extend or not terminate the lease; (ii) defining the initial lease liability to be recorded on the balance sheet to contemplate only those variable lease payments that depend on an index or that are in substance "fixed"; and (iii) a dual approach for determining whether lease expense is recognized on a straight-line or accelerated basis, depending on whether the lessee is expected to consume more than an insignificant portion of the leased asset's economic benefits. The comment period for the Exposure Draft ends on September 13, 2013. If and when effective, this proposed standard will likely have a significant impact on the

Company's consolidated financial statements. However, as the standard-setting process is still ongoing, the Company is unable at this time to determine the impact this proposed change in accounting will have on its consolidated financial statements.

10. Other Current Liabilities and Non-Current Liabilities (in part)

Other non-current liabilities consist of the following:

(Millions)	March 30, 2013	March 31, 2012
Capital lease obligations	$ 38.4	$ 38.3
Deferred rent obligations	189.2	176.9
Deferred income	57.6	78.2
Deferred tax liabilities	29.7	35.2
Other non-current liabilities	47.2	46.7
Total other non-current liabilities	$362.1	$375.3

17. Commitments and Contingencies (in part)

Leases

The Company operates its retail stores under various leasing arrangements. The Company also occupies various office and warehouse facilities and uses certain equipment under numerous lease agreements. Such leasing arrangements are accounted for as either operating leases or capital leases. In this context, capital leases include leases whereby the Company is considered to have the substantive risks of ownership during construction of a leased property. Information on the Company's operating and capital leasing activities is set forth below.

Operating Leases

The Company is typically required to make minimum rental payments, and often contingent rental payments, under its operating leases. Many of the Company's retail store leases provide for contingent rentals based upon sales, and certain rental agreements require payment based solely on a percentage of sales. Terms of the Company's leases generally contain renewal options, rent escalation clauses, and landlord incentives. Rent expense, net of sublease income which was not significant in any period, was approximately $430 million, $427 million, and $317 million in Fiscal 2013, Fiscal 2012, and Fiscal 2011, respectively. Such amounts include contingent rental charges of approximately $174 million, $182 million, and $109 million in Fiscal 2013, Fiscal 2012, and Fiscal 2011, respectively. In addition to such amounts, the Company is normally required to pay taxes, insurance, and occupancy costs relating to the leased real estate properties.

As of March 30, 2013, future minimum rental payments under noncancelable operating leases with lease terms in excess of one year were as follows:

(Millions)	Minimum Operating Lease Payments[a]
Fiscal 2014	$ 279.9
Fiscal 2015	281.6
Fiscal 2016	264.5
Fiscal 2017	241.8
Fiscal 2018	223.9
Fiscal 2019 and thereafter	887.8
Total minimum rental payments	$2,179.5

[a] Net of sublease income, which is not significant in any period.

Capital Leases

Assets under capital leases amounted to approximately $33 million and $31 million at the end of Fiscal 2013 and Fiscal 2012, respectively, net of accumulated amortization of approximately $16 million and $14 million, respectively. Such assets are classified within property and equipment, net in the consolidated balance sheets based on their nature. As of March 30, 2013, future minimum rental payments under noncancelable capital leases with lease terms in excess of one year were as follows:

(Millions)	Minimum Capital Lease Payments[a]
Fiscal 2014	$ 8.1
Fiscal 2015	7.9
Fiscal 2016	7.9
Fiscal 2017	7.3
Fiscal 2018	6.6
Fiscal 2019 and thereafter	26.6
Total	64.4
Less: amount representing interest	(29.8)
Present value of net minimum rental payments	$ 34.6

[a] Net of sublease income, which is not significant in any period.

2.141 OFFICE DEPOT, INC. (DEC)
NOTES TO CONSOLIDATED FINANCIAL STATEMENTS

Note 1. Summary of Significant Accounting Policies (in part)

Leasing Arrangements: The Company conducts a substantial portion of its business in leased properties. Some of the Company's leases contain escalation clauses and renewal options. The Company recognizes rental expense for leases that contain predetermined fixed escalation clauses on a straight-line basis over the expected term of the lease. The difference between the amounts charged to expense and the contractual minimum lease payment is accrued for.

The expected term of a lease is calculated from the date the Company first takes possession of the facility, including any periods of free rent and any option or renewal periods management believes are probable of exercise. This expected term is used in the determination of whether a lease is capital or operating and in the calculation of straight-line rent expense. Rent abatements and escalations are considered in the calculation of minimum lease payments in the Company's capital lease tests and in determining straight-line rent expense for operating leases. Straight-line rent expense is also adjusted to reflect any allowances or reimbursements provided by the lessor. When required under lease agreements, estimated costs to return facilities to original condition are accrued over the lease period.

Note 10. Leases

The Company leases retail stores and other facilities, vehicles, and equipment under operating lease agreements. Facility leases typically are for a fixed non-cancellable term with one or more renewal options. In addition to minimum rentals, the Company is required to pay certain executory costs such as real estate taxes, insurance and common area maintenance on most of the facility leases. Many lease agreements contain tenant improvement allowances, rent holidays, and/or rent escalation clauses. For purposes of recognizing incentives and minimum rental expenses on a straight-line basis over the terms of the leases, the Company uses the date of initial possession to begin amortization. Certain leases contain provisions for additional rent to be paid if sales exceed a specified amount, though such payments have been immaterial during the years presented.

Deferred rent liability for tenant improvement allowances and rent holidays are recognized and amortized over the terms of the related leases as a reduction of rent expense. For scheduled rent escalation clauses during the lease terms or for rental payments commencing at a date other than the date of initial occupancy, the Company records minimum rental expenses on a straight-line basis over the terms of the leases. Rent related accruals totaled approximately $324 million and $263 million at December 28, 2013 and December 29, 2012, respectively. The short-term and long-term components of these liabilities are included in Accrued expenses and other current liabilities and Deferred income taxes and other long-term liabilities, respectively, on the Consolidated Balance Sheets.

Rent expense, including equipment rental, was $458 million, $429 million and $447 million in 2013, 2012, and 2011, respectively. Rent expense was reduced by sublease income of $4 million in 2013, $5 million in 2012, and $3 million in 2011.

Future minimum lease payments due under the non-cancelable portions of leases as of December 28, 2013 include facility leases that were accrued as store closure costs and are as follows.

(In millions)	
2014	$ 726
2015	600
2016	470
2017	341
2018	194
Thereafter	547
	2,878
Less sublease income	56
Total	$2,822

These minimum lease payments do not include contingent rental payments that may be due based on a percentage of sales in excess of stipulated amounts.

As a result of purchase accounting from the Merger, the Company recorded a $44 million favorable lease intangible asset relating to store leases with terms below market value and a $54 million unfavorable lease deferred credit for store leases with terms above market value. The favorable leases and unfavorable leases are included in Other intangible assets and Deferred income taxes and other long-term liabilities in the Consolidated Balance Sheets, respectively. The asset and liability are amortized on a straight-line basis over the lives of the leases. In 2013, the net amortization of these items reduced rent expense by approximately $1 million. Refer to Note 5 for further details on favorable leases amortization. Unfavorable leases estimated future amortization is as follows:

(In millions)	
2014	$16
2015	13
2016	10
2017	7
2018	4
Thereafter	2
Total	$52

The Company has capital lease obligations primarily related to buildings and equipment. Refer to Note 8 for further details on amounts due related to capital lease obligations.

LESSOR LEASES

2.142 VERIZON COMMUNICATIONS INC. (DEC)
NOTES TO CONSOLIDATED FINANCIAL STATEMENTS

Note 7—Leasing Arrangements (in part)

As Lessor

We are the lessor in leveraged and direct financing lease agreements for commercial aircraft and power generating facilities, which comprise the majority of our leasing portfolio along with telecommunications equipment, commercial real estate property and other equipment. These leases have remaining terms of up to 37 years as of December 31, 2013. In addition, we lease space on certain of our cell towers to other wireless carriers. Minimum lease payments receivable represent unpaid rentals, less principal and interest on third-party nonrecourse debt relating to leveraged lease transactions. Since we have no general liability for this debt, which is secured by a senior security interest in the leased equipment and rentals, the related principal and interest have been offset against the minimum lease payments receivable in accordance with U.S. GAAP. All recourse debt is reflected in our consolidated balance sheets.

At each reporting period, we monitor the credit quality of the various lessees in our portfolios. Regarding the leveraged lease portfolio, external credit reports are used where available and where not available we use internally developed indicators. These indicators or internal credit risk grades factor historic loss experience, the value of the underlying collateral, delinquency trends, and industry and general economic conditions. The credit quality of our lessees varies from AAA to CCC $+$. For each reporting period the leveraged leases within the portfolio are reviewed for indicators of impairment where it is probable the rent due according to the contractual terms of the lease will not be collected. All significant accounts, individually or in the aggregate, are current and none are classified as impaired.

Finance lease receivables, which are included in Prepaid expenses and other and Other assets in our consolidated balance sheets, are comprised of the following:

| (Dollars in millions) | At December 31, | | | | | |
| | 2013 | | | 2012 | | |
	Leveraged Leases	Direct Finance Leases	Total	Leveraged Leases	Direct Finance Leases	Total
Minimum lease payments receivable	$1,069	$16	$1,085	$1,253	$58	$1,311
Estimated residual value	780	5	785	923	6	929
Unearned income	(589)	(4)	(593)	(654)	(10)	(664)
Total	$1,260	$17	$1,277	$1,522	$54	$1,576
Allowance for doubtful accounts			(90)			(99)
Finance lease receivables, net			$1,187			$1,477
Prepaid expenses and other			$5			$22
Other assets			1,182			1,455
			$1,187			$1,477

Accumulated deferred taxes arising from leveraged leases, which are included in Deferred income taxes, amounted to $1.0 billion at December 31, 2013 and $1.2 billion at December 31, 2012.

The following table is a summary of the components of income from leveraged leases:

(Dollars in millions) Years Ended December 31,	2013	2012	2011
Pre-tax income	$34	$30	$61
Income tax expense	12	12	24

The future minimum lease payments to be received from noncancelable capital leases (direct financing and leveraged leases), net of nonrecourse loan payments related to leveraged leases and allowances for doubtful accounts, along with expected receipts relating to operating leases for the periods shown at December 31, 2013, are as follows:

(Dollars in millions) Years	Capital Leases	Operating Leases
2014	$ 34	$197
2015	46	170
2016	114	142
2017	38	50
2018	56	23
Thereafter	797	19
Total	$1,085	$601

Other Noncurrent Liabilities

PRESENTATION

2.143 FASB ASC 210 indicates that liabilities classified as noncurrent (that is, beyond the operating cycle) include long-term deferments of the delivery of goods or services, such as the issuance of a long-term warranty or the advance receipt by a lessor of rental for the final period of a 10-year lease. Similarly, a loan on a life insurance policy with the intent that it will not be paid but will be liquidated by deduction from the proceeds of the policy upon maturity or cancellation should be excluded from current liabilities.

2.144 FASB ASC 480, *Distinguishing Liabilities from Equity*, requires that an issuer classify certain financial instruments with characteristics of both liabilities and equity as liabilities. Some issuances of stock, such as mandatorily redeemable preferred stock, impose unconditional obligations requiring the issuer to transfer assets or issue its equity shares. FASB ASC 480 requires an issuer to classify such financial instruments as liabilities, not present them between the "Liabilities" and "Equity" sections of the balance sheet. Rule 5-02 of Regulation S-X includes matters related to redeemable preferred stocks to be stated on the face of the balance sheet or included in the notes.

2.145 Rule 5-02 of Regulation S-X requires that any item not classed in another Regulation S-X liability caption and in excess of 5 percent of total liabilities be stated separately on the balance sheet or disclosed in the notes. Regulation S-X also requires that deferred income taxes, deferred tax credits, and material items of deferred income be stated separately in the balance sheet.

PRESENTATION AND DISCLOSURE EXCERPTS

DEFERRED INCOME TAXES

2.147 ARMSTRONG WORLD INDUSTRIES, INC. (DEC)
CONSOLIDATED BALANCE SHEETS (in part)

(Amounts in millions, except share data)

	December 31, 2013	December 31, 2012
Liabilities and Shareholders' Equity (in part)		
Current liabilities:		
Current installments of long-term debt	$ 23.9	$ 33.0
Accounts payable and accrued expenses	383.6	346.3
Income tax payable	2.7	4.1
Deferred income taxes	0.7	1.3
Total current liabilities	410.9	384.7
Long-term debt, less current installments	1,042.6	1,038.0
Postretirement benefit liabilities	234.2	248.5
Pension benefit liabilities	225.5	247.9
Other long-term liabilities	67.5	86.6
Income taxes payable	81.7	63.3
Deferred income taxes	181.0	66.2
Total noncurrent liabilities	1,832.5	1,750.5

NOTES TO CONSOLIDATED FINANCIAL STATEMENTS

(Dollar amounts in millions)

Note 2. Summary of Significant Accounting Policies (in part)

Taxes. The provision for income taxes has been determined using the asset and liability approach of accounting for income taxes to reflect the expected future tax consequences of events recognized in the financial statements. Deferred income tax assets and liabilities are recognized by applying enacted tax rates to temporary differences that exist as of the balance sheet date which result from differences in the timing of reported taxable income between tax and financial reporting.

We reduce the carrying amounts of deferred tax assets by a valuation allowance if, based on the available evidence, it is more likely than not that such assets will not be realized. The need to establish valuation allowances for deferred tax assets is assessed quarterly. In assessing the requirement for, and amount of, a valuation allowance in accordance with the more likely than not standard, we give appropriate consideration to all positive and negative evidence related to the realization of the deferred tax assets. This assessment considers, among other matters, the nature, frequency and severity of current and cumulative losses, forecasts of future profitability and foreign source income, the duration of statutory carryforward periods, and our experience with operating loss and tax credit carryforward expirations. A history of cumulative losses is a significant piece of negative evidence used in our assessment. If a history of cumulative losses is incurred for a tax jurisdiction, forecasts of future profitability are not used as positive evidence related to the realization of the deferred tax assets in the assessment.

We recognize the tax benefits of an uncertain tax position if those benefits are more likely than not to be sustained based on existing tax law. Additionally, we establish a reserve for tax positions that are more likely than not to be sustained based on existing tax law, but uncertain in the ultimate benefit to be sustained upon examination by the relevant taxing authorities. Unrecognized tax benefits are subsequently recognized at the time the more likely than not recognition threshold is met, the tax matter is effectively settled or the statute of limitations for the relevant taxing authority to examine and challenge the tax position has expired, whichever is earlier.

Taxes collected from customers and remitted to governmental authorities are reported on a net basis.

Recently Issued Accounting Standards (in part)

In July 2013, the FASB issued ASU 2013-11 *"Income Taxes — Presentation of an Unrecognized Tax Benefit When a Net Operating Loss Carryforward, a Similar Tax Loss, or a Tax Credit Carryforward Exists"* which is part of ASC 740: Income Taxes. The new guidance requires an entity to present an unrecognized tax benefit and a net operating loss ("NOL") carryforward, a similar tax loss, or a tax credit carryforward on a net basis as part of a deferred tax asset, unless the unrecognized tax benefit is not available to reduce the deferred tax asset component or would not be utilized for that purpose, then a liability would be recognized. The guidance is to be applied prospectively and will be effective for us beginning January 1, 2014. Since this guidance impacts presentation only, it will have no effect on our financial condition, results of operations or cash flows.

Note 16. Income Taxes (in part)

The tax effects of principal temporary differences between the carrying amounts of assets and liabilities and their tax bases are summarized in the following table. Management believes it is more likely than not that the results of future operations will generate sufficient taxable income and foreign source income to realize deferred tax assets, net of valuation allowances. In arriving at this conclusion, we considered the profit before tax generated for the years 2011 through 2013, as well as future reversals of existing taxable temporary differences and projections of future profit before tax and foreign source income.

We reduce the carrying amounts of deferred tax assets by a valuation allowance if, based on the available evidence, it is more likely than not that such assets will not be realized. The need to establish valuation allowances for deferred tax assets is assessed quarterly. In assessing the requirement for, and amount of, a valuation allowance in accordance with the more likely than not standard for all periods, we give appropriate consideration to all positive and negative evidence related to the realization of the deferred tax assets. This assessment considers, among other matters, the nature, frequency and severity of current and cumulative losses, forecasts of future profitability and foreign source income, the duration of statutory carryforward periods, and our experience with operating loss and tax credit carryforward expirations. A history of cumulative losses is a significant piece of negative evidence used in our assessment. If a history of cumulative losses is incurred for a tax jurisdiction, forecasts of future profitability are not used as positive evidence related to the realization of the deferred tax assets in the assessment.

We have established a valuation allowance in the amount of $228.4 million consisting of $25.3 million for federal capital loss carryovers and statutorily limited operating loss carryovers, $9.4 million for state deferred tax assets, primarily operating loss carryovers, and $193.7 million for foreign deferred tax assets, primarily foreign operating loss carryovers.

We have $1,067.3 million of state net operating loss ("NOL") carryforwards with expirations between 2014 and 2033. In addition, we have $643.5 million of foreign NOL carryforwards, of which $576.0 million are available for carryforward indefinitely and $67.5 million expire between 2014 and 2028. We also have U.S. foreign tax credit ("FTC") carryforwards of $94.4 million expiring between 2014 and 2022.

Our valuation allowances at December 31, 2013 increased from December 31, 2012 by a net amount of $22.9 million. This includes net increases for certain foreign deferred tax assets of $20.4 million and $9.3 million for federal deferred tax assets. There was a net decrease of $6.8 million for certain deferred state income tax assets. The increase in the valuation allowance for deferred foreign income tax assets was primarily due to additional foreign losses and other deferred tax assets, partially offset by the impact of current year income and carryforward expirations. The increase in the valuation allowance for deferred federal income tax assets of $9.3 million was primarily due to an increase in a valuation allowance for certain statutorily limited federal losses of $10.3 million offset by a decrease of the valuation allowance on capital loss carryforwards of $1.0 million. The decrease in the valuation allowance for certain deferred state income tax assets of $6.8 million was primarily due to carryover expirations and an increase in projected utilization. We estimate we will need to generate future federal taxable income of $269.8 million, including foreign source income of $36.1 million, to fully realize the FTCs before they expire in 2022. We estimate we will need to generate future taxable income of approximately $1,286.6 million for state income tax purposes during the respective realization periods (ranging from 2014 to 2033) in order to fully realize the net deferred income tax assets discussed above.

The Internal Revenue Code and some states impose limitations on a corporation's ability to utilize tax attributes, including NOLs and FTCs, if it experiences an "ownership change." An ownership change may result from transactions increasing the ownership of certain shareholders by more than 50 percentage points over a three-year period. There have been no ownership changes as defined in the Internal Revenue Code subsequent to our bankruptcy emergence. Future ownership changes could have an impact on our ability to realize the deferred tax assets discussed above.

	December 31, 2013	December 31, 2012
Deferred Income Tax Assets (Liabilities)		
Postretirement benefits	$ 102.8	$ 105.9
Pension benefit liabilities	21.4	30.7
Net operating losses	230.2	218.6
Foreign tax credit carryforwards	94.4	119.1
Other	100.5	104.2
Total deferred income tax assets	549.3	578.5
Valuation allowances	(228.4)	(205.5)
Net deferred income tax assets	320.9	373.0
Intangibles	(239.3)	(245.6)
Accumulated depreciation	(91.5)	(83.8)
Prepaid pension costs	(44.2)	—
Inventories	(15.7)	(20.8)
Other	(9.8)	(5.3)
Total deferred income tax liabilities	(400.5)	(355.5)
Net deferred income tax (liabilities) assets	($79.6)	$ 17.5
Deferred income taxes have been classified in the Consolidated Balance Sheet as:		
Deferred income tax assets—current	$ 72.0	$ 49.9
Deferred income tax assets—noncurrent	30.1	35.1
Deferred income tax liabilities—current	(0.7)	(1.3)
Deferred income tax liabilities—noncurrent	(181.0)	(66.2)
Net deferred income tax (liabilities) assets	($79.6)	$ 17.5

	2013	2012	2011
Details of Taxes			
Earnings (loss) before income taxes:			
Domestic	$186.2	$188.6	$221.2
Foreign	(14.3)	31.9	(3.9)
Eliminations of dividends from foreign subsidiaries	—	—	(23.5)
Total	$171.9	$220.5	$193.8
Income tax expense (benefit):			
Current:			
Federal	$ 18.7	$ 24.1	$ 3.1
Foreign	8.1	13.1	16.7
State	3.3	4.4	2.7
Total current	30.1	41.6	22.5
Deferred:			
Federal	40.1	27.2	55.0
Foreign	2.3	1.8	(1.6)
State	(1.1)	5.5	5.1
Total deferred	41.3	34.5	58.5
Total income tax expense	$ 71.4	$ 76.1	$ 81.0

We are currently expanding international operations by constructing a plant in Russia and increasing our investments in emerging markets.

During 2013, we reviewed our position with regards to foreign unremitted earnings and determined that unremitted earnings would continue to be permanently reinvested. Accordingly we have not recorded U.S. income or foreign withholding taxes on approximately $293.1 million of undistributed earnings of foreign subsidiaries that could be subject to taxation if remitted to the U.S. because we currently plan to keep these amounts permanently invested overseas. It is not practical to calculate the residual income tax which would result if these basis differences reversed due to the complexities of the tax law and the hypothetical nature of the calculations.

	2013	2012	2011
Reconciliation to U.S. Statutory Tax Rate			
Continuing operations tax at statutory rate	$ 60.2	$ 77.2	$ 67.8
State income tax expense, net of federal benefit	5.9	6.2	7.7
(Decrease) in valuation allowances on deferred domestic income tax assets	(2.9)	(0.7)	(0.8)
Increase in valuation allowances on deferred foreign income tax assets	32.4	14.9	14.7
Tax on foreign and foreign-source income	(13.8)	(8.2)	(2.8)
Domestic production activities	(9.0)	(2.3)	—
Permanent book/tax differences	3.5	1.4	0.6
IRS audit settlement	—	2.2	—
Net benefit due to increase in foreign tax credits	—	(15.7)	(6.6)
Research and development credits	(4.4)	—	—
Other	(0.5)	1.1	0.4
Tax expense at effective rate	$ 71.4	$ 76.1	$ 81.0

During 2010 and 2011, we recorded $169.6 million of dividends from our foreign subsidiaries related to unremitted foreign earnings for which we previously recorded a net deferred tax liability as the earnings were not considered permanently reinvested. The receipt of the foreign dividends in 2011 provided an opportunity to elect to credit foreign taxes that were previously deducted. In 2011, we increased the deferred tax assets by $21.1 million offset by a valuation allowance of $15.7 million, for a net tax benefit of $5.4 million to reflect the net impact of the foreign tax credit over the tax deduction for the foreign taxes.

In 2012, we released the valuation allowance with respect to the foreign tax credits of $15.7 million.

We recognize the tax benefits of an uncertain tax position only if those benefits are more likely than not to be sustained based on existing tax law. Additionally, we establish a reserve for tax positions that are more likely than not to be sustained based on existing tax law, but uncertain in the ultimate benefit to be sustained upon examination by the relevant taxing authorities. Unrecognized tax benefits are subsequently recognized at the time the more likely than not recognition threshold is met, the tax matter is effectively settled or the statute of limitations for the relevant taxing authority to examine and challenge the tax position has expired, whichever is earlier.

We have $145.2 million of Unrecognized Tax Benefits ("UTB") as of December 31, 2013, $92.4 million ($90.0 million, net of federal benefit) of this amount, if recognized in future periods, would impact the reported effective tax rate.

It is reasonably possible that certain UTB's may increase or decrease within the next twelve months due to tax examination changes, settlement activities, expirations of statute of limitations, or the impact on recognition and measurement considerations related to the results of published tax cases or other similar activities. Over the next twelve months, we estimate that UTB's may decrease by $0.7 million due to statutes expiring and increase by $6.0 million due to uncertain tax positions expected to be taken on tax returns.

We account for all interest and penalties on uncertain income tax positions as income tax expense. We reported $1.7 million of interest and penalty exposure as accrued income tax in the Consolidated Balance Sheet as of December 31, 2013.

We had the following activity for UTB's for the years ended December 31, 2013, 2012 and 2011:

	2013	2012	2011
Unrecognized tax benefits balance at January 1,	$138.4	$127.2	$126.3
Gross change for current year positions	8.5	10.2	4.1
Increases for prior period positions	1.4	7.8	1.4
Decrease for prior period positions	(2.1)	(6.1)	(3.9)
Decrease due to statute expirations	(1.0)	(0.7)	(0.7)
Unrecognized tax benefits balance at December 31,	$145.2	$138.4	$127.2

2.148 RALPH LAUREN CORPORATION (MAR)
CONSOLIDATED BALANCE SHEETS (in part)

(Millions)	March 30, 2013	March 31, 2012
Liabilities and Equity (in part)		
Current liabilities:		
Current portion of long-term debt	$ 266.6	$ —
Accounts payable	146.9	180.6
Income tax payable	43.2	71.9
Accrued expenses and other current liabilities	664.6	693.7
Total current liabilities	1,121.3	946.2
Long-term debt	—	274.4
Non-current liability for unrecognized tax benefits	150.2	168.0
Other non-current liabilities	362.1	375.3
Commitments and contingencies (Note 17)		
Total liabilities	1,633.6	1,763.9

NOTES TO CONSOLIDATED FINANCIAL STATEMENTS

3. Summary of Significant Accounting Policies (in part)

Income Taxes

Income taxes are provided using the asset and liability method. Under this method, income taxes (i.e., deferred tax assets and liabilities, current taxes payable/refunds receivable, and tax expense) are recorded based on amounts refundable or payable in the current year and include the results of any difference between U.S. GAAP and tax reporting. Deferred income taxes reflect the tax effect of certain net operating loss, capital loss, and general business credit carryforwards and the net tax effects of temporary differences between the carrying amount of assets and liabilities for financial statement and income tax purposes, as determined under enacted tax laws and rates. The Company accounts for the financial effect of changes in tax laws or rates in the period of enactment.

In addition, valuation allowances are established when management determines that it is more likely than not that some portion or all of a deferred tax asset will not be realized. Tax valuation allowances are analyzed periodically and adjusted as events occur or circumstances change that warrant adjustments to those balances.

In determining the income tax provision for financial reporting purposes, the Company establishes a reserve for uncertain tax positions. If the Company considers that a tax position is more likely than not of being sustained upon audit, based solely on the technical merits of the position, it recognizes the tax benefit. The Company measures the tax benefit by determining the largest amount that is greater than 50% likely of being realized upon settlement, presuming that the tax position is examined by the appropriate taxing authority that has full knowledge of all relevant information. These assessments can be complex and the Company often obtains assistance from external advisors. To the extent that the Company's estimates change or the final tax outcome of these matters is different than the amounts recorded, such differences will impact the income tax provision in the period in which such determinations are made. If the initial assessment fails to result in the recognition of a tax benefit, the Company regularly monitors its position and subsequently recognizes the tax benefit if (i) there are changes in tax law or analogous case law that sufficiently raise the likelihood of prevailing on the technical merits of the position to "more likely than not"; (ii) the statute of limitations expires; or (iii) there is a completion of an audit resulting in a settlement of that tax year with the appropriate agency. Uncertain tax positions are classified as current only when the Company expects to pay cash within the next twelve months. Interest and penalties, if any, are recorded within the provision for income taxes in the Company's consolidated statements of income and are classified on the consolidated balance sheets together with the related liability for unrecognized tax benefits.

See Note 13 for further discussion of the Company's income taxes.

13. Income Taxes (in part)

Uncertain Income Tax Benefits

Fiscal 2013, Fiscal 2012, and Fiscal 2011 Activity

A reconciliation of the beginning and ending amounts of unrecognized tax benefits, excluding interest and penalties, for Fiscal 2013, Fiscal 2012, and Fiscal 2011 is presented below:

(Millions)	Fiscal Years Ended		
	March 30, 2013	**March 31, 2012**	**April 2, 2011**
Unrecognized tax benefits beginning balance	$129.0	$125.0	$ 96.2
Additions related to current period tax positions	4.1	3.5	2.2
Additions related to prior period tax positions	11.6	7.8	45.6
Reductions related to prior period tax positions	(31.9)	(3.5)	(18.0)
Reductions related to expiration of statutes of limitations	(0.9)	(1.5)	(1.4)
Reductions related to settlements with taxing authorities	(10.4)	—	(2.4)
Additions (reductions) related to foreign currency translation	(1.6)	(2.3)	2.8
Unrecognized tax benefits ending balance	$ 99.9	$129.0	$125.0

The Company classifies interest and penalties related to unrecognized tax benefits as part of its provision for income taxes. A reconciliation of the beginning and ending amounts of accrued interest and penalties related to unrecognized tax benefits for Fiscal 2013, Fiscal 2012, and Fiscal 2011 is presented below:

(Millions)	Fiscal Years Ended		
	March 30, 2013	**March 31, 2012**	**April 2, 2011**
Accrued interest and penalties beginning balance	$39.0	$31.4	$29.8
Net additions charged to expense	22.6[a]	8.3	1.2
Reductions related to prior period tax positions	(9.9)	(0.3)	—
Reductions related to settlements with taxing authorities	(1.2)	—	—
Additions (reductions) related to foreign currency translation	(0.2)	(0.4)	0.4
Accrued interest and penalties ending balance	$50.3	$39.0	$31.4

[a] Includes a reserve of $16.8 million for an interest assessment on a prior year withholding tax. No underlying tax exposure exists. The interest assessed was not material to the Company's consolidated financial statements in any prior fiscal period and is not material for Fiscal 2013.

The total amount of unrecognized tax benefits, including interest and penalties, was $150.2 million and $168.0 million as of as of March 30, 2013 and March 31, 2012, respectively, and is included within the non-current liability for unrecognized tax benefits in the consolidated balance sheets. The total amount of unrecognized tax benefits that, if recognized, would affect the Company's effective tax rate was $115.1 million and $119.8 million as of March 30, 2013 and March 31, 2012, respectively.

Future Changes in Unrecognized Tax Benefits

The total amount of unrecognized tax benefits relating to the Company's tax positions is subject to change based on future events including, but not limited to, the settlements of ongoing tax audits and assessments and the expiration of applicable statutes of limitations. Although the outcomes and timing of such events are highly uncertain, the Company does not anticipate that the balance of gross unrecognized tax benefits, excluding interest and penalties, will change significantly during the next twelve months. However, changes in the occurrence, expected outcomes, and timing of those events could cause the Company's current estimate to change materially in the future.

During the third quarter of Fiscal 2013, the Company reached a settlement agreement with respect to a tax examination for the taxable years ended March 29, 2008 through April 3, 2010. In connection with this agreement, the Company recognized a tax benefit of $15.4 million. The Company's unrecognized tax benefits declined by approximately $33.7 million, excluding interest and penalties, as a result of this settlement.

The Company files tax returns in the U.S. federal and various state, local, and foreign jurisdictions. With few exceptions for those tax returns, the Company is no longer subject to examinations by the relevant tax authorities for years prior to Fiscal 2004.

2.149 WASTE MANAGEMENT, INC. (DEC)
CONSOLIDATED BALANCE SHEETS (in part)

(In Millions, Except Share and Par Value Amounts)

	December 31,	
	2013	2012
Liabilities and Equity (in part)		
Current liabilities:		
Accounts payable	$ 744	$ 842
Accrued liabilities	1,069	986
Deferred revenues	475	465
Current portion of long-term debt	726	743
Total current liabilities	3,014	3,036
Long-term debt, less current portion	9,500	9,173
Deferred income taxes	1,842	1,947
Landfill and environmental remediation liabilities	1,518	1,459
Other liabilities	727	807
Total liabilities	16,601	16,422

NOTES TO CONSOLIDATED FINANCIAL STATEMENTS

Years Ended December 31, 2013, 2012 and 2011

3. Summary of Significant Accounting Policies (in part)

Insured and Self-Insured Claims

We have retained a significant portion of the risks related to our health and welfare, automobile, general liability and workers' compensation claims programs. The exposure for unpaid claims and associated expenses, including incurred but not reported losses, generally is estimated with the assistance of external actuaries and by factoring in pending claims and historical trends and data. The gross estimated liability associated with settling unpaid claims is included in "Accrued liabilities" in our Consolidated Balance Sheets if expected to be settled within one year, or otherwise is included in long-term "Other liabilities." Estimated insurance recoveries related to recorded liabilities are reflected as current "Other receivables" or long-term "Other assets" in our Consolidated Balance Sheets when we believe that the receipt of such amounts is probable.

11. Commitments and Contingencies (in part)

Insurance (in part)—We carry insurance coverage for protection of our assets and operations from certain risks including automobile liability, general liability, real and personal property, workers' compensation, directors' and officers' liability, pollution legal liability and other coverages we believe are customary to the industry. Our exposure to loss for insurance claims is generally limited to the per incident deductible under the related insurance policy. Our exposure, however, could increase if our insurers are unable to meet their commitments on a timely basis.

We have retained a significant portion of the risks related to our automobile, general liability and workers' compensation claims programs. "General liability" refers to the self-insured portion of specific third party claims made against us that may be covered under our commercial General Liability Insurance Policy. For our self-insured retentions, the exposure for unpaid claims and associated expenses, including incurred but not reported losses, is based on an actuarial valuation and internal estimates. The accruals for these liabilities could be revised if future occurrences or loss development significantly differ from our assumptions used. As of December 31, 2013, our commercial General Liability Insurance Policy carried self-insurance exposures of up to $2.5 million per incident and our workers' compensation insurance program carried self-insurance exposures of up to $5 million per incident. As of December 31, 2013, our auto liability insurance program included a per-incident base deductible of $5 million, subject to additional deductibles of $4.8 million in the $5 million to $10 million layer. Self-insurance claims reserves acquired as part of our acquisition of WM Holdings in July 1998 were discounted at 3.0% at December 31, 2013, 1.75% at December 31, 2012 and 2.0% at December 31, 2011. The changes to our net insurance liabilities for the three years ended December 31, 2013 are summarized below (in millions):

	Gross Claims Liability	Receivables Associated with Insured Claims[a]	Net Claims Liability
Balance, December 31, 2010	$ 523	$(170)	$ 353
Self-insurance expense (benefit)	176	(14)	162
Cash (paid) received	(188)	23	(165)
Balance, December 31, 2011	511	(161)	350
Self-insurance expense (benefit)	222	(59)	163
Cash (paid) received	(164)	18	(146)
Balance, December 31, 2012	569	(202)	367
Self-insurance expense (benefit)	177	(5)	172
Cash (paid) received	(156)	10	(146)
Balance, December 31, 2013[b]	$ 590	$(197)	$ 393
Current portion at December 31, 2013	$ 121	$ (23)	$ 98
Long-term portion at December 31, 2013	$ 469	$(174)	$ 295

[a] Amounts reported as receivables associated with insured claims are related to both paid and unpaid claims liabilities.
[b] We currently expect substantially all of our net claims liability to be settled in cash over the next five years.

DISCONTINUED OPERATIONS

2.150 DOVER CORPORATION (DEC)

CONSOLIDATED BALANCE SHEETS (in part)

(In thousands, except share and per share amounts)

	December 31, 2013	December 31, 2012
Current Liabilities:		
Notes payable and current maturities of long-term debt	$ 229,278	$ 610,766
Accounts payable	692,565	651,358
Accrued compensation and employee benefits	317,035	334,634
Accrued insurance	93,000	103,318
Other accrued expenses	260,911	255,632
Federal and other taxes on income	22,791	30,920
Total current liabilities	1,615,580	1,986,628
Long-term debt	2,599,201	2,189,350
Deferred income taxes	549,283	462,244
Other liabilities	514,086	677,533
Liabilities of discontinued operations	182,626	208,958

NOTES TO CONSOLIDATED FINANCIAL STATEMENTS

(Amounts in thousands except share data and where otherwise indicated)

1. Description of Business and Summary of Significant Accounting Policies (in part)

Principles of Consolidation —The consolidated financial statements include the accounts of the Company and its wholly-owned subsidiaries. Intercompany accounts and transactions have been eliminated in consolidation. The results of operations of purchased businesses are included from the dates of acquisitions. As discussed in Note 4. Disposed and Discontinued Operations, the Company is reporting certain businesses that are held for sale at December 31, 2013 as discontinued operations. The assets, liabilities, results of operations, and cash flows of all discontinued operations have been separately reported as discontinued operations for all periods presented. In addition, the results of operations, financial condition and cash flows for the businesses to be included in the spin-off of certain businesses within the Communication Technologies segment, are, and will continue to be, presented within Dover's consolidated financial statements as continuing operations within the Communication Technologies segment, until the spin-off becomes effective, upon which the financial presentation of these businesses will be included within Dover's discontinued operations.

4. Disposed and Discontinued Operations (in part)

Management evaluates Dover's businesses periodically for their strategic fit within Dover's operations. Accordingly, in 2012, the Company announced its intention to divest DEK International and Everett Charles Technologies (including the Multitest business, collectively "ECT") within the Printing & Identification segment, which serve the electronic assembly and test markets. These businesses were reclassified to discontinued operations in the fourth quarter of 2012.

2013 —In 2013, in connection with a change in goodwill reporting units within discontinued operations resulting from the Company's expected manner of disposing of its electronic test and assembly businesses, the Company was required to allocate goodwill to these individual reporting units based upon relative current fair values. This process resulted in a benefit of $25,520 in the discontinued operations deferred income tax provision for 2013 as a result of the elimination of certain deferred tax liabilities. The Company recorded a goodwill impairment charge of $54,532 ($44,188 after tax) at ECT in 2013 in connection with the anticipated sale of this business. This charge was a write-down of the carrying value to fair value, based on the current estimated sales price.

The Company completed the sale of ECT in the fourth quarter of 2013 for total proceeds of $92,694, which resulted in an after-tax loss on sale of $2,804. Included in the sale proceeds is a note receivable from the buyer of $20,000, which the Company expects to collect within the next five years. This receivable is reflected in Other assets and deferred charges on the Consolidated Balance Sheet at December 31, 2013.

In 2013, the Company signed a definitive agreement to sell DEK. Based on the anticipated proceeds from this sale, the Company recognized an impairment loss of $14,001 in the fourth quarter of 2013, which includes goodwill impairment of the related reporting unit of $9,251, of which none is deductible for tax purposes. Management plans to complete the sale of this business in the first half of 2014.

The net earnings from operations of $72,797 reflects the net earnings of DEK and ECT prior to sale, as well as $54,827 of discrete tax benefits principally related to the conclusion of certain federal, state and international tax audits and $18,279 of interest on tax obligations in foreign jurisdictions.

2012 —The net earnings from operations of $28,769 reflects net earnings from operations generated by these two businesses, as well as various expense and accrual adjustments relating to other discontinued operations. This activity was more than offset by a goodwill impairment charge determined in connection with the anticipated sale of ECT, at which time the Company recognized a goodwill impairment charge of $63,819 ($51,854 after tax), representing a write-down of the reporting unit's carrying value of goodwill to its fair value.

2011 —In 2011, the Company sold three businesses, Paladin Brands, Crenlo LLC, and Heil Trailer International, that had operated within the Engineered Systems segment for total cash proceeds of $512,122. These businesses were reclassified to discontinued operations in the third and fourth quarters of 2011. The 2011 net earnings from discontinued operations reflects net operating earnings generated by the two businesses discontinued in 2012 and the three business sold in 2011, coupled with tax benefits of $17,960 relating primarily to discrete tax items settled or resolved during the year.

Net earnings from discontinued operations also includes a $4,743 loss on the 2011 sale of the three businesses, inclusive of a after-tax goodwill impairment charge of $76,072, representing a write-down of the carrying value of the associated reporting unit's goodwill to its fair value.

Assets and liabilities of discontinued operations are summarized below:

	December 31, 2013	December 31, 2012
Assets of Discontinued Operations		
Accounts receivable[1]	$121,094	$ 63,229
Inventories, net	17,779	51,252
Prepaid and other current assets	28,381	10,263
Total current assets	167,254	124,744
Property, plant and equipment, net	6,468	31,935
Goodwill and intangible assets, net	145,681	238,657
Other assets and deferred charges	1,319	2,209
Total assets	$320,722	$397,545
Liabilities of Discontinued Operations		
Accounts payable[1]	$108,772	$ 22,613
Other current liabilities	21,445	34,592
Total current liabilities	130,217	57,205
Deferred income taxes	14,783	64,853
Other liabilities	37,626	86,900
Total liabilities	$182,626	$208,958

[1] Amounts include estimated credits and liabilities associated with tax obligations in foreign jurisdictions resulting from value-added tax for the Multitest business within ECT. Accounts receivable includes $93,598 of credits. Accounts payable includes $76,443 of liabilities and $18,279 of interest. This matter is expected to be resolved in 2014.

At December 31, 2013 and December 31, 2012, the assets and liabilities of discontinued operations relate primarily to DEK and ECT, coupled with tax-related accruals and unrecognized benefits, as well as other accruals for compensation, legal, environmental, and warranty contingencies.

WARRANTY

2.151 DELL INC. (JAN)
CONSOLIDATED STATEMENTS OF FINANCIAL POSITION (in part)

(In millions)

Liabilities and Stockholders' Equity (in part)	February 1, 2013	February 3, 2012
Current liabilities:		
Short-term debt	$ 3,843	$ 2,867
Accounts payable	11,579	11,656
Accrued and other	3,644	3,740
Short-term deferred revenue	4,373	3,738
Total current liabilities	23,439	22,001
Long-term debt	5,242	6,387
Long-term deferred revenue	3,971	3,855
Other non-current liabilities	4,187	3,373
Total liabilities	36,839	35,616

NOTES TO CONSOLIDATED FINANCIAL STATEMENTS

Note 1—Description of Business and Summary of Significant Accounting Policies (in part)

Standard Warranty Liabilities—Dell records warranty liabilities for its standard limited warranty at the time of sale for the estimated costs that may be incurred under its limited warranty. The liability for standard warranties is included in accrued and other current and other non-current liabilities on the Consolidated Statements of Financial Position. The specific warranty terms and conditions vary depending upon the product sold and the country in which Dell does business, but generally includes technical support, parts, and labor over a period ranging from one to three years. Factors that affect Dell's warranty liability include the number of installed units currently under warranty, historical and anticipated rates of warranty claims on those units, and cost per claim to satisfy Dell's warranty obligation. The anticipated rate of warranty claims is the primary factor impacting the estimated warranty obligation. The other factors are less significant due to the fact that the average remaining aggregate warranty period of the covered installed base is approximately 16 months, repair parts are generally already in stock or available at pre-determined prices, and labor rates are generally arranged at pre-established amounts with service providers. Warranty claims are relatively predictable based on historical experience of failure rates. If actual results differ from the estimates, Dell revises its estimated warranty liability. Each quarter, Dell reevaluates its estimates to assess the adequacy of its recorded warranty liabilities and adjusts the amounts as necessary.

Deferred Revenue—Deferred revenue represents amounts received in advance for extended warranty services, amounts due or received from customers under a legally binding commitment prior to services being rendered, deferred revenue related to Dell-owned software offerings, as well as other deferred revenue. Other deferred revenue primarily consists of deferred profit on third-party software offerings. See Note 16 of the Notes to the Consolidated Financial Statements for further information on deferred revenue.

Note 9—Warranty and Deferred Extended Warranty Revenue

Dell records liabilities for its standard limited warranties at the time of sale for the estimated costs that may be incurred. The liability for standard warranties is included in accrued and other current liabilities and other non-current liabilities on the Consolidated Statements of Financial Position. Revenue from the sale of extended warranties is recognized over the term of the contract or when the service is completed, and the costs associated with these contracts are recognized as incurred. Deferred extended warranty revenue is included in deferred revenue on the Consolidated Statements of Financial Position. Changes in Dell's liabilities for standard limited warranties and deferred services revenue related to extended warranties are presented in the following tables for the periods indicated:

	Fiscal Year Ended		
(In millions)	February 1, 2013	February 3, 2012	January 28, 2011
Warranty Liability:			
Warranty liability at beginning of period	$ 888	$ 895	$ 912
Costs accrued for new warranty contracts and changes in estimates for pre-existing warranties[(a)(b)]	992	1,025	1,046
Service obligations honored	(1,118)	(1,032)	(1,063)
Warranty liability at end of period	$ 762	$ 888	$ 895
Current portion	$ 492	$ 572	$ 575
Non-current portion	270	316	320
Warranty liability at end of period	$ 762	$ 888	$ 895

(In millions)	Fiscal Year Ended		
	February 1, 2013	February 3, 2012	January 28, 2011
Deferred Extended Warranty Revenue:			
Deferred extended warranty revenue at beginning of period	$ 7,002	$ 6,416	$ 5,910
Revenue deferred for new extended warranties[b]	4,130	4,301	3,877
Revenue recognized	(4,029)	(3,715)	(3,371)
Deferred extended warranty revenue at end of period	$ 7,103	$ 7,002	$ 6,416
Current portion	$ 3,400	$ 3,265	$ 2,959
Non-current portion	3,703	3,737	3,457
Deferred extended warranty revenue at end of period	$ 7,103	$ 7,002	$ 6,416

[a] Changes in cost estimates related to pre-existing warranties are aggregated with accruals for new standard warranty contracts. Dell's warranty liability process does not differentiate between estimates made for pre-existing warranties and new warranty obligations.

[b] Includes the impact of foreign currency exchange rate fluctuations.

ENVIRONMENTAL

2.152 REPUBLIC SERVICES, INC. (DEC)

CONSOLIDATED BALANCE SHEETS (in part)

(In millions, except per share data)

	December 31, 2013	December 31, 2012
Liabilities and Stockholders' Equity (in part)		
Current liabilities:		
Accounts payable	$ 511.4	$ 474.5
Notes payable and current maturities of long-term debt	15.7	19.4
Deferred revenue	301.8	313.2
Accrued landfill and environmental costs, current portion	178.7	195.5
Accrued interest	68.2	68.8
Other accrued liabilities	641.3	623.6
Total current liabilities	1,717.1	1,695.0
Long-term debt, net of current maturities	7,002.4	7,051.1
Accrued landfill and environmental costs, net of current portion	1,464.3	1,420.6
Deferred income taxes and other long-term tax liabilities	1,185.4	1,232.7
Self-insurance reserves, net of current portion	294.9	290.9
Other long-term liabilities	379.0	220.9
Commitments and contingencies		

NOTES TO CONSOLIDATED FINANCIAL STATEMENTS

2. Summary of Significant Accounting Policies (in part)

Landfill and Environmental Costs (in part)

Environmental Liabilities

We are subject to an array of laws and regulations relating to the protection of the environment, and we remediate sites in the ordinary course of our business. Under current laws and regulations, we may be responsible for environmental remediation at sites that we either own or operate, including sites that we have acquired, or sites where we have (or a company that we have acquired has) delivered waste. Our environmental remediation liabilities primarily include costs associated with remediating groundwater, surface water and soil contamination, as well as controlling and containing methane gas migration and the related legal costs. To estimate our ultimate liability at these sites, we evaluate several factors, including the nature and extent of contamination at each identified site, the required remediation methods, the apportionment of responsibility among the potentially responsible parties and the financial viability of those parties. We accrue for costs associated with environmental remediation obligations when such costs are probable and reasonably estimable in accordance with accounting for loss contingencies. We periodically review the status of all environmental matters and update our estimates of the likelihood of and future expenditures for remediation as necessary. Changes in the liabilities resulting from these reviews are recognized currently in earnings in the period in which the adjustment is known. Adjustments to estimates are reasonably possible in the near term and may result in changes to recorded amounts. With the exception of those obligations assumed in the acquisition of Allied, environmental obligations are recorded on an undiscounted basis. Environmental obligations assumed in the acquisition of Allied, which were initially estimated on a discounted basis, are accreted to full value over time through charges to interest expense. Adjustments arising from changes in amounts and timing of estimated costs and settlements may result in increases or decreases in these obligations and are calculated on a discounted basis as they were initially estimated on a discounted basis. These adjustments are charged to operating income when they are known. We perform a comprehensive review of our environmental obligations annually and also review changes in facts and circumstances associated with these obligations at least quarterly. We have not reduced the liabilities we have recorded for recoveries from other potentially responsible parties or insurance companies.

8. Landfill and Environmental Costs (in part)

As of December 31, 2013, we owned or operated 190 active solid waste landfills with total available disposal capacity of approximately 4.9 billion in-place cubic yards. Additionally, we currently have post-closure responsibility for 124 closed landfills.

A summary of our accrued landfill and environmental liabilities as of December 31 is as follows:

	2013	2012
Landfill final capping, closure and post-closure liabilities	$1,091.3	$1,052.4
Environmental remediation	551.7	563.7
Total accrued landfill and environmental costs	1,643.0	1,616.1
Less: current portion	(178.7)	(195.5)
Long-term portion	$1,464.3	$1,420.6

Environmental Remediation Liabilities

We accrue for remediation costs when they become probable and can be reasonably estimated. There can sometimes be a range of reasonable estimates of the costs associated with remediation of a site. In these cases, we use the amount within the range that constitutes our best estimate. If no amount within the range appears to be a better estimate than any other, we use the amount that is at the low end of such range. It is reasonably possible that we will need to adjust the liabilities recorded for remediation to reflect the effects of new or additional information, to the extent such information impacts the costs, timing or duration of the required actions. If we used the reasonably possible high ends of our ranges, our aggregate potential remediation liability as of December 31, 2013 would be approximately $446 million higher than the amounts recorded. Future changes in our estimates of the cost, timing or duration of the required actions could have a material adverse effect on our consolidated financial position, results of operations or cash flows.

The following table summarizes the activity in our environmental remediation liabilities for the years ended December 31:

	2013	2012	2011
Environmental remediation liabilities, beginning of year	$ 563.7	$543.7	$552.1
Net additions charged to expense	83.7	62.4	3.6
Payments	(122.5)	(73.1)	(45.0)
Accretion expense (non-cash interest expense)	26.8	30.7	33.0
Environmental remediation liabilities, end of year	551.7	563.7	543.7
Less: Current portion	(85.1)	(85.1)	(99.0)
Long-term portion	$ 466.6	$478.6	$444.7

The expected undiscounted future payments for remediation costs as of December 31, 2013 are as follows:

2014	$ 85.1
2015	49.8
2016	44.6
2017	35.6
2018	42.3
Thereafter	349.0
	$606.4

The following is a discussion of certain of our significant remediation matters:

Bridgeton Landfill. In June 2013, we recorded an environmental remediation charge at our closed Bridgeton Landfill in Missouri of $108.7 million to manage the remediation area and monitor the site. As of December 31, 2013, the remediation liability recorded for this site is $93.9 million, of which $30.9 million is expected to be paid during the next twelve months. We believe the remaining reasonably possible range of loss for remediation costs is $63 million to $342 million.

Countywide Landfill. In September 2009, Republic Services of Ohio II, LLC entered into Final Findings and Orders with the Ohio Environmental Protection Agency that require us to implement a comprehensive operation and maintenance program to manage the remediation area at the Countywide Recycling and Disposal Facility (Countywide). The remediation liability for Countywide recorded as of December 31, 2013 is $47.0 million, of which $4.6 million is expected to be paid during during the next twelve months. We believe the reasonably possible range of loss for remediation costs is $46 million to $67 million.

Congress Landfill. In August 2010, Congress Development Company agreed with the State of Illinois to have a Final Consent Order (Final Order) entered by the Circuit Court of Illinois, Cook County. Pursuant to the Final Order, we have agreed to continue to implement certain remedial activities at the Congress Landfill. The remediation liability recorded as of December 31, 2013 is $82.7 million, of which $9.9 million is expected to be paid during the next twelve months. We believe the reasonably possible range of loss for remediation costs is $53 million to $153 million.

It is reasonably possible that we will need to adjust the liabilities noted above to reflect the effects of new or additional information, to the extent that such information impacts the costs, timing or duration of the required actions. Future changes in our estimates of the costs, timing or duration of the required actions could have a material adverse effect on our consolidated financial position, results of operations or cash flows.

ASSET RETIREMENT OBLIGATIONS

2.153 MURPHY OIL CORPORATION (DEC)
CONSOLIDATED BALANCE SHEETS (in part)

	December 31	
(Thousands of dollars)	2013	2012
Liabilities and Stockholders' Equity (in part)		
Current liabilities		
Current maturities of long-term debt	$ 26,249	46
Accounts payable	2,158,485	2,803,268
Income taxes payable	222,930	219,847
Other taxes payable	7,059	172,962
Other accrued liabilities	170,168	162,876
Deferred income taxes	0	2,611
Liabilities associated with assets held for sale	639,140	47,471
Total current liabilities	3,224,031	3,409,081
Long-term debt, including capital lease obligation in 2013	2,936,563	2,245,201
Deferred income taxes	1,466,100	1,544,336
Asset retirement obligations	852,488	724,273
Deferred credits and other liabilities	339,028	516,540
Liabilities associated with assets held for sale	95,544	141,177

NOTES TO CONSOLIDATED FINANCIAL STATEMENTS

Note A—Significant Accounting Policies (in part)

PROPERTY, PLANT AND EQUIPMENT (in part)—The Company records a liability for asset retirement obligations (ARO) equal to the fair value of the estimated cost to retire an asset. The ARO liability is initially recorded in the period in which the obligation meets the definition of a liability, which is generally when a well is drilled or the asset is placed in service. The ARO liability is estimated by the Company's engineers using existing regulatory requirements and anticipated future inflation rates.

When the liability is initially recorded, the Company increases the carrying amount of the related long-lived asset by an amount equal to the original liability. The liability is increased over time to reflect the change in its present value, and the capitalized cost is depreciated over the useful life of the related long-lived asset. The Company reevaluates the adequacy of its recorded ARO liability at least annually. Actual costs of asset retirements such as dismantling oil and gas production facilities and site restoration are charged against the related liability. Any difference between costs incurred upon settlement of an asset retirement obligation and the recorded liability is recognized as a gain or loss in the Company's earnings.

Note G—Asset Retirement Obligations

The asset retirement obligations liabilities (ARO) recognized by the Company at December 31, 2013 and 2012 are related to the estimated costs to dismantle and abandon its producing oil and gas properties and related equipment.

The Company has not recorded an ARO for its refining and marketing assets in the U.K. because sufficient information is presently not available to estimate a range of potential settlement dates for the obligation. These assets are held for sale at December 31, 2013. If these assets are not sold as anticipated, the ARO obligation will be initially recognized in the period in which sufficient information exists to estimate the liability.

A reconciliation of the beginning and ending aggregate carrying amount of the asset retirement obligation for 2013 and 2012 is shown in the following table.

(Thousands of dollars)	2013	2012
Balance at beginning of year	$751,583	615,545
Accretion expense	48,996	39,341[1]
Liabilities incurred	172,048	184,439
Revision of previous estimates	(4,856)	10,468
Liabilities settled	(51,647)	(40,434)
Liabilities assumed by Murphy USA Inc. upon separation	(15,401)	0
U.K. oil and gas asset obligations reclassified to liabilities associated with assets held for sale in 2012	0	(64,355)
Changes due to translation of foreign currencies	(20,720)	6,579
Balance at end of year	880,003	751,583
Current portion of liability at end of year[2]	(27,515)	(27,310)
Noncurrent portion of liability at end of year	$852,488	724,273

[1] Includes $980 reclassified to discontinued operations associated with U.S. downstream operations.
[2] Included in Other Accrued Liabilities on the Consolidated Balance Sheet.

The estimation of future ARO is based on a number of assumptions requiring professional judgment. The Company cannot predict the type of revisions to these assumptions that may be required in future periods due to the availability of additional information such as: prices for oil field services, technological changes, governmental requirements and other factors.

LITIGATION

2.154 CRANE CO. (DEC)

CONSOLIDATED BALANCE SHEETS (in part)

	Balance at December 31,	
(In thousands, except shares and per share data)	2013	2012
Liabilities and Equity (in part)		
Current liabilities:		
Short-term borrowings	$125,826	$ 1,123
Accounts payable	229,828	182,731
Current asbestos liability	88,038	91,670
Accrued liabilities	223,148	220,678
U.S. and foreign taxes on income	2,062	15,686
Total current liabilities	668,902	511,888
Long-term debt	749,170	399,092
Accrued pension and postretirement benefits	151,133	233,603
Long-term deferred tax liability	76,041	36,853
Long-term asbestos liability	610,530	704,195
Other liabilities	89,158	76,871
Commitments and Contingencies (Note 11)		

NOTES TO CONSOLIDATED FINANCIAL STATEMENTS

Note 11—Commitments and Contingencies (in part)

Asbestos Liability (in part)

Information Regarding Claims and Costs in the Tort System

As of December 31, 2013, the Company was a defendant in cases filed in numerous state and federal courts alleging injury or death as a result of exposure to asbestos. Activity related to asbestos claims during the periods indicated was as follows:

For the Year Ended December 31,	2013	2012	2011
Beginning claims	56,442	58,658	64,839
New claims	2,950	3,542	3,748
Settlements	(1,142)	(1,030)	(1,117)
Dismissals	(6,762)	(4,919)	(11,059)
MARDOC claims*	2	191	2,247
Ending claims	51,490	56,442	58,658

* As of January 1, 2010, the Company was named in 36,448 maritime actions which had been administratively dismissed by the United States District Court for the Eastern District of Pennsylvania ("MARDOC claims"), and therefore were not classified as active claims. In addition, the Company was named in 8 new maritime actions in 2010 (also not classified as active claims). Through December 31, 2013, pursuant to an ongoing review process initiated by the Court, 26,562 claims were permanently dismissed, and 3,393 claims were classified as active, of which 2,980 claims were subsequently dismissed, 225 claims were subsequently settled and 188 claims remain active (and have been added to "Ending claims"). By settlement agreement of December 30, 2013, the Company resolved all of the remaining MARDOC claims with plaintiffs' counsel. The agreement will result in the dismissal of all MARDOC claims against the Company.

Of the 51,490 pending claims as of December 31, 2013, approximately 19,000 claims were pending in New York, approximately 9,700 claims were pending in Texas, approximately 5,300 claims were pending in Mississippi, and approximately 600 claims were pending in Ohio, all jurisdictions in which legislation or judicial orders restrict the types of claims that can proceed to trial on the merits.

Substantially all of the claims the Company resolves are either dismissed or concluded through settlements. To date, the Company has paid two judgments arising from adverse jury verdicts in asbestos matters. The first payment, in the amount of $2.54 million, was made on July 14, 2008, approximately two years after the adverse verdict in the *Joseph Norris* matter in California, after the Company had exhausted all post-trial and appellate remedies. The second payment, in the amount of $0.02 million, was made in June 2009 after an adverse verdict in the *Earl Haupt* case in Los Angeles, California on April 21, 2009.

The Company has tried several cases resulting in defense verdicts by the jury or directed verdicts for the defense by the court, one of which, the *Patrick O'Neil* claim in Los Angeles, was reversed on appeal. In an opinion dated January 12, 2012, the California Supreme Court reversed the decision of the Court of Appeal and instructed the trial court to enter a judgment of nonsuit in favor of the defendants.

On March 14, 2008, the Company received an adverse verdict in the *James Baccus* claim in Philadelphia, Pennsylvania, with compensatory damages of $2.45 million and additional damages of $11.9 million. The Company's post-trial motions were denied by order dated January 5, 2009. The case was concluded by settlement in the fourth quarter of 2010 during the pendency of the Company's appeal to the Superior Court of Pennsylvania.

On May 16, 2008, the Company received an adverse verdict in the *Chief Brewer* claim in Los Angeles, California. The amount of the judgment entered was $0.68 million plus interest and costs. The Company pursued an appeal in this matter, and on August 2, 2012 the California Court of Appeal reversed the judgment and remanded the matter to the trial court for entry of judgment notwithstanding the verdict in favor of the Company on the ground that this claim could not be distinguished factually from the *Patrick O'Neil* case decided in the Company's favor by the California Supreme Court.

On February 2, 2009, the Company received an adverse verdict in the *Dennis Woodard* claim in Los Angeles, California. The jury found that the Company was responsible for one-half of one percent (0.5%) of plaintiffs' damages of $16.93 million; however, based on California court rules regarding allocation of damages, judgment was entered against the Company in the amount of $1.65 million, plus costs. Following entry of judgment, the Company filed a motion with the trial court requesting judgment in the Company's favor notwithstanding the jury's verdict, and on June 30, 2009, the court advised that the Company's motion was granted and judgment was entered in favor of the Company. The trial court's ruling was affirmed on appeal by order dated August 25, 2011. The plaintiffs appealed that ruling to the Supreme Court of California, which dismissed the appeal on February 29, 2012; the matter is now finally determined in the Company's favor.

On March 23, 2010, a Philadelphia, Pennsylvania, state court jury found the Company responsible for a 1/11th share of a $14.5 million verdict in the *James Nelson* claim, and for a 1/20th share of a $3.5 million verdict in the *Larry Bell* claim. On February 23, 2011, the court entered judgment on the verdicts in the amount of $0.2 million against the Company, only, in *Bell*, and in the amount of $4.0 million, jointly, against the Company and two other defendants in Nelson, with additional interest in the amount of $0.01 million being assessed against the Company, only, in *Nelson*. All defendants, including the Company, and the plaintiffs took timely appeals of certain aspects of those judgments. The Company resolved the Bell appeal by settlement, which is reflected in the settled claims for 2012. On September 5, 2013, a panel of the Pennsylvania Superior Court, in a 2–1 decision, vacated the *Nelson* verdict against all defendants, reversing and remanding for a new trial. Plaintiffs have requested a rehearing in the Superior Court, which the defendants, including the Company, have opposed. By order dated November 18, 2013, the Superior Court vacated the panel opinion, and granted en banc reargument at a date to be scheduled.

On August 17, 2011, a New York City state court jury found the Company responsible for a 99% share of a $32 million verdict on the *Ronald Dummitt* claim. The Company filed post-trial motions seeking to overturn the verdict, to grant a new trial, or to reduce the damages, which the Company argued were excessive under New York appellate case law governing awards for non-economic losses. The Court held oral argument on these motions on October 18, 2011 and issued a written decision on August 21, 2012 confirming the jury's liability findings but reducing the award of damages to $8 million. At plaintiffs' request, the Court entered a judgment in the amount of $4.9 million against the Company, taking into account settlement offsets and accrued interest under New York law. The Company has appealed.

On March 9, 2012, a Philadelphia, Pennsylvania, state court jury found the Company responsible for a 1/8th share of a $123,000 verdict in the *Frank Paasch* claim. The Company and plaintiffs filed post-trial motions. On May 31, 2012, on plaintiffs' motion, the Court entered an order dismissing the claim against the Company, with prejudice, and without any payment.

On August 29, 2012, the Company received an adverse verdict in the *William Paulus* claim in Los Angeles, California. The jury found that the Company was responsible for ten percent (10%), of plaintiffs' non-economic damages of $6.5 million, plus a portion of plaintiffs' economic damages of $0.4 million. Based on California court rules regarding allocation of damages, judgment was entered in the amount of $0.8

million against the Company. The Company filed post-trial motions requesting judgment in the Company's favor notwithstanding the jury's verdict, which were denied. The Company has appealed.

On October 23, 2012, the Company received an adverse verdict in the *Gerald Suttner* claim in Buffalo, New York. The jury found that the Company was responsible for four percent (4%) of plaintiffs' damages of $3 million. The Company filed post-trial motions requesting judgment in the Company's favor notwithstanding the jury's verdict, which were denied. The court entered a judgment of $0.1 million against the Company. The Company has appealed.

On November 28, 2012, the Company received an adverse verdict in the *James Hellam* claim in Oakland, CA. The jury found that the Company was responsible for seven percent (7%) of plaintiffs' non-economic damages of $4.5 million, plus a portion of their economic damages of $0.9 million. Based on California court rules regarding allocation of damages, judgment was entered against the Company in the amount of $1.282 million. The Company filed post-trial motions requesting judgment in the Company's favor notwithstanding the jury's verdict and also requesting that settlement offsets be applied to reduce the judgment in accordance with California law. On January 31, 2013, the court entered an order disposing partially of that motion. On March 1, 2013, the Company filed an appeal regarding the portions of the motion that were denied. The court entered judgment against the Company in the amount of $1.1 million. The Company appealed.

On February 25, 2013, a Philadelphia, Pennsylvania, state court jury found the Company responsible for a 1/10th share of a $2.5 million verdict in the *Thomas Amato* claim and a 1/5th share of a $2.3 million verdict in the *Frank Vinciguerra* claim, which were consolidated for trial. The Company filed post-trial motions requesting judgments in the Company's favor notwithstanding the jury's verdicts or new trials, and also requesting that settlement offsets be applied to reduce the judgment in accordance with Pennsylvania law. These motions were denied. The Company has appealed.

On March 1, 2013, a New York City state court jury entered a $35 million verdict against the Company in the *Ivo Peraica* claim. The Company filed post-trial motions seeking to overturn the verdict, to grant a new trial, or to reduce the damages, which the Company argues were excessive under New York appellate case law governing awards for non-economic losses and further were subject to settlement offsets. After the trial court remitted the verdict to $18 million, but otherwise denied the Company's post-trial motion, judgment also entered against the Company in the amount of $10.6 million (including interest). The Company has appealed. The Company has taken a separate appeal of the trial court's denial of its summary judgment motion.

On July 31, 2013, a Buffalo, New York state court jury entered a $3.1 million verdict against the Company in the *Lee Holdsworth* claim. The Company plans to file post-trial motions seeking to overturn the verdict, to grant a new trial, or to reduce the damages, which the Company argues were excessive under New York appellate case law governing awards for non-economic losses and further were subject to settlement offsets. Plaintiffs have requested judgment in the amount of $1.1 million. Post-trial motions remain pending. The Company plans to pursue an appeal if necessary.

On September 11, 2013, a Columbia, South Carolina state court jury in the *Lloyd Garvin* claim entered an $11 million verdict for compensatory damages against the Company and two other defendants jointly, and also awarded exemplary damages against the Company in the amount of $11 million. The jury also awarded exemplary damages against both other defendants. The Company has filed post-trial motions seeking to overturn the verdict, to grant a new trial, or to reduce the damages. The Company plans to pursue an appeal if necessary.

On September 17, 2013, a Fort Lauderdale, Florida state court jury in the *Richard DeLisle* claim found the Company responsible for 16 percent of an $8 million verdict. The trial court denied all parties' post-trial motions, and entered judgment against the Company in the amount of $1.3 million. The Company has appealed.

Such judgment amounts are not included in the Company's incurred costs until all available appeals are exhausted and the final payment amount is determined.

The gross settlement and defense costs incurred (before insurance recoveries and tax effects) for the Company for the years ended December 31, 2013, 2012 and 2011 totaled $ 90.8 million, $ 96.1 million and $ 105.5 million, respectively. In contrast to the recognition of settlement and defense costs, which reflect the current level of activity in the tort system, cash payments and receipts generally lag the tort system activity by several months or more, and may show some fluctuation from quarter to quarter. Cash payments of settlement amounts are not made until all releases and other required documentation are received by the Company, and reimbursements of both settlement amounts and defense costs by insurers may be uneven due to insurer payment practices, transitions from one insurance layer to the next excess layer and the payment terms of certain reimbursement agreements. The Company's total pre-tax payments for settlement and defense costs, net of funds received from insurers, for the years ended December 31, 2013, 2012 and 2011 totaled $ 62.8 million, $ 78.0 million and $ 79.3 million, respectively. Detailed below are the comparable amounts for the periods indicated.

(In millions)	For the year ended December 31,		
	2013	**2012**	**2011**
Settlement / indemnity costs incurred[1]	$ 31.6	$ 37.5	$ 50.2
Defense costs incurred[1]	59.1	58.7	55.3
Total costs incurred	$ 90.8	$ 96.1	$105.5
Settlement / indemnity payments	$ 37.8	$ 38.0	$ 55.0
Defense payments	59.5	59.8	56.5
Insurance receipts	(34.5)	(19.8)	(32.2)
Pre-tax cash payments	$ 62.8	$ 78.0	$ 79.3

[1] Before insurance recoveries and tax effects.

The amounts shown for settlement and defense costs incurred, and cash payments, are not necessarily indicative of future period amounts, which may be higher or lower than those reported.

Cumulatively through December 31, 2013, the Company has resolved (by settlement or dismissal) approximately 100,000 claims, not including the MARDOC claims referred to above. The related settlement cost incurred by the Company and its insurance carriers is approximately $399 million, for an average settlement cost per resolved claim of approximately $4,000. The average settlement cost per claim resolved during the years ended December 31, 2013, 2012 and 2011 was $3,300, $6,300 and $4,123 respectively. Because claims are sometimes dismissed in large groups, the average cost per resolved claim, as well as the number of open claims, can fluctuate significantly from period to period. In addition to large group dismissals, the nature of the disease and corresponding settlement amounts for each claim resolved will also drive changes from period to period in the average settlement cost per claim. Accordingly, the average cost per resolved claim is not considered in the Company's periodic review of its estimated asbestos liability. For a discussion regarding the four most significant factors affecting the liability estimate, see "Effects on the Consolidated Financial Statements".

Effects on the Consolidated Financial Statements

The Company has retained the firm of Hamilton, Rabinovitz & Associates, Inc. ("HR&A"), a nationally recognized expert in the field, to assist management in estimating the Company's asbestos liability in the tort system. HR&A reviews information provided by the Company concerning claims filed, settled and dismissed, amounts paid in settlements and relevant claim information such as the nature of the asbestos-related disease asserted by the claimant, the jurisdiction where filed and the time lag from filing to disposition of the claim. The methodology used by HR&A to project future asbestos costs is based largely on the Company's experience during a base reference period of eleven quarterly periods (consisting of the two full preceding calendar years and three additional quarterly periods to the estimate date) for claims filed, settled and dismissed. The Company's experience is then compared to the results of widely used previously conducted epidemiological studies estimating the number of individuals likely to develop asbestos-related diseases. Those studies were undertaken in connection with national analyses of the population of workers believed to have been exposed to asbestos. Using that information, HR&A estimates the number of future claims that would be filed against the Company and estimates the aggregate settlement or indemnity costs that would be incurred to resolve both pending and future claims based upon the average settlement costs by disease during the reference period. This methodology has been accepted by numerous courts. After discussions with the Company, HR&A augments its liability estimate for the costs of defending asbestos claims in the tort system using a forecast from the Company which is based upon discussions with its defense counsel. Based on this information, HR&A compiles an estimate of the Company's asbestos liability for pending and future claims, based on claim experience during the reference period and covering claims expected to be filed through the indicated forecast period. The most significant factors affecting the liability estimate are (1) the number of new mesothelioma claims filed against the Company, (2) the average settlement costs for mesothelioma claims, (3) the percentage of mesothelioma claims dismissed against the Company and (4) the aggregate defense costs incurred by the Company. These factors are interdependent, and no one factor predominates in determining the liability estimate. Although the methodology used by HR&A can be applied to show claims and costs for periods subsequent to the indicated period (up to and including the endpoint of the asbestos studies referred to above), management believes that the level of uncertainty regarding the various factors used in estimating future asbestos costs is too great to provide for reasonable estimation of the number of future claims, the nature of such claims or the cost to resolve them for years beyond the indicated estimate.

In the Company's view, the forecast period used to provide the best estimate for asbestos claims and related liabilities and costs is a judgment based upon a number of trend factors, including the number and type of claims being filed each year; the jurisdictions where such claims are filed, and the effect of any legislation or judicial orders in such jurisdictions restricting the types of claims that can proceed to trial on the merits; and the likelihood of any comprehensive asbestos legislation at the federal level. In addition, the dynamics of asbestos litigation in the tort system have been significantly affected over the past five to ten years by the substantial number of companies that have filed for bankruptcy protection, thereby staying any asbestos claims against them until the conclusion of such proceedings, and the establishment of a number of post-bankruptcy trusts for asbestos claimants, which are estimated to provide $36 billion for payments to current and future claimants. These trend factors have both positive and negative effects on the dynamics of asbestos litigation in the tort system and the related best estimate of the Company's asbestos liability, and these effects do not move in a linear fashion but rather change over multi-year periods. Accordingly, the Company's management continues to monitor these trend factors over time and periodically assesses whether an alternative forecast period is appropriate.

Each quarter, HR&A compiles an update based upon the Company's experience in claims filed, settled and dismissed during the updated reference period (consisting of the preceding eleven quarterly periods) as well as average settlement costs by disease category (mesothelioma, lung cancer, other cancer, and non-malignant conditions including asbestosis) during that period. In addition to this claims experience, the Company also considers additional quantitative and qualitative factors such as the nature of the aging of pending claims, significant appellate rulings and legislative developments, and their respective effects on expected future settlement values. As part of this process, the Company also takes into account trends in the tort system such as those enumerated above. Management considers all these factors in conjunction with the liability estimate of HR&A and determines whether a change in the estimate is warranted.

Liability Estimate. With the assistance of HR&A, effective as of December 31, 2011, the Company updated and extended its estimate of the asbestos liability, including the costs of settlement or indemnity payments and defense costs relating to currently pending claims and future claims projected to be filed against the Company through 2021. The Company's previous estimate was for asbestos claims filed or projected to be filed through 2017. As a result of this updated estimate, the Company recorded an additional liability of $285 million as of December 31, 2011. The Company's decision to take this action at such date was based on several factors which contribute to the Company's ability to reasonably estimate this liability for the additional period noted. First, the number of mesothelioma claims (which although constituting approximately 8% of the Company's total pending asbestos claims, have accounted for approximately 90% of the Company's aggregate settlement and defense costs) being filed against the Company and associated settlement costs have recently stabilized. In the Company's opinion, the outlook for mesothelioma claims expected to be filed and resolved in the forecast period is reasonably stable. Second, there have been favorable developments in the trend of case law which has been a contributing factor in stabilizing the asbestos claims activity and related settlement costs. Third, there have been significant actions taken by certain state legislatures and courts over the past several years that have reduced the number and types of claims that can proceed to trial, which has been a significant factor in stabilizing the asbestos claims activity. Fourth, the Company has now entered into coverage-in-place agreements with almost all of its excess insurers, which enables the Company to project a more stable relationship between settlement and defense costs paid by the Company and reimbursements from its insurers. Taking all of these factors into account, the Company believes that it can reasonably estimate the asbestos liability for pending claims and future claims to be filed through 2021. While it is probable that the Company will incur additional charges for asbestos liabilities and defense costs in excess of the amounts currently provided, the Company does not believe that any such amount can be reasonably estimated beyond 2021. Accordingly, no accrual has been recorded for any costs which may be incurred for claims which may be made subsequent to 2021.

Management has made its best estimate of the costs through 2021 based on the analysis by HR&A completed in January 2012. Through December 31, 2013, the Company's actual experience during the updated reference period for mesothelioma claims filed and dismissed generally approximated the assumptions in the Company's liability estimate. In addition to this claims experience, the Company considered additional quantitative and qualitative factors such as the nature of the aging of pending claims, significant appellate rulings and legislative developments, and their respective effects on expected future settlement values. Based on this evaluation, the Company determined that no change in the estimate was warranted for the period ended December 31, 2013. Nevertheless, if certain factors show a pattern of sustained increase or decrease, the liability could change materially; however, all the assumptions used in estimating the asbestos liability are interdependent and no single factor predominates in determining the liability estimate. Because of the uncertainty with regard to and the interdependency of such factors used in the calculation of its asbestos liability, and since no one factor predominates, the Company believes that a range of potential liability estimates beyond the indicated forecast period cannot be reasonably estimated.

A liability of $894 million was recorded as of December 31, 2011 to cover the estimated cost of asbestos claims now pending or subsequently asserted through 2021, of which approximately 80% is attributable to settlement and defense costs for future claims projected to be filed through 2021. The liability is reduced when cash payments are made in respect of settled claims and defense costs. The liability was $699 million as of December 31, 2013. It is not possible to forecast when cash payments related to the asbestos liability will be fully expended; however, it is expected such cash payments will continue for a number of years past 2021, due to the significant proportion of future claims included in the estimated asbestos liability and the lag time between the date a claim is filed and when it is resolved. None of these estimated costs have been discounted to present value due to the inability to reliably forecast the timing of payments. The current portion of the total estimated liability at December 31, 2013 was $88 million and represents the Company's best estimate of total asbestos costs expected to be paid during the twelve-month period. Such amount is based upon the HR&A model together with the Company's prior year payment experience for both settlement and defense costs.

2.155 BOSTON SCIENTIFIC CORPORATION (DEC)

CONSOLIDATED BALANCE SHEETS (in part)

	As of December 31,	
In millions, except share and per share data	2013	2012
Liabilities and Stockholders' Equity (in part)		
Current liabilities:		
Current debt obligations	$ 3	$ 4
Accounts payable	246	232
Accrued expenses	1,348	1,284
Other current liabilities	227	252
Total current liabilities	1,824	1,772
Long-term debt	4,237	4,252
Deferred income taxes	1,402	1,713
Other long-term liabilities	2,569	2,547
Commitments and contingencies		

NOTES TO THE CONSOLIDATED FINANCIAL STATEMENTS

Note A—Significant Accounting Policies (in part)

Financial Instruments

We recognize all derivative financial instruments in our consolidated financial statements at fair value in accordance with ASC Topic 815, *Derivatives and Hedging*, and we present assets and liabilities associated with our derivative financial instruments on a gross basis in our financial statements. In accordance with Topic 815, for those derivative instruments that are designated and qualify as hedging instruments, the hedging instrument must be designated, based upon the exposure being hedged, as a fair value hedge, cash flow hedge, or a hedge of a net investment in a foreign operation. The accounting for changes in the fair value (i.e. gains or losses) of a derivative instrument depends on whether it has been designated and qualifies as part of a hedging relationship and, further, on the type of hedging relationship. Our derivative instruments do not subject our earnings or cash flows to material risk, as gains and losses on these derivatives generally offset losses and gains on the item being hedged. We do not enter into derivative transactions for speculative purposes and we do not have any non-derivative instruments that are designated as hedging instruments pursuant to Topic 815. Refer to *Note E—Fair Value Measurements* for more information on our derivative instruments.

Note E—Fair Value Measurements (in part)

Derivative Instruments and Hedging Activities

We develop, manufacture and sell medical devices globally and our earnings and cash flows are exposed to market risk from changes in foreign currency exchange rates and interest rates. We address these risks through a risk management program that includes the use of derivative financial instruments, and operate the program pursuant to documented corporate risk management policies. We recognize all derivative financial instruments in our consolidated financial statements at fair value in accordance with ASC Topic 815, *Derivatives and Hedging*. In accordance with Topic 815, for those derivative instruments that are designated and qualify as hedging instruments, the hedging instrument must be designated, based upon the exposure being hedged, as a fair value hedge, cash flow hedge, or a hedge of a net investment in a foreign operation. The accounting for changes in the fair value (i.e. gains or losses) of a derivative instrument depends on whether it has been designated and qualifies as part of a hedging relationship and, further, on the type of hedging relationship. Our derivative instruments do not subject our earnings or cash flows to material risk, as gains and losses on these derivatives generally offset losses and gains on the item being hedged. We do not enter into derivative transactions for speculative purposes and we do not have any non-derivative instruments that are designated as hedging instruments pursuant to Topic 815.

Currency Hedging

We are exposed to currency risk consisting primarily of foreign currency denominated monetary assets and liabilities, forecasted foreign currency denominated intercompany and third-party transactions and net investments in certain subsidiaries. We manage our exposure to changes in foreign currency exchange rates on a consolidated basis to take advantage of offsetting transactions. We use both derivative instruments (currency forward and option contracts), and non-derivative transactions (primarily European manufacturing and distribution operations) to reduce the risk that our earnings and cash flows associated with these foreign currency denominated balances and transactions will be adversely affected by foreign currency exchange rate changes.

Designated Foreign Currency Hedges

All of our designated currency hedge contracts outstanding as of December 31, 2013 and December 31, 2012 were cash flow hedges under Topic 815 intended to protect the U.S. dollar value of our forecasted foreign currency denominated transactions. We record the effective portion of any change in the fair value of foreign currency cash flow hedges in other comprehensive income until the related third-party transaction occurs. Once the related third-party transaction occurs, we reclassify the effective portion of any related gain or loss on the foreign currency cash flow hedge to earnings. In the event the hedged forecasted transaction does not occur, or it becomes no longer probable that it will occur, we reclassify the amount of any gain or loss on the related cash flow hedge to earnings at that time. We had currency derivative instruments designated as cash flow hedges outstanding in the contract amount of $2.564 billion as of December 31, 2013 and $2.469 billion as of December 31, 2012.

We recognized net gains of $36 million during 2013 on our cash flow hedges, as compared to $39 million of net losses during 2012, and $95 million of net losses during 2011. All currency cash flow hedges outstanding as of December 31, 2013 mature within 36 months. As of December 31, 2013, $139 million of net gains, net of tax, were recorded in accumulated other comprehensive income (AOCI) to recognize the effective portion of the fair value of any currency derivative instruments that are, or previously were, designated as foreign currency cash flow hedges, as compared to net gains of $31 million as of December 31, 2012. As of December 31, 2013, $75 million of net gains, net of tax, may be reclassified to earnings within the next twelve months.

The success of our hedging program depends, in part, on forecasts of transaction activity in various currencies (primarily Japanese yen, Euro, British pound sterling, Australian dollar and Canadian dollar). We may experience unanticipated currency exchange gains or losses to the extent that there are differences between forecasted and actual activity during periods of currency volatility. In addition, changes in foreign currency exchange rates related to any unhedged transactions may impact our earnings and cash flows.

Non-designated Foreign Currency Contracts

We use currency forward contracts as a part of our strategy to manage exposure related to foreign currency denominated monetary assets and liabilities. These currency forward contracts are not designated as cash flow, fair value or net investment hedges under Topic 815; are marked-to-market with changes in fair value recorded to earnings; and are entered into for periods consistent with currency transaction exposures, generally less than one year. We had currency derivative instruments not designated as hedges under Topic 815 outstanding in the contract amount of $1.952 billion as of December 31, 2013 and $1.942 billion as of December 31, 2012.

Interest Rate Hedging

Our interest rate risk relates primarily to U.S. dollar borrowings, partially offset by U.S. dollar cash investments. We have historically used interest rate derivative instruments to manage our earnings and cash flow exposure to changes in interest rates by converting floating-rate debt into fixed-rate debt or fixed-rate debt into floating-rate debt.

We designate these derivative instruments either as fair value or cash flow hedges under Topic 815. We record changes in the value of fair value hedges in interest expense, which is generally offset by changes in the fair value of the hedged debt obligation. Interest payments made or received related to our interest rate derivative instruments are included in interest expense. We record the effective portion of any change in the fair value of derivative instruments designated as cash flow hedges as unrealized gains or losses in OCI, net of tax, until the hedged cash flow occurs, at which point the effective portion of any gain or loss is reclassified to earnings. We record the ineffective portion of our cash flow hedges in interest expense. In the event the hedged cash flow does not occur, or it becomes no longer probable that it will occur, we reclassify the amount of any gain or loss on the related cash flow hedge to interest expense at that time.

In the fourth quarter of 2013, we entered into interest rate derivative contracts having a notional amount of $450 million to convert fixed-rate debt into floating-rate debt, which we designated as fair value hedges, and had $450 million outstanding as of December 31, 2013. We assessed at inception, and re-assess on an ongoing basis, whether the interest rate derivative contracts are highly effective in offsetting changes in the fair value of the hedged fixed rate debt. We recognized in interest expense, a $7 million gain on our hedged debt obligation, and an $8 million loss on the related interest rate derivative contract during 2013, resulting in a $1 million net loss recorded in earnings due to ineffectiveness. We had no interest rate derivative contracts outstanding as of December 31, 2012.

In prior years, we terminated certain interest rate derivative contracts, including fixed-to-floating interest rate contracts, designated as fair value hedges, and floating-to-fixed treasury locks designated as cash flow hedges. We amortize the gains and losses of these derivative instruments upon termination into earnings as a reduction of interest expense over the remaining term of the hedged debt, in accordance with Topic 815. The carrying amount of certain of our senior notes included unamortized gains of $54 million as of December 31, 2013 and

$64 million as of December 31, 2012, and unamortized losses of $2 million as of December 31, 2013 and $3 million as of December 31, 2012, related to the fixed-to-floating interest rate contracts. In addition, we had pre-tax net gains within AOCI related to terminated floating-to-fixed treasury locks of $3 million as of December 31, 2013 and $4 million as of December 31, 2012. The gains that we recognized in earnings related to previously terminated interest rate derivatives were $10 million in 2013, $11 million in 2012, and were not material in 2011. As of December 31, 2013, $9 million of net gains may be reclassified to earnings within the next twelve months from amortization of our previously terminated interest rate derivative contracts.

Counterparty Credit Risk

We do not have significant concentrations of credit risk arising from our derivative financial instruments, whether from an individual counterparty or a related group of counterparties. We manage our concentration of counterparty credit risk on our derivative instruments by limiting acceptable counterparties to a diversified group of major financial institutions with investment grade credit ratings, limiting the amount of credit exposure to each counterparty, and by actively monitoring their credit ratings and outstanding fair values on an on-going basis. Furthermore, none of our derivative transactions are subject to collateral or other security arrangements and none contain provisions that are dependent on our credit ratings from any credit rating agency.

We also employ master netting arrangements that reduce our counterparty payment settlement risk on any given maturity date to the net amount of any receipts or payments due between us and the counterparty financial institution. Thus, the maximum loss due to credit risk by counterparty is limited to the unrealized gains in such contracts net of any unrealized losses should any of these counterparties fail to perform as contracted. Although these protections do not eliminate concentrations of credit risk, as a result of the above considerations, we do not consider the risk of counterparty default to be significant.

Fair Value of Derivative Instruments (in part)

Topic 815 requires all derivative instruments to be recognized at their fair values as either assets or liabilities on the balance sheet. We determine the fair value of our derivative instruments using the framework prescribed by ASC Topic 820, *Fair Value Measurements and Disclosures*, by considering the estimated amount we would receive or pay to transfer these instruments at the reporting date and by taking into account current interest rates, foreign currency exchange rates, the creditworthiness of the counterparty for assets, and our creditworthiness for liabilities. In certain instances, we may utilize financial models to measure fair value. Generally, we use inputs that include quoted prices for similar assets or liabilities in active markets; quoted prices for identical or similar assets or liabilities in markets that are not active; other observable inputs for the asset or liability; and inputs derived principally from, or corroborated by, observable market data by correlation or other means. As of December 31, 2013, we have classified all of our derivative assets and liabilities within Level 2 of the fair value hierarchy prescribed by Topic 820, as discussed below, because these observable inputs are available for substantially the full term of our derivative instruments.

The following are the balances of our derivative assets and liabilities as of December 31, 2013 and December 31, 2012:

(In millions)	Location in Balance Sheet[1]	As of	
		December 31, 2013	December 31, 2012
Derivative Assets:			
Designated Hedging Instruments			
Currency hedge contracts	Prepaid and other current assets	$117	$ 25
Currency hedge contracts	Other long-term assets	120	63
Interest rate contracts	Prepaid and other current assets	1	—
		238	88
Non-Designated Hedging Instruments			
Currency hedge contracts	Prepaid and other current assets	27	33
Total Derivative Assets		$265	$121
Derivative Liabilities:			
Designated Hedging Instruments			
Currency hedge contracts	Other current liabilities	$ 13	$ 20
Currency hedge contracts	Other long-term liabilities	19	10
Interest rate contracts	Other long-term liabilities	8	—
		40	30
Non-Designated Hedging Instruments			
Currency hedge contracts	Other current liabilities	23	27
Total Derivative Liabilities		$ 63	$ 57

[1] We classify derivative assets and liabilities as current when the remaining term of the derivative contract is one year or less.

DEFERRED GAIN

2.156 CSX CORPORATION (DEC)

CONSOLIDATED BALANCE SHEETS (in part)

(Dollars in Millions)

	December 2013	December 2012[a]
Liabilities and Shareholders' Equity (in part)		
Current Liabilities:		
Accounts Payable	$ 957	$ 948
Labor and Fringe Benefits Payable	587	468
Casualty, Environmental and Other Reserves (Note 5)	151	140
Current Maturities of Long-term Debt (Note 9)	533	780
Income and Other Taxes Payable	91	169
Other Current Liabilities	105	140
Total Current Liabilities	2,424	2,645
Casualty, Environmental and Other Reserves (Note 5)	300	337
Long-term Debt (Note 9)	9,022	9,052
Deferred Income Taxes (Note 11)	8,662	8,096
Other Long-term Liabilities	870	1,457
Total Liabilities	21,278	21,587

[a] See the revision of prior period financial statements in Note 1. Nature of Operations and Significant Accounting Policies.

NOTES TO CONSOLIDATED FINANCIAL STATEMENTS

Note 6. Properties (in part)

Significant Property Disposition

In November 2011, the Company sold 61 miles of operating rail corridor to the Florida Department of Transportation. This corridor will be used by the state of Florida for its new commuter rail operation known as SunRail, which is expected to alleviate highway congestion. The Company diverted a portion of the corridor's existing rail traffic and relocated terminal operations to an adjacent rail corridor in Florida. As part of the transaction, the Company received $173 million in proceeds ($148 million in cash and a $25 million receivable, held in escrow and payable no later than April 2014) and up to $259 million in government grants. These grants are related to reimbursable capital expenditure projects in Florida and are recorded as a reduction of the carrying value of the related asset as received. This agreement also obligated the Company to invest a total of $ 500 million in routine capital expenditures and maintenance related to transportation capacity, facilities or equipment in Florida, including diversion and relocation costs related to this transaction within an eight year period following the transaction. The Company invested $142 million, $311 million and $47 million in 2013, 2012 and 2011, respectively. The required investment obligation was fulfilled during the second quarter of 2013.

This transaction contains multiple elements with separate accounting recognition for the sale of real estate and receipt of the grants. The proceeds related to the sale of real estate approximate fair value. Fair value was determined by management in accordance with the *Fair Value Measurement Topic* in the ASC using level 3 measurements and with the assistance of an independent third-party appraiser.

In accordance with the *Real Estate Sales Topic* in the ASC, this sale of real estate resulted in a deferred gain of $160 million. The deferred gain is primarily recognized into income ratably as the investment obligation is fulfilled. The Company recognized a gain of $43 million, $94 million and $14 million in 2013, 2012 and 2011, respectively. This gain is included in materials, supplies and other in the consolidated income statements. Going forward, the Company expects no further material gains. The deferred gain balance included in the consolidated balance sheets is in the table below.

	Deferred Gain as of	
(Dollars in Millions)	December 2013	December 2012
Current portion, included in Other Current Liabilities	$9	$43
Long term portion, included in Other Long-Term Liabilities	—	9
Total	$9	$52

Accumulated Other Comprehensive Income

PRESENTATION

2.157 FASB ASC 220, *Comprehensive Income*, requires that a separate caption for accumulated other comprehensive income be presented in the "Equity" section of a balance sheet. An entity should disclose accumulated balances for each classification in that separate component of equity on the face of a balance sheet or in notes to the financial statements.

PRESENTATION AND DISCLOSURE EXCERPTS

ACCUMULATED OTHER COMPREHENSIVE INCOME—EQUITY SECTION OF BALANCE SHEET

2.158 BOSTON SCIENTIFIC CORPORATION (DEC)

CONSOLIDATED BALANCE SHEETS

	As of December 31,	
In millions, except share and per share data	2013	2012
Assets		
Current assets:		
Cash and cash equivalents	$ 217	$ 207
Trade accounts receivable, net	1,307	1,217
Inventories	897	884
Deferred income taxes	288	433
Prepaid expenses and other current assets	302	281
Total current assets	3,011	3,022
Property, plant and equipment, net	1,546	1,564
Goodwill	5,693	5,973
Other intangible assets, net	5,950	6,289
Other long-term assets	371	306
Total Assets	$16,571	$17,154
Liabilities and Stockholders' Equity		
Current liabilities:		
Current debt obligations	$ 3	$ 4
Accounts payable	246	232
Accrued expenses	1,348	1,284
Other current liabilities	227	252
Total current liabilities	1,824	1,772
Long-term debt	4,237	4,252
Deferred income taxes	1,402	1,713
Other long-term liabilities	2,569	2,547
Commitments and contingencies		
Stockholders' equity:		
Preferred stock, $0.01 par value—authorized 50,000,000 shares, none issued and outstanding		
Common stock, $0.01 par value—authorized 2,000,000,000 shares; issued 1,560,302,634 shares as of December 31, 2013 and 1,542,347,188 shares as of December 31, 2012	16	15
Treasury stock, at cost—238,006,570 shares as of December 31, 2013 and 186,635,532 shares as of December 31, 2012	(1,592)	(1,092)
Additional paid-in capital	16,579	16,429
Accumulated deficit	(8,570)	(8,449)
Accumulated other comprehensive loss, net of tax:		
Foreign currency translation adjustment	(16)	(26)
Unrealized gain on derivative financial instruments	141	34
Unrealized costs associated with certain retirement plans	(19)	(41)
Total stockholders' equity	6,539	6,870
Total Liabilities And Stockholders' Equity	$16,571	$17,154

2.159 VERIZON COMMUNICATIONS INC. (DEC)

CONSOLIDATED STATEMENTS OF CHANGES IN EQUITY

	Years Ended December 31,					
	2013		2012		2011	
(Dollars in millions, except per share amounts, and shares in thousands)	Shares	Amount	Shares	Amount	Shares	Amount
Common Stock						
Balance at beginning of year	2,967,610	$ 297	2,967,610	$ 297	2,967,610	$ 297
Balance at end of year	2,967,610	297	2,967,610	297	2,967,610	297
Contributed Capital						
Balance at beginning of year		37,990		37,919		37,922
Other		(51)		71		(3)
Balance at end of year		37,939		37,990		37,919
Reinvested Earnings (Accumulated Deficit)						
Balance at beginning of year		(3,734)		1,179		4,368
Net income attributable to Verizon		11,497		875		2,404
Dividends declared ($2.09, $2.03, $1.975) per share		(5,981)		(5,788)		(5,593)
Balance at end of year		1,782		(3,734)		1,179
Accumulated Other Comprehensive Income						
Balance at beginning of year attributable to Verizon		2,235		1,269		1,049
Foreign currency translation adjustments		60		69		(119)
Unrealized gains (losses) on cash flow hedges		25		(68)		30
Unrealized gains (losses) on marketable securities		16		29		(7)
Defined benefit pension and postretirement plans		22		936		316
Other comprehensive income		123		966		220
Balance at end of year attributable to Verizon		2,358		2,235		1,269
Treasury Stock						
Balance at beginning of year	(109,041)	(4,071)	(133,594)	(5,002)	(140,587)	(5,267)
Shares purchased	(3,500)	(153)	—	—	—	—
Employee plans (Note 15)	6,835	260	11,434	433	6,982	265
Shareowner plans (Note 15)	96	3	13,119	498	11	—
Balance at end of year	(105,610)	(3,961)	(109,041)	(4,071)	(133,594)	(5,002)
Deferred Compensation-ESOPs and Other						
Balance at beginning of year		440		308		200
Restricted stock equity grant		152		196		146
Amortization		(171)		(64)		(38)
Balance at end of year		421		440		308
Noncontrolling Interests						
Balance at beginning of year		52,376		49,938		48,343
Net income attributable to noncontrolling interests		12,050		9,682		7,794
Other comprehensive income (loss)		(15)		10		1
Total comprehensive income		12,035		9,692		7,795
Distributions and other		(7,831)		(7,254)		(6,200)
Balance at end of year		56,580		52,376		49,938
Total Equity		$95,416		$85,533		$85,908

NOTES TO CONSOLIDATED FINANCIAL STATEMENTS

Note 14—Comprehensive Income

Comprehensive income consists of net income and other gains and losses affecting equity that, under U.S. GAAP, are excluded from net income. Significant changes in the components of Other comprehensive income, net of provision for income taxes are described below.

Accumulated Other Comprehensive Income

The changes in the balances of Accumulated other comprehensive income by component are as follows:

(Dollars in millions)	Foreign Currency Translation Adjustments	Unrealized Gain on Cashflow Hedges	Unrealized Gain on Marketable Securities	Defined Benefit Pension and Postretirement Plans	Total
Balance at January 1, 2013	$793	$ 88	$101	$1,253	$2,235
Other comprehensive income	60	50	33	—	143
Amounts reclassified to net income	—	(25)	(17)	22	(20)
Net other comprehensive income	60	25	16	22	123
Balance at December 31, 2013	$853	$113	$117	$1,275	$2,358

The amounts presented above in net other comprehensive income are net of taxes and noncontrolling interests, which are not significant. For the year ended December 31, 2013, the amounts reclassified to net income related to defined benefit pension and postretirement plans in the table above are included in Cost of services and sales and Selling, general and administrative expense on our consolidated statements of income. For the year ended December 31, 2013, all other amounts reclassified to net income in the table above are included in Other income, net on our consolidated statements of income.

Foreign Currency Translation Adjustments

The change in Foreign currency translation adjustments during 2013, 2012 and 2011 was primarily related to our investment in Vodafone Omnitel N.V. and was primarily driven by the movements of the U.S. dollar against the Euro.

Net Unrealized Gains (Losses) on Cash Flow Hedges

During 2013, 2012 and 2011, Unrealized gains (losses) on cash flow hedges included in Other comprehensive income (loss) attributable to noncontrolling interests, primarily reflect activity related to a cross currency swap (see Note 9). Reclassification adjustments for gains (losses) realized in net income were not significant.

Net Unrealized Gains (Losses) on Marketable Securities

During 2013, 2012 and 2011, reclassification adjustments on marketable securities for gains (losses) realized in net income were not significant.

Defined Benefit Pension and Postretirement Plans

The change in Defined benefit pension and postretirement plans at December 31, 2013 was not significant.

The change in Defined benefit pension and postretirement plans of $0.9 billion, net of taxes of $0.6 billion at December 31, 2012 was primarily a result of plan amendments.

ACCUMULATED OTHER COMPREHENSIVE INCOME—NOTES TO CONSOLIDATED FINANCIAL STATEMENTS

2.160 THE ESTEE LAUDER COMPANIES INC. (JUN)
NOTES TO CONSOLIDATED FINANCIAL STATEMENTS

Note 17—Accumulated Other Comprehensive Income (Loss)

The components of Accumulated OCI ("AOCI") included in the accompanying consolidated balance sheets consist of the following:

	Year Ended June 30		
(In millions)	**2013**	**2012**	**2011**
Net unrealized investment gains (losses), beginning of year	$ 0.5	$ 0.5	$ 0.2
Unrealized investment gains (losses)	0.4	0.1	0.4
Benefit (provision) for deferred income taxes	(0.1)	(0.1)	(0.1)
Net unrealized investment gains, end of year	0.8	0.5	0.5
Net derivative instruments, beginning of year	17.4	(0.7)	14.3
Gain (loss) on derivative instruments	10.3	40.2	(38.0)
Benefit (provision) for deferred income taxes on derivative instruments	(3.6)	(14.3)	13.4
Reclassification to earnings during the year:			
Foreign currency forward contracts	(8.8)	(11.7)	15.1
Settled interest rate-related derivatives	(0.3)	(0.3)	(0.3)
Benefit (provision) for deferred income taxes on reclassification	3.3	4.2	(5.2)
Net derivative instruments, end of year	18.3	17.4	(0.7)

(In millions)	Year Ended June 30		
	2013	**2012**	**2011**
Net pension and post-retirement adjustments, beginning of year	(293.5)	(199.0)	(217.6)
Changes in plan assets and benefit obligations:			
Net actuarial gains (losses) recognized	92.8	(176.9)	30.7
Net prior service credit (cost) recognized	—	2.0	(10.6)
Translation adjustments	3.5	7.6	(16.4)
Benefit (provision) for deferred income taxes	(36.8)	60.4	(5.9)
Amortization of amounts included in net periodic benefit cost:			
Net actuarial (gains) losses	28.9	14.7	26.3
Net prior service cost (credit)	4.3	4.3	3.1
Net transition asset (obligation)	(0.1)	—	—
Benefit (provision) for deferred income taxes on reclassification	(12.8)	(6.6)	(8.6)
Net pension and post-retirement adjustments, end of year	(213.7)	(293.5)	(199.0)
Cumulative translation adjustments, beginning of year	62.7	216.9	6.4
Translation adjustments	(24.5)	(156.6)	213.2
Benefit (provision) for deferred income taxes	(1.1)	2.4	(2.7)
Cumulative translation adjustments, end of year	37.1	62.7	216.9
Accumulated other comprehensive income (loss)	$(157.5)	$(212.9)	$17.7

Of the $18.3 million, net of tax, derivative instrument gain recorded in AOCI at June 30, 2013, $10.9 million in gains, net of tax, related to foreign currency forward contracts, which the Company will reclassify to earnings through March 2015. Also included in the net derivative instrument gain recorded in AOCI was $7.9 million, net of tax, related to the October 2003 gain from the settlement of the treasury lock agreements upon the issuance of the Company's 2033 Senior Notes, which is being reclassified to earnings as an offset to interest expense over the life of the debt. These gains were partially offset by $0.5 million, net of tax, related to a loss from the settlement of a series of forward-starting interest rate swap agreements upon the issuance of the Company's 2037 Senior Notes, which is being reclassified to earnings as an addition to interest expense over the life of the debt.

Refer to Note 12—Pension, Deferred Compensation and Post-retirement Benefit Plans for the discussion regarding the net pension and post-retirement adjustments.

Income Statement Format

PRESENTATION

3.01 Either a single-step or multi-step form is acceptable for preparing a statement of income. In a single-step format, the operating and non-operating revenues are grouped and totaled and the operating and non-operating expenses are grouped and totaled. Then there is one subtraction of the combined expenses from the combined revenues. In a multi-step format, either costs are deducted from sales to show the gross margin or costs and expenses are deducted from sales to show operating income. The multi-step income statement is divided into two main sections: the operating section and the non-operating sections. Net income should reflect all items of profit and loss recognized during the period, except for certain entities (investment companies, insurance entities, and certain not-for-profit entities) and with the sole exception of error corrections, as discussed in Financial Accounting Standards Board (FASB) *Accounting Standards Codification* (ASC) 250, *Accounting Changes and Error Corrections*.

3.02 FASB ASC 220, *Comprehensive Income*, requires that comprehensive income and its components be reported in a financial statement. Comprehensive income and its components can be reported in an income statement or a separate statement of comprehensive income.

PRESENTATION AND DISCLOSURE EXCERPT

RECLASSIFICATIONS

3.03 JABIL CIRCUIT, INC. (AUG)
NOTES TO CONSOLIDATED FINANCIAL STATEMENTS

12. Derivative Financial Instruments and Hedging Activities (in part)

All derivative instruments are recorded gross on the Consolidated Balance Sheets at their respective fair values. The accounting for changes in the fair value of a derivative instrument depends on the intended use and designation of the derivative instrument. For derivative instruments that are designated and qualify as a fair value hedge, the gain or loss on the derivative and the offsetting gain or loss on the hedged item attributable to the hedged risk are recognized in current earnings. For derivative instruments that are designated and qualify as a cash flow hedge, the effective portion of the gain or loss on the derivative instrument is initially reported as a component of accumulated other comprehensive income ("AOCI"), net of tax, and is subsequently reclassified into the line item within the Consolidated Statements of Operations in which the hedged items are recorded in the same period in which the hedged item affects earnings. The ineffective portion of the gain or loss is recognized immediately in current earnings. For derivative instruments that are not designated as hedging instruments, gains and losses from changes in fair values are recognized in earnings.

For derivatives accounted for as hedging instruments, the Company formally designates and documents, at inception, the financial instruments as a hedge of a specific underlying exposure, the risk management objective and the strategy for undertaking the hedge transaction. In addition, the Company formally performs an assessment, both at inception and at least quarterly thereafter, to determine whether the financial instruments used in hedging transactions are effective at offsetting changes in the cash flows on the related underlying exposures.

a. Foreign Currency Risk Management (in part)

The following tables present the impact that changes in fair value of derivatives utilized for foreign currency risk management purposes and designated as hedging instruments had on AOCI and earnings during fiscal years 2013 and 2012 (in thousands):

Derivatives in Cash Flow Hedging Relationship for the Fiscal Year Ended August 31, 2013	Amount of Gain (Loss) Recognized in OCI on Derivative (Effective Portion)	Location of Gain (Loss) Reclassified from AOCI into Income (Effective Portion)	Amount of Gain (Loss) Reclassified from AOCI into Income (Effective Portion)	Location of Gain (Loss) Recognized in Income on Derivative (Ineffective Portion and Amount Excluded from Effectiveness Testing)	Amount of Gain (Loss) Recognized in Income on Derivative (Ineffective Portion and Amount Excluded from Effectiveness Testing)
Forward foreign exchange contracts	$(2,392)	Revenue	$(1,919)	Revenue	$ 225
Forward foreign exchange contracts	$ 2,721	Cost of revenue	$ 3,717	Cost of revenue	$ 8,996
Forward foreign exchange contracts	$ (511)	Selling, general and administrative	$ (133)	Selling, general and administrative	$ 263

Derivatives in Cash Flow Hedging Relationship for the Fiscal Year Ended August 31, 2012	Amount of Gain (Loss) Recognized in OCI on Derivative (Effective Portion)	Location of Gain (Loss) Reclassified from AOCI into Income (Effective Portion)	Amount of Gain (Loss) Reclassified from AOCI into Income (Effective Portion)	Location of Gain (Loss) Recognized in Income on Derivative (Ineffective Portion and Amount Excluded from Effectiveness Testing)	Amount of Gain (Loss) Recognized in Income on Derivative (Ineffective Portion and Amount Excluded from Effectiveness Testing)
Forward foreign exchange contracts	$ 2,858	Revenue	$ 2,642	Revenue	$ —
Forward foreign exchange contracts	$ 1,644	Cost of revenue	$ 2,717	Cost of revenue	$(1,345)
Forward foreign exchange contracts	$(1,864)	Selling, general and administrative	$(2,790)	Selling, general and administrative	$ 194

As of August 31, 2013, the Company estimates that it will reclassify into earnings during the next 12 months existing losses related to foreign currency risk management hedging arrangements of approximately $1.1 million from the amounts recorded in AOCI as the hedged item affects earnings.

b. Interest Rate Risk Management (in part)

Cash Flow Hedges

During the fourth quarter of fiscal year 2007, the Company entered into forward interest rate swap transactions to hedge the fixed interest rate payments for an anticipated debt issuance, which was the issuance of the 8.250% Senior Notes. The swaps were accounted for as a cash flow hedge and had a notional amount of $400.0 million. Concurrently with the pricing of the 8.250% Senior Notes, the Company settled the swaps by its payment of $43.1 million. The ineffective portion of the swaps was immediately recorded to interest expense within the Consolidated Statements of Operations. The effective portion of the swaps is recorded on the Company's Consolidated Balance Sheets as a component of AOCI and is being amortized to interest expense within the Company's Consolidated Statements of Operations over the life of the 8.250% Senior Notes, which is through March 15, 2018.

The following tables present the impact that changes in the fair value of the derivative utilized for interest rate risk management and designated as a hedging instrument had on AOCI and earnings during fiscal years 2013 and 2012 (in thousands):

Derivatives in Cash Flow Hedging Relationship for the Fiscal Year Ended August 31, 2013	Amount of Gain (Loss) Recognized in OCI on Derivative (Effective Portion)	Location of Gain (Loss) Reclassified from Accumulated OCI into Income (Effective Portion)	Amount of Gain or (Loss) Reclassified from Accumulated OCI into Income (Effective Portion)	Location of Gain or (Loss) Recognized in Income on Derivative (Ineffective Portion and Amount Excluded from Effectiveness Testing)	Amount of Gain or (Loss) Recognized in Income on Derivative (Ineffective Portion and Amount Excluded from Effectiveness Testing)
Interest rate swap	$—	Interest expense	$(3,950)	Interest expense	$—

Derivatives in Cash Flow Hedging Relationship for the Fiscal Year Ended August 31, 2012	Amount of Gain (Loss) Recognized in OCI on Derivative (Effective Portion)	Location of Gain (Loss) Reclassified from Accumulated OCI into Income (Effective Portion)	Amount of Gain or (Loss) Reclassified from Accumulated OCI into Income (Effective Portion)	Location of Gain or (Loss) Recognized in Income on Derivative (Ineffective Portion and Amount Excluded from Effectiveness Testing)	Amount of Gain or (Loss) Recognized in Income on Derivative (Ineffective Portion and Amount Excluded from Effectiveness Testing)
Interest rate swap	$—	Interest expense	$(3,950)	Interest expense	$—

As of August 31, 2013, the Company estimates that it will reclassify into earnings during the next 12 months existing losses related to interest rate risk management hedging arrangements of approximately $4.0 million from the amounts recorded in AOCI as the hedged item affects earnings.

The changes related to cash flow hedges (both forward foreign exchange contracts and interest rate swaps) included in AOCI net of tax are as follows (in thousands):

Accumulated comprehensive loss August 31, 2011	$(11,172)
Changes in fair value of derivative instruments	2,637
Reclassification of net losses realized and included in net income related to derivative instruments	1,382
Accumulated comprehensive loss, August 31, 2012	$ (7,153)
Changes in fair value of derivative instruments	(182)
Reclassification of net losses realized and included in net income related to derivative instruments	2,285
Accumulated comprehensive loss, August 31, 2013	$ (5,050)

Revenues and Gains

Author's Note

In May 2014, FASB issued Accounting Standards Update (ASU) No. 2014-09, *Revenue from Contracts with Customers (Topic 606)*, which creates FASB ASC 606, Revenue from Contracts with Customers, and supersedes the revenue recognition requirements in FASB ASC 605, Revenue Recognition, including most industry-specific revenue recognition guidance throughout the industry topics of the codification. In addition, the ASU supersedes the cost guidance in FASB ASC 605-35 and creates FASB ASC 340-40. The core principle of FASB ASC 606 is that an entity recognizes revenue to depict the transfer of promised goods or services to customers in an amount that reflects the consideration to which the entity expects to be entitled in exchange for those goods or services. Entities are required to apply the amendments in this Update for annual reporting periods beginning on or December 15, 2016, including interim periods within that reporting period. Early adoption is not permitted. For nonpublic entities, the amendments are effective for annual reporting periods beginning after December 15, 2017, and interim periods within annual periods beginning after December 15, 2018. A nonpublic entity may elect to apply this guidance earlier, however only as of the following:

1. An annual reporting period beginning after December 15, 2016, including interim period within that reporting period
2. An annual reporting period beginning after December 15, 2016, and interim periods within annual periods beginning after December 15, 2017
3. An annual reporting period beginning after December 15, 2017, including interim periods within that reporting period.

Given the effective date of this Update, no survey entity will have adopted these requirements in its 2013 financial statements.

RECOGNITION AND MEASUREMENT

3.04 As explained by FASB ASC 605-10-25-1, the recognition of revenue and gains of an entity during a period involves consideration of the following two factors, with sometimes one and sometimes the other being the more important consideration:

- *Being realized or realizable.* Revenue and gains generally are not recognized until realized or realizable. Paragraph 83(a) of FASB Concepts Statement No. 5, *Recognition and Measurement in Financial Statements of Business Enterprises*, states that revenue and gains are realized when products (goods or services), merchandise, or other assets are exchanged for cash or claims to cash. That paragraph states that revenue and gains are realizable when related assets received or held are readily convertible to known amounts of cash or claims to cash.
- *Being earned.* Paragraph 83(b) of FASB Concepts Statement No. 5 states that revenue is not recognized until earned. That paragraph states that an entity's revenue-earning activities involve delivering or producing goods, rendering services, or other activities that constitute its ongoing major or central operations, and revenues are considered to have been earned when the entity has substantially accomplished what it must do to be entitled to the benefits represented by the revenues. That paragraph states that gains commonly result from transactions and other events that involve no earning process, and for recognizing gains, being earned is generally less significant than being realized or realizable.

3.05 FASB ASC 605-25 contains guidance on segmenting of transactions, referred to as *multiple element arrangements*, for both recognition and measurement. FASB ASC 605-25-25-2 requires that an entity should divide revenue arrangements with multiple deliverables into separate units of accounting if both the delivered item(s) have value to the customer on a standalone basis and, if the arrangement includes a general right of return, delivery and performance of the undelivered item(s) is probable and substantially in the vendor's control. FASB ASC 605-25-30-2 requires an entity to allocate the arrangement consideration at the inception of the arrangement to all deliverables based on their relative selling price (relative selling price method), except when another Topic in the FASB ASC requires a unit of accounting in the arrangement to be recorded at fair value or the amount that can be allocated to a unit of accounting is limited to an amount that is not contingent on delivery of additional deliverables or specified performance conditions. When a vendor applies the relative selling price method, an entity should determine the selling price using vendor-specific objective evidence of selling price, if it exists. Otherwise, the vendor should use its best estimate of selling price for that deliverable. Vendors should not ignore information that is reasonably available without undue cost or effort.

DISCLOSURE

3.06 FASB ASC 605-25-50-1 requires an entity to provide specific disclosures regarding multiple element arrangements, including the accounting policy for such arrangements (for example, whether deliverables are separable into units of accounting) and the nature of such arrangements (for example, provisions for performance, termination, or cancellation of the arrangement). FASB ASC 605-25-50-1 explains that the objective of the disclosure guidance is to provide both qualitative and quantitative information about a vendor's revenue arrangements and about the significant judgments made about the application of FASB ASC 605-25, changes in those judgments, or the application of FASB ASC 605-25 that may significantly affect the timing or amount of revenue recognition. Therefore, in addition to the required disclosures, a vendor shall also disclose other qualitative and quantitative information as necessary to comply with this objective. FASB ASC 605-25-50-2 requires a vendor to disclose specific information by similar arrangements including the nature of multiple deliverable arrangements; significant deliverables and the general timing of delivery or performance of service; contract provisions including performance, termination, and refund-type; discussion of significant factors, inputs, assumptions, and methods used to determine selling price; information about whether significant deliverables qualify as separate units of accounting; general timing of revenue recognition for significant deliverables; and effects of changes in selling price or methods for determining selling price.

PRESENTATION AND DISCLOSURE EXCERPTS

REVENUES

3.07 BMC SOFTWARE, INC. (DEC)
CONSOLIDATED STATEMENTS OF COMPREHENSIVE INCOME (in part)

(In millions, except per share data)

	Year Ended March 31,		
	2013	**2012**	**2011**
Revenue:			
License	$ 838.5	$ 877.8	$ 864.5
Maintenance	1,139.1	1,080.4	1,024.2
Professional services	223.8	213.8	176.6
Total revenue	2,201.4	2,172.0	2,065.3

NOTES TO CONSOLIDATED FINANCIAL STATEMENTS

(1) Summary of Significant Accounting Policies (in part)

Revenue Recognition

We derive revenue principally from software-related arrangements consisting of software license and maintenance offerings, non-software arrangements consisting of our software-as-a-service (SaaS) offerings as well as the associated professional services for each of these types of arrangements. We commence revenue recognition when all of the following core revenue recognition criteria are satisfied: i) persuasive evidence of an arrangement exists; ii) delivery of the license or service has occurred or is occurring; iii) the arrangement fee is fixed or determinable and iv) collection of the arrangement fee is probable.

Software License and Maintenance Arrangements

Software license revenue is recognized when the core revenue recognition criteria above are satisfied and vendor-specific objective evidence (VSOE) of the fair value of undelivered elements exists. As substantially all of our software licenses are sold in multiple-element arrangements that include either maintenance or both maintenance and professional services, we use the residual method to determine the amount of license revenue to be recognized. Under the residual method, consideration is allocated to undelivered elements based upon VSOE of the fair value of those elements, with the residual of the arrangement fee allocated to and recognized as license revenue. We have established VSOE of the fair value of our maintenance offerings through independent maintenance renewals. These demonstrate a consistent relationship of pricing maintenance as a percentage of either the net license fee or the discounted or undiscounted license list price. VSOE of the fair value of professional services is established based on daily rates when sold on a stand-alone basis, as well as management-approved pricing for certain new offerings.

We are unable to establish VSOE of fair value for all undelivered elements in certain arrangements that include multiple software products for which the associated maintenance pricing is based on a combination of undiscounted license list prices, net license fees or discounted license list prices. We are also unable to establish VSOE of fair value for all undelivered elements in certain arrangements that include unlimited licensing rights and certain arrangements that contain rights to future unspecified software products as part of the maintenance offering. If VSOE of fair value of one or more undelivered elements does not exist, license revenue is deferred and recognized upon delivery of those elements or when VSOE of fair value exists for all remaining undelivered elements, or if the deferral is due to the factors described above, license revenue is recognized ratably over the longest expected delivery period of undelivered elements in the arrangement, which is typically the longest maintenance term.

In our time-based license agreements, we are unable to establish VSOE of fair value for undelivered maintenance elements because the contractual maintenance terms in these arrangements are the same duration as the license terms, and VSOE of fair value of maintenance cannot be established. Accordingly, license fees in time-based license arrangements are recognized ratably over the term of the arrangements.

Maintenance revenue is recognized ratably over the contractual terms of the maintenance arrangements, which primarily range from one to three years and in some instances can extend up to five or more years.

Professional Services Arrangements

Professional services revenue, which principally relates to implementation, integration and education services associated with our products, is derived under both time-and-material and fixed fee arrangements and in most instances is recognized on a proportional performance basis based on days of effort. If no discernible customer deliverable exists until the completion of the professional services, we apply the completed performance method and defer the recognition of professional services revenue until completion of the services, which is typically evidenced by a signed completion letter from the customer. Services that are sold in connection with software license arrangements generally qualify for separate accounting from the license elements because they do not involve significant production, modification or customization of our products and are not otherwise considered to be essential to the functionality of such products. In arrangements where the professional services do not qualify for separate accounting from the license elements, the combined software license and professional services revenue are recognized based on contract accounting using either the percentage-of-completion or completed-contract method.

SaaS Arrangements

SaaS subscription fees are recognized ratably over the contractual terms of the subscription arrangements beginning on the date that the service is made available to customers. Additional professional services fees, principally related to optional services engagements that are not essential to the functionality of our core SaaS offerings and are considered to have standalone value, are generally recognized on a proportional performance basis based on days of effort. In our consolidated financial statements, SaaS subscription revenue and optional professional services revenue are included in maintenance and professional services revenue, respectively. To date, SaaS and related professional services revenues have not represented a significant percentage of our total revenue in any period since our SaaS offerings were first introduced to the market in late fiscal 2010.

Other Revenue Recognition Considerations

In arrangements containing both software and non-software (e.g., SaaS) elements, which to date have been infrequent, we allocate the arrangement consideration first into software and non-software units of accounting based on a relative selling price hierarchy and then apply the applicable software and non-software revenue recognition criteria to each unit of accounting. To date, we have determined the relative selling price of software and non-software units of accounting based on management's best estimate of selling price as other means of determining relative selling price (e.g., VSOE or other third-party evidence) have not been available with respect to all of the components in bundled software and non-software arrangements.

We also execute arrangements through resellers, distributors and systems integrators (collectively, channel partners) in which the channel partners act as the principals in the transactions with the end users of our products and services. In license arrangements with channel partners, title and risk of loss pass to the channel partners upon execution of our arrangements with them and the delivery of our products to the channel partner or the end user. We recognize revenue from transactions with channel partners on a net basis (the amount actually received by us from the channel partners) when all other revenue recognition criteria are satisfied. We do not offer right of return, product rotation or price protection to any of our channel partners.

Revenue from financed customer transactions are generally recognized in the same manner as those requiring current payment, as we have a history of offering installment contracts to customers and successfully enforcing original payment terms without making concessions. In arrangements where the fees are not considered to be fixed or determinable, we recognize revenue when payments become due under the arrangement. If we determine that a transaction is not probable of collection or a risk of concession exists, we do not recognize revenue in excess of the amount of cash received.

We are required to charge certain taxes on our revenue transactions. These amounts are not included in revenue. Instead, we record a liability when the amounts are collected and relieve the liability when payments are made to the applicable government agency.

In our consolidated statements of comprehensive income, revenue is categorized as license, maintenance or professional services revenue. We allocate revenue from arrangements containing multiple elements to each of these categories based on the VSOE of fair value for elements in each revenue arrangement and the application of the residual method for arrangements in which we have established VSOE of fair value for all undelivered elements. In arrangements where we are not able to establish VSOE of fair value for all undelivered elements, we first allocate revenue to any undelivered elements for which VSOE of fair value has been established, then allocate revenue to any undelivered elements for which VSOE of fair value has not been established based upon management's best estimate of fair value of those undelivered elements and apply a residual method to determine the license fee. Management's best estimate of fair value of undelivered elements for which VSOE of fair value has not been established is based upon the VSOE of similar offerings and other objective criteria.

INTEREST

3.08 CITIGROUP INC. (DEC)
CONSOLIDATED STATEMENT OF INCOME (in part)

(In millions of dollars, except per share amounts)	Years Ended December 31,		
	2013	2012	2011
Revenues			
Interest revenue	$62,970	$67,298	$71,858
Interest expense	16,177	20,612	24,209
Net interest revenue	$46,793	$46,686	$47,649

NOTES TO CONSOLIDATED FINANCIAL STATEMENTS

1. Summary of Significant Accounting Policies (in part)

Investment Securities (in part)

Investments include fixed income and equity securities. Fixed income instruments include bonds, notes and redeemable preferred stocks, as well as certain loan-backed and structured securities that are subject to prepayment risk. Equity securities include common and nonredeemable preferred stock.

Investment securities are classified and accounted for as follows:
- Fixed income securities classified as "held-to-maturity" represent securities that the Company has both the ability and the intent to hold until maturity and are carried at amortized cost. Interest income on such securities is included in *Interest revenue.*

- Fixed income securities and marketable equity securities classified as "available-for-sale" are carried at fair value with changes in fair value reported in *Accumulated other comprehensive income (loss)*, a component of *Stockholders' equity*, net of applicable income taxes and hedges. As described in more detail in Note 14 to the Consolidated Financial Statements, declines in fair value that are determined to be other-than-temporary are recorded in earnings immediately. Realized gains and losses on sales are included in income primarily on a specific identification cost basis. Interest and dividend income on such securities is included in *Interest revenue*.

For investments in fixed income securities classified as held-to-maturity or available-for-sale, accrual of interest income is suspended for investments that are in default or on which it is likely that future interest payments will not be made as scheduled.

Trading Account Assets and Liabilities (in part)

Trading account assets include debt and marketable equity securities, derivatives in a receivable position, residual interests in securitizations and physical commodities inventory. In addition, as described in Note 26 to the Consolidated Financial Statements, certain assets that Citigroup has elected to carry at fair value under the fair value option, such as loans and purchased guarantees, are also included in *Trading account assets*.

Trading account liabilities include securities sold, not yet purchased (short positions), and derivatives in a net payable position, as well as certain liabilities that Citigroup has elected to carry at fair value (as described in Note 26 to the Consolidated Financial Statements).

Other than physical commodities inventory, all trading account assets and liabilities are carried at fair value. Revenues generated from trading assets and trading liabilities are generally reported in *Principal transactions* and include realized gains and losses as well as unrealized gains and losses resulting from changes in the fair value of such instruments. Interest income on trading assets is recorded in *Interest revenue* reduced by interest expense on trading liabilities.

Securities Borrowed and Securities Loaned (in part)

Securities borrowing and lending transactions generally do not constitute a sale of the underlying securities for accounting purposes, and are treated as collateralized financing transactions. Such transactions are recorded at the amount of proceeds advanced or received plus accrued interest. As described in Note 26 to the Consolidated Financial Statements, the Company has elected to apply fair value accounting to a number of securities borrowing and lending transactions. Fees paid or received for all securities lending and borrowing transactions are recorded in *Interest expense* or *Interest revenue* at the contractually specified rate.

Repurchase and Resale Agreements (in part)

Securities sold under agreements to repurchase (repos) and securities purchased under agreements to resell (reverse repos) generally do not constitute a sale for accounting purposes of the underlying securities and are treated as collateralized financing transactions. As described in Note 26 to the Consolidated Financial Statements, the Company has elected to apply fair value accounting to a majority of such transactions, with changes in fair value reported in earnings. Any transactions for which fair value accounting has not been elected are recorded at the amount of cash advanced or received plus accrued interest. Irrespective of whether the Company has elected fair value accounting, interest paid or received on all repo and reverse repo transactions is recorded in *Interest expense* or *Interest revenue* at the contractually specified rate.

Loans (in part)

Loans are reported at their outstanding principal balances net of any unearned income and unamortized deferred fees and costs except that credit card receivable balances also include accrued interest and fees. Loan origination fees and certain direct origination costs are generally deferred and recognized as adjustments to income over the lives of the related loans.

As described in Note 26 to the Consolidated Financial Statements, Citi has elected fair value accounting for certain loans. Such loans are carried at fair value with changes in fair value reported in earnings. Interest income on such loans is recorded in *Interest revenue* at the contractually specified rate.

4. Interest Revenue and Expense

For the years ended December 31, 2013, 2012 and 2011, respectively, *Interest revenue* and *Interest expense* consisted of the following:

(In millions of dollars)	2013	2012	2011
Interest Revenue			
Loan interest, including fees	$45,580	$47,712	$49,466
Deposits with banks	1,026	1,261	1,742
Federal funds sold and securities borrowed or purchased under agreements to resell	2,566	3,418	3,631
Investments, including dividends	6,919	7,525	8,320
Trading account assets[1]	6,277	6,802	8,186
Other interest	602	580	513
Total interest revenue	$62,970	$67,298	$71,858
Interest Expense			
Deposits[2]	$ 6,236	$ 7,690	$ 8,531
Federal funds purchased and securities loaned or sold under agreements to repurchase	2,339	2,817	3,197
Trading account liabilities[1]	169	190	408
Short-term borrowings	597	727	650
Long-term debt	6,836	9,188	11,423
Total interest expense	$16,177	$20,612	$24,209
Net interest revenue	$46,793	$46,686	$47,649
Provision for loan losses	7,604	10,458	11,336
Net interest revenue after provision for loan losses	$39,189	$36,228	$36,313

[1] Interest expense on *Trading account liabilities* of *ICG* is reported as a reduction of interest revenue from *Trading account assets*.
[2] Includes deposit insurance fees and charges of $1,132 million, $1,262 million and $1,332 million for 2013, 2012 and 2011, respectively.

FRANCHISE FEES

3.09 WYNDHAM WORLDWIDE CORPORATION (DEC)
CONSOLIDATED STATEMENTS OF INCOME (in part)

(In millions, except per share amounts)

	Year Ended December 31,		
	2013	2012	2011
Net Revenues			
Service and membership fees	$2,329	$2,005	$2,012
Vacation ownership interest sales	1,379	1,323	1,150
Franchise fees	599	583	522
Consumer financing	426	421	415
Other	276	202	155
Net revenues	5,009	4,534	4,254

NOTES TO CONSOLIDATED FINANCIAL STATEMENTS

(Unless otherwise noted, all amounts are in millions, except share and per share amounts)

2. Summary of Significant Accounting Policies (in part)

Revenue Recognition (in part)

Lodging (in part)

The principal source of revenues from franchising hotels is ongoing franchise fees, which are primarily comprised of royalty, marketing and reservation fees. Royalty, marketing and reservation fees are typically a percentage of gross room revenues of each franchised hotel and are recognized as revenue upon becoming due from the franchisee. An estimate of uncollectible ongoing royalty fees is charged to bad debt expense and included in operating expenses on the Consolidated Statements of Income. Lodging revenues also include initial franchise fees, which are recognized as revenues when all material services or conditions have been substantially performed, which is either when a franchised hotel opens for business or when a franchise agreement is terminated after it has been determined that the franchised hotel will not open.

The Company's franchise agreements also require the payment of marketing and reservation fees, which are intended to reimburse the Company for expenses associated with operating an international, centralized, brand-specific reservations system, e-commerce channels such as the Company's brand.com websites, as well as access to third-party distribution channels, such as online travel agents, advertising and marketing programs, global sales efforts, operations support, training and other related services. Marketing and reservation fees are recognized as revenue upon becoming due from the franchisee. An estimate of uncollectible ongoing marketing and reservation fees is charged to bad debt expense and included in marketing and reservation expenses in the Consolidated Statements of Income.

The Company is contractually obligated to expend the marketing and reservation fees it collects from franchisees in accordance with the franchise agreements; as such, revenues earned in excess of costs incurred are accrued as a liability for future marketing or reservation costs. Costs incurred in excess of revenues earned are expensed as incurred. In accordance with its franchise agreements, the Company includes an allocation of costs required to carry out marketing and reservation activities within marketing and reservation expenses.

The Company also earns revenues from its Wyndham Rewards loyalty program when a member stays at a participating hotel. These revenues are derived from a fee the Company charges which are a percentage of room revenues generated from such stay. This fee is recognized as revenue upon becoming due from the franchisee. Since the Company is committed to expend the fees it collects from franchisees, revenues earned in excess of costs incurred are accrued as a liability for future costs to support the program.

The Company also provides management services for hotels under management contracts, which offer all the benefits of a global brand and a full range of management, marketing and reservation services. In addition to the standard franchise services described above, the Company's hotel management business provides hotel owners with professional oversight and comprehensive operations support services such as hiring, training and supervising the managers and employees that operate the hotels as well as annual budget preparation, financial analysis and extensive food and beverage services. The Company's standard management agreement typically has a term of up to 25 years. The Company's management fees are comprised of base fees, which are typically a specified percentage of gross revenues from hotel operations, and incentive fees, which are typically a specified percentage of a hotel's gross operating profit. Management fee revenues are recognized when earned in accordance with the terms of the contract and recorded as a component of franchise fee revenues on the Consolidated Statements of Income. Management fee revenues were $8 million, $7 million and $7 million during 2013, 2012 and 2011, respectively. The Company also recognizes as revenue reimbursable payroll costs for operational employees at certain of the Company's managed hotels. Although these costs are funded by hotel owners, accounting guidance requires the Company to report these fees on a gross basis as both revenues and expenses. The revenues are recorded as a component of service and membership fees while the offsetting expenses are reflected as a component of operating expenses on the Consolidated Statements of Income. As such, there is no effect on the Company's operating income. Revenues related to these payroll costs were $129 million, $91 million and $79 million in 2013, 2012 and 2011, respectively.

EARNINGS FROM EQUITY INVESTMENTS

3.10 KINDER MORGAN, INC. (DEC)
CONSOLIDATED STATEMENTS OF INCOME (in part)

(In Millions, Except Per Share Amounts)

	Year Ended December 31,		
	2013	2012	2011
Revenues			
Natural gas sales	$ 3,605	$ 2,511	$3,305
Services	6,677	5,013	3,050
Product sales and other	3,788	2,449	1,588
Total revenues	14,070	9,973	7,943
Operating Costs, Expenses and Other			
Costs of sales	5,253	3,057	3,278
Operations and maintenance	2,112	1,702	1,491
Depreciation, depletion and amortization	1,806	1,419	1,068
General and administrative	613	929	515
Taxes, other than income taxes	395	286	174
Other income, net	(99)	(13)	(6)
Total operating costs, expenses and other	10,080	7,380	6,520
Operating income	3,990	2,593	1,423
Other Income (Expense)			
Earnings from equity investments	327	153	226
Amortization of excess cost of equity investments	(39)	(23)	(7)
Interest, net	(1,675)	(1,399)	(682)
Gain (loss) on remeasurement of previously held equity investments to fair value (Note 3)	558	—	(167)
Gain on sale of investments in Express pipeline system (Note 3)	224	—	—
Other, net	53	19	17
Total other income (Expense)	(552)	(1,250)	(613)
Income from continuing operations before income taxes	3,438	1,343	810

2. Summary of Significant Accounting Policies (in part)

Equity Method of Accounting

We account for investments—which we do not control, but do have the ability to exercise significant influence—by the equity method of accounting. Under this method, our equity investments are carried originally at our acquisition cost, increased by our proportionate share of the investee's net income and by contributions made, and decreased by our proportionate share of the investee's net losses and by distributions received.

6. Investments (in part)

Our investments primarily consist of equity investments where we hold significant influence over investee actions and which we account for under the equity method of accounting. As of December 31, 2013 and 2012 our investments consisted of the following (in millions):

	December 31,	
	2013	2012
Citrus Corporation	$1,875	$1,966
Ruby Pipeline Holding Company, L.L.C.	1,153	1,185
Midcontinent Express Pipeline LLC	602	633
Gulf LNG Holdings Group, LLC	578	596
Plantation Pipe Line Company	307	313
EagleHawk	272	208
Red Cedar Gathering Company	176	172
Fort Union Gas Gathering L.L.C.	161	—
Double Eagle Pipeline LLC	144	—
Fayetteville Express Pipeline LLC	144	159
Parkway Pipeline LLC	131	58
Watco Companies, LLC	103	103
Cortez Pipeline Company	12	11
Eagle Ford		151
NGPL Holdco LLC	—	68
All others	285	173
Total equity investments	5,943	5,796
Bond investments	8	8
Total investments	$5,951	$5,804

The overall change in the carrying amount of our equity investments, including those of KMP, since December 31, 2012, related primarily to the increases and decreases associated with KMP's May 1, 2013 Copano acquisition. As part of this acquisition, KMP acquired an approximate 37% equity ownership interest in Fort Union Gas Gathering L.L.C., a 50% equity ownership interest in Double Eagle Pipeline LLC and the remaining 50% equity ownership interest in Eagle Ford that KMP did not already own (KMP exchanged its status as an owner of an equity investment in Eagle Ford for a full controlling financial interest, and KMP began accounting for its investment under the full consolidation method).

As shown in the table above, our remaining significant equity investments, including those of KMP (excluding the three investments described above), as of December 31, 2013 consisted of the following:
- Citrus Corporation—We operate and own a 50% interest in Citrus Corporation, the sole owner of Florida Gas Transmission Company, L.L.C. (Florida Gas). Florida Gas transports natural gas to cogeneration facilities, electric utilities, independent power producers, municipal generators, and local distribution companies through a 5,300-mile natural gas pipeline. The remaining 50% interest is owned by Energy Transfer Partners L.P.;
- Ruby Pipeline Holding Company, L.L.C.—We operate and own a 50% interest in Ruby Pipeline Holding Company, L.L.C., the sole owner of Ruby Pipeline natural gas transmission system. The remaining 50% interest is owned by Global Infrastructure Partners as convertible preferred interests;
- Midcontinent Express Pipeline LLC—KMP operates and owns a 50% interest in MEP, the sole owner of the Midcontinent Express natural gas pipeline system. The remaining 50% ownership interest is owned by subsidiaries of Regency Energy Partners L.P.;
- Gulf LNG Holdings Group, LLC—We operate and own a 50% interest in Gulf LNG Holdings Group, LLC, the owner of a LNG receiving, storage and regasification terminal near Pascagoula, Mississippi, as well as pipeline facilities to deliver vaporized natural gas into third party pipelines for delivery into various markets around the country. The remaining 50% ownership interests are wholly and partially owned by the subsidiaries of GE Financial Services;
- Plantation—KMP operates and owns a 51.17% interest in Plantation, the sole owner of the Plantation refined petroleum products pipeline system. A subsidiary of Exxon Mobil Corporation owns the remaining interest. Each investor has an equal number of directors

on Plantation's board of directors, and board approval is required for certain corporate actions that are considered participating rights; therefore, KMP does not control Plantation, and it accounts for its investment under the equity method;

- BHP Billiton Petroleum (Eagle Ford Gathering) LLC, f/k/a EagleHawk Field Services LLC and referred to in this report as EagleHawk—KMP owns a 25% interest in EagleHawk, the sole owner of a natural gas gathering system serving the producers of the Eagle Ford shale formation. A subsidiary of BHP Billiton operates EagleHawk and owns the remaining 75% ownership interest;
- Red Cedar Gathering Company—KMP owns a 49% interest in the Red Cedar, the sole owner of the Red Cedar natural gas gathering, compression and treating system. The remaining 51% interest is owned by the Southern Ute Indian Tribe;
- Fayetteville Express Pipeline LLC—KMP owns a 50% interest in Fayetteville Express Pipeline LLC, the sole owner of the Fayetteville Express natural gas pipeline system. Energy Transfer Partners, L.P. owns the remaining 50% interest and serves as operator of Fayetteville Express Pipeline LLC;
- Parkway Pipeline LLC—KMP operates and owns a 50% interest in Parkway, the sole owner of the Parkway Pipeline refined petroleum products pipeline system. Valero Energy Corp. owns the remaining 50% interest;
- Watco Companies, LLC—KMP holds a preferred equity investment in Watco Companies, LLC, the largest privately held short line railroad company in the U.S. KMP owns 100,000 Class A preferred shares and pursuant to the terms of its investment, it receives priority, cumulative cash distributions from the preferred shares at a rate of 3.25% per quarter, and participates partially in additional profit distributions at a rate equal to 0.5%. The preferred shares have no conversion features and hold no voting powers, but do provide KMP certain approval rights, including the right to appoint one of the members to Watco's Board of Managers;
- Cortez Pipeline Company—KMP operates and owns a 50% interest in the Cortez Pipeline Company, the sole owner of the Cortez carbon dioxide pipeline system. A subsidiary of Exxon Mobil Corporation owns a 37% interest and Cortez Vickers Pipeline Company owns the remaining 13% interest; and
- NGPL Holdco LLC—KMI operates and owns a 20% interest in NGPL Holdco LLC, the owner of NGPL and certain affiliates, collectively referred to in this report as NGPL, a major interstate natural gas pipeline and storage system.

During 2012 and 2013, continued deteriorating natural gas market conditions characterized by excess gas supply, low commodity prices, reduced basis spreads and low volatility have negatively impacted NGPL's operating results and its cash flows. We also determined that these market conditions would likely not improve in the near future. Therefore, these events caused us to evaluate the carrying value of our investment utilizing market conditions and have resulted in us recording impairments on our investment in NGPL Holdco LLC in 2012 and 2013. We recognized $200 million of pre-tax, non-cash impairment charges in 2012, and in 2013, we recognized $65 million of pre-tax, non-cash impairment charges writing down our remaining investment to its estimated fair value of zero.

Both 2013 and 2012 non-cash impairment charges are included in the caption "Earnings from equity investments" in our accompanying consolidated statements of income.

Our earnings (losses) from equity investments were as follows (in millions):

	Year Ended December 31,		
	2013	2012	2011
Citrus Corporation[a]	$ 84	$ 53	$ —
Fayetteville Express Pipeline LLC	55	55	24
Gulf LNG Holdings Group, LLC[a]	47	22	—
Midcontinent Express Pipeline LLC	40	42	43
Plantation Pipe Line Company	35	32	28
Red Cedar Gathering Company	31	32	32
Cortez Pipeline Company	24	25	24
Eagle Ford[b]	14	34	11
Watco Companies, LLC	13	13	6
Fort Union Gas Gathering L.L.C.	11	—	—
EagleHawk	9	11	3
Parkway Pipeline LLC	1	—	—
Double Eagle Pipeline LLC	1	—	—
KinderHawk[c]	—	—	22
Ruby Pipeline Holding Company, L.L.C.[a]	(6)	(5)	—
NGPL Holdco LLC[d]	(66)	(198)	19
All others	34	37	14
Total	$327	$153	$226
Amortization of excess costs	$ (39)	$ (23)	$ (7)

[a] 2012 amounts are for the period from May 25, 2012 through December 31, 2012.

[b] Effective May 1, 2013, KMP acquired the remaining 50% equity ownership interest in Eagle Ford that KMP did not already own and KMP changed its method of accounting from the equity method to full consolidation.

[c] Effective July 1, 2011, KMP acquired the remaining 50% equity ownership interest in KinderHawk that KMP did not already own and KMP changed its method of accounting from the equity method to full consolidation.

[d] 2013 and 2012 amounts include non-cash investment impairment charges, which we recorded in the amount of $65 million and $200 million (pre-tax), respectively, as discussed above.

Summarized combined financial information for our significant equity investments (listed or described above) is reported below (in millions; amounts represent 100% of investee financial information):

	Year Ended December 31,		
Income Statement	**2013**	**2012**	**2011**
Revenues	$3,615	$3,681	$3,145
Costs and expenses	2,803	3,194	3,287
Net income (loss)	$ 812	$ 487	$ (142)

FOREIGN EXCHANGE CONTRACTS

3.11 MASTERCARD INCORPORATED (DEC)
NOTES TO CONSOLIDATED FINANCIAL STATEMENTS

Note 20. Foreign Exchange Risk Management

The Company enters into foreign currency forward contracts to manage risk associated with anticipated receipts and disbursements which are either transacted in a non-functional currency or valued based on a currency other than its functional currency. The Company also enters into foreign currency derivative contracts to offset possible changes in value due to foreign exchange fluctuations of earnings, assets and liabilities denominated in currencies other than the functional currency of the entity. The objective of these activities is to reduce the Company's exposure to gains and losses resulting from fluctuations of foreign currencies against its functional and reporting currencies.

The Company does not designate foreign currency derivatives as hedging instruments pursuant to the accounting guidance for derivative instruments and hedging activities. The Company records the change in the estimated fair value of the outstanding derivatives at the end of the reporting period to its consolidated balance sheet and consolidated statement of operations.

As of December 31, 2013, all forward contracts to purchase and sell foreign currency had been entered into with customers of MasterCard. MasterCard's derivative contracts are summarized below:

	December 31, 2013		December 31, 2012	
(In millions)	Notional	Estimated Fair Value	Notional	Estimated Fair Value
Commitments to purchase foreign currency	$ 23	$ (1)	$ 76	$ (1)
Commitments to sell foreign currency	1,722	1	1,571	(2)
Balance Sheet Location:				
Accounts Receivable*		$ 13		$ 12
Other Current Liabilities*		(13)		(15)

* The fair values of derivative contracts are presented on a gross basis on the balance sheet and are subject to enforceable master netting arrangements, which contain various netting and setoff provisions.

The amount of gain (loss) recognized in income for the contracts to purchase and sell foreign currency are summarized below:

	Year Ended December 31,		
(In millions)	2013	2012	2011
Foreign currency derivative contracts			
General and administrative	$48	$22	$(6)
Net revenue	4	(6)	(3)
Total	$52	$16	$(9)

The fair value of the foreign currency forward contracts generally reflects the estimated amounts that the Company would receive (or pay), on a pre-tax basis, to terminate the contracts at the reporting date based on broker quotes for the same or similar instruments. The terms of the foreign currency forward contracts are generally less than 18 months. The Company had no deferred gains or losses related to foreign exchange in accumulated other comprehensive income as of December 31, 2013 and 2012 as there were no derivative contracts accounted for under hedge accounting.

The Company's derivative financial instruments are subject to both market and counterparty credit risk. Market risk is the risk of loss due to the potential change in an instrument's value caused by fluctuations in interest rates and other variables related to currency exchange rates. The effect of a hypothetical 10% adverse change in foreign currency rates could result in a fair value loss of approximately $189 million on the Company's foreign currency derivative contracts outstanding at December 31, 2013 related to the hedging program. Counterparty credit risk is the risk of loss due to failure of the counterparty to perform its obligations in accordance with contractual terms. To mitigate counterparty credit risk, the Company enters into derivative contracts with selected financial institutions based upon their credit ratings and other factors. Generally, the Company does not obtain collateral related to derivatives because of the high credit ratings of the counterparties.

GAIN ON ASSET DISPOSALS

3.12 GREIF, INC. (OCT)
CONSOLIDATED STATEMENTS OF INCOME (in part)

(Dollars in millions, except per share amounts)

	For the Years Ended October 31,		
	2013	**2012**	**2011**
Net sales	$4,353.4	$4,269.5	$4,248.2
Costs of products sold	3,520.8	3,489.9	3,449.9
Gross profit	832.6	779.6	798.3
Selling, general and administrative expenses	477.3	468.4	449.2
Restructuring charges	8.8	33.4	30.5
Timberland gains	(17.5)	—	—
Asset impairment charges	30.0	2.6	4.5
Gain on disposal of properties, plants and equipment, net	(5.6)	(7.6)	(16.1)
Operating profit	339.6	282.8	330.2

NOTES TO CONSOLIDATED FINANCIAL STATEMENTS

Note 1—Basis of Presentation and Summary of Significant Accounting Policies (in part)

Properties, Plants and Equipment

Properties, plants and equipment are stated at cost. Depreciation on properties, plants and equipment is provided on the straight-line method over the estimated useful lives of the assets as follows:

	Years
Buildings	30–45
Machinery and equipment	3–19

Depreciation expense was $131.9 million, $131.4 million and $122.7 million, in 2013, 2012 and 2011, respectively. Expenditures for repairs and maintenance are charged to expense as incurred. When properties are retired or otherwise disposed of, the cost and accumulated depreciation are eliminated from the asset and related allowance accounts. Gains or losses are credited or charged to income as incurred.

The Company capitalizes interest on long-term fixed asset projects using a rate that approximates the weighted average cost of borrowing. As of October 31, 2013, 2012, and 2011, the Company capitalized interest costs of $1.7 million, $2.7 million, and $3.8 million, respectively.

The Company tests for impairment of properties, plants and equipment at least annually, or more frequently if certain indicators are present to suggest that impairment may exist.

The Company owns timber properties in the southeastern United States and in Canada. With respect to the Company's United States timber properties, which consisted of approximately 252,475 acres as of October 31, 2013, depletion expense on timber properties is computed on the basis of cost and the estimated recoverable timber. Depletion expense was $4.3 million, $2.9 million and $2.7 million in 2013, 2012 and 2011, respectively. The Company's land costs are maintained by tract. The Company begins recording pre-merchantable timber costs at the time the site is prepared for planting. Costs capitalized during the establishment period include site preparation by aerial spray, costs of seedlings, planting costs, herbaceous weed control, woody release, labor and machinery use, refrigeration rental and trucking for the seedlings. The Company does not capitalize interest costs in the process. Property taxes are expensed as incurred. New road construction costs are capitalized as land improvements and depreciated over 20 years. Road repairs and maintenance costs are expensed as incurred. Costs after establishment of the seedlings, including management costs, pre-commercial thinning costs and fertilization costs, are expensed as incurred. Once the timber becomes merchantable, the cost is transferred from the pre-merchantable timber category to the merchantable timber category in the depletion block.

Merchantable timber costs are maintained by five product classes, pine sawtimber, pine chip-n-saw, pine pulpwood, hardwood sawtimber and hardwood pulpwood, within a depletion block, with each depletion block based upon a geographic district or subdistrict. Currently, the Company has eight depletion blocks. These same depletion blocks are used for pre-merchantable timber costs. Each year, the Company estimates the volume of the Company's merchantable timber for the five product classes by each depletion block. These estimates are based on the current state in the growth cycle and not on quantities to be available in future years. The Company's estimates do not include costs to be incurred in the future. The Company then projects these volumes to the end of the year. Upon acquisition of a new timberland tract, the Company records separate amounts for land, merchantable timber and pre-merchantable timber allocated as a percentage of the values being purchased. These acquisition volumes and costs acquired during the year are added to the totals for each product class within the appropriate depletion block(s). The total of the beginning, one-year growth and acquisition volumes are divided by the total undepleted historical cost to arrive at a depletion rate, which is then used for the current year. As timber is sold, the Company multiplies the volumes sold by the depletion rate for the current year to arrive at the depletion cost.

For 2013, the Company recorded a gain of $17.5 million relating to the sale of timberland.

The Company's Canadian timber properties, which consisted of approximately 10,300 as of October 31, 2013, are not actively managed at this time, and therefore, no depletion expense is recorded.

Note 5—Net Assets Held For Sale

As of October 31, 2013, there were two asset groups in the Flexible Products & Services segment with assets held for sale. As of October 31, 2012, there was one asset group in the Rigid Industrial Packaging & Services segment and one location in the Flexible Products & Services segment with assets held for sale. During 2013, one asset group was added in the Rigid Industrial Packaging Products & Services segment and subsequently sold in the same period. Additionally, two asset groups were added in the Flexible Products & Services segment. One asset group in the Rigid Industrial Packaging and Services segment and one asset group in the Flexible Products & Services segment were placed back in service for purposes of GAAP and depreciation was resumed. As a result of placing these locations back in service in 2013, the 2012 consolidated balance sheet has been reclassified for such locations to conform to the current year presentation. The reclassification of these asset groups to properties, plants and equipment within the consolidated balance sheets was done in accordance with ASC 360, but these assets are still being marketed for sale. The net assets held for sale are being marketed for sale and it is the Company's intention to complete the sales of these assets within the upcoming year.

For the year ended October 31, 2013, the Company recorded a gain on disposal of PP&E, net of $5.6 million. There were sales of HBU and surplus properties which resulted in gains of $1.2 million in the Land Management segment, a sale of equipment in the Paper Packaging segment that resulted in a gain of $0.6 million, a disposal of equipment in the Rigid Industrial Packaging & Services segment that resulted in a gain of $2.5 million, a sale of property that was previously classified as held for sale in the Rigid Industrial Packaging & Services segment that resulted in a gain of $0.6 million, a sale of land adjacent to our corporate offices that resulted in a gain of $0.8 million, a sale of equipment that resulted in a loss of $0.9 million and sales of other miscellaneous equipment which resulted in aggregate gains of $0.8 million.

For the year ended October 31, 2012, the Company recorded a gain on disposal of PP&E, net of $7.6 million. There were sales of HBU and surplus properties which resulted in gains of $5.5 million in the Land Management segment, a sale of equipment in the Rigid Industrial Packaging & Services segment which resulted in a gain of $0.6 million, a sale of miscellaneous equipment in the Paper Packaging segment which resulted in a gain of $0.5 million and sales of other miscellaneous equipment which resulted in aggregate gains of $1.0 million.

For the year ended October 31, 2011, the Company recorded a gain on disposal of PP&E, net of $16.1 million. There were sales in the Rigid Industrial Packaging & Services segment which resulted in a $3.2 million gain, sales in the Paper Packaging segment which resulted in a $0.9 million gain, sales in the Land Management segment of HBU and surplus properties which resulted in a $11.4 million gain and sales of other miscellaneous equipment which resulted in a $0.6 million gain.

BARGAIN PURCHASE GAIN

3.13 CENVEO, INC. (DEC)
CONSOLIDATED STATEMENTS OF OPERATIONS AND COMPREHENSIVE INCOME (LOSS) (in part)

(In thousands, except per share data)

	For the Years Ended		
	2013	2012	2011
Net sales	$1,777,808	$1,738,293	$1,844,371
Cost of sales	1,485,931	1,417,147	1,498,202
Selling, general and administrative expenses	206,085	182,980	213,296
Amortization of intangible assets	9,962	9,881	9,899
Restructuring and other charges	13,100	27,100	17,812
Impairment of intangible assets	33,367	—	—
Operating income	29,363	101,185	105,162
Gain on bargain purchase	(17,262)	—	(11,720)
Interest expense, net	112,677	114,755	115,968
Loss (gain) on early extinguishment of debt, net	11,324	12,487	(4,011)
Other (income) expense, net	(5,602)	(1,249)	9,074
Loss from continuing operations before income taxes	(71,774)	(24,808)	(4,149)

2. Acquisitions (in part)

The Company accounts for business combinations under the provisions of the Business Combination Topic of the Financial Accounting Standards Board's Accounting Standards Codification ("ASC") 805. Acquisitions are accounted for by the purchase method, and accordingly, the assets and liabilities of the acquired businesses have been recorded at their estimated fair value on the acquisition date with the excess of the purchase price over their estimated fair value recorded as goodwill. In the event the estimated fair value of the assets and liabilities acquired exceeds the purchase price paid, a bargain purchase gain is recorded in the statement of operations.

Acquisition-related costs are expensed as incurred. Acquisition-related costs, including integration costs, are included in selling, general and administrative expenses in the Company's consolidated statement of operations and were $8.7 million, $1.5 million and $6.0 million for the years ended 2013, 2012 and 2011, respectively.

2013

National Envelope

On September 16, 2013, the Company acquired certain assets of National. National's accounts receivable and inventory were purchased by unrelated third parties in conjunction with the Company's acquisition. National manufactured and distributed envelope products for the wholesale, billing, financial, direct mail and office products markets and had approximately 1,600 employees. The Company believes the acquisition of certain assets of National will enhance the Company's manufacturing capabilities and reduce capacity in the envelope industry. The preliminary purchase price was $34.1 million, of which $6.0 million was Cenveo common stock, and was preliminarily allocated to the tangible and identifiable intangible assets acquired and liabilities assumed based on their estimated fair values at the acquisition date, and was assigned to the Company's envelope segment. The acquisition of certain assets of National resulted in a preliminary bargain purchase gain of approximately $17.3 million, exclusive of $6.8 million of tax expense, which was recognized in the Company's consolidated statement of operations. Prior to the recognition of the bargain purchase gain, the Company reassessed the fair value of the tangible and identifiable intangible assets acquired and liabilities assumed in the acquisition. The Company believes it was able to acquire those assets of National for less than their fair value due to National's bankruptcy prior to the Company's acquisition. The acquired identifiable intangible asset relates to a leasehold interest with a fair value of $3.8 million, which is being amortized over the remaining lease term of 20 years, which includes renewal periods.

National's results of operations and cash flows are included in the Company's consolidated statement of operations and cash flows from September 16, 2013. As a result of the Company's integration of certain assets of National into the Company's existing envelope operations, it is impracticable to disclose the amounts of revenues and operating income of National since the acquisition date.

Preliminary Purchase Price Allocation

The following table summarizes the preliminary allocation of the purchase price of National to the assets acquired and liabilities assumed in the acquisition (in thousands):

	As of September 16, 2013
Property, plant and equipment	$54,900
Other intangible assets	3,780
Total assets acquired	58,680
Accounts payable	967
Accrued compensation and related liabilities	1,210
Other current liabilities	1,351
Other liabilities	1,292
Note payable	2,536
Total liabilities assumed	7,356
Net assets acquired	51,324
Cost of the acquisition of certain assets of National	34,062
Gain on bargain purchase	$17,262

Property, plant and equipment values were estimated based on discussions with machinery and equipment brokers, internal expertise related to the equipment and current marketplace conditions. The value of the leasehold interest acquired was determined based on the present value of the difference between the contractual amounts to be paid pursuant to the lease and management's estimate of current market lease rates for the corresponding lease, measured over the remaining lease term and renewal periods.

The fair values of property, plant and equipment and the intangible asset acquired from National were determined to be Level 3 under the fair value hierarchy.

Unaudited Pro Forma Financial Information

The following supplemental pro forma consolidated summary financial information of the Company for the years ended 2013 and 2012 herein have been prepared by adjusting the historical data as set forth in its statements of operations to give effect to the acquisition of certain assets of National as if it had been made as of January 1, 2012 (in thousands, except per share amounts).

	For the Years Ended	
	2013	2012
Net sales		
As reported	$1,777,808	$1,738,293
Pro forma	$2,027,799	$2,154,956
Loss from continuing operations		
As reported	$ (85,527)	$ (80,528)
Pro forma	$ (114,127)	$ (125,724)
Loss per share from continuing operations—basic		
As reported	$ (1.32)	$ (1.27)
Pro forma	$ (1.73)	$ (1.92)
Loss per share from continuing operations—diluted		
As reported	$ (1.32)	$ (1.27)
Pro forma	$ (1.73)	$ (1.92)

The supplemental pro forma consolidated summary financial information is presented for comparative purposes only and does not purport to be indicative of the Company's actual consolidated results of operations had the acquisition of certain assets of National been consummated as of the beginning of the period noted above, or of the Company's expected future results of operations. The adjustments related to the supplemental pro forma consolidated summary financial information above include the removal of $7.5 million in acquisition-related expenses incurred during 2013, as well as the removal of a bargain purchase gain of $17.3 million in 2013, and the related $6.8 million of tax expense.

The Company has performed its assessment of the preliminary purchase price allocation by identifying and estimating the fair value of intangible and tangible assets, comprised of a leasehold interest and property, plant and equipment. Pro forma adjustments have been made to depreciation and amortization expense related to these estimated fair values, and to reflect the Company's borrowing rate in the above supplemental pro forma consolidated summary financial information. The pro forma operating results do not include any anticipated synergies related to combining these operations.

LITIGATION

3.14 THE DOW CHEMICAL COMPANY (DEC)
CONSOLIDATED STATEMENTS OF INCOME (in part)

	For the Years Ended December 31		
(In millions, except per share amounts)	2013	2012	2011
Net sales	$57,080	$56,786	$59,985
Cost of sales	47,594	47,792	51,029
Research and development expenses	1,747	1,708	1,646
Selling, general and administrative expenses	3,024	2,861	2,788
Amortization of intangibles	461	478	496
Goodwill impairment loss	—	220	—
Restructuring charges (credits)	(22)	1,343	—
Acquisition-related integration expenses	—	—	31
Equity in earnings of nonconsolidated affiliates	1,034	536	1,223
Sundry income (expense)—net	2,554	(27)	(316)
Interest income	41	41	40
Interest expense and amortization of debt discount	1,101	1,269	1,341
Income before income taxes	6,804	1,665	3,601
Provision for income taxes	1,988	565	817
Net income	4,816	1,100	2,784

Note 14—Commitments and Contingent Liabilities (in part)

K-Dow Arbitration

In February 2009, the Company initiated arbitration proceedings against Petrochemical Industries Company (K.S.C.) ("PIC") alleging that PIC breached the Joint Venture Formation Agreement related to the establishment of K-Dow, a proposed 50:50 global petrochemical joint venture with PIC, by failing to close the transaction. In May 2012, the International Court of Arbitration of the International Chamber of Commerce ("ICC") awarded the Company $2.161 billion in damages ("Partial Award"), not including pre- and post-award interest and arbitration costs. On March 4, 2013 the ICC released the Final Award in the arbitration case covering the Company's claim for pre- and post-award interest and arbitration costs and awarded the Company $318 million, as of February 28, 2013. On May 6, 2013, the Company and PIC entered into a Deed providing for payment of the Company's claims against PIC under the K-Dow arbitration. On May 7, 2013, the Company confirmed the receipt of a $2.195 billion cash payment from PIC, which included the Partial Award of $2.161 billion as well as recovery of Dow's costs incurred in the arbitration, including legal fees. In addition, Kuwait Petroleum Corporation provided assurances that no retaliatory or punitive actions would be taken against the Company and its affiliates as a result of the Deed and payment. In the second quarter of 2013, the Company recorded a pretax gain of $2.195 billion, of which $2.161 billion is included in "Sundry income (expense)—net" and $34 million is included in "Cost of sales" in the consolidated statements of income and reflected in Corporate. The K-Dow arbitration is considered final and settled in full.

GAIN ON ACQUISITION OF CONTROLLING INTEREST

3.15 AXIALL CORPORATION (DEC)
CONSOLIDATED STATEMENTS OF INCOME (in part)

	Year Ended December 31,		
(In millions, except per share data)	**2013**	**2012**	**2011**
Net sales	$4,666.0	$3,325.8	$3,222.9
Operating costs and expenses:			
Cost of sales	3,924.5	2,865.4	2,919.6
Selling, general and administrative expenses	299.1	203.5	168.2
Transaction related costs and other, net	35.6	38.9	3.3
Long-lived asset impairment charges (recoveries), net	36.0	(0.8)	8.3
Gain on sale of assets, net	—	(19.3)	(1.1)
Total operating costs and expenses	4,295.2	3,087.7	3,098.3
Operating income	370.8	238.1	124.6
Interest expense	(77.6)	(57.5)	(65.6)
Loss on redemption and other debt costs	(78.5)	(2.7)	(4.9)
Gain on acquisition of controlling interest	25.9	—	—
Foreign exchange loss	—	(0.6)	(0.9)
Interest income	1.0	0.4	0.3
Income before income taxes	241.6	177.7	53.5
Provision for (benefit from) income taxes	73.6	57.2	(4.2)
Consolidated net income	168.0	120.5	57.7

2. Merger with the PPG Chemicals Business

On January 28, 2013, Axiall Corporation ("Axiall") completed a series of transactions that resulted in our acquisition of substantially all the assets and liabilities of PPG Industries, Inc.'s ("PPG") business related to the production of chlorine, caustic soda and related chemicals, ("the Merged Business") and the related financings (collectively the "Transactions"). The operations of the Merged Business are included in our financial results from January 28, 2013, the closing date of the merger.

The purchase price of the Merged Business of approximately $2.8 billion consists of: (i) shares of our common stock received by PPG shareholders valued at approximately $1.8 billion, based on the closing stock sale price of $50.24 on the last trade date prior to the closing date of the merger; (ii) debt assumed of approximately $967.0 million; and (iii) the assumption of other liabilities, including pension liabilities and other post-retirement obligations. We manage the Merged Business as part of our chlorovinyls business, and have reported the results of operations of the Merged Business as part of our chlorovinyls reporting segment since January 28, 2013.

In connection with the Transactions, through December 31, 2013, we have paid approximately $56.3 million in fees and expenses, which included: (i) approximately $30.3 million of debt issuance costs, of which approximately $19.3 million was deferred; and (ii) approximately $26.0 million of related professional and legal fees.

Goodwill recognized from the acquisition of the Merged Business is primarily due to the increase in size and economies of scale of the merged companies, a significant increase in chlorine production flexibility, an increase in natural gas integration and strategic, geographic and product synergies. Approximately $5.9 million of the goodwill recognized in the merger is expected to be deductible for tax purposes. The fair value of the noncontrolling interest in TCI was estimated based on the present value of estimated future cash flows from TCI attributable to our minority partner's ownership percentage of TCI. The allocation of the purchase price to assets acquired and liabilities assumed, is set forth in the table below:

(In millions)	Amounts Recognized as of the Aquisition Date	Measurement Period Adjustments[1]	Final Allocation as of December 31, 2013
Cash and cash equivalents	$ 26.7	$ —	$ 26.7
Receivables	236.7	(2.4)	234.3
Inventories	72.0	5.1	77.1
Prepaid expenses and other	11.9	(4.3)	7.6
Property, plant and equipment	957.3	(30.4)[2]	926.9
Goodwill	1,454.3	118.4	1,572.7
Intangible assets	1,224.2	(18.4)[3]	1,205.8
Other assets	42.5	(0.3)	42.2
Accounts payable	(97.8)	1.2	(96.6)
Income taxes payable	(4.7)	—	(4.7)
Accrued compensation	(20.6)	—	(20.6)
Other accrued taxes	(12.1)	11.9	(0.2)
Other accrued liabilities	(58.0)	(4.5)	(62.5)
Deferred income taxes	(614.9)	(66.5)[4]	(681.4)
Pensions and other postretirement benefits	(279.0)	26.7[5]	(252.3)
Other non-current liabilities	(67.9)	(10.6)	(78.5)
Debt assumed	(967.0)	—	(967.0)
Noncontrolling interest	(130.3)	0.3	(130.0)
Total net assets acquired	$1,773.3	$ 26.2[6]	$1,799.5

[1] The measurement period adjustments did not have a significant impact on our consolidated net income for the quarters within the year ended December 31, 2013. Therefore, we did not retrospectively adjust those prior periods.
[2] Primarily consists of the adjustments to the fair value of location-specific property, plant and equipment.
[3] Primarily consists of the fair value of supply contracts, offset by adjustments to customer relationship intangible assets.
[4] Deferred income taxes resulting from the revaluation of acquired assets and liabilities.
[5] Primarily relates to the fair value of pension related assets that are being transferred with the merger and the resulting impact on the funded status of the pension liability.
[6] Primarily relates to additional consideration based on the final funding status of certain pension plans, partly offset by a favorable net working capital settlement.

Summary Pro Forma Information. The following unaudited pro forma information reflects our consolidated results of operations as if the Transactions had taken place on January 1, 2012. The pro forma information includes primarily adjustments for depreciation based on the estimated fair value of the property, plant and equipment acquired in the merger, amortization of acquired intangible assets and interest expense on the debt we incurred to finance the Transactions. The pro forma information is not necessarily indicative of the results of operations that we would have reported had the Transactions closed on January 1, 2012, nor is it necessarily indicative of future results.

	Year Ended December 31,	
(In millions, except per share data)	2013	2012
Net sales	$4,773.7	$4,977.4
Net income attributable to Axiall	$ 162.7[a]	$ 271.8[b]
Earnings per share from net income attributable to Axiall:		
Basic	$ 2.33	$ 3.88
Diluted	$ 2.31	$ 3.87

[a] In addition to the normal pro forma adjustments associated with the Transactions, this amount excludes: (i) the $25.9 million gain on acquisition of controlling interest in PHH; (ii) $13.4 million related to the inventory fair value purchase accounting adjustment; and (iii) $11.0 million related to the expensing of financing fees related to a $688.0 million bridge loan used in the Transactions.
[b] In addition to the normal pro forma adjustments associated with the Transactions, this amount includes: (i) the $25.9 million gain on acquisition of controlling interest in PHH; (ii) $13.4 million related to the inventory fair value purchase accounting adjustment; and (iii) $11.0 million related to the expensing of financing fees related to a $688.0 million bridge loan used in the Transactions.

Disclosure of revenues and earnings of the Merged Business since January 28, 2013 on a stand-alone basis is not practicable as the Merged Business is not being operated as a stand-alone business.

Increase of Authorized Shares of Common Stock. In connection with the Transactions and effective January 28, 2013, the Company increased the number of authorized shares of Company common stock from 100 million shares to 200 million shares.

15. Investments and Related Party Transactions (in part)

Chlorovinyls (in part)

We have joint ventures that are accounted for using the equity method. Through the merger, we acquired, as part of the Merged Business, the remaining 50 percent interest that we did not previously own of PHH Monomers LLC ("PHH"), a joint venture between us and PPG. PHH is a manufacturing joint venture that consists primarily of plant and equipment and the fair value was estimated based on the replacement cost of assets in similar condition. Prior to the merger, we owned 50 percent of PHH and accounted for our ownership interest as an equity method investment. We recognized a gain of $25.9 million as a result of remeasuring the equity interest we held in PHH before the merger. The estimated fair value of our prior equity interest in PHH before the merger was $27.6 million.

DERIVATIVES

3.16 CONSTELLATION BRANDS, INC. (FEB)
CONSOLIDATED STATEMENTS OF COMPREHENSIVE INCOME (in part)

(In millions, except per share data)

| | For the Years Ended | | |
	February 28, 2013	February 29, 2012	February 28, 2011
Sales	$ 3,171.4	$ 2,979.1	$ 4,096.7
Less—excise taxes	(375.3)	(324.8)	(764.7)
Net sales	2,796.1	2,654.3	3,332.0
Cost of product sold	(1,687.8)	(1,592.2)	(2,141.9)
Gross profit	1,108.3	1,062.1	1,190.1
Selling, general and administrative expenses	(584.7)	(521.5)	(640.9)
Restructuring charges	(0.7)	(16.0)	(23.1)
Impairment of intangible assets	—	(38.1)	(23.6)
Operating income	522.9	486.5	502.5

NOTES TO CONSOLIDATED FINANCIAL STATEMENTS

1. Summary of Significant Accounting Policies (in part)

Derivative Instruments—

As a multinational company, the Company is exposed to market risk from changes in foreign currency exchange rates, diesel fuel prices and interest rates that could affect the Company's results of operations and financial condition. The amount of volatility realized will vary based upon the effectiveness and level of derivative instruments outstanding during a particular period of time, as well as the currency, fuel pricing and interest rate market movements during that same period.

The Company enters into derivative instruments, primarily interest rate swaps, foreign currency forward and option contracts, and diesel fuel swaps, to manage interest rate, foreign currency and diesel fuel pricing risks, respectively. In accordance with the FASB guidance for derivatives and hedging, the Company recognizes all derivatives as either assets or liabilities on its Consolidated Balance Sheets and measures those instruments at fair value (see Note 4, Note 5). The fair values of the Company's derivative instruments change with fluctuations in interest rates, currency rates and/or fuel prices and are expected to offset changes in the values of the underlying exposures. The Company's derivative instruments are held solely to hedge economic exposures. The Company follows strict policies to manage interest rate, foreign currency and diesel fuel pricing risks, including prohibitions on derivative market-making or other speculative activities.

To qualify for hedge accounting treatment under the FASB guidance for derivatives and hedging, the details of the hedging relationship must be formally documented at inception of the arrangement, including the risk management objective, hedging strategy, hedged item, specific risk that is being hedged, the derivative instrument, how effectiveness is being assessed and how ineffectiveness will be measured. The derivative must be highly effective in offsetting either changes in the fair value or cash flows, as appropriate, of the risk being hedged. Effectiveness is evaluated on a retrospective and prospective basis based on quantitative measures.

Certain of the Company's derivative instruments do not qualify for hedge accounting treatment under the FASB guidance for derivatives and hedging; for others, the Company chooses not to maintain the required documentation to apply hedge accounting treatment. These undesignated instruments are primarily used to economically hedge the Company's exposure to fluctuations in the value of foreign currency denominated receivables and payables; foreign currency investments, primarily consisting of loans to subsidiaries; and cash flows related primarily to repatriation of those loans or investments. Foreign currency contracts, generally less than 12 months in duration, are used to hedge some of these risks. The Company's derivative policy permits the use of undesignated derivatives when the derivative instrument is settled within the fiscal quarter or offsets a recognized balance sheet exposure. In these circumstances, the mark to fair value is reported currently through earnings in selling, general and administrative expenses on the Company's Consolidated Statements of Comprehensive Income. As of February 28, 2013, and February 29, 2012, the Company had undesignated foreign currency contracts outstanding with a notional value of $355.1 million and $148.6 million, respectively. In addition, the Company had offsetting undesignated interest rate swap agreements with an absolute notional amount of $1.0 billion outstanding as of February 28, 2013 (see Note 10). The Company had no undesignated interest rate swap agreements outstanding as of February 29, 2012.

Furthermore, when the Company determines that a derivative instrument which qualified for hedge accounting treatment has ceased to be highly effective as a hedge, the Company discontinues hedge accounting prospectively. The Company also discontinues hedge accounting prospectively when (i) a derivative expires or is sold, terminated, or exercised; (ii) it is no longer probable that the forecasted transaction will occur; or (iii) management determines that designating the derivative as a hedging instrument is no longer appropriate.

Cash flow hedges:

The Company is exposed to foreign denominated cash flow fluctuations in connection with third party and intercompany sales and purchases and, historically, third party financing arrangements. The Company primarily uses foreign currency forward and option contracts to hedge certain of these risks. In addition, the Company utilizes interest rate swaps to manage its exposure to changes in interest rates and diesel fuel swaps to manage its exposure to changes in diesel fuel prices. Derivatives managing the Company's cash flow exposures generally mature within three years or less, with a maximum maturity of five years. Throughout the term of the designated cash flow hedge relationship on at least a quarterly basis, a retrospective evaluation and prospective assessment of hedge effectiveness is performed. All components of the Company's derivative instruments' gains or losses are included in the assessment of hedge effectiveness. In the event the relationship is no longer effective, the Company recognizes the change in the fair value of the hedging derivative instrument from the date the hedging derivative instrument became no longer effective immediately on the Company's Consolidated Statements of Comprehensive Income. In conjunction with its effectiveness testing, the Company also evaluates ineffectiveness associated with the hedge relationship. Resulting ineffectiveness, if any, is recognized immediately on the Company's Consolidated Statements of Comprehensive Income in selling, general and administrative expenses.

The Company records the fair value of its foreign currency contracts, interest rate swap contracts and diesel fuel swap contracts qualifying for cash flow hedge accounting treatment on its Consolidated Balance Sheets with the effective portion of the related gain or loss on those contracts deferred in stockholders' equity (as a component of AOCI). These deferred gains or losses are recognized on the Company's Consolidated Statements of Comprehensive Income in the same period in which the underlying hedged items are recognized and on the same line item as the underlying hedged items. However, to the extent that any derivative instrument is not considered to be highly effective in offsetting the change in the value of the hedged item, the hedging relationship is terminated and the amount related to the ineffective portion of such derivative instrument is immediately recognized on the Company's Consolidated Statements of Comprehensive Income in selling, general and administrative expenses.

As of February 28, 2013, and February 29, 2012, the Company had cash flow designated foreign currency contracts outstanding with a notional value of $220.3 million and $353.7 million, respectively. In addition, as of February 28, 2013, and February 29, 2012, the Company had cash flow designated interest rate swap agreements outstanding with a notional value of $500.0 million (see Note 10). Lastly, as of February 28, 2013, the Company had cash flow designated diesel fuel swap contracts outstanding with a notional value of $17.4 million. The Company had no cash flow designated diesel fuel swap contracts outstanding as of February 29, 2012. The Company expects $4.6 million of net losses, net of income tax effect, to be reclassified from AOCI to earnings within the next 12 months.

Fair value hedges:

Fair value hedges are hedges that offset the risk of changes in the fair values of recorded assets and liabilities, and firm commitments. The Company records changes in fair value of derivative instruments, which are designated and deemed effective as fair value hedges, in earnings offset by the corresponding changes in the fair value of the hedged items. The Company did not designate any derivative instruments as fair value hedges for the years ended February 28, 2013, February 29, 2012, and February 28, 2011.

Net investment hedges:

Net investment hedges are hedges that use derivative instruments or non-derivative instruments to hedge the foreign currency exposure of a net investment in a foreign operation. Historically, the Company has managed currency exposures resulting from certain of its net investments in foreign subsidiaries principally with debt denominated in the related foreign currency. Accordingly, gains and losses on these instruments were recorded as foreign currency translation adjustments in AOCI. The Company did not designate any derivative or non-derivative instruments as net investment hedges for the years ended February 28, 2013, February 29, 2012, and February 28, 2011. As a result of the January 2011 CWAE Divestiture, for the year ended February 28, 2011, the Company reclassified $17.8 million of net gains, net of income tax effect, from AOCI to earnings related to its prior net investment hedges of its U.K. subsidiary (See Note 4). There were no such amounts recognized for the years ended February 28, 2013, and February 29, 2012.

Credit risk:

The Company enters into master agreements with its bank derivative trading counterparties that allow netting of certain derivative positions in order to manage credit risk. The Company's derivative instruments are not subject to credit rating contingencies or collateral requirements. As of February 28, 2013, the fair value of derivative instruments in a net liability position due to counterparties was $45.1 million. If the Company were required to settle the net liability position under these derivative instruments on February 28, 2013, the Company would have had sufficient availability under its revolving credit facility to satisfy this obligation.

Counterparty credit risk:

Counterparty credit risk relates to losses the Company could incur if a counterparty defaults on a derivative contract. The Company manages exposure to counterparty credit risk by requiring specified minimum credit standards and diversification of counterparties. The Company enters into master agreements with its bank derivative trading counterparties that allow netting of certain derivative positions in order to manage counterparty credit risk. As of February 28, 2013, all of the Company's counterparty exposures are with financial institutions which have investment grade ratings. The Company has procedures to monitor counterparty credit risk for both current and future potential credit exposures. As of February 28, 2013, the fair value of derivative instruments in a net receivable position due from counterparties was $9.5 million.

4. Derivative Instruments (in part)

The effect of the Company's derivative instruments designated in cash flow hedging relationships on its Consolidated Statements of Comprehensive Income, as well as its Other Comprehensive Income ("OCI"), net of income tax effect, for the years ended February 28, 2013, February 29, 2012, and February 28, 2011, is as follows. As a result of the CWAE Divestiture, the Company recognized net gains of $6.3 million, net of income tax effect, for the year ended February 28, 2011, related to the discontinuance of cash flow hedge accounting due to the probability that the original forecasted transaction would not occur by the end of the originally specified time period (or within the two months following). There were no such amounts recognized for the years ended February 28, 2013, and February 29, 2012.

Derivative Instruments in Designated Cash Flow Hedging Relationships (In millions)	Net Gain (Loss) Recognized in OCI (Effective portion)	Location of Net Gain (Loss) Reclassified from AOCI to Income (Effective portion)	Net Gain (Loss) Reclassified from AOCI to Income (Effective portion)
For the Year Ended February 28, 2013			
Foreign currency contracts	$ 3.1	Sales	$ 2.4
Foreign currency contracts	—	Cost of product sold	2.0
Diesel fuel swap contracts	0.7	Cost of product sold	0.5
Interest rate swap contracts	(6.3)	Interest expense, net	(8.0)
Total	$ (2.5)	Total	$(3.1)
For the Year Ended February 29, 2012			
Foreign currency contracts	$ 5.8	Sales	$ 6.4
Foreign currency contracts	3.1	Cost of product sold	1.6
Interest rate swap contracts	(27.2)	Interest expense, net	(3.8)
Total	$(18.3)	Total	$ 4.2
For the Year Ended February 28, 2011			
Foreign currency contracts	$11.2	Sales	$13.6
Foreign currency contracts	0.6	Cost of product sold	9.5
Interest rate swap contracts	(2.7)	Interest expense, net	—
Total	$ 9.1	Total	$23.1

Derivative Instruments in Designated Cash Flow Hedging Relationships (In millions)	Location of Net Gain Recognized in Income (Ineffective portion)	Net Gain Recognized in Income (Ineffective portion)
For the Year Ended February 28, 2013		
Foreign currency contracts	Selling, general and administrative expenses	$0.3
For the Year Ended February 29, 2012		
Foreign currency contracts	Selling, general and administrative expenses	$2.2
For the Year Ended February 28, 2011		
Foreign currency contracts	Selling, general and administrative expenses	$1.4

Non-Derivative Instruments in Designated Net Investment Hedging Relationships (In millions)	Net Gain (Loss) Recognized in OCI (Effective portion)	Location of Net Gain Reclassified from AOCI to Income (Effective portion)	Net Gain Reclassified from AOCI to Income (Effective portion)
For the Year Ended February 28, 2011			
Sterling Senior Debt Instrument	$—	Selling, general and administrative expenses	$17.8

The effect of the Company's undesignated derivative instruments on its Consolidated Statements of Comprehensive Income for the years ended February 28, 2013, February 29, 2012, and February 28, 2011, is as follows:

Derivative Instruments not Designated as Hedging Instruments (In millions)	Location of Net (Loss) Gain Recognized in Income	Net (Loss) Gain Recognized in Income
For the Year Ended February 28, 2013		
Foreign currency contracts	Selling, general and administrative expenses	$(3.8)
Interest rate swap contracts	Interest expense, net	(0.5)
		$(4.3)
For the Year Ended February 29, 2012		
Foreign currency contracts	Selling, general and administrative expenses	$(1.9)
For the Year Ended February 28, 2011		
Foreign currency contracts	Selling, general and administrative expenses	$ 4.3

CHANGE IN VALUE OF INVESTMENTS

3.17 BERKSHIRE HATHAWAY INC. (DEC)

CONSOLIDATED STATEMENTS OF EARNINGS (in part)

(Dollars in millions except per-share amounts)

	Year Ended December 31,		
	2013	2012	2011
Revenues:			
Insurance and Other:			
Insurance premiums earned	$ 36,684	$ 34,545	$ 32,075
Sales and service revenues	94,806	83,268	72,803
Interest, dividend and other investment income	4,939	4,534	4,792
Investment gains/losses	3,881	990	1,065
	140,310	123,337	110,735
Railroad, Utilities and Energy:			
Operating revenues	34,649	32,383	30,721
Other	108	199	118
	34,757	32,582	30,839
Finance and Financial Products:			
Interest, dividend and other investment income	1,469	1,572	1,618
Investment gains/losses	184	472	209
Derivative gains/losses	2,608	1,963	(2,104)
Other	2,822	2,537	2,391
	7,083	6,544	2,114
	182,150	162,463	143,688

(1) Significant accounting policies and practices (in part)

(d) Investments

We determine the appropriate classification of investments in fixed maturity and equity securities at the acquisition date and re-evaluate the classification at each balance sheet date. Held-to-maturity investments are carried at amortized cost, reflecting the ability and intent to hold the securities to maturity. Trading investments are securities acquired with the intent to sell in the near term and are carried at fair value. All other securities are classified as available-for-sale and are carried at fair value with net unrealized gains or losses reported as a component of accumulated other comprehensive income. Substantially all of our investments in equity and fixed maturity securities are classified as available-for-sale.

We utilize the equity method to account for investments when we possess the ability to exercise significant influence, but not control, over the operating and financial policies of the investee. The ability to exercise significant influence is presumed when an investor possesses more than 20% of the voting interests of the investee. This presumption may be overcome based on specific facts and circumstances that demonstrate that the ability to exercise significant influence is restricted. We apply the equity method to investments in common stock and to other investments when such other investments possess substantially identical subordinated interests to common stock.

In applying the equity method, we record the investment at cost and subsequently increase or decrease the carrying amount of the investment by our proportionate share of the net earnings or losses and other comprehensive income of the investee. We record dividends or other equity distributions as reductions in the carrying value of the investment. In the event that net losses of the investee reduce the carrying amount to zero, additional net losses may be recorded if other investments in the investee are at-risk, even if we have not committed to provide financial support to the investee. Such additional equity method losses, if any, are based upon the change in our claim on the investee's book value.

Investment gains and losses arise when investments are sold (as determined on a specific identification basis) or are other-than-temporarily impaired. If a decline in the value of an investment below cost is deemed other than temporary, the cost of the investment is written down to fair value, with a corresponding charge to earnings. Factors considered in determining whether an impairment is other than temporary include: the financial condition, business prospects and creditworthiness of the issuer, the relative amount of the decline, our ability and intent to hold the investment until the fair value recovers and the length of time that fair value has been less than cost. With respect to an investment in a fixed maturity security, we recognize an other-than-temporary impairment if we (a) intend to sell or expect to be required to sell the security before its amortized cost is recovered or (b) do not expect to ultimately recover the amortized cost basis even if we do not intend to sell the security. We recognize losses under (a) in earnings and under (b) we recognize the credit loss component in earnings and the difference between fair value and the amortized cost basis net of the credit loss in other comprehensive income.

(7) Investment Gains/Losses

Investment gains/losses, including other-than-temporary impairment ("OTTI") losses, for each of the three years ending December 31, 2013 are summarized below (in millions).

	2013	2012	2011
Fixed maturity securities—			
Gross gains from sales and other disposals	$1,783	$ 188	$ 310
Gross losses from sales and other disposals	(139)	(354)	(10)
Equity securities—			
Gross gains from sales and redemptions	1,253	1,468	1,889
Gross losses from sales and redemptions	(62)	(12)	(36)
OTTI losses	(228)	(337)	(908)
Other	1,458	509	29
	$4,065	$1,462	$1,274

Investment gains from fixed maturity investments in 2013 included a gain of $680 million related to Mars/Wrigley's repurchase of the Wrigley subordinated notes as well as gains from the dispositions and conversions of corporate bonds. Other investment gains/losses in 2013 included $1.4 billion related to the changes in the valuations of the GE and GS warrants. Investment gains from equity securities in 2011 included $1.8 billion with respect to the redemptions of our GS and GE preferred stock investments.

We record investments in equity and fixed maturity securities classified as available-for-sale at fair value and record the difference between fair value and cost in other comprehensive income. OTTI losses recognized in earnings represent reductions in the cost basis of the investment, but not the fair value. Accordingly, such losses that are included in earnings are generally offset by a corresponding credit to other comprehensive income and therefore have no net effect on shareholders' equity as of the balance sheet date.

We recorded OTTI losses on bonds issued by Texas Competitive Electric Holdings ("TCEH") of $228 million in 2013, $337 million in 2012 and $390 million in 2011. In 2011, OTTI losses also included $337 million with respect to 103.6 million shares of our investment in Wells Fargo & Company ("Wells Fargo") common stock. These shares had an aggregate original cost of $3.6 billion. On March 31, 2011, when we recorded the losses, we also held an additional 255.4 million shares of Wells Fargo which were acquired at an aggregate cost of $4.4 billion and which had unrealized gains of $3.7 billion. However, the unrealized gains were not reflected in earnings but were instead recorded directly in shareholders' equity as a component of accumulated other comprehensive income.

GAINS ON EXTINGUISHMENT OF DEBT

3.18 SERVICE CORPORATION INTERNATIONAL (DEC)
CONSOLIDATED STATEMENT OF OPERATIONS (in part)

	Years Ended December 31,		
(In thousands, except per share amounts)	**2013**	**2012**	**2011**
Revenues	$ 2,556,382	$ 2,410,481	$ 2,316,040
Costs and expenses	(2,006,813)	(1,887,268)	(1,839,538)
Gross profits	549,569	523,213	476,502
General and administrative expenses	(155,136)	(121,891)	(101,826)
Losses on divestitures and impairment charges, net	(6,263)	(1,533)	(10,977)
Operating income	388,170	399,789	363,699
Interest expense	(142,360)	(135,068)	(133,782)
Gains (losses) on early extinguishment of debt, net	468	(22,706)	(3,509)
Other (expense) income, net	(559)	3,668	(772)
Income from continuing operations before income taxes	245,719	245,683	225,636
Provision for income taxes	(96,615)	(91,548)	(79,404)
Net income	149,104	154,135	146,232

NOTES TO CONSOLIDATED FINANCIAL STATEMENTS

10. Debt (in part)

Debt Extinguishments and Reductions

In addition to repaying $86.6 million of outstanding cash advances on our previous credit facility during 2013, we paid an aggregate of $31.8 million to repay our remaining $4.8 million 7.875% Debenture due February 2013, to retire $26.4 million in capital lease obligations and to extinguish $0.6 million in other debt. Certain of the above transactions resulted in the recognition of a gain $0.5 million recorded in gains on early extinguishment of debt, net in our Consolidated Statement of Operations. As mentioned above, we have paid down a total of $167.0 million in debt including $107.9 million in principal and premiums associated with our 3.125% Senior Convertible Notes due July 2014 and $59.1 million in principal and premiums associated with our 3.375% Senior Convertible Notes due July 2016. We did not incur any gains or losses as a result of these transactions.

During 2012, we paid an aggregate of $206.6 million, to redeem our 7.375% Senior Notes due October 2014 with a principal amount of $180.7 million and to retire $25.8 million in capital lease obligations. Certain of the above transactions resulted in the recognition of a loss of $22.7 million recorded in *(Losses) gains on early extinguishment of debt, net* in our Consolidated Statement of Operations, which represents the write-off of unamortized deferred loan costs of $1.3 million and $21.4 million in a make-whole provision paid in cash upon retiring our 7.375% Senior Notes due October 2014. This refinancing allowed the Company to replace 7.375% debt due in 2014 with 4.5% debt due in 2020.

Expenses and Losses

PRESENTATION

3.19 Paragraphs 80 and 83 of FASB Concepts Statement No. 6, *Elements of Financial Statements—a replacement of FASB Concepts Statement No. 3 (incorporating an amendment of FASB Concepts Statement No. 2)*, define expenses and losses as follows:

80. Expenses are outflows or other using up of assets or incurrences of liabilities (or a combination of both) from delivering or producing goods, rendering services, or carrying out other activities that constitute the entity's ongoing major or central operations.

83. Losses are decreases in equity (net assets) from peripheral or incidental transactions of an entity and from all other transactions and other events and circumstances affecting the entity except those that result from expenses or distributions to owners.

PRESENTATION AND DISCLOSURE EXCERPTS

SELLING, GENERAL, AND ADMINISTRATIVE

3.20 KOHL'S CORPORATION (JAN)
CONSOLIDATED STATEMENTS OF INCOME (in part)

(In Millions, Except per Share Data)

	2012	2011	2010
Net sales	$19,279	$18,804	$18,391
Cost of merchandise sold (exclusive of depreciation shown separately below)	12,289	11,625	11,359
Gross margin	6,990	7,179	7,032
Operating expenses:			
Selling, general, and administrative	4,267	4,243	4,190
Depreciation and amortization	833	778	750
Operating income	1,890	2,158	2,092

NOTES TO CONSOLIDATED FINANCIAL STATEMENTS

1. Business and Summary of Accounting Policies (in part)

Cost of Merchandise Sold and Selling, General and Administrative Expenses

The following table illustrates the primary costs classified in Cost of Merchandise Sold and Selling, General and Administrative Expenses:

Cost of Merchandise Sold	Selling, General and Administrative Expenses
• Total cost of products sold including product development costs, net of vendor payments other than reimbursement of specific, incremental and identifiable costs • Inventory shrink • Markdowns • Freight expenses associated with moving merchandise from our vendors to our distribution centers • Shipping and handling expenses of E-Commerce sales • Terms cash discount	• Compensation and benefit costs including: —Stores —Corporate headquarters, including buying and merchandising —Distribution centers • Occupancy and operating costs of our retail, distribution and corporate facilities • Net revenues from the Kohl's credit card program • Freight expenses associated with moving merchandise from our distribution centers to our retail stores, and among distribution and retail facilities • Advertising expenses, offset by vendor payments for reimbursement of specific, incremental and identifiable costs • Costs incurred prior to new store openings, such as advertising, hiring and training costs for new employees, processing and transporting initial merchandise, and rent expense • Other administrative revenues and expenses

The classification of these expenses varies across the retail industry.

Vendor Allowances

We receive consideration for a variety of vendor-sponsored programs, such as markdown allowances, volume rebates and promotion and advertising support. The vendor consideration is recorded as earned either as a reduction of inventory costs or Selling, General and Administrative ("SG&A") expenses based on the application of Accounting Standards Codification ("ASC") No. 605, Subtopic 50, "Customer Payments and Incentives." Promotional and advertising allowances are intended to offset our advertising costs to promote vendors' merchandise. Markdown allowances and volume rebates are recorded as a reduction of inventory costs.

RESEARCH AND DEVELOPMENT

3.21 JOHNSON & JOHNSON (DEC)
CONSOLIDATED STATEMENTS OF EARNINGS (in part)

(Dollars and Shares in Millions Except Per Share Amounts) (Note 1)

	2013	2012	2011
Sales to Customers	$71,312	67,224	65,030
Cost of products sold	22,342	21,658	20,360
Gross profit	48,970	45,566	44,670
Selling, marketing and administrative expenses	21,830	20,869	20,969
Research and development expense	8,183	7,665	7,548
In-process research and development	580	1,163	—
Interest income	(74)	(64)	(91)
Interest expense, net of portion capitalized (Note 4)	482	532	571
Other (income) expense, net	2,498	1,626	2,743
Restructuring (Note 22)	—	—	569
Earnings before provision for taxes on income	15,471	13,775	12,361

NOTES TO CONSOLIDATED FINANCIAL STATEMENTS

1. Summary of Significant Accounting Policies (in part)

Research and Development

Research and development expenses are expensed as incurred. Upfront and milestone payments made to third parties in connection with research and development collaborations are expensed as incurred up to the point of regulatory approval. Payments made to third parties subsequent to regulatory approval are capitalized and amortized over the remaining useful life of the related product. Amounts capitalized for such payments are included in other intangibles, net of accumulated amortization.

The Company enters into collaborative arrangements, typically with other pharmaceutical or biotechnology companies, to develop and commercialize drug candidates or intellectual property. These arrangements typically involve two (or more) parties who are active participants in the collaboration and are exposed to significant risks and rewards dependent on the commercial success of the activities. These collaborations usually involve various activities by one or more parties, including research and development, marketing and selling and distribution. Often, these collaborations require upfront, milestone and royalty or profit share payments, contingent upon the occurrence of certain future events linked to the success of the asset in development. Amounts due from collaborative partners related to development activities are generally reflected as a reduction of research and development expense because the performance of contract development services is not central to the Company's operations. In general, the income statement presentation for these collaborations is as follows:

Nature/Type of Collaboration	Statement of Earnings Presentation
Third-party sale of product	Sales to customers
Royalties/milestones paid to collaborative partner (post-regulatory approval)*	Cost of goods sold
Royalties received from collaborative partner	Other income (expense), net
Upfront payments & milestones paid to collaborative partner (pre-regulatory approval)	Research and development expense
Research and development payments to collaborative partner	Research and development expense
Research and development payments received from collaborative partner	Reduction of Research and development expense
* Milestones are capitalized as intangible assets and amortized to cost of goods sold over the useful life.	

For all years presented, there was no individual project that represented greater than 5% of the total annual consolidated research and development expense.

EXPLORATION

3.22 HESS CORPORATION (DEC)
STATEMENT OF CONSOLIDATED INCOME (in part)

(In millions, except per share amounts)	**Years Ended December 31,**		
	2013	**2012**	**2011**
Revenues and Non-Operating Income			
Sales (excluding excise taxes) and other operating revenues	$22,284	$23,381	$21,451
Loss from equity investment in HOVENSA L.L.C.	—	—	(1,073)
Gains on asset sales, net	2,174	584	446
Other, net	(37)	121	32
Total revenues and non-operating income	24,421	24,086	20,856
Costs and Expenses			
Cost of products sold (excluding items shown separately below)	11,368	11,500	10,528
Operating costs and expenses	2,116	2,202	1,876
Production and severance taxes	372	550	476
Marketing expenses	867	802	814
Exploration expenses, including dry holes and lease impairment	1,031	1,070	1,195
General and administrative expenses	709	613	613
Interest expense	406	419	383
Depreciation, depletion and amortization	2,770	2,922	2,373
Asset impairments	289	582	358
Total costs and expenses	19,928	20,660	18,616
Income from continuing operations before income taxes	4,493	3,426	2,240

NOTES TO CONSOLIDATED FINANCIAL STATEMENTS

1. Summary of Significant Accounting Policies (in part)

Exploration and Development Costs: E&P activities are accounted for using the successful efforts method. Costs of acquiring unproved and proved oil and gas leasehold acreage, including lease bonuses, brokers' fees and other related costs, are capitalized. Annual lease rentals, exploration expenses and exploratory dry hole costs are expensed as incurred. Costs of drilling and equipping productive wells, including development dry holes, and related production facilities are capitalized. In production operations, costs of injected CO_2 for tertiary recovery are expensed as incurred.

The costs of exploratory wells that find oil and gas reserves are capitalized pending determination of whether proved reserves have been found. Exploratory drilling costs remain capitalized after drilling is completed if (1) the well has found a sufficient quantity of reserves to justify completion as a producing well and (2) sufficient progress is being made in assessing the reserves and the economic and operational viability of the project. If either of those criteria is not met, or if there is substantial doubt about the economic or operational viability of a project, the capitalized well costs are charged to expense. Indicators of sufficient progress in assessing reserves and the economic and operating viability of a project include commitment of project personnel, active negotiations for sales contracts with customers, negotiations with governments, operators and contractors, firm plans for additional drilling and other factors.

ADVERTISING COSTS

3.23 JACK IN THE BOX INC. (SEP)
CONSOLIDATED STATEMENTS OF EARNINGS (in part)

(In thousands, except per share data)

	Fiscal Year		
	2013	**2012**	**2011**
Revenues:			
Company restaurant sales	$1,143,780	$1,183,483	$1,350,759
Franchise revenues	346,087	325,812	282,066
	1,489,867	1,509,295	1,632,825
Operating Costs and Expenses, Net:			
Company restaurant costs:			
Food and packaging	372,685	389,235	452,033
Payroll and employee benefits	320,384	338,210	400,529
Occupancy and other	255,586	266,440	318,546
Total company restaurant costs	948,655	993,885	1,171,108

(continued)

	Fiscal Year		
	2013	**2012**	**2011**
Franchise costs	173,567	166,078	136,148
Selling, general and administrative expenses	220,641	224,852	222,950
Impairment and other charges, net	13,439	32,809	12,546
Gains on the sale of company-operated restaurants	(4,640)	(29,145)	(61,125)
	1,351,662	1,388,479	1,481,627
Earnings from operations	138,205	120,816	151,198

NOTES TO CONSOLIDATED FINANCIAL STATEMENTS

1. Nature of Operations and Summary of Significant Accounting Policies (in part)

Advertising costs—We administer marketing funds which include contractual contributions. In fiscal years 2013, 2012 and 2011 the marketing funds were approximately 5% and 1% of sales at all franchise and company-operated Jack in the Box and Qdoba restaurants, respectively. We record contributions from franchisees as a liability included in accrued liabilities in the accompanying consolidated balance sheets until such funds are expended. The contributions to the marketing funds are designated for advertising and we act as an agent for the franchisees with regard to these contributions. Therefore, we do not reflect franchisee contributions to the funds in our consolidated statements of earnings or cash flows.

Production costs of commercials, programming and other marketing activities are charged to the marketing funds when the advertising is first used for its intended purpose, and the costs of advertising are charged to operations as incurred. Total contributions and other marketing expenses, are included in selling, general, and administrative expenses in the accompanying consolidated statements of earnings. The following table provides a summary of advertising costs related to company-operated restaurants in each year. Qdoba advertising costs in fiscal years 2012 and 2011 have been reclassified to conform to the fiscal 2013 presentation (*in thousands*):

	2013	**2012**	**2011**
Jack in the Box	$46,739	$49,757	$63,094
Qdoba	16,123	13,135	10,061
Total	$62,862	$62,892	$73,155

TAXES OTHER THAN INCOME TAXES

3.24 EXXON MOBIL CORPORATION (DEC)
CONSOLIDATED STATEMENT OF INCOME (in part)

(Millions of dollars)	Note Reference Number	2013	2012	2011
Revenues and other income				
Sales and other operating revenue[1]		420,836	451,509	467,029
Income from equity affiliates	7	13,927	15,010	15,289
Other income		3,492	14,162	4,111
Total revenues and other income		438,255	480,681	486,429
Costs and other deductions				
Crude oil and product purchases		244,156	263,535	266,534
Production and manufacturing expenses		40,525	38,521	40,268
Selling, general and administrative expenses		12,877	13,877	14,983
Depreciation and depletion		17,182	15,888	15,583
Exploration expenses, including dry holes		1,976	1,840	2,081
Interest expense		9	327	247
Sales-based taxes[1]	19	30,589	32,409	33,503
Other taxes and duties	19	33,230	35,558	39,973
Total costs and other deductions		380,544	401,955	413,172
Income before income taxes		57,711	78,726	73,257

NOTES TO CONSOLIDATED FINANCIAL STATEMENTS

1. Summary of Accounting Policies (in part)

Sales-Based Taxes. The Corporation reports sales, excise and value-added taxes on sales transactions on a gross basis in the Consolidated Statement of Income (included in both revenues and costs).

19. Income, Sales-Based and Other Taxes (in part)

(Millions of dollars)	2013 U.S.	2013 Non-U.S.	2013 Total	2012 U.S.	2012 Non-U.S.	2012 Total	2011 U.S.	2011 Non-U.S.	2011 Total
Income tax expense									
Federal and non-U.S.									
Current	1,073	22,115	23,188	1,791	25,650	27,441	1,547	28,849	30,396
Deferred—net	(116)	757	641	1,097	1,816	2,913	1,577	(1,417)	160
U.S. tax on non-U.S. operations	37	—	37	89	—	89	15	—	15
Total federal and non-U.S.	994	22,872	23,866	2,977	27,466	30,443	3,139	27,432	30,571
State	397	—	397	602	—	602	480	—	480
Total income tax expense	1,391	22,872	24,263	3,579	27,466	31,045	3,619	27,432	31,051
Sales-based taxes	5,992	24,597	30,589	5,785	26,624	32,409	5,652	27,851	33,503
All other taxes and duties									
Other taxes and duties	955	32,275	33,230	1,406	34,152	35,558	1,539	38,434	39,973
Included in production and manufacturing expenses	1,318	1,182	2,500	1,242	1,308	2,550	1,342	1,425	2,767
Included in SG&A expenses	150	516	666	154	595	749	181	623	804
Total other taxes and duties	2,423	33,973	36,396	2,802	36,055	38,857	3,062	40,482	43,544
Total	9,806	81,442	91,248	12,166	90,145	102,311	12,333	95,765	108,098

All other taxes and duties include taxes reported in production and manufacturing and selling, general and administrative (SG&A) expenses. The above provisions for deferred income taxes include net credits of $310 million in 2013 and $330 million in 2011 and a net charge of $244 million in 2012 for the effect of changes in tax laws and rates.

PROVISION FOR LOSSES

3.25 GENERAL ELECTRIC COMPANY (DEC)
STATEMENT OF EARNINGS (in part)

(In millions; per-share amounts in dollars)	General Electric Company and Consolidated Affiliates For the Years Ended December 31 2013	2012	2011
Revenues and other Income			
Sales of goods	$71,873	$72,991	$66,874
Sales of services	28,669	27,158	27,648
Other income (Note 17)	3,108	2,563	5,063
GECC earnings from continuing operations	—	—	—
GECC revenues from services (Note 18)	42,395	43,972	46,957
Total revenues and other income	146,045	146,684	146,542
Costs and Expenses (Note 19)			
Cost of goods sold	57,867	56,785	51,455
Cost of services sold	19,274	17,525	16,823
Interest and other financial charges	10,116	12,407	14,422
Investment contracts, insurance losses and insurance annuity benefits	2,676	2,857	2,912
Provision for losses on financing receivables (Note 6)	4,818	3,832	3,930
Other costs and expenses	35,143	35,897	36,841
Total costs and expenses	129,894	129,303	126,383
Earnings from continuing operations before income taxes	16,151	17,381	20,159

NOTES TO CONSOLIDATED FINANCIAL STATEMENTS

Note 1. Basis of Presentation and Summary of Significant Accounting Policies (in part)

Losses on Financing Receivables

Losses on financing receivables are recognized when they are incurred, which requires us to make our best estimate of probable losses inherent in the portfolio. The method for calculating the best estimate of losses depends on the size, type and risk characteristics of the related financing receivable. Such an estimate requires consideration of historical loss experience, adjusted for current conditions, and judgments about the probable effects of relevant observable data, including present economic conditions such as delinquency rates, financial health of specific customers and market sectors, collateral values (including housing price indices as applicable), and the present and expected future levels of interest rates. The underlying assumptions, estimates and assessments we use to provide for losses are updated periodically to reflect our view of current conditions and are subject to the regulatory examination process, which can result in changes to our assumptions. Changes in such estimates can significantly affect the allowance and provision for losses. It is possible that we will experience credit losses that are different from our current estimates. Write-offs are deducted from the allowance for losses when we judge the principal to be uncollectible and subsequent recoveries are added to the allowance at the time cash is received on a written-off account.

"Impaired" loans are defined as larger-balance or restructured loans for which it is probable that the lender will be unable to collect all amounts due according to the original contractual terms of the loan agreement.

"Troubled debt restructurings" (TDRs) are those loans for which we have granted a concession to a borrower experiencing financial difficulties where we do not receive adequate compensation. Such loans are classified as impaired, and are individually reviewed for specific reserves.

"Nonaccrual financing receivables" are those on which we have stopped accruing interest. We stop accruing interest at the earlier of the time at which collection of an account becomes doubtful or the account becomes 90 days past due, with the exception of consumer credit card accounts, for which we continue to accrue interest until the accounts are written off in the period that the account becomes 180 days past due. Although we stop accruing interest in advance of payments, we recognize interest income as cash is collected when appropriate provided the amount does not exceed that which would have been earned at the historical effective interest rate. Recently restructured financing receivables are not considered delinquent when payments are brought current according to the restructured terms, but may remain classified as nonaccrual until there has been a period of satisfactory payment performance by the borrower and future payments are reasonably assured of collection.

"Nonearning financing receivables" are a subset of nonaccrual financing receivables for which cash payments are not being received or for which we are on the cost recovery method of accounting (i.e., any payments are accounted for as a reduction of principal). This category excludes loans purchased at a discount (unless they have deteriorated post acquisition). These loans are initially recorded at fair value and accrete interest income over the estimated life of the loan based on reasonably estimable cash flows even if the underlying loans are contractually delinquent at acquisition.

Beginning in the fourth quarter of 2013, we revised our methods for classifying financing receivables as nonaccrual and nonearning to more closely align with regulatory guidance. Under the revised methods, we continue to accrue interest on consumer credit cards until the accounts are written off in the period the account becomes 180 days past due. Previously, we stopped accruing interest on consumer credit cards when the account became 90 days past due. In addition, the revised methods limit the use of the cash basis of accounting for nonaccrual financing receivables.

As a result of these revisions, consumer credit card receivables of $1,051 million that were previously classified as both nonaccrual and nonearning were returned to accrual status in the fourth quarter of 2013. In addition, $1,524 million of Real Estate and CLL financing receivables previously classified as nonaccrual, paying in accordance with contractual terms and accounted for on the cash basis, were returned to accrual status, while $2,174 million of financing receivables previously classified as nonaccrual and accounted for on the cash basis (primarily in Real Estate and CLL) were placed into the nonearning category based on our assessment of the short-term outlook for resolution through payoff or refinance.

Given that the revised methods result in nonaccrual and nonearning amounts that are substantially the same, we plan to discontinue the reporting of nonearning financing receivables, one of our internal performance metrics, and report selected ratios related to nonaccrual financing receivables, in the first quarter of 2014.

"Delinquent" receivables are those that are 30 days or more past due based on their contractual terms.

The same financing receivable may meet more than one of the definitions above. Accordingly, these categories are not mutually exclusive and it is possible for a particular loan to meet the definitions of a TDR, impaired loan, nonaccrual loan and nonearning loan and be included in each of these categories. The categorization of a particular loan also may not be indicative of the potential for loss.

Our consumer loan portfolio consists of smaller-balance, homogeneous loans, including credit card receivables, installment loans, auto loans and leases and residential mortgages. We collectively evaluate each portfolio for impairment quarterly. The allowance for losses on these receivables is established through a process that estimates the probable losses inherent in the portfolio based upon statistical analyses of portfolio data. These analyses include migration analysis, in which historical delinquency and credit loss experience is applied to the current aging of the portfolio, together with other analyses that reflect current trends and conditions. We also consider our historical loss experience to date based on actual defaulted loans and overall portfolio indicators including nonearning loans, trends in loan volume and lending terms, credit policies and other observable environmental factors such as unemployment rates and home price indices.

Our commercial loan and lease portfolio consists of a variety of loans and leases, including both larger-balance, non-homogeneous loans and leases and smaller-balance homogeneous loans and leases. Losses on such loans and leases are recorded when probable and estimable. We routinely evaluate our entire portfolio for potential specific credit or collection issues that might indicate an impairment.

For larger-balance, non-homogeneous loans and leases, we consider the financial status, payment history, collateral value, industry conditions and guarantor support related to specific customers. Any delinquencies or bankruptcies are indications of potential impairment requiring further assessment of collectibility. We routinely receive financial as well as rating agency reports on our customers, and we elevate for further attention those customers whose operations we judge to be marginal or deteriorating. We also elevate customers for further attention when we observe a decline in collateral values for asset-based loans. While collateral values are not always available, when we observe such a decline, we evaluate relevant markets to assess recovery alternatives—for example, for real estate loans, relevant markets are local; for commercial aircraft loans, relevant markets are global.

Measurement of the loss on our impaired commercial loans is based on the present value of expected future cash flows discounted at the loan's effective interest rate or the fair value of collateral, net of expected selling costs, if the loan is determined to be collateral dependent. We determine whether a loan is collateral dependent if the repayment of the loan is expected to be provided solely by the underlying collateral. Our review process can often result in reserves being established in advance of a modification of terms or designation as a TDR. After providing for specific incurred losses, we then determine an allowance for losses that have been incurred in the balance of the portfolio but cannot yet be identified to a specific loan or lease. This estimate is based upon various statistical analyses considering historical and projected default rates and loss severity and aging, as well as our view on current market and economic conditions. It is prepared by each respective line of business. For Real Estate, this includes assessing the probability of default and the loss given default based on loss history of our portfolio for loans with similar loan metrics and attributes.

We consider multiple factors in evaluating the adequacy of our allowance for losses on Real Estate financing receivables, including loan-to-value ratios, collateral values at the individual loan level, debt service coverage ratios, delinquency status, and economic factors including interest rate and real estate market forecasts. In addition to these factors, we evaluate a Real Estate loan for impairment classification if its projected loan-to-value ratio at maturity is in excess of 100%, even if the loan is currently paying in accordance with its contractual terms. Substantially all of the loans in the Real Estate portfolio are considered collateral dependent and are measured for impairment based on the fair value of collateral. If foreclosure is deemed probable or if repayment is dependent solely on the sale of collateral, we also include estimated selling costs in our reserve. Collateral values for our Real Estate loans are determined based upon internal cash flow estimates discounted at an appropriate rate and corroborated by external appraisals, as appropriate. Collateral valuations are routinely monitored and updated annually, or more frequently for changes in collateral, market and economic conditions. Further discussion on determination of fair value is in the Fair Value Measurements section below.

Experience is not available for new products; therefore, while we are developing that experience, we set loss allowances based on our experience with the most closely analogous products in our portfolio.

Our loss mitigation strategy intends to minimize economic loss and, at times, can result in rate reductions, principal forgiveness, extensions, forbearance or other actions, which may cause the related loan to be classified as a TDR.

We utilize certain loan modification programs for borrowers experiencing temporary financial difficulties in our Consumer loan portfolio. These loan modification programs are primarily concentrated in our non-U.S. residential mortgage and non-U.S. installment and revolving portfolios and include short-term (three months or less) interest rate reductions and payment deferrals, which were not part of the terms of the original contract. We sold our U.S. residential mortgage business in 2007 and, as such, do not participate in the U.S. government-sponsored mortgage modification programs.

Our allowance for losses on financing receivables on these modified consumer loans is determined based upon a formulaic approach that estimates the probable losses inherent in the portfolio based upon statistical analyses of the portfolio. Data related to redefault experience is also considered in our overall reserve adequacy review. Once the loan has been modified, it returns to current status (re-aged) only after receipt of at least three consecutive minimum monthly payments or the equivalent cumulative amount, subject to a re-aging limitation of once a year, or twice in a five-year period in accordance with the Federal Financial Institutions Examination Council guidelines on Uniform Retail Credit Classification and Account Management policy issued in June 2000. We believe that the allowance for losses would not be materially different had we not re-aged these accounts.

For commercial loans, we evaluate changes in terms and conditions to determine whether those changes meet the criteria for classification as a TDR on a loan-by-loan basis. In Commercial Lending and Leasing (CLL), these changes primarily include: changes to covenants, short-term payment deferrals and maturity extensions. For these changes, we receive economic consideration, including additional fees and/or increased interest rates, and evaluate them under our normal underwriting standards and criteria. Changes to Real Estate's loans primarily include maturity extensions, principal payment acceleration, changes to collateral terms, and cash sweeps, which are in addition to, or sometimes in lieu of, fees and rate increases. The determination of whether these changes to the terms and conditions of our commercial loans meet the TDR criteria includes our consideration of all of the relevant facts and circumstances. When the borrower is experiencing financial difficulty, we carefully evaluate these changes to determine whether they meet the form of a concession. In these circumstances, if the change is deemed to be a concession, we classify the loan as a TDR.

When we repossess collateral in satisfaction of a loan, we write down the receivable against the allowance for losses. Repossessed collateral is included in the caption "All other assets" in the Statement of Financial Position and carried at the lower of cost or estimated fair value less costs to sell.

For Consumer loans, we write off unsecured closed-end installment loans when they are 120 days contractually past due and unsecured open-ended revolving loans at 180 days contractually past due. We write down consumer loans secured by collateral other than residential real estate when such loans are 120 days past due. Consumer loans secured by residential real estate (both revolving and closed-end loans) are written down to the fair value of collateral, less costs to sell, no later than when they become 180 days past due. Unsecured consumer loans in bankruptcy are written off within 60 days of notification of filing by the bankruptcy court or within contractual write-off periods, whichever occurs earlier.

Write-offs on larger-balance impaired commercial loans are based on amounts deemed uncollectible and are reviewed quarterly. Write-offs are determined based on the consideration of many factors, such as expectations of the workout plan or restructuring of the loan, valuation of the collateral and the prioritization of our claim in bankruptcy. Write-offs are recognized against the allowance for losses at the earlier of transaction confirmation (for example, discounted pay-off, restructuring, foreclosure, etc.) or not later than 360 days after initial recognition of a specific reserve for a collateral dependent loan. If foreclosure is probable, the write-off is determined based on the fair value of the collateral less costs to sell. Smaller-balance, homogeneous commercial loans are written off at the earlier of when deemed uncollectible or at 180 days past due.

Note 6. GECC Financing Receivables, Allowance for Losses on Financing Receivables and Supplemental Information on Credit Quality (in part)

	December 31	
(In millions)	2013	2012
Loans, net of deferred income[a]	$231,268	$240,634
Investment in financing leases, net of deferred income	26,939	32,471
	258,207	273,105
Less allowance for losses	(5,178)	(4,944)
Financing receivables—net[b]	$253,029	$268,161

[a] Deferred income was $2,013 million and $2,184 million at December 31, 2013 and 2012, respectively.

[b] Financing receivables at December 31, 2013 and 2012 included $544 million and $750 million, respectively, relating to loans that had been acquired in a transfer but have been subject to credit deterioration since origination.

GECC financing receivables include both loans and financing leases. Loans represent transactions in a variety of forms, including revolving charge and credit, mortgages, installment loans, intermediate-term loans and revolving loans secured by business assets. The portfolio includes loans carried at the principal amount on which finance charges are billed periodically, and loans carried at gross book value, which includes finance charges.

Investment in financing leases consists of direct financing and leveraged leases of aircraft, railroad rolling stock, autos, other transportation equipment, data processing equipment, medical equipment, commercial real estate and other manufacturing, power generation, and commercial equipment and facilities.

For federal income tax purposes, the leveraged leases and the majority of the direct financing leases are leases in which GECC depreciates the leased assets and is taxed upon the accrual of rental income. Certain direct financing leases are loans for federal income tax purposes. For these transactions, GECC is taxed only on the portion of each payment that constitutes interest, unless the interest is tax-exempt (e.g., certain obligations of state governments).

Investment in direct financing and leveraged leases represents net unpaid rentals and estimated unguaranteed residual values of leased equipment, less related deferred income. GECC has no general obligation for principal and interest on notes and other instruments representing third-party participation related to leveraged leases; such notes and other instruments have not been included in liabilities but have been offset against the related rentals receivable. The GECC share of rentals receivable on leveraged leases is subordinate to the share of other participants who also have security interests in the leased equipment. For federal income tax purposes, GECC is entitled to deduct the interest expense accruing on non-recourse financing related to leveraged leases.

Net Investment in Financing Leases

(In millions)	Total Financing Leases 2013	Total Financing Leases 2012	Direct Financing Leases[a] 2013	Direct Financing Leases[a] 2012	Leveraged Leases[b] 2013	Leveraged Leases[b] 2012
			December 31			
Total minimum lease payments receivable	$29,970	$36,451	$24,571	$29,416	$5,399	$7,035
Less principal and interest on third-party non-recourse debt	(3,480)	(4,662)	—	—	(3,480)	(4,662)
Net rentals receivables	26,490	31,789	24,571	29,416	1,919	2,373
Estimated unguaranteed residual value of leased assets	5,073	6,346	3,067	4,272	2,006	2,074
Less deferred income	(4,624)	(5,664)	(3,560)	(4,453)	(1,064)	(1,211)
Investment in financing leases, net of deferred income	26,939	32,471	24,078	29,235	2,861	3,236
Less amounts to arrive at net investment						
Allowance for losses	(202)	(198)	(192)	(193)	(10)	(5)
Deferred taxes	(4,075)	(4,506)	(1,783)	(2,245)	(2,292)	(2,261)
Net investment in financing leases	$22,662	$27,767	$22,103	$26,797	$559	$970

[a] Included $317 million and $330 million of initial direct costs on direct financing leases at December 31, 2013 and 2012, respectively.

[b] Included pre-tax income of $31 million and $81 million and income tax of $11 million and $32 million during 2013 and 2012, respectively. Net investment credits recognized on leveraged leases during 2013 and 2012 were insignificant.

Contractual Maturities

(In millions)	Total Loans	Net rentals Receivable
Due in		
2014	$ 54,971	$ 8,184
2015	19,270	6,114
2016	19,619	4,209
2017	17,281	2,733
2018	14,714	1,798
2019 and later	43,121	3,452
	168,976	26,490
Consumer revolving loans	62,292	—
Total	$231,268	$26,490

We expect actual maturities to differ from contractual maturities.

The following tables provide additional information about our financing receivables and related activity in the allowance for losses for our Commercial, Real Estate and Consumer portfolios.

(In millions)	2013	2012
	December 31	
Commercial		
CLL		
Americas	$ 68,585	$ 72,517
Europe[a]	37,962	37,037
Asia	9,469	11,401
Other[a]	451	603
Total CLL	116,467	121,558
Energy Financial Services	3,107	4,851
GE Capital Aviation Services (GECAS)	9,377	10,915
Other	318	486
Total Commercial	129,269	137,810
Real Estate	19,899	20,946
Consumer		
Non-U.S. residential mortgages	30,501	33,350
Non-U.S. installment and revolving credit	13,677	17,816
U.S. installment and revolving credit	55,854	50,853
Non-U.S. auto	2,054	4,260
Other	6,953	8,070
Total Consumer	109,039	114,349
Total financing receivables	258,207	273,105
Less allowance for losses	(5,178)	(4,944)
Total financing receivables—net	$253,029	$268,161

[a] During 2013, we transferred our European equipment services portfolio from CLL Other to CLL Europe. Prior-period amounts were reclassified to conform to the current period presentation.

Allowance for Losses on Financing Receivables

(In millions)	Balance at January 1, 2013	Provision Charged to Operations	Other[a]	Gross Write-Offs[b]	Recoveries[b]	Balance at December 31, 2013
Commercial						
CLL						
Americas	$ 490	$ 292	$ (1)	$ (422)	$ 114	$ 473
Europe	445	321	12	(441)	78	415
Asia	80	124	(11)	(115)	12	90
Other	6	(3)	—	(3)	—	—
Total CLL	1,021	734	—	(981)	204	978
Energy Financial Services	9	(1)	—	—	—	8
GECAS	8	9	—	—	—	17
Other	3	(1)	—	(2)	2	2
Total Commercial	1,041	741	—	(983)	206	1,005
Real Estate	320	28	(4)	(163)	11	192
Consumer						
Non-U.S. residential mortgages	480	269	10	(458)	57	358
Non-U.S. installment and revolving credit	582	589	(93)	(967)	483	594
U.S. installment and revolving credit	2,282	3,006	(51)	(2,954)	540	2,823
Non-U.S. auto	67	58	(13)	(126)	70	56
Other	172	127	11	(236)	76	150
Total Consumer	3,583	4,049	(136)	(4,741)	1,226	3,981
Total	$4,944	$4,818	$(140)	$(5,887)	$1,443	$5,178

[a] Other primarily included dispositions and the effects of currency exchange.

[b] Net write-offs (gross write-offs less recoveries) in certain portfolios may exceed the beginning allowance for losses as a result of losses that are incurred subsequent to the beginning of the fiscal year due to information becoming available during the current year, which may identify further deterioration on existing financing receivables.

(In millions)	Balance at January 1, 2012	Provision Charged to Operations	Other[a]	Gross Write-Offs[b]	Recoveries[b]	Balance at December 31, 2012
Commercial						
CLL						
Americas	$ 889	$ 109	$ (51)	$ (568)	$ 111	$ 490
Europe	400	374	(3)	(390)	64	445
Asia	157	37	(3)	(134)	23	80
Other	4	13	(1)	(10)	—	6
Total CLL	1,450	533	(58)	(1,102)	198	1,021
Energy Financial Services	26	4	—	(24)	3	9
GECAS	17	4	—	(13)	—	8
Other	37	1	(20)	(17)	2	3
Total Commercial	1,530	542	(78)	(1,156)	203	1,041
Real Estate	1,089	72	(44)	(810)	13	320
Consumer						
Non-U.S. residential mortgages	545	112	8	(261)	76	480
Non-U.S. installment and revolving credit	690	290	24	(974)	552	582
U.S. installment and revolving credit	2,008	2,666	(24)	(2,906)	538	2,282
Non-U.S. auto	101	18	(4)	(146)	98	67
Other	199	132	18	(257)	80	172
Total Consumer	3,543	3,218	22	(4,544)	1,344	3,583
Total	$6,162	$3,832	$(100)	$(6,510)	$1,560	$4,944

[a] Other primarily included transfers to held-for-sale and the effects of currency exchange.

[b] Net write-offs (gross write-offs less recoveries) in certain portfolios may exceed the beginning allowance for losses as a result of losses that are incurred subsequent to the beginning of the fiscal year due to information becoming available during the current year, which may identify further deterioration on existing financing receivables.

(In millions)	Balance at January 1, 2011	Provision Charged to Operations[a]	Other[b]	Gross Write-Offs[c]	Recoveries[c]	Balance at December 31, 2011
Commercial						
CLL						
Americas	$1,288	$ 281	$ (96)	$ (700)	$ 116	$ 889
Europe	429	195	(5)	(286)	67	400
Asia	222	105	13	(214)	31	157
Other	6	3	(3)	(2)	—	4
Total CLL	1,945	584	(91)	(1,202)	214	1,450
Energy Financial Services	22	—	(1)	(4)	9	26
GECAS	20	—	—	(3)	—	17
Other	58	23	—	(47)	3	37
Total Commercial	2,045	607	(92)	(1,256)	226	1,530
Real Estate	1,488	324	2	(747)	22	1,089
Consumer						
Non-U.S. residential mortgages	688	116	(13)	(295)	49	545
Non-U.S. installment and revolving credit	898	470	(29)	(1,198)	549	690
U.S. installment and revolving credit	2,333	2,241	1	(3,095)	528	2,008
Non-U.S. auto	168	30	(4)	(216)	123	101
Other	259	142	(20)	(272)	90	199
Total Consumer	4,346	2,999	(65)	(5,076)	1,339	3,543
Total	$7,879	$3,930	$(155)	$(7,079)	$1,587	$6,162

[a] Included a provision of $77 million at Consumer related to the July 1, 2011 adoption of ASU 2011–02.

[b] Other primarily included transfers to held-for-sale and the effects of currency exchange.

[c] Net write-offs (gross write-offs less recoveries) in certain portfolios may exceed the beginning allowance for losses as a result of losses that are incurred subsequent to the beginning of the fiscal year due to information becoming available during the current year, which may identify further deterioration on existing financing receivables.

Credit Quality Indicators

We provide further detailed information about the credit quality of our Commercial, Real Estate and Consumer financing receivables portfolios. For each portfolio, we describe the characteristics of the financing receivables and provide information about collateral, payment performance, credit quality indicators, and impairment. We manage these portfolios using delinquency and nonearning data as key performance indicators. The categories used within this section such as impaired loans, TDR and nonaccrual financing receivables are defined by the authoritative guidance and we base our categorization on the related scope and definitions contained in the related standards. The categories of nonearning and delinquent are defined by us and are used in our process for managing our financing receivables. Definitions of these categories are provided in Note 1.

Past Due Financing Receivables

The following tables display payment performance of Commercial, Real Estate, and Consumer financing receivables.

	December 31			
	2013		2012	
	Over 30 Days Past Due	Over 90 Days Past Due[a]	Over 30 Days Past Due	Over 90 Days Past Due
Commercial				
CLL				
Americas	1.1%	0.5%	1.1%	0.5 %
Europe	3.8	2.1	3.7	2.1
Asia	0.5	0.3	0.9	0.6
Other	—	—	0.1	—
Total CLL	1.9	1.0	1.9	1.0
Energy Financial Services	—	—	—	—
GECAS	—	—	—	—
Other	0.1	0.1	2.8	2.8
Total Commercial	1.7	0.9	1.7	0.9
Real Estate	1.2	1.1	2.3	2.2

U.S. GAAP Financial Statements—Best Practices in Presentation and Disclosure | 3. Income Statement | 3.25 | **373**

	December 31			
	2013		2012	
	Over 30 Days Past Due	Over 90 Days Past Due[a]	Over 30 Days Past Due	Over 90 Days Past Due
Consumer				
Non-U.S. residential mortgages[b]	11.2	6.9	12.0	7.5
Non-U.S. installment and revolving credit	3.7	1.1	3.8	1.1
U.S. installment and revolving credit	4.4	2.0	4.6	2.0
Non-U.S. auto	4.4	0.7	3.1	0.5
Other	2.5	1.4	2.8	1.7
Total Consumer	6.1	3.2	6.5	3.4
Total	3.5%	1.9%	3.7%	2.1%

[a] Included $1,197 million of Consumer loans at December 31, 2013, which are over 90 days past due and continue to accrue interest until the accounts are written off in the period that the account becomes 180 days past due.

[b] Consumer loans secured by residential real estate (both revolving and closed-end loans) are written down to the fair value of collateral, less costs to sell, no later than when they become 180 days past due.

Nonaccrual Financing Receivables

	December 31			
	Nonaccrual Financing receivables[a]		Nonearning Financing receivables[a]	
(Dollars in millions)	2013	2012	2013	2012
Commercial				
CLL				
Americas	$ 1,275	$ 1,951	$1,243	$1,333
Europe	1,046	1,740	1,046	1,299
Asia	413	395	413	193
Other	—	52	—	52
Total CLL	2,734	4,138	2,702	2,877
Energy Financial Services	4	—	4	—
GECAS	—	3	—	—
Other	6	25	6	13
Total Commercial	2,744[b]	4,166[b]	2,712	2,890
Real Estate	2,551[c]	4,885[c]	2,301	444
Consumer				
Non-U.S. residential mortgages	2,161	2,598	1,766	2,567
Non-U.S. installment and revolving credit	88	213	88	213
U.S. installment and revolving credit	2	1,026	2	1,026
Non-U.S. auto	18	24	18	24
Other	351	427	345	351
Total Consumer	2,620[d]	4,288[d]	2,219	4,181
Total	$ 7,915	$13,339	$7,232	$7,515
Allowance for Losses Percentage				
Commercial	36.6%	25.0%	37.1%	36.0%
Real Estate	7.5	6.6	8.3	72.1
Consumer	151.9	83.6	179.4	85.7
Total	65.4%	37.1%	71.6%	65.8%

[a] During the fourth quarter of 2013, we revised our methods for classifying financing receivables as nonaccrual and nonearning to more closely align with regulatory guidance. Given that the revised methods result in nonaccrual and nonearning amounts that are substantially the same, we plan to discontinue the reporting of nonearning financing receivables in the first quarter of 2014. Further information on our nonaccrual and nonearning financing receivables is provided in Note 1 to the consolidated financial statements.

[b] Included $1,397 million and $2,647 million at December 31, 2013 and 2012, respectively, that are currently paying in accordance with their contractual terms.

[c] Included $2,308 million and $4,461 million at December 31, 2013 and 2012, respectively, that are currently paying in accordance with their contractual terms.

[d] Included $527 million and $734 million at December 31, 2013 and 2012, respectively, that are currently paying in accordance with their contractual terms.

WARRANTY

3.26 KB HOME (NOV)
NOTES TO CONSOLIDATED FINANCIAL STATEMENTS

Note 1. Summary of Significant Accounting Policies (in part)

Warranty Costs. We provide a limited warranty on all of our homes. We estimate the costs that may be incurred under each limited warranty and record a liability in the amount of such costs at the time the revenue associated with the sale of each home is recognized. Our primary assumption in estimating the amounts we accrue for warranty costs is that historical claims experience is a strong indicator of future claims experience. Factors that affect our warranty liability include the number of homes delivered, historical and anticipated rates of warranty claims, and cost per claim. We periodically assess the adequacy of our accrued warranty liability and adjust the amount as necessary based on our assessment.

Note 15. Commitments and Contingencies (in part)

Warranty. We provide a limited warranty on all of our homes. The specific terms and conditions of our limited warranty program vary depending upon the markets in which we do business. We generally provide a structural warranty of 10 years, a warranty on electrical, heating, cooling, plumbing and certain other building systems each varying from two to five years based on geographic market and state law, and a warranty of one year for other components of the home. Our limited warranty program is ordinarily how we respond to and account for homeowners' requests to local division offices seeking repairs, including claims where we could have liability under applicable state statutes or tort law for a defective condition in or damages to a home.

We estimate the costs that may be incurred under each limited warranty and record a liability in the amount of such costs at the time the revenue associated with the sale of each home is recognized. Our primary assumption in estimating the amounts we accrue for warranty costs is that historical claims experience is a strong indicator of future claims experience. Factors that affect our warranty liability include the number of homes delivered, historical and anticipated rates of warranty claims, and cost per claim. We periodically assess the adequacy of our accrued warranty liability, which is included in accrued expenses and other liabilities in our consolidated balance sheets, and adjust the amount as necessary based on our assessment. Our assessment includes the review of our actual warranty costs incurred to identify trends and changes in our warranty claims experience, and considers our home construction quality and customer service initiatives and outside events. While we believe the warranty liability currently reflected in our consolidated balance sheets to be adequate, unanticipated changes or developments in the legal environment, local weather, land or environmental conditions, quality of materials or methods used in the construction of homes or customer service practices and the results of our investigation of and the repair efforts related to homes in central and southwest Florida affected by water intrusion-related issues could have a significant impact on our actual warranty costs in the future and such amounts could differ from our current estimates.

The changes in our warranty liability are as follows (in thousands):

	Years Ended November 30,		
	2013	**2012**	**2011**
Balance at beginning of year	$47,822	$67,693	$93,988
Warranties issued[a]	14,261	8,416	4,852
Payments	(45,338)	(19,701)	(25,024)
Adjustments[b]	31,959	(8,586)	(6,123)
Balance at end of year	$48,704	$47,822	$67,693

[a] The year-over-year increase in the expense associated with warranties issued in 2013 and 2012 reflected higher housing revenues in each of those years. Additionally, in 2013, we increased the warranty accrual rate per home based on our historical claims experience.

[b] Adjustments in 2013 were comprised of charges associated with water intrusion-related issues in central and southwest Florida, while in 2012, favorable warranty adjustments were partly offset by such water intrusion-related charges. In 2011, favorable warranty adjustments were partly offset by the impact of our consolidation of a previously unconsolidated joint venture.

Central and Southwest Florida Claims. During 2012, we received warranty claims from homeowners in certain of our communities in central and southwest Florida that primarily involved framing, stucco, roofing and/or sealant matters on homes we delivered between 2003 and 2009, many of which have resulted in water intrusion-related issues. While we initially believed these issues were isolated, after additional investigation we determined in the fourth quarter of 2012 that more homes and communities may have been affected. Throughout 2013, we continued our investigation in an effort to identify the scope of the issues, to fully understand the causes and to address them as quickly and completely as possible, and we encountered an evolving and at times unexpected range of varied and complex conditions and repairs. As a result, during 2013, the number of identified affected homes and our estimate of the total repair costs associated with those homes were revised upward. In addition, prior to the second quarter of 2013 we were unable to estimate the number of similarly affected homes likely to be identified in the future and the repair costs associated with those homes. As our assessment process and our continued efforts to identify, examine and repair affected homes progressed during the second, third and fourth quarters of 2013, we believed we had accumulated adequate experience with these water intrusion-related issues to be able to reasonably estimate as of the end of each respective period the number of similarly affected homes that we believed were likely to be identified in the future and the probable repair costs associated with such similarly affected homes, in addition to revising the number of identified affected homes and our estimate of the repair costs associated with such identified affected homes. Based on the status of our ongoing investigation and repair efforts, our overall warranty liability at November 30, 2013 included $28.9 million for estimated remaining repair costs associated with homes in central and southwest Florida that have been identified as having water intrusion-related issues and estimated repair costs associated with similarly affected homes in central and southwest Florida that we believe are likely to be identified in the future. As of November 30, 2013, this amount encompasses what we believe is the probable overall cost of the repair effort remaining before insurance and other recoveries.

However, our actual costs to fully resolve repairs on affected homes could differ from the overall costs we have estimated, and the difference could be material to our consolidated financial statements.

As of November 30, 2013, we had identified a total of 1,464 affected homes requiring more than minor repairs and resolved repairs on 754 of them. During 2013, we paid $32.7 million to repair such homes. As of November 30, 2013, we had paid $36.7 million of the total estimated repair costs of $65.6 million associated with the affected homes that have been identified and similarly affected homes that we believe are likely to be identified in the future. Approximately half of the total estimated repair costs as of November 30, 2013 related to two attached-home communities. We consider warranty-related repairs for homes to be resolved when all repairs are complete and all repair costs are fully paid. We anticipate resolving repairs on homes affected by the water intrusion-related issues by the end of 2014.

As discussed below, largely due to the scope and nature of the water intrusion-related issues that we encountered, we recorded charges, net of estimated probable recoveries, during 2013 to increase our overall warranty liability for all of our previously delivered homes that are covered under our limited warranty program, including any such homes in central and southwest Florida that have been identified as having water intrusion-related issues and similarly affected homes in central and southwest Florida that we believe are likely to be identified in the future. In addition to reflecting the remaining estimated repair costs associated with homes in central and southwest Florida that have been identified as having water intrusion-related issues, the charges recorded in 2013 included estimated repair costs associated with similarly affected homes in central and southwest Florida that we believe are likely to be identified in the future. Our investigation and repair efforts in central and southwest Florida remain ongoing. While we have been able to make a determination of the probable overall cost of the repair effort, depending on the number of additional affected homes that are identified and the actual costs we incur in future periods to repair identified affected homes, we may revise the estimated amount of our liability with respect to this matter, which could result in an increase or decrease in our overall warranty liability.

As of November 30, 2013, based on our investigation into the central and southwest Florida water intrusion-related issues, we believe it is probable that we will recover a portion of our total estimated repair costs associated with affected homes from various sources, including subcontractors involved with the original construction of the homes and their insurers, and our direct insurers. Our investigation into the water intrusion-related issues, including the process of determining potentially responsible parties and our efforts to obtain recoveries, is ongoing, and as a result, our estimate of probable recoveries may change as additional information is obtained.

Allegedly Defective Drywall Material Claims. During the years ended November 30, 2013, 2012 and 2011, we paid $.5 million, $2.9 million and $13.7 million, respectively, to repair homes identified as affected or potentially affected by allegedly defective drywall manufactured in China. These homes are located in Florida and were primarily delivered in 2006 and 2007. The drywall used in the construction of our homes is purchased and installed by subcontractors. Our subcontractors obtained drywall material from multiple domestic and foreign sources through late 2008. In late 2008, we directed our subcontractors to obtain only domestically sourced drywall. Based on the significantly reduced warranty claim rate on the issue (only a nominal number of additional homes were identified in 2013 and 2012 as containing or potentially containing allegedly defective drywall manufactured in China), previous community-wide reviews we have conducted, and the domestic sourcing of drywall material since late 2008, we believe that we have identified substantially all affected homes and will receive at most only nominal additional claims in future periods.

As of November 30, 2013, we were a defendant in two lawsuits relating to allegedly defective drywall manufactured in China. One of the lawsuits is an "omnibus" class action purportedly filed on behalf of numerous homeowners asserting claims for damages against drywall manufacturers, homebuilders and other parties in the supply chain of the allegedly defective drywall material. This class action is now in the process of being dismissed pursuant to a final global settlement of claims approved in February 2013 by the federal court judge overseeing a multidistrict litigation case—*In re: Chinese Manufactured Drywall Products Liability Litigation (MDL-2047)*. We were also a defendant in one lawsuit brought in Florida state court by individual homeowners. Except for the Florida state court case, the global settlement resolved all current claims against us, including the remaining omnibus class action (and those that have been previously dismissed) in which we were named as a defendant, and bars any future claims against all participating defendants, including us. Our total obligation as a participating defendant under the global settlement was $.3 million, which we paid on March 25, 2013. We also expect to receive certain amounts under the global settlement in 2014 based on repairs we made to homes of certain settlement class members. The plaintiffs in the Florida state court case opted out of the global settlement, and we settled the case with those plaintiffs in the third quarter of 2013. The case was submitted to the court for dismissal in the first quarter of 2014.

Other Claims. With respect to potential recoveries on claims regarding other homes previously delivered, we have tendered claims with responsible liability insurance carriers, seeking reimbursement of costs we incurred to make repairs and to handle claims. During 2012, we recognized insurance recoveries of $26.5 million as a reduction to construction and land costs in our consolidated statements of operations, representing amounts we received from one of our insurance carriers for a portion of the claims we have tendered. We intend to continue to undertake efforts, including legal proceedings, to obtain reimbursement from various sources, including subcontractors, suppliers and their insurers, for the costs we have incurred or expect to incur to investigate and complete repairs and to defend ourselves in litigation. Given uncertainties in the potential outcomes of these efforts, we have not recorded any amounts for potential future recoveries as of November 30, 2013.

Overall Warranty Liability Assessment. In assessing our overall warranty liability at a reporting date, we evaluate the costs for warranty-related items on a combined basis for all of our previously delivered homes that are under our limited warranty program, which would include any such homes in central and southwest Florida that have been identified as having water intrusion-related issues and similarly affected homes in central and southwest Florida that we believe are likely to be identified in the future. In 2013, based on our assessment of our overall warranty liability, we recorded adjustments to increase our warranty liability by $32.0 million with a corresponding charge to construction and land costs in our consolidated statements of operations. The adjustments reflected the remaining estimated repair costs associated with homes in central and southwest Florida that have been identified as having water intrusion-related issues and the estimated repair costs associated with similarly affected homes in central and southwest Florida that we believe are likely to be identified in the future, net of estimated probable recoveries of such repair costs and other adjustments.

These adjustments, which were made in each quarter of 2013 as our assessment process continued and we gained more experience and knowledge of the scope and nature of the water intrusion-related issues and the associated repair efforts and costs, were largely related to one attached-home community in Florida. At this particular community, we determined in each of the third and fourth quarters of 2013 that additional significant and previously unanticipated repair work would need to be undertaken, and that the costs for certain items, including framing material and labor, stucco and windows, would be substantially higher than previously expected. The adjustments we made in 2013 also reflected the identification of 687 additional affected homes at other communities in central and southwest Florida, and our estimate of the total number of affected homes that we believe are likely to be identified in the future.

Depending on the number of additional affected homes in central and southwest Florida that are identified as having water intrusion-related issues, and the actual costs we incur in future periods to repair identified affected homes, our estimate of costs to repair similarly affected homes in central and southwest Florida that we believe are likely be identified in the future, and/or actual or estimated costs to repair homes affected by other issues, including costs to provide affected homeowners with temporary housing, we may revise the amount of our estimated liability, which could result in an increase or decrease in our overall warranty liability. Based on our investigation of these water intrusion-related issues, we believe that our warranty liability is adequate to cover the estimated probable total repair costs on these affected homes, similarly affected homes that we believe are likely to be identified in the future and homes affected by other issues, though we believe it is reasonably possible that our loss associated with water intrusion-related issues could exceed the amount accrued as of November 30, 2013 by up to $6 million.

In 2012 and 2011, notwithstanding our actual or estimated remaining repair costs related to the allegedly defective drywall material and water intrusion-related issues, we had experienced favorable trends in our actual warranty costs incurred for the previous several years with respect to claims relating to other warranty-related items, reflecting, among other things, our ongoing focus on construction quality and customer service. Based on our assessments of these and other relevant factors on a combined basis, we determined that our overall warranty liability at the end of each year was sufficient to cover our overall warranty obligations on previously delivered homes that are under our limited warranty program. Additionally, based on our assessment of the trends in our warranty claims experience, and taking into account the decrease in the overall number of homes we had delivered over the past several years before 2012 and the steady reduction in our estimated remaining repair costs and actual repair costs incurred for homes identified as affected or potentially affected by the allegedly defective drywall, we recorded favorable warranty adjustments of $11.2 million in 2012 and $7.4 million in 2011 as reductions to construction and land costs in our consolidated statements of operations in those periods. However, as of November 30, 2012, based on our assessment of our overall warranty liability on a combined basis for all of our previously delivered homes that were under our limited warranty, including the homes identified as affected or potentially affected by the allegedly defective drywall and the increased number of homes potentially affected by water intrusion-related issues, we recorded an adjustment to increase our overall warranty liability by $2.6 million in the fourth quarter of 2012 with a corresponding charge to construction and land costs in our consolidated statements of operations.

INTEREST

3.27 CACI INTERNATIONAL INC (JUN)
CONSOLIDATED STATEMENTS OF OPERATIONS (in part)

(amounts in thousands, except per share data)

	Fiscal Year Ended June 30,		
	2013	2012	2011
Revenue	$3,681,990	$3,774,473	$3,577,780
Costs of revenue:			
Direct costs	2,535,606	2,598,890	2,528,660
Indirect costs and selling expenses	821,465	819,772	741,652
Depreciation and amortization	54,078	55,962	56,067
Total costs of revenue	3,411,149	3,474,624	3,326,379
Income from operations	270,841	299,849	251,401
Interest expense and other, net	25,818	24,101	23,144
Income before income taxes	245,023	275,748	228,257

NOTES TO CONSOLIDATED FINANCIAL STATEMENTS

Note 13. Long Term Debt (in part)

Convertible Notes Payable (in part)

The Company separately accounts for the liability and the equity (conversion option) components of the Notes and recognizes interest expense on the Notes using an interest rate in effect for comparable debt instruments that do not contain conversion features. The effective interest rate for the Notes excluding the conversion option was determined to be 6.9 percent.

The fair value of the liability component of the Notes was calculated to be $221.9 million at May 16, 2007, the date of issuance. The excess of the $300.0 million of gross proceeds over the $221.9 million fair value of the liability component, or $78.1 million, represents the fair value of the equity component, which was recorded, net of income tax effect, as additional paid-in capital within shareholders' equity. This $78.1 million difference represents a debt discount that is amortized over the seven-year term of the Notes as a non-cash component of interest expense. The components of interest expense related to the Notes were as follows (in thousands):

	Year Ended June 30,		
	2013	2012	2011
Coupon interest	$ 6,375	$ 6,375	$ 6,375
Non-cash amortization of discount	12,868	12,024	11,235
Amortization of issuance costs	820	820	820
Total	$20,063	$19,219	$18,430

The balance of the unamortized discount as of June 30, 2013 and 2012, was $11.4 million and $24.3 million, respectively. The balance as of June 30, 2013 will be amortized as additional, non-cash interest expense over the remaining term of the Notes (through May 1, 2014) using the effective interest method.

The fair value of the Notes as of June 30, 2013 was $333.0 million based on quoted market values. The value of the Notes over the principal amount would have been $48.4 million as of June 30, 2013, if the Notes were converted as of that date.

The contingently issuable shares that may result from the conversion of the Notes were included in CACI's diluted share count for the fiscal years ended June 30, 2013, 2012 and 2011 because CACI's average stock price during the first, third and fourth quarters of the year ended June 30, 2013, during the third quarter of the year ended June 30, 2012, and during the third and fourth quarters of the year ended June 30, 2011 was above the conversion price of $54.65 per share. Of total debt issuance costs of $7.8 million, $5.8 million is being amortized to interest expense over seven years. The remaining $2.0 million of debt issuance costs attributable to the embedded conversion option was recorded in additional paid-in capital. Upon closing of the sale of the Notes, $45.5 million of the net proceeds was used to concurrently repurchase one million shares of CACI's common stock.

In connection with the issuance of the Notes, the Company purchased in a private transaction at a cost of $84.4 million call options (the Call Options) to purchase approximately 5.5 million shares of its common stock at a price equal to the conversion price of $54.65 per share. The cost of the Call Options was recorded as a reduction of additional paid-in capital. The Call Options allow CACI to receive shares of its common stock from the counterparties equal to the amount of common stock related to the excess conversion value that CACI would pay the holders of the Notes upon conversion.

For income tax reporting purposes, the Notes and the Call Options are integrated. This created an original issue discount for income tax reporting purposes, and therefore the cost of the Call Options is being accounted for as interest expense over the term of the Notes for income tax reporting purposes. The associated income tax benefit of $32.8 million to be realized for income tax reporting purposes over the term of the Notes was recorded as an increase in additional paid-in capital and a long-term deferred tax asset. The majority of this deferred tax asset is offset in the Company's balance sheet by the $30.7 million deferred tax liability associated with the non-cash interest expense to be recorded for financial reporting purposes.

Note 17. Investments in Joint Ventures (in part)

AC FIRST LLC

In July 2009, the Company entered into a joint venture with AECOM Government Services, Inc. (AGS), a division of AECOM Technology Corporation, called AC FIRST LLC (AC FIRST). The companies partnered in the venture to jointly pursue work under a U.S. Army contract. The Company owns 49 percent of AC FIRST and AGS owns 51 percent. The Company accounts for its interest in AC FIRST using the equity method of accounting. The Company's investment in AC FIRST as of June 30, 2013 and 2012 was $9.7 million and $11.9 million, respectively, and is included in other long-term assets on the Company's consolidated balance sheets. The Company's maximum exposure to loss cannot be determined as any losses incurred by AC FIRST would be allocated to each partner based on the joint venture agreement, however, AC FIRST has not experienced any losses to date. During the years ended June 30, 2013 and 2012, the Company's share of the net income of AC FIRST was $2.6 million and $1.7 million, respectively. These amounts are included in interest expense and other, net on the accompanying consolidated statements of operations. During the year ended June 30, 2013, the Company received $6.2 million in cash distributions and made $1.4 million in capital contributions. The Company made no cash contributions and received no cash distributions during the year ended June 30, 2012. The Company has determined that the primary beneficiary of AC FIRST is AGS as AGS owns the majority of AC FIRST and controls its operations.

INTEREST AND PENALTIES RELATED TO UNRECOGNIZED TAX BENEFITS

3.28 VIACOM INC. (SEP)
NOTES TO CONSOLIDATED FINANCIAL STATEMENTS (in part)

Note 2. Summary of Significant Accounting Policies (in part)

Provision for Income Taxes

Our provision for income taxes includes the current tax owed on the current period earnings, as well as a deferred provision which reflects the future tax consequences attributable to differences between the financial statement carrying amounts of existing assets and liabilities and their respective income tax bases. Deferred tax assets and liabilities are measured using enacted tax rates expected to apply to taxable income in the years in which those temporary differences are expected to be recovered or settled. Changes in existing tax laws and rates, their related interpretations, as well as the uncertainty generated by the prospect of tax legislation in the future may affect the amounts of deferred tax liabilities or the realizability of deferred tax assets.

For tax positions we have taken or expect to take in a tax return, we apply a more likely than not assessment (i.e., there is a greater than 50 percent chance) about whether the tax position will be sustained upon examination by the appropriate tax authority with full knowledge of all relevant information. Amounts recorded for uncertain tax positions are periodically assessed, including the evaluation of new facts and circumstances, to ensure sustainability of the position. Interest and penalties related to uncertain tax positions are included in the *Provision for income taxes* in the Consolidated Statements of Earnings. Liabilities for uncertain tax positions are classified as *Other liabilities—current* or *noncurrent* in the Consolidated Balance Sheets based on when they are expected to be paid.

Note 14. Income Taxes (in part)

A reconciliation of the beginning and ending amounts of unrecognized tax benefits, excluding interest and penalties, is as follows:

Unrecognized Tax Benefits	Year Ended September 30,		
(In millions)	2013	2012	2011
Balance at beginning of the period	$207	$212	$304
Gross additions based on tax positions related to the current year	29	28	17
Gross additions for tax positions of prior years	5	24	3
Gross reductions for tax positions of prior years	(50)	(44)	(97)
Settlements	(25)	(2)	(11)
Expiration of the statute of limitation	(7)	(11)	(4)
Balance at end of the period	$159	$207	$212

The total amount of unrecognized tax benefits at September 30, 2013, if recognized, would favorably affect the effective tax rate.

As discussed in Note 2, we recognize interest and penalties accrued related to unrecognized tax benefits as a component of the *Provision for income taxes* in the Consolidated Statements of Earnings. We recognized interest and penalties of $9 million in 2013, $15 million in 2012 and $14 million in 2011. We had accruals of $35 million and $66 million related to interest and penalties recorded as a component of *Other liabilities—current* and *noncurrent* in the Consolidated Balance Sheets at September 30, 2013 and 2012, respectively. The reduction in the accrual for interest and penalties during the year was related to the release of certain effectively settled tax positions as well as settlements.

We and our subsidiaries file income tax returns with the Internal Revenue Service ("IRS") and various state and international jurisdictions. The IRS concluded its examination of our U.S. consolidated income tax returns through 2008 in 2013. Currently, there are no material potential income tax liabilities still in dispute with respect to the IRS examination of 2009. We anticipate the IRS will begin its examination of our 2010 and 2011 U.S. consolidated federal income tax returns in the first quarter of fiscal 2014. Tax authorities are also conducting examinations of Viacom subsidiaries in various state and local jurisdictions, including New York City. Due to potential resolution of unrecognized tax positions involving multiple tax periods and jurisdictions, it is reasonably possible that a reduction of up to $75 million of unrecognized income tax benefits may occur within 12 months, some of which, depending on the nature of the settlement, may affect our income tax provision and therefore benefit the resulting effective tax rate. The majority of these uncertain tax positions, when recognized in the financial statements, would be recorded in the Consolidated Statements of Earnings as part of the *Provision for income taxes*. The actual amount could vary significantly depending on the ultimate timing and nature of any settlements.

ACCRETION ON ASSET RETIREMENT OBLIGATION

3.29 NOBLE ENERGY, INC. (DEC)
CONSOLIDATED STATEMENTS OF OPERATIONS (in part)

(Millions, except per share amounts)

	Year Ended December 31,		
	2013	2012	2011
Revenues			
Oil, gas and NGL sales	$4,809	$4,037	$3,179
Income from equity method investees	206	186	193
Other revenues	—	—	32
Total revenues	5,015	4,223	3,404
Costs and Expenses			
Production expense	850	673	558
Exploration expense	415	409	277
Depreciation, depletion and amortization	1,568	1,370	878
General and administrative	433	384	339
Gain on divestitures	(36)	(154)	(25)
Asset impairments	86	104	757
Other operating (Income) expense, net	43	25	86
Total operating expenses	3,359	2,811	2,870
Operating income	1,656	1,412	534

Note 1. Summary of Significant Accounting Policies

Property, Plant and Equipment (in part) —Significant accounting policies for our property, plant and equipment are as follows:

Asset Retirement Obligations—Asset retirement obligations consist of estimated costs of dismantlement, removal, site reclamation and similar activities associated with our oil and gas properties. We recognize the fair value of a liability for an ARO in the period in which it is incurred when we have an existing legal obligation associated with the retirement of our oil and gas properties that can reasonably be estimated, with the associated asset retirement cost capitalized as part of the carrying cost of the oil and gas asset. The asset retirement cost is determined at current costs and is inflated into future dollars using an inflation rate that is based on the consumer price index. The future projected cash flows are then discounted to their present value using a credit-adjusted risk-free rate. After initial recording, the liability is increased for the passage of time, with the increase being reflected as accretion expense and included in our DD&A expense in the statement of operations. Subsequent adjustments in the cost estimate are reflected in the liability and the amounts continue to be amortized over the useful life of the related long-lived asset. See Note 9. Asset Retirement Obligations.

Note 9. Asset Retirement Obligations

Asset retirement obligations (ARO) consist primarily of estimated costs of dismantlement, removal, site reclamation and similar activities associated with our oil and gas properties. Changes in asset retirement obligations were as follows

	Year Ended December 31,	
(Millions)	**2013**	**2012**
Asset retirement obligations, beginning balance	$402	$377
Liabilities incurred	90	43
Liabilities settled	(41)	(112)
Revision of estimate	156	102
Accretion expense	28	22
Other	(49)	(30)
Asset retirement obligations, ending balance	$586	$402

For the Year Ended December 31, 2013

Liabilities incurred were due to new wells and facilities and included $68 million for deepwater Gulf of Mexico, $15 million for onshore US development, and $7 million for Eastern Mediterranean.

Liabilities settled of $41 million primarily related to deepwater Gulf of Mexico abandonment activities and non-core, onshore US assets sold.

Revisions were primarily due to changes in estimated costs for future abandonment activities and acceleration of timing and included $86 million for DJ Basin, $36 million for deepwater Gulf of Mexico, $10 million for Equatorial Guinea, and $7 million for Eastern Mediterranean. Increased US costs are due primarily to more stringent abandonment standards impacting procedures and materials.

Other includes $17 million for non-core, onshore US, and $32 million for China ARO liabilities transferred to liabilities associated with assets held for sale.

For the Year Ended December 31, 2012

Liabilities incurred were due to new wells and facilities and included $6 million for onshore US development, $8 million for deepwater Gulf of Mexico, and $29 million for offshore Israel.

Liabilities settled primarily included $20 million related to non-core, onshore US assets sold, $55 million related to North Sea assets sold, and $34 million related to the Leviathan-2 appraisal well, offshore Israel.

Revisions were due to changes in estimated costs for future abandonment activities and included $54 million for onshore US, $6 million for deepwater Gulf of Mexico, $26 million for offshore Israel, and $16 million for offshore China.

Other includes North Sea ARO liabilities transferred to liabilities associated with assets held for sale.

See Note 2. Additional Financial Statement Information and Note 3. Property Transactions.

Accretion expense is included in DD&A expense in the consolidated statements of operations.

WRITE-DOWN OF ASSETS

3.30 HOVNANIAN ENTERPRISES, INC. (OCT)
CONSOLIDATED STATEMENTS OF OPERATIONS (in part)

	Year Ended		
(In thousands except per share data)	October 31, 2013	October 31, 2012	October 31, 2011
Revenues:			
Homebuilding:			
Sale of homes	$1,784,327	$1,405,580	$1,072,474
Land sales and other revenues	19,199	41,038	32,952
Total homebuilding	1,803,526	1,446,618	1,105,426
Financial services	47,727	38,735	29,481
Total revenues	1,851,253	1,485,353	1,134,907
Expenses:			
Homebuilding:			
Cost of sales, excluding interest	1,442,044	1,179,801	913,901
Cost of sales interest	52,230	54,538	74,676
Inventory impairment loss and land option write-offs	4,965	12,530	101,749
Total cost of sales	1,499,239	1,246,869	1,090,326
Selling, general and administrative	165,809	142,087	161,456
Total homebuilding expenses	1,665,048	1,388,956	1,251,782
Financial services	29,059	23,648	21,371
Corporate general and administrative	54,357	48,232	49,938
Other interest	91,344	97,895	97,169
Other operations	790	4,205	4,805
Total expenses	1,840,598	1,562,936	1,425,065
(Loss) gain on extinguishment of debt	(760)	(29,066)	7,528
Income (loss) from unconsolidated joint ventures	12,040	5,401	(8,958)
Income (loss) before income taxes	21,935	(101,248)	(291,588)

NOTES TO CONSOLIDATED FINANCIAL STATEMENTS

3. Summary of Significant Accounting Policies (in part)

Inventories (in part)—Inventories consist of land, land development, home construction costs, capitalized interest, construction overhead and property taxes. Construction costs are accumulated during the period of construction and charged to cost of sales under specific identification methods. Land, land development, and common facility costs are allocated based on buildable acres to product types within each community, then charged to cost of sales equally based upon the number of homes to be constructed in each product type.

We record inventories in our consolidated balance sheets at cost unless the inventory is determined to be impaired, in which case the inventory is written down to its fair value. Our inventories consist of the following three components: (1) sold and unsold homes and lots under development, which includes all construction, land, capitalized interest, and land development costs related to started homes and land under development in our active communities; (2) land and land options held for future development or sale, which includes all costs related to land in our communities in planning or mothballed communities; and (3) consolidated inventory not owned, which includes all costs related to specific performance options, variable interest entities, and other options, which consists primarily of model homes financed with an investor and inventory related to land banking arrangements.

We have decided to mothball (or stop development on) certain communities; we do so when we determine that current performance does not justify further investment at that time. When we decide to mothball a community, the inventory is reclassified from "Sold and unsold homes and lots under development" to "Land and land options held for future development or sale". We regularly review communities to determine if mothballing is appropriate. During fiscal 2013, we mothballed one community, re-activated three previously mothballed communities and sold one mothballed community. As of October 31, 2013, the net book value of our 50 total mothballed communities was $115.9 million, which was net of impairment charges recorded in prior periods of $431.6 million.

The recoverability of inventories and other long-lived assets is assessed in accordance with the provisions of ASC 360-10, "Property, Plant and Equipment—Overall". ASC 360-10 requires long-lived assets, including inventories, held for development to be evaluated for impairment based on undiscounted future cash flows of the assets at the lowest level for which there are identifiable cash flows. As such, we evaluate inventories for impairment at the individual community level, the lowest level of discrete cash flows that we measure.

We evaluate inventories of communities under development and held for future development for impairment when indicators of potential impairment are present. Indicators of impairment include, but are not limited to, decreases in local housing market values, decreases in gross margins or sales absorption rates, decreases in net sales prices (base sales price net of sales incentives), or actual or projected operating or cash flow losses. The assessment of communities for indication of impairment is performed quarterly, primarily by completing detailed budgets for all of our communities and identifying those communities with a projected operating loss for any projected fiscal year or for the entire projected community life. For those communities with projected losses, we estimate the remaining undiscounted future cash flows and compare those to the carrying value of the community, to determine if the carrying value of the asset is recoverable.

The projected operating profits, losses, or cash flows of each community can be significantly impacted by our estimates of the following:
- future base selling prices;
- future home sales incentives;
- future home construction and land development costs; and
- future sales absorption pace and cancellation rates.

These estimates are dependent upon specific market conditions for each community. While we consider available information to determine what we believe to be our best estimates as of the end of a quarterly reporting period, these estimates are subject to change in future reporting periods as facts and circumstances change. Local market-specific conditions that may impact our estimates for a community include:
- the intensity of competition within a market, including available home sales prices and home sales incentives offered by our competitors, including foreclosed homes where they have an impact on our ability to sell homes;
- the current sales absorption pace for both our communities and competitor communities;
- community-specific attributes, such as location, availability of lots in the market, desirability and uniqueness of our community, and the size and style of homes currently being offered;
- potential for alternative product offerings to respond to local market conditions;
- changes by management in the sales strategy of the community;
- current local market economic and demographic conditions and related trends and forecasts; and
- existing home inventory supplies, including foreclosures and short sales.

These and other local market-specific conditions that may be present are considered by management in preparing projection assumptions for each community. The sales objectives can differ between our communities, even within a given market. For example, facts and circumstances in a given community may lead us to price our homes with the objective of yielding a higher sales absorption pace, while facts and circumstances in another community may lead us to price our homes to minimize deterioration in our gross margins, although it may result in a slower sales absorption pace. In addition, the key assumptions included in our estimate of future undiscounted cash flows may be interrelated. For example, a decrease in estimated base sales price or an increase in homes sales incentives may result in a corresponding increase in sales absorption pace. Additionally, a decrease in the average sales price of homes to be sold and closed in future reporting periods for one community that has not been generating what management believes to be an adequate sales absorption pace may impact the estimated cash flow assumptions of a nearby community. Changes in our key assumptions, including estimated construction and development costs, absorption pace and selling strategies, could materially impact future cash flow and fair value estimates. Due to the number of possible scenarios that would result from various changes in these factors, we do not believe it is possible to develop a sensitivity analysis with a level of precision that would be meaningful to an investor.

If the undiscounted cash flows are more than the carrying amount of the community, then the carrying amount is recoverable, and no impairment adjustment is required. However, if the undiscounted cash flows are less than the carrying amount, then the community is deemed impaired and is written-down to its fair value. We determine the estimated fair value of each community by determining the present value of its estimated future cash flows at a discount rate commensurate with the risk of the respective community, or in limited circumstances, prices for land in recent comparable sale transactions, market analysis studies, which include the estimated price a willing buyer would pay for the land (other than in a forced liquidation sale), and recent bona fide offers received from outside third parties. Our discount rates used for all impairments recorded from October 31, 2011 to October 31, 2013 range from 16.8% to 19.8%. The estimated future cash flow assumptions are virtually the same for both our recoverability and fair value assessments. Should the estimates or expectations used in determining estimated cash flows or fair value, including discount rates, decrease or differ from current estimates in the future, we may be required to recognize additional impairments related to current and future communities. The impairment of a community is allocated to each lot on a relative fair value basis.

From time to time, we write off deposits and approval, engineering and capitalized interest costs when we determine that it is no longer probable that we will exercise options to buy land in specific locations or when we redesign communities and/or abandon certain engineering costs. In deciding not to exercise a land option, we take into consideration changes in market conditions, the timing of required land takedowns, the willingness of land sellers to modify terms of the land option contract (including timing of land takedowns), and the availability and best use of our capital, among other factors. The write-off is recorded in the period that it is not deemed probable that the optioned property will be acquired. In certain instances, we have been able to recover deposits and other pre-acquisition costs that were previously written off. These recoveries have not been significant in comparison to the total costs written off.

Land and land options held for sale includes land parcels on which we have decided not to build homes and are reported at the lower of carrying amount or fair value less costs to sell. In determining the fair value of land held for sale, management considers, among other things, prices for land in recent comparable sale transactions, market analysis studies, which include the estimated price a willing buyer would pay for the land (other than in a forced liquidation sale) and recent bona fide offers received from outside third parties. At October 31, 2013, land and land options held for sale had a carrying value of $2.7 million.

Land Options—Costs incurred to obtain options to acquire improved or unimproved home sites are capitalized. Such amounts are either included as part of the purchase price if the land is acquired or charged to "Inventory impairments loss and land option write-offs" if we determine we will not exercise the option. If the options are with variable interest entities and we are the primary beneficiary, we record the land under option on the Consolidated Balance Sheets under "Consolidated inventory not owned" with an offset under "Liabilities from inventory not owned." If the option obligation is to purchase under specific performance or has terms that require us to record it as financing, then we record the option on the Consolidated Balance Sheets under "Consolidated inventory not owned" with an offset under "Liabilities from inventory not owned". In accordance with ASC 810-10 "Consolidation—Overall", we record costs associated with other options on the Consolidated Balance Sheets under "Land and land options held for future development or sale."

Unconsolidated Homebuilding and Land Development Joint Ventures—Investments in unconsolidated homebuilding and land development joint ventures are accounted for under the equity method of accounting. Under the equity method, we recognize our proportionate share of earnings and losses earned by the joint venture upon the delivery of lots or homes to third parties. Our ownership interests in the joint ventures vary but our voting interests are generally 50% or less. In determining whether or not we must consolidate joint ventures where we are the managing member of the joint venture, we assess whether the other partners have specific rights to overcome the presumption of control by us as the manager of the joint venture. In most cases, the presumption is overcome because the joint venture agreements require that both partners agree on establishing the significant operating and capital decisions of the partnership, including budgets, in the ordinary course of business. The evaluation of whether or not we control a venture can require significant judgment. In accordance with ASC 323-10, "Investments—Equity Method and Joint Ventures—Overall", we assess our investments in unconsolidated joint ventures for recoverability, and if it is determined that a loss in value of the investment below its carrying amount is other than temporary, we write down the investment to its fair value. We evaluate our equity investments for impairment based on the joint venture's projected cash flows. This process requires significant management judgment and estimates. There were no write-downs in fiscal 2011, 2012 or 2013.

13. Reduction of Inventory to Fair Value

We record impairment losses on inventories related to communities under development and held for future development when events and circumstances indicate that they may be impaired and the undiscounted cash flows estimated to be generated by those assets are less than their related carrying amounts. If the expected undiscounted cash flows are less than the carrying amount, then the community is written down to its fair value. We estimate the fair value of each impaired community by determining the present value of the estimated future cash flows at a discount rate commensurate with the risk of the respective community. For the year ended October 31, 2013, our discount rates used for the impairments recorded ranged from 18.0% to 19.3%. Should the estimates or expectations used in determining cash flows or fair value decrease or differ from current estimates in the future, we may need to recognize additional impairments.

During the years ended October 31, 2013 and 2012, we evaluated inventories of all 388 and 331 communities under development and held for future development, respectively, for impairment indicators through preparation and review of detailed budgets or other market indicators of impairment. We performed detailed impairment calculations during the years ended October 31, 2013 and 2012 for 33 and 54 of those communities (i.e., those with a projected operating loss or other impairment indicators), respectively, with an aggregate carrying value of $85.0 million and $ 77.7 million, respectively, (8 and 31 were in the fourth quarter of fiscal 2013 and 2012, respectively, with an aggregate carrying value of $21.8 million and $47.4 million, respectively). As impairment indicators are assessed on a quarterly basis, some of the communities evaluated during the years ended October 31, 2013 and 2012 were evaluated in more than one quarterly period. Of those communities tested for impairment during the years ended October 31, 2013 and 2012, four and 17 communities, respectively, with an aggregate carrying value of $4.5 million and $31.6 million, respectively, had undiscounted future cash flows that only exceeded the carrying amount by less than 20%. As a result of our impairment analysis, we recorded impairment losses, which are included in the

Consolidated Statement of Operations and deducted from inventory, of $2.4 million, $9.8 million, and $77.5 million for the years ended October 31, 2013, 2012, and 2011, respectively.

The following table represents impairments by segment for fiscal 2013, 2012, and 2011:

(Dollars in millions)	Year Ended October 31, 2013		
	Number of Communities	Dollar Amount of Impairment[2]	Pre-Impairment Value[1]
Northeast	4	$2.4	$7.7
Mid-Atlantic	1	—	0.1
Midwest	—	—	—
Southeast	1	—	0.4
Southwest	—	—	—
West	—	—	—
Total	6	$2.4	$8.2

(Dollars in millions)	Year Ended October 31, 2012		
	Number of Communities	Dollar Amount of Impairment	Pre-Impairment Value[1]
Northeast	10	$2.8	$19.6
Mid-Atlantic	3	0.4	0.8
Midwest	2	1.6	4.5
Southeast	12	2.8	8.3
Southwest	—	—	—
West	5	2.2	4.9
Total	32	$9.8	$38.1

(Dollars in millions)	Year Ended October 31, 2011		
	Number of Communities	Dollar Amount of Impairment	Pre-Impairment Value[1]
Northeast	11	$54.9	$179.9
Mid-Atlantic	5	3.4	17.3
Midwest	7	1.1	4.2
Southeast	11	1.5	5.1
Southwest	1	0.1	0.3
West	6	16.5	45.2
Total	41	$77.5	$252.0

[1] Represents carrying value, net of prior period impairments, if any, at the time of recording the applicable period's impairments.
[2] During year ended October 31, 2013, the Mid-Atlantic had an impairment totaling $2 thousand and the Southeast had an impairment totaling $17 thousand.

The Consolidated Statements of Operations line entitled "Homebuilding-Inventory impairment loss and land option write-offs" also includes write-offs of options and approval, engineering and capitalized interest costs that we record when we redesign communities and/or abandon certain engineering costs and we do not exercise options in various locations because the communities' pro forma profitability is not projected to produce adequate returns on investment commensurate with the risk. The total aggregate write-offs were $2.6 million, $2.7 million, and $24.3 million for the years ended October 31, 2013, 2012, and 2011, respectively. Occasionally, these write-offs are offset by recovered deposits (sometimes through legal action) that had been written off in a prior period as walk-away costs. Historically, these recoveries have not been significant in comparison to the total costs written off.

The following table represents write-offs of such costs by segment for fiscal 2013, 2012, and 2011:

(In millions)	Year Ended October 31,		
	2013	2012	2011
Northeast	$0.7	$0.7	$13.4
Mid-Atlantic	0.1	0.6	6.1
Midwest	0.2	0.2	0.5
Southeast	0.2	0.7	0.8
Southwest	1.4	0.4	0.4
West	—	0.1	3.1
Total	$2.6	$2.7	$24.3

RESTRUCTURING

3.31 WORTHINGTON INDUSTRIES, INC. (MAY)
CONSOLIDATED STATEMENTS OF EARNINGS (in part)

(In thousands, except per share amounts)

	Fiscal Years Ended May 31,		
	2013	2012	2011
Net sales	$2,612,244	$2,534,701	$2,442,624
Cost of goods sold	2,215,601	2,201,833	2,086,467
Gross margin	396,643	332,868	356,157
Selling, general and administrative expense	258,324	225,069	235,198
Impairment of long-lived assets	6,488	355	4,386
Restructuring and other expense	3,293	5,984	2,653
Joint venture transactions	(604)	(150)	(10,436)
Operating income	129,142	101,610	124,356

NOTES TO CONSOLIDATED FINANCIAL STATEMENTS

Note D—Restructuring and Other Expense

In fiscal 2008, we initiated a Transformation Plan (the "Transformation Plan") with the overall goal to improve our sustainable earnings potential, asset utilization and operational performance. The Transformation Plan focuses on cost reduction, margin expansion and organizational capability improvements and, in the process, seeks to drive excellence in three core competencies: sales; operations; and supply chain management. The Transformation Plan is comprehensive in scope and includes aggressive diagnostic and implementation phases. As a result of the Transformation Plan and its related efforts, we have incurred certain asset impairments which have been included within restructuring and other expense in our consolidated statements of earnings. Asset impairment charges that are not a result of these efforts have been included within impairment of long-lived assets in our consolidated statements of earnings, except for the impairment charges incurred in connection with the formations of the unconsolidated joint ventures, ArtiFlex and ClarkDietrich, during the fourth quarter of fiscal 2011. These impairment charges were recognized within the joint venture transactions caption in our consolidated statements of earnings.

To date, we have completed the transformation phases in each of the core facilities within our Steel Processing operating segment, including the facilities of our Mexican joint venture. We also substantially completed the transformation phases at our metal framing facilities prior to their contribution to ClarkDietrich. Transformation efforts within our Pressure Cylinders operating segment, which began during the first quarter of fiscal 2012, are ongoing. In addition, during the first quarter of fiscal 2013, we initiated the diagnostics phase of the Transformation Plan in our Engineered Cabs operating segment.

When this process began, we retained a consulting firm to assist in the development and implementation of the Transformation Plan. As the Transformation Plan progressed, we formed internal teams dedicated to this effort, and they ultimately assumed full responsibility for executing the Transformation Plan. Although the consulting firm was again engaged as we rolled out the Transformation Plan in our Pressure Cylinders operating segment, most of the work is now being done by our internal teams. These internal teams are now an integral part of our business and constitute what we refer to as the Centers of Excellence ("COE"). The COE will continue to monitor the performance metrics and new processes instituted across our transformed operations and drive continuous improvements in all areas of our operations. The majority of the expenses related to the COE will be included in selling, general and administrative expense going forward, except where they relate to a first time diagnostics phase of the Transformation Plan.

A progression of the liabilities associated with our restructuring activities, combined with a reconciliation to the restructuring and other expense line in our consolidated statement of earnings for fiscal 2013, is summarized as follows:

(In thousands)	Beginning Balance	Expense	Payments	Adjustments	Ending Balance
Early retirement and severance	$4,892	$2,228	$(2,388)	$297	$5,029
Facility exit and other costs	691	2,347	(2,378)	540	1,200
	$5,583	4,575	$(4,766)	$837	$6,229
Net gain on dispositions		(1,886)			
Less: joint venture transactions		604			
Restructuring and other expense		$3,293			

Approximately $4,741,000 of the total liability is expected to be paid in fiscal 2014. The remaining liability, which consists of lease termination costs and certain severance benefits, will be paid through September 2016.

During fiscal 2013, the following actions were taken in connection with the Transformation Plan:

- In connection with the wind-down of our former Metal Framing operating segment:
  — Approximately $1,546,000 of facility exit and other costs were incurred in connection with the closure of the retained facilities.
  — The severance accrual was adjusted downward, resulting in a $264,000 credit to earnings.
  — Certain assets of the retained facilities classified as held for sale were disposed of for cash proceeds of $5,637,000 resulting in a net gain of $1,886,000.

These items were recognized within the "joint venture transactions" financial statement caption in our consolidated statement of earnings to correspond with amounts previously recognized in connection with the formation of ClarkDietrich and the subsequent wind-down of our former Metal Framing operating segment.

- In connection with the closure of our commercial stairs business, we incurred net charges of approximately $1,530,000, consisting of $1,624,000 of facility exit and other costs and a $94,000 credit to severance expense.
- In connection with certain organizational changes impacting our former Global Group operating segment, we accrued approximately $98,000 of employee severance. For further information regarding these organizational changes, refer to "NOTE N—Segment Data."
- In connection with the sale of our Pressure Cylinders operations in Czech Republic, we recognized approximately $177,000 of facility exit and other costs.
- In connection with the previously-announced consolidation of the BernzOmatic hand torch manufacturing operation in Medina, New York into the existing Pressure Cylinders' facility in Chilton, Wisconsin, we recognized a $2,488,000 accrual for expected employee severance costs.

A progression of the liabilities associated with our restructuring activities, combined with a reconciliation to the restructuring and other expense line in our consolidated statement of earnings for fiscal 2012, is summarized as follows:

(In thousands)	Beginning Balance	Expense	Payments	Adjustments	Ending Balance
Early retirement and severance	$7,220	$ 245	$ (3,824)	$1,251	$4,892
Facility exit and other costs	409	9,116	(9,630)	796	691
Professional fees	—	4,758	(4,758)	—	—
	$7,629	14,119	$(18,212)	$2,047	$5,583
Net gain on dispositions		(8,285)			
Joint venture transactions		150			
Restructuring and other expense		$5,984			

The adjustment to the early retirement and severance line item above relates primarily to the reclassification of severance costs to be reimbursed by MISA in connection with the ClarkDietrich formation to the assets section of the balance sheet during fiscal 2012.

During fiscal 2012, the following actions were taken in connection with the Transformation Plan:

- In connection with the wind-down of our metal framing business:
  — Approximately $9,116,000 of facility exit and other costs were incurred in connection with the closure of the retained facilities.
  — The severance accrual was adjusted downward, resulting in a $998,000 credit to earnings.
  — Certain assets of the retained facilities classified as held for sale were disposed of for cash proceeds of approximately $14,005,000 resulting in a net gain of approximately $5,417,000.
  — The assets of our Vinyl division, which were also classified as held for sale, were sold to our unconsolidated affiliate, ClarkDietrich, for cash proceeds of approximately $6,125,000 resulting in a gain of approximately $766,000.
  — Certain steel processing assets acquired in connection with the formation of ClarkDietrich and classified as held for sale were disposed of for cash proceeds of approximately $10,948,000 resulting in a gain of approximately $2,102,000.

These items were recognized within the joint venture transactions caption in our consolidated statements of earnings to correspond with amounts previously recognized in connection with the formation of ClarkDietrich and the subsequent wind-down of our Metal Framing operating segment.

- We engaged a consulting firm to assist with the ongoing transformation efforts within our Pressure Cylinders operating segment. As a result, we incurred professional fees of $4,758,000, which were classified as restructuring and other expense in our consolidated statements of earnings. Services provided included assistance through diagnostic tools, performance improvement technologies, project management techniques, benchmarking information and insights that directly related to the Transformation Plan.
- During the fourth quarter of fiscal 2012, we announced the closure of our commercial stairs business and accrued $1,143,000 of employee severance.

3.32 TUPPERWARE BRANDS CORPORATION (DEC)

CONSOLIDATED STATEMENTS OF INCOME (in part)

	Year Ended		
(In millions, except per share amounts)	December 28, 2013	December 29, 2012	December 31, 2011
Net sales	$2,671.6	$2,583.8	$2,585.0
Cost of products sold	889.8	856.4	862.5
Gross margin	1,781.8	1,727.4	1,722.5
Delivery, sales and administrative expense	1,369.7	1,329.5	1,340.0
Re-engineering and impairment charges	9.3	22.4	7.9
Impairment of goodwill and intangible assets	—	76.9	36.1
Gains on disposal of assets	0.7	7.9	3.8
Operating income	403.5	306.5	342.3

NOTES TO THE CONSOLIDATED FINANCIAL STATEMENTS

Note 1: Summary of Significant Accounting Policies (in part)

Intangible Assets. Intangible assets are recorded at their fair market values at the date of acquisition and definite lived intangibles are amortized over their estimated useful lives. The intangible assets included in the Company's Consolidated Financial Statements at December 28, 2013 and December 29, 2012 were related to the acquisition of the Sara Lee direct-to-consumer businesses in December 2005. The weighted average estimated useful lives of the Company's intangible assets were as follows:

	Weighted Average Estimated Useful Life
Indefinite-lived trademarks and tradenames	Indefinite
Definite-lived trademarks and tradenames	10 years
Sales force relationships	6–10 years

The Company's indefinite lived tradename intangible assets are evaluated for impairment annually similarly to goodwill. The annual process for assessing the carrying value of indefinite-lived tradename intangible assets begins with a qualitative assessment that is similar to the assessment performed for goodwill. When the Company determines it is necessary, the quantitative impairment test for the Company's indefinite-lived tradenames involves comparing the estimated fair value of the assets to the carrying amounts, to determine if fair value is lower and a write-down required. If the carrying amount of a tradename exceeds its estimated fair value, an impairment charge is recognized in an amount equal to the excess. When necessary, the fair value of these assets is determined using the relief from royalty method, which is a form of the income approach. In this method, the value of the asset is calculated by selecting royalty rates, which estimate the amount a company would be willing to pay for the use of the asset. These rates are applied to the Company's projected revenue, tax affected and discounted to present value using an appropriate rate.

The Company's definite lived intangible assets consist of the value of the acquired independent sales forces, as well as the Fuller tradename since August 2013. The sales force relationships are amortized to reflect the estimated turnover rates of the sales forces acquired and the Fuller tradename is amortized to reflect the period that it is estimated that the tradename will contribute directly the Company's revenue. Definite lived intangible assets are reviewed for impairment in a similar manner as property, plant and equipment as discussed above. Amortization related to definite lived intangible assets is included in DS&A on the Consolidated Statements of Income.

Intangible assets are further discussed in Note 6 to the Consolidated Financial Statements.

Note 6: Goodwill and Intangible Assets (in part)

In August of 2013, the Company concluded it should reclassify its Fuller tradename from indefinite lived to definite lived. This conclusion was primarily reached in light of a long-term transition in the Fuller Mexico business to a new brand name. As a result of this transition, the Company has estimated that the Fuller tradename has a 10 year useful life with amortization to be recorded on a straight-line basis. Amortization expense recorded in 2013 related to the Fuller tradename was $3.4 million.

The reclassification of the Fuller tradename from an indefinite-lived to definite-lived asset triggered an impairment review similar to that performed during an annual assessment, as described above. The results of the impairment test demonstrated that the current estimated fair value of the Fuller tradename exceeded its carrying value. The fair value of the Fuller tradenames was determined using the relief from royalty method, which is a form of the income approach. In this method, the value of the asset is calculated using a royalty rate of 4.5 percent, which is an estimate of the amount a company would be willing to pay for the use of the asset. This rate was applied to the asset's projected revenue, tax affected and discounted to present value. The royalty rate used was selected by reviewing comparable trademark licensing agreements in the market. In estimating the fair value of the tradename, the Company applied a discount rate of 16.9 percent, and revenue growth ranging from 3 to 7 percent, with an average growth rate of 6 percent, and a long-term terminal growth rate of 3 percent.

The gross carrying amount and accumulated amortization of the Company's intangible assets, other than goodwill, were as follows:

	December 28, 2013		
(In millions)	Gross Carrying Value	Accumulated Amortization	Net
Indefinite-lived trademarks and tradenames	$ 25.0	$ —	$ 25.0
Definite-lived trademarks and tradenames	104.1	3.4	$100.7
Sales force relationships	55.3	52.1	3.2
Total intangible assets	$184.4	$55.5	$128.9

	December 29, 2012		
(In millions)	Gross Carrying Value	Accumulated Amortization	Net
Indefinite-lived trademarks and tradenames	$138.4	$—	$138.4
Sales force relationships	60.9	55.9	5.0
Total intangible assets	$199.3	$55.9	$143.4

A summary of the identifiable intangible asset account activity is as follows:

	Year Ending	
(In millions)	December 28, 2013	December 29, 2012
Beginning balance	$199.3	$219.9
Impairment of intangible assets	—	(22.8)
Effect of changes in exchange rates	(14.9)	2.2
Ending balance	$184.4	$199.3

Amortization expense was $4.8 million, $2.0 million and $2.9 million in 2013, 2012 and 2011, respectively. The estimated annual amortization expense associated with the above intangibles for each of the five succeeding years is $12.1 million, $12.0 million, $10.4 million, $10.4 million and $10.4 million, respectively.

SOFTWARE AMORTIZATION

3.33 UNIFI, INC. (JUN)
CONSOLIDATED STATEMENTS OF INCOME (in part)

(Amounts in thousands, except per share amounts)

	For the Fiscal Years Ended		
	June 30, 2013	June 24, 2012	June 26, 2011
Net sales	$713,962	$705,086	$712,812
Cost of sales	640,858	650,690	638,160
Gross profit	73,104	54,396	74,652
Selling, general and administrative expenses	47,386	43,482	44,659
(Benefit) provision for bad debts	(154)	211	(304)
Other operating expense, net	3,409	2,071	1,605
Operating income	22,463	8,632	28,692

2. Summary of Significant Accounting Policies (in part)

Property, Plant and Equipment (in part)

Property, plant and equipment ("PP&E") are stated at historical cost less accumulated depreciation. Additions and any improvements that substantially extend the useful life of a particular asset are capitalized. Depreciation is calculated primarily utilizing the straight-line method over the following useful lives:

Asset Categories	Useful Lives in Years
Land improvements	Twenty
Buildings and improvements	Fifteen to Forty
Machinery and equipment	Seven to Fifteen
Computer, software and office equipment	Three to Seven
Internal software development costs	Three
Other assets	Three to Seven

Leasehold improvements are depreciated over the lesser of their estimated useful lives or the remaining term of the lease. Assets under capital leases are amortized on a straight-line basis over the lesser of their estimated useful lives or the lease term.

The Company capitalizes its costs of developing internal software when the software is used as an integral part of its manufacturing or business processes and the technological feasibility has been established. Internal software costs are amortized over a period of three years and, in accordance with the project type, charged to cost of sales or selling, general and administrative ("SG&A") expenses.

Fully depreciated assets are retained in cost and accumulated depreciation accounts until they are removed from service. In the case of disposals, asset costs and related accumulated depreciation amounts are removed from the accounts, and the net amounts, less proceeds from disposal, are included in the determination of net income and presented within Other operating expense, net.

Repair and maintenance costs related to PP&E which do not significantly increase the useful life of an existing asset or do not significantly alter, modify or change the capabilities or production capacity of an existing asset are expensed as incurred.

8. Property, Plant and Equipment, Net (in part)

Property, plant and equipment, net consists of the following:

	June 30, 2013	June 24, 2012
Land	$ 2,949	$ 3,095
Land improvements	11,676	11,426
Buildings and improvements	144,833	146,232
Assets under capital leases	1,234	9,520
Machinery and equipment	526,910	530,319
Computers, software and office equipment	16,647	16,350
Transportation equipment	4,866	4,722
Construction in progress	5,691	1,774
Gross property, plant and equipment	714,806	723,438
Less: accumulated depreciation	(599,592)	(587,146)
Less: accumulated amortization—capital lease	(50)	(9,202)
Total property, plant and equipment, net	$ 115,164	$ 127,090

Internal software development costs within PP&E consist of the following:

	June 30, 2013	June 24, 2012
Internal software development costs	$ 2,166	$ 2,014
Accumulated amortization	(1,932)	(1,804)
Net internal software development costs	$ 234	$ 210

Depreciation expense, internal software development costs amortization, repairs and maintenance expenses and capitalized interest were as follows:

	For the Fiscal Years Ended		
	June 30, 2013	June 24, 2012	June 26, 2011
Depreciation expense	$21,597	$23,650	$22,671
Internal software development costs amortization	128	236	368
Repair and maintenance expenses	18,649	16,270	18,638
Capitalized interest	36	—	—

LITIGATION

3.34 MEDTRONIC, INC. (APR)

CONSOLIDATED STATEMENTS OF EARNINGS (in part)

	Fiscal Year		
(In millions, except per share data)	2013	2012	2011
Net sales	$16,590	$16,184	$15,508
Costs and expenses:			
Cost of products sold	4,126	3,889	3,700
Research and development expense	1,557	1,490	1,472
Selling, general, and administrative expense	5,698	5,623	5,427
Restructuring charges, net	172	87	259
Certain litigation charges, net	245	90	245
Acquisition-related items	(49)	12	14
Amortization of intangible assets	331	335	339
Other expense, net	108	364	110
Interest expense, net	151	149	278
Total costs and expenses	12,339	12,039	11,844
Earnings from continuing operations before income taxes	4,251	4,145	3,664

NOTES TO CONSOLIDATED FINANCIAL STATEMENTS

2. Certain Litigation Charges, Net

The Company classifies material litigation reserves and gains recognized as certain litigation charges, net.

During fiscal year 2013, the Company recorded certain litigation charges, net of $245 million related to probable and reasonably estimated damages resulting from patent litigation with Edwards Lifesciences, Inc. Refer to Note 17 for additional information.

During fiscal year 2012, the Company recorded certain litigation charges, net of $90 million related to the agreement to settle the federal securities class action initiated in December 2008 by the Minneapolis Firefighters' Relief Association. During the fourth quarter of fiscal year 2012, Medtronic settled all of these class claims for $85 million and incurred $5 million in additional litigation fees.

During fiscal year 2011, the Company recorded certain litigation charges, net of $245 million related primarily to a $221 million settlement involving the Sprint Fidelis family of defibrillation leads and charges for certain Other Matters litigation. The Sprint Fidelis settlement related to the resolution of certain outstanding product liability litigation related to the Sprint Fidelis family of defibrillation leads that were subject to a field action announced October 15, 2007. During the third quarter of fiscal year 2012, the Company paid out the settlement for both the Sprint Fidelis settlement and for certain Other Matters litigation. Refer to Note 17 for additional information.

17. Contingencies (in part)

Litigation with Edwards Lifesciences, Inc. (in part)

On March 19, 2010, the U.S. District Court for the District of Delaware added Medtronic CoreValve LLC (CoreValve) as a party to litigation pending between Edwards Lifesciences, Inc. (Edwards) and CoreValve, Inc. In the litigation, Edwards asserted that CoreValve's transcatheter aortic valve replacement product infringed three U.S. "Andersen" patents owned by Edwards. Before trial, the court granted summary judgment to Medtronic as to two of the three patents. Following a trial, on April 1, 2010 a jury found that CoreValve willfully infringed a claim on the remaining "Andersen" patent and awarded total lost profit and royalty damages, as of that time, of $74 million. On November 13, 2012, the U.S. Court of Appeals for the Federal Circuit upheld the jury verdict. Medtronic filed a petition for certiorari to the United States

Supreme Court on May 6, 2013. Medtronic recorded an expense of $245 million related to probable and reasonably estimated damages for this matter in the second quarter of fiscal year 2013, of which $84 million was paid on February 28, 2013.

EQUITY IN LOSSES OF INVESTEES

3.35 PEABODY ENERGY CORPORATION (DEC)

CONSOLIDATED STATEMENTS OF OPERATIONS (in part)

(Dollars in millions, except per share data)	Year Ended December 31,		
	2013	**2012**	**2011**
Revenues			
Sales	$6,380.0	$7,041.7	$7,013.0
Other revenues	633.7	1,035.8	882.9
Total revenues	7,013.7	8,077.5	7,895.9
Costs and Expenses			
Operating costs and expenses (exclusive of items shown separately below)	5,736.1	5,932.7	5,477.6
Depreciation, depletion and amortization	740.3	663.4	474.3
Asset retirement obligation expenses	66.5	67.0	52.6
Selling and administrative expenses	249.1	268.8	268.2
Acquisition costs related to Macarthur Coal Limited	—	—	85.2
Other operating (income) loss:			
Net gain on disposal or exchange of assets	(52.6)	(17.1)	(76.9)
Asset impairment and mine closure costs	528.3	929.0	—
Settlement charges related to the Patriot bankruptcy reorganization	30.6	—	—
Loss from equity affiliates	40.2	61.2	19.2
Operating (loss) profit	(324.8)	172.5	1,595.7

NOTES TO CONSOLIDATED FINANCIAL STATEMENTS

(1) Summary of Significant Accounting Policies (in part)

Equity and Cost Method Investments

The Company accounts for its investments in less than majority owned corporate joint ventures under either the equity or cost method. The Company applies the equity method to investments in joint ventures when it has the ability to exercise significant influence over the operating and financial policies of the joint venture. Investments accounted for under the equity method are initially recorded at cost and any difference between the cost of the Company's investment and the underlying equity in the net assets of the joint venture at the investment date is amortized over the lives of the related assets that gave rise to the difference. The Company's pro-rata share of the operating results of joint ventures and basis difference amortization is reported in the consolidated statements of operations in "Loss from equity affiliates." Similarly, the Company's pro-rata share of the cumulative foreign currency translation adjustment of its equity method investments whose functional currency is not the U.S. dollar is reported in the consolidated balances sheet as a component of "Accumulated other comprehensive (loss) income," with periodic changes thereto reflected in the consolidated statements of comprehensive income.

The Company monitors its equity and cost method investments for indicators that a decrease in investment value has occurred that is other than temporary. Examples of such indicators include a sustained history of operating losses and adverse changes in earnings and cash flow outlook. In the absence of quoted market prices for an investment, discounted cash flow projections are used to assess fair value, the underlying assumptions to which are generally considered unobservable Level 3 inputs under the fair value hierarchy. If the fair value of an investment is determined to be below its carrying value and that loss in fair value is deemed other than temporary, an impairment loss is recognized. Refer to Note 2. "Asset Impairment and Mine Closure Costs" and Note 5. "Investments" for details regarding other-than-temporary impairment losses of $43.2 million and $39.4 million recorded during the years ended December 31, 2013 and 2012, respectively, related to certain of the Company's equity and cost method investments. No such impairment losses were recorded during the year ended December 31, 2011.

(5) Investments (in part)

Equity Method Investments

The Company's equity method investments include its joint venture interest in the Middlemount, which was acquired in connection with the 2011 acquisition of PEA-PCI (formerly Macarthur Coal Limited), in addition to certain other equity method investments. The table below summarizes the book value of those investments, which is reported in "Investments and other assets" in the consolidated balance sheets, and the related loss from equity affiliates:

(Dollars in millions)	Book Value at December 31,		Loss from Equity Affiliates for the Year Ended December 31,		
	2013	2012	2013	2012	2011
Equity interest in Middlemount Coal Pty Ltd	$173.4	$295.9	$33.5	$52.1	$ 7.3
Other equity method investments	6.7	2.7	6.7	9.1	11.9
Total equity method investments	$180.1	$298.6	$40.2	$61.2	$19.2

Due to sustained weakness in seaborne metallurgical coal prices that have persisted longer than the Company previously anticipated, a history of operating losses at the mine and the magnitude of the difference between the estimated fair value and the carrying value of its equity investment, the Company determined the carrying value of its equity investment in Middlemount to be other-than-temporarily impaired as of December 31, 2013, in spite of a successful owner-operator conversion completed in 2013 and an ongoing series of operational efficiency initiatives being conducted at the site aimed at improving Middlemount's cost structure. Correspondingly, the Company recorded an impairment charge of $43.2 million during the year ended December 31, 2013 to write down the carrying value of its equity investment, which has been reflected in "Asset impairment and mine closure costs" in the consolidated statement of operations for that period.

The reset carrying value of the Company's equity interest in Middlemount Coal Pty Ltd, reflected in the table above, includes a remaining unamortized difference between the carrying value of that investment and the underlying equity in the net assets of the joint venture of $100.4 million as of December 31, 2013.

In addition to its equity method investment, the Company periodically makes loans to Middlemount pursuant to the related shareholders' agreement. Refer to Note 8. "Financing Receivables" for addition details surrounding those loans.

ENVIRONMENTAL

3.36 FMC CORPORATION (DEC)
NOTES TO CONSOLIDATED FINANCIAL STATEMENTS

Note 1: Principal Accounting Policies and Related Financial Information (in part)

Environmental obligations . We provide for environmental-related obligations when they are probable and amounts can be reasonably estimated. Where the available information is sufficient to estimate the amount of liability, that estimate has been used. Where the information is only sufficient to establish a range of probable liability and no point within the range is more likely than any other, the lower end of the range has been used.

Estimated obligations to remediate sites that involve oversight by the United States Environmental Protection Agency ("EPA"), or similar government agencies, are generally accrued no later than when a Record of Decision ("ROD"), or equivalent, is issued, or upon completion of a Remedial Investigation/Feasibility Study ("RI/FS"), or equivalent, that is submitted by us and the appropriate government agency or agencies. Estimates are reviewed quarterly and, if necessary, adjusted as additional information becomes available. The estimates can change substantially as additional information becomes available regarding the nature or extent of site contamination, required remediation methods, and other actions by or against governmental agencies or private parties.

Our environmental liabilities for continuing and discontinued operations are principally for costs associated with the remediation and/or study of sites at which we are alleged to have released hazardous substances into the environment. Such costs principally include, among other items, RI/FS, site remediation, costs of operation and maintenance of the remediation plan, management costs, fees to outside law firms and consultants for work related to the environmental effort, and future monitoring costs. Estimated site liabilities are determined based upon existing remediation laws and technologies, specific site consultants' engineering studies or by extrapolating experience with environmental issues at comparable sites.

Included in our environmental liabilities are costs for the operation, maintenance and monitoring of site remediation plans (OM&M). Such reserves are based on our best estimates for these OM&M plans. Over time we may incur OM&M costs in excess of these reserves. However, we are unable to reasonably estimate an amount in excess of our recorded reserves because we cannot reasonably estimate the period for which such OM&M plans will need to be in place or the future annual cost of such remediation, as conditions at these environmental sites change over time. Such additional OM&M costs could be significant in total but would be incurred over an extended period of years.

Included in the environmental reserve balance, other assets balance and disclosure of reasonably possible loss contingencies are amounts from third party insurance policies which we believe are probable of recovery.

Provisions for environmental costs are reflected in income, net of probable and estimable recoveries from named Potentially Responsible Parties ("PRPs") or other third parties. Such provisions incorporate inflation and are not discounted to their present values.

In calculating and evaluating the adequacy of our environmental reserves, we have taken into account the joint and several liability imposed by Comprehensive Environmental Remediation, Compensation and Liability Act ("CERCLA") and the analogous state laws on all PRPs and have considered the identity and financial condition of the other PRPs at each site to the extent possible. We have also considered the identity and financial condition of other third parties from whom recovery is anticipated, as well as the status of our claims against such parties. Although we are unable to forecast the ultimate contributions of PRPs and other third parties with absolute certainty, the degree of uncertainty with respect to each party is taken into account when determining the environmental reserve on a site-by-site basis. Our liability includes our best estimate of the costs expected to be paid before the consideration of any potential recoveries from third parties. We believe that any recorded recoveries related to PRPs are realizable in all material respects. Recoveries are recorded as either an offset in "Environmental liabilities, continuing and discontinued" or as "Other assets" in our consolidated balance sheets in accordance with U.S. accounting literature.

Note 7: Restructuring and Other Charges (Income) (in part)

Other Charges (Income), Net

(In millions)	Year Ended December 31,		
	2013	2012	2011
Environmental charges, net	$ 6.2	$5.8	$3.1
Other, net	32.1	4.0	0.9
Other charges (Income), net	$38.3	$9.8	$4.0

Environmental Charges, Net

Environmental charges represent the net charges associated with environmental remediation at continuing operating sites, see Note 10 for additional details.

Note 10: Environmental Obligations (in part)

We are subject to various federal, state, local and foreign environmental laws and regulations that govern emissions of air pollutants, discharges of water pollutants, and the manufacture, storage, handling and disposal of hazardous substances, hazardous wastes and other toxic materials and remediation of contaminated sites. We are also subject to liabilities arising under the Comprehensive Environmental Response, Compensation and Liability Act ("CERCLA") and similar state laws that impose responsibility on persons who arranged for the disposal of hazardous substances, and on current and previous owners and operators of a facility for the clean-up of hazardous substances released from the facility into the environment. We are also subject to liabilities under the Resource Conservation and Recovery Act ("RCRA") and analogous state laws that require owners and operators of facilities that have treated, stored or disposed of hazardous waste pursuant to a RCRA permit to follow certain waste management practices and to clean up releases of hazardous substances into the environment associated with past or present practices. In addition, when deemed appropriate, we enter certain sites with potential liability into voluntary remediation compliance programs, which are also subject to guidelines that require owners and operators, current and previous, to clean up releases of hazardous substances into the environment associated with past or present practices.

We have been named a Potentially Responsible Party ("PRP") at 31 sites on the federal government's National Priorities List ("NPL"), at which our potential liability has not yet been settled. In addition, we received notice from the EPA or other regulatory agencies that we may be a PRP, or PRP equivalent, at other sites, including 37 sites at which we have determined that it is reasonably possible that we have an environmental liability. In cooperation with appropriate government agencies, we are currently participating in, or have participated in, a Remedial Investigation/Feasibility Study ("RI/FS"), or equivalent, at most of the identified sites, with the status of each investigation varying from site to site. At certain sites, a RI/FS has only recently begun, providing limited information, if any, relating to cost estimates, timing, or the involvement of other PRPs; whereas, at other sites, the studies are complete, remedial action plans have been chosen, or a Record of Decision ("ROD") has been issued.

Environmental liabilities consist of obligations relating to waste handling and the remediation and/or study of sites at which we are alleged to have released or disposed of hazardous substances. These sites include current operations, previously operated sites, and sites associated with discontinued operations. We have provided reserves for potential environmental obligations that we consider probable and for which a reasonable estimate of the obligation can be made. Accordingly, total reserves of $225.7 million and $236.5 million, respectively, before recoveries, existed at December 31, 2013 and 2012.

The estimated reasonably possible environmental loss contingencies, net of expected recoveries, exceed amounts accrued by approximately $170 million at December 31, 2013. This reasonably possible estimate is based upon information available as of the date of the filing and the actual future losses may be higher given the uncertainties regarding the status of laws, regulations, enforcement policies, the impact of potentially responsible parties, technology and information related to individual sites.

Additionally, although potential environmental remediation expenditures in excess of the reserves and estimated loss contingencies could be significant, the impact on our future consolidated financial results is not subject to reasonable estimation due to numerous uncertainties concerning the nature and scope of possible contamination at many sites, identification of remediation alternatives under constantly changing requirements, selection of new and diverse clean-up technologies to meet compliance standards, the timing of potential expenditures and the allocation of costs among PRPs as well as other third parties. The liabilities arising from potential environmental obligations that have not been reserved for at this time may be material to any one quarter's or year's results of operations in the future. However, we believe any liability arising from such potential environmental obligations is not likely to have a material adverse effect on our liquidity or financial condition as it may be satisfied over many years.

The table below is a roll forward of our total environmental reserves, continuing and discontinued, from December 31, 2010 to December 31, 2013.

(In millions)	Operating and Discontinued Sites Total
Total environmental reserves, net of recoveries at December 31, 2010	$224.9
2011	
Provision	45.2
Spending, net of recoveries	(43.2)
Net change	2.0
Total environmental reserves, net of recoveries at December 31, 2011	$226.9
2012	
Provision	31.2
Spending, net of recoveries	(42.1)
Net change	(10.9)
Total environmental reserves, net of recoveries at December 31, 2012	$216.0
2013	
Provision	48.2
Spending, net of recoveries	(59.5)
Net change	(11.3)
Total environmental reserves, net of recoveries at December 31, 2013	$204.7

To ensure we are held responsible only for our equitable share of site remediation costs, we have initiated, and will continue to initiate, legal proceedings for contributions from other PRPs. At December 31, 2013 and 2012, we have recorded recoveries representing probable realization of claims against U.S. government agencies, insurance carriers and other third parties. Recoveries are recorded as either an offset to the "Environmental liabilities, continuing and discontinued" or as "Other assets" in the consolidated balance sheets.

The table below is a roll forward of our total recorded recoveries from December 31, 2011 to December 31, 2013:

(In millions)	December 31, 2011	Increase in Recoveries	Cash Received	December 31, 2012	Increase in Recoveries	Cash Received	December 31, 2013
Environmental liabilities, continuing and discontinued	$24.3	$2.2	$ 6.0	$20.5	$4.5	$ 4.0	$21.0
Other assets[1]	58.3	5.0	11.7	51.6	4.7	20.8	35.5
Total	$82.6	$7.2	$17.7	$72.1	$9.2	$24.8	$56.5

[1] The amounts are included within "Prepaid and other current assets" and "Other assets". See Note 21 for more details.

The table below provides detail of current and long-term environmental reserves, continuing and discontinued.

	December 31,	
(In millions)	2013	2012
Environmental reserves, current, net of recoveries[1]	$ 29.5	$ 15.8
Environmental reserves, long-term continuing and discontinued, net of recoveries[2]	175.2	200.2
Total environmental reserves, net of recoveries	$204.7	$216.0

[1] "Current" includes only those reserves related to continuing operations. These amounts are included within "Accrued and other liabilities" on the consolidated balance sheets.

[2] These amounts are included in "Environmental liabilities, continuing and discontinued" on the consolidated balance sheets.

Our net environmental provisions relate to costs for the continued cleanup of both operating sites and for certain discontinued manufacturing operations from previous years. The net provisions are comprised as follows:

(In millions)	Year Ended December 31,		
	2013	2012	2011
Continuing operations[1]	$ 6.2	$ 5.8	$ 3.1
Discontinued operations[2]	37.3	20.4	25.4
Net environmental provision	$43.5	$26.2	$28.5

[1] Recorded as a component of "Restructuring and other charges (income)" on our consolidated statements of income. See Note 7.
[2] Recorded as a component of "Discontinued operations, net" on our consolidated statements of income. See Note 9.

On our consolidated balance sheets, the net environmental provisions affect assets and liabilities as follows:

(In millions)	Year Ended December 31,		
	2013	2012	2011
Environmental reserves[1]	$48.2	$31.2	$45.2
Other assets[2]	(4.7)	(5.0)	(16.7)
Net environmental provision	$43.5	$26.2	$28.5

[1] See above roll forward of our total environmental reserves as presented on our consolidated balance sheets.
[2] Represents certain environmental recoveries. See Note 21 for details of Other assets as presented on our consolidated balance sheets.

SALE OF RECEIVABLES

3.37 ARCHER-DANIELS-MIDLAND COMPANY (DEC)
CONSOLIDATED STATEMENTS OF EARNINGS (in part)

(In millions, except per share amounts)	Year Ended December 31		Six Months Ended December 31		Year Ended June 30	
	2013	2012 (Unaudited)	2012	2011 (Unaudited)	2012	2011
Revenues	$89,804	$90,559	$46,729	$45,208	$89,038	$80,676
Cost of products sold	85,915	86,936	44,927	43,361	85,370	76,376
Gross profit	3,889	3,623	1,802	1,847	3,668	4,300
Selling, general and administrative expenses	1,759	1,665	869	830	1,626	1,611
Asset impairment, exit, and restructuring costs	259	243	146	352	449	—
Interest expense	413	445	213	209	441	482
Equity in earnings of unconsolidated affiliates	(411)	(476)	(255)	(251)	(472)	(542)
Interest income	(102)	(109)	(59)	(62)	(112)	(136)
Other (income) expense—net	(53)	(126)	(109)	(12)	(29)	(130)
Earnings before income taxes	2,024	1,981	997	781	1,765	3,015

NOTES TO CONSOLIDATED FINANCIAL STATEMENTS

Note 20. Sale of Accounts Receivable

Since March 2012, the Company has an accounts receivable securitization program (the "Program") with certain commercial paper conduit purchasers and committed purchasers (collectively, the "Purchasers"). Under the Program, certain U.S.-originated trade accounts receivable are sold to a wholly-owned bankruptcy-remote entity, ADM Receivables, LLC ("ADM Receivables"). ADM Receivables in turn transfers such purchased accounts receivable in their entirety to the Purchasers pursuant to a receivables purchase agreement. In exchange for the transfer of the accounts receivable, ADM Receivables receives a cash payment of up to $1.1 billion and an additional amount upon the collection of the accounts receivable (deferred consideration). ADM Receivables uses the cash proceeds from the transfer of receivables to the Purchasers and other consideration to finance the purchase of receivables from the Company and the ADM subsidiaries originating the receivables. The Company accounts for these transfers as sales. The Company has no retained interests in the transferred receivables, other than collection and administrative responsibilities and its right to the deferred consideration. At December 31, 2013, and 2012, the Company did not record a servicing asset or liability related to its retained responsibility, based on its assessment of the servicing fee, market values for similar transactions and its cost of servicing the receivables sold. The Program terminates on June 28, 2014, unless extended.

As of December 31, 2013, the fair value of trade receivables transferred to the Purchasers under the Program and derecognized from the Company's consolidated balance sheet was $1.9 billion. In exchange for the transfer, the Company received cash of $1.1 billion and recorded a $0.8 billion receivable for deferred consideration included in other current assets. Cash collections from customers on receivables sold were $39.8 billion, $30.8 billion, $21.9 billion, and $8.9 billion for the years ended December 31, 2013 and 2012, the six months ended December 31, 2012, and the year ended June 30, 2012, respectively. All of the cash collections from customers on receivables sold were applied to the deferred consideration. Deferred consideration is paid to the Company in cash on behalf of the Purchasers as receivables are collected; however, as this is a revolving facility, cash collected from the Company's customers is reinvested by the Purchasers daily in new receivable purchases under the Program.

The Company's risk of loss following the transfer of accounts receivable under the Program is limited to the deferred consideration outstanding. The Company carries the deferred consideration at fair value determined by calculating the expected amount of cash to be received and is principally based on observable inputs (a Level 2 measurement under the applicable accounting standards) consisting mainly of the face amount of the receivables adjusted for anticipated credit losses and discounted at the appropriate market rate. Payment of deferred consideration is not subject to significant risks other than delinquencies and credit losses on accounts receivable transferred under the program which have historically been insignificant.

Transfers of receivables under the Program during the years ended December 31, 2013 and 2012, the six months ended December 31, 2012, and the year ended June 30, 2012 resulted in an expense for the loss on sale of $4 million, $8 million, $4 million, and $4 million, respectively, which is classified as selling, general, and administrative expenses in the consolidated statements of earnings.

The Company reflects all cash flows related to the Program as operating activities in its consolidated statements of cash flows because the cash received from the Purchasers upon both the sale and collection of the receivables is not subject to significant interest rate risk given the short-term nature of the Company's trade receivables.

MERGERS AND ACQUISITIONS

3.38 AMERICAN GREETINGS CORPORATION (FEB)
CONSOLIDATED STATEMENT OF INCOME (in part)

Thousands of dollars except share and per share amounts

	2013	2012	2011
Net sales	$1,842,544	$1,663,281	$1,565,539
Other revenue	26,195	31,863	32,355
Total revenue	1,868,739	1,695,144	1,597,894
Material, labor and other production costs	817,740	741,645	682,368
Selling, distribution and marketing expenses	653,935	533,827	483,553
Administrative and general expenses	298,569	250,691	260,476
Goodwill impairment	—	27,154	—
Other operating expense (income)—net	4,330	(8,200)	(6,669)
Operating income	94,165	150,027	178,166
Interest expense	17,896	53,073	25,389
Interest income	(471)	(982)	(853)
Other non-operating (income) expense—net	(9,174)	121	(2,377)
Income before income tax expense	85,914	97,815	156,007

NOTES TO CONSOLIDATED FINANCIAL STATEMENTS

Note 2—Acquisitions (in part)

Clinton Cards Acquisition

During the first quarter of 2013, the Corporation acquired all of the outstanding senior secured debt of Clinton Cards for $56,560 (£35,000) through Lakeshore Lending Limited ("Lakeshore"), a wholly-owned subsidiary of the Corporation organized under the laws of the United Kingdom. Subsequently, on May 9, 2012, Clinton Cards was placed into administration, a procedure similar to Chapter 11 bankruptcy in the United States. Prior to entering into administration, Clinton Cards had approximately 750 stores and annual revenues of approximately $600,000 across its two primary retail brands, Clinton Cards and Birthdays. The legacy Clinton Cards business had been an important customer to the Corporation's international business for approximately forty years and was one of the Corporation's largest customers.

As part of the administration process, the administrators ("Administrators") of Clinton Cards and certain of its subsidiaries (the "Sellers") conducted an auction of certain assets of the business of the Sellers that they believed constituted a viable ongoing business. Lakeshore bid $37,168 (£23,000) for certain of these remaining assets. The bid took the form of a "credit bid," where the Corporation used a portion of the outstanding senior secured debt owed to Lakeshore by Clinton Cards to pay the purchase price for the assets. The bid was accepted by the Administrators and on June 6, 2012 the Corporation entered into an agreement with the Sellers and the Administrators for the purchase of certain assets and the related business of the Sellers.

Under the terms of the agreement, the Corporation expects to acquire approximately 400 stores from the Sellers, together with related inventory and overhead, as well as the Clinton Cards and related brands. The asset acquisition is expected to result in a net increase in the Corporation's annual revenues of approximately $280,000, although the final number will depend on the ultimate number of stores acquired, which is subject to further negotiations with landlords at each respective location. The landlords must generally consent to the assignment of the leases for such stores on terms that are acceptable to the Corporation. If the Corporation cannot negotiate acceptable lease assignments, or if the applicable landlord withholds consent to the assignment of its store lease, then the Corporation may close the store, the store lease will be placed back into the administration process, and the Sellers will be responsible for any further obligations under the store lease. As of February 28, 2013, the Corporation has completed 295 lease assignments. The estimated future minimum rental payments for noncancelable operating leases related to these lease assignments are $255,381. In addition, assuming that the remaining landlords consent to terms proposed by the Corporation and the Corporation is able to successfully complete assignments for all of the approximately 400 stores, the estimated future minimum rental payments for noncancelable operating leases will be approximately $105,000 higher, resulting in a total estimated future minimum rental payments for noncancelable operating leases of approximately $360,000 related to acquired stores. Subsequent to year-end, we have completed an additional 62 lease assignments. As such, the total number of lease assignments was 357 as of April 24, 2013. The negotiations with landlords are expected to take approximately twelve months from the closing of the transaction on June 6, 2012.

The stores and assets not acquired by the Corporation remain part of the administration process. It is anticipated that these remaining assets not purchased by the Corporation will be liquidated and proceeds will be used to repay the creditors of the Sellers, including the Corporation. The Corporation will seek to recover the $19,392 (£12,000) remaining senior secured debt claim held by it through the liquidation process. However, based on the estimated recovery information provided by the Administrators, the Corporation recorded an aggregate charge of $8,106 relating to the senior secured debt it acquired in the current year's first fiscal quarter. The remaining balance of the senior secured debt is included in "Prepaid expenses and other" on the Consolidated Statement of Financial Position. The liquidation process was originally expected to take approximately twelve months from the closing of the transaction on June 6, 2012. The process is currently expected to be completed by December 31, 2013.

Separate from the acquired senior secured debt, the Corporation had unsecured accounts receivable exposure to Clinton Cards. Based on the expected recovery shortfall on the senior secured debt described above, a majority of the unsecured accounts receivable is not expected to be collected. Accordingly, the Corporation recorded bad debt expense of $16,514 in 2013 relating to the unsecured accounts receivable. In addition, with the May 2012 announcement by the Administrators that all of Clinton Cards' Birthdays ("Birthdays") branded retail stores would be liquidated, the Corporation recorded an impairment charge of $3,981 for the deferred costs related to the Birthdays stores.

The charges incurred in 2013 associated with the aforementioned acquisition are reflected on the Consolidated Statement of Income as follows:

	Contract Asset Impairment	Bad Debt Expense	Legal and Advisory Fees	Impairment of Debt Purchased	Total
Net sales	$3,981	$ —	$ —	$ —	$ 3,981
Administrative and general expenses	—	16,514	7,129	—	23,643
Other operating expense (income)—net	—	—	—	8,106	8,106
	$3,981	$16,514	$7,129	$8,106	$35,730

These charges are reflected in the Corporation's reportable segments as follows:

	Contract Asset Impairment	Bad Debt Expense	Legal and Advisory Fees	Impairment of Debt Purchased	Total
International Social Expression Products	$3,981	$16,514	$ —	$ —	$20,495
Unallocated	—	—	7,129	8,106	15,235
	$3,981	$16,514	$7,129	$8,106	$35,730

The total cost of the acquisition has been allocated to the assets acquired and the liabilities assumed based upon their estimated fair values at the date of the acquisition. The estimated purchase price allocation is preliminary and subject to revision as valuation work and other analyses are still being conducted. The following represents the preliminary purchase price allocation:

Purchase price (in millions):	
Credit bid	$37.2
Effective settlement of pre-existing relationships with the legacy Clinton Cards business	6.4
Cash acquired	(0.6)
	$43.0
Allocation (in millions):	
Inventory	$ 5.5
Property, plant and equipment	19.3
Intangible assets	21.7
Current liabilities assumed	(3.5)
	$43.0

The financial results of this acquisition are included in the Corporation's consolidated results from the date of acquisition. Pro forma results of operations have not been presented because the effect of this acquisition was not deemed material at the date of acquisition. The acquired business is included in the Corporation's Retail Operations segment.

CHANGE IN FAIR VALUE OF DERIVATIVES

3.39 NOBLE ENERGY, INC. (DEC)
CONSOLIDATED STATEMENTS OF OPERATIONS (in part)

(Millions, except per share amounts)

	Year Ended December 31,		
	2013	2012	2011
Revenues			
Oil, Gas and NGL Sales	$4,809	$4,037	$3,179
Income from Equity Method Investees	206	186	193
Other Revenues	—	—	32
Total Revenues	5,015	4,223	3,404
Costs and Expenses			
Production Expense	850	673	558
Exploration Expense	415	409	277
Depreciation, Depletion and Amortization	1,568	1,370	878
General and Administrative	433	384	339
Gain on Divestitures	(36)	(154)	(25)
Asset Impairments	86	104	757
Other Operating (Income) Expense, Net	43	25	86
Total Operating Expenses	3,359	2,811	2,870
Operating Income	1,656	1,412	534
Other (Income) Expense			
(Gain) Loss on Commodity Derivative Instruments	133	(75)	(42)
Interest, Net of Amount Capitalized	158	125	65
Other Non-Operating (Income) Expense, Net	21	6	9
Total Other (Income) Expense	312	56	32
Income from Continuing Operations Before Income Taxes	1,344	1,356	502

NOTES TO CONSOLIDATED FINANCIAL STATEMENTS

Note 1. Summary of Significant Accounting Policies (in part)

Derivative Instruments and Hedging Activities All derivative instruments (including certain derivative instruments embedded in other contracts) are recorded in our consolidated balance sheets as either an asset or liability and measured at fair value. Changes in the derivative instrument's fair value are recognized currently in earnings, unless the derivative instrument has been designated as a cash flow hedge and specific cash flow hedge accounting criteria are met. Under cash flow hedge accounting, unrealized gains and losses are reflected in shareholders' equity as accumulated other comprehensive loss (AOCL) until the forecasted transaction occurs. The derivative's gains or losses are then offset against related results on the hedged transaction in the statements of operations.

A company must formally document, designate and assess the effectiveness of transactions that receive hedge accounting. Only derivative instruments that are expected to be highly effective in offsetting anticipated gains or losses on the hedged cash flows and that are subsequently documented to have been highly effective can qualify for hedge accounting. Effectiveness must be assessed both at inception of the hedge and on an ongoing basis. Any ineffectiveness in hedging instruments whereby gains or losses do not exactly offset anticipated gains or losses of hedged cash flows is measured and recognized in earnings in the period in which it occurs. When using hedge accounting, we assess hedge effectiveness quarterly based on total changes in the derivative instrument's fair value by performing regression analysis. A hedge is considered effective if certain statistical tests are met. We record hedge ineffectiveness in (gain) loss on commodity derivative instruments.

Accounting for Commodity Derivative Instruments. We account for our commodity derivative instruments using mark-to-market accounting and recognize all gains and losses in earnings during the period in which they occur. Our consolidated statements of cash flows includes the non-cash unrealized gain and loss on commodity derivative instruments, which represented the difference between the total gain and loss on commodity derivative instruments and the cash received or paid on settlements of commodity derivative instruments during the period.

We offset the fair value amounts recognized for derivative instruments and the fair value amounts recognized for the right to reclaim cash collateral or the obligation to return cash collateral. The cash collateral (commonly referred to as a "margin") must arise from derivative instruments recognized at fair value that are executed with the same counterparty under a master arrangement with netting clauses.

Accounting for Interest Rate Derivative Instruments. We designate interest rate derivative instruments as cash flow hedges. Changes in fair value of interest rate swaps or interest rate "locks" used as cash flow hedges are reported in AOCL, to the extent the hedge is effective, until the forecasted transaction occurs, at which time they are recorded as adjustments to interest expense over the term of the related notes. See Note 8. Derivative Instruments and Hedging Activities.

Note 8. Derivative Instruments and Hedging Activities (in part)

Objective and Strategies for Using Derivative Instruments. In order to mitigate the effect of commodity price volatility and enhance the predictability of cash flows relating to the marketing of our crude oil and natural gas, we enter into crude oil and natural gas price hedging arrangements with respect to a portion of our expected production. The derivative instruments we use may include variable to fixed price commodity swaps, two-way and three-way collars, basis swaps and put options.

The fixed price swap and two-way collar contracts entitle us (floating price payor) to receive settlement from the counterparty (fixed price payor) for each calculation period in amounts, if any, by which the settlement price for the scheduled trading days applicable for each calculation period is less than the fixed strike price or floor price. We would pay the counterparty if the settlement price for the scheduled trading days applicable for each calculation period is more than the fixed strike price or ceiling price. The amount payable by us, if the floating price is above the fixed or ceiling price, is the product of the notional quantity per calculation period and the excess of the floating price over the fixed or ceiling price in respect of each calculation period. The amount payable by the counterparty, if the floating price is below the fixed or floor price, is the product of the notional quantity per calculation period and the excess of the fixed or floor price over the floating price in respect of each calculation period.

A three-way collar consists of a two-way collar contract combined with a put option contract sold by us with a strike price below the floor price of the two-way collar. We receive price protection at the purchased put option floor price of the two-way collar if commodity prices are above the sold put option strike price. If commodity prices fall below the sold put option strike price, we receive the cash market price plus the delta between the two put option strike prices. This type of instrument allows us to capture more value in a rising commodity price environment, but limits our benefits in a downward commodity price environment.

For put options, we typically pay a premium to the counterparty in exchange for the sale of the instrument. If the index price is below the floor price of the put option, we receive the difference between the floor price and the index price multiplied by the contract volumes less the option premium at the time of settlement. If the index price settles at or above the floor price of the put option, we pay only the put option premium at the time of settlement. We had no outstanding put options as of December 31, 2013.

We also may enter into forward contracts to hedge anticipated exposure to interest rate risk associated with public debt financing.

While these instruments mitigate the cash flow risk of future reductions in commodity prices or increases in interest rates, they may also curtail benefits from future increases in commodity prices or decreases in interest rates.

See Note 13. Fair Value Measurements and Disclosures for a discussion of methods and assumptions used to estimate the fair values of our derivative instruments.

Counterparty Credit Risk. Derivative instruments expose us to counterparty credit risk. Our commodity derivative instruments are currently with a diversified group of major banks or market participants, and we monitor and manage our level of financial exposure. Our commodity derivative contracts are executed under master agreements which allow us, in the event of default, to elect early termination of all contracts with the defaulting counterparty. If we choose to elect early termination, all asset and liability positions with the defaulting counterparty would be net settled at the time of election.

We monitor the creditworthiness of our commodity derivatives counterparties. However, we are not able to predict sudden changes in counterparties' creditworthiness. In addition, even if such changes are not sudden, we may be limited in our ability to mitigate an increase in counterparty credit risk.

Possible actions would be to transfer our position to another counterparty or request a voluntary termination of the derivative contracts resulting in a cash settlement. Should one of these financial counterparties not perform, we may not realize the benefit of some of our derivative instruments under lower commodity prices or higher interest rates, and could incur a loss.

Interest Rate Derivative Instrument. In January 2010, we entered into an interest rate forward starting swap to effectively fix the cash flows related to interest payments on our anticipated March 2011 debt issuance. During first quarter 2011, the net liability position on the swap was reduced in our mark to market calculation, and we recognized a corresponding gain of $23 million, net of tax, in AOCL. On February 15,

2011 we settled the interest rate swap, which had a net liability position of $40 million at the time of settlement. Approximately $26 million, net of tax, was recorded in accumulated other comprehensive loss (AOCL) and is being reclassified to interest expense over the term of the notes. The ineffective portion of the interest rate swap was de minimis.

Unsettled Derivative Instruments. As of December 31, 2013, we had entered into the following crude oil derivative instruments:

				Swaps	Collars		
Settlement Period	Type of Contract	Index	Bbls Per Day	Weighted Average Fixed Price	Weighted Average Short Put Price	Weighted Average Floor Price	Weighted Average Ceiling Price
Instruments Entered Into as of December 31, 2013							
2014	Swaps	NYMEX WTI	37,000	$ 92.67	$ —	$ —	$ —
2014	Swaps	Dated Brent	13,000	103.21	—	—	—
2014	Three-Way Collars	NYMEX WTI	12,000	—	75.67	90.67	100.88
2014	Three-Way Collars	Dated Brent	8,000	—	84.38	98.25	121.56
2015	Swaps	NYMEX WTI	16,000	87.66	—	—	—
2015	Swaps	Dated Brent	8,000	100.20	—	—	—
2015	Three-Way Collars	NYMEX WTI	15,000	—	70.67	88.00	94.78
2015	Three-Way Collars	Dated Brent	11,000	—	76.36	95.27	109.26

As of December 31, 2013, we had entered into the following natural gas derivative instruments:

				Swaps	Collars		
Settlement Period	Type of Contract	Index	MMBtu Per Day	Weighted Average Fixed Price	Weighted Average Short Put Price	Weighted Average Floor Price	Weighted Average Ceiling Price
Instruments Entered Into as of December 31, 2013							
2014	Swaps	NYMEX HH	60,000	$4.24	$ —	$ —	$ —
2014	Three-Way Collars	NYMEX HH	230,000	—	2.83	3.75	4.98
2015	Swaps	NYMEX HH	80,000	4.32	—	—	—
2015	Three-Way Collars	NYMEX HH	120,000	—	3.54	4.25	5.06

Fair Value Amounts and Gains and Losses on Derivative Instruments. The fair values of derivative instruments in our consolidated balance sheets were as follows:

	Fair Value of Derivative Instruments							
	Asset Derivative Instruments				Liability Derivative Instruments			
	December 31, 2013		December 31, 2012		December 31, 2013		December 31, 2012	
(Millions)	Balance Sheet Location	Fair Value	Balance Sheet Location	Fair Value	Balance Sheet Location	Fair Value	Balance Sheet Location	Fair Value
Commodity derivative instruments	Current assets	$ 1	Current assets	$63	Current liabilities	$65	Current liabilities	$ 7
	Noncurrent assets	16	Noncurrent assets	21	Noncurrent liabilities	10	Noncurrent liabilities	3
Total		$17		$84		$75		$10

The effect of derivative instruments on our consolidated statements of operations was as follows:

	Year Ended December 31,		
(Millions)	2013	2012	2011
Realized Mark-to-Market (Gain) Loss[1]			
Crude Oil	$ 52	$ 83	$ 44
Natural Gas	(50)	(49)	(108)
Total Realized Mark-to-Market (Gain) Loss	2	34	(64)
Unrealized Mark-to-Market (Gain) Loss[1]			
Crude Oil	87	(120)	5
Natural Gas	44	11	17
Total Unrealized Mark-to-Market (Gain) Loss	131	(109)	22
Total (Gain) Loss on Commodity Derivative Instruments	$133	$ (75)	$ (42)

[1] Gains and losses on commodity derivative instruments included in net income include both pre-tax realized gains and losses, which equals the cash settlements during the period, and pre-tax, unrealized, non-cash gains or losses, which are due to the change in the mark-to-market value of our commodity contracts. Many factors impact our gain and loss on commodity derivative instruments including: increases and decreases in the commodity forward curves compared to our executed hedging arrangements; increases and decreases in hedged future volumes; and the mix of hedge arrangements between NYMEX WTI, Dated Brent and NYMEX HH commodities. Unrealized mark-to-market gains or losses recognized in the current period will be realized in the future when cash settlement occurs.

IMPAIRMENT OF INVESTMENTS

3.40 WASTE MANAGEMENT, INC. (DEC)
CONSOLIDATED STATEMENTS OF OPERATIONS (in part)

(In Millions, Except per Share Amounts)

	Years Ended December 31,		
	2013	**2012**	**2011**
Operating Revenues:			
Service revenues	$12,566	$12,327	$11,852
Tangible product revenues	1,417	1,322	1,526
Total operating revenues	13,983	13,649	13,378
Costs and Expenses:			
Operating costs (exclusive of depreciation and amortization shown below):			
Cost of services	7,880	7,765	7,254
Cost of tangible products	1,232	1,114	1,287
Total operating costs	9,112	8,879	8,541
Selling, general and administrative	1,468	1,472	1,551
Depreciation and amortization	1,333	1,297	1,229
Restructuring	18	67	19
Goodwill impairments	509	4	1
(Income) expense from divestitures, asset impairments (other than goodwill) and unusual items	464	79	9
	12,904	11,798	11,350
Income from operations	1,079	1,851	2,028
Other Income (Expense):			
Interest expense	(481)	(488)	(481)
Interest income	4	4	8
Equity in net losses of unconsolidated entities	(34)	(46)	(31)
Other, net	(74)	(18)	(4)
	(585)	(548)	(508)
Income before income taxes	494	1,303	1,520

NOTES TO CONSOLIDATED FINANCIAL STATEMENTS

3. Summary of Significant Accounting Policies (in part)

Investments in Unconsolidated Entities

Investments in unconsolidated entities over which the Company has significant influence are accounted for under the equity method of accounting. Investments in entities in which the Company does not have the ability to exert significant influence over the investees' operating and financing activities are accounted for under the cost method of accounting. In addition to equity investments in unconsolidated subsidiaries, we support these ventures through loans and advances. These loans and advances are included as a component of "Other" within the "Net cash provided by investing activities" in our Consolidated Statement of Cash Flows. The following table summarizes our equity and cost method investments as of December 31 (in millions):

	2013	2012
Equity investments[a]	$437	$443
Cost investments	154	224
Investments in unconsolidated entities	$591	$667

[a] The amount reported in 2013 includes $177 million attributable to our 2010 investment in Shanghai Environment Group ("SEG"), which is part of our Wheelabrator business. Based on our intent to sell our investment in SEG within the next 12 months, this investment has been classified as a current asset and reflected in "Investment in unconsolidated entity" in our Consolidated Balance Sheet as of December 31, 2013.

We monitor and assess the carrying value of our investments throughout the year for potential impairment and write them down to their fair value when other-than-temporary declines exist. Fair value is generally based on (i) other third-party investors' recent transactions in the securities; (ii) other information available regarding the current market for similar assets and/or (iii) a market or income approach as deemed appropriate.

13. Asset Impairments and Unusual Items (in part)

Other Income (Expense)

During the year ended December 31, 2013, we recognized impairment charges of $71 million relating to other-than-temporary declines in the value of investments in waste diversion technology companies accounted for under the cost method. We wrote down the carrying value of our investments to their fair value, which was primarily determined using an income approach based on estimated future cash flow projections obtained in the fourth quarter of 2013 and, to a lesser extent, third-party investors' recent transactions in these securities. Partially offsetting these charges was a $4 million gain on the sale of a similar investment recognized in the second quarter of 2013.

During the year ended December 31, 2012, we recognized an impairment charge of $16 million relating to an other-than-temporary decline in the value of another investment in a waste diversion technology company accounted for under the cost method. We wrote down the carrying value of our investment to its fair value based on other third-party investors' recent transactions in these securities, which are considered to be the best evidence of fair value currently available.

These net charges are recorded in "Other, net" in our Consolidated Statement of Operations.

IMPAIRMENT OF GOODWILL AND INTANGIBLE ASSETS

3.41 BOSTON SCIENTIFIC CORPORATION (DEC)

CONSOLIDATED STATEMENTS OF OPERATIONS (in part)

	Year Ended December 31,		
(In millions, except per share data)	**2013**	**2012**	**2011**
Net sales	$7,143	$ 7,249	$7,622
Cost of products sold	2,174	2,349	2,659
Gross profit	4,969	4,900	4,963
Operating expenses:			
Selling, general and administrative expenses	2,674	2,535	2,487
Research and development expenses	861	886	895
Royalty expense	140	153	172
Amortization expense	410	395	421
Goodwill impairment charges	423	4,350	697
Intangible asset impairment charges	53	142	21
Contingent consideration expense (benefit)	4	(6)	7
Restructuring charges	101	136	89
Litigation-related charges	221	192	48
Gain on divestiture	(38)	(15)	(778)
	4,849	8,768	4,059
Operating income (loss)	120	(3,868)	904

NOTES TO THE CONSOLIDATED FINANCIAL STATEMENTS

Note A—Significant Accounting Policies (in part)

Indefinite-Lived Intangibles, Including In-Process Research and Development

Our indefinite-lived intangible assets that are not subject to amortization primarily include acquired balloon and other technology, which is foundational to our continuing operations within the Cardiovascular market and other markets within interventional medicine, and in-process research and development intangible assets acquired in a business combination. Our in-process research and development represents intangible assets acquired in a business combination that are used in research and development activities but have not yet reached technological feasibility, regardless of whether they have alternative future use. The primary basis for determining the technological feasibility or completion of these projects is obtaining regulatory approval to market the underlying products in an applicable geographic region. We classify in-process research and development acquired in a business combination as an indefinite-lived intangible asset until the completion or abandonment of the associated research and development efforts. Upon completion of the associated research and development efforts, we will determine the useful life of the technology and begin amortizing the assets to reflect their use over their remaining lives. Upon permanent abandonment, we would write-off the remaining carrying amount of the associated in-process research and development intangible asset. We test our indefinite-lived intangible assets at least annually for impairment and reassess their classification as indefinite-lived assets. We assess qualitative factors to determine whether the existence of events and circumstances indicate that it is more likely than not that our indefinite-lived intangible assets are impaired. If we conclude that it is more likely than not that the asset is impaired, we then determine the fair value of the intangible asset and perform the quantitative impairment test by comparing the fair value with the carrying value in accordance with ASC Topic 350, *Intangibles—Goodwill and Other*. If the carrying value exceeds the fair value of the indefinite-lived intangible asset, we write the carrying value down to the fair value.

We use the income approach to determine the fair values of our in-process research and development. This approach calculates fair value by estimating the after-tax cash flows attributable to an in-process project over its useful life and then discounting these after-tax cash flows back to a present value. We base our revenue assumptions on estimates of relevant market sizes, expected market growth rates, expected trends in technology and expected levels of market share. In arriving at the value of the in-process projects, we consider, among other factors: the in-process projects' stage of completion; the complexity of the work completed as of the acquisition date; the costs already incurred; the projected costs to complete; the contribution of other acquired assets; the expected regulatory path and introduction dates by region; and the estimated useful life of the technology. We apply a market-participant risk-adjusted discount rate to arrive at a present value as of the date of acquisition.

We test our in-process research and development intangible assets acquired in a business combination for impairment at least annually during the third quarter, and more frequently if events or changes in circumstances indicate that the assets may be impaired.

For asset purchases outside of business combinations, we expense any purchased research and development assets as of the acquisition date.

Amortization and Impairment of Intangible Assets

We record intangible assets at historical cost and amortize them over their estimated useful lives. We use a straight-line method of amortization, unless a method that better reflects the pattern in which the economic benefits of the intangible asset are consumed or otherwise used up can be reliably determined. The approximate useful lives for amortization of our intangible assets are as follows: patents and licenses, two to 20 years; definite-lived technology-related, five to 25 years; customer relationships, five to 25 years; other intangible assets, various.

We review intangible assets subject to amortization quarterly to determine if any adverse conditions exist or a change in circumstances has occurred that would indicate impairment or a change in the remaining useful life. Conditions that may indicate impairment include, but are not limited to, a significant adverse change in legal factors or business climate that could affect the value of an asset, a product recall, or an adverse action or assessment by a regulator. If an impairment indicator exists, we test the intangible asset for recoverability. For purposes of the recoverability test, we group our amortizable intangible assets with other assets and liabilities at the lowest level of identifiable cash flows if the intangible asset does not generate cash flows independent of other assets and liabilities. If the carrying value of the intangible asset (asset group) exceeds the undiscounted cash flows expected to result from the use and eventual disposition of the intangible asset (asset group), we will write the carrying value down to the fair value in the period identified.

We generally calculate fair value of our intangible assets as the present value of estimated future cash flows we expect to generate from the asset using a risk-adjusted discount rate. In determining our estimated future cash flows associated with our intangible assets, we use estimates and assumptions about future revenue contributions, cost structures and remaining useful lives of the asset (asset group). See *Note D—Goodwill and Other Intangible Assets* for more information related to impairments of intangible assets during 2013, 2012, and 2011.

For patents developed internally, we capitalize costs incurred to obtain patents, including attorney fees, registration fees, consulting fees, and other expenditures directly related to securing the patent.

Goodwill Valuation

Effective as of January 1, 2013, we reorganized our business from geographic regions to fully operationalized global business units. Our reorganization changed our reporting structure and changed the composition of our reporting units for goodwill impairment testing purposes. Following the reorganization, based on information regularly reviewed by our chief operating decision maker, we have three new global reportable segments consisting of: Cardiovascular, Rhythm Management, and MedSurg. We determined our new global reporting units by identifying our operating segments and assessing whether any components of these segments constituted a business for which discrete financial information is available and whether segment management regularly reviews the operating results of any components. Through this process, we identified the following new global reporting units as of January 1, 2013: Interventional Cardiology, Peripheral Interventions, Cardiac Rhythm Management, Electrophysiology, Endoscopy, Urology and Women's Health, and Neuromodulation. The discussion below for 2013 relates to our global business reporting units and for 2012 and prior periods relates to our former regional reporting units.

We allocate any excess purchase price over the fair value of the net tangible and identifiable intangible assets acquired in a business combination to goodwill. We test our goodwill balances during the second quarter of each year for impairment, or more frequently if indicators are present or changes in circumstances suggest that impairment may exist. In performing the assessment, we utilize the two-step approach prescribed under ASC Topic 350, *Intangibles—Goodwill and Other* (Topic 350). The first step requires a comparison of the carrying value of the reporting units, as defined, to the fair value of these units. We assess goodwill for impairment at the reporting unit level, which is defined as an operating segment or one level below an operating segment, referred to as a component. We determine our reporting units by first identifying our operating segments, and then assess whether any components of these segments constitute a business for which discrete financial information is available and where segment management regularly reviews the operating results of that component. We aggregate components within an operating segment that have similar economic characteristics. For our 2013 annual impairment assessment we identified seven reporting units, including Interventional Cardiology, Peripheral Interventions, Cardiac Rhythm Management, Electrophysiology, Endoscopy, Urology and Women's Health and Neuromodulation. For our 2012 and 2011 impairment assessments, we identified six reporting units within the U.S., including our CRM, Neuromodulation, Endoscopy, Urology and Women's Health, Electrophysiology, and Cardiovascular (consisting of Interventional Cardiology and Peripheral Interventions) franchises, which in aggregate make up the U.S. reportable segment. In addition, we identified four international reporting units, including EMEA, Japan, Asia Pacific and the Americas.

When allocating goodwill from business combinations to our reporting units, we assign goodwill to the reporting units that we expect to benefit from the respective business combination at the time of acquisition. In addition, for purposes of performing our goodwill impairment tests, assets and liabilities, including corporate assets, which relate to a reporting unit's operations, and would be considered in determining its fair value, are allocated to the individual reporting units. We allocate assets and liabilities not directly related to a specific reporting unit, but from which the reporting unit benefits, based primarily on the respective revenue contribution of each reporting unit.

During 2013, 2012, and 2011, we used only the income approach, specifically the DCF method, to derive the fair value of each of our reporting units in preparing our goodwill impairment assessments. This approach calculates fair value by estimating the after-tax cash flows attributable to a reporting unit and then discounting these after-tax cash flows to a present value using a risk-adjusted discount rate. We selected this method as being the most meaningful in preparing our goodwill assessments because we believe the income approach most appropriately measures our income producing assets. We have considered using the market approach and cost approach but concluded they are not appropriate in valuing our reporting units given the lack of relevant market comparisons available for application of the market approach and the inability to replicate the value of the specific technology-based assets within our reporting units for application of the cost approach. Therefore, we believe that the income approach represents the most appropriate valuation technique for which sufficient data are available to determine the fair value of our reporting units.

In applying the income approach to our accounting for goodwill, we make assumptions about the amount and timing of future expected cash flows, terminal value growth rates and appropriate discount rates. The amount and timing of future cash flows within our DCF analysis is based on our most recent operational budgets, long range strategic plans and other estimates. The terminal value growth rate is used to calculate the value of cash flows beyond the last projected period in our DCF analysis and reflects our best estimates for stable, perpetual growth of our reporting units. We use estimates of market-participant risk-adjusted WACC as a basis for determining the discount rates to apply to our reporting units' future expected cash flows.

If the carrying value of a reporting unit exceeds its fair value, we then perform the second step of the goodwill impairment test to measure the amount of impairment loss, if any. If the carrying value of a reporting unit is zero or negative, we evaluate whether it is more likely than not that a goodwill impairment exists. If we determine adverse qualitative factors exist that would indicate it is more likely than not an impairment exists, we then perform the second step of the goodwill test. The second step of the goodwill impairment test compares the estimated fair value of a reporting unit's goodwill to its carrying value. If we were unable to complete the second step of the test prior to the issuance of our financial statements and an impairment loss was probable and could be reasonably estimated, we would recognize our best estimate of the loss in our current period financial statements and disclose that the amount is an estimate. We would then recognize any adjustment to that estimate in subsequent reporting periods, once we have finalized the second step of the impairment test. See *Note D—Goodwill and Other Intangible Assets* for discussion of our goodwill impairment charges.

Note D—Goodwill and Other Intangible Assets

The gross carrying amount of goodwill and other intangible assets and the related accumulated amortization for intangible assets subject to amortization and accumulated write-offs of goodwill as of December 31, 2013 and 2012 is as follows:

(In millions)	As of December 31, 2013		As of December 31, 2012	
	Gross Carrying Amount	Accumulated Amortization/Write-Offs	Gross Carrying Amount	Accumulated Amortization/Write-Offs
Amortizable Intangible Assets				
Technology-related	$ 8,272	$(3,342)	$ 8,020	$(3,005)
Patents	513	(326)	559	(352)
Other intangible assets	845	(479)	810	(428)
	$ 9,630	$(4,147)	$ 9,389	$(3,785)
Unamortizable Intangible Assets				
Goodwill	$15,593	$(9,900)	$15,450	$(9,477)
Technology-related	197		242	
	$15,790	$(9,900)	$15,692	$(9,477)

In addition, we had $270 million and $443 million of in-process research and development intangible assets as of December 31, 2013 and December 31, 2012, respectively. During the third quarter of 2013, we reclassified approximately $45 million of core technology not previously subject to amortization to amortizable intangible assets due to projected changes in the market for this technology. We tested the intangible asset for impairment prior to this reclassification and determined that the asset was not impaired.

2013 Reorganization

We assess goodwill for impairment at the reporting unit level, which is defined as an operating segment or one level below an operating segment, referred to as a component. Effective as of January 1, 2013, we reorganized our business from geographic regions to fully operationalized global business units. Our reorganization changed our reporting structure and changed the composition of our reporting units for goodwill impairment testing purposes. Following the reorganization, based on information regularly reviewed by our chief operating decision maker, we have three new global reportable segments consisting of: Cardiovascular, Rhythm Management, and MedSurg. We determined our new global reporting units by identifying our operating segments and assessing whether any components of these segments constituted a business for which discrete financial information is available and whether segment management regularly reviews the operating results of any components. Through this process, we identified the following new global reporting units effective as of January 1, 2013: Interventional Cardiology, Peripheral Interventions, Cardiac Rhythm Management, Electrophysiology, Endoscopy, Urology and Women's Health, and Neuromodulation. The discussion below for 2013 relates to our global business reporting units and for 2012 and prior periods, relates to our former regional reporting units. For our 2012 and 2011 assessments, we identified (i) six reporting units within the U.S., which included our CRM, Neuromodulation, Endoscopy, Urology and Women's Health, Electrophysiology, and Cardiovascular (consisting of Interventional Cardiology and Peripheral Interventions) franchises, and (ii) four international reporting units, including EMEA, Japan, Asia Pacific and the Americas.

To determine the amount of goodwill within our new global reporting units, on a relative fair value basis we reallocated $1.764 billion of goodwill previously allocated to our former Europe, Middle East and Africa (EMEA), Asia Pacific, Japan, and Americas international reporting units to our new global reporting units. In addition, we reallocated the goodwill previously allocated to the former U.S. divisional reporting units to each respective new global reporting unit, with the exception of the goodwill allocated to the former U.S. Cardiovascular reporting unit. The $2.380 billion of goodwill allocated to the former U.S. Cardiovascular reporting unit was reallocated between the new global Interventional Cardiology and global Peripheral Interventions reporting units on a relative fair value basis.

The following represents our goodwill balance by new global reportable segment. We restated the prior period information to conform to the current presentation:

(In millions)	Cardiovascular	Rhythm Management	MedSurg	Total
Balance as of December 31, 2011	$ 4,542	$ 1,661	$ 3,558	$ 9,761
Purchase price adjustments	—	(1)	—	(1)
Goodwill acquired	186	327	50	563
Goodwill written off	(1,479)	(1,410)	(1,461)	(4,350)
Balance as of December 31, 2012	$ 3,249	$ 577	$ 2,147	$ 5,973
Purchase price adjustments	3	—	—	3
Goodwill acquired	—	140	—	140
Goodwill written off	—	(423)	—	(423)
Balance as of December 31, 2013	$ 3,252	$ 294	$ 2,147	$ 5,693

The 2012 and 2013 purchase price adjustments relate primarily to adjustments in taxes payable and deferred income taxes, including changes in the liability for unrecognized tax benefits.

Goodwill Impairment Testing and Charges

2013 Charges

We test our goodwill balances during the second quarter of each year for impairment, or more frequently if indicators are present or changes in circumstances suggest that impairment may exist. Following our reorganization from regions to global business units and our reallocation of goodwill on a relative fair value basis, we conducted the first step of the goodwill impairment test for all new global reporting units as of January 1, 2013. The first step requires a comparison of the carrying value of the reporting units to the fair value of these units. The fair value of each new global reporting unit exceeded its carrying value, with the exception of the global CRM reporting unit. The global CRM reporting unit carrying value exceeded its fair value primarily due to the carrying value of its amortizable intangible assets. The carrying value of amortizable intangible assets allocated to the global CRM reporting unit was $4.636 billion as of January 1, 2013. In accordance with ASC Topic 350, *Intangibles—Goodwill and Other,* we tested the global CRM amortizable intangible assets for impairment in conjunction with the interim goodwill impairment test of our global CRM reporting unit. We performed the impairment analysis of the amortizable intangible assets on an undiscounted cash flow basis, and concluded that these assets were not impaired.

The second step of the goodwill impairment test compares the estimated fair value of a reporting unit's goodwill to its carrying value. We performed the second step of the goodwill impairment test on the global CRM reporting unit and recorded a non-cash goodwill impairment charge of $423 million ($421 million after-tax) to write-down the goodwill to its implied fair value as of January 1, 2013. The primary driver of this impairment charge was our reorganization from geographic regions to global business units as of January 1, 2013, which changed the composition of our reporting units. As a result of the reorganization, any goodwill allocated to the global CRM reporting unit was no longer supported by the cash flows of other businesses. Under our former reporting unit structure, the goodwill allocated to our regional reporting units was supported by the cash flows from all businesses in each international region. The hypothetical tax structure of the global CRM business and the global CRM business discount rate applied were also contributing factors to the goodwill impairment charge. We finalized the second step of the global CRM goodwill impairment test during the second quarter of 2013, in accordance with ASC Topic 350, *Intangibles—Goodwill and Other*, and determined that no adjustments to the charge were required. After recording the impairment charge in the first quarter of 2013, there was no remaining goodwill allocated to the global CRM reporting unit.

The goodwill impairment charge taken during the first quarter of 2013 was determined on a global CRM basis pursuant to our new organizational structure. We used the income approach, specifically the DCF method, to derive the fair value of the global CRM reporting unit. We completed a DCF model associated with our new global CRM business, including the amount and timing of future expected cash flows, tax attributes, the terminal value growth rate of approximately two percent and the appropriate market-participant risk-adjusted weighted average cost of capital (WACC) of approximately 12 percent.

In the second quarter of 2013, we performed our annual goodwill impairment test for all of our reporting units. In conjunction with our annual test, the fair value of each reporting unit exceeded its carrying value except CRM, for which no goodwill remains. Therefore, it was deemed not necessary to proceed to the second step of the impairment test. We have identified our global Neuromodulation reporting unit as being at higher risk of potential failure of the first step of the goodwill impairment test in future reporting periods. Our global Neuromodulation reporting unit holds $1.356 billion of allocated goodwill. The level of excess fair value over carrying value for this reporting unit identified during our annual goodwill impairment test was approximately 16 percent. Future changes in our reporting units or in the structure of our business as a result of future reorganizations, acquisitions or divestitures of assets or businesses could result in future impairments of goodwill within our reporting units including global CRM. Further, the recoverability of our CRM-related amortizable intangibles ($4.374 billion globally as of December 31, 2013) is sensitive to future cash flow assumptions and our global CRM business performance. The $4.374 billion of CRM-related amortizable intangibles are at higher risk of potential failure of the first step of the amortizable intangible recoverability test in future reporting periods. An impairment of a material portion of our CRM-related amortizable intangibles carrying value would occur if the second step of the amortizable intangible test is required in a future reporting period. Refer to *Critical Accounting Policies and Estimates* within our Management's Discussion and Analysis of Financial Condition and Results of Operations contained in Item 7 of this Annual Report on Form 10-K for a discussion of key assumptions used in our testing.

On a quarterly basis, we monitor the key drivers of fair value to detect events or other changes that would warrant an interim impairment test of our goodwill and intangible assets. The key variables that drive the cash flows of our reporting units and amortizable intangibles are estimated revenue growth rates and levels of profitability. Terminal value growth rate assumptions, as well as the WACC rate applied are additional key variables for reporting unit cash flows. These assumptions are subject to uncertainty, including our ability to grow revenue and improve profitability levels. Relatively small declines in the future performance and cash flows of a reporting unit or asset group or small changes in other key assumptions may result in the recognition of significant asset impairment charges. For example, keeping all other variables constant, an increase in the WACC applied of 80 basis points or a 200 basis point decrease in the terminal value growth rate would require that we perform the second step of the goodwill impairment test for the global Neuromodulation reporting unit. The estimates used for our future cash flows and discount rates represent management's best estimates, which we believe to be reasonable, but future declines in business performance may impair the recoverability of our goodwill and intangible asset balances.

Future events that could have a negative impact on the levels of excess fair value over carrying value of our reporting units and/or amortizable intangible assets include, but are not limited to:

- decreases in estimated market sizes or market growth rates due to greater-than-expected declines in procedural volumes, pricing pressures, reductions in reimbursement levels, product actions, and/or competitive or disruptive technology developments;
- declines in our market share and penetration assumptions due to increased competition, an inability to develop or launch new and next-generation products and technology features in line with our commercialization strategies, and market and/or regulatory conditions that may cause significant launch delays or product recalls;
- decreases in our forecasted profitability due to an inability to successfully implement and achieve timely and sustainable cost improvement measures consistent with our expectations, increases in our market-participant tax rate, and/or changes in tax laws;
- negative developments in intellectual property litigation that may impact our ability to market certain products or increase our costs to sell certain products;
- the level of success of on-going and future research and development efforts, including those related to recent acquisitions, and increases in the research and development costs necessary to obtain regulatory approvals and launch new products;
- the level of success in managing the growth of acquired companies, achieving sustained profitability consistent with our expectations, establishing government and third-party payer reimbursement, supplying the market, and increases in the costs and time necessary to integrate acquired businesses into our operations successfully;
- changes in our reporting units or in the structure of our business as a result of future reorganizations, acquisitions or divestitures of assets or businesses; and
- increases in our market-participant risk-adjusted WACC.

Negative changes in one or more of these factors, among others, could result in additional impairment charges.

2012 Charges

In the second quarter of 2012, we performed our annual goodwill impairment test for all of our reporting units and concluded that the goodwill within our former EMEA reporting unit was impaired and recorded a charge of $3.602 billion ($3.579 billion after-tax). As a result of revised estimates developed during our annual strategic planning process and analysis performed in conjunction with our annual goodwill impairment test, we concluded that the revenue growth rates projected for the EMEA reporting unit were slightly lower than our previous estimates primarily driven by macro-economic factors and our performance in the European market. We updated short-term operating projections based on our most recent strategic plan for EMEA prepared by management. We reduced the EMEA long-term growth rates and terminal value growth rate projections and increased the discount rate within our 15-year DCF model for EMEA by approximately 100 basis points due to increased risk associated with our projections in this market primarily as a result of economic uncertainty in Europe. In addition, our expectations for future growth and profitability were lowered as compared to our previous estimates and reflected declines in average selling prices and volume pressures due to austerity measures. We finalized the second step of the EMEA goodwill impairment test during the third quarter of 2012, in accordance with ASC Topic 350, *Intangibles—Goodwill and Other*, and there were no adjustments to the charge upon finalization.

In the third quarter of 2012, we performed an interim goodwill impairment test and recorded a non-cash $748 million (pre- and after-tax) charge associated with our former U.S. Cardiac Rhythm Management (U.S. CRM) reporting unit, primarily driven by a reduction in the estimated size of the U.S. CRM market, related adjustments to our business and other competitive factors, which led to lower projected U.S. CRM results compared to prior forecasts. The U.S. CRM market is dynamic, highly competitive and difficult to forecast; in the third quarter of 2012, we lowered our projections for the U.S. CRM market size and our future revenue levels within this market, primarily to reflect changes in expectations of average selling prices and unit growth, adjustments to our business and other competitive factors. The increased pricing pressure and lower unit volumes were primarily due to physician alignment with hospitals, efforts to reduce health care costs, focus on appropriate device usage, replacement volumes and competition, and were more impactful to the U.S. CRM business than previously estimated. In addition, we adjusted certain elements of our business and shifted investments to focus on areas expected to provide the highest future growth and financial return. As a result of these factors, we reduced the compound annual revenue growth rate of our 15 year DCF model for the U.S. CRM reporting unit by approximately 250 basis points. We finalized the second step of the U.S. CRM goodwill impairment test during the fourth quarter of 2012, in accordance with ASC Topic 350, *Intangibles—Goodwill and Other*, and there were no adjustments to the charge upon finalization.

2011 Charge

Based on market information that became available to us toward the end of the first quarter of 2011, we concluded that there was a reduction in the estimated size of the U.S. ICD market, which led to lower projected U.S. CRM results compared to prior forecasts and created an indication of potential impairment of the goodwill balance attributable to our former U.S. CRM business unit. Therefore, we performed an interim impairment test in accordance with U.S. GAAP and our accounting policies and recorded a non-deductible goodwill impairment charge of $697 million, on both a pre-tax and after-tax basis, associated with this business unit during the first quarter of 2011.

The following is a rollforward of accumulated goodwill write-offs by global reportable segment:

(In millions)	Cardiovascular	Rhythm Management	MedSurg	Total
Accumulated write-offs as of December 31, 2011	$ —	$(5,127)	$ —	(5,127)
Goodwill written off	(1,479)	(1,410)	(1,461)	(4,350)
Accumulated write-offs as of December 31, 2012	$(1,479)	$(6,537)	(1,461)	$(9,477)
Goodwill written off	—	(423)	—	(423)
Accumulated write-offs as of December 31, 2013	$(1,479)	$(6,960)	$(1,461)	$(9,900)

Intangible Asset Impairment Charges

On a quarterly basis, we monitor for events or other potential indicators of impairment that would warrant an interim impairment test of our intangible assets. The recoverability of our CRM-related amortizable intangibles ($4.374 billion globally as of December 31, 2013) are sensitive to changes in future cash flow assumptions and our global CRM business performance. The $4.374 billion of CRM-related amortizable intangibles are at higher risk of potential failure of the first step of the amortizable intangible recoverability test in future reporting periods. An impairment of a material portion of our CRM-related amortizable intangibles carrying value would occur if the second step of the amortizable intangible test is required in a future reporting period. See *Goodwill Impairment Charges* above for discussion of future events that could have a negative impact on the levels of excess fair value over carrying value of our CRM-related amortizable intangible assets.

2013 Charges

During the third quarter of 2013, we performed our annual impairment test of all in-process research and development projects, and our indefinite lived core technology assets, and recorded no impairments based on the results of our testing.

During the second quarter of 2013 as a result of revised estimates developed in conjunction with our annual strategic planning process and annual goodwill impairment test, we performed an interim impairment test of our in-process research and development projects associated with certain of our acquisitions. Based on the results of our impairment analyses, we revised our expectations of the market size related to Sadra Medical, Inc. (Sadra), and the resulting timing and amount of future revenue and cash flows associated with the technology acquired from Sadra. As a result of these changes, we recorded pre-tax impairment charges of $51 million to write-down the balance of these intangible assets to their fair value during the second quarter of 2013. During the second quarter of 2013, we also recorded an additional $2 million intangible asset impairment charge associated with changes in the amount of the expected cash flows related to certain other acquired in-process research and development projects.

In-process research and development fair value is measured using projected revenues, projected expenses, discount rates, and probability of expected launch. The nonrecurring Level 3 fair value measurements of the impairment analysis performed in the second quarter of 2013 included the following significant unobservable inputs:

Intangible Asset	Fair Value as of Second Quarter 2013	Valuation Technique	Unobservable Input	Rate
In-Process R&D	$178 million	Income Approach-Excess Earnings Method	Discount Rate	16.5%

2012 Charges

During the third quarter of 2012, we performed our annual impairment test of all in-process research and development projects, and our indefinite lived core technology assets. Based on the results of our annual test, we recorded total impairment charges of $13 million ($10 million after-tax) to write-down the balances of certain in-process projects to their fair value. These charges were primarily due to increased expectations in the cost to bring an in-process project to market in a certain geographic region and lower future revenue expectations associated with an in-process project.

In-process research and development fair value is measured using projected revenues, projected expenses, discount rates, and probability of expected launch. The nonrecurring Level 3 fair value measurements of the impairment charges taken in the third quarter of 2012 included the following significant unobservable inputs:

Intangible Asset	Fair Value as of Third Quarter 2012	Valuation Technique	Unobservable Input	Range
In-Process R&D	$26 million	Income Approach-Excess Earnings Method	Discount Rate	20%–25%

During the second quarter of 2012, as a result of revised estimates developed in conjunction with our annual strategic planning process and annual goodwill impairment test, we performed an interim impairment test of our in-process research and development projects associated with our acquisition of Sadra Medical, Inc. Based on our impairment analysis, we revised our expectations of the required effort, time and cost involved in completing the in-process projects and bringing the related products to market. As a result of these changes, we recorded an impairment charge of $129 million ($110 million after-tax) to write-down the balance of these intangible assets to their fair value during the second quarter of 2012.

The nonrecurring Level 3 fair value measurements of the impairment charges taken in the second quarter of 2012 included the following significant unobservable inputs:

Intangible Asset	Fair Value as of Second Quarter 2012	Valuation Technique	Unobservable Input	Range
In-Process R&D	$184 million	Income Approach-Excess Earnings Method	Discount Rate	20%

2011 Charges

During the third quarter of 2011, we recorded a $9 million intangible asset impairment charge attributable to lower projected cash flows associated with certain technologies. During the second quarter of 2011, we recorded a $12 million intangible asset impairment charge associated with changes in the timing and amount of the expected cash flows related to certain in-process research and development projects.

The intangible asset category and associated write downs recorded in 2013, 2012 and 2011 were as follows:

(In millions)	Year Ended December 31,		
	2013	**2012**	**2011**
Technology-related	$—	$—	$ 9
Purchased research and development	53	142	12
	$ 53	142	$21

Estimated amortization expense for each of the five succeeding fiscal years based upon our intangible asset portfolio as of December 31, 2013 is as follows:

Fiscal Year	Estimated Amortization Expense (in millions)
2014	$433
2015	441
2016	441
2017	440
2018	441

Our technology-related intangible assets that are not subject to amortization represent technical processes, intellectual property and/or institutional understanding acquired through business combinations that are fundamental to the on-going operations of our business and have no limit to their useful life. Our technology-related intangible assets that are not subject to amortization are comprised primarily of certain acquired balloon and other technology, which is foundational to our continuing operations within the Cardiovascular market and other markets within interventional medicine. We assess our indefinite-lived intangible assets at least annually for impairment and reassess their classification as indefinite-lived assets. We assess qualitative factors to determine whether the existence of events and circumstances indicate that it is more likely than not that our indefinite-lived intangible assets are impaired. If we conclude that it is more likely than not that the asset is impaired, we then determine the fair value of the intangible asset and perform the quantitative impairment test by comparing the fair value with the carrying value in accordance with ASC Topic 350, *Intangibles—Goodwill and Other.*

LOSS ON EXTINGUISHMENT OF DEBT

3.42 AVON PRODUCTS, INC. (DEC)

CONSOLIDATED STATEMENTS OF INCOME (in part)

(In millions, except per share data)	Years Ended December 31		
	2013	**2012**	**2011**
Net sales	$9,764.4	$10,405.3	$10,935.4
Other revenue	190.6	156.1	164.1
Total revenue	9,955.0	10,561.4	11,099.5
Costs, expenses and other:			
Cost of sales	3,772.5	4,103.1	4,065.0
Selling, general and administrative expenses	5,713.2	5,889.3	5,942.5
Impairment of goodwill and intangible asset	42.1	44.0	—
Operating profit	427.2	525.0	1,092.0
Interest expense	120.6	104.3	92.9
Loss on extinguishment of debt	86.0	—	—
Interest income	(25.9)	(15.1)	(16.4)
Other expense, net	83.9	7.1	35.4
Total other expenses	264.6	96.3	111.9
Income from continuing operations, before taxes	162.6	428.7	980.1

NOTES TO CONSOLIDATED FINANCIAL STATEMENTS

(U.S. dollars in millions, except per share and share data)

Note 5. Debt and Other Financing (in part)

Term Loan Agreement

On June 29, 2012, we entered into a $500.0 term loan agreement (the "term loan agreement"). Subsequently on August 2, 2012, we borrowed an incremental $50.0 of principal from subscriptions by new lenders under the term loan agreement. Pursuant to the term loan agreement, we are required to repay an amount equal to 25% of the aggregate remaining principal amount of the term loan on June 29, 2014, and the remaining outstanding principal amount of the term loan on June 29, 2015. Amounts repaid or prepaid under the term loan agreement may not be reborrowed. Borrowings under the term loan agreement bear interest, at our option, at a rate per annum equal to LIBOR plus an applicable margin or a floating base rate plus an applicable margin, in each case subject to adjustment based on our credit ratings. The term loan agreement also provides for mandatory prepayments and voluntary prepayments. Subject to certain exceptions (including the issuance of commercial paper and draw-downs on our revolving credit facility), we are required to prepay the term loan in an amount equal to 50% of the net cash proceeds received from any incurrence of debt for borrowed money in excess of $500.

In March 2013, we entered into the first amendment to the term loan agreement. This amendment primarily related to (i) adding a provision whereby the lenders may, at our discretion, decline receipt of prepayments, and (ii) adding a subsidiary debt covenant and conforming the interest coverage ratio and leverage ratio covenants to those contained in the revolving credit facility (discussed below under "Debt Covenants"). Later in March 2013, we repaid $380.0 of the outstanding principal amount of the term loan agreement with a portion of the proceeds from the issuance of the Notes (as defined below under "Public Notes"), which repayment resulted in a loss in the first quarter of 2013 of $1.6 on extinguishment of debt associated with the write-off of debt issuance costs related to the term loan agreement. On July 25, 2013, we prepaid $117.5 of the outstanding principal balance under the term loan agreement, without prepayment penalties. At December 31, 2013, there was $52.5 outstanding under the term loan agreement. Based on amounts outstanding at December 31, 2013, $13.1 is required to be repaid on June 29, 2014 and was included within debt maturing within one year, and the remaining $39.4 is required to be repaid on June 29, 2015 and was included within long-term debt, in the Consolidated Balance Sheets.

Private Notes

On November 23, 2010, we issued, in a private placement exempt from registration under the Securities Act of 1933, as amended, $142.0 principal amount of 2.60% Senior Notes, Series A, due November 23, 2015, $290.0 principal amount of 4.03% Senior Notes, Series B, due November 23, 2020, and $103.0 principal amount of 4.18% Senior Notes, Series C, due November 23, 2022 (collectively, the "Private Notes"). The proceeds from the sale of the Private Notes were used to repay existing debt and for general corporate purposes.

On March 29, 2013, we prepaid our Private Notes. The prepayment price was equal to 100% of the principal amount of $535.0, plus accrued interest of $6.9 and a make-whole premium of $68.0. In connection with the prepayment of our Private Notes, we incurred a loss on extinguishment of debt of $71.4 in the first quarter of 2013, which included the make-whole premium and the write-off of $3.4 of debt issuance costs related to the Private Notes.

Public Notes (in part)

In March 2009, we issued $850.0 principal amount of notes payable in a public offering. $500.0 of the notes bear interest at a per annum rate equal to 5.625%, payable semi-annually, and were scheduled to mature on March 1, 2014 (the "2014 Notes").

$350.0 of the notes bear interest at a per annum rate equal to 6.50%, payable semi-annually, and mature on March 1, 2019 (the "2019 Notes"). The net proceeds from the offering of $837.6 were used to repay indebtedness outstanding under our commercial paper program and for general corporate purposes. On April 15, 2013 we prepaid the 2014 Notes at a prepayment price equal to 100% of the principal amount of $500.0, plus accrued interest of $3.4 and a make-whole premium of $21.7. In connection with the prepayment of our 2014 Notes, we incurred a loss on extinguishment of debt of $13.0 in the second quarter of 2013 consisting of the $21.7 make-whole premium for the 2014 Notes and the write-off of $1.1 of debt issuance costs and discounts related to the initial issuance of the 2014 Notes, partially offset by a deferred gain of $9.8 associated with the January 2013 interest-rate swap agreement termination. See Note 8, Financial Instruments and Risk Management for more information. At December 31, 2012, the carrying value of the 2014 Notes represented the $500.0 principal amount, net of the unamortized discount to face value of $.6. The carrying value of the 2019 Notes represented the $350.0 principal amount, net of the unamortized discount to face value of $2.3 at December 31, 2013 and $2.7 at December 31, 2012.

Pensions and Other Postretirement Benefits

RECOGNITION AND MEASUREMENT

3.43 FASB ASC 715, *Compensation—Retirement Benefits*, requires that an entity recognize the overfunded or underfunded status of a single-employer defined benefit postretirement plan as an asset or a liability in its statement of financial position, recognize changes in that funded status in comprehensive income, and disclose in the notes to the financial statements additional information about net periodic benefit cost. FASB ASC 715 requires an entity to recognize as components of other comprehensive income the gains or losses and prior service costs or credits that arise during a period but are not recognized in the income statement as components of net periodic benefit cost of a period. Those amounts recognized in accumulated other comprehensive income are adjusted as they are subsequently recognized in the income statement as components of net periodic benefit cost. Additionally, FASB ASC 715 requires that an entity measure plan assets and benefit obligations as of the date of its fiscal year-end statement of financial position. An employer whose equity securities are publicly traded is required to initially recognize the funded status of a defined benefit postretirement plan.

DISCLOSURE

3.44 FASB ASC 715 states the disclosure requirements for pensions and other postretirement benefits, including disclosures about the assets, obligations, cash flows, investment strategy, and net periodic benefit cost of defined pension and postretirement plans. FASB ASC 715 also includes disclosures related to multiemployer plans. FASB ASC 715-20 calls for different disclosures about defined benefit plans for public and nonpublic entities.

3.45 The disclosure requirements of FASB ASC 715 include, but are not limited to, the actuarial gains and losses, the assumed health care cost trend rate for other postretirement benefits, the allocation by major category of plan assets, the inputs and valuation techniques used to measure the fair value of plan assets, the effect of fair value measurements using significant unobservable inputs (level 3) on changes in plan assets for the period, and significant concentrations of risk within plan assets.

3.46 FASB ASC 715-80 explains the additional disclosures required for multiemployer plans. An entity should include details in these disclosures, including plan names and identifying numbers for significant multiemployer plans, the level of employers' participation in the plans, the financial health of the plans, and the nature of the employer commitments to the plans.

PRESENTATION AND DISCLOSURE EXCERPTS

PENSIONS AND OTHER POSTRETIREMENT BENEFITS

3.47 CENTURYLINK, INC. (DEC)
NOTES TO CONSOLIDATED FINANCIAL STATEMENTS

(1) Basis of Presentation and Summary of Significant Accounting Policies (in part)

Pension and Post-Retirement Benefits

We recognize the underfunded status of our defined benefit and post-retirement plans as an asset or a liability on our balance sheet. Each year's actuarial gains or losses are a component of our other comprehensive income (loss), which is then included in our accumulated other comprehensive loss. Pension and post-retirement benefit expenses are recognized over the period in which the employee renders service and becomes eligible to receive benefits. We make significant assumptions (including the discount rate, expected rate of return on plan assets and health care trend rates) in computing the pension and post-retirement benefits expense and obligations. See Note 8—Employee Benefits for additional information.

(8) Employee Benefits (in part)

Pension, Post-Retirement and Other Post-Employment Benefits

We sponsor several defined benefit pension plans, which in the aggregate cover a substantial portion of our employees including separate plans for Legacy CenturyLink, Legacy Qwest and Legacy Embarq employees. Until such time as we elect to integrate the Qwest and Embarq benefit plans with ours, we plan to continue to operate these plans independently. Pension benefits for participants of these plans who are represented by a collective bargaining agreement are based on negotiated schedules. All other participants' pension benefits are based on each individual participant's years of service and compensation. We use a December 31 measurement date for all our plans. In addition to these tax qualified pension plans, we also maintain non-qualified pension plans for certain current and former highly compensated employees. We maintain post-retirement benefit plans that provide health care and life insurance benefits for certain eligible retirees. We also provide other post-employment benefits for eligible former employees.

Pension Benefits

In connection with the acquisition of Qwest on April 1, 2011, we assumed defined benefit pension plans sponsored by Qwest for its employees. Based on a valuation analysis, we recognized a $490 million net liability at April 1, 2011 for the unfunded status of the Qwest pension plans, reflecting projected benefit obligations of $8.3 billion in excess of the $7.8 billion fair value of plan assets.

Current funding laws require a company with a plan shortfall to fund the annual cost of benefits earned in addition to a seven-year amortization of the shortfall. Our funding policy for the pension plans is to make contributions with the objective of accumulating sufficient assets to pay all qualified pension benefits when due under the terms of the plans. The accounting unfunded status of our qualified pension plans was $995 million as of December 31, 2013.

In 2013, we made cash contributions of approximately $146 million in to our qualified pension plans and paid approximately $5 million of benefits directly to participants of our non-qualified pension plans. Based on current laws and circumstances, our required contributions to our qualified pension plans for 2014 is $123 million, and we estimate that we will pay approximately $5 million of benefits to participants of our non-qualified pension plans.

Post-Retirement Benefits

Our post-retirement health care plans provide post-retirement benefits to qualified retirees. The post-retirement health care plans we assumed as part of our acquisitions of Qwest and Embarq provide post-retirement benefits to qualified retirees and allow (i) eligible employees retiring before certain dates to receive benefits at no or reduced cost and (ii) eligible employees retiring after certain dates to receive benefits on a shared cost basis. The post-retirement health care plans are primarily funded by us and we expect to continue funding these post-retirement obligations as benefits are paid.

In connection with the acquisition of Qwest on April 1, 2011, we assumed post-retirement benefit plans sponsored by Qwest for certain of its employees. At April 1, 2011, we recognized a $2.5 billion liability for the unfunded status of Qwest's post-retirement benefit plans, reflecting estimated accumulated post-retirement benefit obligations of $3.3 billion in excess of the $762 million fair value of the plan assets.

No contributions were made to the post-retirement trusts in 2013, and we do not expect to make a contribution in 2014. However, in 2013 we paid approximately $157 million of benefits (net of participant contributions and direct subsidies) that were not payable by the trusts, and we estimate that in 2014 we will pay approximately $182 million of benefits (net of participant contributions and direct subsidies) that are not payable by the trusts.

A change of 100 basis points in the assumed initial health care cost trend rate would have had the following effects in 2013:

(Dollars in millions)	100 Basis Points Change	
	Increase	(Decrease)
Effect on the aggregate of the service and interest cost components of net periodic post-retirement benefit expense (consolidated statement of operations)	$ 3	(3)
Effect on benefit obligation (consolidated balance sheet)	87	(80)

We expect our health care cost trend rate to decrease by 0.25% per year from 6.50% in 2014 to an ultimate rate of 4.50% in 2022. Our post-retirement health care expense, for certain eligible Legacy Qwest retirees and certain eligible Legacy CenturyLink retirees, is capped at a set dollar amount. Therefore, those health care benefit obligations are not subject to increasing health care trends after the effective date of the caps.

Expected Cash Flows

The qualified pension, non-qualified pension and post-retirement health care benefit payments and premiums and life insurance premium payments are paid by us or distributed from plan assets. The estimated benefit payments provided below are based on actuarial assumptions using the demographics of the employee and retiree populations and have been reduced by estimated participant contributions.

(Dollars in millions)	Pension Plans	Post-Retirement Benefit Plans	Medicare Part D Subsidy Receipts
Estimated future benefit payments:			
2014	$1,036	352	(13)
2015	1,002	341	(10)
2016	990	329	(10)
2017	977	319	(10)
2018	962	308	(10)
2019–2023	4,559	1,369	(40)

Net Periodic Benefit Expense

The actuarial assumptions used to compute the net periodic benefit expense for our qualified pension, non-qualified pension and post-retirement benefit plans are based upon information available as of the beginning of the year, as presented in the following table.

	Pension Plans			Post-Retirement Benefit Plans		
	2013	2012	2011[1]	2013	2012	2011[2]
Actuarial assumptions at beginning of year:						
Discount rate	3.50%–4.20%	4.25%–5.10%	5.00%–5.50%	3.60%	4.60%–4.80%	5.30%
Rate of compensation increase	3.25%	3.25%	3.25%	N/A	N/A	N/A
Expected long-term rate of return on plan assets	7.50%	7.50%	7.50%–8.00%	7.30%	6.00%–7.50%	7.25%
Initial health care cost trend rate	N/A	N/A	N/A	6.50%–7.00%	8.00%	8.50%
Ultimate health care cost trend rate	N/A	N/A	N/A	4.50%	5.00%	5.00%
Year ultimate trend rate is reached	N/A	N/A	N/A	2022	2018	2018

N/A-Not applicable

[1] This column does not consider Qwest's actuarial assumptions for its pension plan as of the beginning of the year due to the acquisition date of April 1, 2011. Qwest had the following actuarial assumptions as of April 1, 2011: discount rate of 5.40%; expected long-term rate of return on plan assets 7.50%; and a rate of compensation increase of 3.50%.

[2] This column does not consider Qwest's actuarial assumptions for its post-retirement benefit plan as of the beginning of the year due to the acquisition date of April 1, 2011. Qwest had the following actuarial assumptions as of April 1, 2011: discount rate of 5.30%; expected long-term rate of return on plan assets of 7.50%; initial health care cost trend rate of 7.50% and ultimate health care trend rate of 5.00% to be reached in 2016.

Net periodic pension benefit (income) expense, which includes the effects of the Qwest acquisition subsequent to April 1, 2011, included the following components:

	Pension Plans		
	Years Ended December 31,		
(Dollars in millions)	2013	2012	2011[1]
Service cost	$ 91	87	70
Interest cost	544	625	560
Expected return on plan assets	(896)	(847)	(709)
Settlements	—	—	1
Amortization of unrecognized prior service cost	5	4	2
Amortization of unrecognized actuarial loss	84	35	13
Net periodic pension benefit (income) expense	$(172)	(96)	(63)

[1] Includes $58 million of income related to the Qwest plans subsequent to the April 1, 2011 acquisition date.

Net periodic post-retirement benefit expense (income), which includes the effects of the Qwest acquisition subsequent to April 1, 2011, included the following components:

	Post-Retirement Plans		
	Years Ended December 31,		
(Dollars in millions)	2013	2012	2011[1]
Service cost	$ 24	22	18
Interest cost	140	173	152
Expected return on plan assets	(39)	(45)	(41)
Amortization of unrecognized prior service cost	—	—	(2)
Amortization of unrecognized actuarial loss	4	—	—
Net periodic post-retirement benefit expense (income)	$129	150	127

[1] Includes $92 million related to the Qwest plans subsequent to the April 1, 2011 acquisition date.

Benefit Obligations

The actuarial assumptions used to compute the funded status for the plans are based upon information available as of December 31, 2013 and 2012 and are as follows:

	Pension Plans		Post-Retirement Benefit Plans	
	December 31,		December 31,	
	2013	2012	2013	2012
Actuarial assumptions at end of year:				
Discount rate	4.20%–5.10%	3.25%–4.20%	4.50%	3.60%
Rate of compensation increase	3.25%	3.25%	N/A	N/A
Initial health care cost trend rate	N/A	N/A	6.50%/7.00%	6.75%/7.50%
Ultimate health care cost trend rate	N/A	N/A	4.50%	4.50%
Year ultimate trend rate is reached	N/A	N/A	2022/2024	2022/2024

N/A-Not applicable

The following table summarizes the change in the benefit obligations for the pension and post-retirement benefit plans:

	Pension Plans		
	Years Ended December 31,		
(Dollars in millions)	2013	2012	2011
Change in benefit obligation			
Benefit obligation at beginning of year	$14,881	13,596	4,534
Service cost	91	87	70
Interest cost	544	625	560
Plan amendments	—	14	12
Acquisitions	—	—	8,267
Actuarial (gain) loss	(1,179)	1,565	930
Benefits paid by company	(5)	(5)	(16)
Benefits paid from plan assets	(931)	(1,001)	(761)
Benefit obligation at end of year	$13,401	14,881	13,596

(Dollars in millions)	Post-Retirement Benefit Plans Years Ended December 31,		
	2013	**2012**	**2011**
Change in benefit obligation			
Benefit obligation at beginning of year	$4,075	3,930	558
Service cost	24	22	18
Interest cost	140	173	152
Participant contributions	96	86	64
Plan amendments	141	—	31
Acquisitions	—	—	3,284
Direct subsidy receipts	13	19	22
Actuarial (gain) loss	(399)	260	153
Benefits paid by company	(266)	(268)	(219)
Benefits paid from plan assets	(136)	(147)	(133)
Benefit obligation at end of year	$3,688	4,075	3,930

Our aggregate benefit obligation as of December 31, 2013, 2012 and 2011 was $17.089 billion, $18.956 billion and $17.499 billion, respectively.

Plan Assets

We maintain plan assets for our qualified pension plans and certain post-retirement benefit plans. The qualified pension plan assets are used for the payment of pension benefits and certain eligible plan expenses. The post-retirement benefit plan's assets are used to pay health care benefits and premiums on behalf of eligible retirees and to pay certain eligible plan expenses. The expected rate of return on plan assets is the long-term rate of return we expect to earn on the plans' assets. The rate of return is determined by the strategic allocation of plan assets and the long-term risk and return forecast for each asset class. The forecasts for each asset class are generated primarily from an analysis of the long-term expectations of various third party investment management organizations. The expected rate of return on plan assets is reviewed annually and revised, as necessary, to reflect changes in the financial markets and our investment strategy. The following tables summarize the change in the fair value of plan assets for the pension and post-retirement benefit plans:

(Dollars in millions)	Pension Plans Years Ended December 31,		
	2013	**2012**	**2011**
Change in plan assets			
Fair value of plan assets at beginning of year	$12,321	11,814	3,732
Return on plan assets	810	1,476	479
Acquisitions	—	—	7,777
Employer contributions	146	32	587
Benefits paid from plan assets	(931)	(1,001)	(761)
Fair value of plan assets at end of year	$12,346	12,321	11,814

(Dollars in millions)	Post-Retirement Benefit Plans Years Ended December 31,		
	2013	**2012**	**2011**
Change in plan assets			
Fair value of plan assets at beginning of year	$ 626	693	54
Actual gain on plan assets	45	80	4
Acquisitions	—	—	768
Benefits paid from plan assets	(136)	(147)	(133)
Fair value of plan assets at end of year	$ 535	626	693

Pension Plans: Our investment objective for the pension plan assets is to achieve an attractive risk-adjusted return over time that will provide for the payment of benefits and minimize the risk of large losses. Our pension plan investment strategy is designed to meet this objective by broadly diversifying plan assets across numerous strategies with differing expected returns, volatilities and correlations. The pension plan assets have target allocations of 55.5% to interest rate sensitive investments and 44.5% to investments designed to provide higher expected returns than the interest rate sensitive investments. Interest rate sensitive investments include 36% of plan assets targeted primarily to long-duration investment grade bonds, 13.5% targeted to high yield, emerging market bonds and convertible bonds and 6% targeted to diversified strategies, which primarily have exposures to global government, corporate and inflation-linked bonds, as well as some exposures to global stocks and commodities. Assets expected to provide higher returns than the interest rate sensitive assets include broadly diversified equity investments with targets of approximately 14% to U.S. stocks and 14% to developed and emerging market non-U.S. stocks. Approximately 11.5% is allocated to other private markets investments including funds primarily invested in private equity, private debt and hedge funds. Real estate investments are targeted at 5% of plan assets. At the beginning of 2014, our expected annual long-term rate of return on pension assets is assumed to be 7.5%.

Post-Retirement Benefit Plans: Our investment objective for the post-retirement benefit plan assets is to achieve an attractive risk-adjusted return and minimize the risk of large losses over the expected life of the assets. Investment risk is managed by broadly diversifying assets across numerous strategies with differing expected returns, volatilities and correlations. Our investment strategy is designed to be consistent with the investment objective, with particular focus on providing liquidity for the reimbursement of our union-represented employees post-retirement health care costs. The post-retirement benefit plan assets have target allocations of 37% to equities and 63% to non-equity investments. Specific target allocations within these broad categories are allowed to vary to provide liquidity in order to meet reimbursement requirements. Equity investments are broadly diversified with exposure to publicly traded U.S., non-U.S. and emerging market stocks and private equity. While no new private equity investments have been made in recent years, the percent allocation to existing private equity investments is expected to increase as liquid, publicly traded stocks are drawn down for the reimbursement of health care costs. The 63% non-equity allocation includes investment grade bonds, high yield bonds, convertible bonds, emerging market debt, real estate, hedge funds, private debt and diversified strategies. At the beginning of 2014, our expected annual long-term rate of return on post-retirement benefit plan assets is assumed to be 7.3%.

Permitted investments: Plan assets are managed consistent with the restrictions set forth by the Employee Retirement Income Security Act of 1974, as amended, which requires diversification of assets and also generally prohibits defined benefit and welfare plans from investing more than 10% of their assets in securities issued by the sponsor company. At December 31, 2013 and 2012, the pension and post-retirement benefit plans did not directly own any shares of our common stock or any of our debt.

Derivative instruments: Derivative instruments are used to reduce risk as well as provide return. The pension and post-retirement benefit plans use exchange traded futures to gain exposure to equity and Treasury markets consistent with target asset allocations. Interest rate swaps are used in the pension plans to reduce risk relative to measurement of the benefit obligation, which is sensitive to interest rate changes. Foreign exchange forward contracts are used to manage currency exposures. Credit default swaps are used to manage credit risk exposures in a cost effective and targeted manner relative to transacting with physical corporate fixed income securities. Options are currently used to manage interest rate exposure taking into account the implied volatility and current pricing of the specific underlying market instrument. Some derivative instruments subject the plans to counterparty risk. The external investment managers, along with Plan Management, monitor counterparty exposure and mitigate this risk by diversifying the exposure among multiple high credit quality counterparties, requiring collateral and limiting exposure by periodically settling contracts.

The gross notional exposure of the derivative instruments directly held by the plans is shown below. The notional amount of the derivatives corresponds to market exposure but does not represent an actual cash investment.

	Gross Notional Exposure			
	Pension Plans		Post-Retirement Benefit Plans	
	Years Ended December 31,			
(Dollars in millions)	2013	2012	2013	2012
Derivative Instruments:				
Exchange-traded U.S. equity futures	$ 95	302	16	30
Exchange-traded non-U.S. equity futures	—	1	—	—
Exchange-traded Treasury futures	3,011	1,763	—	—
Interest rate swaps	556	1,471	—	—
Credit default swaps	253	495	—	—
Foreign exchange forwards	938	726	29	21
Options	261	768	—	—

Fair Value Measurements: Fair value is defined as the price that would be received to sell an asset or paid to transfer a liability in an orderly transaction between independent and knowledgeable parties who are willing and able to transact for an asset or liability at the measurement date. We use valuation techniques that maximize the use of observable inputs and minimize the use of unobservable inputs when determining fair value and then we rank the estimated values based on the reliability of the inputs used following the fair value hierarchy set forth by the FASB. For additional information on the fair value hierarchy, see Note 11—Fair Value Disclosure.

At December 31, 2013, we used the following valuation techniques to measure fair value for assets. There were no changes to these methodologies during 2013:
- Level 1—Assets were valued using the closing price reported in the active market in which the individual security was traded.
- Level 2—Assets were valued using quoted prices in markets that are not active, broker dealer quotations, net asset value of shares held by the plans and other methods by which all significant input were observable at the measurement date.
- Level 3—Assets were valued using unobservable inputs in which little or no market data exists as reported by the respective institutions at the measurement date.

The tables below presents the fair value of plan assets by category and the input levels used to determine those fair values at December 31, 2013. It is important to note that the asset allocations do not include market exposures that are gained with derivatives.

(Dollars in millions)	Fair Value of Pension Plan Assets at December 31, 2013			
	Level 1	Level 2	Level 3	Total
Investment grade bonds (a)	$ 813	1,504	—	$ 2,317
High yield bonds (b)	—	1,265	26	1,291
Emerging market bonds (c)	196	367	—	563
Convertible bonds (d)	—	389	—	389
Diversified strategies (e)	—	723	—	723
U.S. stocks (f)	1,408	92	—	1,500
Non-U.S. stocks (g)	1,159	299	—	1,458
Emerging market stocks (h)	—	110	—	110
Private equity (i)	—	—	721	721
Private debt (j)	—	—	436	436
Market neutral hedge funds (k)	—	867	99	966
Directional hedge funds (k)	—	582	32	614
Real estate (l)	—	306	265	571
Derivatives (m)	—	(34)	—	(34)
Cash equivalents and short-term investments (n)	—	721	—	721
Total investments	$3,576	7,191	1,579	12,346
Accrued expenses				—
Total pension plan assets				$12,346

(Dollars in millions)	Fair Value of Post-Retirement Plan Assets at December 31, 2013			
	Level 1	Level 2	Level 3	Total
Investment grade bonds (a)	$ 21	56	—	$ 77
High yield bonds (b)	—	56	—	56
Emerging market bonds (c)	—	37	—	37
Diversified strategies (e)	—	86	—	86
U.S. stocks (f)	56	—	—	56
Non-U.S. stocks (g)	58	—	—	58
Emerging market stocks (h)	—	12	—	12
Private equity (i)	—	—	40	40
Private debt (j)	—	—	5	5
Market neutral hedge funds (k)	—	35	—	35
Directional hedge funds (k)	—	14	—	14
Real estate (l)	—	22	12	34
Cash equivalents and short-term investments (n)	—	24	—	24
Total investments	$135	342	57	534
Contribution Receivable				1
Total post-retirement plan assets				$535

The tables below presents the fair value of plan assets by category and the input levels used to determine those fair values at December 31, 2012. It is important to note that the asset allocations do not include market exposures that are gained with derivatives. Investments include dividend and interest receivable, pending trades, trades payable and accrued expenses.

(Dollars in millions)	Fair Value of Pension Plan Assets at December 31, 2012			
	Level 1	Level 2	Level 3	Total
Investment grade bonds (a)	$ 830	1,555	—	$ 2,385
High yield bonds (b)	—	1,303	59	1,362
Emerging market bonds (c)	199	396	—	595
Convertible bonds (d)	—	374	—	374
Diversified strategies (e)	—	655	—	655
U.S. stocks (f)	1,225	119	—	1,344
Non-U.S. stocks (g)	1,212	178	—	1,390
Emerging market stocks (h)	111	193	—	304
Private equity (i)	—	—	711	711
Private debt (j)	—	—	465	465
Market neutral hedge funds (k)	—	906	—	906
Directional hedge funds (k)	—	340	194	534
Real estate (l)	—	223	337	560
Derivatives (m)	(5)	3	—	(2)
Cash equivalents and short-term investments (n)	—	750	—	750
Total investments	$3,572	6,995	1,766	12,333
Accrued expenses				(12)
Total pension plan assets				$12,321

(Dollars in millions)	Fair Value of Post-Retirement Plan Assets at December 31, 2012			
	Level 1	Level 2	Level 3	Total
Investment grade bonds (a)	$ 22	86	—	$108
High yield bonds (b)	—	90	—	90
Emerging market bonds (c)	—	40	—	40
Convertible bonds (d)	—	2	—	2
Diversified strategies (e)	—	72	—	72
U.S. stocks (f)	55	—	—	55
Non-U.S. stocks (g)	58	1	—	59
Emerging market stocks (h)	—	20	—	20
Private equity (i)	—	—	45	45
Private debt (j)	—	—	6	6
Market neutral hedge funds (k)	—	41	—	41
Directional hedge funds (k)	—	24	—	24
Real estate (l)	—	21	28	49
Cash equivalents and short-term investments (n)	5	21	—	26
Total investments	$140	418	79	637
Accrued expenses				(1)
Reimbursement accrual				(10)
Total post-retirement plan assets				$626

The plans' assets are invested in various asset categories utilizing multiple strategies and investment managers. For several of the investments in the tables above and discussed below, the plans own units in commingled funds and limited partnerships that invest in various types of assets. Interests in commingled funds are valued using the net asset value ("NAV") per unit of each fund. The NAV reported by the fund manager is based on the market value of the underlying investments owned by each fund, minus its liabilities, divided by the number of shares outstanding. Commingled funds held by the plans that can be redeemed at NAV within a year of the financial statement date are generally classified as Level 2. Investments in limited partnerships represent long-term commitments with a fixed maturity date, typically ten years. Valuation inputs for these limited partnership interests are generally based on assumptions and other information not observable in the market and are classified as Level 3 investments. The assumptions and valuation methodologies of the pricing vendors, account managers, fund managers and partnerships are monitored and evaluated for reasonableness. Below is an overview of the asset categories, the underlying strategies and valuation inputs used to value the assets in the preceding tables:

(a) *Investment grade bonds* represent investments in fixed income securities as well as commingled bond funds comprised of U.S. Treasury securities, agencies, corporate bonds, mortgage-backed securities, asset-backed securities and commercial mortgage-backed securities. Treasury securities are valued at the bid price reported in the active market in which the security is traded and are classified as Level 1. The valuation inputs of other investment grade bonds primarily utilize observable market information and are based on a spread to U.S. Treasury securities and consider yields available on comparable securities of issuers with similar credit ratings. The primary observable inputs include references to the new issue market for similar securities, the secondary trading markets and dealer quotes. Option adjusted spread models are utilized to evaluate securities such as asset backed securities that have early redemption features. These securities are classified as Level 2. The commingled funds are valued at NAV based on the market value of the underlying fixed income securities using the same valuation inputs described above. The commingled funds can be redeemed at NAV within a year of the financial statement date and are classified as Level 2.

(b) *High yield bonds* represent investments in below investment grade fixed income securities as well as commingled high yield bond funds. The valuation inputs for the securities primarily utilize observable market information and are based on a spread to U.S. Treasury securities and consider yields available on comparable securities of issuers with similar credit ratings. These securities are classified as Level 2. The commingled funds are valued at NAV based on the market value of the underlying high yield instruments using the same valuation inputs described above. Commingled funds that can be redeemed at NAV within a year of the financial statement date are classified as Level 2. Commingled funds that cannot be redeemed at NAV or that cannot be redeemed at NAV within a year of the financial statement date are classified as Level 3.

(c) *Emerging market bonds* represent investments in securities issued by governments and other entities located in developing countries as well as registered mutual funds and commingled emerging market bond funds. The valuation inputs for the securities utilize observable market information and are primarily based on dealer quotes or a spread relative to the local government bonds. These securities are classified as Level 2. The commingled funds are valued at NAV based on the market value of the underlying emerging market bonds using the same valuation inputs described above. The commingled funds can be redeemed at NAV within a year of the financial statement date and are classified as Level 2. The registered mutual funds trade at the daily NAV, as determined by the market value of the underlying investments, and are classified as Level 1.

(d) *Convertible bonds* primarily represent investments in corporate debt securities that have features that allow the debt to be converted into equity securities under certain circumstances. The valuation inputs for the individual convertible bonds primarily utilize observable market information including a spread to U.S. Treasuries and the value and volatility of the underlying equity security. Convertible bonds are classified as Level 2.

(e) *Diversified strategies* represent an investment in a commingled fund that primarily has exposures to global government, corporate and inflation linked bonds, global stocks and commodities. The commingled fund is valued at NAV based on the market value of the underlying investments. The valuation inputs utilize observable market information including published prices for exchange traded securities, bid prices for government bonds, and spreads and yields available for comparable fixed income securities with similar credit ratings. This fund can be redeemed at NAV within a year of the financial statement date and is classified as Level 2.

(f) *U.S. stocks* represent investments in stocks of U.S. based companies as well as commingled U.S. stock funds. The valuation inputs for U.S. stocks are based on the last published price reported on the major stock market on which the securities are traded and are classified as Level 1. The commingled funds are valued at NAV based on the market value of the underlying investments using the same valuation inputs described above. These commingled funds can be redeemed at NAV within a year of the financial statement date and are classified as Level 2.

(g) *Non-U.S. stocks* represent investments in stocks of companies based in developed countries outside the U.S. as well as commingled funds. The valuation inputs for non-U.S. stocks are based on the last published price reported on the major stock market on which the securities are traded and are classified as Level 1. The commingled funds are valued at NAV based on the market value of the underlying investments using the same valuation inputs described above. These commingled funds can be redeemed at NAV within a year of the financial statement date and are classified as Level 2.

(h) *Emerging market stocks* represent investments in a registered mutual fund and commingled funds comprised of stocks of companies located in developing markets. Registered mutual funds trade at the daily NAV, as determined by the market value of the underlying investments, and are classified as Level 1. The commingled funds are valued at NAV based on the market value of the underlying investments using the same valuation inputs described previously for individual stocks. These commingled funds can be redeemed at NAV within a year of the financial statement date and are classified as Level 2.

(i) *Private equity* represents non-public investments in domestic and foreign buy out and venture capital funds. Private equity funds are structured as limited partnerships and are valued according to the valuation policy of each partnership, subject to prevailing accounting and other regulatory guidelines. The partnerships use valuation methodologies that give consideration to a range of factors, including but not limited to the price at which investments were acquired, the nature of the investments, market conditions, trading values on comparable public securities, current and projected operating performance, and financing transactions subsequent to the acquisition of the investments. These valuation methodologies involve a significant degree of judgment. Private equity investments are classified as Level 3.

(j) *Private debt* represents non-public investments in distressed or mezzanine debt funds. Mezzanine debt instruments are debt instruments that are subordinated to other debt issues and may include embedded equity instruments such as warrants. Private debt funds are structured as limited partnerships and are valued according to the valuation policy of each partnership, subject to prevailing accounting and other regulatory guidelines. The valuation of underlying fund investments are based on factors including the issuer's current and projected credit worthiness, the security's terms, reference to the securities of comparable companies, and other market factors. These valuation methodologies involve a significant degree of judgment. Private debt investments are classified as Level 3.

(k) *Market neutral hedge funds* hold investments in a diversified mix of instruments that are intended in combination to exhibit low correlations to market fluctuations. These investments are typically combined with futures to achieve uncorrelated excess returns over various markets. *Directional hedge funds*—This asset category represents investments that may exhibit somewhat higher correlations to market fluctuations than the market neutral hedge funds. Investments in hedge funds include both direct investments and investments in diversified funds of funds. Hedge Funds are valued at NAV based on the market value of the underlying investments which include publicly traded equity and fixed income securities and privately negotiated debt securities. The hedge funds are valued by third party administrators using the same valuation inputs previously described. Hedge funds that can be redeemed at NAV within a year of the financial statement date are classified as Level 2. Hedge fund investments that cannot be redeemed at NAV or that cannot be redeemed at NAV within a year of the financial statement date are classified as Level 3.

(l) *Real estate* represents investments in commingled funds and limited partnerships that invest in a diversified portfolio of real estate properties. These investments are valued at NAV according to the valuation policy of each fund or partnership, subject to prevailing accounting and other regulatory guidelines. The valuation inputs of the underlying properties are generally based on third-party appraisals that use comparable sales or a projection of future cash flows to determine fair value. Real estate investments that can be redeemed at NAV within a year of the financial statement date are classified as Level 2. Real estate investments that cannot be redeemed at NAV or that cannot be redeemed at NAV within a year of the financial statement date are classified as Level 3.

(m) *Derivatives* include the market value of exchange traded futures contracts which are classified as Level 1, as well as privately negotiated over-the-counter swaps and options that are valued based on the change in interest rates or a specific market index and classified as Level 2. The market values represent gains or losses that occur due to fluctuations in interest rates, foreign currency exchange rates, security prices, or other factors.

(n) *Cash equivalents and short-term investments* represent investments that are used in conjunction with derivatives positions or are used to provide liquidity for the payment of benefits or other purposes. U.S. Treasury Bills are valued at the bid price reported in the active market in which the security is traded and are classified as Level 1. The valuation inputs of other securities are based on a spread to U.S. Treasury Bills, the Federal Funds Rate, or London Interbank Offered Rate and consider yields available on comparable securities of issuers with similar credit ratings and are classified as Level 2. The commingled funds are valued at NAV based on the market value of the underlying investments using the same valuation inputs described above. These commingled funds can be redeemed at NAV within a year of the financial statement date and are classified as Level 2.

Concentrations of Risk: Investments, in general, are exposed to various risks, such as significant world events, interest rate, credit, foreign currency and overall market volatility risk. These risks are managed by broadly diversifying assets across numerous asset classes and strategies with differing expected returns, volatilities and correlations. Risk is also broadly diversified across numerous market sectors and individual companies. Financial instruments that potentially subject the plans to concentrations of counterparty risk consist principally of investment contracts with high quality financial institutions. These investment contracts are typically collateralized obligations and/or are actively managed, limiting the amount of counterparty exposure to any one financial institution. Although the investments are well diversified, the value of plan assets could change materially depending upon the overall market volatility, which could affect the funded status of the plans.

The table below presents a rollforward of the pension plan assets valued using Level 3 inputs:

(Dollars in millions)	Pension Plan Assets Valued Using Level 3 Inputs						
	High Yield Bonds	Private Equity	Private Debt	Market Neutral Hedge Fund	Directional Hedge Funds	Real Estate	Total
Balance at December 31, 2011	$ 79	791	461	188	183	535	2,237
Net transfers	(12)	—	—	(188)	—	(105)	(305)
Acquisitions	1	70	120	—	—	18	209
Dispositions	(11)	(109)	(102)	—	—	(121)	(343)
Actual return on plan assets:							
Gains relating to assets sold during the year	—	3	1	—	—	—	4
Gains (losses) relating to assets still held at year-end	2	(44)	(15)	—	11	10	(36)
Balance at December 31, 2012	59	711	465	—	194	337	1,766
Net transfers	—	—	—	—	(165)	—	(165)
Acquisitions	5	82	71	100	—	9	267
Dispositions	(43)	(179)	(144)	—	(1)	(97)	(464)
Actual return on plan assets:							
Gains relating to assets sold during the year	12	68	18	—	—	11	109
(Losses) gains relating to assets still held at year-end	(7)	39	26	(1)	4	5	66
Balance at December 31, 2013	$ 26	721	436	99	32	265	1,579

The table below presents a rollforward of the post-retirement plan assets valued using Level 3 inputs:

(Dollars in millions)	Post-Retirement Plan Assets Valued Using Level 3 Inputs			
	Private Equity	Private Debt	Real Estate	Total
Balance at December 31, 2011	$ 60	8	26	94
Acquisitions	1	—	—	1
Dispositions	(15)	(3)	(1)	(19)
Actual return on plan assets:				
Gains (losses) relating to assets sold during the year	4	2	(1)	5
(Losses) gains relating to assets still held at year-end	(5)	(1)	4	(2)
Balance at December 31, 2012	45	6	28	79
Acquisitions	1	—	—	1
Dispositions	(11)	(1)	(18)	(30)
Actual return on plan assets:				
Gains (losses) relating to assets sold during the year	4	—	(1)	3
Gains relating to assets still held at year-end	1	—	3	4
Balance at December 31, 2013	$ 40	5	12	57

Certain gains and losses are allocated between assets sold during the year and assets still held at year-end based on transactions and changes in valuations that occurred during the year. These allocations also impact our calculation of net acquisitions and dispositions.

For the year ended December 31, 2013, the investment program produced actual gains on qualified pension and post-retirement plan assets of $855 million as compared to the expected returns of $935 million for a difference of $80 million. For the year ended December 31, 2012, the investment program produced actual gains on pension and post-retirement plan assets of $1.556 billion as compared to the expected returns of $892 million for a difference of $664 million. The short-term annual returns on plan assets will almost always be different from the expected long-term returns and the plans could experience net gains or losses, due primarily to the volatility occurring in the financial markets during any given year.

Unfunded Status

The following table presents the unfunded status of the pensions and post-retirement benefit plans:

| | Pension Plans | | Post-Retirement Benefit Plans | |
| | Years Ended December 31, | | Years Ended December 31, | |
(Dollars in millions)	2013	2012	2013	2012
Benefit obligation	$(13,401)	(14,881)	(3,688)	(4,075)
Fair value of plan assets	12,346	12,321	535	626
Unfunded status	(1,055)	(2,560)	(3,153)	(3,449)
Current portion of unfunded status	$ (5)	(6)	(154)	(160)
Non-current portion of unfunded status	$ (1,050)	(2,554)	(2,999)	(3,289)

The current portion of our post-retirement benefit obligations is recorded on our consolidated balance sheets in accrued expenses and other current liabilities-salaries and benefits.

Accumulated Other Comprehensive Loss-Recognition and Deferrals

The following tables present cumulative items not recognized as a component of net periodic benefits expense as of December 31, 2012, items recognized as a component of net periodic benefits expense in 2013, additional items deferred during 2013 and cumulative items not recognized as a component of net periodic benefits expense as of December 31, 2013. The items not recognized as a component of net periodic benefits expense have been recorded on our consolidated balance sheets in accumulated other comprehensive loss:

| | As of and for the Years Ended December 31, | | | | |
(Dollars in millions)	2012	Recognition of Net Periodic Benefits Expense	Deferrals	Net Change in AOCI	2013
Accumulated other comprehensive loss:					
Pension plans:					
Net actuarial (loss) gain	$(2,236)	84	1,094	1,178	(1,058)
Prior service (cost) benefit	(38)	5	—	5	(33)
Deferred income tax benefit (expense)	875	(34)	(419)	(453)	422
Total pension plans	(1,399)	55	675	730	(669)
Post-retirement benefit plans:					
Net actuarial (loss) gain	(446)	4	405	409	(37)
Prior service (cost) benefit	(22)	—	(141)	(141)	(163)
Deferred income tax benefit (expense)	179	(1)	(100)	(101)	78
Total post-retirement benefit plans	(289)	3	164	167	(122)
Total accumulated other comprehensive loss	$(1,688)	58	839	897	(791)

The following table presents estimated items to be recognized in 2014 as a component of net periodic benefit expense of the pension, non-qualified pension and post-retirement benefit plans:

(Dollars in millions)	Pension Plans	Post-Retirement Plans
Estimated recognition of net periodic benefit expense in 2014:		
Net actuarial loss	$(17)	—
Prior service cost	(5)	(17)
Deferred income tax benefit	8	6
Estimated net periodic benefit expense to be recorded in 2014 as a component of other comprehensive income (loss)	$(14)	(11)

DEFINED CONTRIBUTION PLANS

3.48 ALLIANT TECHSYSTEMS INC. (MAR)
NOTES TO THE CONSOLIDATED FINANCIAL STATEMENTS

(Amounts in thousands except share and per share data and unless otherwise indicated)

10. Employee Benefit Plans (in part)

	Pension Benefits	Other Postretirement Benefits
2014	$172,771	$13,134
2015	176,081	12,741
2016	179,049	12,376
2017	185,806	12,113
2018	190,050	11,810
2019 through 2023	1,038,643	51,685

Defined Contribution Plan

ATK also sponsors a defined contribution plan. Participation in this plan is available to substantially all U.S. employees. The defined contribution plan is a 401(k) plan, with an employee stock ownership ("ESOP") feature; to which employees may contribute up to 50% of their pay (highly compensated employees are subject to limitations). Employee contributions are invested, at the employees' direction, among a variety of investment alternatives including an ATK common stock fund. Participants may transfer amounts into and out of the investment alternatives at any time. Any dividends declared on ATK common stock can be either reinvested within the ATK common stock fund or provided as a cash payment. Effective January 1, 2013 employees no longer had the option to invest in the ATK common stock fund. Balances in the fund prior to January 1, 2013 remained in the fund unless distributed or transferred. Effective January 1, 2004, the ATK matching contribution and non-elective contribution to this plan depends on a participant's years of service, pension plan participation, and certain other factors. Participants receive:
- a matching contribution of 100% of the first 3% of the participant's contributed pay plus 50% of the next 2% of the participant's contributed pay, or
- a matching contribution of 50% of the first 6% of the participant's contributed pay or,
- a matching contribution of 100% of the first 3% of the participant's contributed pay plus 50% of the next 3% of the participant's contributed pay (subject to one year vesting) and a non-elective contribution based on recognized compensation, age and service (subject to three year vesting), or
- an automatic enrollment of a 6% pre-tax contribution rate (of which the participant can either change or opt out) along with a matching contribution of 100% of the first 3% of the participant's contributed pay plus 50% of the next 3% of the participant's contributed pay (subject to one year vesting) and a non-elective contribution based on recognized compensation, age and service (subject to three year vesting), or
- a non-elective contribution based on the recognized compensation, age, and service (subject to three year vesting), or
- no matching contribution.

ATK's contributions to the plan were $37,377 in fiscal 2013, $35,993 in fiscal 2012, and $36,479 in fiscal 2011.

As of March 31, 2013, ATK had approximately 14,000 U.S. employees eligible under the plan. Less than 10% of these employees were covered by collective bargaining agreements ("CBA"). ATK has union-represented employees at four locations. One locations has two separate bargaining units with collective bargaining agreements that both expire in calendar year 2013. The other CBA's expire in 2014, 2015, and 2016.

3.49 ARROW ELECTRONICS, INC. (DEC)
NOTES TO THE CONSOLIDATED FINANCIAL STATEMENTS

(Dollars in thousands except per share data)

13. Employee Benefit Plans (in part)

The company maintains an unfunded Arrow supplemental executive retirement plan ("SERP") under which the company will pay supplemental pension benefits to certain employees upon retirement. As of December 31, 2013, there were 10 current and 16 former corporate officers participating in this plan. The Board determines those employees who are eligible to participate in the Arrow SERP.

The Arrow SERP, as amended, provides for the pension benefits to be based on a percentage of average final compensation, based on years of participation in the Arrow SERP. The Arrow SERP permits early retirement, with payments at a reduced rate, based on age and years of service subject to a minimum retirement age of 55. Participants whose accrued rights under the Arrow SERP, prior to the 2002 amendment, which were adversely affected by the amendment, will continue to be entitled to such greater rights.

Additionally, as part of the company's acquisition of Wyle Electronics ("Wyle") in 2000, Wyle provided retirement benefits for certain employees under a defined benefit plan. Benefits under this plan were frozen as of December 31, 2000.

The company uses a December 31 measurement date for the Arrow SERP and the Wyle defined benefit plan. Pension information for the years ended December 31 is as follows:

	Arrow SERP		Wyle Defined Benefit Plan	
	2013	2012	2013	2012
Accumulated benefit obligation	$ 67,320	$ 63,584	$ 126,481	$ 128,771
Changes in projected benefit obligation:				
Projected benefit obligation at beginning of year	$ 73,327	$ 61,690	$ 128,771	$ 118,191
Service cost	2,126	2,064	—	—
Interest cost	2,846	3,031	5,038	5,442
Actuarial loss (gain)	301	9,780	(1,158)	10,808
Benefits paid	(3,288)	(3,238)	(6,170)	(5,670)
Projected benefit obligation at end of year	$ 75,312	$ 73,327	$ 126,481	$ 128,771
Changes in plan assets:				
Fair value of plan assets at beginning of year	$ —	$ —	$ 92,976	$ 81,719
Actual return on plan assets	—	—	17,608	11,477
Company contributions	—	—	300	5,450
Benefits paid	—	—	(6,170)	(5,670)
Fair value of plan assets at end of year	$ —	$ —	$ 104,714	$ 92,976
Funded status	$ (75,312)	$ (73,327)	$ (21,767)	$ (35,795)
Amounts recognized in the company's consolidated balance sheets:				
Current liabilities	$ (3,531)	$ (3,483)	$ —	$ —
Noncurrent liabilities	(71,781)	(69,844)	(21,767)	(35,795)
Net assets (liabilities) at end of year	$ (75,312)	$ (73,327)	$ (21,767)	$ (35,795)
Components of net periodic pension cost:				
Service cost	$ 2,126	$ 2,064	$ —	$ —
Interest cost	2,846	3,031	5,038	5,442
Expected return on plan assets	—	—	(6,516)	(6,200)
Amortization of net loss	2,707	2,013	1,956	1,745
Amortization of prior service cost	42	42	—	—
Net periodic pension cost	$ 7,721	$ 7,150	$ 478	$ 987
Weighted-average assumptions used to determine benefit obligation:				
Discount rate	4.50 %	4.00 %	4.50 %	4.00 %
Rate of compensation increase	5.00 %	5.00 %	N/A	N/A
Expected return on plan assets	N/A	N/A	6.75 %	7.25 %
Weighted-average assumptions used to determine net periodic pension cost:				
Discount rate	4.00 %	4.75 %	4.00 %	4.75 %
Rate of compensation increase	5.00 %	5.00 %	N/A	N/A
Expected return on plan assets	N/A	N/A	7.25 %	7.50 %

The amounts reported for net periodic pension cost and the respective benefit obligation amounts are dependent upon the actuarial assumptions used. The company reviews historical trends, future expectations, current market conditions, and external data to determine the assumptions. The discount rate represents the market rate for a high-quality corporate bond. The rate of compensation increase is determined by the company, based upon its long-term plans for such increases. The expected return on plan assets is based on current and expected asset allocations, historical trends, and projected returns on those assets. The actuarial assumptions used to determine the net periodic pension cost are based upon the prior year's assumptions used to determine the benefit obligation.

Benefit payments are expected to be paid as follows:

	Arrow SERP	Wyle Defined Benefit Plan
2014	$ 3,602	$ 6,755
2015	3,564	6,804
2016	3,617	6,980
2017	3,568	7,053
2018	4,054	7,089
2019–2023	25,890	37,572

MULTI-EMPLOYER PLANS

3.50 ARKANSAS BEST CORPORATION (DEC)
NOTES TO CONSOLIDATED FINANCIAL STATEMENTS

Note J—Employee Benefit Plans (in part)

Multiemployer Plans (in part)

ABF Freight contributes to multiemployer pension and health and welfare plans to provide benefits for its contractual employees. ABF Freight's contributions generally are based on the time worked by its contractual employees, in accordance with the ABF NMFA, its collective bargaining agreement with the IBT, and other related supplemental agreements. As of December 2013, approximately 76% of ABF Freight's employees were covered under ABF NMFA. ABF Freight recognizes as expense the contractually required contributions for each period and recognizes as a liability any contributions due and unpaid. The ABF NMFA and the related supplemental agreements which were implemented on November 3, 2013, provide for continued contributions to various multiemployer health, welfare, and pension plans maintained for the benefit of ABF Freight's employees who are members of the IBT. Rate increases under the ABF NMFA were applied retroactively to August 1, 2013. The combined contribution rates for health, welfare, and pension benefits under the ABF NMFA may increase up to $1.00 per hour each August 1 providing that the plans evidence any necessary increase.

The multiemployer plans to which ABF Freight contributes, which have been established pursuant to the Taft-Hartley Act, are jointly-trusteed (half of the trustees of each plan are selected by the participating employers, the other half by the IBT) and cover collectively-bargained employees of multiple unrelated employers. Due to the inherent nature of multiemployer plans, there are risks associated with participation in these plans that differ from single-employer plans. Assets received by the plans are not segregated by employer, and contributions made by one employer can be and are used to provide benefits to current and former employees of other employers. If a participating employer to a multiemployer plan no longer contributes to the plan, the unfunded obligations of the plan may be borne by the remaining participating employers. If a participating employer in a multiemployer pension plan completely withdraws from the plan, it owes to the plan its proportionate share of the plan's unfunded vested benefits, referred to as a withdrawal liability. A complete withdrawal generally occurs when the employer permanently ceases to contribute to the plan. A withdrawal liability is also owed in the event the employer withdraws from a plan in connection with a mass withdrawal, which generally occurs when all or substantially all employers withdraw from the plan pursuant to an agreement in a relatively short period of time. Were ABF Freight to completely withdraw from certain multiemployer pension plans, whether in connection with a mass withdrawal or otherwise, under current law, the Company would have material liabilities for its share of the unfunded vested liabilities of each such plan. However, ABF Freight currently has no intention to withdraw from any such plan, which generally would be effected through collective bargaining.

Pension Plans

The 25 multiemployer pension plans to which ABF Freight contributes vary greatly in size and in funded status. ABF Freight's contribution obligations to these plans are specified in the ABF NMFA, which was implemented on November 3, 2013 and will remain in effect through March 31, 2018. The funding obligations to the pension plans are intended to satisfy the requirements imposed by the PPA. Among other things, the PPA requires that "endangered" (generally less than 80% funded and commonly called "yellow zone") plans adopt "funding improvement plans" and that "critical" (generally less than 65% funded and commonly called "red zone") plans adopt "rehabilitation plans" that are intended to improve the plan's funded status over time. Through the term of its current collective bargaining agreement, ABF Freight's contribution obligations generally will be satisfied by making the specified contributions when due. However, the Company cannot determine with any certainty the contributions that will be required under future collective bargaining agreements for its contractual employees. In addition, notwithstanding any collective bargaining agreement, employer contribution obligations to multiemployer pension plans can be increased if the plan enters reorganization status or becomes insolvent. In those events, the contribution increase generally cannot exceed 7% per year. ABF Freight has not received notification of any plan reorganization or plan insolvency.

Based on the most recent annual funding notices the Company has received, most of which are for plan years ended December 31, 2012, approximately 63% of ABF Freight's contributions to multiemployer pension plans, including the Central States, Southeast and Southwest Areas Pension Plan (the "Central States Pension Plan") discussed below, were made to plans that were in "critical status" and approximately 3% of ABF Freight's contributions to multiemployer pension plans were made to plans that were in "endangered status," each as defined by the PPA. ABF Freight's participation in multiemployer pension plans is summarized in the table below. The multiemployer pension plans listed separately in the table represent plans that are individually significant to ABF Freight based on the amount of plan contributions. The severity of a plan's underfunded status was also considered in ABF Freight's analysis of individually significant funds to be separately disclosed.

Significant multiemployer pension plans and key participation information were as follows:

Legal Name of Plan	EIN/Pension Plan Number[a]	Pension Protection Act Zone Status[b] 2013	Pension Protection Act Zone Status[b] 2012	FIP/RP Status Pending/ Implemented[c]	Contributions[d] (In thousands) 2013	Contributions[d] (In thousands) 2012	Contributions[d] (In thousands) 2011	Surcharge Imposed[e]
Central States, Southeast and Southwest Areas Pension Plan[1][2]	36-6044243	Red	Red	Implemented[3]	$ 70,020	$ 68,683	$ 70,579	No
Western Conference of Teamsters Pension Plan[2]	91-6145047	Green	Green	No[4]	20,601	20,774	20,807	No
Central Pennsylvania Teamsters Defined Benefit Plan[1][2]	23-6262789	Green[5]	Yellow[5]	Implemented[5]	12,143	11,170	12,022	No
I. B. of T. Union Local No. 710 Pension Fund[7][8]	36-2377656	Green[6]	Green[6]	No	10,001	9,567	9,265	No
All other plans in the aggregate					23,468	21,701	20,168	
Total multiemployer pension contributions paid[9]					$136,233	$131,895	$132,841	

Table Heading Definitions

[a] The "EIN/Pension Plan Number" column provides the Federal Employer Identification Number (EIN) and the three-digit plan number, if applicable.

[b] Unless otherwise noted, the most recent PPA zone status available in 2013 and 2012 is for the plan's year-end status at December 31, 2012 and 2011, respectively. The zone status is based on information ABF Freight received from the plan and was certified by the plan's actuary.

[c] The "FIP/RP Status Pending/Implemented" column indicates if a funding improvement plan (FIP) or a rehabilitation plan (RP), if applicable, is pending or has been implemented.

[d] Amounts reflect contributions made by ABF Freight in the respective year and differ from amounts expensed during the year.

[e] The surcharge column indicates if a surcharge was paid by the employer to the plan.

[1] ABF Freight was listed by the plan as providing more than 5% of the total contributions to the plan for the plan years ended December 31, 2012 and 2011.

[2] Information for this plan was obtained from the annual funding notice, other notices received from the plan, and the Forms 5500 filed for the plan years ended December 31, 2012 and 2011.

[3] Adopted a rehabilitation plan effective March 25, 2008, as updated. Utilized amortization extension effective December 31, 2003.

[4] Utilized funding relief elections under the Pension Relief Act to determine the zone status beginning with the January 1, 2011 actuarial valuation.

[5] Certified as "neither endangered nor critical" status for the plan year beginning January 1, 2013. The plan was certified as "endangered" for the plan year beginning January 1, 2012, and a funding improvement plan was adopted in December 2012.

[6] PPA zone status relates to plan years February 1, 2012–January 31, 2013 and February 1, 2011 – January 31, 2012.

[7] ABF Freight was listed by the plan as providing more than 5% of the total contributions to the plan for the plan years ended January 31, 2013 and 2012.

[8] Information for this plan was obtained from the annual funding notice, other notices received from the plan, and the Forms 5500 filed for the plan years ended January 31, 2013 and 2012.

[9] Contribution levels can be impacted by several factors such as changes in business levels and the related time worked by contractual employees, contractual rate increases for pension benefits, and the specific funding structure, which differs among plans. The pension contribution rate for contractual employees increased an average of 2.0%, 2.3%, and 3.6% effective primarily on August 1, 2013, 2012, and 2011, respectively. The Supplemental Negotiating Committee for the Central States Pension Plan approved no pension contribution increase effective August 1, 2013, 2012, and 2011. The Supplemental Negotiating Committee for the Western Conference of Teamsters Pension Plan approved no pension contribution increase effective August 1, 2013 and 2012. The year-over-year changes in multiemployer pension plan contributions presented above were also influenced by changes in ABF Freight's business levels.

For 2013, 2012, and 2011, 50% to 55% of ABF Freight's multiemployer pension contributions were made to the Central States Pension Plan. The funded percentage of the Central States Pension Plan, as set forth in information provided by the Central States Plan, was 47.6%, 53.9%, and 58.9% as of January 1, 2013, 2012, and 2011, respectively. In 2005, the IRS granted an extension of the period of time over which the Central States Pension Plan amortizes unfunded liabilities by ten years subject to the condition that a targeted funding ratio will be maintained by the plan. Based on information currently available to the Company, the Central States Pension Plan has not received notice of revocation of the ten-year amortization extension granted by the IRS. In the unlikely event that the IRS revokes the extension, the revocation would apply retroactively to the 2004 plan year, which would result in a material liability for ABF Freight's share of the resulting funded deficiency, the extent of which is currently unknown to the Company. The Company believes that the occurrence of a revocation that would require recognition of liabilities for ABF Freight's share of a funded deficiency is remote.

PLAN AMENDMENT

3.51 COLGATE-PALMOLIVE COMPANY (DEC)
NOTES TO CONSOLIDATED FINANCIAL STATEMENTS

(Dollars in Millions Except Share and Per Share Amounts)

10. Retirement Plans and Other Retiree Benefits (in part)

Retirement Plans

The Company and certain of its U.S. and overseas subsidiaries maintain defined benefit retirement plans. Benefits under these plans are based primarily on years of service and employees' career earnings.

During 2013, the Company announced changes to the way it will provide future retirement benefits to substantially all of its U.S.-based employees participating in its defined benefit retirement plan. Effective January 1, 2014, the Company will provide future retirement benefits for these U.S.-based employees through the Company's defined contribution plan. As a result, no future service will be considered for future accruals in the U.S. defined benefit retirement plans. Participants in the Company's U.S. defined benefit retirement plan whose retirement benefit was determined under the cash balance formula will continue to earn interest on their vested balances as of December 31, 2013. Participants whose retirement benefit was determined under the final average earnings formula will continue to have their final average earnings adjusted for pay increases until retirement. These changes resulted in a curtailment charge of $91 as all of the previously unamortized prior service costs recorded in Accumulated other comprehensive income (loss) was recognized in 2013.

In the Company's principal U.S. plans and certain funded overseas plans, funds are contributed to trusts in accordance with regulatory limits to provide for current service and for any unfunded projected benefit obligation over a reasonable period. The target asset allocation for the Company's defined benefit plans are as follows:

Asset Category	United States	International
Equity securities	27%	39%
Fixed income securities	53	48
Real estate and other investments	20	13
Total	100%	100%

At December 31, 2013 the allocation of the Company's plan assets and the level of valuation input for each major asset category was as follows:

	Level of Valuation Input	Pension Plans		Other Retiree Benefits
		United States	International	
Investments:				
Cash & cash equivalents	Level 1	$ 97	$ 23	$ 3
U.S. common stocks	Level 1	127	—	3
International common stocks	Level 1	51	—	1
Fixed income securities (a)	Level 2	433	—	8
Common/collective trust funds (b):	Level 2			
Equity index funds		359	229	9
Emerging market equity index funds		33	9	1
Other common stock funds		123	75	3
Fixed income funds: U.S. or foreign government and agency securities		149	73	3
Fixed income funds: investment grade corporate bonds		203	71	5
Fixed income funds: high yield corporate bonds and other		119	1	4
Guaranteed investment contracts (c)	Level 2	2	56	—
Real estate funds (d)	Level 3	40	21	1
Total Investments at fair value		$1,736	$558	$41

At December 31, 2012 the allocation of the Company's plan assets and the level of valuation input for each major asset category was as follows:

Investments:	Level of Valuation Input	Pension Plans United States	Pension Plans International	Other Retiree Benefits
Cash & cash equivalents	Level 1	$ 45	$ 9	$ 1
U.S. common stocks	Level 1	258	—	6
International common stocks	Level 1	93	—	2
Fixed income securities[a]	Level 2	142	—	—
Common/collective trust funds[b]:	Level 2			
Equity index funds		444	199	11
Emerging market equity index funds		65	12	2
Other common stock funds		40	65	1
Fixed income funds: U.S. or foreign government and agency securities		227	59	6
Fixed income funds: investment grade corporate bonds		26	72	1
Fixed income funds: high yield corporate bonds and other		185	1	5
Guaranteed investment contracts[c]	Level 2	2	49	—
Real estate funds[d]	Level 3	70	20	2
Total Investments at fair value		$1,597	$486	$37

[a] The fixed income securities are traded over the counter and certain of these securities lack daily pricing or liquidity and as such are classified as Level 2. As of December 31, 2013 and 2012, approximately 50% of the fixed income portfolio was invested in U.S. treasury or agency securities, with the remainder invested in other government bonds and corporate bonds.

[b] Interests in common/collective trust funds are valued using the net asset value (" NAV ") per unit in each fund. The NAV is based on the value of the underlying investments owned by each trust, minus its liabilities, divided by the number of shares outstanding.

[c] The guaranteed investment contracts (" GICs ") represent contracts with insurance companies measured at the cash surrender value of each contract. The Level 2 valuation reflects that the cash surrender value is based principally on a referenced pool of investment funds with active redemption.

[d] Real estate is valued using the NAV per unit of funds that are invested in real estate property. The investment value of the real estate property is determined quarterly using independent market appraisals as determined by the investment manager. Since the appraisals include unobservable inputs, these investments are classified as Level 3. These unobservable inputs may include items such as annual gross rents, projected vacancy rates, collection losses and recovery rates, yield rates, growth assumptions and risk adjusted discount rates.

The following table presents a reconciliation of Level 3 plan assets measured at fair value for the year ended December 31:

	2013 United States Real Estate Fund	2013 International Real Estate Fund	2012 United States Real Estate Fund	2012 International Real Estate Fund
Beginning balance as of January 1	$ 72	$ 20	$ 64	$ 18
Earned income, net of management expenses	2	—	6	—
Unrealized gain on investment	9	—	2	1
Purchases, sales, issuances and settlements, net	(42)	1	—	1
Ending balance as of December 31	$ 41	$ 21	$ 72	$ 20

Equity securities in the U.S. plans include investments in the Company's common stock representing 6% of U.S. plan assets at December 31, 2013 and 11% of U.S. plan assets at December 31, 2012. In 2013, the U.S. plans sold 1,540,215 shares of the Company's common stock to the Company. No shares of the Company's common stock were purchased or sold by the plans in 2012. The plans received dividends on the Company's common stock of $3 in 2013 and $4 in 2012.

Other Retiree Benefits (in part)

The Company uses a December 31 measurement date for its defined benefit and other retiree benefit plans. Summarized information for the Company's defined benefit and other retiree benefit plans are as follows:

	Pension Benefits 2013 United States	Pension Benefits 2012 United States	Pension Benefits 2013 International	Pension Benefits 2012 International	Other Retiree Benefits 2013	Other Retiree Benefits 2012
Change in Benefit Obligations						
Benefit obligations at beginning of year	$2,227	$2,025	$ 888	$ 760	$ 875	$ 776
Service cost	24	24	19	12	11	9
Interest cost	90	97	34	35	38	40
Participants' contributions	1	1	3	3	—	—
Acquisitions/plan amendments	40	—	2	21	—	(27)
Actuarial loss (gain)	(148)	200	(1)	103	(101)	119
Foreign exchange impact	—	—	12	21	(5)	1
Termination benefits[1]	11	—	—	—	6	—
Curtailments and settlements	(12)	—	(21)	(23)	—	—
Benefit payments	(131)	(128)	(41)	(45)	(32)	(40)
Other	—	8	(1)	1	—	(3)
Benefit obligations at end of year	$2,102	$2,227	$ 894	$ 888	$ 792	$ 875

(continued)

	Pension Benefits				Other Retiree Benefits	
	2013	2012	2013	2012	2013	2012
	United States		International			
Change in Plan Assets						
Fair value of plan assets at beginning of year	$1,597	$1,426	$ 486	$ 437	$ 37	$ 32
Actual return on plan assets	148	173	59	47	4	5
Company contributions	121	125	61	57	32	40
Participants' contributions	1	1	3	3	—	—
Foreign exchange impact	—	—	2	13	—	—
Settlements	—	—	(11)	(21)	—	—
Benefit payments	(131)	(128)	(41)	(45)	(32)	(40)
Other	—	—	(1)	(5)	—	—
Fair value of plan assets at end of year	$1,736	$1,597	$ 558	$ 486	$ 41	$ 37
Funded Status						
Benefit obligations at end of year	$2,102	$2,227	$ 894	$ 888	$ 792	$ 875
Fair value of plan assets at end of year	1,736	1,597	558	486	41	37
Net amount recognized	$ (366)	$ (630)	$(336)	$(402)	$(751)	$(838)
Amounts Recognized in Balance Sheet						
Noncurrent assets	$ 16	$ —	$ 12	$ 2	$ —	$ —
Current liabilities	(19)	(17)	(36)	(29)	(39)	(40)
Noncurrent liabilities	(363)	(613)	(312)	(375)	(712)	(798)
Net amount recognized	$ (366)	$ (630)	$(336)	$(402)	$(751)	$(838)
Amounts Recognized in Accumulated Other Comprehensive Income (Loss)						
Actuarial loss	$ 674	$ 932	$ 181	$ 235	$ 296	$ 421
Transition/prior service cost	3	63	23	26	1	2
	$ 677	$ 995	$ 204	$ 261	$ 297	$ 423
Accumulated benefit obligation	$1,995	$2,093	$ 802	$ 798	$ —	$ —
Weighted-Average Assumptions Used to Determine Benefit Obligations						
Discount rate	4.96%	4.14%	3.99%	3.57%	5.24%	4.32%
Long-term rate of return on plan assets	6.80%	7.30%	5.50%	5.39%	6.80%	7.30%
Long-term rate of compensation increase	3.50%	3.50%	3.02%	2.80%	—%	—%
ESOP growth rate	—%	—%	—%	—%	10.00%	10.00%
Medical cost trend rate of increase	—%	—%	—%	—%	7.00%	7.50%

[1] Represents pension and other retiree benefit enhancements incurred in 2013 pursuant to the 2012 Restructuring Program.

The overall investment objective of the plans is to balance risk and return so that obligations to employees are met. The Company evaluates its long-term rate of return on plan assets on an annual basis. In determining the long-term rate of return, the Company considers the nature of the plans' investments and the historical rates of return. The assumed rate of return as of December 31, 2013 for the U.S. plans was 6.80%. Average annual rates of return for the U.S. plans for the most recent 1-year, 5-year, 10-year, 15-year and 25-year periods were 9%, 11%, 7%, 6%, and 8%, respectively. Similar assessments were performed in determining rates of return on international pension plan assets to arrive at the Company's 2013 weighted-average rate of return of 5.50%.

The medical cost trend rate of increase assumed in measuring the expected cost of benefits is projected to decrease from 7.0% in 2014 to 5.0% by 2020, remaining at 5.0% for the years thereafter. Changes in the assumed rate can have a significant effect on amounts reported. A 1% change in the assumed medical cost trend rate would have the following approximate effect:

	One Percentage Point	
	Increase	Decrease
Accumulated postretirement benefit obligation	$109	$(88)
Total of service and interest cost components	9	(7)

Plans with projected benefit obligations in excess of plan assets and plans with accumulated benefit obligations in excess of plan assets as of December 31 consist of the following:

	Years Ended December 31,	
	2013	2012
Benefit Obligation Exceeds Fair Value of Plan Assets		
Projected benefit obligation	$1,130	$3,112
Fair value of plan assets	402	2,080
Accumulated benefit obligation	700	2,855
Fair value of plan assets	66	2,044

Summarized information regarding the net periodic benefit costs for the Company's defined benefit and other retiree benefit plans is as follows:

	Pension Benefits						Other Retiree Benefits		
	2013	2012	2011	2013	2012	2011	2013	2012	2011
	United States			International					
Components of Net Periodic Benefit Cost									
Service cost	$ 24	$ 24	$ 24	$ 19	$ 12	$ 19	$13	$11	$12
Interest cost	90	97	100	34	35	36	38	40	39
Annual ESOP allocation	—	—	—	—	—	—	(2)	(2)	(2)
Expected return on plan assets	(118)	(112)	(110)	(26)	(26)	(27)	(3)	(3)	(3)
Amortization of transition & prior service costs (credits)	9	9	9	2	2	3	1	3	2
Amortization of actuarial loss	68	62	46	10	9	9	21	18	16
Net periodic benefit cost	$ 73	$ 80	$ 69	$ 39	$ 32	$ 40	$68	$67	$64
Other postretirement charges	102	—	—	3	9	3	6	1	1
Total pension cost	$ 175	$ 80	$ 69	$ 42	$ 41	$ 43	$74	$68	$65
Weighted-Average Assumptions Used to Determine Net Periodic Benefit Cost									
Discount rate	4.14%	4.90%	5.30%	3.57%	4.59%	5.04%	4.32%	5.26%	5.30%
Long-term rate of return on plan assets	7.30%	7.75%	8.00%	5.39%	5.91%	6.23%	7.30%	7.75%	8.00%
Long-term rate of compensation increase	3.50%	4.00%	4.00%	2.80%	2.87%	3.05%	—%	—%	—%
ESOP growth rate	—%	—%	—%	—%	—%	—%	10.00%	10.00%	10.00%
Medical cost trend rate of increase	—%	—%	—%	—%	—%	—%	7.50%	8.00%	8.33%

Other postretirement charges in 2013 primarily relate to a curtailment charge of $91 resulting from changes to the Company's defined benefit retirement plans in the U.S. and certain other one-time pension and other retiree benefit enhancements incurred pursuant to the 2012 Restructuring Program.

Other postretirement charges in 2012 primarily relate to the sale of land in Mexico.

The Company made voluntary contributions of $101, $101 and $178 in 2013, 2012 and 2011, respectively, to its U.S. retirement plans.

The estimated actuarial loss and the estimated transition/prior service cost for defined benefit and other retiree benefit plans that will be amortized from Accumulated other comprehensive income (loss) into net periodic benefit cost over the next fiscal year is as follows:

	Pension Benefits	Other Retiree Benefits
Net actuarial loss	$39	$15
Net transition & prior service cost	2	—

Expected Contributions & Benefit Payments

Management does not expect to make a voluntary contribution to U.S. pension plans for the year ending December 31, 2014. Actual funding may differ from current estimates depending on the variability of the market value of the assets as compared to the obligation and other market or regulatory conditions.

Total benefit payments to be paid to participants for the year ending December 31, 2014 from the Company's assets are estimated to be approximately $98. Total benefit payments expected to be paid to participants from plan assets, or payments directly from the Company's assets to participants in unfunded plans, are as follows:

Years Ended December 31,	Pension Benefits		Other Retiree Benefits	Total
	United States	International		
2014	$172	$ 70	$ 40	$ 282
2015	136	55	41	232
2016	135	47	43	225
2017	136	54	44	234
2018	135	50	45	230
2019–2023	691	273	232	1,196

Postemployment Benefits

RECOGNITION AND MEASUREMENT

3.52 FASB ASC 712, *Compensation—Nonretirement Postemployment Benefits*, requires that entities providing postemployment benefits to their employees accrue the cost of such benefits. FASB ASC 712 does not require that the amount of other postemployment benefits be disclosed.

PRESENTATION AND DISCLOSURE EXCERPT

POSTEMPLOYMENT BENEFITS

3.53 CLIFFS NATURAL RESOURCES INC. (DEC)
STATEMENTS OF CONSOLIDATED FINANCIAL POSITION (in part)

	December 31,	
(In millions)	2013	2012
Liabilities		
Current Liabilities		
Accounts payable	$ 345.5	$ 555.5
Accrued employment costs	129.0	135.6
Income taxes payable	61.7	28.3
State and local taxes payable	61.7	65.9
Current portion of debt	20.9	94.1
Accrued expenses	206.4	258.9
Accrued royalties	57.3	48.1
Other current liabilities	203.0	195.1
Total Current Liabilities	1,085.5	1,381.5
Postemployment Benefit Liabilities		
Pensions	197.5	403.8
Other postretirement benefits	96.5	214.5
Total Postemployment Benefit Liabilities	294.0	618.3
Environmental and Mine Closure Obligations	309.7	252.8
Deferred Income Taxes	1,146.5	1,108.1
Long-Term Debt	3,022.6	3,960.7
Other Liabilities	379.3	492.6
Total Liabilities	6,237.6	7,814.0

NOTES TO CONSOLIDATED FINANCIAL STATEMENTS

Note 1—Basis of Presentation and Significant Accounting Policies (in part)

Pensions and Other Postretirement Benefits

We offer defined benefit pension plans, defined contribution pension plans and other postretirement benefit plans, primarily consisting of retiree healthcare benefits, to most employees in North America as part of a total compensation and benefits program. We do not have employee pension or post-retirement benefit obligations at our Asia Pacific Iron Ore operations.

We recognize the funded or unfunded status of our postretirement benefit obligations on our December 31, 2013 and 2012 Statements of Consolidated Financial Position based on the difference between the market value of plan assets and the actuarial present value of our retirement obligations on that date, on a plan-by-plan basis. If the plan assets exceed the retirement obligations, the amount of the surplus is recorded as an asset; if the retirement obligations exceed the plan assets, the amount of the underfunded obligations are recorded as a liability. Year-end balance sheet adjustments to postretirement assets and obligations are recorded as *Accumulated other comprehensive loss*.

The actuarial estimates of the PBO and APBO retirement obligations incorporate various assumptions including the discount rates, the rates of increases in compensation, healthcare cost trend rates, mortality, retirement timing and employee turnover. For the U.S. and Canadian plans, the discount rate is determined based on the prevailing year-end rates for high-grade corporate bonds with a duration matching the expected cash flow timing of the benefit payments from the various plans. The remaining assumptions are based on our estimates of future events by incorporating historical trends and future expectations. The amount of net periodic cost that is recorded in the Statements of Consolidated Operations consists of several components including service cost, interest cost, expected return on plan assets, and amortization of previously unrecognized amounts. Service cost represents the value of the benefits earned in the current year by the participants. Interest cost represents the cost associated with the passage of time. Certain items, such as plan amendments, gains and/or losses resulting from differences between actual and assumed results for demographic and economic factors affecting the obligations and assets of the plans, and changes in other assumptions are subject to deferred recognition for income and expense purposes. The expected return on plan assets is determined utilizing the weighted average of expected returns for plan asset investments in various asset categories based on historical performance, adjusted for current trends. See NOTE 13—PENSIONS AND OTHER POSTRETIREMENT BENEFITS for further information.

Note 13—Pensions and Other Postretirement Benefits (in part)

We offer defined benefit pension plans, defined contribution pension plans and other postretirement benefit plans, primarily consisting of retiree healthcare benefits, to most employees in North America as part of a total compensation and benefits program. We do not have employee retirement benefit obligations at our Asia Pacific Iron Ore operations. The defined benefit pension plans largely are noncontributory and benefits generally are based on employees' years of service and average earnings for a defined period prior to retirement or a minimum formula.

On November 9, 2012, the USW ratified 37 month labor contracts, which replaced the labor agreements that expired on September 1, 2012. The agreements cover approximately 2,400 USW-represented employees at our Empire and Tilden mines in Michigan and our United Taconite and Hibbing mines in Minnesota, or 32.0 percent of our total workforce. The new agreement set temporary monthly postretirement OPEB caps for participants who retire prior to January 1, 2015. These premium maximums will expire at the end of the contract period and revert to increasing premiums based on the terms of the 2004 bargaining agreement. Also agreed to was an OPEB cap that will limit the amount of contributions that we have to make toward medical insurance coverage for each retiree and spouse of a retiree per calendar year after it goes into effect. The amount of the annual OPEB cap will be based upon the costs we incur in 2014. The OPEB cap will apply to employees who retire on or after January 1, 2015 and will not apply to surviving spouses. In addition, the bargaining agreement renewed the lump sum special payments for certain employees retiring in the near future. The changes also included renewal of and an increase in payments to surviving spouses of certain retirees, as well as, an increase in the temporary supplemental benefit amount paid to certain retirees. The agreements also provide that we and our partners fund an estimated $65.7 million into the bargaining unit VEBA plans during the term of the agreements unless funding obligations have been reached. These agreements are effective through September 30, 2015.

In August 2013, we entered into a new labor agreement with the USW covering our represented employees at Bloom Lake. It has a three-year term that runs from September 1, 2013 through August 31, 2016. The new agreement provides us with significant workforce flexibility.

In November 2013, we entered into a new labor agreement the USW covering our represented employees at our Pointe Noire facility, which is part of our Wabush operations. It has a six-year term and runs from March 1, 2014 to February 28, 2020. It provides for a 26.0 percent increase in the cost of employment over the life of the contract. We also obtained the USW's consent to an application we had made to the Canadian Industrial Relations Board to have this workforce governed by Canadian federal labor law. Following entrance of this agreement, the CIRB granted our application, providing us with significantly more flexibility to manage any future labor disruptions.

In addition, we currently provide various levels of retirement health care and OPEB to most full-time employees who meet certain length of service and age requirements (a portion of which is pursuant to collective bargaining agreements). Most plans require retiree contributions and have deductibles, co-pay requirements and benefit limits. Most bargaining unit plans require retiree contributions and co-pays for major medical and prescription drug coverage. There is an annual limit on our cost for medical coverage under the U.S. salaried plans. The annual limit applies to each covered participant and equals $7,000 for coverage prior to age 65 and $3,000 for coverage after age 65, with the retiree's participation adjusted based on the age at which the retiree's benefits commence. For participants at our Northshore operation, the annual limit ranges from $4,020 to $4,500 for coverage prior to age 65, and equals $2,000 for coverage after age 65. Covered participants pay an amount for coverage equal to the excess of (i) the average cost of coverage for all covered participants, over (ii) the participant's individual limit, but in no event will the participant's cost be less than 15.0 percent of the average cost of coverage for all covered participants. For Northshore participants, the minimum participant cost is a fixed dollar amount. We do not provide OPEB for most U.S. salaried employees hired after January 1, 1993. Retiree healthcare coverage is provided through programs administered by insurance companies whose charges are based on benefits paid.

Our North American Coal segment is required under an agreement with the UMWA to pay amounts into the UMWA pension trusts based principally on hours worked by UMWA-represented employees. This agreement covers approximately 800 UMWA-represented employees at our Pinnacle Complex in West Virginia and our Oak Grove mine in Alabama, or 11.0 percent of our total workforce. These multi-employer pension trusts provide benefits to eligible retirees through a defined benefit plan. The UMWA 1993 Benefit Plan is a defined contribution plan that was created as the result of negotiations for the NBCWA of 1993. The plan provides healthcare insurance to orphan UMWA retirees who are not eligible to participate in the UMWA Combined Benefit Fund or the 1992 Benefit Fund or whose last employer signed the 1993 or later NBCWA and who subsequently goes out of business. Contributions to the trust were at a rate of $8.10 per hour worked in both 2013 and 2012 and $6.50 per hour worked in 2011. These amounted to $14.9 million in both 2013 and 2012 and $9.5 million in 2011, respectively. Our Pinnacle and Oak Grove mines are signatories to labor agreements with the UMWA, making them participants in the UMWA 1974 Pension Plan (the "1974 PP"). As of the most recent estimate, Pinnacle and Oak Grove's combined share of this underfunded liability was estimated to be approximately $342 million. If Pinnacle or Oak Grove were to withdraw from the 1974 PP or if a mass withdrawal were to occur, we would become obligated to pay this amount to the 1974 PP.

In December 2003, The Medicare Prescription Drug, Improvement, and Modernization Act of 2003 was enacted. This act introduced a prescription drug benefit under Medicare Part D as well as a federal subsidy to sponsors of retiree healthcare benefit plans that provide a benefit that at least actuarially is equivalent to Medicare Part D. Our measures of the accumulated postretirement benefit obligation and net periodic postretirement benefit cost as of December 31, 2004 and for periods thereafter reflect amounts associated with the subsidy. We elected to adopt the retroactive transition method for recognizing the cost reduction in 2004. The following table summarizes the annual expense recognized related to the retirement plans for 2013, 2012 and 2011 :

(In millions)	2013	2012	2011
Defined benefit pension plans	$52.1	$55.2	$37.8
Defined contribution pension plans	6.8	6.7	5.7
Other postretirement benefits	17.4	28.1	26.8
Total	$76.3	$90.0	$70.3

The following tables and information provide additional disclosures for our consolidated plans.

Obligations and Funded Status

The following tables and information provide additional disclosures for the December 31, 2013 and 2012 :

	Pension Benefits		Other Benefits	
(In millions)	2013	2012	2013	2012
Change in Benefit Obligations:				
Benefit obligations—beginning of year	$ 1,244.3	$ 1,141.4	$ 459.8	$ 488.4
Service cost (excluding expenses)	38.9	32.0	12.3	14.7
Interest cost	45.9	48.4	17.3	20.6
Plan amendments	0.8	2.8	—	(58.3)
Actuarial (gain) loss	(121.8)	84.3	(103.3)	11.3
Benefits paid	(72.9)	(71.0)	(28.0)	(26.9)
Participant contributions	—	—	5.6	4.6
Federal subsidy on benefits paid	—	—	0.5	0.8
Exchange rate (gain) loss	(17.2)	6.4	(8.0)	4.6
Benefit obligations—end of year	$ 1,118.0	$ 1,244.3	$ 356.2	$ 459.8
Change in Plan Assets:				
Fair value of plan assets—beginning of year	$ 838.7	$ 744.1	$ 237.0	$ 193.5
Actual return on plan assets	109.5	92.5	11.0	26.1
Participant contributions	—	—	1.8	1.7
Employer contributions	53.7	67.7	20.7	23.3
Benefits paid	(72.9)	(71.0)	(18.7)	(7.6)
Exchange rate gain (loss)	(13.7)	5.4	—	—
Fair value of plan assets—end of year	$ 915.3	$ 838.7	$ 251.8	$ 237.0

(continued)

(In millions)	Pension Benefits		Other Benefits	
	2013	2012	2013	2012
Funded Status at December 31:				
Fair value of plan assets	$ 915.3	$ 838.7	$ 251.8	$ 237.0
Benefit obligations	(1,118.0)	(1,244.3)	(356.2)	(459.8)
Funded status (plan assets less benefit obligations)	$ (202.7)	$ (405.6)	$(104.4)	$(222.8)
Amount recognized at December 31	$ (202.7)	$ (405.6)	$(104.4)	$(222.8)
Amounts Recognized in Statements of Financial Position:				
Current liabilities	$ (5.2)	$ (1.8)	$ (7.9)	$ (8.3)
Noncurrent liabilities	(197.5)	(403.8)	(96.5)	(214.5)
Net amount recognized	$ (202.7)	$ (405.6)	$(104.4)	$(222.8)
Amounts Recognized in Accumulated Other Comprehensive Income:				
Net actuarial loss	$ 230.6	$ 429.2	$ 67.0	$ 176.8
Prior service cost	14.9	17.2	(45.4)	(48.8)
Transition asset	—	—	—	—
Net amount recognized	$ 245.5	$ 446.4	$ 21.6	$ 128.0
The Estimated Amounts that will be Amortized from Accumulated other Comprehensive Income into Net Periodic Benefit Cost in 2014:				
Net actuarial loss	$ 14.2		$ 4.6	
Prior service cost	2.7		(3.6)	
Net amount recognized	$ 16.9		$ 1.0	

	2013							
	Pension Plans					Other Benefits		
(In millions)	Salaried	Hourly	Mining	SERP	Total	Salaried	Hourly	Total
Fair value of plan assets	$ 357.4	$ 552.7	$ 5.2	$ —	$ 915.3	$ —	$ 251.8	$ 251.8
Benefit obligation	(427.2)	(674.8)	(6.8)	(9.2)	(1,118.0)	(53.6)	(302.6)	(356.2)
Funded status	$ (69.8)	$(122.1)	$(1.6)	$(9.2)	$ (202.7)	$(53.6)	$ (50.8)	$(104.4)

	2012							
	Pension Plans					Other Benefits		
(In millions)	Salaried	Hourly	Mining	SERP	Total	Salaried	Hourly	Total
Fair value of plan assets	$ 328.2	$ 506.4	$ 4.1	$ —	$ 838.7	$ —	$ 237.0	$ 237.0
Benefit obligation	(464.4)	(764.8)	(6.4)	(8.7)	(1,244.3)	(72.6)	(387.2)	(459.8)
Funded status	$ (136.2)	$(258.4)	$(2.3)	$(8.7)	$ (405.6)	$(72.6)	$(150.2)	$(222.8)

The accumulated benefit obligation for all defined benefit pension plans was $1,091.4 million and $1,204.7 million at December 31, 2013 and 2012, respectively. The decrease in the accumulated benefit obligation primarily is a result of an increase in the discount rates.

Components of Net Periodic Benefit Cost

	Pension Benefits			Other Benefits		
(In millions)	2013	2012	2011	2013	2012	2011
Service cost	$ 38.9	$32.0	$ 23.6	$ 12.3	$ 14.7	$ 11.1
Interest cost	45.9	48.4	51.4	17.3	20.6	22.3
Expected return on plan assets	(65.6)	(59.5)	(61.2)	(20.1)	(17.7)	(16.1)
Amortization:						
Net asset	—	—	—	—	(3.0)	(3.0)
Prior service costs (credits)	3.0	3.9	4.4	(3.6)	1.9	3.7
Net actuarial gains	29.9	30.4	19.6	11.5	11.6	8.8
Net periodic benefit cost	$ 52.1	$55.2	$ 37.8	$ 17.4	$ 28.1	$ 26.8
Acquired through business combinations	—	—	—	—	—	—
Current year actuarial (gain)/loss	(168.8)	53.1	165.3	(95.2)	3.2	46.8
Amortization of net loss	(29.9)	(30.4)	(19.6)	(11.5)	(11.6)	(8.8)
Current year prior service cost	0.8	2.8	—	—	(58.3)	—
Amortization of prior service (cost) credit	(3.0)	(3.9)	(4.4)	3.6	(1.9)	(3.7)
Amortization of transition asset	—	—	—	—	3.0	3.0
Total recognized in other comprehensive income	$(200.9)	$21.6	$141.3	$(103.1)	$(65.6)	$ 37.3
Total recognized in net periodic cost and other comprehensive income	$(148.8)	$76.8	$179.1	$ (85.7)	$(37.5)	$ 64.1

Additional Information

	Pension Benefits			Other Benefits		
(In millions)	2013	2012	2011	2013	2012	2011
Effect of change in mine ownership & noncontrolling interest	$ 46.5	$54.8	$53.3	$ 4.8	$ 8.6	$12.5
Actual return on plan assets	109.5	92.5	10.8	11.0	26.1	1.9

Assumptions

For our U.S. pension and other postretirement benefit plans, we used a discount rate as of December 31, 2013 of 4.57 percent, compared with a discount rate of 3.70 percent as of December 31, 2012. The U.S. discount rates are determined by matching the projected cash flows used to determine the PBO and APBO to a projected yield curve of 494 Aa graded bonds in the 10th to 90th percentiles. These bonds are either noncallable or callable with make-whole provisions. The duration matching produced rates ranging from 4.36 percent to 4.66 percent for our plans. Based upon these results, we selected a December 31, 2013 discount rate of 4.57 percent for our plans. This methodology is consistent with the calculation of the prior-year discount rate.

For our Canadian plans, we used a discount rate as of December 31, 2013 of 4.50 percent for the pension plans and 4.75 percent for the other postretirement benefit plans. Similar to the U.S. plans, the Canadian discount rates are determined by matching the projected cash flows used to determine the PBO and APBO to a projected yield curve of 334 corporate bonds in the 10th to 90th percentiles. The corporate bonds are either Aa graded, or (for maturities of 10 or more years) A or Aaa graded with an appropriate credit spread adjustment. These bonds are either noncallable or callable with make whole provisions. This methodology is consistent with the calculation of the prior-year discount rate.

Weighted-average assumptions used to determine benefit obligations at December 31 were:

	Pension Benefits		Other Benefits	
	2013	2012	2013	2012
U.S. plan discount rate	4.57%	3.70%	4.57%	3.70%
Canadian plan discount rate	4.50	3.75	4.75	4.00
Salaried rate of compensation increase	4.00	4.00	4.00	4.00
Hourly rate of compensation increase (ultimate)	3.00	4.00	N/A	N/A
U.S. expected return on plan assets	8.25	8.25	7.00	8.25
Canadian expected return on plan assets	7.25	7.25	N/A	N/A

Weighted-average assumptions used to determine net benefit cost for the years 2013, 2012 and 2011 were:

	Pension Benefits			Other Benefits		
	2013	2012	2011	2013	2012	2011
U.S. plan discount rate	3.70%	4.28%	5.11%	3.70%	4.28/3.51%[1]	5.11%
Canadian plan discount rate	3.75	4.00	5.00	4.00	4.25	5.00
U.S. expected return on plan assets	8.25	8.25	8.50	8.25	8.25	8.50
Canadian expected return on plan assets	7.25	7.25	7.50	N/A	N/A	7.50
Salaried rate of compensation increase	4.00	4.00	4.00	4.00	4.00	4.00
Hourly rate of compensation increase	4.00	4.00	4.00	N/A	N/A	N/A

[1] 4.28 percent for the Salaried Plan. For the Hourly Plan, 4.28 percent from January 1, 2012 through October 31, 2012, and 3.51 percent from November 1, 2012 through December 31, 2012.

Assumed health care cost trend rates at December 31 were:

	2013	2012
U.S. plan health care cost trend rate assumed for next year	7.25%	7.50%
Canadian plan health care cost trend rate assumed for next year	4.00	7.50
Ultimate health care cost trend rate	5.00	5.00
U.S. plan year that the ultimate rate is reached	2023	2023
Canadian plan year that the ultimate rate is reached	2018	2018

The Canadian plan health care cost trend rate assumed for next year decreased as we have experienced lower than expected Canadian plan health care costs in recent years.

Assumed health care cost trend rates have a significant effect on the amounts reported for the health care plans. A change of one percentage point in assumed health care cost trend rates would have the following effects:

(In millions)	Increase	Decrease
Effect on total of service and interest cost	$ 5.4	$ (4.1)
Effect on postretirement benefit obligation	38.2	(31.3)

Plan Assets (in part)

Our financial objectives with respect to our pension and VEBA plan assets are to fully fund the actuarial accrued liability for each of the plans, to maximize investment returns within reasonable and prudent levels of risk, and to maintain sufficient liquidity to meet benefit obligations on a timely basis.

Our investment objective is to outperform the expected Return on Asset ("ROA") assumption used in the plans' actuarial reports over a full market cycle, which is considered a period during which the U.S. economy experiences the effects of both an upturn and a downturn in the level of economic activity. In general, these periods tend to last between three and five years. The expected ROA takes into account historical returns and estimated future long-term returns based on capital market assumptions applied to the asset allocation strategy.

The asset allocation strategy is determined through a detailed analysis of assets and liabilities by plan, which defines the overall risk that is acceptable with regard to the expected level and variability of portfolio returns, surplus (assets compared to liabilities), contributions and pension expense.

The asset allocation review process involves simulating the effect of financial market performance for various asset allocation scenarios and factoring in the current funded status and likely future funded status levels by taking into account expected growth or decline in the contributions over time. The modeling is then adjusted by simulating unexpected changes in inflation and interest rates. The process also includes quantifying the effect of investment performance and simulated changes to future levels of contributions, determining the appropriate asset mix with the highest likelihood of meeting financial objectives and regularly reviewing our asset allocation strategy.

The asset allocation strategy varies by plan. The following table reflects the actual asset allocations for pension and VEBA plan assets as of December 31, 2013 and 2012, as well as the 2014 weighted average target asset allocations as of December 31, 2013. Equity investments include securities in large-cap, mid-cap and small-cap companies located in the U.S. and worldwide. Fixed income investments primarily include corporate bonds and government debt securities. Alternative investments include hedge funds, private equity, structured credit and real estate.

| | Pension Assets | | | VEBA Assets | | |
| | 2014 Target | Percentage of Plan Assets at December 31, | | 2014 Target | Percentage of Plan Assets at December 31, | |
	Allocation	2013	2012	Allocation	2013	2012
Asset Category						
Equity securities	46.9%	51.5%	45.9%	10.9%	10.4%	42.6%
Fixed income	28.4%	26.7%	29.5%	69.4%	66.6%	32.9%
Hedge funds	6.5%	6.3%	10.2%	8.0%	9.8%	9.8%
Private equity	5.8%	3.2%	3.5%	2.7%	2.4%	2.6%
Structured credit	6.2%	6.7%	6.7%	4.0%	5.4%	5.3%
Real estate	6.2%	4.5%	3.5%	5.0%	5.3%	6.7%
Cash	—%	1.1%	0.7%	—%	0.1%	0.1%
Total	100.0%	100.0%	100.0%	100.0%	100.0%	100.0%

Pension

The fair values of our pension plan assets at December 31, 2013 and 2012 by asset category are as follows:

| | December 31, 2013 | | | |
(In millions)	Quoted Prices in Active Markets for Identical Assets/Liabilities (Level 1)	Significant Other Observable Inputs (Level 2)	Significant Unobservable Inputs (Level 3)	Total
Asset Category				
Equity securities:				
U.S. large-cap	$261.5	$ —	$ —	$261.5
U.S. small/mid-cap	60.8	—	—	60.8
International	149.3	—	—	149.3
Fixed income	214.8	30.1	—	244.9
Hedge funds	—	—	57.6	57.6
Private equity	—	—	29.1	29.1
Structured credit	—	—	61.0	61.0
Real estate	—	—	40.9	40.9
Cash	10.2	—	—	10.2
Total	$696.6	$30.1	$188.6	$915.3

(In millions)	December 31, 2012 Quoted Prices in Active Markets for Identical Assets/Liabilities (Level 1)	Significant Other Observable Inputs (Level 2)	Significant Unobservable Inputs (Level 3)	Total
Asset Category				
Equity securities:				
U.S. large-cap	$231.1	$ —	$ —	$231.1
U.S. small/mid-cap	39.2	—	—	39.2
International	114.5	—	—	114.5
Fixed income	209.1	38.4	—	247.5
Hedge funds	—	—	85.6	85.6
Private equity	—	—	29.3	29.3
Structured credit	—	—	56.2	56.2
Real estate	—	—	29.4	29.4
Cash	5.9	—	—	5.9
Total	$599.8	$38.4	$200.5	$838.7

Following is a description of the inputs and valuation methodologies used to measure the fair value of our plan assets.

Equity Securities

Equity securities classified as Level 1 investments include U.S. large-, small- and mid-cap investments and international equity. These investments are comprised of securities listed on an exchange, market or automated quotation system for which quotations are readily available. The valuation of these securities is determined using a market approach, and is based upon unadjusted quoted prices for identical assets in active markets.

Fixed Income

Fixed income securities classified as Level 1 investments include bonds and government debt securities. These investments are comprised of securities listed on an exchange, market or automated quotation system for which quotations are readily available. The valuation of these securities is determined using a market approach, and is based upon unadjusted quoted prices for identical assets in active markets. Also included in Fixed Income is a portfolio of U.S. Treasury STRIPS, which are zero-coupon bearing fixed income securities backed by the full faith and credit of the U.S. government. The securities sell at a discount to par because there are no incremental coupon payments. STRIPS are not issued directly by the Treasury, but rather are created by a financial institution, government securities broker or government securities dealer. Liquidity on the issue varies depending on various market conditions; however, in general the STRIPS market is slightly less liquid than that of the U.S. Treasury Bond market. The STRIPS are priced daily through a bond pricing vendor and are classified as Level 2.

Hedge Funds

Hedge funds are alternative investments comprised of direct or indirect investment in offshore hedge funds of funds with an investment objective to achieve an attractive risk-adjusted return with moderate volatility and moderate directional market exposure over a full market cycle. The valuation techniques used to measure fair value attempt to maximize the use of observable inputs and minimize the use of unobservable inputs. Considerable judgment is required to interpret the factors used to develop estimates of fair value. Valuations of the underlying investment funds are obtained and reviewed. The securities that are valued by the funds are interests in the investment funds and not the underlying holdings of such investment funds. Thus, the inputs used to value the investments in each of the underlying funds may differ from the inputs used to value the underlying holdings of such funds.

In determining the fair value of a security, the fund managers may consider any information that is deemed relevant, which may include one or more of the following factors regarding the portfolio security, if appropriate: type of security or asset; cost at the date of purchase; size of holding; last trade price; most recent valuation; fundamental analytical data relating to the investment in the security; nature and duration of any restriction on the disposition of the security; evaluation of the factors that influence the market in which the security is purchased or sold; financial statements of the issuer; discount from market value of unrestricted securities of the same class at the time of purchase; special reports prepared by analysts; information as to any transactions or offers with respect to the security; existence of merger proposals or tender offers affecting the security; price and extent of public trading in similar securities of the issuer or compatible companies and other relevant matters; changes in interest rates; observations from financial institutions; domestic or foreign government actions or pronouncements; other recent events; existence of shelf registration for restricted securities; existence of any undertaking to register the security; and other acceptable methods of valuing portfolio securities.

Hedge fund investments in the SEI Special Situations Fund are valued quarterly and recorded on a one-month lag. For alternative investment values reported on a lag, current market information is reviewed for any material changes in values at the reporting date. Share repurchases for the SEI Special Situations Fund are considered semi-annually subject to notice of 95 days.

Private Equity Funds

Private equity funds are alternative investments that represent direct or indirect investments in partnerships, venture funds or a diversified pool of private investment vehicles (fund of funds).

Investment commitments are made in private equity funds of funds based on an asset allocation strategy, and capital calls are made over the life of the funds to fund the commitments. As of December 31, 2013, remaining commitments total $8.7 million for both our pension and other benefits. Committed amounts are funded from plan assets when capital calls are made. Investment commitments are not pre-funded in reserve accounts. Refer to the valuation methodologies for equity securities above for further information.

The valuation of investments in private equity funds of funds initially is performed by the underlying fund managers. In determining the fair value, the fund managers may consider any information that is deemed relevant, which may include: type of security or asset; cost at the date of purchase; size of holding; last trade price; most recent valuation; fundamental analytical data relating to the investment in the security; nature and duration of any restriction on the disposition of the security; evaluation of the factors that influence the market in which the security is purchased or sold; financial statements of the issuer; discount from market value of unrestricted securities of the same class at the time of purchase; special reports prepared by analysts; information as to any transactions or offers with respect to the security; existence of merger proposals or tender offers affecting the security; price and extent of public trading in similar securities of the issuer or compatible companies and other relevant matters; changes in interest rates; observations from financial institutions; domestic or foreign government actions or pronouncements; other recent events; existence of shelf registration for restricted securities; existence of any undertaking to register the security; and other acceptable methods of valuing portfolio securities.

The valuations are obtained from the underlying fund managers, and the valuation methodology and process is reviewed for consistent application and adherence to policies. Considerable judgment is required to interpret the factors used to develop estimates of fair value.

Private equity investments are valued quarterly and recorded on a one-quarter lag. For alternative investment values reported on a lag, current market information is reviewed for any material changes in values at the reporting date. Capital distributions for the funds do not occur on a regular frequency. Liquidation of these investments would require sale of the partnership interest.

Structured Credit

Structured credit investments are alternative investments comprised of collateralized debt obligations and other structured credit investments that are priced based on valuations provided by independent, third-party pricing agents, if available. Such values generally reflect the last reported sales price if the security is actively traded. The third-party pricing agents may also value structured credit investments at an evaluated bid price by employing methodologies that utilize actual market transactions, broker-supplied valuations, or other methodologies designed to identify the market value of such securities. Such methodologies generally consider such factors as security prices, yields, maturities, call features, ratings and developments relating to specific securities in arriving at valuations. Securities listed on a securities exchange, market or automated quotation system for which quotations are readily available are valued at the last quoted sale price on the primary exchange or market on which they are traded. Debt obligations with remaining maturities of 60 days or less may be valued at amortized cost, which approximates fair value.

Structured credit investments are valued monthly and recorded on a one-month lag. For alternative investment values reported on a lag, current market information is reviewed for any material changes in values at the reporting date. Redemption requests are considered quarterly subject to notice of 90 days.

Real Estate

The real estate portfolio for the pension plans is an alternative investment comprised of three funds with strategic categories of real estate investments. All real estate holdings are appraised externally at least annually, and appraisals are conducted by reputable, independent appraisal firms that are members of the Appraisal Institute. All external appraisals are performed in accordance with the Uniform Standards of Professional Appraisal Practices. The property valuations and assumptions of each property are reviewed quarterly by the investment advisor and values are adjusted if there has been a significant change in circumstances relating to the property since the last external appraisal. The valuation methodology utilized in determining the fair value is consistent with the best practices prevailing within the real estate appraisal and real estate investment management industries, including the Real Estate Information Standards, and standards promulgated by the National Council of Real Estate Investment Fiduciaries, the National Association of Real Estate Investment Fiduciaries, and the National Association of Real Estate Managers. In addition, the investment advisor may cause additional appraisals to be performed. Two of the funds' fair values are updated monthly, and there is no lag in reported values. Redemption requests for these two funds are considered on a quarterly basis, subject to notice of 45 days.

Effective October 1, 2009, one of the real estate funds began an orderly wind-down over a three to four year period. The decision to wind down the fund primarily was driven by real estate market factors that adversely affected the availability of new investor capital. Third-party appraisals of this fund's assets were eliminated; however, internal valuation updates for all assets and liabilities of the fund are prepared quarterly. The fund's asset values are recorded on a one-quarter lag, and current market information is reviewed for any material changes in values at the reporting date. Distributions from sales of properties will be made on a pro-rata basis. Repurchase requests will not be honored during the wind-down period.

During 2011, a new real estate fund of funds investment was added for the Empire, Tilden, Hibbing and United Taconite VEBA plans as a result of the asset allocation review process. This fund invests in pooled investment vehicles that in turn invest in commercial real estate properties. Valuations are performed quarterly and financial statements are prepared on a semi-annual basis, with annual audited statements. Asset values for this fund are reported with a one-quarter lag and current market information is reviewed for any material changes in values at the reporting date. In most cases, values are based on valuations reported by underlying fund managers or other independent third-party sources, but the fund has discretion to use other valuation methods, subject to compliance with ERISA. Valuations are typically estimates only and subject to upward or downward revision based on each underlying fund's annual audit. Withdrawals are permitted on the last business day of each quarter subject to a 65 -day prior written notice.

The following represents the effect of fair value measurements using significant unobservable inputs (Level 3) on changes in plan assets for the years ended December 31, 2013 and 2012:

(In millions)	Year Ended December 31, 2013				
	Hedge Funds	Private Equity Funds	Structured Credit Fund	Real Estate	Total
Beginning balance—January 1, 2013	$85.6	$29.3	$56.2	$29.4	$200.5
Actual return on plan assets:					
Relating to assets still held at the reporting date	4.5	(2.1)	33.5	5.1	41.0
Relating to assets sold during the period	(1.2)	5.2	(28.7)	(0.4)	(25.1)
Purchases	66.0	14.7	27.5	36.8	145.0
Sales	(97.3)	(18.0)	(27.5)	(30.0)	(172.8)
Ending balance—December 31, 2013	$57.6	$29.1	$61.0	$40.9	$188.6

(In millions)	Year Ended December 31, 2012				
	Hedge Funds	Private Equity Funds	Structured Credit Fund	Real Estate	Total
Beginning balance—January 1, 2012	$100.7	$30.1	$44.9	$16.5	$192.2
Actual return on plan assets:					
Relating to assets still held at the reporting date	4.2	1.4	11.3	4.9	21.8
Relating to assets sold during the period	(0.3)	—	—	(0.5)	(0.8)
Purchases	—	2.2	—	12.2	14.4
Sales	(19.0)	(4.4)	—	(3.7)	(27.1)
Ending balance—December 31, 2012	$ 85.6	$29.3	$56.2	$29.4	$200.5

The expected return on plan assets takes into account historical returns and the weighted average of estimated future long-term returns based on capital market assumptions for each asset category. The expected return is net of investment expenses paid by the plans.

Assets for other benefits include VEBA trusts pursuant to bargaining agreements that are available to fund retired employees' life insurance obligations and medical benefits. The fair values of our other benefit plan assets at December 31, 2013 and 2012 by asset category are as follows:

| (In millions) | December 31, 2013 | | | |
	Quoted Prices in Active Markets for Identical Assets/Liabilities (Level 1)	Significant Other Observable Inputs (Level 2)	Significant Unobservable Inputs (Level 3)	Total
Asset Category				
Equity securities:				
U.S. large-cap	$ 15.7	$ —	$ —	$ 15.7
U.S. small/mid-cap	2.7	—	—	2.7
International	7.8	—	—	7.8
Fixed income	134.4	33.7	—	168.1
Hedge funds	—	—	24.6	24.6
Private equity	—	—	6.0	6.0
Structured credit	—	—	13.5	13.5
Real estate	—	—	13.2	13.2
Cash	0.2	—	—	0.2
Total	$160.8	$33.7	$57.3	$251.8

| (In millions) | December 31, 2012 | | | |
	Quoted Prices in Active Markets for Identical Assets/Liabilities (Level 1)	Significant Other Observable Inputs (Level 2)	Significant Unobservable Inputs (Level 3)	Total
Asset Category				
Equity securities:				
U.S. large-cap	$ 58.2	$ —	$ —	$ 58.2
U.S. small/mid-cap	10.3	—	—	10.3
International	32.3	—	—	32.3
Fixed income	78.1	—	—	78.1
Hedge funds	—	—	23.2	23.2
Private equity	—	—	6.2	6.2
Structured Credit	—	—	12.5	12.5
Real estate	—	—	15.9	15.9
Cash	0.3	—	—	0.3
Total	$179.2	$ —	$57.8	$237.0

Refer to the pension asset discussion above for further information regarding the inputs and valuation methodologies used to measure the fair value of each respective category of plan assets.

The following represents the effect of fair value measurements using significant unobservable inputs (Level 3) on changes in plan assets for the year ended December 31, 2013 and 2012 :

| (In millions) | Year Ended December 31, 2013 | | | | |
	Hedge Funds	Private Equity Funds	Structured Credit Fund	Real Estate	Total
Beginning balance—January 1	$23.2	$6.2	$12.5	$15.9	$57.8
Actual return on plan assets:					
Relating to assets still held at the reporting date	2.1	0.2	2.4	2.8	7.5
Relating to assets sold during the period	(0.7)	0.4	(1.4)	(0.7)	(2.4)
Purchases	22.5	0.3	11.0	14.2	48.0
Sales	(22.5)	(1.1)	(11.0)	(19.0)	(53.6)
Ending balance—December 31	$24.6	$6.0	$13.5	$13.2	$57.3

| (In millions) | Year Ended December 31, 2012 | | | | |
	Hedge Funds	Private Equity Funds	Structured Credit Fund	Real Estate	Total
Beginning balance—January 1	$28.3	$6.8	$ —	$10.2	$45.3
Actual return on plan assets:					
Relating to assets still held at the reporting date	0.9	0.3	1.5	1.3	4.0
Purchases	—	0.2	11.0	4.4	15.6
Sales	(6.0)	(1.1)	—	—	(7.1)
Ending balance—December 31	$23.2	$6.2	$12.5	$15.9	$57.8

The expected return on plan assets takes into account historical returns and the weighted average of estimated future long-term returns based on capital market assumptions for each asset category. The expected return is net of investment expenses paid by the plans.

Contributions

Annual contributions to the pension plans are made within income tax deductibility restrictions in accordance with statutory regulations. In the event of plan termination, the plan sponsors could be required to fund additional shutdown and early retirement obligations that are not included in the pension obligations. The Company currently has no intention to shutdown, terminate or withdraw from any of its employee benefit plans.

(In millions)	Pension Benefits	Other Benefits		Total
		VEBA	Direct Payments	
Company Contributions				
2012	$67.7	$17.4	$21.6	$39.0
2013	53.7	14.6	10.9	25.5
2014 (Expected)*	68.2	—	7.9	7.9

* Pursuant to the bargaining agreement, benefits can be paid from VEBA trusts that are at least 70 percent funded (all VEBA trusts are 70 percent funded at December 31, 2013). Funding obligations are suspended when Hibbing's, UTAC's, Tilden's and Empire's share of the value of their respective trust assets reaches 90 percent of their obligation.

VEBA plans are not subject to minimum regulatory funding requirements. Amounts contributed are pursuant to bargaining agreements.

Contributions by participants to the other benefit plans were $5.6 million for the year ended December 31, 2013 and $4.6 million for the year ended December 31, 2012.

Estimated Cost for 2014

For 2014, we estimate net periodic benefit cost as follows:

(In millions)	
Defined benefit pension plans	$28.0
Other postretirement benefits	8.3
Total	$36.3

Estimated Future Benefit Payments

(In millions)	Pension Benefits	Other Benefits		
		Gross Company Benefits	Less Medicare Subsidy	Net Company Payments
2014	$81.7	$23.7	$1.0	$22.7
2015	77.9	24.9	1.1	23.8
2016	78.6	24.8	1.2	23.6
2017	79.6	25.0	1.4	23.6
2018	81.6	25.0	1.5	23.5
2019–2023	414.6	119.6	9.4	110.2

Other Potential Benefit Obligations

While the foregoing reflects our obligation, our total exposure in the event of non-performance is potentially greater. Following is a summary comparison of the total obligation:

(In millions)	December 31, 2013	
	Defined Benefit Pensions	Other Benefits
Fair value of plan assets	$ 915.3	$ 251.8
Benefit obligation	(1,118.0)	(356.2)
Underfunded status of plan	$ (202.7)	$(104.4)
Additional shutdown and early retirement benefits	$ (15.4)	$ (53.6)

Employee Compensatory Plans

RECOGNITION AND MEASUREMENT

3.54 FASB ASC 718, *Compensation—Stock Compensation*, establishes accounting and reporting standards for share-based payment transactions with employees, including awards classified as equity, awards classified as liabilities, employee stock ownership plans, and employee stock purchase plans. FASB ASC 718 requires that share-based payment transactions be accounted for using a fair-value-based method. Thus, entities are required to recognize the cost of employee services received in exchange for award of equity instruments based on the grant-date fair value of those awards or the fair value of the liabilities incurred. FASB ASC 718 provides clarification and expanded guidance in several areas, including measuring fair value, classifying an award as equity or a liability, and attributing compensation cost to reporting periods.

PRESENTATION AND DISCLOSURE EXCERPTS

STOCK OPTION PLANS

3.55 AUTODESK, INC. (JAN)
NOTES TO CONSOLIDATED FINANCIAL STATEMENTS

(Tables in millions of dollars, except per share data, unless otherwise indicated)

3. Employee and Director Stock Plans (in part)

Stock Plans

As of January 31, 2013, Autodesk maintained two active stock option plans for the purpose of granting equity awards to employees and to non-employee members of Autodesk's Board of Directors: the 2012 Employee Stock Plan ("2012 Employee Plan"), which is available only to employees, and the Autodesk 2012 Outside Directors' Stock Plan ("2012 Directors' Plan"), which is available only to non-employee directors. Additionally, there are eight expired or terminated plans with options outstanding. The exercise price of all stock options granted under these plans was equal to the fair market value of the stock on the grant date.

The 2012 Employee Plan was approved by Autodesk's stockholders and became effective on January 6, 2012. The 2012 Employee Plan replaced the 2008 Employee Stock Plan, as amended ("2008 Plan") and no further equity awards may be granted under the 2008 Plan. The 2012 Employee Plan reserves up to 21.2 million shares which includes 15.2 million shares reserved upon the effectiveness of the 2012 Employee Plan as well as up to 6.0 million shares forfeited under certain prior employee stock plans during the life of the 2012 Employee Plan. The 2012 Employee Plan permits the grant of stock options, restricted stock units and restricted stock awards. Each restricted stock unit or restricted stock award granted will be counted against the shares authorized for issuance under the 2012 Employee Plan as 1.79 shares. If a granted option, restricted stock unit or restricted stock award expires or becomes unexercisable for any reason, the unpurchased or forfeited shares that were granted may be returned to the 2012 Employee Plan and may become available for future grant under the 2012 Employee Plan. As of January 31, 2013, 7.0 million shares subject to options or restricted stock awards have been granted under the 2012 Employee Plan. Options and restricted stock that were granted under the 2012 plan vest over periods ranging from immediately upon grant to over a three year period and options expire 10 years from the date of grant. The 2012 Employee Plan will expire on June 30, 2022. At January 31, 2013, 11.6 million shares were available for future issuance under the 2012 Employee Plan.

The 2012 Director's Plan was approved by Autodesk's stockholders and became effective on January 6, 2012. The 2012 Directors' Plan replaced the 2010 Outside Directors' Stock Plan, as amended ("2010 Plan"). The 2012 Directors' Plan permits the grant of stock options, restricted stock units and restricted stock awards to non-employee members of Autodesk's Board of Directors. Each restricted stock unit or restricted stock award granted will be counted against the shares authorized for issuance under the 2012 Directors' Plan as 2.11 shares. As of January 31, 2013, 0.2 million shares subject to restricted stock unit awards have been granted under the 2012 Directors' Plan. Restricted stock units that were granted under the 2012 Outside Directors' Plan vest over one year from the date of grant. The 2012 Directors' Plan reserved 2.6 million shares of Autodesk common stock. The 2012 Directors' Plan will expire on June 30, 2022. At January 31, 2013, 2.4 million shares were available for future issuance under the 2012 Director's Plan.

The following sections summarize activity under Autodesk's stock plans.

Stock Options:

A summary of stock option activity for the fiscal year ended January 31, 2013 is as follows:

	Number of Shares (in millions)	Weighted Average Exercise Price Per Share	Weighted Average Remaining Contractual Term (in years)	Aggregate Intrinsic Value [2] (in millions)
Options outstanding at January 31, 2012	28.4	$31.39		
Granted	0.1	36.59		
Exercised	(6.6)	24.67		
Canceled	(2.9)	38.38		
Options outstanding at January 31, 2013	19.0	$32.69	3.8	153.4
Options vested and exercisable at January 31, 2013	13.2	$31.80	2.7	120.8
Options vested and exercisable as of January 31, 2013 and expected to vest thereafter[1]	18.8	$32.63	3.7	153.0
Options available for grant at January 31, 2013	14.0			

[1] Options expected to vest reflect an estimated forfeiture rate.

[2] Represents the total pre-tax intrinsic value, based on Autodesk's closing stock price of $38.88 per share as of January 31, 2013, which would have been received by the option holders had all option holders exercised their options as of that date.

As of January 31, 2013, total compensation cost of $ 34.8 million related to non-vested options is expected to be recognized over a weighted average period of 1.0 year. The following table summarizes information about the pre-tax intrinsic value of options exercised, and the weighted average grant date fair value per share of options granted, during the fiscal years ended January 31, 2013, 2012 and 2011 :

	Fiscal Year Ended January 31,		
	2013	2012	2011
Intrinsic value of options exercised[1]	$ 90.9	$ 85.7	$61.9
Weighted average grant date fair value per share of stock options granted[2]	$13.39	$14.04	$9.30

[1] The intrinsic value of options exercised is calculated as the difference between the exercise price of the option and the market value of the stock on the date of exercise.

[2] The weighted average grant date fair value per share of stock options granted is calculated, as of the stock option grant date, using the BSM option pricing model.

The following table summarizes information about options vested and exercisable, and outstanding at January 31, 2013 :

	Options Vested and Exercisable				Options Outstanding			
	Number of Shares (In millions)	Weighted Average Contractual Life (In years)	Weighted Average Exercise Price Per Share	Aggregate Intrinsic Value[1] (In millions)	Number of Shares (In millions)	Weighted Average Contractual Life (In years)	Weighted Average Exercise Price Per Share	Aggregate Intrinsic Value[1] (In millions)
Range of per-share exercise prices:								
$2.28–$20.69	3.3		$14.59		3.9		$14.85	
$21.89–$29.50	2.4		28.54		4.5		28.92	
$29.56–$41.62	3.9		35.98		6.5		37.93	
$42.39–$48.72	3.4		45.36		3.9		45.16	
$49.80–$49.80	0.2		49.80		0.2		49.80	
	13.2	2.7	$31.80	$120.8	19.0	3.8	$32.69	$153.4

[1] Represents the total intrinsic value, based on Autodesk's closing stock price of $38.88 per share as of January 31, 2013, which would have been received by the option holders had all option holders exercised their options as of that date.

These options will expire if not exercised at specific dates ranging through September 2022.

Restricted Stock:

A summary of restricted stock award and restricted stock unit activity for the fiscal year ended January 31, 2013 is as follows:

	Unreleased Restricted Stock (In thousands)	Weighted Average Grant Date Fair Value
Unreleased restricted stock at January 31, 2012	2,184.1	$36.65
Granted	3,975.5	33.32
Released	(889.5)	37.82
Canceled	(249.3)	34.97
Unreleased restricted stock at January 31, 2013	5,020.8	$33.89

During the fiscal year ended January 31, 2013, Autodesk granted approximately 3.4 million restricted stock units. The restricted stock units vest over periods ranging from immediately upon grant to a pre-determined date that is typically within three years from the date of grant. Restricted stock units are not considered outstanding stock at the time of grant, as the holders of these units are not entitled to any of the rights of a stockholder, including voting rights. The fair value of the restricted stock units is expensed ratably over the vesting period. Autodesk recorded stock-based compensation expense related to restricted stock units of $ 70.5 million, $ 29.1 million and $ 8.9 million during fiscal years ended January 31, 2013, 2012 and 2011, respectively. Included in the $ 70.5 million, Autodesk incurred $ 16.6 million relating to the acceleration of vesting of equity awards held in Socialcam for Socialcam employees immediately prior to the acquisition. As of January 31, 2013, total compensation cost not yet recognized of $ 93.0 million related to non-vested awards, is expected to be recognized over a weighted average period of 1.8 years. At January 31, 2013, the number of units granted but unreleased was 4.5 million.

During the fiscal year ended January 31, 2013, Autodesk granted 0.5 million performance restricted stock units. The majority of the performance restricted stock units that were granted had performance criteria based solely upon the attainment of predetermined goals relative to company revenue growth and non-GAAP operating margin performance for fiscal 2013 as calculated under a pre-established performance matrix. If the performance criteria is achieved, the performance restricted stock units would vest ratably on an annual cliff basis from March 2013 through March 2015. In addition, during fiscal 2013, Autodesk granted an additional performance-based restricted stock unit award to our CEO, the value of which would be realized only if he satisfies certain specified strategic corporate, and talent management performance objectives as established by the Compensation Committee of Autodesk's Board of Directors.

Performance stock units are not considered outstanding stock at the time of grant, as the holders of these units are not entitled to any of the rights of a stockholder, including voting rights. The fair value of the performance restricted stock units is expensed using the accelerated attribution method over the vesting period. Autodesk recorded stock-based compensation expense related to performance restricted stock units of $ 8.1 million during fiscal year ended January 31, 2013. Autodesk recorded no stock-based compensation related to performance restricted stock units during the fiscal years ended January 31, 2012 and 2011. As of January 31, 2013, total compensation cost not yet recognized of $ 5.8 million related to non-vested performance restricted stock units, is expected to be recognized over a weighted average period of 1.1 years. At January 31, 2013, the number of performance restricted stock units granted but unreleased was 0.5 million.

STOCK AWARD PLANS

3.56 THE COCA-COLA COMPANY (DEC)
NOTES TO CONSOLIDATED FINANCIAL STATEMENTS

Note 12: Stock Compensation Plans (in part)

Restricted Stock Award Plans

Under The Coca-Cola Company 1989 Restricted Stock Award Plan and The Coca-Cola Company 1983 Restricted Stock Award Plan (the "Restricted Stock Award Plans"), 80 million and 48 million shares of restricted common stock, respectively, were originally available to be granted to certain officers and key employees of our Company. As of December 31, 2013, 25 million shares remain available for grant under the Restricted Stock Award Plans. The Company issues restricted stock to employees as a result of performance share unit awards, time-based awards and performance-based awards.

For awards prior to January 1, 2008, under the 1983 Restricted Stock Award Plan, participants are reimbursed by our Company for income taxes imposed on the award, but not for taxes generated by the reimbursement payment. The 1983 Restricted Stock Award Plan has been amended to eliminate this tax reimbursement for awards after January 1, 2008. The shares are subject to certain transfer restrictions and may be forfeited if a participant leaves our Company for reasons other than retirement, disability or death, absent a change in control of our Company.

Performance Share Unit Awards

In 2003, the Company established a program to grant performance share units under The Coca-Cola Company 1989 Restricted Stock Award Plan to executives. In 2008, the Company expanded the program to award a mix of stock options and performance share units to eligible employees in addition to executives. The number of shares earned is determined at the end of each performance period, generally three years, based on the actual performance criteria predetermined by the Board of Directors at the time of grant. If the performance criteria are met, the award results in a grant of restricted stock or restricted stock units, which are then generally subject to a holding period in order for the restricted stock to be released. For performance share units granted before 2008, this holding period is generally two years. For performance share units granted in 2008 and after, this holding period is generally one year. Restrictions on such stock generally lapse at the end of the holding period. Performance share units generally do not pay dividends or allow voting rights during the performance period. For awards granted prior to 2011, participants generally receive dividends or dividend equivalents once the performance criteria have been certified and the restricted stock or restricted stock units have been issued. For awards granted in 2011 and later, participants generally receive dividends or dividend equivalents once the shares have been released. Accordingly, the fair value of the performance share units is the quoted market value of the Company stock on the grant date less the present value of the expected dividends not received during the relevant period. In the period it becomes probable that the minimum performance criteria specified in the plan will be achieved, we recognize expense for the proportionate share of the total fair value of the performance share units related to the vesting period that has already lapsed. The remaining cost of the grant is expensed on a straight-line basis over the balance of the vesting period. In the event the Company determines it is no longer probable that we will achieve the minimum performance criteria specified in the plan, we reverse all of the previously recognized compensation expense in the period such a determination is made.

Performance share units under The Coca-Cola Company 1989 Restricted Stock Award Plan require achievement of certain financial measures, primarily compound annual growth in earnings per share or economic profit. These financial measures are adjusted for certain items approved and certified by the Audit Committee of the Board of Directors. The purpose of these adjustments is to ensure a consistent year to year comparison of the specific performance criteria. Economic profit is our net operating profit after tax less the cost of the capital used in our business. In the event the financial results equal the predefined target, the Company will grant the number of restricted shares equal to the target award in the underlying performance share unit agreements. In the event the financial results exceed the predefined target, additional shares up to the maximum award may be granted. In the event the financial results fall below the predefined target, a reduced number of shares may be granted. If the financial results fall below the threshold award performance level, no shares will be granted. Performance share units are generally settled in stock, except for certain circumstances such as death or disability, where former employees or their beneficiaries are provided a cash equivalent payment. As of December 31, 2013, performance share units of 5,365,000, 6,487,000 and 6,122,000 were outstanding for the 2011–2013, 2012–2014 and 2013–2015 performance periods, respectively, based on the target award amounts in the performance share unit agreements.

The following table summarizes information about performance share units based on the target award amounts in the performance share unit agreements:

	Share Units (In thousands)	Weighted-Average Grant Date Fair Value
Outstanding on January 1, 2013	17,584	$28.01
Granted	6,425	32.67
Conversions of restricted stock units[1]	(5,220)	25.17
Paid in cash equivalent	(55)	32.25
Canceled/forfeited	(760)	30.33
Outstanding on December 31, 2013[2]	17,974	$30.41

[1] Represents the target amount of performance share units converted to restricted stock units based on the financial results for the 2010–2012 performance period. The vesting of restricted stock units is subject to the terms of the performance share unit agreements.

[2] The outstanding performance share units as of December 31, 2013, at the threshold award and maximum award levels were 9.0 million and 27.0 million, respectively.

The weighted-average grant date fair value of performance share units granted was $32.67 in 2013, $29.95 in 2012 and $25.58 in 2011. The Company converted performance share units of 54,999 in 2013, 16,267 in 2012 and 19,462 in 2011 to cash equivalent payments of $ 1.8 million, $ 0.6 million and $ 0.7 million, respectively, to former employees who were ineligible for restricted stock grants due to certain events such as death or disability.

The following table summarizes information about the conversions of performance share units to restricted stock and restricted stock units:

	Share Units (In thousands)	Weighted-Average Grant Date Fair Value[1]
Nonvested on January 1, 2013[2]	98	$26.54
Conversions of restricted stock units[3]	7,830	25.17
Vested and released	(406)	25.52
Canceled/forfeited	(508)	25.17
Nonvested on December 31, 2013[2]	7,014	$25.17

[1] The weighted-average grant date fair value is based on the fair values of the performance share units granted.

[2] The nonvested shares as of January 1, 2013, and December 31, 2013, are presented at the performance share units' certified award level.

[3] The converted shares are presented at the performance share units' certified award level of 150 percent.

The total intrinsic value of restricted shares that were vested and released was $ 16 million, $ 148 million and $ 72 million in 2013, 2012 and 2011, respectively. The total restricted share units vested and released in 2013 were 405,963 at the certified award level. In 2012 and 2011, the total restricted share units vested and released were 4,301,732 and 2,084,912, respectively.

Replacement performance share unit awards issued by the Company in connection with our acquisition of CCE's former North America business are not included in the tables or discussions above and were originally granted under the Coca-Cola Enterprises Inc. 2007 Incentive Award Plan. These awards were converted into equivalent share units of the Company's common stock on the acquisition date and entitle the participant to dividend equivalents (which vest, in some cases, only if the restricted share units vest), but not the right to vote. Accordingly, the fair value of these units was the quoted value of the Company's stock at the grant date.

On the acquisition date, the Company issued 3.3 million replacement performance share unit awards at target with a weighted-average grant date price of $ 29.56 per share that were either projected to pay out at, or previously certified at a payout rate of 200 percent. In accordance with accounting principles generally accepted in the United States, the portion of the fair value of the replacement awards related to services provided prior to the acquisition was included in the total purchase price. The portion of the fair value associated with future service was recognized as expense in the fourth quarter of 2010. As of January 1, 2011, there were 3.8 million shares subject to release under these plans based on the 200 percent payout. During 2011, the Company released 3.1 million shares at the 200 percent payout with an intrinsic value of $ 98 million. During 2012, the Company released 0.6 million shares at the 200 percent payout with an intrinsic value of $ 22 million. During 2013, the Company released 0.1 million shares at the 200 percent payout with an intrinsic value of $5 million. As of December 31, 2013, the Company had no remaining outstanding replacement performance share units.

Time-Based and Performance-Based Restricted Stock and Restricted Stock Unit Awards

The Coca-Cola Company 1989 Restricted Stock Award Plan allows for the grant of time-based and performance-based restricted stock and restricted stock units. The performance-based restricted awards are released only upon the achievement of specific measurable performance criteria. These awards pay dividends during the performance period. The majority of awards have specific performance targets for achievement. If the performance targets are not met, the awards will be canceled. In the period it becomes probable that the performance criteria will be achieved, we recognize expense for the proportionate share of the total fair value of the grant related to the vesting period that has already lapsed. The remaining cost of the grant is expensed on a straight-line basis over the balance of the vesting period.

For time-based and performance-based restricted stock awards, participants are entitled to vote and receive dividends on the restricted shares. The Company also awards time-based and performance-based restricted stock units for which participants may receive payments of dividend equivalents but are not entitled to vote. As of December 31, 2013, the Company had outstanding nonvested time-based and performance-based restricted stock awards, including restricted stock units, of 700,000 and 81,000, respectively. Time-based and performance-based restricted stock awards were not significant to our consolidated financial statements.

In 2010, the Company issued time-based restricted stock replacement awards, including restricted stock units, in connection with our acquisition of CCE's former North America business. These awards were converted into equivalent shares of the Company's common stock. These restricted share awards entitle the participant to dividend equivalents (which vest, in some cases, only if the restricted share unit vests), but not the right to vote. As of December 31, 2013, the Company had 59,000 outstanding nonvested time-based restricted stock replacement awards, including restricted stock units. These time-based restricted awards were not significant to our consolidated financial statements.

SAVINGS AND INVESTMENT PLANS

3.57 MONSANTO COMPANY (AUG)
NOTES TO THE CONSOLIDATED FINANCIAL STATEMENTS

Note 20. Employee Savings Plans

Monsanto-Sponsored Plans

The U.S. tax-qualified Monsanto Savings and Investment Plan (Monsanto SIP) was established in June 2001 as a successor to a portion of the Pharmacia Corporation Savings and Investment Plan. The Monsanto SIP is a defined contribution profit-sharing plan with an individual account for each participant. Employees who are 18 years of age or older are generally eligible to participate in the plan. The Monsanto SIP provides for voluntary contributions, generally ranging from 1 percent to 25 percent of an employee's eligible pay. Prior to July 8, 2012, Monsanto satisfied its matching contribution obligations under the Monsanto SIP with shares released from the leveraged employee stock ownership plan (Monsanto ESOP). Effective July 8, 2012, Monsanto satisfies its matching contribution obligations, and its new non-elective contribution for employees hired on or after July 8, 2012, with cash. The Monsanto ESOP was leveraged by debt due to Monsanto. The debt, which was repaid in full in December 2012 and has a zero balance as of Aug. 31, 2013, was repaid primarily through company contributions and dividends paid on Monsanto common stock held in the ESOP. The Monsanto ESOP debt was restructured in December 2004 to level out the future allocation of stock in an impartial manner intended to ensure equitable treatment for and generally to be in the best interests of current and future plan participants consistent with the level of benefits that Monsanto intended for the plan to provide to participants. To that end, the terms of the restructuring were determined pursuant to an arm's length negotiation between Monsanto and an independent trust company as fiduciary for the plan. In this role, the independent fiduciary determined that the restructuring, including certain financial commitments and enhancements that were or will be made in the future by Monsanto to benefit participants and beneficiaries of the plan, including the increased diversification rights that were provided to certain participants, was completed in accordance with the best interests of plan participants. As a result of these enhancements related to the 2004 restructuring, a liability of $55 million was recorded as of Aug. 31, 2012, to reflect the 2004 ESOP enhancements. The entire balance of the liability was considered short term and is included in accrued compensation and benefits on the Statements of Consolidated Financial Position at Aug. 31, 2012. The liability related to the 2004 ESOP refinancing was required to be paid no later than Dec. 31, 2017. Monsanto matching contributions made in cash have been applied towards satisfaction of the 2004 ESOP enhancements, resulting in no liability at Aug. 31, 2013.

The Monsanto ESOP debt was again restructured in November 2008. The terms of the restructuring were determined pursuant to an arm's length negotiation between Monsanto and an independent trust company as fiduciary for the plan. In this role, the independent fiduciary determined that the restructuring, including certain financial commitments and enhancements that were or will be made in the future by Monsanto to benefit participants and beneficiaries of the plan, was in the best interests of participants in the plan's ESOP component. As a result of these enhancements related to the 2008 ESOP restructuring, Monsanto committed to funding an additional $8 million to the plan, above the number of shares currently scheduled for release under the restructured debt schedule. Pursuant to the agreement, a $4 million Special Allocation was allocated proportionately to eligible participants in May 2009 and funded using plan forfeitures and dividends on Monsanto common stock held in the ESOP suspense account. A $5.7 million Special Allocation was allocated proportionately to eligible participants in August 2013 and funded with cash. This Monsanto cash contribution to the SIP was applied towards satisfying the 2008 ESOP enhancements, resulting in no liability at Aug. 31, 2013. As of Aug. 31, 2012, a liability of $5 million was recorded to reflect the 2008 ESOP enhancements, of which $1 million was considered short term and is included in accrued compensation and benefits, while the long term balance is included in other liabilities on the Statements of Consolidated Financial Position. The liability related to the 2008 ESOP refinancing was required to be paid no later than December 31 of the fifth year following the loan repayment date and in no case later than Dec. 31, 2032.

As of Aug. 31, 2013, the Monsanto ESOP held 5.1 million shares of Monsanto common stock (allocated). The unallocated shares of Monsanto common stock held by the ESOP were allocated each year to employee savings accounts as matching contributions in accordance with the terms of the Monsanto SIP. During fiscal year 2013, the remaining less than 0.1 million Monsanto shares were allocated specifically to Monsanto participants, leaving zero shares of Monsanto common stock remaining in the Monsanto ESOP and unallocated as of Aug. 31, 2013.

Contributions to the plan are required annually in amounts sufficient to fund ESOP debt repayment. Dividends paid on the shares held by the Monsanto ESOP were less than $0.1 million in 2013, $8 million in 2012, and $8 million in 2011. These dividends were greater than the cost of the shares allocated to the participants resulting in total ESOP expense of less than $1 million in 2013, 2012 and 2011. In 2013, the Monsanto SIP recognized expense of $18.4 million for matching contributions made in cash over and above the amount required to reduce the ESOP enhancements liabilities to zero, and $0.2 million for new non-elective contributions made in cash for employees hired on or after July 8, 2012, was recognized in 2013.

EMPLOYEE STOCK PURCHASE PLANS (ESPP)

3.58 GUESS?, INC. (JAN)
NOTES TO CONSOLIDATED FINANCIAL STATEMENTS

(17) Share-Based Compensation (in part)

The Company has four share-based compensation plans. The Guess?, Inc. 2004 Equity Incentive Plan (the "Plan") provides that the Board of Directors may grant stock options and other equity awards to officers, key employees and certain consultants and advisors to the Company or any of its subsidiaries. The Plan authorizes the issuance of up to 20,000,000 shares of common stock. At February 2, 2013 and January 28, 2012, there were 12,835,693 and 13,429,837 shares available for grant under the Plan, respectively. Stock options granted under the Plan have ten -year terms and typically vest and become fully exercisable in increments of one-fourth of the shares granted on each anniversary from the date of grant. The three most recent annual grants have initial vesting periods of nine months, nine months and ten months, respectively, followed by three annual vesting periods. The Guess?, Inc. Employee Stock Purchase Plan ("ESPP") allows for qualified employees to participate in the purchase of designated shares of the Company's common stock at a price equal to 85% of the lower of the closing price at the beginning or end of each quarterly stock purchase period. The Guess?, Inc. 2006 Non-Employee Directors' Stock Grant and Stock Option Plan (the "Director Plan") provides for the grant of equity awards to non-employee directors. The Director Plan authorizes the issuance of up to 2,000,000 shares of common stock which consists of 1,000,000 shares that were initially approved for issuance on July 30, 1996 plus an additional 1,000,000 shares that were approved for issuance effective May 9, 2006. At February 2, 2013 and January 28, 2012, there were 899,931 and 930,338 shares available for grant under this plan, respectively. In addition, the Guess?, Inc. 1996 Equity Incentive Plan, under which equity grants have not been permitted since the approval of the Plan in 2004, continues to govern outstanding awards previously made thereunder.

Compensation expense for nonvested stock options and stock awards is recognized on a straight-line basis over the vesting period. The Company estimates forfeitures in calculating the expense relating to share-based compensation as opposed to recognizing forfeitures as an expense reduction as they occur.

The following table summarizes the share-based compensation expense recognized under all of the Company's stock plans during fiscal 2013, fiscal 2012 and fiscal 2011 (in thousands):

	Year Ended Feb 2, 2013	Year Ended Jan 28, 2012	Year Ended Jan 29, 2011
Stock options	$ 4,633	$ 7,123	$ 7,755
Nonvested stock awards/units	11,337	20,584	21,199
ESPP	315	393	358
Total share-based compensation expense	$16,285	$28,100	$29,312

ESPP

In January 2002, the Company established an ESPP, the terms of which allow for qualified employees (as defined) to participate in the purchase of designated shares of the Company's common stock at a price equal to 85% of the lower of the closing price at the beginning or end of each quarterly stock purchase period. Prior to March 4, 2009, the ESPP was a straight purchase plan with no holding period requirement. Effective March 4, 2009, the ESPP was amended to require participants to hold any shares purchased under the ESPP after April 1, 2009 for a minimum period of six months after purchase. In addition, all Company employees are subject to the terms of the Company's securities trading policy which generally prohibits the purchase or sale of any Company securities during the two weeks before the end of each fiscal quarter through two days after the public announcement by the Company of its earnings for that period. On January 23, 2002, the Company filed with the SEC a Registration Statement on Form S-8 registering 4,000,000 shares of common stock for the ESPP. Effective March 12, 2012, the ESPP was amended and restated to extend the term for an additional ten years.

During fiscal 2013, fiscal 2012 and fiscal 2011, 50,013 shares, 47,456 shares and 42,695 shares of the Company's common stock were issued pursuant to the ESPP at an average price of $23.72, $29.00 and $30.69 per share, respectively.

The fair value of stock compensation expense associated with the Company's ESPP was estimated on the date of grant using the Black-Scholes option-pricing valuation model and the following weighted-average assumptions for grants during fiscal 2013, fiscal 2012 and fiscal 2011.

Valuation Assumptions	Year Ended Feb 2, 2013	Year Ended Jan 28, 2012	Year Ended Jan 29, 2011
Risk-free interest rate	0.1 %	0.1 %	0.1%
Expected stock price volatility	46.4 %	49.0 %	43.4%
Expected dividend yield	2.8 %	2.2 %	1.6%
Expected life of ESPP options (in months)	3	3	3

The weighted-average grant-date fair value of ESPP options granted during fiscal 2013, fiscal 2012 and fiscal 2011 was $6.84, $9.35 and $9.39, respectively.

DEFERRED COMPENSATION PLANS

3.59 SYNNEX CORPORATION (NOV)

NOTES TO CONSOLIDATED FINANCIAL STATEMENTS

(currency and share amounts in thousands, except per share amounts)

Note 2—Summary of Significant Accounting Policies (in part)

Investments (in part)

The Company classifies its investments in marketable securities as trading and available-for-sale. Marketable securities related to its deferred compensation plan are classified as trading and are recorded at fair value, based on quoted market prices, and unrealized gains and losses are included in "Other income (expense), net" in the Company's financial statements. All other securities are classified as available-for-sale and are recorded at fair market value, based on quoted market prices, and unrealized gains and losses are included in "Accumulated other comprehensive income," a component of stockholders' equity. Realized gains and losses on available-for-sale securities, which are calculated based on the specific identification method, and declines in value judged to be other-than-temporary, if any, are recorded in "Other income (expense), net" as incurred.

Note 7—Investments (in part)

The carrying amount of the Company's investments is shown in the table below:

	As of November 30, 2013			As of November 30, 2012		
	Cost Basis	Unrealized (Losses)/Gains	Carrying Value	Cost Basis	Unrealized (Losses)/Gains	Carrying Value
Short-term investments:						
Trading	$ 3,857	$871	$ 4,728	$ 5,636	$ 73	$ 5,709
Available-for-sale securities	—	—	—	—	44	44
Held-to-maturity investments	8,753	—	8,753	8,297	—	8,297
Cost method securities	1,653	—	1,653	1,883	—	1,883
	$14,263	$871	$15,134	$15,816	$117	$15,933
Long-term investments in other assets:						
Available-for-sale securities	$ 909	$366	$ 1,275	$ 1,095	$ 22	$ 1,117
Cost-method investments	4,981	—	4,981	3,313	—	3,313

Short-term trading securities generally consist of equity securities relating to the Company's deferred compensation plan. Short-term and long-term available-for-sale securities primarily consist of investments in other companies' equity securities. Held-to-maturity investments primarily consist of term deposits with maturities from the date of purchase greater than three months and less than one year. These term deposits are held until the maturity date and are not traded. Cost-method securities primarily consist of investments in a hedge fund and a private equity fund under the Company's deferred compensation plan.

Trading securities and available-for-sale securities are recorded at fair value in each reporting period and therefore the carrying value of these securities equals their fair value. For cost-method securities and investments, the Company records an impairment charge when the decline in fair value is determined to be other-than-temporary. The fair value of the cost-method investments is based on (i) the published fund values, (ii) a valuation model developed internally based on the published value of the securities held by the fund or (iii) an internal valuation of the investee.

Note 17—Deferred Compensation Plan

The Company has a deferred compensation plan for certain directors and officers. The plan is designed to permit eligible officers and directors to accumulate additional income through a non-qualified deferred compensation plan that enables the officer or director to make elective deferrals of compensation to which he or she will become entitled in the future.

An account is maintained for each participant for the purpose of recording the current value of his or her elective contributions, including earnings credited thereto. The participant may designate one or more investments as the measure of investment return on the participant's account. On January 4, 2012, the Compensation Committee approved an amendment to the deferred compensation plan to prospectively limit designated investments as the measure of investment return to actively traded securities reported on recognized exchanges, bank deposits, and other investments with readily verifiable valuations. The participant's account is adjusted monthly to reflect earnings and losses on the participant's designated investments. The Company pays interest on the uninvested portion of deferred compensation.

The amount credited to the participant's account will be distributed as soon as practicable after the earlier of the participant's termination of employment or attainment of age sixty-five. The distribution of benefits to the participant will be made in accordance with the election made by the participant in a lump sum or in equal monthly or annual installments over a period not to exceed fifteen years. The distribution of account balances subject to Section 409A of the Tax Code upon termination of employment of an officer is subject to a six-month delay. In the event the participant requests an early distribution other than a hardship distribution, a 10% withdrawal penalty will be levied. Such distribution will be in the form of a lump sum cash payment. Such early distribution elections are available only with respect to vested account balances as of December 31, 2004.

As of November 30, 2013 and 2012, the deferred compensation liability balances were $13,013 and $13,870, respectively. Of the above deferred balances, $6,381 and $7,593, respectively, have been invested in equity securities, hedge funds and private equity funds. The Company has recorded a gain of $1,868, a gain of $2,585 and a loss of $1,101 for the fiscal years ended November 30, 2013, 2012 and 2011, respectively.

INCENTIVE COMPENSATION PLANS

3.60 INTERNATIONAL PAPER COMPANY (DEC)
NOTES TO CONSOLIDATED FINANCIAL STATEMENTS

Note 18—Incentive Plans

International Paper currently has an Incentive Compensation Plan (ICP) which, upon the approval by the Company's shareholders in May 2009, replaced the Company's Long-Term Incentive Compensation Plan (LTICP). The ICP authorizes grants of restricted stock, restricted or deferred stock units, performance awards payable in cash or stock upon the attainment of specified performance goals, dividend equivalents, stock options, stock appreciation rights, other stock-based awards, and cash-based awards at the discretion of the Management Development and Compensation Committee of the Board of Directors (the Committee) that administers the ICP. Additionally, restricted stock, which may be deferred into RSU's, may be awarded under a Restricted Stock and Deferred Compensation Plan for Non-Employee Directors.

Stock Option Program

International Paper accounts for stock options in accordance with guidance under ASC 718, "Compensation—Stock Compensation." Compensation expense is recorded over the related service period based on the grant-date fair market value. Since all outstanding options were vested as of July 14, 2005, only replacement option grants are expensed. No replacement options were granted in 2011.

During each reporting period, diluted earnings per share is calculated by assuming that "in-the-money" options are exercised and the exercise proceeds are used to repurchase shares in the marketplace. When options are actually exercised, option proceeds are credited to equity and issued shares are included in the computation of earnings per common share, with no effect on reported earnings. Equity is also increased by the tax benefit that International Paper will receive in its tax return for income reported by the employees in their individual tax returns.

Under the program, upon exercise of an option, a replacement option may be granted under certain circumstances with an exercise price equal to the market price at the time of exercise and with a term extending to the expiration date of the original option.

The Company has discontinued the issuance of stock options for all eligible U.S. and non-U.S. employees. In the United States, the stock option program was replaced with a performance-based restricted share program to more closely tie long-term incentive compensation to Company performance on two key performance drivers: return on investment (ROI) and total shareholder return (TSR).

The following summarizes the status of the Stock Option Program and the changes during the three years ending December 31, 2013:

	Options [a,b]	Weighted Average Exercise Price	Weighted Average Remaining Life (Years)	Aggregate Intrinsic Value (Thousands)
Outstanding at December 31, 2010	18,245,253	$37.73	2.30	$ —
Exercised	(1,850)	32.54		
Forfeited	(21,070)	35.21		
Expired	(2,665,547)	35.45		
Outstanding at December 31, 2011	15,556,786	38.13	1.55	—
Granted	2,513	35.94		
Exercised	(3,200,642)	33.62		
Expired	(3,222,597)	40.71		
Outstanding at December 31, 2012	9,136,060	38.79	1.15	1,077
Granted	4,744	48.11		
Exercised	(7,317,825)	38.57		
Expired	(70,190)	37.15		
Outstanding at December 31, 2013	1,752,789	$39.80	0.67	$16,175

[a] The table does not include Continuity Award tandem stock options described below. No fair market value is assigned to these options under ASC 718. The tandem restricted shares accompanying these options are expensed over their vesting period.

[b] The table includes options outstanding under an acquired company plan under which options may no longer be granted.

Performance Share Plan

Under the Performance Share Plan (PSP), contingent awards of International Paper common stock are granted by the Committee. The PSP awards are earned over a three-year period. For the 2011 grant, one-fourth of the award is earned during each twelve-month period, with the final one-fourth segment earned over the full three-year period. Beginning with the 2012 grant, the award is earned evenly over a thirty-six-month period. PSP awards are earned based on the achievement of defined performance rankings of ROI and TSR compared to ROI and TSR peer groups of companies. Awards are weighted 75% for ROI and 25% for TSR for all participants except for officers for whom the awards are weighted 50% for ROI and 50% for TSR. The ROI component of the PSP awards is valued at the closing stock price on the day prior to the grant date. As the ROI component contains a performance condition, compensation expense, net of estimated forfeitures, is recorded over the requisite service period based on the most probable number of awards expected to vest. The TSR component of the PSP awards is valued using a Monte Carlo simulation as the TSR component contains a market condition. The Monte Carlo simulation estimates the fair value of the TSR component based on the expected term of the award, a risk-free rate, expected dividends, and the expected volatility for the Company and its competitors. The expected term is estimated based on the vesting period of the awards, the risk-free rate is based on the yield on U.S. Treasury securities matching the vesting period, and the volatility is based on the Company's historical volatility over the expected term.

PSP grants are made in performance-based restricted stock units (PSU's). PSP awards issued to certain members of senior management are accounted for as liability awards, which are remeasured at fair value at each balance sheet date. The valuation of these PSP liability awards is computed based on the same methodology as the PSP equity awards.

The following table sets forth the assumptions used to determine compensation cost for the market condition component of the PSP plan:

	Twelve Months Ended December 31, 2013
Expected volatility	25.30%–62.58%
Risk-free interest rate	0.13%–0.99%

The following summarizes PSP activity for the three years ending December 31, 2013:

	Share/Units	Weighted Average Grant Date Fair Value
Outstanding at December 31, 2010	6,812,594	$23.31
Granted	4,314,376	28.04
Shares issued	(2,565,971)	32.43
Forfeited	(500,940)	25.07
Outstanding at December 31, 2011	8,060,059	22.83
Granted	3,641,911	31.57
Shares issued	(2,871,367)	16.83
Forfeited	(169,748)	28.89
Outstanding at December 31, 2012	8,660,855	28.37
Granted	3,148,445	40.76
Shares issued[a]	(3,262,760)	32.48
Forfeited	(429,051)	34.58
Outstanding at December 31, 2013	8,117,489	$31.20

[a] Includes 356,542 units related to retirements or terminations that are held for payout until the end of the performance period.

Executive Continuity and Restricted Stock Award Programs

The Executive Continuity Award program provides for the granting of tandem awards of restricted stock and/or nonqualified stock options to key executives. Grants are restricted and awards conditioned on attainment of a specified age. The awarding of a tandem stock option results in the cancellation of the related restricted shares.

The service-based Restricted Stock Award program (RSA), designed for recruitment, retention and special recognition purposes, also provides for awards of restricted stock to key employees.

The following summarizes the activity of the Executive Continuity Award program and RSA program for the three years ending December 31, 2013:

	Shares	Weighted Average Grant Date Fair Value
Outstanding at December 31, 2010	167,500	$26.95
Granted	21,500	27.01
Shares issued	(55,083)	24.84
Forfeited	(5,000)	26.78
Outstanding at December 31, 2011	128,917	27.86
Granted	88,715	31.91
Shares issued	(61,083)	27.13
Forfeited	(5,000)	28.91
Outstanding at December 31, 2012	151,549	30.49
Granted	67,100	44.41
Shares issued	(88,775)	32.30
Forfeited	(17,500)	37.75
Outstanding at December 31, 2013	112,374	$36.24

At December 31, 2013, 2012 and 2011 a total of 17.8 million, 19.3 million and 18.6 million shares, respectively, were available for grant under the ICP.

Stock-based compensation expense and related income tax benefits were as follows:

In millions	2013	2012	2011
Total stock-based compensation expense (included in selling and administrative expense)	$137	$116	$84
Income tax benefits related to stock-based compensation	74	48	34

At December 31, 2013, $116 million of compensation cost, net of estimated forfeitures, related to unvested restricted performance shares, executive continuity awards and restricted stock attributable to future performance had not yet been recognized. This amount will be recognized in expense over a weighted-average period of 1.7 years.

EMPLOYEE STOCK OWNERSHIP PLANS (ESOP)

3.61 STANLEY BLACK & DECKER, INC. (DEC)

CONSOLIDATED STATEMENTS OF CHANGES IN SHAREOWNERS' EQUITY (in part)

(Millions of Dollars, Except Per Share Amounts)

	Common Stock	Additional Paid In Capital	Retained Earnings	Accumulated Other Comprehensive Loss	ESOP	Treasury Stock	Non-Controlling Interests	Shareowners' Equity
Balance January 1, 2011	$440.7	$4,885.7	$2,301.8	$(116.3)	$(74.5)	$ (420.4)	$ 52.7	$ 7,069.7
Net earnings	—	—	674.6	—	—	—	(0.1)	674.5
Other comprehensive loss				(232.9)				(232.9)
Cash dividends declared—$1.64 per share			(271.3)					(271.3)
Issuance of common stock		(22.4)				123.7		101.3
Forward obligation to purchase treasury shares		(350.0)						(350.0)
Equity purchase contracts—stock issuance		(0.4)						(0.4)
Net premium paid and settlement of equity option		(19.4)				(0.2)		(19.6)
Repurchase of common stock (164,710 shares)						(11.1)		(11.1)
Non-controlling interests of acquired businesses							10.6	10.6
Other, stock-based compensation related		68.9						68.9
Tax benefit related to stock options exercised		18.9						18.9
ESOP and related tax benefit			2.2		6.0			8.2
Balance December 31, 2011	$440.7	$4,581.3	$2,707.3	$(349.2)	$(68.5)	$ (308.0)	$ 63.2	$ 7,066.8

(continued)

	Common Stock	Additional Paid In Capital	Retained Earnings	Accumulated Other Comprehensive Loss	ESOP	Treasury Stock	Non-Controlling Interests	Shareowners' Equity
Net earnings			883.8				(0.8)	883.0
Other comprehensive loss				(38.8)				(38.8)
Cash dividends declared—$1.80 per share			(293.8)				(1.0)	(294.8)
Issuance of common stock		(52.7)				161.4		108.7
Convertible equity-hedge share receipt		46.9				(46.9)		—
Delivery to Convertible note holder	1.6	(1.6)						—
Net premium paid on equity option		(29.5)						(29.5)
Repurchase of common stock (12,613,068 shares)		(170.0)				(903.9)		(1,073.9)
Non-controlling interest buyout		(8.3)					(13.3)	(21.6)
Non-controlling interests of acquired businesses							11.9	11.9
Stock-based compensation related		89.7						89.7
Tax benefit related to stock options exercised		17.7						17.7
ESOP and related tax benefit			2.2		5.7			7.9
Balance December 29, 2012	$442.3	$4,473.5	$3,299.5	$(388.0)	$(62.8)	$(1,097.4)	$ 60.0	$ 6,727.1
Net earnings			490.3				(1.0)	489.3
Other comprehensive loss				(111.0)				(111.0)
Cash dividends declared—$1.98 per share			(307.1)				—	(307.1)
Issuance of common stock		(115.6)				250.1		134.5
Settlement of forward share repurchase contract		350.0				(350.0)		—
Equity units—non-cash stock contract fees		(40.2)						(40.2)
Equity units—offering fees		(9.2)						(9.2)
Net premium paid on equity option		(83.2)						(83.2)
Repurchase of common stock (2,225,732 shares)		217.9				(257.1)		(39.2)
Non-controlling interest buyout		(1.1)					(15.2)	(16.3)
Non-controlling interests of acquired businesses							37.5	37.5
Stock-based compensation related		66.4						66.4
Tax benefit related to stock options exercised		20.1						20.1
ESOP and related tax benefit			2.2		9.6			11.8
Balance December 28, 2013	$442.3	$4,878.6	$3,484.9	$(499.0)	$(53.2)	$(1,454.4)	$ 81.3	$ 6,880.5

NOTES TO CONSOLIDATED FINANCIAL STATEMENTS

L. Employee Benefit Plans (in part)

EMPLOYEE STOCK OWNERSHIP PLAN ("ESOP "). Most U.S. employees, including Black & Decker employees beginning on January 1, 2011, may contribute from 1% to 25% of their eligible compensation to a tax-deferred 401(k) savings plan, subject to restrictions under tax laws. Employees generally direct the investment of their own contributions into various investment funds. An employer match benefit is provided under the plan equal to one-half of each employee's tax-deferred contribution up to the first 7% of their compensation. Participants direct the entire employer match benefit such that no participant is required to hold the Company's common stock in their 401(k) account. The employer match benefit totaled $18.8 million, $19.1 million and $17.7 million in 2013, 2012 and 2011, respectively.

In addition, approximately 6,900 U.S. salaried and non-union hourly employees are eligible to receive a non-contributory benefit under the Core benefit plan. Core benefit allocations range from 2% to 6% of eligible employee compensation based on age. Approximately 4,200 U.S. employees also receive a Core transition benefit, allocations of which range from 1% to 2% of eligible compensation based on age and date of hire. Approximately 1,700 U.S. employees are eligible to receive an additional average 1% contribution actuarially designed to replace previously curtailed pension benefits. Allocations for benefits earned under the Core plan were $21.1 million in 2013, $29.4 million million in 2012 and $33.0 million in 2011. Assets held in participant Core accounts are invested in target date retirement funds which have an age-based allocation of investments.

Shares of the Company's common stock held by the ESOP were purchased with the proceeds of borrowings from the Company in 1991 ("1991 internal loan"). Shareowners' equity reflects a reduction equal to the cost basis of unearned (unallocated) shares purchased with the internal borrowings. In October 2013, the Company made an additional contribution to the ESOP for $9.5 million, which was used by the ESOP to make an additional payment on the 1991 internal loan. This payment triggered the release of 219,900 shares of unallocated stock.

The Company accounts for the ESOP under ASC 718–40, *"Compensation—Stock Compensation—Employee Stock Ownership Plans"*. Net ESOP activity recognized is comprised of the cost basis of shares released, the cost of the aforementioned Core and 401(k) match defined contribution benefits, less the fair value of shares released and dividends on unallocated ESOP shares. The Company's net ESOP activity resulted in expense of $1.9 million in 2013, $25.9 million in 2012 and $28.4 million in 2011. The decrease in net ESOP expense in 2013 is related to the release of 219,900 additional shares discussed above. ESOP expense is affected by the market value of the Company's common stock on the monthly dates when shares are released. The market value of shares released averaged $80.71 in 2013, $70.98 per share in 2012 and $68.12 per share in 2011.

Unallocated shares are released from the trust based on current period debt principal and interest payments as a percentage of total future debt principal and interest payments. Dividends on both allocated and unallocated shares may be used for debt service and to credit participant accounts for dividends earned on allocated shares. Dividends paid on the shares acquired with the 1991 internal loan were used solely to pay internal loan debt service in all periods. Dividends on ESOP shares, which are charged to shareowners' equity as declared, were $12.3 million in 2013, $12.4 million in 2012 and $12.2 million in 2011, net of the tax benefit which is recorded within equity. Dividends on ESOP shares were utilized entirely for debt service in all years. Interest costs incurred by the ESOP on the 1991 internal loan, which have no earnings impact, were $6.1 million, $6.7 million and $7.2 million for 2013, 2012 and 2011, respectively. Both allocated and unallocated ESOP shares are treated as outstanding for purposes of computing earnings per share. As of December 28, 2013, the cumulative number of ESOP shares allocated to participant accounts was 12,699,476, of which participants held 2,885,480 shares, and the number of unallocated shares was 2,865,580. At December 28, 2013, there were no released shares in the ESOP trust holding account pending allocation. The Company made cash contributions totaling $30.7 million in 2013, $36.6 million in 2012 and $16.2 million in 2011.

PROFIT SHARING PLANS

3.62 RALPH LAUREN CORPORATION (MAR)
NOTES TO CONSOLIDATED FINANCIAL STATEMENTS

21. Employee Benefit Plans (in part)

Profit Sharing Retirement Savings Plans

The Company sponsors defined contribution benefit plans covering substantially all eligible employees in the U.S. and Puerto Rico who are not covered by a collective bargaining agreement. The plans include a savings plan feature under Section 401(k) of the Internal Revenue Code. The Company makes discretionary matching contributions to the plans, which historically were equal to 50% of the first 6% of salary contributed by an eligible employee. On November 7, 2011, the Company's Board of Directors approved a supplemental discretionary matching contribution for plan years beginning with Fiscal 2012, whereby if the Company achieves a "stretch" or a "maximum" performance target based on certain goals established at the beginning of each fiscal year, the matching contribution will be increased to 75% or 100%, respectively, of the first 6% of salary contributed by eligible employees, not to exceed the maximum contribution permitted by the plan.

Under the terms of the plans, a participant becomes 100% vested in the Company's matching contributions after five years of credited service. Contributions made by the Company under these plans were approximately $10 million in each of Fiscal 2013 and Fiscal 2012, and $8 million in Fiscal 2011.

Other Compensation Plans

The Company has a non-qualified supplemental retirement plan for certain highly compensated employees whose benefits under the 401(k) profit sharing retirement savings plans were expected to be constrained by the operation of certain Internal Revenue Code limitations. These supplemental benefits vest over time and the related compensation expense is recognized over the vesting period. Effective August 2008, the Company amended this plan, resulting in a suspension of the annual contributions for substantially all plan participants. Further, affected participants were provided with a one-time election to either withdraw all benefits vested in the plan in a lump sum amount or remain in the plan and receive future distributions of benefits vested over a three-year period. As of both March 30, 2013 and March 31, 2012, amounts accrued under this plan totaled approximately $9 million and were classified within other non-current liabilities in the consolidated balance sheets. Total compensation expense recognized related to these benefits was $0.2 million in each of the three fiscal years presented.

Additionally, the Company has deferred compensation arrangements for certain key executives which generally provide for payments upon retirement, death, or termination of employment. The amounts accrued under these plans were approximately $3 million and $2 million as of March 30, 2013 and March 31, 2012, respectively, and were classified within other non-current liabilities in the consolidated balance sheets. Total compensation expense related to these compensation arrangements was $0.2 million in each of Fiscal 2013 and Fiscal 2012, and $0.3 million in Fiscal 2011. The Company funds a portion of these obligations through the establishment of trust accounts on behalf of the executives participating in the plans. The trust accounts are classified within other non-current assets in the consolidated balance sheets.

Depreciation Expense

RECOGNITION AND MEASUREMENT

3.63 FASB ASC 360, *Property, Plant, and Equipment*, defines *depreciation accounting* (the process of allocating the cost of productive facilities over the expected useful lives of the facilities) as a system of accounting that aims to distribute the cost or other basic value of tangible capital assets, less salvage (if any), over the estimated useful life of the unit, which may be a group of assets, in a systematic and rational manner. It is a process of allocation, not valuation.

3.64 FASB ASC 250 requires that a change in depreciation, amortization, or depletion method for long-lived, nonfinancial assets be accounted for as a change in accounting estimate effected by a change in accounting principle. Changes in accounting estimate are accounted for prospectively, not retrospectively as is required for changes in accounting principle.

DISCLOSURE

3.65 FASB ASC 360 stipulates that both the amount of depreciation expense and method(s) of depreciation should be disclosed in the financial statements or notes thereto.

PRESENTATION AND DISCLOSURE EXCERPTS

STRAIGHT-LINE AND ACCELERATED METHODS

3.66 ALLIANCE ONE INTERNATIONAL, INC. (MAR)

STATEMENTS OF CONSOLIDATED OPERATIONS (in part)

	Years Ended March 31,		
(In thousands, except per share data)	**2013**	**2012**	**2011**
Sales and other operating revenues	$2,243,816	$2,150,767	$2,094,062
Cost of goods and services sold	1,958,570	1,863,115	1,817,243
Gross profit	285,246	287,652	276,819
Selling, general and administrative expenses	145,750	147,558	157,920
Other income	20,721	15,725	37,442
Restructuring and asset impairment charges (recoveries)	(55)	1,006	23,467
Operating income	160,272	154,813	132,874

NOTES TO CONSOLIDATED FINANCIAL STATEMENTS

(In thousands)

Note 1—Significant Accounting Policies (in part)

Property, Plant and Equipment

Property, plant and equipment at March 31, 2013 and 2012, are summarized as follows:

	2013	2012
Land	$ 28,752	$ 27,991
Buildings	196,601	202,153
Machinery and equipment	207,717	187,026
Total	433,070	417,170
Less accumulated depreciation	162,092	157,491
Total property, plant and equipment, net	$270,978	$259,679

Property, plant and equipment is stated at cost less accumulated depreciation. Provisions for depreciation are computed on a straight-line basis at annual rates calculated to amortize the cost of depreciable properties over their estimated useful lives. Buildings and machinery and equipment are depreciated over ranges of 20 to 30 years and 3 to 10 years, respectively. The consolidated financial statements do not include fully depreciated assets. Depreciation expense recorded in Cost of Goods and Services Sold for the years ended March 31, 2013, 2012 and 2011 was $25,939, $24,712 and $20,699, respectively. Depreciation expense recorded in Selling, General and Administrative Expense for the years ended March 31, 2013, 2012 and 2011 was $3,112, $3,717 and $2,915, respectively. Total property and equipment purchases, including internally developed software intangibles, were $42,803 for the year ended March 31, 2013 of which $2,743 was unpaid at March 31, 2013 and included in Accounts Payable; $42,347 for the year ended March 31, 2012 of which $776 was unpaid at March 31, 2012 and included in Accounts Payable; and $70,608 for the year ended March 31, 2011 of which $3,141 was unpaid at March 31, 2011 and included in Accounts Payable. Included in fiscal 2011 purchases is $43,775 for a new tobacco processing facility in the State of Santa Catarina by the Company's subsidiary in Brazil.

Estimated useful lives are periodically reviewed and changes are made to the estimated useful lives when necessary. Long-lived assets are reviewed for indicators of impairment whenever events or changes in circumstances indicate that the carrying amount may not be recoverable. The evaluation is performed at the lowest level of identifiable cash flows. An impairment loss would be recognized when estimated undiscounted future cash flows from the use of the asset and its eventual disposition are less than its carrying amount. Measurement of an impairment loss would be based on the excess of the carrying amount of the asset over its fair value. Fair value is the amount at which the asset could be bought or sold in a current transaction between willing parties and may be estimated using a number of techniques, including quoted market prices or valuations, present value techniques based on estimates of cash flows, or multiples of earnings or revenue performance measures.

3.67 CLIFFS NATURAL RESOURCES INC. (DEC)
NOTES TO CONSOLIDATED FINANCIAL STATEMENTS

Note 1—Basis of Presentation and Significant Accounting Policies (in part)

Property, Plant and Equipment

U.S. Iron Ore and Eastern Canadian Iron Ore

U.S. Iron Ore and Eastern Canadian Iron Ore properties are stated at the lower of cost less accumulated depreciation or fair value. Depreciation of plant and equipment is computed principally by the straight-line method based on estimated useful lives, not to exceed the mine lives. The Northshore, United Taconite, Empire, Tilden and Wabush operations use the double-declining balance method of depreciation for certain mining equipment. Depreciation is provided over the following estimated useful lives:

Asset Class	Basis	Life
Buildings	Straight line	45 Years
Mining equipment	Straight line/Double declining balance	10 to 20 Years
Processing equipment	Straight line	15 to 45 Years
Information technology	Straight line	2 to 7 Years

Depreciation continues to be recognized when operations temporarily are idled.

Asia Pacific Iron Ore

Our Asia Pacific Iron Ore properties are stated at cost. Depreciation is calculated by the straight-line method or production output basis, not to exceed the mine life, provided over the following estimated useful lives:

Asset Class	Basis	Life
Plant and equipment—non-mining assets	Straight line	5 to 10 Years
Plant and equipment—mining assets	Production output	6 Years
Motor vehicles, furniture & equipment	Straight line	3 to 5 Years

The costs capitalized and classified as *Land rights and mineral rights* represent lands where we own the surface and/or mineral rights.

Our Asia Pacific Iron Ore, Bloom Lake, Wabush, and United Taconite operations' interests in iron ore reserves and mineralized materials were valued when acquired using a discounted cash flow method. The fair value was estimated based upon the present value of the expected future cash flows from iron ore operations over the economic lives of the respective mines. Refer to NOTE 5—PROPERTY, PLANT AND EQUIPMENT for further information.

North American Coal

North American Coal properties are stated at cost. Depreciation is provided over the estimated useful lives, not to exceed the mine lives and is calculated by the straight-line method. Depreciation is provided over the following estimated useful lives:

Asset Class	Basis	Life
Buildings	Straight line	30 Years
Mining equipment	Straight line	2 to 22 Years
Processing equipment	Straight line	2 to 30 Years
Information technology	Straight line	2 to 3 Years

Our North American Coal operation leases coal mining rights from third parties through lease agreements. The lease agreements are for varying terms and extend through the earlier of their lease termination date or until all merchantable and mineable coal has been extracted. Our interest in coal reserves and non-reserve coal was valued when acquired using a discounted cash flow method. The fair value was estimated based upon the present value of the expected future cash flows from coal operations over the life of the reserves acquired.

Refer to NOTE 5—PROPERTY, PLANT AND EQUIPMENT for further information.

Note 5—Property, Plant and Equipment (in part)

The following table indicates the value of each of the major classes of our consolidated depreciable assets as of December 31, 2013 and 2012:

	December 31,	
(In millions)	2013	2012
Land rights and mineral rights	$7,819.6	$7,920.8
Office and information technology	125.7	92.4
Buildings	255.2	162.0
Mining equipment	1,600.3	1,290.7
Processing equipment	2,148.6	1,937.4
Railroad equipment	219.0	240.8
Electric power facilities	114.3	58.7
Port facilities	99.4	114.3
Interest capitalized during construction	23.8	20.8
Land improvements	69.3	43.9
Other	104.4	39.0
Construction in-progress	991.3	1,123.9
	13,570.9	13,044.7
Allowance for depreciation and depletion	(2,417.5)	(1,837.4)
	$11,153.4	$11,207.3

We recorded depreciation expense of $366.9 million, $293.5 million and $237.8 million in the Statements of Consolidated Operations for the years ended December 31, 2013, 2012 and 2011, respectively.

UNITS-OF-PRODUCTION METHOD

3.68 ALCOA INC. (DEC)
STATEMENT OF CONSOLIDATED OPERATIONS (in part)

(in millions, except per-share amounts)

For the Year Ended December 31,	2013	2012	2011
Sales (Q)	$23,032	$23,700	$24,951
Cost of goods sold (exclusive of expenses below)	19,286	20,401	20,480
Selling, general administrative, and other expenses	1,008	997	1,027
Research and development expenses	192	197	184
Provision for depreciation, depletion, and amortization	1,421	1,460	1,479
Impairment of goodwill (A & E)	1,731	—	—
Restructuring and other charges (D)	782	172	281
Interest expense (V)	453	490	524
Other income, net (O)	(25)	(341)	(87)
Total costs and expenses	24,848	23,376	23,888
(Loss) income from continuing operations before income taxes	(1,816)	324	1,063

(Dollars in millions, except per-share amounts)

A. Summary of Significant Accounting Policies (in part)

Properties, Plants, and Equipment. Properties, plants, and equipment are recorded at cost. Depreciation is recorded principally on the straight-line method at rates based on the estimated useful lives of the assets. For greenfield assets, which refer to the construction of new assets on undeveloped land, the units of production method is used to record depreciation. These assets require a significant period (generally greater than one-year) to ramp-up to full production capacity. As a result, the units of production method is deemed a more systematic and rational method for recognizing depreciation on these assets. Depreciation is recorded on temporarily idled facilities until such time management approves a permanent shutdown. The following table details the weighted-average useful lives of structures and machinery and equipment by reporting segment (numbers in years):

Segment	Structures	Machinery and Equipment
Alumina:		
Alumina refining	30	26
Bauxite mining	31	17
Primary Metals:		
Aluminum smelting	35	21
Power generation	30	21
Global Rolled Products	32	21
Engineered Products and Solutions	29	18

Gains or losses from the sale of assets are generally recorded in other income or expenses (see policy below for assets classified as held for sale and discontinued operations). Repairs and maintenance are charged to expense as incurred. Interest related to the construction of qualifying assets is capitalized as part of the construction costs.

Properties, plants, and equipment are reviewed for impairment whenever events or changes in circumstances indicate that the carrying amount of such assets (asset group) may not be recoverable. Recoverability of assets is determined by comparing the estimated undiscounted net cash flows of the operations related to the assets (asset group) to their carrying amount. An impairment loss would be recognized when the carrying amount of the assets (asset group) exceeds the estimated undiscounted net cash flows. The amount of the impairment loss to be recorded is calculated as the excess of the carrying value of the assets (asset group) over their fair value, with fair value determined using the best information available, which generally is a discounted cash flow (DCF) model. The determination of what constitutes an asset group, the associated estimated undiscounted net cash flows, and the estimated useful lives of assets also require significant judgments.

GROUP-LIFE METHOD OF DEPRECIATION

3.69 CSX CORPORATION (DEC)
CONSOLIDATED INCOME STATEMENTS (in part)

(Dollars in Millions, Except Per Share Amounts)

	Fiscal Years		
	2013	**2012**[a]	**2011**[a]
Revenue	$12,026	$11,763	$11,795
Expense			
Labor and fringe	3,138	3,020	3,073
Materials, supplies and other	2,275	2,156	2,229
Fuel	1,656	1,672	1,668
Depreciation	1,104	1,059	976
Equipment and other rents	380	392	379
Total expense	8,553	8,299	8,325
Operating income	3,473	3,464	3,470

Note 6. Properties (in part)

A detail of the Company's net properties are as follows:

(Dollars in millions) December 2013	Cost	Accumulated Depreciation	Net Book Value	Annual Depreciation Rate	Depreciation Method	Estimated Useful Life
Road						
Rail and other track material	$ 6,452	$(1,270)	$ 5,182	2.9%	Group Life	
Ties	4,534	(947)	3,587	4.0%	Group Life	
Grading	2,425	(448)	1,977	1.5%	Group Life	
Ballast	2,612	(645)	1,967	2.8%	Group Life	
Bridges, trestles, and culverts	2,008	(250)	1,758	1.6%	Group Life	
Signals and interlockers	1,922	(291)	1,631	3.4%	Group Life	
Buildings	1,011	(355)	656	2.5%	Group Life	
Other	3,654	(1,386)	2,268	4.7%	Group Life	
Total road	24,618	(5,592)	19,026			6–80 Years
Equipment						
Locomotive	4,987	(2,176)	2,811	3.6%	Group Life	
Freight cars	3,111	(1,135)	1,976	3.1%	Group Life	
Work equipment and other	1,666	(914)	752	7.1%	Group Life	
Total equipment	9,764	(4,225)	5,539			5–38 Years
Land	1,842	—	1,842	N/A	N/A	N/A
Construction in progress	854	—	854	N/A	N/A	N/A
Other	106	(76)	30	N/A	Straight Line	4–30 Years
Total properties	$37,184	$(9,893)	$27,291			

(Dollars in millions) December 2012	Cost	Accumulated Depreciation	Net Book Value	Annual Depreciation Rate	Depreciation Method	Estimated Useful Life
Road						
Rail and other track material	$ 6,177	$(1,131)	$ 5,046	2.9%	Group Life	
Ties	4,287	(861)	3,426	4.0%	Group Life	
Grading	2,407	(414)	1,993	1.5%	Group Life	
Ballast	2,528	(624)	1,904	2.8%	Group Life	
Bridges, trestles, and culverts	1,962	(224)	1,738	1.6%	Group Life	
Signals and interlockers	1,787	(302)	1,485	3.4%	Group Life	
Buildings	926	(316)	610	2.5%	Group Life	
Other	3,345	(1,281)	2,064	4.7%	Group Life	
Total road	23,419	(5,153)	18,266			6–80 Years
Equipment						
Locomotive	4,747	(2,079)	2,668	3.6%	Group Life	
Freight Cars	3,088	(1,119)	1,969	3.1%	Group Life	
Work equipment and other	1,466	(810)	656	7.1%	Group Life	
Total equipment	9,301	(4,008)	5,293			5–38 Years
Land	1,745	—	1,745	N/A	N/A	N/A
Construction in progress	602	—	602	N/A	N/A	N/A
Other	212	(68)	144	N/A	Straight Line	4–30 Years
Total properties	$35,279	$(9,229)	$26,050			

Railroad Assets

The Company depreciates its rail assets, including main-line track, locomotives and freight cars, using the group-life method of accounting. Assets depreciated under the group-life method of accounting comprise over 86% of total fixed assets of $37 billion on a gross basis as of December 2013. All other depreciable assets of the Company are depreciated on a straight-line basis. The group-life method aggregates assets with similar lives and characteristics into groups and depreciates each of these groups as a whole. When using the group-life method, an underlying assumption is that each group of assets, as a whole, is used and depreciated to the end of its recoverable life.

The Company currently utilizes more than 130 different depreciable asset categories to account for depreciation expense for the railroad assets that are depreciated under the group-life method of accounting. Examples of depreciable asset categories include 18 different categories for crossties due to the different combinations of density classifications and asset types. By utilizing various depreciable categories, the Company can more accurately account for the use of its assets. All assets of the Company are depreciated on a time or life basis.

The Company believes the group-life method of depreciation closely approximates the straight-line method of depreciation. Additionally, due to the nature of most of its assets (e.g. track is one contiguous, connected asset) the Company believes that this is the most effective way to properly depreciate its assets.

Under the group-life method of accounting, the service lives and salvage values for each group of assets are determined by completing periodic depreciation studies and applying management's assumptions regarding the service lives of its properties. A depreciation study (also referred to as a life study) is the periodic review of asset service lives, salvage values, accumulated depreciation, and other related factors for group assets conducted by a third-party specialist, analyzed by the Company's management and approved by the Surface Transportation Board ("STB"), the regulatory board that has broad jurisdiction over railroad practices. The STB requires depreciation studies be performed for equipment assets every three years and for road (e.g. bridges and signals) and track (e.g. rail, ties and ballast) assets every six years. The Company believes the frequency currently required by the STB provides adequate review of asset service lives and that a more frequent review would not result in a material change due to the long-lived nature of most of the assets.

The results of the depreciation study process determine the service lives for each asset group under the group-life method. Road assets, including main-line track, have estimated service lives ranging from six years for system roadway machinery to 80 years for grading (construction of protection for the roadway, tracks and embankments). Equipment assets, including locomotives and freight cars, have estimated service lives ranging from six years for technology assets to 38 years for work equipment.

Changes in asset service lives due to the results of the depreciation studies are applied on a prospective basis and could significantly impact future periods' depreciation expense, and thus, the Company's results of operations.

There are several factors taken into account during the depreciation study and they include:
- statistical analysis of historical life and salvage data for each group of property;
- statistical analysis of historical retirements for each group of property;
- evaluation of current operations;
- evaluation of technological advances and maintenance schedules;
- previous assessment of the condition of the assets and outlook for their continued use;
- expected net salvage to be received upon retirement; and
- comparison of assets to the same asset groups with other companies.

For retirements or disposals of depreciable rail assets that occur in the ordinary course of business, the asset cost (net of salvage value or sales proceeds) is charged to accumulated depreciation and no gain or loss is recognized. As individual assets within a specific group are retired or disposed of, resulting gains and losses are recorded in accumulated depreciation. As part of the depreciation study, an assessment of the recorded amount of accumulated depreciation is made to determine if it is deficient (or in excess) of the appropriate amount indicated by the study. Any such deficiency (or excess), including any deferred gains or losses, is amortized as a component of depreciation expense over the remaining service life of the asset group until the next required depreciation study. Since the overall assumption with the group-life method of accounting is that the assets within the group on average have the same service life and characteristics, it is therefore concluded that the deferred gains and losses offset over time.

Since the rail network is one contiguous, connected network it is impractical to maintain specific identification records for these assets. For road assets (such as rail and track related items), CSX utilizes a first-in, first-out approach to asset retirements. The historical cost of these replaced assets is estimated using inflation indices published by the Bureau of Labor Statistics applied to the replacement value based on the age of the retired asset. The indices are used because they closely correlate with the major cost of the materials comprising the applicable road assets.

Equipment assets (such as locomotives and freight cars) are specifically identified. When an equipment asset is retired that has been depreciated using the group-life method, the cost is reduced from the cost base and recorded in accumulated depreciation.

In the event that large groups of assets are removed from service as a result of unusual acts or sales, resulting gains and losses are recognized immediately. These acts are not considered to be in the normal course of business and are therefore recognized when incurred. Examples of such acts would be the major destruction of assets due to significant storm damage (e.g. major hurricanes), the sale of a rail line segment or the disposal of an entire class of assets (e.g. disposal of all refrigerated freight cars). Abnormal operating gains were $65 million in 2013, $104 million in 2012 and $14 million in 2011 and all relate to the disposition of operating rail corridors. Each year includes gains from the 2011 sale of an operating rail corridor to the state of Florida. See the Significant Property Disposition section below for further details on the transaction with the state of Florida. In 2013, a gain was recognized for a non-monetary exchange of easements and rail assets, and in 2012, a gain was recognized for a sale of operating rail corridor to the Commonwealth of Massachusetts.

Recent experience with depreciation studies has resulted in depreciation rate changes, which did not materially affect the Company's annual depreciation expense of $1.1 billion, $1.1 billion, and $976 million for 2013, 2012, and 2011, respectively. In 2012, the Company completed a depreciation study for its equipment assets and a technical update (an update to the prior depreciation study) for its road and track assets.

Income Taxes

Author's Note
In July 2013, FASB issued Accounting Standards Update (ASU) No. 2013-11, *Income Taxes (Topic 740): Presentation of an Unrecognized Tax Benefit When a Net Operating Loss Carryforward, a Similar Tax Loss, or a Tax Credit Carryforward Exists (a consensus of the FASB Emerging Issues Task Force)*, because FASB ASC 740, *Income Taxes*, does not include explicit guidance on the financial statement presentation of an unrecognized tax benefit when a net operating loss carryforward, a similar tax loss, or a tax credit carryforward exists. There is diversity in practice in the presentation of unrecognized tax benefits in those instances. Some entities present unrecognized tax benefits as a liability unless the unrecognized tax benefit is directly associated with a tax position taken in a tax year that results in, or that resulted in, the recognition of a net operating loss or tax credit carryforward for that year and the net operating loss or tax credit carryforward has not been utilized. Other entities present unrecognized tax benefits as a reduction of a deferred tax asset for a net operating loss or tax credit carryforward in certain circumstances. The objective of the amendments in this update is to eliminate that diversity in practice. Public entities are required to apply the amendments in this update for annual reporting periods beginning on or after December 15, 2013, and interim periods within those annual periods. For nonpublic entities, the amendments are effective for fiscal years, and interim periods within those years, beginning after December 15, 2014. Early adoption is permitted. The amendments should be applied prospectively to all unrecognized tax benefits that exist at the effective date. Retrospective application is permitted. Given the effective date of this update, no survey entity will have adopted these requirements in its 2013 financial statements.

RECOGNITION AND MEASUREMENT

3.70 FASB ASC 740, *Income Taxes*, clarifies the accounting for tax positions in an entity's financial statements. FASB ASC 740 prescribes a more-likely-than-not recognition threshold and measurement attribute for the financial statement recognition and measurement of a tax position taken or expected to be taken. Under FASB ASC 740, tax positions will be evaluated for recognition, derecognition, and measurement using consistent criteria. In addition, FASB ASC 740 provides guidance on classification and disclosure. FASB ASC 740 requires, except in certain specified situations, that undistributed earnings of a subsidiary included in consolidated income be accounted for as a temporary difference. Finally, the provisions of FASB ASC 740 provide more information about the uncertainty in income tax assets and liabilities.

DISCLOSURE

3.71 FASB ASC 740 sets forth standards for financial presentation and disclosure of income tax liabilities or assets and expense. These requirements vary for public and nonpublic entities. FASB ASC 740 states that amounts and expiration dates of operating loss and tax credit carryforwards for tax purposes should be disclosed. Any portion of the valuation allowance for deferred tax assets for which subsequently recognized tax benefits will be credited directly to contributed capital should also be disclosed. An entity's temporary difference and carryforward information requires additional disclosure, which differs for public and nonpublic entities.

PRESENTATION AND DISCLOSURE EXCERPTS

EXPENSE PROVISION

3.72 AVNET, INC. (JUN)

CONSOLIDATED STATEMENTS OF OPERATIONS (in part)

	Years Ended		
(Thousands, except share amounts)	June 29, 2013	June 30, 2012	July 2, 2011
Sales	$25,458,924	$25,707,522	$26,534,413
Cost of sales	22,479,123	22,656,965	23,426,608
Gross profit	2,979,801	3,050,557	3,107,805
Selling, general and administrative expenses	2,204,319	2,092,807	2,100,650
Restructuring, integration and other charges (Note 17)	149,501	73,585	77,176
Operating income	625,981	884,165	929,979
Other income (expense), net	(74)	(5,442)	10,724
Interest expense	(107,653)	(90,859)	(92,452)
Gain on bargain purchase and other (Note 2)	31,011	2,918	22,715
Income before income taxes	549,265	790,782	870,966
Income tax provision (Note 9)	99,192	223,763	201,897
Net income	$ 450,073	$ 567,019	$ 669,069

NOTES TO CONSOLIDATED FINANCIAL STATEMENTS

1. Summary of Significant Accounting Policies (in part)

Income taxes—The Company follows the asset and liability method of accounting for income taxes. Deferred income tax assets and liabilities are recognized for the estimated future tax impact of differences between the financial statement carrying amounts of assets and liabilities and their respective tax bases. Deferred income tax assets and liabilities are measured using enacted tax rates in effect for the year in which those temporary differences are expected to be recovered or settled. The effect on deferred income tax assets and liabilities of a change in tax rates is recognized in earnings in the period in which the new rate is enacted. Based upon historical and projected levels of taxable income and analysis of other key factors, the Company may record a valuation allowance against its deferred tax assets, as deemed necessary, to state such assets at their estimated net realizable value.

The Company establishes reserves for potentially unfavorable outcomes of positions taken on certain tax matters. These reserves are based on management's assessment of whether a tax benefit is more likely than not to be sustained upon examination by tax authorities. There may be differences between the anticipated and actual outcomes of these matters that may result in reversals of reserves or additional tax liabilities in excess of the reserved amounts. To the extent such adjustments are warranted, the Company's effective tax rate may potentially fluctuate as a result. In accordance with the Company's accounting policy, accrued interest and penalties, if any, related to unrecognized tax benefits are recorded as a component of income tax expense.

No provision for U.S. income taxes has been made for approximately $2.7 billion of cumulative unremitted earnings of foreign subsidiaries at June 29, 2013 because those earnings are expected to be permanently reinvested outside the U.S. A hypothetical calculation of the deferred tax liability, assuming those earnings were remitted, is not practicable.

9. Income Taxes (in part)

The components of the provision for income taxes are indicated in the table below. The tax provision for deferred income taxes results from temporary differences arising principally from inventory valuation, accounts receivable valuation, net operating losses, certain accruals and depreciation, net of any changes to the valuation allowance.

	Years Ended		
(Thousands)	June 29, 2013	June 30, 2012	July 2, 2011
Current:			
Federal	$17,212	$ 94,237	$ 64,476
State and local	7,034	19,466	11,724
Foreign	84,965	98,278	109,731
Total current taxes	109,211	211,981	185,931
Deferred:			
Federal	2,619	6,896	41,029
State and local	2,390	758	5,273
Foreign	(15,028)	4,128	(30,336)
Total deferred taxes	(10,019)	11,782	15,966
Provision for income taxes	$99,192	$223,763	$201,897

The provision for income taxes noted above is computed based upon the split of income before income taxes from U.S. and foreign operations. U.S. income before income taxes was $174,000,000, $320,333,000 and $273,287,000 and foreign income before income taxes was $375,265,000, $470,449,000 and $597,679,000 in fiscal 2013, 2012 and 2011, respectively.

Reconciliations of the federal statutory tax rate to the effective tax rates are as follows:

	Years Ended		
	June 29, 2013	June 30, 2012	July 2, 2011
Federal statutory rate	35.0%	35.0%	35.0%
State and local income taxes, net of federal benefit	1.1	1.8	1.5
Foreign tax rates, net of valuation allowances	(7.2)	(5.4)	(5.3)
Release of valuation allowance, net of U.S. tax expense (as discussed below)	(6.4)	(2.8)	(7.4)
Change in contingency reserves	0.4	0.5	1.4
Tax audit settlements	(6.0)	(1.0)	(0.4)
Other, net	1.2	0.2	(1.6)
Effective tax rate	18.1%	28.3%	23.2%

Foreign tax rates generally consist of the impact of the difference between foreign and federal statutory rates applied to foreign income or loss and also include the impact of valuation allowances against the Company's otherwise realizable foreign loss carry-forwards.

Avnet's effective tax rate on income before income taxes was 18.1% in fiscal 2013 as compared with an effective tax rate of 28.3% in fiscal 2012. Included in the fiscal 2013 effective tax rate is a net tax benefit of $50,376,000, which is comprised of (i) a tax benefit of $41,572,000 for the release of valuation allowance against deferred tax assets that were determined to be realizable, primarily related to a legal entity in EMEA (discussed further below), (ii) net favorable audit settlements resulting in a benefit of $33,182,000, partially offset by (iii) a tax provision of $24,378,000 primarily related to the establishment of a valuation allowance against deferred tax assets that were determined to be unrealizable during fiscal 2013. The fiscal 2013 effective tax rate is lower than the fiscal 2012 effective tax rate primarily due to a favorable impact from audit settlements and, to a lesser extent, a greater impact to the rate from the valuation allowance released in fiscal 2013 (as discussed further below) as compared with the amount released in fiscal 2012 due to the reduced level of income and mix of income in the current year. In fiscal 2012, withholding tax related to legal entity reorganization resulted in an increase to the rate that does not exist in the current year.

During fiscal 2013, the Company had a partial valuation allowance against significant tax assets related to a legal entity in EMEA due to, among several other factors, a history of losses in that entity. Since fiscal 2010, the entity has been experiencing improved earnings, which required the partial release of the valuation allowance to the extent the entity has projected taxable income. In each of fiscal 2013 and 2012, the Company determined a portion of the valuation allowance for this legal entity was no longer required due to the expected continuation of improved earnings in the foreseeable future and, as a result, the Company's effective tax rate was positively impacted (decreased) upon the release of the valuation allowance, net of the U.S. tax expense. In fiscal 2013 and 2012, the valuation allowance released associated with this EMEA legal entity was $27,055,000 and $22,127,000, respectively, net of the U.S. tax expense associated with the release. The Company will continue to evaluate the need for a valuation allowance against these tax assets and will adjust the valuation allowance as deemed appropriate which, when adjusted, will result in an impact to the effective tax rate. Factors that are considered in such an evaluation include historic levels of income, expectations and risk associated with estimates of future taxable income and ongoing prudent and feasible tax planning strategies. Excluding the benefit in both fiscal years related to the release of the tax valuation allowance associated with the EMEA legal entity, the effective tax rate for fiscal 2013 would have been 23.0% as compared with 31.1% for fiscal 2012.

During fiscal 2013, the Company's effective tax rate was favorably impacted primarily by the settlement of two audits by the U.S. Internal Revenue Service ("IRS") for the Company and an acquired company. As a result, the Company recognized a tax benefit of $33,005,000 in fiscal 2013.

Avnet's effective tax rate on income before income taxes was 28.3% in fiscal 2012 as compared with an effective tax rate of 23.2% in fiscal 2011. As compared with fiscal 2011, the fiscal 2012 effective tax rate is higher than the fiscal 2011 effective tax rate primarily due to a lower amount of valuation allowance released in fiscal 2012 as compared with the amount released in fiscal 2011, and, to a lesser extent, a more favorable impact from audit settlements and changes to existing tax positions in fiscal 2012 as compared with fiscal 2011. These favorable impacts were partially offset by withholding tax in fiscal 2012.

3.73 PRUDENTIAL FINANCIAL, INC. (DEC)

CONSOLIDATED STATEMENTS OF OPERATIONS (in part)

(In millions, except per share amounts)

	2013	2012	2011
Revenues			
Premiums	$26,237	$65,354	$24,301
Policy charges and fee income	5,415	4,489	3,924
Net investment income	14,729	13,661	13,124
Asset management fees and other income	286	2,784	4,905
Realized investment gains (losses), net:			
Other-than-temporary impairments on fixed maturity securities	(1,055)	(1,611)	(2,202)
Other-than-temporary impairments on fixed maturity securities transferred to Other Comprehensive Income	856	1,274	1,667
Other realized investment gains (losses), net	(5,007)	(1,104)	3,366
Total realized investment gains (losses), net	(5,206)	(1,441)	2,831
Total revenues	41,461	84,847	49,085
Benefits and Expenses			
Policyholders' benefits	26,733	65,131	23,614
Interest credited to policyholders' account balances	3,111	4,234	4,484
Dividends to policyholders	2,050	2,176	2,723
Amortization of deferred policy acquisition costs	240	1,504	2,695
General and administrative expenses	11,011	11,094	10,605
Total benefits and expenses	43,145	84,139	44,121
Income (Loss) from continuing operations before income taxes and equity in earnings of operating joint ventures	(1,684)	708	4,964
Income taxes:			
Current	34	1,088	447
Deferred	(1,092)	(875)	1,068
Total income tax expense (benefit)	(1,058)	213	1,515
Income (Loss) from continuing operations before equity in earnings of operating joint ventures	(626)	495	3,449
Equity in earnings of operating joint ventures, net of taxes	59	60	182
Income (Loss) from continuing operations	(567)	555	3,631
Income (loss) from discontinued operations, net of taxes	7	15	35
Net income (Loss)	(560)	570	3,666

NOTES TO CONSOLIDATED FINANCIAL STATEMENTS

2. Significant Accounting Policies and Pronouncements (in part)

Income Taxes

The Company and its includible domestic subsidiaries file a consolidated federal income tax return that includes both life insurance companies and non-life insurance companies. Non-includible domestic subsidiaries file separate individual corporate tax returns. Subsidiaries operating outside the U.S. are taxed, and income tax expense is recorded, based on applicable foreign statutes. See Note 19 for a discussion of certain non-U.S. jurisdictions for which the Company assumes repatriation of earnings to the U.S.

Deferred income taxes are recognized, based on enacted rates, when assets and liabilities have different values for financial statement and tax reporting purposes. A valuation allowance is recorded to reduce a deferred tax asset to the amount expected to be realized.

Items required by tax regulations to be included in the tax return may differ from the items reflected in the financial statements. As a result, the effective tax rate reflected in the financial statements may be different than the actual rate applied on the tax return. Some of these differences are permanent such as expenses that are not deductible in the Company's tax return, and some differences are temporary, reversing over time, such as valuation of insurance reserves. Temporary differences create deferred tax assets and liabilities. Deferred tax assets generally represent items that can be used as a tax deduction or credit in future years for which the Company has already recorded the tax benefit in the Company's income statement. Deferred tax liabilities generally represent tax expense recognized in the Company's financial statements for which payment has been deferred, or expenditures for which the Company has already taken a deduction in the Company's tax return but have not yet been recognized in the Company's financial statements.

The application of U.S. GAAP requires the Company to evaluate the recoverability of the Company's deferred tax assets and establish a valuation allowance if necessary to reduce the Company's deferred tax assets to an amount that is more likely than not to be realized. Considerable judgment is required in determining whether a valuation allowance is necessary, and if so, the amount of such valuation allowance. In evaluating the need for a valuation allowance the Company may consider many factors, including: (1) the nature of the deferred tax assets and liabilities; (2) whether they are ordinary or capital; (3) in which tax jurisdictions they were generated and the timing of their reversal; (4) taxable income in prior carryback years as well as projected taxable earnings exclusive of reversing temporary differences and carryforwards; (5) the length of time that carryovers can be utilized in the various taxing jurisdictions; (6) any unique tax rules that would impact the utilization of the deferred tax assets; and (7) any tax planning strategies that the Company would employ to avoid a tax benefit from expiring unused. Although realization is not assured, management believes it is more likely than not that the deferred tax assets, net of valuation allowances, will be realized.

U.S. GAAP prescribes a comprehensive model for how a company should recognize, measure, present, and disclose in its financial statements uncertain tax positions that a company has taken or expects to take on tax returns. The application of this guidance is a two-step process, the first step being recognition. The Company determines whether it is more likely than not, based on the technical merits, that the tax position will be sustained upon examination. If a tax position does not meet the more likely than not recognition threshold, the benefit of that position is not recognized in the financial statements. The second step is measurement. The Company measures the tax position as the largest amount of benefit that is greater than 50 percent likely of being realized upon ultimate resolution with a taxing authority that has full knowledge of all relevant information. This measurement considers the amounts and probabilities of the outcomes that could be realized upon ultimate settlement using the facts, circumstances, and information available at the reporting date.

The Company's liability for income taxes includes the liability for unrecognized tax benefits, interest and penalties which relate to tax years still subject to review by the Internal Revenue Service ("IRS") or other taxing jurisdictions. Audit periods remain open for review until the statute of limitations has passed. Generally, for tax years which produce net operating losses, capital losses or tax credit carryforwards ("tax attributes"), the statute of limitations does not close, to the extent of these tax attributes, until the expiration of the statute of limitations for the tax year in which they are fully utilized. The completion of review or the expiration of the statute of limitations for a given audit period could result in an adjustment to the liability for income taxes. The Company classifies all interest and penalties related to tax uncertainties as income tax expense. See Note 19 for additional information regarding income taxes.

19. Income Taxes (in part)

The components of income tax expense (benefit) for the years ended December 31 were as follows:

(In millions)	2013	2012	2011
Current tax expense (benefit)			
U.S.	$ (292)	$ 674	$ 73
State and local	16	27	2
Foreign	310	387	372
Total	34	1,088	447
Deferred tax expense (benefit)			
U.S.	44	(437)	771
State and local	0	(5)	12
Foreign	(1,136)	(433)	285
Total	(1,092)	(875)	1,068
Total income tax expense (benefit) on continuing operations before equity in earnings of operating joint ventures	(1,058)	213	1,515
Income tax expense on equity in earnings of operating joint ventures	19	19	79
Income tax expense on discontinued operations	3	8	18
Income tax expense (benefit) reported in equity related to:			
Other comprehensive income	(582)	2,667	1,301
Stock-based compensation programs	(32)	(56)	(19)
Total income taxes	$(1,650)	$2,851	$2,894

The Company's actual income tax expense on continuing operations before equity in earnings of operating joint ventures for the years ended December 31 differs from the expected amount computed by applying the statutory federal income tax rate of 35% to income from continuing operations before income taxes and equity in earnings of operating joint ventures for the following reasons:

(In millions)	2013	2012	2011
Expected federal income tax expense (benefit)	$ (589)	$248	$1,737
Non-taxable investment income	(319)	(302)	(247)
Low income housing and other tax credits	(105)	(78)	(80)
Reversal of acquisition opening balance sheet deferred tax items	55	384	221
Medicare Part D	(43)	(1)	(2)
Minority interest	(37)	(17)	(11)
Foreign taxes at other than U.S. rate	(36)	(51)	(37)
State taxes	10	15	0
Other	6	15	(66)
Total income tax expense (benefit) on continuing operations before equity in earnings of operating joint ventures	$(1,058)	$213	$1,515

The dividends received deduction ("DRD") reduces the amount of dividend income subject to U.S. tax and is the primary component of the non-taxable investment income shown in the table above, and, as such, is a significant component of the difference between the Company's effective tax rate and the federal statutory tax rate of 35%. The DRD for the current period was estimated using information from 2012 and current year results, and was adjusted to take into account the current year's equity market performance. The actual current year DRD can vary from the estimate based on factors such as, but not limited to, changes in the amount of dividends received that are eligible for the DRD, changes in the amount of distributions received from mutual fund investments, changes in the account balances of variable life and annuity contracts, and the Company's taxable income before the DRD.

OPERATING LOSS AND TAX CREDIT CARRYFORWARDS

3.74 CITIGROUP INC. (DEC)
MANAGEMENT'S DISCUSSION AND ANALYSIS OF FINANCIAL CONDITION AND RESULTS OF OPERATIONS

Executive Summary (in part)

Overview (in part)

2013—Steady Progress on Execution Priorities and Strategy Despite Continued Challenging Operating Environment (in part)

2013 represented a continued challenging operating environment for Citigroup in several respects, including:
- changing expectations regarding the Federal Reserve Board's tapering of quantitative easing and the impact of this uncertainty on the markets, trading environment and customer activity;
- the increasing costs of legal settlements across the financial services industry as Citi continued to work through its legacy legal issues; and
- a continued low interest rate environment.

These issues significantly impacted Citi's results of operations, particularly during the second half of 2013. Despite these challenges, however, Citi made progress on its execution priorities as identified in early 2013, including:
- Efficient resource allocation, including disciplined expense management—During 2013, Citi completed the significant repositioning actions announced in the fourth quarter of 2012, which resulted in the exit of markets that do not fit Citi's strategy and contributed to the reduction in its operating expenses year-over-year (see discussion below).
- Continued focus on the wind down of Citi Holdings and getting Citi Holdings closer to "break even"—Citi Holdings' assets declined by $39 billion, or 25%, during 2013, and the net loss for this segment improved by approximately 49% (see discussion below). Citi also was able to resolve certain of its legacy legal issues during 2013, including entering into agreements with Fannie Mae and Freddie Mac relating to residential mortgage representation and warranty repurchase matters.
- Utilization of deferred tax assets (DTAs)—Citi utilized approximately $2.5 billion of its DTAs during 2013, including $700 million in the fourth quarter.

1. Summary of Significant Accounting Policies (in part)

Income Taxes

The Company is subject to the income tax laws of the U.S. and its states and municipalities, and the foreign jurisdictions in which it operates. These tax laws are complex and subject to different interpretations by the taxpayer and the relevant governmental taxing authorities. In establishing a provision for income tax expense, the Company must make judgments and interpretations about the application of these inherently complex tax laws. The Company must also make estimates about when in the future certain items will affect taxable income in the various tax jurisdictions, both domestic and foreign.

Disputes over interpretations of the tax laws may be subject to review and adjudication by the court systems of the various tax jurisdictions or may be settled with the taxing authority upon examination or audit. The Company treats interest and penalties on income taxes as a component of *Income tax expense*.

Deferred taxes are recorded for the future consequences of events that have been recognized for financial statements or tax returns, based upon enacted tax laws and rates. Deferred tax assets are recognized subject to management's judgment that realization is more-likely-than-not. FASB Interpretation No. 48, "Accounting for Uncertainty in Income Taxes" (FIN 48) (now incorporated into ASC 740, *Income Taxes*), sets out a consistent framework to determine the appropriate level of tax reserves to maintain for uncertain tax positions. This interpretation uses a two-step approach wherein a tax benefit is recognized if a position is more-likely-than-not to be sustained. The amount of the benefit is then measured to be the highest tax benefit that is greater than 50% likely to be realized. FIN 48 also sets out disclosure requirements to enhance transparency of an entity's tax reserves.

See Note 9 to the Consolidated Financial Statements for a further description of the Company's tax provision and related income tax assets and liabilities.

Future Application of Accounting Standards (in part)

Presentation of an Unrecognized Tax Benefit When a Net Operating Loss Carry-forward, a Similar Tax Loss, or a Tax Credit Carry-forward Exists

In July 2013, the FASB issued ASU No. 2013-11, *Income Taxes (Topic 740): Presentation of an Unrecognized Tax Benefit When a Net Operating Loss Carry-forward, a Similar Tax Loss, or a Tax Credit Carry-forward Exists (a consensus of the FASB Emerging Issues Task Force)*. As a result of applying this ASU, an unrecognized tax benefit should be presented as a reduction of a deferred tax asset for a net operating loss (NOL) or other tax credit carry-forward when settlement in this manner is available under the tax law. The assessment of whether settlement is available under the tax law would be based on facts and circumstances as of the balance sheet reporting date and would not consider future events (e.g., upcoming expiration of related NOL carry-forwards). This classification should not affect an entity's analysis of the realization of its deferred tax assets. Gross presentation in the rollforward of unrecognized tax positions in the notes to the financial statements would still be required.

This ASU is effective for Citi in its 2014 fiscal year, and may be applied on a prospective basis to all unrecognized tax benefits that exist at the effective date. Citi has the option to apply the ASU retrospectively. Early adoption is also permitted. The impact of adopting this ASU is not expected to be material to Citi.

9. Income Taxes

Details of the Company's income tax provision for the years ended December 31 are presented in the table below:

Income Taxes

(In millions of dollars)	2013	2012	2011
Current			
Federal	$ (260)	$ (71)	$ (144)
Foreign	3,788	3,869	3,552
State	(41)	300	241
Total current income taxes	$3,487	$4,098	$3,649

(continued)

(In millions of dollars)	2013	2012	2011
Deferred			
Federal	$ 2,550	$(4,943)	$ (793)
Foreign	(716)	900	628
State	546	(48)	91
Total deferred income taxes	$ 2,380	$(4,091)	$ (74)
Provision (benefit) for income tax on continuing operations before noncontrolling interests[1]	$ 5,867	$ 7	$3,575
Provision (benefit) for income taxes on discontinued operations	(244)	(52)	12
Provision (benefit) for income taxes on cumulative effect of accounting changes	—	(58)	—
Income tax expense (benefit) reported in stockholders' equity related to:			
Foreign currency translation	5	(709)	(609)
Investment securities	(1,353)	369	1,495
Employee stock plans	28	265	297
Cash flow hedges	625	311	(92)
Benefit Plans	698	(390)	(235)
Income taxes before noncontrolling interests	$ 5,626	$ (257)	$4,443

[1] Includes the effect of securities transactions and other-than-temporary-impairment losses resulting in a provision (benefit) of $262 million and $(187) million in 2013, $1,138 million and $(1,740) million in 2012 and $699 million and $(789) million in 2011, respectively.

Tax Rate

The reconciliation of the federal statutory income tax rate to the Company's effective income tax rate applicable to income from continuing operations (before noncontrolling interests and the cumulative effect of accounting changes) for the years ended December 31 was as follows:

	2013	2012	2011
Federal statutory rate	35.0 %	35.0 %	35.0 %
State income taxes, net of federal benefit	1.7	3.0	1.5
Foreign income tax rate differential	(2.2)	(4.6)	(8.4)
Audit settlements[1]	(0.6)	(11.8)	—
Effect of tax law changes[2]	(0.3)	(0.1)	2.0
Basis difference in affiliates	—	(9.2)	—
Tax advantaged investments	(4.2)	(12.4)	(6.0)
Other, net	0.7	0.2	0.2
Effective income tax rate	30.1%	0.1%	24.3%

[1] For 2013, relates to the settlement of U.S. federal issues for 2003–2005 at IRS appeals. For 2012, relates to the conclusion of the audit of various issues in the Company's 2006–2008 U.S. federal tax audits and the conclusion of a New York City tax audit for 2006–2008.

[2] For 2011, includes the results of the Japan tax rate change which resulted in a $300 million DTA charge.

As set forth in the table above, Citi's effective tax rate for 2013 was 30.1%, which included a tax benefit of $127 million for the resolution of certain tax items during the year. This compared to an effective tax rate for 2012 of 0.1% due to the effect of permanent differences on the comparably lower level of pretax income. 2012 included a $925 million tax benefit, also related to the resolution of certain tax audit items during the year.

As previously disclosed, during 2013, Citi decided that earnings in certain foreign subsidiaries would no longer be indefinitely reinvested outside the U.S. (as asserted under ASC 740, *Income Taxes*). This decision increased Citi's 2013 tax provision on these foreign subsidiary earnings to the higher U.S. tax rate and thus increased Citi's effective tax rate for 2013 and reduced its after-tax earnings. For additional information on Citi's foreign earnings, see "Foreign Earnings" below.

Deferred Income Taxes

Deferred income taxes at December 31 related to the following:

(In millions of dollars)	2013	2012
Deferred Tax Assets		
Credit loss deduction	$ 8,356	$10,947
Deferred compensation and employee benefits	4,067	4,890
Restructuring and settlement reserves	1,806	1,645
Unremitted foreign earnings	6,910	5,114
Investment and loan basis differences	4,409	3,878
Cash flow hedges	736	1,361
Tax credit and net operating loss carry-forwards	26,097	28,087

(continued)

(In millions of dollars)	2013	2012
Fixed assets and leases	666	—
Debt Issuances	—	614
Other deferred tax assets	2,734	1,964
Gross deferred tax assets	$55,781	$58,500
Valuation allowance	—	—
Deferred tax assets after valuation allowance	$55,781	$58,500
Deferred Tax Liabilities		
Deferred policy acquisition costs and value of insurance in force	$(455)	$(495)
Fixed assets and leases	—	(623)
Intangibles	(1,076)	(1,517)
Debt issuances	(811)	—
Other deferred tax liabilities	(640)	(543)
Gross deferred tax liabilities	$(2,982)	$(3,178)
Net deferred tax assets	$52,799	$55,322

Unrecognized Tax Benefits

The following is a roll-forward of the Company's unrecognized tax benefits.

(In millions of dollars)	2013	2012	2011
Total unrecognized tax benefits at January 1	$ 3,109	$ 3,923	$4,035
Net amount of increases for current year's tax positions	58	136	193
Gross amount of increases for prior years' tax positions	251	345	251
Gross amount of decreases for prior years' tax positions	(716)	(1,246)	(507)
Amounts of decreases relating to settlements	(1,115)	(44)	(11)
Reductions due to lapse of statutes of limitation	(15)	(3)	(38)
Foreign exchange, acquisitions and dispositions	2	(2)	—
Total unrecognized tax benefits at December 31	$ 1,574	$ 3,109	$3,923

The total amounts of unrecognized tax benefits at December 31, 2013, 2012 and 2011 that, if recognized, would affect Citi's effective tax rate, are $0.8 billion, $1.3 billion and $2.2 billion, respectively. The remaining uncertain tax positions have offsetting amounts in other jurisdictions or are temporary differences, except for $0.4 billion at December 31, 2013, which would be booked directly to *Retained earnings*.

Interest and penalties (not included in "unrecognized tax benefits" above) are a component of the *Provision for income taxes*.

	2013		2012		2011	
(In millions of dollars)	Pretax	Net of Tax	Pretax	Net of Tax	Pretax	Net of Tax
Total interest and penalties in the Consolidated Balance Sheet at January 1	$ 492	$315	$404	$261	$348	$223
Total interest and penalties in the Consolidated Statement of Income	(108)	(72)	114	71	61	41
Total interest and penalties in the Consolidated Balance Sheet at December 31[1]	277	173	492	315	404	261

[1] Includes $2 million, $10 million and $14 million for foreign penalties in 2013, 2012 and 2011, respectively. Also includes $4 million for state penalties in 2013, 2012 and 2011.

Citi currently is under audit by the Internal Revenue Service and other major taxing jurisdictions around the world. It is thus reasonably possible that significant changes in the gross balance of unrecognized tax benefits may occur within the next 12 months, although Citi does not expect such audits to result in amounts that would cause a significant change to its effective tax rate, other than as discussed below.

Citi expects to conclude its IRS audit for the 2009–2011 cycle within the next 12 months. The gross uncertain tax positions at December 31, 2013 for the items that may be resolved are as much as $520 million. Because of the number and nature of the issues remaining to be resolved, the potential tax benefit to continuing operations could be anywhere from $0 to $150 million, while the potential tax benefit to retained earnings could be from $0 to $350 million. In addition, Citi may conclude certain state and local tax audits within the next 12 months. The gross uncertain tax positions at December 31, 2013 are as much as $170 million. The potential tax benefit to continuing operations could be anywhere between $0 and $110 million, excluding interest.

The following are the major tax jurisdictions in which the Company and its affiliates operate and the earliest tax year subject to examination:

Jurisdiction	Tax Year
United States	2009
Mexico	2008
New York State and City	2005
United Kingdom	2012
India	2009
Brazil	2009
Singapore	2007
Hong Kong	2007
Ireland	2010

Foreign Earnings

Foreign pretax earnings approximated $13.1 billion in 2013, $14.7 billion in 2012 and $13.1 billion in 2011 (of which $0.1 billion, $0.0 billion and $0.1 billion, respectively, are in *Discontinued operations*). As a U.S. corporation, Citigroup and its U.S. subsidiaries are subject to U.S. taxation on all foreign pretax earnings earned by a foreign branch. Pretax earnings of a foreign subsidiary or affiliate are subject to U.S. taxation when effectively repatriated. The Company provides income taxes on the undistributed earnings of non-U.S. subsidiaries except to the extent that such earnings are indefinitely reinvested outside the United States.

At December 31, 2013, $43.8 billion of accumulated undistributed earnings of non-U.S. subsidiaries was indefinitely invested. At the existing U.S. federal income tax rate, additional taxes (net of U.S. foreign tax credits) of $11.7 billion would have to be provided if such earnings were remitted currently. The current year's effect on the income tax expense from continuing operations is included in the "Foreign income tax rate differential" line in the reconciliation of the federal statutory rate to the Company's effective income tax rate in the table above.

Income taxes are not provided for the Company's "savings bank base year bad debt reserves" that arose before 1988, because under current U.S. tax rules, such taxes will become payable only to the extent such amounts are distributed in excess of limits prescribed by federal law. At December 31, 2013, the amount of the base year reserves totaled approximately $358 million (subject to a tax of $125 million).

DTAs

As of December 31, 2013 and 2012, Citi had no valuation allowance on its DTAs.

(In billions of dollars) Jurisdiction/component	DTAs Balance December 31, 2013	DTAs Balance December 31, 2012
U.S. federal[1]		
Net operating losses (NOLs)[2]	$ 1.4	$ 0.8
Foreign tax credits (FTCs)[3]	19.6	22.0
Consolidated tax return general business credits (GBCs)	2.5	2.6
Future tax deductions and credits	21.5	22.0
Other	—	0.1
Total U.S. federal	$45.0	$47.5
State and Local		
New York NOLs	$ 1.4	$ 1.3
Other state NOLs	0.5	0.6
Future tax deductions	2.4	2.6
Total state and local	$ 4.3	$ 4.5
Foreign		
APB 23 subsidiary NOLs	$ 0.2	$ 0.2
Non-APB 23 subsidiary NOLs	1.2	1.2
Future tax deductions	2.1	1.9
Total foreign	$ 3.5	$ 3.3
Total	$52.8	$55.3

[1] Included in the net U.S. federal DTAs of $45.0 billion as of December 31, 2013 were deferred tax liabilities of $2 billion that will reverse in the relevant carry-forward period and may be used to support the DTAs.

[2] Includes $0.6 billion and $0.8 billion for 2013 and 2012, respectively, of NOL carry-forwards related to non-consolidated tax return companies that are expected to be utilized separately from Citigroup's consolidated tax return and $0.8 billion of non-consolidated tax return NOL carry-forwards for 2013 that are eventually expected to be utilized in Citigroup's consolidated tax return.

[3] Includes $0.7 billion of non-consolidated tax return FTC carry-forwards that are eventually expected to be utilized in Citigroup's consolidated tax return.

The following table summarizes the amounts of tax carry-forwards and their expiration dates as of December 31, 2013:

(In billions of dollars) Year of Expiration	Amount	
	December 31, 2013	December 31, 2012
U.S. Tax Return Foreign Tax Credit Carry-Forwards		
2016	$ —	$ 0.4
2017	4.7	6.6
2018	5.2	5.3
2019	1.2	1.3
2020	3.1	2.3
2021	1.4	1.9
2022	3.3	4.2
2023[1]	0.7	—
Total U.S. tax return foreign tax credit carry-forwards	$19.6	$22.0
U.S. Tax Return General Business Credit Carry-Forwards		
2027	$ —	$ 0.3
2028	0.4	0.4
2029	0.4	0.4
2030	0.4	0.5
2031	0.4	0.5
2032	0.5	0.5
2033	0.4	—
Total U.S. tax return general business credit carry-forwards	$ 2.5	$ 2.6
U.S. Subsidiary Separate Federal NOL Carry-Forwards		
2027	$ 0.2	$ 0.2
2028	0.1	0.1
2030	0.3	0.3
2031	1.7	1.8
2033	1.7	—
Total U.S. subsidiary separate federal NOL carry-forwards[2]	$ 4.0	$ 2.4
New York State NOL Carry-Forwards		
2027	$ 0.1	$ 0.1
2028	6.5	7.2
2029	2.0	1.9
2030	0.1	0.4
2032	0.9	—
Total New York State NOL carry-forwards[2]	$ 9.6	$ 9.6
New York City NOL Carry-Forwards		
2027	$ 0.1	$ 0.1
2028	3.9	3.7
2029	1.5	1.6
2032	0.6	0.2
Total New York City NOL carry-forwards[2]	$ 6.1	$ 5.6
APB 23 Subsidiary NOL Carry-Forwards		
Various	$ 0.2	$ 0.2
Total APB 23 subsidiary NOL carry-forwards	$ 0.2	$ 0.2

[1] The $0.7 billion in FTC carry-forwards that expires in 2023 is in a non-consolidated tax return entity but is eventually expected to be utilized in Citigroup's consolidated tax return.

[2] Pretax.

While Citi's net total DTAs decreased year-over-year, the time remaining for utilization has shortened, given the passage of time, particularly with respect to the FTC component of the DTAs. Realization of the DTAs will continue to be driven by Citi's ability to generate U.S. taxable earnings in the carry-forward periods, including through actions that optimize Citi's U.S. taxable earnings.

Although realization is not assured, Citi believes that the realization of the recognized net DTAs of $52.8 billion at December 31, 2013 is more likely than not based upon expectations as to future taxable income in the jurisdictions in which the DTAs arise and available tax planning strategies (as defined in ASC 740, *Income Taxes*) that would be implemented, if necessary, to prevent a carry-forward from expiring. In general, Citi would need to generate approximately $98 billion of U.S. taxable income during the FTC carry-forward periods to prevent this most time sensitive component of Citi's DTAs from expiring. Citi's net DTAs will decline primarily as additional domestic GAAP taxable income is generated.

Citi has concluded that two components of positive evidence support the full realization of its DTAs. First, Citi forecasts sufficient U.S. taxable income in the carry-forward periods, exclusive of ASC 740 tax planning strategies. Citi's forecasted taxable income, which will continue to be subject to overall market and global economic conditions, incorporates geographic business forecasts and taxable income adjustments to those forecasts (e.g., U.S. tax exempt income, loan loss reserves deductible for U.S. tax reporting in subsequent years), and actions intended to optimize its U.S. taxable earnings.

Second, Citi has sufficient tax planning strategies available to it under ASC 740 that would be implemented to prevent a carry-forward from expiring. These strategies include: repatriating low taxed foreign source earnings for which an assertion that the earnings have been indefinitely reinvested has not been made; accelerating U.S. taxable income into, or deferring U.S. tax deductions out of, the latter years of the carry-forward period (e.g., selling appreciated intangible assets, electing straight-line depreciation); accelerating deductible temporary differences outside the U.S.; and selling certain assets that produce tax-exempt income, while purchasing assets that produce fully taxable income. In addition, the sale or restructuring of certain businesses can produce significant U.S. taxable income within the relevant carry-forward periods.

Based upon the foregoing discussion, Citi believes the U.S. federal and New York state and city NOL carry-forward period of 20 years provides enough time to fully utilize the DTAs pertaining to the existing NOL carry-forwards and any NOL that would be created by the reversal of the future net deductions that have not yet been taken on a tax return.

The U.S. FTC carry-forward period is 10 years and represents the most time-sensitive component of Citi's DTAs.

Utilization of FTCs in any year is restricted to 35% of foreign source taxable income in that year. However, overall domestic losses that Citi has incurred of approximately $64 billion as of December 31, 2013 are allowed to be reclassified as foreign source income to the extent of 50% of domestic source income produced in subsequent years. Such resulting foreign source income would cover the FTCs being carried forward. As such, Citi believes the foreign source taxable income limitation will not be an impediment to the FTC carry-forward usage, as long as Citi can generate sufficient domestic taxable income within the 10-year carry-forward period.

As noted in the tables above, Citi's FTC carry-forwards were $19.6 billion as of December 31, 2013, compared to $22.0 billion as of December 31, 2012. This decrease represented $2.4 billion of the $2.5 billion decrease in Citi's overall DTAs during 2013. Citi believes that it will generate sufficient U.S. taxable income within the 10-year carry-forward period referenced above to be able to fully utilize the FTC carry-forward, in addition to any FTCs produced in such period, which must be used prior to any carry-forward utilization.

3.75 THE PNC FINANCIAL SERVICES GROUP, INC. (DEC)
NOTES TO CONSOLIDATED FINANCIAL STATEMENTS

Note 1—Accounting Policies (in part)

Income Taxes

We account for income taxes under the asset and liability method. Deferred tax assets and liabilities are determined based on differences between the financial reporting and tax bases of assets and liabilities and are measured using the enacted tax rates and laws that we expect will apply at the time when we believe the differences will reverse. The recognition of deferred tax assets requires an assessment to determine the realization of such assets. Realization refers to the incremental benefit achieved through the reduction in future taxes payable or refunds receivable from the deferred tax assets, assuming that the underlying deductible differences and carryforwards are the last items to enter into the determination of future taxable income. We establish a valuation allowance for tax assets when it is more likely than not that they will not be realized, based upon all available positive and negative evidence.

Note 21—Income Taxes

The components of Income taxes are as follows:

Table 145: Components of Income Taxes

	Year Ended December 31		
(in millions)	**2013**	**2012**	**2011**
Current			
Federal	$ 117	$343	$191
State	17	29	(33)
Total current	134	372	158
Deferred			
Federal	1,129	522	783
State	78	48	57
Total deferred	1,207	570	840
Total	$1,341	$942	$998

Significant components of deferred tax assets and liabilities are as follows:

Table 146: Deferred Tax Assets and Liabilities

	December 31	
(in millions)	2013	2012
Deferred Tax Assets		
Allowance for loan and lease losses	$1,343	$1,681
Compensation and benefits	581	790
Basis difference in loans		284
Loss and credit carryforward	797	766
Accrued expenses	575	835
Other	536	650
Total gross deferred tax assets	3,832	5,006
Valuation allowance	(61)	(54)
Total deferred tax assets	3,771	4,952
Deferred Tax Liabilities		
Leasing	1,498	1,396
Goodwill and intangibles	342	363
Basis difference in loans	48	
Fixed assets	397	398
Net unrealized gains on securities and financial instruments	391	939
BlackRock basis difference	2,031	1,874
Other	730	543
Total deferred tax liabilities	5,437	5,513
Net deferred tax liability	$1,666	$ 561

A reconciliation between the statutory and effective tax rates follows:

Table 147: Reconciliation of Statutory and Effective Tax Rates

	Year Ended December 31		
	2013	2012	2011
Statutory tax rate	35.0%	35.0%	35.0%
Increases (decreases) resulting from			
State taxes net of federal benefit	1.1	1.3	.4
Tax-exempt interest	(2.0)	(2.4)	(1.7)
Life insurance	(1.7)	(2.3)	(2.0)
Dividend received deduction	(1.3)	(1.7)	(1.6)
Tax credits	(5.4)	(6.5)	(5.1)
Other	(1.6)	.5	(.5)
Effective tax rate	24.1%	23.9%	24.5%

The net operating loss carryforwards at December 31, 2013 and 2012 follow:

Table 148: Net Operating Loss Carryforwards and Tax Credit Carryforwards

(In millions)	December 31, 2013	December 31, 2012
Net Operating Loss Carryforwards:		
Federal	$1,116	$1,698
State	2,958	2,468
Tax Credit Carryforwards:		
Federal	$ 221	$ 29
State	7	4

The federal net operating loss carryforwards expire from 2028 to 2032. The state net operating loss carryforwards will expire from 2014 to 2031. The majority of the tax credit carryforwards expire in 2033.

The federal net operating loss carryforwards and tax credit carryforwards above are substantially from the 2012 acquisition of RBC Bank (USA) and are subject to a federal annual Section 382 limitation of $119 million under the Internal Revenue Code of 1986, as amended; and acquired state operating loss carryforwards are subject to similar limitations that exist for state tax purposes. The decrease in federal net operating loss carryforwards is primarily attributable to the final settlement with RBC based on RBC's final federal income tax return as filed. The majority of the increase to state net operating loss carryforwards is attributable to a state tax audit settlement. It is anticipated that the company will be able to fully utilize its carryforwards for federal tax purposes, but a valuation allowance of $61 million has been recorded against certain state tax carryforwards as of December 31, 2013.

During 2013, PNC made an assertion under ASC 740—Income Taxes that the earnings of certain non-U.S. subsidiaries were indefinitely reinvested. As of December 31, 2013, the company had approximately $46 million of earnings and $39 million of foreign currency translation attributed to foreign subsidiaries that have been indefinitely reinvested abroad for which no incremental U.S. income tax provision has been recorded. If a U.S. deferred tax liability were to be recorded, the estimated tax liability on those undistributed earnings and foreign currency translation would be approximately $29 million.

Retained earnings at both December 31, 2013 and 2012 included $117 million in allocations for bad debt deductions of former thrift subsidiaries for which no income tax has been provided. Under current law, if certain subsidiaries use these bad debt reserves for purposes other than to absorb bad debt losses, they will be subject to Federal income tax at the current corporate tax rate.

The Company had a liability for unrecognized tax benefits of $110 million at December 31, 2013 and $176 million at December 31, 2012. At December 31, 2013, $87 million of unrecognized tax benefits, if recognized, would favorably impact the effective income tax rate.

A reconciliation of the beginning and ending balance of the liability for unrecognized tax benefits is as follows:

Table 149: Changes in Liability for Unrecognized Tax Benefits

(In millions)	2013	2012	2011
Balance of gross unrecognized tax benefits at January 1	$176	$209	$238
Increases:			
Positions taken during a prior period	11	23	65
Positions taken during the current period		1	1
Decreases:			
Positions taken during a prior period	(22)	(51)	(62)
Settlements with taxing authorities	(48)	(1)	(10)
Reductions resulting from lapse of statute of limitations	(7)	(5)	(23)
Balance of gross unrecognized tax benefits at December 31	$110	$176	$209

It is reasonably possible that the liability for unrecognized tax benefits could increase or decrease in the next twelve months due to completion of tax authorities' exams or the expiration of statutes of limitations. Management estimates that the liability for unrecognized tax benefits could decrease by $63 million within the next twelve months.

Examinations are substantially completed for PNC's consolidated federal income tax returns for 2007 and 2008 and there are no outstanding unresolved issues. The Internal Revenue Service (IRS) is currently examining PNC's 2009 and 2010 returns. National City's consolidated federal income tax returns through 2008 have been audited by the IRS. Certain adjustments remain under review by the IRS Appeals Division for years 2003 through 2008.

PNC files tax returns in most states and some non-U.S. jurisdictions each year and is under continuous examination by various state taxing authorities. With few exceptions, we are no longer subject to state and local and non-U.S. income tax examinations by taxing authorities for periods before 2007. For all open audits, any potential adjustments have been considered in establishing our reserve for unrecognized tax benefits as of December 31, 2013.

Our policy is to classify interest and penalties associated with income taxes as income tax expense. For 2013, we had a benefit of $41 million of gross interest and penalties, decreasing income tax expense. The total accrued interest and penalties at December 31, 2013 and December 31, 2012 was $45 million and $93 million, respectively.

TAXES ON UNDISTRIBUTED EARNINGS

3.76 AVON PRODUCTS, INC. (DEC)
NOTES TO CONSOLIDATED FINANCIAL STATEMENTS

(U.S. dollars in millions, except per share and share data)

Note 1. Description of the Business and Summary of Significant Accounting Policies (in part)

Deferred Income Taxes

Deferred income taxes have been provided on items recognized for financial reporting purposes in different periods than for income tax purposes using tax rates in effect for the year in which the differences are expected to reverse. A valuation allowance is provided to reduce our deferred tax assets to an amount that is "more likely than not" to be realized. The ultimate realization of our deferred tax assets depends upon generating sufficient future taxable income during the periods in which our temporary differences become deductible or before our net operating loss and tax credit carryforwards expire.

With respect to our deferred tax assets, at December 31, 2013, we had recognized deferred tax assets relating to tax loss carryforwards of $756.1, primarily from foreign jurisdictions, for which a valuation allowance of $717.6 has been provided. We also had recognized deferred tax assets of $585.4 relating to excess foreign tax credit carryforwards that will expire in the 2018–2023 period.

We have concluded that the deferred tax assets associated with the excess foreign tax credits are "more likely than not" to be realized prior to expiration. Our conclusion is based on forecasted future U.S. taxable income, including domestic profitability, royalties received from foreign subsidiaries, and the potential impact of possible tax planning strategies, including the repatriation of foreign earnings and the acceleration of royalties. Assumptions embedded in our forecasted future U.S. taxable income include continued international growth, the stabilization of the U.S. business and the reduction of corporate expenses. To the extent U.S. taxable income is less favorable than currently projected, our ability to utilize these foreign tax credits may be negatively affected.

With respect to our deferred tax liability, during the fourth quarter of 2012, as a result of the uncertainty of our financing arrangements and our domestic liquidity profile at that time, we determined that we may repatriate offshore cash to meet certain domestic funding needs. Accordingly, we asserted that these undistributed earnings of foreign subsidiaries were no longer indefinitely reinvested and, therefore, recorded an additional provision for income taxes of $168.3 on such earnings. At December 31, 2012, we had a deferred tax liability in the amount of $224.8 for the U.S. tax cost on the undistributed earnings of subsidiaries outside of the U.S. of $3.1 billion.

At December 31, 2013, we continue to assert that our foreign earnings are not indefinitely reinvested, as a result of our domestic liquidity profile. Accordingly, we adjusted our deferred tax liability to account for our 2013 undistributed earnings of foreign subsidiaries and for earnings that were actually repatriated to the U.S. during the year. Additionally, the deferred tax liability was reduced due to the lower cost to repatriate the undistributed earnings of our foreign subsidiaries compared to 2012. The net impact on the deferred tax liability associated with the Company's undistributed earnings is a reduction of $81.9, resulting in a deferred tax liability balance of $142.8 related to the incremental U.S. tax cost on $2.6 billion of undistributed foreign earnings at December 31, 2013. This deferred income tax liability amount is net of the estimated foreign tax credits that would be generated upon the repatriation of such earnings. The repatriation of foreign earnings should result in the utilization of foreign tax credits in the year of repatriation; therefore, the utilization of foreign tax credits is dependent on the amount and timing of repatriations, as well as the jurisdictions involved. We have not included the undistributed earnings of our subsidiary in Venezuela in the calculation of this deferred income tax liability as local regulations restrict cash distributions denominated in U.S. dollars.

Note 7. Income Taxes (in part)

At December 31, 2013, we had recognized deferred tax assets relating to tax loss carryforwards of $756.1 primarily from foreign jurisdictions, for which a valuation allowance of $717.6 has been provided. We also had recognized deferred tax assets of $585.4 relating to excess foreign tax credit carryforwards that will expire in the 2018–2023 period. We have concluded that the deferred tax assets associated with the excess foreign tax credits are "more likely than not" to be realized prior to expiration.

During the fourth quarter of 2012, as a result of the uncertainty of our financing arrangements and our domestic liquidity profile at that time, we determined that we may repatriate offshore cash to meet certain domestic funding needs. Accordingly, we asserted that these undistributed earnings of foreign subsidiaries were no longer indefinitely reinvested and, therefore, recorded an additional provision for income taxes of $168.3 on such earnings. At December 31, 2012, we had a deferred tax liability in the amount of $224.8 for the U.S. tax cost on the undistributed earnings of subsidiaries outside of the U.S. of $3.1 billion.

At December 31, 2013, we continue to assert that our foreign earnings are not indefinitely reinvested, as a result of our domestic liquidity profile. Accordingly, we adjusted our deferred tax liability to account for our 2013 undistributed earnings of foreign subsidiaries and for earnings that were actually repatriated to the U.S. during the year. Additionally, the deferred tax liability was reduced due to the lower cost to repatriate the undistributed earnings of our foreign subsidiaries compared to 2012. The net impact on the deferred tax liability associated with the Company's undistributed earnings is a reduction of $81.9, resulting in a deferred tax liability balance of $142.8 related to the incremental U.S. tax cost on $2.6 billion of undistributed foreign earnings at December 31, 2013. This deferred income tax liability amount is net of the estimated foreign tax credits that would be generated upon the repatriation of such earnings. The repatriation of foreign earnings should result in the utilization of foreign tax credits in the year of repatriation; therefore, the utilization of foreign tax credits is dependent on the amount and timing of repatriations, as well as the jurisdictions involved. We have not included the undistributed earnings of our subsidiary in Venezuela in the calculation of this deferred income tax liability as local regulations restrict cash distributions denominated in U.S. dollars.

Construction-Type and Production-Type Contracts

RECOGNITION AND MEASUREMENT

3.77 Accounting and disclosure requirements for construction-type and production-type contracts are discussed in FASB ASC 605-35. Two accounting methods commonly followed by contractors are the percentage-of-completion method and the completed-contract method. The two methods should be used in specific circumstances and should not be used as acceptable alternatives for the same circumstances. The use of either of the two generally accepted methods involves, to a greater or lesser extent, three key areas of estimates and uncertainties, including the extent of progress toward completion, contract revenues, and contract costs.

PRESENTATION AND DISCLOSURE EXCERPTS

CONSTRUCTION- AND PRODUCTION-TYPE CONTRACTS

3.78 URS CORPORATION (DEC)
CONSOLIDATED STATEMENTS OF OPERATIONS (in part)

(In millions, except per share data)

	Year Ended		
	January 3, 2014	December 28, 2012	December 30, 2011
Revenues	$ 10,990.7	$ 10,972.5	$ 9,545.0
Cost of revenues	(10,416.0)	(10,294.5)	(8,988.8)
General and administrative expenses	(77.5)	(83.6)	(79.5)
Acquisition-related expenses (Note 8)	—	(16.1)	(1.0)
Restructuring costs (Note 17)	—	—	(5.5)
Goodwill impairment (Note 9)	—	—	(351.3)
Equity in income of unconsolidated joint ventures	93.6	107.6	132.2
Operating income	590.8	685.9	251.1

NOTES TO CONSOLIDATED FINANCIAL STATEMENTS

Note 1. Business, Basis of Presentation, and Accounting Policies (in part)

Revenue Recognition

We recognize revenues from engineering, construction and construction-related contracts using the percentage-of-completion method as project progress occurs. Service-related contracts, including operations and maintenance services and a variety of technical assistance services, are accounted for using the proportionate performance method as project progress occurs.

Percentage of Completion. Under the percentage-of-completion method, revenue is recognized as contract performance progresses. We estimate the progress towards completion to determine the amount of revenue and profit to recognize. We generally utilize a cost-to-cost approach in applying the percentage-of-completion method, where revenue is earned in proportion to total costs incurred, divided by total costs expected to be incurred. Costs are generally determined from actual hours of labor effort expended at per-hour labor rates calculated using a labor dollar multiplier that includes direct labor costs and allocable overhead costs. Direct non-labor costs are charged as incurred plus any mark-up permitted under the contract.

Under the percentage-of-completion method, recognition of profit is dependent upon the accuracy of a variety of estimates, including engineering progress, materials quantities, and achievement of milestones, incentives, penalty provisions, labor productivity, cost estimates and others. Such estimates are based on various professional judgments we make with respect to those factors and are subject to change as the project proceeds and new information becomes available.

Proportional Performance. Our service contracts, primarily performed by our Federal Services Division, are accounted for using the proportional performance method, under which revenue is recognized in proportion to the number of service activities performed, in proportion to the direct costs of performing the service activities, or evenly across the period of performance depending upon the nature of the services provided.

Revenues from all contracts may vary based on the actual number of labor hours worked and other actual contract costs incurred. If actual labor hours and other contract costs exceed the original estimate agreed to by our client, we generally obtain a change order, contract modification or successfully prevail in a claim in order to receive and recognize additional revenues relating to the additional costs (see "Change Orders and Claims" below).

If estimated total costs on any contract indicate a loss, we charge the entire estimated loss to operations in the period the loss becomes known. The cumulative effect of revisions to revenue, estimated costs to complete contracts, including penalties, incentive awards, change orders, claims, anticipated losses, and others are recorded in the accounting period in which the events indicating a loss or change in estimates are known and the loss can be reasonably estimated. Such revisions could occur at any time and the effects may be material.

We have a history of making reasonably dependable estimates of the extent of progress towards completion, contract revenue and contract completion costs on our long-term engineering and construction contracts. However, due to uncertainties inherent in the estimation process, it is possible that actual completion costs may vary from estimates.

Change Orders and Claims. Change orders and/or claims occur when changes are experienced once contract performance is underway, and may arise under any of the contract types described below.

Change orders are modifications of an original contract that effectively change the existing provisions of the contract without adding new scope or terms. Change orders may include changes in specifications or designs, manner of performance, facilities, equipment, materials, sites and period of completion of the work. Either we or our clients may initiate change orders. Client agreement as to the terms of change orders is, in many cases, reached prior to work commencing; however, sometimes circumstances require that work progress without obtaining client agreement. Costs related to change orders are recognized as incurred. Revenues attributable to change orders that are unapproved as to price or scope are recognized to the extent that costs have been incurred if the amounts can be reliably estimated and their realization is probable. Revenues in excess of the costs attributable to change orders that are unapproved as to price or scope are recognized only when realization is assured beyond a reasonable doubt. Change orders that are unapproved as to both price and scope are evaluated as claims.

Claims are amounts in excess of agreed contract prices that we seek to collect from our clients or others for customer-caused delays, errors in specifications and designs, contract terminations, change orders that are either in dispute or are unapproved as to both scope and price, or other causes of unanticipated additional contract costs. Claims are included in total estimated contract revenues when the contract or other evidence provides a legal basis for the claim, when the additional costs are caused by circumstances that were unforeseen at the contract date and are not the result of the deficiencies in the contract performance, when the costs associated with the claim are identifiable, and when the evidence supporting the claim is objective and verifiable. Revenue on claims is recognized only to the extent that contract costs related to the claims have been incurred and when it is probable that the claim will result in a bona fide addition to contract value which can be reliably estimated. No profit is recognized on claims until final settlement occurs. As a result, costs may be recognized in one period while revenues may be recognized when client agreement is obtained or claims resolution occurs, which can be in subsequent periods.

"At-risk" and "Agency" Contracts. The amount of revenues we recognize also depends on whether the contract or project represents an at-risk or an agency relationship between the client and us. Determination of the relationship is based on characteristics of the contract or the relationship with the client. For at-risk relationships where we act as the principal to the transaction, the revenue and the costs of materials, services, payroll, benefits, and other costs are recognized at gross amounts. For agency relationships, where we act as an agent for our client, only the fee revenue is recognized, meaning that direct project costs and the related reimbursement from the client are netted. Revenues from agency contracts and collaborative arrangements were not a material part of revenues for any period presented.

In classifying contracts or projects as either at-risk or agency, we consider the following primary characteristics to be indicative of at-risk relationships: (i) we acquire the related goods and services using our procurement resources, (ii) we assume the risk of loss under the contract and (iii) we are responsible for insurance coverage, employee-related liabilities and the performance of subcontractors.

We consider the following primary characteristics to be indicative of agency relationships: (i) our client owns the work facilities utilized under the contract, (ii) we act as a procurement agent for goods and services acquired with client funds, (iii) our client is invoiced for our fees, (iv) our client is exposed to the risk of loss and maintains insurance coverage, and (v) our client is responsible for employee-related benefit plan liabilities and any remaining liabilities at the end of the contract.

Contract Types

Our contract types include cost-plus, target-price, fixed-price, and time-and-materials contracts. Revenue recognition is determined based on the nature of the service provided, irrespective of the contract type, with engineering, construction and construction-related contracts accounted for under the percentage-of-completion method and service-related contracts accounted for under the proportional performance method.

Cost-Plus Contracts. We enter into four major types of cost-plus contracts. Revenue for the majority of our cost-plus contracts is recognized using the percentage-of-completion method:

Cost-Plus Fixed Fee. Under cost-plus fixed fee contracts, we charge our clients for our costs, including both direct and indirect costs, plus a fixed negotiated fee.

Cost-Plus Fixed Rate. Under our cost-plus fixed rate contracts, we charge clients for our direct costs plus negotiated rates based on our indirect costs.

Cost-Plus Award Fee. Some cost-plus contracts provide for award fees or penalties based on performance criteria in lieu of a fixed fee or fixed rate. Other contracts include a base fee component plus a performance-based award fee. In addition, we may share award fees with subcontractors and/or our employees. We accrue fee sharing as related award fee revenue is earned. We take into consideration the award fee or penalty on contracts when estimating revenues and profit rates, and we record revenues related to the award fees when there is sufficient information to assess anticipated contract performance. On contracts that represent higher than normal risk or technical difficulty, we defer all award fees until an award fee letter is received. Once an award fee letter is received, the estimated or accrued fees are adjusted to the actual award amount.

Cost-Plus Incentive Fee. Some of our cost-plus contracts provide for incentive fees based on performance against contractual milestones. The amount of the incentive fees varies, depending on whether we achieve above-, at- or below-target results. We recognize incentive fees revenues as milestones are achieved, assuming that we will achieve at-target results, unless our estimates indicate our cost at completion to be significantly above or below target.

Target-Price Contracts. Under our target-price contracts, project costs are reimbursable. Our fee is established against a target budget that is subject to changes in project circumstances and scope. Should the project costs exceed the target budget within the agreed-upon scope, we generally degrade a portion of our fee or profit to mitigate the excess cost; however, the customer reimburses us for the costs that we incur if costs continue to escalate beyond our expected fee. If the project costs are less than the target budget, we generally recover a portion of the project cost savings as additional fee or profit. We recognize revenues on target-price contracts using the percentage-of-completion method.

Fixed-Price Contracts. We enter into two major types of fixed-price contracts:

Firm Fixed-Price ("FFP"). Under FFP contracts, our clients pay us an agreed fixed-amount negotiated in advance for a specified scope of work. We generally recognize revenues on FFP contracts using the percentage-of-completion method. If the nature or circumstances of the contract prevent us from preparing a reliable estimate at completion, we will delay profit recognition until adequate information about the contract's progress becomes available. Prior to completion, our recognized profit margins on any FFP contract depend on the accuracy of our estimates and will increase to the extent that our current estimates of aggregate actual costs are below amounts previously estimated. Conversely, if our current estimated costs exceed prior estimates, our profit margins will decrease and we may realize a loss on a project.

Fixed-Price Per Unit ("FPPU"). Under our FPPU contracts, clients pay us a set fee for each service or production transaction that we complete. We recognize revenues under FPPU contracts as we complete the related service or production transactions for our clients generally using the proportional performance method. Some of our FPPU contracts are subject to maximum contract values.

Time-and-Materials Contracts. Under our time-and-materials contracts, we negotiate hourly billing rates and charge our clients based on the actual time that we spend on a project. In addition, clients reimburse us for our actual out-of-pocket costs of materials and other direct incidental expenditures that we incur in connection with our performance under the contract. The majority of our time-and-material contracts are subject to maximum contract values and, accordingly, revenues under these contracts are generally recognized under the percentage-of-completion method. However, time-and-materials contracts that are service-related contracts are accounted for utilizing the proportional performance method. Revenues on contracts that are not subject to maximum contract values are recognized based on the actual number of hours we spend on the projects plus any actual out-of-pocket costs of materials and other direct incidental expenditures that we incur on the projects. Our time-and-materials contracts also generally include annual billing rate adjustment provisions.

3.79 B/E AEROSPACE, INC. (DEC)
CONSOLIDATED STATEMENTS OF EARNINGS AND COMPREHENSIVE INCOME (in part)

(In millions, except per share data)

	Years Ended December 31,		
	2013	2012	2011
Revenues	$3,483.7	$3,085.3	$2,499.8
Cost of sales	2,154.8	1,921.2	1,563.5
Selling, general and administrative	478.7	432.4	349.7
Research, development and engineering	220.9	191.7	158.6
Operating earnings	629.3	540.0	428.0
Interest expense	122.5	124.4	105.0
Debt prepayment costs	—	82.1	—
Earnings before income taxes	506.8	333.5	323.0
Income tax expense	141.2	99.8	95.2
Net earnings	365.6	233.7	227.8

NOTES TO CONSOLIDATED FINANCIAL STATEMENTS

(In millions, except share and per share data)

1. Summary of Significant Accounting Policies (in part)

Revenue Recognition—Sales of products are recorded when the earnings process is complete. This generally occurs when the products are shipped to the customer in accordance with the contract or purchase order, risk of loss and title has passed to the customer, collectability is reasonably assured and pricing is fixed and determinable. In instances where title does not pass to the customer upon shipment, the Company recognizes revenue upon delivery or customer acceptance, depending on the terms of the sales contract.

Service revenues primarily consist of engineering activities and logistics related services, including revenue from oilfield rental equipment and services, and are recorded when services are performed.

Revenues and costs under certain long-term contracts are recognized using contract accounting under the percentage-of-completion method in accordance with the Financial Accounting Standards Board ("FASB") Accounting Standards Codification ("ASC") 605-35, *Construction–Type and Production–Type Contracts* ("ASC 605-35"), with the majority of the contracts accounted for under the cost-to-cost method. Under the cost-to-cost method, the revenues related to the long-term contracts are recognized based on the ratio of actual costs incurred to total estimated costs to be incurred. The Company uses the units-of-delivery method to account for certain contracts, principally with The Boeing Company and Airbus. Under the units-of delivery method, revenues are recognized based on the contract price of units delivered.

The percentage-of-completion method requires the use of estimates of costs to complete long-term contracts. Due to the duration of these contracts as well as the technical nature of the products involved, the estimation of these costs requires management's judgment in connection with assumptions and projections related to the outcome of future events. Management's assumptions include future labor performance and rates and projections relative to material and overhead costs, as well as the quantity and timing of product deliveries. The Company reevaluates its contract estimates periodically and reflects changes in estimates in the current period using the cumulative catch-up method. Revenues associated with any contractual claims are recognized when it is probable that the claim will result in additional contract revenue and the amount can be reasonably estimated. For the years ended December 31, 2013, 2012 and 2011, approximately 16%, 15% and 15% of our revenues, respectively, were derived from contracts accounted for using percentage-of-completion accounting. Net costs and estimated earnings in excess of billings on uncompleted contracts were $81.9 and $95.9 at December 31, 2013 and 2012, respectively, and recorded as work in process inventory. Excess over average costs on long-term contracts accounted for using the units-of-delivery method of accounting were $213.4 and $134.4 at December 31, 2013 and 2012, respectively and recorded as work in process inventory. Anticipated losses on contracts are recognized in the period in which the losses become evident and determinable. Advance payments and engineering development costs on certain long-term contracts are deferred and included in revenues and research, development and engineering, respectively, when the products are shipped.

3.80 L-3 COMMUNICATIONS HOLDINGS, INC. (DEC)
CONSOLIDATED STATEMENTS OF OPERATIONS (in part)

(in millions, except per share data)

	Year Ended December 31,		
	2013	2012	2011
Net sales:			
Products	$ 7,192	$ 7,535	$ 7,552
Services	5,437	5,611	5,606
Total net sales	12,629	13,146	13,158
Cost of sales:			
Products	(6,409)	(6,724)	(6,673)
Services	(4,962)	(5,071)	(5,043)
Total cost of sales	(11,371)	(11,795)	(11,716)
Impairment charge	—	—	(43)
Operating income	1,258	1,351	1,399

NOTES TO CONSOLIDATED FINANCIAL STATEMENTS

2. Summary of Significant Accounting Policies (in part)

Revenue Recognition: Substantially all of the Company's sales are generated from written contractual (revenue) arrangements. The sales price for the Company's revenue arrangements are either fixed-price, cost-plus or time-and-material type. Depending on the contractual scope of work, the Company utilizes either contract accounting standards or accounting standards for revenue arrangements with commercial customers to account for these contracts. Approximately 47% of the Company's 2013 sales were accounted for under contract accounting standards, of which approximately 38% were fixed-price type contracts and approximately 9% were cost-plus type contracts. For contracts that are accounted for under contract accounting standards, sales and profits are recognized based on: (1) a Percentage-of-Completion (POC) method of accounting (fixed-price contracts), (2) allowable costs incurred plus the estimated profit on those costs (cost-plus contracts), or (3) direct labor hours expended multiplied by the contractual fixed rate per hour plus incurred costs for material (time-and-material contracts). Aggregate net changes in contract estimates increased operating income by $106 million, or 8%, for the year ended December 31, 2013, $78 million, or 6%, for the year ended December 31, 2012, and $73 million, or 5%, for the year ended December 31, 2011.

Sales and profits on fixed-price type contracts covered by contract accounting standards are substantially recognized using POC methods of accounting. Sales and profits on fixed-price production contracts under which units are produced and delivered in a continuous or sequential process are recorded as units are delivered based on their contractual selling prices (the "units-of-delivery" method). Sales and profits on each fixed-price production contract under which units are not produced and delivered in a continuous or sequential process, or under which a relatively few number of units are produced, are recorded based on the ratio of actual cumulative costs incurred to the total estimated costs at completion of the contract, multiplied by the total estimated contract revenue, less cumulative sales recognized in prior periods (the "cost-to-cost" method). Under both POC methods of accounting, a single estimated total profit margin is used to recognize profit for each contract over its entire period of performance, which can exceed one year. Losses on contracts are recognized in the period in which they become evident. The impact of revisions of contract estimates, which may result from contract modifications, performance or other reasons, are recognized on a cumulative catch-up basis in the period in which the revisions are made.

Sales and profits on cost-plus type contracts covered by contract accounting standards are recognized as allowable costs are incurred on the contract, at an amount equal to the allowable costs plus the estimated profit on those costs. The estimated profit on a cost-plus type contract is fixed or variable based on the contractual fee arrangement. Incentive and award fees are the primary variable fee contractual arrangements. Incentive and award fees on cost-plus type contracts are included as an element of total estimated contract revenues and are recorded as sales when a basis exists for the reasonable prediction of performance in relation to established contractual targets and the Company is able to make reasonably dependable estimates for them.

Sales and profits on time-and-material type contracts are recognized on the basis of direct labor hours expended multiplied by the contractual fixed rate per hour, plus the actual costs of materials and other direct non-labor costs.

Sales on arrangements for (1) fixed-price type contracts that require us to perform services that are not related to the production of tangible assets (Fixed-Price Service Contracts) and (2) certain commercial customers are recognized in accordance with accounting standards for revenue arrangements with commercial customers. Sales for the Company's businesses whose customers are primarily commercial business enterprises are substantially all generated from single element revenue arrangements. Sales are recognized when there is persuasive evidence of an arrangement, delivery has occurred or services have been performed, the selling price to the buyer is fixed or determinable and collectability is reasonably assured. Sales for Fixed-Price Service Contracts that do not contain measurable units of work performed are generally recognized on a straight-line basis over the contractual service period, unless evidence suggests that the revenue is earned, or obligations fulfilled, in a different manner. Sales for Fixed-Price Service Contracts that contain measurable units of work performed are generally recognized when the units of work are completed. Sales and profit on cost-plus and time-and-material type contracts to perform services are recognized in the same manner as those within the scope of contract accounting standards, except for incentive and award fees. Cost-based incentive fees are recognized when they are realizable in the amount that would be due under the contractual termination provisions as if the contract was terminated. Performance based incentive fees and award fees are recorded as sales when awarded by the customer.

For contracts with multiple deliverables, the Company applies the separation and allocation guidance under the accounting standard for revenue arrangements with multiple deliverables, unless all the deliverables are covered by contract accounting standards, in which case the Company applies the separation and allocation guidance under contract accounting standards. Revenue arrangements with multiple deliverables are evaluated to determine if the deliverables should be separated into more than one unit of accounting. The Company recognizes revenue for each unit of accounting based on the revenue recognition policies discussed above.

Sales and profit in connection with contracts to provide services to the U.S. Government that contain collection risk because the contracts are incrementally funded and subject to the availability of funds appropriated, are deferred until a contract modification is obtained, indicating that adequate funds are available to the contract or task order.

Contracts in Process: Contracts in process include unbilled contract receivables and inventoried contract costs for which sales and profits are recognized primarily using a POC method of accounting. Unbilled Contract Receivables represent accumulated incurred costs and earned profits on contracts in process that have been recorded as sales, primarily using the cost-to-cost method, but have not been billed to customers. Inventoried Contract Costs primarily represent incurred costs on contracts using the units-of-delivery method of accounting and include direct costs and indirect costs, including overhead costs, and materials acquired for U.S. Government service contracts. As discussed in Note 5, the Company's inventoried contract costs for U.S. Government contracts, and contracts with prime contractors or subcontractors of the U.S. Government include allocated general and administrative costs (G&A), IRAD costs and B&P costs. Contracts in Process contain amounts relating to contracts and programs with long performance cycles, a portion of which may not be realized within one year. For contracts in a loss position, the unrecoverable costs expected to be incurred in future periods are recorded in Estimated Costs in Excess of Estimated Contract Value to Complete Contracts in Process in a Loss Position, which is a component of Other Current Liabilities. Under the terms of certain revenue arrangements (contracts) with the U.S. Government, the Company is entitled to receive progress payments as costs are incurred or milestone payments as work is performed. The U.S. Government has a security interest in the Unbilled Contract Receivables and Inventoried Contract Costs to which progress payments have been applied, and such progress payments are reflected as a reduction of the related amounts. Milestone payments that have been received in excess of contract costs incurred and related estimated profits are reported on the Company's balance sheet as Advance Payments and Billings in Excess of Costs Incurred.

The Company values its acquired contracts in process in connection with business acquisitions on the date of acquisition at contract value less the Company's estimated costs to complete the contract and a reasonable profit allowance on the Company's completion effort commensurate with the profit margin that the Company earns on similar contracts.

5. Contracts in Process (in part)

The components of contracts in process are presented in the table below. The unbilled contract receivables, inventoried contract costs and unliquidated progress payments principally relate to contracts with the U.S. Government and prime contractors or subcontractors of the U.S. Government. In connection with contracts in process assumed by the Company in its business acquisitions, the underlying contractual customer relationships are separately recognized as identifiable intangible assets at the date of acquisition, and are discussed and presented in Note 7.

(In millions)	December 31,	
	2013	2012
Unbilled contract receivables, gross	$ 2,547	$ 2,879
Unliquidated progress payments	(1,035)	(1,255)
Unbilled contract receivables, net	1,512	1,624
Inventoried contract costs, gross	1,093	1,101
Unliquidated progress payments	(81)	(128)
Inventoried contract costs, net	1,012	973
Total contracts in process	$ 2,524	$ 2,597

Unbilled Contract Receivables. Unbilled contract receivables represent accumulated incurred costs and earned profits on contracts (revenue arrangements), which have been recorded as sales, but have not yet been billed to customers. Unbilled contract receivables arise from the cost-to-cost method of revenue recognition that is used to record sales on certain fixed-price contracts. Unbilled contract receivables from fixed-price type contracts are converted to billed receivables when amounts are invoiced to customers according to contractual billing terms, which generally occur when deliveries or other performance milestones are completed. Unbilled contract receivables also arise from cost-plus type contracts and time-and-material type contracts, for revenue amounts that have not been billed by the end of the accounting period due to the timing of preparation of invoices to customers. The Company believes that approximately 95% of the unbilled contract receivables at December 31, 2013 will be billed and collected within one year.

Unliquidated Progress Payments. Unliquidated progress payments arise from fixed-price type contracts with the U.S. Government that contain progress payment clauses, and represent progress payments on invoices that have been collected in cash, but have not yet been liquidated. Progress payment invoices are billed to the customer as contract costs are incurred at an amount generally equal to 75% to 80% of incurred costs. Unliquidated progress payments are liquidated as deliveries or other contract performance milestones are completed, at an amount equal to a percentage of the contract sales price for the items delivered or work performed, based on a contractual liquidation rate. Therefore, unliquidated progress payments are a contra asset account, and are classified against unbilled contract receivables if revenue for the underlying contract is recorded using the cost-to-cost method, and against inventoried contract costs if revenue is recorded using the units-of-delivery method.

Inventoried Contract Costs. In accordance with contract accounting standards, the Company's U.S. Government contractor businesses account for the portion of their G&A, IRAD and B&P costs that are allowable and reimbursable indirect contract costs under U.S. Government procurement regulations on their U.S. Government contracts (revenue arrangements) as inventoried contract costs. G&A, IRAD and B&P costs are allocated to contracts for which the U.S. Government is the end customer and are charged to costs of sales when sales on the related contracts are recognized. The Company's U.S. Government contractor businesses record the unallowable portion of their G&A, IRAD and B&P costs to expense as incurred, and do not include them in inventoried contract costs.

The table below presents a summary of G&A, IRAD and B&P costs included in inventoried contract costs and the changes to them, including amounts charged to cost of sales by the Company's U.S. Government contractor businesses for the periods presented.

(in millions)	Year Ended December 31,		
	2013	2012	2011
Amounts included in inventoried contract costs at beginning of the year	$ 110	$ 91	$ 97
IRAD and B&P costs incurred	296	336	327
Other G&A costs incurred	893	891	843
Total contract costs incurred	1,189	1,227	1,170
Amounts charged to cost of sales	(1,161)	(1,208)	(1,176)
Amounts included in inventoried contract costs at end of the year	$ 138	$ 110	$ 91

Discontinued Operations

RECOGNITION AND MEASUREMENT

3.81 FASB ASC 205-20 sets forth the financial accounting and reporting requirements for discontinued operations of a component of an entity. A *component of an entity* comprises operations and cash flows that can be clearly distinguished, operationally and for financial reporting purposes, from the rest of the entity. A component of an entity may be a reportable or an operating segment, a reporting unit, a subsidiary, or an asset group.

3.82 FASB ASC 205-20 uses a single accounting model to account for all long-lived assets to be disposed of (by sale, abandonment, or distribution to owners). This includes asset disposal groups meeting the criteria for presentation as a discontinued operation, as specified in FASB ASC 205-20. A long-lived asset group classified as held for sale should be measured at the lower of its carrying amount or fair value less cost to sell. Additionally, in accordance with FASB ASC 360, a loss shall be recognized for any write-down to fair value less cost to sell. A gain shall be recognized for any subsequent recovery of cost. Lastly, a gain or loss not previously recognized that results from the sale of the asset disposal group should be recognized at the date of sale.

PRESENTATION

3.83 The conditions for determining whether discontinued operations treatment is appropriate and the required income statement presentation are stated in FASB ASC 205-20-45-1, as follows:

> The results of operations of a component of an entity that either has been disposed of or is classified as held for sale . . . [should] be reported in discontinued operations . . . if both of the following conditions are met:
> a. The operations and cash flows of the component have been (or will be) eliminated from the ongoing operations of the entity as a result of the disposal transaction.
> b. The entity will not have any significant continuing involvement in the operations of the component after the disposal transaction.

3.84 FASB ASC 205-20-45-3 explains that in a period in which a component of an entity either has been disposed of or is classified as held for sale, the income statement of a business entity or statement of activities of a not-for-profit entity for current and prior periods should report the results of operations of the component, including any gain or loss recognized from the sale or write-down, in discontinued operations. The results of operations of a component classified as held for sale should be reported in discontinued operations in the period(s) in which they occur. The results of discontinued operations, less applicable income taxes (benefit), should be reported as a separate component of income before extraordinary items (if applicable). For example, the results of discontinued operations may be reported in the income statement of a business entity as follows:

Income from continuing operations before income taxes	$XXXX	
Income taxes	XXX	
Income from continuing operations		$XXXX
Discontinued operations (Note X):		
Loss from operations of discontinued component X (including loss on disposal of $XXX)	$XXXX	
Income tax benefit	XXXX	
Loss on discontinued operations		XXXX
Net income		$XXXX

A gain or loss recognized on the disposal should be disclosed either on the face of the income statement or in the notes to the financial statements.

3.85 Illustrations of transactions that should and should not be accounted for as business segment disposals are presented in the implementation guidance and illustrations of FASB ASC 205-20-55.

PRESENTATION AND DISCLOSURE EXCERPTS

BUSINESS COMPONENT DISPOSALS

3.86 ALLEGHENY TECHNOLOGIES INCORPORATED (DEC)
CONSOLIDATED STATEMENTS OF INCOME

(In millions, except per share amounts)

For the Years Ended December 31,	2013	2012	2011
Sales	$4,043.5	$4,666.9	$4,812.3
Costs and expenses:			
Cost of sales	3,790.9	4,041.4	4,075.5
Selling and administrative expenses	276.4	321.6	323.0
Restructuring costs	67.5	—	—
Income (loss) before interest, other income and income taxes	(91.3)	303.9	413.8
Interest expense, net	(65.2)	(71.6)	(92.3)
Other income, net	1.7	—	0.6
Income (loss) from continuing operations before income taxes	(154.8)	232.3	322.1
Income tax provision (benefit)	(63.6)	72.4	110.4
Income (loss) from continuing operations	(91.2)	159.9	211.7
Income from discontinued operations, net of tax	252.8	7.9	11.4
Net income	161.6	167.8	223.1
Less: Net income attributable to noncontrolling interests	7.6	9.4	8.8
Net income attributable to ATI	$ 154.0	$ 158.4	$ 214.3
Basic Net Income (Loss) Per Common Share			
Continuing operations attributable to ATI per common share	$(0.93)	$1.42	$1.98
Discontinued operations attributable to ATI per common share	2.37	0.07	0.11
Basic net income attributable to ATI per common share	$ 1.44	$ 1.49	$ 2.09
Diluted Net Income (Loss) Per Common Share			
Continuing operations attributable to ATI per common share	$ (0.93)	$ 1.36	$ 1.87
Discontinued operations attributable to ATI per common share	2.37	0.07	0.10
Diluted net income attributable to ATI per common share	$ 1.44	$ 1.43	$ 1.97
Amounts Attributable to ATI Common Stockholders			
Income (loss) from continuing operations, net of tax	$ (98.8)	$ 150.5	$ 202.9
Income from discontinued operations, net of tax	252.8	7.9	11.4
Net income	$ 154.0	$ 158.4	$ 214.3

NOTES TO CONSOLIDATED FINANCIAL STATEMENTS

Note 2. Discontinued Operations

On November 4, 2013, the Company completed the sale of its tungsten materials business, which produces tungsten powder, tungsten heavy alloys, tungsten carbide materials, and carbide cutting tools. The Company received cash proceeds, net of transaction costs, of $600.9 million on the sale of this business and recognized a $428.3 million pre-tax ($261.4 million after tax) gain which has been recorded in discontinued operations.

Also, during the third quarter of 2013, the Company completed a strategic review of its iron castings and fabricated components businesses. Based on current and forecasted results, these businesses were not projected to meet the Company's long-term profitable growth and return on capital employed expectations. As a result of this review, the Company closed its fabricated components business and recorded $8.1 million of pre-tax exit costs, including $7.3 million of non-cash impairment charges for long-lived assets, and $0.8 million primarily related to lease exit costs. The Company expects the cash requirements associated with lease-related exit costs to be approximately $4 million, to be incurred over the next four years. The planned divestiture of the iron castings business, which is held for sale at December 31, 2013, resulted in a $11.3 million pre-tax, non-cash long-lived asset impairment charge based on an analysis of the estimated fair value of the business, which represents Level 3 unobservable information in the fair value hierarchy.

The tungsten materials, iron castings and fabricated components businesses were all previously reported as part of the Company's former Engineered Products segment. The net assets of the iron castings and fabricated components businesses were classified as held for sale as of the end of fiscal year 2013 and the operating results of all three of these businesses have been included in discontinued operations in the Company's consolidated statements of income for all periods presented. Results of discontinued operations for 2013 include $19.5 million pre-tax ($11.9 million after-tax) of charges associated with the iron castings and fabricated components divestitures. Results of discontinued operations for 2012 include a $13.0 million pre-tax ($8.8 million after-tax) charge to write down the value of the long-lived assets with the closing of the Alpena, MI iron casting facility.

The following table presents summarized results for these discontinued operations (in millions):

	2013	2012	2011
Sales	$268.2	$364.6	$370.7
Income before income tax provision	$414.2	$ 11.7	$ 17.3

Net assets of discontinued operations were $4.2 million at December 31, 2013 and consisted of the following items (in millions):

	2013
Accounts receivable, net of allowances for doubtful accounts	$2.9
Inventories, net	3.1
Prepaid expenses and other current assets	0.1
Property, plant and equipment, net	3.7
Total Assets	9.8
Accounts payable	1.8
Accrued liabilities	3.1
Long-term liabilities	0.7
Total Liabilities	5.6
Net Assets	$4.2

SEPARATION OF BUSINESS

3.87 VALERO ENERGY CORPORATION (DEC)
NOTES TO CONSOLIDATED FINANCIAL STATEMENTS

3. Dispositions Of Businesses (in part)

Separation of Retail Business

On May 1, 2013, we completed the separation of our retail business by creating an independent public company named CST Brands, Inc. (CST) and distributing 80 percent of the outstanding shares of CST common stock to our stockholders. Each Valero stockholder received one share of CST common stock for every nine shares of Valero common stock held at the close of business on the record date of April 19, 2013. Fractional shares of CST common stock were not distributed, but instead were aggregated and sold in the open market at prevailing rates with net cash proceeds then distributed pro rata to each Valero stockholder who was entitled to receive fractional shares.

In connection with the separation, we received an aggregate of $1.05 billion in cash, consisting of $550 million from the issuance of short-term debt to a third-party financial institution on April 16, 2013 and $500 million distributed to us by CST on May 1, 2013. The cash distributed to us by CST was borrowed by CST on May 1, 2013 under its senior secured credit facility. See Note 11 for further discussion of that credit facility. Also on May 1, 2013, CST issued $550 million of its senior unsecured bonds to us, and we exchanged those bonds with the third-party financial institution in satisfaction of our short-term debt. Immediately prior to May 1, 2013, subsidiaries of CST held $315 million of cash, and CST retained that cash following the distribution on May 1, 2013. Also in connection with the separation, we incurred a tax liability of approximately $189 million primarily related to the manner in which the transaction is treated for tax purposes in Canada; the majority of this liability was paid during 2013 and the remaining amounts will be paid in the first quarter of 2014. Therefore, the cash we received as a result of the separation, net of our tax liability, was $546 million. We also incurred $30 million in costs during the three months ended June 30, 2013 to effect the separation, which are included in general and administrative expenses.

We also entered into long-term motor fuel supply agreements with CST in the U.S. and Canada. The nature and significance of our agreements to supply motor fuel to CST through 2028 represents a continuation of activities with CST for accounting purposes. As such, the historical results of operations of our retail business have not been reported as discontinued operations in our statements of income.

On November 14, 2013, we disposed of our 20 percent retained interest in CST by transferring all remaining shares of CST common stock owned by us to a third-party financial institution in exchange for $467 million of our short-term debt and recognized a $325 million nontaxable gain, as further described in Note 11.

Selected historical results of operations of our retail business prior to the separation are disclosed in Note 18. Subsequent to May 1, 2013 and through November 14, 2013, our share of CST's results of operations is reflected in "other income, net." Our share of income taxes incurred directly by CST during this period is reported in the equity in earnings from CST, and as such is not included in income taxes in our statements of income.

The following table presents the carrying values of the major categories of assets and liabilities of our retail business, immediately preceding its separation on May 1, 2013, which are excluded from our consolidated balance sheet as of December 31, 2013 (in millions):

Assets	
Cash and temporary cash investments	$ 315
Credit card receivables from Valero	44
Other receivables, net	109
Inventories	170
Deferred income taxes	14
Prepaid expenses and other	13
Total current assets	665
Property, plant, and equipment, at cost	1,891
Accumulated depreciation	(611)
Property, plant, and equipment, net	1,280
Intangible assets, net	38
Deferred charges and other assets, net	191
Total assets	$2,174
Liabilities	
Current portion of capital lease obligations	$2
Trade payable to Valero	242
Other accounts payable	96
Accrued expenses	31
Taxes other than income taxes	20
Total current liabilities	391
Debt and capital lease obligations, less current portion	1,053
Deferred income taxes	83
Other long-term liabilities	112
Total liabilities	$1,639

We retained certain environmental and other liabilities related to our former retail business and we have indemnified CST for certain self-insurance liabilities related to its employees and property.

Extraordinary Items

RECOGNITION AND MEASUREMENT

3.88 FASB ASC 225-20 defines *extraordinary items* as events and transactions that are distinguished by their unusual nature and by the infrequency of their occurrence. Both of the following criteria should be met to classify an event or a transaction as an extraordinary item:

- *Unusual nature.* The underlying event or transaction should possess a high degree of abnormality and be of a type clearly unrelated to, or only incidentally related to, the ordinary and typical activities of the entity, taking into account the environment in which the entity operates.
- *Infrequency of occurrence.* The underlying event or transaction should be of a type that would not reasonably be expected to recur in the foreseeable future, taking into account the environment in which the entity operates.

PRESENTATION

3.89 FASB ASC 225-20 also addresses the presentation and disclosure of unusual and infrequently occurring items that do not meet the extraordinary criteria. Such items are reported as a separate component of continuing operations either on the face of the income statement or in the notes. FASB ASC 225-20-55 illustrates events and transactions that should and should not be classified as extraordinary items.

PRESENTATION AND DISCLOSURE EXCERPTS

EXTRAORDINARY ITEMS

3.90 HUNTSMAN CORPORATION (DEC)
CONSOLIDATED STATEMENTS OF OPERATIONS

(In Millions, Except Per Share Amounts)

	Year Ended December 31,		
	2013	2012	2011
Revenues:			
Trade sales, services and fees, net	$10,847	$10,964	$11,041
Related party sales	232	223	180
Total revenues	11,079	11,187	11,221
Cost of goods sold	9,326	9,153	9,381
Gross profit	1,753	2,034	1,840
Operating Expenses:			
Selling, general and administrative	942	951	921
Research and development	140	152	166
Other operating expense (income)	10	(6)	(20)
Restructuring, impairment and plant closing costs	151	92	167
Total expenses	1,243	1,189	1,234
Operating income	510	845	606
Interest expense, net	(190)	(226)	(249)
Equity in income of investment in unconsolidated affiliates	8	7	8
Loss on early extinguishment of debt	(51)	(80)	(7)
Other income	2	1	2
Income from continuing operations before income taxes	279	547	360
Income tax expense	(125)	(169)	(109)
Income from continuing operations	154	378	251
Loss from discontinued operations	(5)	(7)	(1)
Income before extraordinary gain	149	371	250
Extraordinary gain on the acquisition of a business, net of tax of nil	—	2	4
Net income	149	373	254
Net income attributable to noncontrolling interests	(21)	(10)	(7)
Net income attributable to Huntsman Corporation	$ 128	$ 363	$ 247

	Year Ended December 31,		
	2013	2012	2011
Basic Income (Loss) Per Share:			
Income from continuing operations attributable to Huntsman Corporation common stockholders	$ 0.55	$ 1.55	$ 1.03
Loss from discontinued operations attributable to Huntsman Corporation common stockholders, net of tax	(0.02)	(0.03)	—
Extraordinary gain on the acquisition of a business attributable to Huntsman Corporation common stockholders, net of tax	—	0.01	0.01
Net income attributable to Huntsman Corporation common stockholders	$ 0.53	$ 1.53	$ 1.04
Weighted average shares	239.7	237.6	237.6
Diluted Income (Loss) Per Share:			
Income from continuing operations attributable to Huntsman Corporation common stockholders	$ 0.55	$ 1.53	$ 1.01
Loss from discontinued operations attributable to Huntsman Corporation common stockholders, net of tax	(0.02)	(0.03)	—
Extraordinary gain on the acquisition of a business attributable to Huntsman Corporation common stockholders, net of tax	—	0.01	0.01
Net income attributable to Huntsman Corporation common stockholders	$ 0.53	$ 1.51	$ 1.02
Weighted average shares	242.4	240.6	241.7
Amounts Attributable to Huntsman Corporation Common Stockholders:			
Income from continuing operations	$133	$368	$244
Loss from discontinued operations, net of tax	(5)	(7)	(1)
Extraordinary gain on the acquisition of a business, net of tax	—	2	4
Net income	$ 128	$ 363	$ 247
Dividends per share	$ 0.50	$ 0.40	$ 0.40

3. Business Combinations and Dispositions (in part)

Textile Effects Acquisition

On June 30, 2006, we acquired Ciba's textile effects business and accounted for the Textile Effects Acquisition using the purchase method. As such, we analyzed the fair value of tangible and intangible assets acquired and liabilities assumed and determined the excess of fair value of net assets over cost. Because the fair value of the acquired assets and liabilities assumed exceeded the purchase price, the value of the long-lived assets acquired was reduced to zero. Accordingly, no basis was assigned to property, plant and equipment or any other non-current nonfinancial assets and the remaining excess was recorded as an extraordinary gain. During 2012 and 2011, we recorded an additional extraordinary gain on the acquisition of $2 million and $4 million, respectively, related to settlement of contingent purchase price consideration, the reversal of accruals for certain restructuring and employee termination costs recorded in connection with the Textile Effects Acquisition and a reimbursement by Ciba of certain costs pursuant to the acquisition agreements.

UNUSUAL ITEMS

3.91 GENCORP INC. (NOV)
NOTES TO CONSOLIDATED FINANCIAL STATEMENTS

Note 11. Operating Segments and Related Disclosures

The Company's operations are organized into two operating segments based on different products and customer bases: Aerospace and Defense, and Real Estate. The accounting policies of the operating segments are the same as those described in the summary of significant accounting policies (see Note 1).

The Company evaluates its operating segments based on several factors, of which the primary financial measure is segment performance. Segment performance represents net sales from continuing operations less applicable costs, expenses and provisions for unusual items relating to the segment operations. Segment performance excludes corporate income and expenses, legacy income or expenses, provisions for unusual items not related to the segment operations, interest expense, interest income, and income taxes.

Selected financial information for each reportable segment was as follows:

(In millions)	Year Ended		
	2013	**2012**	**2011**
Net Sales:			
Aerospace and Defense	$1,377.4	$986.1	$909.7
Real Estate	5.7	8.8	8.4
Total	$1,383.1	$994.9	$918.1
Segment Performance:			
Aerospace and Defense	$ 147.6	$115.5	$108.6
Environmental remediation provision adjustments	(4.6)	(11.4)	(8.9)
Retirement benefit plan expense	(44.2)	(18.9)	(21.0)
Unusual items (see Note 15)	(1.6)	(0.7)	(4.1)
Aerospace and Defense Total	97.2	84.5	74.6
Real Estate	3.8	3.7	5.6
Total	$ 101.0	$ 88.2	$ 80.2
Reconciliation of Segment Performance to (Loss) Income from Continuing Operations Before Income Taxes:			
Segment Performance	$ 101.0	$ 88.2	$ 80.2
Interest expense	(48.7)	(22.3)	(30.8)
Interest income	0.2	0.6	1.0
Stock-based compensation	(14.1)	(6.5)	(3.7)
Corporate retirement benefit plan expense	(20.8)	(22.1)	(25.4)
Corporate and other expenses	(20.9)	(12.7)	(10.8)
Corporate unusual items (see Note 15)	(22.9)	(12.0)	(1.5)
(Loss) income from continuing operations before income taxes	$ (26.2)	$ 13.2	$ 9.0
Aerospace and Defense	$ 63.2	$ 37.2	$ 21.1
Real Estate	—	—	—
Corporate	—	—	—
Capital Expenditures	$ 63.2	$ 37.2	$ 21.1
Aerospace and Defense	$ 43.1	$ 21.7	$ 24.3
Real Estate	0.7	0.6	0.3
Corporate	—	—	—
Depreciation and Amortization	$ 43.8	$ 22.3	$ 24.6

(In millions)	As of November 30,	
	2013	**2012**
Aerospace and Defense[1]	$1,349.1	$637.6
Real Estate	109.3	82.3
Identifiable assets	1,458.4	719.9
Corporate	296.9	199.4
Assets	$1,755.3	$919.3

[1] The Aerospace and Defense operating segment had $159.6 million and $94.9 million of goodwill as of November 30, 2013 and 2012, respectively. In addition, as of November 30, 2013 and 2012 intangible assets balances were $135.7 million and $13.9 million, respectively, for the Aerospace and Defense operating segment.

The Company's continuing operations are located in the United States. Inter-area sales are not significant to the total sales of any geographic area. Unusual items included in segment performance pertained only to the United States.

Note 14. Assets Held for Sale

As of November 30, 2012, the Company classified its LDACS program as assets held for sale, as at that time the Company expected that it would be required to divest the LDACS product line in order to consummate the Acquisition. For operating segment reporting, the LDACS program has been reported as a part of the Aerospace and Defense segment. The components of assets and liabilities held for sale in the consolidated balance sheet as of November 30, 2012 were as follows:

Accounts receivable	$3.5
Equipment	0.1
Estimated costs to divest	(3.6)
Assets held for sale	$—
Accounts payable	$0.1
Other liabilities	1.0
Liabilities held for sale	$1.1

As of May 31, 2013, the Company believed that it would not be required to divest the LDACS product line in order to consummate the Acquisition based on conversations with the FTC. On June 10, 2013, the FTC announced that it closed its investigation into the Acquisition under the Hart-Scott-Rodino Antitrust Improvements Act of 1976, as amended, and the Company was not required to divest its LDACS business. The Company expensed $3.6 million, recorded as part of unusual items, in fiscal 2012 for the estimated costs to divest the LDACS program. The Company recorded a benefit of $3.6 million, as part of unusual items, in the second quarter of fiscal 2013 as the Company believed that the FTC would not require the divestiture of the LDACS program.

Note 15. Unusual Items

Total unusual items expense, a component of other expense, net in the consolidated statements of operations was as follows:

(In millions)	Year Ended		
	2013	**2012**	**2011**
Aerospace and Defense:			
(Gain) loss on legal matters and settlements	$(1.0)	$0.7	$4.1
Rocketdyne Business acquisition related costs	2.6	—	—
Aerospace and defense unusual items	1.6	0.7	4.1
Corporate:			
Rocketdyne Business acquisition related costs	17.4	11.6	—
Loss on debt repurchased	5.0	0.4	0.2
Loss on legal settlement	0.5		
Loss on bank amendment	—	—	1.3
Corporate unusual items	22.9	12.0	1.5
Total unusual items	$24.5	$12.7	$5.6

Fiscal 2013 Activity:

The Company recorded a charge of $0.5 million related to a legal settlement.

The Company recorded ($1.0) million for gains and interest associated with the failure to register with the SEC the issuance of certain of the Company's common shares under the defined contribution 401(k) employee benefit plan.

The Company incurred expenses of $20.0 million, including internal labor costs of $1.4 million, related to the Rocketdyne Business acquisition.

A summary of the Company's losses on the 4 1 / 16% Debentures repurchased during fiscal 2013 is as follows (in millions):

Principal amount repurchased	$ 5.2
Cash repurchase price	(10.1)
Write-off of the deferred financing costs	(0.1)
Loss on 4 1 / 16% Debentures repurchased	$ (5.0)

Fiscal 2012 Activity:

The Company recorded $0.7 million for losses and interest associated with the failure to register with the SEC the issuance of certain of the Company's common shares under the defined contribution 401(k) employee benefit plan.

The Company incurred expenses of $11.6 million, including internal labor costs of $2.0 million, related to the Rocketdyne Business acquisition announced in July 2012.

The Company redeemed $75.0 million of its 9 1 / 2% Notes at a redemption price of 100% of the principal amount. The redemption resulted in a charge of $0.4 million associated with the write-off of the 9 1 / 2% Notes deferred financing costs.

Fiscal 2011 Activity:

The Company recorded a charge of $3.3 million related to a legal settlement and $0.8 million for losses and interest associated with the failure to register with the SEC the issuance of certain of its common shares under the defined contribution 401(k) employee benefit plan.

During fiscal 2011, the Company repurchased $22.0 million principal amount of its 2 1 / 4% Debentures at various prices ranging from 99.0% of par to 99.6% of par resulting in a loss of $0.2 million.

In addition, during fiscal 2011, the Company recorded $1.3 million of losses related to an amendment to the Senior Credit Facility.

3.92 BEAM INC. (DEC)
NOTES TO CONSOLIDATED FINANCIAL STATEMENTS

23. Quarterly Financial Data (Unaudited)

Selected quarterly financial data for the years ended December 31, 2013 and 2012 are as follows (in millions, except per share data):

	2013			
	First Quarter [a][g]	Second Quarter [b]	Third Quarter [c]	Fourth Quarter [d]
Net sales	$571.5	$637.6	$598.7	$739.5
Gross profit	347.3	374.1	343.4	414.6
Income from continuing operations	114.4	74.6	84.9	91.6
(Loss) income from discontinued operations	(1.3)	(0.3)	(0.1)	(1.3)
Net income	113.1	74.3	84.8	90.3
Basic earnings (loss) per Beam Inc. common share				
Continuing operations	$ 0.71	$ 0.46	$ 0.52	$ 0.56
Discontinued operations	(0.01)	—	—	(0.01)
Net income	$ 0.70	$ 0.46	$ 0.52	$ 0.55
Diluted earnings (loss) per Beam Inc. common share				
Continuing operations	$ 0.71	$ 0.46	$ 0.52	$ 0.56
Discontinued operations	(0.01)	—	—	(0.01)
Net income	$ 0.70	$ 0.46	$ 0.52	$ 0.55

(continued)

	2012			
	First Quarter [(g)]	Second Quarter [(e)]	Third Quarter	Fourth Quarter [(f)(g)]
Net sales	$526.8	$597.0	$626.7	$709.2
Gross profit	312.0	347.6	371.0	405.4
Income from continuing operations	76.3	101.9	98.4	126.8
Income (loss) from discontinued operations	0.7	(0.8)	(2.2)	(15.9)
Net income	77.0	101.1	96.2	110.9
Basic earnings (loss) per Beam Inc. common share				
Continuing operations	$ 0.49	$ 0.64	$ 0.62	$ 0.80
Discontinued operations	—	(0.01)	(0.01)	(0.10)
Net income	$ 0.49	$ 0.63	$ 0.61	$ 0.70
Diluted earnings (loss) per Beam Inc. common share				
Continuing operations	$ 0.48	$ 0.63	$ 0.61	$ 0.79
Discontinued operations	—	(0.01)	(0.01)	(0.10)
Net income	$ 0.48	$ 0.62	$ 0.60	$ 0.69

[(a)] Unusual items impacting the quarter ended March 31, 2013 include: a $12.8 million (pre-tax) gain on sale of brands and related assets mostly related to the sale of certain non-strategic, economy brands and related inventory in January 2013 and a $5.9 million income tax benefit related to our decision to participate in a tax amnesty program resulting in adjustment to uncertain tax positions.

[(b)] Unusual items impacting the quarter ended June 30, 2013 include a $43.1 million pre-tax loss on early extinguishment of debt related to a tender offer (Note 13).

[(c)] Unusual items impacting the quarter ended September 30, 2013 include (on a pre-tax basis): a $13.8 million loss on early extinguishment of debt related to our redemption of outstanding senior notes, a $12.2 million decrease in the fair value of estimated contingent consideration for our Skinnygirl ready-to-serve cocktail business based on revised estimated sales levels, and $11.2 million of charges primarily related to an organizational restructuring plan to improve efficiency and effectiveness across the organization.

[(d)] Unusual items impacting the quarter ended December 31, 2013 include: $49.5 million (pre-tax) non-cash impairment of the DYC trade name, tax expense of $9.7 million in connection with a foreign tax law enacted during the quarter, and a $7.8 million benefit arising from the resolution of certain foreign income tax return matters.

[(e)] Unusual items impacting the quarter ended June 30, 2012 include: $18.0 million (pre-tax) tax indemnification income related to the resolution of routine foreign tax audits, $13.8 million (pre-tax) for business separation costs, $12.1 million (pre-tax) for acquisition and integration-related charges incurred in connection with the May 2012 acquisition of the Pinnacle assets, and a $5.8 million income tax benefit related to the favorable resolution of foreign tax audit examinations.

[(f)] Unusual items impacting the quarter ended December 31, 2012 include: $22 million of excess net foreign tax credits related to U.S. taxes applicable to repatriation of 2012 foreign earnings, a $9 million net tax benefit related to the resolution of certain foreign and U.S. federal tax audits, and $15.6 million (pre-tax) non-cash impairment of the Larios trade name.

[(g)] As discussed in Note 1, during the second quarter of 2013 and in 2012 the Company identified errors impacting prior interim periods. The following are the impacts of these revisions to quarterly financial statements that have not yet been reflected in Quarterly Reports on Form 10-Q previously filed with the SEC:

- For the three months ended March 31, 2013, the correction of these errors resulted in a decrease to net sales, gross profit and income from continuing operations before taxes of $6.2 million, $1.8 million, and $1.8 million, respectively. The impact of these error corrections was a decrease of $0.01 in earnings per share.
- For the three months ended March 31, 2012, the correction of these errors resulted in a decrease to net sales, gross profit and income from continuing operations before taxes of $7.0 million, $2.7 million, and $2.7 million, respectively. The impact of these error corrections was a decrease of $0.01 in earnings per share.
- For the three months ended December 31, 2012, the correction of errors related to continuing operations resulted in a $0.1 million increase to net sales and gross profit and a $0.01 increase in basic earnings per share from continuing operations. In addition, the correction of errors related to discontinued operations resulted in a $15.4 million increase in loss from discontinued operations (net of tax) ($0.10 per share). The discontinued operations revision relates to pre-fourth quarter 2012 errors that were identified and corrected in the fourth quarter of 2012. As previously disclosed (refer to 2012 10-K), these errors related to our discontinued Golf business (primarily relating to the 2011 tax return filing process). The combined impact of the corrections was a decrease to net income of $15.4 million ($0.09 and $0.10 per basic and diluted share, respectively).

Earnings Per Share

PRESENTATION

3.93 The computation, presentation, and disclosure requirements for earnings per share (EPS) for entities with publicly held common stock or potential common stock are stated in FASB ASC 260, *Earnings Per Share*. The objective of basic EPS is to measure the performance of an entity over the reporting period. The objective of diluted EPS, which is consistent with that of basic EPS, is to measure the performance of an entity over the reporting period, while giving effect to all dilutive potential common shares that were outstanding during the period. FASB ASC 260 also discusses the application of EPS guidance to master limited partnerships.

PRESENTATION AND DISCLOSURE EXCERPTS

EARNINGS PER SHARE

3.94 RAYTHEON COMPANY (DEC)

CONSOLIDATED STATEMENTS OF OPERATIONS

(In millions, except per share amounts) Years Ended December 31:	2013	2012	2011
Net sales			
Products	$19,855	$20,380	$20,725
Services	3,851	4,034	4,066
Total net sales	23,706	24,414	24,791
Operating expenses			
Cost of sales—products	15,292	15,712	16,245
Cost of sales—services	3,240	3,380	3,419
General and administrative expenses	2,236	2,333	2,297
Total operating expenses	20,768	21,425	21,961
Operating income	2,938	2,989	2,830
Non-operating (income) expense, net			
Interest expense	210	201	172
Interest income	(12)	(9)	(14)
Other (income) expense, net	(17)	18	12
Total non-operating (income) expense, net	181	210	170
Income from continuing operations before taxes	2,757	2,779	2,660
Federal and foreign income taxes	808	878	782
Income from continuing operations	1,949	1,901	1,878
Income (loss) from discontinued operations, net of tax	64	(1)	18
Net income	2,013	1,900	1,896
Less: Net income attributable to noncontrolling interests in subsidiaries	17	12	30
Net income attributable to Raytheon Company	$ 1,996	$ 1,888	$ 1,866
Basic earnings per share attributable to Raytheon Company common stockholders:			
Income from continuing operations	$ 5.97	$ 5.67	$ 5.25
Income (loss) from discontinued operations, net of tax	0.20	—	0.05
Net income	6.17	5.67	5.30
Diluted earnings per share attributable to Raytheon Company common stockholders:			
Income from continuing operations	$ 5.96	$ 5.65	$ 5.22
Income (loss) from discontinued operations, net of tax	0.20	—	0.05
Net income	6.16	5.65	5.28
Amounts attributable to Raytheon Company common stockholders:			
Income from continuing operations	$ 1,932	$ 1,889	$ 1,848
Income (loss) from discontinued operations, net of tax	64	(1)	18
Net income	$ 1,996	$ 1,888	$ 1,866

NOTES TO CONSOLIDATED FINANCIAL STATEMENTS

Note 1: Summary of Significant Accounting Policies (in part)

Earnings per Share (EPS)— We compute basic EPS attributable to Raytheon Company common stockholders by dividing income from continuing operations attributable to Raytheon Company common stockholders, income (loss) from discontinued operations attributable to Raytheon Company common stockholders, and net income attributable to Raytheon Company, by our weighted-average common shares outstanding, including participating securities outstanding, as described below, during the period. Diluted EPS reflects the potential dilution beyond shares for basic EPS that could occur if securities or other contracts to issue common stock were exercised, converted into common stock, or resulted in the issuance of common stock that would have shared in our earnings. We compute basic and diluted EPS using actual income from continuing operations attributable to Raytheon Company common stockholders, income (loss) from discontinued operations attributable to Raytheon Company common stockholders, net income attributable to Raytheon Company, and our actual weighted-average shares and participating securities outstanding rather than the numbers presented within our consolidated financial statements, which are rounded to the nearest million. As a result, it may not be possible to recalculate EPS as presented in our consolidated financial statements. Furthermore, it may not be possible to recalculate EPS attributable to Raytheon Company common stockholders by adjusting EPS from continuing operations by EPS from discontinued operations.

We include all unvested stock awards that contain non-forfeitable rights to dividends or dividend equivalents, whether paid or unpaid, in the number of shares outstanding in our basic and diluted EPS calculations. As a result, we have included all of our outstanding unvested restricted stock and Long-Term Performance Plan (LTPP) awards that meet the retirement eligible criteria in our calculation of basic and diluted EPS. We disclose EPS for common stock and unvested share-based payment awards, and separately disclose distributed and undistributed earnings. Distributed earnings represent common stock dividends and dividends earned on unvested share-based payment awards of retirement eligible employees. Undistributed earnings represent earnings that were available for distribution but were not distributed. Common stock and unvested share-based payment awards earn dividends equally.

Note 11: Stockholders' Equity (in part)

Earnings Per Share (EPS)

EPS from continuing operations attributable to Raytheon Company common stockholders and unvested share-based payment awards was as follows:

	2013	2012	2011
Basic EPS attributable to Raytheon Company common stockholders:			
Distributed earnings	$2.19	$1.98	$1.71
Undistributed earnings	3.78	3.69	3.54
Total	$5.97	$5.67	$5.25
Diluted EPS attributable to Raytheon Company common stockholders:			
Distributed earnings	$2.18	$1.98	$1.70
Undistributed earnings	3.78	3.67	3.52
Total	$5.96	$5.65	$5.22

Basic and diluted EPS from discontinued operations attributable to Raytheon Company common stockholders and unvested share-based payment awards were earnings of $0.20, a loss of less than of $0.01 and earnings of $0.05 for 2013, 2012 and 2011, respectively.

Income attributable to participating securities was as follows:

(In millions)	2013	2012	2011
Income from continuing operations attributable to participating securities	$38	$36	$31
Income (loss) from discontinued operations, net of tax attributable to participating securities[1]	1	—	—
Net income attributable to participating securities	$39	$36	$31

[1] Income (loss) from discontinued operations, net of tax attributable to participating securities was a loss of less than $1 million for 2012 and income of less than $1 million for 2011.

The weighted-average shares outstanding for basic and diluted EPS were as follows:

(In millions)	2013	2012	2011
Shares for basic EPS (including 6.4 participating securities for 2013, 6.3 for 2012, and 5.8 for 2011)	323.4	333.2	351.7
Dilutive effect of stock options and LTPP	0.8	1.0	1.4
Dilutive effect of warrants	—	—	0.5
Shares for diluted EPS	324.2	334.2	353.6

There were no stock options with exercise prices greater than the average market price (anti-dilutive) that were excluded from our calculation of diluted EPS in 2013, 2012 and 2011. Stock options to purchase the following number of shares of common stock had exercise prices that were less than the average market price (dilutive) of our common stock and were included in our calculations of diluted EPS:

(In millions)	2013	2012	2011
Stock options included in the calculation of EPS (dilutive)	0.1	0.9	4.4

Our Board of Directors is authorized to issue up to 200 million shares of preferred stock, $0.01 par value per share, in multiple series with terms as determined by them. There were no shares of preferred stock outstanding at December 31, 2013 and December 31, 2012.

Warrants to purchase shares of our common stock with an exercise price of $37.50 per share, were included in our calculations of diluted EPS at December 31, 2011. These warrants expired in June 2011.

CONSOLIDATED STATEMENTS OF OPERATIONS

(Dollars in millions, except per share data)	Year Ended December 31,		
	2013	**2012**	**2011**
Revenues			
Sales	$6,380.0	$7,041.7	$7,013.0
Other revenues	633.7	1,035.8	882.9
Total revenues	7,013.7	8,077.5	7,895.9
Costs and Expenses			
Operating costs and expenses (exclusive of items shown separately below)	5,736.1	5,932.7	5,477.6
Depreciation, depletion and amortization	740.3	663.4	474.3
Asset retirement obligation expenses	66.5	67.0	52.6
Selling and administrative expenses	249.1	268.8	268.2
Acquisition costs related to Macarthur Coal Limited	—	—	85.2
Other operating (income) loss:			
Net gain on disposal or exchange of assets	(52.6)	(17.1)	(76.9)
Asset impairment and mine closure costs	528.3	929.0	—
Settlement charges related to the Patriot bankruptcy reorganization	30.6	—	—
Loss from equity affiliates	40.2	61.2	19.2
Operating (loss) profit	(324.8)	172.5	1,595.7
Interest expense	425.2	405.6	238.6
Interest income	(15.7)	(24.5)	(18.9)
(Loss) income from continuing operations before income taxes	(734.3)	(208.6)	1,376.0
Income tax (benefit) provision	(448.3)	262.3	363.2
(Loss) income from continuing operations, net of income taxes	(286.0)	(470.9)	1,012.8
Loss from discontinued operations, net of income taxes	(226.6)	(104.2)	(66.5)
Net (loss) income	(512.6)	(575.1)	946.3
Less: Net income (loss) attributable to noncontrolling interests	12.3	10.6	(11.4)
Net (loss) income attributable to common stockholders	$ (524.9)	$ (585.7)	$ 957.7
(Loss) Income from Continuing Operations			
Basic (loss) earnings per share	$ (1.12)	$ (1.80)	$ 3.78
Diluted (loss) earnings per share	$ (1.12)	$ (1.80)	$ 3.77
Net (loss) income attributable to common stockholders			
Basic (loss) earnings per share	$ (1.97)	$ (2.19)	$ 3.53
Diluted (loss) earnings per share	$ (1.97)	$ (2.19)	$ 3.52
Dividends declared per share	$ 0.34	$ 0.34	$ 0.34

NOTES TO CONSOLIDATED FINANCIAL STATEMENTS

(21) Earnings per Share (EPS)

Basic and diluted EPS are computed using the two-class method, which is an earnings allocation that determines EPS for each class of common stock and participating securities according to dividends declared and participation rights in undistributed earnings. The Company's restricted stock awards are considered participating securities because holders are entitled to receive non-forfeitable dividends during the vesting term. Diluted EPS includes securities that could potentially dilute basic EPS during a reporting period, for which the Company includes share-based compensation awards and the Debentures. Dilutive securities are not included in the computation of loss per share when the Company reports a net loss from continuing operations as the impact would be anti-dilutive.

For all but the performance units, the potentially dilutive impact of the Company's share-based compensation awards is determined using the treasury stock method. Under the treasury stock method, awards are treated as if they had been exercised, with any proceeds used to repurchase common stock at the average market price during the period. Any incremental difference between the assumed number of shares issued and purchased is included in the diluted share computation. For the Company's performance units, their contingent features result in an assessment for any potentially dilutive common stock by using the end of the reporting period as if it were the end of the contingency period for all units granted. For further discussion of the Company's share-based compensation awards, see Note 18. "Share-Based Compensation."

A conversion of the Debentures may result in payment for any conversion value in excess of the principal amount of the Debentures in the Company's common stock. For diluted EPS purposes, potential common stock is calculated based on whether the market price of the Company's common stock at the end of each reporting period is in excess of the conversion price of the Debentures. For a full discussion of the conditions under which the Debentures may be converted, the conversion rate to common stock and the conversion price, see Note 12. "Long-term Debt." The effect of the Debentures was excluded from the calculation of diluted EPS for all periods presented because to do so would have been anti-dilutive for those periods.

The computation of diluted EPS also excluded aggregate stock options and restricted stock awards of approximately 2.3 million, 1.2 million and 0.1 million for the years ended December 31, 2013, 2012 and 2011, respectively, because to do so would have been anti-dilutive for those periods. The potential dilutive impact of such share-based compensation awards is calculated under the treasury stock method. Anti-dilution generally occurs when the exercise prices or unrecognized compensation costs per share of such awards are higher than the Company's average stock price during the applicable period.

The following illustrates the earnings allocation method utilized in the calculation of basic and diluted EPS:

(In millions, except per share amounts)	Year Ended December 31,		
	2013	2012	2011
EPS numerator:			
(Loss) income from continuing operations, net of income taxes	$(286.0)	$(470.9)	$1,012.8
Less: Net income (loss) attributable to noncontrolling interests	12.3	10.6	(11.4)
(Loss) income from continuing operations attributable to common stockholders before allocation of earnings to participating securities	(298.3)	(481.5)	1,024.2
Less: Earnings allocated to participating securities	0.8	0.7	5.3
(Loss) income from continuing operations attributable to common stockholders, after earnings allocated to participating securities[1]	(299.1)	(482.2)	1,018.9
Loss from discontinued operations, net of income taxes	(226.6)	(104.2)	(66.5)
Less: Loss from discontinued operations allocated to participating securities	—	—	(0.4)
Loss from discontinued operations attributable to common stockholders, after allocation of earnings to participating securities[1]	$(226.6)	$(104.2)	$ (66.1)
Net (loss) income attributable to common stockholders, after earnings allocated to participating securities[1]	$(525.7)	$(586.4)	$ 952.8
EPS denominator:			
Weighted average shares outstanding—basic	267.1	268.0	269.1
Impact of dilutive securities	—	—	1.2
Weighted average shares outstanding—diluted	267.1	268.0	270.3
Basic EPS attributable to common stockholders:			
(Loss) income from continuing operations	$ (1.12)	$ (1.80)	$ 3.78
Loss from discontinued operations	(0.85)	(0.39)	(0.25)
Net (loss) income attributable to common stockholders	$ (1.97)	$ (2.19)	$ 3.53
Diluted EPS attributable to common stockholders:			
(Loss) income from continuing operations	$ (1.12)	$ (1.80)	$ 3.77
Loss from discontinued operations	(0.85)	(0.39)	(0.25)
Net (loss) income attributable to common stockholders	$ (1.97)	$ (2.19)	$ 3.52

[1] The reallocation adjustment for participating securities to arrive at the numerator used to calculate diluted EPS was less than $0.1 million for the periods presented.

Comprehensive Income in Annual Filings

RECOGNITION AND MEASUREMENT

4.01 Financial Accounting Standards Board (FASB) *Accounting Standards Codification* (ASC) 220, *Comprehensive Income*, requires that items included in other comprehensive income should be classified based on their nature. Other comprehensive income includes the following: foreign currency items, changes in the fair value of certain derivatives, unrealized gains and losses on certain securities, and certain pension or other postretirement benefit items.

PRESENTATION

4.02 FASB ASC 220 requires entities that provide a full set of general-purpose financial statements (that is, financial position, results of operations, and cash flows) to report comprehensive income and its components either in a single continuous financial statement or in two separate but consecutive financial statements. The FASB ASC glossary defines *comprehensive income* as the change in equity (net assets) of a business entity during a period from transactions and other events and circumstances from nonowner sources. It includes all changes in equity during a period except those resulting from investments by owners and distributions to owners. *Other comprehensive income* is defined as revenues, expenses, gains, and losses that under generally accepted accounting principles are included in comprehensive income but excluded from net income. If an entity has only net income, it is not required to report comprehensive income. All items that meet the definition of components of comprehensive income must be reported in a financial statement for the period in which they are recognized. Further, a total amount for comprehensive income should be displayed in the financial statement when the components of other comprehensive income are reported.

4.03 FASB ASC 220-10-45-5 states that if an entity has an outstanding noncontrolling interest, amounts for both net income and comprehensive income attributable to the parent and net income and comprehensive income attributable to the noncontrolling interest in a less-than-wholly-owned subsidiary shall be reported on the face of the financial statement(s) in which net income and comprehensive income are presented in addition to presenting consolidated net income and comprehensive income.

4.04 FASB ASC 220-10-45-12 also states that an entity should disclose the amount of income tax expense or benefit allocated to each component of other comprehensive income, including reclassification adjustments, either on the face of the statement in which those components are displayed or in the notes thereto. Also, FASB ASC 810, *Consolidation*, states that if an entity has an outstanding noncontrolling interest (minority interest), the components of both net income and other comprehensive income attributable to the parent and noncontrolling interest in a less-than-wholly-owned subsidiary are required to be reported on the face of the financial statement in which net income and comprehensive income are presented, in addition to presenting consolidated comprehensive income.

4.05 FASB ASC 220-10-45-15 also requires that adjustments should be made to avoid double counting in comprehensive income items that are displayed as part of net income for a period that also had been displayed as part of other comprehensive income in that period or earlier periods. For example, gains on investment securities that were realized and included in net income of the current period that also had been included in other comprehensive income as unrealized holding gains in the period in which they arose must be deducted through other comprehensive income of the period in which they are included in net income to avoid including them in comprehensive income twice. These adjustments are called *reclassification adjustments*. An entity may display reclassification adjustments on the face of the financial statement in which comprehensive income is reported, or it may disclose them in the notes to the financial statements (that is, either a gross display on the face of the financial statement or a net display on the face of the financial statement and disclosure of the gross change in the notes to the financial statements). FASB ASC 220-10-45-14A also requires an entity to present the changes in the accumulated balances for each component of other comprehensive income. Both before-tax and net-of-tax presentations are permitted provided the requirements of FASB ASC 220-10-45-12 are met.

COMBINED STATEMENT OF INCOME AND COMPREHENSIVE INCOME

4.06 ALLIANT TECHSYSTEMS INC. (MAR)
CONSOLIDATED STATEMENTS OF COMPREHENSIVE INCOME

	Years Ended March 31		
(Amounts in thousands except per share data)	**2013**	**2012**	**2011**
Sales	$4,362,145	$4,613,399	$4,842,264
Cost of sales	3,421,276	3,618,503	3,840,698
Gross profit	940,869	994,896	1,001,566
Operating expenses:			
Research and development	64,678	66,403	64,960
Selling	162,359	169,984	164,063
General and administrative	244,189	262,923	246,817
Income before interest, loss on extinguishment of debt, income taxes, and noncontrolling interest	469,643	495,586	525,726
Interest expense	(65,924)	(89,296)	(87,612)
Interest income	538	676	560
Loss on extinguishment of debt	(11,773)	—	—
Income before income taxes and noncontrolling interest	392,484	406,966	438,674
Income tax provision	120,243	143,762	124,963
Net income	272,241	263,204	313,711
Less net income attributable to noncontrolling interest	436	592	536
Net income attributable to Alliant Techsystems Inc.	$ 271,805	$ 262,612	$ 313,175
Alliant Techsystems Inc. earnings per common share:			
Basic	$ 8.38	$ 7.99	$ 9.41
Diluted	$ 8.34	$ 7.93	$ 9.32
Cash dividends paid per share	$ 0.92	$ 0.80	$ 0.20
Alliant Techsystems Inc. weighted-average number of common shares outstanding:			
Basic	32,447	32,874	33,275
Diluted	32,608	33,112	33,615
Net Income (from above)	$ 272,241	$ 263,204	$ 313,711
Other comprehensive income (loss), net of tax:			
Pension and other postretirement benefit liabilities:			
Reclassification of prior service credits for pension and postretirement benefit plans recorded to net income, net of tax benefit of $3,366, $3,370, and $3,600	(5,406)	(5,392)	(5,785)
Reclassification of net actuarial loss for pension and postretirement benefit plans recorded to net income, net of tax expense of $(49,192), $(38,042), and $(33,962)	78,062	60,864	54,569
Valuation adjustment for pension and postretirement benefit plans, net of tax (expense) benefit of $(9,575), $94,968, and $4,009	15,456	(152,066)	(4,844)
Change in fair value of derivatives, net of tax expense of $3,586, $17,060, and $6,078, respectively	(5,608)	(26,683)	(9,607)
Change in fair value of available-for-sale securities, net of tax benefit of $135, $156, and $205, respectively	(210)	(244)	(324)
Total other comprehensive income (loss)	$ 82,294	$ (123,521)	$ 34,009
Comprehensive income	354,535	139,683	347,720
Less comprehensive income attributable to noncontrolling interest	436	592	536
Comprehensive income attributable to Alliant Techsystems Inc.	$ 354,099	$ 139,091	$ 347,184

SEPARATE STATEMENT OF COMPREHENSIVE INCOME

4.07 AUTOZONE, INC. (AUG)
CONSOLIDATED STATEMENTS OF INCOME

	Year Ended		
(In thousands, except per share data)	August 31, 2013 (53 Weeks)	August 25, 2012 (52 Weeks)	August 27, 2011 (52 Weeks)
Net sales	$9,147,530	$8,603,863	$8,072,973
Cost of sales, including warehouse and delivery expenses	4,406,595	4,171,827	3,953,510
Gross profit	4,740,935	4,432,036	4,119,463
Operating, selling, general and administrative expenses	2,967,837	2,803,145	2,624,660
Operating profit	1,773,098	1,628,891	1,494,803
Interest expense, net	185,415	175,905	170,557
Income before income taxes	1,587,683	1,452,986	1,324,246
Income tax expense	571,203	522,613	475,272
Net income	$1,016,480	$ 930,373	$ 848,974
Weighted average shares for basic earnings per share	35,943	38,696	42,632
Effect of dilutive stock equivalents	638	929	971
Adjusted weighted average shares for diluted earnings per share	36,581	39,625	43,603
Basic earnings per share	$ 28.28	$ 24.04	$ 19.91
Diluted earnings per share	$ 27.79	$ 23.48	$ 19.47

CONSOLIDATED STATEMENTS OF COMPREHENSIVE INCOME

	Year Ended		
(In thousands)	August 31, 2013 (53 Weeks)	August 25, 2012 (52 Weeks)	August 27, 2011 (52 Weeks)
Net income	$1,016,480	$930,373	$848,974
Other comprehensive income (loss):			
Pension liability adjustments, net of taxes[1]	43,106	(17,262)	(17,346)
Foreign currency translation adjustments	(12,216)	(13,866)	8,347
Unrealized loss on marketable securities, net of taxes[2]	(376)	(128)	(171)
Net derivative activity, net of taxes[3]	711	(1,066)	(4,053)
Total other comprehensive income (loss)	31,225	(32,322)	(13,223)
Comprehensive income	$1,047,705	$898,051	$835,751

[1] Pension liability adjustments are presented net of taxes of $27,972 in 2013, $29,744 in 2012, and $3,998 in 2011.
[2] Unrealized losses on marketable securities are presented net of taxes of $202 in 2013, $69 in 2012 and $91 in 2011.
[3] Net derivative activities are presented net of taxes of $440 in 2013, $4,800 in 2012, and $0 in 2011.

TAX EFFECT DISCLOSURE IN THE NOTES

4.08 SYSCO CORPORATION (JUN)
CONSOLIDATED STATEMENTS OF COMPREHENSIVE INCOME

	Year Ended		
(In thousands)	June 29, 2013	June 30, 2012	July 2, 2011
Net earnings	$ 992,427	$1,121,585	$1,152,030
Other comprehensive income (loss):			
Foreign currency translation adjustment	(33,191)	(81,003)	122,217
Items presented net of tax:			
Amortization of cash flow hedges	386	426	428
Settlement of cash flow hedge	—	445	—
Amortization of prior service cost	11,310	3,093	2,553
Amortization of actuarial loss (gain), net	44,610	36,860	49,013
Amortization of transition obligation	88	93	93
Prior service cost arising in current year	(33,203)	(5,363)	(5,692)
Actuarial gain (loss), net arising in current year	225,929	(357,459)	51,681
Total other comprehensive income (loss)	215,929	(402,908)	220,293
Comprehensive income	$1,208,356	$ 718,677	$1,372,323

16. Comprehensive Income (in part)

Comprehensive income is net earnings plus certain other items that are recorded directly to shareholders' equity, such as foreign currency translation adjustments, amounts related to cash flow hedging arrangements and certain amounts related to pension and other postretirement plans. Comprehensive income was $ 1,208.4 million, $718.7 million and $1,372.3 million in fiscal 2013, 2012 and 2011, respectively.

A summary of the components of other comprehensive income (loss) and the related tax effects for each of the years presented is as follows:

	2013		
(In thousands)	Before Tax Amount	Tax	Net of Tax Amount
Foreign currency translation adjustment	$ (33,191)	$ —	$ (33,191)
Amortization of cash flow hedges	626	240	386
Amortization of prior service cost	18,360	7,050	11,310
Amortization of actuarial loss (gain), net	72,421	27,811	44,610
Amortization of transition obligation	141	53	88
Prior service cost arising in current year	(53,902)	(20,699)	(33,203)
Actuarial gain (loss), net arising in current year	366,769	140,840	225,929
Total other comprehensive income (loss)	$371,224	$155,295	$215,929

	2012		
(In thousands)	Before Tax Amount	Tax	Net of Tax Amount
Foreign currency translation adjustment	$ (81,003)	$ —	$ (81,003)
Amortization of cash flow hedges	692	266	426
Settlement of cash flow hedge	722	277	445
Amortization of prior service cost	5,021	1,928	3,093
Amortization of actuarial loss (gain), net	59,835	22,975	36,860
Amortization of transition obligation	153	60	93
Prior service cost arising in current year	(8,706)	(3,343)	(5,363)
Actuarial gain (loss), net arising in current year	(580,291)	(222,832)	(357,459)
Total other comprehensive income (loss)	$(603,577)	$(200,669)	$(402,908)

	2011		
(In thousands)	Before Tax Amount	Tax	Net of Tax Amount
Foreign currency translation adjustment	$122,217	$ —	$122,217
Amortization of cash flow hedge	696	268	428
Amortization of prior service cost	4,145	1,592	2,553
Amortization of actuarial loss (gain), net	79,564	30,551	49,013
Amortization of transition obligation	153	60	93
Prior service cost arising in current year	(9,239)	(3,547)	(5,692)
Actuarial gain (loss), net arising in current year	83,898	32,217	51,681
Total other comprehensive income (loss)	$281,434	$61,141	$220,293

TOTAL AMOUNT OF TAX EFFECT DISCLOSED IN THE NOTES

4.09 PFIZER INC. (DEC)
CONSOLIDATED STATEMENTS OF COMPREHENSIVE INCOME

	Year Ended December 31,		
(Millions)	2013	2012	2011
Net income before allocation to noncontrolling interests	$22,072	$14,598	$10,049
Foreign currency translation adjustments	$ (535)	$ (811)	$ 796
Reclassification adjustments[a]	144	(207)	(127)
	(391)	(1,018)	669
Unrealized holding gains/(losses) on derivative financial instruments	488	745	(726)
Reclassification adjustments for realized (gains)/losses[b]	(94)	(616)	537
	394	129	(189)
Unrealized holding gains on available-for-sale securities	151	74	81
Reclassification adjustments for realized (gains)/losses[b]	(237)	356	(283)
	(86)	430	(202)

(continued)

(Millions)	Year Ended December 31,		
	2013	**2012**	**2011**
Benefit plans: actuarial gains/(losses), net	3,714	(2,136)	(2,246)
Reclassification adjustments related to amortization[c]	581	473	284
Reclassification adjustments related to settlements, net[c]	175	221	140
Other	48	22	(98)
	4,518	(1,420)	(1,920)
Benefit plans: prior service credits and other	151	25	106
Reclassification adjustments related to amortization[c]	(58)	(69)	(69)
Reclassification adjustments related to curtailments, net[c]	1	(130)	(91)
Other	(8)	(3)	3
	86	(177)	(51)
Other comprehensive income/(loss), before tax	4,521	(2,056)	(1,693)
Tax provision/(benefit) on other comprehensive income/(loss)[d]	1,928	(225)	(959)
Other comprehensive income/(loss) before allocation to noncontrolling interests	$ 2,593	$ (1,831)	$ (734)
Comprehensive income before allocation to noncontrolling interests	$24,665	$12,767	$ 9,315
Less: Comprehensive income/(loss) attributable to noncontrolling interests	7	21	(5)
Comprehensive income attributable to Pfizer Inc.	$24,658	$12,746	$ 9,320

[a] Reclassified into *Gain on disposal of discontinued operations—net of tax* in the consolidated statements of income.

[b] Reclassified into *Other (income)/deductions—net* in the consolidated statements of income.

[c] Generally reclassified, as part of net periodic pension cost, into *Cost of sales, Selling, informational and administrative expenses,* and/or *Research and development expenses,* as appropriate, in the consolidated statements of income. For additional information, see *Note 11. Pension and Postretirement Benefit Plans and Defined Contribution Plans.*

[d] See *Note 5E. Tax Matters: Taxes on Items of Other Comprehensive Income/(Loss).*

NOTES TO CONSOLIDATED FINANCIAL STATEMENTS

Note 5. Tax Matters (in part)

E. Taxes on Items of Other Comprehensive Income/(Loss)

The following table provides the components of the tax provision/(benefit) on *Other comprehensive income/(loss)* :

(Millions of dollars)	Year Ended December 31,		
	2013	**2012**	**2011**
Foreign currency translation adjustments[a]	$ 111	$ 110	$ (61)
Unrealized holding gains/(losses) on derivative financial instruments	217	251	(220)
Reclassification adjustments for realized (gains)/losses	(63)	(144)	135
	154	107	(85)
Unrealized holding gains/(losses) on available-for-sale securities	57	15	(4)
Reclassification adjustments for realized (gains)/losses	(57)	47	(38)
	—	62	(42)
Benefit plans: actuarial gains/(losses), net	1,422	(721)	(993)
Reclassification adjustments related to amortization	205	171	99
Reclassification adjustments related to settlements, net	2	105	118
Foreign currency translation adjustments and other	2	15	29
	1,631	(430)	(747)
Benefit plans: prior service credits and other	56	7	41
Reclassification adjustments related to amortization	(23)	(27)	(27)
Reclassification adjustments related to curtailments, net	(1)	(51)	(35)
Other	—	(3)	(3)
	32	(74)	(24)
Tax provision/(benefit) on other comprehensive income/(loss)	$1,928	$(225)	$(959)

[a] Taxes are not provided for foreign currency translation adjustments relating to investments in international subsidiaries that will be held indefinitely.

TAX EFFECT DISCLOSURE ON THE FACE OF THE FINANCIAL STATEMENTS

4.10 ABM INDUSTRIES INCORPORATED (OCT)

CONSOLIDATED STATEMENTS OF COMPREHENSIVE INCOME

	Year Ended October 31,								
	2013			2012			2011		
(In thousands)	Pre-Tax Amounts	Tax Expense / (Benefit)	After-Tax Amounts	Pre-Tax Amounts	Tax Expense / (Benefit)	After-Tax Amounts	Pre-Tax Amounts	Tax Expense / (Benefit)	After-Tax Amounts
Net income			$72,900			$62,582			$68,504
Other comprehensive income:									
Unrealized Gains on Auction Rate Securities:									
Unrealized gains on auction rate securities	$214	$ 88	$ 126	$2,110	$866	$ 1,244	$ 499	$ 193	$ 306
Reclassification adjustment for credit losses recognized in earnings	—	—	—	313	126	187	—	—	—
Net unrealized gains on auction rate securities	214	88	126	2,423	992	1,431	499	193	306
Unrealized (Losses) Gains on Interest Rate Swaps:									
Unrealized losses arising during the period	(381)	(156)	(225)	(125)	(51)	(74)	(245)	(101)	(144)
Reclassification adjustment for loss included in interest expense	445	182	263	164	67	97	436	177	259
Net unrealized gains on interest rate swaps	64	26	38	39	16	23	191	76	115
Foreign currency translation	(183)	—	(183)	(85)	—	(85)	214	—	214
Defined and postretirement benefit plans adjustments:									
Actuarial gains (losses) arising during the current year	675	276	399	(1,660)	(678)	(982)	(2,669)	(1,094)	(1,575)
Reclassification adjustment for amortization of actuarial losses	138	56	82	97	40	57	114	46	68
Reclassification adjustment for settlement losses	70	29	41	107	44	63	126	52	74
Net defined and postretirement benefit plans adjustments	883	361	522	(1,456)	(594)	(862)	(2,429)	(996)	(1,433)
Total other comprehensive income (loss)	$978	$475	$503	$ 921	$414	$507	$(1,525)	$(727)	$(798)
Comprehensive income			$73,403			$63,089			$67,706

FOREIGN CURRENCY TRANSLATION

4.11 GUESS?, INC. (JAN)

CONSOLIDATED STATEMENTS OF COMPREHENSIVE INCOME

(In thousands)

	Year Ended Feb 2, 2013	Year Ended Jan 28, 2012	Year Ended Jan 29, 2011
Net earnings	$181,486	$270,650	$294,503
Other comprehensive income (loss):			
Foreign currency translation adjustment	22,347	(17,453)	(1,440)
Net unrealized gain (loss) on hedges			
Net gains (losses) arising during the period	(7,097)	7,218	(4,033)
Less income tax effect	1,056	(1,170)	399
Net unrealized gain (loss) on investments			
Net gains (losses) arising during the period	224	(67)	188
Less income tax effect	(85)	24	(72)
Supplemental Executive Retirement Plan ("SERP")			
Actuarial gain (loss)	3,508	(9,342)	(8,361)
Actuarial loss amortization	3,340	2,048	619
Prior service cost amortization	620	940	1,195
Curtailment	—	1,242	5,819
Less income tax effect	(2,855)	2,057	251
Total comprehensive income	202,544	256,147	289,068
Less comprehensive income attributable to noncontrolling interests:			
Net earnings	2,742	5,150	4,995
Foreign currency translation adjustment	322	116	191
Amounts attributable to noncontrolling interests	3,064	5,266	5,186
Comprehensive income attributable to Guess?, Inc.	$199,480	$250,881	$283,882

(1) Summary of Significant Accounting Policies and Practices (in part)

Foreign Currency

Foreign Currency Translation

The local selling currency is typically the functional currency for all of the Company's significant international operations. In accordance with authoritative guidance, assets and liabilities of the Company's foreign operations are translated from foreign currencies into U.S. dollars at period-end rates, while income and expenses are translated at the weighted-average exchange rates for the period. The related translation adjustments are reflected as a foreign currency translation adjustment in accumulated other comprehensive income (loss) within stockholders' equity. In addition, the Company records foreign currency translation adjustments related to its noncontrolling interests within stockholders' equity. The total foreign currency translation adjustment increased stockholders' equity by $22.3 million, from an accumulated foreign currency translation loss of $11.6 million as of January 28, 2012 to an accumulated foreign currency translation gain of $10.7 million as of February 2, 2013.

Foreign Currency Transaction Gains and Losses

Transaction gains and losses that arise from exchange rate fluctuations on transactions denominated in a currency other than the functional currency, including gains and losses on foreign currency contracts (see below), are included in the consolidated statements of income. Net foreign currency transaction gains (losses) included in the determination of net earnings were $8.6 million, $(6.8) million and $10.1 million for fiscal 2013, fiscal 2012 and fiscal 2011, respectively.

Forward Contracts Designated as Cash Flow Hedges

The Company operates in foreign countries, which exposes it to market risk associated with foreign currency exchange rate fluctuations. Various transactions that occur in Canada, Europe and South Korea are denominated in U.S. dollars and British pounds and thus are exposed to earnings risk as a result of exchange rate fluctuations when converted to their functional currencies. These types of transactions include U.S. dollar denominated purchases of merchandise and U.S. dollar and British pound denominated intercompany liabilities. In addition, certain operating expenses and tax liabilities are denominated in Swiss francs and are exposed to earnings risk as a result of exchange rate fluctuations when converted to the functional currency. The Company has entered into certain forward contracts to hedge the risk of a portion of these anticipated foreign currency transactions against foreign currency rate fluctuations. The Company has elected to apply the hedge accounting rules in accordance with authoritative guidance for certain of these hedges. The Company does not hedge all transactions denominated in foreign currency.

Changes in the fair values of the U.S. dollar/euro and U.S. dollar/Canadian dollar forward contracts for anticipated U.S. dollar merchandise purchases designated as cash flow hedges are recorded as a component of accumulated other comprehensive income (loss) within stockholders' equity and are recognized in cost of product sales in the period which approximates the time the hedged merchandise inventory is sold. Changes in the fair value of U.S. dollar/euro forward contracts for U.S. dollar intercompany royalties designated as cash flow hedges are recorded as a component of accumulated other comprehensive income (loss) within stockholders' equity and are recognized in other income and expense in the period in which the royalty expense is incurred.

Forward Contracts Not Designated as Cash Flow Hedges

The Company also has forward contracts that are not designated as cash flow hedges for accounting purposes. Changes in fair value of forward contracts not qualifying as cash flow hedges are reported in net earnings as part of other income and expense.

Comprehensive Income

Comprehensive income consists of net earnings, Supplemental Executive Retirement Plan ("SERP") prior service cost amortization, curtailment and actuarial valuation gains or losses and related amortization, unrealized gains or losses on available-for-sale investments, foreign currency translation adjustments and the effective portion of the change in the fair value of cash flow hedges. Comprehensive income is presented in the consolidated statements of comprehensive income.

PENSION AND POSTRETIREMENT PLANS

4.12 TENET HEALTHCARE CORPORATION (DEC)

CONSOLIDATED STATEMENTS OF OTHER COMPREHENSIVE INCOME (LOSS)

Dollars in Millions

	Years Ended December 31,		
	2013	2012	2011
Net income (loss)	$(104)	$133	$94
Other comprehensive income (loss):			
Adjustments for defined benefit plans	68	(25)	(15)
Unrealized gains on securities held as available-for-sale	1	0	0
Reclassification adjustments for realized losses included in net income	0	0	0
Other comprehensive income (loss) before income taxes	69	(25)	(15)
Income tax benefit (expense) related to items of other comprehensive loss	(25)	9	6
Total other comprehensive income (loss), net of tax	44	(16)	(9)
Comprehensive income (loss)	(60)	117	85
Less: Preferred stock dividends	0	11	24
Less: Comprehensive income (loss) attributable to noncontrolling interests	30	(19)	12
Comprehensive income (loss) attributable to Tenet Healthcare Corporation common shareholders	$ (90)	$125	$49

NOTES TO CONSOLIDATED FINANCIAL STATEMENTS

Note 8. Employee Benefit Plans (in part)

Employee Retirement Plans (in part)

Substantially all of our employees, upon qualification, are eligible to participate in one of our defined contribution 401(k) plans. Under the plans, employees may contribute a portion of their eligible compensation, and we match such contributions annually up to a maximum percentage for participants actively employed, as defined by the plan documents. Employer matching contributions will vary by plan. Plan expenses, primarily related to our contributions to the plan, were approximately $35 million, $32 million and $32 million for the years ended December 31, 2013, 2012 and 2011, respectively. Such amounts are reflected in salaries, wages and benefits in the accompanying Consolidated Statements of Operations.

We maintain one active and two frozen non-qualified defined benefit pension plans ("SERPs") that provide supplemental retirement benefits to certain of our current and former executives. These plans are not funded, and plan obligations for these plans are paid from our working capital. Pension benefits are generally based on years of service and compensation. Upon completing the acquisition of Vanguard on October 1, 2013, we assumed a frozen qualified defined benefit plan ("DMC Pension Plan") covering substantially all of the employees of our Detroit market that were hired prior to June 1, 2003. The benefits paid under the DMC Pension Plan are primarily based on years of service and final average earnings. The following tables summarize the balance sheet impact, as well as the benefit obligations, funded status and rate assumptions associated with the SERPs and the DMC Pension Plan based on actuarial valuations prepared as of December 31, 2013 and 2012:

	December 31,	
	2013	2012
Reconciliation of funded status of plans and the amounts included in the Consolidated Balance Sheets:		
Projected benefit obligations[(1)]		
Beginning obligations	$ (312)	$(285)
Assumed from acquisition	(1,037)	(0)
Service cost	(2)	(2)
Interest cost	(25)	(14)
Actuarial gain(loss)	44	(30)
Plan changes	(2)	(0)
Benefits paid/employer contributions	31	19
Ending obligations	(1,303)	(312)

(continued)

	December 31,	
	2013	**2012**
Fair value of plans assets		
Beginning obligations	(0)	(0)
Assumed from acquisition	863	(0)
Gain on plan assets	34	(0)
Benefits paid	(11)	(0)
Ending plan assets	886	(0)
Funded status of plans	$ (417)	$(312)
Amounts recognized in the Consolidated Balance Sheets consist of:		
Other current liability	$ (19)	$ (20)
Other long-term liability	(398)	(292)
Accumulated other comprehensive loss	22	90
	$ (395)	$(222)
SERP Assumptions:		
Discount rate	5.00%	4.00%
Compensation increase rate	3.00%	3.00%
Measurement date	December 31, 2013	December 31, 2012
DMC Pension Plan Assumptions:		
Discount rate	5.18%	n/a
Compensation increase rate	Frozen	n/a
Measurement date	December 31, 2013	n/a

(1) The accumulated benefit obligation at December 31, 2013 and 2012 was approximately $1,297 million and $308 million, respectively.

The components of net periodic benefit costs and related assumptions are as follows:

	Years Ended December 31,		
	2013	**2012**	**2011**
Service costs	$ 2	$ 2	$ 2
Interest costs	25	14	14
Amortization of prior-year service costs	(15)	0	0
Amortization of net actuarial loss	7	5	3
Net periodic benefit cost	$ 19	$21	$19
SERP Assumptions:			
Discount rate	4.00%	5.00%	5.50%
Long-term rate of return on assets	n/a	n/a	n/a
Compensation increase rate	3.00%	3.00%	3.00%
Measurement date	January 1, 2013	January 1, 2012	January 1, 2011
Census date	January 1, 2013	January 1, 2012	January 1, 2011
DMC Pension Plan Assumptions:			
Discount rate	5.01%	n/a	n/a
Long-term rate of return on assets	7.00%	n/a	n/a
Compensation increase rate	Frozen	n/a	n/a
Measurement date	October 1, 2013	n/a	n/a
Census date	January 1, 2013	n/a	n/a

Net periodic benefit costs for the current year are based on assumptions determined at the valuation date of the prior year for the SERPs and at the date of acquisition for the DMC Pension Plan.

We recorded gain/(loss) adjustments of $68 million, ($25) million and ($15) million in other comprehensive income (loss) in the years ended December 31, 2013, 2012 and 2011, respectively, to recognize changes in the funded status of our SERPs and the DMC Pension Plan. Changes in the funded status are recorded as a direct increase or decrease to shareholders' equity through accumulated other comprehensive loss. Net actuarial gains/(losses) of $63 million, ($30) million and ($19) million during the years ended December 31, 2013, 2012 and 2011, respectively, and the amortization of net prior service costs of less than $1 million for the years ended December 31, 2013, 2012 and 2011 were recognized in other comprehensive income (loss). Cumulative net actuarial losses of $21 million, $90 million and $65 million as of December 31, 2013, 2012 and 2011, respectively, and unrecognized prior service costs of less than $1 million as of each of the years ended December 31, 2013, 2012 and 2011, have not yet been recognized as components of net periodic benefit costs.

4.13 WELLPOINT, INC. (DEC)

CONSOLIDATED STATEMENTS OF COMPREHENSIVE INCOME

| | Years Ended December 31 | | |
	2013	2012	2011
(In millions)			
Net income	$2,489.7	$2,655.5	$2,646.7
Other Comprehensive (Loss) Income, Net of Tax:			
Change in net unrealized gains/losses on investments	(294.7)	189.9	20.6
Change in non-credit component of other-than-temporary impairment losses on investments	1.7	4.5	(0.7)
Change in net unrealized gains/losses on cash flow hedges	3.0	0.1	(10.0)
Change in net periodic pension and postretirement costs	172.7	(10.9)	(119.8)
Foreign currency translation adjustments	1.4	0.6	0.2
Other comprehensive (loss) income	(115.9)	184.2	(109.7)
Total comprehensive income	$2,373.8	$2,839.7	$2,537.0

NOTES TO CONSOLIDATED FINANCIAL STATEMENTS

(In Millions, Except Per Share Data or As Otherwise Stated Herein)

2. Basis of Presentation and Significant Accounting Policies (in part)

Investments: Certain FASB other-than-temporary impairment, or FASB OTTI, guidance applies to fixed maturity securities and provides guidance on the recognition and presentation of other-than-temporary impairments. In addition, this FASB OTTI guidance requires disclosures related to other-than-temporary impairments. If a fixed maturity security is in an unrealized loss position and we have the intent to sell the fixed maturity security, or it is more likely than not that we will have to sell the fixed maturity security before recovery of its amortized cost basis, the decline in value is deemed to be other-than-temporary and is recorded to other-than-temporary impairment losses recognized in income in our consolidated income statements. For impaired fixed maturity securities that we do not intend to sell or it is more likely than not that we will not have to sell such securities, but we expect that we will not fully recover the amortized cost basis, the credit component of the other-than-temporary impairment is recognized in other-than-temporary impairment losses recognized in income in our consolidated income statements and the non-credit component of the other-than-temporary impairment is recognized in other comprehensive income. Furthermore, unrealized losses entirely caused by non-credit related factors related to fixed maturity securities for which we expect to fully recover the amortized cost basis continue to be recognized in accumulated other comprehensive income, or AOCI.

The credit component of an other-than-temporary impairment is determined by comparing the net present value of projected future cash flows with the amortized cost basis of the fixed maturity security. The net present value is calculated by discounting our best estimate of projected future cash flows at the effective interest rate implicit in the fixed maturity security at the date of acquisition. For mortgage-backed and asset-backed securities, cash flow estimates are based on assumptions regarding the underlying collateral including prepayment speeds, vintage, type of underlying asset, geographic concentrations, default rates, recoveries and changes in value. For all other debt securities, cash flow estimates are driven by assumptions regarding probability of default, including changes in credit ratings, and estimates regarding timing and amount of recoveries associated with a default.

The unrealized gains or losses on our current and long-term equity securities classified as available-for-sale are included in accumulated other comprehensive income as a separate component of shareholders' equity, unless the decline in value is deemed to be other-than-temporary and we do not have the intent and ability to hold such equity securities until their full cost can be recovered, in which case such equity securities are written down to fair value and the loss is charged to other-than-temporary impairment losses recognized in income.

We maintain various rabbi trusts to account for the assets and liabilities under certain deferred compensation plans. Under these plans, the participants can defer certain types of compensation and elect to receive a return on the deferred amounts based on the changes in fair value of various investment options, primarily a variety of mutual funds. Rabbi trust assets are classified as trading, which are reported in other invested assets, current, in the consolidated balance sheets.

We use the equity method of accounting for investments in companies in which our ownership interest enables us to influence the operating or financial decisions of the investee company. Our proportionate share of equity in net income of these unconsolidated affiliates is reported with net investment income.

For asset-backed securities included in fixed maturity securities, we recognize income using an effective yield based on anticipated prepayments and the estimated economic life of the securities. When estimates of prepayments change, the effective yield is recalculated to reflect actual payments to date and anticipated future payments. The net investment in the securities is adjusted to the amount that would have existed had the new effective yield been applied since the acquisition of the securities. Such adjustments are reported with net investment income.

Investment income is recorded when earned. All securities sold resulting in investment gains and losses are recorded on the trade date. Realized gains and losses are determined on the basis of the cost or amortized cost of the specific securities sold.

We participate in securities lending programs whereby marketable securities in our investment portfolio are transferred to independent brokers or dealers based on, among other things, their creditworthiness in exchange for cash collateral initially equal to at least 102% of the value of the securities on loan and is thereafter maintained at a minimum of 100% of the market value of the securities loaned (calculated as the ratio of initial market value of cash collateral to current market value of the securities on loan). Accordingly, the market value of the securities on loan to each borrower is monitored daily and the borrower is required to deliver additional cash collateral if the market value of the securities on loan exceeds the initial market value of cash collateral delivered. The fair value of the collateral received at the time of the transaction amounted to $969.7 and $564.7 at December 31, 2013 and 2012, respectively. The value of the cash collateral delivered represented 102% of the market value of the securities on loan at December 31, 2013 and 2012. Under FASB guidance related to accounting for transfers and servicing of financial assets and extinguishments of liabilities, we recognize the cash collateral as an asset, which is reported as "securities lending collateral" on our consolidated balance sheets and we record a corresponding liability for the obligation to return the cash collateral to the borrower, which is reported as "securities lending payable." The securities on loan are reported in the applicable investment category on the consolidated balance sheets. Unrealized gains or losses on securities lending collateral are included in accumulated other comprehensive income as a separate component of shareholders' equity.

5. Investments (in part)

A summary of current and long-term investments, available-for-sale, at December 31, 2013 and 2012 is as follows:

	Cost or Amortized Cost	Gross Unrealized Gains	Gross Unrealized Losses		Estimated Fair Value	Non-Credit Component of Other-Than-Temporary Impairments Recognized in AOCI
			Less Than 12 Months	12 Months or Greater		
December 31, 2013:						
Fixed maturity securities:						
United States Government securities	$ 300.8	$ 2.5	$ (3.4)	$ —	$ 299.9	$ —
Government sponsored securities	174.4	0.4	(1.3)	—	173.5	—
States, municipalities and political subdivisions, tax-exempt	5,899.5	202.9	(90.1)	(9.6)	6,002.7	(0.6)
Corporate securities	7,614.1	205.2	(95.2)	(15.5)	7,708.6	(0.1)
Options embedded in convertible securities	89.2	—	—	—	89.2	—
Residential mortgage-backed securities	2,269.4	48.0	(41.4)	(7.1)	2,268.9	—
Commercial mortgage-backed securities	479.0	10.5	(2.6)	(0.3)	486.6	—
Other debt securities	456.2	5.8	(2.5)	(0.8)	458.7	(0.1)
Total fixed maturity securities	17,282.6	475.3	(236.5)	(33.3)	17,488.1	$(0.8)
Equity securities	1,195.9	578.9	(8.0)	—	1,766.8	
Total investments, available-for-sale	$18,478.5	$1,054.2	$(244.5)	$(33.3)	$19,254.9	
December 31, 2012						
Fixed maturity securities:						
United States Government securities	$ 330.3	$ 13.1	$ (0.2)	$—	$ 343.2	$ —
Government sponsored securities	153.6	2.6	—	—	156.2	—
States, municipalities and political subdivisions, tax-exempt	5,501.3	388.2	(5.7)	(1.6)	5,882.2	—
Corporate securities	7,642.0	387.0	(17.0)	(8.0)	8,004.0	(1.7)
Options embedded in convertible securities	67.2	—	—	—	67.2	—
Residential mortgage-backed securities	2,204.7	103.1	(1.1)	(1.9)	2,304.8	(0.4)
Commercial mortgage-backed securities	323.2	22.5	—	—	345.7	—
Other debt securities	236.8	7.6	(0.2)	(3.1)	241.1	(1.3)
Total fixed maturity securities	16,459.1	924.1	(24.2)	(14.6)	17,344.4	$(3.4)
Equity securities	897.0	358.0	(12.5)	—	1,242.5	
Total investments, available-for-sale	$17,356.1	$1,282.1	$ (36.7)	$(14.6)	$18,586.9	

At December 31, 2013, we owned $2,755.5 of mortgage-backed securities and $423.8 of asset-backed securities out of a total available-for-sale investment portfolio of $19,254.9. These securities included sub-prime and Alt-A securities with fair values of $32.2 and $102.4, respectively. These sub-prime and Alt-A securities had accumulated net unrealized gains of $1.7 and $6.4, respectively. The average credit rating of the sub-prime and Alt-A securities was "BB" and "CCC", respectively.

The following tables summarize for fixed maturity securities and equity securities in an unrealized loss position at December 31, 2013 and 2012, the aggregate fair value and gross unrealized loss by length of time those securities have been continuously in an unrealized loss position.

	Less Than 12 Months			12 Months or Greater		
(Securities are whole amounts)	Number of Securities	Estimated Fair Value	Gross Unrealized Loss	Number of Securities	Estimated Fair Value	Gross Unrealized Loss
December 31, 2013:						
Fixed maturity securities:						
United States Government securities	27	$ 179.2	$ (3.4)	—	$ —	$ —
Government sponsored securities	22	73.4	(1.3)	—	—	—
States, municipalities and political subdivisions, tax-exempt	806	2,070.9	(90.1)	42	82.4	(9.6)
Corporate securities	1,448	2,586.6	(95.2)	107	81.3	(15.5)
Residential mortgage-backed securities	605	1,243.0	(41.4)	80	116.2	(7.1)
Commercial mortgage-backed securities	52	177.7	(2.6)	4	5.6	(0.3)
Other debt securities	65	185.3	(2.5)	17	16.2	(0.8)
Total fixed maturity securities	3,025	6,516.1	(236.5)	250	301.7	(33.3)
Equity securities	426	120.8	(8.0)	—	—	—
Total fixed maturity and equity securities	3,451	$6,636.9	$(244.5)	250	$301.7	$(33.3)
December 31, 2012						
Fixed maturity securities:						
United States Government securities	17	$ 48.5	$ (0.2)	—	$ —	$ —
States, municipalities and political subdivisions, tax-exempt	184	420.1	(5.7)	1	46.9	(1.6)
Corporate securities	457	1,066.5	(17.0)	74	52.6	(8.0)
Residential mortgage-backed securities	79	211.0	(1.1)	44	25.5	(1.9)
Commercial mortgage-backed securities	4	10.1	—	3	4.1	—
Other debt securities	7	5.4	(0.2)	21	28.9	(3.1)
Total fixed maturity securities	748	1,761.6	(24.2)	143	158.0	(14.6)
Equity securities	961	149.6	(12.5)	—	—	—
Total fixed maturity and equity securities	1,709	$1,911.2	$ (36.7)	143	$158.0	$(14.6)

The amortized cost and fair value of fixed maturity securities at December 31, 2013, by contractual maturity, are shown below. Expected maturities may differ from contractual maturities because the issuers of the securities may have the right to prepay obligations.

	Amortized Cost	Estimated Fair Value
Due in one year or less	$ 423.9	$ 426.3
Due after one year through five years	4,580.5	4,712.1
Due after five years through ten years	5,105.4	5,196.6
Due after ten years	4,424.4	4,397.6
Mortgage-backed securities	2,748.4	2,755.5
Total available-for-sale fixed maturity securities	$17,282.6	$17,488.1

The major categories of net investment income for the years ended December 31 are as follows:

	2013	2012	2011
Fixed maturity securities	$638.9	$671.2	$692.4
Equity securities	45.9	38.4	34.0
Cash and cash equivalents	1.0	2.5	3.7
Other	19.8	16.2	2.4
Investment income	705.6	728.3	732.5
Investment expense	(46.5)	(42.2)	(28.8)
Net investment income	$659.1	$686.1	$703.7

Net realized investment gains/losses and net change in unrealized appreciation/depreciation in investments for the years ended December 31 are as follows:

	2013	2012	2011
Net realized gains (losses) on investments:			
Fixed maturity securities:			
Gross realized gains from sales	$ 225.9	$ 401.0	$ 289.2
Gross realized losses from sales	(125.7)	(54.8)	(65.1)
Net realized gains from sales of fixed maturity securities	100.2	346.2	224.1
Equity securities:			
Gross realized gains from sales	224.1	82.0	75.4
Gross realized losses from sales	(100.5)	(93.8)	(68.0)
Net realized gains (losses) from sales of equity securities	123.6	(11.8)	7.4
Other realized gains on investments	48.1	0.5	3.6
Net realized gains on investments	271.9	334.9	235.1
Other-than-temporary impairment losses recognized in income:			
Fixed maturity securities	(42.5)	(11.8)	(24.2)
Equity securities	(13.9)	(17.5)	(27.9)
Other invested assets, long-term	(42.5)	(8.5)	(41.2)
Other-than-temporary impairment losses recognized in income	(98.9)	(37.8)	(93.3)
Change in net unrealized (losses) gains on investments:			
Fixed maturity securities	(679.8)	199.8	155.9
Equity securities	225.4	94.7	(124.6)
Total change in net unrealized (losses) gains on investments	(454.4)	294.5	31.3
Deferred income tax benefit (expense)	159.7	(104.6)	(10.7)
Net change in net unrealized (losses) gains on investments	(294.7)	189.9	20.6
Net realized gains on investments, other-than-temporary impairment losses recognized in income and net change in net unrealized (losses) gains on investments	$(121.7)	$ 487.0	$ 162.4

A primary objective in the management of our fixed maturity and equity portfolios is to maximize total return relative to underlying liabilities and respective liquidity needs. In achieving this goal, assets may be sold to take advantage of market conditions or other investment opportunities as well as tax considerations. Sales will generally produce realized gains and losses. In the ordinary course of business, we may sell securities at a loss for a number of reasons, including, but not limited to: (i) changes in the investment environment; (ii) expectations that the fair value could deteriorate further; (iii) desire to reduce exposure to an issuer or an industry; (iv) changes in credit quality; or (v) changes in expected cash flow.

Proceeds from fixed maturity securities, equity securities and other invested assets and the related gross realized gains and gross realized losses for the years ended December 31 are as follows:

	2013	2012	2011
Proceeds	$13,662.8	$15,915.6	$12,654.3
Gross realized gains	498.1	483.5	368.2
Gross realized losses	(226.2)	(148.6)	(133.1)

GAINS AND LOSSES ON DERIVATIVES HELD AS CASH FLOW HEDGES

4.14 CONVERGYS CORPORATION (DEC)
CONSOLIDATED STATEMENTS OF COMPREHENSIVE INCOME

	Year Ended December 31,		
(In millions)	2013	2012	2011
Net Income	$ 60.9	$100.6	$334.8
Other Comprehensive (Loss) Income, Net of Tax:			
Foreign currency translation adjustments	(1.3)	22.3	(3.9)
Change related to pension liability (net of tax (expense) benefit of ($17.1), ($0.6) and $6.7)	26.2	1.0	(7.3)
Unrealized (loss) gain on hedging activities (net of reclassification adjustments and net of tax benefit (expense) of $21.4, ($8.1) and $13.0)	(33.9)	12.9	(20.2)
Total other comprehensive (loss) income	(9.0)	36.2	(31.4)
Total comprehensive income	$ 51.9	$136.8	$303.4

(Amounts in millions except share and per share amounts)

2. Significant Accounting Policies (in part)

Derivative Instruments

The Company's risk management strategy includes the use of derivative instruments to reduce the effects on its operating results and cash flows from fluctuations caused by volatility in currency exchange and interest rates. The Company currently uses only cash flow hedges. These instruments are hedges of forecasted transactions or of the variability of cash flows to be received or paid related to a recognized asset or liability. The Company generally enters into forward exchange contracts expiring within 36 months as hedges of anticipated cash flows denominated in foreign currencies. These contracts are entered into to protect against the risk that the eventual cash flows resulting from such transactions will be adversely affected by changes in exchange rates. In using derivative financial instruments to hedge exposures to changes in exchange rates, the Company exposes itself to counterparty credit risk.

All derivatives, including foreign currency exchange contracts, are recognized in the Consolidated Balance Sheets at fair value. Fair values for the Company's derivative financial instruments are based on quoted market prices of comparable instruments or, if none are available, on pricing models or formulas using current assumptions. On the date the derivative contract is entered into, the Company determines whether the derivative contract qualifies for designation as a hedge. For derivatives that are designated as hedges, the Company further designates the hedge as either a fair value or cash flow hedge; all currently existing hedges have been designated as cash flow hedges. Changes in the fair value of derivatives that are highly effective and designated as fair value hedges would be recorded in the Consolidated Statements of Income along with the loss or gain on the hedged asset or liability. Changes in the fair value of derivatives that are highly effective and designated as cash flow hedges are reported as a component of Other Comprehensive (Loss) Income and reclassified into earnings in the same line-item associated with the forecasted transaction and in the same periods during which the hedged transaction impacts earnings. The Company formally documents all relationships between hedging instruments and hedged items, as well as its risk management objective and strategy for undertaking various hedging activities. This process includes linking all derivatives that are designated as fair value or cash flow hedges to specific assets and liabilities on the balance sheet or to forecasted transactions, respectively. The Company also formally assesses, both at the hedge's inception and on an ongoing basis, whether the derivatives that are used in hedging transactions are highly effective in offsetting changes in fair value or cash flows of hedged items. When it is determined that a derivative is not highly effective as a hedge or that it has ceased to be a highly effective hedge, the Company discontinues hedge accounting prospectively.

The Company also periodically enters into forward exchange contracts and options that are not designated as hedges. The purpose of the majority of these derivative instruments is to protect the Company against foreign currency exposure pertaining to receivables, payables and intercompany transactions that are denominated in currencies different from the functional currencies of the Company or the respective subsidiaries. The Company records changes in the fair value of these derivative instruments in the Consolidated Statements of Income within Other income, net.

12. Financial Instruments (in part)

Derivative Instruments

The Company is exposed to a variety of market risks, including the effects of changes in foreign currency exchange rates and interest rates. Market risk is the potential loss arising from adverse changes in market rates and prices. The Company's risk management strategy includes the use of derivative instruments to reduce the effects on its operating results and cash flows from fluctuations caused by volatility in currency exchange and interest rates.

The Company serves many of its U.S.-based clients using contact center capacity in the Philippines, India, Canada, and Colombia. Although the contracts with these clients are typically priced in U.S. dollars, a substantial portion of the costs incurred to render services under these contracts are denominated in Philippine pesos (PHP), Indian rupees (INR), Canadian dollars (CAD) or Colombian pesos (COP), which represents a foreign exchange exposure. Beginning in 2011, the Company entered into a contract with a client priced in Australian dollars (AUD). The Company has hedged a portion of its exposure related to the anticipated cash flow requirements denominated in these foreign currencies by entering into forward exchange contracts and options with several financial institutions to acquire a total of PHP 31,479.0 at a fixed price of $732.9 at various dates through December 2016, INR 11,006.0 at a fixed price of $181.2 at various dates through December 2016, CAD 20.9 at a fixed price of $20.1 at various dates through December 2015 and COP 20,100.0 at a fixed price of $10.5 at various dates through December 2014, and to sell a total of AUD 20.3 at a fixed price of $20.7 at various dates through September 2014. These instruments mature within the next 36 months and had a notional value of $965.5 at December 31, 2013 and $590.4 at December 31, 2012. The derivative instruments discussed above are designated and are effective as cash flow hedges. The following table reflects the fair values of these derivative instruments:

	At December 31,	
	2013	2012
Forward Exchange Contracts and Options Designated as Hedging Instruments:		
Included within other current assets	$ 4.3	$16.4
Included within other non-current assets	0.2	11.6
Included within other current liabilities	21.2	6.1
Included within other long-term liabilities	19.8	3.5

The Company recorded a deferred tax benefit of $14.1 and deferred tax expense of $7.1 related to these derivatives at December 31, 2013 and 2012, respectively. A total of $22.5 of deferred losses and $11.4 of deferred gains, net of tax, related to these cash flow hedges at December 31, 2013 and 2012, respectively, were included in accumulated other comprehensive loss (OCL). As of December 31, 2013, deferred losses of $16.9 ($10.5 net of tax), on derivative instruments included in accumulated OCL are expected to be reclassified into earnings during the next 12 months. The following tables provide the effect of these derivative instruments on the Company's Consolidated Financial Statements during 2013 and 2012, respectively:

2013:

Derivatives in Cash Flow Hedging Relationships	Gain (Loss) Recognized in OCL on Derivative (Effective Portion)	Gain (Loss) Reclassified From Accumulated OCL into Income (Effective Portion)	Location of Gain (Loss) Reclassified from Accumulated OCL into Income (Effective Portion)
Foreign exchange contracts	$(57.1)	$(2.1)	Cost of providing services and products sold and Selling, general and administrative

2012:

Derivatives in Cash Flow Hedging Relationships	Gain (Loss) Recognized in OCL on Derivative (Effective Portion)	Gain (Loss) Reclassified From Accumulated OCL into Income (Effective Portion)	Location of Gain (Loss) Reclassified from Accumulated OCL into Income (Effective Portion)
Foreign exchange contracts	$35.8	$14.8	Cost of providing services and products sold and Selling, general and administrative

The gain/loss recognized related to the ineffective portion of the derivative instruments was immaterial for the years ended December 31, 2013 and 2012.

During 2013, 2012 and 2011, the Company recorded a net loss of $2.1, and net gains of $14.8 and $11.6, respectively, related to the settlement of forward contracts and options which were designated as cash flow hedges.

The Company also enters into derivative instruments (forwards) to economically hedge the foreign currency impact of assets and liabilities denominated in nonfunctional currencies. During the year ended December 31, 2013, a gain of $2.4 was recognized related to changes in fair value of these derivative instruments not designated as hedges, compared to a loss of $0.4 in the same period in 2012. The gains and losses largely offset the currency gains and losses that resulted from changes in the assets and liabilities denominated in nonfunctional currencies. These gains and losses are classified within other income, net in the accompanying Consolidated Statements of Income. The fair value of these derivative instruments not designated as hedges at December 31, 2013, was a liability of $0.1.

A few of the Company's counterparty agreements related to derivative instruments contain provisions that require that the Company maintain collateral on derivative instruments in net liability positions. The aggregate fair value of all derivative instruments in liability position at December 31, 2013 was $41.5 for which the Company has no posted collateral. Future downgrades in the Company's credit ratings and/or changes in the foreign currency markets could result in collateral to counterparties.

15. Accumulated Other Comprehensive Income (Loss)

The following table summarizes the changes in the accumulated balances for each component of accumulated other comprehensive income (loss):

	Foreign Currency	Derivative Financial Instruments	Pension Liability	Total
Balance at December 31, 2012	$36.4	$ 11.4	$(58.3)	$(10.5)
Other comprehensive (loss) income before reclassifications	(1.3)	(35.1)	10.3	(26.1)
Adjustment of pension and other post employment obligations	—	—	15.9	15.9
Amounts reclassified from accumulated other comprehensive income	—	1.2	—	1.2
Net current-period other comprehensive (loss) income	(1.3)	(33.9)	26.2	(9.0)
Balance at December 31, 2013	$35.1	$(22.5)	$(32.1)	$(19.5)

The following table summarizes the reclassification out of accumulated other comprehensive income (loss) during 2013:

Details about Accumulated Other Comprehensive Income (Loss) Components	Amount Reclassified from Accumulated Other Comprehensive Income (Loss)	Affected Line Item in the Consolidated Statements of Income
Loss on derivative instruments	$ (2.1)	Cost of providing services and products sold and Selling, general and administrative
Tax benefit	0.9	Income tax benefit
Loss on derivative instruments, net of tax	(1.2)	Net of tax
Adjustment of pension and other post employment obligations	(24.9)	Selling, general and administrative
Tax benefit	9.0	Income tax benefit
Adjustment of pension and other post employment obligations, net of tax	(15.9)	Net of tax
Total reclassifications for the period	$(17.1)	

4.15 GILEAD SCIENCES, INC. (DEC)
CONSOLIDATED STATEMENTS OF COMPREHENSIVE INCOME

(in thousands)

	Year Ended December 31,		
	2013	2012	2011
Net income	$3,057,286	$2,573,599	$2,789,059
Other comprehensive income (loss):			
Net foreign currency translation gain (loss), net of tax	(44,440)	11,076	(5,264)
Available-for-sale securities:			
Net unrealized gain (loss), net of tax impact of $3,741, $(703) and $(3,305)	4,867	1,242	(24,067)
Reclassifications to net income, net of tax impact of $(262), $849 and $(11,114)	(462)	33,008	(19,209)
Net change	4,405	34,250	(43,276)
Cash flow hedges:			
Net unrealized gain (loss), net of tax impact of $4,345, $1,566 and $(93)	(59,653)	(62,505)	1,571
Reclassification to net income, net of tax impact of $(1,193), $(2,171) and $4,389	20,857	(86,636)	74,258
Net change	(38,796)	(149,141)	75,829
Other comprehensive income (loss)	(78,831)	(103,815)	27,289
Comprehensive income	2,978,455	2,469,784	2,816,348
Comprehensive loss attributable to noncontrolling interest	17,522	17,967	14,578
Comprehensive income attributable to Gilead	$2,995,977	$2,487,751	$2,830,926

NOTES TO CONSOLIDATED FINANCIAL STATEMENTS

1. Organization and Summary of Significant Accounting Policies (in part)

Foreign Currency Translation, Transaction Gains and Losses, and Hedging Contracts (in part)

We hedge a portion of our foreign currency exposures related to outstanding monetary assets and liabilities as well as forecasted product sales using foreign currency exchange forward and option contracts. In general, the market risk related to these contracts is offset by corresponding gains and losses on the hedged transactions. The credit risk associated with these contracts is driven by changes in interest and currency exchange rates and, as a result, varies over time. By working only with major banks and closely monitoring current market conditions, we seek to limit the risk that counterparties to these contracts may be unable to perform. We also seek to limit our risk of loss by entering into contracts that permit net settlement at maturity. Therefore, our overall risk of loss in the event of a counterparty default is limited to the amount of any unrecognized gains on outstanding contracts (i.e., those contracts that have a positive fair value) at the date of default. We do not enter into derivative contracts for trading purposes, nor do we hedge our net investment in any of our foreign subsidiaries.

Derivative Financial Instruments

We recognize all derivative instruments as either assets or liabilities at fair value in our Consolidated Balance Sheets. Changes in the fair value of derivatives are recorded each period in current earnings or accumulated other comprehensive income (loss), depending on whether a derivative is designated as part of a hedge transaction and, if it is, the type of hedge transaction. We classify the cash flows from these instruments in the same category as the cash flows from the hedged items. We do not hold or issue derivative instruments for trading or speculative purposes.

We assess, both at inception and on an ongoing basis, whether the derivatives that are used in hedging transactions are highly effective in offsetting the changes in cash flows or fair values of the hedged items. We also assess hedge ineffectiveness on a quarterly basis and record the gain or loss related to the ineffective portion to current earnings to the extent significant. If we determine that a forecasted transaction is no longer probable of occurring, we discontinue hedge accounting for the affected portion of the hedge instrument, and any related unrealized gain or loss on the contract is recognized in current earnings.

4. Derivative Financial Instruments (in part)

We operate in foreign countries, which exposes us to market risk associated with foreign currency exchange rate fluctuations between the U.S. dollar and various foreign currencies, the most significant of which is the Euro. In order to manage this risk, we may hedge a portion of our foreign currency exposures related to outstanding monetary assets and liabilities as well as forecasted product sales using foreign currency exchange forward or option contracts. In general, the market risk related to these contracts is offset by corresponding gains and losses on the hedged transactions. The credit risk associated with these contracts is driven by changes in interest and currency exchange rates and, as a result, varies over time. By working only with major banks and closely monitoring current market conditions, we seek to limit the risk that counterparties to these contracts may be unable to perform. We also seek to limit our risk of loss by entering into contracts that permit net settlement at maturity. Therefore, our overall risk of loss in the event of a counterparty default is limited to the amount of any unrecognized gains on outstanding contracts (i.e., those contracts that have a positive fair value) at the date of default. We do not enter into derivative contracts for trading purposes.

We hedge our exposure to foreign currency exchange rate fluctuations for certain monetary assets and liabilities of our foreign subsidiaries that are denominated in a non-functional currency. The derivative instruments we use to hedge this exposure are not designated as hedges, and as a result, changes in their fair value are recorded in other income (expense), net on our Consolidated Statements of Income.

We hedge our exposure to foreign currency exchange rate fluctuations for forecasted product sales that are denominated in a non-functional currency. The derivative instruments we use to hedge this exposure are designated as cash flow hedges and have maturity dates of 18 months or less. Upon executing a hedging contract and quarterly thereafter, we assess prospective hedge effectiveness using a regression analysis which calculates the change in cash flow as a result of the hedge instrument. On a monthly basis, we assess retrospective hedge effectiveness using a dollar offset approach. We exclude time value from our effectiveness testing and recognize changes in the time value of the hedge in other income (expense), net. The effective component of our hedge is recorded as an unrealized gain or loss on the hedging instrument in accumulated other comprehensive income (OCI) within stockholders' equity. When the hedged forecasted transaction occurs, the hedge is de-designated and the unrealized gains or losses are reclassified into product sales. The majority of gains and losses related to the hedged forecasted transactions reported in accumulated OCI at December 31, 2013 will be reclassified to product sales within 12 months.

The cash flow effects of our derivatives contracts for the three years ended December 31, 2013, 2012 and 2011 are included within net cash provided by operating activities in the Consolidated Statements of Cash Flows.

We had notional amounts on foreign currency exchange contracts outstanding of $4.28 billion at December 31, 2013 and $3.39 billion at December 31, 2012.

The following table summarizes the effect of our foreign currency exchange contracts on our Consolidated Statements of Income (in thousands):

	Year Ended December 31,		
	2013	2012	2011
Derivatives designated as hedges:			
Gains (losses) recognized in OCI (effective portion)	$(55,308)	$(62,258)	$ 1,664
Gains (losses) reclassified from accumulated OCI into product sales (effective portion)	$(19,664)	$ 88,807	$(78,647)
Gains (losses) recognized in other income (expense), net (ineffective portion and amounts excluded from effectiveness testing)	$ 1,645	$ (8,444)	$(17,237)
Derivatives not designated as hedges:			
Gains (losses) recognized in other income (expense), net	$(16,550)	$ (1,099)	$ 22,084

From time to time, we may discontinue cash flow hedges and as a result, record related amounts in other income (expense), net on our Consolidated Statements of Income. There were no material amounts recorded in other income (expense), net for the years ended December 31, 2013, 2012 and 2011 as a result of the discontinuance of cash flow hedges.

RECLASSIFICATION ADJUSTMENTS

4.16 YAHOO! INC. (DEC)
CONSOLIDATED STATEMENTS OF COMPREHENSIVE INCOME

	Years Ended December 31,		
(In thousands)	2011	2012	2013
Comprehensive income			
Net income	$1,062,669	$3,950,602	$1,376,566
Available-for-sale securities:			
Unrealized (losses) gains on available-for-sale securities, net of taxes of $8,518, $(86), and $(1,724) for 2011, 2012, and 2013, respectively	(17,244)	7,571	6,776
Reclassification adjustment for realized losses (gains) on available-for-sale securities included in net income, net of taxes of $(648), $(5,197), and $479 for 2011, 2012, and 2013, respectively	972	9,088	(796)
Net change in unrealized gains (losses) on available-for-sale securities, net of tax	(16,272)	16,659	5,980
Foreign currency translation adjustments ("CTA"):			
Foreign CTA gains (losses), net of taxes of $101, $(143), and $496 for 2011, 2012, and 2013, respectively	209,887	(9,334)	(577,711)
Net investment hedge CTA gains (losses), net of taxes of $0 for both of 2011 and 2012 and $(193) million for 2013	—	3,241	317,459
Reclassification adjustment for CTA, net of taxes of $0, $68 million, and $0 for 2011, 2012, and 2013 respectively	—	(137,186)	—
Net foreign CTA gains (losses), net of tax	209,887	(143,279)	(260,252)
Cash flow hedges:			
Unrealized gains (losses) on cash flow hedges, net of taxes of $0 for both of 2011 and 2012, and $(1,199) for 2013	—	—	3,492
Reclassification adjustment for realized (gains) losses on cash flow hedges, net of taxes of $0 for both of 2011 and 2012, and $575 for 2013	—	—	(2,080)
Net change in unrealized gains (losses) on cash flow hedges, net of tax	—	—	1,412
Other comprehensive income (loss)	193,615	(126,620)	(252,860)
Comprehensive income	1,256,284	3,823,982	1,123,706
Less: Comprehensive income attributable to noncontrolling interests	(13,842)	(5,123)	(10,285)
Comprehensive income attributable to Yahoo! Inc.	$1,242,442	$3,818,859	$1,113,421

NOTES TO CONSOLIDATED FINANCIAL STATEMENTS

Note 1—The Company and Summary of Significant Accounting Policies (in part)

Derivative Financial Instruments. The Company uses derivative financial instruments, primarily foreign currency forward contracts, to mitigate certain foreign currency exposures. The Company hedges, on an after-tax basis, a portion of its net investment in Yahoo Japan. The Company has designated these foreign currency forward contracts as net investment hedges, which are accounted for in accordance with ASC 815 "Derivatives and Hedging" ("ASC 815"). The effective portion of changes in fair value is recorded in accumulated other comprehensive income on the Company's consolidated balance sheet and any ineffective portion is recorded in other income, net on the Company's consolidated statements of income. The Company expects the net investment hedges to be effective, on an after-tax basis, as described in ASC 815 and effectiveness will be assessed each quarter. Should any portion of the net investment hedge become ineffective, the ineffective portion will be reclassified to other income, net on the Company's consolidated statements of income. The fair values of the net investment hedges are determined using quoted observable inputs. Gains and losses reported in accumulated other comprehensive income will not be reclassified into earnings until a sale of the Company's underlying investment.

For derivatives designated as cash flow hedges, the effective portion of the unrealized gains or losses on these forward contracts is recorded in accumulated other comprehensive income on the Company's consolidated balance sheets and reclassified into revenue on the consolidated statements of income when the underlying hedged revenue is recognized. If the cash flow hedges were to become ineffective, the ineffective portion would be immediately recorded in other income, net on the Company's consolidated statements of income.

The Company hedges certain of its net recognized foreign currency assets and liabilities with foreign exchange forward contracts to reduce the risk that its earnings and cash flows will be adversely affected by changes in foreign currency exchange rates. These balance sheet hedges are used to partially offset the foreign currency exchange gains and losses generated by the re-measurement of certain assets and liabilities denominated in non-functional currency. Changes in the fair value of these derivatives are recorded in other income, net on the Company's consolidated statements of income. The fair values of the balance sheet hedges are determined using quoted observable inputs.

In October 2013, the Company began hedging a portion of the forecasted revenue of certain international subsidiaries whose functional currencies are not the U.S. dollar. This program attempts to reduce the risk that the Company's revenue denominated in these currencies will be adversely affected by foreign currency exchange rate fluctuations. These derivatives are economic hedges and as such do not qualify for hedge accounting. Changes in the fair value of these derivatives are recorded as a component of revenue in the Company's consolidated statements of income.

The Company recognizes all derivative instruments as other assets or liabilities on the Company's consolidated balance sheets at fair value. See Note 9—"Derivative Financial Instruments" for a full description of the Company's derivative financial instrument activities and related accounting.

Note 3—Consolidated Financial Statement Details (in part)

Reclassifications Out of Accumulated Other Comprehensive Income

Reclassifications out of accumulated other comprehensive income for the period ended December 31, 2012 were as follows (in thousands):

	Amount Reclassified From Accumulated Other Comprehensive Income	Affected Line Item in the Statement of Income
Realized losses on available-for-sale securities, net of tax	$ 9,088	Yahoo!'s share of earnings in equity method investments and Other income, net
Foreign currency translation adjustments ("CTA"):		
Korea business closure CTA reclassification	$ (16,208)	Restructuring charges net
Alibaba Group Initial Repurchase related CTA reclassification, net of $68 million in tax	(120,978)	Other income, net
Total foreign currency translation adjustments, net of tax	$(137,186)	
Total reclassifications for the period	$(128,098)	

Reclassifications out of accumulated other comprehensive income for the period ended December 31, 2013 were as follows (in thousands):

	Amount Reclassified From Accumulated Other Comprehensive Income	Affected Line Item in the Statement of Income
Realized gains on cash flow hedges, net of tax	$(2,080)	Revenue
Realized gains on available-for-sale securities, net of tax	(796)	Other income, net
Total reclassifications for the period	$(2,876)	

Note 9—Derivative Financial Instruments (in part)

The Company uses derivative financial instruments, primarily forward contracts, to mitigate risk associated with adverse movements in foreign currency exchange rates.

The Company generally enters into master netting arrangements, which are designed to reduce credit risk by permitting net settlement of transactions with the same counterparty. The Company presents its derivative assets and liabilities at their gross fair values on the consolidated balance sheets. The Company is not required to pledge, and is not entitled to receive, cash collateral related to these derivative transactions.

Cash Flow Hedges. The Company entered into foreign currency forward contracts designated as cash flow hedges of varying maturities through July 31, 2014. For derivatives designated as cash flow hedges, the effective portion of the unrealized gains or losses on these forward contracts is recorded in accumulated other comprehensive income on the Company's consolidated balance sheets and reclassified into revenue on the consolidated statements of income when the underlying hedged revenue is recognized. If the cash flow hedges were to become ineffective, the ineffective portion would be immediately recorded in other income, net on the Company's consolidated statements of income. The cash flow hedges were considered to be effective as of December 31, 2013. The total notional amount of the foreign currency forward contracts was $56 million as of December 31, 2013. The fair value of the foreign currency forward contract assets was $4 million as of December 31, 2013 which was included in prepaid expenses and other current assets on the Company's consolidated balance sheets. A pre-tax net gain of $2 million was recorded as of December 31, 2013, which was included in accumulated other comprehensive income on the Company's consolidated balance sheets. For year ended December 31, 2013, the Company recorded gains of $2 million, net of tax, for cash flow hedges, which were recorded in revenue in the consolidated statements of income. The Company received $2 million in cash for settlement of certain foreign currency forward contracts during the year ended December 31, 2013. The Company did not enter into any cash flow hedges in the years ended December 31, 2011 and 2012.

4.17 DELL INC. (JAN)
CONSOLIDATED STATEMENTS OF COMPREHENSIVE INCOME

(In millions)

	Fiscal Year Ended		
	February 1, 2013	February 3, 2012	January 28, 2011
Net income	$2,372	$3,492	$2,635
Adjustment to consolidate variable interest entities	—	—	(1)
Other comprehensive income, net of tax			
Foreign currency translation adjustments	(33)	(74)	79
Available-for-sale investments			
Change in unrealized gains (losses)	7	42	—
Reclassification adjustment for net (gains) losses included in net income	(13)	(29)	(1)
Net change	(6)	13	(1)
Cash Flow Hedges			
Change in unrealized gains (losses)	(18)	(119)	(254)
Reclassification adjustment for net (gains) losses included in net income	59	190	142
Net change	41	71	(112)
Total other comprehensive income (loss), net of tax benefit (expense) of $(8), $(1) and $2, respectively	2	10	(34)
Comprehensive income, net of tax	$2,374	$3,502	$2,600

NOTES TO CONSOLIDATED FINANCIAL STATEMENTS

Note 1—Description of Business and Summary of Significant Accounting Policies (in part)

Hedging Instruments—Dell uses derivative financial instruments, primarily forwards, options, and swaps, to hedge certain foreign currency and interest rate exposures. The relationships between hedging instruments and hedged items, as well as the risk management objectives and strategies for undertaking hedge transactions, are formally documented. Dell does not use derivatives for speculative purposes.

All derivative instruments are recognized as either assets or liabilities in the Consolidated Statements of Financial Position and are measured at fair value. Hedge accounting is applied based upon the criteria established by accounting guidance for derivative instruments and hedging activities. Derivatives are assessed for hedge effectiveness both at the onset of the hedge and at regular intervals throughout the life of the derivative. Any hedge ineffectiveness is recognized currently in earnings as a component of interest and other, net. Dell's hedge portfolio includes derivatives designated as both cash flow and fair value hedges.

For derivative instruments that are designated as cash flow hedges, hedge ineffectiveness is measured by comparing the cumulative change in the fair value of the hedge contract with the cumulative change in the fair value of the hedged item, both of which are based on forward rates. Dell records the effective portion of the gain or loss on the derivative instrument in accumulated other comprehensive income (loss) ("OCI"), as a separate component of stockholders' equity and reclassifies the gain or loss into earnings in the period during which the hedged transaction is recognized in earnings.

For derivatives that are designated as fair value hedges, hedge ineffectiveness is measured by calculating the periodic change in the fair value of the hedge contract and the periodic change in the fair value of the hedged item. To the extent that these fair value changes do not fully offset each other, the difference is recorded as ineffectiveness in earnings as a component of interest and other, net.

For derivatives that are not designated as hedges or do not qualify for hedge accounting treatment, Dell recognizes the change in the instrument's fair value currently in earnings as a component of interest and other, net.

Cash flows from derivative instruments are presented in the same category on the Consolidated Statements of Cash Flows as the cash flows from the underlying hedged items. See Note 6 of the Notes to the Consolidated Financial Statements for a description of Dell's derivative financial instrument activities.

Note 6—Derivative Instruments and Hedging Activities (in part)

Derivative Instruments Additional Information

The unrealized net gain or loss for interest rate swaps and foreign currency exchange contracts, recorded as a component of accumulated other comprehensive loss in the Consolidated Statements of Financial Position, was a gain of $1 million and a loss of $40 million as of February 1, 2013 and February 3, 2012, respectively.

Dell has reviewed the existence and nature of credit-risk-related contingent features in derivative trading agreements with its counterparties. Certain agreements contain clauses under which, if Dell's credit ratings were to fall below investment grade upon a change of control of Dell, counterparties would have the right to terminate those derivative contracts where Dell is in a net liability position. As of February 1, 2013, there had been no such triggering events.

Effect of Derivative Instruments on the Consolidated Statements of Financial Position and the Consolidated Statements of Income

Derivatives in Cash Flow Hedging Relationships	Gain (Loss) Recognized in Accumulated OCI, Net of Tax, on Derivatives (Effective Portion)	Location of Gain (Loss) Reclassified From Accumulated OCI into Income (Effective Portion)	Gain (Loss) Reclassified From Accumulated OCI into Income (Effective Portion)	Location of Gain (Loss) Recognized in Income on Derivative (Ineffective Portion)	Gain (Loss) Recognized in Income on Derivative (Ineffective Portion)
		(In millions)			
For the fiscal year ended February 1, 2013					
		Total net revenue	$ (42)		
Foreign exchange contracts	$ (16)	Total cost of net revenue	(15)		
Interest rate contracts	(2)	Interest and other, net	—	Interest and other, net	$(2)
Total	$ (18)		$ (57)		$(2)
For the fiscal year ended February 3, 2012					
		Total net revenue	$(188)		
Foreign exchange contracts	$(122)	Total cost of net revenue	(3)		
Interest rate contracts	3	Interest and other, net	—	Interest and other, net	$ 1
Total	$(119)		$(191)		$ 1

Format of Stockholders' Equity in Annual Filings

PRESENTATION

5.01 *Equity* (sometimes referred to as net assets) is the residual interest in the assets of an entity that remains after deducting its liabilities. As discussed in Financial Accounting Standards Board (FASB) *Accounting Standards Codification* (ASC) 505-10-50-2 if both financial position and results of operations are presented, disclosure of changes in (*a*) the separate accounts comprising stockholders' equity (in addition to retained earnings) and (*b*) the number of shares of equity securities during at least the most recent annual fiscal period and any subsequent interim period presented is required in order to make the financial statements sufficiently informative. Disclosure of such changes may take the form of separate statements or may be made in the basic financial statements or notes thereto. Most public entities present a statement of stockholders' equity to conform with Rule 3-04 of Securities and Exchange Commission (SEC) Regulation S-X.

5.02 FASB ASC 505-10-25-1 explains that additional paid-in capital, however created, should not be used to relieve income of the current or future years of charges that would otherwise be made to the income statement.

5.03 As discussed in FASB ASC 505-20-30-3, in accounting for a stock dividend, a corporation should transfer from retained earnings to the category of capital stock and additional paid-in capital an amount equal to the fair value of the additional shares issued.

5.04 Rule 5-02 of Regulation S-X requires separate captions for additional paid-in capital, other additional capital, and retained earnings. If appropriate, additional paid-in capital and other additional capital may be combined with the stock caption to which it applies.

DISCLOSURE

5.05 FASB ASC 505-10-50-3 states that an entity should explain the pertinent rights and privileges of the various securities outstanding. Examples are dividend and liquidation preferences; contractual rights of security holders to receive dividends or returns from the security issuer's profits, cash flows, or returns on investments; participation rights; call prices and dates; conversion or exercise prices or rates and pertinent dates; sinking-fund requirements; unusual voting rights; and significant terms of contracts to issue additional shares.

5.06 FASB ASC 505-10-50-2 also requires disclosure of changes in the separate accounts comprising shareholders' equity (in addition to retained earnings) and of the changes in the number of shares of equity securities during at least the most recent annual fiscal period. Disclosure of such changes may take the form of separate statements or may be made in the basic financial statements or notes thereto.

PRESENTATION AND DISCLOSURE EXCERPTS

ISSUANCE OF COMMON STOCK UNDER STOCK PLANS

5.07 ST. JUDE MEDICAL, INC. (DEC)
CONSOLIDATED STATEMENTS OF SHAREHOLDERS' EQUITY

(In millions, except share amounts)

	Common Stock		Additional Paid-In Capital	Retained Earnings	Accumulated Other Comprehensive Income	Non-controlling Interest	Total Shareholders' Equity
	Number of Shares	Amount					
Balance at January 1, 2011	329,018,166	$33	$ 156	$4,099	$ 84	$ —	$ 4,372
Net earnings				826		—	826
Other comprehensive loss					(68)	—	(68)
Cash dividends declared				(272)			(272)
Repurchases of common stock	(18,314,774)	(2)	(504)	(269)			(775)
Stock-based compensation			76				76
Common stock issued under employee stock plans and other, net	8,912,573	1	302				303
Tax benefit from stock plans			13				13

(continued)

	Common Stock		Additional Paid-In Capital	Retained Earnings	Accumulated Other Comprehensive Income	Non-controlling Interest	Total Shareholders' Equity
	Number of Shares	Amount					
Balance at December 31, 2011	319,615,965	32	43	4,384	16	—	4,475
Net earnings				752		—	752
Other comprehensive income					30	—	30
Cash dividends declared				(284)			(284)
Repurchases of common stock	(27,670,874)	(3)	(221)	(834)			(1,058)
Stock-based compensation			69				69
Common stock issued under employee stock plans and other, net	3,703,236	1	118				119
Tax shortfall from stock plans			(9)				(9)
Balance at December 29, 2012	295,648,327	30	—	4,018	46	—	4,094
Net earnings				723		(31)	692
Other comprehensive income					—		—
Cash dividends declared				(286)			(286)
Repurchases of common stock	(18,385,436)	(2)	(287)	(519)			(808)
Stock-based compensation			65				65
Common stock issued under employee stock plans and other, net	11,854,461	1	442				443
Additions in noncontrolling ownership interests						2 04	204
Balance at December 28, 2013	289,117,352	$29	$ 220	$3,936	$ 46	$173	$ 4,404

NOTES TO THE CONDENSED CONSOLIDATED FINANCIAL STATEMENTS

Note 1—Summary of Significant Accounting Policies (in part)

Stock-Based Compensation: The Company accounts for stock-based compensation in accordance with ASC Topic 718, *Compensation—Stock Compensation* (ASC Topic 718). Under the fair value recognition provisions of ASC Topic 718, the Company measures stock-based compensation cost at the grant date fair value and recognizes the compensation expense over the requisite service period, which is the vesting period, using a straight-line attribution method.

The amount of stock-based compensation expense recognized during a period is based on the portion of the awards that are ultimately expected to vest. The Company estimates pre-vesting award forfeitures at the time of grant by analyzing historical data and revises those estimates in subsequent periods if actual forfeitures differ from those estimates. Ultimately, the total expense recognized over the vesting period will only be for those awards that vest. The Company's awards are not eligible to vest early in the event of retirement, however, the majority of the Company's awards vest early in the event of a change in control. See Note 8 for further detail on the Company's stock compensation plans.

Note 8—Stock-Based Compensation

Stock Compensation Plans

The Company's stock compensation plans provide for the issuance of stock-based awards, such as stock options, restricted stock units and restricted stock awards, to directors, officers, employees and consultants. Since 2000, all stock option awards granted under these plans have an exercise price equal to the closing stock price on the date of grant, an eight-year contractual life and generally, vest annually over a four-year vesting term. Restricted stock units and restricted stock awards under these plans also generally vest annually over a four-year period. Restricted stock awards are considered issued and outstanding at the grant date and have the same dividend and voting rights as other common stock. Directors can elect to receive half of their entire annual retainer in the form of a restricted stock award with a six-month vesting term. Restricted stock units are not issued and outstanding at the grant date; instead, upon vesting the recipient receives one share of the Company's common stock for each vested restricted stock unit. At December 28, 2013, the Company had 15.7 million shares of common stock available for stock option grants under its stock compensation plans. The Company has the ability to grant a portion of the available shares in the form of restricted stock awards or units. Specifically, in lieu of granting up to 13.9 million stock options under these plans, the Company may grant up to 6.2 million restricted stock awards or units (for certain grants of restricted stock units or awards, the number of shares available are reduced by 2.25 shares). Additionally, in lieu of granting up to 0.1 million stock options under these plans, the Company may grant up to 0.1 million restricted stock awards (for certain grants of restricted stock awards, the number of shares available are reduced by one share). The remaining 1.7 million shares of common stock are available only for stock option grants. At December 28, 2013, there was $149 million of total unrecognized stock-based compensation expense, adjusted for estimated forfeitures, which is expected to be recognized over a weighted average period of approximately 2.9 years and will be adjusted for any future changes in estimated forfeitures.

The Company also has an Employee Stock Purchase Plan (ESPP) that allows participating employees to purchase newly issued shares of the Company's common stock at a discount through payroll deductions. The ESPP consists of a 12-month offering period whereby employees can purchase shares at 85% of the market value at either the beginning of the offering period or the end of the offering period, whichever price is lower. Employees purchased 0.9 million shares each year in fiscal years 2013, 2012 and 2011. At December 28, 2013, 5.8 million shares of common stock were available for future purchases under the ESPP.

The Company's total stock compensation expense for fiscal years 2013, 2012 and 2011 by income statement line item was as follows (in millions):

	2013	2012	2011
Selling, general and administrative expense	$45	$49	$55
Research and development expense	15	15	15
Cost of sales	5	5	6
Total stock compensation expense	$65	$69	$76

Valuation Assumptions

The Company uses the Black-Scholes standard option pricing model (Black-Scholes model) to determine the fair value of stock options and ESPP purchase rights. The determination of the fair value of the awards on the date of grant using the Black-Scholes model is affected by the Company's stock price as well as assumptions of other variables, including projected employee stock option exercise behaviors, risk-free interest rate, expected volatility of the Company's stock price in future periods and expected dividend yield. The fair value of both restricted stock and restricted stock units is based on the Company's closing stock price on the date of grant. The weighted average fair value of restricted stock awards granted during fiscal years 2013, 2012 and 2011 was $42.26, $37.63 and $49.77, respectively. The weighted average fair value of the restricted stock units granted during fiscal years 2013, 2012 and 2011 was $59.04, $35.39 and $35.14, respectively. The weighted average fair value of ESPP purchase rights granted to employees during fiscal years 2013, 2012 and 2011 was $13.06, $9.39 and $10.86, respectively.

The following table provides the weighted average fair value of stock options granted to employees during fiscal years 2013, 2012 and 2011 and the related weighted average assumptions used in the Black-Scholes model:

	2013	2012	2011
Fair value of options granted	$13.83	$7.71	$9.17
Assumptions:			
Expected life (years)	5.4	5.4	5.5
Risk-free interest rate	1.6%	0.7%	0.9%
Volatility	28.6%	31.2%	33.9%
Dividend yield	1.8%	2.5%	2.0%

Expected Life: The Company analyzes historical employee exercise and termination data to estimate the expected life assumption. Annually, the Company updates these assumptions unless circumstances would indicate a more frequent update is necessary.

Risk-free Interest Rate: The rate is based on the U.S. Treasury zero-coupon yield curve on the grant date for a maturity equal to or approximating the expected life of the options.

Volatility: The Company calculates its expected volatility assumption by blending the historical and implied volatility. The historical volatility is based on the daily closing prices of the Company's common stock over a period equal to the expected term of the option. Market-based implied volatility is based on utilizing market data of actively traded options on the Company's stock, from options at- or near-the-money, at a point in time as close to the grant date of the employee options as reasonably practical and with similar terms to the employee share option, or a remaining maturity of at least six months if no similar terms are available. The historical volatility of the Company's common stock price over the expected term of the option is a strong indicator of the expected future volatility. In addition, implied volatility takes into consideration market expectations of how future volatility will differ from historical volatility. The Company does not believe that one estimate is more reliable than the other, and as a result, the Company uses an equal weighting of historical volatility and market-based implied volatility.

Dividend Yield: Beginning in fiscal year 2011, the Company began paying cash dividends. The Company's dividend yield assumption is based on the expected annual dividend yield on the grant date.

Stock Compensation Activity

The following table summarizes stock option activity under all stock compensation plans during the fiscal year ended December 28, 2013:

	Options (In Millions)	Weighted Average Exercise Price	Weighted Average Remaining Contractual Term (In Years)	Aggregate Intrinsic Value (In Millions)
Outstanding at December 29, 2012	28.2	$38.05		
Granted	2.7	59.16		
Exercised	(10.6)	39.83		
Canceled	(1.4)	40.05		
Outstanding at December 28, 2013	18.9	$39.94	5.3	$422
Vested and expected to vest	18.2	$39.70	5.2	$409
Exercisable at December 28, 2013	10.6	$37.07	4.1	$267

The aggregate intrinsic value of options outstanding and options exercisable is based on the Company's closing stock price on the last trading day of the fiscal year for in-the-money options. The aggregate intrinsic value represents the cumulative difference between the fair market value of the underlying common stock and the option exercise prices. The total intrinsic value of options exercised during fiscal years 2013, 2012 and 2011 was $125 million, $14 million and $96 million, respectively.

The following table summarizes activity for restricted stock awards and restricted stock units under all stock compensation plans during the fiscal year ended December 28, 2013:

	Restricted Stock (in millions)	Weighted Average Grant Date Fair Value
Unvested balance at December 29, 2012	1.6	$36.61
Granted	0.7	58.32
Vested	(0.5)	37.45
Canceled	(0.2)	36.96
Unvested balance at December 28, 2013	1.6	$45.98

The total aggregate grant date fair value of restricted stock awards and restricted stock units vested during fiscal years 2013, 2012 and 2011 was $18 million, $11 million and $7 million, respectively.

EXERCISE OF WARRANTS

5.08 LAS VEGAS SANDS CORP. (DEC)
CONSOLIDATED STATEMENTS OF EQUITY

	Las Vegas Sands Corp. Stockholder's Equity							
(In thousands)	Preferred Stock	Common Stock	Capital in Excess of Par Value	Treasury Stock	Accumulated Other Comprehensive Income	Retained Earnings	Noncontrolling Interests	Total
Balance at January 1, 2011	$ 207,356	$708	$5,444,705	$ —	$129,519	$ 880,703	$1,268,197	$ 7,931,188
Net income	—	—	—	—	—	1,560,123	322,996	1,883,119
Currency translation adjustment	—	—	—	—	(35,415)	—	2,622	(32,793)
Exercise of stock options	—	2	24,223	—	—	—	1,280	25,505
Stock-based compensation	—	—	60,363	—	—	—	2,927	63,290
Issuance of restricted stock	—	1	(1)	—	—	—	—	—
Exercise of warrants	(68,380)	22	80,870	—	—	—	—	12,512
Disposition of interest in majority owned subsidiary	—	—	—	—	—	—	829	829
Repurchase and redemption of preferred stock	(138,976)	—	—	—	—	(128,845)	—	(267,821)
Dividends declared, net of amounts previously accrued	—	—	—	—	—	(68,443)	—	(68,443)
Distributions to noncontrolling interests	—	—	—	—	—	—	(10,388)	(10,388)
Accretion to redemption value of preferred stock issued to Principal Stockholder's family	—	—	—	—	—	(80,975)	—	(80,975)
Preferred stock inducement premium	—	—	—	—	—	(16,871)	—	(16,871)

(continued)

(In thousands)				Las Vegas Sands Corp. Stockholder's Equity				
	Preferred Stock	Common Stock	Capital in Excess of Par Value	Treasury Stock	Accumulated Other Comprehensive Income	Retained Earnings	Noncontrolling Interests	Total
Balance at December 31, 2011	—	733	5,610,160	—	94,104	2,145,692	1,588,463	9,439,152
Net income	—	—	—	—	—	1,524,093	357,720	1,881,813
Currency translation adjustment, net of reclassification adjustment	—	—	—	—	168,974	—	3,814	172,788
Exercise of stock options	—	2	40,038	—	—	—	6,200	46,240
Stock-based compensation	—	—	63,102	—	—	—	3,264	66,366
Issuance of restricted stock	—	1	(1)	—	—	—	—	—
Exercise of warrants	—	88	528,820	—	—	—	—	528,908
Acquisition of remaining shares of noncontrolling interest	—	—	(4,631)	—	—	—	4,631	—
Dividends declared	—	—	—	—	—	(3,090,757)	(357,056)	(3,447,813)
Distributions to noncontrolling interests	—	—	—	—	—	—	(10,466)	(10,466)
Deemed distribution to Principal Stockholder	—	—	—	—	—	(18,576)	—	(18,576)
Balance at December 31, 2012	—	824	6,237,488	—	263,078	560,452	1,596,570	8,658,412
Net income	—	—	—	—	—	2,305,997	648,679	2,954,676
Currency translation adjustment	—	—	—	—	(89,295)	—	(681)	(89,976)
Exercise of stock options	—	3	60,065	—	—	—	9,528	69,596
Stock-based compensation	—	—	50,162	—	—	—	4,156	54,318
Repurchase of common stock	—	—	—	(570,520)	—	—	—	(570,520)
Exercise of warrants	—	—	350	—	—	—	—	350
Dividends declared	—	—	—	—	—	(1,153,110)	(411,359)	(1,564,469)
Distributions to noncontrolling interests	—	—	—	—	—	—	(11,858)	(11,858)
Balance at December 31, 2013	$ —	$827	$6,348,065	$(570,520)	$173,783	$ 1,713,339	$1,835,035	$ 9,500,529

NOTES TO CONSOLIDATED FINANCIAL STATEMENTS

Note 9—Equity (in part)

Preferred Stock and Warrants (in part)

In November 2008, the Company issued 10,446,300 shares of its 10% Series A Cumulative Perpetual Preferred Stock (the "Preferred Stock") and warrants to purchase up to an aggregate of approximately 174,105,348 shares of common stock at an exercise price of $6.00 per share and an expiration date of November 16, 2013 (the "Warrants"). Units consisting of one share of Preferred Stock and one Warrant to purchase 16.6667 shares of common stock were sold for $100 per unit. As described further below, the outstanding Preferred Stock was redeemed in whole by the Company on November 15, 2011, at a redemption price of $110 per share. Holders of the Preferred Stock had no rights to exchange or convert such shares into any other securities.

Preferred Stock Issued to Public

Of the 10,446,300 shares of Preferred Stock issued, the Company issued 5,196,300 shares to the public together with Warrants to purchase up to an aggregate of approximately 86,605,173 shares of its common stock and received gross proceeds of $519.6 million ($503.6 million, net of transaction costs). The allocated carrying values of the Preferred Stock and Warrants on the date of issuance (based on their relative fair values) were $298.1 million and $221.5 million, respectively.

During the year ended December 31, 2013, the remaining 3,500 Warrants were exercised to purchase an aggregate of 64,562 shares of the Company's common stock at $6.00 per share and $0.3 million in cash was received as settlement of the Warrant exercise price.

During the year ended December 31, 2012, 39,070 Warrants were exercised to purchase an aggregate of 655,496 shares of the Company's common stock at $6.00 per share and $3.9 million in cash was received as settlement of the Warrant exercise price.

During the year ended December 31, 2011, holders of Preferred Stock exercised 1,317,220 Warrants to purchase an aggregate of 21,953,704 shares of the Company's common stock at $6.00 per share and tendered 1,192,100 shares of Preferred Stock and $12.5 million in cash as settlement of the Warrant exercise price. In conjunction with certain of these transactions, the Company paid $16.9 million in premiums to induce the exercise of Warrants with settlement through tendering Preferred Stock. During the year ended December 31, 2011, the Company also repurchased and retired 736,629 shares of Preferred Stock for $82.3 million.

Preferred Stock Issued to Principal Stockholder's Family (in part)

Of the 10,446,300 shares of Preferred Stock issued, the Company issued 5,250,000 shares to the Principal Stockholder's family together with Warrants to purchase up to an aggregate of approximately 87,500,175 shares of its common stock and received gross proceeds of $525.0 million ($523.7 million, net of transaction costs). The allocated carrying values of the Preferred Stock and Warrants on the date of issuance (based on their relative fair values) were $301.1 million and $223.9 million, respectively. The Preferred Stock amount had been recorded as mezzanine equity as the Principal Stockholder and his family have a greater than 50% ownership of the Company and therefore had the ability to require the Company to redeem their Preferred Stock beginning November 15, 2011.

On March 2, 2012, the Principal Stockholder's family exercised all of their outstanding Warrants to purchase 87,500,175 shares of the Company's common stock for $6.00 per share and paid $525.0 million in cash as settlement of the Warrant exercise price.

Common Stock (in part)

Rollforward of Shares of Common Stock and Preferred Stock Issued to Public

A summary of the outstanding shares of common stock and preferred stock issued to the public is as follows:

	Preferred Stock	Common Stock
Balance as of January 1, 2011	3,614,923	707,507,982
Exercise of stock options	—	2,549,131
Issuance of restricted stock	—	1,250,381
Forfeiture of unvested restricted stock	—	(11,500)
Exercise of warrants	(1,192,100)	21,953,704
Repurchases and redemption of preferred stock	(2,422,823)	—
Balance as of December 31, 2011	—	733,249,698
Exercise of stock options	—	2,387,831
Issuance of restricted stock	—	516,556
Forfeiture of unvested restricted stock	—	(12,000)
Exercise of warrants	—	88,155,671
Balance as of December 31, 2012	—	824,297,756
Exercise of stock options	—	2,777,127
Issuance of restricted stock	—	146,848
Forfeiture of unvested restricted stock	—	(13,076)
Repurchase of common stock	—	(8,570,281)
Exercise of warrants	—	64,562
Balance as of December 31, 2013	—	818,702,936

Note 16—Related Party Transactions (in part)

On November 15, 2011, the Company paid $577.5 million to redeem all of the Preferred Stock held by the Principal Stockholder's family. On March 2, 2012, the Principal Stockholder's family exercised all of their outstanding Warrants to purchase 87,500,175 shares of the Company's common stock for $6.00 per share and paid $525.0 million in cash as settlement of the Warrant exercise price. See "—Note 9—Equity—Preferred Stock and Warrants—Preferred Stock Issued to Principal Stockholder's Family."

STOCK-BASED COMPENSATION

5.09 VALERO ENERGY CORPORATION (DEC)
CONSOLIDATED STATEMENTS OF EQUITY

(Millions of Dollars)

	Valero Energy Corporation Stockholders' Equity						Non-controlling Interests	Total Equity
	Common Stock	Additional Paid-in Capital	Treasury Stock	Retained Earnings	Accumulated Other Comprehensive Income (Loss)	Total		
Balance as of December 31, 2010	$ 7	$7,704	$(6,462)	$13,388	$ 388	$15,025	$ —	$15,025
Net income (loss)	—	—	—	2,090	—	2,090	(1)	2,089
Dividends on common stock	—	—	—	(169)	—	(169)	—	(169)
Stock-based compensation expense	—	57	—	—	—	57	—	57
Tax deduction in excess of stock-based compensation expense	—	22	—	—	—	22	—	22
Transactions in connection with stock-based compensation plans:								
Stock issuances	—	(287)	336	—	—	49	—	49
Stock repurchases	—	(10)	(349)	—	—	(359)	—	(359)
Contributions from noncontrolling interest	—	—	—	—	—	—	23	23
Recognition of noncontrolling interests in Mainline Pipelines Limited in connection with Pembroke Acquisition	—	—	—	—	—	—	5	5
Acquisition of noncontrolling interests in Mainline Pipelines Limited	—	—	—	—	—	—	(5)	(5)
Other comprehensive loss	—	—	—	—	(292)	(292)	—	(292)
Balance as of December 31, 2011	7	7,486	(6,475)	15,309	96	16,423	22	16,445
Net income (loss)	—	—	—	2,083	—	2,083	(3)	2,080
Dividends on common stock	—	—	—	(360)	—	(360)	—	(360)
Stock-based compensation expense	—	57	—	—	—	57	—	57
Tax deduction in excess of stock-based compensation expense	—	29	—	—	—	29	—	29
Transactions in connection with stock-based compensation plans:								
Stock issuances	—	(260)	319	—	—	59	—	59
Stock repurchases	—	10	(163)	—	—	(153)	—	(153)
Stock repurchases under buyback program	—	—	(118)	—	—	(118)	—	(118)
Contributions from noncontrolling interest	—	—	—	—	—	—	44	44
Other comprehensive income	—	—	—	—	12	12	—	12
Balance as of December 31, 2012	7	7,322	(6,437)	17,032	108	18,032	63	18,095
Net income	—	—	—	2,720	—	2,720	8	2,728
Dividends on common stock	—	—	—	(462)	—	(462)	—	(462)
Stock-based compensation expense	—	64	—	—	—	64	—	64
Tax deduction in excess of stock-based compensation expense	—	47	—	—	—	47	—	47
Transactions in connection with stock-based compensation plans:								
Stock issuances	—	(243)	302	—	—	59	—	59
Stock repurchases	—	—	(236)	—	—	(236)	—	(236)
Stock repurchases under buyback program	—	—	(692)	—	—	(692)	—	(692)
Separation of retail business	—	(9)	9	(320)	(159)	(479)	—	(479)
Net proceeds from initial public offering of common units of Valero Energy Partners LP	—	—	—	—	—	—	369	369
Contributions from noncontrolling interests	—	—	—	—	—	—	46	46
Other	—	6	—	—	—	6	—	6
Other comprehensive income	—	—	—	—	401	401	—	401
Balance as of December 31, 2013	$ 7	$7,187	$(7,054)	$18,970	$ 350	$19,460	$486	$19,946

1. Basis of Presentation and Summary of Significant Accounting Policies (in part)

Significant Accounting Policies (in part)

Stock-Based Compensation

Compensation expense for our share-based compensation plans is based on the fair value of the awards granted and is recognized in income on a straight-line basis over the requisite service period of each award. For new grants that have retirement-eligibility provisions, we use the non-substantive vesting period approach, under which compensation cost is recognized immediately for awards granted to retirement-eligible employees or over the period from the grant date to the date retirement eligibility is achieved if that date is expected to occur during the nominal vesting period.

15. Stock-Based Compensation

We maintain the 2011 Omnibus Stock Incentive Plan (the OSIP) under which various stock and stock-based awards are granted to employees and non-employee directors. Awards available under the OSIP include options to purchase shares of common stock, performance awards that vest upon the achievement of an objective performance goal, stock appreciation rights, and restricted stock that vests over a period determined by our compensation committee. The OSIP was approved by our stockholders on April 28, 2011. As of December 31, 2013, 15,340,981 shares of our common stock remained available to be awarded under the OSIP.

We also maintain other stock-based compensation plans under which previously granted equity awards remain outstanding. No additional grants may be awarded under these plans.

In connection with the separation of our retail business on May 1, 2013 (as further described in Note 3), we entered into an employee matters agreement with CST, which provides that employees of CST no longer participate in our benefit plans. Under this agreement, we made certain adjustments to the exercise price and the number of our share-based compensation awards, the effect of which preserved the intrinsic value of the awards immediately prior to the separation; no incremental value resulted from these adjustments. Also upon the separation, awards of restricted stock and performance shares made to Valero employees who became employees of CST were either vested or forfeited. These adjustments are reflected in the activity tables below.

The following table reflects activity related to our stock-based compensation arrangements (in millions):

	Year Ended December 31,		
	2013	**2012**	**2011**
Stock-based compensation expense	$64	$58	$58
Tax benefit recognized on stock-based compensation expense	22	20	20
Tax benefit realized for tax deductions resulting from exercises and vestings	66	45	35
Effect of tax deductions in excess of recognized stock-based compensation expense reported as a financing cash flow	47	27	23

Each of our stock-based compensation arrangements is discussed below.

Stock Options

Under the terms of our various stock-based compensation plans, the exercise price of options granted is not less than the fair market value of our common stock on the date of grant. Stock options become exercisable pursuant to the individual written agreements between the participants and us, usually in three equal annual installments beginning one year after the date of grant, with unexercised options generally expiring seven or ten years from the date of grant.

The fair value of stock options granted during 2013 and 2012 were estimated using the Monte Carlo simulation model, as these options contain both a service condition and a market condition in order to be exercised. Prior to 2012, the fair value of each stock option grant was estimated on the grant date using the Black-Scholes option-pricing model. The expected life of options granted is the period of time from the grant date to the date of expected exercise or other expected settlement. The expected life for each of the years in the table below was calculated using the safe harbor provisions of SEC Staff Accounting Bulletin No. 107 and No. 110 related to share-based payments. Because the stock options granted in 2012 and later contain a market condition, historical exercise patterns did not provide a reasonable basis for estimating the expected life. Expected volatility is based on closing prices of our common stock for periods corresponding to the expected life of options granted. Expected dividend yield is based on annualized dividends at the date of grant. The risk-free interest rate used is the implied yield currently available from the U.S. Treasury zero-coupon issues with a remaining term equal to the expected life of the options at the grant date.

A summary of the weighted-average assumptions used in our fair value measurements is presented in the table below.

	Year Ended December 31,		
	2013	2012	2011
Expected life in years	6.0	6.0	6.0
Expected volatility	49.63%	49.11%	49.30%
Expected dividend yield	2.27%	2.39%	2.28%
Risk-free interest rate	1.77%	0.85%	1.44%

A summary of the status of our stock option awards is presented in the table below.

	Number of Stock Options	Weighted-Average Exercise Price Per Share	Weighted-Average Remaining Contractual Term (In years)	Aggregate Intrinsic Value (In millions)
Outstanding as of January 1, 2013	13,214,728	$28.54		
Granted	201,300	39.67		
Exercised	(3,837,090)	15.21		
Expired	(1,780,113)	49.45		
Options granted on conversion related to separation of retail business	759,268	28.84		
Outstanding as of December 31, 2013	8,558,093	27.88	3.5	$216
Exercisable as of December 31, 2013	8,037,807	27.66	3.1	206

The following table reflects activity related to our stock options granted (in millions, except per share data):

	Year Ended December 31,		
	2013	2012	2011
Weighted average grant-date fair value price per share	$15.83	$10.98	$10.10
Intrinsic value of stock options exercised	101	78	63
Cash received from stock option exercises	59	59	49

As of December 31, 2013, there was $1 million of unrecognized compensation cost related to outstanding unvested stock option awards, which is expected to be recognized over a weighted-average period of approximately two years.

Restricted Stock

Restricted stock is granted to employees and non-employee directors. Restricted stock granted to employees vests in accordance with individual written agreements between the participants and us, usually in equal annual installments over a period of three to five years beginning one year after the date of grant. Restricted stock granted to our non-employee directors generally vests in three years following the date of grant. A summary of the status of our restricted stock awards is presented in the table below.

	Number of Shares	Weighted-Average Grant-Date Fair Value Per Share
Nonvested shares as of January 1, 2013	2,920,288	$24.76
Granted	1,255,742	39.55
Vested	(2,113,647)	23.73
Forfeited	(31,546)	23.73
Shares granted on conversion related to separation of retail business	174,477	23.42
Nonvested shares as of December 31, 2013	2,205,314	32.23

As of December 31, 2013, there was $40 million of unrecognized compensation cost related to outstanding unvested restricted stock awards, which is expected to be recognized over a weighted-average period of approximately two years. The total fair value of restricted stock that vested during the years ended December 31, 2013, 2012, and 2011 was $74 million, $47 million, and $32 million, respectively.

Performance Awards

Performance awards are issued to certain of our key employees and represent rights to receive shares of our common stock upon the achievement by us of an objective performance measure. The objective performance measure is our total shareholder return, which is ranked among the total shareholder returns of a defined peer group of companies. Our ranking determines the rate at which the performance awards convert into our common shares. Conversion rates can range from zero to 200 percent.

Performance awards vest in equal one-third increments (tranches) on an annual basis. Our compensation committee establishes the peer group of companies for each tranche of awards at the beginning of the one year vesting period for that tranche. Therefore, performance awards are not considered to be granted for accounting purposes until our compensation committee establishes the peer group of companies for each tranche of awards. The fair value of each tranche of awards is determined at the time the awards are considered to be granted and is based on the expected conversion rate for those awards and the fair value per share. Fair value per share is equal to the market price of our common stock on the grant date reduced by expected dividends over that tranche's vesting period.

A summary of the status of our performance awards considered granted is presented below.

	Nonvested Awards	Vested Awards
Awards outstanding as of January 1, 2013	989,414	208,916
Granted	415,317	—
Vested	(442,274)	442,274
Converted	—	(534,515)
Forfeited	(50,076)	(116,675)
Shares granted on conversion related to separation of retail business	34,784	—
Awards outstanding as of December 31, 2013	947,165	—

There were three tranches of performance awards granted during the year ended December 31, 2013 as follows:

	Awards Granted	Expected Conversion Rate	Fair Value Per Share
Third tranche of 2011 awards	227,565	100%	$38.77
Second tranche of 2012 awards	105,030	100%	38.77
First tranche of 2013 awards	82,722	100%	38.77
Total	415,317		

As of December 31, 2013, there was $16 million of unrecognized compensation cost related to outstanding unvested performance awards, which will be recognized during 2014. The total fair value of performance awards that vested during the years ended December 31, 2013, 2012, and 2011 was $12 million, $3 million, and $4 million, respectively.

Performance awards converted during the year ended December 31, 2013 were as follows:

	Vested Awards Converted	Actual Conversion Rate	Number of Shares Issued	Awards Forfeited
2010 awards	417,833	100%	417,833	—
2011 awards	233,357	50%	116,682	116,675
Total	651,190		534,515	116,675

5.10 AGCO CORPORATION (DEC)
CONSOLIDATED STATEMENTS OF STOCKHOLDERS' EQUITY

(In millions, except share amounts)

	Common Stock Shares	Common Stock Amount	Additional Paid-in Capital	Retained Earnings	Defined Benefit Pension Plans	Cumulative Translation Adjustment	Deferred (Losses) Gains on Derivatives	Accumulated Other Comprehensive Loss	Noncontrolling Interests	Total Stockholders' Equity	Temporary Equity
						Accumulated Other Comprehensive Loss					
Balance, December 31, 2010	93,143,542	$0.9	$1,051.3	$1,738.3	$(179.1)	$ 48.4	$(1.4)	$(132.1)	$ 0.8	$2,659.2	$ —
Net income	—	—	—	583.3	—	—	—	—	2.0	585.3	
Issuance of restricted stock	12,034	—	0.7	—	—	—	—	—	—	0.7	
Issuance of performance award stock	51,590	—	(1.5)	—	—	—	—	—	—	(1.5)	
Stock options and SSARs exercised	60,992	—	(0.7)	—	—	—	—	—	—	(0.7)	
Stock compensation	—	—	23.7	—	—	—	—	—	—	23.7	
Conversion of 1 3/4% convertible senior subordinated notes	3,926,574	0.1	(0.1)	—	—	—	—	—	—	—	
Investments by noncontrolling interests	—	—	—	—	—	—	—	—	34.6	34.6	
Distribution to noncontrolling interest	—	—	—	—	—	—	—	—	(1.5)	(1.5)	
Change in fair value of noncontrolling interest	—	—	(0.2)	—	—	—	—	—	0.2	—	
Defined benefit pension plans, net of taxes:											
Prior service cost arising during year	—	—	—	—	(5.0)	—	—	(5.0)	—	(5.0)	
Net actuarial loss arising during year	—	—	—	—	(61.8)	—	—	(61.8)	—	(61.8)	
Amortization of prior service cost included in net periodic pension cost	—	—	—	—	0.1	—	—	0.1	—	0.1	
Amortization of net actuarial losses included in net periodic pension cost	—	—	—	—	5.6	—	—	5.6	—	5.6	
Deferred gains and losses on derivatives, net	—	—	—	—	—	—	(5.4)	(5.4)	—	(5.4)	
Deferred gains and losses on derivatives held by affiliates, net	—	—	—	—	—	—	2.5	2.5	—	2.5	
Change in cumulative translation adjustment	—	—	—	—	—	(204.5)	—	(204.5)	(0.1)	(204.6)	
Balance, December 31, 2011	97,194,732	1.0	1,073.2	2,321.6	(240.2)	(156.1)	(4.3)	(400.6)	36.0	3,031.2	—
Net income (loss)	—	—	—	522.1	—	—	—	—	3.0	525.1	(8.7)
Issuance of restricted stock	13,986	—	1.0	—	—	—	—	—	—	1.0	
Stock options and SSARs exercised	16,287	—	(0.3)	—	—	—	—	—	—	(0.3)	
Stock compensation	—	—	35.8	—	—	—	—	—	—	35.8	
Investments by redeemable noncontrolling interest	—	—	—	—	—	—	—	—	—	—	17.6
Distribution to noncontrolling interest	—	—	—	—	—	—	—	—	(1.7)	(1.7)	
Changes in noncontrolling interests	—	—	—	—	—	—	—	—	(4.0)	(4.0)	
Purchases and retirement of common stock	(409,007)	—	(17.6)	—	—	—	—	—	—	(17.6)	
Defined benefit pension plans, net of taxes:											
Prior service cost arising during year	—	—	—	—	(2.5)	—	—	(2.5)	—	(2.5)	
Net actuarial loss arising during year	—	—	—	—	(28.2)	—	—	(28.2)	—	(28.2)	

(continued)

| | Common Stock | | Additional Paid-in Capital | Retained Earnings | **Accumulated Other Comprehensive Loss** | | | | Noncontrolling Interests | Total Stockholders' Equity | Temporary Equity |
	Shares	Amount			Defined Benefit Pension Plans	Cumulative Translation Adjustment	Deferred (Losses) Gains on Derivatives	Accumulated Other Comprehensive Loss			
Amortization of prior service cost included in net periodic pension cost	—	—	—	—	0.4	—	—	0.4	—	0.4	
Amortization of net actuarial losses included in net periodic pension cost	—	—	—	—	7.6	—	—	7.6	—	7.6	
Deferred gains and losses on derivatives, net	—	—	—	—	—	—	5.0	5.0	—	5.0	
Reclassification to temporary equity- Equity component of convertible senior subordinated notes	—	—	(9.2)	—	—	—	—	—	—	(9.2)	9.2
Change in cumulative translation adjustment	—	—	—	—	—	(61.1)	—	(61.1)	—	(61.1)	(1.6)
Balance, December 31, 2012	96,815,998	1.0	1,082.9	2,843.7	(262.9)	(217.2)	0.7	(479.4)	33.3	3,481.5	16.5
Net income (loss)	—	—	—	597.2	—	—	—	—	4.4	601.6	(9.3)
Payment of dividends to shareholders	—	—	—	(38.9)	—	—	—	—	—	(38.9)	
Issuance of restricted stock	12,059	—	0.6	—	—	—	—	—	—	0.6	
Issuance of performance award stock	491,692	—	(14.7)	—	—	—	—	—	—	(14.7)	
SSARs exercised	61,941	—	(2.2)	—	—	—	—	—	—	(2.2)	
Stock compensation	—	—	34.0	—	—	—	—	—	—	34.0	
Excess tax benefit of stock awards	—	—	11.4	—	—	—	—	—	—	11.4	
Conversion of $1\frac{1}{4}$% convertible senior subordinated notes	286										
Distribution to noncontrolling interest	—	—	—	—	—	—	—	—	(3.1)	(3.1)	
Changes in noncontrolling interest	—	—	(2.3)	—	—	—	—	—	—	(2.3)	2.3
Purchases and retirement of common stock	(19,510)	—	(1.0)	—	—	—	—	—	—	(1.0)	
Defined benefit pension plans, net of taxes:											
Net actuarial gain arising during year	—	—	—	—	45.2	—	—	45.2	—	45.2	
Amortization of prior service cost included in net periodic pension cost	—	—	—	—	0.6	—	—	0.6	—	0.6	
Amortization of net actuarial losses included in net periodic pension cost	—	—	—	—	10.7	—	—	10.7	—	10.7	
Deferred gains and losses on derivatives, net	—	—	—	—	—	—	(0.9)	(0.9)	—	(0.9)	
Reclassification from temporary equity-Equity component of convertible senior subordinated notes	—	—	9.2	—	—	—	—	—	—	9.2	(9.2)
Change in cumulative translation adjustment	—	—	—	—	—	(86.9)	—	(86.9)	—	(86.9)	(0.3)
Balance, December 31, 2013	97,362,466	$1.0	$1,117.9	$3,402.0	$(206.4)	$(304.1)	$(0.2)	$(510.7)	$34.6	$4,044.8	$ —

NOTES TO CONSOLIDATED FINANCIAL STATEMENTS

9. Stock Incentive Plan (in part)

Employee Plans

The 2006 Plan encompasses stock incentive plans to Company executives and key managers. The primary long-term incentive plan is a performance share plan that provides for awards of shares of the Company's common stock based on achieving financial targets, such as targets for earnings per share and return on invested capital, as determined by the Company's Board of Directors. The Company's other incentive plan includes the margin growth incentive plan, which provides for awards of shares of the Company's common stock based on achieving operating margin targets as determined by the Company's Board of Directors. The stock awards under the 2006 Plan are earned over a performance period, and the number of shares earned is determined based on the cumulative or average results for the period, depending on the measurement. Performance periods for the long-term incentive plan are consecutive and overlapping three-year cycles, and performance targets are set at the beginning of each cycle. The long-term incentive plan provides for participants to earn 33% to 200% of the target awards depending on the actual performance achieved, with no shares earned if performance is below the established minimum target. The performance period for the margin growth incentive plan is a three—to five-year cycle commencing in January 2011 and performance targets were set at the beginning of the cycle. The margin growth incentive plan provides for participants to earn 33% to 300% of the target awards depending on the actual performance achieved, with no shares earned if performance is below the established minimum target. Awards earned under the 2006 Plan are paid in shares of common stock at the end of each performance period. The compensation expense associated with these awards is amortized ratably over the vesting or performance period based on the Company's projected assessment of the level of performance that will be achieved and earned.

Compensation expense recorded during 2013, 2012 and 2011 with respect to awards granted was based upon the stock price as of the grant date. The weighted average grant-date fair value of performance awards granted under the 2006 Plan during 2013, 2012 and 2011 was $51.51, $52.11 and $52.73, respectively. Based on the level of performance achieved as of December 31, 2013, 622,018 shares were earned under the 2011–2013 performance period and 368,497 shares were issued in 2014, net of 226,721 shares that were withheld for taxes related to the earned awards. Based on the level of performance achieved as of December 31, 2012, 748,137 shares were earned under the 2010–2012 performance period and 473,499 shares were issued in 2013, net of 274,638 shares that were withheld for taxes related to the earned awards. The 2006 Plan allows for the participant to have the option of forfeiting a portion of the shares awarded in lieu of a cash payment contributed to the participant's tax withholding to satisfy the participant's statutory minimum federal, state and employment taxes which would be payable at the time of grant.

During 2013, the Company granted 1,103,494 awards for the three-year performance period commencing in 2013 and ending in 2015, assuming the maximum target level of performance is achieved. In addition, the Company granted 29,158 awards for the three-year performance period commencing in 2012 and ending in 2014, and 8,042 awards for the three-year performance period commencing in 2011 and ending in 2013. These awards were granted on a pro-rated basis and assume maximum target levels of performance are achieved. The Company also granted 11,250 awards during 2013 under the margin growth incentive plan on a prorated basis for a performance period commencing in 2011 and ending in 2015, assuming the maximum target level of performance is achieved for operating margin improvement. Performance award transactions during 2013 were as follows and are presented as if the Company were to achieve its maximum levels of performance under the plan:

Shares awarded but not earned at January 1	2,509,323
Shares awarded	1,151,944
Shares forfeited or unearned	(230,730)
Shares earned	(622,018)
Shares awarded but not earned at December 31	2,808,519

As of December 31, 2013, the total compensation cost related to unearned performance awards not yet recognized, assuming the Company's current projected assessment of the level of performance that will be achieved and earned, was approximately $33.7 million, and the weighted average period over which it is expected to be recognized is approximately two years.

In addition to the performance share plans, certain executives and key managers are eligible to receive grants of SSARs. The SSARs provide a participant with the right to receive the aggregate appreciation in stock price over the market price of the Company's common stock at the date of grant, payable in shares of the Company's common stock. The participant may exercise his or her SSARs at any time after the grant is vested but no later than seven years after the date of grant. The SSARs vest ratably over a four-year period from the date of grant. SSAR award grants made to certain executives and key managers under the 2006 Plan are made with the base price equal to the price of the Company's common stock on the date of grant. The Company recorded stock compensation expense of approximately $4.7 million, $3.8 million and $2.6 million associated with SSAR award grants during 2013, 2012 and 2011, respectively. The compensation expense associated with these awards is being amortized ratably over the vesting period. The Company estimated the fair value of the grants using the Black-Scholes option pricing model.

The weighted average grant-date fair value of SSARs granted under the 2006 Plan and the weighted average assumptions under the Black-Scholes option model were as follows for the years ended December 31, 2013, 2012 and 2011:

	Years Ended December 31,		
	2013	**2012**	**2011**
Weighted average grant-date fair value	$21.10	$22.50	$22.26
Weighted average assumptions under Black-Scholes option model:			
Expected life of awards (years)	5.5	5.5	5.5
Risk-free interest rate	0.9%	0.8%	1.9%
Expected volatility	50.3%	51.0%	49.7%
Expected dividend yield	0.8%	—	—

SSAR transactions during the year ended December 31, 2013 were as follows:

SSARs outstanding at January 1	1,073,087
SSARs granted	335,630
SSARs exercised	(251,536)
SSARs canceled or forfeited	(62,345)
SSARs outstanding at December 31	1,094,836
SSAR price ranges per share:	
Granted	$51.84–63.64
Exercised	21.45–56.98
Canceled or forfeited	21.45–56.98
Weighted average SSAR exercise prices per share:	
Granted	$ 52.96
Exercised	33.74
Canceled or forfeited	49.86
Outstanding at December 31	46.35

At December 31, 2013, the weighted average remaining contractual life of SSARs outstanding was approximately four years. As of December 31, 2013, the total compensation cost related to unvested SSARs not yet recognized was approximately $10.2 million and the weighted-average period over which it is expected to be recognized is approximately three years.

The following table sets forth the exercise price range, number of shares, weighted average exercise price, and remaining contractual lives by groups of similar price as of December 31, 2013:

	SSARs Outstanding			SSARs Exercisable	
Range of Exercise Prices	Number of Shares	Weighted Average Remaining Contractual Life (Years)	Weighted Average Exercise Price	Exercisable as of December 31, 2013	Weighted Average Exercise Price
$21.45–$32.01	159,281	2.1	$21.87	157,656	$21.73
$33.65–$44.55	132,025	3.1	$33.93	90,325	$33.90
$47.89–$63.64	803,530	4.9	$53.24	216,725	$54.25
	1,094,836			464,706	$39.26

The total fair value of SSARs vested during 2013 was approximately $3.6 million. There were 630,130 SSARs that were not vested as of December 31, 2013. The total intrinsic value of outstanding and exercisable SSARs as of December 31, 2013 was $14.2 million and $9.3 million, respectively. The total intrinsic value of SSARs exercised during 2013 was approximately $5.7 million. The Company realized an insignificant tax benefit from the exercise of these SSARs.

The excess tax benefit realized for tax deductions in the United States related to the exercise of SSARs, vesting of performance awards under the 2006 Plan and exercise of stock options under the Company's 1991 Stock Option Plan was approximately $11.4 million for the year ended December 31, 2013. No excess tax benefit was realized for tax deductions for the years ended December 31, 2012 and 2011 in the United States. The Company realized an insignificant tax benefit from the exercise of SSARs, vesting of performance awards and exercise of stock options in certain foreign jurisdictions during the years ended December 31, 2013, 2012 and 2011.

On January 22, 2014, the Company granted 432,300 performance award shares (subject to the Company achieving future target levels of performance) and 296,700 SSARs under the 2006 Plan.

ISSUANCE OF COMMON STOCK IN ACQUISITION

5.11 ECOLAB INC. (DEC)
CONSOLIDATED STATEMENT OF EQUITY

(Millions)	Common Stock	Additional Paid-In Capital	Retained Earnings	Accumulated Other Comprehensive Income (Loss)	Treasury Stock	Total Ecolab Shareholders' Equity	Non-Controlling Interest	Total Equity
				Ecolab Shareholders				
Balance December 31, 2010	$333.1	$1,310.2	$3,279.1	$(271.9)	$(2,521.3)	$2,129.2	$ 3.8	$2,133.0
Net income			462.5			462.5	0.8	463.3
Comprehensive income (loss) activity				(73.0)		(73.0)		(73.0)
Total comprehensive income						389.5	0.8	390.3
Cash dividends declared			(181.7)			(181.7)	(0.6)	(182.3)
Nalco merger		2,573.2			1,300.0	3,873.2	70.4	3,943.6
Stock options and awards	3.0	142.1			1.4	146.5		146.5
Reacquired shares		(44.7)			(645.3)	(690.0)		(690.0)
Balance December 31, 2011	336.1	3,980.8	3,559.9	(344.9)	(1,865.2)	5,666.7	74.4	5,741.1
Net income (loss)			703.6			703.6	(2.3)	701.3
Comprehensive income (loss) activity				(114.8)		(114.8)	(1.9)	(116.7)
Total comprehensive income (loss)						588.8	(4.2)	584.6
Cash dividends declared			(242.9)			(242.9)	(3.9)	(246.8)
Nalco merger		0.3				0.3	16.8	17.1
Stock options and awards	6.0	260.7			7.3	274.0		274.0
Reacquired shares		7.3			(217.2)	(209.9)		(209.9)
Balance December 31, 2012	342.1	4,249.1	4,020.6	(459.7)	(2,075.1)	6,077.0	83.1	6,160.1
Net income			967.8			967.8	5.8	973.6
Comprehensive income (loss) activity				154.5		154.5	(16.0)	138.5
Total comprehensive income (loss)						1,122.3	(10.2)	1,112.1
Cash dividends declared			(289.4)			(289.4)	(11.4)	(300.8)
Champion acquisition		258.1			284.9	543.0	3.6	546.6
Stock options and awards	3.0	184.8			11.2	199.0		199.0
Reacquired shares					(307.6)	(307.6)		(307.6)
Balance December 31, 2013	$345.1	$4,692.0	$4,699.0	$(305.2)	$(2,086.6)	$7,344.3	$ 65.1	$7,409.4

Common Stock Activity

Year Ended December 31 (Shares)	2013 Common Stock	2013 Treasury Stock	2012 Common Stock	2012 Treasury Stock	2011 Common Stock	2011 Treasury Stock
Shares, beginning of year	342,106,581	(47,384,557)	336,088,243	(44,113,799)	333,141,410	(100,628,659)
Stock options, shares	2,206,661	254,680	5,430,997	208,239	2,946,833	93,771
Stock awards, net issuances	787,767	11,008	587,341	(21,257)		114,064
Champion acquisition		6,596,444				
Nalco merger						68,316,283
Reacquired shares		(3,443,405)		(3,457,740)		(12,009,258)
Shares, end of year	345,101,009	(43,965,830)	342,106,581	(47,384,557)	336,088,243	(44,113,799)

NOTES TO CONSOLIDATED FINANCIAL STATEMENTS

4. Acquisitions and Dispositions (in part)

Acquisitions (in part)

Ecolab makes acquisitions that align with the company's strategic business objectives. The assets and liabilities of the acquired entities have been recorded as of the acquisition date, at their respective fair values, and consolidated with the company. The purchase price allocation is based on estimates of the fair value of assets acquired and liabilities assumed. The results of operations related to each acquired entity have been included in the results of the company from the date each entity was acquired. The aggregate purchase price of acquisitions has been reduced for any cash or cash equivalents acquired with the acquisition.

Champion Acquisition

In October 2012, the company entered into an agreement and plan of merger to acquire Champion. Based in Houston, Texas, Champion is a global energy specialty products and services company delivering its offerings to the oil and gas industry.

In November 2012, the company amended the acquisition agreement to provide that Champion's downstream business would not be acquired by the company. Further, in April 2013, the company entered into a consent agreement with the U.S. Department of Justice under which the company agreed to take certain steps designed to ensure continued independent competition utilizing Champion technology for certain U.S. deepwater Gulf of Mexico products and services. The amendment and consent agreement discussed above did not significantly impact the value of the acquisition transaction. On April 10, 2013, the company completed its acquisition of Champion. Champion's sales for the business acquired by the company were approximately $1.3 billion in 2012. The business became part of the company's Global Energy reportable segment in the second quarter of 2013.

Pursuant to the terms of the acquisition agreement, the consideration transferred as of December 31, 2013 to acquire all of Champion's stock was as follows:

Millions, except per share

Cash consideration	$1,425.3
Stock consideration	
Ecolab shares issued at closing	6.6
Ecolab's closing stock price on April 10, 2013	$ 82.31
Total fair value of stock consideration	$ 543.0
Total fair value of cash and stock consideration	$1,968.3

The company deposited approximately $100 million of the above stock consideration in an escrow account to fund post-closing adjustments to the consideration and covenant and other indemnification obligations of the acquired entity's former stockholders for a period of two years following the effective date of the acquisition.

The company incurred certain acquisition and integration costs associated with the transaction that were expensed as incurred and are reflected in the Consolidated Statement of Income. A total of $88.8 million and $19.4 million was incurred during 2013 and 2012, respectively. Amounts included in cost of sales are related to recognition of fair value step-up in Champion international inventory, which is maintained on a FIFO basis, and Champion U.S. inventory which is associated with the adoption of LIFO and integration into an existing LIFO pool. Amounts included in special (gains) and charges are related to acquisition costs, advisory and legal fees and integration costs. Amounts included in net interest expense are related to interest expense through the close date of the Champion transaction of the company's $500 million public debt issuance in December 2012 as well as fees to secure term loans and short-term debt.

The company funded the initial cash component of the merger consideration through a $900 million unsecured term loan, initiated in April 2013, the proceeds from the December 2012 issuance of $500 million 1.450% senior notes and commercial paper borrowings backed by its syndicated credit facility. See Note 6 for further discussion on the company's debt.

The Champion acquisition has been accounted for using the acquisition method of accounting, which requires, among other things, that most assets acquired and liabilities assumed be recognized at fair value as of the acquisition date. Certain estimated values are not yet finalized and are subject to change, which could be significant.

The company has finalized the majority of the purchase price allocation adjustments as of December 31, 2013. Amounts for certain contingent liabilities, certain deferred tax assets and liabilities, income tax uncertainties, certain property, plant and equipment valuations, an estimated indemnification receivable, and goodwill remain subject to change. The company will finalize the amounts recognized as information necessary to complete the analysis is obtained. The company expects to finalize remaining purchase price allocation adjustments no later than one year from the acquisition date.

The following table summarizes the value of Champion assets acquired and liabilities assumed as of the acquisition date. Also summarized in the table, subsequent to the acquisition, net adjustments of $37.1 million have been made to the preliminary purchase price allocation of the assets acquired and liabilities assumed, with a corresponding adjustment to goodwill.

Millions	Preliminary Allocation at Acquisition Date	2013 Adjustments to Fair Value	Updated Allocation at December 31, 2013
Current assets	$ 593.9	$ (1.6)	$ 592.3
Property, plant and equipment	369.3	(11.5)	357.8
Other assets	30.5	(14.3)	16.2
Identifiable intangible assets			
Customer relationships	840.0	—	840.0
Trademarks	120.0	—	120.0
Other technology	36.5	—	36.5
Total assets acquired	1,990.2	(27.4)	1,962.8

(continued)

Millions	Preliminary Allocation At Acquisition Date	2013 Adjustments To Fair Value	Updated Allocation At December 31, 2013
Current liabilities	418.2	(8.7)	409.5
Long-term debt	70.8	—	70.8
Net deferred tax liability	420.3	7.1	427.4
Noncontrolling interests and other liabilities	17.1	13.4	30.5
Total liabilities and noncontrolling interests assumed	926.4	11.8	938.2
Goodwill	993.0	37.1	1,030.1
Total aggregate purchase price	2,056.8	(2.1)	2,054.7
Future consideration payable to sellers	(83.9)	(2.5)	(86.4)
Total consideration transferred	$1,972.9	$ (4.6)	$1,968.3

The adjustments to the purchase price allocation during 2013 primarily relate to an estimated indemnification receivable, income tax liabilities, contingent liabilities, updated property, plant and equipment values and deferred taxes. The $4.6 million adjustment to the consideration transferred relates to post-acquisition working capital adjustments.

In accordance with the acquisition agreement, except under limited circumstances, the company was required to pay an additional amount in cash, up to $100 million in the aggregate, equal to 50% of the incremental tax on the merger consideration as a result of increases in applicable gains and investment taxes after December 31, 2012. Such additional payment was due on January 31, 2014, and was based on 2013 tax rates in effect on January 1, 2014. In January 2014, subsequent to the company's year end, an additional payment of $86.4 million was made to the acquired entity's former stockholders. The balance was classified within other current liabilities as of December 31, 2013.

The customer relationships, trademarks and other technology are being amortized over weighted average lives of 14, 12 and 7 years, respectively. In process research and development associated with the Champion acquisition was not significant.

Goodwill is calculated as the excess of consideration transferred over the fair value of identifiable net assets acquired and represents the expected synergies and other benefits of combining the operations of Champion with the operations of the company's existing Global Energy business. Key areas of cost synergies include leveraging and simplifying the global supply chain, including the reduction of plant and distribution center locations and product line optimization, as well as the reduction of other redundant facilities.

The results of Champion's operations have been included in the company's consolidated financial statements since the close of the acquisition in April 2013. Due to the rapid pace at which the business is being fully integrated with the company's Global Energy segment, including all customer selling activity, discrete financial data specific to the legacy Champion business is not readily available post acquisition.

Based on applicable accounting and reporting guidance, the Champion acquisition is not material to the company's consolidated financial statements; therefore, pro forma financial information has not been presented.

10. Shareholders' Equity (in part)

Champion Acquisition

On April 10, 2013, the company issued 6,596,444 shares of common stock for the stock consideration portion of the Champion acquisition. Of the total shares issued, the company deposited 1,258,115 shares, or approximately $100 million of the total consideration, into an escrow fund to satisfy adjustments to the consideration and indemnification obligations of the acquired company's stockholders. Further information related to the Champion acquisition is included in Note 4.

NONCONTROLLING INTEREST

5.12 MICRON TECHNOLOGY, INC. (AUG)
CONSOLIDATED STATEMENTS OF CHANGES IN EQUITY

(In millions)

	Micron Shareholders						Noncontrolling Interests in Subsidiaries	Total Equity
	Common Stock		Additional Capital	Accumulated Deficit	Accumulated Other Comprehensive Income (Loss)	Total Micron Shareholders' Equity		
	Number Shares	Amount						
Balance at September 2, 2010	994.5	$ 99	$8,446	$ (536)	$ 11	$ 8,020	$1,796	$ 9,816
Net income				167		167	23	190
Other comprehensive income (loss), net					121	121	6	127
Issuance and repurchase of convertible notes			211			211		211
Stock-based compensation expense			76			76		76
Stock issued under stock plans	11.1	1	27			28		28
Contributions from noncontrolling interests						—	8	8
Distributions to noncontrolling interests						—	(225)	(225)
Repurchase and retirement of common stock	(21.3)	(2)	(160)	(1)		(163)		(163)
Acquisition of noncontrolling interests in TECH			67			67	(226)	(159)
Purchase of capped calls			(57)			(57)		(57)
Balance at September 1, 2011	984.3	$ 98	$8,610	$ (370)	$132	$ 8,470	$1,382	$ 9,852
Net loss				(1,032)		(1,032)	1	(1,031)
Other comprehensive income (loss), net					(52)	(52)	(6)	(58)
Contributions from noncontrolling interests						—	197	197
Issuance of convertible notes			191			191		191
Conversion of 2013 Notes	27.3	3	135			138		138
Stock-based compensation expense			87			87		87
Stock issued under stock plans	7.1	1	5			6		6
Acquisition of noncontrolling interest in IMFS						—	(466)	(466)
Distributions to noncontrolling interests						—	(391)	(391)
Purchase and settlement of capped calls			(102)			(102)		(102)
Repurchase and retirement of common stock	(1.0)	—	(6)	—		(6)		(6)
Balance at August 30, 2012	1,017.7	$102	$8,920	$(1,402)	$ 80	$ 7,700	$ 717	$ 8,417
Net income				1,190		1,190	4	1,194
Other comprehensive income (loss), net					(17)	(17)	1	(16)
Acquisition of Elpida						—	168	168
Stock issued under stock plans	27.4	2	148			150		150
Stock-based compensation expense			91			91		91
Issuance and repurchase of convertible notes			57			57		57
Contributions from noncontrolling interests						—	11	11
Distributions to noncontrolling interests						—	(37)	(37)
Purchase and settlement of capped calls			(24)			(24)		(24)
Repurchase and retirement of common stock	(0.7)	—	(5)	—		(5)		(5)
Balance at August 29, 2013	1,044.4	$104	$9,187	$ (212)	$ 63	$ 9,142	$ 864	$10,006

(All tabular amounts in millions except per share amounts)

Acquisition of Elpida Memory, Inc. (in part)

On July 31, 2013, we completed the acquisition of Elpida Memory, Inc., a Japanese corporation, pursuant to the terms and conditions of an Agreement on Support for Reorganization Companies (as amended, the "Sponsor Agreement") that we entered into on July 2, 2012, with the trustees of Elpida and one of its subsidiaries, Akita Elpida Memory, Inc., a Japanese corporation ("Akita" and, together with Elpida, the "Elpida Companies") pursuant to and in connection with the Elpida Companies' corporate reorganization proceedings under the Corporate Reorganization Act of Japan. We paid $615 million for the acquisition of Elpida, of which substantially all was deposited into accounts that are legally restricted for payment to the secured and unsecured creditors of the Elpida Companies in October 2013. As of August 29, 2013, the amount held in the restricted accounts was presented as restricted cash. Of the $615 million paid at closing, $18 million was applied from amounts we had deposited into an escrow account in July 2012 as a condition to the execution of the Sponsor Agreement.

On July 31, 2013, we also completed the acquisition of an additional 24% ownership interest in Rexchip Electronics Corporation ("Rexchip"), a Taiwanese corporation and manufacturing joint venture formed by Elpida and Powerchip Technology Corporation ("Powerchip") from Powerchip and certain of its affiliates (the "Powerchip Group") pursuant to a share purchase agreement. We paid $334 million in cash for the shares. Elpida owns, directly and indirectly through a subsidiary, approximately 65% of Rexchip's outstanding common stock. Therefore, as a result of the consummation of our acquisition of Elpida and the Rexchip shares from the Powerchip Group, we own approximately 89% ownership interest in Rexchip.

Elpida's assets include, among others: a 300 mm DRAM wafer fabrication facility located in Hiroshima, Japan; its approximate 65% ownership interest in Rexchip, whose assets include a 300 mm DRAM wafer fabrication facility located in Taichung City, Taiwan; and a 100% ownership interest in Akita, whose assets include an assembly and test facility located in Akita, Japan. Elpida's semiconductor memory products include mobile DRAM targeted toward mobile phones and tablets. We believe that combining the complementary product portfolios of Micron and Elpida strengthens our position in the memory market and enables us to provide customers with a wider portfolio of high-quality memory solutions. We also believe that our acquisition of Elpida strengthens our market position in the memory industry through increased research and development and manufacturing scale, improved access to core memory market segments, and additional wafer capacity to balance among our DRAM, NAND Flash and NOR Flash memory solutions.

The Elpida Acquisition and Rexchip share purchase are treated as a single business combination because (1) the two transactions were entered into and closed contemporaneously and (2) the Rexchip share purchase was negotiated in contemplation of the Elpida acquisition and its completion was contingent on the closing of the Elpida acquisition.

We estimated the provisional fair value of the assets and liabilities of Elpida and it's subsidiaries (the "Elpida Group") as of the July 31, 2013 acquisition date using an in-use model, which reflects its value through its use in combination with other assets as a group. These provisional amounts could change as additional information becomes available.

The consideration and provisional valuation of assets acquired and liabilities assumed are as follows:

Assets Acquired and Liabilities Assumed:	
Cash and equivalents	$ 999
Receivables	697
Inventories	962
Restricted cash	557
Other current assets	142
Property, plant and equipment	935
Equity method investment	40
Intangible assets	10
Deferred tax assets	811
Other noncurrent assets	66
Accounts payable and accrued expenses	(387)
Equipment purchase contracts	(22)
Current portion of long-term debt	(673)
Long-term debt	(1,461)
Other noncurrent liabilities	(75)
Total net assets acquired	2,601
Noncontrolling interests in Elpida:	168
Consideration	949
Gain on acquisition	$ 1,484

Because the fair value of the net assets acquired less noncontrolling interests exceeded the purchase price, we recognized a gain on the acquisition of $1,484 million. The yen-denominated purchase price was fixed on July 2, 2012 when we entered into the Sponsor Agreement. We believe the fair value exceeded the purchase price because of increases in working capital from improvements in market conditions in the DRAM industry between July 2, 2012 and July 31, 2013, when we completed the acquisition. These conditions resulted in significant increases in U.S. dollar equivalent net assets of Elpida.

The fair value of the noncontrolling interest in the table above primarily relates to Rexchip and was derived based on the purchase price we paid the Powerchip Group for their 24% ownership interest.

CONVERSION OF SHARES

5.13 APACHE CORPORATION (DEC)
STATEMENT OF CONSOLIDATED CHANGES IN EQUITY

(In millions)	Series D Preferred Stock	Common Stock	Paid-In Capital	Retained Earnings	Treasury Stock	Accumulated Other Comprehensive (Loss)	Apache Shareholders' Equity	Non Controlling Interest	Total Equity
Balance at December 31, 2010	$ 1,227	$240	$ 8,864	$14,223	$ (36)	$(141)	$24,377	$ —	$24,377
Net income	—	—	—	4,584	—	—	4,584	—	4,584
Postretirement, net of tax of $7	—	—	—	—	—	(1)	(1)	—	(1)
Commodity hedges, net of tax of $66	—	—	—	—	—	133	133	—	133
Dividends:									
Preferred	—	—	—	(76)	—	—	(76)	—	(76)
Common ($0.60 per share)	—	—	—	(231)	—	—	(231)	—	(231)
Common stock activity, net	—	1	35	—	—	—	36	—	36
Treasury stock activity, net	—	—	2	—	4	—	6	—	6
Compensation expense	—	—	167	—	—	—	167	—	167
Other	—	—	(2)	—	—	—	(2)	—	(2)
Balance at December 31, 2011	$ 1,227	$241	$ 9,066	$18,500	$ (32)	$ (9)	$28,993	$ —	$28,993
Net income	—	—	—	2,001	—	—	2,001	—	2,001
Postretirement, net of tax of $5	—	—	—	—	—	(2)	(2)	—	(2)
Commodity hedges, net of tax of $35	—	—	—	—	—	(120)	(120)	—	(120)
Dividends:									
Preferred	—	—	—	(76)	—	—	(76)	—	(76)
Common ($0.68 per share)	—	—	—	(264)	—	—	(264)	—	(264)
Common shares issued	—	3	598	—	—	—	601	—	601
Common stock activity, net	—	1	(44)	—	—	—	(43)	—	(43)
Treasury stock activity, net	—	—	1	—	2	—	3	—	3
Compensation expense	—	—	238	—	—	—	238	—	238
Balance at December 31, 2012	$ 1,227	$245	$ 9,859	$20,161	$ (30)	$(131)	$31,331	$ —	$31,331
Net income	—	—	—	2,232	—	—	2,232	56	2,288
Postretirement, net of tax of $9	—	—	—	—	—	9	9	—	9
Commodity hedges, net of tax of $4	—	—	—	—	—	7	7	—	7
Dividends:									
Preferred	—	—	—	(44)	—	—	(44)	—	(44)
Common ($0.80 per share)	—	—	—	(317)	—	—	(317)	—	(317)
Common stock activity, net	—	1	(22)	—	—	—	(21)	—	(21)
Treasury stock activity, net	—	—	—	—	(997)	—	(997)	—	(997)
Sale of noncontrolling interest	—	—	1,007	—	—	—	1,007	1,941	2,948
Conversion of Series D preferred stock	(1,227)	9	1,218	—	—	—	—	—	—
Compensation expense	—	—	189	—	—	—	189	—	189
Balance at December 31, 2013	$ —	$255	$12,251	$22,032	$(1,027)	$(115)	$33,396	$1,997	$35,393

10. Capital Stock (in part)

Common Stock Outstanding

	2013	2012	2011
Balance, beginning of year	391,640,770	384,117,643	382,391,742
Shares issued for stock-based compensation plans:			
Treasury shares issued	25,214	60,767	144,313
Common shares issued	929,596	1,189,693	1,581,588
Common shares issued for conversion of preferred shares	14,399,247	—	—
Treasury shares acquired	(11,221,919)	—	—
Cordillera consideration (Note 2)	—	6,272,667	—
Balance, end of year	395,772,908	391,640,770	384,117,643

Preferred Stock (in part)

The Company has 10,000,000 shares of no par preferred stock authorized, of which 25,000 shares have been designated as Series A Junior Participating Preferred Stock (the Series A Preferred Stock). The Company's 6.00 percent Mandatory Convertible Preferred Stock, Series D (the Series D Preferred Stock) were converted to Apache common shares in August 2013.

Series D Preferred Stock

On July 28, 2010, Apache issued 25.3 million depositary shares, each representing a 1/20th interest in a share of Apache's 6.00-percent Mandatory Convertible Preferred Stock, Series D (Preferred Share), or 1.265 million Preferred Shares. Upon conversion of the outstanding Preferred Shares on August 1, 2013, 14.4 million Apache common shares were issued.

SHARE REPURCHASE PROGRAM

5.14 ARROW ELECTRONICS, INC. (DEC)
CONSOLIDATED STATEMENTS OF EQUITY

(In thousands)

	Common Stock at Par Value	Capital in Excess of Par Value	Treasury Stock	Retained Earnings	Accumulated Other Comprehensive Income	Noncontrolling Interests	Total
Balance at December 31, 2010	$125,337	$1,063,461	$(318,494)	$2,174,147	$206,744	$ —	$3,251,195
Consolidated net income	—	—	—	598,810	—	506	599,316
Foreign currency translation adjustment	—	—	—	—	(49,364)	(20)	(49,384)
Unrealized loss on investment securities, net	—	—	—	—	(11,886)	—	(11,886)
Unrealized loss on interest rate swaps designated as cash flow hedges, net	—	—	—	—	(1,855)	—	(1,855)
Employee benefit plan items, net	—	—	—	—	(14,482)	—	(14,482)
Amortization of stock-based compensation	—	39,225	—	—	—	—	39,225
Shares issued for stock-based compensation awards	45	(33,959)	80,579	—	—	—	46,665
Tax benefits related to stock-based compensation awards	—	7,548	—	—	—	—	7,548
Repurchases of common stock	—	—	(197,044)	—	—	—	(197,044)
Acquisition of noncontrolling interests	—	—	—	—	—	5,962	5,962
Balance at December 31, 2011	125,382	1,076,275	(434,959)	2,772,957	129,157	6,448	3,675,260

(continued)

	Common Stock at Par Value	Capital in Excess of Par Value	Treasury Stock	Retained Earnings	Accumulated Other Comprehensive Income	Noncontrolling Interests	Total
Consolidated net income	—	—	—	506,332	—	385	506,717
Foreign currency translation adjustment	—	—	—	—	24,082	(193)	23,889
Unrealized gain on investment securities, net	—	—	—	—	3,679	—	3,679
Unrealized loss on interest rate swaps designated as cash flow hedges, net	—	—	—	—	(4,805)	—	(4,805)
Employee benefit plan items, net	—	—	—	—	(6,976)	—	(6,976)
Amortization of stock-based compensation	—	34,546	—	—	—	—	34,546
Shares issued for stock-based compensation awards	42	(29,632)	42,962	—	—	—	13,372
Tax benefits related to stock-based compensation awards	—	5,076	—	—	—	—	5,076
Repurchases of common stock	—	—	(260,870)	—	—	—	(260,870)
Purchase of subsidiary shares from noncontrolling interest	—	(26)	—	—	—	(2,500)	(2,526)
Balance at December 31, 2012	$125,424	$1,086,239	$(652,867)	$3,279,289	$145,137	$ 4,140	$3,987,362
Consolidated net income	—	—	—	399,420	—	456	399,876
Foreign currency translation adjustment	—	—	—	—	65,793	—	65,793
Unrealized gain on investment securities, net	—	—	—	—	1,027	—	1,027
Unrealized gain on interest rate swaps designated as cash flow hedges, net	—	—	—	—	2,075	—	2,075
Employee benefit plan items, net	—	—	—	—	11,520	—	11,520
Amortization of stock-based compensation	—	36,923	—	—	—	—	36,923
Shares issued for stock-based compensation awards	—	(59,118)	95,132	—	—	—	36,014
Tax benefits related to stock-based compensation awards	—	7,031	—	—	—	—	7,031
Repurchases of common stock	—	—	(362,793)	—	—	—	(362,793)
Balance at December 31, 2013	$125,424	$1,071,075	$(920,528)	$3,678,709	$225,552	$ 4,596	$4,184,828

NOTES TO THE CONSOLIDATED FINANCIAL STATEMENTS

(Dollars in thousands except per share data)

10. Shareholders' Equity (in part)

Common Stock Outstanding Activity

The following table sets forth the activity in the number of shares outstanding (in thousands):

	Common Stock Issued	Treasury Stock	Common Stock Outstanding
Common stock outstanding at December 31, 2010	125,337	10,690	114,647
Shares issued for stock-based compensation awards	45	(2,662)	2,707
Repurchases of common stock	—	5,540	(5,540)
Common stock outstanding at December 31, 2011	125,382	13,568	111,814
Shares issued for stock-based compensation awards	42	(1,326)	1,368
Repurchases of common stock	—	7,181	(7,181)
Common stock outstanding at December 31, 2012	125,424	19,423	106,001
Shares issued for stock-based compensation awards	—	(2,772)	2,772
Repurchases of common stock	—	8,837	(8,837)
Common stock outstanding at December 31, 2013	125,424	25,488	99,936

The company has 2,000,000 authorized shares of serial preferred stock with a par value of one dollar. There were no shares of serial preferred stock outstanding at December 31, 2013 and 2012.

In February 2013, the company's Board of Directors (the "Board") approved the repurchase of up to $200,000 of the company's common stock through a share-repurchase program. In July 2013, the company's Board approved an additional repurchase of up to $200,000 of the company's common stock. As of December 31, 2013, the company repurchased 6,032,892 shares under these programs with a market value of $248,571 at the dates of repurchase.

Common Stock

DISCLOSURE

5.15 Rule 5-02 of Regulation S-X requires stating on the face of the balance sheet the number of shares issued or outstanding, as appropriate, and the dollar amount. The number of shares authorized should be disclosed on the balance sheet or in the notes.

Preferred Stock

PRESENTATION

5.16 FASB ASC 505-10-50-4 requires that if preferred stock or other senior stock has a preference in involuntary liquidation, the entity should disclose the liquidation preference of the stock (the relationship between the preference in liquidation and the par or stated value of the shares). That disclosure should be made in the Equity section of the balance sheet in the aggregate, either parenthetically or in short.

5.17 FASB ASC 480-10-05-1 requires that an issuer classify certain financial instruments with characteristics of both liabilities and equity as liabilities because those financial instruments embody obligations of the issuer. Some issuances of stock, such as mandatorily redeemable preferred stock, impose unconditional obligations requiring the issuer to transfer assets or issue its equity shares.

DISCLOSURE

5.18 FASB ASC 505-10-50-5 requires disclosure of both of the following either on the face of the statement of financial position or in the notes thereto:
- The aggregate or per-share amounts at which preferred stock may be called or is subject to redemption through sinking-fund operations or otherwise
- The aggregate and per-share amounts of arrearages in cumulative preferred dividends

Rule 5-02 of SEC Regulation S-X also calls for disclosure of the number of shares authorized and the number of shares issued or outstanding, as appropriate.

PREFERRED STOCK

5.19 THE GOODYEAR TIRE & RUBBER COMPANY (DEC)
CONSOLIDATED STATEMENTS OF SHAREHOLDERS' EQUITY

(Dollars in millions)	Preferred Stock Shares	Preferred Stock Amount	Common Stock Shares	Common Stock Amount	Capital Surplus	Retained Earnings	Accumulated Other Comprehensive Loss	Goodyear Shareholders' Equity	Minority Shareholders' Equity—Non-Redeemable	Total Shareholders' Equity
Balance at December 31, 2010 (after deducting 7,950,743 common treasury shares)	—	$ —	242,938,949	$243	$2,805	$ 866	$(3,270)	$ 644	$277	$ 921
Comprehensive income (loss):										
Net income						343		343	39	382
Foreign currency translation (net of tax of $0)							(140)	(140)	(27)	(167)
Amortization of prior service cost and unrecognized gains and losses included in net periodic benefit cost (net of tax of $8)							157	157		157
Increase in net actuarial losses (net of tax benefit of $28)							(770)	(770)		(770)
Immediate recognition of prior service cost and unrecognized gains and losses due to curtailments, settlements and divestitures (net of tax of $1)							18	18		18
Deferred derivative gains (net of tax of $1)							3	3		3
Reclassification adjustment for amounts recognized in income (net of tax of $2)							6	6		6
Unrealized investment gains (net of tax of $0)							5	5		5
Other comprehensive income (loss)								(721)	(27)	(748)
Total comprehensive income (loss)								(378)	12	(366)
Dividends declared to minority shareholders									(20)	(20)
Stock-based compensation plans					13			13		13
Preferred stock issued (Note 19)	10,000,000	500			(16)			484		484
Preferred stock dividends declared (Note 19)						(22)		(22)		(22)
Common stock issued from treasury (Note 17)			1,596,892	2	6			8		8
Other									(1)	(1)
Balance at December 31, 2011 (after deducting 6,353,851 common treasury shares)	10,000,000	$500	244,535,841	$245	$2,808	$1,187	$(3,991)	$ 749	$268	$1,017
Comprehensive income (loss):										
Net income						212		212	35	247
Foreign currency translation (net of tax of $0)							51	51	14	65
Amortization of prior service cost and unrecognized gains and losses included in total benefit cost (net of tax of $9)							203	203		203
Increase in net actuarial losses (net of tax benefit of $44)							(898)	(898)		(898)
Immediate recognition of prior service cost and unrecognized gains and losses due to curtailments, settlements and divestitures (net of tax of $1)							9	9		9
Prior service credit from plan amendments (net of tax of $3)							72	72		72
Deferred derivative losses (net of tax of $0)							(4)	(4)		(4)
Reclassification adjustment for amounts recognized in income (net of tax benefit of $3)							(7)	(7)		(7)
Other comprehensive income (loss)								(574)	14	(560)
Total comprehensive income (loss)								(362)	49	(313)

(continued)

(Dollars in millions)	Preferred Stock		Common Stock		Capital Surplus	Retained Earnings	Accumulated Other Comprehensive Loss	Goodyear Shareholders' Equity	Minority Shareholders' Equity— Non-Redeemable	Total Shareholders' Equity
	Shares	Amount	Shares	Amount						
Purchase of subsidiary shares from minority interest					(13)		5	(8)	(47)	(55)
Dividends declared to minority shareholders									(15)	(15)
Stock-based compensation plans					17			17		17
Preferred stock dividends declared (Note 19)						(29)		(29)		(29)
Common stock issued from treasury (Note 17)			704,921	—	3			3		3
Balance at December 31, 2012 (after deducting 5,648,930 common treasury shares)	10,000,000	$500	245,240,762	$245	$2,815	$1,370	$(4,560)	$ 370	$255	$ 625
Comprehensive income (loss):										
Net income						629		629	45	674
Foreign currency translation (net of tax of $0)							(153)	(153)	(21)	(174)
Reclassification adjustment for amounts recognized in income (net of tax of $0)							1	1		1
Amortization of prior service cost and unrecognized gains and losses included in total benefit cost (net of tax of $9)							224	224		224
Decrease in net actuarial losses (net of tax of $33)							498	498		498
Immediate recognition of prior service cost and unrecognized gains and losses due to curtailments, settlements and divestitures (net of tax of $1)							2	2		2
Prior service credit from plan amendments (net of tax of $0)							30	30		30
Deferred derivative gains (net of tax of $1)							1	1		1
Reclassification adjustment for amounts recognized in income (net of tax of $0)							2	2		2
Unrealized investment gains (net of tax of $0)							8	8		8
Other comprehensive income (loss)								613	(21)	592
Total comprehensive income (loss)								1,242	24	1,266
Purchase of subsidiary shares from minority interest					(2)			(2)	(2)	(4)
Dividends declared to minority shareholders									(11)	(11)
Stock-based compensation plans					15			15		15
Dividends declared (Note 19)						(41)		(41)		(41)
Common stock issued from treasury (Note 17)			2,512,267	3	19			22		22
Other								—	(4)	(4)
Balance at December 31, 2013 (after deducting 3,136,663 common treasury shares)	10,000,000	$500	247,753,029	$248	$2,847	$1,958	$(3,947)	$1,606	$262	$1,868

NOTES TO CONSOLIDATED FINANCIAL STATEMENTS

Note 1. Accounting Policies (in part)

Earnings Per Share of Common Stock

Basic earnings per share are computed based on the weighted average number of common shares outstanding. Diluted earnings per share primarily reflects the dilutive impact of outstanding stock options, our mandatory convertible preferred stock and related dividends. All earnings per share amounts in these notes to the consolidated financial statements are diluted, unless otherwise noted. Refer to Note 6.

Note 6. Earnings Per Share

Basic earnings per share are computed based on the weighted average number of common shares outstanding. Diluted earnings per share are calculated to reflect the potential dilution that could occur if securities or other contracts were exercised or converted into common stock.

Basic and diluted earnings per common share are calculated as follows:

(In millions, except per share amounts)	2013	2012	2011
Earnings per share—basic:			
Goodyear net income	$ 629	$ 212	$ 343
Less: Preferred stock dividends	29	29	22
Goodyear net income available to common shareholders	$ 600	$ 183	$ 321
Weighted average shares outstanding	246	245	244
Earnings per common share—basic	$2.44	$0.75	$1.32
Earnings per share—diluted:			
Goodyear net income	$ 629	$ 212	$ 343
Less: Preferred stock dividends	—	29	—
Goodyear net income available to common shareholders	$ 629	$ 183	$ 343
Weighted average shares outstanding	246	245	244
Dilutive effect of mandatory convertible preferred stock	28	—	25
Dilutive effect of stock options and other dilutive securities	3	2	2
Weighted average shares outstanding—diluted	277	247	271
Earnings per common share—diluted	$2.28	$0.74	$1.26

Weighted average shares outstanding—diluted for the year ended December 31, 2012 excludes the effect of approximately 34 million equivalent shares related to the mandatory convertible preferred stock as their inclusion would have been anti-dilutive. In addition, Goodyear net income used to compute earnings per share—diluted for the year ended December 31, 2012 is reduced by $29 million of preferred stock dividends since the inclusion of the related shares of preferred stock would have been anti-dilutive.

Additionally, weighted average shares outstanding—diluted for 2013, 2012 and 2011 excludes approximately 3 million, 11 million and 6 million equivalent shares, respectively, related to options with exercise prices greater than the average market price of our common stock (i.e., "underwater" options).

Note 19. Capital Stock

Mandatory Convertible Preferred Stock

On March 31, 2011, we issued 10,000,000 shares of our 5.875% mandatory convertible preferred stock, without par value and with an initial liquidation preference of $50.00 per share, at a price of $50.00 per share. Quarterly dividends on each share of the mandatory convertible preferred stock accrue at a rate of 5.875% per year on the initial liquidation preference of $50.00 per share. Dividends accrue and accumulate from the date of issuance and, to the extent that we are legally permitted to pay a dividend and the Board of Directors declares a dividend payable, we will pay dividends in cash on January 1, April 1, July 1 and October 1 of each year, commencing on July 1, 2011 and ending on April 1, 2014. The mandatory convertible preferred stock ranks senior to our common stock with respect to distribution rights in the event of any liquidation, winding-up or dissolution of the Company.

Unless converted earlier, each share of the mandatory convertible preferred stock will automatically convert on April 1, 2014 into between 2.7454 and 3.4317 shares of common stock, depending on the market value of our common stock for the 20 consecutive trading day period ending on the third trading day prior to April 1, 2014, subject to customary anti-dilution adjustments (including in connection with the declaration of dividends on our common stock). At any time prior to April 1, 2014, holders may elect to convert shares of the mandatory convertible preferred stock at the minimum conversion rate of 2.7454 shares of common stock, subject to customary anti-dilution adjustments (including in connection with the declaration of dividends on our common stock). If certain fundamental changes involving the Company occur, holders of the mandatory convertible preferred stock may convert their shares into a number of shares of common stock at the fundamental change conversion rate described in our Amended Articles of Incorporation.

Upon conversion, we will pay converting holders all accrued and unpaid dividends, whether or not previously declared, on the converted shares and, in the case of a conversion upon a fundamental change, the present value of the remaining dividend payments on the converted shares. Except as required by law or as specifically set forth in our Amended Articles of Incorporation, the holders of the mandatory convertible preferred stock have no voting rights.

So long as any of the mandatory convertible preferred stock is outstanding, no dividend, except a dividend payable in shares of our common stock, or other shares ranking junior to the mandatory convertible preferred stock, may be paid or declared or any distribution be made on shares of the common stock unless all accrued and unpaid dividends on the then outstanding mandatory convertible preferred stock payable on all dividend payment dates occurring on or prior to the date of such action have been declared and paid or funds sufficient therefor set apart.

Dividends

During 2013, 2012 and 2011, we paid cash dividends of $29 million, $29 million, and $15 million, respectively, on our mandatory convertible preferred stock. On November 21, 2013, the Company's Board of Directors (or a duly authorized committee thereof) declared cash dividends of $0.7344 per share of mandatory convertible preferred stock or $7 million in the aggregate. The dividend was paid on January 2, 2014 to stockholders of record as of the close of business of December 13, 2013.

During 2013, we paid cash dividends of $12 million on our common stock. On January 13, 2014, the Company's Board of Directors (or a duly authorized committee thereof) declared cash dividends of $0.05 per share of our common stock, or approximately $12 million in the aggregate. The cash dividend will be paid on March 3, 2014 to stockholders of record as of the close of business of January 31, 2014.

Dividends

PRESENTATION

5.20 For public entities with respect to any dividends, Rule 3-04 of Regulation S-X requires the amount per share and in the aggregate for each class of shares to be stated. This may be stated on the financial statements or within the note disclosures. Further, Rule 4-08 of Regulation S-X requires disclosure of any restrictions that limit the payment of dividends.

PRESENTATION AND DISCLOSURE EXCERPTS

CASH DIVIDENDS

5.21 CA, INC. (MAR)
CONSOLIDATED STATEMENTS OF STOCKHOLDERS' EQUITY

(In millions, except per share amounts)	Common Stock	Additional Paid-In Capital	Retained Earnings	Accumulated Other Comprehensive Income/(Loss)	Treasury Stock	Total Stockholders' Equity
Balance at March 31, 2010	$59	$3,657	$3,361	$(126)	$(1,964)	$4,987
Net income			827			827
Other comprehensive income				61		61
Comprehensive income						888
Share-based compensation		80				80
Dividends declared			(82)			(82)
Release of restricted stock, exercise of common stock options and other items		(122)			107	(15)
Treasury stock purchased					(238)	(238)
Balance at March 31, 2011	$59	$3,615	$4,106	$ (65)	$(2,095)	$5,620
Net income			951			951
Other comprehensive loss				(43)		(43)
Comprehensive income						908
Share-based compensation		89				89
Dividends declared			(192)			(192)
Release of restricted stock, exercise of common stock options and other items		(88)			110	22
Accelerated share repurchase		(125)			(375)	(500)
Treasury stock purchased					(550)	(550)
Balance at March 31, 2012	$59	$3,491	$4,865	$(108)	$(2,910)	$5,397
Net income			955			955
Other comprehensive loss				(47)		(47)
Comprehensive income						908
Share-based compensation		78				78
Dividends declared			(463)			(463)
Release of restricted stock, exercise of common stock options, ESPP and other items		(101)			126	25
Accelerated share repurchase		125			(125)	—
Treasury stock purchased					(495)	(495)
Balance at March 31, 2013	$59	$3,593	$5,357	$(155)	$(3,404)	$5,450

Note 12—Stockholders' Equity (in part)

Cash Dividends: In January 2012, the Board of Directors approved a $2.5 billion capital allocation program through fiscal year 2014 that includes an increase in the Company's annual dividend from $0.20 to $1.00 per share of common stock as and when declared by the Board of Directors.

The Company's Board of Directors declared the following dividends during fiscal years 2013 and 2012:

Year Ended March 31, 2013:

(In millions, except per share amounts)

Declaration Date	Dividend Per Share	Record Date	Total Amount	Payment Date
May 8, 2012	$0.25	May 22, 2012	$119	June 12, 2012
August 2, 2012	$0.25	August 14, 2012	$116	September 11, 2012
November 7, 2012	$0.25	November 20, 2012	$114	December 11, 2012
February 7, 2013	$0.25	February 21, 2013	$114	March 19, 2013

Year Ended March 31, 2012:

(In millions, except per share amounts)

Declaration Date	Dividend Per Share	Record Date	Total Amount	Payment Date
May 12, 2011	$0.05	May 23, 2011	$ 25	June 16, 2011
August 3, 2011	$0.05	August 16, 2011	$ 25	September 14, 2011
November 9, 2011	$0.05	November 22, 2011	$ 25	December 14, 2011
January 23, 2012	$0.25	February 14, 2012	$117	March 13, 2012

5.22 MURPHY OIL CORPORATION (DEC)
MANAGEMENT'S DISCUSSION AND ANALYSIS OF FINANCIAL CONDITION AND RESULTS OF OPERATIONS

Cash Flows (in part)

Financing activities—During 2013, the Company borrowed additional long-term debt of $350.0 million, and primarily used these borrowings to fund a portion of its capital program. The Company paid $500.0 million in 2013 and $250.0 million in 2012 to repurchase 7.66 million shares and 3.87 million shares, respectively, of its Common stock. The Company received 0.28 million additional shares of its stock in 2014 upon completion of an accelerated share repurchase agreement with a major financial institution that was still open at the end of 2013. Through December 31, 2013, the Company has spent $750.0 million of a $1.0 billion share buyback program approved by the Board of Directors. Cash used for dividends to stockholders was $235.1 million in 2013, $714.4 million in 2012 and $212.8 million in 2011. The Company increased its normal dividend rate by 14% in 2012 as the annualized dividend was raised from $1.10 per share to $1.25 per share effective in the third quarter 2012. Additionally, in December 2012, the Company paid a special dividend of $2.50 per share. At the date of the spin-off, Murphy USA Inc. paid Murphy Oil Corporation cash of $650.0 million, which the Company primarily used to partially repay outstanding debt. However, Murphy USA retained cash of $55.5 million at the time of the separation. At December 31, 2013, the Company's held for sale U.K. downstream business had cash of $301.3 million. This cash is classified within current assets held for sale on the Consolidated Balance Sheet at year-end 2013, effectively removing this amount from the Company's reported cash balance. During 2012, the Company sold $2.0 billion of long-term notes. The proceeds of these notes were primarily used to repay $350.0 million of notes that matured in 2012, to repay other debt, to fund a special dividend totaling $486.1 million, to fund a $250.0 million repurchase of Common stock, and to fund a portion of the Company's development capital expenditures. During 2011, the Company used available cash flow to repay $340.0 million of debt. The debt reduction in 2011 was accomplished with proceeds from sale of the two U.S. refineries. Cash proceeds from stock option exercises and employee stock purchase plans, including income tax benefits received on stock options, amounted to $4.2 million in 2013, $15.0 million in 2012 and $20.4 million in 2011. In 2013, the Company paid $3.3 million of fees to increase the size of its committed credit facility from $1.5 billion to $2.0 billion and to extend the maturity date by one year to June 2017. In 2012, the Company paid $7.0 million of fees and other expenses associated with sales of $2.0 billion of long-term notes. In 2011, the Company used cash of $7.9 million for fees and other expenses associated with renewing its primary $1.5 billion committed credit facility that has now been increased to $2.0 billion of capacity. In 2013, 2012 and 2011, cash of $16.7 million, $3.3 million and $8.0 million, respectively, was used to pay statutory withholding taxes on stock-based incentive awards that vested with a net-of-tax payout.

(Thousands of dollar)	Years Ended December 31		
	2013	2012	2011
Cumulative Preferred Stock—par $100, authorized 400,000 shares, none issued	0	0	0
Common Stock—par $1.00, authorized 450,000,000 shares at December 31, 2013, 2012 and 2011, issued 194,920,155 shares at December 31, 2013, 194,616,470 shares at December 31, 2012 and 193,909,200 shares at December 31, 2011			
Balance at beginning of year	$ 194,616	193,909	193,294
Exercise of stock options	304	483	615
Awarded restricted stock	0	224	0
Balance at end of year	194,920	194,616	193,909
Capital in Excess of Par Value			
Balance at beginning of year	873,934	817,974	767,762
Exercise of stock options, including income tax benefits	563	12,717	21,774
Restricted stock transactions and other	(28,339)	(5,257)	(15,119)
Stock-based compensation	56,622	46,584	42,492
Sale of stock under employee stock purchase plans	(147)	1,916	1,065
Balance at end of year	902,633	873,934	817,974
Retained Earnings			
Balance at beginning of year	7,717,389	7,460,942	6,800,992
Net income for the year	1,123,473	970,876	872,702
Cash dividends—$1.25 per share in 2013, $3.675 per share in 2012 and $1.10 per share in 2011	(235,108)	(714,429)	(212,752)
Distribution of common stock of Murphy USA Inc. to shareholders	(546,962)	0	0
Balance at end of year	8,058,792	7,717,389	7,460,942
Accumulated Other Comprehensive Income			
Balance at beginning of year	408,901	310,420	449,428
Foreign currency translation gains (losses), net of income taxes	(308,300)	117,331	(91,247)
Retirement and postretirement benefit plan adjustments, net of income taxes	69,583	(17,650)	(30,909)
Change in deferred loss on interest rate hedges, net of income taxes	1,935	(1,200)	(16,852)
Balance at end of year	172,119	408,901	310,420
Treasury Stock			
Balance at beginning of year	(252,805)	(4,848)	(11,926)
Purchase of treasury shares	(500,000)	(250,000)	0
Sale of stock under employee stock purchase plans	1,015	2,043	870
Awarded restricted stock, net of forfeitures	19,056	0	6,208
Balance at end of year—11,513,642 shares of Common Stock in 2013, 3,975,153 shares of Common Stock in 2012 and 185,992 shares of Common Stock in 2011	(732,734)	(252,805)	(4,848)
Total stockholders' equity	$8,595,730	8,942,035	8,778,397

NOTES TO CONSOLIDATED FINANCIAL STATEMENTS

Note C—Discontinued Operations (in part)

Separation of U.S. Downstream Business (in part)

On August 30, 2013, Murphy Oil Corporation (the "Company") distributed 100% of the outstanding common stock of Murphy USA Inc. ("MUSA") to its shareholders in a generally tax-free spin-off for U.S. federal income tax purposes. After the close of the New York Stock Exchange on August 30, 2013, the Company's shareholders of record as of 5:00 p.m. Eastern time on August 21, 2013 received one share of MUSA common stock for every four common shares of the Company held by such shareholders. Prior to the separation, MUSA held all of the Company's U.S. downstream operations, including retail gasoline stations and other marketing assets, plus two ethanol production facilities. In connection with the separation, Murphy Oil USA, Inc., MUSA's 100% owned primary operating subsidiary, distributed $650,000,000 to the Company in the form of a cash dividend. These funds were raised from the proceeds of $500,000,000 secured notes issued by Murphy Oil USA, Inc. plus $150,000,000 borrowed under credit facilities entered into by MUSA and Murphy Oil USA, Inc. in connection with the separation. The shares of MUSA common stock are traded on the New York Stock Exchange under the ticker symbol "MUSA." The Company has no continuing involvement with MUSA operations. Accordingly, the operating results and the cash flows for these former U.S. downstream operations have been reported as discontinued operations for all periods presented in the consolidated financial statements. These operations were formerly reported as the U.S. refining and marketing segment in prior years' financial statements.

Note L—Stockholders' Equity (in part)

On December 3, 2012, the Company paid a special dividend of $2.50 per outstanding Common share to shareholders of record on November 16, 2012. This dividend totaled $486,141,000.

Note U—Subsequent Events

On February 5, 2014, the Company entered into a variable term, capped accelerated share repurchase (ASR) transaction with a major financial institution to repurchase a total of $250,000,000 of the Company's Common stock. Through February 28, 2014, the Company has received 4,018,000 shares under the ASR. The total number of shares to be repurchased under the ASR will be determined by references to the Rule 10b-18 volume-weighted price of the Company's Common stock, less a fixed discount. The ASR is expected to be completed within three months of the transaction. Also on February 5, 2014, the Company's Board of Directors declared a quarterly dividend of $0.3125 per share payable on March 3, 2014 to shareholders of record on February 18, 2014.

NON-CASH DIVIDENDS

5.23 COLGATE-PALMOLIVE COMPANY (DEC)
CONSOLIDATED STATEMENTS OF CHANGES IN SHAREHOLDERS' EQUITY

(Dollars in Millions)

	Colgate-Palmolive Company Shareholders' Equity						
	Common Stock	Additional Paid-In Capital	Unearned Compensation	Treasury Stock	Retained Earnings	Accumulated Other Comprehensive Income (Loss)	Noncontrolling Interests
Balance, January 1, 2011	$1,466	$ 399	$(99)	$(11,305)	$14,329	$(2,115)	$ 142
Net income					2,431		123
Other comprehensive income (loss), net of tax						(360)	(7)
Dividends					(1,111)		(92)
Stock-based compensation expense		122					
Shares issued for stock options		88		251			
Shares issued for restricted stock awards		(53)		53			
Treasury stock acquired				(1,806)			
Other		47	39	(1)			
Balance, December 31, 2011	$1,466	$ 603	$(60)	$(12,808)	$15,649	$(2,475)	$ 166
Net income					2,472		159
Other comprehensive income (loss), net of tax						(146)	2
Dividends					(1,168)		(109)
Stock-based compensation expense		120					
Shares issued for stock options		99		297			
Shares issued for restricted stock awards		(70)		70			
Treasury stock acquired				(1,943)			
Other		66	19	(2)			(17)
Balance, December 31, 2012	$1,466	$ 818	$(41)	$(14,386)	$16,953	$(2,621)	$ 201
Net income					2,241		169
Other comprehensive income (loss), net of tax						170	(3)
Dividends					(1,242)		(140)
Stock-based compensation expense		128					
Shares issued for stock options		82		201			
Shares issued for restricted stock awards		(75)		75			
Treasury stock acquired				(1,521)			
Other		51	8	(2)			4
Balance, December 31, 2013	$1,466	$1,004	$(33)	$(15,633)	$17,952	$(2,451)	$ 231

NOTES TO CONSOLIDATED FINANCIAL STATEMENTS

(Dollars in Millions Except Share and Per Share Amounts)

8. Capital Stock and Stock-Based Compensation Plans (in part)

Common Stock Split

On March 7, 2013, the Company's Board of Directors approved a two-for-one stock split of the Company's common stock to be effected through a 100% stock dividend (the "2013 Stock Split"). The record date for the 2013 Stock Split was the close of business on April 23, 2013, and the share distribution occurred on May 15, 2013. As a result of the stock split, shareholders received one additional share of Colgate common stock, par value $1.00, for each share they held as of the record date.

All per share amounts and numbers of shares outstanding in these Consolidated Financial Statements and Notes to the Consolidated Financial Statements are presented on a post-split basis. In addition, the impact on the Balance Sheet as a result of the 2013 Stock Split was an increase of $733 to Common Stock and an offsetting reduction in Additional paid-in capital, which has been retroactively restated.

Stock Splits

RECOGNITION AND MEASUREMENT

5.24 The FASB ASC glossary defines a *stock split* as an issuance by a corporation of its own common shares to its common shareholders without consideration and under conditions indicating that such action is prompted mainly by a desire to increase the number of outstanding shares for the purpose of effecting a reduction in their unit market price and, thereby, of obtaining wider distribution and improved marketability of the shares. It is also sometimes called a stock split-up.

5.25 FASB ASC 505–20 addresses the accounting for stock splits, as well as stock dividends, and provides guidance on determining whether a stock dividend or stock split should be accounted for according to its form or whether it should be accounted for differently.

PRESENTATION AND DISCLOSURE EXCERPTS

STOCK SPLIT

5.26 FLOWERS FOODS, INC. (DEC)
CONSOLIDATED STATEMENTS OF CHANGES IN STOCKHOLDERS' EQUITY

(Amounts in thousands, except share data)	Common Stock		Capital in Excess of Par Value	Retained Earnings	Accumulated Other Comprehensive Loss	Treasury Stock		Total
	Number of Shares Issued	Par Value				Number of Shares	Cost	
Balances at January 1, 2011	101,659,924	$199	$540,294	$503,689	$(33,709)	(11,011,494)	$(214,683)	$795,790
Net income				123,428				123,428
Derivative instruments, net of tax					(38,813)			(38,813)
Pension and postretirement plans, net of tax					(39,525)			(39,525)
Adjustment for 3 for 2 stock split (Note 14)	50,828,084			(39)		(5,375,912)		(39)
Stock repurchases						(1,155,103)	(26,598)	(26,598)
Exercise of stock options			(2,512)			803,090	15,445	12,933
Issuance of performance-contingent restricted stock awards			(4,213)			216,050	4,213	—
Issuance of deferred stock awards			(1,160)			56,505	1,119	(41)
Amortization of share-based compensation awards			12,982					12,982
Income tax benefits related to share-based payments			2,932					2,932
Performance-contingent restricted stock awards forfeitures and cancellations			961			(51,630)	(961)	—
Issuance of deferred compensation			(219)			11,672	219	—
Contingent acquisition consideration			(5,000)					(5,000)
Dividends paid—$0.389 per common share				(79,081)				(79,081)
Balances at December 31, 2011	152,488,008	$199	$544,065	$547,997	$(112,047)	(16,506,822)	$(221,246)	$758,968

(continued)

(Amounts in thousands, except share data)	Common Stock Number of Shares Issued	Par Value	Capital in Excess of Par Value	Retained Earnings	Accumulated Other Comprehensive Loss	Treasury Stock Number of Shares	Cost	Total
Net income				136,121				136,121
Derivative instruments, net of tax					10,808			10,808
Pension and postretirement plans, net of tax					(13,428)			(13,428)
Shares issued for acquisition			16,628			2,178,648	29,259	45,887
Stock repurchases						(935,742)	(18,726)	(18,726)
Exercise of stock options			(329)			1,047,297	14,210	13,881
Issuance of deferred stock awards			(610)			45,405	610	—
Amortization of share-based compensation awards			9,373					9,373
Income tax benefits related to share-based payments			2,225					2,225
Performance-contingent restricted stock awards forfeitures and cancellations			606			(45,252)	(606)	—
Issuance of deferred compensation			(34)			1,647	34	—
Dividends paid on vested performance-contingent restricted stock and deferred share awards				(255)				(255)
Dividends paid—$0.420 per common share				(86,234)				(86,234)
Balances at December 29, 2012	152,488,008	$199	$571,924	$597,629	$(114,667)	(14,214,819)	$(196,465)	$858,620
Net income				230,894				230,894
Derivative instruments, net of tax					(7,316)			(7,316)
Pension and postretirement plans, net of tax					59,468			59,468
Adjustment for 3 for 2 stock split (Note 14)	76,241,577		(52)			(6,860,135)		(52)
Stock repurchases						(367,623)	(8,819)	(8,819)
Exercise of stock options			508			1,158,590	13,177	13,685
Issuance of deferred stock awards			(752)			54,120	752	—
Amortization of share-based compensation awards			14,725					14,725
Income tax benefits related to share-based payments			7,824					7,824
Performance-contingent restricted stock awards supplemental grant for exceeding TSR (Note 15)			(874)			63,232	874	—
Dividends paid on vested performance-contingent restricted stock and deferred share awards				(386)				(386)
Dividends paid—$0.444 per common share				(92,454)				(92,454)
Balances at December 28, 2013	228,729,585	$199	$593,355	$735,631	$(62,515)	(20,166,635)	$(190,481)	$1,076,189

NOTES TO CONSOLIDATED FINANCIAL STATEMENTS

Note 14. Stockholders' Equity (in part)

Stock Split

On May 25, 2011, the board of directors declared a 3-for-2 stock split of the company's common stock. The record date for the split was June 10, 2011 and new shares were issued on June 24, 2011.

On May 22, 2013, the board of directors declared a 3-for-2 stock split of the company's common stock. The record date for the split was June 5, 2013, and new shares were issued on June 19, 2013. All share and per share information has been restated for all prior periods presented giving retroactive effect to the stock split in the accompanying footnotes.

Note 17. Earnings Per Share

On May 22, 2013, the board of directors declared a 3-for-2 stock split of the company's common stock. The record date for the split was June 5, 2013, and new shares were issued on June 19, 2013. All share and per share information has been restated for all prior periods presented giving retroactive effect to the stock split.

The following is a reconciliation of net income and weighted average shares for calculating basic and diluted earnings per common share for fiscal years 2013, 2012, and 2011 (amounts in thousands, except per share data):

	Fiscal 2013	Fiscal 2012	Fiscal 2011
Net income	$230,894	$136,121	$123,428
Basic Earnings Per Common Share:			
Weighted average shares outstanding for common stock	207,935	205,005	203,015
Weighted average shares outstanding for participating securities	—	—	66
Basic weighted average shares outstanding per common share	207,935	205,005	203,081
Basic earnings per common share	$ 1.11	$ 0.66	$ 0.61
Diluted Earnings Per Common Share:			
Basic weighted average shares outstanding per common share	207,935	205,005	203,081
Add: Shares of common stock assumed issued upon exercise of stock options, vesting of performance-contingent restricted stock and deferred stock	3,992	2,669	2,241
Diluted weighted average shares outstanding per common share	211,927	207,674	205,322
Diluted earnings per common share	$ 1.09	$ 0.66	$ 0.60

There were no anti-dilutive shares for fiscal years 2013, 2012, or 2011.

REVERSE STOCK SPLIT

5.27 DEAN FOODS COMPANY (DEC)

CONSOLIDATED STATEMENTS OF STOCKHOLDERS' EQUITY (DEFICIT)

	Dean Foods Company Stockholders						
	Common Stock		Additional Paid-In Capital	Retained Earnings (Accumulated Deficit)	Accumulated Other Comprehensive Income (Loss)	Non-controlling Interest	Total Stock-holders' Equity (Deficit)
(Dollars in thousands, except share data)	Shares	Amount					
Balance, January 1, 2011	91,127,667	$912	$1,062,164	$ 583,102	$(146,653)	$ 14,543	$ 1,514,068
Issuance of common stock, net of tax impact of share-based compensation	745,228	7	(5,850)	—	—	—	(5,843)
Share-based compensation expense	—	—	31,408	—	—	—	31,408
Capital contribution from non-controlling interest	—	—	—	—	—	6,754	6,754
Net loss attributable to non-controlling interest	—	—	—	—	—	(16,550)	(16,550)
Net loss attributable to Dean Foods Company	—	—	—	(1,575,621)	—	—	(1,575,621)
Other comprehensive income (loss) (Note 14):							
Change in fair value of derivative instruments, net of tax benefit of $38,527	—	—	—	—	(58,797)	—	(58,797)
Amounts reclassified to statement of operations related to hedging activities, net of tax of $23,156	—	—	—	—	35,235	—	35,235
Cumulative translation adjustment	—	—	—	—	(12,738)	—	(12,738)
Pension liability adjustment, net of tax benefit of $10,694	—	—	—	—	(16,567)	—	(16,567)
Balance, December 31, 2011	91,872,895	$919	$1,087,722	$ (992,519)	$(199,520)	$ 4,747	$ (98,651)
Issuance of common stock, net of tax impact of share-based compensation	908,872	9	(233)	—	—	—	(224)
Share-based compensation expense	—	—	24,247	—	—	—	24,247
Sale of former subsidiary shares to non-controlling interest	—	—	265,004	—	4,469	98,067	367,540
Share-based compensation expense for former subsidiary shares	—	—	—	—	—	1,167	1,167
Wind-down of former subsidiary joint venture	—	—	—	—	—	(4,747)	(4,747)
Net income attributable to non-controlling interest	—	—	—	—	—	2,419	2,419
Net income attributable to Dean Foods Company	—	—	—	158,622	—	—	158,622

(continued)

(Dollars in thousands, except share data)	Common Stock Shares	Common Stock Amount	Additional Paid-In Capital	Retained Earnings (Accumulated Deficit)	Accumulated Other Comprehensive Income (Loss)	Non-controlling Interest	Total Stockholders' Equity (Deficit)
					Dean Foods Company Stockholders		
Other comprehensive income (loss) (Note 14):							
Change in fair value of derivative instruments, net of tax benefit of $12,682	—	—	—	—	(19,780)	(13)	(19,793)
Amounts reclassified to statement of operations related to hedging activities, net of tax of $16,239	—	—	—	—	24,964	—	24,964
Cumulative translation adjustment	—	—	—	—	10,354	933	11,287
Pension liability adjustment, net of tax benefit of $4,493	—	—	—	—	(7,071)	(132)	(7,203)
Balance, December 31, 2012	92,781,767	$928	$1,376,740	$ (833,897)	$(186,584)	$ 102,441	$ 459,628
Issuance of common stock, net of tax impact of share-based compensation	2,049,610	20	19,900	—	—	—	19,920
Share-based compensation expense	—	—	11,718	—	—	—	11,718
Share-based compensation expense for former subsidiary shares	—	—	—	—	—	7,733	7,733
Net income attributable to non-controlling interest	—	—	—	—	—	6,179	6,179
Net income attributable to Dean Foods Company	—	—	—	813,178	—	—	813,178
Other comprehensive income (loss) (Note 14):							
Change in fair value of derivative instruments, net of tax benefit of $21	—	—	—	—	(91)	10	(81)
Amounts reclassified to statement of operations related to hedging activities, net of tax of $37,017	—	—	—	—	58,784	—	58,784
Cumulative translation adjustment	—	—	—	—	(9,393)	(1,398)	(10,791)
Pension liability adjustment, net of tax of $29,474	—	—	—	—	47,069	4	47,073
Spin-Off of The WhiteWave Foods Company	—	—	(617,082)	—	33,025	(114,969)	(699,026)
Balance, December 31, 2013	94,831,377	$948	$ 791,276	$ (20,719)	$ (57,190)	$ —	$ 714,315

[1] Common Stock and Additional Paid-In Capital at January 1, 2011, December 31, 2011 and December 31, 2012 have been adjusted retroactively to reflect a 1-for-2 reverse stock split effected August 26, 2013.

NOTES TO CONSOLIDATED FINANCIAL STATEMENTS

1. Summary of Significant Accounting Policies (in part)

Basis of Presentation and Consolidation (in part)—Our Consolidated Financial Statements are prepared in accordance with U.S. generally accepted accounting principles ("GAAP") and include the accounts of our wholly-owned subsidiaries.

On August 26, 2013, we effected a 1-for-2 reverse stock split of our issued common stock. Each stockholder's percentage ownership and proportional voting power generally remained unchanged as a result of the reverse stock split. All applicable share data, per share amounts and related information in the Consolidated Financial Statements and notes thereto have been adjusted retroactively to give effect to the 1-for-2 reverse stock split. See Note 13.

12. Common Stock and Share-Based Compensation (in part)

Our authorized shares of capital stock include one million shares of preferred stock and 500 million shares of common stock with a par value of $0.01 per share.

1-for-2 Reverse Stock Split—At the 2013 Annual Stockholders' Meeting, which was held on May 15, 2013, our stockholders approved an amendment to our restated certificate of incorporation, as amended, to effect a reverse stock split of our issued common stock by a ratio of not less than 1-for-2 and not more than 1-for-8. The approval of the amendment was conditioned upon the successful completion of the WhiteWave spin-off, which was completed on May 23, 2013. On August 26, 2013, we effected a 1-for-2 reverse stock split of our issued common stock. The reverse stock split ratio and the implementation and timing of the reverse stock split were determined by our Board of Directors. The reverse stock split did not change the authorized number of shares or par value of our common stock or preferred stock, but did effect a proportionate adjustment to the per share exercise price and the number of shares of common stock issuable upon the exercise of outstanding stock options, the number of shares of common stock issuable upon the vesting of restricted stock awards, and the number of shares of common stock eligible for issuance under our 2007 Stock Incentive Plan (the "2007 Plan"). No fractional shares were issued in connection with the reverse stock split. Each stockholder's percentage ownership and proportional voting power generally remained unchanged as a result of the reverse stock split.

All applicable outstanding equity awards discussed below have been adjusted retroactively for the 1-for-2 reverse stock split.

Changes to Retained Earnings

RECOGNITION AND MEASUREMENT

5.28 The retained earnings account is affected by direct charges and credits. Examples of direct charges to retained earnings are net loss for the year, losses on treasury stock transactions, and cash or stock dividends; an example of a direct credit to retained earnings is net income for the year.

PRESENTATION

5.29 In addition to direct charges and credits, the retained earnings account is also affected by opening balance adjustments. Reasons for which the opening balance of retained earnings is properly restated include certain changes in accounting principles, changes in the reporting entity, and corrections of an error in previously issued financial statements.

5.30 FASB ASC 250-10-05-2 requires, unless impracticable or otherwise specified by applicable authoritative guidance, retrospective application to prior periods' financial statements of a change in accounting principle. *Retrospective application* is the application of a different accounting principle to prior accounting periods as if that principle had always been used. More specifically, FASB ASC 250-10-45-5 explains that retrospective application involves the following:
- The cumulative effect of the change on periods prior to those presented should be reflected in the carrying amounts of assets and liabilities as of the beginning of the first period presented.
- An offsetting adjustment, if any, shall be made to the opening balance of retained earnings or other appropriate components of equity or net assets in the statement of financial position for that period.
- Financial statements for each individual prior period presented should be adjusted to reflect the period-specific effects of applying the new accounting principle.

5.31 FASB ASC 250-10-45-23 also requires any accounting error in the financial statements of a prior period discovered after the financial statements are issued or are available to be issued to be reported as an error correction by restating the prior period financial statements. Restatement involves similar requirements as those specified for retrospective application of a change in accounting principle.

5.32 SEC Staff Accounting Bulletin (SAB) No. 108 provides guidance on the consideration of the effects of prior year misstatements in quantifying current year misstatements for the purpose of assessing materiality. SAB No. 108 requires that registrant entities determine the quantitative effect of a financial statement misstatement by using both an income statement ("rollover") and a balance sheet ("iron curtain") approach and evaluate whether, under either approach, the error is material after considering all relevant quantitative and qualitative factors.

CHANGE IN ACCOUNTING PRINCIPLE

5.33 PVH CORP. (JAN)

CONSOLIDATED STATEMENTS OF CHANGES IN STOCKHOLDERS' EQUITY—AS ADJUSTED

(In thousands, except share and per share data)

	Preferred Stock	Common Stock Shares	Common Stock $1 par Value	Additional Paid In Capital-Common Stock	Retained Earnings	Accumulated Other Comprehensive Income	Treasury Stock	Stock-holders' Equity
January 31, 2010		57,139,230	$57,139	$ 596,344	$ 713,633	$ 2,201	$(200,764)	$1,168,553
Net income					54,377			54,377
Amortization of prior service credit related to pension and postretirement plans, net of tax (benefit) of $(310)						(578)		(578)
Foreign currency translation adjustments, net of tax (benefit) of $(149)						147,574		147,574
Liquidation of foreign operation, net of tax expense of $318						523		523
Net unrealized and realized loss on effective hedges, net of tax (benefit) of $(256)						(11,899)		(11,899)
Total comprehensive income								189,997
Common stock offering, including the sale of 5,250,000 treasury shares		500,000	500	162,573			201,456	364,529
Issuance of restricted stock		350,861	351	(351)				—
Issuance of common stock in connection with the acquisition of Tommy Hilfiger		7,872,980	7,873	467,734				475,607
Issuance of 8,000 preferred shares	$ 188,595							188,595
Exercise of warrant, net of withholding of 140,207 treasury shares		320,000	320	8,640			(8,960)	—
Settlement of awards under stock plans		1,051,496	1,052	22,887				23,939
Tax benefits from awards under stock plans				10,539				10,539
Stock-based compensation expense				33,281				33,281
Cash dividends					(10,015)			(10,015)
Acquisition of 41,868 treasury shares							(2,481)	(2,481)
January 30, 2011	188,595	67,234,567	67,235	1,301,647	757,995	137,821	(10,749)	2,442,544
Net income					275,697			275,697
Amortization of prior service credit related to pension and postretirement plans, net of tax (benefit) of $(344)						(535)		(535)
Foreign currency translation adjustments, net of tax (benefit) of $(1,070)						(82,062)		(82,062)
Net unrealized and realized gain on effective hedges, net of tax (benefit) of $(2,822)						18,611		18,611
Total comprehensive income								211,711
Settlement of awards under stock plans		1,063,206	1,063	23,394				24,457
Tax benefits from awards under stock plans				11,943				11,943
Stock-based compensation expense				40,938				40,938
Cash dividends					(10,874)			(10,874)
Acquisition of 80,638 treasury shares							(5,270)	(5,270)
January 29, 2012	188,595	68,297,773	68,298	1,377,922	1,022,818	73,835	(16,019)	2,715,449
Net income					433,840			433,840
Amortization of prior service credit related to pension and postretirement plans, net of tax (benefit) of $(338)						(542)		(542)
Foreign currency translation adjustments, net of tax expense of $469						86,492		86,492
Net unrealized and realized (loss) on effective hedges, net of tax expense of $2,681						(19,903)		(19,903)
Total comprehensive income								499,887
Settlement of awards under stock plans		837,360	837	12,434				13,271
Tax benefits from awards under stock plans				15,332				15,332
Stock-based compensation expense				33,599				33,599
Conversion of convertible preferred stock	(188,595)	4,189,358	4,189	184,406				—
Cash dividends					(10,985)			(10,985)
Acquisition of 164,065 treasury shares							(13,984)	(13,984)
February 3, 2013	$ —	73,324,491	$73,324	$1,623,693	$1,445,673	$139,882	$ (30,003)	$3,252,569

(Currency and share amounts in thousands, except per share data)

1. Summary of Significant Accounting Policies (in part)

Change in Accounting for Pension and Other Postretirement Plans—During the fourth quarter of 2012, the Company changed its method of accounting for actuarial gains and losses for its pension and other postretirement plans. Historically, the Company recognized actuarial gains and losses for its pension and other postretirement obligations and pension plan assets as a component of other comprehensive income in the periods in which they arose. As set forth in FASB guidance for pension and other postretirement plans, the Company amortized actuarial gains and losses (to the extent they exceeded a 10% corridor) in future periods over the average remaining service period of active employees or, if substantially all plan participants were inactive, over the average remaining life expectancy of inactive participants, as a component of its net periodic benefit cost. The Company elected in the fourth quarter of 2012 to begin to immediately recognize actuarial gains and losses in its operating results in the year in which they occur. These gains and losses are measured at least annually as of the end of the Company's fiscal year and, as such, will generally be recognized during the fourth quarter of each year. Additionally, the Company will no longer calculate expected return on plan assets using a permitted averaging technique for market-related value of plan assets but instead will use the fair value of plan assets. The Company believes the accounting policy changes improve the transparency of the Company's operational performance by recognizing in current period earnings the financial statement effects of changes in assumptions on the Company's pension and other postretirement obligations and changes in fair value of pension plan assets. The financial data for all prior periods presented has been retrospectively adjusted to reflect the effect of these accounting changes. The cumulative effect of the changes on retained earnings as of February 1, 2010, was a reduction of $ 82,649, with an offset to AOCI. Please see Note 10, "Retirement and Benefit Plans" for a further discussion of the Company's pension and other postretirement plans.

The following table presents the Company's results under its historical method and as adjusted to reflect the effect of these accounting changes:

	2012			2011			2010		
	Recognized Under Previous Method	Adjustments	Recognized Under New Method	As Originally Reported in Form 10-K in 2011	Adjustments	As Retrospectively Adjusted	As Originally Reported in Form 10-K in 2010	Adjustments	As Retrospectively Adjusted
Income Statement Information:									
Selling, general and administrative expenses	$2,584,257	$10,058	$2,594,315	$2,481,370	$68,480	$2,549,850	$2,071,416	$365	$2,071,781
Income before interest and taxes	670,420	(10,058)	660,362	559,653	(68,480)	491,173	203,395	(365)	203,030
Income tax expense	113,136	(3,864)	109,272	113,684	(26,296)	87,388	22,768	(937)	21,831
Net income	440,034	(6,194)	433,840	317,881	(42,184)	275,697	53,805	572	54,377
Basic net income per common share	6.07	(0.09)	5.98	4.46	(0.60)	3.86	0.82	0.01	0.83
Diluted net income per common share	5.96	(0.09)	5.87	4.36	(0.58)	3.78	0.80	0.01	0.81

	2012			2011		
	Recognized Under Previous Method	Adjustments	Recognized Under New Method	As Originally Reported in Form 10-K in 2011	Adjustments	As Retrospectively Adjusted
Balance Sheet Information:						
Retained earnings	$1,576,128	$(130,455)	$1,445,673	$1,147,079	$(124,261)	$1,022,818
AOCI	9,427	130,455	139,882	(50,426)	124,261	73,835

5.34 THE NEW YORK TIMES COMPANY (DEC)

CONSOLIDATED STATEMENTS OF CHANGES IN STOCKHOLDERS' EQUITY

(In thousands, except share and per share data)	Capital Stock Class A and Class B Common	Additional Paid-in Capital	Retained Earnings	Common Stock Held in Treasury, at Cost	Accumulated Other Comprehensive Loss, Net of Income Taxes	Total New York Times Company Stockholders' Equity	Non-controlling Interest	Total Stockholders' Equity
Balance, December 26, 2010, as reported	$15,012	$ 40,155	$1,126,294	$(134,463)	$(387,071)	$ 659,927	$4,149	$ 664,076
Cumulative prior period adjustment	—	—	5,957	—	14,476	20,433	—	20,433
Balance, December 26, 2010	15,012	40,155	1,132,251	(134,463)	(372,595)	680,360	4,149	684,509
Net loss	—	—	(37,648)	—	—	(37,648)	(555)	(38,203)
Other comprehensive loss	—	—	—	—	(124,463)	(124,463)	(445)	(124,908)
Issuance of shares:								
Employee stock purchase plan—603,114 Class A shares	60	4,258	—	—	—	4,318	—	4,318
Stock options—100,200 Class A shares	11	353	—	—	—	364	—	364
Stock conversions—240 Class B shares to Class A shares	—	—	—	—	—	—	—	—
Restricted stock units vested—210,769 Class A shares	—	(6,250)	—	4,965	—	(1,285)	—	(1,285)
401(k) Company stock match—781,088 Class A shares	—	(11,800)	—	18,524	—	6,724	—	6,724
Stock-based compensation	—	9,410	—	—	—	9,410	—	9,410
Income tax shortfall related to share-based payments	—	(4,102)	—	—	—	(4,102)	—	(4,102)
Balance, December 25, 2011	15,083	32,024	1,094,603	(110,974)	(497,058)	533,678	3,149	536,827
Net income	—	—	135,847	—	—	135,847	166	136,013
Other comprehensive loss	—	—	—	—	(15,508)	(15,508)	(4)	(15,512)
Issuance of shares:								
Stock options—176,400 Class A shares	18	712	—	—	—	730	—	730
Stock conversions—500 Class B shares to Class A shares	—	—	—	—	—	—	—	—
Restricted stock units vested—92,847 Class A shares	8	(656)	—	147	—	(501)	—	(501)
401(k) Company stock match—490,031 Class A shares	—	(10,785)	—	14,549	—	3,764	—	3,764
Stock-based compensation	—	5,329	—	—	—	5,329	—	5,329
Income tax shortfall related to share-based payments	—	(1,014)	—	—	—	(1,014)	—	(1,014)
Balance, December 30, 2012	15,109	25,610	1,230,450	(96,278)	(512,566)	662,325	3,311	665,636
Net income/(loss)	—	—	65,105	—	—	65,105	(249)	64,856
Dividends	—	—	(12,037)	—	—	(12,037)	—	(12,037)
Other comprehensive income	—	—	—	—	109,955	109,955	562	110,517
Issuance of shares:								
Stock options—914,272 Class A shares	92	4,994	—	—	—	5,086	—	5,086
Stock conversions—324 Class B shares to Class A shares	—	—	—	—	—	—	—	—
Restricted stock units vested—104,054 Class A shares	10	(756)	—	—	—	(746)	—	(746)
401(k) Company stock match—303,066 Class A shares	—	(6,571)	—	10,025	—	3,454	—	3,454
Stock-based compensation	—	6,813	—	—	—	6,813	—	6,813
Income tax benefit related to share-based payments	—	2,955	—	—	—	2,955	—	2,955
Balance, December 29, 2013	$15,211	$ 33,045	$1,283,518	$ (86,253)	$(402,611)	$ 842,910	$3,624	$ 846,534

NOTES TO THE CONSOLIDATED FINANCIAL STATEMENTS

3. Prior Period Adjustments

During the second quarter of 2013, we determined that due to an error in the actuarial valuation of accrued benefits for approximately 800 participants primarily in The New York Times Companies Pension Plan, our pension benefit obligation was overstated by approximately $50.4 million as of December 31, 2012 and $50.9 million as of March 31, 2013. The New York Times Companies Pension Plan (which was frozen as of December 31, 2009) provides for certain offsetting credits for plan participants who are also entitled to benefits under another qualified pension plan to which we contribute, primarily from The New York Times Newspaper Guild Pension Plan or the Boston Globe

Retirement Plan for employees represented by the Boston Newspaper Guild. We determined that those offsetting credits were not properly recorded in prior interim and annual periods, on our balance sheet from December 30, 2007 through March 31, 2013 and on our income statement from the fiscal year ended December 28, 2008 through the quarter ended March 31, 2013.

In accordance with the provisions of SEC Staff Accounting Bulletin No. 108, we assessed the impact of these adjustments on prior period financial statements and concluded that these errors were not material individually or in the aggregate to any of the prior reporting periods from an income statement and balance sheet perspective. However, the correction of the error in the second quarter of 2013 would have been considered material and would impact comparisons to prior periods.

Accordingly, we have adjusted our consolidated financial statements for the periods ended December 25, 2011 through March 31, 2013 to correct the errors and will make adjustments for future Form 10-Q filings that include financial statements for the periods affected. The adjustment primarily resulted in a reduction in pension expense, other comprehensive income and pension liability in each of the periods presented.

The cumulative effect, net of tax, on the opening retained earnings and opening accumulated comprehensive income as of December 27, 2010 were $6.0 million and $14.5 million, respectively. There was no impact on cash flows for the periods indicated. The following tables show the adjusted financial statements for those periods indicated:

		2012 by Quarter			
(In thousands) **As Previously Reported:**	March 31, 2013	December 30, 2012	September 23, 2012	June 24, 2012	March 25, 2012
Condensed Consolidated Balance Sheets					
Assets					
Current assets					
Cash and cash equivalents	$ 308,014	$ 820,490	$ 334,374	$ 290,292	$ 206,468
Short-term marketable securities	366,805	134,820	279,740	279,858	224,878
Accounts receivable (net of allowances)	159,344	197,589	160,998	170,904	180,406
Inventories:					
Newsprint and magazine paper	6,952	5,608	9,857	9,695	12,129
Other inventory	1,697	1,729	1,689	1,954	2,076
Total inventories	8,649	7,337	11,546	11,649	14,205
Deferred income taxes	58,214	58,214	73,055	73,055	73,055
Other current assets	49,824	42,068	45,491	42,886	59,404
Assets held for sale	127,529	137,050	356,030	361,358	550,836
Total current assets	1,078,379	1,397,568	1,261,234	1,230,002	1,309,252
Other assets					
Long-term marketable securities	190,841	4,444	—	—	—
Investments in joint ventures	38,409	40,872	41,401	41,809	43,420
Property, plant and equipment (less accumulated depreciation and amortization)	757,507	773,469	789,147	804,189	819,586
Goodwill (less accumulated impairment losses)	120,275	122,691	121,251	118,825	123,061
Deferred income taxes	322,222	322,767	365,666	369,439	316,446
Miscellaneous assets	165,202	166,214	168,470	173,880	227,088
Total assets	$2,672,835	$2,828,025	$2,747,169	$2,738,144	$2,838,853
Liabilities and stockholders' equity					
Current liabilities					
Accounts payable	$80,687	$88,990	$86,104	$80,754	$83,192
Accrued payroll and other related liabilities	52,288	86,772	87,753	72,641	66,826
Unexpired subscriptions	59,549	57,336	57,050	55,725	57,870
Accrued expenses and other	112,316	118,753	197,934	198,719	198,809
Accrued income taxes	—	38,932	—	—	—
Liabilities held for sale	33,302	32,373	34,611	36,479	41,407
Total current liabilities	338,142	423,156	463,452	444,318	448,104
Other liabilities					
Long-term debt and capital lease obligations	697,920	696,752	701,518	700,614	699,349
Pension benefits obligation	714,505	788,268	830,868	848,669	860,836
Postretirement benefits obligation	109,500	110,347	100,248	101,397	102,689
Other	166,434	173,690	175,949	176,305	171,944
Total other liabilities	1,688,359	1,769,057	1,808,583	1,826,985	1,834,818
Stockholders' equity					
Common stock of $.10 par value:					
Class A	15,045	15,027	15,023	15,009	15,005
Class B	82	82	82	82	82
Additional paid-in capital	27,656	25,610	31,181	34,278	35,820
Retained earnings	1,222,936	1,219,798	1,042,888	1,040,606	1,128,755
Common stock held in treasury, at cost	(93,506)	(96,278)	(102,690)	(107,572)	(110,827)

(continued)

| (In thousands) As Previously Reported: | March 31, 2013 | 2012 by Quarter | | | |
		December 30, 2012	September 23, 2012	June 24, 2012	March 25, 2012
Accumulated other comprehensive loss, net of income taxes:					
Foreign currency translation adjustments	9,858	11,327	10,418	8,286	12,382
Unrealized (loss)/gain on available-for-sale security	(1,242)	(431)	732)	2,102	4,109
Funded status of benefit plans	(537,557)	(542,634)	(525,548)	(529,019)	(532,491)
Total accumulated other comprehensive loss, net of income taxes	(528,941)	(531,738)	(514,398)	(518,631)	(516,000)
Total New York Times Company stockholders' equity	643,272	632,501	472,086	463,772	552,835
Noncontrolling interest	3,062	3,311	3,048	3,069	3,096
Total stockholders' equity	646,334	635,812	475,134	466,841	555,931
Total liabilities and stockholders' equity	$2,672,835	$2,828,025	$2,747,169	$2,738,144	$2,838,853

| (In thousands) Adjustments: | March 31, 2013 | 2012 by Quarter | | | |
		December 30, 2012	September 23, 2012	June 24, 2012	March 25, 2012
Condensed Consolidated Balance Sheets					
Assets					
Current assets					
Cash and cash equivalents	$ —	$ —	$ —	$ —	$ —
Short-term marketable securities	—	—	—	—	—
Accounts receivable (net of allowances)	—	—	—	—	—
Inventories:					
Newsprint and magazine paper	—	—	—	—	—
Other inventory	—	—	—	—	—
Total inventories	—	—	—	—	—
Deferred income taxes	—	—	—	—	—
Other current assets	—	—	—	—	—
Assets held for sale	—	—	—	—	—
Total current assets	—	—	—	—	—
Other assets					
Long-term marketable securities	—	—	—	—	—
Investments in joint ventures	—	—	—	—	—
Property, plant and equipment (less accumulated depreciation and amortization)	—	—	—	—	—
Goodwill (less accumulated impairment losses)	—	—	—	—	—
Deferred income taxes	(20,438)	(20,555)	(19,862)	(19,493)	(19,185)
Miscellaneous assets	—	—	—	—	—
Total assets	$(20,438)	$(20,555)	$(19,862)	$(19,493)	$(19,185)
Liabilities and Stockholders' Equity					
Current liabilities					
Accounts payable	$ —	$ —	$ —	$ —	$ —
Accrued payroll and other related liabilities	—	—	—	—	—
Unexpired subscriptions	—	—	—	—	—
Accrued expenses and other	—	—	—	—	—
Accrued income taxes	360	—	—	—	—
Liabilities held for sale	—	—	—	—	—
Total current liabilities	360	—	—	—	—
Other liabilities					
Long-term debt and capital lease obligations	—	—	—	—	—
Pension benefits obligation	(50,888)	(50,379)	(48,515)	(47,723)	(46,931)
Postretirement benefits obligation	—	—	—	—	—
Other	—	—	—	—	—
Total other liabilities	(50,888)	(50,379)	(48,515)	(47,723)	(46,931)
Stockholders' equity					
Common stock of $.10 par value:					
Class A	—	—	—	—	—
Class B	—	—	—	—	—
Additional paid-in capital	—	—	—	—	—
Retained earnings	11,087	10,652	9,439	8,974	8,448
Common stock held in treasury, at cost	—	—	—	—	—
Accumulated other comprehensive gain, net of income taxes:					
Foreign currency translation adjustments	—	—	—	—	—
Unrealized (loss)/gain on available-for-sale security	—	—	—	—	—
Funded status of benefit plans	19,003	19,172	19,214	19,256	19,298
Total accumulated other comprehensive gain, net of income taxes	19,003	19,172	19,214	19,256	19,298
Total New York Times Company stockholders' equity	30,090	29,824	28,653	28,230	27,746
Noncontrolling interest	—	—	—	—	—
Total stockholders' equity	30,090	29,824	28,653	28,230	27,746
Total liabilities and stockholders' equity	$(20,438)	$(20,555)	$(19,862)	$(19,493)	$(19,185)

(In thousands)		2012 by Quarter			
As adjusted:	March 31, 2013	December 30, 2012	September 23, 2012	June 24, 2012	March 25, 2012
Condensed Consolidated Balance Sheets					
Assets					
Current assets					
Cash and cash equivalents	$ 308,014	$ 820,490	$ 334,374	$ 290,292	$ 206,468
Short-term marketable securities	366,805	134,820	279,740	279,858	224,878
Accounts receivable (net of allowances)	159,344	197,589	160,998	170,904	180,406
Inventories:					
Newsprint and magazine paper	6,952	5,608	9,857	9,695	12,129
Other inventory	1,697	1,729	1,689	1,954	2,076
Total inventories	8,649	7,337	11,546	11,649	14,205
Deferred income taxes	58,214	58,214	73,055	73,055	73,055
Other current assets	49,824	42,068	45,491	42,886	59,404
Assets held for sale	127,529	137,050	356,030	361,358	550,836
Total current assets	1,078,379	1,397,568	1,261,234	1,230,002	1,309,252
Other assets					
Long-term marketable securities	190,841	4,444	—	—	—
Investments in joint ventures	38,409	40,872	41,401	41,809	43,420
Property, plant and equipment (less accumulated depreciation and amortization)	757,507	773,469	789,147	804,189	819,586
Goodwill (less accumulated impairment losses)	120,275	122,691	121,251	118,825	123,061
Deferred income taxes	301,784	302,212	345,804	349,946	297,261
Miscellaneous assets	165,202	166,214	168,470	173,880	227,088
Total assets	$2,652,397	$2,807,470	$2,727,307	$2,718,651	$2,819,668
Liabilities and Stockholders' Equity					
Current liabilities					
Accounts payable	$80,687	$88,990	$86,104	$80,754	$83,192
Accrued payroll and other related liabilities	52,288	86,772	87,753	72,641	66,826
Unexpired subscriptions	59,549	57,336	57,050	55,725	57,870
Accrued expenses and other	112,316	118,753	197,934	198,719	198,809
Accrued income taxes	360	38,932	—	—	—
Liabilities held for sale	33,302	32,373	34,611	36,479	41,407
Total current liabilities	338,502	423,156	463,452	444,318	448,104
Other liabilities					
Long-term debt and capital lease obligations	697,920	696,752	701,518	700,614	699,349
Pension benefits obligation	663,617	737,889	782,353	800,946	813,905
Postretirement benefits obligation	109,500	110,347	100,248	101,397	102,689
Other	166,434	173,690	175,949	176,305	171,944
Total other liabilities	1,637,471	1,718,678	1,760,068	1,779,262	1,787,887
Stockholders' equity					
Common stock of $.10 par value:					
Class A	15,045	15,027	15,023	15,009	15,005
Class B	82	82	82	82	82
Additional paid-in capital	27,656	25,610	31,181	34,278	35,820
Retained earnings	1,234,023	1,230,450	1,052,327	1,049,580	1,137,203
Common stock held in treasury, at cost	(93,506)	(96,278)	(102,690)	(107,572)	(110,827)
Accumulated other comprehensive loss, net of income taxes:					
Foreign currency translation adjustments	9,858	11,327	10,418	8,286	12,382
Unrealized (loss)/gain on available-for-sale security	(1,242)	(431)	732	2,102	4,109
Funded status of benefit plans	(518,554)	(523,462)	(506,334)	(509,763)	(513,193)
Total accumulated other comprehensive loss, net of income taxes	(509,938)	(512,566)	(495,184)	(499,375)	(496,702)
Total New York Times Company stockholders' equity	673,362	662,325	500,739	492,002	580,581
Noncontrolling interest	3,062	3,311	3,048	3,069	3,096
Total stockholders' equity	676,424	665,636	503,787	495,071	583,677
Total liabilities and stockholders' equity	$2,652,397	$2,807,470	$2,727,307	$2,718,651	$2,819,668

| (In thousands, except per share data)
As Previously Reported: | March 31, 2013 | Full Year 2012 | 2012 by Quarter | | | | Full Year 2011 |
			December 30, 2012	September 23, 2012	June 24, 2012	March 25, 2012	
Condensed Consolidated Statements of Operations							
Revenues	$380,675	$1,595,341	$468,114	$355,337	$ 387,841	$384,049	$1,554,574
Operating costs							
Production costs	157,341	653,883	178,116	158,003	158,802	158,962	642,374
Selling, general and administrative costs	177,060	712,001	186,686	169,689	173,057	182,569	688,344
Depreciation and amortization	18,938	78,980	18,492	19,594	20,212	20,682	83,833
Total operating costs	353,339	1,444,864	383,294	347,286	352,071	362,213	1,414,551
Pension settlement expense	—	48,729	48,729	—	—	—	
Other expense	—	2,620	2,620	—	—	—	4,500
Impairment of assets	—	—	—	—	—	—	7,458
Pension withdrawal expense	—	—	—	—	—	—	4,228
Operating profit	27,336	99,128	33,471	8,051	35,770	21,836	123,837
Gain on sale of investment	—	220,275	164,630	—	37,797	17,848	71,171
Impairment of investments	—	5,500	—	600	—	4,900	—
(Loss)/income from joint ventures	(2,870)	2,936	847	1,010	1,064	15	(270)
Premium on debt redemption	—	—	—	—	—	—	46,381
Interest expense, net	14,071	62,808	16,402	15,490	15,464	15,452	85,243
Income/(loss) from continuing operations before income taxes	10,395	254,031	182,546	(7,029)	59,167	19,347	63,114
Income tax expense/(benefit)	4,721	92,765	65,449	(3,587)	25,443	5,460	20,539
Income/(loss) from continuing operations	5,674	161,266	117,097	(3,442)	33,724	13,887	42,575
(Loss)/income from discontinued operations, net of income taxes	(2,785)	(27,927)	60,080	5,703	(121,900)	28,190	(82,799)
Net income/(loss)	2,889	133,339	177,177	2,261	(88,176)	42,077	(40,224)
Net loss/(income) attributable to the noncontrolling interest	249	(166)	(267)	21	27	53	555
Net income/(loss) attributable to The New York Times Company common stockholders	$ 3,138	$ 133,173	$176,910	$ 2,282	$ (88,149)	$ 42,130	$ (39,669)
Amounts attributable to The New York Times Company common stockholders:							
Income/(loss) from continuing operations	$ 5,923	$ 161,100	$116,830	$ (3,421)	$ 33,751	$ 13,940	$ 43,130
(Loss)/income from discontinued operations, net of income taxes	(2,785)	(27,927)	60,080	5,703	(121,900)	28,190	(82,799)
Net income/(loss)	$ 3,138	$ 133,173	$176,910	$ 2,282	$ (88,149)	$ 42,130	$ (39,669)
Average number of common shares outstanding:							
Basic	148,710	148,147	148,461	148,254	148,005	147,867	147,190
Diluted	155,270	152,693	154,685	148,254	149,799	151,468	152,007
Basic earnings per share attributable to The New York Times Company common stockholders:							
Income/(loss) from continuing operations	$ 0.04	$ 1.09	$ 0.79	$ (0.02)	$ 0.22	$ 0.09	$ 0.29
(Loss)/income from discontinued operations, net of income taxes	(0.02)	(0.19)	0.40	0.04	(0.82)	0.19	(0.56)
Net income/(loss)	$ 0.02	$ 0.90	$ 1.19	$ 0.02	$ (0.60)	$ 0.28	$ (0.27)
Diluted earnings per share attributable to The New York Times Company common stockholders:							
Income/(loss) from continuing operations	$ 0.04	$ 1.05	$ 0.76	$ (0.02)	$ 0.23	$ 0.09	$ 0.28
(Loss)/income from discontinued operations, net of income taxes	(0.02)	(0.18)	0.39	0.04	(0.81)	0.19	(0.54)
Net income/(loss)	$ 0.02	$ 0.87	$ 1.15	$ 0.02	$ (0.58)	$ 0.28	$ (0.26)

(In thousands, except per share data) Adjustments:	March 31, 2013	Full Year 2012	2012 by Quarter				Full Year 2011
			December 30, 2012	September 23, 2012	June 24, 2012	March 25, 2012	
Condensed Consolidated Statements of Operations							
Revenues	$ —	$ —	$ —	$ —	$ —	$ —	$ —
Operating costs							
Production costs	(607)	(2,565)	(676)	(633)	(628)	(628)	(2,113)
Selling, general and administrative costs	(188)	(889)	(185)	(230)	(237)	(237)	(786)
Depreciation and amortization	—	—	—	—	—	—	—
Total operating costs	(795)	(3,454)	(861)	(863)	(865)	(865)	(2,899)
Pension settlement expense	—	(1,072)	(1,072)	—	—	—	—
Other expense	—	—	—	—	—	—	—
Impairment of assets	—	—	—	—	—	—	—
Pension withdrawal expense	—	—	—	—	—	—	—
Operating profit	795	4,526	1,933	863	865	865	2,899
Gain on sale of investment	—	—	—	—	—	—	—
Impairment of investments	—	—	—	—	—	—	—
(Loss)/income from joint ventures	—	—	—	—	—	—	—
Premium on debt redemption	—	—	—	—	—	—	—
Interest expense, net	—	—	—	—	—	—	—
Income from continuing operations before income taxes	795	4,526	1,933	863	865	865	2,899
Income tax expense	361	1,852	722	400	338	392	878
Income from continuing operations	434	2,674	1,211	463	527	473	2,021
(Loss)/income from discontinued operations, net of income taxes	—	—	—	—	—	—	—
Net income	434	2,674	1,211	463	527	473	2,021
Net loss/(income) attributable to the noncontrolling interest	—	—	—	—	—	—	—
Net income attributable to The New York Times Company common stockholders	$ 434	$ 2,674	$ 1,211	$ 463	$ 527	$ 473	$ 2,021
Amounts attributable to The New York Times Company common stockholders:							
Income from continuing operations	$ 434	$ 2,674	$ 1,211	$ 463	$ 527	$ 473	$ 2,021
(Loss)/income from discontinued operations, net of income taxes	—	—	—	—	—	—	—
Net income	$ 434	$ 2,674	$ 1,211	$ 463	$ 527	$ 473	$ 2,021
Average number of common shares outstanding:							
Basic	148,710	148,147	148,461	148,254	148,005	147,867	147,190
Diluted	155,270	152,693	154,685	148,254	149,799	151,468	152,007
Basic earnings per share attributable to The New York Times Company common stockholders:							
Income from continuing operations	$ —	$ 0.02	$ 0.01	$ —	$ 0.01	$ —	$ 0.01
(Loss)/income from discontinued operations, net of income taxes	—	—	—	—	—	—	—
Net income	$ —	$ 0.02	$ 0.01	$ —	$ 0.01	$ —	$ 0.01
Diluted earnings per share attributable to The New York Times Company common stockholders:							
Income from continuing operations	$ —	$ 0.02	$ —	$ —	$ —	$ —	$ 0.01
(Loss)/income from discontinued operations, net of income taxes	—	—	—	—	—	—	—
Net income	$ —	$ 0.02	$ —	$ —	$ —	$ —	$ 0.01

| (In thousands, except per share data) As Adjusted: | March 31, 2013 | Full Year 2012 | 2012 by Quarter | | | | Full Year 2011 |
			December 30, 2012	September 23, 2012	June 24, 2012	March 25, 2012	
Condensed Consolidated Statements of Operations							
Revenues	$380,675	$1,595,341	$468,114	$355,337	$ 387,841	$384,049	$1,554,574
Operating costs							
Production costs	156,734	651,318	177,440	157,370	158,174	158,334	640,261
Selling, general and administrative costs	176,872	711,112	186,501	169,459	172,820	182,332	687,558
Depreciation and amortization	18,938	78,980	18,492	19,594	20,212	20,682	83,833
Total operating costs	352,544	1,441,410	382,433	346,423	351,206	361,348	1,411,652
Pension settlement expense	—	47,657	47,657	—	—	—	—
Other expense	—	2,620	2,620	—	—	—	4,500
Impairment of assets	—	—	—	—	—	—	7,458
Pension withdrawal expense	—	—	—	—	—	—	4,228
Operating profit	28,131	103,654	35,404	8,914	36,635	22,701	126,736
Gain on sale of investment	—	220,275	164,630	—	37,797	17,848	71,171
Impairment of investments	—	5,500	—	600	—	4,900	—
(Loss)/income from joint ventures	(2,870)	2,936	847	1,010	1,064	15	(270)
Premium on debt redemption	—	—	—	—	—	—	46,381
Interest expense, net	14,071	62,808	16,402	15,490	15,464	15,452	85,243
Income/(loss) from continuing operations before income taxes	11,190	258,557	184,479	(6,166)	60,032	20,212	66,013
Income tax expense/(benefit)	5,082	94,617	66,171	(3,187)	25,781	5,852	21,417
Income/(loss) from continuing operations	6,108	163,940	118,308	(2,979)	34,251	14,360	44,596
(Loss)/income from discontinued operations, net of income taxes	(2,785)	(27,927)	60,080	5,703	(121,900)	28,190	(82,799)
Net income/(loss)	3,323	136,013	178,388	2,724	(87,649)	42,550	(38,203)
Net loss/(income) attributable to the noncontrolling interest	249	(166)	(267)	21	27	53	555
Net income/(loss) attributable to The New York Times Company common stockholders	$ 3,572	$ 135,847	$178,121	$ 2,745	$ (87,622)	$ 42,603	$ (37,648)
Amounts attributable to The New York Times Company common stockholders:							
Income/(loss) from continuing operations	$ 6,357	$ 163,774	$118,041	$ (2,958)	$ 34,278	$ 14,413	$ 45,151
(Loss)/income from discontinued operations, net of income taxes	(2,785)	(27,927)	60,080	5,703	(121,900)	28,190	(82,799)
Net income/(loss)	$ 3,572	$ 135,847	$178,121	$ 2,745	$ (87,622)	$ 42,603	$ (37,648)
Average number of common shares outstanding:							
Basic	148,710	148,147	148,461	148,254	148,005	147,867	147,190
Diluted	155,270	152,693	154,685	148,254	149,799	151,468	152,007
Basic earnings per share attributable to The New York Times Company common stockholders:							
Income/(loss) from continuing operations	$ 0.04	$ 1.11	$ 0.80	$ (0.02)	$ 0.23	$ 0.10	$ 0.31
(Loss)/income from discontinued operations, net of income taxes	(0.02)	(0.19)	0.40	0.04	(0.82)	0.19	(0.57)
Net income/(loss)	$ 0.02	$ 0.92	$ 1.20	$ 0.02	$ (0.59)	$ 0.29	$ (0.26)
Diluted earnings per share attributable to The New York Times Company common stockholders:							
Income/(loss) from continuing operations	$ 0.04	$ 1.07	$ 0.76	$ (0.02)	$ 0.23	$ 0.10	$ 0.30
(Loss)/income from discontinued operations, net of income taxes	(0.02)	(0.18)	0.39	0.04	(0.81)	0.18	(0.55)
Net income/(loss)	$ 0.02	$ 0.89	$ 1.15	$ 0.02	$ (0.58)	$ 0.28	$ (0.25)

(In thousands) **As Previously Reported:**	March 31, 2013	Full Year 2012	**2012 by Quarter** December 30, 2012	September 23, 2012	June 24, 2012	March 25, 2012	Full Year 2011
Condensed Consolidated Statements of Comprehensive Income/(Loss)							
Net income/(loss)	$ 2,889	$133,339	$177,177	$ 2,261	$(88,176)	$ 42,077	$ (40,224)
Other comprehensive income/(loss), before tax:							
Foreign currency translation adjustments	(2,477)	536	1,684	3,251	(6,712)	2,313	(523)
Unrealized derivative gain on cash-flow hedge of equity method investment	—	1,143	—	—	—	1,143	839
Unrealized (loss)/gain on available-for-sale security	(1,374)	(729)	(1,980)	(2,338)	(3,425)	7,014	—
Pension and postretirement benefits obligation	8,546	(26,938)	(28,507)	5,888	5,888	(10,207)	(219,590)
Other comprehensive income/(loss), before tax	4,695	(25,988)	(28,803)	6,801	(4,249)	263	(219,274)
Income tax expense/(benefit)	1,897	(10,643)	(11,458)	2,568	(1,618)	(135)	(89,502)
Other comprehensive income/(loss), net of tax	2,798	(15,345)	(17,345)	4,233	(2,631)	398	(129,772)
Comprehensive income/(loss)	5,687	117,994	159,832	6,494	(90,807)	42,475	(169,996)
Comprehensive loss/(income) attributable to the noncontrolling interest	249	(162)	(263)	21	27	53	1,000
Comprehensive income/(loss) attributable to The New York Times Company common stockholders	$ 5,936	$117,832	$159,569	$ 6,515	$(90,780)	$ 42,528	$(168,996)

(In thousands) **Adjustments:**	March 31, 2013	Full Year 2012	**2012 by Quarter** December 30, 2012	September 23, 2012	June 24, 2012	March 25, 2012	Full Year 2011
Condensed Consolidated Statements of Comprehensive Income/(Loss)							
Net income	$ 434	$2,674	$1,211	$463	$527	$473	$2,021
Other comprehensive income, before tax:							
Foreign currency translation adjustments	—	—	—	—	—	—	—
Unrealized derivative gain on cash-flow hedge of equity method investment	—	—	—	—	—	—	—
Unrealized (loss)/gain on available-for-sale security	—	—	—	—	—	—	—
Pension and postretirement benefits obligation	(287)	(284)	(71)	(71)	(71)	(71)	8,301
Other comprehensive (loss)/income, before tax	(287)	(284)	(71)	(71)	(71)	(71)	8,301
Income tax expense/(benefit)	(117)	(117)	(34)	(29)	(29)	(25)	3,437
Other comprehensive (loss)/income, net of tax	(170)	(167)	(37)	(42)	(42)	(46)	4,864
Comprehensive income	264	2,507	1,174	421	485	427	6,885
Comprehensive loss/(income) attributable to the noncontrolling interest	—	—	—	—	—	—	—
Comprehensive income attributable to The New York Times Company common stockholders	$ 264	$2,507	$1,174	$421	$485	$427	$6,885

(In thousands) **As Adjusted:**	March 31, 2013	Full Year 2012	**2012 by Quarter** December 30, 2012	September 23, 2012	June 24, 2012	March 25, 2012	Full Year 2011
Condensed Consolidated Statements of Comprehensive Income/(Loss)							
Net income/(loss)	$ 3,323	$136,013	$178,388	$ 2,724	$(87,649)	$ 42,550	$ (38,203)
Other comprehensive income/(loss), before tax:							
Foreign currency translation adjustments	(2,477)	536	1,684	3,251	(6,712)	2,313	(523)
Unrealized derivative gain on cash-flow hedge of equity method investment	—	1,143	—	—	—	1,143	839
Unrealized (loss)/gain on available-for-sale security	(1,374)	(729)	(1,980)	(2,338)	(3,425)	7,014	—
Pension and postretirement benefits obligation	8,259	(27,222)	(28,578)	5,817	5,817	(10,278)	(211,289)
Other comprehensive income/(loss), before tax	4,408	(26,272)	(28,874)	6,730	(4,320)	192	(210,973)
Income tax expense/(benefit)	1,780	(10,760)	(11,492)	2,539	(1,647)	(160)	(86,065)
Other comprehensive income/(loss), net of tax	2,628	(15,512)	(17,382)	4,191	(2,673)	352	(124,908)
Comprehensive income/(loss)	5,951	120,501	161,006	6,915	(90,322)	42,902	(163,111)
Comprehensive loss/(income) attributable to the noncontrolling interest	249	(162)	(263)	21	27	53	1,000
Comprehensive income/(loss) attributable to The New York Times Company common stockholders	$ 6,200	$120,339	$160,743	$ 6,936	$(90,295)	$ 42,955	$(162,111)

5.35 THE CHILDREN'S PLACE RETAIL STORES, INC. (JAN)
CONSOLIDATED STATEMENTS OF CHANGES IN STOCKHOLDERS' EQUITY

(In thousands)

	Common Stock		Additional Paid-In Capital	Deferred Compen-sation	Retained Earnings	Accumulated Other Comprehensive Income	Treasury Stock		Total Stockholders' Equity
	Shares	Amount					Shares	Value	
Balance, January 30, 2010 (As adjusted)	27,475	$2,747	$204,646	$ —	$396,131	$ 7,601	—	$ —	$611,125
Exercise of stock options	366	37	11,886						11,923
Excess tax benefits from stock-based compensation			692						692
Vesting of stock awards	242	24	(24)						—
Stock-based compensation Expense			8,045						8,045
Purchase and retirement of shares	(1,947)	(195)	(15,285)		(75,143)				(90,623)
Change in cumulative translation adjustment						5,698			5,698
Net income					79,297				79,297
Balance, January 29, 2011 (As adjusted)	26,136	2,613	209,960	—	400,285	13,299	—	—	626,157
Exercise of stock options	188	19	6,806						6,825
Excess tax benefits from stock-based compensation			532						532
Vesting of stock awards	331	34	(34)						—
Stock-based compensation Expense			9,286						9,286
Purchase and retirement of shares	(1,944)	(195)	(16,391)		(75,171)				(91,757)
Change in cumulative translation adjustment						(419)			(419)
Deferral of common stock into deferred compensation plan				598			(14)	(598)	—
Net income					74,345				74,345
Balance, January 28, 2012 (As adjusted)	24,711	2,471	210,159	598	399,459	12,880	(14)	(598)	624,969
Exercise of stock options	68	6	2,179						2,185
Excess tax benefits from stock-based compensation			4,941						4,941
Vesting of stock awards	200	20	(20)						—
Stock-based compensation Expense			14,253						14,253
Purchase and retirement of shares	(1,800)	(179)	(15,821)		(73,020)				(89,020)
Change in cumulative translation adjustment						378			378
Deferral of common stock into deferred compensation plan				521			(10)	(521)	—
Net income					63,243				63,243
Balance, February 2, 2013	23,179	$2,318	$215,691	$1,119	$389,682	$13,258	(24)	$(1,119)	$620,949

NOTES TO CONSOLIDATED FINANCIAL STATEMENTS

1. Basis of Presentation and Summary of Significant Accounting Policies (in part)

Treasury Stock

Treasury stock is recorded at acquisition cost. Gains and losses on disposition are recorded as increases or decreases to additional paid-in capital with losses in excess of previously recorded gains charged directly to retained earnings. When treasury shares are retired and returned to authorized but unissued status, the carrying value in excess of par is allocated to additional paid-in capital and retained earnings on a pro rata basis.

3. Stockholders' Equity

On August 18, 2010, the Company's Board of Directors authorized a share repurchase program in the amount of $100 million (the "2010 Share Repurchase Program"), on March 3, 2011 another share repurchase program was authorized in the amount of $100 million (the "2011 Share Repurchase Program"), on March 7, 2012 another share repurchase program was authorized in the amount of $50.0 million (the "2012 $50 Million Share Repurchase Program") and on November 26, 2012 another share repurchase program was authorized in the amount of $100.0 million (the "2012 $100 Million Share Repurchase Program"). At February 2, 2013, there was approximately $80.4 million remaining on the 2012 $100 Million Share Repurchase Program. The 2010 Share Repurchase Program, 2011 Share Repurchase Program and 2012 $50 Million Share Repurchase Program have been completed. Under the 2012 $100 Million Share Repurchase Program, the Company may repurchase shares in the open market at current market prices at the time of purchase or in privately negotiated transactions. The timing and actual number of shares repurchased under the program will depend on a variety of factors including price, corporate and regulatory requirements, and other market and business conditions. The Company may suspend or discontinue the program at any time, and may thereafter reinstitute purchases, all without prior announcement.

Pursuant to restrictions imposed by the Company's equity plan during black-out periods, the Company withholds and retires shares of vesting stock awards in exchange for payments to satisfy the withholding tax requirements of certain recipients. The Company's payment of the withholding taxes in exchange for the shares constitutes a purchase of its common stock.

The Company acquires shares of its common stock in conjunction with liabilities owed under a deferred compensation plan, which are held in treasury. The following table summarizes the Company's share repurchases (in thousands):

	Fiscal Year Ended					
	February 2, 2013		January 28, 2012		January 29, 2011	
	Shares	Value	Shares	Value	Shares	Value
Share repurchases related to:						
2010 Share buyback program	—	—	213	10,102	1,933	89,898
2011 Share buyback program	377	19,236	1,712	80,764	—	—
2012 $50 Million Share buyback program	1,001	50,000	—	—	—	—
2012 $100 Million Share buyback program[1]	420	19,638	—	—	—	—
Withholding taxes	2	146	19	891	14	725
Shares acquired and held in treasury	10	521	14	598	—	—

[1] Subsequent to February 2, 2013 and through March 26, 2013, the Company repurchased an additional 0.1 million shares for approximately $5.9 million.

In accordance with the "Equity" topic of the FASB ASC, the par value of the shares retired is charged against common stock and the remaining purchase price is allocated between additional paid-in capital and retained earnings. The portion charged against additional paid-in capital is done using a pro rata allocation based on total shares outstanding. Related to all shares retired for Fiscal 2012 and Fiscal 2011, approximately $73.0 million and $75.2 million was charged to retained earnings, respectively.

OTHER CHANGES IN RETAINED EARNINGS—STOCK SPLIT AND CASH DIVIDENDS

5.36 BROWN-FORMAN CORPORATION (APR)
SELECTED FINANCIAL DATA

The following selected financial data for each of the fiscal years in the ten-year period ended April 30, 2013, should be read in conjunction with Item 7. Management's Discussion and Analysis of Financial Condition and Results of Operations and our Consolidated Financial Statements and Notes thereto contained in Item 8. Financial Statements and Supplementary Data of this report on Form 10-K.

(Dollars in millions, except per share amounts)

Year Ended April 30,	2004	2005	2006	2007	2008	2009	2010	2011	2012	2013
Continuing Operations:										
Net sales	$1,992	2,195	2,412	2,806	3,282	3,192	3,226	3,404	3,614	3,784
Gross profit	$1,024	1,156	1,308	1,481	1,695	1,577	1,611	1,724	1,795	1,955
Operating income	$ 383	445	563	602	685	661	710	855	788	898
Net income	$ 243	339	395	400	440	435	449	572	513	591
Weighted average shares used to calculate earnings per share										
— Basic	227.5	228.3	228.9	230.4	229.6	225.7	221.8	218.4	214.5	213.4
— Diluted	228.7	229.7	231.4	232.8	231.6	227.1	222.9	219.8	216.1	215.0
Earnings per share from continuing operations										
— Basic	$ 1.07	1.49	1.73	1.74	1.91	1.92	2.02	2.61	2.39	2.77
— Diluted	$ 1.06	1.48	1.71	1.72	1.89	1.91	2.01	2.60	2.37	2.75
Gross margin	51.4%	52.7%	54.2%	52.8%	51.6%	49.4%	50.0%	50.7%	49.7%	51.7%
Operating margin	19.2%	20.3%	23.3%	21.5%	20.9%	20.7%	22.0%	25.1%	21.8%	23.7%
Effective tax rate	33.1%	32.6%	29.3%	31.7%	31.7	31.1%	34.1%	31.0%	32.5%	31.7%
Average invested capital	$1,392	1,535	1,863	2,431	2,747	2,893	2,825	2,711	2,803	2,834
Return on average invested capital	18.5%	23.0%	21.9%	17.4%	17.2%	15.9%	16.6%	21.8%	19.1%	21.7%

(continued)

Year Ended April 30,	2004	2005	2006	2007	2008	2009	2010	2011	2012	2013
Total Company:										
Cash dividends declared per common share	$ 0.43	0.49	0.56	0.62	0.69	0.75	0.78	1.49	0.89	4.98
Average stockholders' equity	$ 936	1,198	1,397	1,700	1,668	1,793	1,870	1,904	2,046	1,879
Total assets at April 30	$2,376	2,649	2,728	3,551	3,405	3,475	3,383	3,712	3,477	3,626
Long-term debt at April 30	$ 630	351	351	422	417	509	508	504	503	997
Total debt at April 30	$ 679	630	576	1,177	1,006	999	699	759	510	1,002
Cash flow from operations	$ 304	396	343	355	534	491	545	527	516	537
Return on average stockholders' equity	27.1%	25.7%	22.9%	22.9%	26.4%	24.2%	24.0%	30.0%	25.1%	31.4%
Total debt to total capital	38.3%	32.5%	26.9%	42.8%	36.8%	35.5%	26.9%	26.9%	19.8%	38.1%
Dividend payout ratio	38.2%	36.1%	40.0%	36.8%	35.8%	38.9%	38.7%	57.0%	37.4%	179.8%

1. Includes the consolidated results of Swift & Moore, Chambord, and Casa Herradura since their acquisitions in February 2006, May 2006, and January 2007, respectively. Includes the results of our Hopland-based wine brands, which were sold in April 2011 but retained in our portfolio as agency brands through December 2011.
2. Weighted average shares, earnings per share, and cash dividends declared per common share have been adjusted for a 2-for-1 stock split in January 2004, a 5-for-4 stock split in October 2008, and a 3-for-2 stock split in August 2012.
3. Cash dividends declared per common share include special cash dividends of $0.67 per share in fiscal 2011 and $4.00 per share in fiscal 2013.
4. We define return on average invested capital as the sum of net income (excluding extraordinary items) and after-tax interest expense, divided by average invested capital. Invested capital equals assets less liabilities, excluding interest-bearing debt.
5. We define return on average stockholders' equity as net income applicable to common stock divided by average stockholders' equity.
6. We define total debt to total capital as total debt divided by the sum of total debt and stockholders' equity.
7. We define dividend payout ratio as cash dividends divided by net income.

CONSOLIDATED STATEMENTS OF STOCKHOLDERS' EQUITY

(Dollars in millions, except per share amounts)

Year Ended April 30,	2011	2012	2013
Class A common stock:			
Balance at beginning of year	$ 9	$ 9	$ 9
Stock split	—	—	4
Balance at end of year	9	9	13
Class B Common Stock:			
Balance at beginning of year	15	15	15
Stock split	—	—	6
Balance at end of year	15	15	21
Additional paid-in capital:			
Balance at beginning of year	59	55	49
Stock-based compensation expense	9	9	11
Loss on issuance of treasury stock issued under compensation plans	(21)	(23)	(6)
Excess tax benefits from stock-based awards	8	8	17
Balance at end of year	55	49	71
Retained earnings:			
Balance at beginning of year	2,464	2,710	3,031
Stock split	—	—	(18)
Net income	572	513	591
Cash dividends ($1.49, $0.89, and $4.98 per share in 2011, 2012, and 2013, respectively)	(326)	(192)	(1,063)
Loss on issuance of treasury stock issued under compensation plans	—	—	(41)
Balance at end of year	2,710	3,031	2,500
Accumulated other comprehensive (Loss) Income, net of tax:			
Balance at beginning of year	(176)	(131)	(230)
Net other comprehensive (loss) income	45	(99)	19
Balance at end of year	(131)	(230)	(211)
Treasury stock, at cost:			
Balance at beginning of year	(476)	(598)	(805)
Stock split	—	—	8
Acquisition of treasury stock	(136)	(220)	—
Stock issued under compensation plans	14	13	31
Balance at end of year	(598)	(805)	(766)
Total stockholders' equity	$ 2,060	$ 2,069	$ 1,628

(continued)

Year Ended April 30,	2011	2012	2013
Class A common shares outstanding (in thousands):			
Balance at beginning of year	56,601	56,561	56,251
Stock split	—	—	28,149
Acquisition of treasury stock	(40)	(310)	—
Stock issued under compensation plans	—	—	46
Balance at end of year	56,561	56,251	84,446
Class B common shares outstanding (in thousands):			
Balance at beginning of year	90,362	88,429	85,823
Stock split	—	—	42,951
Acquisition of treasury stock	(2,200)	(2,851)	—
Stock issued under compensation plans	267	245	487
Balance at end of year	88,429	85,823	129,261
Total common shares outstanding (in thousands)	144,990	142,074	213,707

NOTES TO CONSOLIDATED FINANCIAL STATEMENTS

(Dollars in Millions, except Per Share Data)

16. Cash Dividends

We paid total cash dividends per share of $1.49, $0.89, and $4.98 during 2011, 2012, and 2013, respectively. Those amounts included special cash dividends per share of $0.67 in 2011 and $4.00 in 2013. The remaining amounts consisted of regular quarterly cash dividends.

17. Stock Split

On June 14, 2012, our Board of Directors authorized a 3-for-2 stock split for outstanding shares of the Company's Class A and Class B common stock, subject to stockholder approval of an amendment to the Company's Restated Certificate of Incorporation to increase the number of authorized shares of Class A and Class B common stock. The amendment, which was approved by stockholders on July 26, 2012, increased the authorized number of Class A Common Stock to 85,000,000 from 57,000,000 and the authorized number of Class B Common Stock to 400,000,000 from 100,000,000.

The stock split, which was effected as a stock dividend, resulted in the Company issuing one new share of Class A common stock for each two shares of Class A common stock outstanding and one new share of Class B common stock for each two shares of Class B common stock outstanding. The stock split was paid on August 10, 2012, to stockholders of record as of August 3, 2012. The stock split was not applied to the Company's treasury shares.

As a result of the stock split, we reclassified approximately $10 from the Company's retained earnings account to its common stock accounts during 2013. The $10 represents the $0.15 par value per share of the new shares issued in the stock split. Also, we adjusted retained earnings and treasury stock by approximately $8 to reflect the book value (at cost) of treasury shares issued in connection with the stock split.

Previously reported share and per share amounts have been restated in the accompanying financial statements and related notes to reflect the stock split.

Spinoffs

RECOGNITION AND MEASUREMENT

5.37 The distributions of nonmonetary assets that constitute a business to owners of an entity are commonly referred to as spinoffs. A *business* is defined as an integrated set of activities and assets that is capable of being conducted and managed for the purpose of providing a return in the form of dividends, lower costs, or other economic benefits directly to investors or other owners, members, or participants. Spinoffs are discussed in FASB ASC 505-60.

5.38 FASB ASC 505-60-25-2 requires that the accounting for the distribution of nonmonetary assets to owners of an entity in a spinoff be based on the recorded amount (after reduction, if appropriate, for an indicated impairment of value). An entity's distribution of the shares of a wholly owned or consolidated subsidiary to its shareholders should be recorded based on the carrying value of the subsidiary. Regardless of whether the spun-off operations will be sold immediately after the spinoff, the transaction should not be accounted for as a sale of the accounting spinnee followed by a distribution of the proceeds. In order to determine the required accounting and reporting in a spinoff transaction, an entity needs to determine which party is the accounting spinnor and which is the accounting spinnee. The accounting spinnee should be reported as a discontinued operation by the accounting spinnor if the spinnee is a component of an entity and meets the conditions for such reporting.

PRESENTATION AND DISCLOSURE EXCERPT

SPINOFFS

5.39 DEAN FOODS COMPANY (DEC)
CONSOLIDATED STATEMENTS OF STOCKHOLDERS' EQUITY (DEFICIT)

| | Dean Foods Company Stockholders | | | | | | |
| | Common Stock | | Additional Paid-In | Retained Earnings (Accumulated | Accumulated Other Comprehensive | Non-controlling | Total Stockholders' Equity |
(Dollars in thousands, except share data)	Shares	Amount	Capital	Deficit)	Income (Loss)	Interest	(Deficit)
Balance, January 1, 2011	91,127,667	$912	$1,062,164	$ 583,102	$(146,653)	$ 14,543	$ 1,514,068
Issuance of common stock, net of tax impact of share-based compensation	745,228	7	(5,850)	—	—	—	(5,843)
Share-based compensation expense	—	—	31,408	—	—	—	31,408
Capital contribution from non-controlling interest	—	—	—	—	—	6,754	6,754
Net loss attributable to non-controlling interest	—	—	—	—	—	(16,550)	(16,550)
Net loss attributable to Dean Foods Company	—	—	—	(1,575,621)	—	—	(1,575,621)
Other comprehensive income (loss) (Note 14):							
Change in fair value of derivative instruments, net of tax benefit of $38,527	—	—	—	—	(58,797)	—	(58,797)
Amounts reclassified to statement of operations related to hedging activities, net of tax of $23,156	—	—	—	—	35,235	—	35,235
Cumulative translation adjustment	—	—	—	—	(12,738)	—	(12,738)
Pension liability adjustment, net of tax benefit of $10,694	—	—	—	—	(16,567)	—	(16,567)

(continued)

(Dollars in thousands, except share data)	Common Stock Shares	Common Stock Amount	Additional Paid-In Capital	Retained Earnings (Accumulated Deficit)	Accumulated Other Comprehensive Income (Loss)	Non-controlling Interest	Total Stockholders' Equity (Deficit)
	Dean Foods Company Stockholders						
Balance, December 31, 2011	91,872,895	$919	$1,087,722	$ (992,519)	$(199,520)	$ 4,747	$ (98,651)
Issuance of common stock, net of tax impact of share-based compensation	908,872	9	(233)	—	—	—	(224)
Share-based compensation expense	—	—	24,247	—	—	—	24,247
Sale of former subsidiary shares to non-controlling interest	—	—	265,004	—	4,469	98,067	367,540
Share-based compensation expense for former subsidiary shares	—	—	—	—	—	1,167	1,167
Wind-down of former subsidiary joint venture	—	—	—	—	—	(4,747)	(4,747)
Net income attributable to non-controlling interest	—	—	—	—	—	2,419	2,419
Net income attributable to Dean Foods Company	—	—	—	158,622	—	—	158,622
Other comprehensive income (loss) (Note 14):							
Change in fair value of derivative instruments, net of tax benefit of $12,682	—	—	—	—	(19,780)	(13)	(19,793)
Amounts reclassified to statement of operations related to hedging activities, net of tax of $16,239	—	—	—	—	24,964	—	24,964
Cumulative translation adjustment	—	—	—	—	10,354	933	11,287
Pension liability adjustment, net of tax benefit of $4,493	—	—	—	—	(7,071)	(132)	(7,203)
Balance, December 31, 2012	92,781,767	$928	$1,376,740	$ (833,897)	$(186,584)	$ 102,441	$ 459,628
Issuance of common stock, net of tax impact of share-based compensation	2,049,610	20	19,900	—	—	—	19,920
Share-based compensation expense	—	—	11,718	—	—	—	11,718
Share-based compensation expense for former subsidiary shares	—	—	—	—	—	7,733	7,733
Net income attributable to non-controlling interest	—	—	—	—	—	6,179	6,179
Net income attributable to Dean Foods Company	—	—	—	813,178	—	—	813,178
Other comprehensive income (loss) (Note 14):							
Change in fair value of derivative instruments, net of tax benefit of $21	—	—	—	—	(91)	10	(81)
Amounts reclassified to statement of operations related to hedging activities, net of tax of $37,017	—	—	—	—	58,784	—	58,784
Cumulative translation adjustment	—	—	—	—	(9,393)	(1,398)	(10,791)
Pension liability adjustment, net of tax of $29,474	—	—	—	—	47,069	4	47,073
Spin-Off of The WhiteWave Foods Company	—	—	(617,082)	—	33,025	(114,969)	(699,026)
Balance, December 31, 2013	94,831,377	$948	$ 791,276	$ (20,719)	$ (57,190)	$ —	$ 714,315

(1) Common Stock and Additional Paid-In Capital at January 1, 2011, December 31, 2011 and December 31, 2012 have been adjusted retroactively to reflect a 1-for-2 reverse stock split effected August 26, 2013.

NOTES TO CONSOLIDATED FINANCIAL STATEMENTS

1. Summary of Significant Accounting Policies (in part)

Basis of Presentation and Consolidation (in part)

As discussed in Note 2, in October 2012, The WhiteWave Foods Company ("WhiteWave") completed its initial public offering (the "WhiteWave IPO"). Upon completion of the WhiteWave IPO, we owned an 86.7% economic interest, and a 98.5% voting interest, in WhiteWave. On May 1, 2013, our Board of Directors declared a dividend of an aggregate of 47,686,000 shares of Class A common stock and 67,914,000 shares of Class B common stock of WhiteWave to holders of record of Dean Foods common stock at the close of business on May 17, 2013, the record date. The dividend was distributed on May 23, 2013. Upon completion of the WhiteWave spin-off, we ceased to own a controlling financial interest in WhiteWave, and WhiteWave's results of operations have been reclassified as discontinued operations for all periods presented herein. See Note 3. Subsequent to the WhiteWave spin-off, we retained ownership of 34,400,000 shares of WhiteWave's Class A common stock, or approximately 19.9% of the economic interest of WhiteWave, which we disposed of in July 2013 in a tax-free debt-for-equity exchange transaction as set forth in more detail in Note 2 below. Upon completion of the offering, we no longer owned any shares of WhiteWave common stock. WhiteWave's common stock is listed on the New York Stock Exchange ("NYSE") under the symbol "WWAV".

Beginning in the first quarter of 2013, we combined the results of our legacy Fresh Dairy Direct business and the corporate items previously categorized as "Corporate and Other" into a single reportable segment, as all of our corporate activities now directly support our ongoing dairy operations. This change reflects the manner in which our Chief Executive Officer, who is our chief operating decision maker, determines strategy and investment plans for our business given the changes to our operating structure as a result of the WhiteWave spin-off and the Morningstar sale. All operating results herein have been recast to present results on a comparable basis. These changes had no impact on consolidated net sales and operating income.

2. Whitewave Spin-Off Transaction and Disposition of Remaining Ownership of Whitewave Common Stock (in part)

WhiteWave IPO and Spin-Off Transaction—On October 31, 2012, WhiteWave completed the WhiteWave IPO, and sold 23 million shares of its Class A common stock at a price to the public of $17 per share. Prior to completion of the WhiteWave IPO, we contributed the capital stock of WWF Operating Company ("WWF Opco"), another wholly-owned subsidiary of ours that held substantially all of the assets and liabilities associated with our WhiteWave segment, to WhiteWave in exchange for 150 million shares of Class B common stock of WhiteWave.

The WhiteWave IPO was accounted for as an equity transaction in accordance with ASC 810 and no gain or loss was recognized as we retained the controlling financial interest immediately upon completion of the transaction. The WhiteWave IPO increased our equity attributable to non-controlling interest by $98.1 million, which represented the carrying value of the non-controlling interest, increased our additional paid-in capital by $265 million and reduced our accumulated other comprehensive loss by $4.5 million.

WhiteWave contributed $282 million of the net proceeds from the WhiteWave IPO to WWF Opco, which used those proceeds, together with substantially all of the net proceeds of the initial borrowings described in Note 10 to the Consolidated Financial Statements included in our 2012 Annual Report on Form 10-K, to repay then-outstanding obligations under intercompany notes owed to Dean Foods Company. Dean Foods Company subsequently utilized these proceeds to prepay a portion of the outstanding indebtedness under our prior senior secured credit facility. The remaining net proceeds of approximately $86 million were used to repay indebtedness under WhiteWave's inaugural senior secured credit facilities.

Upon completion of the WhiteWave IPO, we owned no shares of WhiteWave Class A common stock and 150 million shares of WhiteWave's Class B common stock, which represented 100% of the outstanding shares of WhiteWave's Class B common stock. The rights of the holders of the shares of Class A common stock and Class B common stock were identical, except with respect to voting and conversion. Each share of Class A common stock is entitled to one vote per share, and each share of class B common stock was, at that time, entitled to ten votes per share, subject to reduction in accordance with the terms of WhiteWave's amended and restated certificate of incorporation, on all matters presented to WhiteWave stockholders. Upon completion of the WhiteWave IPO, we owned an 86.7% economic interest, and a 98.5% voting interest, in WhiteWave.

On May 1, 2013, our Board of Directors approved the distribution to our stockholders of a portion of our remaining equity interest in WhiteWave and announced the approximate distribution ratios, record date and distribution date for the WhiteWave spin-off. On May 23, 2013, we completed our previously announced spin-off of WhiteWave through a tax-free distribution to our stockholders of an aggregate of 47,686,000 shares of WhiteWave Class A common stock and 67,914,000 shares of WhiteWave Class B common stock as a pro rata dividend on the shares of Dean Foods common stock outstanding at the close of business on the record date of May 17, 2013. Each share of Dean Foods common stock received 0.25544448 shares of WhiteWave Class A common stock and 0.36380189 shares of WhiteWave Class B common stock in the distribution.

Fractional shares of WhiteWave Class A common stock and WhiteWave Class B common stock were not distributed to Dean Foods stockholders; instead, the fractional shares were aggregated and sold in the open market, with the net proceeds distributed on a pro rata basis in the form of cash payments to Dean Foods stockholders who would otherwise have held WhiteWave fractional shares. The WhiteWave spin-off qualified as a tax-free distribution to Dean Foods stockholders for U.S. federal tax purposes; however, the cash received in lieu of fractional shares was taxable.

Additionally, on May 1, 2013, we announced that we had consented to the reduction in the voting rights of WhiteWave Class B common stock effective upon the completion of the WhiteWave spin-off. At such time, each share of WhiteWave Class B common stock became entitled to ten votes with respect to the election and removal of directors and one vote with respect to all other matters submitted to a vote of WhiteWave's stockholders. On the distribution date, we provided notice to WhiteWave of the conversion of 82,086,000 shares of WhiteWave Class B common stock owned by us into 82,086,000 shares of WhiteWave Class A common stock, of which 47,686,000 shares of WhiteWave Class A common stock were distributed in the WhiteWave spin-off. The conversion was effective at the close of business on the distribution date.

In connection with the WhiteWave spin-off, we recorded a $617.1 million reduction to additional paid-in capital. The distribution was recorded through additional paid-in capital rather than through retained earnings, as we were in an accumulated deficit position at the time of the WhiteWave spin-off. Upon completion of the WhiteWave spin-off, we have reclassified WhiteWave's results of operations as discontinued operations for all periods presented. See Note 3. We retained ownership of 34,400,000 shares of WhiteWave's Class A common stock, or approximately 19.9% of the economic interest of WhiteWave, which we disposed of in July 2013 in a tax-free transaction as set forth in more detail below. From the completion of the WhiteWave spin-off through the date of disposition in July 2013, we accounted for our investment in WhiteWave common stock using the fair value method of accounting for available-for-sale securities, which requires the investment to be marked to market with unrealized gains and losses recorded in accumulated other comprehensive income until realized or until losses are deemed to be other-than-temporary.

Disposition of Remaining Ownership of WhiteWave Common Stock—On July 11, 2013, in connection with the anticipated monetization of our remaining shares of Class A common stock of WhiteWave, we entered into a loan agreement with certain lenders, pursuant to which we were provided with two term loans in an aggregate principal amount of $626.75 million, consisting of a $545 million term loan required to be repaid no later than August 12, 2013, and an $81.75 million term loan required to be repaid no later than September 9, 2013. We will use the proceeds from the credit facility for general corporate purposes. Loans outstanding under the credit facility bore interest at the Adjusted LIBO Rate (as defined in the loan agreement) plus a margin of 2.50%. We were permitted to make optional prepayments of the loans, in whole or in part, without premium or penalty (other than any applicable LIBOR breakage costs).

The credit facility was unsecured and was guaranteed by our existing and future domestic material restricted subsidiaries (as defined in the loan agreement), which are substantially all of our wholly-owned U.S. subsidiaries other than our receivables securitization subsidiaries. The loan agreement contained certain representations, warranties and covenants, including, but not limited to specified restrictions on acquisitions and payment of dividends, as well as maintenance of certain liquidity levels. The loan agreement also contained customary events of default and related cure provisions. We were required to comply with a maximum consolidated net leverage ratio initially set at 4.00 to 1.00 and a minimum consolidated interest coverage ratio set at 3.00 to 1.00.

On July 25, 2013, we announced the closing of a secondary public offering of 34.4 million shares of Class A common stock of WhiteWave owned by us at a public offering price of $17.75 per share. Following the closing of the offering, we no longer owned any shares of WhiteWave common stock.

Immediately prior to the closing of the offering, we exchanged our shares of WhiteWave Class A common stock in partial satisfaction of the two term loans, which loans were held by two of the underwriters in the offering, as described more fully above. The underwriters subsequently sold these shares of WhiteWave's Class A common stock in the offering. Following the closing of the debt-for-equity exchange, we repaid the non-exchanged balance of the two term loans in full and terminated the loan agreement. The debt-for-equity exchange resulted in total cash proceeds, net of underwriting fees, of $589.2 million. We recorded a gain in continuing operations of $415.8 million in the third quarter of 2013 related to the disposition of our investment in WhiteWave common stock. The gain represents the excess of the value of the exchanged shares of WhiteWave Class A common stock over our cost basis in such shares. As the debt-for-equity exchange qualified as a tax-free transaction pursuant to the terms of our private letter ruling from the IRS, we did not incur, nor did we record, any income tax expense associated with the transaction.

3. Discontinued Operations and Divestitures (in part)

WhiteWave and Morningstar

WhiteWave Spin-Off—As discussed in Note 2, on May 23, 2013, we completed the WhiteWave spin-off through a tax-free distribution to our stockholders. Following the WhiteWave spin-off, we retained 34.4 million shares of WhiteWave's Class A common stock, or approximately 19.9% of WhiteWave's economic interest. While we are a party to a separation and distribution agreement and various other agreements relating to the separation, including a transitional services agreement, an amended and restated tax matters agreement, an employee matters agreement and certain other commercial agreements, we have determined that the continuing cash flows generated by these agreements (which generally are not expected to extend beyond December 2014), and the retention and subsequent monetization of our investment in WhiteWave common stock in July 2013 as discussed in Note 2 and below, did not constitute significant continuing involvement in the operations of WhiteWave. Accordingly, the net assets, operating results and cash flows of WhiteWave, previously reported in the WhiteWave segment, were reclassified to discontinued operations beginning in the second quarter of 2013 and have accordingly been separately reflected as discontinued operations for all periods presented herein.

No gain or loss was recognized in connection with the WhiteWave spin-off, but subsequent unrealized gains or losses on our investment in WhiteWave common stock through the date of disposition of our remaining interest in WhiteWave common stock on July 25, 2013 were recognized as a component of other comprehensive income (see Note 14). No related deferred tax impact was recorded as the disposition of our remaining investment in WhiteWave common stock was completed in July 2013 in the tax-free debt-for-equity transaction described in Note 2 and Note 10. Following the closing of the debt-for-equity exchange, we no longer owned any shares of WhiteWave's common stock.

During the third quarter of 2013, as a result of the tax-free disposition of our investment in WhiteWave common stock, we recorded a gain in continuing operations of $415.8 million, which included $385.6 million of unrealized holding gains that were previously recorded as a component of accumulated other comprehensive income as of June 30, 2013. The gain was recorded in the gain on disposition of WhiteWave common stock line item in our Consolidated Statements of Operations.

From January 1, 2013 through May 23, 2013 (the date of the WhiteWave spin-off), our net sales to WhiteWave totaled $10.3 million and our purchases from WhiteWave totaled $33.2 million. These transactions, which were previously eliminated in consolidation prior to the spin-off, are now reflected as third-party transactions in our Consolidated Statements of Operations. At December 31, 2013, accounts receivable from, and accounts payable to, WhiteWave are presented as third-party balances in our Consolidated Balance Sheets.

WhiteWave is a stand-alone public company which separately reports its financial results. Due to differences between the basis of presentation for discontinued operations and the basis of presentation as a stand-alone company, the financial results of WhiteWave included within discontinued operations may not be indicative of the actual financial results of WhiteWave as a stand-alone company.

Treasury Stock

PRESENTATION

5.40 Repurchased common stock is often referred to as treasury stock or treasury shares. FASB ASC 505-30-45-1 discusses the balance sheet presentation of treasury stock and states that if a corporation's stock is acquired for purposes other than retirement (formal or constructive), or if ultimate disposition has not yet been decided, the cost of acquired stock may be shown separately as a deduction from the total of capital stock, additional paid-in capital, and retained earnings or may be accorded the accounting treatment appropriate for retired stock.

5.41 A repurchase of shares at a price significantly in excess of the current market price creates a presumption that the repurchase price includes amounts attributable to items other than the shares repurchased. FASB ASC 505-30-30-2 explains that a repurchase of shares at a price significantly in excess of the current market price may require an entity to allocate amounts to other elements of the transaction.

PRESENTATION AND DISCLOSURE EXCERPTS

TREASURY STOCK

5.42 FLOWERS FOODS, INC. (DEC)
CONSOLIDATED STATEMENTS OF CHANGES IN STOCKHOLDERS' EQUITY

(Amounts in thousands, except share data)	Common Stock Number of Shares Issued	Par Value	Capital in Excess of Par Value	Retained Earnings	Accumulated Other Comprehensive Loss	Treasury Stock Number of Shares	Cost	Total
Balances at January 1, 2011	101,659,924	$199	$540,294	$503,689	$ (33,709)	(11,011,494)	$(214,683)	$ 795,790
Net income				123,428				123,428
Derivative instruments, net of tax					(38,813)			(38,813)
Pension and postretirement plans, net of tax					(39,525)			(39,525)
Adjustment for 3 for 2 stock split (Note 14)	50,828,084			(39)		(5,375,912)		(39)
Stock repurchases						(1,155,103)	(26,598)	(26,598)
Exercise of stock options			(2,512)			803,090	15,445	12,933
Issuance of performance-contingent restricted stock awards			(4,213)			216,050	4,213	—
Issuance of deferred stock awards			(1,160)			56,505	1,119	(41)
Amortization of share-based compensation awards			12,982					12,982
Income tax benefits related to share-based payments			2,932					2,932
Performance-contingent restricted stock awards forfeitures and cancellations			961			(51,630)	(961)	—
Issuance of deferred compensation			(219)			11,672	219	—
Contingent acquisition consideration			(5,000)					(5,000)
Dividends paid—$0.389 per common share				(79,081)				(79,081)

(continued)

| (Amounts in thousands, except share data) | Common Stock | | Capital in Excess of Par Value | Retained Earnings | Accumulated Other Comprehensive Loss | Treasury Stock | | Total |
	Number of Shares Issued	Par Value				Number of Shares	Cost	
Balances at December 31, 2011	152,488,008	$199	$544,065	$547,997	$(112,047)	(16,506,822)	$(221,246)	$ 758,968
Net income				136,121				136,121
Derivative instruments, net of tax					10,808			10,808
Pension and postretirement plans, net of tax					(13,428)			(13,428)
Shares issued for acquisition			16,628			2,178,648	29,259	45,887
Stock repurchases						(935,742)	(18,726)	(18,726)
Exercise of stock options			(329)			1,047,297	14,210	13,881
Issuance of deferred stock awards			(610)			45,405	610	—
Amortization of share-based compensation awards			9,373					9,373
Income tax benefits related to share-based payments			2,225					2,225
Performance-contingent restricted stock awards forfeitures and cancellations			606			(45,252)	(606)	—
Issuance of deferred compensation			(34)			1,647	34	—
Dividends paid on vested performance-contingent restricted stock and deferred share awards				(255)				(255)
Dividends paid—$0.420 per common share				(86,234)				(86,234)
Balances at December 29, 2012	152,488,008	$199	$571,924	$597,629	$(114,667)	(14,214,819)	$(196,465)	$ 858,620
Net income				230,894				230,894
Derivative instruments, net of tax					(7,316)			(7,316)
Pension and postretirement plans, net of tax					59,468			59,468
Adjustment for 3 for 2 stock split (Note 14)	76,241,577		(52)			(6,860,135)		(52)
Stock repurchases						(367,623)	(8,819)	(8,819)
Exercise of stock options			508			1,158,590	13,177	13,685
Issuance of deferred stock awards			(752)			54,120	752	—
Amortization of share-based compensation awards			14,725					14,725
Income tax benefits related to share-based payments			7,824					7,824
Performance-contingent restricted stock awards supplemental grant for exceeding TSR (Note 15)			(874)			63,232	874	—
Dividends paid on vested performance-contingent restricted stock and deferred share awards				(386)				(386)
Dividends paid—$0.444 per common share				(92,454)				(92,454)
Balances at December 28, 2013	228,729,585	$199	$593,355	$735,631	$ (62,515)	(20,166,635)	$(190,481)	$1,076,189

NOTES TO CONSOLIDATED FINANCIAL STATEMENTS

Note 2. Summary of Significant Accounting Policies (in part)

Treasury Stock. The company records acquisitions of its common stock for treasury at cost. Differences between proceeds for reissuances of treasury stock and average cost are credited or charged to capital in excess of par value to the extent of prior credits and thereafter to retained earnings. See Note 14, *Stockholders' Equity*, for additional disclosure.

Note 14. Stockholders' Equity (in part)

Flowers Foods' articles of incorporation provide that its authorized capital consist of 500,000,000 shares of common stock having a par value of $0.01 per share and 1,000,000 shares of preferred stock. The preferred stock of which (a) 200,000 shares have been designated by the Board of Directors as Series A Junior Participating Preferred Stock, having a par value per share of $100 and (b) 800,000 shares of preferred stock, having a par value per share of $0.01, has not been designated by the Board of Directors. No shares of preferred stock have been issued by Flowers Foods.

Common Stock

The holders of Flowers Foods common stock are entitled to one vote for each share held of record on all matters submitted to a vote of shareholders. Subject to preferential rights of any issued and outstanding preferred stock, including the Series A Preferred Stock, holders of common stock are entitled to receive ratably such dividends, if any, as may be declared by the Board of Directors of the company out of funds legally available. In the event of a liquidation, dissolution, or winding-up of the company, holders of common stock are entitled to share ratably in all assets of the company, if any, remaining after payment of liabilities and the liquidation preferences of any issued and outstanding preferred stock, including the Series A Preferred Stock. Holders of common stock have no preemptive rights, no cumulative voting rights, and no rights to convert their shares of common stock into any other securities of the company or any other person.

Preferred Stock

The Board of Directors has the authority to issue up to 1,000,000 shares of preferred stock in one or more series and to fix the designations, relative powers, preferences, rights, qualifications, limitations, and restrictions of all shares of each such series, including without limitation, dividend rates, conversion rights, voting rights, redemption and sinking fund provisions, liquidation preferences, and the number of shares constituting each such series, without any further vote or action by the holders of our common stock. Although the Board of Directors does not presently intend to do so, it could issue shares of preferred stock, with rights that could adversely affect the voting power and other rights of holders of our common stock without obtaining the approval of our shareholders. In addition, the issuance of preferred shares could delay or prevent a change in control of the company without further action by our shareholders.

Stock Repurchase Plan

Our Board of Directors has approved a plan that authorized stock repurchases of up to 67.5 million shares of the company's common stock. Under the plan, the company may repurchase its common stock in open market or privately negotiated transactions at such times and at such prices as determined to be in the company's best interest. The company repurchases its common stock primarily for issuance under the company's stock compensation plans and to fund possible future acquisitions. These purchases may be commenced or suspended without prior notice depending on the then-existing business or market conditions and other factors. As of December 28, 2013, 58,541,104 shares at a cost of $458.3 million have been purchased under this plan. Included in these amounts are 435,935 shares at a cost of $8.8 million purchased during fiscal 2013.

Other Components of Stockholders' Equity

PRESENTATION

5.43 For public entities, Rule 3–04 of Regulation S-X requires that an analysis of the changes in each caption of stockholders' equity and noncontrolling interests presented in the balance sheets be given in a note or separate statement. This analysis should be presented in the form of a reconciliation of the beginning balance to the ending balance for each period for which an income statement is required to be filed, with all significant reconciling items described by appropriate captions.

5.44 Many of the survey entities present accounts other than capital stock, additional paid-in capital, retained earnings, accumulated other comprehensive income, and treasury stock in the "Stockholders' Equity" section of the balance sheet. Other stockholders' equity accounts appearing on the balance sheets of the survey entities include, but are not limited to, guarantees of employee stock ownership plan debt, unearned or deferred compensation related to employee stock award plans, and amounts owed to an entity by employees for loans to buy company stock, in each instance pursuant to relevant FASB ASC requirements. Other items, such as foreign currency translation adjustments, unrealized gains and losses on certain investments in debt and equity securities, and defined benefit postretirement plan adjustments, are considered components of other comprehensive income. FASB ASC 220-10-45-14 provides guidance for reporting other comprehensive income in the Equity section of a statement of financial position.

DISCLOSURE

5.45 Rule 3–04 of SEC Regulation S-X requires an SEC registrant to disclose an analysis of the changes in each caption of other stockholders' equity and noncontrolling interests presented in the balance sheets in a note or separate statement (see also FASB ASC 505-10-S99-1).

5.46 FASB ASC 810, *Consolidation*, establishes accounting and reporting standards for the noncontrolling interest in a subsidiary. It clarifies that a noncontrolling interest in a subsidiary is an ownership interest in the consolidated entity that should be reported as equity in the consolidated financial statements but separate from the parent's equity, and clearly identified and labeled. In addition, FASB ASC 810 requires expanded disclosures in the consolidated financial statements that clearly identify and distinguish between the interests of the parent's owners and the interests of the noncontrolling owners of a subsidiary. Those expanded disclosures include a reconciliation of the beginning and ending balances of the equity attributable to the parent and noncontrolling owners and a schedule showing the effects of changes in a parent's ownership interest in a subsidiary on the equity attributable to the parent.

PRESENTATION AND DISCLOSURE EXCERPTS

UNEARNED COMPENSATION

5.47 GENERAL MILLS, INC. (MAY)
CONSOLIDATED STATEMENTS OF TOTAL EQUITY AND REDEEMABLE INTEREST

(In Millions, Except per Share Data)

| | $.10 Par Value Common Stock (One Billion Shares Authorized) | | | | | | | | | |
| | Issued | | Additional Paid-In Capital | Treasury | | Retained Earnings | Accumulated Other Comprehensive Income (Loss) | Non-controlling Interests | Total Equity | Redeemable Interest |
	Shares	Par Amount		Shares	Amount					
Balance as of May 30, 2010	754.6	75.5	1,307.1	(98.1)	(2,615.2)	8,122.4	(1,486.9)	245.1	5,648.0	
Total comprehensive income						1,798.3	476.1	5.9	2,280.3	
Cash dividends declared ($1.12 per share)						(729.4)			(729.4)	
Shares purchased				(31.8)	(1,163.5)				(1,163.5)	
Stock compensation plans (includes income tax benefits of $106.2)			(22.2)	20.1	568.4				546.2	
Unearned compensation related to restricted stock unit awards			(70.4)						(70.4)	
Earned compensation			105.3						105.3	
Distributions to noncontrolling interest holders								(4.3)	(4.3)	
Balance as of May 29, 2011	754.6	75.5	1,319.8	(109.8)	(3,210.3)	9,191.3	(1,010.8)	246.7	6,612.2	
Total comprehensive income (loss)						1,567.3	(732.9)	(44.3)	790.1	(86.1)
Cash dividends declared ($1.22 per share)						(800.1)			(800.1)	
Shares purchased				(8.3)	(313.0)				(313.0)	
Stock compensation plans (includes income tax benefits of $63.1)			3.2	12.0	346.3				349.5	
Unearned compensation related to restricted stock unit awards			(93.4)						(93.4)	
Earned compensation			108.3						108.3	
Addition of redeemable and noncontrolling interest from acquisitions								263.8	263.8	904.4
Increase in redemption value of redeemable interest			(29.5)						(29.5)	29.5
Distributions to noncontrolling interest holders								(5.2)	(5.2)	
Balance as of May 27, 2012	754.6	$75.5	$1,308.4	(106.1)	$(3,177.0)	$ 9,958.5	$(1,743.7)	$461.0	$ 6,882.7	$847.8
Total comprehensive income						1,855.2	158.4	18.3	2,031.9	42.8
Cash dividends declared ($1.70 per share)						(1,111.1)			(1,111.1)	
Shares purchased				(30.0)	(24.2) (1,014.9)				(1,044.9)	
Stock compensation plans (includes income tax benefits of $103.0)			(38.6)	16.5	504.7				466.1	
Unearned compensation related to restricted stock unit awards			(80.5)						(80.5)	
Earned compensation			100.4						100.4	
Increase in redemption value of redeemable interest			(93.1)						(93.1)	93.1
Distributions to redeemable and noncontrolling interest holders								(23.0)	(23.0)	(16.2)
Balance as of May 26, 2013	754.6	$75.5	$1,166.6	(113.8)	$(3,687.2)	$10,702.6	$(1,585.3)	$456.3	$ 7,128.5	$967.5

NOTES TO CONSOLIDATED FINANCIAL STATEMENTS

Note 2. Summary of Significant Accounting Policies (in part)

Stock-based Compensation

We generally measure compensation expense for grants of restricted stock units using the value of a share of our stock on the date of grant. We estimate the value of stock option grants using a Black-Scholes valuation model. Stock compensation is recognized straight line over the vesting period. Our stock compensation expense is recorded in selling, general and administrative (SG&A) expenses and cost of sales in the Consolidated Statements of Earnings and allocated to each reportable segment in our segment results.

Certain equity-based compensation plans contain provisions that accelerate vesting of awards upon retirement, termination or death of eligible employees and directors. We consider a stock-based award to be vested when the employee's retention of the award is no longer contingent on providing subsequent service. Accordingly, the related compensation cost is recognized immediately for awards granted to retirement-eligible individuals or over the period from the grant date to the date retirement eligibility is achieved, if less than the stated vesting period.

We report the benefits of tax deductions in excess of recognized compensation cost as a financing cash flow, thereby reducing net operating cash flows and increasing net financing cash flows.

Note 11. Stock Plans

We use broad-based stock plans to help ensure that management's interests are aligned with those of our stockholders. As of May 26, 2013, a total of 35,492,790 shares were available for grant in the form of stock options, restricted stock, restricted stock units, and shares of unrestricted stock under the 2011 Stock Compensation Plan (2011) Plan) and the 2011 Compensation Plan for Non-Employee Directors. The 2011 Plan also provides for the issuance of cash-settled share-based units, stock appreciation rights, and performance awards. Stock-based awards now outstanding include some granted under the 1998 (employee), 2001, 2003, 2005, 2006, 2007, and 2009 stock plans and the Executive Incentive Plan (EIP), under which no further awards may be granted. The stock plans provide for accelerated vesting of awards upon retirement, termination, or death of eligible employees and directors.

Stock Options

The estimated fair values of stock options granted and the assumptions used for the Black-Scholes option-pricing model were as follows:

	Fiscal Year		
	2013	2012	2011
Estimated fair values of stock options granted	$3.65	$5.88	$4.12
Assumptions:			
Risk-free interest rate	1.6%	2.9%	2.9%
Expected term	9.0 years	8.5 years	8.5 years
Expected volatility	17.3%	17.6%	18.5%
Dividend yield	3.5%	3.3%	3.0%

The valuation of stock options is a significant accounting estimate that requires us to use judgments and assumptions that are likely to have a material impact on our financial statements. Annually, we make predictive assumptions regarding future stock price volatility, employee exercise behavior, dividend yield, and the forfeiture rate.

We estimate the fair value of each option on the grant date using a Black-Scholes option-pricing model, which requires us to make predictive assumptions regarding future stock price volatility, employee exercise behavior, and dividend yield. We estimate our future stock price volatility using the historical volatility over the expected term of the option, excluding time periods of volatility we believe a marketplace participant would exclude in estimating our stock price volatility. We also have considered, but did not use, implied volatility in our estimate, because trading activity in options on our stock, especially those with tenors of greater than 6 months, is insufficient to provide a reliable measure of expected volatility.

Our expected term represents the period of time that options granted are expected to be outstanding based on historical data to estimate option exercises and employee terminations within the valuation model. Separate groups of employees have similar historical exercise behavior and therefore were aggregated into a single pool for valuation purposes. The weighted-average expected term for all employee groups is presented in the table above. The risk-free interest rate for periods during the expected term of the options is based on the U.S. Treasury zero-coupon yield curve in effect at the time of grant.

Any corporate income tax benefit realized upon exercise or vesting of an award in excess of that previously recognized in earnings (referred to as a windfall tax benefit) is presented in the Consolidated Statements of Cash Flows as a financing cash flow.

Realized windfall tax benefits are credited to additional paid-in capital within the Consolidated Balance Sheets. Realized shortfall tax benefits (amounts which are less than that previously recognized in earnings) are first offset against the cumulative balance of windfall tax benefits, if any, and then charged directly to income tax expense, potentially resulting in volatility in our consolidated effective income tax rate. We calculated a cumulative memo balance of windfall tax benefits for the purpose of accounting for future shortfall tax benefits.

Options may be priced at 100 percent or more of the fair market value on the date of grant, and generally vest four years after the date of grant. Options generally expire within 10 years and one month after the date of grant.

Information on stock option activity follows:

	Options Exercisable (Thousands)	Weighted-Average Exercise Price Per Share	Options Outstanding (Thousands)	Weighted-Average Exercise Price Per Share
Balance as of May 30, 2010	47,726.6	22.89	81,104.6	25.17
Granted			5,234.3	37.38
Exercised			(18,665.4)	22.59
Forfeited or expired			(126.2)	31.26
Balance as of May 29, 2011	39,221.7	23.78	67,547.3	26.82
Granted			4,069.0	37.29
Exercised			(10,279.3)	24.12
Forfeited or expired			(394.3)	27.88
Balance as of May 27, 2012	39,564.9	25.27	60,942.7	27.96
Granted			3,407.7	38.15
Exercised			(16,534.6)	23.49
Forfeited or expired			(143.7)	34.06
Balance as of May 26, 2013	29,290.3	$27.69	47,672.1	$30.22

Stock-based compensation expense related to stock option awards was $17.5 million in fiscal 2013, $23.9 million in fiscal 2012, and $26.8 million in fiscal 2011.

Net cash proceeds from the exercise of stock options less shares used for withholding taxes and the intrinsic value of options exercised were as follows:

	Fiscal Year		
(In Millions)	2013	2012	2011
Net cash proceeds	$300.8	$233.5	$410.4
Intrinsic value of options exercised	$297.2	$156.7	$275.6

Restricted Stock, Restricted Stock Units, and Cash-Settled Share-Based Units

Stock and units settled in stock subject to a restricted period and a purchase price, if any (as determined by the Compensation Committee of the Board of Directors), may be granted to key employees under the 2011 Plan. Certain restricted stock and restricted stock unit awards require the employee to deposit personally owned shares (on a one-for-one basis) during the restricted period. Restricted stock and restricted stock units generally vest and become unrestricted four years after the date of grant. Participants are entitled to dividends on such awarded shares and units, but only receive those amounts if the shares or units vest. The sale or transfer of these shares and units is restricted during the vesting period. Participants holding restricted stock, but not restricted stock units, are entitled to vote on matters submitted to holders of common stock for a vote.

Information on restricted stock unit and cash-settled share-based units activity follows:

	Equity Classified		Liability Classified			
	Share-Settled Units (Thousands)	Weighted-Average Grant-Date Fair Value	Share-Settled Units (Thousands)	Weighted-Average Grant-Date Fair Value	Cash-Settled Share-Based Units (Thousands)	Weighted-Average Grant-Date Fair Value
Non-vested as of May 27, 2012	8,551.8	$33.79	397.1	$32.68	3,991.5	$31.58
Granted	2,330.4	38.42	74.5	38.15	—	—
Vested	(2,495.0)	32.05	(73.0)	31.68	(1,638.2)	31.64
Forfeited or expired	(345.0)	36.00	(10.4)	35.60	(65.5)	32.31
Non-vested as of May 26, 2013	8,042.2	$35.89	388.2	$32.60	2,287.8	$38.41

	Fiscal Year		
	2013	2012	2011
Number of units granted (thousands)	2,404.9	2,785.7	3,751.6
Weighted average price per unit	$ 38.41	$ 37.29	$ 36.16

The total grant-date fair value of restricted stock unit awards that vested during fiscal 2013 was $134.1 million, and $106.0 million vested during fiscal 2012.

As of May 26, 2013, unrecognized compensation expense related to non-vested stock options and restricted stock units was $125.4 million. This expense will be recognized over 17 months, on average.

Stock-based compensation expense related to restricted stock units and cash-settled share-based payment awards was $128.9 million for fiscal 2013, $124.3 million for fiscal 2012, and $141.2 million for fiscal 2011.

DEFERRED COMPENSATION

5.48 THE CHILDREN'S PLACE RETAIL STORES, INC. (JAN)
CONSOLIDATED STATEMENTS OF CHANGES IN STOCKHOLDERS' EQUITY

(In thousands)

	Common Stock		Additional Paid-In Capital	Deferred Compensation	Retained Earnings	Accumulated Other Comprehensive Income	Treasury Stock		Total Stockholders' Equity
	Shares	Amount					Shares	Value	
Balance, January 30, 2010 (As adjusted)	27,475	$2,747	$204,646	$ —	$396,131	$ 7,601	—	$ —	$611,125
Exercise of stock options	366	37	11,886						11,923
Excess tax benefits from stock-based compensation			692						692
Vesting of stock awards	242	24	(24)						—
Stock-based compensation expense			8,045						8,045
Purchase and retirement of shares	(1,947)	(195)	(15,285)		(75,143)				(90,623)
Change in cumulative translation adjustment						5,698			5,698
Net income					79,297				79,297
Balance, January 29, 2011 (As adjusted)	26,136	2,613	209,960	—	400,285	13,299	—	—	626,157
Exercise of stock options	188	19	6,806						6,825
Excess tax benefits from stock-based compensation			532						532
Vesting of stock awards	331	34	(34)						—
Stock-based compensation expense			9,286						9,286
Purchase and retirement of shares	(1,944)	(195)	(16,391)		(75,171)				(91,757)
Change in cumulative translation adjustment						(419)			(419)
Deferral of common stock into deferred compensation plan				598			(14)	(598)	—
Net income					74,345				74,345
Balance, January 28, 2012 (As adjusted)	24,711	2,471	210,159	598	399,459	12,880	(14)	(598)	624,969
Exercise of stock options	68	6	2,179						2,185
Excess tax benefits from stock-based compensation			4,941						4,941
Vesting of stock awards	200	20	(20)						—
Stock-based compensation expense			14,253						14,253
Purchase and retirement of shares	(1,800)	(179)	(15,821)		(73,020)				(89,020)
Change in cumulative translation adjustment						378			378
Deferral of common stock into deferred compensation plan				521			(10)	(521)	—
Net income					63,243				63,243
Balance, February 2, 2013	23,179	$2,318	$215,691	$1,119	$389,682	$13,258	(24)	$(1,119)	$620,949

NOTES TO CONSOLIDATED FINANCIAL STATEMENTS

1. Basis of Presentation and Summary of Significant Accounting Policies (in part)

Earnings (Loss) per Common Share

The Company reports its earnings (loss) per share in accordance with the *"Earnings Per Share"* topic of the FASB ASC, which requires the presentation of both basic and diluted earnings (loss) per share on the statements of operations. The diluted weighted average common shares includes adjustments for the potential effects of outstanding stock options, Deferred Awards and Performance Awards, but only in the periods in which such effect is dilutive under the treasury stock method. Included in our basic and diluted weighted average common shares are those shares due to participants in the deferred compensation plan, which are held in treasury stock. Antidilutive stock awards are comprised of stock options and unvested deferred, restricted and performance shares which would have been antidilutive in the application of the treasury stock method in accordance with "Earnings Per Share" topic of FASB ASC.

In accordance with this topic, the following table reconciles income (loss) and share amounts utilized to calculate basic and diluted net income (loss) per common share (in thousands):

	Fiscal Year Ended		
	February 2, 2013	January 28, 2012	January 29, 2011
Income from continuing operations	$63,243	$74,345	$79,760
(Loss) from discontinued operations, net of taxes	—	—	(463)
Net income	$63,243	$74,345	$79,297
Basic weighted average common shares	24,092	25,459	27,084
Dilutive effect of stock awards	184	209	352
Diluted weighted average common shares	24,276	25,668	27,436
Antidilutive stock awards	10	80	103

3. Stockholders' Equity (in part)

On August 18, 2010, the Company's Board of Directors authorized a share repurchase program in the amount of $100 million (the "2010 Share Repurchase Program"), on March 3, 2011 another share repurchase program was authorized in the amount of $100 million (the "2011 Share Repurchase Program"), on March 7, 2012 another share repurchase program was authorized in the amount of $50.0 million (the "2012 $50 Million Share Repurchase Program") and on November 26, 2012 another share repurchase program was authorized in the amount of $100.0 million (the "2012 $100 Million Share Repurchase Program"). At February 2, 2013, there was approximately $80.4 million remaining on the 2012 $100 Million Share Repurchase Program. The 2010 Share Repurchase Program, 2011 Share Repurchase Program and 2012 $50 Million Share Repurchase Program have been completed. Under the 2012 $100 Million Share Repurchase Program, the Company may repurchase shares in the open market at current market prices at the time of purchase or in privately negotiated transactions. The timing and actual number of shares repurchased under the program will depend on a variety of factors including price, corporate and regulatory requirements, and other market and business conditions. The Company may suspend or discontinue the program at any time, and may thereafter reinstitute purchases, all without prior announcement.

Pursuant to restrictions imposed by the Company's equity plan during black-out periods, the Company withholds and retires shares of vesting stock awards in exchange for payments to satisfy the withholding tax requirements of certain recipients. The Company's payment of the withholding taxes in exchange for the shares constitutes a purchase of its common stock.

The Company acquires shares of its common stock in conjunction with liabilities owed under a deferred compensation plan, which are held in treasury. The following table summarizes the Company's share repurchases (in thousands):

	Fiscal Year Ended					
	February 2, 2013		January 28, 2012		January 29, 2011	
	Shares	Value	Shares	Value	Shares	Value
Share repurchases related to:						
2010 Share buyback program	—	—	213	10,102	1,933	89,898
2011 Share buyback program	377	19,236	1,712	80,764	—	—
2012 $50 Million Share buyback program	1,001	50,000	—	—	—	—
2012 $100 Million Share buyback program[1]	420	19,638	—	—	—	—
Withholding taxes	2	146	19	891	14	725
Shares acquired and held in treasury	10	521	14	598	—	—

[1] Subsequent to February 2, 2013 and through March 26, 2013, the Company repurchased an additional 0.1 million shares for approximately $5.9 million.

In accordance with the "Equity" topic of the FASB ASC, the par value of the shares retired is charged against common stock and the remaining purchase price is allocated between additional paid-in capital and retained earnings. The portion charged against additional paid-in capital is done using a pro rata allocation based on total shares outstanding. Related to all shares retired for Fiscal 2012 and Fiscal 2011, approximately $73.0 million and $75.2 million was charged to retained earnings, respectively.

13. Retirement and Savings Plans (in part)

Deferred Compensation Plan

The Company has a deferred compensation plan (the "Deferred Compensation Plan"), which is a nonqualified, unfunded plan, for eligible senior level employees. Under the plan, participants may elect to defer up to 80% of his or her base salary and/or up to 100% of his or her bonus to be earned for the year following the year in which the deferral election is made. The Deferred Compensation Plan also permits members of the Board of Directors to elect to defer payment of all or a portion of their retainer and other fees to be earned for the year following the year in which a deferral election is made. In addition, eligible employees and directors of the Company may also elect to defer payment of any shares of Company stock that is earned with respect to deferred stock awards. The Company may, but is not required to, credit participants with additional Company contribution amounts. Deferred amounts are not subject to forfeiture and are deemed invested among investment funds offered under the Deferred Compensation Plan, as directed by each participant. Payments of deferred amounts (as adjusted for earnings and losses) are payable following separation from service or at a date or dates elected by the participant at the time the deferral is elected. Payments of deferred amounts are generally made in either a lump sum or in annual installments over a period not exceeding 15 years. During Fiscal 2010, the Deferred Compensation Plan was amended to allow for cash deferrals made by members of the Board of Directors to be invested in shares of the Company's common stock. Such elections are irrevocable and will be settled in shares of common stock. All other deferred amounts are payable in the form in which they were made; cash deferrals are payable in cash and stock deferrals are payable in stock. Earlier distributions are not permitted except in the case of an unforeseen hardship.

The Company has established a rabbi trust that serves as an investment to shadow the Deferred Compensation Plan liability; however, the assets of the rabbi trust are general assets of the Company and as such, would be subject to the claims of creditors in the event of bankruptcy or insolvency. The investments of the rabbi trust consist of company-owned life insurance policies ("COLIs") and Company stock. The Deferred Compensation Plan liability, excluding Company stock, is included in other long-term liabilities and changes in the balance are recognized as compensation expense. The cash surrender values of the COLIs are included in other assets and related earnings and losses are recognized as investment income or loss, which is included in selling, general and administrative expenses. Company stock deferrals are included in the equity section of the Company's consolidated balance sheet as treasury stock and as a deferred compensation liability. Deferred stock is recorded at fair market value at the time of deferral and any subsequent changes in fair market value are not recognized.

The Deferred Compensation Plan liability, excluding Company stock, at fair value, was approximately $0.7 million and $0.7 million at February 2, 2013 and January 28, 2012, respectively. The cash surrender value of the COLIs, which reflects the underlying assets at fair value, was approximately $0.7 million and $0.7 million and at February 2, 2013 and January 28, 2012, respectively. Company stock was $1.1 million and $0.6 million at February 2, 2013 and January 28, 2012, respectively. Prior to Fiscal 2011, there was no Company stock in the Deferred Compensation Plan.

WARRANTS

5.49 THE STANDARD REGISTER COMPANY (DEC)
CONSOLIDATED STATEMENTS OF SHAREHOLDERS' DEFICIT

(In thousands, except per share amounts)

	2013	2012	2011
Common Stock			
Beginning balance	$ 6,922	$ 6,889	$ 6,843
Dividend reinvestment plan	—	—	11
Exercise of warrants	2,646	—	—
Exercise of stock options	1	—	—
Issuance of vested shares	84	33	35
Ending balance	$ 9,653	$ 6,922	$ 6,889
Class A Stock	$ 945	$ 945	$ 945
Capital in Excess of Par Value			
Beginning balance	$ 91,266	$ 88,587	$ 86,565
Share-based compensation expense	2,310	2,706	1,905
Issuance of warrants	6,509	—	—
Exercise of warrants	(2,646)	—	—
Exercise of stock options	3	—	—
Issuance of vested shares	(84)	(33)	(35)
Other	(68)	6	152
Ending balance	$ 97,290	$ 91,266	$ 88,587
Accumulated Other Comprehensive Losses			
Beginning balance	$ (39,454)	$ (37,413)	$ (7,875)
Cumulative translation adjustment	(169)	138	(204)
Change in net actuarial losses	14,390	(2,179)	(15,696)
Change in net prior service credit	—	—	(13,638)
Ending balance	$ (25,233)	$ (39,454)	$ (37,413)
Accumulated Deficit			
Beginning balance	$(136,303)	$(107,836)	$ 23,493
Net loss	(7,413)	(28,476)	(125,433)
Dividends declared, $1.00 per share	—	—	(5,896)
Other	—	9	—
Ending balance	$(143,716)	$(136,303)	$(107,836)
Treasury Stock at Cost			
Beginning balance	$ (50,236)	$ (50,225)	$ (50,167)
Treasury stock acquired	—	(11)	(58)
Ending balance	$ (50,236)	$ (50,236)	$ (50,225)
Total shareholders' deficit	$(111,297)	$(126,860)	$ (99,053)

(Dollars in thousands, except per share amounts)

Note 3—Acquisition (in part)

On August 1, 2013, the Company acquired all of the outstanding membership interests of WorkflowOne for a total purchase price of one dollar (the "Acquisition"). In connection with the Acquisition, the Company also assumed $210,000 of WorkflowOne's existing debt under two secured credit facilities (the "First Lien Term Loan" and "Second Lien Term Loan") and issued warrants with an estimated fair value of $6,509 that were subsequently converted into 2,645,945 shares of the Company's Common Stock in October 2013. The exercise price of each warrant was $0.00001 per common share. The estimated fair value of the warrants issued was calculated based on the closing market price of the Company's stock on July 31, 2013, with an estimated discount for lack of marketability due to certain restrictions.

NONCONTROLLING INTEREST

5.50 VALERO ENERGY CORPORATION (DEC)
CONSOLIDATED STATEMENTS OF EQUITY

(Millions of Dollars)

	Valero Energy Corporation Stockholders' Equity						Non-controlling Interests	Total Equity
	Common Stock	Additional Paid-in Capital	Treasury Stock	Retained Earnings	Accumulated Other Comprehensive Income (Loss)	Total		
Balance as of December 31, 2010	$ 7	$7,704	$(6,462)	$13,388	$ 388	$15,025	$ —	$15,025
Net income (loss)	—	—	—	2,090	—	2,090	(1)	2,089
Dividends on common stock	—	—	—	(169)	—	(169)	—	(169)
Stock-based compensation expense	—	57	—	—	—	57	—	57
Tax deduction in excess of stock-based compensation expense	—	22	—	—	—	22	—	22
Transactions in connection with stock-based compensation plans:								
Stock issuances	—	(287)	336	—	—	49	—	49
Stock repurchases	—	(10)	(349)	—	—	(359)	—	(359)
Contributions from noncontrolling interest	—	—	—	—	—	—	23	23
Recognition of noncontrolling interests in Mainline Pipelines Limited in connection with Pembroke Acquisition	—	—	—	—	—	—	5	5
Acquisition of noncontrolling interests in Mainline Pipelines Limited	—	—	—	—	—	—	(5)	(5)
Other comprehensive loss	—	—	—	—	(292)	(292)	—	(292)
Balance as of December 31, 2011	7	7,486	(6,475)	15,309	96	16,423	22	16,445
Net income (loss)	—	—	—	2,083	—	2,083	(3)	2,080
Dividends on common stock	—	—	—	(360)	—	(360)	—	(360)
Stock-based compensation expense	—	57	—	—	—	57	—	57
Tax deduction in excess of stock-based compensation expense	—	29	—	—	—	29	—	29
Transactions in connection with stock-based compensation plans:								
Stock issuances	—	(260)	319	—	—	59	—	59
Stock repurchases	—	10	(163)	—	—	(153)	—	(153)
Stock repurchases under buyback program	—	—	(118)	—	—	(118)	—	(118)
Contributions from noncontrolling interest	—	—	—	—	—	—	44	44
Other comprehensive income	—	—	—	—	12	12	—	12

(continued)

| | Valero Energy Corporation Stockholders' Equity | | | | | | | |
	Common Stock	Additional Paid-in Capital	Treasury Stock	Retained Earnings	Accumulated Other Comprehensive Income (Loss)	Total	Non-controlling Interests	Total Equity
Balance as of December 31, 2012	7	7,322	(6,437)	17,032	108	18,032	63	18,095
Net income	—	—	—	2,720	—	2,720	8	2,728
Dividends on common stock	—	—	—	(462)	—	(462)	—	(462)
Stock-based compensation expense	—	64	—	—	—	64	—	64
Tax deduction in excess of stock-based compensation expense	—	47	—	—	—	47	—	47
Transactions in connection with stock-based compensation plans:								
Stock issuances	—	(243)	302	—	—	59	—	59
Stock repurchases	—	—	(236)	—	—	(236)	—	(236)
Stock repurchases under buyback program	—	—	(692)	—	—	(692)	—	(692)
Separation of retail business	—	(9)	9	(320)	(159)	(479)	—	(479)
Net proceeds from initial public offering of common units of Valero Energy Partners LP	—	—	—	—	—	—	369	369
Contributions from noncontrolling interests	—	—	—	—	—	—	46	46
Other	—	6	—	—	—	6	—	6
Other comprehensive income	—	—	—	—	401	401	—	401
Balance as of December 31, 2013	$ 7	$7,187	$(7,054)	$18,970	$ 350	$19,460	$486	$19,946

NOTES TO CONSOLIDATED FINANCIAL STATEMENTS

1. Basis of Presentation and Summary of Significant Accounting Policies (in part)

Significant Accounting Policies (in part)

Principles of Consolidation

General

These financial statements include the accounts of Valero and subsidiaries in which Valero has a controlling interest. Intercompany balances and transactions have been eliminated in consolidation. Investments in significant noncontrolled entities are accounted for using the equity method.

Noncontrolling Interests

Because of our controlling financial interest in each of the following entities, we have included their financial statements in our financial statements and have separately disclosed the related noncontrolling interests.
- Valero Energy Partners LP (VLP) is a master limited partnership formed in July 2013 to own, operate, develop, and acquire primarily fee-based crude oil and refined petroleum product pipelines and terminals. As further described in Note 5, VLP completed an initial public offering of its common units on December 16, 2013 and we owned a 70.6 percent controlling financial interest in VLP as of December 31, 2013.
- Diamond Green Diesel Holdings LLC (DGD Holdings) is a 50/50 joint venture with Darling Green Energy LLC, a subsidiary of Darling International, Inc., that constructed and now operates a biomass- based diesel unit having a design feed capacity of 10,000 barrels per day that processes animal fats, used cooking oils, and other vegetable oils into renewable green diesel. As of December 31, 2013, we had loaned $221 million to a subsidiary of DGD Holdings to finance a portion of the construction costs of the unit. The unit began operations in June 2013.
- PI Dock Facilities LLC (PI Dock) is a 50/50 joint venture with TGSD PI, LLC that will construct and operate crude oil docks and related facilities near our Port Arthur Refinery. In December 2012, we agreed to lend PI Dock up to $90 million to finance the construction of the initial crude dock, which is expected to be completed in late third quarter or early fourth quarter of 2014. As of December 31, 2013, we had loaned PI Dock $13 million to finance its construction projects.

5. Initial Public Offering of Valero Energy Partners LP

In July 2013, we formed VLP, a master limited partnership, to own, operate, develop, and acquire crude oil and refined petroleum products pipelines, terminals, and other transportation and logistics assets. On December 16, 2013, VLP completed its initial public offering (the Offering) of 17,250,000 common units at a price of $23.00 per unit, which included a 2,250,000 common unit over-allotment option that was fully exercised by the underwriters. VLP received $369 million in net proceeds from the sale of the units, after deducting underwriting fees, structuring fees, and other offering costs. VLP's assets include crude oil and refined petroleum products pipeline and terminal systems in the U.S Gulf Coast and U.S. Mid-Continent regions that are integral to the operations of our Port Arthur, McKee and Memphis Refineries.

As of December 31, 2013, we owned a 68.6 percent limited partner interest and a 2 percent general partner interest in VLP, and the public owned a 29.4 percent limited partner interest. VLP's cash and temporary cash investments was $375 million as of December 31, 2013, which can be used only to settle its obligations. The public's ownership interest in VLP of $370 million is reflected in noncontrolling interests as of December 31, 2013.

The following table is a reconciliation of net proceeds from the Offering (in millions):

Total proceeds from the Offering	$397
Less offering costs	(28)
Net proceeds from the Offering	$369

We have agreements with VLP, which establish fees for certain general and administrative services, and operational and maintenance services provided by us. In addition, we have a master transportation services agreement and a master terminal services agreement with VLP where VLP provides commercial transportation and terminaling services to us. These transactions are eliminated in consolidation.

General

PRESENTATION

6.01 Financial Accounting Standards Board (FASB) *Accounting Standards Codification* (ASC) 230, *Statement of Cash Flows*, requires entities to present a statement of cash flows that classifies cash receipts and payments by operating, investing, and financing activities. The information provided in a statement of cash flows, if used with related disclosures and information in the other financial statements, should help investors, creditors, and others assess the following:
- The entity's ability to generate positive future net cash flows
- The entity's ability to meet its obligations, its ability to pay dividends, and its needs for external financing
- The reasons for differences between net income and associated cash receipts and payments
- The effects on an entity's financial position of both its cash and noncash investing and financing transactions during the period

6.02 Paragraphs 4–6 of FASB ASC 230-10-45 provide that the statement of cash flows explains the change in cash and cash equivalents during a period. *Cash equivalents* are defined by the FASB ASC glossary to be short-term, highly liquid investments that have both of the following characteristics:
- Readily convertible to known amounts of cash
- So near their maturity that they present an insignificant risk of changes in value because of changes in interest rates

Generally, only investments with original maturities of three months or less qualify under that definition. *Original maturity* means original maturity to the entity holding the investment.

6.03 FASB ASC 230-10-45-4 states that the amount of cash and cash equivalents at the beginning and end of the period reported on a statement of cash flows should agree with the amount of cash and cash equivalents reported on a statement of financial position. Because not all investments that qualify are required to be treated as cash equivalents, an entity should establish a policy concerning which short-term, highly liquid investments that satisfy the definition of *cash equivalents* are treated as such.

6.04 Paragraphs 7–9 of FASB ASC 230-10-45 explain that generally, cash receipts and payments should be reported separately and not netted. For certain items, the turnover is quick, the amounts are large, and the maturities are short. For certain other items, such as demand deposits of a bank and customer accounts payable of a broker-dealer, the entity is substantively holding or disbursing cash on behalf of its customers. Only the net changes during the period in assets and liabilities with those characteristics need be reported because knowledge of the gross cash receipts and payments related to them may not be necessary to understand the entity's operating, investing, and financing activities. Specifically, provided that the original maturity of the asset or liability is three months or less, cash receipts and payments pertaining to investments (other than cash equivalents), loans receivable, and debt qualify for net reporting based on this rationale.

6.05 FASB ASC 830-230-45-1 specifies that the effect of exchange rate changes on cash balances held in foreign currencies be reported as a separate part of the reconciliation of the change in cash and cash equivalents during the period in the statement of cash flows. Further, a statement of cash flows of an entity with foreign exchange transactions or foreign operations should report the reporting currency equivalent of foreign currency cash flows using the exchange rates in effect at the time of the cash flows. An appropriately weighted average exchange rate for the period may be used for translation if the result is substantially the same as if the rates at the dates of the cash flows were used.

DISCLOSURE

6.06 FASB ASC 230-10-50-1 explains that an entity should disclose its policy regarding cash equivalent classification, and any change to that policy is a change in accounting principle that should be affected by restating financial statements for earlier years presented for comparative purposes. FASB ASC 230-10-50-2 specifies that if the indirect method is used, amounts of interest (net of capitalized amounts) and income tax payments during the period are required to be disclosed.

PRESENTATION AND DISCLOSURE EXCERPTS

CASH AND CASH EQUIVALENTS

6.08 JABIL CIRCUIT, INC. (AUG)

MANAGEMENT'S DISCUSSION AND ANALYSIS OF FINANCIAL CONDITION AND RESULTS OF OPERATIONS

Liquidity and Capital Resources

At August 31, 2013, we had cash and cash equivalent balances totaling $1.0 billion, total notes payable, long-term debt and capital lease obligations of $1.9 billion, $1.1 billion in available liquidity under our revolving credit facilities and up to $192.3 million in available liquidity under our trade accounts receivable securitization and committed and uncommitted sale programs. We can offer no assurance under the uncommitted sales programs that if we attempt to draw on such programs in the future that we will receive funding from the associated banks which would require us to utilize other available sources of liquidity, including our revolving credit facilities.

Cash Flows

The following table sets forth, for the fiscal years ended August 31 selected consolidated cash flow information (in thousands):

	Fiscal Year Ended August 31,		
	2013	**2012**	**2011**
Net cash provided by operating activities	$ 1,213,889	$ 634,226	$ 828,009
Net cash used in investing activities	(1,374,462)	(605,870)	(426,278)
Net cash (used in) provided by financing activities	(22,993)	317,358	(267,722)
Effect of exchange rate changes on cash	(22,317)	(17,069)	10,273
Net (decrease) increase in cash and cash equivalents	$ (205,883)	$ 328,645	$ 144,282

Net cash provided by operating activities for fiscal year 2013 was approximately $1.2 billion. This resulted primarily from net income of $370.1 million, a $486.0 million increase in accounts payable and accrued expenses, $418.1 million in non-cash depreciation and amortization expense, $68.4 million in stock-based compensation expense and a $50.2 million decrease in inventories; which were partially offset by $123.2 million in deferred income taxes and an $82.8 million increase in prepaid expenses and other current assets. The increase in accounts payable and accrued expenses was primarily driven by the timing of purchases and cash payments. The decrease in inventories was primarily a result of a continued focus on inventory management. The increase in prepaid expenses and other current assets was primarily due to increases in the deferred purchase price receivable under our asset-backed securitization programs due to higher levels of sales and the timing of cash funding provided by the unaffiliated conduits and financial institutions as well as an increase in advanced deposits.

Net cash used in investing activities for fiscal year 2013 was $1.4 billion. This consisted primarily of capital expenditures of $736.9 million principally for machinery and equipment for new business, particularly within our DMS segment and maintenance levels of machinery and equipment and $650.1 million of net cash paid for business acquisitions.

Net cash used in financing activities for fiscal year 2013 was $23.0 million. This resulted from our receipt of approximately $5.8 billion of proceeds from borrowings under existing debt agreements, which primarily included $5.4 billion of borrowings under the Amended and Restated Credit Facility and $362.4 million of borrowings under various credit facilities with foreign facilities. This was offset by repayments in an aggregate amount of approximately $5.6 billion during fiscal year 2013, which primarily included an aggregate of $5.2 billion of repayments under the Amended and Restated Credit Facility and approximately $370.4 million of repayments under various credit facilities with foreign subsidiaries. In addition, we paid $129.3 million to repurchase 7,342,904 of our common shares, $67.2 million in dividends to stockholders and $20.3 million to the IRS on behalf of certain employees to satisfy minimum tax obligations related to the vesting of certain restricted stock awards (as consideration for these payments to the IRS, we withheld $20.3 million of employee-owned common stock related to this vesting) during the fiscal year ended August 31, 2013.

Sources

We may need to finance day-to-day working capital needs, as well as future growth and any corresponding working capital needs, with additional borrowings under our Amended and Restated Credit Facility (which is further discussed in the following paragraphs) and our other revolving credit facilities described below, as well as additional public and private offerings of our debt and equity. Currently, we have a shelf registration statement with the SEC registering the potential sale of an indeterminate amount of debt and equity securities in the future, from time-to-time over the three years following the registration, to augment our liquidity and capital resources. The current shelf registration statement will expire in the first quarter of fiscal year 2015 at which time we currently anticipate filing a new shelf registration statement. Any future sale or issuance of equity or convertible debt securities could result in dilution to current or future shareholders. Further, we may issue debt securities that have rights and privileges senior to those of holders of ordinary shares, and the terms of this debt could impose restrictions on operations, increase debt service obligations, limit our flexibility as a result of debt service requirements and restrictive covenants, potentially negatively affect our credit ratings, and limit our ability to access additional capital or execute our business strategy. We continue to assess our capital structure and evaluate the merits of redeploying available cash to reduce existing debt or repurchase common shares.

We regularly sell designated pools of trade accounts receivable under two asset-backed securitization programs, a factoring program, a committed trade accounts receivable sale program and two uncommitted trade accounts receivable sale programs (collectively referred to herein as the "programs"). Transfers of the receivables under the programs are accounted for as sales and, accordingly, net receivables sold under the programs are excluded from accounts receivable on the Consolidated Balance Sheets and are reflected as cash provided by operating activities on the Consolidated Statements of Cash Flows. Discussion of each of the programs is included in the following paragraphs. In addition, refer to Note 2—"Trade Accounts Receivable Securitization and Sale Programs" to the Consolidated Financial Statements for further details on the programs.

a. Asset-Backed Securitization Programs

We continuously sell designated pools of trade accounts receivable under our asset-backed securitization programs to special purpose entities, which in turn sell 100% of the receivables to conduits administered by unaffiliated financial institutions (for the North American asset-backed securitization program) and an unaffiliated financial institution (for the foreign asset-backed securitization program). Any portion of the purchase price for the receivables which is not paid in cash upon the sale taking place is recorded as a deferred purchase price receivable, which is paid from available cash as payments on the receivables are collected. Net cash proceeds up to a maximum of $300.0 million for the North American asset-backed securitization program, currently scheduled to expire on October 21, 2014, and $200.0 million for the foreign asset-backed securitization program, currently scheduled to expire on May 15, 2015, are available at any one time.

In connection with our asset-backed securitization programs, at August 31, 2013, we had sold $886.3 million of eligible trade accounts receivable, which represents the face amount of total sold outstanding receivables at that date. In exchange, we received cash proceeds of $345.1 million, and a deferred purchase price receivable. At August 31, 2013, the deferred purchase price receivable in connection with the asset-backed securitization programs totaled approximately $541.2 million. The deferred purchase price receivable was recorded initially at fair value as prepaid expenses and other current assets on the Consolidated Balance Sheets.

b. Trade Accounts Receivable Factoring Agreement

In connection with a factoring agreement, we transfer ownership of eligible trade accounts receivable of a foreign subsidiary without recourse to a third party purchaser in exchange for cash. Proceeds from the transfer reflect the face value of the account less a discount. In April 2013, the factoring agreement was extended through September 30, 2013, at which time it was automatically renewed for an additional six-month period.

During the fiscal year ended August 31, 2013, we sold $31.2 million of trade accounts receivable and received cash proceeds of $31.2 million.

c. Trade Accounts Receivable Sale Programs

In connection with three separate trade accounts receivable sale agreements with unaffiliated financial institutions, we may elect to sell, at a discount, on an ongoing basis, up to a maximum of $200.0 million, $150.0 million and $40.0 million, respectively, of specific trade accounts receivable at any one time. The $200.0 million trade accounts receivable sale agreement is a committed facility that was renewed during the third quarter of fiscal year 2013 and is scheduled to expire on November 30, 2013. The $150.0 million trade accounts receivable sale agreement is an uncommitted facility scheduled to expire on November 28, 2013. The $40.0 million trade accounts receivable sale agreement is an uncommitted facility and is scheduled to expire no later than June 1, 2015, though either party may elect to cancel the agreement by giving prior written notification to the other party of no less than 30 days.

During the fiscal year ended August 31, 2013, we sold $2.4 billion of trade accounts receivable under these programs and we received cash proceeds of $2.4 billion.

Notes payable, long-term debt and capital lease obligations outstanding at August 31, 2013 and 2012 are summarized below (in thousands):

	August 31, 2013	August 31, 2012
7.750% Senior Notes due 2016[a]	$ 306,940	$ 305,221
8.250% Senior Notes due 2018[b]	398,284	397,903
5.625% Senior Notes due 2020[c]	400,000	400,000
4.700% Senior Notes due 2022[d]	500,000	500,000
Borrowings under credit facilities[e]	200,000	8,000
Borrowings under loans[f]	58,447	55,870
Capital lease obligations[g]	35,468	166
Fair value adjustment related to terminated interest rate swaps on the 7.750% Senior Notes[h]	6,823	9,197
Total notes payable, long-term debt and capital lease obligations	1,905,962	1,676,357
Less current installments of notes payable, long-term debt and capital lease obligations	215,536	18,031
Notes payable, long-term debt and capital lease obligations, less current installments	$1,690,426	$1,658,326

[a] During the fourth quarter of fiscal year 2009, we issued the 7.750% Senior Notes at 96.1% of par, resulting in net proceeds of approximately $300.0 million. The 7.750% Senior Notes mature on July 15, 2016 and pay interest semiannually on January 15 and July 15. Also, the 7.750% Senior Notes are our senior unsecured obligations and rank equally with all other existing and future senior unsecured debt obligations. We are subject to covenants such as limitations on our and/or our subsidiaries' ability to: consolidate or merge with, or convey, transfer or lease all or substantially all of our assets to, another person; create certain liens; enter into sale and leaseback transactions; create, incur, issue, assume or guarantee funded debt (which only applies to our "restricted subsidiaries"); and guarantee any of our indebtedness (which only applies to our subsidiaries). We are also subject to a covenant requiring our repurchase of the 7.750% Senior Notes upon a "change of control repurchase event."

[b] During the second and third quarters of fiscal year 2008, we issued $250.0 million and $150.0 million, respectively, of ten-year, unregistered 8.250% notes at 99.965% of par and 97.5% of par, respectively, resulting in net proceeds of approximately $245.7 million and $148.5 million, respectively. On July 18, 2008, we completed an exchange whereby all of the outstanding unregistered 8.250% Notes were exchanged for the 8.250% Senior Notes that are substantially identical to the unregistered notes except that the 8.250% Senior Notes are registered under the Securities Act and do not have any transfer restrictions, registration rights or rights to additional special interest.

The 8.250% Senior Notes mature on March 15, 2018 and pay interest semiannually on March 15 and September 15. The interest rate payable on the 8.250% Senior Notes is subject to adjustment from time to time if the credit ratings assigned to the 8.250% Senior Notes increase or decrease, as provided in the 8.250% Senior Notes. The 8.250% Senior Notes are our senior unsecured obligations and rank equally with all other existing and future senior unsecured debt obligations.

We are subject to covenants such as limitations on our and/or our subsidiaries' ability to: consolidate or merge with, or convey, transfer or lease all or substantially all of our assets to, another person; create certain liens; enter into sale and leaseback transactions; create, incur, issue, assume or guarantee any funded debt (which only applies to our "restricted subsidiaries"); and guarantee any of our indebtedness (which only applies to our subsidiaries). We are also subject to a covenant requiring our repurchase of the 8.250% Senior Notes upon a "change of control repurchase event."

[c] During the first quarter of fiscal year 2011, we issued the 5.625% Senior Notes at par. The net proceeds from the offering of $400.0 million were used to fully repay the term portion of the Old Credit Facility and partially repay amounts outstanding under our foreign asset-backed securitization program. The 5.625% Senior Notes mature on December 15, 2020. Interest on the 5.625% Senior Notes is payable semiannually on June 15 and December 15 of each year, beginning on June 15, 2011. The 5.625% Senior Notes are our senior unsecured obligations and rank equally with all other existing and future senior unsecured debt obligations. We are subject to covenants such as limitations on our and/or our subsidiaries' ability to: consolidate or merge with, or convey, transfer or lease all or substantially all of our assets to, another person; create certain liens; enter into sale and leaseback transactions; create, incur, issue, assume or guarantee any funded debt (which only applies to our "restricted subsidiaries"); and guarantee any of our indebtedness (which only applies to our subsidiaries). We are also subject to a covenant requiring our repurchase of the 5.625% Senior Notes upon a "change of control repurchase event."

[d] During the fourth quarter of fiscal year 2012, we issued the 4.700% Senior Notes at 99.992% of par. The net proceeds from the offering of $500.0 million were used to repay outstanding borrowings under our revolving Amended and Restated Credit Facility and for general corporate purposes. The 4.700% Senior Notes mature on September 15, 2022 and pay interest semiannually on March 15 and September 15 of each year, beginning on March 15, 2013. The 4.700% Senior Notes are our senior unsecured obligations and rank equally with all other existing and future senior unsecured debt obligations. We are subject to covenants such as limitations on our and/or our subsidiaries' ability to: consolidate or merge with, or convey, transfer or lease all or substantially all of our assets to, another person; create certain liens; enter into sale and leaseback transactions; create, incur, issue, assume or guarantee any funded debt (which only applies to our "restricted subsidiaries"); and guarantee any of our indebtedness (which only applies to our subsidiaries). We are also subject to a covenant requiring our repurchase of the 4.700% Senior Notes upon a "change of control repurchase event."

[e] As of August 31, 2013, six of our foreign subsidiaries have credit facilities that finance their future growth and any corresponding working capital needs. Four of the credit facilities are denominated in U.S. dollars, one is denominated in Brazilian reais and one is denominated in Taiwan new dollar. The credit facilities incur interest at fixed and variable rates ranging from 1.8% to 10.0%.

During the third quarter of fiscal year 2012, we entered into the Amended and Restated Credit Facility which provides for a revolving credit facility in the initial amount of $1.3 billion. The Amended and Restated Credit Facility may, subject to lenders' discretion, potentially be increased up to $1.6 billion and expires on March 19, 2017. Interest and fees on the Amended and Restated Credit Facility advances are based on our non-credit enhanced long-term senior unsecured debt rating as determined by S&P and Moody's. Interest is charged at a rate equal to either 0.175% to 0.850% above the base rate or 1.175% to 1.850% above the Eurocurrency rate, where the base rate represents the greatest of Citibank, N.A.'s prime rate, 0.50% above the federal funds rate, or 1.0% above one-month LIBOR, and the Eurocurrency rate represents adjusted LIBOR for the applicable interest period, each as more fully described in the Amended and Restated Credit Facility agreement. Fees include a facility fee based on the revolving credit commitments of the lenders and a letter of credit fee based on the amount of outstanding letters of credit. We, along with our subsidiaries, are subject to the following financial covenants: (1) a maximum ratio of (a) Debt (as defined in the Amended and Restated Credit Facility agreement) to (b) Consolidated EBITDA (as defined in the Amended and Restated Credit Facility agreement) and (2) a minimum ratio of (a) Consolidated EBITDA to (b) interest payable on, and amortization of debt discount in respect of, all Debt (as defined in the Amended and Restated Credit Facility agreement) and loss on sale of accounts receivables. In addition, we are subject to other covenants, such as: limitation upon liens; limitation upon mergers, etc.; limitation upon accounting changes; limitation upon subsidiary debt; limitation upon sales, etc. of assets; limitation upon changes in nature of business; payment restrictions affecting subsidiaries; compliance with laws, etc.; payment of taxes, etc.; maintenance of insurance; preservation of corporate existence, etc.; visitation rights; keeping of books; maintenance of properties, etc.; transactions with affiliates; and reporting requirements.

During fiscal year 2013, we borrowed $5.4 billion against the Amended and Restated Credit Facility under multiple draws and paid $5.2 billion under multiple payments. In addition, during the fourth quarter of fiscal year 2013, we borrowed $2.5 billion against the Amended and Restated Credit Facility under multiple draws and repaid $2.3 billion under multiple payments.

(continued)

(f) During the third quarter of fiscal year 2012, we entered into a master lease agreement with a variable interest entity (the "VIE") whereby we sell to and subsequently lease back from the VIE up to $60.0 million in certain machinery and equipment for a period of up to five years. In connection with this transaction, we hold a variable interest in the VIE, which was designed to hold debt obligations payable to third-party creditors. The proceeds from such debt obligations are utilized to finance the purchase of the machinery and equipment that is then leased by us. We are the primary beneficiary of the VIE as we have both the power to direct the activities of the VIE that most significantly impact the VIE's economic performance and the obligation to absorb losses or the right to receive benefits that could potentially be significant to the VIE. Therefore, we consolidate the financial statements of the VIE and eliminate all intercompany transactions. At August 31, 2013, the VIE had approximately $46.6 million of total assets, of which approximately $45.4 million was comprised of a note receivable due from us, and approximately $46.0 million of total liabilities, of which approximately $45.9 million were debt obligations to the third-party creditors (as the VIE has utilized approximately $45.9 million of the $60.0 million debt obligation capacity). The third-party creditors have recourse to our general credit only in the event that we default on our obligations under the terms of the master lease agreement. In addition, the assets held by the VIE can be used only to settle the obligations of the VIE.

    In addition to the loans described above, at August 31, 2013, we have borrowings outstanding to fund working capital needs. These additional loans total approximately $12.1 million, of which $11.9 million are denominated in Euros and $0.2 million are denominated in U.S. dollars.

(g) During the fourth quarter of fiscal year 2013, we acquired various capital lease obligations in connection with the acquisition of Nypro.

(h) This amount represents the fair value hedge accounting adjustment related to the 7.750% Senior Notes. For further discussion of our fair value hedges, see Note 12—"Derivative Financial Instruments and Hedging Activities" to the Consolidated Financial Statements

At August 31, 2013 and 2012, we were in compliance with all covenants under the Amended and Restated Credit Facility, respectively and our securitization programs.

Uses

On October 16, 2012, January 23, 2013 April 15, 2013, and July 18, 2013, our Board of Directors approved payment of a quarterly dividend of $0.08 per share to shareholders of record as of November 15, 2012, February 15, 2013, May 15, 2013, and August 15, 2013, respectively. Of the total cash dividend declared on October 16, 2012 of $17.0 million, $16.2 million was paid on December 3, 2012. Of the total cash dividend declared on January 23, 2013 of $17.0 million, $16.2 million was paid on March 1, 2013. Of the total cash dividend declared on April 15, 2013 of $17.0 million, $16.2 million was paid on June 3, 2013. Of the total cash dividend declared on July 18, 2013 of $17.0 million, $16.2 million was paid on September 3, 2013. The remaining $0.8 million that was not paid during each quarter is related to dividend equivalents on unvested restricted stock units that will be payable at the time the awards vest. We currently expect to continue to declare and pay regular quarterly dividends of an amount similar to our past declarations. However, the declaration and payment of future dividends are discretionary and will be subject to determination by our Board of Directors each quarter following its review of our financial performance.

In the first quarter of fiscal year 2012, our Board of Directors authorized the repurchase of $100.0 million of our common shares. We repurchased $29.0 million worth of shares during the first quarter of fiscal year 2013, which was the remaining amount outstanding of the $100.0 million authorized by our Board of Directors in fiscal year 2012.

In the first quarter of fiscal year 2013, our Board of Directors authorized the repurchase of up to an additional $100.0 million of our common shares during the twelve month period following their authorization. The shares were repurchased during the first quarter of fiscal year 2013 utilizing the entire $100.0 million authorized by our Board of Directors.

Our working capital requirements and capital expenditures could continue to increase in order to support future expansions of our operations through construction of greenfield operations or acquisitions. It is possible that future expansions may be significant and may require the payment of cash. Future liquidity needs will also depend on fluctuations in levels of inventory and shipments, changes in customer order volumes and timing of expenditures for new equipment.

At August 31, 2013, we had approximately $1.0 billion in cash and cash equivalents. As our growth remains predominantly outside of the United States, a significant portion of such cash and cash equivalents are held by our foreign subsidiaries. We estimate that approximately $742.7 million of the cash and cash equivalents held by our foreign subsidiaries could not be repatriated to the United States without potential income tax consequences.

At August 31, 2013, however, we intend to repatriate the Nypro pre-acquisition undistributed foreign earnings of approximately $240.0 million to our U.S. operations. Therefore, we recorded a deferred tax liability of approximately $80.0 million based on the anticipated U.S. income taxes of the repatriation. We intend to indefinitely reinvest the remaining earnings from our foreign subsidiaries.

For discussion of our cash management and risk management policies see "Quantitative and Qualitative Disclosures About Market Risk."

We currently anticipate that during the next 12 months, our capital expenditures will be in the range of $250.0 million to $350.0 million, principally for maintenance levels of machinery and equipment, information technology infrastructure upgrades and investments to support ongoing growth in our DMS operations. We believe that our level of resources, which include cash on hand, available borrowings under our revolving credit facilities, additional proceeds available under our trade accounts receivable securitization programs and committed trade accounts receivable sale program and potentially available under our uncommitted trade accounts receivable sale programs and funds provided by operations, will be adequate to fund these capital expenditures, the payment of any declared quarterly dividends and our working capital requirements for the next 12 months.

As discussed in Note 16—"Business Acquisitions" to the Consolidated Financial Statements, we completed our acquisition of Nypro during the fourth quarter of fiscal year 2013 by acquiring 100% of the issued and outstanding common shares of Nypro for net aggregate consideration of $679.5 million, which was funded from available cash.

Our $300.0 million North American asset-backed securitization program is scheduled to expire on October 21, 2014 and our $200.0 million foreign asset-backed securitization program is scheduled to expire on May 15, 2015, and we may be unable to renew either of these. Our $200.0 million trade accounts receivable sale agreement is a committed facility that amended and restated an existing uncommitted facility during the first quarter of fiscal year 2013 to change the facility to a committed facility and to reduce the capacity from $250.0 million to $200.0 million. Our $200.0 million trade accounts receivable sale agreement was renewed during the third quarter of fiscal year 2013 and is scheduled to expire on November 30, 2013. Our $150.0 million trade accounts receivable sale agreement is an uncommitted facility that was entered into during the first quarter of fiscal year 2013 and is scheduled to expire on November 28, 2013. Our $40.0 million uncommitted trade accounts receivable sale program is scheduled to expire no later than June 1, 2015, though either party can elect to cancel the agreement by giving prior written notification to the other party of no less than 30 days. We can offer no assurance under the uncommitted sales programs that if we attempt to sell receivables under such programs in the future that we will receive funding from the associated banks which would require us to utilize other available sources of liquidity, including our revolving credit facilities.

Should we desire to consummate significant additional acquisition opportunities or undertake significant additional expansion activities, our capital needs would increase and could possibly result in our need to increase available borrowings under our revolving credit facilities or access public or private debt and equity markets. There can be no assurance, however, that we would be successful in raising additional debt or equity on terms that we would consider acceptable. See "Risk Factors—Our amount of debt could significantly increase in the future."

Contractual Obligations

Our contractual obligations for short and long-term debt arrangements and capital lease obligations; future interest on notes payable, long-term debt and capital lease obligations; future minimum lease payments under non-cancelable operating lease arrangements; non-cancelable purchase order obligations for property, plant and equipment; pension and postretirement contributions and payments and capital commitments as of August 31, 2013 are summarized below. While, as disclosed below, we have certain non-cancelable purchase order obligations for property, plant and equipment, we generally do not enter into non-cancelable purchase orders for materials until we receive a corresponding purchase commitment from our customer. Non-cancelable purchase orders do not typically extend beyond the normal lead time of several weeks at most. Purchase orders beyond this time frame are typically cancelable.

(In thousands)		Payments due by Period			
	Total	Less than 1 Year	1–3 Years	4–5 Years	After 5 Years
Notes payable, long-term debt and capital lease obligations[a]	$1,899,139	$215,536	$331,016	$422,346	$ 930,241
Future interest on notes payable, long-term debt and capital lease obligations[b]	629,125	106,957	209,605	147,137	165,426
Operating lease obligations	408,152	89,451	117,522	78,573	122,606
Non-cancelable purchase order obligations[c]	162,699	159,904	2,795	—	—
Pension and postretirement contributions and payments[d]	19,013	5,260	2,043	2,682	9,028
Capital commitments[e]	1,500	1,500	—	—	—
Total contractual cash obligations[f]	$3,119,628	$578,608	$662,981	$650,738	$1,227,301

[a] The above table excludes a $6.8 million fair value adjustment related to the former interest rate swap on the 7.750% Senior Notes.

[b] Certain of our notes payable, long-term debt and capital lease obligations pay interest at variable rates. In the contractual obligations table above, we have elected to apply estimated interest rates to determine the value of these future interest payments.

[c] Consists of purchase commitments entered into as of August 31, 2013 for property, plant and equipment pursuant to legally enforceable and binding agreements.

[d] Includes the estimated company contributions to funded pension plans during fiscal year 2014 and the expected benefit payments for unfunded pension and postretirement plans from fiscal years 2014 through 2023. These future payments are not recorded on the Consolidated Balance Sheets but will be recorded as incurred.

[e] During the first quarter of fiscal year 2009, we committed $10.0 million to an independent private equity limited partnership which invests in companies that address resource limits in energy, water and materials (commonly referred to as the "CleanTech" sector). Of that amount, we have invested $8.5 million as of August 31, 2013.

[f] At August 31, 2013, we have $10.0 million and $80.4 million recorded as a current and a long-term liability, respectively, for uncertain tax positions. We are not able to reasonably estimate the timing of payments, or the amount by which our liability for these uncertain tax positions will increase or decrease over time, and accordingly, this liability has been excluded from the above table.

6.09 ALLERGAN, INC. (DEC)

MANAGEMENT'S DISCUSSION AND ANALYSIS OF FINANCIAL CONDITION AND RESULTS OF OPERATIONS

Results of Continuing Operations

We operate our business on the basis of two reportable segments—specialty pharmaceuticals and medical devices. The specialty pharmaceuticals segment produces a broad range of pharmaceutical products, including: ophthalmic products for dry eye, glaucoma, inflammation, infection, allergy and retinal disease; *Botox®* for certain therapeutic and aesthetic indications; skin care products for acne, psoriasis, eyelash growth and other prescription and physician-dispensed skin care products; and urologics products. The medical devices segment produces a broad range of medical devices, including: breast implants for augmentation, revision and reconstructive surgery and tissue expanders; and facial aesthetics products. We provide global marketing strategy teams to coordinate the development and execution of a consistent marketing strategy for our products in all geographic regions that share similar distribution channels and customers.

Management evaluates our business segments and various global product portfolios on a revenue basis, which is presented below in accordance with GAAP. We also report sales performance using the non-GAAP financial measure of constant currency sales. Constant currency sales represent current period reported sales, adjusted for the translation effect of changes in average foreign exchange rates between the current period and the corresponding period in the prior year. We calculate the currency effect by comparing adjusted current period reported sales, calculated using the monthly average foreign exchange rates for the corresponding period in the prior year, to the actual current period reported sales. We routinely evaluate our net sales performance at constant currency so that sales results can be viewed without the impact of changing foreign currency exchange rates, thereby facilitating period-to-period comparisons of our sales. Generally, when the U.S. dollar either strengthens or weakens against other currencies, the growth at constant currency rates will be higher or lower, respectively, than growth reported at actual exchange rates.

The following table compares net sales by product line within each reportable segment and certain selected pharmaceutical products for the years ended December 31, 2013, 2012 and 2011:

	Year Ended December 31,		Change in Product Net Sales			Percent Change in Product Net Sales		
	2013	**2012**	**Total**	**Performance**	**Currency**	**Total**	**Performance**	**Currency**
			(In millions)					
Net sales by product line:								
Specialty pharmaceuticals:								
Eye care pharmaceuticals	$2,890.3	$2,692.2	$198.1	$216.2	$(18.1)	7.4%	8.0%	(0.6)%
Botox®/Neuromodulator	1,982.2	1,766.3	215.9	233.6	(17.7)	12.2%	13.2%	(1.0)%
Skin care and other	466.5	326.1	140.4	140.9	(0.5)	43.1%	43.2%	(0.1)%
Total specialty pharmaceuticals	5,339.0	4,784.6	554.4	590.7	(36.3)	11.6%	12.3%	(0.7)%
Medical devices:								
Breast aesthetics	377.9	377.1	0.8	2.1	(1.3)	0.2%	0.6%	(0.4)%
Facial aesthetics	477.5	387.6	89.9	93.4	(3.5)	23.2%	24.1%	(0.9)%
Core medical devices	855.4	764.7	90.7	95.5	(4.8)	11.9%	12.5%	(0.6)%
Other	3.1	—	3.1	3.1	—	N/A	N/A	N/A
Total medical devices	858.5	764.7	93.8	98.6	(4.8)	12.3%	12.9%	(0.6)%
Total product net sales	$6,197.5	$5,549.3	$648.2	$689.3	$(41.1)	11.7%	12.4%	(0.7)%
Domestic product net sales	62.0%	60.9%						
International product net sales	38.0%	39.1%						
Selected product net sales[a]:								
Alphagan® P, *Alphagan®* and *Combigan®*	$ 474.1	$ 453.2	$ 20.9	$ 24.1	$ (3.2)	4.6%	5.3%	(0.7)%
Lumigan® Franchise	625.3	622.6	2.7	1.7	1.0	0.4%	0.3%	0.1%
Total glaucoma products	1,108.5	1,085.8	22.7	25.3	(2.6)	2.1%	2.3%	(0.2)%
Restasis®	940.0	792.0	148.0	150.3	(2.3)	18.7%	19.0%	(0.3)%
Latisse®	100.0	97.3	2.7	3.1	(0.4)	2.7%	3.2%	(0.5)%

(continued)

	Year Ended December 31, 2012	2011	Change in Product Net Sales — Total (In millions)	Performance	Currency	Percent Change in Product Net Sales — Total	Performance	Currency
Net sales by product line:								
Specialty pharmaceuticals:								
Eye care pharmaceuticals	$2,692.2	$2,520.2	$172.0	$244.2	$(72.2)	6.8%	9.7%	(2.9)%
Botox®/Neuromodulator	1,766.3	1,594.9	171.4	202.1	(30.7)	10.7%	12.7%	(2.0)%
Skin care and other	326.1	316.9	9.2	9.7	(0.5)	2.9%	3.1%	(0.2)%
Total specialty pharmaceuticals	4,784.6	4,432.0	352.6	456.0	(103.4)	8.0%	10.3%	(2.3)%
Medical devices:								
Breast aesthetics	377.1	349.3	27.8	36.8	(9.0)	8.0%	10.5%	(2.5)%
Facial aesthetics	387.6	362.7	24.9	35.8	(10.9)	6.9%	9.9%	(3.0)%
Total medical devices	764.7	712.0	52.7	72.6	(19.9)	7.4%	10.2%	(2.8)%
Total product net sales	$5,549.3	$5,144.0	$405.3	$528.6	$(123.3)	7.9%	10.3%	(2.4)%
Domestic product net sales	60.9%	60.0%						
International product net sales	39.1%	40.0%						
Selected product net sales[a]:								
Alphagan® P, *Alphagan*® and *Combigan*®	$453.2	$419.4	$33.8	$44.4	$(10.6)	8.1%	10.6%	(2.5)%
Lumigan® Franchise	622.6	612.7	9.9	29.8	(19.9)	1.6%	4.9%	(3.3)%
Total glaucoma products	1,085.8	1,042.9	42.9	74.1	(31.2)	4.1%	7.1%	(3.0)%
Restasis®	792.0	697.1	94.9	97.1	(2.2)	13.6%	13.9%	(0.3)%
Latisse®	97.3	93.6	3.7	4.2	(0.5)	4.0%	4.5%	(0.5)%

[a] Percentage change in selected product net sales is calculated on amounts reported to the nearest whole dollar. Total glaucoma products include the *Alphagan*® and *Lumigan*® franchises.

Product Net Sales (in part)

Foreign currency changes decreased product net sales by $41.1 million in 2013 compared to 2012, primarily due to the weakening of the Brazilian real, Canadian dollar, Australian dollar, Turkish lira and Indian rupee compared to the U.S. dollar, partially offset by the strengthening of the euro compared to the U.S. dollar.

Eye care pharmaceuticals product net sales increased in 2012 compared to 2011 in the United States, Canada, Europe and Asia Pacific. Net sales of eye care pharmaceutical products in Latin America decreased in 2012 compared to 2011 due to the negative translation effect of average foreign currency exchange rates in effect during 2012 compared to 2011. When measured at constant currency, net sales of eye care pharmaceutical products in Latin America increased in 2012 compared to 2011.

Total sales of *Botox*® increased in 2012 compared to 2011 due to strong growth in sales for both therapeutic and cosmetic uses. Sales of *Botox*® for therapeutic use increased in the United States due to strong growth in sales for the prophylactic treatment of headaches in adults with chronic migraine, urinary incontinence in adults with neurological conditions, and upper limb spasticity. Sales of *Botox*® for therapeutic use also increased in Latin America and Asia Pacific. Sales of *Botox*® for cosmetic use increased in all of our principal geographic markets. Sales of *Botox*® in international markets were negatively affected by the translation effect of average foreign currency exchange rates in effect during 2012 compared to 2011. When measured at constant currency, total sales of *Botox*® increased in Europe in 2012 compared to 2011. Based on internal information and assumptions, we estimate in 2012 that *Botox*® therapeutic sales accounted for approximately 52% of total consolidated *Botox*® sales and increased by approximately 13% compared to 2011. In 2012, *Botox*® Cosmetic sales accounted for approximately 48% of total consolidated *Botox*® sales and increased by approximately 8% compared to 2011.

Breast aesthetics product net sales, which consist primarily of sales of silicone gel and saline breast implants and tissue expanders, increased in 2012 compared to 2011 due to increases in sales in all of our principal geographic markets. The increase in sales of breast aesthetics products in the United States was primarily due to higher implant and tissue expander unit volume and favorable product mix due to the continued transition of the U.S. market to higher priced tissue expanders and silicone gel products from lower priced saline products, partially offset by a small decline in market share due to the entrance of a new competitor in the U.S. market. The overall increase in sales of breast aesthetics products in our international markets was primarily due to higher unit volume, offset by the negative translation effect of average foreign currency exchange rates in effect during 2012 compared to 2011.

Facial aesthetics product net sales, which consist primarily of sales of hyaluronic acid-based dermal fillers used to correct facial wrinkles, increased in 2012 compared to 2011 primarily due to strong growth in sales in Europe and Asia Pacific. The increase in international sales of facial aesthetics products was due primarily to the recent launch of *Juvéderm*® *Voluma*™ with lidocaine in a number of countries in Europe and Asia, partially offset by the negative translation effect of average foreign currency exchange rates in effect during 2012 compared to

2011. Sales of facial aesthetics products in the United States increased slightly in 2012 compared to 2011, primarily due to overall growth in unit volume in the dermal filler market, partially offset by increased rebate activity.

Foreign currency changes decreased product net sales by $123.3 million in 2012 compared to 2011, primarily due to the weakening of the euro, Brazilian real, Mexican peso, Canadian dollar, Turkish lira and Indian rupee compared to the U.S. dollar.

U.S. product net sales as a percentage of total product net sales increased by 0.9 percentage points to 60.9% in 2012 compared to U.S. sales of 60.0% in 2011, due primarily to higher sales growth in the U.S. market compared to our international markets for our *Botox*® product line, an increase in sales of our skin care and other products, which are highly concentrated in the United States, and the negative overall translation impact on international sales due to a general weakening of foreign currencies compared to the U.S. dollar in markets where we sold products in 2012 compared to 2011, partially offset by higher sales growth, when measured at constant currency, in international markets compared to the U.S. market for our facial aesthetics, breast aesthetics and eye care pharmaceuticals product lines.

Liquidity and Capital Resources (in part)

Foreign Currency Fluctuations

Approximately 38.0% of our product net sales in 2013 were derived from operations outside the United States, and a portion of our international cost structure is denominated in currencies other than the U.S. dollar. As a result, we are subject to fluctuations in sales and earnings reported in U.S. dollars due to changing currency exchange rates. We routinely monitor our transaction exposure to currency rates and implement certain economic hedging strategies to limit such exposure, as we deem appropriate. The net impact of foreign currency fluctuations on our sales was a decrease of $41.1 million and $123.3 million in 2013 and 2012, respectively. The 2013 sales decrease included $20.1 million related to the Brazilian real, $9.5 million related to the Australian dollar, $7.5 million related to the Canadian dollar, $5.0 million related to the Turkish lira, $4.4 million related to the Indian rupee, $2.3 million related to the U.K. pound and $7.8 million related to other currencies, partially offset by an increase of $15.5 million related to the euro. The 2012 sales decrease included $62.3 million related to the euro, $32.3 million related to the Brazilian real, $6.4 million related to the Indian rupee, $5.0 million related to the Turkish lira, $3.4 million related to the Mexican peso, $2.9 million related to the Canadian dollar, $2.0 million related to the U.K. pound and $9.0 million related to other currencies. See Note 1, "Summary of Significant Accounting Policies," in the notes to the consolidated financial statements listed under Item 15 of Part IV of this report, "Exhibits and Financial Statement Schedules," for a description of our accounting policy on foreign currency translation.

QUANTITATIVE AND QUALITATIVE DISCLOSURES ABOUT MARKET RISK

Foreign Currency Risk

Overall, we are a net recipient of currencies other than the U.S. dollar and, as such, benefit from a weaker dollar and are adversely affected by a stronger dollar relative to major currencies worldwide. Accordingly, changes in exchange rates, and in particular a strengthening of the U.S. dollar, may negatively affect our consolidated revenues or operating costs and expenses as expressed in U.S. dollars.

From time to time, we enter into foreign currency option and forward contracts to reduce earnings and cash flow volatility associated with foreign exchange rate changes to allow our management to focus its attention on our core business issues. Accordingly, we enter into various contracts which change in value as foreign exchange rates change to economically offset the effect of changes in the value of foreign currency assets and liabilities, commitments and anticipated foreign currency denominated sales and operating expenses. We enter into foreign currency option and forward contracts in amounts between minimum and maximum anticipated foreign exchange exposures, generally for periods not to exceed 24 months.

We use foreign currency option contracts, which provide for the sale or purchase of foreign currencies, to economically hedge the currency exchange risks associated with probable but not firmly committed transactions that arise in the normal course of our business. Probable but not firmly committed transactions are comprised primarily of sales of products and purchases of raw material in currencies other than the U.S. dollar. The foreign currency option contracts are entered into to reduce the volatility of earnings generated in currencies other than the U.S. dollar, primarily earnings denominated in the Canadian dollar, Mexican peso, Australian dollar, Brazilian real, euro, Korean won, Turkish lira, Polish zloty, Swiss franc, Russian ruble, Swedish krona, South African rand and Japanese yen. While these instruments are subject to fluctuations in value, such fluctuations are anticipated to offset changes in the value of the underlying exposures. Changes in the fair value of open foreign currency option contracts and any realized gains (losses) on settled contracts are recorded through earnings as "Other, net" in the accompanying consolidated statements of earnings. The premium costs of purchased foreign exchange option contracts are recorded in "Other current assets" and amortized to "Other, net" over the life of the options.

All of our outstanding foreign exchange forward contracts are entered into to offset the change in value of certain intercompany receivables or payables that are subject to fluctuations in foreign currency exchange rates. The realized and unrealized gains and losses from foreign currency forward contracts and the revaluation of the foreign denominated intercompany receivables or payables are recorded through "Other, net" in the accompanying consolidated statements of earnings.

The following table provides information about our foreign currency derivative financial instruments outstanding as of December 31, 2013 and 2012. The information is provided in U.S. dollars, as presented in our consolidated financial statements:

	December 31, 2013		December 31, 2012	
	Notional Amount (In millions)	Average Contract Rate or Strike Amount	Notional Amount (In millions)	Average Contract Rate or Strike Amount
Foreign currency forward contracts:				
(Receive U.S. dollar/pay foreign currency)				
Japanese yen	$ 9.2	103.02	$ 8.3	83.88
Australian dollar	9.3	0.88	17.3	1.05
Russian ruble	16.5	33.42	17.9	31.31
Polish zloty	—	—	1.1	3.14
	$ 35.0		$ 44.6	
Estimated fair value	$ 0.1		$ 0.3	
Foreign currency forward contracts:				
(Pay U.S. dollar/receive foreign currency)				
Euro	$ 41.3	1.38	$ 39.6	1.32
Estimated fair value	$ 0.1		$ —	
Foreign currency sold—put options:				
Canadian dollar	$ 95.4	1.04	$105.6	1.02
Mexican peso	17.7	13.12	17.8	13.10
Australian dollar	44.8	0.92	67.9	1.00
Brazilian real	29.7	2.42	45.5	2.14
Euro	245.5	1.36	168.0	1.29
Korean won	18.5	1,062.71	20.1	1,086.16
Turkish lira	32.7	2.13	27.0	1.83
Polish zloty	9.7	3.08	8.7	3.19
Swiss franc	9.5	0.88	8.6	0.92
Russian ruble	17.0	34.09	10.6	31.74
Swedish krona	6.8	6.57	9.7	6.70
South African rand	11.0	10.72	12.1	8.94
Japanese yen	22.5	102.75	—	—
	$560.8		$501.6	
Estimated fair value	$ 20.2		$ 9.9	

NOTES TO CONSOLIDATED FINANCIAL STATEMENTS

Note 1: Summary of Significant Accounting Policies (in part)

Foreign Currency Translation

The financial position and results of operations of the Company's foreign subsidiaries are generally determined using local currency as the functional currency. Assets and liabilities of these subsidiaries are translated at the exchange rate in effect at each year end. Income statement accounts are translated at the average rate of exchange prevailing during the year. Adjustments arising from the use of differing exchange rates from period to period are included in accumulated other comprehensive loss in equity. Aggregate net realized and unrealized (losses) gains resulting from foreign currency transactions and derivative contracts of approximately $(7.4) million, $(23.4) million and $0.3 million for the years ended December 31, 2013, 2012 and 2011, respectively, are included in "Other, net" in the Company's consolidated statements of earnings.

INTEREST AND INCOME TAX PAYMENTS

6.10 ORACLE CORPORATION (MAY)
CONSOLIDATED STATEMENTS OF CASH FLOWS (in part)

| | Year Ended May 31, | | |
(In millions)	**2013**	**2012**	**2011**
Net cash provided by operating activities	14,224	13,743	11,214
Net cash used for investing activities	(5,956)	(8,381)	(6,081)
Net cash (used for) provided by financing activities	(8,500)	(6,099)	516
Effect of exchange rate changes on cash and cash equivalents	(110)	(471)	600
Net (decrease) increase in cash and cash equivalents	(342)	(1,208)	6,249
Cash and cash equivalents at beginning of period	14,955	16,163	9,914
Cash and cash equivalents at end of period	$14,613	$14,955	$16,163
Non-cash investing and financing transactions:			
Fair value of stock options and restricted stock-based awards assumed in connection with acquisitions	$ 15	$ 29	$ 17
Fair value of contingent consideration payable in connection with acquisition	$ —	$ 346	$ —
(Decrease) increase in unsettled repurchases of common stock	$ (27)	$ 112	$ 12
Supplemental schedule of cash flow data:			
Cash paid for income taxes	$ 2,644	$ 2,731	$ 2,931
Cash paid for interest	$ 781	$ 737	$ 770

6.11 TEXTRON INC. (DEC)
CONSOLIDATED STATEMENTS OF CASH FLOWS (in part)

| | Consolidated | | |
(In millions)	**2013**	**2012**	**2011**
Net cash provided by operating activities	810	927	1,063
Net cash provided by (used in) investing activities	(264)	378	843
Net cash used in financing activities	(742)	(781)	(1,951)
Effect of exchange rate changes on cash and equivalents	(6)	4	(1)
Net increase (decrease) in cash and equivalents	(202)	528	(46)
Cash and equivalents at beginning of year	1,413	885	931
Cash and equivalents at end of year	$1,211	$1,413	$ 885

NOTES TO THE CONSOLIDATED FINANCIAL STATEMENTS

Note 14. Supplemental Cash Flow Information

We have made the following cash payments:

(In millions)	**2013**	**2012**	**2011**
Interest paid:			
Manufacturing group	$124	$135	$135
Finance group	46	64	89
Net taxes paid /(received):			
Manufacturing group	223	(7)	30
Finance group	(49)	43	(65)

Cash paid for interest by the Finance group included amounts paid to the Manufacturing group of $11 million and $26 million in 2012 and 2011, respectively. Cash paid for interest by the Finance group to the Manufacturing group was not significant in 2013.

In 2012, net taxes paid by the Finance group included a payment of $111 million primarily from a settlement related to the IRS's challenge of tax deductions claimed in prior years for certain leveraged lease transactions.

6.12 PFIZER INC. (DEC)

CONSOLIDATED STATEMENTS OF CASH FLOWS (in part)

(Millions)	Year Ended December 31,		
	2013	2012	2011
Net cash provided by operating activities	17,765	16,746	20,240
Net cash provided by/(used in) investing activities	(10,625)	6,154	1,843
Financing Activities			
Proceeds from short-term borrowings	4,323	7,995	12,810
Principal payments on short-term borrowings	(4,234)	(8,177)	(13,276)
Net proceeds from/(payments on) short-term borrowings with original maturities of 90 days or less	3,475	(30)	1,910
Proceeds from issuance of long-term debt[a]	6,618	—	—
Principal payments on long-term debt	(4,146)	(1,513)	(6,986)
Purchases of common stock	(16,290)	(8,228)	(9,000)
Cash dividends paid	(6,580)	(6,534)	(6,234)
Proceeds from exercise of stock options	1,750	568	153
Other financing activities	109	(80)	16
Net cash used in financing activities	(14,975)	(15,999)	(20,607)
Effect of exchange-rate changes on cash and cash equivalents	(63)	(2)	(29)
Net increase/(decrease) in cash and cash equivalents	(7,898)	6,899	1,447
Cash and cash equivalents, beginning	10,081	3,182	1,735
Cash and cash equivalents, end	$ 2,183	$10,081	$ 3,182

	Year Ended December 31,		
	2013	2012	2011
Supplemental Cash Flow Information			
Non-cash transactions:			
Sale of subsidiary common stock (Zoetis) for Pfizer common stock[b]	$11,408	$ —	$ —
Exchange of subsidiary common stock (Zoetis) for the retirement of Pfizer commercial paper issued in 2013[b]	2,479	—	—
Exchange of subsidiary senior notes (Zoetis) for the retirement of Pfizer commercial paper issued in 2012[b]	992	—	—
Transfer of certain product rights to an equity-method investment (Hisun Pfizer)[c]	1,233	—	—
Contribution of an investment in connection with the resolution of a legal matter (Quigley)[d]	447	—	—
Cash paid during the period for:			
Income taxes	$ 2,874	$ 2,409	$ 2,927
Interest	1,729	1,873	2,085

[a] Includes $2.6 billion from the issuance of senior notes by Zoetis (our former Animal Health subsidiary), net of the $1.0 billion non-cash exchange of Zoetis senior notes for the retirement of Pfizer commercial paper issued in 2012. See *Note 2B. Acquisitions, Divestitures, Collaborative Arrangements and Equity-Method Investments: Divestitures.*

[b] Relates to Zoetis (our former Animal Health subsidiary). See *Note 2B. Acquisitions, Divestitures, Collaborative Arrangements and Equity-Method Investments: Divestitures.*

[c] See *Note 2D. Acquisitions, Divestitures, Collaborative Arrangements and Equity-Method Investments: Equity-Method Investments.*

[d] See *Note 17A5. Commitments and Contingencies: Legal Proceedings—Certain Matters Resolved During 2013.*

NOTES TO CONSOLIDATED FINANCIAL STATEMENTS

Note 2. Acquisitions, Divestitures, Collaborative Arrangements and Equity-Method Investments (in part)

B. Divestitures (in part)

Animal Health Business—Zoetis Inc.

On June 24, 2013, we completed the full disposition of our Animal Health business. The full disposition was completed through a series of steps, including the formation of Zoetis, an initial public offering (IPO) of an approximate 19.8% interest in Zoetis and an exchange offer for the remaining 80.2% interest.

Formation of Zoetis—On January 28, 2013, our then wholly owned subsidiary, Zoetis, issued $3.65 billion aggregate principal amount of senior notes. Also, on January 28, 2013, we transferred to Zoetis substantially all of the assets and liabilities of our Animal Health business in exchange for all of the Class A and Class B common stock of Zoetis, $1.0 billion of the $3.65 billion of Zoetis senior notes, and an amount of cash equal to substantially all of the cash proceeds received by Zoetis from the remaining $2.65 billion of senior notes issued. The $1.0 billion of Zoetis senior notes received by Pfizer were exchanged by Pfizer for the retirement of Pfizer commercial paper issued in 2012, and the cash proceeds received by Pfizer of approximately $2.6 billion were used for dividends and stock buybacks.

Initial Public Offering (19.8% Interest)—On February 6, 2013, an IPO of the Class A common stock of Zoetis was completed, pursuant to which we sold 99.015 million shares of Class A common stock of Zoetis (all of the Class A common stock, including shares sold pursuant to the underwriters' overallotment option to purchase additional shares, which was exercised in full) in exchange for the retirement of approximately $2.5 billion of Pfizer commercial paper issued in 2013. The Class A common stock sold in the IPO represented approximately 19.8% of the total outstanding Zoetis shares. The excess of the consideration received over the net book value of our divested interest was approximately $2.3 billion and was recorded in *Additional paid-in capital*.

Exchange Offer (80.2% Interest)—On June 24, 2013, we exchanged all of our remaining interest in Zoetis, 400.985 million shares of Class A common stock of Zoetis (after converting all of our Class B common stock into Class A common stock, representing approximately 80.2% of the total outstanding Zoetis shares), for approximately 405.117 million outstanding shares of Pfizer common stock on a tax-free basis pursuant to an exchange offer made to Pfizer shareholders. The $11.4 billion of Pfizer common stock received in the exchange transaction was recorded in *Treasury stock* and was valued using the opening price of Pfizer common stock on June 24, 2013, the date we accepted the Zoetis shares for exchange. The gain on the sale of the remaining interest in Zoetis was approximately $10.3 billion, net of income taxes resulting from certain legal entity reorganizations, and was recorded in *Gain on disposal of discontinued operations—net of tax* in the consolidated statement of income for the year ended December 31, 2013.

In summary, as a result of the above transactions, we received cash and were relieved of debt obligations in the aggregate amount of approximately $6.1 billion and received shares of Pfizer common stock (held in *Treasury stock*) valued at approximately $11.4 billion.

The operating results of the animal health business are reported as *Income from discontinued operations—net of tax* in the consolidated statements of income through June 24, 2013, the date of disposal. In addition, in the consolidated balance sheet as of December 31, 2012, the assets and liabilities associated with this business are classified as *Assets of discontinued operations and other assets held for sale* and *Liabilities of discontinued operations*, as appropriate. Prior-period financial information has been restated, as appropriate.

In connection with the above transactions, we entered into a transitional services agreement (TSA) and manufacturing and supply agreements (MSAs) with Zoetis that are designed to facilitate the orderly transfer of business operations to the standalone Zoetis entity. The TSA relates primarily to administrative services, which are generally to be provided within 24 months. Under the MSAs, we will manufacture and supply certain animal health products to Zoetis for a transitional period of up to 5 years, with an ability to extend, if necessary, upon mutual agreement of both parties. These agreements are not material and none confers upon us the ability to influence the operating and/or financial policies of Zoetis subsequent to June 24, 2013, the full disposition date.

Total Discontinued Operations

The following table provides the components of *Discontinued operations—net of tax* :

(Millions of dollars)	Year Ended December 31,[a]		
	2013	**2012**	**2011**
Revenues	$ 2,201	$6,587	$6,897
Pre-tax income from discontinued operations[a]	408	1,253	1,310
Provision for taxes on income[b]	100	459	425
Income from discontinued operations—net of tax	308	794	885
Pre-tax gain on sale of discontinued operations	10,446	7,123	1,688
Provision for taxes on income[c]	92	2,340	384
Gain on disposal of discontinued operations—net of tax	10,354	4,783	1,304
Discontinued operations—net of tax	$10,662	$5,577	$2,189

[a] Includes (i) the Animal Health (Zoetis) business through June 24, 2013, the date of disposal, (ii) the Nutrition business through November 30, 2012, the date of disposal and (iii) the Capsugel business through August 1, 2011, the date of disposal.

[b] Includes a deferred tax benefit of $23 million for 2013 and $23 million for 2012, and a deferred tax expense of $28 million for 2011, which is net of a deferred tax expense of $42 million in 2012, and includes a deferred tax expense of $6 million in 2011 related to investments in certain foreign subsidiaries, resulting from our intention not to hold these subsidiaries indefinitely.

[c] For 2013, primarily reflects income tax expense of $122 million resulting from certain legal entity reorganizations. For 2012 and 2011, includes a deferred tax expense of $1.4 billion for 2012 and $190 million for 2011, which includes a deferred tax expense of $2.2 billion for 2012 and $190 million for 2011 on certain current-year funds earned outside the U.S. that will not be indefinitely reinvested overseas. For 2012, also includes a deferred tax benefit reflecting the reversal of net deferred tax liabilities associated with the divested Nutrition assets.

D. Equity-Method Investments (in part)

Investment in Hisun Pfizer Pharmaceuticals Company Limited (Hisun Pfizer)

On September 6, 2012, we and Zhejiang Hisun Pharmaceuticals Co., Ltd., a leading pharmaceutical company in China, formed a new company, Hisun Pfizer, to develop, manufacture, market and sell pharmaceutical products, primarily branded generic products, predominately in China. Hisun Pfizer was established with registered capital of $250 million, of which our portion was $122.5 million. On

January 1, 2013, both parties transferred selected employees to Hisun Pfizer and contributed, among other things, certain rights to commercialized products and products in development, intellectual property rights, and facilities, equipment and distribution/customer contracts. Our contributions in 2013 constituted a business, as defined by U.S. GAAP, and included, among other things, the China rights to certain commercialized products and other products not yet commercialized and all associated intellectual property rights. As a result of the contributions from both parties, Hisun Pfizer holds a broad portfolio of branded generics covering cardiovascular disease, infectious disease, oncology, mental health, and other therapeutic areas. We hold a 49% equity interest in Hisun Pfizer.

We also entered into certain transition agreements designed to ensure and facilitate the orderly transfer of the business operations to Hisun Pfizer, primarily the Pfizer Products Transition Period Agreement and a related supply and promotional services agreement. These agreements provide for a profit margin on the manufacturing services provided by Pfizer to Hisun Pfizer and govern the supply, promotion and distribution of Pfizer products until Hisun Pfizer begins its own manufacturing and distribution. While intended to be transitional, these agreements may be extended by mutual agreement of the parties for several years and, possibly, indefinitely. These agreements are not material to Pfizer, and none confers upon us any additional ability to influence the operating and/or financial policies of Hisun Pfizer.

In connection with our contributions in the first quarter of 2013, we recognized a pre-tax gain of approximately $459 million in *Other (income)/deductions—net*, reflecting the transfer of the business to Hisun Pfizer (including an allocation of goodwill from our Emerging Markets reporting unit as part of the carrying amount of the business transferred). Since we hold a 49% interest in Hisun Pfizer, we have an indirect retained interest in the contributed assets; as such, 49% of the gain, or $225 million, represents the portion of the gain associated with that indirect retained interest.

In valuing our investment in Hisun Pfizer (which includes the indirect retained interest in the contributed assets), we used discounted cash flow techniques, utilizing a 11.5% discount rate, reflecting our best estimate of the various risks inherent in the projected cash flows, and a nominal terminal year growth factor. Some of the more significant estimates and assumptions inherent in this approach include: the amount and timing of the projected net cash flows, which include the expected impact of competitive, legal and/or regulatory forces on the products; the long-term growth rate, which seeks to project the sustainable growth rate over the long-term; and the discount rate, which seeks to reflect the various risks inherent in the projected cash flows, including country risk.

We are accounting for our interest in Hisun Pfizer as an equity-method investment, due to the significant influence we have over the operations of Hisun Pfizer through our board representation, minority veto rights and 49% voting interest. Our investment in Hisun Pfizer is reported as a private equity investment in *Long-term investments*, and our share of Hisun Pfizer's net income is recorded in *Other (income)/deductions—net*. As of December 31, 2013, the carrying value of our investment in Hisun Pfizer is approximately $1.4 billion, and the amount of our underlying equity in the net assets of Hisun Pfizer is approximately $770 million. The excess of the carrying value of our investment over our underlying equity in the net assets of Hisun Pfizer has been allocated, within the investment account, to goodwill and other intangible assets. The amount allocated to other intangible assets is being amortized into *Other (income)/deductions—net* over an average estimated useful life of 25 years.

Note 17. Commitments and Contingencies (in part)

A5. Legal Proceedings—Certain Matters Resolved During 2013 (in part)

During 2013, certain matters, including those discussed below, were resolved or substantially resolved or were the subject of definitive settlement agreements or settlement agreements-in-principle.

Asbestos—Quigley

Quigley Company, Inc. (Quigley or, subsequent to the effectiveness of the amended reorganization plan on November 4, 2013, Reorganized Quigley), a wholly owned subsidiary, was acquired by Pfizer in 1968 and sold products containing small amounts of asbestos until the early 1970s. In September 2004, Pfizer and Quigley took steps that were intended to resolve all pending and future claims against Pfizer and Quigley in which the claimants allege personal injury from exposure to Quigley products containing asbestos, silica or mixed dust. We recorded a charge of $369 million pre-tax ($229 million after-tax) in the third quarter of 2004 in connection with these matters.

In September 2004, Quigley filed a petition in the U.S. Bankruptcy Court for the Southern District of New York seeking reorganization under Chapter 11 of the U.S. Bankruptcy Code. In March 2005, Quigley filed a reorganization plan in the Bankruptcy Court. In connection with that filing, Pfizer entered into settlement agreements with lawyers representing more than 80% of the individuals with claims related to Quigley products against Quigley and Pfizer. The agreements provide for a total of $430 million in payments, of which $215 million became due in December 2005 and has been and is being paid to claimants upon receipt by Pfizer of certain required documentation from each of the claimants. The reorganization plan provided for the establishment of a trust (the Asbestos Personal Injury Trust) for the evaluation and, as appropriate, payment of all unsettled pending claims, as well as any future claims alleging injury from exposure to Quigley products.

In September 2010, the Bankruptcy Court declined to confirm the amended reorganization plan. As a result, Pfizer recorded additional charges for this matter of approximately $1.3 billion pre-tax (approximately $800 million after-tax) in 2010.

In March 2011, Pfizer entered into a settlement agreement with a committee (the Ad Hoc Committee) representing approximately 40,000 claimants in the Quigley bankruptcy proceeding (the Ad Hoc Committee claimants). Pursuant to the settlement agreement and consistent with the charges previously recorded with respect to Quigley, Pfizer, among other things, paid an aggregate of $800 million to the Ad Hoc Committee for the benefit of the Ad Hoc Committee claimants.

In July 2013, the Bankruptcy Court entered an order confirming the amended reorganization plan, and the District Court entered an order issuing an injunction directing pending and future claims alleging asbestos-related personal injury from exposure to Quigley products to the Asbestos Personal Injury Trust, with certain exceptions. The District Court's judgment on its order became final and non-appealable on October 17, 2013. The amended reorganization plan became effective on November 4, 2013, at which time, consistent with the charges previously recorded with respect to Quigley, we contributed an additional amount of cash (approximately $277 million), a money market investment valued at approximately $447 million and non-cash items (including an insurance receivable, insurance policies valued at face value, a business operation and the value of certain debt forgiveness) to Reorganized Quigley and the Asbestos Personal Injury Trust with a total value of approximately $1.08 billion; the value of the non-cash items was finalized and approved by the Bankruptcy Court.

Cash Flows From Operating Activities

PRESENTATION

6.13 FASB ASC 230-10-45 defines those transactions and events that constitute operating cash receipts and payments. Cash inflows from operating activities include the following:
- Cash receipts from sales of goods or services, including receipts from the collection or sale of accounts and both short- and long-term notes receivable from customers arising from those sales. Goods include certain loans and other debt and equity instruments of other entities that are acquired specifically for resale.
- Cash receipts from returns on loans, other debt instruments of other entities, and equity securities—interest and dividends.
- All other cash receipts that do not stem from transactions defined as investing or financing activities, such as amounts received to settle lawsuits; proceeds of insurance settlements, except for those that are directly related to investing or financing activities, such as from destruction of a building; and refunds from suppliers.

Cash outflows from operating activities include the following:
- Cash payments to acquire materials for manufacture or goods for resale, including principal payments on accounts and both short- and long-term notes payable to suppliers for those materials or goods. Goods include certain loans and other debt and equity instruments of other entities that are acquired specifically for resale.
- Cash payments to other suppliers and employees for other goods or services.
- Cash payments to governments for taxes, duties, fines, and other fees or penalties and the cash that would have been paid for income taxes if increases in the value of equity instruments issued under share-based payment arrangements that are not included in the cost of goods or services recognizable for financial reporting purposes also had not been deductible in determining taxable income.
- Cash payments to lenders and other creditors for interest.
- Cash payment made to settle an asset retirement obligation.
- All other cash payments that do not stem from transactions defined as investing or financing activities, such as payments to settle lawsuits, cash contributions to charities, and cash refunds to customers.

6.14 Entities can present operating activities using either the direct or indirect method. However, FASB ASC 230-10-45-30 also requires entities using the direct method to provide a reconciliation of net income to net cash flow from operating activities in a separate schedule.

6.15 FASB ASC 230-10-45-28 also notes that when reconciling net income to net cash flow from operating activities, a business entity should adjust net income to remove past operating cash receipts and payments and accruals of expected future operating cash receipts and payments, including changes during the period in inventory and receivables and payables pertaining to operating activities. Additionally, all items that are included in net income, such as depreciation and amortization expense, that do not affect net cash provided from, or used for, operating activities should be adjusted for.

PRESENTATION AND DISCLOSURE EXCERPTS

DIRECT METHOD

6.16 FIRST SOLAR, INC. (DEC)
CONSOLIDATED STATEMENTS OF CASH FLOWS

(In thousands)

	Years Ended December 31,		
	2013	**2012**	**2011**
Cash Flows from Operating Activities:			
Cash received from customers	$ 3,868,540	$ 3,231,268	$ 2,290,944
Cash paid to suppliers and associates	(2,973,855)	(2,447,337)	(2,159,429)
Interest received	6,599	4,693	10,156
Interest paid	(9,289)	(19,916)	(14,229)
Income tax refunds (payments), net	1,550	21,543	(46,153)
Excess tax benefit from share-based compensation arrangements	(35,076)	(27,373)	(110,836)
Other operating activities	(2,343)	(669)	(3,916)
Net cash provided by (used in) operating activities	856,126	762,209	(33,463)
Cash Flows from Investing Activities:			
Purchases of property, plant and equipment	(282,576)	(379,228)	(731,814)
Proceeds from sale of property, plant and equipment	116,403	5,083	632
Purchases of marketable securities	(435,015)	(29,200)	(331,240)
Proceeds from maturities and sales of marketable securities	93,984	108,663	492,613
Investment in note receivable, affiliate	—	(21,659)	—
Payments received on note receivable, affiliate	17,108	4,498	—
Purchase of restricted investments	—	(80,667)	(62,749)
Change in restricted cash	5,173	16,215	(23,154)
Acquisitions, net of cash acquired	(30,745)	(2,437)	(21,105)
Purchase of equity and cost method investments	(17,905)	(5,000)	—
Other investing activities	(3,533)	—	360
Net cash used in investing activities	(537,106)	(383,732)	(676,457)
Cash Flows from Financing Activities:			
Proceeds from stock option exercises	1,054	176	8,326
Repayment of borrowings under revolving credit facility	(605,000)	(1,305,000)	(450,000)
Proceeds from borrowings under revolving credit facility	335,000	1,375,000	550,000
Repayment of long-term debt	(64,954)	(178,842)	(33,796)
Proceeds from borrowings under long-term debt, net of discount and issuance costs	—	—	370,108
Excess tax benefit from share-based compensation arrangements	35,076	27,373	110,836
(Repayment of) proceeds from economic development funding	(8,315)	(6,820)	16,188
Proceeds from equity offering, net of issuance costs	428,190	—	—
Contingent consideration payments and other financing activities	(19,887)	(996)	(444)
Net cash provided by (used in) financing activities	101,164	(89,109)	571,218
Effect of exchange rate changes on cash and cash equivalents	3,594	6,307	(21,368)
Net increase (decrease) in cash and cash equivalents	423,778	295,675	(160,070)
Cash and cash equivalents, beginning of the period	901,294	605,619	765,689
Cash and cash equivalents, end of the period	$ 1,325,072	$ 901,294	$ 605,619
Supplemental Disclosure of Noncash Investing and Financing Activities:			
Property, plant and equipment acquisitions funded by liabilities	$ 60,677	$ 62,344	$ 74,391
Acquisitions funded by liabilities and contingent consideration	$ 97,885	$ —	$ —
Shares issued for acquisition	$ 83,755	$ —	$ —
Settlement of long-term debt	$ —	$ 4,802	$ —

22. Statement of Cash Flows

The following table presents a reconciliation of net income (loss) to net cash provided by (used in) operating activities for the years ended December 31, 2013, 2012, and 2011 (in thousands):

	2013	2012	2011
Net income (loss)	$ 353,038	$ (96,338)	$ (39,493)
Adjustments to reconcile net income (loss) to cash provided by (used in) operating activities:			
Depreciation, amortization and accretion	234,370	262,716	235,231
Impairment and net loss on disposal of long-lived assets	97,132	356,522	57,414
Impairment of project assets	—	3,253	7,933
Impairment of goodwill	—	—	393,365
Share-based compensation	55,079	36,971	114,428
Remeasurement of monetary assets and liabilities	(15,109)	8,509	(4,701)
Deferred income tax (benefit) expense	(20,878)	14,588	(155,505)
Excess tax benefit from share-based compensation arrangements	(35,076)	(27,373)	(110,836)
Provision for doubtful accounts receivable	2,106	4,471	10,761
Gain on sales of marketable securities and restricted investments, net	—	(16)	(4,581)
Other operating activities	(1,073)	(4,762)	(719)
Changes in operating assets and liabilities:			
Accounts receivable, trade, unbilled and retainage	564,964	(388,039)	(529,809)
Prepaid expenses and other current assets	109,126	(28,854)	(140,961)
Other assets	(1,684)	82,120	(21,908)
Inventories and balance of systems parts	15,394	(75,626)	(348,151)
Project assets and deferred project costs	(316,022)	(174,532)	(368,619)
Accounts payable	(93,259)	174,319	94,674
Income taxes payable	36,307	63,489	95,132
Accrued expenses and other liabilities	(138,937)	506,253	647,162
Accrued solar module collection and recycling liability	10,648	44,538	35,720
Total adjustments	503,088	858,547	6,030
Net cash provided by (used in) operating activities	$ 856,126	$ 762,209	$ (33,463)

INDIRECT/RECONCILIATION METHOD

6.17 XEROX CORPORATION (DEC)

CONSOLIDATED STATEMENTS OF CASH FLOWS

	Year Ended December 31,		
(In millions)	2013	2012	2011
Cash Flows from Operating Activities:			
Net income	$ 1,179	$ 1,223	$ 1,328
Adjustments required to reconcile net income to cash flows from operating activities:			
Depreciation and amortization	1,358	1,301	1,251
Provision for receivables	123	127	154
Provision for inventory	35	30	39
Deferred tax expense	122	96	203
Net (gain) loss on sales of businesses and assets	(45)	2	(9)
Undistributed equity in net income of unconsolidated affiliates	(92)	(90)	(86)
Stock-based compensation	90	125	123
Restructuring and asset impairment charges	116	154	32
Payments for restructurings	(136)	(144)	(218)
Contributions to defined benefit pension plans	(230)	(364)	(426)
Increase in accounts receivable and billed portion of finance receivables	(576)	(776)	(296)
Collections of deferred proceeds from sales of receivables	482	470	380
Increase in inventories	(38)	—	(124)
Increase in equipment on operating leases	(303)	(276)	(298)
Decrease in finance receivables	609	947	90
Collections on beneficial interest from sales of finance receivables	58	—	—
Increase in other current and long-term assets	(145)	(265)	(249)
(Decrease) increase in accounts payable and accrued compensation	(29)	120	82
Decrease in other current and long-term liabilities	(50)	(71)	(22)
Net change in income tax assets and liabilities	3	42	89
Net change in derivative assets and liabilities	(11)	11	39
Other operating, net	(145)	(82)	(121)
Net cash provided by operating activities	2,375	2,580	1,961

(continued)

(In millions)	Year Ended December 31,		
	2013	2012	2011
Cash Flows from Investing Activities:			
Cost of additions to land, buildings and equipment	(346)	(388)	(338)
Proceeds from sales of land, buildings and equipment	86	9	28
Cost of additions to internal use software	(81)	(125)	(163)
Proceeds from sale of businesses	26	—	—
Acquisitions, net of cash acquired	(155)	(276)	(212)
Other investing, net	18	19	10
Net cash used in investing activities	(452)	(761)	(675)
Cash Flows from Financing Activities:			
Net (payments) proceeds on debt	(434)	(108)	49
Payment of liability to subsidiary trust issuing preferred securities	—	—	(670)
Common stock dividends	(272)	(231)	(241)
Preferred stock dividends	(24)	(24)	(24)
Proceeds from issuances of common stock	124	44	44
Excess tax benefits from stock-based compensation	16	10	6
Payments to acquire treasury stock, including fees	(696)	(1,052)	(701)
Repurchases related to stock-based compensation	(57)	(42)	(27)
Distributions to noncontrolling interests	(56)	(69)	(22)
Other financing	(3)	—	—
Net cash used in financing activities	(1,402)	(1,472)	(1,586)
Effect of exchange rate changes on cash and cash equivalents	(3)	(3)	(9)
Increase (decrease) in cash and cash equivalents	518	344	(309)
Cash and cash equivalents at beginning of year	1,246	902	1,211
Cash and Cash Equivalents at End of Year	$ 1,764	$ 1,246	$ 902

ADJUSTMENTS TO RECONCILE NET INCOME—DEPRECIATION AND AMORTIZATION

6.18 VISTEON CORPORATION (DEC)

CONSOLIDATED STATEMENTS OF CASH FLOWS (in part)

(Dollars in millions)	Year Ended December 31		
	2013	2012	2011
Operating Activities			
Net income	$ 775	$ 167	$ 154
Adjustments to reconcile net income to net cash provided from operating activities:			
Depreciation and amortization	262	259	316
Asset impairments	—	24	66
Equity in net income of non-consolidated affiliates, net of dividends remitted	(26)	(122)	(122)
Stock-based compensation	15	25	39
Gain on Yanfeng transactions and sale of other joint ventures	(470)	(19)	—
Other non-cash items	6	26	20
Changes in assets and liabilities:			
Accounts receivable	(21)	(38)	(110)
Inventories	(49)	(26)	(33)
Accounts payable	97	(26)	(25)
Accrued income taxes	(54)	10	1
Other assets and other liabilities	(223)	(41)	(131)
Net cash provided from operating activities	312	239	175

NOTES TO CONSOLIDATED FINANCIAL STATEMENTS

Note 2. Summary of Significant Accounting Policies (in part)

Product Tooling: Product tooling includes molds, dies and other tools used in production of a specific part or parts of the same basic design. It is generally required that non-reimbursable design and development costs for products to be sold under long-term supply arrangements be expensed as incurred and costs incurred for molds, dies and other tools that will be owned by the Company or its customers and used in producing the products under long-term supply arrangements be capitalized and amortized over the shorter of the expected useful life of the assets or the term of the supply arrangement. Contractually reimbursable design and development costs that would otherwise be expensed are recorded as an asset as incurred. Product tooling owned by the Company is capitalized as property and equipment and is amortized to cost of sales over its estimated economic life, generally not exceeding six years.The Company had receivables of $53 million and

$36 million as of December 31, 2013 and 2012, respectively, related to production tools in progress, which will not be owned by the Company and for which there is a contractual agreement for reimbursement from the customer.

Property and Equipment: Property and equipment is stated at cost or fair value for impaired assets. As a result of the adoption of fresh-start accounting, property and equipment was re-measured and adjusted to estimated fair value as of October 1, 2010. Depreciation expense is computed principally by the straight-line method over estimated useful lives for financial reporting purposes and by accelerated methods for income tax purposes in certain jurisdictions. Certain costs incurred in the acquisition or development of software for internal use are capitalized. Capitalized software costs are amortized using the straight-line method over estimated useful lives generally ranging from 3 to 8 years. The net book value of capitalized software costs was approximately $5 million and $13 million at December 31, 2013 and 2012, respectively. Related amortization expense was approximately $6 million for the years ended December 31, 2013, 2012 and 2011. Amortization expense of approximately $2 million, $2 million and $1 million is expected for the annual periods ended December 31, 2014, 2015 and 2016, respectively.

Goodwill and Intangible Assets (in part)

Other indefinite-lived intangible assets are subject to impairment analysis annually or more frequently if an event occurs or circumstances indicate the carrying amount may be impaired. Indefinite-lived intangible assets are tested for impairment by comparing the fair value to the carrying value. If the carrying value exceeds the fair value, the asset is adjusted to fair value. Other definite-lived intangible assets are amortized over their estimated useful lives, and tested for impairment in accordance with the methodology discussed above under "Property and Equipment."

Note 7. Property and Equipment

Property and equipment, net consists of the following:

(Dollars in millions)	December 31 2013	December 31 2012
Land	$ 162	$ 161
Buildings and improvements	301	269
Machinery, equipment and other	1,309	1,137
Construction in progress	145	100
Total property and equipment	1,917	1,667
Accumulated depreciation	(580)	(421)
	1,337	1,246
Product tooling, net of amortization	77	80
Property and equipment, net	$1,414	$1,326

In April 2012, the Company sold its corporate headquarters, consisting of land and building, which had a net book value of approximately $60 million, for cash proceeds of approximately $80 million and entered into an agreement to lease back the corporate offices over a period of 15 years. The gain on the sale of $20 million is being amortized into income on a straight-line basis over the term of the lease.

Property and equipment is depreciated principally using the straight-line method of depreciation over the related asset's estimated useful life. Generally, buildings and improvements are depreciated over a 40-year estimated useful life, leasehold improvements are depreciated on a straight-line basis over the initial lease term period, and machinery, equipment and other are depreciated over estimated useful lives ranging from 3 to 15 years. Product tooling is amortized using the straight-line method over the estimated life of the tool, generally not exceeding six years. Depreciation and amortization expenses for property and equipment, including assets recorded under capital leases, are summarized as follows:

(Dollars in millions)	Year Ended December 31 2013	2012	2011
Depreciation	$207	$209	$254
Amortization	10	10	17
	$217	$219	$271

Note 8. Intangible Assets (in part)

Intangible assets at December 31, 2013 and 2012 were as follows:

(Dollars in millions)	Estimated Weighted Average Useful Life (Years)	December 31, 2013			December 31, 2012		
		Gross Carrying Value	Accumulated Amortization	Net Carrying Value	Gross Carrying Value	Accumulated Amortization	Net Carrying Value
Definite-Lived							
Developed technology	8	$219	$ 88	$131	$209	$ 60	$149
Customer related	10	214	45	169	124	30	94
Other	39	32	9	23	22	5	17
Subtotal		$465	$142	$323	$355	$ 95	$260
Indefinite-Lived							
Goodwill		$ 97	$ —	$ 97	$ 46	$—	$ 46
Trade names		27	—	27	26	—	26
Subtotal		$124	$ —	124	$ 72	$—	72
Total		$589	$142	$447	$427	$ 95	$332

Changes in intangible asset gross carrying values and accumulated amortization are summarized in the table below.

(Dollars in millions)	2013		2012	
	Gross Carrying Value	Accumulated Amortization	Gross Carrying Value	Accumulated Amortization
Balance January 1	$427	$ 95	$404	$ 51
Additions	156	—	11	—
Divestiture	—	—	(5)	—
Amortization	—	45	—	40
Foreign currency	6	2	17	4
Balance December 31	$589	$142	$427	$ 95

Additions to intangible assets for 2013 are primarily attributable to the November 2013 step acquisition of YFVE. In connection with the preliminary purchase price allocation acquired intangible assets were recorded at estimated fair values, including customer related assets of approximately $89 million, land use rights of approximately $9 million and developed technology of approximately $7 million. Additionally, the Company recorded goodwill of approximately $51 million on the YFVE step acquisition for the excess of the purchase price over the net of the fair values of the identifiable assets and liabilities acquired.

The Company recorded approximately $45 million, $40 million and $45 million of amortization expense related to definite-lived intangible assets for the years ended December 31, 2013, 2012 and 2011 respectively. The Company currently estimates annual amortization expense to be $50 million for 2014, $ 49 million for 2015, $48 million for 2016, $46 million for 2017 and $41 million for 2018. Indefinite-lived intangible assets, including goodwill and trade names are not amortized but are tested for impairment at least annually.

ADJUSTMENTS TO RECONCILE NET INCOME—STOCK-BASED COMPENSATION

6.19 ELECTRONIC ARTS INC. (MAR)
CONSOLIDATED STATEMENTS OF CASH FLOWS (in part)

(In millions)	Year Ended March 31,		
	2013	2012	2011
Operating Activities			
Net income (loss)	$ 98	$ 76	$(276)
Adjustments to reconcile net income (loss) to net cash provided by operating activities:			
Depreciation, amortization and accretion, net	264	216	180
Stock-based compensation	164	170	176
Acquisition-related contingent consideration	(64)	11	(17)
Net gains on investments and sale of property and equipment	(37)	(12)	(25)
Non-cash restructuring charges	7	(6)	1
Change in assets and liabilities:			
Receivables, net	56	(14)	(122)
Inventories	16	21	25
Other assets	15	(101)	5
Accounts payable	(78)	(50)	114
Accrued and other liabilities	(106)	13	(4)
Deferred income taxes, net	(7)	(90)	24
Deferred net revenue (online-enabled games)	(4)	43	239
Net cash provided by operating activities	324	277	320

(1) Description of Business and Summary of Significant Accounting Policies (in part)

Stock-Based Compensation

We are required to estimate the fair value of share-based payment awards on the date of grant. We recognize compensation costs for stock-based payment awards to employees based on the grant-date fair value using a straight-line approach over the service period for which such awards are expected to vest.

We determine the fair value of our share-based payment awards as follows:
- *Restricted Stock Units, Restricted Stock, and Performance-Based Restricted Stock Units*. The fair value of restricted stock units, restricted stock, and performance-based restricted stock units (other than market-based restricted stock units) is determined based on the quoted market price of our common stock on the date of grant. Performance-based restricted stock units include grants made (1) to certain members of executive management primarily granted in fiscal year 2009 and (2) in connection with certain acquisitions.
- *Market-Based Restricted Stock Units*. Market-based restricted stock units consist of grants of performance-based restricted stock units to certain members of executive management that vest contingent upon the achievement of pre-determined market and service conditions (referred to herein as "market-based restricted stock units"). The fair value of our market-based restricted stock units is determined using a Monte-Carlo simulation model. Key assumptions for the Monte-Carlo simulation model are the risk-free interest rate, expected volatility, expected dividends and correlation coefficient.
- *Stock Options and Employee Stock Purchase Plan*. The fair value of stock options and stock purchase rights granted pursuant to our equity incentive plans and our 2000 Employee Stock Purchase Plan ("ESPP"), respectively, is determined using the Black-Scholes valuation model based on the multiple-award valuation method. Key assumptions of the Black-Scholes valuation model are the risk-free interest rate, expected volatility, expected term and expected dividends.

The determination of the fair value of market-based restricted stock units, stock options and ESPP is affected by assumptions regarding subjective and complex variables. Generally, our assumptions are based on historical information and judgment is required to determine if historical trends may be indicators of future outcomes.

Employee stock-based compensation expense is calculated based on awards ultimately expected to vest and is reduced for estimated forfeitures. Forfeitures are revised, if necessary, in subsequent periods if actual forfeitures differ from those estimates and an adjustment to stock-based compensation expense will be recognized at that time.

(14) Stock-Based Compensation and Employee Benefit Plans (in part)

Stock-Based Compensation Expense

Employee stock-based compensation expense recognized during the fiscal years ended March 31, 2013, 2012 and 2011 was calculated based on awards ultimately expected to vest and has been reduced for estimated forfeitures. In subsequent periods, if actual forfeitures differ from those estimates, an adjustment to stock-based compensation expense will be recognized at that time.

The following table summarizes stock-based compensation expense resulting from stock options, restricted stock, restricted stock units and the ESPP included in our Consolidated Statements of Operations (in millions):

| | Year Ended March 31, | | |
	2013	2012	2011
Cost of revenue	$ 2	$ 2	$ 2
Research and development[a]	94	103	107
Marketing and sales[a]	30	27	23
General and administrative[a]	38	38	42
Restructuring and other charges	—	—	2
Stock-based compensation expense	$164	$170	$176

[a] During the fourth quarter of fiscal year 2013, we reviewed our operating expenses and reclassified certain amounts, primarily headcount and facilities costs, to align with our current operating structure. As a result, we also reclassified the related prior year stock-based compensation expense amounts within our Consolidated Statements of Operations for comparability purposes. These reclassifications did not affect the Company's total stock-based compensation expense.

During the fiscal years ended March 31, 2013, 2012 and 2011, we did not recognize any provision for or benefit from income taxes related to our stock-based compensation expense.

As of March 31, 2013, our total unrecognized compensation cost related to stock options was $5 million and is expected to be recognized over a weighted-average service period of 2.1 years. As of March 31, 2013, our total unrecognized compensation cost related to restricted stock and restricted stock units (collectively referred to as "restricted stock rights") was $221 million and is expected to be recognized over a weighted-average service period of 1.7 years. Of the $221 million of unrecognized compensation cost, $7 million relates to market-based restricted stock units.

For fiscal year ended March 31, 2013, we recognized $1 million of tax expense from the exercise of stock options, net of $1 million of deferred tax write-offs. There is no tax benefit related to stock-based compensation reported in the financing activities on our Consolidated Statements of Cash Flows. For the fiscal year ended March 31, 2012, we recognized $3 million of tax benefit from the exercise of stock options, net of $1 million of deferred tax write-offs; of this amount $4 million of excess tax benefit related to stock-based compensation was reported in the financing activities on our Consolidated Statements of Cash Flows. For the fiscal year ended March 31, 2011, we recognized $2 million of tax expense from the exercise of stock options, net of $3 million of deferred tax write-offs; of this amount $1 million of excess tax benefit related to stock-based compensation was reported in the financing activities on our Consolidated Statements of Cash Flows.

ADJUSTMENTS TO RECONCILE NET INCOME—ACCRETION OF CONVERTIBLE NOTES DISCOUNT

6.20 YAHOO! INC. (DEC)
CONSOLIDATED STATEMENTS OF CASH FLOWS (in part)

(In thousands)	Years Ended December 31,		
	2011	**2012**	**2013**
Cash Flows from Operating Activities:			
Net income	$1,062,669	$ 3,950,602	$1,376,566
Adjustments to reconcile net income to net cash provided by (used in) operating activities:			
Depreciation	530,516	549,235	532,485
Amortization of intangible assets	117,723	105,366	96,518
Accretion of convertible notes discount	—	—	4,846
Stock-based compensation expense, net	204,172	220,936	278,220
Gains from sales of patents	—	—	(79,950)
Goodwill impairment charge	—	—	63,555
Restructuring charges	990	109,896	547
Gain from sale of Alibaba Group Shares	—	(4,603,322)	—
Loss (gain) from sales of investments, assets, and other, net	4,405	(11,840)	22,397
Earnings in equity interests	(476,920)	(676,438)	(896,675)
Dividend income related to Alibaba Group Preference Shares	—	(20,000)	(35,726)
Tax benefits (detriments) from stock-based awards	33,497	(31,440)	49,061
Excess tax benefits from stock-based awards	(70,680)	(35,844)	(64,407)
Deferred income taxes	70,392	(769,320)	(84,302)
Dividends received from equity investees	75,391	83,648	135,058
Changes in assets and liabilities, net of effects of acquisitions:			
Accounts receivable	38,100	34,752	26,199
Prepaid expenses and other	97,849	78,529	27,401
Accounts payable	(316)	12,747	(7,764)
Accrued expenses and other liabilities	(290,070)	255,799	(98,853)
Deferred revenue	(73,912)	465,140	(149,929)
Net cash provided by (used in) operating activities	1,323,806	(281,554)	1,195,247

NOTES TO CONSOLIDATED FINANCIAL STATEMENTS

Note 11—Convertible Notes (in part)

0.00% Convertible Senior Notes

In 2013, the Company issued the Notes. The Notes were sold under a purchase agreement, dated November 20, 2013, with J.P. Morgan Securities LLC and Goldman, Sachs & Co., as representatives of the several initial purchasers named therein (collectively, the "Initial Purchasers"). The Notes were sold to the Initial Purchasers for resale to qualified institutional buyers pursuant to Rule 144A under the Securities Act of 1933, as amended.

In connection with the issuance of the Notes, the Company entered into an indenture (the "Indenture") with respect to the Notes with The Bank of New York Mellon Trust Company, N.A., as trustee. Under the Indenture, the Notes are senior unsecured obligations of Yahoo! Inc., the Notes will not bear regular interest, and the principal amount of the Notes will not accrete. The Notes will mature on December 1, 2018, unless previously purchased or converted in accordance with their terms prior to such date. The Company may not redeem Notes prior to maturity. However, holders of the Notes may convert them at certain times and upon the occurrence of certain events in the future, as outlined in the Indenture. Holders of the Notes who convert in connection with a "make-whole fundamental change," as defined in the Indenture, may require Yahoo to purchase for cash all or any portion of their Notes at a purchase price equal to 100 percent of the principal amount, plus accrued and unpaid special interest as defined in the Indenture, if any. The Notes will be convertible into shares of Yahoo's common stock at an initial conversion rate of 18.7161 shares per $1,000 principal amount of Notes (which is equivalent to an initial conversion price of approximately $53.43 per share), subject to adjustment upon the occurrence of certain events. Certain corporate events described in the Indenture may increase the conversion rate for holders who elect to convert their Notes in connection with such corporate event should they occur. Upon conversion of the Notes, holders will receive cash, shares of Yahoo's common stock or a combination thereof, at Yahoo's election. The Company's intent is to settle the principal amount of the Notes in cash upon conversion. If the conversion value exceeds the principal amount, the Company would deliver shares of its common stock in respect to the remainder of its conversion obligation in excess of the aggregate principal amount (conversion spread). The conversion spread would be included in the denominator for the computation of diluted net income per common share, using the treasury stock method. As of December 31, 2013, none of the conditions allowing holders of the Notes to convert had been met.

In accounting for the issuance of the Notes, the Company separated the Notes into liability and equity components. The carrying amount of the liability component was calculated by measuring the estimated fair value of a similar liability that does not have an associated convertible feature. The carrying amount of the equity component representing the conversion option was determined by deducting the fair value of the liability component from the face value of the Notes as a whole. The excess of the principal amount of the liability component over its carrying amount ("debt discount") is amortized to interest expense over the term of the Notes using the effective interest method with an effective interest rate of 5.26 percent per annum. The equity component is not remeasured as long as it continues to meet the conditions for equity classification.

In accounting for the transaction costs related to the Note issuance, the Company allocated the total amount incurred to the liability and equity components based on their relative values. Issuance costs attributable to the $1.1 billion liability component are being amortized to expense over the term of the Notes, and issuance costs attributable to the $306 million equity component were included with the equity component in stockholders' equity. Additionally, the Company recorded a deferred tax liability of $37 million on a portion of the equity component transaction costs which are deductible for tax purposes.

The Notes consist of the following (in thousands):

	Year Ended December 31, 2013
Liability component:	
Principal	$1,437,500
Less: note discount	(326,915)
Net carrying amount	$1,110,585
Equity component(*)	$ 305,569

(*) Recorded in the consolidated balance sheet within additional paid-in capital.

The following table sets forth total interest expense recognized related to the Notes (in thousands):

	Year Ended December 31, 2013
Accretion of convertible note discount	$4,846

As of December 31, the fair value of the Notes, which was determined based on inputs that are observable in the market (Level 2) and carrying value of debt instruments (carrying value excludes the equity component of the Company's Notes classified in equity) was as follows:

	2013	
	Fair Value	Carrying Value
Convertible senior notes	$1,111,473	$1,110,585

6.21 COLGATE-PALMOLIVE COMPANY (DEC)

CONSOLIDATED STATEMENTS OF CASH FLOWS (in part)

(Dollars in Millions)

	2013	2012	2011
Operating Activities			
Net income including noncontrolling interests	$2,410	$2,631	$2,554
Adjustments to reconcile net income including noncontrolling interests to net cash provided by operations:			
Depreciation and amortization	439	425	421
Restructuring and termination benefits, net of cash	182	35	103
Venezuela devaluation charge	172	—	—
Gain before tax on sales of non-core product lines	—	—	(207)
Voluntary benefit plan contributions	(101)	(101)	(178)
Stock-based compensation expense	128	120	122
Deferred income taxes	71	63	88
Cash effects of changes in:			
Receivables	(37)	19	(130)
Inventories	(97)	(21)	(130)
Accounts payable and other accruals	24	(5)	199
Other non-current assets and liabilities	13	30	54
Net cash provided by operations	3,204	3,196	2,896

NOTES TO CONSOLIDATED FINANCIAL STATEMENTS

(Dollars in Millions Except Share and Per Share Amounts)

14. Venezuela

Effective January 1, 2010, Venezuela was designated hyper-inflationary and, therefore, the functional currency for the Company's Venezuelan subsidiary (" CP Venezuela ") is the U.S. dollar and Venezuelan currency fluctuations are reported in income.

The Venezuelan government devalued its currency effective February 9, 2013. As a result of the devaluation the official exchange rate changed from 4.30 to 6.30 Venezuelan bolivares fuerte per dollar. The Company incurred a one-time pretax loss of $172 ($111 aftertax loss) in the first quarter of 2013 related to the remeasurement of the net monetary assets included in the local balance sheet at the date of the devaluation. The impact of this one-time aftertax loss of $111 on diluted earnings per common share was $0.12 for the year ended December 31, 2013. The Company remeasured the financial statements of CP Venezuela at the rate at which it expects to remit future dividends, which was 6.30 for 2013 and 4.30 for 2012 and 2011. As the local currency operations in Venezuela translated into fewer U.S. dollars, this had and will continue to have an ongoing adverse effect on the Company's reported results.

For the year ended December 31, 2013, CP Venezuela represented approximately 4% of the Company's consolidated Net sales. At December 31, 2013, CP Venezuela's bolivar fuerte-denominated net monetary asset position, which would be subject to remeasurement in the event of a further devaluation, was approximately $600. This amount does not include $ 233 of devaluation-protected bonds issued by the Venezuelan government, as these bonds provide protection against devaluations by adjusting the amount of bolivares fuerte received at maturity for any devaluation subsequent to issuance. CP Venezuela's local currency-denominated non-monetary assets were approximately $335 at December 31, 2013 and included approximately $225 of fixed assets that could be subject to impairment if the Company continues to be unable to implement price increases to offset the impacts of continued high inflation or further devaluations or if it does not have sufficient access to U.S. dollars to fund imports.

6.22

CENVEO, INC. (DEC)
CONSOLIDATED STATEMENTS OF CASH FLOWS (in part)

(In thousands)

	For the Years Ended		
	2013	**2012**	**2011**
Cash Flows from Operating Activities:			
Net loss	$(68,786)	$(79,887)	$ (8,565)
Adjustments to reconcile net loss to net cash provided by operating activities:			
(Gain) loss on sale of discontinued operations, net of taxes	(14,933)	6,260	—
Income from discontinued operations, net of taxes	(1,808)	(6,901)	(129)
Depreciation	50,534	50,777	52,649
Amortization of intangible assets	9,962	9,881	9,899
Impairment of goodwill related to discontinued operations	—	—	13,500
Non-cash interest expense, net	10,289	8,263	5,277
Deferred income taxes	(28,672)	(1,948)	6,861
Non-cash taxes	40,562	56,500	—
Gain on bargain purchase	(17,262)	—	(11,720)
(Gain) loss on sale of assets	(120)	(2,782)	376
Non-cash restructuring and other charges, net	2,622	11,226	3,853
Impairment of intangible assets	33,367	—	—
Loss (gain) on early extinguishment of debt, net	11,324	12,487	(4,011)
Provisions for bad debts	4,392	2,024	2,284
Provisions for inventory obsolescence	6,523	3,588	3,416
Stock-based compensation provision	3,739	5,333	8,716
Gain on insurance claim	(2,670)	—	—
Changes in operating assets and liabilities, excluding the effects of acquired businesses:			
Accounts receivable	(31,686)	26,594	(8,403)
Inventories	(40,622)	(617)	20,453
Accounts payable and accrued compensation and related liabilities	69,848	(13,291)	13,650
Other working capital changes	4,047	(29,050)	(14,948)
Other, net	(18,335)	(15,613)	(23,529)
Net cash provided by operating activities of continuing operations	22,315	42,844	69,629
Net cash provided by operating activities of discontinued operations	5,878	9,221	10,693
Net cash provided by operating activities	28,193	52,065	80,322

NOTES TO CONSOLIDATED FINANCIAL STATEMENTS

5. Property, Plant and Equipment (in part)

Property, plant and equipment are as follows (in thousands):

	2013	2012
Land and land improvements	$ 14,507	$ 17,283
Buildings and building improvements	97,674	103,326
Machinery and equipment	635,638	579,570
Furniture and fixtures	11,049	11,170
Construction in progress	11,828	7,060
	770,696	718,409
Accumulated depreciation	(465,789)	(439,331)
	$ 304,907	$ 279,078

Proceeds From Long-Lived Assets (in part)

During the first quarter of 2013, a press in the Company's label and packaging segment was destroyed by a fire. The Company's insurance policy provided coverage for business interruption and the replacement cost of the press. The insurance settlement was finalized during the second quarter of 2013 and the Company received cash proceeds of $4.4 million, resulting in a $2.7 million gain. The gain on the insurance settlement represents the difference between the replacement cost and carrying value of the press. The gain is recorded in other (income) expense, net in the Company's consolidated statement of operations.

Cash Flows From Investing Activities

PRESENTATION

6.23 FASB ASC 230 defines those transactions and events that constitute investing cash receipts and payments. Investing activities include making and collecting loans and acquiring and disposing of debt or equity instruments and property, plant, and equipment (PPE) and other productive assets. Paragraphs 20–21 of FASB ASC 230-10-45 explain that investing activities exclude acquiring and disposing of certain loans or other debt or equity instruments that are acquired specifically for resale. Cash flows from purchases, sales, and maturities of available-for-sale securities should be classified as cash flows from investing activities and reported gross in the statement of cash flows. Cash inflows from investing activities include the following:

- Receipts from collections or sales of loans made by the entity and of other entities' debt instruments, other than cash equivalents and certain debt instruments that are acquired specifically for resale, that were purchased by the entity.
- Receipts from sales of equity instruments of other entities, other than certain equity instruments carried in a trading account, and from returns of investment in those instruments.
- Receipts from sales of PPE and other productive assets.
- Receipts from sales of loans that were not specifically acquired for resale. If loans were acquired as investments, cash receipts from sales of those loans shall be classified as investing cash inflows, regardless of a change in the purpose for holding those loans.

Cash outflows from investing activities include the following:

- Disbursements for loans made by the entity and payments to acquire debt instruments of other entities, other than cash equivalents and certain debt instruments that are acquired specifically for resale.
- Payments to acquire equity instruments of other entities, other than certain equity instruments carried in a trading account.
- Payments at the time of purchase or soon before or after purchase to acquire PPE and other productive assets, including interest capitalized as part of the cost of those assets. Generally, only advance payments, the down payment, or other amounts paid at the time of purchase or soon before or after the purchase of PPE and other productive assets are investing cash outflows. However, incurring directly related debt to the seller is a financing transaction; thus, subsequent payments of principal on that debt are financing cash outflows.

PRESENTATION AND DISCLOSURE EXCERPTS

ACQUISITIONS

6.24 ARROW ELECTRONICS, INC. (DEC)
CONSOLIDATED STATEMENTS OF CASH FLOWS (in part)

(In thousands)

	Years Ended December 31,		
	2013	2012	2011
Cash flows from investing activities:			
Cash consideration paid for acquired businesses	(367,940)	(281,918)	(532,568)
Acquisition of property, plant, and equipment	(116,162)	(112,224)	(113,941)
Purchase of cost method investments	(3,000)	(15,000)	—
Net cash used for investing activities	(487,102)	(409,142)	(646,509)

NOTES TO THE CONSOLIDATED FINANCIAL STATEMENTS

(Dollars in thousands except per share data)

2. Acquisitions (in part)

The company accounts for acquisitions using the acquisition method of accounting. The results of operations of acquisitions are included in the company's consolidated results from their respective dates of acquisition. The company allocates the purchase price of each acquisition to the tangible assets, liabilities, and identifiable intangible assets acquired based on their estimated fair values. In certain circumstances, a portion of purchase price may be contingent upon the achievement of certain operating results. The fair values assigned to identifiable intangible assets acquired and contingent consideration were determined primarily by using an income approach which was based on assumptions and estimates made by management. Significant assumptions utilized in the income approach were based on company specific information and projections, which are not observable in the market and are thus considered Level 3 measurements by authoritative guidance (see Note 7). The excess of the purchase price over the fair value of the identified assets and liabilities has been recorded as goodwill. Any change in the estimated fair value of the net assets prior to the finalization of the allocation for acquisitions could change the amount of the purchase price allocable to goodwill. The company is not aware of any information that indicates the final purchase price allocations will differ materially from the preliminary estimates.

2013 Acquisitions

On October 28, 2013, the company acquired CSS Computer Security Solutions Holding GmbH, doing business as ComputerLinks AG ("ComputerLinks"), for a purchase price of approximately $313,209, which included $20,981 of cash acquired. ComputerLinks is a value-added distributor of enterprise computing solutions with a comprehensive offering of IT solutions from many of the world's leading technology suppliers. ComputerLinks has operations in EMEA, North America, and select countries within the Asia Pacific region.

Since the date of the acquisition, ComputerLinks sales for the year ended December 31, 2013 of $208,177 were included in the company's consolidated results of operations.

The following table summarizes the preliminary allocation of the net consideration paid to the fair value of the assets acquired and liabilities assumed for the ComputerLinks acquisition:

Accounts receivable, net	$ 177,700
Inventories	58,041
Other current assets	11,168
Property, plant, and equipment	7,070
Other assets	1,480
Identifiable intangible assets	39,195
Cost in excess of net assets acquired	275,442
Accounts payable	(213,456)
Accrued expenses	(51,270)
Other liabilities	(13,142)
Cash consideration paid, net of cash acquired	$ 292,228

In connection with the ComputerLinks acquisition, the company allocated the following amounts to identifiable intangible assets:

	Weighted-Average Life	
Customer relationships	9 years	$37,125
Other intangible assets	(a)	2,070
Total identifiable intangible assets		$39,195

(a) Consists of non-competition agreements and sales backlog with useful lives ranging from one to two years.

The cost in excess of net assets acquired related to the ComputerLinks acquisition was recorded in the company's global ECS business segment. The intangible assets related to the ComputerLinks acquisition are not expected to be deductible for income tax purposes.

During 2013, the company completed four additional acquisitions. The aggregate consideration for these four acquisitions was $80,210, net of cash acquired, and includes $4,498 of contingent consideration. The impact of these acquisitions was not material, individually or in the aggregate, to the company's consolidated financial position or results of operations.

PURCHASE OF NONCONTROLLING INTEREST

6.25 SCHNITZER STEEL INDUSTRIES, INC. (AUG)
CONSOLIDATED STATEMENTS OF CASH FLOWS (in part)

(In thousands)

	Year Ended August 31,		
	2013	2012	2011
Cash flows from investing activities:			
Capital expenditures	(90,381)	(78,560)	(104,964)
Acquisitions, net of cash acquired	(25,366)	(6,567)	(293,880)
Joint venture payments, net	(2,194)	(92)	(1,587)
Proceeds from sale of assets	5,491	953	530
Purchase of noncontrolling interest	(24,734)	—	—
Net cash used in investing activities	(137,184)	(84,266)	(399,901)

Note 2—Summary of Significant Accounting Policies (in part)

Redeemable Noncontrolling Interest

The Company issued common stock of one of its subsidiaries to the noncontrolling interest holder of that subsidiary that, prior to the Company's purchase of that interest on March 8, 2013, had been redeemable both at the option of the holder and upon the occurrence of an event that was not solely within the Company's control. Since redemption of the noncontrolling interest was outside of the Company's control, this interest was presented on the Consolidated Balance Sheets in the mezzanine section under the caption redeemable noncontrolling interest. If the interest had been redeemed, the Company would have been required to purchase all of such interest at fair value on the date of redemption. Prior to its purchase by the Company on March 8, 2013, the redeemable noncontrolling interest was presented at the greater of its carrying amount (adjusted for the noncontrolling interest's share of the allocation of income or loss of the subsidiary, dividends to and contributions from the noncontrolling interest) or its fair value as of each measurement date. Any adjustments to the carrying amount of the redeemable noncontrolling interest for changes in fair value prior to the Company's purchase of the interest in March 2013 were recorded to retained earnings. See Note 13—Redeemable Noncontrolling Interest for further detail.

Note 13—Redeemable Noncontrolling Interest

In March 2011, the Company, through a wholly-owned acquisition subsidiary, acquired substantially all of the metals recycling business assets of Amix Salvage & Sales Ltd. As part of the purchase consideration, the Company issued the seller common shares equal to 20% of the issued and outstanding capital stock of the Company's acquisition subsidiary. Under the terms of an agreement related to the acquisition, the noncontrolling interest holder has the right to require the Company to purchase its interest in the Company's acquisition subsidiary for fair value. The noncontrolling interest becomes redeemable within 60 days after the later of (i) the third anniversary of the date of the acquisition and (ii) the date on which certain principals of the minority shareholder are no longer employed by the Company.

On March 8, 2013, the Company entered into an agreement with the noncontrolling interest holder for the purchase of all of the outstanding noncontrolling interest in the Company's subsidiary for $25 million. In the second quarter of fiscal 2013, the Company adjusted the redeemable noncontrolling interest to its fair value corresponding to the purchase price of $25 million, with the difference between the adjusted carrying value and fair value recorded as a reduction to retained earnings.

Prior to the second quarter of fiscal 2013, the noncontrolling interest was presented at its adjusted carrying value, which approximated its fair value. The Company determined fair value using Level 3 inputs under the fair value hierarchy using an income approach based on a discounted cash flow analysis. The determination of fair value requires management to apply significant judgment in formulating estimates and assumptions used in the discounted cash flow model, including primarily revenue growth rates driven by future commodity prices and volume expectations, operating margins, capital expenditures, working capital requirements, terminal year growth rates and an appropriate discount rate. The present value of future cash flows was determined using a market-based weighted average cost of capital including a subject-company risk premium. The Company also used a market approach based on earnings multiple data to corroborate the fair value estimates of the noncontrolling interest determined using the discounted cash flow model.

Following is a reconciliation of the changes in the redeemable noncontrolling interest for the years ended August 31 (in thousands):

	2013	2012
Balances—Beginning of period	$ 22,248	$19,053
Net loss attributable to noncontrolling interest	(903)	(1,163)
Currency translation adjustment	(1,030)	350
Capital contributions from noncontrolling interest holder	1,970	4,008
Adjustment to fair value	2,449	—
Purchase	(24,734)	—
Balances—End of period	$ —	$22,248

BUSINESS COMBINATIONS

6.26 GENCORP INC. (NOV)

CONSOLIDATED STATEMENTS OF CASH FLOWS (in part)

	Year Ended		
(In millions)	2013	2012	2011
Investing Activities			
Capital expenditures	(63.2)	(37.2)	(21.1)
Proceeds from sale of land	—	0.6	—
Purchases of marketable securities	—	—	(15.0)
Sales of marketable securities	—	—	41.7
Purchase of Rocketdyne business (see table below)	(411.2)	—	—
Purchases of investments	(0.5)	—	—
Purchase of restricted cash investments	(470.0)	—	—
Sale of restricted cash investments	470.0	—	—
Net cash (used in) provided by investing activities	(474.9)	(36.6)	5.6
Supplemental Disclosures of Cash Flow Information			
Cash refund for income taxes	$ 0.1	$ 6.0	$ 0.2
Cash paid for income taxes	8.5	11.2	3.9
Cash paid for interest	33.7	18.5	22.4
Conversion of debt to common stock	1.6	—	—
Purchase of Rocketdyne Business (see Note 4)			
Total tangible assets	$ 318.0	$ —	$ —
Intangible assets	128.3	—	—
Goodwill	64.7	—	—
Deferred income taxes	12.9	—	—
Liabilities assumed	(112.7)	—	—
Total preliminary purchase price	$ 411.2	$ —	$ —

NOTES TO CONSOLIDATED FINANCIAL STATEMENTS

Note 1. Summary of Significant Accounting Policies (in part)

a. Basis of Presentation and Nature of Operations (in part)

Real Estate (in part)

In July 2012, the Company signed a stock and asset purchase agreement (the "Original Purchase Agreement") with United Technologies Corporation ("UTC") to acquire the Pratt & Whitney Rocketdyne division (the "Rocketdyne Business") from UTC for $550 million (the "Acquisition"). The Rocketdyne Business was the largest liquid rocket propulsion designer, developer, and manufacturer in the U.S. On June 10, 2013, the Federal Trade Commission ("FTC") announced that it closed its investigation into the Acquisition under the Hart-Scott-Rodino Antitrust Improvements Act of 1976, as amended. On June 12, 2013, the Company and UTC entered into an amended and restated stock and asset purchase agreement (the "Amended and Restated Purchase Agreement"), which amended and restated the Original Purchase Agreement, as amended. On June 14, 2013, the Company completed the acquisition of substantially all of the Rocketdyne Business pursuant to the Amended and Restated Purchase Agreement. The aggregate consideration to UTC was $411 million, paid in cash, which represents the initial purchase price of $550 million reduced by $55 million relating to the pending future acquisition of UTC's 50% ownership interest of RD Amross, LLC (a joint venture with NPO Energomash of Khimki, Russia which sells RD-180 engines to RD Amross) and the portion of the UTC business that markets and supports the sale of RD-180 engines. The acquisition of UTC's 50% ownership interest of RD Amross and UTC's related business is contingent upon certain conditions including receipt of certain Russian governmental regulatory approvals, which may not be obtained. Pursuant to the terms of the Amended and Restated Purchase Agreement, either party to such agreement may terminate the obligations to consummate the RDA Acquisition on or after June 12, 2015; provided, however, that such termination date may be extended for up to four additional periods of three months each (with the final termination date extended until June 12, 2016). Subject to the terms of Amended and Restated Purchase Agreement, in order to extend the termination date, either party may request the extension by providing written notice to the other party at least five business days prior to the termination date, provided that the requesting party must have a reasonable belief at the time such notice is given that a certain authorization for completion of the RDA Acquisition from the Russian government will be forthcoming. The purchase price was further adjusted for changes in advance payments on contracts, capital expenditures and other net assets, and is subject further to post-closing adjustments (see Note 4).

Note 4. Acquisition (in part)

In July 2012, the Company signed the Original Purchase Agreement with UTC to acquire the Rocketdyne Business from UTC for $550.0 million. On June 10, 2013, the FTC announced that it closed its investigation into the Acquisition under the Hart-Scott-Rodino Antitrust Improvements Act of 1976, as amended. On June 12, 2013, the Company entered into an Amended and Restated Purchase Agreement with UTC, which amended and restated the Original Purchase Agreement, as amended. On June 14, 2013, the Company completed the Acquisition of substantially all of the Rocketdyne Business pursuant to the Amended and Restated Purchase Agreement.

The aggregate consideration to UTC was $411.2 million, paid in cash, which represents the initial purchase price of $550.0 million reduced by $55.0 million relating to the pending future acquisition of UTC's 50% ownership interest of RD Amross (a joint venture with NPO Energomash of Khimki, Russia which sells RD-180 engines to RD Amross), and the portion of the UTC business that markets and supports the sale of RD-180 engines. The purchase price was further adjusted for changes in advance payments on contracts, capital expenditures and other net assets, and is subject to further post-closing adjustments. The components of the estimated purchase price to UTC are as follows (in millions):

Purchase price	$495.0
Advance payments on contracts adjustment	(57.3)
Capital expenditures adjustment	(29.8)
Target net asset adjustment	3.3
Cash payment to UTC	$411.2

The Company received a revised purchase price computation from UTC on September 12, 2013 and, per the terms and conditions of the Amended and Restated Purchase Agreement, the Company responded with its objections on December 9, 2013. The Company and UTC have 60 days to resolve the disputed items. If unable to do so within the 60 days, the dispute will be resolved by a mutually selected national accounting firm.

On January 28, 2013, the Company issued $460.0 million in aggregate principal amount of its $7\frac{1}{8}$% Notes. The $7\frac{1}{8}$% Notes were sold to qualified institutional buyers in accordance with Rule 144A under the Securities Act of 1933, as amended (the "Securities Act") and outside the U.S. in accordance with Regulation S under the Securities Act. The net proceeds of the $7\frac{1}{8}$% Notes offering were used to fund, in part, the acquisition of the Rocketdyne Business, and to pay related fees and expenses in June 2013 (see Note 6(b)).

The Company incurred substantial expenses in connection with the Acquisition. A summary of the expenses related to the Acquisition recorded in fiscal 2012 ($11.6 million) and fiscal 2013 ($20.0 million) is as follows (in millions):

Legal expenses	$16.4
Professional fees and consulting	8.9
Internal labor	3.4
Costs related to the previously planned divestiture of the LDACS business, including $0.3 million of internal labor	1.7
Other	1.2
	$31.6

The operating results of the Rocketdyne Business are included in the Company's Consolidated Financial Statements since June 13, 2013, the acquisition date, within the Company's Aerospace and Defense segment. Effective June 14, 2013, deposits on leased facilities of $1.8 million and letters of credit of $12.3 million for various financial assurance obligations were issued in conjunction with the Acquisition.

The preliminary purchase price allocation has been developed based on preliminary estimates of the fair value of the assets and liabilities of the Rocketdyne Business that the Company acquired. In addition, the allocation of the preliminary purchase price to acquired intangible assets is based on preliminary fair value estimates.

The following table summarizes the estimated fair values of the assets acquired and liabilities assumed at the acquisition date (in millions):

Current assets	$ 105.3
Property, plant and equipment, net	202.7
Other non-current assets	10.0
Total tangible assets acquired	318.0
Intangible assets acquired	128.3
Deferred income taxes	12.9
Total assets acquired	459.2
Liabilities assumed, current	(105.5)
Liabilities assumed, non-current	(7.2)
Total identifiable net assets acquired	346.5
Goodwill	$ 64.7

The preliminary purchase price allocation resulted in the recognition of $64.7 million in goodwill, all of which is deductible for tax purposes and included within the Company's Aerospace and Defense segment. Goodwill recognized from the Acquisition primarily relates to the expected contributions of the Rocketdyne Business to the Company's overall corporate strategy.

Intangible assets acquired in connection with the Rocketdyne Business included the following:

	Gross Carrying Amount (In millions)	Weighted Average Amortization Period (Years)
Customer related	$ 73.1	8.7
Intellectual property \ trade secrets	34.2	13.0
Non-Compete Agreements	0.5	3.0
Trade name	20.5	30.0
Total intangible assets	$128.3	

Amortization of intangible assets is not recoverable in the future through the Company's U.S. government contracts. Additionally, the Company has a $12.4 million and $20.4 million, respectively, indemnification receivable from and payable to UTC as of November 30, 2013. Pursuant to the terms of the Amended and Restated Purchase Agreement, the Company is indemnified for certain matters.

Net sales and net income of the Rocketdyne Business included in the Company's operating results for fiscal 2013 from the acquisition date of June 14, 2013 were $319.4 million and $18.3 million, respectively.

CAPITALIZED SOFTWARE

6.27 THE WESTERN UNION COMPANY (DEC)
CONSOLIDATED STATEMENTS OF CASH FLOWS (in part)

(In millions)

	Year Ended December 31,		
	2013	2012	2011
Cash Flows from Investing Activities			
Capitalization of contract costs	(119.3)	(174.9)	(96.7)
Capitalization of purchased and developed software	(41.8)	(32.4)	(13.0)
Purchases of property and equipment	(80.2)	(60.9)	(52.8)
Purchases of non-settlement related investments	(100.0)	—	—
Acquisition of businesses, net (Note 4)	—	10.0	(1,218.6)
Net proceeds from settlement of foreign currency forward contracts related to acquisitions	—	—	20.8
Net cash used in investing activities	(341.3)	(258.2)	(1,360.3)

NOTES TO CONSOLIDATED FINANCIAL STATEMENTS

2. Summary of Significant Accounting Policies (in part)

Other Intangible Assets

Other intangible assets primarily consist of acquired contracts, contract costs (primarily amounts paid to agents in connection with establishing and renewing long-term contracts) and software. Other intangible assets are amortized on a straight-line basis over the length of the contract or benefit periods. Included in the Consolidated Statements of Income is amortization expense of $198.6 million, $184.4 million and $131.6 million for the years ended December 31, 2013, 2012 and 2011, respectively.

Acquired contracts include customer and contractual relationships and networks of subagents that are recognized in connection with the Company's acquisitions.

The Company capitalizes initial payments for new and renewed agent contracts to the extent recoverable through future operations or penalties in the case of early termination. The Company's accounting policy is to limit the amount of capitalized costs for a given contract to the lesser of the estimated future cash flows from the contract or the termination fees the Company would receive in the event of early termination of the contract.

The Company purchases and develops software that is used in providing services and in performing administrative functions. Software development costs are capitalized once technological feasibility of the software has been established. Costs incurred prior to establishing technological feasibility are expensed as incurred. Technological feasibility is established when the Company has completed all planning and designing activities that are necessary to determine that a product can be produced to meet its design specifications, including functions, features and technical performance requirements. Capitalization of costs ceases when the product is available for general use. Software development costs and purchased software are generally amortized over a term of three to five years.

The following table provides the components of other intangible assets (in millions):

	December 31, 2013			December 31, 2012	
	Weighted-Average Amortization Period (in Years)	Initial Cost	Net of Accumulated Amortization	Initial Cost	Net of Accumulated Amortization
Acquired contracts	11.2	$ 632.0	$414.3	$ 627.2	$466.2
Capitalized contract costs	5.9	528.5	315.2	457.2	303.7
Internal use software	3.2	264.9	65.1	221.0	54.7
Acquired trademarks	22.7	38.0	25.3	43.4	28.4
Projects in process	3.0	9.6	9.6	15.4	15.4
Other intangibles	2.6	33.1	4.3	34.4	10.5
Total other intangible assets	8.0	$1,506.1	$833.8	$1,398.6	$878.9

The estimated future aggregate amortization expense for existing other intangible assets as of December 31, 2013 is expected to be $210.0 million in 2014, $151.0 million in 2015, $134.0 million in 2016, $102.5 million in 2017, $54.0 million in 2018 and $ 182.3 million thereafter.

Other intangible assets are reviewed for impairment on an annual basis or whenever events or changes in circumstances indicate that their carrying amount may not be recoverable. In such reviews, estimated undiscounted cash flows associated with these assets or operations are compared with their carrying values to determine if a write-down to fair value (normally measured by the present value technique) is required. The Company recorded immaterial impairments related to other intangible assets for the year ended December 31, 2013 and did not record any impairment during the years ended December 31, 2012 and 2011.

RESTRICTED CASH

6.28 WYNDHAM WORLDWIDE CORPORATION (DEC)
CONSOLIDATED STATEMENTS OF CASH FLOWS (in part)

(In millions)

	Year Ended December 31,		
	2013	2012	2011
Investing Activities			
Property and equipment additions	(238)	(208)	(239)
Net assets acquired, net of cash acquired	(129)	(263)	(27)
Development advances	(65)	(14)	(5)
Equity investments and loans	(3)	(42)	(12)
Proceeds from asset sales	6	1	31
Decrease in securitization restricted cash	29	11	6
Increase in escrow deposit restricted cash	(2)	(5)	(5)
Other, net	1	1	(5)
Net cash used in investing activities	(401)	(519)	(256)

NOTES TO CONSOLIDATED FINANCIAL STATEMENTS

(Unless otherwise noted, all amounts are in millions, except share and per share amounts)

2. Summary of Significant Accounting Policies (in part)

Restricted Cash

The largest portion of the Company's restricted cash relates to securitizations. The remaining portion is comprised of cash held in escrow related to the Company's vacation ownership business and cash held in all other escrow accounts.

Securitizations: In accordance with the contractual requirements of the Company's various vacation ownership contract receivable securitizations, a dedicated lockbox account, subject to a blocked control agreement, is established for each securitization. At each month end, the total cash in the collection account from the previous month is analyzed and a monthly servicer report is prepared by the Company, which details how much cash should be remitted to the note holders for principal and interest payments, and any cash remaining is transferred by the trustee back to the Company. Additionally, as required by various securitizations, the Company holds an agreed-upon percentage of the aggregate outstanding principal balances of the VOI contract receivables collateralizing the asset-backed notes in a segregated trust (or reserve) account as credit enhancement. Each time a securitization closes and the Company receives cash from the note holders, a portion of the cash is deposited in the reserve account. Such amounts were $92 million and $121 million, of which $64 million and $65 million is recorded within other current assets and $28 million and $56 million is recorded within other non-current assets as of December 31, 2013 and 2012, respectively, on the Consolidated Balance Sheets.

Escrow Deposits: Laws in most U.S. states require the escrow of down payments on VOI sales, with the typical requirement mandating that the funds be held in escrow until the rescission period expires. As sales transactions are consummated, down payments are collected and are subsequently placed in escrow until the rescission period has expired. Depending on the state, the rescission period can be as short as 3 calendar days or as long as 15 calendar days. In certain states, the escrow laws require that 100% of VOI purchaser funds (excluding interest payments, if any), be held in escrow until the deeding process is complete. Where possible, the Company utilizes surety bonds in lieu of escrow deposits. Escrow deposit amounts were $57 million and $56 million as of December 31, 2013 and 2012, respectively, which is recorded within other current assets on the Consolidated Balance Sheets.

14. Variable Interest Entities (in part)

The Company pools qualifying vacation ownership contract receivables and sells them to bankruptcy-remote entities. Vacation ownership contract receivables qualify for securitization based primarily on the credit strength of the VOI purchaser to whom financing has been extended. Vacation ownership contract receivables are securitized through bankruptcy-remote SPEs that are consolidated within the Consolidated Financial Statements. As a result, the Company does not recognize gains or losses resulting from these securitizations at the time of sale to the SPEs. Interest income is recognized when earned over the contractual life of the vacation ownership contract receivables. The Company services the securitized vacation ownership contract receivables pursuant to servicing agreements negotiated on an arms-length basis based on market conditions. The activities of these SPEs are limited to (i) purchasing vacation ownership contract receivables from the Company's vacation ownership subsidiaries, (ii) issuing debt securities and/or borrowing under a conduit facility to fund such purchases and (iii) entering into derivatives to hedge interest rate exposure. The bankruptcy-remote SPEs are legally separate from the Company. The receivables held by the bankruptcy-remote SPEs are not available to creditors of the Company and legally are not assets of the Company. Additionally, the creditors of these SPEs have no recourse to the Company for principal and interest.

The assets and liabilities of these vacation ownership SPEs are as follows:

	December 31, 2013	December 31, 2012
Securitized contract receivables, gross[a]	$2,204	$2,401
Securitized restricted cash[b]	92	121
Interest receivables on securitized contract receivables[c]	17	19
Other assets[d]	1	2
Total SPE assets[e]	2,314	2,543
Securitized term notes[f]	1,648	1,770
Securitized conduit facilities[f]	262	190
Other liabilities[g]	2	5
Total SPE liabilities	1,912	1,965
SPE assets in excess of SPE liabilities	$ 402	$ 578

[a] Included in current ($222 million and $252 million as of December 31, 2013 and 2012, respectively) and non-current ($1,982 million and $2,149 million as of December 31, 2013 and 2012, respectively) vacation ownership contract receivables on the Consolidated Balance Sheets.

[b] Included in other current assets ($64 million and $65 million as of December 31, 2013 and 2012, respectively) and other non-current assets ($28 million and $56 million as of December 31, 2013 and 2012, respectively) on the Consolidated Balance Sheets.

[c] Included in trade receivables, net on the Consolidated Balance Sheets.

[d] Includes interest rate derivative contracts and related assets; included in other non-current assets on the Consolidated Balance Sheets.

[e] Excludes deferred financing costs of $28 million as of both December 31, 2013 and 2012, related to securitized debt.

[f] Included in current ($184 million and $218 million as of December 31, 2013 and 2012, respectively) and long-term ($1,726 million and $1,742 million as of December 31, 2013 and 2012, respectively) securitized vacation ownership debt on the Consolidated Balance Sheets.

[g] Primarily includes accrued interest on securitized debt ($2 million as of both December 31, 2013 and 2012) which is included in accrued expenses and other current liabilities, and interest rate derivative contracts ($3 million as of December 31, 2012) which is included in other non-current liabilities on the Consolidated Balance Sheets.

Cash Flows From Financing Activities

PRESENTATION

6.29 FASB ASC 230-10-45 defines those transactions and events that constitute financing cash receipts and payments. Cash inflows from financing activities include the following:

- Proceeds from issuing equity instruments.
- Proceeds from issuing bonds, mortgages, and notes and from other short- or long-term borrowing.
- Receipts from contributions and investment income that, by donor stipulation, are restricted for the purposes of acquiring, constructing, or improving PPE or other long-lived assets or establishing or increasing a permanent or term endowment.
- Proceeds received from derivative instruments that include financing elements at inception, regardless of whether the proceeds were received at inception or over the term of the derivative instrument, other than a financing element inherently included in an at-the-market derivative instrument with no prepayments.
- Cash that is recognizable for financial reporting purposes because it is retained as a result of the tax deductibility of increases in the value of equity instruments issued under share-based payment arrangements that are not included in the cost of goods or services. For this purpose, excess tax benefits should be determined on an individual award (or portion thereof) basis.

Cash outflows from financing activities include the following:

- Payments of dividends or other distributions to owners, including outlays to reacquire the entity's equity instruments.
- Repayments of borrowed amounts.
- Other principal payments to creditors who have extended long-term credit.
- Distributions to counterparties of derivative instruments that include financing elements at inception, other than a financing element inherently included in an at-the-market derivative instrument with no prepayments. The distributions may be either at inception or over the term of the derivative instrument.
- Payments for debt issue costs.

PRESENTATION AND DISCLOSURE EXCERPTS

SPIN-OFF

6.30 IDT CORPORATION (JUL)
CONSOLIDATED STATEMENTS OF CASH FLOWS (in part)

	Year Ended July 31		
(In thousands)	2013	2012	2011
Financing Activities			
Cash of subsidiaries deconsolidated as a result of spin-offs	(15,000)	(104,243)	—
Dividends paid	(17,123)	(15,014)	(15,178)
Distributions to noncontrolling interests	(2,245)	(1,580)	(2,010)
Purchases of stock of subsidiary	(1,804)	—	—
Proceeds from sales of stock and exercise of stock options of subsidiary	154	133	—
Proceeds from exercise of stock options	921	—	1,674
Repayments of capital lease obligations	—	(1,781)	(4,821)
Proceeds from revolving credit loan payable	21,062	—	—
Repayments of borrowings	(21,304)	(332)	(4,602)
Repurchases of Class B common stock from Howard S. Jonas	—	—	(7,499)
Repurchases of common stock and Class B common stock	(1,079)	(2,816)	(205)
Net cash used in financing activities	(36,418)	(125,633)	(32,641)

NOTES TO CONSOLIDATED FINANCIAL STATEMENTS

Note 1—Description of Business and Summary of Significant Accounting Policies (in part)

Description of Business (in part)

On July 31, 2013, the Company completed a pro rata distribution of the common stock of the Company's subsidiary, Straight Path Communications Inc. ("Straight Path"), to the Company's stockholders of record as of the close of business on July 25, 2013 (the "Straight Path Spin-Off") (see Note 2). On October 28, 2011, the Company completed a pro rata distribution of the common stock of the Company's subsidiary, Genie Energy Ltd. ("Genie"), to the Company's stockholders of record as of the close of business on October 21, 2011 (the "Genie Spin-Off") (see Note 2). Straight Path and Genie met the criteria to be reported as discontinued operations and accordingly, their assets, liabilities, results of operations and cash flows are classified as discontinued operations for all periods presented.

Note 2—Discontinued Operations (in part)

Straight Path Communications, Inc.

On July 31, 2013, the Company completed a pro rata distribution of the common stock of the Company's subsidiary, Straight Path Communications Inc., to the Company's stockholders of record as of the close of business on July 25, 2013. At the time of the Straight Path Spin-Off, Straight Path owned 100% of Straight Path Spectrum, Inc. (formerly IDT Spectrum, Inc.), which holds, leases and markets fixed wireless spectrum licenses, and 84.5% of Straight Path IP Group, Inc. (formerly Innovative Communications Technologies, Inc.), which holds intellectual property primarily related to communications over the Internet and the licensing and other businesses related to this intellectual property. As of July 31, 2013, each of the Company's stockholders received one share of Straight Path Class A common stock for every two shares of the Company's Class A common stock and one share of Straight Path Class B common stock for every two shares of the Company's Class B common stock held of record date as of the close of business on July 25, 2013. Straight Path and subsidiaries met the criteria to be reported as discontinued operations and accordingly, their assets, liabilities, results of operations and cash flows are classified as discontinued operations for all periods presented.

The Company intends for the Straight Path Spin-Off to be tax-free for the Company and the Company's stockholders for U.S. federal income tax purposes under Section 355 of the Internal Revenue Code of 1986 (the "Code"). The Company received an opinion from Pryor Cashman LLP on the requirements for a tax-free distribution. Specifically, the opinion concluded that the distribution (i) should satisfy the business purpose requirement of the Code for a tax-free distribution, (ii) should not be viewed as being used principally as a device for the distribution of earnings and profits of the distributing corporation or the controlled corporation or both, and (iii) should not be viewed as part of a plan (or series of related transactions) pursuant to which one or more persons will acquire directly or indirectly stock representing a 50 percent or greater interest in the distributing corporation or controlled corporation within the meaning of the relevant section of the Code.

In connection with the Straight Path Spin-Off, the Company funded Straight Path with a total of $15.0 million in aggregate cash and cash equivalents.

DEBT PROCEEDS/REPAYMENTS

6.31 VISHAY INTERTECHNOLOGY, INC. (DEC)
CONSOLIDATED STATEMENTS OF CASH FLOWS (in part)

(In thousands)

	Years Ended December 31,		
	2013	**2012**	**2011**
Continuing Financing Activities			
Proceeds from long-term borrowings	—	150,000	150,000
Issuance costs	(4,558)	(4,827)	(4,429)
Principal payments on long-term debt and capital leases	(28)	(27)	(681)
Net proceeds (payments) on revolving credit lines	25,000	(66,000)	(85,000)
Common stock repurchases	—	(150,000)	(150,000)
Net changes in short-term borrowings	(146)	(115)	(10)
Distributions to noncontrolling interests	(257)	(1,040)	(1,440)
Proceeds from stock options exercised	—	174	9,675
Excess tax benefit from stock options exercised	196	—	555
Other financing activites	(3,638)	—	—
Net cash provided by (used in) continuing financing activities	16,569	(71,835)	(81,330)

(Dollars in thousands, except per share amounts)

Note 6—Long-Term Debt (in part)

Long-term debt consists of the following:

	December 31, 2013	December 31, 2012
Credit facility	$114,000	$ 89,000
Exchangeable unsecured notes, due 2102	38,642	95,042
Convertible senior debentures, due 2040	101,846	100,166
Convertible senior debentures, due 2041	52,264	51,399
Convertible senior debentures, due 2042	58,159	57,324
	364,911	392,931
Less current portion	—	—
	$364,911	$392,931

Credit Facility

The Company maintains a credit facility with a consortium of banks led by JPMorgan Chase Bank, N.A., as administrative agent (the "Credit Facility"). On August 8, 2013, the Company entered into an Amended and Restated Credit Agreement, which provides an aggregate commitment of $ 640,000 of revolving loans available until August 8, 2018. The original credit agreement became effective December 1, 2010 and was scheduled to expire on December 1, 2015. The Credit Facility, as amended and restated, also provides for the ability of Vishay to request up to $ 50,000 of incremental revolving commitments, subject to the satisfaction of certain conditions.

Borrowings under the Credit Facility bear interest at the London Interbank Offered Rate ("LIBOR") plus an interest margin. The applicable interest margin is based on the Company's leverage ratio. Based on the Company's current leverage ratio, borrowings bear interest at LIBOR plus 1.75%. The interest rate on the Company's borrowings will increase to LIBOR plus 2.00% if the Company's leverage ratio equals or exceeds 2.50 to 1 and will decrease to LIBOR plus 1.50% if the Company's leverage ratio decreases below 1.50 to 1. Vishay is also required to pay facility fees on the entire commitment amount based on the Company's leverage ratio. Based on the Company's current leverage ratio, the facility fee is 0.35% per annum. Such facility fee will increase to 0.50% per annum if the Company's leverage ratio equals or exceeds 2.50 to 1 and will decrease to 0.30% per annum if the leverage ratio decreases below 1.50 to 1.

The August 8, 2013 Amended and Restated Credit Agreement also removes certain restrictions related to the incurrence and repayment of certain intercompany indebtedness, mergers, liquidations, and transfers of ownership of wholly owned subsidiaries that were present in the original credit agreement. These changes will enable the Company to streamline its complex subsidiary structure and provide greater operating flexibility.

The borrowings under the Credit Facility are secured by a lien on substantially all assets, including accounts receivable, inventory, machinery and equipment, and general intangibles (but excluding real estate, intellectual property registered or licensed for use in, or arising under the laws of, any country other than the United States, assets located outside of the United States and deposit and securities accounts), of Vishay and certain significant subsidiaries located in the United States, and pledges of stock in certain significant domestic and foreign subsidiaries; and are guaranteed by certain significant subsidiaries. Certain of the Company's subsidiaries are permitted to borrow under the Credit Facility, subject to the satisfaction of specified conditions. Any borrowings by these subsidiaries under the Credit Facility are guaranteed by Vishay and certain subsidiaries. The Credit Facility also limits or restricts the Company and its subsidiaries, from, among other things, incurring indebtedness, incurring liens on its respective assets, making investments and acquisitions, making asset sales, and making other restricted payments, and requires the Company to comply with other covenants, including the maintenance of specific financial ratios.

The Credit Facility permits the Company to repurchase shares of its common stock or pay cash dividends up to a permitted capacity, conditioned upon Vishay maintaining (i) a pro forma leverage ratio of 2.75 to 1.00, (ii) a pro forma interest expense coverage ratio of 2.00 to 1.00, and (iii) $300,000 of available liquidity, as defined in the Credit Facility. The permitted capacity to repurchase shares of the Company's outstanding common stock or pay cash dividends under the Credit Facility increases each quarter by an amount equal to 20% of net income. At December 31, 2013, the Credit Facility allows the Company to repurchase its common stock or pay cash dividends up to $204,596 (See Note 7). The amount and timing of any future stock repurchases or cash dividends remains subject to authorization of the Company's Board of Directors.

The Credit Facility also contains customary events of default, including, but not limited to, failure to pay principal or interest, failure to pay or default under other material debt, material misrepresentation or breach of warranty, violation of certain covenants, a change of control, the commencement of bankruptcy proceedings, the insolvency of Vishay or certain of its significant subsidiaries, and the rendering of a judgment in excess of $ 25,000 against Vishay or certain of its significant subsidiaries. Upon the occurrence of an event of default under the Credit Facility, the Company's obligations under the credit facility may be accelerated and the lending commitments under the credit facility terminated.

At December 31, 2013 and 2012, there was $ 518,345 and $ 431,295, respectively, available under the Credit Facility. Letters of credit totaling $ 7,655 and $ 7,705 were outstanding at December 31, 2013 and 2012, respectively.

PREFERRED STOCK PROCEEDS/PAYMENTS

6.32 THE PNC FINANCIAL SERVICES GROUP, INC. (DEC)
CONSOLIDATED STATEMENT OF CASH FLOWS (in part)

| (In millions) | Year ended December 31 | | |
Unaudited	2013	2012	2011
Financing Activities			
Net change in			
Noninterest-bearing deposits	$ 341	$ 7,149	$ 8,909
Interest-bearing deposits	7,463	902	(4,863)
Federal funds purchased and repurchase agreements	965	(2)	(1,151)
Federal Home Loan Bank borrowings		(1,000)	1,000
Commercial paper	(5,607)	4,762	227
Other borrowed funds	221	(279)	(789)
Sales/issuances			
Federal Home Loan Bank borrowings	16,435	13,000	1,000
Bank notes and senior debt	3,938	2,093	1,244
Subordinated debt	1,986	995	
Commercial paper	12,595	16,480	9,565
Other borrowed funds	695	1,011	460
Preferred stock	496	2,449	988
Common and treasury stock	244	158	72
Repayments/maturities			
Federal Home Loan Bank borrowings	(12,960)	(10,500)	(1,076)
Bank notes and senior debt	(1,420)	(4,037)	(2,612)
Subordinated debt	(731)	(1,769)	(1,942)
Commercial paper	(10,444)	(17,060)	(8,236)
Other borrowed funds	(340)	(1,090)	(741)
Preferred stock	(150)		
Excess tax benefits from share-based payment arrangements	23	18	2
Redemption of noncontrolling interests	(375)	(500)	
Acquisition of treasury stock	(24)	(216)	(73)
Preferred stock cash dividends paid	(237)	(177)	(56)
Common stock cash dividends paid	(911)	(820)	(604)
Net cash provided (used) by financing activities	12,203	11,567	1,324

NOTES TO CONSOLIDATED FINANCIAL STATEMENTS

Note 19—Equity (in part)

Preferred Stock

The following table provides the number of preferred shares issued and outstanding, the liquidation value per share and the number of authorized preferred shares that are available for future use.

Table 141: Preferred Stock—Authorized, Issued and Outstanding

December 31 Shares in Thousands	Liquidation Value Per Share	Preferred Shares 2013	Preferred Shares 2012
Authorized			
$1 par value		16,588	16,588
Issued and outstanding			
Series B	$ 40	1	1
Series K	10,000	50	50
Series L	100,000		2
Series O	100,000	10	10
Series P	100,000	15	15
Series Q	100,000	5	5
Series R	100,000	5	—
Total issued and outstanding		86	83

The following table discloses information related to the preferred stock outstanding as of December 31, 2013.

Table 142: Terms of Outstanding Preferred Stock

Preferred Stock	Issue Date	Number of Depositary Shares Issued	Fractional Interest in a Share of Preferred Stock Represented by Each Depositary Share	Dividend Dates[a]	Annual Per Share Dividend Rate	Optional Redemption Date[b]
Series B[c]	[c]	N/A	N/A	Quarterly from March 10th	$1.80	None
Series K[d]	May 21, 2008	500,000	1/10th	Semi-annually beginning on November 21, 2008 until May 21, 2013 Quarterly beginning on August 21, 2013	8.25% until May 21, 2013 3 Mo. LIBOR plus 4.22% per annum beginning on May 21, 2013	May 21, 2013
Series O[d]	July 27, 2011	1 million	1/100th	Semi-annually beginning on February 1, 2012 until August 1, 2021 Quarterly beginning on November 1, 2021	6.75% until August 1, 2021 3 Mo. LIBOR plus 3.678% per annum beginning on August 1, 2021	August 1, 2021
Series P[d]	April 24, 2012	60 million	1/4,000th	Quarterly beginning on August 1, 2012	6.125% until May 1, 2022 3 Mo. LIBOR plus 4.0675% per annum beginning on May 1, 2022	May 1, 2022
Series Q[d]	September 21, 2012 October 9, 2012	18 million 1.2 million	1/4,000th	Quarterly beginning on December 1, 2012	5.375%	December 1, 2017
Series R[d]	May 7, 2013	500,000	1/100th	Semi-annually beginning on December 1, 2013 until June 1, 2023 Quarterly beginning on September 1, 2023	4.85% until June 1, 2023 3 Mo. LIBOR plus 3.04% per annum beginning June 1, 2023	June 1, 2023

[a] Dividends are payable when, as, and if declared by our Board of Directors or an authorized committee of our Board.

[b] Redeemable at PNC's option on or after the date stated. With the exception of the Series B and Series K preferred stock, redeemable at PNC's option within 90 days of a regulatory capital treatment event as defined in the designations.

[c] Cumulative preferred stock. Holders of Series B preferred stock are entitled to 8 votes per shares, which is equal to the number of full shares of common stock into which the Series B preferred stock is convertible. The Series B preferred stock was issued in connection with the consolidation of Pittsburgh National Corporation and Provident National Corporation in 1983.

[d] Non-Cumulative preferred stock.

Our Series L preferred stock was issued in connection with the National City transaction in exchange for National City's Fixed-to-Floating Rate Non-Cumulative Preferred Stock, Series F. Dividends on the Series L preferred stock were payable if and when declared each 1st of February, May, August and November. Dividends were paid at a rate of 9.875% prior to February 1, 2013 and at a rate of three-month LIBOR plus 633 basis points beginning February 1, 2013. On April 19, 2013, PNC redeemed all 6,000,000 depositary shares representing interests in PNC's Series L preferred stock and all 1,500 shares of Series L preferred stock underlying such depositary shares, resulting in a net outflow of $150 million.

We have authorized but unissued Series H and Series I preferred stock. As described in Note 14 Capital Securities of Subsidiary Trusts and Perpetual Trust Securities, the PNC Preferred Funding Trust II securities that currently qualify as capital for regulatory purposes are automatically exchangeable into shares of PNC Series I preferred stock under certain conditions relating to the capitalization or the financial condition of PNC Bank, N.A. and upon the direction of the Office of the Comptroller of the Currency. The Series A preferred stock of PNC REIT Corp. is also automatically exchangeable under similar conditions into shares of PNC Series H preferred stock. As described in Note 14, on March 15, 2013, we redeemed all $375 million of the PNC Preferred Funding Trust III securities that had been exchangeable under certain conditions into PNC Series J preferred stock.

DIVIDENDS

6.33 CABLEVISION SYSTEMS CORPORATION (DEC)
CONSOLIDATED STATEMENTS OF CASH FLOWS (in part)

(Dollars in thousands)

	2013	2012	2011
Cash flows from financing activities:			
Proceeds from credit facility debt, net of discount	3,296,760	—	1,265,000
Repayment of credit facility debt	(3,445,751)	(519,458)	(580,651)
Proceeds from issuance of senior notes	—	750,000	1,000,000
Redemption and repurchase of senior notes, including premiums and fees	(371,498)	(531,326)	(1,227,307)
Repayment of notes payable	(570)	—	—
Proceeds from collateralized indebtedness	569,561	248,388	307,763
Repayment of collateralized indebtedness and related derivative contracts	(508,009)	(218,754)	(257,913)
Dividend distributions to common stockholders	(159,709)	(163,872)	(162,032)
Proceeds from stock option exercises	18,120	18,722	6,471
Tax withholding associated with shares issued for equity-based compensation	(644)	—	—
Principal payments on capital lease obligations	(13,828)	(13,729)	(3,226)
Deemed repurchases of restricted stock	(12,262)	(19,831)	(35,555)
Purchase of shares of CNYG Class A common stock, pursuant to a share repurchase program, held as treasury shares	—	(188,600)	(555,831)
Excess tax benefit related to share-based awards	1,280	—	—
Additions to deferred financing costs	(27,080)	(21,491)	(25,186)
Distributions to noncontrolling interests, net	(1,424)	(1,588)	(1,311)
Net cash used in financing activities	(655,054)	(661,539)	(269,778)

COMBINED NOTES TO CONSOLIDATED FINANCIAL STATEMENTS

(Dollars in thousands, except per share amounts)

Note 2. Summary of Significant Accounting Policies (in part)

Dividends

Cablevision may pay dividends on its capital stock only from net profits and surplus as determined under Delaware law. If dividends are paid on CNYG common stock, holders of CNYG Class A common stock and CNYG Class B common stock are entitled to receive dividends, and other distributions in cash, stock or property, equally on a per share basis, except that stock dividends with respect to CNYG Class A common stock may be paid only with shares of CNYG Class A common stock and stock dividends with respect to CNYG Class B common stock may be paid only with shares of CNYG Class B common stock.

CSC Holdings may make distributions on its membership interests only if sufficient funds exist as determined under Delaware law.

Cablevision's and CSC Holdings' indentures and CSC Holdings credit agreement restrict the amount of dividends and distributions in respect of any equity interest that can be made.

The Board of Directors of Cablevision declared the following cash dividends to stockholders of record on both its CNYG Class A common stock and CNYG Class B common stock:

Declaration Date	Dividend Per Share	Record Date	Payment Date
November 6, 2013	$ 0.15	November 22, 2013	December 13, 2013
July 30, 2013	$ 0.15	August 15, 2013	September 5, 2013
May 7, 2013	$ 0.15	May 24, 2013	June 14, 2013
February 26, 2013	$ 0.15	March 15, 2013	April 3, 2013
October 24, 2012	$ 0.15	November 7, 2012	November 28, 2012
August 1, 2012	$ 0.15	August 14, 2012	September 4, 2012
May 1, 2012	$ 0.15	May 17, 2012	June 1, 2012
February 22, 2012	$ 0.15	March 9, 2012	March 30, 2012
October 27, 2011	$ 0.15	November 11, 2011	December 2, 2011
August 5, 2011	$ 0.15	August 19, 2011	September 9, 2011
May 4, 2011	$ 0.15	May 16, 2011	June 6, 2011
February 15, 2011	$0.125	February 28, 2011	March 21, 2011

Cablevision paid dividends aggregating $159,709, $163,872 and $162,032 in 2013, 2012 and 2011, respectively, including accrued dividends on vested restricted shares of $3,092, $5,987, and $3,059, respectively, primarily from the proceeds of equity distribution payments from CSC Holdings. In addition, as of December 31, 2013, up to approximately $6,058 will be paid when, and if, restrictions lapse on restricted shares outstanding.

During the years ended December 31, 2013, 2012 and 2011, CSC Holdings made equity distribution cash payments to Cablevision aggregating $501,224, $671,809 and $929,947, respectively. These distribution payments were funded from cash on hand. The proceeds were used to fund:

- Cablevision's dividends paid;
- Cablevision's interest and principal payments on its senior notes;
- Cablevision's payments for the acquisition of treasury shares related to statutory minimum tax withholding obligations upon the vesting of certain restricted shares;
- Cablevision's repurchases of certain outstanding senior notes in 2013; and
- the repurchase of CNYG Class A common stock under Cablevision's share repurchase program in 2012 and 2011 (see Note 19).

Additionally on June 30, 2011, CSC Holdings distributed to Cablevision all of the outstanding common stock of AMC Networks.

ACCOUNTS RECEIVABLE SECURITIZATION FACILITY

6.34 HANESBRANDS INC. (DEC)
CONSOLIDATED STATEMENTS OF CASH FLOWS (in part)

(In thousands)

	Years Ended		
	December 28, 2013	December 29, 2012	December 31, 2011
Financing activities:			
Borrowings on notes payable	101,175	78,036	360,893
Repayments on notes payable	(91,027)	(115,117)	(348,924)
Borrowings on Accounts Receivable Securitization Facility	145,715	177,300	280,629
Repayments on Accounts Receivable Securitization Facility	(137,761)	(170,397)	(203,696)
Borrowings on Revolving Loan Facility	4,053,500	2,938,500	2,890,000
Repayments on Revolving Loan Facility	(3,654,000)	(2,885,500)	(2,875,500)
Redemption of Floating Rate Senior Notes	—	(293,277)	(197,458)
Redemption of debt under 8% Senior Notes	(250,000)	(250,000)	—
Cash dividends paid	(59,442)	—	—
Payments to amend and refinance credit facilities	(5,630)	(2,353)	(3,757)
Proceeds from stock options exercised	5,279	8,752	17,104
Taxes paid related to net shares settlement of equity awards	(41,839)	(4,705)	(5,521)
Excess tax benefit from stock-based compensation	26,784	1,253	1,673
Transactions with Sara Lee Corporation	—	—	(11,403)
Other	1,003	(269)	920
Net cash from financing activities	93,757	(517,777)	(95,040)

NOTES TO CONSOLIDATED FINANCIAL STATEMENTS

(Amounts in thousands, except per share data)

(10) Debt (in part)

The Company had the following debt at December 28, 2013 and December 29, 2012 :

	Interest Rate as of December 28, 2013	Principal Amount		Maturity Date
		December 28, 2013	December 29, 2012	
Senior secured credit facility:				
Revolving loan facility	1.69%	$ 467,000	$ 67,500	July 2018
6.375% Senior Notes	6.38%	1,000,000	1,000,000	December 2020
Accounts receivable securitization facility	1.22%	181,790	173,836	March 2014
8% Senior Notes	—	—	250,000	
		1,648,790	1,491,336	
Less current maturities		181,790	173,836	
		$1,467,000	$1,317,500	

The Company's primary financing arrangements are the senior secured credit facility (the "Senior Secured Credit Facility"), $1,000,000 in aggregate principal amount of 6.375% senior notes (the " 6.375% Senior Notes") and the Accounts Receivable Securitization Facility. The outstanding balances at December 28, 2013 are reported in the "Long-term debt" and "Accounts Receivable Securitization Facility" lines of the Consolidated Balance Sheets.

Total cash paid for interest related to debt in 2013, 2012 and 2011 was $96,434, $124,427 and $140,083, respectively.

Accounts Receivable Securitization Facility

The Accounts Receivable Securitization Facility provides for up to $225,000 in funding accounted for as a secured borrowing, limited to the availability of eligible receivables, and is secured by certain domestic trade receivables. Under the terms of the Accounts Receivable Securitization Facility, the Company and certain of its subsidiaries sell, on a revolving basis, certain domestic trade receivables to HBI Receivables LLC ("Receivables LLC"), a wholly-owned bankruptcy-remote subsidiary that in turn uses the trade receivables to secure the borrowings, which are funded through conduits and financial institutions that are not affiliated with the Company. The commitments of any conduits party to the Accounts Receivable Securitization Facility are funded through the issuance of commercial paper in the short-term market or through committed bank purchasers if the conduits fail to fund. The assets and liabilities of Receivables LLC are fully reflected on the Consolidated Balance Sheet, and the securitization is treated as a secured borrowing for accounting purposes, but the assets of Receivables LLC will be used first to satisfy the creditors of Receivables LLC, not the Company's creditors. The borrowings under the Accounts Receivable Securitization Facility remain outstanding throughout the term of the agreement subject to the Company maintaining sufficient eligible receivables, by continuing to sell trade receivables to Receivables LLC, unless an event of default occurs. The Accounts Receivable Securitization Facility will terminate on March 14, 2014; however, the Company plans to extend the term.

Availability of funding under the Accounts Receivable Securitization Facility depends primarily upon the eligible outstanding receivables balance. As of December 28, 2013, Receivables LLC had $181,790 outstanding under the Accounts Receivable Securitization Facility. The outstanding balance under the Accounts Receivable Securitization Facility is reported on the Consolidated Balance Sheet in the line "Accounts Receivable Securitization Facility." In the case of any creditors party to the Accounts Receivable Securitization Facility that are conduits, unless the conduits fail to fund, the yield on the commercial paper, which is the conduits' cost to issue the commercial paper plus certain dealer fees, is considered a financing cost and is included in interest expense on the Consolidated Statement of Income. If the conduits fail to fund, the Accounts Receivable Securitization Facility would be funded through committed bank purchasers, and the interest rate would be payable at the Company's option at the rate announced from time to time by HSBC Bank USA, N.A. as its prime rate or at the LIBO Rate (as defined in the Accounts Receivable Securitization Facility) plus the applicable margin in effect from time to time. In the case of borrowings from any other creditors party to the Accounts Receivable Securitization Facility that are not conduits or their related committed bank purchasers, the interest rate is payable at the LIBO Rate (as defined in the Accounts Receivable Securitization Facility) or, if this rate is unavailable or otherwise does not accurately reflect the costs to these creditors related to the borrowings, the prime rate. These amounts are also considered financing costs and are included in interest expense on the Consolidated Statement of Income. In addition, Receivables LLC is required to make certain payments to a conduit purchaser, a committed purchaser, or certain entities that provide funding to or are affiliated with them, in the event that assets and liabilities of a conduit purchaser are consolidated for financial and/or regulatory accounting purposes with certain other entities. The average blended interest rate for the outstanding balance as of December 28, 2013 was 1.22%.

The Accounts Receivable Securitization Facility contains customary events of default and requires the Company to maintain the same interest coverage ratio and leverage ratio contained from time to time in the Senior Secured Credit Facility, provided that any changes to such covenants will only be applicable for purposes of the Accounts Receivable Securitization Facility if approved by the Managing Agents or their affiliates. As of December 28, 2013, the Company was in compliance with all financial covenants.

The total amount of receivables used as collateral for the credit facility was $320,192 at December 28, 2013 and is reported on the Company's Consolidated Balance Sheet in trade accounts receivable less allowances.

6.35 MICRON TECHNOLOGY, INC. (AUG)

CONSOLIDATED STATEMENTS OF CASH FLOWS (in part)

(In millions)

For the Year Ended	August 29, 2013	August 30, 2012	September 1, 2011
Cash Flows From Financing Activities			
Proceeds from issuance of debt	1,121	1,065	690
Proceeds from issuance of common stock under equity Plans	150	5	28
Proceeds from equipment sale-leaseback transactions	126	609	268
Cash received from noncontrolling interests	11	197	8
Repayments of debt	(743)	(203)	(1,215)
Payments on equipment purchase contracts	(214)	(172)	(322)
Cash paid for capped call transactions	(48)	(103)	(57)
Distributions to noncontrolling interests	(37)	(391)	(225)
Cash paid to purchase common stock	(5)	(6)	(163)
Acquisition of noncontrolling interests	—	(466)	(159)
Other	(39)	(38)	(48)
Net cash provided by (used for) financing activities	322	497	(1,195)

NOTES TO CONSOLIDATED FINANCIAL STATEMENTS

(All tabular amounts in millions except per share amounts)

Variable Interest Entities (in part)

We have interests in entities that are Variable Interest Entities ("VIEs"). If we are the primary beneficiary of a VIE, we are required to consolidate it. To determine if we are the primary beneficiary, we evaluate whether we have the power to direct the activities that most significantly impact the VIE's economic performance and the obligation to absorb losses or the right to receive benefits of the VIE that could potentially be significant to the VIE. Our evaluation includes identification of significant activities and an assessment of our ability to direct those activities based on governance provisions and arrangements to provide or receive product and process technology, product supply, operations services, equity funding, financing and other applicable agreements and circumstances. Our assessments of whether we are the primary beneficiary of our VIEs require significant assumptions and judgments.

Unconsolidated Variable Interest Entities (in part)

EQUVO Entities: EQUVO HK Limited and EQUVA Capital 1 Pte. Ltd. (together, the "EQUVO Entities") are special purpose entities created to facilitate equipment sale-leaseback financing transactions between us and a consortium of financial institutions that fund the sale-leaseback transactions ("Financing Entities"). Neither we nor the Financing Entities have an equity interest in the EQUVO Entities. The EQUVO Entities are VIEs because their equity is not sufficient to permit them to finance their activities without additional support from the Financing Entities and because the third-party equity holder lacks characteristics of a controlling financial interest. By design, the arrangements with the EQUVO Entities are merely financing vehicles and we do not bear any significant risks from variable interests with the EQUVO Entities. Therefore, we have determined that we do not have the power to direct the activities of the EQUVO Entities that most significantly impact their economic performance and we do not consolidate the EQUVO Entities.

Debt (in part)

Capital Lease Obligations

We have various capital lease obligations due in periodic installments with a weighted-average remaining term of 4.0 years and weighted-average effective interest rates of 4.1% as of 2013 and 4.9% as of 2012. In 2013, we received $126 million in proceeds from equipment sale-leaseback transactions and as a result recorded capital lease obligations aggregating $126 million at a weighted-average effective interest rate of 4.3%, payable in periodic installments through July 2017. On July 31, 2013, in connection with our acquisition of the Elpida Companies and purchase of the Rexchip shares from Powerchip, we recorded $377 million of capital lease obligations at a weighted-average effective interest rate of 3.2%, payable in periodic installments with a weighted-average remaining term of 5.5 years. In 2012, we received $609 million in proceeds from equipment sale-leaseback transactions and as a result recorded capital lease obligations aggregating $609 million at a weighted-average effective interest rate of 4.2%, payable in periodic installments through August, 2016.

LITIGATION ESCROW ACCOUNT

6.36 VISA INC. (SEP)

CONSOLIDATED STATEMENTS OF CASH FLOWS (in part)

(In millions)	For the Years Ended September 30,		
	2013	**2012**	**2011**
Financing Activities			
Repurchase of class A common stock (Note 14)	(5,365)	(710)	(2,024)
Dividends paid (Note 14)	(864)	(595)	(423)
Deposits into litigation escrow account—retrospective responsibility plan (Note 3)	—	(1,715)	(1,200)
Payments from litigation escrow account—retrospective responsibility plan (Note 3)	4,383	140	280
Cash proceeds from exercise of stock options	108	174	99
Restricted stock and performance shares settled in cash for taxes	(64)	—	—
Excess tax benefit for share-based compensation	74	71	18
Payments for earn-out related to PlaySpan acquisition	(12)	(14)	—
Principal payments on capital lease obligations	(6)	(6)	(10)
Principal payments on debt	—	—	(44)
Net cash used in financing activities	(1,746)	(2,655)	(3,304)

NOTES TO CONSOLIDATED FINANCIAL STATEMENTS

Note 1—Summary of Significant Accounting Policies (in part)

Restricted cash—litigation escrow. The Company maintains an escrow account from which settlements of, or judgments in, the covered litigation are paid. See *Note 3—Retrospective Responsibility Plan* and *Note 20—Legal Matters* for a discussion of the covered litigation. The escrow funds are held in money market investments, together with the interest earned, less applicable taxes payable, and classified as restricted cash on the consolidated balance sheets. Interest earned on escrow funds is included in non-operating income, on the consolidated statements of operations.

Financial instruments. The Company considers the following to be financial instruments: cash and cash equivalents, restricted cash-litigation escrow, trading and available-for-sale investment securities, settlement receivable and payable, customer collateral, non-marketable equity investments, settlement risk guarantee, derivative instruments, the Visa Europe put option and the earn-out provision related to the PlaySpan acquisition. See *Note 4—Fair Value Measurements and Investments*.

Note 3—Retrospective Responsibility Plan (in part)

The Company has established several related mechanisms designed to address potential liability under certain litigation referred to as the "covered litigation." These mechanisms are included in and referred to as the retrospective responsibility plan, or the plan, and consist of a litigation escrow agreement, the conversion feature of the Company's shares of class B common stock, the indemnification obligations of the Visa U.S.A. members, an interchange judgment sharing agreement and a loss sharing agreement.

Covered litigation consists of:

- *the Discover Litigation*. Discover Financial Services Inc. v. Visa U.S.A. Inc., Case No. 04-CV-07844 (S.D.N.Y) (settled);
- *the American Express Litigation*. American Express Travel Related Services Co., Inc. v. Visa U.S.A. Inc. et al., No. 04-CV-0897 (S.D.N.Y.), which the Company refers to as the American Express litigation (settled);
- *the Attridge Litigation*. Attridge v. Visa U.S.A. Inc. et al., Case No. CGC-04—436920 (Cal. Super.);
- *the Interchange Multidistrict Litigation*. In re Payment Card Interchange Fee and Merchant Discount Antitrust Litigation, 1:05-md-01720-JG-JO (E.D.N.Y.) or MDL 1720, including all cases currently included in MDL 1720, any other case that includes claims for damages relating to the period prior to the Company's IPO that has been or is transferred for coordinated or consolidated pre-trial proceedings at any time to MDL 1720 by the Judicial Panel on Multidistrict Litigation or otherwise included at any time in MDL 1720 by order of any court of competent jurisdiction and Kendall v. Visa U.S.A., Inc. et al., Case No. C04-4276 JSW (N.D. Cal.); and
- any claim that challenges the reorganization or the consummation thereof; provided that such claim is transferred for coordinated or consolidated pre-trial proceedings at any time to MDL 1720 by the Judicial Panel on Multidistrict Litigation or otherwise included at any time in MDL 1720 by order of any court of competent jurisdiction.

Litigation escrow agreement. In accordance with the litigation escrow agreement, the Company maintains an escrow account, from which settlements of, or judgments in, the covered litigation are paid. The amount of the escrow is determined by the board of directors and the Company's litigation committee, all members of which are affiliated with, or act for, certain Visa U.S.A. members. The escrow funds are held in money market investments along with the interest earned, less applicable taxes, and are classified as restricted cash on the consolidated balance sheets.

The following table sets forth the changes in the litigation escrow account:

(In millions)	Fiscal 2013	Fiscal 2012
Balance at October 1	$ 4,432	$2,857
Payments to settlement funds:[1]		
Class plaintiffs	(4,033)	—
Individual plaintiffs	(350)	—
Payments to American Express	—	(140)
Deposits into the litigation escrow account	—	1,715
Balance at September 30	$ 49	$4,432

[1] These payments are associated with the interchange multidistrict litigation. The settlement with the class plaintiffs in these proceedings is subject to final court approval, which the Company cannot assure will be received, and to the adjudication of any appeals. See *Note 20—Legal Matters.*

An accrual for the covered litigation and a change to the litigation provision are recorded when loss is deemed to be probable and reasonably estimable. In making this determination, the Company evaluates available information, including but not limited to recommendations made by the litigation committee. The accrual related to the covered litigation could be either higher or lower than the litigation escrow account balance. The Company did not record an additional accrual for the covered litigation during fiscal 2013. See *Note 20—Legal Matters.*

Note 20—Legal Matters (in part)

Covered Litigation

Visa Inc., Visa U.S.A. and Visa International are parties to certain legal proceedings that are covered by the retrospective responsibility plan, which the Company refers to as the covered litigation. See *Note 3—Retrospective Responsibility Plan.* An accrual for the covered litigation and a charge to the litigation provision are recorded when loss is deemed to be probable and reasonably estimable. In making this determination, the Company evaluates available information, including but not limited to actions taken by the litigation committee. The total accrual related to the covered litigation could be either higher or lower than the escrow account balance. The Company recorded an additional accrual of $4.1 billion for the covered litigation during fiscal 2012, which increased its total reserve for the covered litigation from $285 million to $4.4 billion. During fiscal 2013, the Company paid approximately $4.4 billion from the litigation escrow account into settlement funds pursuant to settlement agreements with individual and class plaintiffs in the interchange multidistrict litigation.

The Attridge Litigation

On December 8, 2004, a complaint was filed in California state court on behalf of an alleged class of consumers asserting claims against Visa U.S.A., Visa International and MasterCard. The claims in this action, *Attridge v. Visa U.S.A. Inc., et al.*, allege that Visa's bylaw 2.10(e) and MasterCard's Competitive Programs Policy, which prohibited their respective members from issuing American Express or Discover cards, constitute unlawful restraints of trade under California's Unfair Competition Law and the Cartwright Act. On May 19, 2006, the court entered an order dismissing plaintiff's Cartwright Act claims with prejudice but allowing the plaintiff to proceed with his Unfair Competition Law claims, which seek restitution, injunctive relief, and attorneys' fees and costs. On December 14, 2007, the plaintiff amended his complaint to add Visa Inc. as a defendant.

In the separate " Indirect Purchaser" *Credit/Debit Card Tying Cases*, also pending in California state court (see below), Visa entered into a settlement agreement on September 14, 2009 which potentially could have had the effect of releasing the claims asserted in the *Attridge* case, subject to the ruling of the *Attridge* court. On August 23, 2010, final approval of the *Credit/Debit Card Tying Cases* settlement was granted. The plaintiff in *Attridge* and others appealed the final approval order. On February 15, 2011, the court ordered that the *Attridge* case be stayed until 30 days following the final resolution of the appeals in the *Credit/Debit Card Tying Cases*. On January 9, 2012, the appeals court reversed the approval of the *Credit/Debit Card Tying Cases* settlement, and the case was remanded to the trial court for consideration of the fairness and adequacy of the settlement in light of the inclusion of the *Attridge* claims in the release.

The parties in the *Credit/Debit Card Tying Cases* subsequently agreed upon a revised written settlement agreement, which was finally approved by the court on April 11, 2013. Objectors have filed notices of appeal in those cases and the *Attridge* case. On September 18, 2013, in light of the proceedings in the *Credit/Debit Card Tying Cases*, the *Attridge* case was stayed until April 11, 2014.

Interchange Multidistrict Litigation (MDL)

Beginning in May 2005, approximately fifty-five complaints (all but thirteen of which were styled as class actions) were filed in U.S. federal district courts by merchants against Visa U.S.A., Visa International, and/or MasterCard, and in some cases, certain Visa member financial institutions. The complaints challenged, among other things, Visa's and MasterCard's purported setting of interchange reimbursement fees, their "no surcharge" rules, and alleged tying and bundling of transaction fees under the federal antitrust laws, and, in some cases, certain state unfair competition laws. On October 19, 2005, the Judicial Panel on Multidistrict Litigation issued an order transferring the cases to the U.S. District Court for the Eastern District of New York for coordination of pre-trial proceedings in MDL 1720. A group of purported class plaintiffs filed a Second Consolidated Amended Class Action Complaint on January 29, 2009 which, together with the thirteen complaints brought by individual merchants, sought money damages alleged to range in the tens of billions of dollars (subject to trebling), as well as attorneys' fees and injunctive relief. The class plaintiffs also filed a Second Supplemental Class Action Complaint against Visa Inc. and certain member financial institutions challenging Visa's reorganization and IPO under the antitrust laws and seeking unspecified money damages and declaratory and injunctive relief, including an order that the IPO be unwound.

On July 1, 2007, as part of the retrospective responsibility plan, Visa U.S.A. and Visa International entered into an interchange judgment sharing agreement with certain member financial institutions of Visa U.S.A.

On February 7, 2011, Visa entered into an omnibus agreement that confirmed and memorialized the signatories' intentions with respect to the loss sharing agreement, the judgment sharing agreement and other agreements relating to the interchange multidistrict litigation. Under the omnibus agreement, the monetary portion of any settlement of the interchange multidistrict litigation covered by the omnibus agreement would be divided into a MasterCard portion at 33.3333% and a Visa portion at 66.6667%. In addition, the monetary portion of any judgment assigned to Visa-related claims in accordance with the omnibus agreement would be treated as a Visa portion. Visa would have no liability for the monetary portion of any judgment assigned to MasterCard-related claims in accordance with the omnibus agreement, and if a judgment is not assigned to Visa-related claims or MasterCard-related claims in accordance with the omnibus agreement, then any monetary liability would be divided into a MasterCard portion at 33.3333% and a Visa portion at 66.6667%. The Visa portion of a settlement or judgment covered by the omnibus agreement would be allocated in accordance with specified provisions of the Company's retrospective responsibility plan. The litigation provision on the consolidated statements of operations is not impacted by the execution of the omnibus agreement.

On October 19, 2012, the Company and the individual plaintiffs whose claims were consolidated with the MDL (the "Individual Plaintiffs") signed a settlement agreement to resolve the Individual Plaintiffs' claims against the Company for approximately $350 million. This payment was made from the litigation escrow account under the retrospective responsibility plan on October 29, 2012. On November 6, 2012, the court entered an order dismissing the Individual Plaintiffs' claims with prejudice.

In addition, on October 19, 2012, Visa Inc., its wholly-owned subsidiaries Visa U.S.A. and Visa International, MasterCard Incorporated, MasterCard International Incorporated, various U.S. financial institution defendants, and the class plaintiffs signed a settlement agreement (the "Settlement Agreement") to resolve the class plaintiffs' claims.

The terms of the Settlement Agreement include, among other terms:
- A comprehensive release from participating class members for liability arising out of claims asserted in the litigation, and a further release to protect against future litigation regarding default interchange and the other U.S. rules at issue in the MDL;
- Settlement payments from the Company of approximately $4.0 billion, to be paid from the Company's previously funded litigation escrow account established under the retrospective responsibility plan, see *Note 3—Retrospective Responsibility Plan*;
- Distribution to class merchants of an amount equal to 10 basis points of default interchange across all credit rate categories for a period of eight consecutive months, which otherwise would have been paid to issuers and which effectively reduces credit interchange for that period of time. The eight month period for the reduction would begin within 60 days after completion of the court-ordered period during which individual class members may opt out of this settlement;
- Certain modifications to the Company's rules, including modifications to permit surcharging on credit transactions under certain circumstances, subject to a cap and a level playing field with other general purpose card competitors; and
- Agreement that the Company will meet with merchant buying groups that seek to negotiate interchange rates collectively.

The district court entered the preliminary approval order of the Settlement Agreement on November 27, 2012. On November 27, 2012, certain objectors filed a notice of appeal from the preliminary approval order in the U.S. Court of Appeals for the Second Circuit. On December 10, 2012, the court of appeals entered an order deferring briefing for the appeal until after the district court enters an order of final approval and final judgment with respect to the settlement, or otherwise concludes the matters by entry of a final judgment.

On December 10, 2012, Visa paid approximately $4.0 billion from the litigation escrow account into a settlement fund established pursuant to the Settlement Agreement.

Certain merchants in the proposed settlement classes thereafter objected to the settlement, opted out of the damages portion of the class settlement, and/or are seeking to opt out of the rules portion of the class settlement. Details of merchants who have filed an opt-out claim may be found below (see "*Interchange Opt-out Litigation*" below).

Certain competitors and other interested parties have also objected to the class settlement, including Discover, which filed a motion to intervene on May 28, 2013. Discover sought, among other things, to object to the Settlement Agreement and to file a proposed complaint challenging certain aspects of the Settlement Agreement as a restraint of trade in violation of Section 1 of the Sherman Act. On August 16, 2013, defendants responded to Discover's objections. On September 12, 2013, the district court held a hearing on the motion for final approval of the class settlement. Until the Settlement Agreement is finally approved by the court and any appeals are finally adjudicated, no assurance can be provided that the Company will be able to resolve the class plaintiffs' claims as contemplated by the Settlement Agreement.

Under the Settlement Agreement, if class members opt out of the damages portion of the class settlement, the defendants are entitled to receive payments of no more than 25% of the original cash payments made into the settlement fund, based on the percentage of payment card sales volume for a defined period attributable to merchants who opted out (the "takedown payments"). The class administrator has filed an amended report stating that the administrator had received 7,953 requests to opt out of the settlement, some of which may include multiple merchants. Based on the payment card sales volume of merchants requesting to opt out, in the event of final approval, the defendants will receive takedown payments equal to an amount calculated as 25% of the original cash payments made into the settlement fund. Visa's portion of the takedown payments is calculated to be approximately $1.1 billion, and would be deposited into the litigation escrow account.

Presentation in Annual Report

PRESENTATION

7.01 This section reviews the format and content of independent auditors' reports appearing in the annual reports of the 350 survey entities. AU section 508, *Reports on Audited Financial Statements* (AICPA, *PCAOB Standards and Related Rules*, Interim Standards), applies to auditors' reports of issuers issued in connection with audits of historical financial statements that are intended to present financial position, results of operations, and cash flows in conformity with generally accepted accounting principles (GAAP).

7.02 With the adoption of the clarified auditing standards, the following AU-C sections are applicable to the auditor's report:
- AU-C section 560, *Subsequent Events and Subsequently Discovered Facts* (AICPA, *Professional Standards*)
- AU-C section 600, *Special Considerations—Audits of Group Financial Statements (Including the Work of Component Auditors* (AICPA, *Professional Standards*)
- AU-C section 700, *Forming an Opinion and Reporting on Financial Statements* (AICPA, *Professional Standards*)
- AU-C section 705, *Modifications to the Opinion in the Independent Auditor's Report* (AICPA, *Professional Standards*)
- AU-C section 706, *Emphasis-of-Matter Paragraphs and Other-Matter Paragraphs in the Independent Auditor's Report* (AICPA, *Professional Standards*)
- AU-C section 708, *Consistency of Financial Statements* (AICPA, *Professional Standards*)
- AU-C section 800, *Special Considerations—Audits of Financial Statements Prepared in Accordance With Special Purpose Frameworks* (AICPA, *Professional Standards*)
- AU-C section 805, *Special Considerations—Audits of Single Financial Statements and Specific Elements, Accounts, or Items of a Financial Statement* (AICPA, *Professional Standards*)
- AU-C section 810, *Engagements to Report on Summary Financial Statements* (AICPA, *Professional Standards*)
- AU-C section 905, *Alert That Restricts the Use of the Auditor's Written Communication* (AICPA, *Professional Standards*)
- AU-C section 910, *Financial Statements Prepared in Accordance With a Financial Reporting Framework Generally Accepted in Another Country* (AICPA, *Professional Standards*)

As stated, AICPA professional standards apply to audits of nonissuers. PCAOB Auditing Standards apply to audits of issuers.

7.03 Section 103(a) of the Sarbanes-Oxley Act of 2002 authorized the PCAOB to establish auditing and related professional practice standards to be used by public accounting firms registered with the PCAOB. PCAOB Rule 3100, *Compliance With Auditing and Related Professional Practice Standards* (AICPA, *PCAOB Standards and Related Rules*, Select Rules of the Board), requires auditors to comply with all applicable auditing and related professional practice standards of the PCAOB. On an initial, transitional basis, the PCAOB adopted, as interim standards, the generally accepted auditing standards described in AU section 150, *Generally Accepted Auditing Standards* (AICPA, *Professional Standards*), in existence on April 16, 2003, to the extent not superseded or amended by the PCAOB.

Auditors' Reports

PRESENTATION

NONISSUERS

7.04 AU-C section 700 explains and provides examples of the unmodified auditor's report. The report should be written and include
- title,
- addressee,
- introductory paragraph,
- paragraph explaining management's responsibilities for the financial statements,
- auditor's responsibility,
- auditor's opinion,
- other reporting responsibilities (if applicable),
- signature of the auditor,
- auditor's address, and
- date of the auditor's report.

7.05 Paragraph .23 of AU-C section 700 states that the auditor's report should have a title that includes the word *independent* to clearly indicate that it is the report of an independent auditor.

7.06 Paragraph .24 of AU-C section 700 states that the auditor's report should be addressed as required by the circumstances of the engagement.

7.07 The introductory paragraph, as described by paragraph .25 of AU-C section 700, should
- identify the entity whose financial statements have been audited,
- state that the financial statements have been audited,
- identify the title of each statement that the financial statements comprise, and
- specify the date or period covered by each financial statement that the financial statements comprise.

7.08 Paragraphs .26–.28 of AU-C section 700 describe what should be included in the paragraph explaining management's responsibilities for the financial statements. These responsibilities include management's responsibility for the preparation and fair presentation of the financial statements in accordance with the applicable financial reporting framework. The description of management's responsibilities should not reference a separate statement by management if such a statement is included in a document containing the auditor's report.

7.09 Paragraphs .29–.33 of AU-C section 700 explain what should be included in the auditor's responsibility portion of the auditor's report. Included in these responsibilities is that the audit was conducted in accordance with GAAS and determining whether the audit evidence obtained is sufficient and appropriate to provide a basis for the auditor's opinion.

7.10 Paragraphs .34–.36 of AU-C section 700 describe the opinion paragraph of the auditor's report. This paragraph should state that the financial statements present fairly, in all material respects, the financial position of the entity as of the balance sheet date and the results of its operations and its cash flows for the period then ended, in accordance with the applicable financial reporting framework. The auditor's opinion should also identity the applicable financial reporting framework and its origin.

7.11 Paragraph .A58 of AU-C section 700 presents examples of the auditor's standard reports for single year financial statements and comparative two year financial statements. Two of these examples follow.

An Auditor's Report on a Single Year Prepared in Accordance With Accounting Principles Generally Accepted in the United States of America

Circumstances include the following:
- Audit of a complete set of general purpose financial statements (single year).
- The financial statements are prepared in accordance with accounting principles generally accepted in the United States of America.

INDEPENDENT AUDITOR'S REPORT

[Appropriate Addressee]

Report on the Financial Statements[1]

We have audited the accompanying financial statements of ABC Company, which comprise the balance sheet as of December 31, 20X1, and the related statements of income, changes in stockholders' equity, and cash flows for the year then ended, and the related notes to the financial statements.

Management's Responsibility for the Financial Statements

Management is responsible for the preparation and fair presentation of these financial statements in accordance with accounting principles generally accepted in the United States of America; this includes the design, implementation, and maintenance of internal control relevant to the preparation and fair presentation of financial statements that are free from material misstatement, whether due to fraud or error.

Auditor's Responsibility

Our responsibility is to express an opinion on these financial statements based on our audit. We conducted our audit in accordance with auditing standards generally accepted in the United States of America. Those standards require that we plan and perform the audit to obtain reasonable assurance about whether the financial statements are free from material misstatement.

An audit involves performing procedures to obtain audit evidence about the amounts and disclosures in the financial statements. The procedures selected depend on the auditor's judgment, including the assessment of the risks of material misstatement of the financial statements, whether due to fraud or error. In making those risk assessments, the auditor considers internal control relevant to the entity's preparation and fair presentation of the financial statements in order to design audit procedures that are appropriate in the circumstances, but not for the purpose of expressing an opinion on the effectiveness of the entity's internal control.[2] Accordingly, we express no such opinion. An audit also includes evaluating the appropriateness of accounting policies used and the reasonableness of significant accounting estimates made by management, as well as evaluating the overall presentation of the financial statements.

We believe that the audit evidence we have obtained is sufficient and appropriate to provide a basis for our audit opinion.

Opinion

In our opinion, the financial statements referred to above present fairly, in all material respects, the financial position of ABC Company as of December 31, 20X1, and the results of its operations and its cash flows for the year then ended in accordance with accounting principles generally accepted in the United States of America.

Report on Other Legal and Regulatory Requirements

[Form and content of this section of the auditor's report will vary depending on the nature of the auditor's other reporting responsibilities.]

[Auditor's signature]
[Auditor's city and state]
[Date of the auditor's report]

An Auditor's Report on Consolidated Comparative Financial Statements Prepared in Accordance With Accounting Principles Generally Accepted in the United States of America

Circumstances include the following:
- Audit of a complete set of general purpose consolidated financial statements (comparative).
- The financial statements are prepared in accordance with accounting principles generally accepted in the United States of America.

---

[1] The subtitle "Report on the Financial Statements" is unnecessary in circumstances when the second subtitle, "Report on Other Legal and Regulatory Requirements," is not applicable.

[2] In circumstances when the auditor also has responsibility to express an opinion on the effectiveness of internal control in conjunction with the audit of the financial statements, this sentence would be worded as follows: "In making those risk assessments, the auditor considers internal control relevant to the entity's preparation and fair presentation of the financial statements in order to design audit procedures that are appropriate in the circumstances." In addition, the next sentence, "Accordingly, we express no such opinion." would not be included.

INDEPENDENT AUDITOR'S REPORT

[Appropriate Addressee]

Report on the Financial Statements[3]

We have audited the accompanying consolidated financial statements of ABC Company and its subsidiaries, which comprise the consolidated balance sheets as of December 31, 20X1 and 20X0, and the related consolidated statements of income, changes in stockholders' equity, and cash flows for the years then ended, and the related notes to the financial statements.

Management's Responsibility for the Financial Statements

Management is responsible for the preparation and fair presentation of these consolidated financial statements in accordance with accounting principles generally accepted in the United States of America; this includes the design, implementation, and maintenance of internal control relevant to the preparation and fair presentation of consolidated financial statements that are free from material misstatement, whether due to fraud or error.

Auditor's Responsibility

Our responsibility is to express an opinion on these consolidated financial statements based on our audits. We conducted our audits in accordance with auditing standards generally accepted in the United States of America. Those standards require that we plan and perform the audit to obtain reasonable assurance about whether the consolidated financial statements are free from material misstatement.

An audit involves performing procedures to obtain audit evidence about the amounts and disclosures in the consolidated financial statements. The procedures selected depend on the auditor's judgment, including the assessment of the risks of material misstatement of the consolidated financial statements, whether due to fraud or error. In making those risk assessments, the auditor considers internal control relevant to the entity's preparation and fair presentation of the consolidated financial statements in order to design audit procedures that are appropriate in the circumstances, but not for the purpose of expressing an opinion on the effectiveness of the entity's internal control.[4] Accordingly, we express no such opinion. An audit also includes evaluating the appropriateness of accounting policies used and the reasonableness of significant accounting estimates made by management, as well as evaluating the overall presentation of the consolidated financial statements.

We believe that the audit evidence we have obtained is sufficient and appropriate to provide a basis for our audit opinion.

Opinion

In our opinion, the consolidated financial statements referred to above present fairly, in all material respects, the financial position of ABC Company and its subsidiaries as of December 31, 20X1 and 20X0, and the results of their operations and their cash flows for the years then ended in accordance with accounting principles generally accepted in the United States of America.

Report on Other Legal and Regulatory Requirements

[Form and content of this section of the auditor's report will vary depending on the nature of the auditor's other reporting responsibilities.]

[Auditor's signature]
[Auditor's city and state]
[Date of the auditor's report]

7.12 If statements of income, retained earnings, and cash flows are presented on a comparative basis for one of more periods, but the balance sheet(s) as of the end of one or more of the prior period(s) is not presented, the phrase "for the years then ended" should be changed to indicate that the auditor's opinion applies to each period for which statements of income, retained earnings, and cash flows are presented, such as "for each of the three years in the period ended [date of latest balance sheet]."

---

[3] The subtitle "Report on the Financial Statements" is unnecessary in circumstances when the second subtitle, "Report on Other Legal and Regulatory Requirements," is not applicable.

[4] In circumstances when the auditor also has responsibility to express an opinion on the effectiveness of internal control in conjunction with the audit of the financial statements, this sentence would be worded as follows: "In making those risk assessments, the auditor considers internal control relevant to the entity's preparation and fair presentation of the financial statements in order to design audit procedures that are appropriate in the circumstances." In addition, the next sentence, "Accordingly, we express no such opinion." would not be included.

7.13 If periods being audited and reported on are prior to the effective date of the clarified auditing standards, the Clarified Auditing Standards, including the reporting standards mentioned previously, may be used. This issue was taken up by the Technical Issues Committee of the AICPA and is addressed in Technical Questions and Answers (TIS) section 8100.03, "Using Current Auditing Standards of Prior Periods."[5]

7.14 Financial Accounting Standards Board (FASB) *Accounting Standards Codification* (ASC) 220, *Comprehensive Income*, requires entities that provide a full set of general-purpose financial statements (that is, financial position, results of operations, and cash flows) to report comprehensive income and its components either in a single continuous financial statement or in two separate but consecutive financial statements.

7.15 FASB ASC 505-10-50-2 allows for changes in the separate accounts comprising stockholders' equity to be presented either on the face of the basic financial statements or in the form of a separate statement, such as a statement of changes in stockholders' equity.

ISSUERS

7.16 Paragraph .08(a) of AU section 508 states that the title of an auditor's report should include the word *independent*.

7.17 Paragraph .09 of AU section 508 states the following:

> The report may be addressed to the company whose financial statements are being audited or to its board of directors or stockholders. A report on the financial statements of an unincorporated entity should be addressed as circumstances dictate, for example, to the partners, to the general partner, or to the proprietor. Occasionally, an auditor is retained to audit the financial statements of a company that is not a client; in such a case, the report is customarily addressed to the client and not to the directors or stockholders of the company whose financial statements are being audited.

7.18 For audits of public entities (that is, *issuers*, as defined by the Sarbanes-Oxley Act of 2002, and other entities, when prescribed by the rules of the Securities and Exchange Commission [SEC]), PCAOB Auditing Standard No. 1, *References in Auditors' Reports to the Standards of the Public Company Accounting Oversight Board* (AICPA, *PCAOB Standards and Related Rules*, Auditing Standards), directs auditors to state that the engagement was conducted in accordance with "the standards of the Public Company Accounting Oversight Board (United States)" whenever the auditor has performed the engagement in accordance with the PCAOB's standards. An example of a standard independent registered auditor's report presented in the appendix, "Illustrative Reports," of Auditing Standard No. 1 follows:

REPORT OF INDEPENDENT REGISTERED PUBLIC ACCOUNTING FIRM

We have audited the accompanying balance sheets of X Company as of December 31, 20X3 and 20X2, and the related statements of operations, stockholders' equity, and cash flows for each of the three years in the period ended December 31, 20X3. These financial statements are the responsibility of the Company's management. Our responsibility is to express an opinion on these financial statements based on our audits.

We conducted our audits in accordance with the standards of the Public Company Accounting Oversight Board (United States). Those standards require that we plan and perform the audit to obtain reasonable assurance about whether the financial statements are free of material misstatement. An audit includes examining, on a test basis, evidence supporting the amounts and disclosures in the financial statements. An audit also includes assessing the accounting principles used and significant estimates made by management, as well as evaluating the overall financial statement presentation. We believe that our audits provide a reasonable basis for our opinion.

In our opinion, the financial statements referred to above present fairly, in all material respects, the financial position of the company as of [at] December 31, 20X3 and 20X2, and the results of its operations and its cash flows for each of the three years in the period ended December 31, 20X3, in conformity with U.S. generally accepted accounting principles.

[*Signature*]
[*City and State or Country*]
[*Date*]

7.19 For audit requirements on reporting on internal controls over financial reporting, refer to paragraph 7.63.

---

[5] The questions and answers are not sources of established authoritative principles. This material is based on selected practice matters identified by the staff of the AICPA's Technical Hotline and various other bodies within the AICPA and has not been approved, disapproved, or otherwise acted upon by any senior technical committee of the AICPA.

PRESENTATION AND DISCLOSURE EXCERPTS

PRICEWATERHOUSECOOPERS LLP AUDITORS' REPORT

> **Author's Note**
> Although most audit reports use the exact format and order of paragraphs, PricewaterhouseCoopers uses a variation of the standard auditor's report that rearranges the standard auditor report.

7.20 THE KROGER CO. (JAN)
REPORT OF INDEPENDENT REGISTERED PUBLIC ACCOUNTING FIRM

To the Shareowners and Board of Directors of
The Kroger Co.

In our opinion, the accompanying consolidated balance sheets and the related consolidated statements of operations, comprehensive income, cash flows and changes in shareowners' equity present fairly, in all material respects, the financial position of The Kroger Co. and its subsidiaries at February 2, 2013 and January 28, 2012, and the results of their operations and their cash flows for each of the three years in the period ended February 2, 2013 in conformity with accounting principles generally accepted in the United States of America. Also in our opinion, the Company maintained, in all material respects, effective internal control over financial reporting as of February 2, 2013, based on criteria established in *Internal Control—Integrated Framework* issued by the Committee of Sponsoring Organizations of the Treadway Commission (COSO). The Company's management is responsible for these financial statements, for maintaining effective internal control over financial reporting and for its assessment of the effectiveness of internal control over financial reporting, included in Management's Report on Internal Control over Financial Reporting appearing under Item 9A. Our responsibility is to express opinions on these financial statements and on the Company's internal control over financial reporting based on our integrated audits. We conducted our audits in accordance with the standards of the Public Company Accounting Oversight Board (United States). Those standards require that we plan and perform the audits to obtain reasonable assurance about whether the financial statements are free of material misstatement and whether effective internal control over financial reporting was maintained in all material respects. Our audits of the financial statements included examining, on a test basis, evidence supporting the amounts and disclosures in the financial statements, assessing the accounting principles used and significant estimates made by management, and evaluating the overall financial statement presentation. Our audit of internal control over financial reporting included obtaining an understanding of internal control over financial reporting, assessing the risk that a material weakness exists, and testing and evaluating the design and operating effectiveness of internal control based on the assessed risk. Our audits also included performing such other procedures as we considered necessary in the circumstances. We believe that our audits provide a reasonable basis for our opinions.

A company's internal control over financial reporting is a process designed to provide reasonable assurance regarding the reliability of financial reporting and the preparation of financial statements for external purposes in accordance with generally accepted accounting principles. A company's internal control over financial reporting includes those policies and procedures that (i) pertain to the maintenance of records that, in reasonable detail, accurately and fairly reflect the transactions and dispositions of the assets of the company; (ii) provide reasonable assurance that transactions are recorded as necessary to permit preparation of financial statements in accordance with generally accepted accounting principles, and that receipts and expenditures of the company are being made only in accordance with authorizations of management and directors of the company; and (iii) provide reasonable assurance regarding prevention or timely detection of unauthorized acquisition, use, or disposition of the company's assets that could have a material effect on the financial statements.

Because of its inherent limitations, internal control over financial reporting may not prevent or detect misstatements. Also, projections of any evaluation of effectiveness to future periods are subject to the risk that controls may become inadequate because of changes in conditions, or that the degree of compliance with the policies or procedures may deteriorate.

/s/ PricewaterhouseCoopers LLP
Cincinnati, Ohio
April 2, 2013

STATEMENTS OF INCOME AND COMPREHENSIVE INCOME

7.21 WAL-MART STORES, INC. (JAN)
REPORT OF INDEPENDENT REGISTERED PUBLIC ACCOUNTING FIRM

The Board of Directors and Shareholders of
Wal-Mart Stores, Inc.

We have audited the accompanying consolidated balance sheets of Wal-Mart Stores, Inc. as of January 31, 2013 and 2012, and the related consolidated statements of income, comprehensive income, shareholders' equity, and cash flows for each of the three years in the period ended January 31, 2013. These financial statements are the responsibility of the Company's management. Our responsibility is to express an opinion on these financial statements based on our audits.

We conducted our audits in accordance with the standards of the Public Company Accounting Oversight Board (United States). Those standards require that we plan and perform the audit to obtain reasonable assurance about whether the financial statements are free of material misstatement. An audit includes examining, on a test basis, evidence supporting the amounts and disclosures in the financial statements. An audit also includes assessing the accounting principles used and significant estimates made by management, as well as evaluating the overall financial statement presentation. We believe that our audits provide a reasonable basis for our opinion.

In our opinion, the financial statements referred to above present fairly, in all material respects, the consolidated financial position of Wal-Mart Stores, Inc. at January 31, 2013 and 2012, and the consolidated results of its operations and its cash flows for each of the three years in the period ended January 31, 2013, in conformity with U.S. generally accepted accounting principles.

We also have audited, in accordance with the standards of the Public Company Accounting Oversight Board (United States), Wal-Mart Stores, Inc.'s internal control over financial reporting as of January 31, 2013, based on criteria established in Internal Control-Integrated Framework issued by the Committee of Sponsoring Organizations of the Treadway Commission and our report dated March 26, 2013 expressed an unqualified opinion thereon.

/s/ Ernst & Young LLP
Rogers, Arkansas
March 26, 2013

STATEMENT OF CHANGES IN STOCKHOLDERS' EQUITY

7.22 WALTER ENERGY, INC. (DEC)
REPORT OF INDEPENDENT REGISTERED PUBLIC ACCOUNTING FIRM

The Board of Directors and Stockholders of
Walter Energy, Inc.

We have audited the accompanying consolidated balance sheets of Walter Energy, Inc. and subsidiaries as of December 31, 2013 and 2012, and the related consolidated statements of operations, comprehensive income, changes in stockholders' equity and cash flows for each of the three years in the period ended December 31, 2013. These financial statements are the responsibility of the Company's management. Our responsibility is to express an opinion on these financial statements based on our audits.

We conducted our audits in accordance with the standards of the Public Company Accounting Oversight Board (United States). Those standards require that we plan and perform the audit to obtain reasonable assurance about whether the financial statements are free of material misstatement. An audit includes examining, on a test basis, evidence supporting the amounts and disclosures in the financial statements. An audit also includes assessing the accounting principles used and significant estimates made by management, as well as evaluating the overall financial statement presentation. We believe that our audits provide a reasonable basis for our opinion.

In our opinion, the financial statements referred to above present fairly, in all material respects, the consolidated financial position of Walter Energy, Inc. and subsidiaries at December 31, 2013 and 2012, and the consolidated results of their operations and their cash flows for each of the three years in the period ended December 31, 2013, in conformity with U.S. generally accepted accounting principles.

We also have audited, in accordance with the standards of the Public Company Accounting Oversight Board (United States), Walter Energy, Inc.'s internal control over financial reporting as of December 31, 2013, based on criteria established in Internal Control—Integrated

Framework issued by the Committee of Sponsoring Organizations of the Treadway Commission (1992Framework) and our report dated February 25, 2014 expressed an unqualified opinion thereon.

/s/ Ernst & Young, LLP
Birmingham, Alabama
February 25, 2014

Reference to the Report of Other Auditors

PRESENTATION

NONISSUERS

7.23 AU-C section 600 establishes requirements and provides guidance for the independent auditor in deciding (*a*) whether he or she may use the work and reports of component auditors who have audited the financial statements of one or more subsidiaries, divisions, branches, components, or investments included in the financial statements presented and (*b*) the form and content of the principal auditor's report in these circumstances.

7.24 Paragraph .25 of AU-C section 600 explains that when the group engagement partner decides to make reference to the component auditor, the following should be true:
- The component's financial statements are prepared using the same financial reporting framework as the group financial statements.
- The component auditor has performed an audit of the financial statements of the component in accordance with generally accepted accounting standards.
- The component auditor has issued an auditor's report that is not restricted as to use.

7.25 As described in paragraph .28 of AU-C section 600, the group financial statements should clearly indicate that the component was not audited by the auditor of the group financial statements but was audited by the component auditor and should include the magnitude of the portion of the financial statement audited by the component auditor. The disclosure of the magnitude of the portion of the financial statements audited by a component auditor may be achieved by stating either the dollar amounts or percentages (whichever most clearly describes the portion of the financial statements audited by a component auditor) of one or more of the following: total assets, total revenues, or other appropriate criteria. When two or more component auditors participate in the audit, the dollar amounts or the percentages covered by the component auditors may be stated in the aggregate. If the group engagement partner decides to name a component auditor in the auditor's report on the group financial statements, then the component auditor's express permission should be obtained and the component's auditor's report should be presented together with that of the auditor's report on the group financial.

7.26 Exhibit A of AU-C section 600 contains an example of appropriate reporting in the auditor's report on the group financial statements when reference is made to the audit of a component auditor.

ISSUERS

7.27 Paragraphs C8–C11 of PCAOB Auditing Standard No. 5, *An Audit of Internal Control Over Financial Reporting That Is Integrated with An Audit of Financial Statements* (AICPA, *PCAOB Standards and Related Rules*, Auditing Standards), provide guidance on opinions based, in part, on the report of another auditor in an audit of internal control over financial reporting. Paragraphs C8–C11 of Auditing Standard No. 5 state the following:
- If the auditor decides it is appropriate to serve as the principal auditor of the financial statements, then that auditor also should be the principal auditor of the company's internal control over financial reporting. When serving as the principal auditor of internal control over financial reporting, the auditor should decide whether to make reference in the report on internal control over financial reporting to the audit of internal control over financial reporting performed by the other auditor. In these circumstances, the auditor's decision is based on factors analogous to those of the auditor who uses the work and reports of other independent auditors when reporting on a company's financial statements.
- The decision about whether to make reference to another auditor in the report on the audit of internal control over financial reporting might differ from the corresponding decision as it relates to the audit of the financial statements. For example, the audit report on the financial statements may make reference to the audit of a significant equity investment performed by another independent auditor, but the report on internal control over financial reporting might not make a similar reference because management's assessment of internal control over financial reporting ordinarily would not extend to controls at the equity method investee.

- When the auditor decides to make reference to the report of the other auditor as a basis, in part, for his or her opinion on the company's internal control over financial reporting, the auditor should refer to the report of the other auditor when describing the scope of the audit and expressing the opinion.

7.28 When the principal auditor decides not to make reference to the audit of the other auditor, he or she must obtain and review and retain the following information from the other auditor, as prescribed in PCAOB AU section 508, *Reports on Audited Financial Statements* (AICPA, *PCAOB Standards and Related Rules*, Interim Standards):

- An engagement completion document consistent with paragraphs 12–13 of PCAOB Auditing Standard No. 3, *Audit Documentation* (AICPA, *PCAOB Standards and Related Rules,* Auditing Standards). This engagement completion document should include all cross-referenced supporting audit documentation.
- A list of significant risks, the auditor's responses, and the results of the auditor's related procedures.
- Sufficient information relating to significant findings or issues that are inconsistent with or contradict the auditor's final conclusions, as described in paragraph 8 of Auditing Standard No. 3.
- Any findings affecting the consolidating or combining of accounts in the consolidated financial statements.
- Sufficient information to enable the office issuing the auditor's report to agree or reconcile the financial statement amounts audited by the other firm to the information underlying the consolidated financial statements.
- A schedule of accumulated misstatements, including a description of the nature and cause of each accumulated misstatement, and an evaluation of uncorrected misstatements, including the quantitative and qualitative factors the auditor considered to be relevant to the evaluation.
- All significant deficiencies and material weaknesses in internal control over financial reporting, including a clear distinction between those two categories.
- Letters of representations from management.
- All matters to be communicated to the audit committee.

PRESENTATION AND DISCLOSURE EXCERPT

REFERENCE TO OTHER AUDITORS

7.29 LEE ENTERPRISES, INCORPORATED (SEP)
REPORT OF INDEPENDENT REGISTERED PUBLIC ACCOUNTING FIRM

The Board of Directors and Stockholders
Lee Enterprises, Incorporated:

We have audited the accompanying consolidated balance sheets of Lee Enterprises, Incorporated and subsidiaries (the Company) as of September 29, 2013 and September 30, 2012, and the related consolidated statements of operations and comprehensive income (loss), stockholders' equity (deficit), and cash flows for the 52-week period ended September 29, 2013, the 53-week period ended September 30, 2012, and the 52-week period ended September 25, 2011. These consolidated financial statements are the responsibility of the Company's management. Our responsibility is to express an opinion on these consolidated financial statements based on our audits. We did not audit the consolidated balance sheet of Madison Newspapers, Inc., and Subsidiary (MNI), a 50% owned investee company, as of September 29, 2013, and the related consolidated statement of income, stockholders' equity, and cash flows for the year ended September 29, 2013. The Company's investment in MNI at September 29, 2013 was $21,011,000 and its equity in earnings of MNI was $3,509,000 for the 52-week period ended September 29, 2013. The consolidated financial statements of MNI for the year ended September 29, 2013 were audited by other auditors whose report has been furnished to us, and our opinion, insofar as it relates to the amounts included for MNI for the 52-week period ended September 29, 2013, is based solely on the report of the other auditors.

We conducted our audits in accordance with the standards of the Public Company Accounting Oversight Board (United States). Those standards require that we plan and perform the audit to obtain reasonable assurance about whether the financial statements are free of material misstatement. An audit includes examining, on a test basis, evidence supporting the amounts and disclosures in the financial statements. An audit also includes assessing the accounting principles used and significant estimates made by management, as well as evaluating the overall financial statement presentation. We believe that our audits provide a reasonable basis for our opinion.

In our opinion, based on our audits and the report of other auditors, the consolidated financial statements referred to above present fairly, in all material respects, the financial position of Lee Enterprises, Incorporated and subsidiaries as of September 29, 2013 and September 30, 2012, and the results of their operations and their cash flows for the 52-week period ended September 29, 2013, the 53-week period ended September 30, 2012, and the 52-week period ended September 25, 2011, in conformity with U.S. generally accepted accounting principles.

We also have audited, in accordance with the standards of the Public Company Accounting Oversight Board (United States), Lee Enterprises, Incorporated and subsidiaries internal control over financial reporting as September 29, 2013, based on criteria established in *Internal Control—Integrated Framework* issued by the Committee of Sponsoring Organizations of the Treadway Commission (COSO), and our report dated December 13, 2013 expressed an unqualified opinion on the effectiveness of the Company's internal control over financial reporting.

/s/ KPMG LLP
Chicago, Illinois
December 13, 2013

REPORT OF INDEPENDENT REGISTERED PUBLIC ACCOUNTING FIRM

Board of Directors
Madison Newspapers, Inc.
Madison, Wisconsin

We have audited the accompanying consolidated balance sheet of Madison Newspapers, Inc. and Subsidiary (the "Company") as of September 29, 2013, and the related consolidated statements of income, stockholders' equity, and cash flows for the year then ended. These consolidated financial statements are the responsibility of the Company's management. Our responsibility is to express an opinion on these consolidated financial statements based on our audit.

We conducted our audit in accordance with the standards of the Public Company Accounting Oversight Board (United States). Those standards require that we plan and perform the audit to obtain reasonable assurance about whether the consolidated financial statements are free of material misstatement. The Company is not required to have, nor were we engaged to perform, an audit of its internal control over financial reporting. Our audit included consideration of its internal control over financial reporting as a basis for designing audit procedures that are appropriate in the circumstances, but not for the purpose of expressing an opinion on the effectiveness of the Company's internal control over financial reporting. Accordingly, we express no such opinion. An audit includes examining, on a test basis, evidence supporting the amounts and disclosures in the consolidated financial statements. An audit also includes assessing the accounting principles used and significant estimates made by management, as well as evaluating the overall consolidated financial statement presentation. We believe that our audit provides a reasonable basis for our opinion.

In our opinion, the consolidated financial statements referred to above present fairly, in all material respects, the financial position of the Company as of September 29, 2013, and the results of their operations and their cash flows for the year then ended, in conformity with U.S. generally accepted accounting principles.

/s/ BAKER TILLY VIRCHOW KRAUSE, LLP
Madison, Wisconsin
November 22, 2013

Uncertainties

PRESENTATION

NONISSUERS

7.30 Paragraph .A13 of AU-C section 705 explains that an audit includes an assessment of whether the audit evidence related to uncertainties supports management's analysis. Absence of the existence of information related to the outcome of an uncertainty does not necessarily lead to a conclusion that the audit evidence supporting management's assertion is not sufficient. Rather, the auditor's professional judgment regarding the sufficiency of the audit evidence is based on the audit evidence that is, or should be, available. This does not apply to uncertainties related to going concern situations, for which AU-C section 570, *The Auditor's Consideration of an Entity's Ability to Continue as a Going Concern* (AICPA, *Professional Standards*), provides guidance.

ISSUERS

7.31 Paragraph .30 of AU section 508 does not require an explanatory paragraph for *uncertainties*, as defined in paragraph .29 of AU section 508. This does not apply to uncertainties related to going concern situations, for which AU section 341, *The Auditor's Consideration of an Entity's Ability to Continue as a Going Concern* (AICPA, *PCAOB Standards and Related Rules,* Interim Standards), provides guidance.

PRESENTATION AND DISCLOSURE EXCERPTS

GOING CONCERN

7.32 EXIDE TECHNOLOGIES (MAR)
REPORT OF INDEPENDENT REGISTERED PUBLIC ACCOUNTING FIRM

The Board of Directors and Stockholders of
Exide Technologies:

We have audited the accompanying consolidated balance sheet of Exide Technologies and subsidiaries (the "Company") as of March 31, 2013, and the related consolidated statements of operations, comprehensive loss, stockholders' equity, and cash flows for the year ended March 31, 2013. In connection with our audit of the consolidated financial statements, we also have audited the financial statement schedule for 2013 listed in the accompanying index. We also have audited Exide Technologies' internal control over financial reporting as of March 31, 2013, based on criteria established in Internal Control—Integrated Framework issued by the Committee of Sponsoring Organizations of the Treadway Commission (COSO). Exide Technologies' management is responsible for these consolidated financial statements and financial statement schedule, for maintaining effective internal control over financial reporting, and for its assessment of the effectiveness of internal control over financial reporting, included in the accompanying Management's Report on Internal Control over Financial Reporting. Our responsibility is to express an opinion on these consolidated financial statements and financial statement schedule and an opinion on Exide Technologies' internal control over financial reporting based on our audits.

We conducted our audits in accordance with the standards of the Public Company Accounting Oversight Board (United States). Those standards require that we plan and perform the audits to obtain reasonable assurance about whether the financial statements are free of material misstatement and whether effective internal control over financial reporting was maintained in all material respects. Our audit of the consolidated financial statements included examining, on a test basis, evidence supporting the amounts and disclosures in the financial statements, assessing the accounting principles used and significant estimates made by management, and evaluating the overall financial statement presentation. Our audit of internal control over financial reporting included obtaining an understanding of internal control over financial reporting, assessing the risk that a material weakness exists, and testing and evaluating the design and operating effectiveness of internal control based on the assessed risk. Our audits also included performing such other procedures as we considered necessary in the circumstances. We believe that our audits provide a reasonable basis for our opinions.

A company's internal control over financial reporting is a process designed to provide reasonable assurance regarding the reliability of financial reporting and the preparation of financial statements for external purposes in accordance with generally accepted accounting principles. A company's internal control over financial reporting includes those policies and procedures that (1) pertain to the maintenance of records that, in reasonable detail, accurately and fairly reflect the transactions and dispositions of the assets of the company; (2) provide reasonable assurance that transactions are recorded as necessary to permit preparation of financial statements in accordance with generally accepted accounting principles, and that receipts and expenditures of the company are being made only in accordance with authorizations of management and directors of the company; and (3) provide reasonable assurance regarding prevention or timely detection of unauthorized acquisition, use, or disposition of the company's assets that could have a material effect on the financial statements.

Because of its inherent limitations, internal control over financial reporting may not prevent or detect misstatements. Also, projections of any evaluation of effectiveness to future periods are subject to the risk that controls may become inadequate because of changes in conditions, or that the degree of compliance with the policies or procedures may deteriorate.

In our opinion, the consolidated financial statements referred to above present fairly, in all material respects, the financial position of Exide Technologies and subsidiaries as of March 31, 2013, and the results of their operations and their cash flows for the year ended March 31, 2013, in conformity with U.S. generally accepted accounting principles. Also in our opinion, the related financial statement schedule for 2013, when considered in relation to the basic consolidated financial statements taken as a whole, presents fairly, in all material respects, the information set forth therein. Also in our opinion, Exide Technologies maintained, in all material respects, effective internal control over financial reporting as of March 31, 2013, based on criteria established in Internal Control—Integrated Framework issued by the Committee of Sponsoring Organizations of the Treadway Commission.

The accompanying consolidated financial statements and financial statement schedule have been prepared assuming that the Company will continue as a going concern. As discussed in note 1 to the consolidated financial statements, the Company's bankruptcy filing and related matters raise substantial doubt about the Company's ability to continue as a going concern. Management's plans in regard to these matters are also described in note 1. The consolidated financial statements do not include any adjustments that might result from the outcome of this uncertainty.

/s/ KPMG LLP
Atlanta, Georgia
June 14, 2013

NOTES TO CONSOLIDATED FINANCIAL STATEMENTS

(1) Proceedings Under Chapter 11 of the Bankruptcy Code

The Consolidated Financial Statements include the accounts of Exide Technologies (referred to together with its subsidiaries, unless the context requires otherwise, as "Exide" or the "Company") and all of its majority-owned subsidiaries. The Consolidated Financial Statements are prepared in accordance with U.S. generally accepted accounting principles ("GAAP"). Unless otherwise indicated or unless the context otherwise requires, references to "fiscal year" refer to the period ended March 31 of that year (e.g. " fiscal 2013 " refers to the period beginning April 1, 2012 and ending March 31, 2013).

On June 10, 2013 ("Petition Date") Exide Technologies (the "Debtor") filed voluntary petitions for reorganization under Chapter 11 of the federal bankruptcy laws ("Bankruptcy Code" or "Chapter 11") in the United States Bankruptcy Court for the District of Delaware ("Bankruptcy Court") under the caption *In re Exide Technologies*, case number 13-11482. The Debtor is currently operating the Company's business as debtors-in-possession pursuant to the Bankruptcy Code. The Company's subsidiaries, foreign and domestic, have been excluded from the Chapter 11 proceedings and continue to operate their businesses without supervision from the Bankruptcy Court and are not subject to the requirements of the Bankruptcy Code.

The Company filed for reorganization under Chapter 11 as it offered the most efficient alternative to restructure the Company's balance sheet and access new working capital while continuing to operate in the ordinary course of business. The Company has a significant debt burden including $55.8 million of convertible notes ("Convertible Notes") coming due on September 18, 2013. Other factors leading to the reorganization included the impact of economic conditions on the Company's markets, particularly the U.S. and European markets, ongoing competitive pressures, loss of key customers over several years, unplanned production shut down in certain facilities, higher commodity costs including lead and purchased spent batteries. These factors contributed to higher costs and lower revenues and have resulted in significant operating losses and material adverse reductions in cash flows, severely impacting the Company's financial condition and its ability to make debt payments coming due. Lastly, recent downgrades of the Company's credit rating as previously announced and loss of credit insurance used by certain suppliers adversely affected supplier trade credit terms, further impacting the Company's liquidity

As debtors-in-possession, the Debtors are authorized to continue to operate as an ongoing business, but may not engage in transactions outside the ordinary course of business without the approval of the Bankruptcy Court.

On June 11, 2013 Exide received Bankruptcy Court approval for among other things, on an interim basis, access to $395.0 million of a $500.0 million debtor-in-possession financing facility ("DIP Credit Facility"), the ability to pay pre-petition and post-petition employee wages, salaries and benefits and to honor customer warranty, sales returns and rebate obligations.

The DIP Credit Facility will be used to supplement cash flows from operations during the reorganization process including the payment of post-petition ordinary course trade and other payables, the payment of certain permitted pre-petition claims, working capital needs, letter of credit requirements and other general corporate purposes. The DIP Credit Facilities continue certain financial covenants. Failure to maintain compliance with these covenants would result in an event of default which would restrict the Company's availability to funds necessary to maintain the Company's operations and assist in funding the Company's reorganization plans.

The Chapter 11 petitions triggered defaults on substantially all debt obligations of the Debtor and as a result, the Senior Secured Notes, Convertible Notes and ABL facility described below have been accelerated and are due and payable. Under Section 362 of the Bankruptcy Code, actions to collect pre-petition indebtedness, as well as most other pending litigation, are stayed. Absent an order of the Bankruptcy Court, substantially all prepetition liabilities are subject to settlement under a plan of reorganization approved by the Bankruptcy Court. Although the Debtors expect to file a reorganization plan that provides for emergence from bankruptcy as a going concern, there can be no assurance that a reorganization plan will be proposed by the Debtors or confirmed by the Bankruptcy Court, or that any such plan will be successfully implemented.

Under the Bankruptcy Code, the Debtors may also assume or reject executory contracts, including lease obligations, subject to the approval of the Bankruptcy Court and certain other conditions. Parties affected by these rejections may file claims with the Bankruptcy Court in accordance with the reorganization process. Due to the timing of the Chapter 11 proceedings, the Company cannot currently estimate or anticipate what impact the rejection and subsequent claims of executory contracts may have in the reorganization process.

On August 9, 2013, the Company expects to file with the Bankruptcy Court schedules and statements of financial affairs setting forth, among other things, the assets and liabilities of the Debtors as shown by the Company's books and records on the petition date, subject to the assumptions contained in certain notes filed in connection therewith. All of the schedules will be subject to further amendment or modification. In Addition, the Bankruptcy Code provides for a claims reconciliation and resolution process, although a bar date for filing claims has not yet been established. As the ultimate number and amount of allowed claims is not presently known and, because any settlement terms of such allowed claims are subject to a confirmed plan of reorganization, the ultimate distribution with respect to allowed claims is not presently ascertainable.

At this time, it is not possible to predict the ultimate effect of the Chapter 11 reorganization on our business, various creditors and security holders or when it may be possible to emerge from Chapter 11. Our future results are dependent upon our confirming and implementing, on a timely basis, a plan of reorganization. The Company believes, however, that under any reorganization plan, the Company's common stock would likely be substantially if not completely diluted or cancelled as a result of the conversion of debt to equity or with respect to any other compromise of interest. Further it is also expected that the Company's senior secured notes and convertible senior subordinated notes will suffer substantial impairment.

The consolidated financial statements have been prepared on a going concern basis, which assumes continuity of operations and realization of assets and satisfaction of liabilities in the ordinary course of business. The ability of the Company to continue as a going concern is predicated upon, among other things, the confirmation of a reorganization plan, compliance with the provisions of the DIP Credit Facility, the ability of the Company to generate cash flows from operations, and where necessary, obtaining financing sources sufficient to satisfy future obligations. As a result of the Chapter 11 filing, and consideration of various strategic alternatives, including possible assets sales, the Company expects that any reorganization plan will likely result in material changes to the carrying amount of assets and liabilities in the consolidated financial statements.

The consolidated financial statements do not include adjustments, if any, to reflect the possible future effects on the recoverability and classification of recorded assets or the amounts and classifications of liabilities that may result from the outcome of these uncertainties. In addition, since the Debtors filed for protection under the Bankruptcy Code subsequent to March 31, 2013, the accompanying fiscal 2013 consolidated financial statements have not been prepared to reflect the impact of the bankruptcy filing, and do not include disclosures of liabilities subject to compromise. Financial statements prepared subsequent to the filing date under Chapter 11 will be prepared reflecting such amounts subject to compromise.

EMERGENCE FROM BANKRUPTCY

7.33 W. R. GRACE & CO. (DEC)
REPORT OF INDEPENDENT REGISTERED PUBLIC ACCOUNTING FIRM

To the Shareholders and Board of Directors of
W. R. Grace & Co.:

In our opinion, the accompanying consolidated balance sheets and the related consolidated statements of operations, of comprehensive income, of equity (deficit), and of cash flows present fairly, in all material respects, the financial position of W. R. Grace & Co. and its subsidiaries (the "Company") at December 31, 2013 and December 31, 2012, and the results of their operations and their cash flows for each of the three years in the period ended December 31, 2013 in conformity with accounting principles generally accepted in the United States of America. Also in our opinion, the Company maintained, in all material respects, effective internal control over financial reporting as of December 31, 2013, based on criteria established in *Internal Control—Integrated Framework (1992)* issued by the Committee of Sponsoring Organizations of the Treadway Commission (COSO). The Company's management is responsible for these financial statements, for maintaining effective internal control over financial reporting and for its assessment of the effectiveness of internal control over financial reporting, included in the accompanying Management's Report on Internal Control over Financial Reporting. Our responsibility is to express opinions on these financial statements and on the Company's internal control over financial reporting based on our integrated audits. We conducted our audits in accordance with the standards of the Public Company Accounting Oversight Board (United States). Those standards require that we plan and perform the audits to obtain reasonable assurance about whether the financial statements are free of material misstatement and whether effective internal control over financial reporting was maintained in all material respects. Our audits of the financial statements included examining, on a test basis, evidence supporting the amounts and disclosures in the financial statements, assessing the accounting principles used and significant estimates made by management, and evaluating the overall financial statement presentation. Our audit of internal control over financial reporting included obtaining an understanding of internal control over financial reporting, assessing the risk that a material weakness exists, and testing and evaluating the design and operating effectiveness of internal control based on the assessed risk. Our audits also included performing such other procedures as we considered necessary in the circumstances. We believe that our audits provide a reasonable basis for our opinions.

As discussed in Note 2 to the consolidated financial statements, the Company emerged from bankruptcy on February 3, 2014. As discussed in Note 1 to the consolidated financial statements, the Company changed the manner in which it accounts for defined benefit pension plans in 2013.

A company's internal control over financial reporting is a process designed to provide reasonable assurance regarding the reliability of financial reporting and the preparation of financial statements for external purposes in accordance with generally accepted accounting principles. A company's internal control over financial reporting includes those policies and procedures that (i) pertain to the maintenance of records that, in reasonable detail, accurately and fairly reflect the transactions and dispositions of the assets of the company; (ii) provide reasonable assurance that transactions are recorded as necessary to permit preparation of financial statements in accordance with generally accepted accounting principles, and that receipts and expenditures of the company are being made only in accordance with authorizations of management and directors of the company; and (iii) provide reasonable assurance regarding prevention or timely detection of unauthorized acquisition, use, or disposition of the company's assets that could have a material effect on the financial statements.

Because of its inherent limitations, internal control over financial reporting may not prevent or detect misstatements. Also, projections of any evaluation of effectiveness to future periods are subject to the risk that controls may become inadequate because of changes in conditions, or that the degree of compliance with the policies or procedures may deteriorate.

/s/ PricewaterhouseCoopers LLP
PricewaterhouseCoopers LLP
McLean, Virginia
February 27, 2014

NOTES TO CONSOLIDATED FINANCIAL STATEMENTS

1. Basis of Presentation and Summary of Significant Accounting and Financial Reporting Policies (in part)

Chapter 11 Proceedings   During 2000 and the first quarter of 2001, Grace experienced several adverse developments in its asbestos-related litigation, including: a significant increase in personal injury claims, higher than expected costs to resolve personal injury and certain property damage claims, and class action lawsuits alleging damages from Zonolite® Attic Insulation ("ZAI"), a former Grace attic insulation product.

After a thorough review of these developments, Grace's Board of Directors concluded that a federal court-supervised bankruptcy process provided the best forum available to achieve fairness in resolving these claims and on April 2, 2001 (the "Filing Date"), Grace and 61 of its United States subsidiaries and affiliates filed voluntary petitions for reorganization (the "Filing") under Chapter 11 of the United States Bankruptcy Code in the United States Bankruptcy Court for the District of Delaware (the "Bankruptcy Court").

Under Chapter 11, Grace operated its businesses under court supervision, while using the Chapter 11 process to develop and implement a plan for addressing the asbestos-related claims.

In September 2008, Grace and other parties filed a joint plan of reorganization with the Bankruptcy Court to address all pending and future asbestos-related claims and all other pre-petition claims as outlined therein (as subsequently amended, the "Joint Plan"). Following the confirmation of the Joint Plan in 2011 by the Bankruptcy Court and in 2012 by a U.S. District Court, and the resolution of all appeals, Grace emerged from bankruptcy on February 3, 2014. (See Note 2 for Chapter 11 information.)

2. Chapter 11 and Joint Plan of Reorganization (in part)

On April 2, 2001, Grace and 61 of its United States subsidiaries and affiliates filed voluntary petitions for reorganization under Chapter 11 of the Bankruptcy Code. The cases were consolidated under case number 01-01139 (the "Chapter 11 Cases"). Grace's non-U.S. subsidiaries and certain of its U.S. subsidiaries were not included in the filing.

In September 2008, Grace and other parties filed the Joint Plan with the Bankruptcy Court to address all pending and future asbestos-related claims and all other pre-petition claims as outlined therein. On January 31, 2011, the Bankruptcy Court issued an order (the "Confirmation Order") confirming the Joint Plan. On January 31, 2012, the United States District Court for the District of Delaware (the

"District Court") issued an order affirming the Confirmation Order and confirming the Joint Plan in its entirety. On February 3, 2014 (the "Effective Date"), the U.S. Court of Appeals for the Third Circuit (the "Third Circuit") dismissed the sole remaining appeal challenging the Confirmation Order and the Joint Plan became effective.

Under the Joint Plan, two asbestos trusts have been established and funded under Section 524(g) of the Bankruptcy Code. The Confirmation Order contains a channeling injunction which provides that all pending and future asbestos-related personal injury claims and demands ("PI Claims") are to be channeled for resolution to an asbestos personal injury trust (the "PI Trust") and all pending and future asbestos-related property damage claims and demands ("PD Claims"), including PD Claims related to Grace's former attic insulation product ("ZAI PD Claims"), are to be channeled to a separate asbestos property damage trust (the "PD Trust"). Canadian ZAI PD Claims are channeled to a separate Canadian claims fund. The trusts are the sole recourse for holders of asbestos-related claims; the channeling injunctions prohibit holders of asbestos-related claims from asserting such claims directly against Grace.

Accounting Impact   The accompanying Consolidated Financial Statements have been prepared in accordance with ASC 852 "Reorganizations". ASC 852 requires that financial statements of debtors-in-possession be prepared on a going concern basis, which contemplates continuity of operations and realization of assets and liquidation of liabilities in the ordinary course of business.

Pursuant to ASC 852, Grace's pre-petition and post-petition liabilities that are subject to compromise are required to be reported separately on the balance sheet at an estimate of the amount that will ultimately be allowed by the Bankruptcy Court. As of December 31, 2013, such pre-petition liabilities include fixed obligations (such as debt and contractual commitments), as well as estimates of costs related to contingent liabilities (such as asbestos-related litigation, environmental remediation and other claims). Obligations of Grace subsidiaries not covered by the Filing continue to be classified on the Consolidated Balance Sheets based upon maturity dates or the expected dates of payment. ASC 852 also requires separate reporting of certain expenses, realized gains and losses, and provisions for losses related to the Filing as reorganization items. Grace presents reorganization items as "Chapter 11 expenses, net of interest income," a separate caption in its Consolidated Statements of Operations.

Grace has not recorded the benefit of the assets available to fund asbestos-related and other liabilities under the Fresenius settlement and the Sealed Air settlement as provided by the Joint Plan, as these assets were transferred directly to the PI Trust and the PD Trust on the Effective Date. The estimated fair value available under the Fresenius settlement and the Sealed Air settlement as measured at December 31, 2013, was $1,653 million composed of $115 million in cash from Fresenius and $1,538 million in cash and stock from Cryovac.

Grace's Consolidated Balance Sheets separately identify the liabilities that are "subject to compromise" as a result of the Chapter 11 proceedings. In Grace's case, "liabilities subject to compromise" represent both pre-petition and post-petition liabilities as determined under U.S. GAAP. Changes to pre-petition liabilities subsequent to the Filing Date reflect: (1) cash payments under approved court orders; (2) the terms of the Joint Plan, as discussed above, including the accrual of interest on pre-petition debt and other fixed obligations; (3) accruals for employee-related programs; and (4) changes in estimates related to other pre-petition contingent liabilities.

Components of liabilities subject to compromise are as follows:

(In millions)	December 31, 2013	December 31, 2012	Filing Date (Unaudited)
Asbestos-related contingencies	$2,092.4	$2,065.0	$1,002.8
Pre-petition bank debt plus accrued interest	1,100.0	937.2	511.5
Environmental contingencies	134.5	140.5	164.8
Unfunded special pension arrangements	129.4	137.1	70.8
Income tax contingencies	76.6	87.6	242.1
Postretirement benefits other than pension	57.2	63.9	185.4
Drawn letters of credit plus accrued interest	37.8	36.1	—
Accounts payable	34.3	31.3	43.0
Retained obligations of divested businesses	29.9	29.0	43.5
Other accrued liabilities	94.3	102.3	102.1
Reclassification to current liabilities[(1)]	(10.3)	(10.1)	—
Total liabilities subject to compromise	$3,776.1	$3,619.9	$2,366.0

[(1)] As of December 31, 2013 and 2012, approximately $10.3 million and $10.1 million, respectively, of certain pension and postretirement benefit obligations subject to compromise have been presented in "other current liabilities" in the Consolidated Balance Sheets in accordance with ASC 715 "Compensation—Retirement Benefits".

Note that the unfunded special pension arrangements reflected above exclude non-U.S. pension plans and qualified U.S. pension plans that became underfunded subsequent to the Filing.

Change in Liabilities Subject to Compromise

The following table is a reconciliation of the changes in pre-filing date liability balances for the period from the Filing Date through December 31, 2013 .

(In millions) (Unaudited)	Cumulative Since Filing
Balance, filing date April 2, 2001	$2,366.0
Cash Disbursements and/or Reclassifications Under Bankruptcy Court Orders:	
Payment of environmental settlement liability	(252.0)
Freight and distribution order	(5.7)
Trade accounts payable order	(9.1)
Resolution of contingencies subject to Chapter 11	(130.0)
Other court orders for payments of certain operating expenses	(374.9)
Expense (Income) Items:	
Interest on pre-petition liabilities	682.5
Employee-related accruals	127.6
Provision for asbestos-related contingencies	1,137.2
Provision for environmental contingencies	362.0
Release of income tax contingencies	(91.5)
Balance sheet reclassifications	(36.0)
Balance, end of period	$3,776.1

For the holders of pre-petition bank credit facilities, beginning January 1, 2006, Grace agreed to pay interest on pre-petition bank debt at the prime rate, adjusted for periodic changes, and compounded quarterly. The effective rate for the years ended December 31, 2013 and 2012, was 3.25%. From the Filing Date through December 31, 2005, Grace accrued interest on pre-petition bank debt at a negotiated fixed annual rate of 6.09%, compounded quarterly. The pre-petition bank debt holders argued that they were entitled to post-petition interest at the default rate specified under the terms of the underlying credit agreements, which they asserted was more than an additional $210 million in interest. The Bankruptcy Court and the District Court overruled this assertion and the pre-petition bank debt holders appealed these rulings to the Third Circuit Court of Appeals. On December 23, 2013, Grace and the pre-petition bank debt holders settled this appeal. Under the terms of the settlement, Grace agreed to pay an additional $129.0 million of interest above the amount provided for under the Joint Plan as of December 31, 2013, with interest to continue to accrue at 3.25% through January 31, 2014, and at 5.00% thereafter. The principal and all accrued interest on the pre-petition bank debt was paid in full on the Effective Date.

For the holders of claims who, but for the Filing, would be entitled under a contract or otherwise to accrue or be paid interest on such claim in a non-default (or non-overdue payment) situation under applicable non-bankruptcy law, Grace accrued interest at the rate provided in the contract between the Grace entity and the claimant or such rate as may otherwise apply under applicable non-bankruptcy law.

For all other holders of allowed general unsecured claims, Grace accrued interest at a rate of 4.19% per annum, compounded annually, unless otherwise negotiated during the claim settlement process.

Chapter 11 Expenses

(In millions)	Year Ended December 31,		
	2013	**2012**	**2011**
Legal and financial advisory fees	$17.1	$17.4	$20.6
Interest (income) expense	(1.8)	(0.8)	(0.6)
Chapter 11 expenses, net of interest income	$15.3	$16.6	$20.0

Pursuant to ASC 852, interest income earned on the Debtors' cash balances must be offset against Chapter 11 expenses.

Condensed Financial Information of the Debtors

W. R. Grace & Co.—Chapter 11 Filing Entities
Debtor-in-Possession Statements of Operations

(In millions) (Unaudited)	Year Ended December 31,		
	2013	**2012**	**2011**
Net sales, including intercompany	$1,425.4	$1,512.6	$1,479.4
Cost of goods sold, including intercompany, exclusive of depreciation and amortization shown separately below	882.2	951.3	919.1
Selling, general and administrative expenses	178.1	274.9	334.5
Depreciation and amortization	69.1	67.3	68.3
Chapter 11 expenses, net of interest income	15.3	16.6	20.0
Default interest settlement	129.0	—	—
Asbestos and bankruptcy-related charges, net	21.9	384.6	—
Research and development expenses	37.8	35.9	39.7
Interest expense and related financing costs	37.7	41.5	40.0
Other income, net	(75.7)	(93.2)	(75.3)
	1,295.4	1,678.9	1,346.3
Income (loss) before income taxes and equity in net income of non-filing entities	130.0	(166.3)	133.1
Benefit from (provision for) income taxes	(53.2)	48.4	(50.8)
Income (loss) before equity in net income of non-filing entities	76.8	(117.9)	82.3
Equity in net income of non-filing entities	179.3	157.9	137.4
Net income attributable to W. R. Grace & Co. shareholders	$ 256.1	$ 40.0	$ 219.7

In the above table, for 2013, Asbestos and bankruptcy-related charges, net, primarily includes adjustments made to reflect the emergence-date value of the deferred payment obligations and adjustments to record the final allowed claims listing, partially offset by adjustments for interest per the terms of the Joint Plan. For 2012, Asbestos and bankruptcy-related charges, net, includes adjustments made to our asbestos-related liability and to accrue for the Libby Medical Program settlement.

W. R. Grace & Co.—Chapter 11 Filing Entities
Debtor-in-Possession Statements of Cash Flows

(In millions) (Unaudited)	Year Ended December 31,		
	2013	**2012**	**2011**
Operating Activities			
Net income attributable to W. R. Grace & Co. shareholders	$ 256.1	$ 40.0	$ 219.7
Reconciliation to Net Cash Provided by Operating Activities:			
Depreciation and amortization	69.1	67.3	68.3
Asbestos and bankruptcy-related charges, net	21.9	384.6	—
Default interest settlement	129.0	—	—
Equity in net income of non-filing entities	(179.3)	(157.9)	(137.4)
Provision for (benefit from) income taxes	53.2	(48.4)	50.8
Income taxes (paid), net of refunds	13.5	(33.9)	(13.2)
Tax benefits from stock-based compensation	35.4	(36.8)	—
Defined benefit pension (income) expense	(51.8)	82.0	111.6
Payments under defined benefit pension arrangements	(55.6)	(114.9)	(251.4)
Repatriation of cash from foreign entities	29.7	21.6	30.3
Changes in assets and liabilities, excluding the effect of foreign currency translation and business acquired:			
Trade accounts receivable	(6.2)	(7.1)	(26.2)
Inventories	(23.0)	66.7	(66.4)
Accounts payable	21.9	(15.1)	37.5
All other items, net	31.1	75.9	13.4
Net cash provided by operating activities	345.0	324.0	37.0
Investing Activities			
Capital expenditures	(94.1)	(82.6)	(77.7)
Business acquired, net of cash acquired	(510.4)	—	—
Transfer to restricted cash and cash equivalents	(222.2)	(35.4)	(8.4)
Other	—	—	10.0
Net cash used for investing activities	(826.7)	(118.0)	(76.1)
Borrowings under credit arrangements	0.3	—	—
Repayments under credit arrangements	(0.8)	(0.6)	—
Proceeds from exercise of stock options	34.4	32.2	12.1
Excess tax benefits from stock-based compensation	(35.4)	36.8	—
Other financing activities	4.1	1.2	28.4
Net cash provided by financing activities	2.6	69.6	40.5
Net (decrease) increase in cash and cash equivalents	(479.1)	275.6	1.4
Cash and cash equivalents, beginning of period	1,064.2	788.6	787.2
Cash and cash equivalents, end of period	$ 585.1	$1,064.2	$ 788.6

(In millions) (Unaudited)	December 31,	
	2013	2012
Assets		
Current assets		
Cash and cash equivalents	$ 585.1	$1,064.2
Restricted cash and cash equivalents	340.5	118.3
Trade accounts receivable, net	138.8	132.6
Accounts receivable—unconsolidated affiliate	10.9	14.1
Receivables from non-filing entities, net	173.0	160.5
Inventories	138.9	115.9
Other current assets	69.3	58.5
Total current assets	1,456.5	1,664.1
Properties and equipment, net	484.5	433.5
Goodwill	279.9	26.8
Technology and other intangible assets, net	249.1	9.6
Deferred income taxes	817.3	933.3
Asbestos-related insurance	500.0	500.0
Loans receivable from non-filing entities, net	283.8	282.1
Investment in non-filing entities	531.3	442.3
Investment in unconsolidated affiliate	96.2	85.5
Other assets	16.5	10.8
Total assets	$4,715.1	$4,388.0
Liabilities and Equity		
Liabilities not subject to compromise		
Current liabilities (including $17.5 due to unconsolidated affiliate) (2012—$6.0)	$ 247.4	$ 244.7
Underfunded defined benefit pension plans	52.2	156.9
Other liabilities (including $24.3 due to unconsolidated affiliate) (2012—$22.4)	78.7	56.5
Total liabilities not subject to compromise	378.3	458.1
Liabilities subject to compromise	3,776.1	3,619.9
Total liabilities	4,154.4	4,078.0
Total W. R. Grace & Co. shareholders' equity	560.6	309.9
Noncontrolling interests in Chapter 11 filing entities	0.1	0.1
Total equity	560.7	310.0
Total liabilities and equity	$4,715.1	$4,388.0

In addition to Grace's financial reporting obligations as prescribed by the SEC, during the Chapter 11 proceeding, Grace was required, under the rules and regulations of the Bankruptcy Code, to periodically file certain statements and schedules with the Bankruptcy Court. This information is available to the public through the Bankruptcy Court. This information was prepared in a format that may not be comparable to information in Grace's quarterly and annual financial statements as filed with the SEC. These statements and schedules are not audited and do not purport to represent the financial position or results of operations of Grace on a consolidated basis.

This summary of the terms of various agreements does not purport to be complete and is qualified in its entirety by reference to the Joint Plan, the Confirmation Order, the Asbestos Trust Agreements, the Asbestos Insurance Transfer Agreement, the Deferred Payment Agreements, the Guarantee Agreements, the Share Issuance Agreement, the Warrant Agreement, the Warrant Implementation Letter, and the Warrant Registration Rights Agreement, which have been filed with the SEC.

3. Subsequent Event—Chapter 11 Emergence

Grace emerged from bankruptcy on February 3, 2014. Grace paid approximately $1,900 million in emergence-related claims and other costs. This included payments to the PI Trust and the PD Trust, pre-petition bank debt, drawn letters of credit, environmental settlements, income tax settlements, amounts due to vendors, and other non-asbestos claims, plus accrued interest for certain of these items as well as other emergence costs. Grace will satisfy all other liabilities previously subject to compromise as they become due and payable after emergence.

Grace funded these payments through a combination of approximately $1,360 million of cash on hand and approximately $900 million in exit financing. The exit financing consisted of a $700 million term loan and a €150 million term loan. See Note 8 for a discussion of Grace's exit financing.

Pro forma Information (Unaudited)   The below table presents the pro forma consolidated balance sheet of Grace as of December 31, 2013, reflecting the accounting effects of the Joint Plan as if it became effective on that date. The income tax effects of the pro forma adjustments have been computed at a 37.41% U.S. Federal and state income tax rate. Grace is not required to adopt fresh-start accounting at emergence since existing shareholders continue to retain a majority interest in the Company on the Effective Date, and Grace is not balance sheet insolvent. Following is a description of the pro forma adjustments:

1. **Borrowings Under New Credit Agreements**—Reflects $900 million of debt borrowed on the Effective Date. Cash proceeds were approximately $873 million after approximately $27 million of origination fees and other costs of the exit financing, including original issue discount.

2. **Consideration to the Asbestos Trusts**—Reflects the transfer by Grace to the PI Trust and the PD Trust of (i) cash (including restricted cash) of approximately $512 million, (ii) the PI Deferred Payment Obligations, (iii) the PD Deferred Payment Obligation, (iv) the warrant, and (v) rights to proceeds from Grace's asbestos-related insurance coverage. See Note 2 for a discussion of this consideration. The related deferred income tax assets are reclassified from temporary differences to NOL carryforward.

    Grace expects to recognize income tax deductions on the Deferred Payments when cash payments are made. Grace has determined that payments of the U.S. ZAI contingent payments are not probable, and no such payments are included in this pro forma.

3. **Payment of Remaining Pre-Petition Liabilities and Adjustment for Additional Expenses**—Reflects the payment of pre-petition bank debt, drawn letters of credit, environmental settlements, income tax settlements, amounts due to vendors and other non-asbestos claims, accrued interest for certain of these items, and other emergence costs on the Effective Date. The related deferred income tax assets are reclassified from temporary differences to NOL carryforward. Also reflects approximately $12 million of emergence costs, which are assumed fully deductible for tax purposes.

4. **NOLs and Future Tax Deductions**—Reflects U.S. Federal and state income tax deductions attributable to the payment of certain bankruptcy claims. U.S. Federal and state NOL carryforwards are assumed to increase to approximately $670 million (tax effected at approximately $252 million). In addition, under current U.S. Federal and state income tax law, future deductions are expected in the amount of $1,580 million when the deferred payments are made and $490 million when the warrant is settled.

    These future payments are expected to create additional NOL carryforwards in the years paid. It is expected that use of these U.S. Federal tax benefits will be unrestricted and that a valuation allowance will not be established. U.S. state tax benefits associated with these future payments may have some restrictions and a partial valuation allowance may be recorded. The realization of the tax benefits depends on the amount and timing of future U.S. taxable income and the avoidance of limitation events that would apply in the event that Grace undergoes an "ownership change" (as defined by the Internal Revenue Code).

5. **Reclassification of Liabilities Subject to Compromise**—Reflects certain items that were classified as Liabilities Subject to Compromise as of December 31, 2013, and were not paid at emergence, which were reclassified to the appropriate liability accounts at emergence. This includes income tax contingencies, postretirement benefits, and environmental contingencies that will be paid as they come due after emergence.

W. R. Grace and Co. and Subsidiaries
Pro forma Consolidated Balance Sheet (unaudited)

(In millions, except par value and shares)	December 31, 2013 Reported	Pro Forma Adjustments				December 31, 2013 Pro Forma
		Borrowings Under New Credit Agreements	Consideration to the Asbestos Trusts	Payment of Remaining Pre-Petition Liabilities and Adjustment for Additional Expenses	Reclassifications at Emergence	
Assets						
Current assets						
Cash and cash equivalents	$ 964.8	$873.0	$ (269.6)	$(1,370.6)	$ 153.2	$ 350.8
Restricted cash and cash equivalents	395.4	—	(242.2)	—	(153.2)	—
Trade accounts receivable, less allowance of $6.0	469.5	—	—	—	—	469.5
Accounts receivable—unconsolidated affiliate	12.3	—	—	—	—	12.3
Inventories	295.3	—	—	—	—	295.3
Deferred income taxes	58.1	—	—	—	—	58.1
Other current assets	99.0	—	—	—	—	99.0
Total current assets	2,294.4	873.0	(511.8)	(1,370.6)	—	1,285.0

(continued)

(In millions, except par value and shares)	December 31, 2013 Reported	Pro Forma Adjustments Borrowings Under New Credit Agreements	Consideration to the Asbestos Trusts	Payment of Remaining Pre-Petition Liabilities and Adjustment for Additional Expenses	Reclassifications at Emergence	December 31, 2013 Pro Forma
Properties and equipment, net of accumulated depreciation and amortization of $1,876.8	829.9	—	—	—	—	829.9
Goodwill	457.5	—	—	—	—	457.5
Technology and other intangible assets, net	315.5	—	—	—	—	315.5
Deferred income taxes:						
Net operating loss carryforward	—	—	111.0	141.2	—	252.2
Temporary differences	845.9	—	(111.0)	(134.1)	—	600.8
Asbestos-related insurance	500.0	—	(500.0)	—	—	—
Overfunded defined benefit pension plans	16.7	—	—	—	—	16.7
Investment in unconsolidated affiliate	96.2	—	—	—	—	96.2
Other assets	40.0	27.0	—	—	—	67.0
Total assets	$5,396.1	$900.0	$(1,011.8)	$(1,363.5)	$ —	$3,920.8
Liabilities and Equity						
Liabilities not subject to compromise						
Current liabilities						
Debt payable within one year	$ 76.6	$ 9.0	$ —	$ —	$ —	$ 85.6
Debt payable—unconsolidated affiliate	4.5	—	—	—	—	4.5
Accounts payable	249.5	—	—	—	—	249.5
Accounts payable—unconsolidated affiliate	13.0	—	—	—	—	13.0
PI warrant liability	—	—	490.0	—	—	490.0
Other current liabilities	292.0	—	—	7.2	38.8	338.0
Total current liabilities	635.6	9.0	490.0	7.2	38.8	1,180.6
Debt payable after one year	5.3	891.0	—	—	—	896.3
Debt payable—unconsolidated affiliate	24.3	—	—	—	—	24.3
Deferred payment obligations	—	—	594.5	—	—	594.5
Deferred income taxes	18.2	—	—	—	—	18.2
Income tax contingencies	—	—	—	—	76.6	76.6
Underfunded defined benefit pension plans	66.2	—	—	—	—	66.2
Unfunded pay-as-you-go defined benefit pension plans	233.4	—	—	—	95.9	329.3
Other liabilities	65.8	—	—	—	105.2	171.0
Total liabilities not subject to compromise	1,048.8	900.0	1,084.5	7.2	316.5	3,357.0
Liabilities subject to compromise						
Debt plus accrued interest	1,137.8	—	—	(1,135.7)	(2.1)	—
Income tax contingencies	76.6	—	—	—	(76.6)	—
Asbestos-related contingencies	2,092.4	—	(2,084.1)	—	(8.3)	—
Environmental contingencies	134.5	—	—	(77.5)	(57.0)	—
Postretirement benefits	176.3	—	—	(27.7)	(148.6)	—
Other liabilities and accrued interest	158.5	—	(12.2)	(122.4)	(23.9)	—
Total liabilities subject to compromise	3,776.1	—	(2,096.3)	(1,363.3)	(316.5)	—
Total liabilities	4,824.9	900.0	(1,011.8)	(1,356.1)	—	3,357.0
Equity						
Common stock issued, par value $0.01; 300,000,000 shares authorized; outstanding: 77,046,143 (2012—75,565,409)	0.8	—	—	—	—	0.8
Paid-in capital	533.4	—	—	—	—	533.4
Retained earnings	15.8	—	—	(7.4)	—	8.4
Treasury stock, at cost: shares: 0 (2012—1,414,351)	—	—	—	—	—	—
Accumulated other comprehensive loss	10.6	—	—	—	—	10.6
Total W. R. Grace & Co. shareholders' equity	560.6	—	—	(7.4)	—	553.2
Noncontrolling interests	10.6	—	—	—	—	10.6
Total equity	571.2	—	—	(7.4)	—	563.8
Total liabilities and equity	$5,396.1	$900.0	$(1,011.8)	$(1,363.5)	$ —	$3,920.8

Lack of Consistency

PRESENTATION

NONISSUERS

7.34 As required by paragraph .08 of AU-C section 708, if there has been a change in accounting principles or the method of their application that has a material effect on the comparability of the company's financial statements, the auditor should refer to the change in an emphasis-of-matter paragraph in the report. Such paragraph should follow the opinion paragraph and identify the nature of the change and refer the reader to the note in the financial statements that discusses the change in detail.

7.35 Paragraph .09 of AU-C section 708 states that the auditor should include an emphasis-of-matter paragraph relating to a change in accounting principle in reports on financial statements in the period of the change, and in subsequent periods, until the new accounting principle is applied in all periods presented. If the change in accounting principle is accounted for by retrospective application to the financial statements of all prior periods presented, the emphasis-of-matter paragraph is needed only in the period of such change.

ISSUERS

7.36 Although the information in paragraphs 7.34–.35 apply to issuers as well, PCAOB Auditing Standard No. 6, *Evaluating Consistency of Financial Statements* (AICPA, *PCAOB Standards and Related Rules*, Auditing Standards), further states that the auditor should evaluate a change in accounting principle to determine whether the
  * newly adopted accounting principle is a generally accepted accounting principle (GAAP).
  * method of accounting for the effect of the change is in conformity with GAAP.
  * disclosures related to the accounting change are adequate.
  * company has justified that the alternative accounting principle is preferable.

7.37 Auditing Standard No. 6 further states that if the auditor concludes that the criteria in paragraph 7.36 for a change in accounting principle are not met, the auditor should consider the matter to be a departure from GAAP and, if the effect of the change in accounting principle is material, should issue a qualified or an adverse opinion.

7.38 In addition to a change in accounting principle, a lack of consistency can also be the result of a correction of a material misstatement in previously issued financial statements. Paragraphs .18A–.18C of PCAOB AU section 508 state that the correction of a material misstatement in previously issued financial statements should be recognized in the auditor's report on the audited financial statements through the addition of an explanatory paragraph following the opinion paragraph.

7.39 The explanatory paragraph should include a
  * statement that the previously issued financial statements have been restated for the correction of a misstatement in the respective period.
  * reference to the company's disclosure of the correction of the misstatement.

7.40 This type of explanatory paragraph in the auditor's report should be included in reports on financial statements when the related financial statements are restated to correct the prior material misstatement. The paragraph need not be repeated in subsequent years.

PRESENTATION AND DISCLOSURE EXCERPTS

SEPARATION OF BUSINESS SEGMENT

7.41 ABBOTT LABORATORIES (DEC)
REPORT OF INDEPENDENT REGISTERED PUBLIC ACCOUNTING FIRM

To the Board of Directors and Shareholders of
Abbott Laboratories:

We have audited the accompanying consolidated balance sheets of Abbott Laboratories and subsidiaries (the "Company") as of December 31, 2013 and 2012, and the related consolidated statements of earnings, comprehensive income, shareholders' investment, and cash flows for each of the three years in the period ended December 31, 2013. These financial statements are the responsibility of the Company's management. Our responsibility is to express an opinion on these financial statements based on our audits.

We conducted our audits in accordance with the standards of the Public Company Accounting Oversight Board (United States). Those standards require that we plan and perform the audit to obtain reasonable assurance about whether the financial statements are free of material misstatement. An audit includes examining, on a test basis, evidence supporting the amounts and disclosures in the financial statements. An audit also includes assessing the accounting principles used and significant estimates made by management, as well as evaluating the overall financial statement presentation. We believe that our audits provide a reasonable basis for our opinion.

In our opinion, such consolidated financial statements present fairly, in all material respects, the financial position of the Company as of December 31, 2013 and 2012, and the results of its operations and its cash flows for each of the three years in the period ended December 31, 2013, in conformity with accounting principles generally accepted in the United States of America.

As discussed in Note 2 to the consolidated financial statements, on January 1, 2013, the Company distributed all of the outstanding shares of AbbVie Inc., which encompasses the Company's research-based pharmaceuticals business, to the Company's shareholders. Also, as discussed in Note 1, in 2011 the Company changed the year end of its foreign subsidiaries from a November 30 fiscal year end to a December 31 calendar year end.

We also have audited, in accordance with the standards of the Public Company Accounting Oversight Board (United States), the Company's internal control over financial reporting as of December 31, 2013, based on criteria established in *Internal Control—Integrated Framework (1992)* issued by the Committee of Sponsoring Organizations of the Treadway Commission and our report dated February 21, 2014 expressed an unqualified opinion on the Company's internal control over financial reporting.

/s/ Deloitte & Touche LLP
Chicago, Illinois
February 21, 2014

NOTES TO CONSOLIDATED FINANCIAL STATEMENTS

Note 2—Separation of AbbVie Inc.

On November 28, 2012, Abbott's board of directors declared a special dividend distribution of all of the outstanding shares of common stock of AbbVie Inc. (AbbVie), the company formed to hold Abbott's research-based proprietary pharmaceuticals business. For each Abbott common share held at the close of business on December 12, 2012, Abbott shareholders received one share of AbbVie stock on January 1, 2013. Abbott has received a ruling from the Internal Revenue Service that the separation qualifies as a tax-free distribution to Abbott and its U.S. shareholders for U.S. federal income tax purposes.

The historical operating results of the research-based proprietary pharmaceuticals business prior to separation are excluded from Earnings from Continuing Operations and are presented on the Earnings from Discontinued Operations line. Discontinued operations include the results of AbbVie's business except for certain corporate overhead costs and certain costs associated with transition services that will be provided by Abbott to AbbVie. Discontinued operations also includes other costs incurred by Abbott to separate AbbVie as well as an allocation of interest assuming a uniform ratio of consolidated debt to equity for all of Abbott's historical operations. The assets, liabilities, and cash flows of the research-based proprietary pharmaceuticals business are included in Abbott's Consolidated Balance Sheet and its Consolidated Statements of Cash Flows for periods prior to January 1, 2013.

The following is a summary of the assets and liabilities transferred to AbbVie as part of the separation on January 1, 2013:

(In billions)	
Assets:	
Cash and cash equivalents	$ 5.9
Investments	2.2
Trade receivables, less allowances	3.2
Inventories	0.7
Prepaid expenses, deferred income taxes, and other current receivables	2.9
Net property and equipment	2.2
Intangible assets, net of amortization	2.3
Goodwill	6.1
Deferred income taxes and other assets	1.1
	26.6

(continued)

(In billions)	
Liabilities:	
Short-term borrowings	1.0
Trade accounts payable and other current liabilities	5.2
Long-term debt	14.6
Post-employment obligations, deferred income taxes and other long-term liabilities	3.1
	23.9
Net assets transferred to AbbVie Inc.	$ 2.7

In addition, approximately $1 billion of accumulated other comprehensive losses, net of income taxes, primarily related to the pension and other benefit plan net liabilities as well as foreign translation was transferred to AbbVie.

In 2013, there are no operating results related to discontinued operations other than a favorable adjustment to tax expense of $193 million as a result of the resolution of various tax positions related to AbbVie's operations prior to separation. Summarized financial information for discontinued operations for 2012 and 2011 is as follows:

	Year Ended December 31	
(In millions)	**2012**	**2011**
Net sales	$18,380	$17,444
Earnings before taxes	5,958	3,963
Taxes on earnings	574	361
Net earnings	5,384	3,602

Abbott and AbbVie entered into transitional services agreements prior to the separation pursuant to which Abbott and AbbVie are providing various services to each other on an interim transitional basis. Transition services may be provided for up to 24 months with an option for a one-year extension by the recipient. Services being provided by Abbott include certain information technology and back office support. Billings by Abbott under these transitional services agreements are recorded as a reduction of the costs to provide the respective service in the applicable expense category in the Consolidated Statement of Earnings. This transitional support will enable AbbVie to establish its stand-alone processes for various activities that were previously provided by Abbott and does not constitute significant continuing support of AbbVie's operations.

For a small portion of AbbVie's operations, the legal transfer of AbbVie's assets (net of liabilities) did not occur with the separation of AbbVie on January 1, 2013 due to the time required to transfer marketing authorizations and other regulatory requirements in each of these countries. Under the terms of the separation agreement with Abbott, AbbVie is subject to the risks and entitled to the benefits generated by these operations and assets. The majority of these operations were transferred to AbbVie in 2013 with the remainder transferring in 2014. These assets and liabilities have been presented as held for disposition in the Consolidated Balance Sheet. At December 31, 2013, the assets and liabilities held for disposition consist of inventories of $243 million, trade accounts receivable of $163 million, other current assets of $32 million, equipment of $28 million, other assets of $38 million, trade accounts payable and accrued liabilities of $386 million and other liabilities of $7 million. Abbott's obligation to transfer the net assets held for disposition to AbbVie of $111 million is included in Other accrued liabilities.

Abbott has retained all liabilities for all U.S. federal and foreign income taxes on income prior to the separation, as well as certain non-income taxes attributable to AbbVie's business. AbbVie generally will be liable for all other taxes attributable to its business. In connection with the separation, Abbott has adjusted its employee stock compensation awards and separated its defined benefit programs for pensions and post-employment medical and dental benefit plans. See notes 8 and 12 for additional information.

INVENTORY

7.42 JOHNSON CONTROLS, INC. (SEP)
REPORT OF INDEPENDENT REGISTERED PUBLIC ACCOUNTING FIRM

To the Board of Directors and Shareholders of
Johnson Controls, Inc.

In our opinion, the consolidated financial statements listed in the accompanying index present fairly, in all material respects, the financial position of Johnson Controls, Inc. and its subsidiaries at September 30, 2013 and 2012, and the results of their operations and their cash flows for each of the three years in the period ended September 30, 2013 in conformity with accounting principles generally accepted in the United States of America. In addition, in our opinion, the financial statement schedule listed in the accompanying index presents fairly, in all material respects, the information set forth therein when read in conjunction with the related consolidated financial statements. Also in our opinion, the Company maintained, in all material respects, effective internal control over financial reporting as of September 30, 2013, based on criteria established in *Internal Control—Integrated Framework (1992)* issued by the Committee of Sponsoring Organizations of the Treadway Commission (COSO). The Company's management is responsible for these financial statements and financial statement schedule, for maintaining effective internal control over financial reporting and for its assessment of the effectiveness of internal control over financial reporting, included in Management's Report on Internal Control Over Financial Reporting appearing under Item 9A. Our responsibility is to express opinions on these financial statements, on the financial statement schedule, and on the Company's internal control over financial reporting based on our integrated audits. We conducted our audits in accordance with the standards of the Public Company Accounting Oversight Board (United States). Those standards require that we plan and perform the audits to obtain reasonable assurance about whether the financial statements are free of material misstatement and whether effective internal control over financial reporting was maintained in all material respects. Our audits of the financial statements included examining, on a test basis, evidence supporting the amounts and disclosures in the financial statements, assessing the accounting principles used and significant estimates made by management, and evaluating the overall financial statement presentation. Our audit of internal control over financial reporting included obtaining an understanding of internal control over financial reporting, assessing the risk that a material weakness exists, and testing and evaluating the design and operating effectiveness of internal control based on the assessed risk. Our audits also included performing such other procedures as we considered necessary in the circumstances. We believe that our audits provide a reasonable basis for our opinions.

As discussed in Note 1 to the consolidated financial statements, in 2013 the Company changed their inventory costing method for certain inventories. All periods have been retroactively revised for this accounting change.

A company's internal control over financial reporting is a process designed to provide reasonable assurance regarding the reliability of financial reporting and the preparation of financial statements for external purposes in accordance with generally accepted accounting principles. A company's internal control over financial reporting includes those policies and procedures that (i) pertain to the maintenance of records that, in reasonable detail, accurately and fairly reflect the transactions and dispositions of the assets of the company; (ii) provide reasonable assurance that transactions are recorded as necessary to permit preparation of financial statements in accordance with generally accepted accounting principles, and that receipts and expenditures of the company are being made only in accordance with authorizations of management and directors of the company; and (iii) provide reasonable assurance regarding prevention or timely detection of unauthorized acquisition, use, or disposition of the company's assets that could have a material effect on the financial statements.

Because of its inherent limitations, internal control over financial reporting may not prevent or detect misstatements. Also, projections of any evaluation of effectiveness to future periods are subject to the risk that controls may become inadequate because of changes in conditions, or that the degree of compliance with the policies or procedures may deteriorate.

/s/ PricewaterhouseCoopers LLP
PricewaterhouseCoopers LLP
Milwaukee, Wisconsin
November 21, 2013

NOTES TO CONSOLIDATED FINANCIAL STATEMENTS

1. Summary of Significant Accounting Policies (in part)

Inventories

Inventories are stated at the lower of cost or market. Finished goods and work-in-process inventories include material, labor and manufacturing overhead costs.

In the fourth quarter of fiscal 2013, the Company changed its method of inventory costing for certain inventory in its Power Solutions business to the first-in first-out (FIFO) method from the last-in first-out (LIFO) method. The Company's other businesses also determine costs using the FIFO method. Prior to the change, Power Solutions utilized two methods of inventory costing: LIFO for inventories in the U.S. and FIFO for inventories in other countries. The Company believes that the FIFO method is preferable as it better reflects the current value of inventory on the Company's consolidated statement of financial position, provides better matching of revenues and expenses, results in uniformity across the Company's global operations with respect to the method of inventory accounting and improves comparability with the Company's peers. The change has been reported through retrospective application of the new accounting policy to all periods presented and resulted in a $5 million increase (less than $0.01 per diluted share), $16 million increase ($0.03 per diluted share) and $21 million decrease ($0.03 per diluted share) to net income attributable to Johnson Controls, Inc. for the quarters ended December 31, 2012, March 31, 2013 and June 30, 2013, respectively.

The impact of all adjustments made to the consolidated financial statements presented is summarized in the following table (in millions, except per share data):

	2013		
	Previous Method	As Reported	Effect of Change
Consolidated Statement of Income			
Cost of sales			
Products and systems	$29,207	$29,196	$(11)
Gross profit	6,767	6,778	11
Income before income taxes	2,454	2,465	11
Provision for income taxes	1,164	1,168	4
Net income	1,290	1,297	7
Net income attributable to Johnson Controls, Inc.	1,171	1,178	7
Earnings per share			
Basic	1.71	1.72	0.01
Diluted	1.70	1.71	0.01
Consolidated Statement of Comprehensive Income (Loss)			
Net income	$ 1,290	$ 1,297	$ 7
Total comprehensive income	1,251	1,258	7
Consolidated Statement of Financial Position			
Inventories	$ 2,198	$ 2,325	$ 127
Other current assets	2,358	2,308	(50)
Retained earnings	9,251	9,328	77
Consolidated Statement of Cash Flows			
Cash provided by operating activities			
Net income attributable to Johnson Controls, Inc.	$ 1,171	$ 1,178	$ 7
Net income	1,290	1,297	7
Deferred income taxes	269	273	4
Inventories	(86)	(97)	(11)
Consolidated Statement of Shareholders' Equity Attributable to Johnson Controls, Inc.			
Retained earnings at September 30, 2012	$ 8,541	$ 8,611	$ 70
Retained earnings at September 30, 2013	9,251	9,328	77

	2012		
	Previously Reported	Revised	Effect of Change
Consolidated Statement of Income			
Cost of sales			
Products and systems	$28,839	$28,909	$ 70
Gross profit	6,218	6,148	(70)
Income before income taxes	1,590	1,520	(70)
Provision for income taxes	237	209	(28)
Net income	1,353	1,311	(42)
Net income attributable to Johnson Controls, Inc.	1,226	1,184	(42)
Earnings per share			
Basic	1.80	1.74	(0.06)
Diluted	1.78	1.72	(0.06)
Consolidated Statement of Comprehensive Income (Loss)			
Net income	$ 1,353	$ 1,311	$(42)
Total comprehensive income	1,161	1,119	(42)
Consolidated Statement of Financial Position			
Inventories	$ 2,227	$ 2,343	$ 116
Other current assets	2,873	2,827	(46)
Retained earnings	8,541	8,611	70
Consolidated Statement of Cash Flows			
Cash provided by operating activities			
Net income attributable to Johnson Controls, Inc.	$ 1,226	$ 1,184	$ (42)
Net income	1,353	1,311	(42)
Deferred income taxes	(206)	(234)	(28)
Inventories	39	109	70
Consolidated Statement of Shareholders' Equity Attributable to Johnson Controls, Inc.			
Retained earnings at September 30, 2011	$ 7,838	$ 7,950	$ 112
Retained earnings at September 30, 2012	8,541	8,611	70

(continued)

	2011		
	Previously Reported	Revised	Effect of Change
Consolidated Statement of Income			
Cost of sales			
Products and systems	$27,675	$27,674	$ (1)
Gross profit	6,058	6,059	1
Income before income taxes	1,789	1,790	1
Provision for income taxes	257	258	1
Net income	1,532	1,532	—
Net income attributable to Johnson Controls, Inc.	1,415	1,415	—
Earnings per share			
Basic	2.09	2.09	—
Diluted	2.06	2.06	—
Consolidated Statement of Comprehensive Income (Loss)			
Net income	$ 1,532	$ 1,532	$—
Total comprehensive income	1,382	1,382	—
Consolidated Statement of Cash Flows			
Cash provided by operating activities			
Net income attributable to Johnson Controls, Inc.	$ 1,415	$ 1,415	$—
Net income	1,532	1,532	—
Deferred income taxes	(257)	(256)	1
Inventories	(387)	(388)	(1)
Consolidated Statement of Shareholders' Equity Attributable to Johnson Controls, Inc.			
Retained earnings at September 30, 2010	$ 6,890	$ 7,002	$112
Retained earnings at September 30, 2011	7,838	7,950	112

EMPLOYEE BENEFITS

7.43 SPX CORPORATION (DEC)
REPORT OF INDEPENDENT REGISTERED PUBLIC ACCOUNTING FIRM

To the Shareholders and Board of Directors of
SPX Corporation:

We have audited the accompanying Consolidated Balance Sheets of SPX Corporation and subsidiaries (the "Company") as of December 31, 2013 and 2012, and the related Consolidated Statements of Operations, Comprehensive Income, Equity, and Cash Flows for each of the three years in the period ended December 31, 2013. These financial statements are the responsibility of the Company's management. Our responsibility is to express an opinion on these financial statements based on our audits. We did not audit the consolidated financial statements of EGS Electrical Group, LLC and subsidiaries ("EGS") for the fiscal years ended September 30, 2013, 2012 and 2011, the Company's investment that is accounted for by use of the equity method (see Note 9 to the Company's consolidated financial statements). The Company's equity in income of EGS for the fiscal years ended September 30, 2013, 2012 and 2011 was $41.9 million, $39.0 million, and $28.7 million, respectively. The consolidated financial statements of EGS were audited by other auditors whose report has been furnished to us, and our opinion, insofar as it relates to the amounts included for EGS, is based solely on the report of the other auditors.

We conducted our audits in accordance with the standards of the Public Company Accounting Oversight Board (United States). Those standards require that we plan and perform the audit to obtain reasonable assurance about whether the financial statements are free of material misstatement. An audit includes examining, on a test basis, evidence supporting the amounts and disclosures in the financial statements. An audit also includes assessing the accounting principles used and significant estimates made by management, as well as evaluating the overall financial statement presentation. We believe that our audits and the report of the other auditors provide a reasonable basis for our opinion.

In our opinion, based on our audits and the report of the other auditors, such consolidated financial statements present fairly, in all material respects, the financial position of SPX Corporation and subsidiaries at December 31, 2013 and 2012, and the results of their operations and their cash flows for each of the three years in the period ended December 31, 2013, in conformity with accounting principles generally accepted in the United States of America.

As discussed in Note 1 to the consolidated financial statements, the Company has elected to change its methods of accounting for defined benefit pension and other postretirement benefit plan costs in 2013. Such changes are reflected in the accompanying consolidated balance sheets as of December 31, 2013 and 2012, and the related consolidated statements of operations, comprehensive income, equity, and cash flows for each of the three years in the period ended December 31, 2013.

We have also audited, in accordance with the standards of the Public Company Accounting Oversight Board (United States), the Company's internal control over financial reporting as of December 31, 2013, based on the criteria established in *Internal Control—Integrated Framework (1992)* issued by the Committee of Sponsoring Organizations of the Treadway Commission and our report dated February 21, 2014 expressed an unqualified opinion on the Company's internal control over financial reporting based on our audit.

/s/ Deloitte & Touche LLP
Charlotte, North Carolina
February 21, 2014

NOTES TO CONSOLIDATED FINANCIAL STATEMENTS

(All currency and share amounts are in millions, except per share and par value data)

(1) Summary of Significant Accounting Policies (in part)

Pension and Postretirement—In the fourth quarter of 2013, we elected to change our accounting methods for recognizing expense associated with all of our pension and postretirement benefit plans. Historically, actuarial gains and losses in excess of 10% of the greater of the market-related value of plan assets or the plans' projected benefit obligations (the "corridor") were recognized as a component of accumulated other comprehensive income ("AOCI") within our consolidated balance sheet and, depending on the benefit plan, we amortized these gains and losses to earnings either over the remaining average service period for the active participants or the average remaining life expectancy of the inactive participants. Additionally, for our domestic qualified pension plan, we used a calculated value of plan assets reflecting changes in the fair value of plan assets over a five-year period and we applied a fair value method for our foreign pension plans. Under our new accounting methods, we recognize changes in the fair value of plan assets and actuarial gains and losses in earnings during the fourth quarter of each year as a component of net periodic benefit expense (and we no longer apply a corridor and, therefore, no longer defer any gains or losses). These new accounting methods result in changes in the fair value of plan assets and actuarial gains and losses being recognized in earnings faster than under our previous methods of accounting. We believe the new methods of accounting are preferable as these methods recognize the effects of plan investment performance, interest rate changes, and changes in actuarial assumptions as a component of earnings in the year in which they occur. These changes have been reported through retrospective application of the new accounting methods to all periods presented. The remaining components of pension/postretirement expense, primarily service and interest costs and expected return on plan assets, will continue to be recorded on a quarterly basis. See Note 10 for further discussion of our pension and postretirement benefits and Note 19 for the impact of the above changes on our consolidated financial statements for the years ended December 31, 2013, 2012 and 2011.

(19) Effect of Accounting Changes

As described in Note 1, we have retrospectively applied the new accounting methods for recognizing changes in the fair value of plan assets and actuarial gains and losses associated with our pension and postretirement benefit plans. Accordingly, we recorded a cumulative reduction in retained earnings as of January 1, 2011 of $416.2, with a corresponding offset to AOCI. The impact of these changes on the accompanying consolidated financial statements is summarized below:

	2013			2012			2011		
	New Method[3]	Historical Method[2]	Effect of Change	As Adjusted[3]	As Revised and Restated[1]	Effect of Change	As Adjusted[3]	As Revised and Restated[1]	Effect of Change
Consolidated Statements of Operations:									
Cost of products sold	$3,359.6	$3,388.4	$ (28.8)	$3,517.4	$3,511.6	$ 5.8	$3,066.4	$3,065.6	$ 0.8
Selling, general and administrative	956.0	1,370.5	(414.5)	1,112.6	999.1	113.5	897.4	882.1	15.3
Operating income (loss)[4]	329.6	(113.7)	443.3	(142.4)	(23.1)	(119.3)	237.0	253.1	(16.1)
Income (loss) from continuing operations before income taxes	256.1	(187.2)	443.3	(197.9)	(78.6)	(119.3)	120.4	136.5	(16.1)
Income tax (provision) benefit	(54.8)	115.8	(170.6)	21.3	(21.0)	42.3	12.3	8.2	4.1
Income (loss) from continuing operations	201.3	(71.4)	272.7	(176.6)	(99.6)	(77.0)	132.7	144.7	(12.0)
Income from discontinued operations, net of tax	11.3	8.2	3.1	359.8	360.2	(0.4)	43.5	51.6	(8.1)
Net income (loss)	212.6	(63.2)	275.8	183.2	260.6	(77.4)	176.2	196.3	(20.1)
Net income (loss) attributable to SPX common shareholders	210.2	(65.6)	275.8	180.4	257.8	(77.4)	171.2	191.3	(20.1)
Amounts attributable to SPX Corporation common shareholders:									
Income (loss) from continuing operations, net of tax	199.1	(73.6)	272.7	(179.6)	(102.6)	(77.0)	127.7	139.7	(12.0)
Income from discontinued operations, net of tax	11.1	8.0	3.1	360.0	360.4	(0.4)	43.5	51.6	(8.1)
Net income (loss)	210.2	(65.6)	275.8	180.4	257.8	(77.4)	171.2	191.3	(20.1)
Basic income (loss) per share of common stock:									
Continuing operations	$ 4.39	$ (1.62)	$ 6.01	$ (3.59)	$ (2.05)	$ (1.54)	$ 2.53	$ 2.77	$ (0.24)
Discontinued operations	0.24	0.17	0.07	7.20	7.20	—	0.86	1.02	(0.16)
Net income (loss)	$ 4.63	$ (1.45)	$ 6.08	$ 3.61	$ 5.15	$ (1.54)	$ 3.39	$ 3.79	$ (0.40)
Diluted income (loss) per share of common stock:									
Continuing operations	$ 4.33	$ (1.62)	$ 5.95	$ (3.59)	$ (2.05)	$ (1.54)	$ 2.51	$ 2.74	$ (0.23)
Discontinued operations	0.24	0.17	0.07	7.20	7.20	—	0.85	1.01	(0.16)
Net income (loss)	$4.57	$(1.45)	$ 6.02	$3.61	$5.15	$ (1.54)	$3.36	$3.75	$ (0.39)
Consolidated Statements of Comprehensive Income:									
Net income (loss)	$ 212.6	$ (63.2)	$ 275.8	$ 183.2	$ 260.6	$ (77.4)	$ 176.2	$ 196.3	$ (20.1)
Pension liability adjustment, net of tax	(2.2)	(278.0)	(275.8)	(1.0)	(80.3)	79.3	(2.1)	(21.7)	19.6
Consolidated Balance Sheets/Consolidated Statements of Equity:									
Retained earnings	$2,303.1	$2,541.0	$(237.9)	$2,138.4	$2,652.1	$(513.7)	$2,008.9	$2,445.2	$(436.3)
Accumulated other comprehensive income (loss)	287.5	49.6	237.9	284.8	(228.9)	513.7	189.8	(246.5)	436.3
Consolidated Statements of Cash Flows:									
Net income (loss)	$ 212.6	$ (63.2)	$ 275.8	$ 183.2	$ 260.6	$ (77.4)	$ 176.2	$ 196.3	$ (20.1)
Less: Income from discontinued operations, net of tax	11.3	8.2	3.1	359.8	360.2	(0.4)	43.5	51.6	(8.1)
Income (loss) from continuing operations	201.3	(71.4)	272.7	(176.6)	(99.6)	(77.0)	132.7	144.7	(12.0)
Deferred and other income taxes	95.0	(75.6)	170.6	(43.6)	(1.3)	(42.3)	(39.8)	(35.7)	(4.1)
Pension and other employee benefits	(0.1)	443.2	(443.3)	176.1	56.8	119.3	72.3	56.2	16.1

[1] "As Revised and Restated" for 2012 and 2011 represents amounts as previously reported in our 2012 Annual Report on Form 10-K (as amended), revised and restated to reflect (i) the reclassification of certain prior period amounts, including the results of discontinued operations (see Note 4), as well as (ii) the correction of prior period misstatements within our income tax accounts (see Notes 1, 11 and 18 for further information).

[2] Reflects amounts we would have reported had we not changed our accounting methods for recognizing changes in the fair value of plan assets and actuarial gains and losses.

[3] Reflects amounts reported in the accompanying consolidated financial statements as of and for the years ended December 31, 2013, 2012 and 2011.

[4] Under our historical methods of accounting for our pension and postretirement benefit plans, our pension and postretirement benefit expense for 2013 would have been a pre-tax charge of $425.6 as compared to pension and postretirement benefit income of $17.7 recognized under our new methods. The pre-tax charge under our historical methods reflects the effects of a $399.4 charge that would have been recognized as a result of the settlement of approximately 61% of the Plan's projected benefit obligation as of November 12, 2013, due primarily to the transfer of the retiree pension obligations of the Plan to Mass Mutual, as previously described.

7.44 THE PROCTER & GAMBLE COMPANY (JUN)
REPORT OF INDEPENDENT REGISTERED PUBLIC ACCOUNTING FIRM

To the Board of Directors and Stockholders of
The Procter & Gamble Company

We have audited the accompanying Consolidated Balance Sheets of The Procter & Gamble Company and subsidiaries (the "Company") as of June 30, 2013 and 2012, and the related Consolidated Statements of Earnings, Comprehensive Income, Shareholders' Equity and Cash Flows for each of the three years in the period ended June 30, 2013. These financial statements are the responsibility of the Company's management. Our responsibility is to express an opinion on these financial statements based on our audits.

We conducted our audits in accordance with the standards of the Public Company Accounting Oversight Board (United States). Those standards require that we plan and perform the audit to obtain reasonable assurance about whether the financial statements are free of material misstatement. An audit includes examining, on a test basis, evidence supporting the amounts and disclosures in the financial statements. An audit also includes assessing the accounting principles used and significant estimates made by management, as well as evaluating the overall financial statement presentation. We believe that our audits provide a reasonable basis for our opinion.

In our opinion, such Consolidated Financial Statements present fairly, in all material respects, the financial position of the Company at June 30, 2013 and 2012, and the results of its operations and cash flows for each of the three years in the period ended June 30, 2013, in conformity with accounting principles generally accepted in the United States of America.

As discussed in Note 1 to the Consolidated Financial Statements, the Company adopted the new accounting guidance in ASU 2011–05, *Comprehensive Income (Topic 220)—Presentation of Comprehensive Income*, and ASU 2013-02, *Comprehensive Income (Topic 220)—Reporting of Amounts Reclassified out of Accumulated Other Comprehensive Income*.

We have also audited, in accordance with the standards of the Public Company Accounting Oversight Board (United States), the Company's internal control over financial reporting as of June 30, 2013, based on the criteria established in *Internal Control—Integrated Framework (1992)* issued by the Committee of Sponsoring Organizations of the Treadway Commission and our report dated August 8, 2013 expressed an unqualified opinion on the Company's internal control over financial reporting.

/s/ Deloitte & Touche LLP
Cincinnati, Ohio
August 8, 2013

NOTES TO CONSOLIDATED FINANCIAL STATEMENTS

Amounts in millions of dollars except per share amounts or as otherwise specified

Note 1—Summary of Significant Accounting Policies (in part)

New Accounting Pronouncements and Policies

Other than as described below, no new accounting pronouncement issued or effective during the fiscal year had or is expected to have a material impact on the Consolidated Financial Statements.

During fiscal 2013, the Company adopted ASU 2011-05, "Comprehensive Income (Topic 220)—Presentation of Comprehensive Income", and ASU 2013-02, "Comprehensive Income (Topic 220)—Reporting of Amounts Reclassified out of Accumulated Other Comprehensive Income". This guidance eliminates the option to present the components of OCI as part of the statement of shareholders' equity and requires entities to present the components of net earnings and OCI in either a single continuous statement of comprehensive income or two separate but consecutive statements. We chose to present net earnings and OCI in two separate but consecutive statements. This guidance also requires entities to provide information about the amounts reclassified out of accumulated other comprehensive income (AOCI) by component and to present, either on the face of the statement where net income is presented or in the notes, significant amounts reclassified out of AOCI by the respective line items of net income. We chose to present the requirements in the notes to the financial statements (see Note 6). The adoption of this guidance had no impact on our consolidated financial position, results of operations or cash flows.

Note 6—Accumulated Other Comprehensive Income/(Loss)

The tables below present the changes in accumulated other comprehensive income/(loss) by component and the reclassifications out of accumulated other comprehensive income/(loss):

Changes in Accumulated Other Comprehensive Income/(Loss) by Component					
	Hedges	Investment Securities	Pension and Other Retiree Benefits	Financial Statement Translation	Total
Balance at June 30, 2012	$(3,673)	$ (3)	$(5,300)	$(357)	$(9,333)
OCI before reclassifications[1]	363	(24)	731	710	1,780
Amounts reclassified from AOCI	(219)	—	273	—	54
Net current period OCI	144	(24)	1,004	710	1,834
Balance at June 30, 2013	(3,529)	(27)	(4,296)	353	(7,499)

[1] Net of tax of $94, $5 and $496 for gains and losses on hedges, investment securities and pension and other retiree benefit items, respectively.

Reclassifications out of Accumulated Other Comprehensive Income/(Loss)	
Year Ended June 30	2013
Hedges[1]	
Interest rate contracts	$ 6
Foreign exchange contracts	215
Total before-tax	221
Tax (expense)/benefit	(2)
Net of tax	219
Pension and Other Retiree Benefits[2]	
Amortization of deferred amounts	2
Recognized net actuarial gains/(losses)	(412)
Curtailments and settlements	(4)
Total before-tax	(414)
Tax (expense)/benefit	141
Net of tax	(273)
Total reclassifications, net of tax	(54)

[1] See Note 5 for classification of these items in the Consolidated Statement of Earnings.

[2] Reclassified from AOCI into costs of products sold and SG&A. These components are included in the computation of net periodic pension cost (see Note 9 for additional details).

PRESENTATION OF INVESTMENTS

7.45 TIME WARNER INC. (DEC)
REPORT OF INDEPENDENT REGISTERED PUBLIC ACCOUNTING FIRM

The Board of Directors and Shareholders of
Time Warner Inc.

We have audited the accompanying consolidated balance sheets of Time Warner Inc. ("Time Warner") as of December 31, 2013 and 2012, and the related consolidated statements of operations, comprehensive income, cash flows and equity for each of the three years in the period ended December 31, 2013. Our audits also included the Supplementary Information and Financial Statement Schedule II listed in the Index at Item 15(a). These financial statements, supplementary information and schedule are the responsibility of Time Warner's management. Our responsibility is to express an opinion on these financial statements, supplementary information and schedule based on our audits.

We conducted our audits in accordance with the standards of the Public Company Accounting Oversight Board (United States). Those standards require that we plan and perform the audit to obtain reasonable assurance about whether the financial statements are free of material misstatement. An audit includes examining, on a test basis, evidence supporting the amounts and disclosures in the financial statements. An audit also includes assessing the accounting principles used and significant estimates made by management, as well as evaluating the overall financial statement presentation. We believe that our audits provide a reasonable basis for our opinion.

In our opinion, the financial statements referred to above present fairly, in all material respects, the consolidated financial position of Time Warner at December 31, 2013 and 2012, and the consolidated results of its operations and its cash flows for each of the three years in the period ended December 31, 2013, in conformity with U.S. generally accepted accounting principles. Also, in our opinion, the related

Supplementary Information and Financial Statement Schedule, when considered in relation to the basic financial statements taken as a whole, present fairly in all material respects the information set forth therein.

As described in Note 1 to the Company's consolidated financial statements, during the year ended December 31, 2013, Time Warner recast its historical financial results to reflect the presentation of its investment in the Class A common stock and Series A convertible preferred stock (which is convertible into Class A common stock and votes with the Class A common stock on an as-adjusted basis) of Central European Media Enterprises Ltd. under the equity method of accounting on a retrospective basis resulting in revision of the December 31, 2012 consolidated balance sheet, and the related consolidated statements of operations, comprehensive income, cash flows and equity for each of the two years in the period ended December 31, 2012.

We also have audited, in accordance with the standards of the Public Company Accounting Oversight Board (United States), Time Warner's internal control over financial reporting as of December 31, 2013, based on criteria established in Internal Control-Integrated Framework issued by the Committee of Sponsoring Organizations of the Treadway Commission (1992 framework) and our report dated February 26, 2014 expressed an unqualified opinion thereon.

/s/ Ernst & Young LLP
New York, NY
February 26, 2014

NOTES TO CONSOLIDATED FINANCIAL STATEMENTS

1. Description of Business, Basis of Presentation and Summary of Significant Accounting Policies (in part)

Basis of Presentation (in part)

Recast of Historical Financial Results—CME Investment

During the quarter ended June 30, 2013, the Company recast its historical financial results to reflect the presentation of its investment in the Class A common stock and Series A convertible preferred stock (which is convertible into Class A common stock and votes with the Class A common stock on an as-adjusted basis) of Central European Media Enterprises Ltd. ("CME") under the equity method of accounting for all prior periods from the date of the Company's initial investment in CME in May 2009.For more information, see Note 3, "Investments."

3. Dispositions and Acquisitions (in part)

Acquisitions (in part)

CME

Central European Media Enterprises Ltd. ("CME") is a publicly-traded broadcasting company operating leading networks in six Central and Eastern European countries. Since the Company's initial investment in CME in May 2009, CME founder and Non-Executive Chairman Ronald S. Lauder had controlled the voting rights associated with the Company's shares in CME pursuant to a voting agreement between the parties. During the second quarter of 2013, the voting agreement ended and the Company assumed control of the voting rights associated with its shares of Class A common stock and Series A convertible preferred stock. Prior to the second quarter of 2013, the Company accounted for its investment in CME under the cost method of accounting. However, as a result of the end of the voting agreement with Mr. Lauder, the Company began accounting for its investment in the Class A common stock and Series A convertible preferred stock of CME under the equity method of accounting. In accordance with applicable accounting guidance, the Company has recast its historical financial results to reflect the presentation of its investment in the Class A common stock and Series A convertible preferred stock of CME under the equity method of accounting for all prior periods from the date of the Company's initial investment in CME in May 2009. The recast resulted in an increase in net income of $34 million for the three months ended March 31, 2013 and a decrease in net income of $94 million for the year ended December 31, 2012.

During the second quarter of 2013, CME conducted a public offering of shares of its Class A common stock in which the Company purchased approximately 28.5 million shares for approximately $78 million in cash. As of December 31, 2013, the Company owned 61.4 million shares of CME's Class A common stock and 1 share of Series A convertible preferred stock, which is convertible into 11.2 million shares of CME's Class A common stock and votes with the Class A common stock on an as-converted basis. The combination of these holdings provides the Company with a 49.9% voting interest in CME's common stock.

In addition, on June 25, 2013, the Company purchased $200 million of CME's newly-issued, non-voting Series B convertible redeemable preferred shares. The Series B convertible redeemable preferred shares will accrete in value through the third anniversary of closing at an annual rate of 7.5% compounded quarterly and from the third anniversary to the fifth anniversary of closing at an annual rate of 3.75% compounded quarterly. Thereafter, the Series B convertible redeemable preferred shares will no longer accrete in value. CME has the right from the third anniversary to pay a cash dividend to the Company in lieu of further accretion. Each Series B convertible redeemable preferred share may be converted into shares of Class A common stock at the Company's option at any time after the third anniversary of the closing. The number of shares of Class A common stock received upon conversion would be determined by dividing the accreted value of the Series B convertible redeemable preferred shares (including any accrued but unpaid dividends) by the conversion price of $3.1625. The Series B convertible redeemable preferred shares will also be redeemable at the option of CME at any time after the third anniversary of the closing; however, upon notice from CME of a proposed redemption, the Company may elect to receive cash or shares of Class A common stock. The Company accounts for its investment in the Series B convertible redeemable preferred shares of CME under the cost method of accounting.

In 2012 and 2011, the Company acquired additional interests in CME for $165 million and $61 million, respectively. During 2011, the Company recorded a $131 million noncash impairment related to its investment in CME.

Emphasis of a Matter

PRESENTATION

NONISSUERS

7.46 Paragraph .06 of AU-C section 706 explains that if the auditor considers it necessary to draw users' attention to a matter appropriately presented or disclosed in the financial statements, the auditor should include an emphasis-of-matter paragraph. Paragraph .07 of AU-C section 706 states that the emphasis-of-matter paragraph should

- be included immediately after the opinion paragraph in the auditor's report,
- use the heading "Emphasis of Matter" or other appropriate heading,
- include in the paragraph a clear reference to the matter being emphasized and to where relevant disclosures that fully describe the matter can be found in the financial statements, and
- indicate that the auditor's opinion is not modified with respect to the matter emphasized.

7.47 Other-matter paragraphs should be included in the auditor's report when the auditor considers it necessary to communicate matters other than those that are presented or disclosed in the financial statements, as described in paragraph .08 of AU-C section 706. The paragraph should be included immediately after the opinion paragraph and any emphasis-of-matter paragraph or elsewhere in the auditor's report if the content of the other-matter paragraph is relevant to the "Other Reporting Responsibilities" section.

ISSUERS

7.48 Paragraph .19 of AU section 508 states the following:

In any report on financial statements, the auditor may emphasize a matter regarding the financial statements. Such explanatory information should be presented in a separate paragraph of the auditor's report. Phrases such as "with the foregoing [following] explanation" should not be used in the opinion paragraph if an emphasis paragraph is included in the auditor's report. Emphasis paragraphs are never required; they may be added solely at the auditor's discretion. Examples of matters the auditor may wish to emphasize are—

- That the entity is a component of a larger business enterprise.
- That the entity has had significant transactions with related parties.
- Unusually important subsequent events.
- Accounting matters, other than those involving a change or changes in accounting principles, affecting the comparability of the financial statements with those of the preceding period.

PRESENTATION AND DISCLOSURE EXCERPT

EMPHASIS OF A MATTER

7.49 SPRINT CORPORATION (DEC)
REPORT OF INDEPENDENT REGISTERED PUBLIC ACCOUNTING FIRM

The Board of Directors and Stockholders of
Sprint Corporation
Overland Park, Kansas

We have audited the accompanying Successor consolidated balance sheets of Sprint Corporation and subsidiaries (the "Company") as of December 31, 2013 and 2012, and the related Successor consolidated statements of comprehensive loss, the statement of stockholders' equity and the statement of cash flows for the period from October 5, 2012 (date of incorporation) through December 31, 2012 and the year ended December 31, 2013. We also have audited the Company's internal control over financial reporting as of December 31, 2013, based on criteria established in Internal Control—Integrated Framework (1992) issued by the Committee of Sponsoring Organizations of the Treadway Commission. The Company's management is responsible for these consolidated financial statements, for maintaining effective internal control over financial reporting, and for its assessment of the effectiveness of internal control over financial reporting, included in the accompanying Management's Report on Internal Control over Financial Reporting. Our responsibility is to express an opinion on these consolidated financial statements and an opinion on the Company's internal control over financial reporting based on our audits.

We conducted our audits in accordance with the standards of the Public Company Accounting Oversight Board (United States). Those standards require that we plan and perform the audits to obtain reasonable assurance about whether the consolidated financial statements are free of material misstatement and whether effective internal control over financial reporting was maintained in all material respects. Our audits of the consolidated financial statements included examining, on a test basis, evidence supporting the amounts and disclosures in the financial statements, assessing the accounting principles used and significant estimates made by management, and evaluating the overall financial statement presentation. Our audit of internal control over financial reporting included obtaining an understanding of internal control over financial reporting, assessing the risk that a material weakness exists, and testing and evaluating the design and operating effectiveness of internal control based on the assessed risk. Our audits also included performing such other procedures as we considered necessary in the circumstances. We believe that our audits provide a reasonable basis for our opinions.

A company's internal control over financial reporting is a process designed by, or under the supervision of, the company's principal executive and principal financial officers, or persons performing similar functions, and effected by the company's board of directors, management, and other personnel to provide reasonable assurance regarding the reliability of financial reporting and the preparation of financial statements for external purposes in accordance with generally accepted accounting principles. A company's internal control over financial reporting includes those policies and procedures that (1) pertain to the maintenance of records that, in reasonable detail, accurately and fairly reflect the transactions and dispositions of the assets of the company; (2) provide reasonable assurance that transactions are recorded as necessary to permit preparation of financial statements in accordance with generally accepted accounting principles, and that receipts and expenditures of the company are being made only in accordance with authorizations of management and directors of the company; and (3) provide reasonable assurance regarding prevention or timely detection of unauthorized acquisition, use, or disposition of the company's assets that could have a material effect on the financial statements.

Because of the inherent limitations of internal control over financial reporting, including the possibility of collusion or improper management override of controls, material misstatements due to error or fraud may not be prevented or detected on a timely basis. Also, projections of any evaluation of the effectiveness of the internal control over financial reporting to future periods are subject to the risk that the controls may become inadequate because of changes in conditions, or that the degree of compliance with the policies or procedures may deteriorate.

In our opinion, the consolidated financial statements referred to above present fairly, in all material respects, the financial position of Sprint Corporation and subsidiaries as of December 31, 2013 and 2012, and the related Successor results of their operations and their cash flows for the period from October 5, 2012 (date of incorporation) through December 31, 2012 and the year ended December 31, 2013 in conformity with accounting principles generally accepted in the United States of America. Also, in our opinion, the Company maintained, in all material respects, effective internal control over financial reporting as of December 31, 2013, based on criteria established in Internal Control—Integrated Framework (1992) issued by the Committee of Sponsoring Organizations of the Treadway Commission.

As discussed in Notes 1 and 3 to the consolidated financial statements, on July 10, 2013, SoftBank Corp. completed a merger with Sprint Communications, Inc. (formerly Sprint Nextel Corporation) by which Sprint Corporation was the acquiring company of Sprint Communications, Inc. and applied the acquisition method of accounting as of the merger date.

Kansas City, Missouri
February 24, 2014

NOTES TO THE CONSOLIDATED FINANCIAL STATEMENTS

Note 1. Description of Operations (in part)

On July 10, 2013, SoftBank Corp. and certain of its wholly-owned subsidiaries (together, "SoftBank") completed the merger (SoftBank Merger) with Sprint Nextel Corporation (Sprint Nextel) contemplated by the Agreement and Plan of Merger, dated as of October 15, 2012 (as amended, the Merger Agreement) and the Bond Purchase Agreement, dated as of October 15, 2012 (as amended, the Bond Agreement). As a result of the SoftBank Merger, Starburst II, Inc. (Starburst II), a wholly-owned subsidiary of SoftBank became the parent company of Sprint Nextel. Immediately thereafter, Starburst II changed its name to Sprint Corporation and Sprint Nextel changed its name to Sprint Communications, Inc. In addition, in connection with the closing of the SoftBank Merger, Sprint Corporation became the successor registrant to Sprint Nextel under Rule 12g-3 of the Securities Exchange Act of 1934 (Exchange Act) and is the entity subject to the reporting requirements of the Exchange Act for filings with the Securities and Exchange Commission (SEC) subsequent to the close of the SoftBank Merger. In addition, in order to align with SoftBank's reporting schedule, our Board of Directors have approved a change in our fiscal year end to March 31, effective March 31, 2014. As a result, we expect to file an additional Annual Report on Form 10-K for the transition period from January 1, 2014 to March 31, 2014. See *Note 3. Significant Transactions* for additional information regarding the SoftBank Merger and related transactions. Unless the context otherwise requires, references to "Sprint," "we," "us," "our" and the "Company" mean Sprint Corporation and its consolidated subsidiaries for all periods presented, inclusive of Successor and Predecessor periods described below, and references to "Sprint Communications" are to Sprint Communications, Inc. and its consolidated subsidiaries.

In connection with the change of control, as a result of the SoftBank Merger, Sprint Communications' assets and liabilities were adjusted to fair value on the closing date of the SoftBank Merger. The consolidated financial statements distinguish between the predecessor period (Predecessor) relating to Sprint Communications for periods prior to the SoftBank Merger and the successor period (Successor) relating to Sprint Corporation, formerly known as Starburst II, for periods subsequent to the incorporation of Starburst II on October 5, 2012. The Successor financial information includes the activity and accounts of Sprint Corporation as of and for the year ended December 31, 2013, which includes the activity and accounts of Sprint Communications, inclusive of the consolidation of Clearwire Corporation (Clearwire), prospectively for the 174-day period following completion of the SoftBank Merger (Post-merger period), beginning on July 11, 2013. The accounts and operating activity for the Successor periods from October 5, 2012 (date of inception) to December 31, 2012 and from January 1, 2013 to July 10, 2013 consist solely of the activity of Starburst II prior to the close of the SoftBank Merger, which primarily related to merger expenses that were incurred in connection with the SoftBank Merger (recognized in selling, general and administrative expense) and interest related to the $3.1 billion convertible bond (Bond) Sprint Communications, Inc. issued to Starburst II. The Predecessor financial information represents the historical basis of presentation for Sprint Communications for all periods prior to the SoftBank Merger. As a result of the preliminary valuation of assets acquired and liabilities assumed at fair value at the time of the SoftBank Merger, the financial statements for the Successor period are presented on a measurement basis different than the Predecessor period (Sprint Communications historical cost) and are, therefore, not comparable. *See Note 3. Significant Transactions* for additional information regarding the SoftBank Merger.

On July 9, 2013, Sprint Communications completed the acquisition of the remaining equity interests in Clearwire that it did not already own for approximately $3.5 billion, net of cash acquired, or $5.00 per share (Clearwire Acquisition). The consideration paid was allocated to assets acquired and liabilities assumed based on their estimated preliminary fair values at the time of the Clearwire Acquisition. The effects of the Clearwire Acquisition are included in the Predecessor period financial information and are therefore included in the allocation of the consideration transferred at the closing date of the SoftBank Merger.

Note 3. Significant Transactions (in part)

SoftBank Transaction

As discussed above, the SoftBank Merger was completed on July 10, 2013 (SoftBank Merger Date). Sprint Communications, Inc. stockholders received consideration in a combination of both cash and stock, subject to proration. Cash consideration paid in the SoftBank Merger was $14.1 billion, net of cash acquired of $2.5 billion and the estimated fair value of the 22% interest in Sprint Corporation issued to the then existing stockholders of Sprint Communications, Inc. SoftBank provided an equity contribution of $1.9 billion to Sprint at the close of the SoftBank Merger, which was not distributed to the then existing stockholders and is intended to be used for general corporate purposes.

In addition, pursuant to the Bond Agreement, on October 15, 2012, Sprint Communications, Inc. issued a Bond to Starburst II with a principal amount of $3.1 billion, interest rate of 1%, and maturity date of October 15, 2019, which was converted into 590,476,190 shares of Sprint

Communications, Inc. common stock at $5.25 per share immediately prior to the close of the SoftBank Merger. As a result of the completion of the SoftBank Merger and subsequent open market stock purchases, SoftBank owns approximately 80% of the outstanding voting common stock of Sprint Corporation and other Sprint stockholders own the remaining approximately 20% as of December 31, 2013, which consisted of common shares issued pursuant to the Merger Agreement.

Consideration Transferred

The fair value of consideration transferred, which is measured at the estimated fair value of each element of consideration transferred as of the SoftBank Merger Date, was determined as the sum of (a) cash transferred to Sprint Communications stockholders, (b) the number of shares of Sprint issued to Sprint Communications stockholders and (c) share-based payment awards (replacement awards) exchanged for awards held by Sprint employees. The fair value of the consideration transferred was based on the most reliable measure for each element of consideration, which was determined to be the market price of Sprint common shares as of July 11, 2013 for all non-cash consideration. The estimated fair value of the consideration transferred, based on the market price of Sprint common stock, as determined using the closing price of Sprint common stock on the New York Stock Exchange as of July 11, 2013, and the investments by SoftBank consisted of the following:

Consideration Transferred and Investments by Softbank (In millions):	
Cash consideration paid to Sprint Communications stockholders	$16,640
Issuance of Sprint Corporation common stock to former Sprint Communications stockholders	5,344
Estimated value of Sprint Corporation equity awards issued to holders of Sprint Communications equity awards for service provided in the pre-combination period	193
Total purchase price to be allocated	22,177
Convertible Bond	3,100
Additional capital contribution made by SoftBank	1,900
Total consideration transferred and investments by SoftBank	$27,177

The fair value of the investments by SoftBank was determined based on the cash transferred, including $3.1 billion to purchase the Bond and $1.9 billion at the close of the SoftBank Merger. Merger-related costs (included in selling, general and administrative in the results of operations) for the SoftBank Merger totaled approximately $129 million, of which $32 million were recognized in 2012 and $97 million were recognized in the 2013 Successor period.

Preliminary Purchase Price Allocation

The consideration transferred has been preliminarily allocated to assets acquired and liabilities assumed based on their estimated fair values as of the SoftBank Merger Date, inclusive of the Clearwire Acquisition described above. The preliminary allocation of consideration transferred was based on management's judgment after evaluating several factors, including a preliminary valuation assessment. Additional analysis, including, but not limited to, the value of intangible assets, and any associated tax impacts, could result in a change in the total amount of goodwill. The preliminary allocation represents management's current best estimate of fair value, but these amounts could change as additional information is obtained and evaluated. In addition, because approximately $46 million of certain merger-related fees of Sprint Communications, the acquiree, were contingent upon the closing of the SoftBank Merger, these fees were not recorded as an expense subsequent to the close of the transaction. However, these fees are reflected in the preliminary purchase price allocation. Of the total acquisition-related costs, approximately $73 million of contingent merger-related costs paid by, or incurred by SoftBank on behalf of, the accounting acquirer, formerly Starburst II, were recorded as an expense in the 2013 Successor period. Adjustments made since the initial purchase price allocation decreased recorded goodwill by approximately $385 million. Indefinite-lived intangible assets increased by approximately $254 million due to additional analysis performed by management during the fourth quarter of 2013 related to the value assigned to certain FCC licenses. Deferred tax liabilities decreased approximately $126 million primarily due to adjustments related to FCC licenses. The remaining adjustments were insignificant.

The following table summarizes the preliminary purchase price allocation of consideration transferred:

Preliminary Purchase Price Allocation (In millions):	
Current assets	$ 8,517
Investments	133
Property, plant and equipment	14,558
Identifiable intangibles	50,626
Goodwill	6,434
Other assets	227
Current liabilities	(10,711)
Long-term debt	(29,481)
Deferred tax liabilities	(14,131)
Other liabilities	(3,995)
Net assets acquired, prior to conversion of the Bond	22,177
Conversion of Bond	3,100
Net assets acquired, after conversion of the Bond	$ 25,277

The excess of the consideration transferred over the estimated fair values of assets acquired and liabilities assumed was recorded as goodwill. Goodwill includes expected synergies such as cost synergies related to scaled purchasing and other additional cost savings. Goodwill resulting from the SoftBank Merger is allocated to the Wireless segment, substantially all of which is not expected to be deductible for income tax purposes. Gross contractual receivables acquired and included within current assets above totaled approximately $3.4 billion for which the estimated fair value is $3.2 billion. The difference is the estimated amount of Sprint Communication's allowance for doubtful accounts at the SoftBank Merger Date.

Identifiable intangible assets acquired in the SoftBank Merger include the following:

(In millions)	Estimated Fair Value	Weighted Average Useful Life
Indefinite-Lived Intangible Assets:		
FCC licenses	$35,723	n/a
Trademarks	5,935	n/a
Intangible Assets Subject to Amortization:		
Customer relationships	6,923	8
Other definite-lived intangible assets		
Favorable spectrum leases	884	23
Favorable tower leases	589	6
Trademarks	520	34
Other	52	10
	$50,626	

Indefinite-lived intangible assets consist of 1.9 GHz, 800 megahertz (MHz), 900 MHz, and 2.5 GHz FCC licenses as well as the Sprint and Boost Mobile trademarks. Intangible assets subject to amortization consist of customer relationships, favorable spectrum and tower leases resulting from the favorable difference between the terms of the tower and spectrum leases acquired and the current market terms for those leases at the SoftBank Merger date, and the Virgin Mobile trade name *(see Note 7. Intangible Assets).*

Pro Forma Financial Information

The following unaudited pro forma consolidated results of operations assume that the SoftBank Merger and Clearwire Acquisition were completed as of January 1, 2012 for 2013 and 2012, respectively.

	Years Ended December 31,	
(In millions)	2013	2012
Net operating revenues	$35,953	$35,918
Net loss	$ (4,290)	$ (5,141)
Basic loss per common share	$ (1.12)	$ (1.35)

The unaudited pro forma financial information was prepared to illustrate the pro forma effect of the combination of Sprint, Sprint Communications and Clearwire using the consideration transferred as of each acquisition date as though the acquisition date for each transaction occurred on January 1, 2012. The preparation of the pro forma financial information also assumed a preliminary purchase price allocation of the consideration transferred among the assets acquired and liabilities assumed for each acquiree. The pro forma financial information adjusts the actual combined results for items that are recurring in nature and directly attributable to the Clearwire Acquisition and SoftBank Merger. The pro forma net loss provided excludes certain non-recurring items such as Sprint's gain on its previously held interest in Clearwire and transaction costs associated with the Clearwire Acquisition and SoftBank Merger. As a result, the pro forma financial information presented above excludes a net gain of $1.4 billion *(See Note 4. Investments)* and acquisition related costs of approximately $169 million.

This pro forma financial information has been prepared based on estimates and assumptions, which management believes are reasonable, and is not necessarily indicative of the consolidated financial position or results of operations that Sprint would have achieved had the Clearwire Acquisition and/or the SoftBank Merger actually occurred at January 1, 2012 or at any other historical date, nor is it reflective of our expected actual financial positions or results of operations for any future period.

Departures From Unmodified (Unqualified) Opinions

PRESENTATION

> **Author's Note**
> The clarified auditing standards use the term *unmodified opinions*, and the extant standards as adopted by the PCAOB use the term *unqualified opinions*.

NONISSUERS

7.50 Paragraph .07 of AU-C section 705 states that the auditor should modify the opinion in the auditor's report when the auditor concludes the financial statements as a whole are materially misstated or when the auditor is unable to obtain sufficient appropriate audit evidence to conclude that the financial statements as a whole are free from material misstatement.

ISSUERS

7.51 AU section 508 does not require auditors to express qualified opinions about the effects of uncertainties or lack of consistency. Under AU section 508, departures from unqualified opinions include opinions qualified because of a scope limitation or departure from GAAP, including inadequate disclosures; adverse opinions; and disclaimers of opinion. Paragraphs .20–.63 of AU section 508 discuss these departures. None of the auditors' reports issued in connection with the financial statements of the survey entities contained a *departure*, as defined by AU section 508.

Reports on Comparative Financial Statements

PRESENTATION

NONISSUERS

7.52 AU-C section 700 discusses reports on comparative statements. Paragraph .53 of AU-C section 700 states that when reporting on prior period financial statements in connection with the current period's audit, if the auditor's opinion on such prior period financial statements differs from the opinion the auditor, the auditor should disclose the following in an emphasis-of-matter or other-matter paragraph, in accordance with AU-C section 706:
- The date of the auditor's previous report
- The type of opinion previously expressed
- The substantive reasons for the different opinion
- That the auditor's opinion on the amended financial statements is different from the auditor's previous opinion

ISSUERS

7.53 Paragraphs .65–.74 of AU section 508 discuss reports on comparative financial statements.

7.54 LAS VEGAS SANDS CORP. (DEC)

REPORT OF INDEPENDENT REGISTERED PUBLIC ACCOUNTING FIRM

To the Board of Directors and Stockholders of
Las Vegas Sands Corp.

We have audited the accompanying consolidated balance sheet of Las Vegas Sands Corp. and subsidiaries (the "Company") as of December 31, 2013, and the related consolidated statement of operations, comprehensive income, equity, and cash flows for the year then ended. Our audit also included the 2013 financial information in the financial statement schedule listed in the Index at Item 15(a)(2). These financial statements and the financial statement schedule are the responsibility of the Company's management. Our responsibility is to express an opinion on these financial statements and financial statement schedule based on our audit. The consolidated financial statements of the Company for the years ended December 31, 2012 and 2011, before the effects of the retrospective adjustments to the Condensed Consolidating Financial Information for a change in the composition of the Restricted Subsidiaries discussed in Note 18 to the consolidated financial statements, were audited by other auditors whose report, dated March 1, 2013, expressed an unqualified opinion on those statements. We conducted our audit in accordance with the standards of the Public Company Accounting Oversight Board (United States). Those standards require that we plan and perform the audit to obtain reasonable assurance about whether the financial statements are free of material misstatement. An audit includes examining, on a test basis, evidence supporting the amounts and disclosures in the financial statements. An audit also includes assessing the accounting principles used and significant estimates made by management, as well as evaluating the overall financial statement presentation. We believe that our audit provides a reasonable basis for our opinion.

In our opinion, such 2013 consolidated financial statements present fairly, in all material respects, the financial position of Las Vegas Sands Corp. and subsidiaries as of December 31, 2013, and the results of their operations and their cash flows for the year then ended, in conformity with accounting principles generally accepted in the United States of America. Also, in our opinion, the 2013 information in the financial statement schedule, when considered in relation to the basic 2013 consolidated financial statements taken as a whole, presents fairly, in all material respects, the information set forth therein.

We have also audited the adjustments to Note 18 of the 2012 and 2011 consolidated financial statements to retrospectively adjust the Condensed Consolidating Financial Information for a change in the composition of Restricted Subsidiaries in 2013, as discussed in Note 18 to the consolidated financial statements. Our procedures included (1) comparing the previously reported consolidating financial information to previously issued consolidating financial information in Note 18, (2) comparing the adjustments to the consolidating financial information to the Company's underlying analysis, and (3) testing the mathematical accuracy of the underlying analysis and the recast consolidating financial information. In our opinion, such retrospective adjustments are appropriate and have been properly applied. However, we were not engaged to audit, review, or apply any procedures to the 2012 and 2011 consolidated financial statements of the Company other than with respect to such adjustments and, accordingly, we do not express an opinion or any form of assurance on the 2012 and 2011 consolidated financial statements taken as a whole. We have also audited, in accordance with the standards of the Public Company Accounting Oversight Board (United States), the Company's internal control over financial reporting as of December 31, 2013, based on the criteria established in Internal Control—Integrated Framework (1992) issued by the Committee of Sponsoring Organizations of the Treadway Commission and our report dated February 28, 2014 expressed an unqualified opinion on the Company's internal control over financial reporting.

/s/ Deloitte & Touche LLP
Las Vegas, Nevada
February 28, 2014

REPORT OF INDEPENDENT REGISTERED PUBLIC ACCOUNTING FIRM

To the Directors and Shareholders of
Las Vegas Sands Corp.

In our opinion, the consolidated balance sheet as of December 31, 2012 and the related consolidated statements of operations, comprehensive income, of equity and cash flows for each of the two years in the period ended December 31, 2012, before the effects of the adjustments to retrospectively reflect the change in the group of subsidiaries that are the Restricted Subsidiaries described in Note 18, present fairly, in all material respects, the financial position of Las Vegas Sands Corp. and its subsidiaries (the "Company") at December 31, 2012, and the results of their operations and their cash flows for each of the two years in the period ended December 31, 2012, in conformity with accounting principles generally accepted in the United States of America (the 2012 financial statements before the effects of the adjustments discussed in Note 18 are not presented herein). In addition, in our opinion, the financial statement schedule for each of the two years in the period ended December 31, 2012 presents fairly, in all material respects, the information set forth therein when read in conjunction with the related consolidated financial statements before the effects of the adjustments described above. These financial statements and financial statement schedule are the responsibility of the Company's management. Our responsibility is to express an opinion on these financial statements and financial statement schedule based on our audits. We conducted our audits, before the effects of the adjustments described above, of these statements in accordance with the standards of the Public Company Accounting Oversight Board (United States). Those standards require that we plan and perform the audit to obtain reasonable assurance about whether the financial statements are free of material misstatement. An audit includes examining, on a test basis, evidence supporting the amounts and disclosures in the financial statements, assessing the accounting principles used and significant estimates made by management, and evaluating the overall financial statement presentation. We believe that our audits provide a reasonable basis for our opinion.

We were not engaged to audit, review, or apply any procedures to the adjustments to retrospectively reflect the change in the group of subsidiaries that are the Restricted Subsidiaries described in Note 18 and accordingly, we do not express an opinion or any other form of assurance about whether such adjustments are appropriate and have been properly applied. Those adjustments were audited by other auditors.

/s/ PricewaterhouseCoopers LLP
Florham Park, New Jersey
March 1, 2013

NOTES TO CONSOLIDATED FINANCIAL STATEMENTS

Note 18—Condensed Consolidating Financial Information

LVSLLC, as the issuer and primary obligor of the 2013 U.S. Credit Facility, VCR, Venetian Marketing, Inc., Sands Expo & Convention Center, Inc. (formerly Interface Group-Nevada, Inc.) and Sands Pennsylvania, Inc. (collectively, the "Restricted Subsidiaries"), are all guarantors under the 2013 U.S. Credit Facility. The noncontrolling interest amounts included in the Restricted Subsidiaries' condensed consolidating financial information are related to non-voting preferred stock of one of the subsidiaries held by third parties.

In February 2008, all of the capital stock of Phase II Mall Subsidiary, LLC (a subsidiary of VCR), was sold to GGP; however, the sale is not complete from an accounting perspective due to the Company's continuing involvement in the transaction related to the participation in certain potential future revenues earned by GGP. Certain of the assets, liabilities and operating results related to the ownership and operation of the mall by Phase II Mall Subsidiary, LLC subsequent to the sale will continue to be accounted for by the Restricted Subsidiaries, and therefore are included in the "Restricted Subsidiaries" columns in the following condensed consolidating financial information. As a result, net liabilities of $29.3 million (consisting of $239.3 million of property and equipment, offset by $268.6 million of liabilities consisting primarily of deferred proceeds from the sale) and $17.3 million (consisting of $250.8 million of property and equipment, offset by $268.1 million of liabilities consisting primarily of deferred proceeds from the sale) as of December 31, 2013 and 2012, respectively, and a net loss (consisting primarily of depreciation expense) of $12.9 million, $15.1 million and $19.5 million for the years ended December 31, 2013, 2012 and 2011, respectively, related to the mall and are being accounted for by the Restricted Subsidiaries. These balances and amounts are not collateral for the 2013 U.S. Credit Facility.

In connection with the refinancing of the Senior Secured Credit Facility, there has been a change in the group of subsidiaries that are the Restricted Subsidiaries, to exclude Palazzo Condo Tower, LLC, LVS (Nevada) International Holdings, Inc. and LVS Management Services, LLC. Accordingly, the Company has reclassified the prior periods to conform with the current presentation of the Restricted Subsidiaries.

The following condensed consolidating financial information of LVSC, a non-guarantor parent; the Restricted Subsidiaries, including LVSLLC as the issuer; and the non-restricted subsidiaries on a combined basis as of December 31, 2013 and 2012, and for each of the three years in the period ended December 31, 2013, is being presented in order to meet the reporting requirements under the 2013 U.S. Credit Facility, and is not intended to comply with SEC Regulation S-X 3—10 (in thousands):

Condensed Consolidating Balance Sheets

December 31, 2013

	LVSC (Non-Guarantor Parent)	Restricted Subsidiaries	Non-Restricted Subsidiaries	Consolidating/ Eliminating Entries	Total
Cash and cash equivalents	$ 50,180	$ 315,489	$ 3,234,745	$ —	$ 3,600,414
Restricted cash and cash equivalents	—	—	6,839	—	6,839
Intercompany receivables	271,993	236,259	—	(508,252)	—
Intercompany notes receivables	—	—	251,537	(251,537)	—
Accounts receivable, net	11,815	295,333	1,454,962	—	1,762,110
Inventories	3,895	12,609	25,442	—	41,946
Deferred income taxes, net	7,509	37,233	—	(44,742)	—
Prepaid expenses and other	21,311	11,592	71,327	—	104,230
Total current assets	366,703	908,515	5,044,852	(804,531)	5,515,539
Property and equipment, net	155,806	3,056,678	12,146,469	—	15,358,953
Investments in subsidiaries	7,568,252	6,112,507	—	(13,680,759)	—
Deferred financing costs, net	181	30,737	155,046	—	185,964
Intercompany receivables	483	38,931	—	(39,414)	—
Intercompany notes receivable	—	1,081,710	—	(1,081,710)	—
Deferred income taxes, net	—	—	—	13,821	13,821
Leasehold interests in land, net	—	—	1,428,819	—	1,428,819
Intangible assets, net	690	—	101,391	—	102,081
Other assets, net	264	22,288	96,535	—	119,087
Total assets	$8,092,379	$11,251,366	$18,973,112	$(15,592,593)	$22,724,264
Accounts payable	$ 8,381	$ 25,679	$ 85,134	$ —	$ 119,194
Construction payables	2,161	3,226	236,173	—	241,560
Intercompany payables	—	278,309	229,943	(508,252)	—
Intercompany notes payable	251,537	—	—	(251,537)	—
Accrued interest payable	77	224	6,250	—	6,551
Other accrued liabilities	54,071	224,759	1,916,036	—	2,194,866
Income taxes payable	—	17	176,661	—	176,678
Deferred income taxes	—	—	58,051	(44,742)	13,309
Current maturities of long-term debt	3,688	24,892	348,927	—	377,507
Total current liabilities	319,915	557,106	3,057,175	(804,531)	3,129,665
Other long-term liabilities	3,775	10,175	98,245	—	112,195
Intercompany payables	—	—	39,414	(39,414)	—
Intercompany notes payable	—	—	1,081,710	(1,081,710)	—
Deferred income taxes	39,523	54,668	65,199	13,821	173,211
Deferred amounts related to mall transactions	—	425,912	—	—	425,912
Long-term debt	63,672	2,823,269	6,495,811	—	9,382,752
Total liabilities	426,885	3,871,130	10,837,554	(1,911,834)	13,223,735
Total Las Vegas Sands Corp. stockholders' equity	7,665,494	7,379,831	6,300,928	(13,680,759)	7,665,494
Noncontrolling interests	—	405	1,834,630	—	1,835,035
Total equity	7,665,494	7,380,236	8,135,558	(13,680,759)	9,500,529
Total liabilities and equity	$8,092,379	$11,251,366	$18,973,112	$(15,592,593)	$22,724,264

Condensed Consolidating Balance Sheets

December 31, 2012

	LVSC (Non-Guarantor Parent)	Restricted Subsidiaries	Non-Restricted Subsidiaries	Consolidating/ Eliminating Entries	Total
Cash and cash equivalents	$ 7,962	$ 182,402	$ 2,322,402	$ —	$ 2,512,766
Restricted cash and cash equivalents	—	1	4,520	—	4,521
Intercompany receivables	209,961	256,409	—	(466,370)	—
Intercompany notes receivable	—	1,100,000	237,161	(1,337,161)	—
Accounts receivable, net	6,646	259,691	1,552,923	—	1,819,260
Inventories	3,501	13,081	27,293	—	43,875
Deferred income taxes, net	5,687	36,900	—	(40,288)	2,299
Prepaid expenses and other	13,257	12,223	69,313	—	94,793
Total current assets	247,014	1,860,707	4,213,612	(1,843,819)	4,477,514

(continued)

	LVSC (Non-Guarantor Parent)	Restricted Subsidiaries	Non-Restricted Subsidiaries	Consolidating/ Eliminating Entries	Total
Property and equipment, net	173,065	3,157,605	12,436,078	—	15,766,748
Investments in subsidiaries	7,045,198	4,675,328	—	(11,720,526)	—
Deferred financing costs, net	238	12,528	201,699	—	214,465
Restricted cash and cash equivalents	—	—	1,938	—	1,938
Intercompany receivables	6,109	56,302	—	(62,411)	—
Intercompany notes receivable	—	928,728	—	(928,728)	—
Deferred income taxes, net	3,665	—	—	39,615	43,280
Leasehold interests in land, net	—	—	1,458,741	—	1,458,741
Intangible assets, net	690	—	69,928	—	70,618
Other assets, net	243	18,403	111,702	—	130,348
Total assets	$7,476,222	$10,709,601	$18,493,698	$(14,515,869)	$22,163,652
Accounts payable	$ 9,948	$ 25,007	$ 71,543	$ —	$ 106,498
Construction payables	5,318	7,646	330,408	—	343,372
Intercompany payables	—	173,893	292,477	(466,370)	—
Intercompany notes payable	237,161	—	1,100,000	(1,337,161)	—
Accrued interest payable	82	1,050	14,410	—	15,542
Other accrued liabilities	42,318	235,889	1,617,276	—	1,895,483
Income taxes payable	—	4	164,122	—	164,126
Deferred income taxes	—	—	40,288	(40,288)	—
Current maturities of long-term debt	3,688	90,649	3,465	—	97,802
Total current liabilities	298,515	534,138	3,633,989	(1,843,819)	2,622,823
Other long-term liabilities	48,506	9,776	75,654	—	133,936
Intercompany payables	—	—	62,411	(62,411)	—
Intercompany notes payable	—	—	928,728	(928,728)	—
Deferred income taxes	—	39,643	106,687	39,615	185,945
Deferred amounts related to mall transactions	—	430,271	—	—	430,271
Long-term debt	67,359	2,753,745	7,311,161	—	10,132,265
Total liabilities	414,380	3,767,573	12,118,630	(2,795,343)	13,505,240
Total Las Vegas Sands Corp. stockholders' equity	7,061,842	6,941,623	4,778,903	(11,720,526)	7,061,842
Noncontrolling interests	—	405	1,596,165	—	1,596,570
Total equity	7,061,842	6,942,028	6,375,068	(11,720,526)	8,658,412
Total liabilities and equity	$7,476,222	$10,709,601	$18,493,698	$(14,515,869)	$22,163,652

Condensed Consolidating Statements of Operations

For the Year Ended December 31, 2013

	LVSC (Non-Guarantor Parent)	Restricted Subsidiaries	Non-Restricted Subsidiaries	Consolidating/ Eliminating Entries	Total
Revenues:					
Casino	$ —	$ 584,372	$10,802,545	$ —	$11,386,917
Rooms	—	472,518	908,163	—	1,380,681
Food and beverage	—	197,371	532,888	—	730,259
Mall	—	—	481,400	—	481,400
Convention, retail and other	—	310,276	377,791	(172,888)	515,179
	—	1,564,537	13,102,787	(172,888)	14,494,436
Less—promotional allowances	(1,455)	(91,217)	(629,994)	(1,885)	(724,551)
Net revenues	(1,455)	1,473,320	12,472,793	(174,773)	13,769,885
Operating expenses:					
Casino	—	314,966	6,171,744	(2,992)	6,483,718
Rooms	—	157,497	114,449	(4)	271,942
Food and beverage	—	90,507	283,366	(4,303)	369,570
Mall	—	—	73,358	—	73,358
Convention, retail and other	—	106,242	238,296	(26,669)	317,869
Provision for doubtful accounts	—	29,977	207,809	—	237,786
General and administrative	—	341,659	988,927	(846)	1,329,740
Corporate	164,926	1,264	163,287	(139,942)	189,535
Pre-opening	—	911	12,428	—	13,339
Development	15,207	—	619	(17)	15,809
Depreciation and amortization	26,165	186,871	794,432	—	1,007,468
Amortization of leasehold interests in land	—	—	40,352	—	40,352
(Gain) loss on disposal of assets	(12,641)	1,823	21,974	—	11,156
	193,657	1,231,717	9,111,041	(174,773)	10,361,642

(continued)

	LVSC (Non-Guarantor Parent)	Restricted Subsidiaries	Non-Restricted Subsidiaries	Consolidating/ Eliminating Entries	Total
Operating income (loss)	(195,112)	241,603	3,361,752	—	3,408,243
Other income (expense):					
Interest income	1,155	173,203	18,189	(176,210)	16,337
Interest expense, net of amounts capitalized	(4,269)	(88,972)	(354,180)	176,210	(271,211)
Other income (expense)	(5,282)	(2,322)	11,925	—	4,321
Loss on modification or early retirement of debt	—	(14,178)	—	—	(14,178)
Income from equity investments in subsidiaries	2,416,604	2,119,936	—	(4,536,540)	—
Income before income taxes	2,213,096	2,429,270	3,037,686	(4,536,540)	3,143,512
Income tax benefit (expense)	92,901	(133,519)	(148,218)	—	(188,836)
Net income	2,305,997	2,295,751	2,889,468	(4,536,540)	2,954,676
Net income attributable to noncontrolling interests	—	(2,894)	(645,785)	—	(648,679)
Net income attributable to Las Vegas Sands Corp.	$2,305,997	$2,292,857	$ 2,243,683	$(4,536,540)	$ 2,305,997

Condensed Consolidating Statements of Operations

For the Year Ended December 31, 2012

	LVSC (Non-Guarantor Parent)	Restricted Subsidiaries	Non-Restricted Subsidiaries	Consolidating/ Eliminating Entries	Total
Revenues:					
Casino	$ —	$ 512,647	$ 8,495,511	$ —	$ 9,008,158
Rooms	—	446,241	707,783	—	1,154,024
Food and beverage	—	173,111	455,417	—	628,528
Mall	—	—	396,927	—	396,927
Convention, retail and other	—	294,047	359,342	(156,357)	497,032
	—	1,426,046	10,414,980	(156,357)	11,684,669
Less—promotional allowances	(1,109)	(84,613)	(466,177)	(1,638)	(553,537)
Net revenues	(1,109)	1,341,433	9,948,803	(157,995)	11,131,132
Operating expenses:					
Casino	—	288,999	4,841,526	(2,489)	5,128,036
Rooms	—	138,356	98,951	(4)	237,303
Food and beverage	—	85,206	250,258	(4,254)	331,210
Mall	—	—	68,763	—	68,763
Convention, retail and other	—	84,957	239,904	(20,598)	304,263
Provision for doubtful accounts	—	28,987	210,345	—	239,332
General and administrative	—	268,834	793,916	(815)	1,061,935
Corporate	188,187	413	148,243	(129,813)	207,030
Pre-opening	—	1,909	141,893	(7)	143,795
Development	19,973	—	—	(15)	19,958
Depreciation and amortization	19,921	222,096	650,029	—	892,046
Amortization of leasehold interests in land	—	—	40,165	—	40,165
Impairment loss	—	—	143,674	—	143,674
(Gain) loss on disposal of assets	(1)	389	1,852	—	2,240
	228,080	1,120,146	7,629,519	(157,995)	8,819,750
Operating income (loss)	(229,189)	221,287	2,319,284	—	2,311,382
Other income (expense):					
Interest income	281	135,153	21,700	(133,882)	23,252
Interest expense, net of amounts capitalized	(4,841)	(91,870)	(295,735)	133,882	(258,564)
Other income (expense)	(47)	792	4,995	—	5,740
Loss on modification or early retirement of debt	(2,831)	(1,599)	(14,804)	—	(19,234)
Income from equity investments in subsidiaries	1,705,354	1,430,459	—	(3,135,813)	—
Income before income taxes	1,468,727	1,694,222	2,035,440	(3,135,813)	2,062,576
Income tax benefit (expense)	55,366	(78,240)	(157,889)	—	(180,763)
Net income	1,524,093	1,615,982	1,877,551	(3,135,813)	1,881,813
Net income attributable to noncontrolling interests	—	(2,733)	(354,987)	—	(357,720)
Net income attributable to Las Vegas Sands Corp.	$1,524,093	$1,613,249	$ 1,522,564	$(3,135,813)	$ 1,524,093

Condensed Consolidating Statements of Operations

For the Year Ended December 31, 2011

	LVSC (Non-Guarantor Parent)	Restricted Subsidiaries	Non-Restricted Subsidiaries	Consolidating/ Eliminating Entries	Total
Revenues:					
Casino	$ —	$ 430,758	$7,006,244	$ —	$7,437,002
Rooms	—	450,487	549,548	—	1,000,035
Food and beverage	—	186,894	411,929	—	598,823
Mall	—	—	325,123	—	325,123
Convention, retail and other	—	280,349	362,050	(141,048)	501,351
	—	1,348,488	8,654,894	(141,048)	9,862,334
Less—promotional allowances	(720)	(75,238)	(374,060)	(1,571)	(451,589)
Net revenues	(720)	1,273,250	8,280,834	(142,619)	9,410,745
Operating expenses:					
Casino	—	266,203	3,744,193	(2,509)	4,007,887
Rooms	—	136,416	73,636	—	210,052
Food and beverage	—	88,485	223,807	(4,846)	307,446
Mall	—	—	59,183	—	59,183
Convention, retail and other	—	87,779	274,582	(24,252)	338,109
Provision for doubtful accounts	—	14,532	135,924	—	150,456
General and administrative	—	254,139	583,472	(687)	836,924
Corporate	165,120	265	130,623	(110,314)	185,694
Pre-opening	—	—	65,833	(8)	65,825
Development	11,312	—	—	(3)	11,309
Depreciation and amortization	18,493	227,400	548,511	—	794,404
Amortization of leasehold interests in land	—	—	43,366	—	43,366
(Gain) loss on disposal of assets	7,662	2,590	(49)	—	10,203
	202,587	1,077,809	5,883,081	(142,619)	7,020,858
Operating income (loss)	(203,307)	195,441	2,397,753	—	2,389,887
Other income (expense):					
Interest income	3,702	112,218	9,867	(111,393)	14,394
Interest expense, net of amounts capitalized	(13,856)	(95,993)	(284,493)	111,393	(282,949)
Other income (expense)	171	(1,946)	(2,180)	—	(3,955)
Loss on modification or early retirement of debt	—	(503)	(22,051)	—	(22,554)
Income from equity investments in subsidiaries	1,716,119	1,442,967	—	(3,159,086)	—
Income before income taxes	1,502,829	1,652,184	2,098,896	(3,159,086)	2,094,823
Income tax benefit (expense)	57,294	(57,336)	(211,662)	—	(211,704)
Net income	1,560,123	1,594,848	1,887,234	(3,159,086)	1,883,119
Net income attributable to noncontrolling interests	—	(2,495)	(320,501)	—	(322,996)
Net income attributable to Las Vegas Sands Corp.	$1,560,123	$1,592,353	$1,566,733	$(3,159,086)	$1,560,123

Condensed Consolidating Statements of Comprehensive Income

For the Year Ended December 31, 2013

	LVSC (Non-Guarantor Parent)	Restricted Subsidiaries	Non-Restricted Subsidiaries	Consolidating/ Eliminating Entries	Total
Net income	$2,305,997	$2,295,751	$2,889,468	$(4,536,540)	$2,954,676
Currency translation adjustment, before and after tax	(89,295)	(75,797)	(89,976)	165,092	(89,976)
Total comprehensive income	2,216,702	2,219,954	2,799,492	(4,371,448)	2,864,700
Comprehensive income attributable to noncontrolling interests	—	(2,894)	(645,104)	—	(647,998)
Comprehensive income attributable to Las Vegas Sands Corp.	$2,216,702	$2,217,060	$2,154,388	$(4,371,448)	$2,216,702

Condensed Consolidating Statements of Comprehensive Income

For the Year Ended December 31, 2012

	LVSC (Non-Guarantor Parent)	Restricted Subsidiaries	Non-Restricted Subsidiaries	Consolidating/ Eliminating Entries	Total
Net income	$1,524,093	$1,615,982	$1,877,551	$(3,135,813)	$1,881,813
Currency translation adjustment, net of reclassification adjustment and before and after tax	168,974	143,570	172,788	(312,544)	172,788
Total comprehensive income	1,693,067	1,759,552	2,050,339	(3,448,357)	2,054,601
Comprehensive income attributable to noncontrolling interests	—	(2,733)	(358,801)	—	(361,534)
Comprehensive income attributable to Las Vegas Sands Corp.	$1,693,067	$1,756,819	$1,691,538	$(3,448,357)	$1,693,067

Condensed Consolidating Statements of Comprehensive Income

For the Year Ended December 31, 2011

	LVSC (Non-Guarantor Parent)	Restricted Subsidiaries	Non-Restricted Subsidiaries	Consolidating/ Eliminating Entries	Total
Net income	$1,560,123	$1,594,848	$1,887,234	$(3,159,086)	$1,883,119
Currency translation adjustment, before and after tax	(35,415)	(28,876)	(32,793)	64,291	(32,793)
Total comprehensive income	1,524,708	1,565,972	1,854,441	(3,094,795)	1,850,326
Comprehensive income attributable to noncontrolling interests	—	(2,495)	(323,123)	—	(325,618)
Comprehensive income attributable to Las Vegas Sands Corp.	$1,524,708	$1,563,477	$1,531,318	$(3,094,795)	$1,524,708

Condensed Consolidating Statements of Cash Flows

For the Year Ended December 31, 2013

	LVSC (Non-Guarantor Parent)	Restricted Subsidiaries	Non-Restricted Subsidiaries	Consolidating/ Eliminating Entries	Total
Net cash generated from operating activities	$ 1,693,766	$ 1,892,021	$ 4,255,589	$(3,401,964)	$ 4,439,412
Cash flows from investing activities:					
Change in restricted cash and cash equivalents	—	1	(383)	—	(382)
Capital expenditures	(29,901)	(91,900)	(776,310)	—	(898,111)
Proceeds from disposal of property and equipment	31,000	121	1,034	—	32,155
Acquisition of intangible assets	—	—	(45,871)	—	(45,871)
Repayments of receivable from non-restricted subsidiaries	—	1,357	—	(1,357)	—
Notes receivable to Las Vegas Sands Corp.	—	—	(251,537)	251,537	—
Repayments of receivable from Las Vegas Sands Corp.	—	—	237,161	(237,161)	—
Dividends received from non-restricted subsidiaries	—	1,383,116	—	(1,383,116)	—
Capital contributions to subsidiaries	(68)	(1,292,416)	—	1,292,484	—
Net cash generated from (used in) investing activities	1,031	279	(835,906)	(77,613)	(912,209)
Cash flows from financing activities:					
Proceeds from exercise of stock options	50,223	—	19,373	—	69,596
Repurchase of common stock	(561,150)	—	—	—	(561,150)
Proceeds from exercise of warrants	350	—	—	—	350
Dividends paid	(1,152,690)	—	(411,359)	—	(1,564,049)
Distributions to noncontrolling interests	—	(2,894)	(8,964)	—	(11,858)
Dividends paid to Las Vegas Sands Corp.	—	(1,732,152)	(108,570)	1,840,722	—
Dividends paid to Restricted Subsidiaries	—	—	(2,944,358)	2,944,358	—
Capital contributions received	—	—	1,292,484	(1,292,484)	—
Borrowings from non-restricted subsidiaries	251,537	—	—	(251,537)	—
Repayments on borrowings from Restricted Subsidiaries	—	—	(1,357)	1,357	—
Repayments on borrowings from non-restricted subsidiaries	(237,161)	—	—	237,161	—

(continued)

	LVSC (Non-Guarantor Parent)	Restricted Subsidiaries	Non-Restricted Subsidiaries	Consolidating/ Eliminating Entries	Total
Proceeds from 2013 U.S. credit facility	—	2,828,750	—	—	2,828,750
Proceeds from senior secured credit facility	—	250,000	—	—	250,000
Proceeds from 2012 Singapore credit facility	—	—	104,357	—	104,357
Repayments on senior secured credit facility	—	(3,073,038)	—	—	(3,073,038)
Repayments on 2012 Singapore credit facility	—	—	(430,504)	—	(430,504)
Repayments on airplane financings	(3,688)	—	—	—	(3,688)
Repayments on HVAC equipment lease and other long-term debt	—	(2,350)	(3,452)	—	(5,802)
Payments of deferred financing costs	—	(27,529)	(7,885)	—	(35,414)
Net cash used in financing activities	(1,652,579)	(1,759,213)	(2,500,235)	3,479,577	(2,432,450)
Effect of exchange rate on cash	—	—	(7,105)	—	(7,105)
Increase in cash and cash equivalents	42,218	133,087	912,343	—	1,087,648
Cash and cash equivalents at beginning of year	7,962	182,402	2,322,402	—	2,512,766
Cash and cash equivalents at end of year	$ 50,180	$ 315,489	$ 3,234,745	$ —	$ 3,600,414

Condensed Consolidating Statements of Cash Flows

For the Year Ended December 31, 2012

	LVSC (Non-Guarantor Parent)	Restricted Subsidiaries	Non-Restricted Subsidiaries	Consolidating/ Eliminating Entries	Total
Net cash generated from operating activities	$ 2,544,296	$ 2,177,182	$ 2,894,423	$(4,558,144)	$ 3,057,757
Cash flows from investing activities:					
Change in restricted cash and cash equivalents	—	(1)	694	—	693
Capital expenditures	(50,903)	(155,936)	(1,242,395)	—	(1,449,234)
Proceeds from disposal of property and equipment	—	454	2,455	—	2,909
Intercompany receivable to non-restricted subsidiaries	(20,297)	—	—	20,297	—
Repayments of receivable from non-restricted subsidiaries	—	683	—	(683)	—
Notes receivable to Las Vegas Sands Corp.	—	—	(237,161)	237,161	—
Notes receivable to non-restricted subsidiaries	—	(9,773)	—	9,773	—
Dividends received from non-restricted subsidiaries	—	2,564,500	—	(2,564,500)	—
Capital contributions to subsidiaries	(64)	(2,485,000)	—	2,485,064	—
Net cash used in investing activities	(71,264)	(85,073)	(1,476,407)	187,112	(1,445,632)
Cash flows from financing activities:					
Proceeds from exercise of stock options	34,668	—	11,572	—	46,240
Proceeds from exercise of warrants	528,908	—	—	—	528,908
Dividends paid	(3,085,256)	—	(357,056)	—	(3,442,312)
Distributions to noncontrolling interests	—	(2,733)	(7,733)	—	(10,466)
Deemed distribution to Principal Stockholder	—	—	(18,576)	—	(18,576)
Dividends paid to Las Vegas Sands Corp.	—	(2,568,900)	(181,191)	2,750,091	—
Dividends paid to Restricted Subsidiaries	—	—	(4,372,553)	4,372,553	—
Capital contributions received	—	—	2,485,064	(2,485,064)	—
Borrowings from Las Vegas Sands Corp.	—	—	20,297	(20,297)	—
Borrowings from Restricted Subsidiaries	—	—	9,773	(9,773)	—
Borrowings from non-restricted subsidiaries	237,161	—	—	(237,161)	—
Repayments on borrowings from Restricted Subsidiaries	—	—	(683)	683	—
Proceeds from 2012 Singapore credit facility	—	—	3,951,486	—	3,951,486
Proceeds from senior secured credit facility	—	400,000	—	—	400,000
Repayments on Singapore credit facility	—	—	(3,635,676)	—	(3,635,676)
Repayments on senior secured credit facility	—	(425,555)	—	—	(425,555)
Redemption of senior notes	(189,712)	—	—	—	(189,712)
Repayments on ferry financing	—	—	(140,337)	—	(140,337)
Repayments on airplane financings	(3,688)	—	—	—	(3,688)
Repayments on HVAC equipment lease and other long-term debt	—	(2,161)	(2,569)	—	(4,730)
Payments of deferred financing costs	—	—	(100,888)	—	(100,888)
Net cash used in financing activities	(2,477,919)	(2,599,349)	(2,339,070)	4,371,032	(3,045,306)
Effect of exchange rate on cash	—	—	43,229	—	43,229
Decrease in cash and cash equivalents	(4,887)	(507,240)	(877,825)	—	(1,389,952)
Cash and cash equivalents at beginning of year	12,849	689,642	3,200,227	—	3,902,718
Cash and cash equivalents at end of year	$ 7,962	$ 182,402	$ 2,322,402	$ —	$ 2,512,766

Condensed Consolidating Statements of Cash Flows

For the Year Ended December 31, 2011

	LVSC (Non-Guarantor Parent)	Restricted Subsidiaries	Non-Restricted Subsidiaries	Consolidating/ Eliminating Entries	Total
Net cash generated from (used in) operating activities	$ (42,087)	$ 404,624	$ 2,503,697	$(203,738)	$ 2,662,496
Cash flows from investing activities:					
Change in restricted cash and cash equivalents	—	2,285	802,109	—	804,394
Capital expenditures	(21,355)	(47,560)	(1,439,578)	—	(1,508,493)
Proceeds from disposal of property and equipment	—	—	6,093	—	6,093
Acquisition of intangible assets	(100)	—	—	—	(100)
Repayments of receivable from non-restricted subsidiaries	—	1,200	—	(1,200)	—
Notes receivable to non-restricted subsidiaries	—	(50,766)	—	50,766	—
Dividends received from non-restricted subsidiaries	—	94,472	—	(94,472)	—
Capital contributions to subsidiaries	(50,026)	—	—	50,026	—
Net cash used in investing activities	(71,481)	(369)	(631,376)	5,120	(698,106)
Cash flows from financing activities:					
Proceeds from exercise of stock options	23,238	—	2,267	—	25,505
Proceeds from exercise of warrants	12,512	—	—	—	12,512
Dividends paid	(75,297)	—	—	—	(75,297)
Distributions to noncontrolling interests	—	(2,495)	(7,893)	—	(10,388)
Dividends paid to Las Vegas Sands Corp.	—	(143,738)	—	143,738	—
Dividends paid to Restricted Subsidiaries	—	—	(154,472)	154,472	—
Capital contributions received	—	50,000	26	(50,026)	—
Borrowings from Restricted Subsidiaries	—	—	50,766	(50,766)	—
Repayments on borrowings from Restricted Subsidiaries	—	—	(1,200)	1,200	—
Proceeds from 2011 VML credit facility	—	—	3,201,535	—	3,201,535
Repayments on senior secured credit facility	—	(28,937)	—	—	(28,937)
Repayments on VML credit facility	—	—	(2,060,819)	—	(2,060,819)
Repayments on VOL credit facility	—	—	(749,660)	—	(749,660))
Repayments on Singapore credit facility	—	—	(418,564)	—	(418,564)
Repayments on ferry financing	—	—	(35,002)	—	(35,002)
Repayments on airplane financings	(3,688)	—	—	—	(3,688)
Repayments on HVAC equipment lease and other long-term debt	—	(1,669)	(1,971)	—	(3,640)
Repurchases and redemption of preferred stock	(845,321)	—	—	—	(845,321)
Payments of preferred stock inducement premium	(16,871)	—	—	—	(16,871)
Payments of deferred financing costs	—	—	(84,826)	—	(84,826)
Net cash used in financing activities	(905,427)	(126,839)	(259,813)	198,618	(1,093,461)
Effect of exchange rate on cash	—	—	(5,292)	—	(5,292)
Increase (decrease) in cash and cash equivalents	(1,018,995)	277,416	1,607,216	—	865,637
Cash and cash equivalents at beginning of year	1,031,844	412,226	1,593,011	—	3,037,081
Cash and cash equivalents at end of year	$ 12,849	$ 689,642	$ 3,200,227	$ —	$ 3,902,718

CHANGE IN AUDITORS

7.55 SYNNEX CORPORATION (NOV)
REPORT OF INDEPENDENT REGISTERED PUBLIC ACCOUNTING FIRM

The Board of Directors and Stockholders
SYNNEX Corporation:

We have audited the accompanying consolidated balance sheets of SYNNEX Corporation and subsidiaries (theCompany) as of November 30, 2013 and 2012, and the related consolidated statements of operations, comprehensive income, stockholders' equity, and cash flows for the years ended November 30, 2013 and 2012. In connection with our audits of the consolidated financial statements, we also have audited the financial statement schedule of valuation and qualifying accounts as listed in the accompanying index. We also have audited the Company's internal control over financial reporting as of November 30, 2013, based on criteria established in *Internal Control—Integrated Framework (1992)* issued by the Committee of Sponsoring Organizations of the Treadway Commission (COSO). The Company's management is responsible for these consolidated financial statements and financial statement schedule, for maintaining effective internal control over financial reporting, and for its assessment of the effectiveness of internal control over financial reporting, included in the accompanying Management's Report on Internal Control over Financial Reporting appearing under Item 9A. Our responsibility is to express an opinion on these consolidated financial statements and financial statement schedule, and an opinion on the Company's internal control over financial reporting based on our audits.

We conducted our audits in accordance with the standards of the Public Company Accounting Oversight Board (United States). Those standards require that we plan and perform the audits to obtain reasonable assurance about whether the financial statements are free of material misstatement and whether effective internal control over financial reporting was maintained in all material respects. Our audits of the consolidated financial statements included examining, on a test basis, evidence supporting the amounts and disclosures in the financial statements, assessing the accounting principles used and significant estimates made by management, and evaluating the overall financial statement presentation. Our audit of internal control over financial reporting included obtaining an understanding of internal control over financial reporting, assessing the risk that a material weakness exists, and testing and evaluating the design and operating effectiveness of internal control based on the assessed risk. Our audits also included performing such other procedures as we considered necessary in the circumstances. We believe that our audits provide a reasonable basis for our opinion.

A company's internal control over financial reporting is a process designed to provide reasonable assurance regarding the reliability of financial reporting and the preparation of financial statements for external purposes in accordance with generally accepted accounting principles. A company's internal control over financial reporting includes those policies and procedures that (1) pertain to the maintenance of records that, in reasonable detail, accurately and fairly reflect the transactions and dispositions of the assets of the company; (2) provide reasonable assurance that transactions are recorded as necessary to permit preparation of financial statements in accordance with generally accepted accounting principles, and that receipts and expenditures of the company are being made only in accordance with authorizations of management and directors of the company; and (3) provide reasonable assurance regarding prevention or timely detection of unauthorized acquisition, use, or disposition of the company's assets that could have a material effect on the financial statements.

Because of its inherent limitations, internal control over financial reporting may not prevent or detect misstatements. Also, projections of any evaluation of effectiveness to future periods are subject to the risk that controls may become inadequate because of changes in conditions, or that the degree of compliance with the policies or procedures may deteriorate.

In our opinion, the consolidated financial statements referred to above present fairly, in all material respects, the financial position of SYNNEX Corporation and subsidiaries as of November 30, 2013 and 2012, and the results of their operations and their cash flows for the years ended November 30, 2013 and 2012, in conformity with U.S. generally accepted accounting principles. Also in our opinion, the related financial statement schedule, when considered in relation to the basic consolidated financial statements taken as a whole, presents fairly, in all material respects, the information set forth therein. Also in our opinion, SYNNEX Corporation maintained, in all material respects, effective internal control over financial reporting as of November 30, 2013, based on criteria established in *Internal Control—Integrated Framework (1992)* issued by the Committee of Sponsoring Organizations of the Treadway Commission.

/s/ KPMG LLP
Santa Clara, California
January 27, 2014

REPORT OF INDEPENDENT REGISTERED PUBLIC ACCOUNTING FIRM

To the Board of Directors and Stockholders of
SYNNEX Corporation:

In our opinion, the consolidated statements of operations, comprehensive income, stockholders equity and cash flows for the year ended November 30, 2011 present fairly, in all material respects, the results of operations and cash flows of SYNNEX Corporation and its subsidiaries for the year ended November 30, 2011, in conformity with accounting principles generally accepted in the United States of America. In addition, in our opinion, the financial statement schedule for the year ended November 30, 2011 presents fairly, in all material respects, the information set forth therein when read in conjunction with the related consolidated financial statements. These financial statements and financial statement schedule are the responsibility of the Company's management. Our responsibility is to express an opinion on these financial statements and financial statement schedule based on our audit. We conducted our audit of these statements in accordance with the standards of the Public Company Accounting Oversight Board (United States). Those standards require that we plan and perform the audit to obtain reasonable assurance about whether the financial statements are free of material misstatement. An audit includes examining, on a test basis, evidence supporting the amounts and disclosures in the financial statements, assessing the accounting principles used and significant estimates made by management, and evaluating the overall financial statement presentation. We believe that our audit provides a reasonable basis for our opinion.

/s/ PricewaterhouseCoopers LLP
PricewaterhouseCoopers LLP
San Jose, California
January 27, 2012

Opinion Expressed on Supplementary Financial Information

PRESENTATION

> **Author's Note**
> Because the report on supplementary financial information is applicable only for issuers, the following guidance is not intended for nonissuers.

7.56 Annual reports to security holders may be combined with the required information of SEC Form 10-K and are suitable for filing with the SEC if certain conditions are satisfied. Accordingly, many survey entities prepare an integrated annual report or simply provide to stockholders a copy of Form 10-K in lieu of the annual report. Form 10-K requires inclusion of certain supplementary financial information, including schedules (Article 12 of Regulation S-X), that must be audited. The report on the audit of schedules may be a separate report or combined with the report on the audit of the basic financial statements.

PRESENTATION AND DISCLOSURE EXCERPTS

SUPPLEMENTARY FINANCIAL INFORMATION

7.57 AUTOMATIC DATA PROCESSING, INC. (JUN)
REPORT OF INDEPENDENT REGISTERED PUBLIC ACCOUNTING FIRM

To the Board of Directors and Stockholders of
Automatic Data Processing, Inc.
Roseland, New Jersey

We have audited the accompanying consolidated balance sheets of Automatic Data Processing, Inc. and subsidiaries (the "Company") as of June 30, 2013 and 2012, and the related statements of consolidated earnings, comprehensive income, stockholders' equity, and cash flows for each of the three years in the period ended June 30, 2013. Our audits also included the consolidated financial statement schedule listed in the Index at Item 15(a) 2. These financial statements and financial statement schedule are the responsibility of the Company's management. Our responsibility is to express an opinion on the consolidated financial statements and consolidated financial statement schedule based on our audits.

We conducted our audits in accordance with the standards of the Public Company Accounting Oversight Board (United States). Those standards require that we plan and perform the audit to obtain reasonable assurance about whether the financial statements are free of material misstatement. An audit includes examining, on a test basis, evidence supporting the amounts and disclosures in the financial statements. An audit also includes assessing the accounting principles used and significant estimates made by management, as well as evaluating the overall financial statement presentation. We believe that our audits provide a reasonable basis for our opinion.

In our opinion, such consolidated financial statements present fairly, in all material respects, the financial position of Automatic Data Processing, Inc. and subsidiaries as of June 30, 2013 and 2012, and the results of their operations and their cash flows for each of the three years in the period ended June 30, 2013, in conformity with accounting principles generally accepted in the United States of America. Also, in our opinion, the consolidated financial statement schedule, when considered in relation to the basic consolidated financial statements taken as a whole, present fairly, in all material respects, the information set forth therein.

We have also audited, in accordance with the standards of the Public Company Accounting Oversight Board (United States), the Company's internal control over financial reporting as of June 30, 2013, based on the criteria established in Internal Control-Integrated Framework (1992) issued by the Committee of Sponsoring Organizations of the Treadway Commission and our report dated August 19, 2013 expressed an unqualified opinion on the Company's internal control over financial reporting.

/s/ Deloitte & Touche LLP
Parsippany, New Jersey
August 19, 2013

(a) Financial Statements and Financial Statement Schedules

1. Financial Statements

The following report and consolidated financial statements of the Company are contained in Part II, Item 8 hereof:
- Report of Independent Registered Public Accounting Firm
- Statements of Consolidated Earnings—years ended June 30, 2013, 2012 and 2011
- Consolidated Balance Sheets—June 30, 2013 and 2012
- Statements of Consolidated Stockholders' Equity—years ended June 30, 2013, 2012 and 2011
- Statements of Consolidated Cash Flows—years ended June 30, 2013, 2012 and 2011
- Notes to Consolidated Financial Statements

2. Financial Statement Schedules

	Page in Form 10-K
Schedule II—Valuation and Qualifying Accounts	76

All other Schedules have been omitted because they are inapplicable or are not required or the information is included elsewhere in the financial statements or notes thereto.

SCHEDULE II—VALUATION AND QUALIFYING ACCOUNTS

(In thousands)

	Column B	Column C Additions		Column D	Column E
Column A	Balance at Beginning of Period	(1) Charged to Costs and Expenses	(2) Charged to Other Accounts	Deductions	Balance at End of Period
Year ended June 30, 2013:					
Allowance for doubtful accounts:					
Current	$46,132	$19,713	$ —	$(14,930)(A)	$50,915
Long-term	$ 8,812	$ 2,687	$ —	$ (2,466)(A)	$ 9,033
Deferred tax valuation allowance	$54,755	$ 3,887	$ (850)(B)	$ (8,393)	$49,399
Year ended June 30, 2012:					
Allowance for doubtful accounts:					
Current	$50,164	$24,088	$ —	$(28,120)(A)	$46,132
Long-term	$ 9,438	$ 2,106	$ —	$ (2,732)(A)	$ 8,812
Deferred tax valuation allowance	$62,700	$ 4,003	$(5,454)(B)	$ (6,494)	$54,755
Year ended June 30, 2011:					
Allowance for doubtful accounts:					
Current	$48,543	$22,976	$ —	$(21,355)(A)	$50,164
Long-term	$16,048	$ 2,954	$ —	$ (9,564)(A)	$ 9,438
Deferred tax valuation allowance	$61,883	$ 3,399	$ 2,507(B)	$ (5,089)	$62,700

(A) Doubtful accounts written off, less recoveries on accounts previously written off.
(B) Includes amounts related to foreign exchange fluctuation.

7.58 THE JONES GROUP INC. (DEC)
REPORT OF INDEPENDENT REGISTERED PUBLIC ACCOUNTING FIRM

Board of Directors and Stockholders
The Jones Group Inc.
New York, New York

The audits referred to in our report dated February 18, 2014 relating to the consolidated financial statements of The Jones Group Inc., which is contained in Item 8 of this Form 10-K also included the audit of the financial statement schedule listed in the accompanying index. This financial statement schedule is the responsibility of the Company's management. Our responsibility is to express an opinion on this financial statement schedule based on our audits.

In our opinion such financial statement schedule, when considered in relation to the basic consolidated financial statements taken as a whole, present fairly, in all material respects, the information set forth therein.

BDO USA, LLP
New York, New York
February 18, 2014

SCHEDULE II

The Jones Group Inc.

Valuation and Qualifying Accounts

Years Ended December 31, 2011, 2012 and 2013

(In Millions)

	Column B	Column C Additions		Column D	Column E
	Balance at	Charged Against	Charged		Balance at
	Beginning	Revenues or to	to Other		End of
Column A	of Period	Costs and Expenses	Accounts	Deductions	Period
Accounts receivable allowances					
Allowance for doubtful accounts					
For the year ended December 31:					
2011	$ 1.8	$ 1.3	$—	$ 0.2[1]	$ 2.9
2012	2.9	0.3	—	0.4[1]	2.8
2013	2.8	0.6	—	0.4[1]	3.0
Allowance for sales returns					
For the year ended December 31:					
2011	7.9	38.4	—	36.4[3]	9.9
2012	9.9	40.1	—	41.2[3]	8.8
2013	8.8	70.2	(0.1)[2]	66.3[3]	12.6
Allowance for sales discounts					
For the year ended December 31:					
2011	7.1	69.3	—	69.9[3]	6.5
2012	6.5	59.0	—	59.5[3]	6.0
2013	6.0	49.5	—	50.8[3]	4.7
Allowance for co-op advertising					
For the year ended December 31:					
2011	11.7	22.3	—	25.0[3]	9.0
2012	9.0	28.7	—	27.9[3]	9.8
2013	9.8	22.9	(0.1)[2]	21.3[3]	11.3
Deferred tax valuation allowance					
For the year ended December 31:					
2011	5.8	2.3	—	—	8.1
2012	8.1	0.7	—	—	8.8
2013	8.8	3.4	—	—	12.2

[1] Doubtful accounts written off against accounts receivable.
[2] Represents effects of foreign currency translation.
[3] Deductions taken by customers written off against accounts receivable.

Dating of Report

PRESENTATION

NONISSUERS

7.59 Dating of the auditor's report is discussed in both AU-C section 700 and AU-C section 560. Paragraph .41 of AU-C section 700 states that the auditor's report should be dated no earlier than the date on which the auditors has obtained sufficient appropriate audit evidence

on which to base the auditor's opinion, including evidence that
- the audit documentation has been reviewed;
- all statements that the financial statements comprise, including related notes, have been prepared; and
- management has asserted that it has taken responsibility for those financial statements.

7.60 Paragraph .13 of AU-C section 560 states that if management revises the financial statements, the auditor should perform the audit procedures necessary in the circumstances on the revision. The auditor also should either
- date the auditor's report as of a later date or
- include an additional date in the auditor's report on the revised financial statements that is limited to the revision (that is, dual-date the auditor's report for that revision), thereby indicating that the auditor's procedures subsequent to the original date of the auditor's report are limited solely to the revision of the financial statements described in the relevant note to the financial statements.

ISSUERS

7.61 Paragraphs .01 and .05 of PCAOB AU section 530, *Dating of the Independent Auditor's Report* (AICPA, *PCAOB Standards and Related Rules*, Interim Standards), state the following:

.01 The auditor should date the audit report no earlier than the date on which the auditor has obtained sufficient appropriate evidence to support the auditor's opinion. Paragraph .05 describes the procedure to be followed when a subsequent event occurring after the report date is disclosed in the financial statements.

Note: When performing an integrated audit of financial statements and internal control over financial reporting, the auditor's reports on the company's financial statements and on internal control over financial reporting should be dated the same date.

Note: If the auditor concludes that a scope limitation will prevent the auditor from obtaining the reasonable assurance necessary to express an opinion on the financial statements, then the auditor's report date is the date that the auditor has obtained sufficient appropriate evidence to support the representations in the auditor's report.

.05 The independent auditor has two methods for dating the report when a subsequent event disclosed in the financial statements occurs after the auditor has obtained sufficient appropriate evidence on which to base his or her opinion, but before the issuance of the related financial statements. The auditor may use "dual dating," for example, "February 16, 20___, except for Note___, as to which the date is March 1, 20___," or may date the report as of the later date. In the former instance, the responsibility for events occurring subsequent to the original report date is limited to the specific event referred to in the note (or otherwise disclosed). In the latter instance, the independent auditor's responsibility for subsequent events extends to the later report date and, accordingly, the procedures outlined in section 560.12 generally should be extended to that date.

PRESENTATION AND DISCLOSURE EXCERPT

DATING OF REPORT

7.62 BARNES & NOBLE, INC. (APR)
REPORT OF INDEPENDENT REGISTERED PUBLIC ACCOUNTING FIRM

Board of Directors and Stockholders
Barnes & Noble, Inc.
New York, New York

We have audited the accompanying consolidated balance sheet of Barnes & Noble, Inc., as of April 28, 2012 and the related consolidated statements of operations, comprehensive income (loss), changes in shareholders' equity and cash flows for each of the two fiscal years ended April 28, 2012. These financial statements are the responsibility of the Company's management. Our responsibility is to express an opinion on these financial statements based on our audits.

We conducted our audits in accordance with the standards of the Public Company Accounting Oversight Board (United States). Those standards require that we plan and perform the audit to obtain reasonable assurance about whether the financial statements are free of material misstatement. An audit includes examining, on a test basis, evidence supporting the amounts and disclosures in the financial statements, assessing the accounting principles used and significant estimates made by management, as well as evaluating the overall financial statement presentation. We believe that our audits provide a reasonable basis for our opinion.

In our opinion, the consolidated financial statements referred to above present fairly, in all material respects, the financial position of Barnes & Noble, Inc. as of April 28, 2012 and the results of its operations and its cash flows for each of the two fiscal years ended April 28, 2012, in conformity with accounting principles generally accepted in the United States of America.

As discussed in Note 2, certain restatements have been made to the previously issued consolidated financial statements for each of two fiscal years ended April 28, 2012.

/s/ BDO USA, LLP
BDO USA, LLP
New York, New York
June 27, 2012, except for Note 2, as to which the date is July 26, 2013

NOTES TO CONSOLIDATED FINANCIAL STATEMENTS

(Thousands of dollars, except per share data)

2. Restatement of Prior Period Financial Statements

The Company has restated its previously reported consolidated financial statements for the years ended April 28, 2012 and April 30, 2011, including the opening stockholders' equity balance, in order to correct certain previously reported amounts.

In fiscal 2013, management determined that the Company had incorrectly overstated certain accruals for the periods prior to April 27, 2013, as a result of inadequate controls over its Distribution Center accrual reconciliation process. In accordance with ASC 250–10–S99–2, *Considering the Effects of Prior Year Misstatements when Quantifying Misstatements in Current Year Financial Statements* (ASC 250), the Company recorded an adjustment to decrease cost of sales by $6,700 ($4,027 after tax) and $8,460 ($5,084 after tax) to correctly present the statement of operations for fiscal 2012 and 2011, respectively. The Company also decreased accounts payable by $89,500 and $96,200 at April 30, 2011 and April 28, 2012, respectively; increased income taxes payable included in Accrued Liabilities in the consolidated Balance Sheets by $14,939 and $18,598 at April 30, 2011 and April 28, 2012, respectively; and increased retained earnings by $74,561 and $78,588, net of tax at April 30, 2011 and April 28, 2012, respectively.

In addition, in reviewing the Company's components of deferred income tax assets and liabilities, management determined that deferred income tax liability in the amount of $26,026, net, was related to a transaction in which gain was reported for both accounting and tax purposes prior to 2010. Accordingly, management concluded that this deferred income tax liability should be reversed. In accordance with ASC 250, the Company recorded an adjustment to decrease deferred tax liability and increase retained earnings by $26,026 at May 1, 2010. The cumulative effect of these adjustments increased previously reported retained earnings by $95,503 at May 1, 2010.

In fiscal 2013, management determined that the Company had not accrued a tenant allowance related to one of its properties in fiscal 2012. The Company recorded an adjustment to increase receivable, net and other long-term liabilities by $9,450 in fiscal 2012.

The following tables set forth the correction to each of the individual affected line items in the consolidated balance sheets as of April 30, 2011 and April 28, 2012 and the consolidated statement of operations for fiscal 2011 and 2012. The restated amounts presented below reflect the impact of these corrections, as well as adjustments of $52,072 and $47,026 related to the current portion of deferred rent and tenant allowances on the April 30, 2011 and April 28, 2012 balance sheet, respectively. The Company did not present tables for the adjustments within the consolidated cash flow statement since all of the adjustments were within the operating section of the consolidated cash flow statement. The above corrections and adjustments did not effect total cash flows from operating activities, financing activities or investing activities for any period presented.

The financial information included in the accompanying financial statements and notes thereto reflect the affects of the corrections and other adjustments described in the preceding discussion and tables.

Balance Sheet Data:

(In thousands, except per share data)	As Previously Reported	Corrections	Other Adjustments	Restated
	As of April 30, 2011			
Assets				
Current assets:				
Cash and cash equivalents	$ 59,429	—	—	$ 59,429
Receivables, net	150,294	—	—	150,294
Merchandise inventories, net	1,375,362	—	—	1,375,362
Prepaid expenses and other current assets	161,936	—	—	161,936
Total current assets	$ 1,747,021	—	—	$ 1,747,021
Property and equipment:				
Land and land improvements	8,617	—	—	8,617
Buildings and leasehold improvements	1,204,108	—	—	1,204,108
Fixtures and equipment	1,670,488	—	—	1,670,488
	2,883,213	—	—	2,883,213
Less accumulated depreciation and amortization	2,178,562	—	—	2,178,562
Net property and equipment	704,651	—	—	704,651
Goodwill	524,113	—	—	524,113
Intangible assets, net	566,578	—	—	566,578
Other noncurrent assets	54,103	—	—	54,103
Total assets	$ 3,596,466	—	—	$ 3,596,466
Liabilities and Shareholders' Equity				
Current liabilities:				
Accounts payable	$ 949,010	(89,500)	—	$ 859,510
Accrued liabilities	474,575	14,939	52,072	541,586
Gift card liabilities	311,092	—	—	311,092
Total current liabilities	1,734,677	(74,561)	52,072	1,712,188
Long-term debt	313,100	—	—	313,100
Deferred taxes	280,132	(26,026)	—	254,106
Other long-term liabilities	448,647	—	(52,072)	396,575
Shareholders' equity:				
Common stock; $.001 par value; 300,000 shares authorized; 90,465 shares issued	90	—	—	90
Additional paid-in capital	1,323,263	—	—	1,323,263
Accumulated other comprehensive loss	(11,630)	—	—	(11,630)
Retained earnings	562,379	100,587	—	662,966
Treasury stock, at cost, 33,410 shares	(1,054,192)	—	—	(1,054,192)
Total Shareholders' equity	819,910	100,587	—	920,497
Commitments and contingencies	—	—	—	—
Total liabilities and shareholders' equity	$ 3,596,466	—	—	$ 3,596,466

Balance Sheet Data:

(In thousands, except per share data)	As Previously Reported	Corrections	Other Adjustments	Restated
	As of April 28, 2012			
Assets				
Current assets:				
Cash and cash equivalents	$ 54,131	—	—	$ 54,131
Receivables, net	160,497	9,450	—	169,947
Merchandise inventories, net	1,561,841	—	—	1,561,841
Prepaid expenses and other current assets	221,324	—	—	221,324
Total current assets	$ 1,997,793	9,450	—	$2,007,243
Property and equipment:				
Land and land improvements	2,541	—	—	2,541
Buildings and leasehold improvements	1,196,764	—	—	1,196,764
Fixtures and equipment	1,784,492	—	—	1,784,492
	2,983,797	—	—	2,983,797
Less accumulated depreciation and amortization	2,361,142	—	—	2,361,142
Net property and equipment	622,655	—	—	622,655
Goodwill	519,685	—	—	519,685
Intangible assets, net	564,054	—	—	564,054
Other noncurrent assets	61,062	—	—	61,062
Total assets	$ 3,765,249	9,450	—	$3,774,699

(continued)

As of April 28, 2012

(In thousands, except per share data)	As Previously Reported	Corrections	Other Adjustments	Restated
Liabilities and Shareholders' Equity				
Current liabilities:				
Accounts payable	$ 959,423	(96,200)	—	$ 863,223
Accrued liabilities	546,495	18,598	47,026	612,119
Gift card liabilities	321,362	—	—	321,362
Total current liabilities	1,827,280	(77,602)	47,026	1,796,704
Long-term debt	324,200	—	—	324,200
Deferred taxes	268,774	(26,026)	—	242,748
Other long-term liabilities	405,065	8,464	(47,026)	366,503
Redeemable Preferred Shares; $.001 par value; 5,000 shares authorized; 204 shares issued	192,273	—	—	192,273
Shareholders' equity:				
Common stock; $.001 par value; 300,000 shares authorized; 91,376 shares issued	91	—	—	91
Additional paid-in capital	1,340,909	—	—	1,340,909
Accumulated other comprehensive loss	(16,635)	—	—	(16,635)
Retained earnings	481,574	104,614	—	586,188
Treasury stock, at cost, 33,722 shares	(1,058,282)	—	—	(1,058,282)
Total Shareholders' equity	747,657	104,614	—	852,271
Commitments and contingencies	—	—	—	—
Total liabilities and shareholders' equity	$ 3,765,249	9,450	—	$ 3,774,699

Statement of Operations Data:

(In thousands, except per share data)	Fiscal 2011 As Previously Reported	Corrections	Restated
Sales	$6,998,565	—	$6,998,565
Cost of sales and occupancy	5,205,712	(8,460)	5,197,252
Gross profit	1,792,853	8,460	1,801,313
Selling and administrative expenses	1,629,465	—	1,629,465
Depreciation and amortization	228,647	—	228,647
Operating income (loss)	(65,259)	8,460	(56,799)
Interest expense, net and amortization of deferred financing fees	(57,350)	—	(57,350)
Income (loss) before income taxes (benefit)	(122,609)	8,460	(114,149)
Income taxes (benefit)	(48,652)	3,376	(45,276)
Net income (loss)	(73,957)	5,084	(68,873)
Net loss attributable to noncontrolling interests	37	—	37
Net income (loss) attributable to Barnes & Noble, Inc.	$ (73,920)	5,084	$ (68,836)
Diluted income (loss) per common share			
Net income (loss) attributable to Barnes & Noble, Inc.	$ (1.31)	0.09	$ (1.22)

Statement of Operations Data:

(In thousands, except per share data)	Fiscal 2012 As Previously Reported	Corrections	Restated
Sales	$7,129,199	—	$7,129,199
Cost of sales and occupancy	5,218,383	(6,700)	5,211,683
Gross profit	1,910,816	6,700	1,917,516
Selling and administrative expenses	1,739,452	—	1,739,452
Depreciation and amortization	232,667	—	232,667
Operating income (loss)	(61,303)	6,700	(54,603)
Interest expense, net and amortization of deferred financing fees	(35,304)	—	(35,304)
Income (loss) before income taxes (benefit)	(96,607)	6,700	(89,907)
Income taxes (benefit)	(27,740)	2,673	(25,067)
Net income (loss)	$ (68,867)	4,027	$ (64,840)
Diluted income (loss) per common share			
Net income (loss)	$ (1.41)	0.07	$ (1.34)

Auditors' Reports on Internal Control Over Financial Reporting

PRESENTATION

> **Author's Note**
> Because the report on internal control over financial reporting is required only for issuers, the following guidance is not applicable for nonissuers.

7.63 Section 404(a) of the Sarbanes-Oxley Act of 2002 requires that management of a public entity assess the effectiveness of the entity's internal control over financial reporting as of the end of the entity's most recent fiscal year and include in the entity's annual report management's conclusions about the effectiveness of the entity's internal control structure and procedures. Management is required to state a direct conclusion about whether the entity's internal control over financial reporting is effective. Management's report on internal control over financial reporting is required to include the following:

- A statement of management's responsibility for establishing and maintaining adequate internal control over financial reporting for the entity
- A statement identifying the framework used by management to conduct the required assessment of the effectiveness of the entity's internal control over financial reporting
- An assessment of the effectiveness of the entity's internal control over financial reporting as of the end of the entity's most recent fiscal year, including an explicit statement about whether that internal control over financial reporting is effective
- A statement that the registered public accounting firm that audited the financial statements included in the annual report has issued an attestation report on management's assessment of the entity's internal control over financial reporting

7.64 Under Section 404(b) of the Sarbanes-Oxley Act of 2002, the auditor who audits the public entity's financial statements included in the annual report is required to audit the entity's internal control over financial reporting. In addition, the auditor is required to audit and report on management's assessment of the effectiveness of internal control over financial reporting. Under PCAOB Auditing Standard No. 5, *An Audit of Internal Control Over Financial Reporting That is Integrated with an Audit of Financial Statements* (AICPA, *PCAOB Standards and Related Rules*, Auditing Standards), the auditor's objective in an audit of internal control over financial reporting is to express an opinion on the effectiveness of the entity's internal control over financial reporting. The audit of internal control over financial reporting should be integrated with the audit of the financial statements. Accordingly, independent auditors engaged to audit the financial statements of such entities also are required to audit and report on the entity's internal control over financial reporting as of the end of such fiscal year. Further, if the auditor determines that elements of management's annual report on internal control over financial reporting are incomplete or improperly presented, the auditor should modify the report to include an explanatory paragraph describing the reasons for this determination and identify and fairly describe any material weakness. Paragraph 86 of Auditing Standard No. 5 allows the auditor to issue a combined report (that is, one report containing both an opinion on the financial statements and an opinion on internal control over financial reporting) or separate reports on the entity's financial statements and on internal control over financial reporting.

7.65 In September 2010, the SEC approved a final rule related to the Dodd-Frank Wall Street Reform and Consumer Protection Act (Dodd-Frank Act). The Dodd-Frank Act provides that Section 404(b) of the Sarbanes-Oxley Act of 2002 shall not apply with respect to any audit report prepared for an issuer that is neither an accelerated filer nor a large accelerated filer. Prior to the Dodd-Frank Act, a nonaccelerated filer would have been required, under existing SEC rules, to include an attestation report of its registered public accounting firm on internal control over financial reporting in the filer's annual report filed with the SEC for fiscal years ending on or after June 15, 2010.

PRESENTATION AND DISCLOSURE EXCERPTS

SEPARATE REPORT ON INTERNAL CONTROL

7.66 ACUITY BRANDS, INC. (AUG)
REPORT OF INDEPENDENT REGISTERED PUBLIC ACCOUNTING FIRM

The Board of Directors and Stockholders
Acuity Brands, Inc.

We have audited the accompanying consolidated balance sheets of Acuity Brands, Inc. as of August 31, 2013 and 2012, and the related consolidated statements of comprehensive income, stockholders' equity, and cash flows for each of the three years in the period ended August 31, 2013. Our audits also included the financial statement schedule listed in the Index at Item 15(a). These consolidated financial statements and schedule are the responsibility of the Company's management. Our responsibility is to express an opinion on these consolidated financial statements and schedule based on our audits.

We conducted our audits in accordance with the standards of the Public Company Accounting Oversight Board (United States). Those standards require that we plan and perform the audit to obtain reasonable assurance about whether the financial statements are free of material misstatement. An audit includes examining, on a test basis, evidence supporting the amounts and disclosures in the financial statements. An audit also includes assessing the accounting principles used and significant estimates made by management, as well as evaluating the overall financial statement presentation. We believe that our audits provide a reasonable basis for our opinion.

In our opinion, the financial statements referred to above present fairly, in all material respects, the consolidated financial position of Acuity Brands, Inc. at August 31, 2013 and 2012, and the consolidated results of its operations and its cash flows for each of the three years in the period ended August 31, 2013, in conformity with U.S. generally accepted accounting principles. Also, in our opinion, the related financial statement schedule, when considered in relation to the basic financial statements taken as a whole, presents fairly in all material respects the information set forth therein.

We also have audited, in accordance with the standards of the Public Company Accounting Oversight Board (United States), Acuity Brands, Inc.'s internal control over financial reporting as of August 31, 2013, based on criteria established in Internal Control-Integrated Framework issued by the Committee of Sponsoring Organizations of the Treadway Commission (1992Framework) and our report dated October 29, 2013 expressed an unqualified opinion thereon.

/s/ Ernst & Young LLP
Atlanta, Georgia
October 29, 2013

REPORT OF INDEPENDENT REGISTERED PUBLIC ACCOUNTING FIRM ON INTERNAL CONTROL OVER FINANCIAL REPORTING

The Board of Directors and Stockholders
Acuity Brands, Inc.

We have audited Acuity Brands, Inc.'s internal control over financial reporting as of August 31, 2013, based on criteria established in Internal Control—Integrated Framework issued by the Committee of Sponsoring Organizations of the Treadway Commission (1992Framework) (the COSO criteria). Acuity Brands, Inc.'s management is responsible for maintaining effective internal control over financial reporting, and for its assessment of the effectiveness of internal control over financial reporting included in the accompanying Management's Report on Internal Control Over Financial Reporting. Our responsibility is to express an opinion on the company's internal control over financial reporting based on our audit.

We conducted our audit in accordance with the standards of the Public Company Accounting Oversight Board (United States). Those standards require that we plan and perform the audit to obtain reasonable assurance about whether effective internal control over financial reporting was maintained in all material respects. Our audit included obtaining an understanding of internal control over financial reporting, assessing the risk that a material weakness exists, testing and evaluating the design and operating effectiveness of internal control based on the assessed risk, and performing such other procedures as we considered necessary in the circumstances. We believe that our audit provides a reasonable basis for our opinion.

A company's internal control over financial reporting is a process designed to provide reasonable assurance regarding the reliability of financial reporting and the preparation of financial statements for external purposes in accordance with generally accepted accounting principles. A company's internal control over financial reporting includes those policies and procedures that (1) pertain to the maintenance of records that, in reasonable detail, accurately and fairly reflect the transactions and dispositions of the assets of the company; (2) provide reasonable assurance that transactions are recorded as necessary to permit preparation of financial statements in accordance with generally accepted accounting principles, and that receipts and expenditures of the company are being made only in accordance with authorizations of management and directors of the company; and (3) provide reasonable assurance regarding prevention or timely detection of unauthorized acquisition, use, or disposition of the company's assets that could have a material effect on the financial statements.

Because of its inherent limitations, internal control over financial reporting may not prevent or detect misstatements. Also, projections of any evaluation of effectiveness to future periods are subject to the risk that controls may become inadequate because of changes in conditions, or that the degree of compliance with the policies or procedures may deteriorate.

In our opinion, Acuity Brands, Inc. maintained, in all material respects, effective internal control over financial reporting as of August 31, 2013, based on the COSO criteria.

We also have audited, in accordance with the standards of the Public Company Accounting Oversight Board (United States), the consolidated balance sheets of Acuity Brands, Inc. as of August 31, 2013 and 2012, and the related consolidated statements of comprehensive income, stockholders' equity, and cash flows for each of the three years in the period ended August 31, 2013 of Acuity Brands, Inc. and our report dated October 29, 2013 expressed an unqualified opinion thereon.

/s/ Ernst & Young LLP
Atlanta, Georgia
October 29, 2013

COMBINED REPORT ON FINANCIAL STATEMENTS AND INTERNAL CONTROL

7.67 CISCO SYSTEMS, INC. (JUL)
REPORT OF INDEPENDENT REGISTERED PUBLIC ACCOUNTING FIRM

To the Board of Directors and Shareholders of
Cisco Systems, Inc.:

In our opinion, the accompanying consolidated balance sheets and the related consolidated statements of operations, of comprehensive income, of cash flows and of equity listed in the accompanying index present fairly, in all material respects, the financial position of Cisco Systems, Inc. and its subsidiaries at July 27, 2013 and July 28, 2012, and the results of their operations and their cash flows for each of the three years in the period ended July 27, 2013 in conformity with accounting principles generally accepted in the United States of America. In addition, in our opinion, the financial statement schedule appearing under Item 15(a)(2) presents fairly, in all material respects, the information set forth therein when read in conjunction with the related consolidated financial statements. Also in our opinion, the Company maintained, in all material respects, effective internal control over financial reporting as of July 27, 2013, based on criteria established in *Internal Control—Integrated Framework* issued by the Committee of Sponsoring Organizations of the Treadway Commission (COSO). The Company's management is responsible for these financial statements and financial statement schedule, for maintaining effective internal control over financial reporting and for its assessment of the effectiveness of internal control over financial reporting, included in the accompanying Management's Report on Internal Control over Financial Reporting. Our responsibility is to express opinions on these financial statements, on the financial statement schedule, and on the Company's internal control over financial reporting based on our integrated audits. We conducted our audits in accordance with the standards of the Public Company Accounting Oversight Board (United States). Those standards require that we plan and perform the audits to obtain reasonable assurance about whether the financial statements are free of material misstatement and whether effective internal control over financial reporting was maintained in all material respects. Our audits of the financial statements included examining, on a test basis, evidence supporting the amounts and disclosures in the financial statements, assessing the accounting principles used and significant estimates made by management, and evaluating the overall financial statement presentation. Our audit of internal control over financial reporting included obtaining an understanding of internal control over financial reporting, assessing the risk that a material weakness exists, and testing and evaluating the design and operating effectiveness of internal control based on the assessed risk. Our audits also included performing such other procedures as we considered necessary in the circumstances. We believe that our audits provide a reasonable basis for our opinions.

A company's internal control over financial reporting is a process designed to provide reasonable assurance regarding the reliability of financial reporting and the preparation of financial statements for external purposes in accordance with generally accepted accounting principles. A company's internal control over financial reporting includes those policies and procedures that (i) pertain to the maintenance of records that, in reasonable detail, accurately and fairly reflect the transactions and dispositions of the assets of the company; (ii) provide reasonable assurance that transactions are recorded as necessary to permit preparation of financial statements in accordance with generally accepted accounting principles, and that receipts and expenditures of the company are being made only in accordance with authorizations of management and directors of the company; and (iii) provide reasonable assurance regarding prevention or timely detection of unauthorized acquisition, use, or disposition of the company's assets that could have a material effect on the financial statements.

Because of its inherent limitations, internal control over financial reporting may not prevent or detect misstatements. Also, projections of any evaluation of effectiveness to future periods are subject to the risk that controls may become inadequate because of changes in conditions, or that the degree of compliance with the policies or procedures may deteriorate.

/s/ PricewaterhouseCoopers LLP
San Jose, California
September 10, 2013

REPORT ON INTERNAL CONTROL NOT PRESENTED

7.68 THE STANDARD REGISTER COMPANY (DEC)
REPORT OF INDEPENDENT REGISTERED PUBLIC ACCOUNTING FIRM

Board of Directors and Shareholders
The Standard Register Company
Dayton, Ohio

We have audited the accompanying consolidated balance sheets of The Standard Register Company and subsidiaries (the Company) as of December 29, 2013 and December 30, 2012, and the related consolidated statements of income, comprehensive income, cash flows, and shareholders' deficit for each of the three fiscal years in the period ended December 29, 2013. These financial statements are the responsibility of the Company's management. Our responsibility is to express an opinion on these financial statements based on our audits.

We conducted our audits in accordance with the standards of the Public Company Accounting Oversight Board (United States). Those standards require that we plan and perform the audit to obtain reasonable assurance about whether the financial statements are free of material misstatement. An audit includes examining, on a test basis, evidence supporting the amounts and disclosures in the financial statements, assessing the accounting principles used and significant estimates made by management, as well as evaluating the overall financial statement presentation. We believe that our audits provide a reasonable basis for our opinion.

The Company is not required to have, nor were we engaged to perform, an audit of its internal control over financial reporting. Our audits included consideration of internal control over financial reporting as a basis for designing audit procedures that are appropriate in the circumstances, but not for the purpose of expressing an opinion on the effectiveness of the Company's internal control over financial reporting. Accordingly, we express no such opinion.

In our opinion, the consolidated financial statements referred to above present fairly, in all material respects, the financial position of the Company as of December 29, 2013 and December 30, 2012, and the results of its operations and its cash flows for each of the three fiscal years in the period ended December 29, 2013, in conformity with accounting principles generally accepted in the United States of America.

As discussed in Note 2 to the consolidated financial statements, the Company has elected to change its method of accounting for defined benefit pension plan costs. Such changes are reflected in the consolidated financial statements through retrospective application to all periods presented.

/S/ BATTELLE RIPPE KINGSTON LLP
Dayton, Ohio
March 3, 2014

REPORT ON INTERNAL CONTROL WITH SPECIFIC ITEMS EXCLUDED

7.69 CONAGRA FOODS, INC. (MAY)

REPORT OF INDEPENDENT REGISTERED PUBLIC ACCOUNTING FIRM

The Board of Directors and Stockholders
ConAgra Foods, Inc.:

We have audited the internal control over financial reporting of ConAgra Foods, Inc. and subsidiaries (the Company) as of May 26, 2013, based on the criteria established in *Internal Control-Integrated Framework* issued by the Committee of Sponsoring Organizations of the Treadway Commission (COSO). The Company's management is responsible for maintaining effective internal control over financial reporting and for its assessment of the effectiveness of internal control over financial reporting, included in the accompanying Management's Annual Report on Internal Control Over Financial Reporting. Our responsibility is to express an opinion on the Company's internal control over financial reporting based on our audit.

We conducted our audit in accordance with the standards of the Public Company Accounting Oversight Board (United States). Those standards require that we plan and perform the audit to obtain reasonable assurance about whether effective internal control over financial reporting was maintained in all material respects. Our audit included obtaining an understanding of internal control over financial reporting, assessing the risk that a material weakness exists, and testing and evaluating the design and operating effectiveness of internal control based on the assessed risk. Our audit also included performing such other procedures as we considered necessary in the circumstances. We believe that our audit provides a reasonable basis for our opinion.

A company's internal control over financial reporting is a process designed to provide reasonable assurance regarding the reliability of financial reporting and the preparation of financial statements for external purposes in accordance with generally accepted accounting principles. A company's internal control over financial reporting includes those policies and procedures that (1) pertain to the maintenance of records that, in reasonable detail, accurately and fairly reflect the transactions and dispositions of the assets of the company; (2) provide reasonable assurance that transactions are recorded as necessary to permit preparation of financial statements in accordance with generally accepted accounting principles, and that receipts and expenditures of the company are being made only in accordance with authorizations of management and directors of the company; and (3) provide reasonable assurance regarding prevention or timely detection of unauthorized acquisition, use, or disposition of the company's assets that could have a material effect on the financial statements.

Because of its inherent limitations, internal control over financial reporting may not prevent or detect misstatements. Also, projections of any evaluation of effectiveness to future periods are subject to the risk that controls may become inadequate because of changes in conditions, or that the degree of compliance with the policies or procedures may deteriorate.

In our opinion, ConAgra Foods, Inc. and subsidiaries maintained, in all material respects, effective internal control over financial reporting as of May 26, 2013, based on the criteria established in *Internal Control-Integrated Framework* issued by the Committee of Sponsoring Organizations of the Treadway Commission.

ConAgra Foods, Inc. acquired Ralcorp Holdings, Inc. (Ralcorp) during the year ended May 26, 2013, and management excluded from its assessment of the effectiveness of the Company's internal control over financial reporting as of May 26, 2013, Ralcorp's internal control over financial reporting associated with total assets of $8.18 billion and total net sales of $1.25 billion included in the consolidated financial statements of the Company as of and for the year ended May 26, 2013. Our audit of internal control over financial reporting also excluded an evaluation of the internal control over financial reporting of Ralcorp.

We also have audited, in accordance with the standards of the Public Company Accounting Oversight Board (United States), the consolidated balance sheets of the Company as of May 26, 2013, and May 27, 2012, and the related consolidated statements of earnings, comprehensive income, common stockholders' equity, and cash flows for each of the years in the three-year period ended May 26, 2013, and our report dated July 19, 2013 expressed an unqualified opinion on those consolidated financial statements.

/s/ KPMG LLP
Omaha, Nebraska
July 19, 2013

7.70 GREIF, INC. (OCT)
CONTROLS AND PROCEDURES

Changes in Internal Control Over Financial Reporting

As previously disclosed in Item 9A of the 2012Form 10-K (the "preceding Form 10-K"), management had then concluded that there was a material weakness in internal controls over financial reporting related to the financial statement close process and oversight in the Rigid Industrial Packaging & Services business unit in Brazil. In response, management has changed and added personnel in the Brazil business unit and in its corporate accounting function and has strengthened internal controls to provide more rigorous reconciliation and analytical review procedures. Management has concluded that, as of October 31, 2013, the above identified material weakness has been fully remediated.

As previously disclosed in the preceding Form 10-K, management had then concluded that there was a material weakness in internal controls over financial reporting related to accounting for non-routine or complex transactions. Remedial actions have been and are being implemented to address these controls, including improving processes and communications around non-routine or complex transactions, supplementing the technical competence of our accounting staff with additional internal and, as needed, contract resources and improving, from a holistic standpoint, the documentation of the review of the accounting, presentation and disclosure of such transactions. Once all remedial actions have been implemented and in operation for a sufficient period of time, these actions will be fully tested to determine whether they are operating effectively. Therefore, management concluded that, as of October 31, 2013, there was a material weakness over financial reporting related to accounting for non-routine or complex transactions.

As previously disclosed in our Quarterly Report on Form 10-Q for the fiscal quarter ended July 31, 2013, management had then concluded there was a material weakness in internal controls over financial reporting related to accounting for withholding taxes on subsidiary financing transactions. These errors were not material to any individual prior period, but the correction of these errors would have been material to the current period consolidated statements of operations, consolidated balance sheets and consolidated statements of cash flows. Actions were implemented to remediate the above identified material weakness, including the improvement of the technical competency of the staff through continuing education and revised accounting policies, improvement of the processes for accruing withholding tax expense, alignment of withholding tax accrual with the related interest income accrual, simplification of the Company's subsidiary loan portfolio through enhanced design and maintenance, enhancements to the periodic tax reporting packages, and strengthening of the underlying process and analysis (Treasury, Accounting and Tax) that supports subsidiary financing decisions and procedures. These actions are in the process of being tested; however, as of October 31, 2013, the controls and processes documented and implemented have not been in place long enough to provide sufficient assurances to support the conclusion that the above identified material weakness has been fully remediated. Once in operation for a sufficient period of time, these actions will be fully tested to determine whether they are operating effectively. Therefore, management concluded that, as of October 31, 2013, there was a material weakness over financial reporting related to accounting for withholding taxes on subsidiary financing transactions.

Notwithstanding the identified material weaknesses, management believes the consolidated financial statements included in this Form 10-K fairly represent in all material respects our financial condition, results of operations and cash flows at and for the periods presented in accordance with U.S. GAAP.

Except as noted in the preceding paragraphs, there has been no change in our internal control over financial reporting that occurred during the most recent quarter that has materially affected, or is reasonably likely to materially affect, our internal control over financial reporting.

Disclosure Controls and Procedures

With the participation of our principal executive officer and principal accounting officer, our management has evaluated the effectiveness of our disclosure controls and procedures (as defined in Rule 13a-15(e) under the Securities Exchange Act of 1934, as amended (the "Exchange Act")), as of the end of the period covered by this report. Based upon that evaluation, our principal executive officer and principal financial officer have concluded that, as of the end of the period covered by this report:
  - Information required to be disclosed by us in the reports that we file or submit under the Exchange Act is recorded, processed, summarized and reported within the time periods specified in the rules and forms of the Securities and Exchange Commission;
  - Information required to be disclosed by us in the reports that we file or submit under the Exchange Act is accumulated and communicated to our management, including our principal executive officer and principal financial officer, as appropriate to allow timely decisions regarding required disclosure; and

- Management has concluded that, because of a material weakness over financial reporting related to accounting for non-routine or complex transactions and a material weakness in internal controls over financial reporting related accounting for withholding taxes on subsidiary financing transactions, our disclosure controls and procedures were not effective.

Management's Annual Report on Internal Control over Financial Reporting

Management's annual report on internal control over financial reporting required by Item 308(a) of Regulation S-K follows. The report of the independent registered public accounting firm required by Item 308(b) of Regulation S-K is found under the caption "Report of Independent Registered Public Accounting Firm" below.

The following report is provided by our management on our internal control over financial reporting (as defined in Rule 13a-15(f) of the Exchange Act):

1. Our management is responsible for establishing and maintaining adequate internal control over our financial reporting as such term is defined in Exchange Act Rule 13a-15(f).
2. Our management has used the Committee of Sponsoring Organizations of the Treadway Commission ("COSO") framework to evaluate the effectiveness of our internal control over financial reporting. Management believes that the COSO framework is a suitable framework for its evaluation of our internal control over financial reporting because it is free from bias, permits reasonably qualitative and quantitative measurements of our internal controls, is sufficiently complete so that those relevant factors that would alter a conclusion about the effectiveness of our internal controls are not omitted and is relevant to an evaluation of internal control over financial reporting.
3. As previously disclosed in Item 9A of the 2012Form 10-K, management had concluded that there was a material weakness in internal controls over financial reporting related to accounting for non-routine or complex transactions.
4. As previously disclosed in our Quarterly Report on Form 10-Q for the fiscal quarter ended July 31, 2013, management had concluded that there was a material weakness in internal controls over financial reporting related to accounting for withholding taxes on subsidiary financing transactions.
5. Management has assessed the effectiveness of our internal control over financial reporting as of October 31, 2013, and has concluded that, because of a material weakness in internal controls over financial reporting related to accounting for non-routine or complex transactions and a material weakness in internal controls over financial reporting related to accounting for withholding taxes on subsidiary financing transactions, our disclosure controls and procedures were not effective.

Our internal control over financial reporting as of October 31, 2013, has been audited by Ernst & Young LLP, an independent registered public accounting firm, as stated in their report, which follows below.

REPORT OF INDEPENDENT REGISTERED PUBLIC ACCOUNTING FIRM

The Board of Directors and Shareholders of
Greif, Inc. and subsidiary companies:

We have audited Greif, Inc. and subsidiary companies' internal control over financial reporting as of October 31, 2013 based on criteria established in Internal Control—Integrated Framework issued by the Committee of Sponsoring Organizations of the Treadway Commission (1992 framework) (the COSO criteria). Greif, Inc. and subsidiary companies' management is responsible for maintaining effective internal control over financial reporting, and for its assessment of the effectiveness of internal control over financial reporting included in the Management's Annual Report on Internal Control over Financial Reporting. Our responsibility is to express an opinion on the company's internal control over financial reporting based on our audit.

We conducted our audit in accordance with the standards of the Public Company Accounting Oversight Board (United States). Those standards require that we plan and perform the audit to obtain reasonable assurance about whether effective internal control over financial reporting was maintained in all material respects. Our audit included obtaining an understanding of internal control over financial reporting, assessing the risk that a material weakness exists, testing and evaluating the design and operating effectiveness of internal control based on the assessed risk, and performing such other procedures as we considered necessary in the circumstances. We believe that our audit provides a reasonable basis for our opinion.

A company's internal control over financial reporting is a process designed to provide reasonable assurance regarding the reliability of financial reporting and the preparation of financial statements for external purposes in accordance with generally accepted accounting principles. A company's internal control over financial reporting includes those policies and procedures that (1) pertain to the maintenance of records that, in reasonable detail, accurately and fairly reflect the transactions and dispositions of the assets of the company; (2) provide reasonable assurance that transactions are recorded as necessary to permit preparation of financial statements in accordance with generally accepted accounting principles, and that receipts and expenditures of the company are being made only in accordance with authorizations of management and directors of the company; and (3) provide reasonable assurance regarding prevention or timely detection of unauthorized acquisition, use, or disposition of the company's assets that could have a material effect on the financial statements.

Because of its inherent limitations, internal control over financial reporting may not prevent or detect misstatements. Also, projections of any evaluation of effectiveness to future periods are subject to the risk that controls may become inadequate because of changes in conditions, or that the degree of compliance with the policies or procedures may deteriorate.

A material weakness is a deficiency, or combination of deficiencies, in internal control over financial reporting, such that there is a reasonable possibility that a material misstatement of the company's annual or interim financial statements will not be prevented or detected on a timely basis. The following material weaknesses have been identified and included in management's assessment. Management has identified material weaknesses in internal controls over financial reporting relating to accounting for non-routine or complex transactions and the identification and recording of withholding taxes on subsidiary financing transactions. We also have audited, in accordance with the standards of the Public Company Accounting Oversight Board (United States), the balance sheets of Greif, Inc. and subsidiary companies as of October 31, 2013 and 2012, and the related consolidated statements of income, comprehensive income, shareholders' equity, and cash flows for each of the three years in the period ended October 31, 2013. These material weaknesses were considered in determining the nature, timing and extent of audit tests applied in our audit of the October 31, 2013 financial statements, and this report does not affect our report dated December 23, 2013, which expressed an unqualified opinion on those financial statements.

In our opinion, because of the effect of the material weaknesses described above on the achievement of the objectives of the control criteria, Greif, Inc. and subsidiary companies has not maintained effective internal control over financial reporting as of October 31, 2013, based on the COSO criteria.

/s/ Ernst & Young LLP
Columbus, Ohio
December 23, 2013

General Management and Special-Purpose Committee Reports

PRESENTATION

7.71 Some survey entities presented a report of management on financial statements. These reports may include the following:
- Description of management's responsibility for preparing the financial statements
- Identification of independent auditors
- Statement about management's representations to the independent auditors
- Statement about financial records and related data made available to the independent auditors
- Description of special-purpose committees of the board of directors
- General description of the entity's system of internal control
- Description of the entity's code of conduct

Occasionally, survey entities presented a report of a special-purpose committee, such as the audit committee or compensation committee.

PRESENTATION AND DISCLOSURE EXCERPTS

REPORTS OF MANAGEMENT

7.72 CAMPBELL SOUP COMPANY (JUL)
REPORTS OF MANAGEMENT

Management's Report on Financial Statements

The accompanying financial statements have been prepared by the company's management in conformity with generally accepted accounting principles to reflect the financial position of the company and its operating results. The financial information appearing throughout this Report is consistent with the financial statements. Management is responsible for the information and representations in such financial statements, including the estimates and judgments required for their preparation. The financial statements have been audited by PricewaterhouseCoopers LLP, an independent registered public accounting firm, as stated in their report, which appears herein.

The Audit Committee of the Board of Directors, which is composed entirely of Directors who are not officers or employees of the company, meets regularly with the company's worldwide internal auditing department, other management personnel, and the independent registered public accounting firm. The independent registered public accounting firm and the internal auditing department have had, and continue to have, direct access to the Audit Committee without the presence of other management personnel, and have been directed to discuss the results of their audit work and any matters they believe should be brought to the Committee's attention. The internal auditing department and the independent registered public accounting firm report directly to the Audit Committee.

Management's Report on Internal Control Over Financial Reporting

The company's management is responsible for establishing and maintaining adequate internal control over financial reporting. Internal control over financial reporting is a process designed to provide reasonable assurance regarding the reliability of financial reporting and the preparation of financial statements for external purposes in accordance with generally accepted accounting principles in the United States of America.

The company's internal control over financial reporting includes those policies and procedures that:
- pertain to the maintenance of records that, in reasonable detail, accurately and fairly reflect the transactions and dispositions of the assets of the company;
- provide reasonable assurance that transactions are recorded as necessary to permit preparation of financial statements in accordance with generally accepted accounting principles, and that receipts and expenditures of the company are being made only in accordance with authorizations of management and Directors of the company; and
- provide reasonable assurance regarding prevention or timely detection of unauthorized acquisition, use, or disposition of the company's assets that could have a material effect on the financial statements.

Because of its inherent limitations, internal control over financial reporting may not prevent or detect misstatements. Also, projections of any evaluation of effectiveness to future periods are subject to the risk that controls may become inadequate because of changes in conditions, or that the degree of compliance with the policies or procedures may deteriorate.

The company's management assessed the effectiveness of the company's internal control over financial reporting as of July 28, 2013. In making this assessment, management used the criteria set forth by the Committee of Sponsoring Organizations of the Treadway Commission (COSO) in *Internal Control—Integrated Framework*. Based on this assessment using those criteria, management concluded that the company's internal control over financial reporting was effective as of July 28, 2013.

The effectiveness of the company's internal control over financial reporting as of July 28, 2013 has been audited by PricewaterhouseCoopers LLP, an independent registered public accounting firm, as stated in their report, which appears herein.

REPORT OF THE AUDIT COMMITTEE

7.73 PFIZER INC. (DEC)
AUDIT COMMITTEE REPORT

The Audit Committee reviews the Company's financial reporting process on behalf of the Board of Directors. Management has the primary responsibility for the financial statements and the reporting process, including the system of internal controls.

In this context, the Committee has met and held discussions with management and the independent registered public accounting firm regarding the fair and complete presentation of the Company's results and the assessment of the Company's internal control over financial reporting. The Committee has discussed significant accounting policies applied by the Company in its financial statements, as well as, when applicable, alternative accounting treatments. Management has represented to the Committee that the Company's consolidated financial statements were prepared in accordance with accounting principles generally accepted in the United States of America, and the Committee has reviewed and discussed the consolidated financial statements with management and the independent registered public accounting firm. The Committee has discussed with the independent registered public accounting firm matters required to be discussed under applicable Public Company Accounting Oversight Board standards.

In addition, the Committee has reviewed and discussed with the independent registered public accounting firm the auditor's independence from the Company and its management. As part of that review, the Committee has received the written disclosures and the letter required by applicable requirements of the Public Company Accounting Oversight Board regarding the independent accountant's communications with the Audit Committee concerning independence, and the Committee has discussed the independent registered public accounting firm's independence from the Company.

The Committee also has considered whether the independent registered public accounting firm's provision of non-audit services to the Company is compatible with the auditor's independence. The Committee has concluded that the independent registered public accounting firm is independent from the Company and its management.

As part of its responsibilities for oversight of the Company's Enterprise Risk Management process, the Committee has reviewed and discussed Company policies with respect to risk assessment and risk management, including discussions of individual risk areas, as well as an annual summary of the overall process.

The Committee has discussed with the Company's Internal Audit Department and independent registered public accounting firm the overall scope of and plans for their respective audits. The Committee meets with the Chief Internal Auditor, Chief Compliance and Risk Officer and representatives of the independent registered public accounting firm, in regular and executive sessions to discuss the results of their examinations, the evaluations of the Company's internal controls, and the overall quality of the Company's financial reporting and compliance programs.

In reliance on the reviews and discussions referred to above, the Committee has recommended to the Board of Directors, and the Board has approved, that the audited financial statements be included in the Company's Annual Report on Form 10-K for the year ended December 31, 2013, for filing with the SEC. The Committee has selected, and the Board of Directors has ratified, the selection of the Company's independent registered public accounting firm for 2014.

List of 350 Survey Entities and Where in the Text Excerpts From Their Annual Reports Can Be Found

The following table lists the 350 entities surveyed in alphabetical order, as well as where in the text their annual reports are excerpted.

Company Name	Month of Fiscal Year End	Accounting Technique Illustration
3M Company	December	1.48
A. O. Smith Corporation	December	
Abbott Laboratories	December	7.41
ABM Industries Incorporated	October	4.10
Acuity Brands, Inc.	August	7.66
AGCO Corporation	December	1.47, 2.76, 5.10
Air Products and Chemicals, Inc.	September	
Airgas, Inc.	March	
AK Steel Holding Corporation	December	1.64, 2.130
Alcoa Inc.	December	2.63, 2.75, 3.68
Allegheny Technologies Incorporated	December	3.86
Allergan, Inc.	December	6.09
Alliance One International, Inc.	March	2.32, 2.46, 2.135, 3.66
Alliant Techsystems Inc.	March	1.80, 3.48, 4.06
Altria Group, Inc.	December	
American Greetings Corporation	February	1.20, 2.134, 3.38
American International Group, Inc.	December	1.102, 2.19
AMETEK, Inc.	December	
Amkor Technology, Inc.	December	
Amphenol Corporation	December	
Anadarko Petroleum Corporation	December	1.78
Analog Devices, Inc.	October	
Ann Inc.	January	
Apache Corporation	December	5.13
Apple Inc.	September	
Applied Materials, Inc.	October	2.81
Archer-Daniels-Midland Company	December	3.37
Arkansas Best Corporation	December	3.50
Armstrong World Industries, Inc.	December	2.147
Arrow Electronics, Inc.	December	3.49, 5.14, 6.24
Ashland Inc.	September	
AT&T Inc.	December	
Atmel Corporation	December	
Autodesk, Inc.	January	3.55
Automatic Data Processing, Inc.	June	2.67, 7.57
AutoNation, Inc.	December	1.71
AutoZone, Inc.	August	4.07
Avnet, Inc.	June	3.72
Avon Products, Inc.	December	3.42, 3.76
Axiall Corporation	December	3.15
B/E Aerospace, Inc.	December	3.79
Badger Meter, Inc.	December	
Baker Hughes Incorporated	December	
Ball Corporation	December	

Company Name	Month of Fiscal Year End	Accounting Technique Illustration
Barnes & Noble, Inc.	April	1.52, 7.62
Bassett Furniture Industries, Incorporated	November	2.114
Baxter International Inc.	December	
BB&T Corporation	December	1.22
Beam Inc.	December	3.92
Becton, Dickinson and Company	September	
Berkshire Hathaway Inc.	December	3.17
Best Buy Co., Inc.	January	
BMC Software, Inc.	March	1.9, 3.07
Boeing Company, The	December	2.103
Bon-Ton Stores, Inc., The	January	2.41, 2.131
Boston Scientific Corporation	December	2.122, 2.155, 2.158, 3.41
Briggs & Stratton Corporation	June	2.104
Brink's Company, The	December	1.119
Brown Shoe Company, Inc.	January	
Brown-Forman Corporation	April	5.36
Brunswick Corporation	December	
CA, Inc.	March	2.120, 5.21
Cablevision Systems Corporation	December	1.114, 6.33
Cabot Corporation	September	
CACI International Inc	June	3.27
Campbell Soup Company	July	7.72
Cardinal Health, Inc.	June	
Career Education Corporation	December	2.118
Carlisle Companies Incorporated	December	1.34
Carpenter Technology Corporation	June	
Caterpillar Inc.	December	1.83, 2.84
CBS Corporation	December	
CenturyLink, Inc.	December	2.77, 3.47
Cenveo, Inc.	December	3.13, 6.22
CF Industries Holdings, Inc.	December	
Chesapeake Energy Corporation	December	1.72
Chevron Corporation	December	2.58
Children's Place Retail Stores, Inc., The	January	1.45, 2.88, 5.35, 5.48
Cisco Systems, Inc.	July	1.23, 2.25, 7.67
Citigroup Inc.	December	1.19, 1.63, 2.21, 3.08, 3.74
Cliffs Natural Resources Inc.	December	1.116, 3.53, 3.67
Clorox Company, The	June	
Coach, Inc.	June	1.109
Coca-Cola Company, The	December	2.90, 3.56
Coca-Cola Enterprises, Inc.	December	2.57
Coherent, Inc.	September	
Colgate-Palmolive Company	December	3.51, 5.23, 6.21
Commercial Metals Company	August	
Computer Sciences Corporation	March	1.53
ConAgra Foods, Inc.	May	7.69
ConocoPhillips	December	
Constellation Brands, Inc.	February	2.62, 3.16
Convergys Corporation	December	4.14
Cooper Tire & Rubber Company	December	2.116
Corning Incorporated	December	1.43
Covance Inc.	December	
Crane Co.	December	2.26, 2.154
CSX Corporation	December	1.25, 2.156, 3.69
Cummins Inc.	December	
CVS Caremark Corporation	December	2.125
Dana Holding Corporation	December	
Danaher Corporation	December	
Darden Restaurants, Inc.	May	
Dean Foods Company	December	5.27, 5.39
Deere & Company	October	2.34, 2.96
Dell Inc.	January	1.111, 2.151, 4.17
DIRECTV	December	
Discovery Communications, Inc.	December	

Company Name	Month of Fiscal Year End	Accounting Technique Illustration
Domino's Pizza, Inc.	December	
Donaldson Company, Inc.	July	
Dover Corporation	December	2.150
Dow Chemical Company, The	December	3.14
Dun & Bradstreet Corporation, The	December	2.91
E. W. Scripps Company, The	December	
Eastman Chemical Company	December	2.121
eBay Inc.	December	
Ecolab Inc.	December	5.11
Electronic Arts Inc.	March	1.73, 6.19
Eli Lilly and Company	December	
EMC Corporation	December	
EMCOR Group, Inc.	December	2.117
Emerson Electric Co.	September	
Energizer Holdings, Inc.	September	
Equifax Inc.	December	
Estee Lauder Companies Inc., The	June	2.160
Exide Technologies	March	7.32
Express Scripts Holding Company	December	
Exxon Mobil Corporation	December	3.24
FedEx Corporation	May	
Fidelity National Information Services, Inc.	December	
First Solar, Inc.	December	2.86, 6.16
Flowers Foods, Inc.	December	5.26, 5.42
Fluor Corporation	December	
FMC Corporation	December	3.36
Foot Locker, Inc.	January	
Ford Motor Company	December	
Fred's, Inc.	January	2.43
Freeport-McMoRan Copper & Gold Inc.	December	2.126
GameStop Corp.	January	
GenCorp Inc.	November	1.28, 1.97, 3.91, 6.26
General Cable Corporation	December	2.42, 2.132
General Dynamics Corporation	December	2.51
General Electric Company	December	3.25
General Mills, Inc.	May	5.47
Genuine Parts Company	December	
Gilead Sciences, Inc.	December	4.15
Goldman Sachs Group, Inc., The	December	
Goodyear Tire & Rubber Company, The	December	5.19
Google Inc.	December	
Graham Holdings Company	December	
Greif, Inc.	October	1.70, 3.12, 7.70
Griffon Corporation	September	
Guess?, Inc.	January	3.58, 4.11
Halliburton Company	December	
Hanesbrands Inc.	December	2.92, 6.34
Harley-Davidson, Inc.	December	2.105
Harman International Industries, Incorporated	June	
Harris Corporation	June	1.51, 2.79
Hasbro, Inc.	December	
Health Net, Inc.	December	
Hershey Company, The	December	
Hess Corporation	December	3.22
Hewlett-Packard Company	October	
Hill-Rom Holdings, Inc.	September	
Hormel Foods Corporation	October	
Hovnanian Enterprises, Inc.	October	3.30
Humana Inc.	December	
Huntsman Corporation	December	3.90
IAC/InterActiveCorp	December	1.79, 2.108
IDT Corporation	July	6.30
Illinois Tool Works Inc.	December	2.113
Ingram Micro Inc.	December	

Company Name	Month of Fiscal Year End	Accounting Technique Illustration
Ingredion Incorporated	December	
Insperity, Inc.	December	2.87
Intel Corporation	December	2.78
International Business Machines Corporation	December	2.49
International Flavors & Fragrances Inc.	December	
International Paper Company	December	3.60
Interpublic Group of Companies, Inc., The	December	
Iron Mountain Incorporated	December	
ITT Corporation	December	
J. C. Penney Company, Inc.	January	1.18
J. M. Smucker Company, The	April	
Jabil Circuit, Inc.	August	3.03, 6.08
Jack in the Box Inc.	September	3.23
Jarden Corporation	December	
JDS Uniphase Corporation	June	
Johnson & Johnson	December	1.82, 3.21
Johnson Controls, Inc.	September	2.47, 7.42
Jones Group Inc., The	December	7.58
Joy Global Inc.	October	
JPMorgan Chase & Co.	December	1.27
Juniper Networks, Inc.	December	
KB Home	November	3.26
Kellogg Company	December	
Kimberly-Clark Corporation	December	
Kinder Morgan, Inc.	December	3.10
KLA-Tencor Corporation	June	
Kohl's Corporation	January	3.20
Kraft Foods Group, Inc.	December	
Kroger Co., The	January	7.20
L.S. Starrett Company, The	June	
L-3 Communications Holdings, Inc.	December	3.80
Lam Research Corporation	June	
Las Vegas Sands Corp.	December	5.08, 7.54
La-Z-Boy Incorporated	April	
Lear Corporation	December	
Lee Enterprises, Incorporated	September	7.29
Leggett & Platt, Incorporated	December	
Lennar Corporation	November	
Lockheed Martin Corporation	December	
Louisiana-Pacific Corporation	December	1.112
Lowe's Companies, Inc.	January	
LSI Corporation	December	
Macy's Inc	January	
Manitowoc Company, Inc., The	December	
Marriott International, Inc.	December	2.64
MasterCard Incorporated	December	2.123, 3.11
McClatchy Company, The	December	
McKesson Corporation	March	
Medtronic, Inc.	April	1.44, 3.34
Merck & Co., Inc.	December	1.95
Meritor, Inc.	September	
MetLife, Inc.	December	
Micron Technology, Inc.	August	5.12, 6.35
Microsoft Corporation	June	
Molex Incorporated	June	
Molson Coors Brewing Company	December	2.111
Monsanto Company	August	3.57
Morgan Stanley	December	
Mosaic Company, The	May	
Motorola Solutions, Inc.	December	
Mueller Industries, Inc.	December	
Murphy Oil Corporation	December	2.153, 5.22
NACCO Industries, Inc.	December	
National Oilwell Varco, Inc.	December	

Company Name	Month of Fiscal Year End	Accounting Technique Illustration
NetApp, Inc.	April	
New York Times Company, The	December	5.34
Newell Rubbermaid Inc.	December	
NewMarket Corporation	December	
Noble Energy, Inc.	December	3.29, 3.39
Northrop Grumman Corporation	December	2.89
NVR, Inc.	December	
Office Depot, Inc.	December	2.141
Oracle Corporation	May	6.10
Owens-Illinois, Inc.	December	
PACCAR Inc	December	1.21
Parker-Hannifin Corporation	June	
Peabody Energy Corporation	December	3.35, 3.95
PepsiCo, Inc.	December	
PerkinElmer, Inc.	December	
Pfizer Inc.	December	4.09, 6.12, 7.73
Pilgrim's Pride Corporation	December	
Pitney Bowes Inc.	December	
Plum Creek Timber Company, Inc.	December	1.94
PNC Financial Services Group, Inc., The	December	3.75, 6.32
Polaris Industries Inc.	December	
PolyOne Corporation	December	
PPG Industries, Inc.	December	
Praxair, Inc.	December	
Precision Castparts Corp.	March	
priceline.com Incorporated	December	2.06
Procter & Gamble Company, The	June	7.44
Prudential Financial, Inc.	December	1.46, 2.20, 3.73
PulteGroup, Inc.	December	1.81
PVH Corp.	January	5.33
RadioShack Corporation	December	
Ralph Lauren Corporation	March	2.140, 2.148, 3.62
Raytheon Company	December	3.94
Regal Beloit Corporation	December	2.124
Regal Entertainment Group	December	
Republic Services, Inc.	December	2.152
Reynolds American Inc.	December	
Rite Aid Corporation	February	
Rock-Tenn Company	September	
Rockwell Automation, Inc.	September	
Rockwell Collins, Inc.	September	
Safeway Inc.	December	1.50
Schnitzer Steel Industries, Inc.	August	1.33, 6.25
Scotts Miracle-Gro Company, The	September	1.74, 2.33
Seaboard Corporation	December	
Sealed Air Corporation	December	1.11
Service Corporation International	December	1.26, 3.18
Sherwin-Williams Company, The	December	
Smithfield Foods, Inc.	April	
Snap-on Incorporated	December	
Spectrum Brands Holdings, Inc.	September	1.24, 1.67, 2.45
Sprint Corporation	December	7.49
SPX Corporation	December	7.43
St. Jude Medical, Inc.	December	5.07
Standard Pacific Corp.	December	
Standard Register Company, The	December	5.49, 7.68
Stanley Black & Decker, Inc.	December	1.17, 3.61
Steel Dynamics, Inc.	December	
Steelcase Inc.	February	
SYNNEX Corporation	November	3.59, 7.55
Sysco Corporation	June	4.08
Target Corporation	January	
Teleflex Incorporated	December	
Tempur Sealy International, Inc.	December	1.68

Company Name	Month of Fiscal Year End	Accounting Technique Illustration
Tenet Healthcare Corporation	December	4.12
Tenneco Inc.	December	2.31
Terex Corporation	December	2.40
Texas Instruments Incorporated	December	
Textron Inc.	December	2.68, 6.11
Thermo Fisher Scientific Inc.	December	
Tiffany & Co.	January	
Time Warner Inc.	December	7.45
Toll Brothers, Inc.	October	
TRW Automotive Holdings Corp.	December	
Tupperware Brands Corporation	December	3.32
Tutor Perini Corporation	December	
Unifi, Inc.	June	3.33
Unisys Corporation	December	
United Continental Holdings, Inc.	December	
United Parcel Service, Inc.	December	
United States Steel Corporation	December	
United Health Group Incorporated	December	
Universal Corporation	March	
Universal Forest Products, Inc.	December	
Universal Health Services, Inc.	December	1.84, 2.119
URS Corporation	December	2.48, 3.78
Valero Energy Corporation	December	3.87, 5.09, 5.50
Varian Medical Systems, Inc.	September	2.115
Verizon Communications Inc.	December	2.80, 2.142, 2.159
Viacom Inc.	September	1.115, 3.28
Visa Inc.	September	2.24, 6.36
Vishay Intertechnology, Inc.	December	6.31
Visteon Corporation	December	6.18
Vulcan Materials Company	December	
W. R. Grace & Co.	December	7.33
Wal-Mart Stores, Inc.	January	7.21
Walter Energy, Inc.	December	7.22
Waste Management, Inc.	December	2.149, 3.40
Weis Markets, Inc.	December	
WellPoint, Inc.	December	2.85, 4.13
Wendy's Company, The	December	
Werner Enterprises, Inc.	December	
Western Union Company, The	December	6.27
Weyerhaeuser Company	December	
Williams-Sonoma, Inc.	January	2.50
Winnebago Industries, Inc.	August	
Worthington Industries, Inc.	May	3.31
Wyndham Worldwide Corporation	December	3.09, 6.28
Wynn Resorts, Limited	December	
Xerox Corporation	December	6.17
Xilinx, Inc.	March	
Yahoo! Inc.	December	4.16, 6.20
YUM! Brands, Inc.	December	
Zimmer Holdings, Inc.	December	

List of Industries Represented by the 350 Survey Entities

The following table lists the industries represented by the 350 survey entities and lists the entities within each industry classification.*

Industry Classification	Company Name
Basic Materials/Agricultural Inputs	CF Industries Holdings, Inc.
	Monsanto Company
	Scotts Miracle-Gro Company, The
Basic Materials/Aluminum	Alcoa Inc.
Basic Materials/Building Materials	Armstrong World Industries, Inc.
	Griffon Corporation
	Vulcan Materials Company
Basic Materials/Chemicals	Air Products and Chemicals, Inc.
	Ashland Inc.
	Axiall Corporation
	Dow Chemical Company, The
	Eastman Chemical Company
	FMC Corporation
	Huntsman Corporation
	International Flavors & Fragrances Inc.
	PolyOne Corporation
Basic Materials/Coal	Peabody Energy Corporation
	Walter Energy, Inc.
Basic Materials/Copper	Freeport-McMoRan Copper & Gold Inc.
Basic Materials/Industrial Metals & Minerals	Cliffs Natural Resources Inc.
Basic Materials/Lumber & Wood Production	Louisiana-Pacific Corporation
	Universal Forest Products, Inc.
Basic Materials/Paper & Paper Products	Cenveo, Inc.
	International Paper Company
Basic Materials/Specialty Chemicals	Cabot Corporation
	Mosaic Company, The
	NewMarket Corporation
	PPG Industries, Inc.
	Praxair, Inc.
	W. R. Grace & Co.
Basic Materials/Steel	AK Steel Holding Corporation
	Carpenter Technology Corporation
	Commercial Metals Company
	Schnitzer Steel Industries, Inc.
	Steel Dynamics, Inc.
	Worthington Industries, Inc.
Communication Services/Pay TV	Cablevision Systems Corporation
	DIRECTV
Communication Services/Telecom Services	AT&T Inc.
	CenturyLink, Inc.
	IDT Corporation
	Sprint Corporation
	Verizon Communications Inc.
Consumer Cyclical/Advertising Agencies	Interpublic Group of Companies, Inc., The

* Industry classifications according to Morningstar, Inc. (www.morningstar.com).

Industry Classification	Company Name
Consumer Cyclical/Apparel Manufacturing	Guess?, Inc.
	Hanesbrands Inc.
	Jones Group Inc., The
	PVH Corp.
	Ralph Lauren Corporation
Consumer Cyclical/Apparel Stores	Ann Inc.
	Children's Place Retail Stores, Inc., The
Consumer Cyclical/Auto & Truck Dealerships	AutoNation, Inc.
Consumer Cyclical/Auto Manufacturers	Ford Motor Company
Consumer Cyclical/Auto Parts	AutoZone, Inc.
	Dana Holding Corporation
	Johnson Controls, Inc.
	Lear Corporation
	Tenneco Inc.
	TRW Automotive Holdings Corp.
	Visteon Corporation
Consumer Cyclical/Broadcasting—TV	CBS Corporation
Consumer Cyclical/Department Stores	Bon-Ton Stores, Inc., The
	J. C. Penney Company, Inc.
	Kohl's Corporation
	Macy's Inc
Consumer Cyclical/Footwear & Accessories	Brown Shoe Company, Inc.
	Foot Locker, Inc.
Consumer Cyclical/Home Furnishings & Fixtures	Bassett Furniture Industries, Incorporated
	Jarden Corporation
	La-Z-Boy Incorporated
	Leggett & Platt, Incorporated
	Tempur Sealy International, Inc.
Consumer Cyclical/Home Improvement Stores	Lowe's Companies, Inc.
Consumer Cyclical/Leisure	Brunswick Corporation
	Hasbro, Inc.
	priceline.com Incorporated
	Regal Entertainment Group
Consumer Cyclical/Lodging	Marriott International, Inc.
	Wyndham Worldwide Corporation
Consumer Cyclical/Luxury Goods	Coach, Inc.
	Tiffany & Co.
Consumer Cyclical/Media—Diversified	Discovery Communications, Inc.
	Time Warner Inc.
	Viacom Inc.
Consumer Cyclical/Packaging & Containers	Ball Corporation
	Greif, Inc.
	Owens-Illinois, Inc.
	Rock-Tenn Company
	Sealed Air Corporation
Consumer Cyclical/Personal Services	American Greetings Corporation
	Service Corporation International
	Western Union Company, The
Consumer Cyclical/Publishing	E. W. Scripps Company, The
	Lee Enterprises, Incorporated
	McClatchy Company, The
	New York Times Company, The
Consumer Cyclical/Recreational Vehicles	Harley-Davidson, Inc.
	Polaris Industries Inc.
	Winnebago Industries, Inc.
Consumer Cyclical/Residential Construction	Hovnanian Enterprises, Inc.
	KB Home
	Lennar Corporation
	NVR, Inc.
	PulteGroup, Inc.
	Standard Pacific Corp.
	Toll Brothers, Inc.
Consumer Cyclical/Resorts & Casinos	Las Vegas Sands Corp.
	Wynn Resorts, Limited

Industry Classification	Company Name
Consumer Cyclical/Restaurants	Darden Restaurants, Inc.
	Domino's Pizza, Inc.
	Jack in the Box Inc.
	Wendy's Company, The
	YUM! Brands, Inc.
Consumer Cyclical/Rubber & Plastics	Carlisle Companies Incorporated
	Cooper Tire & Rubber Company
	Goodyear Tire & Rubber Company, The
Consumer Cyclical/Specialty Retail	Barnes & Noble, Inc.
	Best Buy Co., Inc.
	eBay Inc.
	GameStop Corp.
	Office Depot, Inc.
	RadioShack Corporation
	Sherwin-Williams Company, The
	Williams-Sonoma, Inc.
Consumer Cyclical/Textile Manufacturing	Unifi, Inc.
Consumer Defensive/Beverages—Brewers	Molson Coors Brewing Company
Consumer Defensive/Beverages—Soft Drinks	Coca-Cola Company, The
	Coca-Cola Enterprises, Inc.
	PepsiCo, Inc.
Consumer Defensive/Beverages—Wineries & Distilleries	Beam Inc.
	Brown-Forman Corporation
	Constellation Brands, Inc.
Consumer Defensive/Confectioners	Hershey Company, The
Consumer Defensive/Discount Stores	Fred's, Inc.
	Target Corporation
	Wal-Mart Stores, Inc.
Consumer Defensive/Education & Training Services	Career Education Corporation
	Graham Holdings Company
Consumer Defensive/Farm Products	Archer-Daniels-Midland Company
	Hormel Foods Corporation
	Pilgrim's Pride Corporation
	Seaboard Corporation
Consumer Defensive/Food Distribution	Sysco Corporation
Consumer Defensive/Grocery Stores	Kroger Co., The
	Safeway Inc.
	Weis Markets, Inc.
Consumer Defensive/Household & Personal Products	Avon Products, Inc.
	Clorox Company, The
	Colgate-Palmolive Company
	Energizer Holdings, Inc.
	Estee Lauder Companies Inc., The
	Kimberly-Clark Corporation
	Newell Rubbermaid Inc.
	Procter & Gamble Company, The
	Tupperware Brands Corporation
Consumer Defensive/Packaged Foods	Campbell Soup Company
	ConAgra Foods, Inc.
	Dean Foods Company
	Flowers Foods, Inc.
	General Mills, Inc.
	Ingredion Incorporated
	J. M. Smucker Company, The
	Kellogg Company
	Kraft Foods Group, Inc.
	Smithfield Foods, Inc.
Consumer Defensive/Pharmaceutical Retailers	CVS Caremark Corporation
	Rite Aid Corporation
Consumer Defensive/Tobacco	Alliance One International, Inc.
	Altria Group, Inc.
	Reynolds American Inc.
	Universal Corporation

Industry Classification	Company Name
Energy/Oil & Gas E&P	Apache Corporation
	Chesapeake Energy Corporation
	Noble Energy, Inc.
Energy/Oil & Gas Equipment & Services	Baker Hughes Incorporated
	Halliburton Company
	National Oilwell Varco, Inc.
Energy/Oil & Gas Integrated	Chevron Corporation
	ConocoPhillips
	Exxon Mobil Corporation
	Hess Corporation
	Murphy Oil Corporation
Energy/Oil & Gas Midstream	Kinder Morgan, Inc.
Energy/Oil & Gas Refining & Marketing	Valero Energy Corporation
Financial Services/Banks—Global	Citigroup Inc.
	JPMorgan Chase & Co.
Financial Services/Banks—Regional—US	BB&T Corporation
	PNC Financial Services Group, Inc., The
Financial Services/Capital Markets	Goldman Sachs Group, Inc., The
	Morgan Stanley
Financial Services/Credit Services	MasterCard Incorporated
	Visa Inc.
Financial Services/Insurance—Diversified	American International Group, Inc.
	Berkshire Hathaway Inc.
Financial Services/Insurance—Life	MetLife, Inc.
	Prudential Financial, Inc.
Healthcare/Biotechnology	Gilead Sciences, Inc.
Healthcare/Diagnostics & Research	Covance Inc.
Healthcare/Drug Manufacturers—Major	Abbott Laboratories
	Allergan, Inc.
	Eli Lilly and Company
	Johnson & Johnson
	Merck & Co., Inc.
	Pfizer Inc.
Healthcare/Health Care Plans	Express Scripts Holding Company
	Health Net, Inc.
	UnitedHealth Group Incorporated
	WellPoint, Inc.
Healthcare/Medical Care	Tenet Healthcare Corporation
	Universal Health Services, Inc.
Healthcare/Medical Devices	Medtronic, Inc.
	St. Jude Medical, Inc.
	Teleflex Incorporated
	Zimmer Holdings, Inc.
Healthcare/Medical Distribution	Cardinal Health, Inc.
	McKesson Corporation
Healthcare/Medical Instruments & Supplies	Baxter International Inc.
	Becton, Dickinson and Company
	Boston Scientific Corporation
	Hill-Rom Holdings, Inc.
	PerkinElmer, Inc.
	Thermo Fisher Scientific Inc.
	Varian Medical Systems, Inc.
Industrials/Aerospace & Defense	Alliant Techsystems Inc.
	B/E Aerospace, Inc.
	Boeing Company, The
	GenCorp Inc.
	General Dynamics Corporation
	L-3 Communications Holdings, Inc.
	Lockheed Martin Corporation
	Raytheon Company
	Rockwell Collins, Inc.
Industrials/Airlines	United Continental Holdings, Inc.
Industrials/Business Equipment	Pitney Bowes Inc.
	Standard Register Company, The
	Steelcase Inc.
	Xerox Corporation

Industry Classification	Company Name
Industrials/Business Services	ABM Industries Incorporated
	Automatic Data Processing, Inc.
	Dun & Bradstreet Corporation, The
	Ecolab Inc.
	Equifax Inc.
	Fidelity National Information Services, Inc.
	Humana Inc.
	Iron Mountain Incorporated
	SYNNEX Corporation
Industrials/Conglomerates	Northrop Grumman Corporation
	Spectrum Brands Holdings, Inc.
Industrials/Diversified Industrials	3M Company
	A. O. Smith Corporation
	Airgas, Inc.
	AMETEK, Inc.
	Anadarko Petroleum Corporation
	Briggs & Stratton Corporation
	Crane Co.
	Danaher Corporation
	Donaldson Company, Inc.
	Dover Corporation
	Emerson Electric Co.
	Exide Technologies
	General Cable Corporation
	General Electric Company
	Illinois Tool Works Inc.
	ITT Corporation
	Parker-Hannifin Corporation
	Regal Beloit Corporation
	Rockwell Automation, Inc.
	SPX Corporation
	Textron Inc.
Industrials/Engineering & Construction	EMCOR Group, Inc.
	Fluor Corporation
	Tutor Perini Corporation
	URS Corporation
Industrials/Farm & Construction Equipment	AGCO Corporation
	Caterpillar Inc.
	Deere & Company
	Joy Global Inc.
	Manitowoc Company, Inc., The
	NACCO Industries, Inc.
	Terex Corporation
Industrials/Industrial Distribution	Genuine Parts Company
Industrials/Integrated Shipping & Logistics	FedEx Corporation
	United Parcel Service, Inc.
Industrials/Metal Fabrication	Allegheny Technologies Incorporated
	Mueller Industries, Inc.
	Precision Castparts Corp.
	United States Steel Corporation
Industrials/Railroads	CSX Corporation
Industrials/Security & Protection Services	Brink's Company, The
Industrials/Staffing & Outsourcing Services	Insperity, Inc.
Industrials/Tools & Accessories	L.S. Starrett Company, The
	Snap-on Incorporated
	Stanley Black & Decker, Inc.
Industrials/Truck Manufacturing	Cummins Inc.
	PACCAR Inc
Industrials/Trucking	Arkansas Best Corporation
	Werner Enterprises, Inc.
Industrials/Waste Management	Republic Services, Inc.
	Waste Management, Inc.
Real Estate/REIT—Industrial	Plum Creek Timber Company, Inc.
	Weyerhaeuser Company

Industry Classification	Company Name
Technology/Communications Equipment	Cisco Systems, Inc.
	Harris Corporation
	JDS Uniphase Corporation
	Juniper Networks, Inc.
	Motorola Solutions, Inc.
Technology/Computer Distribution	Ingram Micro Inc.
Technology/Computer Systems	Apple Inc.
	Dell Inc.
	Hewlett-Packard Company
	International Business Machines Corporation
Technology/Consumer Electronics	Harman International Industries, Incorporated
Technology/Contract Manufacturers	Jabil Circuit, Inc.
Technology/Data Storage	EMC Corporation
	NetApp, Inc.
Technology/Electronic Components	Acuity Brands, Inc.
	Amphenol Corporation
	Corning Incorporated
	Molex Incorporated
	Vishay Intertechnology, Inc.
Technology/Electronic Gaming & Multimedia	Electronic Arts Inc.
Technology/Electronics Distribution	Arrow Electronics, Inc.
	Avnet, Inc.
Technology/Information Technology Services	CACI International Inc
	Computer Sciences Corporation
	Unisys Corporation
Technology/Internet Content & Information	Google Inc.
	IAC/InterActiveCorp
	Yahoo! Inc.
Technology/Scientific & Technical Instruments	Badger Meter, Inc.
	Coherent, Inc.
Technology/Semiconductor Equipment & Materials	Applied Materials, Inc.
	KLA-Tencor Corporation
	Lam Research Corporation
Technology/Semiconductor Memory	Micron Technology, Inc.
Technology/Semiconductors	Amkor Technology, Inc.
	Analog Devices, Inc.
	Atmel Corporation
	Intel Corporation
	LSI Corporation
	Meritor, Inc.
	Texas Instruments Incorporated
	Xilinx, Inc.
Technology/Software—Application	Autodesk, Inc.
	BMC Software, Inc.
	Convergys Corporation
Technology/Software—Infrastructure	CA, Inc.
	Microsoft Corporation
	Oracle Corporation
Technology/Solar	First Solar, Inc.

Index of Authoritative Accounting & Auditing Guidance 707

Subject Index

A

Accelerated depreciation method, 3.66–3.67

Accounting changes and error corrections
    changes in accounting estimates, 1.40, 1.51–1.52
    changes in accounting principle. *See* Accounting principles, changes in
    comprehensive income, 1.47
    errors, correction of, 1.52–1.53
    incentive fee revenue, 1.46
    inventory, 1.45
    investments, 1.44
    lack of consistency in independent auditors' report, 7.34–7.40
    presentation, 1.35–1.41
    prior period adjustments, 1.41
    restatement, 7.39–7.40
    retained earnings, 5.31, 5.32, 5.34

Accounting corrections. *See* Accounting changes and error corrections

Accounting estimates
    changes in, 1.40, 1.51–1.52
    critical accounting policies, 1.23
    depreciation expense, 3.64
    prospective application, 1.39
    use of, 1.26

Accounting policies
    critical accounting policies, 1.23
    summary of significant, 1.24

Accounting principles
    changes in. *See* Accounting principles, changes in
    comprehensive income, 1.47
    cumulative translation adjustment, 1.50
    employee retirement plans, 1.43
    exceptions, 1.37
    incentive fee revenue, 1.46
    inventory, 1.45
    investments, 1.44
    nonauthoritative accounting guidance sources, 1.04
    offsetting assets and liabilities, 1.48–1.49
    retained earnings, 5.33
    retrospective application, 1.38, 5.30–5.31

Accounting principles, changes in
    changes in, generally, 1.45–1.52. *See also* Accounting changes and
      error corrections
    changes in, when permitted, 1.37
    distinguishing from change in accounting estimates, 1.40
    evaluating, independent auditors' report, 7.36–7.40
    retained earnings, 5.33

Accounting standards, new, 1.21

Accounting Standards Board (ASB), clarified auditing standards, 7.01

Accounts payable. *See* Payables

Accounts receivable. *See* Current receivables; Receivables; Receivables
    sold or collateralized

Accretion
    on asset retirement obligations, 3.29
    of convertible notes discount, 6.20

Accrued earnings, in excess of billings, 2.48

Accumulated depreciation, 2.56

Accumulated other comprehensive income. *See also* Comprehensive
      income; Other comprehensive income
    balance sheet, 2.157–2.160
    in equity section of balance sheet, 2.168
    in notes to consolidated financial statements, 2.160
    pension plans, recognition and measurement, 3.43
    presentation, 2.157
    statement of changes in equity, 2.159

Acquisitions. *See also* Business combinations
    cash flows from investing activities, 6.24
    of controlling interest, gain on, 3.15
    expenses and losses, 3.38
    issuance of common stock, 5.11
    subsequent events, 1.112

Actuarial gains and losses, pension plan disclosures, 3.45

Additional paid-in capital, credits and charges to, 5.02–5.04

Address of auditor, auditors' report, 7.04, 7.11

Addressee of auditors' report, 7.04, 7.06

Administrative expenses, 3.20

Advances, 2.46

Advertising
    expenses, 3.23
    marketing agreement, 1.74
    royalty and licensing agreements, 1.73

Allowances for doubtful accounts, 2.23

Amendments to pension plans, 3.51

Amortization
    adjustments to reconcile net income, 6.18
    depreciation expense, 3.64
    intangible assets, 2.69, 3.32
    of software, 3.33

Annual filings, comprehensive income in, 4.01–4.18

Annual reports
    auditors' report, presentation in, 7.01–7.03
    required contents, 1.09–1.11
    stockholders' equity, 5.01–5.14

Asset retirement obligations
    accretion on, 3.29
    other current liabilities, 2.126
    other noncurrent liabilities, 2.153

adjustments to reconcile net income, 6.18–6.22
amortization, 6.18
cash inflows/outflows, 6.13
currency devaluation charge, 6.21
depreciation, 6.18
direct method to report, 6.14, 6.16
gain on insurance claim, 6.22
indirect/reconciliation method to report, 6.14, 6.17
presentation, 6.13–6.15
reporting methods, 6.14–6.15
statement of cash flows, 6.13–6.22

Forward-looking information, 1.19

Franchise fees, 3.09

G

Gain contingencies, 1.75, 1.76, 1.84

Gains. *See also* Revenues and gains
  actuarial gains, pension plan disclosures, 3.45
  on asset disposals, 3.12
  debt extinguishment, 3.18
  derivatives, 1.91, 1.92, 4.14–4.15
  discontinued operations, 3.82, 3.84
  on insurance claim, 6.22
  unrealized, net change on available-for-sale securities, 4.13
  unrealized, on marketable securities, 2.10, 2.18

General management committee reports
  audit committee report, 7.73
  independent auditors' report, 7.71–7.73
  management report on financial statements, 7.17, 7.72
  management report on internal control, 7.70
  presentation, 7.71

Going concern, 7.32

Goodwill. *See also* Intangible assets
  business combinations, 1.65
  impairment of, 3.41
  intangible assets, 2.75
  presentation, 2.73
  recognition and measurement, 2.69

Government matters, contingencies, 1.82

Group-life method of depreciation, 3.69

Guarantees
  contingencies, 1.83
  financial, 1.94

H

Hedging instruments. *See also* Derivative financial instruments
  plain English references, 1.07
  recognition and measurement, 1.85

Held for disposal, 2.56

Held for sale
  discontinued operations, 3.82, 3.83, 3.84
  long-term assets, 3.82
  other current assets, 2.47
  other noncurrent assets, 2.84

Held-to-maturity securities, 2.10, 2.20

Highest and best use, fair value, 1.99

Hybrid financial instruments, 1.85

I

Impairment
  of goodwill, 3.41

of intangibles, 2.69–2.71, 3.41
of investments, 2.11, 3.40
testing intangible assets, 2.69–2.71

Incentive employee compensation plans, 3.60

Incentive fee revenue, changes in accounting principle, 1.46

Income, comprehensive. *See* Comprehensive income

Income statement
  annual report requirements, 1.09, 1.10
  changes to retained earnings, 5.32
  combined statement of income and comprehensive income, 4.06
  construction-type and production-type contracts, 3.77–3.80
  depreciation expense, 3.63–3.69
  discontinued operations, 3.81–3.87
  earnings per share, 3.93–3.95
  employee compensatory plans, 3.54–3.62
  expenses and losses, 3.19–3.51
  extraordinary items, 3.88–3.92
  format, 3.01–3.03
  incomes taxes, 3.70–3.76
  pensions and other postretirement benefits, 3.43–3.51
  postemployment benefits, 3.52–3.53
  presentation, 3.01–3.03
  reclassifications, 3.03
  revenues and gains, 3.04–3.18

Income tax liability
  balance sheet, 2.106–2.108
  presentation, 2.106

Income tax receivables, 2.24

Income taxes
  credit provision, 3.73
  deferred, 2.88, 2.115, 2.147
  expense provisions, 3.72
  expenses other than income taxes, 3.24
  income statement, 3.70–3.76
  as liability. *See* Income tax liability
  operating loss and tax credit carryforwards, 3.74–3.75
  payment of, 6.10–6.11
  presentation on statement of cash flows, 6.10–6.11
  recognition and measurement, 3.70
  on undistributed earnings, 3.76

Increasing-rate debt, 2.93

Indebtedness. *See* Debt

Indemnifications, 1.94

"Independent," in title of auditors' report, 7.05, 7.16

Independent auditors' report
  address of auditor, 7.04, 7.11
  addressee of auditors' report, 7.04, 7.06, 7.17
  audit committee report, 7.73
  auditor's opinions, 7.04, 7.10, 7.11, 7.12
  auditor's responsibilities, 7.04, 7.09, 7.11
  audits of public entities, 7.18
  change in auditors, 7.55
  comparative financial statement report, 7.52–7.55
  date of auditor's report, 7.11
  dating of report, 7.59–7.62
  departures from unmodified opinions, 7.50–7.51
  emergence from bankruptcy, 7.33
  emphasis of a matter, 7.46–7.49
  evaluating changes in accounting principle, 7.36–7.40
  general management and special-purpose committee reports, 7.71–7.73
  generally, 7.01

issuers, 7.36–7.40
nonissuers, 7.34–7.35
presentation, 7.35–7.40
presentation of investments, 7.45
separation of business segment, 7.41

Land, 2.82. *See also* Property, plant, and equipment

Last-in, first-out (LIFO) inventory, 2.38–2.39, 2.41

Lawsuits. *See* Litigation

Leases
agreements as commitments, 1.72
lease agreements, 1.72
lessee leases, 2.140–2.141
lessor leases, 2.142
long-term. *See* Long-term leases
operating leases, 2.136, 2.138, 2.139

Legal matters, contingencies, 1.78

Lessee leases, 2.140–2.141

Lessor leases, 2.142

Letters of credit, 1.69

Liabilities
contingent liabilities, 2.146
current liabilities, 2.100, 2.127
employee compensatory plans, 3.54
fair value measurement, 1.100, 1.101
noncurrent liabilities, 2.100
offsetting with assets, 1.12
other current. *See* Other current liabilities
other noncurrent. *See* Other noncurrent liabilities
pension plan disclosures, 3.44
preferred stock classified as, 5.17
servicing liabilities, fair value, 2.28

Licenses and licensing, 2.80

Licenses and licensing agreements, 1.73

Life insurance
cash surrender value, 2.89
group-life method of depreciation, 3.69

LIFO. *See* Last-in, first-out (LIFO) inventory

Line of credit, 1.94

Liquidation, involuntary, 5.16

Liquidity, 1.20

Litigation
escrow account, cash flows from financing activities, 6.36
expenses and losses, 3.34
other current liabilities, 2.123
other noncurrent liabilities, 2.154
revenues and gains, 3.14
subsequent events, 1.110

Loans. *See also* Credit agreements; Debt
due-on-demand arrangements, 2.93
loans payable, 2.95

Long-term assets held for sale. *See* Held for sale

Long-term debt
balance sheet, 2.127–2.132
collateralized, 2.131
convertible, 2.132
current amount, 2.111
presentation, 2.127
unsecured, 2.130

Long-term leases
balance sheet, 2.136–2.142
commitments, 1.69
lessee leases, 2.140–2.141
lessor leases, 2.142
presentation, 2.137–2.138
recognition and measurement, 2.136

Long-term prepayments, 2.82

Long-term receivables, 2.67

Loss carryforward, contingencies, 3.74–3.75

Loss contingencies, 1.75, 1.76

Losses. *See also* Expenses and losses
actuarial gains, pension plan disclosures, 3.45
debt extinguishment, 3.42
defined, 3.19
derivative changes in fair value, 3.39
derivatives, 1.91, 1.92
derivatives held as cash flow hedges, 4.14–4.15
discontinued operations, 3.82, 3.84
impairment of investments, 2.11
operating loss carryforward, 3.74–3.75
provision for, 3.25
unrealized, net change on available-for-sale securities, 4.13
unrealized, on marketable securities, 2.10

M

Management's discussion and analysis (MD&A), financial condition and results of operations, 1.09

Management's reports
on financial statements, 7.17, 7.72
general management committee reports, 7.71–7.73
on internal control, 7.70
segment reporting approaches, 1.31

Management's responsibilities, auditors' report, 7.04, 7.08, 7.11

Mandatorily redeemable preferred stock, 2.144, 5.17

Market method of inventory, 2.35

Market risk information, 1.22

Marketable securities. *See also* Trading securities
available-for-sale securities, 2.10, 2.12, 2.19, 4.13, 6.23
balance sheet, 2.09–2.21
classification of, 2.10
held-to-maturity securities, 2.10, 2.20
presentation, 2.12
recognition and measurement, 2.09–2.11
trading, 2.21

Marketing
advertising costs, 3.23
marketing agreement, 1.74
royalty and licensing agreements, 1.73

Master limited partnerships, 3.92

Materiality, related party transactions, 1.113

MD&A. *See* Management's discussion and analysis

MEPP. *See* Multi-employer pension plans

Merger agreements, 1.111. *See also* Acquisitions; Business combinations

Minority interest. *See* Noncontrolling interest

S

AICPA® Online Professional Library

Powerful Online Research Tools

The AICPA Online Professional Library offers the most current access to comprehensive accounting and auditing literature, as well business and practice management information, combined with the power and speed of the Web. Through your online subscription, you'll get:

• Cross-references within and between titles — smart links give you quick access to related information and relevant materials
• First available updates — no other research tool offers access to new AICPA standards and conforming changes more quickly, guaranteeing that you are always current with all of the authoritative guidance!
• Robust search engine — helps you narrow down your research to find your results quickly
• And much more...

Choose from two comprehensive libraries or select only the titles you need!

With the *Essential A&A Research Collection*, you gain access to the following:
• AICPA Professional Standards
• AICPA Technical Practice Aids
• PCAOB Standards & Related Rules
• All current AICPA Audit and Accounting Guides
• All current Audit Risk Alerts
One-year individual online subscription
Item # ORS-XX

OR

***Premium A&A Research Collection* and get everything from the *Essential A&A Research Collection* plus:**
• AICPA Audit & Accounting Manual
• All current Checklists & Illustrative Financial Statements
• eXacct: Financial Reporting Tools & Techniques
• IFRS Accounting Trends & Techniques
One-year individual online subscription
Item # WAL-BY

You can also add the FASB *Accounting Standards Codification*™ and the GASB Library to either collection.

Take advantage of a 30-day free trial!
See for yourself how these powerful online libraries can improve your productivity and simplify your accounting research.

Visit **cpa2biz.com/library** for details or to subscribe.

Additional Publications

Audit Risk Alerts/Financial Reporting Alerts
Find out about current economic, regulatory and professional developments before you perform your audit engagement. AICPA industry-specific Audit Risk Alerts will make your audit planning process more efficient by giving you concise, relevant information that shows you how current developments may impact your clients and your audits. For financial statement preparers, AICPA also offers a series of Financial Reporting Alerts. For a complete list of Audit Risk Alerts available from the AICPA, please visit **cpa2biz.com/ara**.

Checklists and Illustrative Financial Statements
Updated to reflect recent accounting and auditing standards, these industry-specific practice aids are invaluable tools to both financial statement preparers and auditors. For a complete list of Checklists available from the AICPA, please visit **cpa2biz.com/checklists**.